LET'S
Isra
& Egypt

"Lighthearted and sophisticated, informative and fun to read. *[Let's Go]* helps the novice traveler navigate like a knowledgeable old hand."
—Atlanta Journal-Constitution

"The guides are aimed not only at young budget travelers but at the independent traveler, a sort of streetwise cookbook for traveling alone."
—The New York Times

▓ Let's Go writers travel on your budget.

"Retains the spirit of the student-written publication it is: candid, opinionated, resourceful, amusing info for the traveler of limited means but broad curiosity."
—Mademoiselle

"The writers seem to have experienced every rooster-packed bus and lunar-surfaced mattress about which they write."
—The New York Times

"All the dirt, dirt cheap."
—People

▓ Great for independent travelers.

"A world-wise traveling companion—always ready with friendly advice and helpful hints, all sprinkled with a bit of wit."
—The Philadelphia Inquirer

"Lots of valuable information for any independent traveler."
—The Chicago Tribune

▓ Let's Go is completely revised each year.

"Unbeatable: good sight-seeing advice; up-to-date info on restaurants, hotels, and inns; a commitment to money-saving travel; and a wry style that brightens nearly every page."
—The Washington Post

"Its yearly revision by a new crop of Harvard students makes it as valuable as ever."
—The New York Times

▓ All the important information you need.

"Enough information to satisfy even the most demanding of budget travelers...*Let's Go* follows the creed that you don't have to toss your life's savings to the wind to travel—unless you want to."
—The Salt Lake Tribune

"Value-packed, unbeatable, accurate, and comprehensive."
—The Los Angeles Times

Let's Go Publications

Let's Go: Alaska & the Pacific Northwest 1998
Let's Go: Australia 1998 **New title!**
Let's Go: Austria & Switzerland 1998
Let's Go: Britain & Ireland 1998
Let's Go: California 1998
Let's Go: Central America 1998
Let's Go: Eastern Europe 1998
Let's Go: Ecuador & the Galápagos Islands 1998
Let's Go: Europe 1998
Let's Go: France 1998
Let's Go: Germany 1998
Let's Go: Greece & Turkey 1998
Let's Go: India & Nepal 1998
Let's Go: Ireland 1998
Let's Go: Israel & Egypt 1998
Let's Go: Italy 1998
Let's Go: London 1998
Let's Go: Mexico 1998
Let's Go: New York City 1998
Let's Go: New Zealand 1998 **New title!**
Let's Go: Paris 1998
Let's Go: Rome 1998
Let's Go: Southeast Asia 1998
Let's Go: Spain & Portugal 1998
Let's Go: USA 1998
Let's Go: Washington, D.C. 1998

Let's Go Map Guides

Berlin	New Orleans
Boston	New York City
Chicago	Paris
London	Rome
Los Angeles	San Francisco
Madrid	Washington, D.C.

Coming Soon: Amsterdam, Florence

Let's Go
Publications

LET'S GO
Israel
& Egypt
1998

Taya Lynn Weiss
Editor

Adam B. Stein
Associate Editor

Jennifer R. Weiss
Assistant Editor

Macmillan

HELPING LET'S GO

If you want to share your discoveries, suggestions, or corrections, please drop us a line. We read every piece of correspondence, whether a postcard, a 10-page email, or a coconut. Please note that mail received after May 1998 may be too late for the 1999 book, but will be kept for future editions. **Address mail to:**

**Let's Go: Israel & Egypt
67 Mount Auburn Street
Cambridge, MA 02138
USA**

Visit Let's Go at **http://www.letsgo.com,** or send email to:

**fanmail@letsgo.com
Subject: "Let's Go: Israel & Egypt"**

In addition to the invaluable travel advice our readers share with us, many are kind enough to offer their services as researchers or editors. Unfortunately, our charter enables us to employ only currently enrolled Harvard-Radcliffe students.

❧

Published in Great Britain 1998 by Macmillan, an imprint of Macmillan General Books, 25 Eccleston Place, London SW1W 9NF and Basingstoke.

Maps by David Lindroth copyright © 1998, 1997, 1996, 1995, 1994, 1993, 1992, 1991, 1990, 1989, 1988 by St. Martin's Press, Inc.

Map revisions pp. 1, 71, 88, 89, 133, 149, 181, 187, 203, 231, 241, 247, 269, 280, 281, 285, 323, 337, 353, 365, 375, 377, 381, 391, 407, 429, 439, 451, 459, 469, 491, 537, 544, 545, 555, 563 by Let's Go, Inc.

Published in the United States of America by St. Martin's Press, Inc.

ISBN: 0 333 71175 0

First edition
10 9 8 7 6 5 4 3 2 1

Let's Go: Israel & Egypt is written by Let's Go Publications, 67 Mount Auburn Street, Cambridge, MA 02138, USA.

Let's Go® and the thumb logo are trademarks of Let's Go, Inc. Printed in the USA on recycled paper with biodegradable soy ink.

About Let's Go

THIRTY-EIGHT YEARS OF WISDOM

Back in 1960, a few students at Harvard University banded together to produce a 20-page pamphlet offering a collection of tips on budget travel in Europe. This modest, mimeographed packet, offered as an extra to passengers on student charter flights to Europe, met with instant popularity. The following year, students traveling to Europe researched the first, full-fledged edition of *Let's Go: Europe,* a pocket-sized book featuring honest, irreverent writing and a decidedly youthful outlook on the world. Throughout the 60s, our guides reflected the times; the 1969 guide to America led off by inviting travelers to "dig the scene" at San Francisco's Haight-Ashbury. During the 70s and 80s, we gradually added regional guides and expanded coverage into the Middle East and Central America. With the addition of our in-depth city guides, handy map guides, and extensive coverage of Asia and Australia, the 90s are also proving to be a time of explosive growth for Let's Go, and there's certainly no end in sight. The first editions of *Let's Go: Australia* and *Let's Go: New Zealand* hit the shelves this year, expanding our coverage to six continents, and research for next year's series has already begun.

We've seen a lot in 38 years. *Let's Go: Europe* is now the world's bestselling international guide, translated into seven languages. And our new guides bring Let's Go's total number of titles, with their spirit of adventure and their reputation for honesty, accuracy, and editorial integrity, to 40. But some things never change: our guides are still researched, written, and produced entirely by students who know first-hand how to see the world on the cheap.

HOW WE DO IT

Each guide is completely revised and thoroughly updated every year by a well-traveled set of over 200 students. Every winter, we recruit over 140 researchers and 60 editors to write the books anew. After several months of training, Researcher-Writers hit the road for seven weeks of exploration, from Anchorage to Adelaide, Estonia to El Salvador, Iceland to Indonesia. Hired for their rare combination of budget travel sense, writing ability, stamina, and courage, these adventurous travelers know that train strikes, stolen luggage, food poisoning, and marriage proposals are all part of a day's work. Back at our offices, editors work from spring to fall, massaging copy written on Himalayan bus rides into witty yet informative prose. A student staff of typesetters, cartographers, publicists, and managers keeps our lively team together. In September, the collected efforts of the summer are delivered to our printer, who turns them into books in record time, so that you have the most up-to-date information available for your vacation. And even as you read this, work on next year's editions is well underway.

WHY WE DO IT

We don't think of budget travel as the last recourse of the destitute; we believe that it's the only way to travel. Living cheaply and simply brings you closer to the people and places you've been saving up to visit. Our books will ease your anxieties and answer your questions about the basics—so you can get off the beaten track and explore. Once you learn the ropes, we encourage you to put *Let's Go* down now and then to strike out on your own. As any seasoned traveler will tell you, the best discoveries are often those you make yourself. When you find something worth sharing, drop us a line. We're Let's Go Publications, 67 Mount Auburn Street, Cambridge, MA 02138, USA (email fanmail@letsgo.com).

HAPPY TRAVELS!

BEST AIRLINE TO THE MIDDLE EAST:
1. **El Al**
2. British Airways
3. TWA
4. Lufthansa
5. Swissair

1992

BEST AIRLINE TO THE MIDDLE EAST:
1. **El Al**
2. British Airways
3. TWA
4. Lufthansa
5. Swissair

1993

BEST AIRLINE TO THE MIDDLE EAST:
1. **El Al**
2. British Airways
3. TWA
4. Lufthansa
5. Swissair

1994

BEST AIRLINE TO THE MIDDLE EAST:
1. British Airways
2. **El Al**
3. TWA
4. Lufthansa/Gulf Air/Swissair
5. Emirates

1995

BEST AIRLINE TO THE MIDDLE EAST:
1. **El Al**
2. British Airways
3. TWA
4. Emirates
5. Lufthansa

1996

Hey, nobody's perfect.

It's not just an airline. It's Israel.

Contents

About Let's Go v
Let's Go Picks ix
Maps xi
Acknowledgments xiii
Researcher-Writers xv
How to Use This Book xvi

ESSENTIALS 1

Planning Your Trip 2
Getting There 37
Once There 41
Introduction to the Region 46

EGYPT 71

Once There 72
Life and Times 80

Cairo **86**
Pyramids at Giza 132

Mediterranean Coast **148**
Alexandria 148
West of Alexandria 163

Nile Valley **175**
Luxor 179
Aswan 203

Western Desert Oases **215**

Suez Canal **230**

Red Sea Coast **237**
Hurghada 239

Sinai **245**

ISRAEL 267

Once There 267
Life and Times 273

Jerusalem **278**

Tel Aviv-Jaffa **321**
Near Tel Aviv 338

Mediterranean Coast **343**
Haifa 351

Galilee **374**
Nazareth 374
Tiberias 379
Tzfat (Safed) 389

Golan Heights **400**

The Negev **406**
The Dead Sea 406
Central Negev 414
Eilat 428

WEST BANK 438

Once There 438
Life and Times 441
Bethlehem   444
Jericho 450

JORDAN 457

Once There 457
Life and Times 463
Amman   467
Near Amman 480
South of Amman   485
Petra 492
Aqaba 498
North of Amman   505
Jerash 505

SYRIA 513

Once There 513
Life and Times 517
Damascus   521
Northwest Syria   531
Palmyra 531
Aleppo 540

LEBANON 549

Once There 549
Life and Times 552
Beirut   557
Beit ed Din 564
Jeita Grotto 565
Tripoli 565
Near Tripoli 567
Saida (Sidon) 568
Sur (Tyre) 569
Baalbeck 569

APPENDIX 571

Holidays and Festivals 571
Climate 572
Time Zones 573
Measurements 573
Telephone Codes 573
Arabic 574
Phrasebook 575
Hebrew 577
Phrasebook 577

INDEX 581

Let's Go Picks

From the halls of Tutankhamun, to the shores of Tripoli; if we weren't typing Let's Go Picks, this is where we'd be:

Natural Favorites: The most spectacular sunrises in the world can be seen from the top of **Mount Sinai**; believe it or not, the pilgrim hordes make the scene more enjoyable—after their rented camels parade up the mountain, they gently serenade the coming of the sun (p. 251). Frolicking with the **dolphin** in **Nuweiba'** is a magically life-changing experience, and not nearly as cheesy as it sounds (p. 263). All visitors to **Wadi Rum** are impressed by the grandeur of the monumental rock formations, but desert overnighters become stunned by the echoing sound of silence (p. 503).

Food, Glorious Food: Nine thousand years of culinary evolution have created some pretty good eats. Everyone loves the *fuul* at **Muhammad Ahmed Fuul** in Alexandria, and for good reason—it's simply the best (p. 156). Get your kicks with some creamy licks at **El 'Abd**—at 3 cool scoops for E£1.50, it's a budget traveler's ice cream dream (p. 128). **Aswan Panorama** is the best of the Nile's legendary floating restaurants—its spiced Bedouin tea, served on hot coals, is the little-known eighth wonder of the world (p. 207). If you're tired of the same old thing, the **fried sloth** in Aqaba is always something to write home about (p. 502).

Stay Hydrated...Drink More: Everyone likes to kick back and relax; everyone likes to kick off their shoes and boogie down. **The Cellar** jazz bar in Amman is a hip 'n' mellow place to hear some of the best tunes this side of New Orleans (p. 479). Need to wash those socks, but don't want to give up an evening? Practical partiers head to **The Embassy** in Tel Aviv, where you can fill the dryer with shekels and the mouth with beer (p. 335). Beirut's **Orange Mechanique** is the Levant's hottest club and one of the few that tend to attract gay patrons; spinning a melange of New York techno, acid jazz, and rave, the dance floor gets lit on fire by one professional dancer after another (p. 562). Can you keep up?

I Think I'm Seeing Things: The train from **Nahariya** (p. 369) to **Tel Aviv** (p. 321) runs south along Israel's Mediterranean Coast, lulling riders with beautiful watery views and the train's smooth chugging. On a clear day, you can see **Gibraltar**. **Qal'at Ibn Maan** (p. 534) in Palmyra, Syria, is perched on a hill that affords unsurpassed views of the ruins at sunset. If you're lucky enough to get caught in one of the area's periodic desert rainstorms, rainbows stretch from horizon to horizon as the clouds disperse. The world's best views from a toilet seat are in **Petra's bathrooms** (p. 496). Windows from the stalls overlook the rose-red ruins and will make you want to take your time.

The Best of the Alternative Lifestyles: Crossroads of civilization, birthplace of culture: the Middle East is still finding new ways to do things. One man's garbage is another man's palatial residence at the astounding **Hermit's House** in Herzliya (p. 344). The peaceful village of **Dimona** is home to the Hebrew Israelite Community, a unique sect of Jewish, African-ex-American vegans, and their fascinating cultural and artistic innovations (p. 421). The **Basata** camp ("Basata" is Arabic for "simplicity"), on the Gulf of Aqaba Coast, combines a family atmosphere with ecological friendliness and trusting hospitality (p. 265). Still not satisfied? Follow in the footsteps of Eli Avivi, and form your own country—a visit to **Akhzibland** will put ideas in your head and a stamp in your passport (p. 371).

Maps

Eastern Mediterranean 1
Egypt 71
Cairo 88-89
Downtown Cairo 91
Islamic Cairo 93
Cairo Environs 133
Giza 135
Alexandria 149
Marsa Matrouh 167
Nile Valley (Lower and Upper) 177
Luxor 181
Karnak 187
Aswan 203
Port Said 231
Suez and Port Tewfik 237
Hurghada 241
Sinai 247
Israel and the West Bank 269
Jerusalem 280-281
Jerusalem Old City 285
Tel Aviv 323
Jaffa (Yafo) 337
Haifa 353
Akko (Acre) 365
Galilee 375
Nazareth 377
Tiberias 381
Sea of Galilee 387
Tzfat 391
The Negev 407
Masada 413
Be'er Sheva 415
Eilat 429
Central Israel & the West Bank 439
Bethlehem 445
Jericho 451
Jordan 459
Amman 469
Petra 491
Aqaba 499
Syria 515
Damascus and Surrounding Area 522-523
Palmyra 533
Aleppo 541
Lebanon 551
Beirut 558-559
Hamra District 561

Acknowledgments

I&E thanks best-ever-ME Kate for loving guidance and tireless text-tweaking; Jake for keeping a concerned eye out; Sarah & Map Men for Viae Dolorosae. *Shukran* to the Nite Train: Katie, Little Clint, Ian, Rachel, and Derek. Expats always welcome at Club I&E: Nick (for SOS), Bede (thanks for waking up for SOS), Amir, and Lukie. "No one belongs here more than you." Måns and Alex, thanks for sharing. Thanks to Krzys for the camel, and to the whole office for the last-minute proofing *blitzkreig*.—I&E

To Adam, my creative partner in crime, for the backrubs, flips, and other inspiration: to Jenny, for "hitting the floor" in between long, in-depth bouts with text, and for adding her unique spirit to my life. I'll miss our chemistry. To Katie for guerilla interview tactics. To my family and friends in Lebanon for your caring and assistance. Jon & Karen sustained me, Chris & Nate listened, and Christine ventured to the edge. Couldn't have done it without Tabasco. To Hayat, Joe, and Puff, thank you for being my fountain of love. To Seth for understanding, friendship, and snugglefish.—TLW

Taya: a giving reservoir of intelligence, energy, humor, and head-scratching. Jenny: a good friend, an astoundingly dedicated worker, and a completely insane professional dancer. Nick—we'll always have Palm Beach. *A los dos cititos*, SF & NJ; to new friends. Corman and the Cewgrz, format office hours, and Getz/Gilberto. NYC for a great birthday. Dan for his sensitivity; Sonesh for his humor. Danny, Mike, and the folks at PSWD—thanks for continuing to always be there. My aunts, uncles, cousins, and the rest of the lovable, playful clan. Grandma and Grandpa for love and support. Bea & David for their love of life & for looking after me. Mom, Dad, Elana—the love, stability, and memories you've given me have made my life. I love you.—ABS

Thank you, Taya, not my sister but fearless leader; Adam, font of creativity and voice of reason; Kate for constant kindness; to Nick, Bede, Luke, and all who gave me hospitality and/or stability. Thank you, FAP, for food, company, and housing; Raleigh, N.C. *Money Magazine*'s 1994 Best Place to Live in America. Lonne, I wish you could have been here with me. To my parents, practically perfect in every way. And to the men and women of *Let's Go* for a sweet opportunity and a smooth cruise.—JRW

Editor	Taya Lynn Weiss
Associate Editor	Adam Benjamin Stein
Assistant Editor	Jennifer R. Weiss
Managing Editor	Kate Galbraith
Publishing Director	John R. Brooks
Production Manager	Melanie Quintana Kansil
Associate Production Manager	David Collins
Cartography Manager	Sara K. Smith
Editorial Manager	Melissa M. Reyen
Editorial Manager	Emily J. Stebbins
Financial Manager	Krzysztof Owerkowicz
Personnel Manager	Andrew E. Nieland
Publicity Manager	Nicholas Corman
Publicity Manager	Kate Galbraith
New Media Manager	Daniel O. Williams
Associate Cartographer	Joseph E. Reagan
Associate Cartographer	Luke Z. Fenchel
Office Coordinators	Emily Bowen, Chuck Kapelke
	Laurie Santos
Director of Advertising Sales	Todd L. Glaskin
Senior Sales Executives	Matthew R. Hillery, Joseph W. Lind
	Peter J. Zakowich, Jr.
President	Amit Tiwari
General Manager	Richard Olken
Assistant General Manager	Anne E. Chisholm

Researcher-Writers

Leah Altman   *Tel Aviv, Israeli Mediterranean Coast, Golan, Galilee*
Leah revealed Israel's many personalities with magical wit and an incurable habit of
finding adventure in unlikely places. She experimented with excess in Tel Aviv, got
mystical in Tzfat, befriended the Hermit, and separated the *shishlik* from the chaff in
the north's tiny towns. Leah's whimsical turn-of-phrase and insightful insiders' tips
made her copy almost as exciting as her adventures. Whether mastering the public
transportation system or fending off sassy *sabras*, it is clear to us that trendy Sheinkin
and environs have never seen anything better.

Peter Currie   *Cairo and environs, Alexandria, Mediterranean Coast, Siwa*
Peter was an unstoppable research turbo-engine. Dodging Cairo traffic at all hours in
search of local haunts, he was determined not to rest until he found the best *fuul*
joints, sweetest *sheesha* smokes, and jazziest jazzercise studios the cities have to
offer. Peter's determination breezed him through Cairo's ancient sprawl and Siwa's
ancient calm with equal ease; his immaculately detailed prose and unflagging attention to detail left no grain of sand unturned.

Waqaas Fahmawi   *Jordan, Syria, Lebanon*
No stranger to the international jet-setting scene, Waqaas blazed an unforgettable trail
through Jordan and Syria, surviving it all to report in on skyrocketing *bakhsheesh*
rates and how best to bargain them down. Days after the U.S. travel ban to Lebanon
was lifted, our faithful correspondent was on a flight to Beirut, with an impossible
itinerary in hand—in one outstanding night, Waqaas hit every club in and around Lebanon's capital city (next day, Tripoli!). His nuanced nightlife write-ups made already
colorful copy groove to the beat of the Levant's undiscovered, underground party.

Richard Knapp   *Suez Canal, Sinai Peninsula, Eilat, Aqaba*
When he could get through on the phone, Rich's effusive and confident voice was an
spellbinding source of traveler's tales. A true backpacker and a dedicated outdoors-
man, Rich made us itch to strap on our hiking boots and start saving those reefs. We
had always expected Rich to find us a Gulf-full of natural gems, but we didn't realize
that when he turned his perceptive eye towards the oh-so-hip southern cities that
things would click so well. He ate his way through Hurghada, crossed borders with a
smile, and trekked to places that the tourist officials had never heard of...advanced
seekers of obscure places, beware.

Willow Lawson   *Nile Valley, Western Desert Oases*
A degree in archaeology and a personal collection of Pyramids paraphernalia (including the inevitable pop-up book or two) finally landed Willow in her spiritual home.
Soaked with fascinating detail and dripping sweat, her copy overhauled our coverage
of Egypt's ancient sites, Osiris bless her heart. On the road, she talked her way into
current digging projects, casually hobnobbed with heavyweight dealers at the Daraw
camel market, and laughed in Michael Jackson's face. Willow loved Egypt and Egypt
loved her—so did we.

Sharmila Sohoni   *Negev Desert, Jerusalem, West Bank, Galilee*
You might have heard of Sharmila—everyone else traveling through the Middle East
has. Sharp-sighted and with a puckish passion for perfect wordplay, she charmed
everyone she met (and she met everyone). A nightclub *masseuse,* a famous photogra-
pher, and the Indian ambassador to Israel all tried to make her acquaintance. Sharmila's real attachment, though, was to Jerusalem; her sensitivity to detail, her
effervescent prose, and her constant craving for internet access improved our book
wherever she set her pen. Braving both the West Bank and the Arizona with confidence and natural narrative insight, Sharmie never let us down.

How to Use This Book

A good guidebook is like a good camel. Both of them should go where you want to go, but both can lead when you're not quite sure where you're going. A guidebook should be intelligent, dependable, and reliably up-to-date; a camel should be intelligent, dependable, and able to hold lots of water. Both are always a delightful shade of yellow.

Let's Go is very excited about this new edition. We've added twelve new maps and expanded coverage in every country to bring you more of those out-of-the-way gems *Let's Go* is famous for. This book also has the most recent coverage of **Lebanon,** completed shortly after the U.S. travel ban was lifted. As always, our researchers scoured the region, checking every price and phone number and keeping us up to date on the hottest spots, best deals, and most spectacular sights. Our history section keeps you informed about **This Year's News,** always important to travelers in the Middle East. For millennia, the area between the Nile and the Euphrates has been a crossroads of cultures, and we demystify those pesky border crossings so you too can follow in the footsteps of the Greeks and the Mamluks. We've even expanded special shopping sections in Cairo and Jerusalem and filled them with tips that will help you bargain like a pro. This is no decrepit, flea-bitten camel you're riding.

Before we travel the Middle East with you, let's show you around the book. The **Essentials** section is full of the details that everyone needs for a successful trip; we share our thoughts on when to go, how to get a cheap flight, the best places to study abroad, and what to do when you get diarrhea. This is the section where we list resources for senior citizens, women traveling alone, gay and lesbian travelers, travelers with small children, and others who might have **special concerns.** The second part of the Essentials section is the **Introduction to the Region,** where we describe the 9000 years of religion and history that have enriched the Middle East.

After the Essentials section, this camel gets serious. We start with **Egypt** and proceed roughly northeast, cycling counter-clockwise through **Israel,** the **West Bank, Jordan, Syria,** and **Lebanon.** Handy black tabs mark the edge of each page for easy browsing and quick reference. Each country begins with its own useful Essentials section, followed by **Life and Times,** which is chock-full of cultural tidbits about the government, arts, history, and food of the place you'll be visiting. After that, each country's coverage begins with the capital city and radiates outward.

Orientation sections help the maps help you to get your bearings in a strange place. Look to the **Practical Information** section for…well…practical information—things like emergency phone numbers, currency exchange, internet access, and late-night pharmacies. Camels retain such pragmatic details in their humps as well as they hold water. **Accommodations** and **Food** sections come next—these listings have been ranked in order of preference by our researchers. The low-down on the city's **Sights** follows, and in **Entertainment,** we let you know the best places to kick back for a drink or take in a symphony. Don't neglect the back of the book, because the **Appendix** can tell you when Ramadan starts or how to say "I'm not a dumb tourist" in Arabic (*Ana mish khawaga*).

Camels are infallible; guidebooks aren't. Please write to us and let us know what you think. Enjoy the book, but enjoy your adventures more.

A NOTE TO OUR READERS

The information for this book is gathered by *Let's Go*'s researchers from late May through August. Each listing is derived from the assigned researcher's opinion based upon his or her visit at a particular time. The opinions are expressed in a candid and forthright manner. Other travelers might disagree. Those traveling at a different time may have different experiences since prices, dates, hours, and conditions are always subject to change. You are urged to check beforehand to avoid inconvenience and surprises. Travel always involves a certain degree of risk, especially in low-cost areas. When traveling, especially on a budget, always take particular care to ensure your safety.

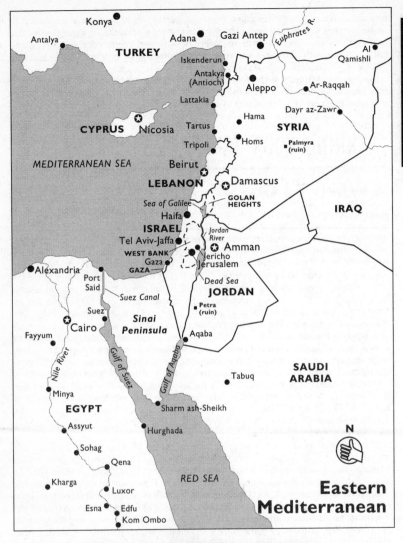

Eastern
Mediterranean

ESSENTIALS

This guide covers one of the world's most fascinating regions. Written alphabets began here, monotheism developed into three dynamic faiths, and people engineered massive constructions that continue to astound and mystify visitors 3000 years later. Ancient civilizations came, conquered, and were conquered, leaving behind records of human achievement that still remain undiscovered. The region is dotted with *tel*s, a word used in both Arabic and Hebrew to denote a hill formed by level after level of habitation. These physical reminders of the passage of time often contain more than a dozen different layers of civilization. In Israel, Egypt, Jordan, Syria, Lebanon, and the West Bank, 20th-century apartments mingle with 12th-cen-

1

ESSENTIALS

tury monasteries, and stones taken from thousand-year-old ruins pave the streets of modern cities. The natural backdrop for this history is remarkable: eerie deserts dotted with verdant oases, flourishing groves of olive and citrus trees, mountains and hills carpeted with pine trees and traversed by streams, moonscaped caves and canyons, and psychedelic underwater worlds.

No less awe-inspiring is the tradition of Middle Eastern hospitality. Although you may gape at the region's natural and historical beauty, your most powerful memories will most likely be of a shared cup of coffee with a vendor in a *souq* or a spirited discussion with a gregarious bus driver.

PLANNING YOUR TRIP

■ When To Go

HOLIDAYS

Arrange your itinerary with an awareness of **holidays** (for a comprehensive listing of religious and national holidays for Israel, Egypt, Jordan, Syria, and Lebanon see the **Appendix,** p. 571). In Muslim countries, many businesses are closed on Friday, the day of prayer. On holidays, they may close during the afternoon, but are generally open in the morning. Holiday dates are difficult to pin down ahead of time, as Islamic holidays are based on a lunar calendar. Approximate dates for 1998 follow: **Ras as-Sana** (Apr. 28) is the Islamic New Year's Day, and **Mawlid an-Nabi** (July 7) celebrates Muhammad's birthday. The most important event and the one most likely to complicate travel is **Ramadan** (Dec. 31, 1997 to Jan. 30, 1998), the annual month-long fast during which Muslims abstain from food and drink, dawn to sunset. During this time, most restaurants close up shop until sundown. Shops may open for a few hours in the morning and a short time after *iftar*, the breaking of the fast; government services are either closed entirely or open only in the morning. It would be rude to eat in public at this time. The celebratory, three-day **'Eid al-Fitr** (Jan. 30) feast marks the end of Ramadan. **'Eid al-Adha** (Apr. 8), commemorates Abraham's intended sacrifice of his son Ishmael and coincides with the *hajj* (pilgrimage) to Mecca, the fifth pillar of Islam (see **Islam,** p. 66 for more detail).

In Israel, most businesses close Friday afternoon for **Shabbat,** the Jewish sabbath, and reopen at sundown on Saturday. They also close for Jewish holy days, which begin at sunset on the previous day. 1998 dates follow: **Pesaḥ,** or Passover (April 11-17), celebrates the exodus of the Jews from Egypt. Observant Jews refrain from eating bread and pastries; products made with regular flour and leavening agents may be hard to come by in Jewish areas. **Shavu'ot** (May 31) celebrates the giving of the Torah. **Rosh Ha-Shana** (the Jewish New Year; Sept. 21-22) is only slightly less holy than **Yom Kippur** (Sept. 30), the holiest day of the Jewish calendar; observant Jews fast in atonement for their sins and Israel shuts down entirely. **Sukkot** (Oct. 5-11), the festival of the harvest, commemorates the Israelites' wilderness wanderings and culminates with **Simḥat Torah** on October 12.

Secular Israeli holidays include **Yom Ha-Sho'ah** (Holocaust Day, April 22), **Yom Ha-Zikaron** (Memorial Day, April 29), and **Yom Ha'Atzma'ut** (Independence Day, April 30). On both *Yom Ha-Sho'ah* and *Yom Ha-Zikaron,* sirens signal moments of silence. Refer to the **Appendix** for more holidays and dates. Israel also has a plethora of cultural festivals. The **Israel Festival** takes place in Jerusalem (May-June), followed by the **Jerusalem Film Festival** (later in June). Other noteworthy events include the rocking **Hebrew Music Festival** in Arad (mid-July), attracting mostly young crowds and the internationally acclaimed **Jazz in the Red Sea** festival in Eilat (late Aug.).

In addition to holidays, it would be wise to think about when everyone else in the region is vacationing. Egypt's high and low seasons depend partly on the region: Cairo is a year-round mob scene, while summertime is partytime in Alexandria and on the Mediterranean and Red Sea Beaches. In the Sinai, Oases, and Upper Egypt, reasonable temperatures make winter the high season, especially for wealthier tourists, but younger travelers revel in summertime bargains. North Americans and students favor summer for visiting Israel and the West Bank; Europeans prefer winter. Jordan's peak seasons are spring and autumn, while Syria and Lebanon receive many visitors in the summer. If you can stand the climate, off-season travel means smaller crowds, lower prices, and greater local hospitality, not to mention more falafel.

CLIMATE

In southern **Egypt,** summer temperatures often reach 49°C (120°F) and can push 54°C (129°F). Fortunately, it's dry—your body's cooling system should know what to do. Winter is perfect. In arid Cairo, pollution makes summer afternoons hellish. Alexandria is temperate year-round, but the humidity might wilt your new papyrus. The Red Sea coast is comfortably warm in winter and hot but dry in summer; higher elevations in the Sinai can be freezing in winter and on summer nights.

In **Israel,** the coastal plain is a sweaty steambath in summer. Cacti love Eilat and the Jordan Valley, where it's mild in winter and hot and dry (except on the humid Dead Sea) in summer. The Negev Desert is not as hot; it has cool nights that actually qualify as cold. Summer in Jerusalem is hot and dry with mild evenings; winter is crisp and cool, but occasionally rainy and even snowy. The landlocked, hilly **West Bank** is spared the summer humidity of the Mediterranean coast, but not the heat. Summer afternoons blister; mild nights invite long walks. Winters can be cold, rainy, and sometimes snowy.

Most attractions in **Jordan** are in the mountain region, where summer days could melt a cheap wig but evenings are deliciously cool. Winters are cold, with frequent rain. Aqaba enjoys balmy winter weather. **Syria** and **Lebanon** have widely varying Mediterranean climates: semi-arid, with sunny days and cool nights. Refer to the **Appendix** (p. 572) for a chart of average temperatures and rainfall for major Middle Eastern cities.

■ Useful Information

TOURIST AND INFORMATION OFFICES

Egyptian Tourist Authority: Canada: 1253 McGill College Ave. #250, Montreal, Que. H3B 2Y5 (tel. (514) 861-4420; fax 861-8071). **U.K.:** 170 Piccadilly, London W1V 9DD (tel. (0171) 493 52 82 or 83; fax 408 02 95). **U.S.:** 630 5th Ave. #1706, New York, NY 10111 (tel. (212) 332-2570; fax 956-6439); Wilshire San Vicente Plaza, 83-83 Wilshire Blvd. #215, Beverly Hills, CA 90211 (tel. (213) 653-8815; fax 653-8961); 645 N. Michigan Ave. #829, Chicago, IL 60611 (tel. (312) 280-4666; fax 280-4788).

Israel Government Tourist Office (IGTO): Australia: Tourism Department, 395 New South Head Road, Double Bay, Sydney, N.S.W. 2028 (tel (02) 9326 1700; fax 9326 1676). **Canada:** 180 Bloor St. W #700, Toronto, Ont. M5S 2V6 (tel. (416) 964-3784; fax 961-3962). **South Africa:** Nedbank Gardens 5th floor, 33 Bath Ave., Rosebank P.O. Box 52560, Saxonwold 2132, Johannesburg (tel. (11) 788 1700; fax 447 3104). **U.K.:** 18 Great Marlborough St., London W1V 1AF (tel. (0171) 434 36 51; fax 437 05 27). **U.S.:** 800 2nd Ave., New York, NY 10117 (tel. (212) 499-5600 or (800) 596-1199; fax 499-5645); 6380 Wilshire Blvd. #1718, Los Angeles, CA 90048 (tel. (213) 658-6543; fax 658-7462/3); other offices in Chicago and Dallas.

Jordan Information Bureau: Canada: 100 Bronson Ave. #701, Ottawa K1R 6G8 (tel (613) 238-8090; fax 232-3341). **U.K.:** 11/12 Buckingham Gate, London SW1E 6LB (tel. (0171) 630 92 77; fax 937 87 95). **U.S.:** 2319 Wyoming Ave. NW, Washington, D.C. 20008 (tel. (202) 265-1606; fax 667-0777).

Palestinian Embassies and Information Offices: Australia: Office 27, State Circle, Deakin ACT 2600, P.O. Box 646, Kingston ACT 2604 (tel. (02) 6273 3711; fax 6273 3903). **U.K.:** 5 Galena Rd. Hammersmith, London W6OLT (tel. (0181) 563 00 08;

fax 563 0058). **U.S.:** 1730 K St. NW #1004, Washington, D.C. 20006 (tel. (202) 785-8394; fax 887-5337).

TRAVEL ORGANIZATIONS

Council on International Educational Exchange (CIEE), 205 East 42nd St., New York, NY 10017-5706 (tel. (888)-COUNCIL (268-6245); fax (212) 822-2699; http://www.ciee.org). A private, not-for-profit organization; administers work, volunteer, academic, internship, and professional programs around the world. Offers identity cards, (including the ISIC and the GO25) and a range of publications, among them the useful magazine *Student Travels* (free). Call or write for further information.

Federation of International Youth Travel Organizations (FIYTO), Bredgade 25H, DK-1260 Copenhagen K, Denmark (tel. (45) 33 33 96 00; fax 33 93 96 76; email mailbox@fiyto.org; http://www.fiyto.org). An international organization promoting educational, cultural and social travel for young people. Member organizations include language schools, educational travel companies, national tourist boards, accommodation centers and other suppliers of travel services to youth and students. FIYTO sponsors the GO25 Card (http://www.go25.org).

USEFUL PUBLICATIONS

Adventurous Traveler Bookstore, P.O. Box 1468, Williston, VT 05495 (tel. (801) 282-3963; fax 677-1821; email books@atbook.com; http://www.AdventurousTraveler.com). Free 40-page catalogue upon request; or browse the web site. Specializes in outdoor adventure travel books and maps.

Blue Guides, published in Britain by A&C Black Limited, 35 Bedford Row, London WC1R 4JH; in the U.S. by W.W. Norton & Co. Inc., 500 5th Ave., New York, NY 10110; in Canada by Penguin Books Canada Ltd., 10 Alcorn Ave., #300, Toronto, Ontario N4V 3B2. Invaluable, unmatched historical and cultural information as well as sight-seeing routes, maps, tourist information, and listings of pricey hotels.

Specialty Travel Index, 305 San Anselmo Ave., #313, San Anselmo, CA 94960 (tel. (415) 459-4900; fax 459-4974; email spectrav@ix.netcom.com; http://www.spectrav.com). Published twice yearly. Extensive listing of "off the beaten track" and specialty travel options. One copy US$6, one-year subscription (2 copies) US$10.

Travel Books & Language Center, Inc., 4931 Cordell Ave., Bethesda, MD 20814 (tel. (800) 220-2665; fax (301) 951-8546; email travelbks@aol.com). Sells over 75,000 items, including books, cassettes, atlases, dictionaries, and a wide range of specialty travel maps. Offers travel lectures, book signings, newsletter, and free comprehensive catalogue upon request.

INTERNET RESOURCES

Along with everything else in the 90s, budget travel is moving rapidly into the information age. There are a number of ways to access the **Internet.** Most popular are commercial internet providers, such as **America Online** (tel. (800) 827-6364) and **Compuserve** (tel. (800) 433-0389). Many employers and schools also offer gateways to the Internet, often at no cost (unlike the corporate providers above). The following web sites can be wonderful resources for researching and planning your travel dreams. Just make sure you don't forgo your travels for virtual visitations.

ArabNet (http://www.arab.net). An incredible resource for cultural, historical, and travel information on the countries of the Arab world.

The CIA World Factbook (http://www.odci.gov/cia/pubs.html). Lists country-specific vital statistics and some basic travel information. Check it out for an overview of a country's economy, or an explanation of their system of government.

Egypt has it All! (http://its-idsc.gov.eg/tourism), run by the Egyptian Tourist Authority. A glossy travel mag on Egypt. Pictures and information on all the major tourist sites and cities.

InfoTour (http://www.infotour.co.il). The Israel Ministry of Tourism's official page chock full of detailed information sorted by region.

Jordan Online (http://jordan-online.com). Information on recent news, upcoming cultural events, and links to other Jordan- and Arab-related sites.

Let's Go (http://letsgo.com). A spunky page with useful links and an entertaining researcher-writer "Job Simulator."

Rent-A-Wreck's Travel Links Page (http://www.rent-a-wreck.com/raw/travist.htm). An extensive list of additional browsing possibilities.

The United States State Department (http://travel.state.gov) lists current travel advisory warnings, publishes countries' consular fact sheets with information about health, safety, and general travel conditions, and disseminates updates on major terrorism concerns and threats to U.S. tourists.

■ Documents and Formalities

All applications should be filed several weeks or months in advance of your planned departure date. Remember that you are relying on inefficient government agencies to complete these transactions. Demand for passports is highest between January and August, so apply as early as possible. A backlog in processing can spoil your plans.

When you travel, always carry two or more forms of identification on your person, including at least one photo ID. A passport combined with a driver's license or birth certificate usually serves as adequate proof of your identity and citizenship. Many establishments, especially banks, require several IDs before cashing traveler's checks. Never carry all your forms of ID together, however; you risk being left entirely without ID or funds in case of theft or loss. If you plan an extended stay, register your passport with the nearest embassy or consulate.

EMBASSIES AND CONSULATES

Egypt: Australia (Consulate), 112 Glenn Moore, Paddington, Sydney NSW 2028 (tel. (02) 9362 3483; fax 9332 3288). **(Consulate),** 124 Exhibition St., 9th floor, Melbourne, Victoria 3000 (tel. (03) 9654 8634; fax 9650 8362). **Canada (Embassy),** 454 Laurier Ave. E, Ottawa, Ont. K1N 6R3 (tel. (613) 234-4931/5/8; fax 234-9347). **(Consulate),** 3754 1 Place Ville Marie #2617, Montreal, Que. H3H 1V6 (tel. (514) 866-8455). **U.K. (Embassy),** 12 Curzin St., London W1Y 6DD (tel. (0171) 499 2401; fax 355 3568). **(Consulate),** 2 Lowndes St., London SW1 X9ET (tel. (0171) 235 9777). **U.S. (Embassy),** 3521 International Court NW, Washington, D.C. 20008 (tel. (202) 895-5400; fax 244-4319). **(Consulate),** 1110 2nd Ave., #201, New York, NY 10022 (tel. (212) 759-7120/1/2; fax 308-7643). **(Consulate),** 3001 Pacific Ave., San Francisco, CA 94115 (tel. (415) 346-9700; fax 346-9480). More offices in other cities.

Israel: Australia (Embassy), 6 Turrana St., Yarralumla, Canberra ACT 2600 (tel. (02) 6273 2045, 1309, or 1300; fax 6273 42 73). **(Consulate),** 37 York St., 6th floor, Sydney NSW 2000 (tel. (02) 9264 7933; fax 9290 2259). **Canada (Embassy),** 50 O'Connor St., #1005, Ottawa, Ont. K1P 6L2 (tel. (613) 567-6450, 6453, or 6455; fax 237-8865). **(Consulate),** 180 Bloor St., Toronto, Ont. M5S 2V6 (tel. (416) 961-1126; fax 961-7737). **New Zealand (Embassy),** D.B. Tower 111, Terrace, P.O. Box 2171, Wellington (tel. (04) 472 23 62 or 68; fax 499 06 32). **South Africa (Embassy),** 339 Hilda St., Dashing Center-Hatfield, Pretoria (tel. (12) 342 26 93 or 97; fax 342 14 42). **U.K. (Embassy),** 2 Palace Green, London W8 4QB (tel. (0171) 957 95 00; fax 957 95 55). **U.S. (Embassy),** 3514 International Drive NW, Washington, D.C. 20008 (tel. (202) 364-5500; fax 364-5423). **(Consulate),** 800 2nd Ave., New York, NY 10017 (tel. (212) 499-5400; fax 499-5425). **(Consulate),** 6380 Wilshire Blvd. #1700, Los Angeles, CA 90048 (tel. (213) 852-5500; fax 852-5555; email israelinfo@primenet.com). More offices in San Francisco, Miami, Atlanta, Chicago, New Orleans, Boston, Philadelphia, and others.

Jordan: Australia (Embassy), 20 Roebuck St., Red Hill ACT 2603, Canberra (tel. (02) 6295 9951; fax 6239 7236). **Canada (Embassy),** 100 Bronson Ave. #701, Ottawa, Ont. K1R 6G8 (tel. (613) 238-8090; fax 232-3341). **U.K. (Embassy,:** 6 Upper Philimore Gardens, London W8 7HB (tel. (0171) 937 36 85; fax 937 87 95). **U.S. (Embassy),** 3504 International Dr. NW, Washington, D.C. 20008 (tel. (202) 966-2664; fax 966-3110). **(Consulate),** 866 United Nations Plaza #554, New York, NY

10017 (tel. (212) 355-9342; fax 826-0830). **(Consulate),** P.O. Box 3727, Houston, TX 77253 (tel. (713) 224-2911).

Syria: U.K. (Embassy), 8 Belgrave Square, London, SW1 (tel. (0171) 245 90 12). **U.S. (Embassy),** 2215 Wyoming Ave. NW, Washington, D.C. 20008 (tel. (202) 232-6313; fax 234-9548). **(Consulate),** 820 2nd Ave., New York, NY 10017 (tel. (212) 661-1553).

Lebanon: Australia (Embassy), 27 Endeavour St., Red Hill ACT 2603, Canberra (tel. (02) 6295 7378; fax 6239 7024). **(Consulate),** Level 5-70 William St., Sydney NSW 2000. **Canada (Embassy),** 640 Lyons St. Ottawa, Ontario, K1S 3Z5 (tel. (613) 236-5825 or 5855; fax 232-1609). **South Africa (Consulate),** 16th Avenue, No. 7, Lower Houghton, Johannesburg 2198 (tel. (11) 483 11 06 or 07; fax 283 18 10). **U.K. (Embassy),** 21 Kensington Palace Gardens, London W.8 4QM (tel. (0171) 229 72 65 or 66; fax 243 16 99). **U.S. (Embassy),** 2560 28th St. NW, Washington, D.C. 20008 (tel. (202) 939-6300; fax 939-6324). **(Consulate),** 7060 Hollywood Blvd., Suite 510, Hollywood, CA 90028 (tel. (213) 467-1253; fax 467-2935). **(Consulate),** 9 East 76th St., New York, NY 10021 (tel. (212) 744-7905 or 7985; fax 794 1510).

ENTRANCE REQUIREMENTS

Citizens of Australia, Canada, Ireland, New Zealand, South Africa, the U.K., and the U.S. all need valid **passports** to enter all countries in this book and to re-enter their own country. Returning home with an expired passport is illegal, and may result in a fine. The countries covered in this book also require a **visa** (see below).

Upon entering a country, you must declare certain items from abroad and must pay a duty on the value of those articles that exceed the allowance established by that country's **customs** service. Keeping receipts for purchases made abroad will help establish values when you return. It is wise to make a list, including serial numbers, of any valuables that you carry with you from home; if you register this list with customs before your departure and have an official stamp it, you will avoid import duty charges and ensure an easy passage upon your return. Be especially careful to document items manufactured abroad.

When you enter any country, dress neatly and carry proof of your financial independence, such as a visa to the next country on your itinerary, an airplane ticket to depart, enough money to cover the cost of your living expenses, etc. Admission as a visitor does not include the right to work, which is authorized only by a **work permit.** Entering to study may require a special visa depending on the nature of the program, and immigration officers may also want to see proof of acceptance from a school as well as proof that you can support yourself.

PASSPORTS

Before you leave, photocopy the page of your passport that contains your photograph, passport number, and other identifying information. Carry one photocopy in a safe place apart from your passport, and leave another copy at home. These measures will help prove your citizenship and facilitate the issuing of a new passport if you lose the original document. Consulates also recommend that you carry an expired passport or an official copy of your birth certificate in a part of your baggage separate from other documents.

If you lose your passport, immediately notify the local police and the nearest embassy or consulate of your home government. To expedite its replacement, you will need to know all information previously recorded and show identification and proof of citizenship. A replacement may take weeks to process, and it may be valid only for a limited time. Some consulates can issue new passports within 24 hours if you give them proof of citizenship. Any visas stamped in your old passport will be irretrievably lost. In an emergency, ask for immediate temporary traveling papers that will permit you to reenter your home country.

Your passport is a public document belonging to your nation's government. You may have to surrender it to a foreign government official, but if you don't get it back in a reasonable amount of time, inform the nearest mission of your home country.

Australia Citizens must apply for a passport in person at a post office, a passport office, or an Australian diplomatic mission overseas. An appointment may be necessary. Passport offices are located in Adelaide, Brisbane, Canberra City, Darwin, Hobart, Melbourne, Newcastle, Perth, and Sydney. A parent may file an application for a child who is under 18 and unmarried. Adult passports cost AUS$126 (for a 32 page passport) or AUS$188 (64 page), and a child's is AUS$63 (32 page) or AUS$94 (64 page). For more info, call toll-free (in Australia) 13 12 32.

Canada Application forms in English and French are available at all passport offices, Canadian missions, many travel agencies, and Northern Stores in northern communities. Citizens may apply in person at any of 28 regional Passport Offices across Canada. Travel agents can direct applicants to the nearest location. Canadian citizens residing abroad should contact the nearest Canadian embassy or consulate. Children under 16 may be included on a parent's passport. Passports cost CDN$60, are valid for 5 years, and are not renewable. Processing takes approximately five business days for applications in-person; 10 days if by mail. For additional information, contact the **Canadian Passport Office,** Department of Foreign Affairs and International Trade, Ottawa, ON, K1A 0G3 (tel. (613) 994-3500; http://www.dfait-maeci.gc.ca/passport). Travelers may also call (800) 567-6868 (24hr.); in Toronto (416) 973-3251; in Vancouver (604) 775-6250; in Montreal (514) 283-2152. Refer to the booklet *Bon Voyage, But...,* free at any passport office or by calling InfoCentre at (800) 267-8376, for further help and a list of Canadian embassies and consulates abroad. You may also find entry and background information for various countries by contacting the Consular Affairs Bureau in Ottawa (tel. (800) 267-6788 (24hr.) or (613) 944-6788).

Ireland Citizens can apply for a passport by mail to either the **Department of Foreign Affairs,** Passport Office, Setanta Centre, Molesworth St., Dublin 2 (tel. (01) 671 1633), or the **Passport Office,** Irish Life Building, 1A South Mall, Cork (tel. (021) 272 525). Obtain an application at a local Garda station or request one from a passport office. The **Passport Express Service,** available through post offices, allows citizens to get a passport in 2 weeks for an extra IR£3. Passports cost IR£45 and are valid for 10 years. Citizens under 18 or over 65 can request a 3-year passport that costs IR£10.

New Zealand Application forms for passports are available in New Zealand from travel agents and Department of Internal Affairs Link Centres in the main cities and towns. Overseas, forms and passport services are provided by New Zealand embassies, high commissions, and consulates. Applications may also be forwarded to the **Passport Office,** P.O. Box 10526, Wellington, New Zealand. Standard processing time in New Zealand is 10 working days for correct applications. The fees are adult NZ$80, and child NZ$40. An urgent passport service is also available for an extra NZ$80. Different fees apply at overseas post: nine posts, including London, Sydney, and Los Angeles, offer both standard and urgent services (adult NZ$130, child NZ$65, plus NZ$130 if urgent). The fee at other posts is adult NZ$260, child NZ$195, and a passport will be issued within three working days. Children's names can no longer be endorsed on a parent's passport—they must apply for their own, valid for up to five years. An adult's passport is valid for up to 10 years.

South Africa Citizens can apply for a passport at any **Home Affairs Office** or **South African Mission.** Tourist passports, valid for 10 years, cost SAR80. Children under 16 must be issued their own passports, valid for 5 years, which cost SAR60. If a passport is needed in a hurry, an **emergency passport** may be issued for SAR50. An application for a permanent passport must accompany the emergency passport application. Time for the completion of an application is normally three months or more from the time of submission. Current passports less than 10 years old (counting from date of issuance) may be **renewed** until December 31, 1999; every citizen whose passport's validity does not extend far beyond this date is urged to renew it as soon as possible, to avoid the expected glut of applications as 2000 approaches. Renewal is free, and turnaround time is usually 2 weeks. For further information, contact the nearest Department of Home Affairs Office.

United Kingdom British citizens, British Dependent Territories citizens, British Nationals (overseas), and British Overseas citizens may apply for a **full passport,** valid for 10 years (5 years if under 16). Application forms are available at passport offices, main post offices, many travel agents, and branches of Lloyds Bank and Artac World Choice. Apply in person or by mail to one of the passport offices, located in London, Liverpool, Newport, Peterborough, Glasgow, or Belfast. The fee is UK£18. Children under 16 may be included on a parent's passport. Processing by mail usually takes four to six weeks. The London office offers same-day, walk-in rush service; arrive early. The formerly available **British Visitor's Passport** has been abolished; every traveler over 16 now needs a 10-year, standard passport. The **U.K. Passport Agency** can be reached by phone at (0990) 21 04 10, and information is available on the Internet at http://www.open.gov.uk/ukpass.

United States Citizens may apply for a passport at any federal or state **courthouse** or **post office** authorized to accept passport applications, or at a **U.S. Passport Agency,** located in Boston, Chicago, Honolulu, Houston, Los Angeles, Miami, New Orleans, New York, Philadelphia, San Francisco, Seattle, Stamford, or Washington, D.C. Refer to the "U.S. Government State Department" section of the telephone directory or the local post office for addresses. Parents must apply in person for children under age 13. You must apply in person if this is your first passport, if you're under age 18, or if your current passport is more than 12 years old or was issued before your 18th birthday. Passports are valid for 10 years (5 years if under 18) and cost US$65 (under 18 US$40). Passports may be **renewed** by mail or in person for US$55. Processing takes 3-4 weeks. **Rush service** is available for a surcharge of US$30 with proof of departure within 10 working days (e.g., an airplane ticket or itinerary), or for travelers leaving within three weeks who require visas. Given proof of citizenship, a U.S. embassy or consulate abroad can usually issue a new passport. Report a passport lost or stolen in the U.S. in writing to **Passport Services,** 1425 K St., N.W., U.S. Department of State, Washington D.C., 20524 or to the nearest passport agency. For more information, contact the U.S. Passport Information's **24-hour recorded message** (tel. (202) 647-0518). U.S. citizens may receive consular information sheets, travel warnings, and public announcements at any passport agency, U.S. embassy, or consulate, or by sending a self-addressed stamped envelope to: Overseas Citizens Services, Room 4811, Department of State, Washington, D.C. 20520-4818 (tel. (202) 647-5225; fax 647-3000). Additional information (including publications) about documents, formalities and travel abroad is available through the Bureau of Consular Affairs homepage at http://travel.state.gov or the State Department site at http://www.state.gov.

VISAS AND VISA EXTENSIONS

A **visa** is an endorsement that a foreign government stamps into a passport; it allows the bearer to stay in that country for a specified purpose and period of time. Cost and length-of-stay rules vary. For more information, send for *Foreign Entry Requirements* (US$0.50) from the **Consumer Information Center,** Department 363D, 18th and F St. NW, Room G-142, Washington, D.C. 20405 (tel. (719) 948-4000; http://www.pueblo.gsa.gov), or contact the **Center for International Business and Travel (CIBT),** 25 West 43rd St. #1420, New York, NY 10036 (tel. (800) 925-2428 or (212) 575-2811 from NYC), which secures visas for travel to and from all countries for a variable service charge. If you lose your visa overseas (via a stolen passport, for example), you must get a new one immediately to prove that you are allowed to be there; in Egypt, you will not be permitted to leave the country without a valid Egyptian visa. For a new Egyptian visa, go to the nearest passport office. In Israel, Jordan, and Syria, go to your embassy or consulate.

Visa extensions are normally granted for six months to one year in Egypt, Israel, Jordan, Syria, and Lebanon. Egyptian visa extensions are available in Cairo at the Mugamma' Building or at any passport office, Israeli visa extensions at offices of the Ministry of the Interior, Jordanian visa extensions at the Ministry of the Interior in Amman, Syrian visa extensions at any immigration office, and Lebanese visa extensions at local passport offices. To get an Egyptian visa extension, you must show evidence of having changed at least US$200 into Egyptian pounds..

> Until Syria, Lebanon, and Israel formalize a peace treaty (which could be a while), you will not be allowed to enter Syria or Lebanon if you have an Israeli stamp on your passport. See **Border Crossings,** p. 41.

Egypt Visas can be easily obtained in advance; apply by mail or in person at the nearest Egyptian embassy or consulate. Provide the application and 1) your passport, which must be valid at least six months from the date of issue of your visa; 2) a passport-sized photo; and 3) the fees in cash or a certified check (US$15 for U.S. citizens, more for others). If applying by mail, include a stamped, self-addressed, certified envelope and allow at least 10 days for delivery. If you apply in person the process takes one day. In case of emergencies, visas can be obtained at the airport in Cairo, and with some restrictions at the borders.

Visas are good for entry within six months of the date of issue, valid for one month, and easily extended. An Egyptian visa does not permit the holder to work. When applying, you can request a **multiple-entry visa** for travel in and out of Egypt, allowing you to reenter any number of times while the visa is valid. Visits to Sinai from Israel or Jordan can be made on a two-week **Sinai-only visa,** available at borders.

Israel Visitors' visas are free for U.S., Canadian, British, Irish, Australian, New Zealand, and South African citizens at the point of entry if your passport is valid for at least six months. These visas are valid for three months but are extendable (see below). **Study visas** can be obtained from an Israeli embassy or consulate prior to departure or from an Office of the Interior once in Israel. Show proof of acceptance at an educational institution, proof of sufficient funds, a medical statement, a travel document valid for two years, and two photos; if you are under the age of 18, you also need a letter indicating the consent of both parents. For temporary work in Israel, have your employer in Israel contact the Office of the Interior and arrange a **work visa** before you leave. Cruise ship passengers visiting Israel are issued **landing cards** allowing them to remain in the country as long as the ship is in port. **Collective visas** are issued by Israeli embassies or consulates for groups of five to 50 people.

Jordan Visas may be obtained upon arrival at Queen Alia Airport in Amman, or in person or by mail from any Jordanian embassy or consulate (can take up to five days). Requirements include a passport (valid for at least six months), a completed application form with one photo, and a self-addressed stamped envelope. Visas cost US$20 for U.S. citizens, and at least that for other nationalities. A **group visa** can be issued for tours of 10 persons or more, provided all have valid American passports. These are valid for one month and can be renewed at any police station.

Lebanon To obtain a visa application, send a letter of request to your nearest embassy or consulate, specifying length of stay and the reason for your trip. Completed visa applications must include two 2x2 notarized photos, money (US$20 for a single-entry visa; US$40 for multiple-entry), your passport, and a self-addressed stamped envelope. Since May 3, 1997, citizens of Australia, Canada, Ireland, the U.K., and the U.S. can conveniently obtain tourist visas at the Beirut airport, or at surface-entry border stations upon arrival in Lebanon; costs are the same. Travelers with passports that have an Israeli visa stamp will be refused entry.

Syria Visas must be obtained before arrival in the country. Applications are available from any Syrian embassy. Send two completed applications (not photocopied), your passport (without evidence of a trip to Israel), two signed photos, a self-addressed envelope stamped for US$2, and payment (by money order *only*) to the embassy. Six-month single-entry visas and three-month double-entry visas cost US$15; six-month multiple-entry visas cost US$30. They will return the passport with your tourist visa in it. You may also have luck applying at Syrian embassies in Egypt or Jordan (see **Cairo** and **Amman: Practical Information,** p. 99 and p. 471).

CUSTOMS: GOING HOME

Upon returning home, you must declare all articles you acquired abroad and pay a **duty** on the value that exceeds the allowance established by your country's customs service. Goods and gifts purchased at **duty-free** shops abroad are not exempt from duty or sales tax at your point of return; you must declare these items as well. "Duty-free" merely means that you pay no tax in the country of purchase.

Australia Citizens may import AUS$400 (under 18 AUS$200) of goods duty-free, in addition to 1.125L alcohol and 250 cigarettes or 250g tobacco. You must be over 18 to import alcohol or tobacco. There is no limit to the amount of Australian and/or foreign cash that may be brought into or taken out of the country, but amounts of AUS$10,000 or more, or the equivalent in foreign currency, must be reported. All foodstuffs and animal products must be declared on arrival. For information, contact the Regional Director, Australian Customs Service, GPO Box 8, Sydney NSW 2001 (tel. (02) 9213 2000; fax 9213 4000).

Canada Citizens who remain abroad for at least 1 week may bring back up to CDN$500 worth of goods duty-free any time. Citizens or residents who travel for a period between 48 hours and six days can bring back up to CDN$200. Both of these exemptions may include tobacco and alcohol. You are permitted to ship goods except tobacco and alcohol home under the CDN$500 exemption as long as you declare them when you arrive. Goods under the CDN$200 exemption, as well as all alcohol and tobacco, must be in your hand or checked luggage. Each citizen of legal age (which varies by province) may import up to 200 cigarettes, 50 cigars or cigarillos, 400g loose tobacco, 400 tobacco sticks, 1.14L wine or alcohol, and 24 355mL cans/bottles of beer; the value of these products is included in the CDN$200 or CDN$500. For more info, write to Canadian Customs, 2265 St. Laurent Blvd., Ottawa, Ont. K1G 4K3 (tel. (613) 993-0534), phone the 24-hour Automated Customs Information Service at (800) 461-9999, or visit Revenue Canada at http://www.revcan.ca.

Ireland Citizens must declare everything in excess of IR£142 (IR£73 per traveler under 15 years of age) obtained outside the EU or duty- and tax-free in the EU above the following allowances: 200 cigarettes, 100 cigarillos, 50 cigars, or 250g tobacco; 1L liquor or 2L wine; 2L still wine; 50g perfume; and 250mL toilet water. Goods obtained duty- and tax-paid in another EU country up to a value of IR£460 (IR£115 per traveler under 15) will not be subject to additional customs duties. Travelers under 17 may not import tobacco or alcohol. Contact The Revenue Commissioners, Dublin Castle (tel. (01) 679 27 77; fax 671 20 21; email taxes@iol.ie; http://www.revenue.ie) or The Collector of Customs and Excise, The Custom House, Dublin 1.

New Zealand Citizens may import up to NZ$700 worth of goods duty-free if they are intended for personal use or are unsolicited gifts. The concession is 200 cigarettes (1 carton), 250g tobacco, 50 cigars, or a combination of all three not to exceed 250g. You may also bring in 4.5L of beer or wine and 1.125L of liquor. Only travelers over 17 may import tobacco or alcohol. For more information, contact New Zealand Customs, 50 Anzac Ave., Box 29, Auckland (tel. (09) 377 35 20; fax 309 29 78).

South Africa Citizens may import duty-free: 400 cigarettes, 50 cigars, 250g tobacco, 2L wine, 1L of spirits, 250mL toilet water, 50mL perfume, and other consumable items up to a value of SAR500. Goods up to a value of SAR10,000 over and above this duty-free allowance are dutiable at 20%; such goods are also exempted from payment of VAT. Items acquired abroad and sent to the Republic as unaccompanied baggage do not qualify for any allowances. You may not export or import South African bank notes in excess of SAR2000. For more information, consult the free pamphlet *South African Customs Information,* available in airports or from the Commissioner for Customs and Excise, Private Bag X47, Pretoria 0001 (tel. (12) 314 99 11; fax 328 64 78).

United Kingdom Citizens or visitors arriving in the U.K. from outside the EU must declare goods in excess of the following allowances: 200 cigarettes, 100 cigarillos, 50 cigars, or 250g tobacco; still table wine (2L); strong liquors over 22% volume (1L), fortified or sparkling wine, or other liqueurs (2L); perfume (60 cc/mL); toilet water (250 cc/mL); and UK£136 worth of all other goods including gifts and souvenirs. You must be over 17 to import liquor or tobacco. These allowances also apply to duty-free purchases within the EU, except for the last category, other goods, which then has an allowance of UK£71. Goods obtained duty- and tax-paid for personal use (regulated according to set guide levels) within the EU do not require any further customs duty. For more information, contact Her Majesty's Customs and Excise, Custom House, Nettleton Road, Heathrow Airport, Hounslow, Middlesex TW6 2LA (tel. (0181) 910-3744; fax 910-3765).

United States Citizens may import US$400 worth of accompanying goods duty-free and must pay a 10% tax on the next US$1000. You must declare all purchases, so have sales slips ready. The US$400 personal exemption covers goods purchased for personal or household use (this includes gifts) and cannot include more than 100 cigars, 200 cigarettes (1 carton), and 1L of wine or liquor. You must be over 21 to bring liquor into the U.S. If you mail home personal goods of U.S. origin, you can avoid duty charges by marking the package "American goods returned." For more information, consult the brochure *Know Before You Go,* available from the U.S. Customs Service, Box 7407, Washington D.C. 20044 (tel. (202) 927-6724), or visit the Web (http://www.customs.ustreas.gov).

YOUTH, STUDENT, AND TEACHER IDENTIFICATION

The **International Student Identity Card (ISIC)** is the most widely accepted form of student identification. Flashing this card can procure you discounts for sights, theaters, museums, accommodations, meals, train, ferry, bus, and airplane transportation, and other services. Present the card wherever you go, and ask about discounts even when none are advertised. It also provides insurance benefits, including US$100 per day of in-hospital sickness for a maximum of 60 days, and US$3000 accident-related medical reimbursement for each accident (see **Insurance,** p. 22). In addition, cardholders have access to a toll-free 24-hour ISIC helpline whose multilingual staff can provide assistance in medical, legal, and financial emergencies overseas.

Many student travel agencies around the world issue ISICs, including STA Travel in Australia and New Zealand; Travel CUTS in Canada; USIT in Ireland and Northern Ireland; SASTS in South Africa; Campus Travel and STA Travel in the U.K.; Council Travel, Let's Go Travel, and STA Travel in the U.S.; and any of the other organizations under the auspices of the International Student Travel Confederation (ISTC). When you apply for the card, request a copy of the *International Student Identity Card Handbook,* which lists some of the available discounts in each country. You can also write to Council for a copy. The card is valid from September to December of the following year and costs US$19 or CDN$15. Applicants must be at least 12 years old and degree-seeking students of a secondary or post-secondary school. Because of the proliferation of phony ISICs, many airlines and some other services require other proof of student identity, such as a signed letter from the registrar attesting to your student status and stamped with the school seal or your school ID card. The US$20 **International Teacher Identity Card (ITIC)** offers the same insurance coverage, and similar but limited discounts. For more information on these cards, consult the organization's web site (http://www.istc.org; email isicinfo@istc.org).

Federation of International Youth Travel Organizations (FIYTO) issues a discount card to travelers who are under 26 but not students. Known as the **GO25 Card,** this one-year card offers many of the same benefits as the ISIC, and most organizations that sell the ISIC also sell the GO25 Card. A brochure that lists discounts is free when you purchase the card. To apply, you will need a passport, valid driver's license, or copy of a birth certificate; and a passport-sized photo with your name printed on the back. The fee is US$19, CDN$15, or UK£5. Information is available on the web at http://www.fiyto.org or http://www.go25.org, or by contacting Travel CUTS in Canada, STA Travel in the U.K., Council Travel in the U.S. (see **Budget Travel Services,** p. 37), or FIYTO headquarters in Denmark (see **Travel Organizations,** p. 4).

DRIVING PERMITS AND INSURANCE

An **International Driving Permit (IDP)** is honored for driving in Egypt, Israel, Jordan, Lebanon, and Syria. Your IDP, valid for one year, must be issued in your own country before you depart. An application for an IDP usually needs to be accompanied by one or two photos, a current local license, an additional form of identification, and a fee. **Australians** can obtain an IDP by contacting their local **Royal Automobile Club (RAC),** or the **National Royal Motorist Association (NRMA)** if in NSW or the ACT, where a permit can be obtained for AUS$12. **Canadian** license holders can obtain an IDP (CDN$10) through any **Canadian Automobile Association (CAA)** branch office in Canada, or by writing to CAA Central Ontario, 60 Commerce Valley Drive East, Thornhill, Ontario L3T 7P9 (tel. (416) 221-4300). Citizens of **Ireland** should drop by their nearest **Automobile Association (AA)** office where an IDP can be picked up for IR£4, or phone (01) 283 3555 for a postal application form. In **New Zealand,** contact your local **Automobile Association (AA),** or their main office at 99 Albert Street, PO Box 5, Auckland (tel. (09) 377 4660; fax 309 4564). IDPs cost NZ$8 plus NZ$2 for return postage. In **South Africa,** visit your local **Automobile Association of South Africa** office, where IDPs can be picked up for SAR25, or for more information phone (011) 466 6641, or write to P.O. Box 596, 2000 Johannesburg. In the **U.K.** IDPs are UK£4 and you can either visit your local AA Shop, or call (01256) 49 39 32 and order a postal application form (allow 2-3 weeks). **U.S.** license holders can obtain an IDP (US$10) at any **American Automobile Association (AAA)** office or by writing to AAA Florida, Travel Agency Services Department, 1000 AAA Drive (mail stop 28), Heathrow, FL 32746-5080 (tel. (407) 444-4245; fax 444-4247).

Most credit cards cover standard **insurance.** If you rent, lease, or borrow a car, you will need a **green card,** or **International Insurance Certificate,** to prove that you have liability insurance. Obtain it through your car rental agency, which should include coverage in its prices. If you lease a car, you can obtain a green card from the dealer; some travel agents also offer the card. Verify whether your auto insurance applies abroad; even if it does, you will still need a green card to certify this to foreign officials. If you have a collision abroad, the accident will appear on your domestic records if you report it to your insurance company.

■ Money

CURRENCY AND EXCHANGE

You can easily get by in most cities and towns in this book for less than US$40 per day. Ultra-budgeteers can travel through much of the region for less than US$10. No matter how low your budget, if you plan to travel for more than a couple of days, you will need to keep handy a larger amount of cash than usual. Carrying it around with you, even in a money belt, is risky; personal checks from home will probably not be acceptable no matter how many forms of identification you have.

It is cheaper to buy domestic currency than to buy foreign, so as a rule you should convert money after arriving at your destination. It's a good idea, however, to bring enough foreign currency to last for the first 24-72 hours of a trip, to avoid getting stuck with no money after banking hours or on a holiday.

Observe commission rates closely and check newspapers to get the standard rate of exchange. Often tourist offices, exchange kiosks, or black-market hole-in-the-walls offer the best rates. A good rule of thumb is to go to offices which only have a 5% margin between their buy and sell prices.

You may find it difficult to exchange your home currency abroad. If this is the case, it is a good idea to carry U.S. dollars instead. In many places, Western currency will actually be preferred to local, but throwing dollars around to gain preferential treatment labels you as a foreigner and may invite locals to jack prices up as much as tenfold or more. Even so, U.S. dollars are much easier to exchange than other currency.

TRAVELER'S CHECKS

Traveler's checks are one of the safest means of carrying funds, as they can be refunded if stolen. Several agencies and many banks sell them, usually for face value plus a small percentage commission. (Members of the American Automobile Association, and some banks and credit unions, can get American Express checks commission-free; for contact information see **Driving Permits and Insurance,** above). **American Express** and **Visa** are the most widely recognized, though other major checks are sold, exchanged, cashed, and refunded with almost equal ease. Keep in mind that in small towns, traveler's checks are less readily accepted than in cities with large tourist industries. If you're ordering your checks, do so well in advance, especially if large sums are being requested.

Each agency provides refunds if your checks are lost or stolen, and many provide additional services. (Note that you may need a police report verifying the loss or theft.) Inquire about toll-free refund hotlines in the countries you're visiting and emergency message relay services.

You should expect a fair amount of red tape and delay in the event of theft or loss of traveler's checks. To expedite the refund process, keep your check receipts separate from your checks and store them in a safe place or with a traveling companion, record check numbers when you cash them and leave a list of check numbers with someone at home, and ask for a list of refund centers when you buy your checks (American Express and Bank of America have over 40,000 centers worldwide). Never countersign your checks until you're prepared to cash them, and always bring your passport with you when you plan to use the checks.

Buying traveler's checks in the currency of the country you're visiting can be an exercise in futility in the Middle East. The most readily accepted checks are in U.S. dollars and British pounds; the German mark will sometimes be taken as well. Checks in other currencies won't get you very far—if the place will exchange it, you'll probably get a crummy rate. Be sure to keep cash on hand in less touristed regions.

American Express: Call (800) 25 19 02 in Australia; in New Zealand (0800) 44 10 68; in the U.K. (0800) 52 13 13; in the U.S. and Canada (800) 221-7282). Elsewhere, call the U.S. collect (801) 964-6665. American Express traveler's checks are now available in 10 currencies: Australian, British, Canadian, Dutch, French, German, Japanese, Saudi Arabian, Swiss, and U.S., and soon South African, but the US$ checks will be easiest to exchange abroad. They are the most recognized worldwide and the easiest to replace if lost or stolen. Checks can be purchased for a small fee (1-4%) at American Express Travel Service Offices, banks, and American Automobile Association offices (AAA members can buy the checks commission-free). Cardmembers can also purchase checks at American Express Dispensers at Travel Service Offices at airports and by ordering them via phone (tel. (800) ORDER-TC (673-3782)). American Express offices cash their checks commission-free (except where prohibited by national governments), although they often offer slightly worse rates than banks. You can also buy *Cheques for Two* which can be signed by either of two people travelling together. Request the American Express booklet "Traveler's Companion," which lists travel office addresses and stolen check hotlines for each European country. Visit their online travel offices (http://www.aexp.com).

Citicorp: Call (800) 645-6556 in the U.S. and Canada; in Europe, the Middle East, or Africa (44) 171 508 7007; from elsewhere call to the U.S. collect (813) 623-1709. Sells both Citicorp and Citicorp Visa traveler's checks in U.S., Australian, and Canadian dollars, British pounds, German marks, Spanish pesetas, and Japanese yen. Commission is 1-2% on check purchases. Checkholders are automatically enrolled for 45 days in the Travel Assist Program (hotline (800) 250-4377 or collect (202) 296-8728) which provides travellers with English-speaking doctor, lawyer, and interpreter referrals as well as check refund assistance and general travel information. Citicorp's World Courier Service guarantees hand-delivery of traveler's checks when a refund location is not convenient. Call 24hr. per day, 7 days per week.

Thomas Cook MasterCard: For 24hr. cashing or refund assistance, call (800) 223-9920 in the U.S. and Canada; elsewhere call U.S. collect (609) 987-7300; from the U.K. call (0800) 622 101 free or (1733) 502 995 collect or (1733) 318 950 collect. Offers checks in U.S., Canadian, and Australian dollars, British and Cypriot pounds, French and Swiss francs, German marks, Japanese yen, Dutch guilders, Spanish pesetas, South African rand, and ECUs. Commission 1-2% for purchases. Thomas Cook offices may sell checks for lower commissions and will cash checks commission-free. Thomas Cook MasterCard Traveler's Checks are also available from **Capital Foreign Exchange** (see **Currency and Exchange**) in U.S. or Canadian dollars, French and Swiss francs, British pounds, and German marks.

Visa: Call (800) 227-6811 in the U.S.; in the U.K. (0800) 895 492; from anywhere else in the world call (01733 318 949) and reverse the charges. Any of the above numbers can tell you the location of their nearest office. Any type of Visa traveler's checks can be reported lost at the Visa number.

CREDIT AND CASH CARDS

Credit cards are of limited day-to-day value in the Middle East—usually only places too expensive for the budget traveler will accept them. They are invaluable, however, if you need an instant cash advance. Both **Visa** (800 336-8472) and **MasterCard** (800 999-0454) give cash advances at affiliated banks (usually found in capital cities). Credit card companies get the wholesale exchange rate, generally 5% better than the retail rate used by banks and even better than that used by other currency exchange establishments. **American Express** (tel. (800) 843-2273) cards also work in some ATMs, as well as at AmEx offices and major airports. All such machines require a **Personal Identification Number (PIN).** You must ask American Express, MasterCard, or Visa to assign you one before you leave; without this PIN, you will be unable to withdraw cash with your credit card abroad. Contact your company to find out what additional services they provide; possible benefits include emergency assistance, mail service, and car rental collision insurance. Keep in mind that MasterCard and Visa may have different names elsewhere ("EuroCard" or "Access" for MasterCard and "Carte Bleue" or Barclaycard" for Visa).

Cash cards are a convenient source for cash in Israel. There are now well over 200 **Cirrus** (U.S. tel. (800) 4-CIRRUS or 424-7787) **automated teller machines (ATMs)** available at Bank Ha-Poalim branches, with many also on the PLUS network (U.S. tel. (800) 843-7587). ATMs in Egypt are more common than in Jordan and Syria, but are still relatively rare outside of heavily touristed areas. Lebanon has few ATMs, but the banks in this international banking powerhouse (80 of them in Beirut alone) can arrange a cash advance on your credit card.

Depending on the system that your bank at home uses, you will probably be able to access your own personal bank account whenever you're in need of funds. ATM machines get the same wholesale exchange rate as credit cards. There is often a limit on the amount of money you can withdraw per day, and computer network failures are not uncommon. If your PIN is longer than four digits, be sure to ask your bank whether the first four digits will work, or whether you need a new number.

GETTING MONEY FROM HOME

Try to avoid this horror. Carry a credit card or a separate stash of traveler's checks. Even a single US$50 bill can sustain you for quite some time in the Middle East.

One possibility is to use an **American Express** card. AmEx allows green-card holders to draw cash from their checking accounts at any of its major offices and many of its representatives' offices, up to US$1000 every 21 days (no service charge, no interest). AmEx also offers Express Cash, with over 100,000 ATMs located in airports, hotels, banks, office complexes, and shopping areas around the world. Express Cash withdrawals are automatically debited from the Cardmember's checking account or line of credit. Green card holders may withdraw up to US$1000 in a seven day period. There is a 2% transaction fee for each cash withdrawal, with a US$2.50 minimum/$20 maximum. To enroll in Express Cash, Cardmembers may call (800) CASH NOW (227-4669). Outside the U.S. call collect (904) 565-7875. Unless you are using the AmEx service, avoid cashing checks in foreign currencies; they usually take weeks and a US$30 fee to clear.

Money can also be wired abroad through international money transfer services operated by **Western Union** (800 325-6000). The rate for sending cash is generally US$10 cheaper than with a credit card, and the money is usually available in the destination country within an hour, although this may vary.

In emergencies, U.S. citizens can have money sent via the State Department's **Overseas Citizens Service, American Citizens Services,** Consular Affairs, Room 4811, U.S. Department of State, Washington, D.C. 20520 (tel. (202) 647-5225; nights, Sundays, and holidays (202) 647-4000; fax (on demand only) (202) 647-3000; http://travel.state.gov). For a fee of US$15, the State Department will forward money within hours to the nearest consular office, which will then disburse it according to instructions. The office serves only Americans in the direst of straits abroad; non-American travelers should contact their embassies or information on wiring cash. The quickest way to have the money sent is to cable the State Department through Western Union.

Some people choose to send money abroad in cash via Federal Express to avoid transmission fees and taxes. This method is **illegal,** involves an element of risk, and requires that you remain at a legitimate address for a day or two to wait for the money's arrival. With the strict postal security policies of Middle Eastern countries, it is not likely that you will receive your package intact.

■ Safety and Security

Politics in the Middle East can easily intrude on travel; keep apprised of events. For official **U.S. State Department** travel advisories, call their 24-hour hotline at (202) 647-5225, or check their website (http://travel.state.gov), which provides travel information and publications. Alternatively, order publications, including a free pamphlet entitled *A Safe Trip Abroad,* by writing to Superintendent of Documents, U.S. Government Printing Office, Washington, DC 20402, or by calling them at (202) 512-1800. Official warnings from the **United Kingdom Foreign and Commonwealth Office** are on-line at http://www.fco.gov.uk; you can also call the office at (0171) 238-4503. The **Canadian Department of Foreign Affairs and International Trade (DFAIT)** offers advisories and travel warnings at its web address (http://www.dfait-maeci.gc.ca) and at its phone number ((613) 944-6788 in Ottawa, (800) 267-6788 elsewhere in Canada). Their free publication, *Bon Voyage, But....*, offers travel tips to Canadian citizens; you can receive a copy by calling them at (613) 944-6788 from Ottawa or abroad, or at (800) 267-6788 from Canada.

Travelers are frequently the most obvious targets for crime—they often carry large amounts of cash and they are not as savvy as locals. Do your best to blend in; avoid fumbling about with the tourist map in the middle of the *souq*. Always try to appear confident, even when you lose bodily control. An obviously bewildered bodybuilder is more likely to be harassed than a stern and confident 98-pound weakling.

There is no sure-fire set of precautions that will protect you from all of the situations you might encounter when you travel. A good self-defense course will give you more concrete ways to react to different types of aggression, but it can carry a steep price tag. **Impact Model Mugging** offers local self-defense courses in the United States (tel. (800) 345-KICK or 345-5425). Course prices $50-400. Women's and men's courses. Community colleges also frequently run inexpensive self-defense courses.

Don't put a wallet with money in your back pocket. Never count your money in public and carry as little as possible. If you carry a purse, buy a sturdy one with a secure clasp, and carry it crosswise on the side, away from the street with the clasp against you. Secure packs with small combination padlocks which slip through the two zippers. A **money belt** is the best way to carry cash; you can buy one at most camping supply stores. A nylon, zippered pouch with belt that sits inside the waist of your pants or skirt combines convenience and security. A **neck pouch** is equally safe, although less accessible. Refrain from pulling out your neck pouch in public; if you must, be very discreet. Avoid keeping anything precious in a fanny-pack (even if it's worn on your stomach)—your valuables will be highly visible and easy to steal.

Among the more colorful aspects of these important tourist nations are the **con artists.** Be aware of certain classics: sob stories that require money, rolls of bills "found" on the street, mustard spilled (or saliva spat) onto your shoulder, distracting you for enough time to snatch your bag. Contact the police if a hustler is particularly insistent or aggressive. In Egypt especially, where a thriving tourist industry has existed for years and where tourism is often the only source of income, hustlers have finetuned the con into an art (see **The Pros of Cons in Cairo,** p. 92). Beware of people who have the time and patience to gain your trust over a period of a few days, only to rob you of your valuables the second that you let your guard down.

In cities, and elsewhere, extra vigilance may be wise, but there is never need for paranoia. Stick to busy, well-lit streets. Tourist information, and hotel and hostel managers can be valuable sources of advice on which areas to avoid. If you're in a dorm-style room or have no lock on your door, sleep with all valuables on your person or under your pillow; laying your pack alongside the bed won't do. The same holds for **overnight trains;** steer clear of empty compartments. **Trains** in general are notoriously easy spots for thieving, as are **buses.** Don't check your luggage on trains, as it is often "lost" this way.

TERRORISM

Terrorism is a threat in the Middle East, as it is everywhere, from Oklahoma City to Manchester. Travelers need not feel like powerless bystanders, however. The chances of becoming a victim of terrorism are low, and can be lowered further by taking certain precautions. You should be aware of the possibility of danger, without letting it paralyze you.

For the past several years, Egyptian extremist groups have attacked targets ranging from Egyptian police to tourists. In April 1996, 18 Greek tourists were killed in a terrorist attack in Cairo. However, the overall number of terrorist incidents throughout the country has declined in 1997 due to an increase in government security. By dressing modestly, avoiding large organized tours, and respecting local sensibilities, you will be less conspicuous as a tourist, and less prone to attack. Remember, though, that even the guy with the tour group hat, the Hawaiian shirt, and the camcorder is probably safe. **Middle Egypt,** the region between Beni Suef and Luxor, is worlds away from Cairo and Luxor and is far more dangerous. Tourists should avoid Asyut, the center of the fundamentalist movement, as well as Minya, Sohag, and Qena. Special permission from the Egyptian Ministry of Tourism is required to visit sights near these areas. Tourist police also hover around visitors in many Nile valley towns. They may seem gruff and intrusive, but they are there to protect you.

Terrorists in **Israel** target public transportation and crowded areas. The best defense is to learn the pattern of previous incidents. Most bus bombings in Israel occur in the early morning rush hour. If your plans are flexible, try to avoid bus travel at this time. As terrorism has sadly become a part of life in the country, Israelis look at abandoned purses and backpacks in a different light. Don't leave anything unattended, or it will be snatched up by the police and possibly blown to bits. Alert authorities if you see an abandoned package.

Traveling in the **West Bank** can be dangerous, especially in a car with yellow license plates. Jewish travelers should avoid identifying themselves as such. Simply placing a baseball cap over a *kippah* can prevent stares and hostility. Demonstrations by Palestinians and Israelis in the West Bank have led to confrontations and clashes with the police, and some turn deadly. Stone throwing and other forms of protest can occur without warning and escalate quickly. Be aware of potential unrest in the West Bank by staying up to date with the news and contacting the consular division of the United States Consulate General, located at 27 Nablus Road in East Jerusalem.

There is very little threat of terrorism directed at tourists in **Jordan,** although there have been incidents of violence perpetrated by groups or individuals responding to changes in the Middle East Peace Process. Areas near the border of Israel are more dangerous during times of potential unrest. There is very little threat of terrorism in **Syria,** although it is a good idea to stay apprised of the current situation by getting news from sources outside of Syria, including your home country's embassy.

In **Lebanon,** stay away from the Israeli-controlled military zone in the south and from the Hizbullah-controlled Beqaa Valley, particularly during times of unrest. Americans are in more danger than other nationalities because of the resentment surrounding the United States' increasingly important role in the Peace Process. Kidnapping was once, and still could be, a significant problem, though the U.S. State Department has lifted the ban on U.S. travel to Lebanon. The U.S. travel ban for Americans in Lebanon was meant to protect citizens from kidnapping, but the lifting of the travel restrictions does not necessarily mean that travel in the region is safe. The State Department continues to advise against travel by Americans to Lebanon; contact them for any updates on the current situation (see p. 5).

The United States State Department encourages U.S. citizens who are planning to visit the region for substantial periods of time to register with the U.S. Embassy in each destination country. U.S. citizens who register can obtain updated information on travel and security in specific areas.

ALCOHOL AND DRUGS

Laws vary from country to country, but, needless to say, **illegal drugs** are best avoided altogether. Some countries do not differentiate between "hard" drugs and more mainstream ones such as marijuana. The Islamic law forbidding **alcohol** is like the American law against jaywalking—lots of people do it anyway. You may be asked to purchase alcohol for not-so-devout Muslims that you meet in Arab countries; they won't want to be seen buying it for themselves. The drinking age in Egypt is 21; in Israel, Jordan, Syria, and Lebanon it is 18. Only Israel's restriction is enforced. The U.S. State Department warns that "U.S. citizens are subject to the laws of the country in which they travel." This is true of all other nationalities as well. Penalties for possession, use, or trafficking in **illegal drugs** are severe throughout the Middle East. Both Egypt and Syria may impose the death penalty on anyone convicted of smuggling or selling. Consulates can do no more than bring floral arrangements to the prisoner, provide a list of attorneys, and inform family and friends.

■ Health

Common sense is the simplest prescription for good health while you travel: eat well, drink lots of bottled water, sleep enough, and don't overexert yourself. Travelers complain most often about their feet and their gut, so take precautionary measures. Drinking lots of fluids can often prevent dehydration and constipation, while wearing sturdy shoes with clean socks and using talcum powder can help keep your feet dry. To minimize the effects of jet lag, "reset" your body's clock by adopting the time of your destination immediately upon arrival. Most travelers feel acclimatized to a new time zone after two or three days.

BEFORE YOU GO

Though no amount of planning can guarantee an accident-free trip, preparation can help minimize the likelihood of contracting a disease and maximize the chances of receiving effective health-care in the event of an emergency.

For minor health problems, bring a compact **first-aid kit,** including bandages, aspirin or other pain killer, antibiotic cream, a thermometer, a Swiss Army knife with tweezers, moleskin, a decongestant for colds, motion sickness remedy, medicine for diarrhea or stomach problems, sunscreen, insect repellent, and burn ointment.

In your passport, write the names of any people you wish to be contacted in case of a medical emergency, and also list any allergies or medical conditions that doctors should know to treat you. If you wear glasses or contact lenses, carry an extra prescription and pair of glasses or arrange to have your doctor or a family member send a replacement pair in an emergency. Obtain a full supply of any necessary medication before the trip, since matching a prescription to a foreign equivalent is not always easy, safe, or possible. Carry up-to-date, legible prescriptions or a statement from your doctor, especially if you use insulin, a syringe, or a narcotic. While traveling, be sure to keep all medication with you in carry-on luggage.

Take a look at your **immunization** records before you go; some countries require visitors to carry vaccination certificates. Travelers over two years old should be sure that the following vaccines are up to date: Measles, Mumps, and Rubella (MMR); Diptheria, Tetanus, and Pertussis (DTP or DTap); Polio (OPV); Haemophilus Influenza B (HbCV); and Hepatitis B (HBV). A booster of Tetanus-diptheria (Td) is recommended once every 10 years, and adults should consider an additional dose of Polio vaccine if they have not already had one during their adult years. Hepatitis A vaccine and/or Immune Globulin (IG) is recommended for travelers to the Middle East, as well. If you will be spending more than four weeks in Egypt, Jordan, Lebanon, or Syria, you should consider the typhoid vaccine also. Check with a doctor for guidance through this maze of injections, and try to remember that no matter how bad the needles are, they're better than the diseases they prevent.

If you are concerned about being able to access medical support while traveling, contact one of these two services: **Global Emergency Medical Services (GEMS)** has products called *MedPass* that provide 24-hour international medical assistance and support coordinated through registered nurses who have on-line access to your medical information, your primary physician, and a worldwide network of screened, credentialed English-speaking doctors and hospitals. Subscribers also receive a personal medical record that contains vital information in case of emergencies. For more information call (800) 860-1111, fax (770) 475-0058, or write: 2001 Westside Drive, #120, Alpharetta, GA 30201. The **International Association for Medical Assistance to Travelers (IAMAT)** offers a membership ID card, a directory of English-speaking doctors around the world who treat members for a set fee schedule, and detailed charts on immunization requirements, various tropical diseases, climate, and sanitation. Membership is free, though donations are appreciated and used for further research. Contact chapters in the **U.S.,** 417 Center St., Lewiston, NY 14092 (tel. (716) 754-4883; fax (519) 836-3412; email iamat@sentex.net; http://www.sentex.net/~iamat); **Canada,** 40 Regal Road, Guelph, Ontario, N1K 1B5 (tel. (519) 836-0102) or 1287 St. Clair Avenue West, Toronto, M6E 1B8 (tel. (416) 652-0137; fax (519) 836-3412); or **New Zealand,** P.O. Box 5049, Christchurch 5.

FOOD, WATER, AND DISEASE

The hot temperatures and low sanitation standards of the Middle East can make even the most careful traveler ill. Drink *lots* of water (as much as 10L per day may be necessary to avoid dehydration), always cover your head with something white when you go out in the sun, and ease into street food slowly. Avoid excessive caffeine and alcohol, both of which can cause dehydration. Copious and clear urine is a good sign; if it's close to the color of your *Let's Go* book, you're not drinking enough water. It's a good idea to carry sun block with a high sun protection factor (SPF) and to apply it liberally and often. SPFs of 15 or 20 are strong enough for the fairest skin. This is not the place to work on a tan—even the dark-skinned or pre-tanned are not immune.

To ensure that your food is safe, make sure that everything is cooked properly (deep-fried is good, for once), and be positive the water you drink is clean. Don't order meat "rare," and eggs should be thoroughly cooked, not served sunny-side up.

Never drink unbottled water which you have not treated yourself—the risk of contracting traveler's diarrhea or other diseases is high. To purify your own water, bring it to a rolling boil (simmering isn't enough), or treat it with iodine drops or tablets. Don't brush your teeth with tap water, and don't even rinse your toothbrush under the faucet. Keep your mouth closed in the shower. Don't be fooled by the clever disguise of impure water—the ice-cube. Stay away from salads; uncooked vegetables (including lettuce) are full of untreated water. Other culprits are raw shellfish, unpasteurized milk, and sauces containing raw eggs. Peel all fruits and vegetables yourself, and beware of watermelon, a storehouse of impure water. Watch out for food from markets or street vendors that may have been washed in dirty water—like juices or peeled fruits. Always wash your hands before eating. Your bowels will thank you.

ON THE ROAD AILMENTS

You can minimize the chances of contracting a disease while traveling by taking a few precautionary measures. Always avoid animals with open wounds, beware of touching any animal at all in developing countries. Often dogs are not given shots, so that sweet-faced pooch at your feet might very well be disease-ridden. If you are bitten, be concerned about **rabies**—be sure to clean your wound thoroughly and seek medical help immediately to find out whether you need treatment. The danger of rabies is greatest in rural areas.

Many diseases are transmitted by insects—mainly mosquitoes, fleas, ticks, and lice. Be aware of insects in wet or forested areas, while hiking, and especially while camping. **Mosquitoes** are most active from dusk to dawn. Wear long pants and long sleeves (fabric need not be thick or warm; tropic-weight cottons can keep you comfortable in the heat) and buy a bednet for camping. Wear shoes and socks, and tuck long pants into socks. Use insect repellents; DEET can be bought in spray or liquid form, but use it sparingly, especially on children. Soak or spray your gear with permethrin, which is licensed in the U.S. for use on clothing. Natural repellents can also be useful; taking vitamin B-12 or garlic pills regularly can eventually make you smelly to insects. Still, be sure to supplement your vitamins with repellent Calamine lotion or topical cortisones (like Cortaid) may stop insect bites from itching, as can a bath with a half-cup of baking soda or oatmeal.

Malaria is transmitted by Anopheles mosquitoes which bite during the night. These pesky bloodsuckers are present in almost all tropical and subtropical regions. Preliminary symptoms include fever, chills, aches, and fatigue. Since early stages resemble the flu, you should see a doctor for any flu-like sickness that occurs after travel in a risk area. Treatment drugs are available, but left untreated, malaria can cause anemia, kidney failure, coma, and death. Malaria poses an especially serious threat to pregnant women and their fetuses. The risk is greatest in rural areas. If hiking or staying overnight in certain areas (whether camping or not), you may want to take weekly anti-malarial drugs. Contact your doctor for a prescription. The type of drug you should take depends upon the strain of malaria present in the region.

Dengue Fever is an "urban viral infection" transmitted by Aedes mosquitoes, which bite during the day rather than at night. Dengue has flu-like symptoms and is often indicated by a rash three to four days after the onset of fever. There is no vaccine; the only prevention is to avoid mosquito bites. To treat the symptoms, rest, drink lots of water, and take fever-reducing medication such as acetaminophen (but avoid aspirin). **Filariasis** is a round worm infestation also transmitted by mosquitoes. Infection causes enlargement (elephantitis) of extremities; there is no vaccine.

Typhoid Fever is common in villages and rural areas in the Middle East. Although mostly transmitted through contaminated food and water, it may also be acquired by direct contact with another person. Symptoms include fever, headaches, fatigue, loss of appetite, constipation, and a rash on the abdomen or chest; antibiotics treat typhoid fever. The Center for Disease Control and Prevention recommends vaccinations (70-90% effective) if you will be going off the "usual tourist itineraries"—that is, hiking, camping, and staying in small cities or rural areas.

Parasites (tapeworms, etc.) also hide in unsafe water and food. *Giardia*, for example, is acquired by drinking untreated water from streams or lakes all over the world. It can stay with you for years. Symptoms of parasitic infections in general include swollen glands or lymph nodes, fever, rashes or itchiness, digestive problems, eye problems, and anemia. Boil your water, wear shoes, avoid bugs, and eat cooked food.

Hepatitis A (distinct from B and C) is a high risk in the Middle East. Hepatitis A is a viral infection of the liver acquired primarily through contaminated water, ice, shellfish, or unpeeled fruit, and vegetables (as well as from sexual contact). Symptoms include fatigue, fever, loss of appetite, nausea, dark urine, jaundice, vomiting, aches and pains, and light stools. Ask your doctor about a new vaccine called "Harvix," or ask to get an injection of immune globulin (IG; formerly called Gamma Globulin). Risk is highest in rural areas and the countryside, but is also present in urban areas.

Hepatitis B is a viral infection of the liver transmitted by sharing needles, having unprotected sex, or coming into direct contact with an infected person's lesioned skin. If you think you may be sexually active while traveling or if you are working or living in rural areas, you are typically advised to get the vaccination for Hepatitis B. Vaccination should begin six months before traveling.

Hepatitis C is like Hepatitis B, but the methods of transmission are different. At risk are intravenous drug users, those with occupational exposure to blood, hemodialysis patients, or recipients of a blood transfusion; doctors aren't sure if you can get it through sexual contact.

TRAVELER'S DIARRHEA

Sooner or later, no matter how careful you are, you'll probably get diarrhea, affectionately known among its victims as **"Pharaoh's Revenge."** The Revenge typically strikes 10 to 12 days after arrival, lasts from two to four days if you rest up, and may be accompanied by fever and fatigue. If the nasties hit you, eat quick-energy, non-sugary foods with protein and carbohydrates to keep your strength up. Over-the-counter remedies (such as Pepto-Bismol or Immodium) may counteract the problems, but they can complicate serious infections. Avoid anti-diarrheals if you suspect you have been exposed to contaminated food or water, which puts you at risk for other diseases. The most dangerous side effect of diarrhea is dehydration; the simplest and most effective anti-dehydration formula is 8oz. of (clean) water with half a teaspoon of sugar or honey and a pinch of salt. Also good are soft drinks without caffeine, and salted crackers. Down several of these remedies a day, rest, and wait for the disease to run its course. If you develop a fever or your symptoms don't go away after four or five days, consult a doctor. Also consult a doctor if children develop traveler's diarrhea, since treatment is different.

FEELING THE HEAT

Common sense goes a long way toward preventing **heat exhaustion:** relax in hot weather, drink lots of non-alcoholic fluids, and lie down inside if you feel awful. Continuous heat stress can eventually lead to **heatstroke,** characterized by rising body temperature, severe headache, and cessation of sweating. Wear a hat, sunglasses, and a lightweight, light-colored longsleeve shirt to avoid heatstroke. Heatstroke can occur without direct exposure to the sun. Victims must be cooled off with wet towels and taken to a doctor as soon as possible.

Always drink enough liquids to keep your urine clear. Alcoholic beverages are dehydrating, as are coffee, strong tea, and caffeinated sodas. If you'll be sweating a lot, be sure to eat enough salty food to prevent electrolyte depletion, which causes severe headaches. Less debilitating, but still dangerous, is **sunburn.** If you're prone to sunburn, bring sunscreen with you (it's often more expensive and hard to find when traveling), and apply it liberally and often to avoid burns and risk of skin cancer. If you get sunburned, drink more fluids than usual. See **Food, Water, Disease,** above, for more entreaties to **drink lots of water.**

WOMEN'S HEALTH

Women traveling in unsanitary conditions are vulnerable to urinary tract and bladder infections, common and severely uncomfortable bacterial diseases which cause a burning sensation and painful and sometimes frequent urination. Drink tons of vitamin-C-rich juice, plenty of clean water, and urinate frequently. If you have intercourse, urinate immediately afterward. Untreated, these infections can be fatal. If symptoms persist, see a doctor.

Yeast infections are characterized by an itchy rash and white discharge, and can be avoided by keeping the genital area clean and wearing cotton underwear and loose-fitting pants or skirts. If you're prone to yeast infections, pack an over-the-counter medicine, as treatments may not be readily available in rural Egypt or Syria. Eating plain yogurt or using a lemon or vinegar douche may also help in a pinch. Tampons and pads are hard to find when traveling; your preferred brands may not be available, so take supplies along. Refer to the *Handbook for Women Travellers* by Maggie and Gemma Moss (published by Piatkus Books) or to *Our Bodies, Our Selves* (published by the Boston Women's Health Collective) for more extensive information specific to women's health on the road.

If you are overseas and want an **abortion,** your best bet may be your embassy, which can provide a list of doctors who perform abortions. You can also contact the **National Abortion Federation Hotline** (front desk tel. (202) 667-5881; within the US toll free tel. (800) 772-9100; Mon.-Fri. 9:30am-12:30pm and 1:30-5:30pm EST), 1755 Massachusetts Ave. NW, Suite 600, Washington, D.C., 20036. If you don't mind paying for the call, the hotline can answer questions about the abortion procedure and will try to direct you to organizations which provide information on the availability of and techniques for abortion in other countries. For information on contraception, condoms, and abortion worldwide, contact the **International Planned Parenthood Federation,** European Regional Office, Regent's College Inner Circle, Regent's Park, London NW1 4NS (tel. (0171) 487 7900, fax (0171) 487 7950).

AIDS, HIV, STDS, AND BIRTH CONTROL

Acquired Immune Deficiency Syndrome (AIDS) is a growing problem around the world. **The World Health Organization** estimates that there are around 13 million people infected with **the HIV virus**. Well over 90% of adults newly infected with HIV acquired their infection through heterosexual sex; women now represent 50% of all new HIV infections.

The easiest mode of HIV transmission is through direct blood-to-blood contact with an HIV+ person; *never* share intravenous drug, tattooing, or other needles. The most common mode of transmission is sexual intercourse. Health professionals recommend the use of latex condoms; follow the instructions on the packet. Since it isn't always easy to buy condoms when traveling, take a supply with you before you depart for your trip. Casual contact (including drinking from the same glass or using the same eating utensils as an infected person) is not believed to pose a risk.

Some countries do screen incoming travelers, primarily those planning extended visits for work or study, and deny entrance to HIV positive people. Contact the consulate for information about this policy.

For more information on AIDS, call the **U.S. Center for Disease Control's** 24-hour Hotline at (800) 342-2437. In Europe, write to the **World Health Organization,** attn: Global Program on AIDS, 20 Avenue Appia, 1211 Geneva 27, Switzerland (tel. (22) 791-2111), for statistical material on AIDS internationally. Or write to the **Bureau of**

Consular Affairs, #6831, Department of State, Washington, D.C. 20520 (http://travel.state.gov). Council's brochure, *Travel Safe: AIDS and International Travel,* is available at all Council Travel offices.

Sexually transmitted diseases (STDs) such as gonorrhea, chlamydia, genital warts, syphilis, and herpes are a lot easier to catch than HIV, and can be just as deadly. It's a wise idea to actually *look* at your partner's genitals before you have sex. Warning signs for STDs include: swelling, sores, bumps, or blisters on sex organs, rectum, or mouth; burning and pain during urination and bowel movements; itching around sex organs; swelling or redness in the throat, flu-like symptoms with fever, chills, and aches. If these symptoms develop, see a doctor immediately. When having sex, condoms may protect you from certain STDs, but oral or even tactile contact can lead to transmission.

Stock up on **condoms** before leaving (although in Israel your favorite brand is most likely available). **Contraceptives** are not always available, or safe, in the Middle East; women on the pill should bring all they'll ever need.

■ Insurance

Beware of buying unnecessary travel coverage—your regular insurance policies may well extend to many travel-related accidents. **Medical insurance** (especially university policies) often cover costs incurred abroad, check with your provider. **Medicare's** "foreign travel" coverage is valid only in Canada and Mexico. Canadians are protected by their home province's health insurance plan for up to 90 days after leaving the country; check with the provincial Ministry of Health or Health Plan Headquarters for details. Australia has Reciprocal Health Care Agreements (RHCAs) with several countries; when traveling in these nations Australians are entitled to many of the services that they would receive at home. The Commonwealth Department of Human Services and Health can provide information. Your **homeowners' insurance** (or your family's coverage) often covers theft during travel. Homeowners are generally covered against loss of documents (passport, plane ticket, railpass, etc.) up to US$500.

ISIC and **ITIC** provide basic insurance benefits, including US$100 per day of in-hospital sickness for a maximum of 60 days, and US$3000 of accident-related medical reimbursement (see **Youth, Student, and Teacher Identification,** p. 11). Cardholders have access to a toll-free 24-hour helpline whose multilingual staff can provide assistance in medical, legal, and financial emergencies overseas. **Council** and **STA** offer a range of plans that can supplement your basic insurance coverage, with options covering medical treatment and hospitalization, accidents, baggage loss, and even charter flights missed due to illness. Most **American Express** cardholders receive automatic car rental (collision and theft, but not liability) insurance and travel accident coverage (US$100,000 in life insurance) on flight purchases made with the card (customer service tel. 800) 528-4800).

Remember that insurance companies usually require a copy of the police report for thefts, or evidence of having paid medical expenses (doctor's statements, receipts) before they will honor a claim and may have time limits on filing for reimbursement. Always carry policy numbers and proof of insurance. Check with each insurance carrier for specific restrictions and policies. All of the carriers listed have 24-hour hotlines and deal regularly with youth and budget travelers: **Access America,** 6600 West Broad St., P.O. Box 11188, Richmond, VA 23230 (tel. (800) 284-8300; fax (804) 673-1491); **Avi International,** 90 Rue de la Victoire, 75009 Paris, France (tel. (1) 44 63 51 07; fax (1) 40 82 90 35); **The Berkely Group/Carefree Travel Insurance,** 100 Garden City Plaza, P.O. Box 9366, Garden City, NY 11530-9366 (tel. (800) 323-3149 or (516) 294-0220; fax 294-1096); **Travel Assistance International,** by Worldwide Assistance Services, Inc., 1133 15th St. NW, #400, Washington, D.C. 20005-2710 (tel. (800) 821-2828 or (202) 828-5894; fax (202) 828-5896; email wassist@aol.com); **Travel Guard International,** 1145 Clark St., Stevens Point, WI 54481 (tel. (800) 826-1300; fax (715) 345-0525; http://www.travel-guard.com). Comprehensive insurance programs starting at US$40. Programs cover trip cancellation/interruption, medical coverage abroad, emergency assistance, and lost baggage. 24-hr. hotline, **Travel Insured International, Inc.,** 52-S Oakland Ave., P.O. Box 280568, East Hartford, CT 06128-0568 (tel. (800) 243-3174; fax (203) 528-8005; email travelins@aol.com).

■ Alternatives to Tourism

STUDY

Foreign study programs vary tremendously in expense, academic quality, living conditions, degree of contact with local students, and exposure to local culture and languages. There is a plethora of exchange programs for high school students. Most American undergraduates enroll in programs sponsored by U.S. universities, and many colleges have offices that give advice and information on study abroad. Ask for the names of recent participants in these programs, and get in touch with them in order to judge which program is best for you.

Berlitz Language Centers administer programs of study in Hebrew and Arabic; contact them at 165 Muhammad Farid St., Cairo (tel. (02) 391 50 96); 28 Sa'ad Zaghloul Blvd., Alexandria (tel. (03) 808 226); 37 Sha'ul Ha-Melekh Ave., Tel Aviv 64298 (tel. (03) 695 21 31; fax (03) 695 21 34); 40 W. 51st St., New York, NY 10020 (tel. (212) 765-1000); or at any of their locations world-wide. They also offer cultural training. Check out interactive "Berlitz World" at www.berlitz.com.

Biblical Archaeology Society, 4710 41st St. NW, Washington, D.C. 20016 (tel. (202) 364-3300; fax 364-2636). Organizes travel/study tours that center around archaeological sights. Also publishes the *Biblical Archaeological Review.*

College Semester Abroad, School for International Training, Kipling Rd., P.O. Box 676, Brattleboro, VT 05302 (tel. (800) 336-1616; fax (802) 258-3500). Runs semester- and year-long programs featuring cultural orientation, intensive language study, homestay, and field and independent study in Israel and Jordan (among many others). Programs cost US$9300-11,500, including tuition, room and board, and airfare. Scholarships are available and federal financial aid is usually transferable from home college or university. Write for a brochure.

Institute of International Education (IIE), 809 United Nations Plaza, New York, NY 10017-3580 (tel. (212) 984-5413; fax 984-5358). For book orders: IIE Books, Institute of International Education, P.O. Box 371, Annapolis Junction, MD 20701 (tel. (800) 445-0443; fax (301) 206-9789; email iiebooks@pmds.com). A nonprofit, international and cultural exchange agency, IIE's library of study abroad resources is open to the public Tues.-Thurs. 11am-3:45pm. Publishes *Academic Year Abroad* (US$43, US$5 postage) and *Vacation Study Abroad* (US$37, US$5 postage). Write for a complete list of publications.

International Schools Services, Educational Staffing Program, 15 Roszel Rd., P.O. Box 5910, Princeton, NJ 08543 (tel. (609) 452-0990; fax 452-2690; email edustaffing@iss.edu; http://www.iss.edu). Recruits teachers and administrators to work in schools. All instruction in English. Applicants must have a bachelor's degree and two years of relevant experience. Nonrefundable US$100 application fee. The *ISS Directory of Overseas Schools* (US$35) is also helpful.

Language Immersion Institute, State University of New York at New Paltz, 75 South Manheim Blvd., New Paltz, NY 12561 (tel. (914) 257-3500; fax 257-3569; email lii@newpaltz.edu; http://www.eelab.newpaltz.edu/lii). Provides language instruction at all levels in Arabic and Hebrew. Weekend courses offered at New Paltz and in New York City. They also conduct 2-week summer courses, overseas learning vacations, and customized corporate instruction. Program fees are about US$295 for a weekend and US$625 for a 2-week course. College credit is available.

Peterson's Guides, P.O. Box 2123, Princeton, NJ 08543-2123 (tel. (800) 338-3282; fax (609) 243-9150; http://www.petersons.com). Their comprehensive *Study Abroad* (US$30) annual guide lists programs in countries all over the world and provides essential information on the study abroad experience in general.

Israel! Judaism!

Study it. **Build it** **Hike it.**

Livnot U'Lehibanot

"To Build and To Be Built"

Three months or three weeks of study, service, and hiking in Jerusalem & Tzfat. Designed for young men and women with minimal Jewish background.

* Learn about Judaism and Israel, in an open atmosphere where all questions are invited.
* Work in the community, restoring & rebuilding the land.
* Hire weekly, including a 3-day trek form Sea to Sea.

Programs begin throughout the year.

For more information, contact **LIVNOT U'LEHIBANOT**
Toll free #: 1-888-Livnot-0 **E**-mail: sammyrose@aol.com
Address: 110 East 59th St., New York, NY 10022
Fax: 212-832-2597 **Phone**: 212-752-2390

VOLUNTEERING

Volunteer jobs are readily available almost everywhere. You may receive room and board in exchange for your labor; the work can be fascinating (or stultifying). You can sometimes avoid the high application fees charged by the organizations that arrange placement by contacting the individual workcamps directly; check with the organizations.

The Archaeological Institute of America, 656 Beacon St., Boston, MA 02215-2010 (tel. (617) 353-9361; fax 353-6550; email aia@bu.edu; http://csa.brynmawr.edu/web2/aia.html), puts out the *Archaeological Fieldwork Opportunities Bulletin* (US$11 non-members), which lists over 300 field sites throughout the world. This can be purchased from Kendall/Hunt Publishing, 4050 Westmark Dr., Dubuque, Iowa 52002 (tel. (800) 228-0810).

Council has a Voluntary Services Dept., 205 E. 42nd St., New York, NY 10017 (tel. (888) COUNCIL (268-6245); fax (212) 822-2699; email info@ciee.org; http://www.ciee.org), which offers 2- to 4-week environmental or community services projects in over 30 countries. Participants must be at least 18 years old. Minimum US$295 placement fee; additional fees may also apply for various countries.

Peace Corps, 1990 K St. NW, Room 8508, Washington, D.C. 20526 (tel. (800) 424-8580; fax (202) 606-4469; email msaucier@peacecorps.gov; http://www.peacecorps.gov). Opportunities available in developing nations in agriculture, business, education, the environment, and health; programs are in Jordan and elsewhere. Volunteers must be U.S. citizens, age 18 and over, and willing to make a 2-year commitment. A bachelor's degree is usually required.

WORK

There's no better way to immerse yourself in a foreign culture than to become part of its economy. It's easy to find a **temporary job,** but it will rarely be glamorous and may not even pay for your plane fare, let alone your accommodation. Officially, you can hold a job only with a **work permit.** Your employer must obtain this document, usually by asserting that you have skills that locals lack—not the easiest of tasks. There are, however, ways to make it easier. Friends in your destination country can help expedite work permits or arrange work-for-accommodations swaps. Be an au pair, or advertise to teach English. Many permit-less agricultural workers go untroubled by local authorities. Students can check with their universities' foreign language departments, which may have connections to job openings abroad. Call the consulate or embassy of the country in which you wish to work to get more information about work permits.

Office of Overseas Schools, A/OS Room 245, SA-29, Dept. of State, Washington, D.C. 20522-2902 (tel. (703) 875-7800; http://www.state.gov/www/about_state/schools/). Keeps a list of schools abroad and agencies that arrange placement for Americans to teach abroad.

Transitions Abroad Publishing, Inc., 18 Hulst Rd., P.O. Box 1300, Amherst, MA 01004-1300 (tel. (800) 293-0373; fax (413) 256-0373; email trabroad@aol.com; http://www.transabroad.com). Publishes *Transitions Abroad*, a bi-monthly magazine listing opportunities and printed resources for those seeking to study, work, or travel abroad. For subscriptions (U.S. US$25 for 6 issues, Canada US$30, other countries US$38), contact them at *Transitions Abroad,* Dept. TRA, Box 3000, Denville, NJ 07834 or call (800) 293-0373. Publishes *The Alternative Travel Directory,* with truly exhaustive listings for the "active international traveler."

Vacation Work Publications, 9 Park End St., Oxford OX1 1HJ, U.K. (tel. (01865) 24 19 78; fax 79 08 85). Publishes a wide variety of guides and directories with job listings and info for the working traveler, including *Teaching English Abroad* (UK£10, UK£2.50 postage, UK£1.50 within U.K.).

EGYPT

Study

The **American University of Cairo (AUC)** offers semester, year, and summer programs for study abroad, intensive Arabic, and graduate degree study. Instruction is in English. Popular topics include Arabic language, Egyptology, and Middle East studies. Tuition and fees for 1997-98 are US$5030 per semester; US$2495 for the summer session. AUC is located in the center of modern Cairo, just off Tahrir Square at 113 Qasr el-Aini St. For more information, write to Office of Student Affairs, American University in Cairo, 420 Fifth Avenue, 3rd Floor, New York, NY 10018 (tel. (212) 838-1100; fax 838-1155; email aucegypt@aucnyo.edu).

Al-Azhar University, El Nasr Rd., Cairo (tel. (02) 262 32 78 or 79) also offers programs for foreign students. Those interested should contact the Department of International Students, **Egyptian Cultural and Educational Bureau,** 1303 New Hampshire Ave. NW, Washington, D.C. 20036 (tel. (202) 296-3888; fax 296-3891), or for more information on placement with a program, contact **AmidEast** (1730 M St. NW Suite 1100, Washington, D.C., 20036; tel (202) 776-9601; fax 822-6563).

Work and Volunteer

Some people look for temporary jobs upon arrival in Na'ama Bay or Alexandria. The **American Chamber of Commerce** in Cairo at the Marriott Hotel (tel. (02) 340 88 88) will pass your resume along to any interested local companies. Work permits can be obtained through any Egyptian consulate, or from the Ministry of the Interior.

The **Supreme Council for Youth and Sport in Egypt** (Foreign Relations Administration) runs programs in which students of different nationalities spend two to four weeks working together on agricultural or sociological projects. Contact the Council at 26th July St., Oqba Sq., Giza (tel. (02) 346 17 01) or the Egyptian Embassy.

American Field Service (AFS), 198 Madison Ave., 8th Fl., New York, NY 10016 (students tel. (800) AFS-INFO (237-4636); administration (800) 876-2376; fax (503) 241-1653; email afsinfo@afs.org; http://www.afs.org), offers summer-, semester-, and year-long homestay Egypt exchange programs for current students and short-term service projects for adults. Has programs for nearly every country of origin. Financial aid is available.

ISRAEL

The University Student Department of the **American Zionist Youth Foundation (USD/AZYF)** is a clearinghouse for many programs, offering tours and study or work/volunteer/archaeological dig programs. University programs offer classes in English or Hebrew. There are fully accredited programs in Jerusalem, Tel Aviv, Haifa, and Be'er Sheva. Contact the USD/AZYF at University Student Department, Israel Action Center, 110 E. 59th St. 4th floor, New York, NY 10022 (tel. (800) 27-ISRAEL (274-7723) or (212) 339-6940; fax 755-4781).

Work and Apprenticeships

Unemployment in Israel is high, greatly limiting work opportunities; foreigners must also compete with new immigrants from the Soviet Union. American or European companies with branches in Israel are a possible source of employment. Another option is volunteer work in exchange for room and board. Some people look for temporary jobs in Eilat upon arrival, where high tourism provides openings for foreigners to work in hotels and restaurants. Be wary of scams that exploit foreigners' unfamiliarity with the laws in order to get free labor.

The **Jewish Agency** is a good clearinghouse for work and volunteer opportunities throughout the country. Their representatives will help you find a kibbutz, a place to study Hebrew, or a volunteer organization. The multilingual staff is trained to work with immigrants and long-term visitors. English speakers should ask for Tziki Aud.

Write to the Information and Service Center, P.O. Box 31677, Jerusalem 91030 (tel. (02) 623 20 99 or 18 23, or 624 65 22; fax 623 53 28).

Kibbutzim

Israel's 250 kibbutzim (singular kibbutz), communal settlements whose members divide work and profits equally, are often eager for volunteers. Kibbutzim vary greatly in size, wealth, number of volunteers, and ideological basis. Volunteers generally work six eight-hour days per week, with a few days off per month, and receive a small monthly allowance in addition to room and board and various other benefits; the work is generally physical, in agriculture, industry, or service. Prior knowledge of Hebrew is helpful, but certainly not necessary; non-speakers can even study Hebrew through combined work/study Ulpan programs (see **Ulpanim,** p. 31). Accommodations are most often in dormitory settings. Kibbutz life can be seductive in its routine, and many volunteers find themselves staying longer than planned. Getting a written promise of placement on a specific kibbutz before arriving in Israel will help with passport authorities.

To apply for any kibbutz program, contact your local Kibbutz Aliya Desk or the main office at 110 E. 59th St., 4th floor, New York, NY 10022 (tel. (800) 247-7852; fax (212) 318-6134; email: kibbutzdsk@aol.com; http://www.webflex.com/kibbutz.htm). Applicants must be age 18-35 with no children; there is a two-month minimum commitment and no maximum stay length. After being interviewed and given the appropriate application and medical forms, you will be sent to the **Kibbutz Program Center, Volunteer Office** in Tel Aviv, 18 Frishman St., Center Ben Yehuda, 3rd floor, Tel Aviv 61030 (tel. (03) 527 88 74 or 524 61 56; fax 523 99 66), where you will be assigned to a kibbutz. For information and listings, get a copy of the 1997 edition of *Kibbutz Volunteer,* Vacation Work Publications, 9 Park End St., Oxford, OX1 1HJ, U.K. (tel. (01865) 241 978, UK£7.99 plus UK£2.50 shipping). **Project 67,** 94 Ben-Yehuda St., Tel Aviv 63345 (tel. (03) 523 01 40), places volunteers on Kibbutzim and *moshavim* for two to four months.

These agencies provide official volunteer appointments, but kibbutz volunteering can be arranged through informal trial-and-error as well. Many find that visiting a kibbutz, seeking out the volunteer leader, and asking if they need help is a preferable method, one that allows the would-be volunteer to test the environment rather than having to cope with a blind assignment (it also avoids registration fees). On the other hand, working through the agencies provides the security of a prompt match.

Moshavim

Moshavim, agricultural communities in which farms and homes are privately owned and operated, provide a somewhat different work experience from kibbutzim. You will receive free lodging either with a family or in a house with other workers. In return, you work a six-day week, at least eight hours per day. Workers are paid about US$300 per month, and are expected to pay for their own food. Applicants must be ages 18-35 and physically fit. Write the organizations listed above for kibbutzim or contact **Volunteers Moshavim Movement,** 19 Leonardo da Vinci St., Tel Aviv (tel. (03) 695 84 73; fax 691 89 96).

Archaeological Digs

Work on archaeological digs consists largely of digging pits, shoveling shards, and hauling baskets of dirt for eight to ten hours per day in searing heat—beginning at 5am; don't dream of discovering ancient treasures.

The "Dig for a Day" program by Archaeological Seminars is designed for the curious tourist. The three-hour program at the Beit Guvrin National Park includes a short seminar on the history of the area, excavation, a crawl through an unexcavated cave system, and a tour of the park (US$22). Individuals are taken on Fridays; the rest of the week is for groups. Reservations are a good idea. Write to P.O. Box 14002, Jaffa Gate, Jerusalem 91140 (tel. (02) 627 35 15; fax (02) 627 26 60).

Volunteer

Shatil, a project of the New Israel Fund, places volunteers with organizations working in areas such as civil and human rights, Jewish-Arab coexistence, the status of women, and religious tolerance. Contact them at the **New Israel Fund,** 1625 K St. NW #3500, Washington, D.C. 20006 (tel. (202) 223-3333), or at 9 Yad Ha-Rutzim St., Jerusalem 91534 (tel. (02) 672 30 95; fax 672 30 99).

The **Volunteers for Israel** program places participants in non-combat support jobs in the Israeli military. The three-week program involves menial work such as washing dishes or mending equipment. You will wear army fatigues, army boots, and sleep in army barracks, but don't expect to carry an Uzi or keep the uniform afterwards. The program offers reduced airfare on El Al or Tower Air, provided you fulfill your commitment. There may also be a special fare for those under 24. Contact: Volunteers for Israel, 330 W. 42nd St. #1618, New York, NY 10036 (tel. (212) 643-4848; fax 643-4855). The application includes a US$100 non-refundable registration fee.

Living Experiences

Project Otzma is a 10-month volunteer leadership development program for young adults ages 20-24 (college graduates preferred), which provides its participants with the opportunity to live and work in kibbutzim, youth *aliya* villages, immigrant absorbtion centers and areas of urban renewal. Participants also study, travel throughout the country, and live with host families. Contact: Council of Jewish Federations, 730 Broadway, New York, NY 10003 (tel. (212) 598-3532; fax 529-5842).

Livnot U'Lehibanot: To Build and To Be Built offers three-week or three-month study and work experiences in Jerusalem and Tzfat. Four hours per day of discussion-oriented classes and seminars exploring Jewish heritage and the land of Israel, and four hours per day of building and community service projects, plus hikes throughout the country. Open to ages 21-30. Contact: Livnot U'Lehibanot, at 110 E. 59th St. 3rd fl., New York, NY 10022 (tel. (212) 752-2390; fax 832-2597), or at 27 Ben-Zakkai, Katamon, Jerusalem 93585 (tel. (02) 679 34 91; fax 679 34 92; email livnot@jer1.org.il).

Study

Ulpanim

An *ulpan* is a five-month program providing intensive Hebrew and Jewish culture instruction. Israel has about 100 *ulpanim*. **Kibbutz Ulpanim** offer instruction together with work. Contact the **Kibbutz Aliya Desk** (see Kibbutzim, above).

The **Municipality of Jerusalem Department of Culture** can place in you in any *ulpan* in the city. They're located at 11 Bezalel St. (tel. (02) 563 37 18). Two of the city's better known *ulpanim* are **Beit Ha-Noar Ha'Ivri,** 105 Ha-Rav Herzog, Jerusalem 92622 (tel. (02) 678 94 41; fax 678 86 42) and **Mo'adon Ha'Oleh,** 9 Alkalai St., Jerusalem (tel. (02) 563 37 18).

Ulpan Akiva, Netanya, offers a live-in program at its seaside campus for students from around the world—Jews, non-Jews, Israelis, and new immigrants. The daily program includes five hours of Hebrew study, social and cultural activities, tours, trips, and special *Shabbat* activities. Three-, eight-, 12-, and 20-week courses are accredited by several universities. Costs vary. Contact: **Ulpan Akiva Netanya,** P.O. Box 6086, Netanya 42160, Israel (tel. (09) 835 23 12 or 13 or 14; fax 865 29 19), or **JCC Ulpan Center,** 15 W 65 St., 8th floor, New York, NY 10023 (tel. (212) 580-0099).

Universities

Programs for foreign students range in length from one summer to four years. **Year-abroad** programs usually begin with a four- to nine-week *ulpan* to learn Hebrew before the semester begins in October. Courses are usually in English; those who know Hebrew have the option of taking regular university courses. University programs are usually preceded by a *mekhina* (see **Mekhinot,** below). Admission for undergraduates requires proficiency in Hebrew and often at least one year of college. For all programs contact: **Israel Student Authority,** 15 Hillel St., Jerusalem (tel. (02) 624 11 21) or the New York consulate's Office of Academic Affairs.

Ben-Gurion University, Center for International Student Programs, Office of Student Services/NA, 342 Madison Ave. #1224, New York, NY 10173 (tel. (212) 687-7721; fax 370-0686; email bguosp@haven.ios.com). In Israel, contact: Center for International Student Programs, P.O. Box 653, Beer Sheva 84105 (tel. (07) 646 11 44; fax 647 29 48; email osp@bgumail.bgu.ac.il). Students must be enrolled at an accredited college or university.

American Society of Haifa University, 352 7th Ave., New York, NY 10001 (tel. (800) 334-0755, or (212) 631-7471; fax 631-7472; email university-of-haifa@worldnet.att.net), or Mt. Carmel Haifa 31905 (tel. (04) 824 07 66; fax 824 03 91; email rcbs702@uvm.haifa.ac.il; http://www.haifa.ac.il).

Hebrew University of Jerusalem, 11 E. 69th St., New York, NY 10021 (tel. (212) 472-2288; fax 517-4548). Friends of the Hebrew University, 3 St. Johns Wood Road, London NW8 8RB (tel (0171) 266 32 14; fax (0171) 289 55 49). In Israel, Mount Scopus, Jerusalem 91905 (tel. (02) 588 21 11).

Technion-Israel Institute of Technology, contact the American Technion Society National Office, 810 7th Ave., New York, NY 10019 (tel. (212) 262-6200; fax 765-1723) or the Institute directly at Technion City, Haifa, 32000 (tel. (04) 829 29 64).

Tel Aviv University, Office of Academic Affairs, 360 Lexington Ave., New York, NY 10017 (tel. (212) 687-5651; fax 687-4085), or Ramat Aviv, Tel Aviv 69978 (tel. (03) 640 81 11; fax (03) 640 95 98).

Mekhinot

Students who are not proficient in Hebrew but wish to enter a full undergraduate degree program usually first enroll in mekhina (preparation) programs, providing a year of intensive Hebrew and a chance to develop study plans. *Mekhinot* are offered by the universities and other schools of post-secondary education. Note that *mekhina* participation does not guarantee acceptance to a university; students must still take entrance examinations.

WEST BANK

During much of the *intifada,* all four West Bank universities—Birzeit, Bethlehem, Hebron, and An-Najah—were closed by the Israeli authorities as security threats. Today, most West Bank schools are still only open sporadically. **Birzeit University,** north of Ramallah, runs a Palestine and Arab Studies Program, with courses in Modern Standard Arabic, Colloquial Arabic, and the social sciences and arts. Semesters are in spring, summer, and fall. Courses cost US$500 each ($600 for language courses) plus food and lodging. For information, contact the Student Affairs Office, Birzeit University, P.O. Box 14, Birzeit, West Bank, Palestine (tel. (02) 998 20 00; fax 995 76 56 or 43 83; email pas-isp@admin.birzeit.edu; http://www.birzeit.edu/pas). Berzeit may also be able to provide up-to-date information on other organizations that administer programs in the West Bank or East Jerusalem (see more information about Birzeit and environs on p. 455).

JORDAN

Work

It's difficult for foreigners to find jobs in Jordan, although English skills are in demand. A combination of perfect English and business or banking skills is optimal. Positions must be arranged before arrival in order to get a work visa. **Work permits** can be secured from the Ministry of Labor. **Residence permits** are required for stays of more than three months. Volunteers for **archaeological digs** are in demand. The Peace Corps (see p. 25) currently operates in Jordan.

Study

Two Jordanian universities are open to foreign students. The **University of Jordan Language Centre** (Al-Jubaiha, Amman) offers a five-level intensive program in Arabic (classical and spoken) for non-native speakers. All levels are offered regularly and concurrently during the fall (Sept.-Jan.), spring (Feb.-May), and summer (June-Aug.). Tuition fees for the fall and spring are JD340, for the summer JD205. Write to Director, Language Centre, University of Jordan, Amman 11942, Jordan, for application forms (tel. (06) 843 555, ext. 3436 or 3427; fax 832 318). **Yarmouk University** in Irbid (tel. (02) 271 100) has a more conservative atmosphere (although you shouldn't plan on wearing shorts at either). The courses for foreign students at Yarmouk will be offered only if there are enough people interested in enrolling. Both schools guarantee dormitory housing for women. A Jordanian embassy, consulate, or information bureau (see p. 3 and 5) can provide further information on either school.

SYRIA

As in Jordan, work for foreigners is scarce in Syria. A **residence permit** is required, as visitors on tourist visas are not allowed to work; bureaucratic nightmares abound. Tutoring or teaching English as a second language are your best bets for employment. Archaeological digs offer hard work for no pay; volunteers are generally welcome. Few Westerners study in Syria. Universities are state-run, so the curricula do not vary, but graduate students and lecturers can individualize their course of study to a degree. Contact the Syrian Embassy for assistance and information.

LEBANON

The **American University of Beirut (AUB),** chartered in 1863 by the state of New York, is located in Beirut's Hamra District (Ras Beirut) and is a centerpiece of the youth culture and social life of the city. The university offers a wide range of academic and technical programs, from philosophy to poultry science. Tuition costs are about L£5,000,000 per semester (12 credits); L£400,000 per credit during the summer session. Admissions criteria are rigorous, but applications to the university are "open to all who wish to learn, regardless of color, sex, nationality, political belief, or religious persuasion." All courses are conducted in English. Their web page at http://www.aub.ac.lb can give more detailed information on applications, programs, housing, and everything else. To get questions answered, write to Office of the Registrar, American University of Beirut (AUB), P.O. Box 11-0236, Beirut, Lebanon or email to registrar@aub.edu.lb. In the U.S., university officials can be contacted by writing to American University of Beirut, 850 Third Avenue, 18th floor, New York, NY 10022-6297 (fax (212) 478-1995).

People who seek to **work** in Lebanon must acquire a special work visa. Contact the nearest Lebanese embassy for details.

■ Specific Concerns

WOMEN AND TRAVEL

Women can travel safely alone or in groups in Israel, Egypt, Jordan, Lebanon, Syria, and the West Bank. As is true for all travelers in the region, common sense and cultural sensitivity are the best ways to avoid threatening situations. In major cities and at tourist sites, Western codes of dress and behavior are more acceptable than elsewhere. Further from metropolitan areas in Egypt, Jordan, Syria, Lebanon, and the West Bank, and in both the Orthodox Jewish and Arab sections of Israel, however, it is advisable to dress modestly (nothing sleeveless or tight, with skirts and pants well below the knees) and adhere to local standards of behavior as much as possible. Only on or very near beaches of tourist resorts (and dive centers, in the Sinai) are locals used to seeing women in bathing suits.

While foreign women are not expected to behave like locals, it is a good idea to make yourself as inconspicuous as possible by following a few simple guidelines. Don't smoke in public in Arab areas. Avoid cafes with few women. In Islamist-controlled areas, covering your hair in public with a head scarf can sometimes save you from stares and unwanted attention. Covering your hair when taking public transportation in these areas is always wise, especially for longer bus rides or on crowded vehicles. Unfortunately, no matter what you do (short of dressing like a devout Muslim woman), you will be the subject of looks, comments, and in crowded areas, perhaps even touching. Fortunately, violent attacks on foreign women are uncommon in the Middle East.

The best response to harassment is often none at all. Avoiding eye contact, walking confidently, and showing no interest in come-ons is often the most efficient way to navigate. If a situation arises that feels threatening, a sharp rebuke will usually get your point across no matter what language you are speaking. Most Middle Eastern men are easily embarrassed after being publicly confronted. Turn to an older woman or a group of women if the offender is persistent. In general, don't be afraid to yell in any language to call attention to your situation. If it becomes clear that a truly threatening situation will not go away, leave as quickly as possible and inform the tourist police or a comparable authority. Always carry change for the phone and enough extra money for a bus or taxi. *Let's Go* lists emergency, police, and consulate phone numbers in most cities: memorize them or carry them around with you.

Other methods of preventing harassment include strolling arm in arm with another woman, a common Middle Eastern practice, and wearing a wedding ring. The latter is especially smart if you're traveling with a man, as unmarried intimacy between the sexes may be perceived as immoral. Claiming that you are about to meet a male member of your family, like a brother, father, uncle, or husband, is also sure to make even the most persistent man think twice.

When traveling by train, choose compartments occupied by other women or couples. When traveling by *felucca*, it's best to bring along a male companion. In cabs, keep your luggage handy and the door unlocked. *Never* hitchhike—it's especially dangerous in Israel.

Once you've arrived at your destination, consider staying with religious organizations or in hostels with doors that lock from the inside. Forego cheaper places in remote areas of town in favor of popular youth hostels or more centrally located hotels. Avoid walking alone in alleys, dark streets, even near isolated sights. If you lose your way, ask other women or couples for directions. If you think you are being followed, walk quickly and confidently to the nearest public area. A whistle or an airhorn on your keychain is always useful. Consider enrolling in an **Impact Model Mugging** self-defense course for a more in-depth approach to specific tools geared towards women's safety and empowerment (see **Safety and Security,** p. 15).

Don't take unnecessary risks, but don't lose your spirit of adventure! The books listed below and the individual country introductions in this book can offer more information and advice.

A Journey of One's Own, by Thalia Zepatos, (US$17). Interesting and full of good advice, with a bibliography of books and resources. **Adventures in Good Company,** on group travel by the same author, costs US$17. Available from The Eighth Mountain Press, 624 Southeast 29th Ave., Portland, OR 97214 (tel. (503) 233-3936; fax 233-0774; email eightmt@aol.com).

Handbook For Women Travellers by Maggie and Gemma Moss (UK£9). Encyclopedic and well-written. Available from Piatkus Books, 5 Windmill St., London W1P 1HF (tel. (0171) 631 07 10).

Travelin' Woman, 855 Moraga Dr., #14, Los Angeles, CA 90049 (tel. (310) 472-6318) or (800) 871-6409). Monthly newsletter with features, news, and tips, subscription US$48.

OLDER TRAVELERS

Senior citizens are eligible for a wide range of discounts on transportation, museums, movies, theaters, concerts, restaurants, and accommodations. If you don't see a senior citizen price listed, ask and you may be delightfully surprised.

Elderhostel, 75 Federal St., 3rd Fl., Boston, MA 02110-1941 (tel. (617) 426-7788; fax 426-8351; email Cadyg@elderhostel.orghttp://www.elderhostel.org). For those 55 or over (spouse of any age). Programs at colleges, universities, and other learning centers in over 70 countries on varied subjects lasting 1-4 weeks.

National Council of Senior Citizens, 8403 Colesville Rd., Silver Spring, MD 20910 (tel. (301) 578-8800; fax 578-8999). Memberships cost US$13 per year, US$33 for 3 years, or US$175 for a lifetime. Individuals or couples get hotel and auto rental discounts, a senior citizen newspaper, and use of a discount travel agency.

Pilot Books, 127 Sterling Ave., P.O. Box 2102, Greenport, NY 11944 (tel. (516) 477-1094 or (800) 79-PILOT (797-4568); fax (516) 477-0978; email feedback@pilot-books.com; http://www.pilotbooks.com). Publishes many helpful guides including *Doctor's Guide to Protecting Your Health Before, During, and After International Travel* (US$10, postage US$2). Ask for a complete list of titles.

No Problem! Worldwise Tips for Mature Adventurers, by Janice Kenyon. Advice and info on insurance, finances, security, health, packing. Useful appendices. US$16 from Orca Book Publishers, P.O. Box 468, Custer, WA 98240-0468.

BISEXUAL, GAY, AND LESBIAN TRAVELERS

Open expressions of gay affection in Israel are uncommon, and nonexistent in the rest of the Middle East. Israel (particularly Tel Aviv) is a world apart from its Arab neighbors in terms of the public and legal status of gays, lesbians, and bisexuals and the availability of gathering places and support organizations. Homosexuality is completely invisible in the Arab world and **illegal** in Jordan, Syria, and Lebanon, and most Arabs want it to stay that way. Public displays of affection are a bad idea for people of every sexual orientation. What happens behind closed doors (and everything in Arab countries occurs behind closed doors) is another story. There is *no* gay and lesbian assistance in Egypt, Jordan, Syria, or Lebanon. One main organization for gay and lesbian concerns in Israel is the **Society for the Protection of Personal Rights,** P.O. Box 376 04, Tel Aviv 61375 (tel. (03) 629 36 81; fax 525 23 41), or P.O. Box 3592, Haifa (tel. (04) 867 26 65). A community center, library, and coffee shop are located in the basement at 28 Naḥmani St., Tel Aviv. The society's gay and lesbian hotline is the **White Line** (Ha-Kav Ha-Lavan; tel. (03) 629 27 97; operates Sun.-Thurs. 7:30-11:30pm).

International Gay and Lesbian Travel Association, P.O. Box 4974, Key West, FL 33041 (tel. (800) 448-8550; fax (305) 296-6633; email IGTA@aol.com; http://www.rainbow-mall.com/igta). An organization of over 1300 companies serving gay and lesbian travelers worldwide. Call for lists of travel agents, accommodations, and events.

International Lesbian and Gay Association (ILGA), 81 rue Marché-au-Charbon, B-1000 Bruxelles, Belgium (tel./fax 32-2-502-24 71; email ilga@ilga.org). Not a travel service. Provides political information, such as homosexuality laws of individual countries.

Spartacus International Gay Guides (US$33), published by Bruno Gmunder, Postfach 61 01 04, D-10921 Berlin, Germany (tel. (30) 615 00 3-42; fax (30) 615 91 34). Lists bars, restaurants, hotels, and bookstores around the world catering to gays. Also lists hotlines for gays in various countries and homosexuality laws for each country. Available in bookstores and in the U.S. by mail from Lambda Rising, 1625 Connecticut Ave. NW, Washington D.C., 20009-1013 (tel. (202) 462-6969).

DISABLED TRAVELERS

Many areas of the Middle East are not prepared to deal with the special concerns of disabled travelers; travel in these places could be quite difficult. A guided or group tour can be the most rewarding option, depending on the extent of the disability. The following resources can be invaluable in planning or researching trips.

Access Project (PHSP), 39 Bradley Gardens, West Ealing, London W13 8HE, U.K. Publications researched by persons with disabilities. They cover traveling, accommodations, and access to sights and entertainment. Includes a "Loo Guide" with a list of wheelchair-accessible toilets. Sells *Access in Israel* (£5).

American Foundation for the Blind, 11 Penn Plaza, 300, New York, NY 10011 (tel. (212) 502-7600), open Mon.-Fri. 8:30am-4:30pm. Provides information and services for the visually impaired. For a catalogue of products, contact Lighthouse, Enterprises, 36-20 Northern Boulevard, Long Island City, NY 10011 (tel. (800) 829-0500).

Directions Unlimited, 720 N. Bedford Rd., Bedford Hills, NY 10507 (tel. (800) 533-5343; in NY (914) 241-1700; fax 241-0243). Specializes in arranging individual and group vacations, tours, and cruises for the physically disabled. Group tours for blind travelers.

Mobility International, USA (MIUSA), P.O. Box 10767, Eugene, OR 97440 (tel. (514) 343-1284 voice and TDD; fax 343-6812; email info@miusa.org; http://miusa.org). International Headquarters in Brussels, rue de Manchester 25, Brussels, Belgium, B-1070 (tel. (322) 410-6297; fax 410 6874). Contacts in 30 countries. Information on travel programs, international work camps, accommodations, access guides, and organized tours for those with physical disabilities. Membership US$30 per year. Sells the 3rd edition of *A World of Options: A Guide to International Educational Exchange, Community Service, and Travel for Persons with Disabilities* (US$30, nonmembers US$35; organizations US$40).

Yad Sarah, 43 Haneviim St., Jerusalem 95141 (tel. (02) 644 44 44; fax 644 44 93). With 76 branches throughout Israel, it is the country's largest volunteer organization. Free loan of medical and rehabilitative equipment, oxygen service, and transport service for persons in wheelchairs. Call the English speaking P.R. director at least 2 weeks in advance to book airport pick-up and for help with special needs.

TRAVELING WITH CHILDREN

When deciding where to stay, remember the special needs of young children; if you pick a hostel, call ahead and make sure it's child-friendly. If you rent a car, make sure the rental company provides a car seat for younger children. Consider using a papoose-style device to carry your baby on walking trips. Be sure that your child carries some sort of ID in case of an emergency or he or she gets lost, and arrange a reunion spot in case of separation when sight-seeing.

Children under two generally fly for 10% of the adult airfare on international flights (this does not necessarily include a seat). International fares are usually discounted

25% for children from two to 11. Breast-feeding is often a problem while traveling; pack accordingly.

Backpacking with Babies and Small Children (US$10), published by Wilderness Press, 2440 Bancroft Way, Berkeley, CA 94704 (tel. (800) 443-7227 or (510) 843-8080; fax 548-1355; email wpress@ix.netcom.com) offers tips for budget travelers with children.

■ Packing

Fashion is the least of your worries when trekking through the Sinai or searching for the hidden treasures of Palmyra. A general rule is to pack only what you absolutely need, then remove half the clothes and take twice the money.

Decide whether a backpack, light suitcase, or shoulder bag is most suitable for your travels. If you're planning to move around a lot, a sturdy **backpack** is hard to beat. A small **daypack** is indispensable for flights, sight-seeing, and holding your valuables. "Fanny-packs" look silly, label you as an easy mark, and are easily stolen; instead use a hidden moneybelt or neck pouch to store your passport, money, and important documents, which you should keep with you *at all times.*

Natural fibers are better than synthetics in the heat. Dark colors hide dirt, but light colors deflect sun. After a day in an oasis, a little dirt won't be a big deal. In many areas and especially holy sites, both men and women should cover their knees and upper arms to avoid offending local rules of modesty (see **Travel Etiquette,** above). Jeans are heavy and difficult to wash; take khakis or light cotton **trousers** instead. **Shorts** are okay in some touristy areas. Bring one wool sweater (or something with Polartec) for cooler nights; wool is ideal because it is warm and light-weight.

Appropriate shoes are vital: well-cushioned **sneakers** are good for walking. Lace-up leather shoes with firm grips provide better support and social acceptibilty than athletic shoes. For hiking, a pair of **hiking boots,** with good ventilation, is a must. A double pair of socks—light absorbent cotton inside and thick wool outside—will cushion feet, keep them dry, and help prevent blisters. If you only want to bring one pair, the best all-around footwear are **sneakers-cum-hiking boots**. Talcum powder in your shoes and on your feet can prevent sores, and moleskin is great for blisters. Break in your shoes before you leave home. You should also bring a comfortable pair of **sandals** for urban trekking in sweltering climes.

If you plan on camping, remember are warm layers (wool or synthetic, not cotton!), a first-aid kit, high energy food, and water. Your camping list will depend heavily on the duration and destination of your trip, but some essentials should be toted by everybody: a frame backpack for any trip longer than an overnight; a Swiss Army knife; a hat; matches; a sleeping bag rated to the temperature of the coldest night you might encounter; calamine lotion, snake bite medicine, and lotion for sunburns; a sturdy pair of hiking boots; and a camel's worth of water and water-purification tablets. Some other items to consider include a tent, a stove, a plastic groundcloth, a flashlight, and insect repellent.

This book lists laundry options in the city or town coverage, but laundromats are sometimes hard to find; washing clothes in your hotel sink can be a better option. Bring a small bar or tube of **laundry soap, a rubber squash ball** to stop up the sink, and a **travel clothes line.** Also pack deodorant, razors, condoms, tampons, re-hydration and constipation pills, and ibuprofen. **Contact lens** supplies are rare and expensive. Either bring enough saline, etc. for the entire trip or wear your glasses.

Electric current in Israel, Egypt, Jordan, and Syria is 220V. Travelers with appliances designed for 110V (North America) should bring a **converter.** Most outlets are made for round prongs, so even if your machine has a built-in converter, you'll also need an **adapter** to change the plug shape. Get them both before you leave.

Film is generally more expensive abroad. Some foreign airport X-ray machines are film-safe and some are not—better to play it safe and protect your film with a special lead-lined bag available from any photo shop. (Or ask the sometimes unwilling security people to check it by hand.) It is always a good idea to bring along a **first-aid kit.** And finally, bring a small **towel;** hostels and inexpensive hotels don't provide them.

GETTING THERE

■ Budget Travel Services

Students and people under 26 ("youth") with proper ID qualify for enticing reduced airfares. These are rarely available from airlines or travel agents, but instead can be bought from student travel agencies which negotiate special reduced-rate bulk purchase with the airlines, then resell them to the youth market. Return-date change fees also tend to be low (around US$35 per segment through Council or Let's Go Travel). Most flights are on major airlines, though in peak season some agencies may sell seats on less reliable chartered aircraft. Student travel agencies can also help non-students and people over 26, but probably won't be able to get fares as low.

Campus Travel, 52 Grosvenor Gardens, London SW1W 0AG (http://www.campus-travel.co.uk). 46 branches in the U.K. Student and youth fares on plane, train, boat, and bus travel. Skytrekker, flexible airline tickets. Discount and ID cards for students and youths, travel insurance for students and those under 35, and maps and guides. Puts out travel suggestion booklets. Telephone booking service: in Europe call (0171) 730 34 02; in North America call (0171) 730 21 01; worldwide call (0171) 730 81 11; in Manchester call (0161) 273 17 21; in Scotland (0131) 668 33 03.

Council Travel (http://www.ciee.org/travel/index.htm), the travel division of Council, is a full-service travel agency specializing in youth and budget travel. They offer discount airfares on scheduled airlines, railpasses, hosteling cards, low-cost accommodations, guidebooks, budget tours, travel gear, and international student (ISIC), youth (GO25), and teacher (ITIC) identity cards. U.S. offices include: Emory Village, 1561 N. Decatur Rd., **Atlanta,** GA 30307 (tel. (404) 377-9997); 2000 Guadalupe, **Austin,** TX 78705 (tel. (512) 472-4931); 273 Newbury St., **Boston,** MA 02116 (tel. (617) 266-1926); 1153 N. Dearborn, **Chicago,** IL 60610 (tel. (312) 951-0585); 10904 Lindbrook Dr., **Los Angeles,** CA 90024 (tel. (310) 208-3551); 1501 University Ave. SE #300, **New York,** NY 10017 (tel. (212) 822-2700); 530 Bush St., **San Francisco,** CA 94108 (tel. (415) 421-3473); 1314 NE 43rd St. #210, **Seattle,** WA 98105 (tel. (206) 632-2448); 3300 M St. NW, **Washington, D.C.** 20007 (tel. (202) 337-6464). **For U.S. cities not listed,** call 800-2-COUNCIL (226-8624). Also 28A Poland St. (Oxford Circus), **London,** W1V 3DB (tel. (0171) 287 3337); **Paris** (146 55 55 65); and **Munich** (089 39 50 22).

Let's Go Travel, Harvard Student Agencies, 17 Holyoke St., Cambridge, MA 02138 (tel. (617) 495-9649; fax 495-7956; email travel@hsa.net; http://hsa.net/travel). Railpasses, HI-AYH memberships, ISICs, ITICs, FIYTO cards, guidebooks (including every *Let's Go* at a substantial discount), maps, and a complete line of budget travel gear. All items available by mail; call or write for a catalogue (or see the catalogue in center of this publication).

STA Travel, 6560 Scottsdale Rd. #F100, Scottsdale, AZ 85253 (tel. (800) 777-0112) in U.S.; fax (602) 922-0793; http://sta-travel.com). A student and youth travel organization with over 150 offices worldwide offering discount airfares for young travelers, railpasses, accommodations, tours, insurance, and ISICs. 16 offices in the U.S. including: 297 Newbury Street, **Boston,** MA 02115 (tel. (617) 266-6014); 429 S. Dearborn St., **Chicago,** IL 60605 (tel. (312) 786-9050; 7202 Melrose Ave., **Los Angeles,** CA 90046 (tel. (213) 934-8722); 10 Downing St., Ste. G, **New York,** NY 10003 (tel. (212) 627-3111); 4341 University Way NE, **Seattle,** WA 98105 (tel. (206) 633-5000); 2401 Pennsylvania Ave., **Washington, D.C.** 20037 (tel. (202) 887-0912); 51 Grant Ave., **San Francisco,** CA 94108 (tel. (415) 391-8407), **Miami,** FL 33133 (tel. (305) 461-3444). In the U.K., 6 Wrights Ln., **London** W8 6TA (tel. (0171) 938 47 11 for North American travel). In New Zealand, 10 High St., **Auckland** (tel. (09) 309 97 23). In Australia, 222 Faraday St., **Melbourne** VIC 3050 (tel. (03) 349 69 11).

Travel CUTS (Canadian Universities Travel Services Limited), 187 College St., Toronto, Ont. M5T 1P7 (tel. (416) 979-2406; fax 979-8167; email mail@travelcuts.com).

Canada's national student travel bureau and equivalent of Council, with 40 offices across Canada. Also in the U.K., 295-A Regent St., **London** W1R 7YA (tel. (0171) 637 31 61). Discounted domestic and international airfares open to all; special student fares to all destinations with valid ISIC. Issues ISIC, FIYTO, GO25, and HI hostel cards, as well as railpasses. Offers free *Student Traveller* magazine, as well as information on the Student Work Abroad Program (SWAP).

Unitravel, 117 North Warson Rd., St. Louis, MO 63132 (tel. (800) 325 2222; fax (314) 569 2503). Offers discounted airfares on major scheduled airlines from the U.S. to Europe, Africa, and Asia.

■ By Plane

The **airline industry** attempts to squeeze every dollar from customers; finding a cheap airfare will be easier if you understand the airlines' systems. Call every toll-free number and don't be afraid to ask about discounts; if you don't ask, it's unlikely they'll be volunteered. Have knowledgeable **travel agents** guide you; better yet, have an agent who specializes in the Middle East guide you. An agent whose clients fly mostly to Nassau or Miami will not be the best person to hunt down a bargain flight to Cairo. Travel agents may not want to spend time finding the cheapest fares (for which they receive the lowest commissions), but if you travel often, you should definitely find an agent who will cater to you and your needs and track down deals in exchange for your frequent business.

Students and others under 26 should never need to pay full price for a ticket. Seniors can also get great deals; many airlines offer senior traveler clubs or airline passes with few restrictions and discounts for their companions. Outsmart airline reps with the phone-book-sized *Official Airline Guide* (check your local library; at US$359/yr, the tome costs as much as some flights), a monthly guide listing nearly every scheduled flight in the world (with fares, US$479) and toll-free phone numbers for all the airlines which allow you to call in reservations directly. More accessible is

Michael McColl's *The Worldwide Guide to Cheap Airfare* (US$15), an incredibly useful guide for finding cheap airfare.

There is also a steadily increasing amount of travel information to be found on the Internet. The *Official Airline Guide* now also has a website (http://www.oag.com) which allows access to flight schedules, but it costs (one-time hook-up fee US$25 plus 17-47¢/min. user fee). The site also provides information on hotels, cruises, and rail and ferry schedules. **TravelHUB** (http://www.travelhub.com) will help you search for travel agencies on the web. The **Air Traveler's Handbook** (http://www.cis.ohio-state.edu/hypertext/faq/usenet/travel/air/handbook/top.html) is an excellent source of general information on air travel. Marc-David Seidel's **Airlines of the Web** (http://www.itn.net/airlines) provides links to pages and 800 numbers for most of the world's airlines. The newsgroup **rec.travel.air** is a good source of tips on current bargains.

Most airfares peak between mid-June and early September. Midweek (Mon.-Thurs. morning) round-trip flights run cheaper than on weekends; weekend flights, however, are generally less crowded. Return-date flexibility is usually not an option for the budget traveler; traveling with an "open return" ticket can be pricier than fixing a return date and paying to change it. Whenever flying internationally, pick up your ticket well in advance of the departure date, have the flight confirmed within 72 hours of departure, and arrive at the airport at least three hours before your flight.

COMMERCIAL AIRLINES

If you choose to fly with a commercial airline, you'll be paying for reliability and flexibility. **Advanced Purchase Excursion (APEX) Fares,** commercial airlines' lowest regular rates, provide confirmed reservations and "open-jaw" tickets (landing in and returning from different cities). Reservations usually must be made 7 to 21 days in advance with a 7- to 14-day minimum and 30- to 90-day maximum stay. Beware hefty penalties for canceling or altering reservations. Also, be sure to ask for student, youth, or senior fares. You may have to wait until three days before departure to get these fares. Fares shown here were compiled June to August 1997 from the airlines themselves. Prices often vary within the peak three months; keep your eyes open.

Many airlines have flights to the Middle East. European carriers such as **Air France** (tel. (800) 237-2747; http://www.airfrance.fr) and **KLM Royal Dutch Airlines** (tel. (800) 374-7747, in Britain tel. (0181) 750 9000, in Australia tel. (008) 222 747; http://www.klm.nl) fly from New York and London to Tel Aviv, Amman, Damascus, and Cairo with connections in Paris and Amsterdam.

British Airways (tel. (800) 247-9297, in Britain tel. (0345) 222 111; http://british-airways.com). Lowest round-trip prices are London to Amman, Damascus, or Cairo US$976, to Tel Aviv US$310.

EgyptAir (tel. (800) 334-6787). Egypt's national airline. Round-trip New York City to Cairo US$1784 (student fare available). London to Cairo US$976.

El Al (tel. (800) 223-6700; http://www.elal.com). Israel's national airline. Round-trip New York City to Tel Aviv US$1070. Round-trip London to Tel Aviv US$500.

Middle East Air (tel. (212) 664-7310; http://www.mea.com.lb). Round-trip London to Beirut US$550.

Royal Jordanian Airlines (tel. (800) 223-0470; http://www.rjor.com.jo). Jordan's national airline. Round-trip New York City to Amman US$1369. London to Amman US$1289. Tour department (tel. (800) RJTOUR8 (758 6878).

AIRLINE TICKET CONSOLIDATORS

Ticket consolidators resell unsold tickets on commercial and charter airlines at unpublished fares. Consolidator flights are the best deals if you are travelling on short notice or in the peak season, when published fares are jacked way up. Fares sold by consolidators are generally much cheaper; a 30-40% price reduction is not uncommon. There are rarely age constraints or stay limitations, but unlike tickets bought through an airline, you won't be able to use your tickets on another flight if you miss yours, and you will have to go back to the consolidator to get a refund, rather than the airline. Keep in mind that these tickets are often for coach seats on connecting (not direct) flights on foreign airlines, and that frequent-flyer miles may not be credited. Decide what you can and can't live with before shopping.

Not all consolidators deal with the general public; many only sell tickets through travel agents. **Bucket shops** are retail agencies that specialize in getting cheap tickets. Although ticket prices are marked up slightly, bucket shops generally have access to a larger market than would be available to the public and can also get tickets from wholesale consolidators. Look for bucket shops' tiny ads in the travel section of weekend papers; in the U.S., the *Sunday New York Times* is a good source. In London, a call to the **Air Travel Advisory Bureau** (tel. (0171) 636 50 00) can provide names of reliable consolidators and discount flight specialists. Kelly Monaghan's *Consolidators: Air Travel's Bargain Basement* (US$7 plus US$2 shipping) from the Intrepid Traveler, P.O. Box 438, New York, NY 10034 (email intreptrav@aol.com), is an invaluable source for more information.

Dollarwise Travel, 7221 NW 12th St., Miami, FL 33126 (tel. (305) 592-3343), specializes in flights from the U.S. to the Middle East, and **Tourlite International,** 551 Fifth Ave., New York, NY 10176 (tel. (800) 272-7600), specializes in budget flights and tours to the Mediterranean region. For a processing fee, depending on the number of travelers and the itinerary, **Travel Avenue,** Chicago, IL (tel. (800) 333-3335; fax (312) 876-1254; http://www.travelavenue.com) will search for the lowest international airfare available and even give you a rebate on fares over US$300.

CHARTER FLIGHTS

Charters are flights a tour operator contracts with an airline (usually one specializing in charters) to fly extra loads of passengers to peak-season destinations. Charters are often cheaper than flights on scheduled airlines, especially during peak seasons, although fare wars, consolidator tickets, and small airlines can beat charter prices. Some charters operate nonstop, and restrictions on minimum advance-purchase and minimum stay are more lenient. However, charter flights fly less frequently than major airlines, make refunds particularly difficult, and are almost always fully booked. Schedules and itineraries may also change or be cancelled at the last moment (as late as 48 hours before the trip, and without a full refund), and check-in, boarding, and baggage claim are often much slower. As always, pay with a credit card if you can; consider traveler's insurance against trip interruption.

Try **Interworld** (tel. (305) 443-4929, fax 443-0351); **Travac** (tel. (800) 872-8800; fax (212) 714-9063; email mail@travac.com; http://www.travac.com) or **Rebel,** Valencia, CA (tel. (800) 227-3235; fax (805)-294-0981; http://rebeltours.com; email travel@rebeltours.com) or Orlando, FL (tel. (800) 732-3588). Don't be afraid to call every number and hunt for the best deal.

Eleventh-hour **discount clubs** and **fare brokers** offer members savings on charter flights and tour packages. Research your options carefully. **Last Minute Travel Club,** 100 Sylvan Rd., Woburn, MA 01801 (tel. (800) 527-8646 or (617) 267-9800), and **Discount Travel International** New York, NY (tel. (212) 362-3636; fax 362-3236) are among the few travel clubs that don't charge a membership fee. Others include **Moment's Notice,** New York, NY (tel. (718) 234-6295; fax 234 6450; http://www.moments-notice.com), which offers air tickets, tours, and hotels for a US$25 annual fee; **Travelers Advantage,** Stamford, CT (tel. (800) 548-1116; http://www.travelersadvantage.com; US$49 annual fee); and **Travel Avenue** (tel. (800) 333-3335; see **Ticket Consolidators,** above). Study these organizations' contracts closely; you don't want to end up with an unwanted overnight layover.

ONCE THERE

■ Border Crossings

> Overland border crossing policies in the Middle East seem to change with the weather; check with government tourist offices for the latest information. As late as September 1997, neither Syria nor Lebanon would admit travelers with evidence of a visit to Israel in their passports. Israeli officials can give you a detachable visa stamp upon request. Egyptian and Jordanian entry stamps from borders with Israel may also keep you out of Syria and Lebanon.

U.S. citizens can still obtain limited-duration (2yr.) second passports from the State Department: pick up the standard passport-by-mail form at your nearest federal building and send it in along with a detailed written statement explaining why you require a second passport, your present passport, and a fee. Other countries may also issue second passports. For more information, contact your Government Passport Agency (see **Passports**, p. 6).

For all border crossings, we recommend that you have at least US$20 worth of the currency of each country involved, plus the same in U.S. currency. There are exchange facilities at most borders, but they could be closed or out of cash. For more information on border crossings, please see specific crossing sites; check the **index** under **"border crossings"** for page numbers.

■ Accommodations

HOSTELS

For tight budgets and those lonesome traveling blues, hostels can't be beat. Hostels are generally dorm-style accommodations, often in large single-sex rooms with bunk beds, although some hostels do offer private rooms for families and couples. They sometimes have kitchens and utensils for your use, bike or moped rentals, storage areas, and laundry facilities. There can be drawbacks: some hostels close during certain daytime "lock-out" hours, have a curfew, impose a maximum stay, or, less frequently, require that you do chores. Fees range from US$5 to $25 per night and hostels associated with one of the large hostel associations often have lower rates for members. If you have Internet access, check out the Internet Guide to Hostelling (http://hostels.com), which includes hostels from around the world in addition to oodles of information about hostelling and backpacking worldwide. Reservations for over 300 **Hostelling International (HI)** hostels (see listing below) may be made via the International Booking Network (IBN), a computerized system that allows you make hostels reservations months in advance for a nominal fee (tel. (202) 783-6161). Most countries have their own HI branch; if you plan to stay in hostels, consider joining one of these associations:

An Óige (Irish Youth Hostel Association), 61 Mountjoy St., Dublin 7 (tel. (01) 830 4555; fax 830-5808; anoige@iol.ie). One-year membership is IR£7.50, under 18 IR£4, family IR£7.50 for each adult with children under 16 free.

Australian Youth Hostels Association (AYHA), Level 3, 10 Mallett St., Camperdown NSW 2050 (tel. (02) 9565 1699; fax 9565 1325; email YHA@zeta.org.au). Memberships AUS$44, renewal AUS$27; under 18 AUS$13.

Hostelling International-American Youth Hostels (HI-AYH), 733 15th St. NW, #840, Washington, D.C. 20005 (202-783-6161; fax 783-6171; email hiayhserv@hiayh.org; http://www.hiayh.org). Maintains 35 offices in the U.S. Memberships can be purchased at many travel agencies or the national office in Washington, D.C. One year membership US$25, under 18 US$10, over 54 US$15,

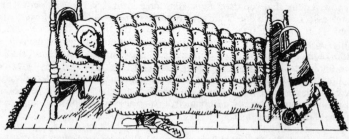

family cards US$35; includes *Hostelling North America: The Official Guide to Hostels in Canada and the United States*. Reserve by letter, phone, fax, or through the International Booking Network (IBN), a computerized reservation system which lets you book from other HI hostels worldwide up to 6 months in advance.

Hostelling International-Canada (HI-C), 400-205 Catherine St., Ottawa, Ontario K2P 1C3, Canada (613-237-7884; fax 237-7868). Maintains 73 hostels throughout Canada. IBN booking centers in Edmonton, Montreal, Ottawa, and Vancouver; expect CDN$9-22.50/night. Membership packages: 1 year, under 18 CDN$12; 1 year, over 18 CDN$25; 2 year, over 18 CDN$35; lifetime CDN$175.

Scottish Youth Hostels Association (SYHA), 7 Glebe Crescent, Stirling FK8 2JA (tel. (01786) 891400; fax 891333; email syha@syha.org.uk; http://www.syha.org.uk). Membership UK£6, under 18 UK£2.50.

Youth Hostels Association of England and Wales (YHA), Trevelyan House, 8 St. Stephen's Hill, St. Albans, Hertfordshire AL1 2DY, England (tel. (01727) 855215; fax 844126). Enrollment fees are: UK£9.50; under 18 UK£3.50; UK£19 for both parents with children under 18 enrolled free; UK£9.50 for 1 parent with children under 18 enrolled free; UK£130 for lifetime membership.

Youth Hostels Association of Northern Ireland (YHANI), 22 Donegall Rd., Belfast BT12 5JN, Northern Ireland (tel. (01232) 324733 or 315435; fax 439699). Annual memberships UK£7, under 18 UK£3, family UK£14 for up to 6 children.

Youth Hostels Association of New Zealand (YHANZ), P.O. Box 436, 173 Gloucester St., Christchurch 1 (tel. (643) 379 9970; fax 365 4476; email info@yha.org.nz; http://www.yha.org.nz). Annual membership NZ$24.

Hostel Association of South Africa, P.O. Box 4402, Cape Town 8000 (tel. (021) 24 2511; fax 24 4119; email hisa@gem.co.za; http://www.gen.com/hisa). Membership SAR45, group SAR120, family SAR90, lifetime SAR250.

Egyptian Youth Hostel Association, 1 El-Ibrahimy St., Garden City, Cairo (tel. (02) 354 05 27; fax 355 03 29).

Israel Youth Hostels Association (ANA), 1 Shazar St., P.O. Box 6001, Jerusalem 91060 (tel. 655 84 00; fax 655 84 30). Youth Travel Bureau organizes tours to Israel, Egypt, and Jordan. Write for *Israel on the Youth Hostel Trail.*

CAMPING

Camping in the Middle East can be an incredibly rich, rewarding experience. It can also be prohibitively difficult and dangerous. Sleeping under the wide-open desert sky, on top of a temple mount, or amid a vibrant oasis, could be the most memorable part of your travels. To make sure that it's memorable for the right reasons, plan ahead. The right **equipment** and up-to-date information from rangers or other travelers are imperative. This book lists camping options and prohibitions around the region.

The three most important things to remember when hiking or camping: stay warm, stay dry, and stay hydrated. The vast majority of life-threatening wilderness problems stem from a failure to follow this advice. If you are going on any hike, overnight or just a day hike, that will take you more than one mile from civilization, you should pack enough equipment to keep you alive should disaster fall. This includes rain gear, warm layers (wool or synthetic, not cotton!), a first-aid kit, high energy food, and water. (For more suggestions on what to pack, see **Packing,** p. 36.)

■ Keeping in Touch

MAIL

Mail can be sent internationally through **Poste Restante** (the international phrase for General Delivery) to most cities and towns; it's well worth using and more reliable than you might think; in most cases it's the only option anyway. Mark the envelope "HOLD" and address it, for example, "Seth <u>GOLDBARG</u>, Poste Restante, City, Country." The recipient's last name should be capitalized and underlined. The mail will go to a special desk in the central post office, unless you specify a post office by street

ESSENTIALS

address or postal code. As a rule, it is best to use the largest post office in the area; sometimes, mail will be sent there regardless of what you write on the envelope.

When picking up your mail, bring your passport or other ID. If the clerks insist that there is nothing for you, have them check under your first name as well. *Let's Go* lists post offices in the **Practical Information** section for each city and notes which offices will hold mail.

Aerogrammes, printed sheets that fold into envelopes and travel via airmail, are available at post offices. It helps to mark "airmail" in the appropriate language if possible, though *par avion* is universally understood. Most post offices will charge exorbitant fees or simply refuse to send Aerogrammes with enclosures. Airmail between the Middle East and the U.S. or Europe usually takes about two weeks. Allow *at least* two weeks for Australia and New Zealand.

American Express travel offices throughout the world will act as a mail service for cardholders if you contact them in advance. Under this free **"Client Letter Service,"** they will hold mail for 30 days, forward upon request, and accept telegrams. Just like Poste Restante, the last name of the person to whom the mail is addressed should be capitalized and underlined. Some offices will offer these services to non-cardholders (especially those who have purchased AmEx Travellers' Cheques), but you must call ahead to make sure. Check the **Practical Information** section of the countries you plan to visit; *Let's Go* lists AmEx office locations for most large cities. A complete list is available free from AmEx (tel. (800) 528-4800) in the booklet *Traveler's Companion* or online at http://www.americanexpress.com/shared/cgi-bin/tsoserve.cgi?travel/index.

TELEPHONES

If you make direct international calls from **pay phones,** you may need to drop your coins as quickly as your words. In Israel, pay phones are card-operated; buy a phone card at post offices, convenience stores, or many other locations. In Egypt, the more reliable phones are card-operated and bright orange, but coin-operated ones are not

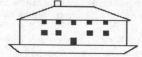

uncommon. In Jordan and Syria, pay phones cannot make international calls; either call from a **telephone office,** or make a friend and use a private phone. See country sections for details.

English-speaking operators are often available for both local and international assistance. Operators in most countries will place **collect calls** for you. It's cheaper to find a pay phone and deposit just enough money to be able to say "Call me" and give your number (though some pay phones can't receive calls).

Some companies, seizing upon this "call-me-back" concept, have created callback phone services. Under these plans, you call a specified number, ring once, and hang up. The company's computer calls back and gives you a dial tone. You can then make as many calls as you want, at rates about 20-60% lower than you'd pay using credit cards or pay phones. This option is most economical for loquacious travelers, as services may include a US$10-25 minimum billing per month. For information, call **America Tele-Fone** (tel. (800) 321-5817), **Globaltel** (tel. (770) 449-1295), **International Telephone** (tel. (800) 638-5558), and **Telegroup** (tel. (800) 338-0225).

A **calling card** may be the best and cheapest alternative; your local long-distance service provider will have a number for you to dial while travelling (either toll-free or charged as a local call) to connect instantly to an operator in your home country. The calls (plus a small surcharge) are then billed either collect or to the calling card. For more information, call **AT&T** about its **USADirect** and **World Connect** services (tel. (888) 288-4685; from abroad call (810) 262-6644 collect), **Sprint** (tel. (800) 877-4646; from abroad, call (913) 624-5335 collect), or **MCI WorldPhone** and **World Reach** (tel. (800) 444-4141; from abroad, dial the country's MCI access number). In Canada, contact Bell Canada's **Canada Direct** (tel. (800) 565 4708); in the U.K., British Telecom **BT Direct** (tel. (800) 34 51 44); in Ireland, Telecom Éireann **Ireland Direct** (tel. (800) 250 250); in Australia, Telstra **Australia Direct** (tel. 13 22 00); in New Zealand, **Telecom New Zealand** (tel. 123); in South Africa, **Telkom South Africa** (tel. 09 03).

OTHER COMMUNICATION

Domestic and international **telegrams** offer an option slower than phone but faster than post. Fill out a form at some post or telephone offices; cables arrive in one or two days. You may wish to consider **faxes** for more immediate, personal, and cheaper communication. Many places have options for sending and receiving faxes.

Daily newspapers, including *The London Times, The Wall Street Journal* (International Edition), *The New York Times,* and *The International Herald Tribune,* are available at train stations and kiosks in major cities in the Middle East. *The Economist* and international versions of *Time* and *Newsweek* are also easy to find.

If you're spending a year abroad and want to keep in touch with friends or colleagues in a college or research institution, **electronic mail (email)** is an attractive option. With a minimum of computer knowledge and a little planning, you can beam messages anywhere for no per-message charges. Look for bureaus that offer access to email for sending individual messages or search through http://www.cyberiacafe.net/cyberia/guide/ccafe.htm to find a list of **cybercafes** around the world, from which you can drink a cup of joe, and email him too. You shouldn't be surprised if you come across an internet cafe in Jerusalem or Beirut—we list them.

■ Travel Etiquette

Standards of dress and behavior are much more conservative in the Arab world than in the West. Egypt, Jordan, Lebanon, Syria, and the West Bank all mix Western and traditional Arab dress. In Egypt and Lebanon, there are some liberal enclaves, though the rise of Islamic fundamentalism is pushing less touristy areas in a conservative direction; Jordan and Syria are as conservative. Public behavior in all these areas should be reserved. Israel, except in some Arab and Jewish-Orthodox regions, is more casual in its dress code than some Western countries. Consult the introductions to individual countries and cities for specific information about proper etiquette.

In holy places, modest dress is the norm. Do not visit sanctuaries during services unless you are worshipping, in which case you are always welcome. Remove your shoes before entering a mosque. Women should completely cover their hair in a mosque (for more information see **Women and Travel,** p. 33); men should cover their heads in a synagogue.

Photography is often forbidden in holy places, archaeological sites, and museums. It is absolutely forbidden at some military installations, border crossings, railroad stations, ports, airfields, and the Aswan High Dam.

INTRODUCTION TO THE REGION

■ History

ANCIENT EGYPT

Around 7000 BCE, hunter-gatherers from the increasingly arid **Sahara** began to settle in the Nile valley. Divided into regional nomes (separate autonomous chiefdoms), the earliest Egyptians developed a variety of relatively advanced cultures and religions. Ancient Egyptian legend tells of **King Menes,** who conquered Lower (northern) Egypt, uniting it with Upper (southern) Egypt and founding one of the most powerful and lasting civilizations of history. The actual task was probably accomplished by **Narmer,** who conquered the Delta region from Upper Egypt around 3000 BCE before he was, as legend has it, eaten by a **hippo.**

The first two dynasties of pharaohs (the **Early Dynastic Period**) ruled from Abydos. Their successors, the pharaohs of the **Old Kingdom** (ca. 2650-2150 BCE) built a new capital, **Memphis,** around 2600 BCE. Successive pharaohs oversaw the construction of complicated irrigation systems and grandiose monuments using only the manual skills of conscripted peasants. Many, including the ancient Egyptians themselves, have viewed this era as the apex of ancient Egyptian civilization. The Old Kingdom elite exploited the faith and labor of the peasantry to live lives of unrestrained hedonism. The all-powerful pharaohs (who were seen as embodiments of the god **Horus**) feared only death; their most magnificent monuments represent attempts to defeat this more-powerful enemy. Two generations after the first step pyramid was built at Saqqara, the pharaohs were organizing skilled builders and tens of thousands of laborers to build the classic, smooth-sided pyramids. At a time when even China had scarcely emerged from the Stone Age, Egyptians had invented writing and **papyrus,** formed a national economy, traded with Canaan and Lebanon, recorded the history of eight dynasties of pharaohs, and crafted extraordinary artworks and a few of humanity's most impressive monumental structures.

The absolute authority of the pharaoh began to wane by the 20th century BCE, and the Old Kingdom drew to an end as local governors regained power. The increasing fragmentation was aggravated by drought, bankruptcy, and the long-lived **Pepi II,** whose death finally ended pharaonic rule. After a century of feuding, famine, and disorder (the **First Intermediate Period**), the princes of Thebes conquered and centralized the whole kingdom. Mentuhotep II of Thebes became the first pharaoh of the 11th dynasty, establishing the **Middle Kingdom** (ca. 2040-1786 BCE).

During the Middle Kingdom, contact with the southern kingdoms of Nubia and Kush spawned subsidiary pharaonic cultures. In Egypt itself, conservatism and order reigned supreme; the Old Kingdom was considered to have been a Golden Age destroyed by innovation, while the First Intermediate Period was seen as an awful, chaotic disruption of an "eternal" order of totalitarian rule by the god-pharaoh (see **Ma'at,** p. 62). Internal political rivalries weakened the Egyptian dynasties in the 18th century BCE. Around 1650 BCE, the **Hyksos** rode in from Asia on their chariots, conquered Egypt, and established the 15th and 16th dynasties. Upon the expulsion of the

Hyksos by the ever-plotting Theban princes almost a century later, Egypt was resuscitated as the **New Kingdom** (ca. 1550-1075 BCE).

The capital at Thebes became the center of a theocratic police state. The high priests of the sun (now embodied in the god **Amun**) wielded exorbitant power, often controlling the pharaoh himself. Egypt "modernized" its formerly primitive army, adapting the bronze weapons and chariots of the Hyksos, and invaded Africa, Palestine, and Syria. Now an empire ruled by warrior kings, Egypt established control over the eastern Mediterranean. Trade in wood, olive oil, and slaves brought stability and prosperity, though the rivalry between the pharaoh and the priests of Amun often brought disruption.

Despite the achievements of aggressive pharaohs like Thutmosis III and Ramses II, the New Kingdom slowly crumbled. The competition between temple and state was won by the priests of Amun, and the state collapsed around 1075 BCE. Lower Egypt was ruled by dynasties centered in the Delta, while Thebes became the theocratic center of Upper Egypt. After a last-ditch attempt by the conservative Kushites (Ethiopians in Sudan) to re-establish centralized Egyptian authority, the Assyrians (670 BCE), followed by the Persians (525 BCE), pounced "like wolves on the fold."

The **Persian dynasty** interrupted pharaonic rule and was, despite a policy of social non-interference, deeply loathed. For the next 200 years the Egyptians struggled to overthrow the Persians; they periodically succeeded, only to be subjugated again. When **Alexander the Great** arrived in 332 BCE, he was received as a liberator. After ousting the Persians, he set off for the oracle of Amun in the distant Siwa Oasis. There, he was promptly declared the Son of Amun and the legitimate pharaoh of Egypt. But after dutifully founding another Alexandria, the new pharaoh went on his way and never returned. Upon Alexander's death, the empire broke up and his general Ptolemy took control of Egypt, becoming the pharaoh **Ptolemy,** Son of God (see p. 62). Alexandria swelled into a cosmopolitan center of trade and learning; its 500,000-volume library contained all of the Greeks' knowledge under one roof.

> **The all-powerful pharaohs feared only death; their most magnificent monuments represent attempts to defeat this enemy.**

In 48 BCE, more than a century after Rome made its first, tentative overtures to the ever-feuding Ptolemies, **Julius Caesar** came to Egypt and fell captive to the allure of **Cleopatra VII,** Queen of Egypt. Cleopatra, facing challenges from other claimants to the throne, accepted an alliance with Caesar that left her secure—until his assassination four years later. Sensing danger as well as opportunity, Cleopatra conspired with **Marc Antony,** one of three successors vying to succeed Caesar. Although these events sparked one of history's most celebrated love affairs, Roman third wheel **Octavian** grabbed the empire for himself, ruthlessly crushing the affair and the Ptolemaic dynasty in 30 BCE.

Political stability and an increasingly entrenched bureaucracy characterized the Egypt of Imperial Rome and Byzantium. During this period, Egypt was the breadbasket of the Mediterranean, supplying most of the grain needed to support the empire's growing urban population. In 451 CE, not quite two centuries after the Byzantine emperors adopted and promoted Christianity, the Coptic Church split from the church of Constantinople due to doctrinal differences.

THE ANCIENT LEVANT

An important trade route between Egypt and **Mesopotamia,** the Levant was periodically conquered by both, as well as by the charioteering Hyksos and Hittites. The Bible begins the recorded history of the area with the story of Abraham, the first of the Patriarchs. The semi-nomadic Amorite tribes' migration to Palestine almost four thousand years ago has been linked with the biblical tradition of Abraham's (Avraham in Hebrew, Ibrahim in Arabic) journey from Chaldea (Genesis 12). These Semitic-speaking people were the ancestors of the people of Palestine. Meticulous Egyptian records (a rarity today) attest to the existence of a troublesome people known as the 'Apiru, who were possibly the ancestors of the **Hebrews.** These semi-nomads frequently troubled Canaan's Egyptian-controlled kings, who pleaded to their overlords for help in the 14th century.

Whether or not the 'Apiru became the Israelites remains a mystery. Some theorize that the Israelites were highlanders who united in opposition to the urban, valley-dwelling Canaanite traders. Others believe that the Israelites were forced from the coastal area by the invading "sea peoples" in the 13th century BCE. The invaders, now believed to be the descendants of the Myceneans of Greece, became known as the Philistines. Their cities included the ports of Gaza, Ashkelon, and Jaffa.

Whatever their origins, evidence shows that the scattered tribes of the Judean and Galilean hills began interacting around 1200 BCE. The next two centuries are known as the Period of Judges. Local leaders, Gideon and Samuel among them, united the Israelite tribes under a new god, Yahweh, to fight off the encroaching Egyptians, Canaanites, and Philistines. Possibly inspired by the arrival of Semitic brethren from Egypt (the Exodus), the Israelites managed to establish their own kingdom under **Saul** at the end of the 11th century BCE.

The Israelite kingdom reached its peak during the reign of Saul's successor, **David,** and that of David's son, **Solomon.** The construction of the Temple of Jerusalem is considered Solomon's most formidable feat, but the cost of the Temple and other civil projects proved a heavy burden for his subjects. After Solomon's death in 922 BCE, social and political unrest split the empire into the Kingdom of Israel in the north, which was never particularly happy to be ruled by Jerusalem-centric southerners, and the Kingdom of Judah in the south. Philistia had been reduced to a small coastal strip around Gaza, though the **Phoenicians,** a sea-faring people from the area between Akko and Tartus, prospered from the decline of the Egyptian Empire.

> **The adoption of Christianity by the Emperor Constantine in 331 created increased interest in the "Holy Land."**

The Assyrians conquered Phoenicia and Israel in the late 8th century BCE. The ten tribes of northern Israel were taken into captivity and never returned. Judah became a vassal state of the Assyrian empire until the Assyrians themselves were crushed by the Babylonians. The Babylonian king **Nebuchadnezzar** conquered Judah, razed the Temple, burned Jerusalem, and deported many Jews to Mesopotamia (the Babylonian Captivity or Exile) in 587 BCE. When the Persians defeated Nebuchadnezzar's successor some 50 years later, King Cyrus permitted the Jews to return to Jerusalem and to build the Second Temple. The Israelites prospered intellectually and economically under the Persians, although an increasing Greek presence, especially in Philistia, encouraged Alexander the Great to conquer the region in 333 BCE. His heirs, the Ptolemies, succeeded in 323 BCE (see **Ancient Egypt,** above).

The Syrian-based **Seleucids** displaced the Ptolemies in 198 BCE and attempted to Hellenize the Jews. Judas Maccabeus, responding to the persecutions of **Antiochus IV,** led a revolt of the Jewish lower-classes. Victorious, the **Maccabees** resanctified the Temple in 164 BCE and founded the **Hasmonean Dynasty.** In spite of potent internal conflict, the Hasmonean Dynasty ruled Palestine for over a century.

The **Nabateans,** originally a nomadic Arab tribe, made their way into the area south of the Dead Sea around the 2nd century BCE, taking advantage of the enmity between the Ptolemies and the Seleucids to establish their hold on those lands. They emerged as an independent kingdom by about 169 BCE. The Nabateans also interacted with the Hasmoneans, sometimes as allies, sometimes as enemies, and took control of at least a part of the Red Sea trade route, which proved to be an important source of income. With **Petra** (in modern Jordan) as its capital, the Nabatean kingdom continued to flourish, even when it became a Roman client state in the first century CE. In 106 CE, the Roman emperor **Trajan** was finally able to conquer Petra. He abolished the kingdom and reorganized its territories into a Roman province.

In 63 BCE, the Roman general **Pompey** swept in, secured much of modern-day Israel, and ruled via Herod the Great. The territory was made into a Roman province (Judea) in 44 CE. Jerusalem rebelled in 65-6 CE. In 70 CE the Roman general **Titus,** faced with the choice of sparing the Temple at great military cost or burning Jerusalem, chose to save his men and burned the Temple with the rest of Jerusalem. Three years later the Romans captured the last Jewish stronghold at **Masada** (see p. 411). The Romans exiled the majority of the population, dispersing them throughout the empire. The reconquered province was dubbed Palestine (after the Philistines).

The **Decapolis,** a loose association of trading cities, thrived as allies of Rome in what is now north Jordan and south Syria. These Hellenistic cities, which included Gerasa (Jerash) and Philadelphia (Amman), shared a common culture and heritage as well as commercial and security interests.

With the division of the empire into Latin West and Byzantine East in 330 CE, Palestine came under the supervision of **Constantinople.** Although little changed administratively, the adoption of Christianity by the Emperor Constantine in 331 created increased interest in what to many was the "Holy Land." Led by proto-pilgrim St. Eleni (Constantine's mother), worshippers and devout financiers built churches and endowed monasteries and schools. The Ghassanids, a Christian Arab client state in northern Syria, acted as a buffer between Palestine and Persia. Behind the frontier, political stability, disrupted only during the Samaritans' revolt in 529 and a brief Persian invasion a few decades later, fostered a new sense of prosperity in the region.

THE RULE OF THE CALIPHS

After the death of the **Prophet Muhammad** in 632 CE, Bedouin armies, inspired by Islam and the prospect of substantial booty, ventured outside their traditional strongholds in central Arabia and, by 642, had conquered Mesopotamia, Palestine, Syria, Persia, and Egypt. The Egyptians, tired of Byzantine taxation and religious rigidity, appreciated the Arabs' relative tolerance, if not Islam itself.

Muhammad's death gave rise to political confusion, as he had designated no successor. Amid vigorous debate as to whether the successor had to be a blood relative, **Abu Bakr,** confidante and father-in-law of Muhammad, was chosen as the first successor (*khalifa,* or caliph). Ruling from 632-34, he was followed by Omar (634-44), Uthman (644-56), and finally Ali (656-61), all based in Medina. The election of Ali, the Prophet's nephew and son-in-law, incited a civil war and produced a lasting schism in Islam between the **Sunni** (the "orthodox," who believe that the caliph should be chosen by the community of believers), and the **Shi'a** (those who supported Ali's claim and who believe that the caliph should be a direct descendant of the prophet). This division notwithstanding, the first four caliphs are known to most Muslims as the **Rashidun** (the Rightly Guided Caliphs). With the advent of the

> Impelled by desires for land, power, and heavenly reward, the Crusaders wreaked havoc.

Umayyad Dynasty, founded by the Caliph Mu'awiya in Damascus in 661, Shi'a opposition was crushed, and a Sunni hereditary caliphate (unrelated to the Prophet) was installed. Eighty years later, the Islamic world stretched from Narbonne to Samarkand. By 750, when the 'Abbasids overthrew the Umayyads on charges of decadence and impiety, the majority of the peasantry had converted to Islam. A mammoth bureaucracy, operating out of Baghdad and composed of everything from tax officials to scribes to Islamic jurists (*ulama*), helped run the empire.

Successive 'Abbasid caliphs, usually based in Baghdad, were never without challenges; the rival Umayyad family had established a potentially troublesome dynasty in Spain, while various Shi'a dynasties flourished on the borders of the 'Abbasid empire. The Shi'a Fatimids, attacking eastward from their domain in Tunisia, expelled the 'Abbasids from Egypt in 969. They established Cairo as their new capital to replace the old 'Abbasid center, Fustat. By 977, the Fatimids had captured most of Palestine, controlled Jerusalem, and were prospering through trade. It was the Fatimid Caliph Al Hakim who broke the long-established trend of Muslim toleration of other faiths and destroyed the **Church of the Holy Sepulchre.**

Europe's internal violence and economic prosperity and rumors of Seljuk policies regarding the treatment of Christian pilgrims prompted western Europeans to launch a series of **Crusades** aimed at the recapture of the Holy Land. Impelled by desires for land, power, and heavenly reward, the Crusaders wreaked havoc. Massacring the

Muslim and Jewish inhabitants of Jerusalem in 1099, the Crusaders established a feudal kingdom under **Godfrey I** and then **Baldwin I.** Consistently outnumbered and outclassed, the second and third Crusades were choked at the hands of the Zengids of Damascus and **Salah ad-Din** (a Kurd), founder of the short-lived Ayyubid Dynasty (1171-1250). Salah ad-Din dethroned the Fatimids in 1192 with a vast army of Turkish slaves (Mamluks). The Fourth through Seventh Crusades did little good to anyone but the Venetians, who thrived on trade with the Middle East. The Crusader States fell one by one, Edessa in 1144, Jerusalem in 1187, Acre in 1291. The Crusaders did, however, manage to capture Christian Byzantium in 1204.

Although Salah ad-Din's victories over the Crusaders made him a hero among his people, his finely disciplined slave armies became a scourge for his successors. Chosen as youths, then trained and equipped by the palace, the **Mamluks** were technically property of the sultan (secular leader) but their collective strength threatened the sultan's authority, which was often tenuous at best. In 1250, **'Izz al-Din,** a Mamluk of the Bahri clan, resolved to dispense with formality as well as the Ayyubids and rule the sultanate directly. Chronic instability and infighting followed. Lifestyles for those at the top were still lavish; life expectancies, however, decreased dramatically. By 1291, Mamluks controlled all of the former Crusader outposts, including Acre, Shobak, and Montfort. They even managed to stop the Mongols at 'Ayn Jalut (1260), though the Horde had already sacked Baghdad and destroyed the 'Abbasid Caliphate (1258), as well as taken Aleppo and Damascus (both in 1260).

THE OTTOMAN CENTURIES

When the **Ottoman Empire,** expanding out from Anatolia, gained formal sovereignty over Egypt and Palestine in the early part of the 16th century, Mamluks still retained most of their political power. But through appointments, bribery, and assassination, the Ottoman sultans maintained real and effective control. Manipulating their local "representatives" and playing them against one another, the Ottoman rulers enjoyed seemingly indelible authority.

When the gates of Vienna stood firm against Ottoman armies in 1683, the Ottomans began worrying about the fate of their increasingly decrepit empire. While European nation states had grown more and more powerful, the Ottoman Empire had languished. The animated ports of Syria, Palestine, and Egypt had once provided the sole access to the East; now, they were relegated to insignificance as Portuguese sailors finagled their way around the Horn of Africa. Egypt's economy—for two centuries buttressed by the Arabian and Yemeni coffee trade—collapsed when European investors cultivated their own, cheaper coffee in the Java Islands and, turning the tables, sold it to Cairene merchants. At the same time, the Spanish discovery of the New World created opportunities for seemingly limitless economic expansion. The once-formidable Ottoman Empire became "the sick man of Europe."

Napoleon's successful 1798 invasion of Egypt surprised even the grumpiest European pessimist. The French occupation of Egypt that followed, although a failure, marked the first intrusion of modern European colonialism into the Middle East. Upon the withdrawal of the French army in 1801, resurgent Mamluks sought to regain their former prerogative. An Ottoman general, **Muhammad Ali** (who ruled 1805-1848), stepped in to prevent this. Born in Greece to an Albanian couple in 1769, Muhammad Ali had served in the Turkish campaign against the French occupation of Egypt and had fought Napoleon's forces in the battle of Abu Kir. In 1805, he took over after the Egyptian revolt against the Turkish *Wali,* crushing his rivals in a bloody, invitation-only dinner party at the Citadel in Cairo. Building upon the administrative apparatus left by the French, Muhammad Ali modernized the civil service, created a regular tax system, and appropriated the vast feudal estates of his Mamluk enemies. He also laid the foundations of the modern Egyptian state, sparked the Europeanization of the country, introduced education in the arts and sciences, and paved the way for an independent dynasty. In lieu of buy-

> The French occupation of Egypt, although a failure, marked the first instrusion of modern European colonialism into the region.

ing more potentially rebellious slaves, Muhammad Ali conscripted peasants to stock his army. Those who managed to avoid the army labored to build a new, massive irrigation network meant to modernize of Egyptian agriculture.

Naturally, a resurgent Egypt led by a nominally faithful "servant" disturbed the Ottoman sultan. Avoiding direct confrontation, the sultan ordered Muhammad Ali to send Egypt's armies to face a Wahhabi revolt in central Arabia and, shortly thereafter, a Greek revolt. The dramatic Greek victory enraged Muhammad Ali far more than it weakened him. By the late 1830s, his violent forays into Palestine, Syria, Lebanon, and Arabia left him with more of the Ottoman Empire than the sultan himself controlled. But when Muhammad Ali began to march on Istanbul—his armies reached central Turkey—France and Britain threatened to intervene to preserve the balance of power, and Muhammad Ali was forced to withdraw to Egypt. The Ottoman sultan responded by granting the Europeans unrestricted access to Egypt's markets but at the same time recognizing Muhammad Ali and his descendants as Khedives (hereditary rulers) of Egypt.

Egypt's situation did not improve much under Muhammad Ali's successors, despite the Ottoman Empire's attempts at reforms (the *tanzimat*). Economic and political crises went unabated. Modernization of the economy (and financing the Egyptian rulers' trips to foreign spas) left Egypt indebted to British and French bankers. At the same time, the developing strategic interest in the newly completed **Suez Canal** made it a focus for British, French, and German foreign ministers.

The Egyptian government's declaration of bankruptcy and stirrings in the Egyptian army prompted the British to send an expeditionary force, which captured Egypt in 1882, defeating the out-gunned Khedieval forces in Alexandria. Although the Egyptian Khedive remained on the throne, all decisions were made by the British Consul General Lord Cromer (alias Evelyn Baring, or "Lord Over-Bearing") who dominated Egypt for almost three decades. Lord Cromer monitored Egyptian finances with a tight fist, salaried the Khedive and the royal family, and made it his task to ensure full payment to British investors.

ZIONISM AND THE BRITISH MANDATE

Although small Jewish communities were present in Palestine over the 18 centuries following the Roman exile, the vast majority of the world's Jews existed in **diaspora** communities in Europe, the Middle East, North Africa, and, more recently, the Americas. Throughout this period, many Jews maintained the hope of someday returning to and rebuilding the ancient homeland. This hoped-for future became the focus of the modern political movement of **Zionism** among European Jews in the late 19th and early 20th centuries

After centuries of persecution, Jews in many European countries were eventually emancipated in the 19th century. Exposed to various contemporary European political movements, some Jews flocked to the banner of revolutionary socialism while others preached complete assimilation. A third group was inspired by nationalism and, unconvinced that European nations would accept Jews as full citizens, preached a Jewish return to Zion (a biblical name for Israel).

In 1882, a group of Jews made *aliya* (or "going up," the term for Jewish immigration to Israel) to the Holy Land, forming agricultural settlements based on private land ownership *(moshavim)*. Many were sponsored by Parisian Baron Edmund de Rothschild. In 1896, Austrian journalist **Theodore Herzl,** who had witnessed the Dreyfus trial in France, published a pamphlet entitled *The Jewish State,* prophesying the establishment of a Jewish homeland as the answer to Jewish persecution. This had been proposed in such earlier works as Leo Pinsker's *Auto-Emancipation,* but never before had a secular, pro-Enlightenment Jew like Herzl articulated such ideas. Herzl initially considered Uganda and South America as sites for the Jewish state. Only the Holy Land, however, had the emotional lure necessary to unite Diaspora Jews.

The second *aliya* (1904-1914) witnessed the development of cooperative agricultural settlements (kibbutzim), led by Jews who shared the socialist principles, sense of urgency, and nationalism needed to sustain the Zionist movement. Zionists acted in two directions: "Political Zionism" sought to gain international support for the establishment of a Jewish state while, "Practical Zionism" sought to build up the Jewish community in Palestine and to develop its economic infrastructure.

During World War I, the British government, at war with the German-allied Ottomans, conducted secret and separate negotiations with both the Arabs and the Zionists to enlist their help. To obtain Arab support, Britain pledged, in 1915-16 correspondence between Sharif Hussein of Mecca (of the Hashemite family) and British High Commissioner in Egypt, Sir Henry McMahon, to back "the independence of the Arabs" in exchange for an Arab declaration of war against Turkey. The Arab revolt started in June 1916, assisted by the dynamic **Lawrence of Arabia,** who led attacks on Ottoman forces throughout what is now Jordan. At the same time, Britain sought political support from Jews worldwide by offering sympathy to the Zionist movement. The November 1917 **Balfour Declaration** stated that Britain viewed "with favour the establishment in Palestine of a national home for the Jewish people, it being clearly understood that nothing shall be done which may prejudice the civil and religious rights of existing non-Jewish communities in Palestine." Many Arabs were outraged, and Hussein's suspicions grew. The vague wording of the Balfour Declaration and the ambiguity of the boundaries agreed upon in the McMahon-Hussein correspondence only complicated the situation.

Meanwhile, the British and French had made a separate deal. The 1916 **Sykes-Picot Agreement** divided the region into zones of permanent British and French influence, giving control neither to Arabs nor to Jews. At the war's end, the various promises made by Britain to the Arabs, the Jews, and the French resulted in a muddled system of mandates: the newly created **League of Nations** awarded the Western European powers control over the territories from which the Ottomans had been expelled with the stated purpose of preparing these countries for independence. Great Britain was thus given a mandate over Palestine (which included modern-day Israel, Jordan, the West Bank, and Gaza) and Iraq, while France was accorded Syria and Lebanon.

France, for its part, drove Sharif Hussein's son Faisal out of Syria, where he had seized control. In 1921, Britain made good on one of its promises: Faisal's younger brother Abdallah was established as *emir* (prince) of Palestine east of the Jordan River, dubbed the Emirate of Transjordan (granted independence in 1946).

Throughout the inter-war years, British and French colonial rule was constantly tested by rising Arab and Jewish nationalism. In Egypt, **Sa'ad Zaghloul** founded the **Wafd party,** which forcefully criticized English rule and the Egyptian monarchy. After a skirmish between British soldiers and Egyptian peasants, Britain granted King Fouad nominal independence, taking care to sign treaties that protected British military bases, economic interests, and the Suez Canal.

In Palestine, the intervening 30 years of British rule saw institutional and economic development under the leadership of David Ben Gurion's Labor Movement. Land was extensively purchased from Arab owners, many of whom resided in neighboring countries, and Jewish immigration to Palestine increased. The Arab population of Palestine grew more anxious that they were in danger of losing their clear majority, and Palestinian Arab nationalist organizations such as the Higher Arab Council were established in an effort to combat Zionist activities and influence British policy. Leaders such as the Grand Mufti of Jerusalem, Haj Amin al-Husseini, sought support abroad for the termination of the British mandate and the cessation of all Zionist activity.

> The British and French had divided the region into zones of British and French influence, giving control neither to Arabs nor to Jews.

The British tried various unsuccessful tactics to appease one side or the other. Several commissions of inquiry were sent to Palestine to calm Arab fears of the growing Jewish presence. Various policy directives, known as "White Papers," restricted Jewish immigration and distinguished the Jewish "national home" pledged by the Balfour Declaration from the sovereign state sought by the Zionists. The clash between Arab and Jewish nationalism, however, was not averted. With the rise of Nazism in Germany, tens of thousands of European Jews sought to enter Palestine by legal or illegal means. Underground Jewish efforts to assist illegal immigration led to greater friction between the *yishuv* and the Mandatory Government. Meanwhile, growing Arab discontent with the developing situation culminated in the Arab Revolt of 1936-39, which the British were only able to put down with considerable military force. With the outbreak of the World War II, Zionist leaders patched up their relationship with the British to support the war effort against Germany.

THE 1948 (INDEPENDENCE) WAR AND THE UNIFICATION OF JORDAN

Shortly after the conclusion of World War II, an exhausted Great Britain submitted the question of Palestine to the newly formed United Nations. The U.N. General Assembly voted in 1947 to partition Palestine into two states, Jewish and Arab. The Jewish leadership accepted the resolution with some reluctance, while Palestinian Arab leaders and the governments of neighboring Arab states rejected the plan completely, denying the U.N.'s authority to divide and distribute territories they considered to be Arab patrimony. As the British prepared to evacuate Palestine in accordance with the partition resolution, Jews and Arabs clashed in sporadic skirmishes, purchased arms overseas, and planned for imminent, full-scale war.

On May 14, 1948, the British mandate over Palestine ended and **David Ben-Gurion** declared the independence of the State of Israel. The next day, a combined army of Syrian, Iraqi, Lebanese, Saudi, Egyptian, and Jordanian troops marched in from the north, west, and south. Few observers gave the new state much chance for survival, but the war's results became clear with the signing of armistices in the spring of 1949. Israel had secured not only its U.N.-allotted territory but also some Arab land designated in the north and in the West Bank designated for Palestine by the U.N. The Gaza Strip, which had also been designated for Palestine, was secured during the war by Egypt, and the West Bank and half of Jerusalem by Jordan. Thousands of Palestinian refugees crowded into camps in the West Bank, Gaza, and bordering Arab states. The dispossessed Palestinians came to bitterly remember the 1948 War as *An-Naqba*, the catastrophe.

> **The dispossessed Palestinians came to bitterly remember the 1948 War as "An-Naqba," the catastrophe.**

On April 9, 1948, the Palestinian village of Dayr Yasin, which had entered into a non-aggression pact with the **Hagana** (one of the Jewish underground fighting organizations), was attacked by the more aggressive and extreme LEHI and Irgun forces. These groups killed about 250 men, women, and children. The massacre was advertised via loudspeakers in Haifa and Jaffa, spurring Arabs to leave the country, figuring that they would return to their homes when the Arab armies won the war.

King Abdallah of Jordan annexed the West Bank in 1950 and declared a unified **Hashemite Kingdom of Jordan;** this move met an icy reception from Palestinians and other Arab governments. Some felt that Jordan was becoming too accommodating of Israel. To the Palestinians, Jordanian rule was not much different from any other foreign occupation. In 1951, Abdallah, praying in Al Aqsa Mosque in Jerusalem, was assassinated by a Palestinian youth. After a six month tenure by Abdallah's eldest son, Talal, who resigned due to schizophrenia, the crown passed to **King Hussein.** Not quite 18 when he assumed the throne—which he holds to this day—Hussein embarked on a bold agenda aimed at raising Jordan's status in the Arab world.

THE SUEZ CRISIS AND THE RISE OF PAN-ARABISM

Egypt, weakened by struggles between Wafdist nationalists and the monarchy, was in a shambles after its 1948 loss to Israel. In 1952, following a bloody confrontation between British soldiers and Egyptian police officers, a group of young army officers led, by charismatic heartthrob Colonel **Gamal Abd an-Nasser,** bloodlessly seized power from the late King Fouad's corrupt son, Farouk. Calling themselves the "Free Officers," Nasser's cabinet instituted major economic reforms and foreign policy changes, while avoiding the bilateral alignments of the Cold War. Drawing from the writings of countless Arab nationalists, Nasser espoused a highly emotional brand of pan-Arabism, hoping to unify the Arabic-speaking masses into one state powerful enough to resist imperial encroachments and to take control of Palestine. When Nasser forced Britain to withdraw from Egypt in 1954, many puppet Arab leaders dependent on foreign assistance became alarmed by his growing popularity.

The United States and other foreign powers, which had undertaken extensive development of the oil fields of Arabia, feared their arrangements with local monarchs would collapse if Nasserism spread. Nasser, alarmed by a British-led alignment of conservative Middle East states (the Baghdad Pact), had begun buying Soviet arms from Czechoslovakia in defiance of a 1950 West-imposed arms control deal. In 1956, the United States clumsily attempted to curtail Nasser's power by withdrawing its offer to finance the Aswan High Dam. Rather than yield to the snub, Nasser nationalized the previously international Suez Canal to use its revenues for the dam.

Israel, Britain, and France devised a scheme to take the canal. Israel would attack Egypt with French logistical support; a Franco-British "peace-keeping" force would follow. Initially, the conspiracy worked well: Israel took the Sinai and dealt Nasser's military a major blow. The Anglo-French force entered Egypt and began the seizure of the canal under the pretext of separating Egyptian and Israeli combatants. The military victors, however, had not considered world reaction to their adventure. The United States and the Soviet Union, both furious, applied intense diplomatic pressure. When Israel, Britain, and France withdrew their troops to placate the U.S., Nasser was heralded as the savior of the Arab world without having won a battle.

> **A group of young army officers led by charismatic heartthrob Colonel Gamal Abd an-Nasser, bloodlessly seized power from Farouk.**

After gaining independence from the British and French in April 1946, Syria experienced civilian government for three years. A military coup took over in March 1949; and by 1954, the pan-Arabist Ba'th party had crept into power. Racked with internal feuding, Syria joined Egypt in 1958 in forming the **United Arab Republic (UAR).** Nasser trumpeted the UAR as a triumph of pan-Arabism, but the Syrians were irritated by its unwieldy and Egypt-dominated government. After the 1961 secession of Syria from the UAR, Nasser remained at the forefront of Arab politics. In 1964, he hosted two Arab summits and helped create the Egypt-based **Palestine Liberation Organization (PLO),** keeping the Palestinian movement under Cairo's suspicious eye. One PLO faction was led by a young Palestinian nationalist, **Yassir Arafat.** His FATAH party (the Arabic acronym for PLO written backwards) would later lead the PLO.

THE 1967 SIX-DAY WAR

In 1963, the Syrian coup which interrupted the Egypto-Syrian joy ride gave way to the Syrian Ba'th party (led by **Hafez al Asad**), which in February 1966 split off from the larger Ba'th party and began focusing its efforts on developing Syrian nationalism (rather than pan-Arabism) and maintaining power.

Meanwhile, from bases sanctioned by the governments of Jordan, Syria, and Lebanon, the PLO raided Israel; in return, Israel hit Palestinian refugee camps. The cycle of raids and reprisals created tension on Israel's northern border, and a Syrian-Israeli air battle took place in April 1967. When Syria's hard-line government turned up the rhetoric, Nasser stepped in, concentrating the Egyptian army in the Sinai and successfully demanding the withdrawal of the U.N. buffer-zone troops stationed there since 1956. Israeli Prime Minister **Levi Eshkol** nervously warned that a blockade of the Straits of Tiran would be taken as an act of aggression. Nasser, under pressure from Syria and Saudi Arabia, initiated a blockade on May 22, 1967.

Jordan, Iraq, and Syria deployed troops along Israel's borders. On June 5, 1967, Israel launched a preemptive strike against air fields in the Sinai, obliterating the Egyptian air force before it ever got off the ground. The U.S., eager to embarrass Soviet-backed Egypt, condoned the attack, after receiving assurances that the attack would eventually bring peace. Eshkol appealed to King Hussein not to get involved; but when it became clear that Jordanian shelling would continue, Israel saw an opportunity: it delayed acceptance of a U.N.-sponsored cease-fire (initially rejected by the Arab nations) until it could take East Jerusalem.

East Jerusalem fell to Israel on June 7, and by June 9 all parties had accepted the cease-fire. Shortly afterwards, Israel annexed East Jerusalem, much to the United State's chagrin. From Egypt, Israel had won the Sinai Peninsula (all the way to the Suez Canal) and the Gaza Strip, from Syria the Golan Heights, and from Jordan the West Bank. Nasser resigned, but a swell of public sympathy prompted him to reclaim his post. Staggered by yet another defeat, the Palestinians decided it was up to them to carry on the struggle. In 1969, Arafat's FATAH took over the PLO from its pro-Nasser leadership and undertook the liberation of Palestine through propaganda and guerilla warfare.

With the U.S. behind Israel and the USSR behind Nasser, any local conflict now raised the threat of superpower confrontation. U.N. Security Council Resolution 242, passed in November 1967 and accepted by all parties, stipulated "withdrawal of Israeli armed forces from territories occupied in the recent conflict" and "acknowledgment of the sovereignty, territorial integrity, and political independence of every State in the area." Bickering over the intentional ambiguity of the document began almost immediately, while the situation on the Israeli-Egyptian border (the Suez Canal) degenerated into what was known as the War of Attrition.

THE PLO AND JORDAN

Among the PLO groups vying for control at the time were the Popular Front for the Liberation of Palestine, begun in 1967 by pan-Arabist Dr. George Habash and backed by Iraq; Ahmad Jibril's Syria-backed FATAH; and Marxist-Leninist Nayif Hawatmeh's Popular Democratic Front for the Liberation of Palestine (PDFLP), also backed by Syria. Among their differences was the fact that FATAH was composed mostly of Sunni Muslims, while Habash, Hawatmeh, and many of their adherents were Christian. In addition, Arafat stressed that Palestinians should not get involved in rivalries among Arab states, while Habash and Hawatmeh sought to radicalize the Arab governments into fighting the West and helping to liberate Palestine. Factionalism became a constant feature of Palestinian politics. The rivalries between factions were manipulated by the various Arab states supporting them, though FATAH consistently sought to maintain contact with all Arab regimes.

> **With the U.S. behind israel and the USSR behind Hasser, any local conflict now raised the threat of superpower confrontation.**

The 1967 War created 400,000 more Palestinian refugees, most of whom went to Jordan. With this influx of Palestinians, the Jordanian government and the PLO were thrown together in a tense relationship: Hussein wanted to hold secret peace negotiations with the Israelis, while the PLO hoped to use Jordan as a base for attacks on Israeli-held territory. Responding to PLO raids, the Israeli army attacked the Jordanian town of Karameh. Though the towns resident Palestinians were defeated, the image of FATAH members standing together (with Jordanian support) against Israeli forces became a tremendously successful propaganda image for FATAH. Young recruits flocked, allowing the PLO increased control over the refugee camps, and threatening Hussein's sovereignty.

In September 1970, Hussein and Arafat's conflicting ambitions exploded. Infuriated by a hard-line PLO faction's hijacking of a number of commercial airliners (to protest the exclusion of Palestinians from negotiations between Israel, Egypt, and Jordan), Hussein declared war on the PLO. Martial law was imposed, and fighting between Jordanian and PLO troops took over 3000 lives. September 1970 became known among Palestinians as **Black September.** After Arab League mediation and Nasser's personal intervention, an agreement was forged, requiring the PLO to reluctantly move its headquarters to Lebanon.

WAR AND PEACE: 1970-1988

Nasser died suddenly of a heart attack that same September. Vice President **Anwar es-Sadat** assumed control of Egypt and promptly began dismantling Nasser's legacy of state socialism. He also announced the *infitah* (opening), a plan to promote foreign investment and revive the economy. Anxious for his own security, Sadat exposed Nasser's extensive secret police network and released political prisoners, including members of the formerly suppressed religious opposition.

President Asad of Syria reassumed his country's reins in February 1971 and was sworn in as President for seven years. Asad, an Alawite Muslim of penurious heritage, had held power for a short time at the beginning of Ba'th monopoly, but had lost his position in 1966. After reassuming office, Asad called for the popular election of a 173-member People's Assembly that would draft a new constitution. Completed in March 1973, the constitution contained a clause requiring the President of Syria to be a follower of Islam. Sunni Muslims used this clause to object to Asad's presidency, holding that Alawites are not true Muslims. It was not until a high-ranking religious authority deemed Alawites devout followers of Islam that the road to domination was cleared for Asad.

Meanwhile, the war of attrition along the Suez Canal was an increasingly heavy burden for Egypt to bear. In order to alleviate his country's financial crisis, Sadat sought to reopen the lucrative canal and reclaim the desperately needed Sinai oil fields. In 1972 Sadat expelled the numerous Soviet military advisors in Egypt and, seeing little hope in negotiations, began making preparations to attack Israel.

On October 6, 1973, when many Israelis were in synagogues for Yom Kippur (the Day of Atonement), Egypt and Syria, eager to regain their lost territories, launched a surprise assault. In the war's first three days, Egypt overwhelmed Israeli defenses in the Sinai and Syrian forces thrust deep into the Golan, threatening Galilee. Because Egypt and Syria's preparatory moves had been perceived by the Israeli government to be bluffs, Israel's reserves had not been activated and it appeared that Israel was on the verge of defeat. Sadat, who had planned only to cross into the Sinai and hold the position, decided to press on with the battle, refusing a U.S.-brokered cease-fire. Accepting America's terms, Israel received formerly withheld U.S arms and, over a number of weeks, pushed the Egyptians and Syrians back.

> **Israel had won, but the aura of invincibility it had earned over the years had dissipated.**

All parties finally agreed to disengage forces in January 1974 in an agreement negotiated by then-U.S. Secretary of State **Henry Kissinger.** The subsequent Sinai I and II agreements returned much of the Sinai to Egypt. Both sides, though, had suffered tremendous losses. Israeli public uproar over the government's unpreparedness prompted Prime Minister **Golda Meir** to resign in April. Israel had won, but the aura of invincibility it had earned over the years had dissipated.

In October 1974, the Arab League declared in Rabat, Morocco that the PLO, not Jordan, was "the sole legitimate representative of the Palestinian people." This incensed King Hussein; but when the other 20 Arab nations assented to PLO representation in the League, he was forced to agree. In November 1974, the U.N. General Assembly voted to give the PLO observer status in the U.N. as representatives of the Palestinian people.

Throughout the 1970s, an increasing number of Israelis began to settle in the occupied territories. On November 11, 1976, the U.N. Security Council condemned this West Bank policy and demanded that Israel follow the Geneva Convention's rules regarding occupied territory. Although Prime Minister Yitzhak Rabin (of the left-leaning Labor party) discouraged permanent West Bank settlement, the next government (after 1977), under Prime Minister Menahem Begin of the right-wing Likud bloc, invested money and effort in new settlements.

Eager to regain the Sinai, Sadat decided to seek a unilateral peace with Israel. In October 1977, he declared that he would even go to Jerusalem to make peace. The next month, Sadat made a historic visit to Jerusalem and was officially welcomed.

By September 1978, Begin and Sadat had forged an agreement with the help of U.S. President Jimmy Carter at Camp David, the presidential retreat in Virginia. The most successful and lasting stipulation was Israel's agreement to relinquish the Sinai in exchange for peace and full diplomatic relations with Egypt. More muddled were the stipulations concerning Israel's control of the West Bank and Gaza. By the time of the signing of the Accords, there was still confusion over ambiguities: Sadat returned to Cairo content that Palestinians in the occupied territories would be granted full personal and territorial sovereignty within the next five years, while Begin maintained that nothing regarding the occupied territories had been agreed upon.

After the Camp David Accords, early hopes that other Arab states would negotiate with Israel evaporated. The PLO, Syria, and Jordan were adamant about guarantees for the Palestinians; more distant Arab states issued statements of disapproval, but felt no need to interfere. Egypt, viewed as a traitor to Palestine by many, was left isolated and turned to the U.S for financial support. Islamists, whom Sadat had courted in his battles against the Nasserist left, objected to this open alliance with the West. In October 1981, in response to cracking down on Fundamentalists, Sadat was assassinated. The Egyptian government acted swiftly to crush an Islamist riot in Assyut, and **Hosni Mubarak,** Sadat's Vice President, was sworn in.

Though sticking to the terms of the 1979 Camp David peace treaty, Mubarak held Egypt at arm's length from Israel, keeping the diplomatic air cool for most of the 1980s in an attempt to reintegrate Egypt with the rest of the Arab world. In 1984, Egypt restored relations with the Soviet Union and was readmitted to the Islamic Conference, and by 1988, the Arab League had invited Egypt to rejoin and dropped demands that Egypt sever ties with Israel.

THE ISRAELI INVASION OF LEBANON

It had long been apparent that the June 6, 1982 Israeli invasion of Lebanon, dubbed Operation Peace for Galilee by Defense Minister Ariel Sharon, was intended not simply to create a protective buffer zone, but to wipe out PLO forces operating from Palestinian refugee camps that had been attacking northern Israel. When the Israeli army, after surrounding the PLO in Beirut, began shelling the city at an enormous civilian cost, Israeli citizens joined in the world-wide chorus of condemnation. With the massacre of civilians at the Sabra and Shatila refugee camps by Lebanese Christian Phalangists operating in Israeli-controlled territory, the Israeli government's position eroded even further. Under an agreement negotiated by the U.S., most fighting ended in 1983. Israel, worried about the continued Syrian presence and active Shi'a militia in Lebanon, did not fully withdraw until 1985 and continues to maintain a strip of southern Lebanese territory as a security zone.

THE INTIFADA

On December 8, 1987, an Israeli armored transport and several Arab cars collided in Gaza; four Palestinians were killed and several injured in the crash. The Palestinians' despair after 20 years of Israeli military occupation and frustration with Israel's unwillingness to negotiate over Palestinian autonomy turned demonstrations at the victims' funerals into an upheaval that spread to the West Bank. The Palestinian *intifada,* or uprising, was a tremendous shock to everyone, the PLO (at this point relocated to Tunis) included. At first, Israeli authorities viewed the *intifada* ("throwing off" or "shaking off" in Arabic) as a short-lived affair which would dissolve much as earlier agitations had. But after Palestinians in the territories began establishing networks to coordinate their hitherto sporadic civil disobedience and strikes, the *intifada* came alive, and gained a shadowy leadership all its own.

By mid-1988 it became apparent that the *intifada* was not abating. The Israeli Defense Forces made frequent television appearances as they violently suppressed demonstrators, and reconsideration of Israel's Palestinian policies began around the world. U.S. Secretary of State George Schultz proposed an international peace conference to be attended by the permanent members of the U.N. Security Council. The

Americans and the Israelis, however, refused to allow the PLO to attend until the organization renounced terrorism and accepted Israel's right to exist.

In the summer of 1988, King Hussein suddenly dropped his claims to the West Bank and ceased assisting in the administration of the territories, which Jordan had been doing since 1967. Hussein's move left Israel and the United States without a negotiating partner, since they refused to negotiate with the PLO. Arafat seized the opportunity to secure a PLO role in negotiations by renouncing terrorism, recognizing Israel's right to exist, and proposing an independent Palestinian state. Israeli Prime Minister Yitzhak Shamir (Likud) presented his own proposal (actually formulated by then-Defense Minister Rabin), promising elections in the territories but insisting that neither the PLO nor PLO-sponsored candidates take part. This seemed ridiculous to those who considered all Palestinians members of the PLO. Nonetheless, the United States and Egypt began trying to draw up a list of acceptable candidates. Shamir then qualified his proposal by insisting that Arab residents of East Jerusalem be barred from participation. The PLO, local Palestinians, and Egypt could not stomach any recognition of the decades-old Israeli claim that Jerusalem, whole and undivided, was Israel's eternal capital, nor that Palestinian refugees living outside the occupied territories should not be allowed to return.

Many Palestinians became convinced, by late 1989, that Yassir Arafat had weakened the position the Palestinians had gained as a result of the *intifada*. They were also worried by the increasing numbers of Soviet Jews immigrating to Israel and the growing number of Israeli settlements in the West Bank. A PLO faction launched an attack against Israeli hotels on the coast near Tel Aviv. The raid was foiled before it inflicted any damage, and Israel, backed by the United States, pressured Arafat to denounce the incident. His refusal to do so attested to FATAH's waning power relative to more militant factions. The United States and the PLO terminated their discussions that summer.

THE GULF WAR

The Gulf Crisis began when Iraqi troops marched into Kuwait on August 2, 1990. Early on, Iraqi President **Saddam Hussein** had slyly suggested "linkage" as a way of solving the Gulf crisis—that is, he would withdraw from Kuwait when Israel withdrew from the West Bank, Gaza, and Golan, and when Syria withdrew from Lebanon. This gesture, along with promises to liberate Palestine, won Saddam the support of Palestinians. In fighting that lasted from January 16 to February 28, 1991, a coalition formed by the United States, various European countries, Egypt, Syria, Saudi Arabia, and the other Gulf states disabled Baghdad and forced Iraq to withdraw from Kuwait. During the conflict, 39 Iraqi SCUD missiles fell on Tel Aviv and Haifa. Israel, under pressure from the U.S., and fearful of an Arab-Israeli conflagration and chaos in Jordan, did not retaliate.

The war damaged the Jordanian economy, burdening it with approximately 300,000 Palestinians no longer welcome in the Gulf countries. Across the river, Israel's demographics were also in flux, as the collapse of regimes brought in 450,000 Jewish immigrants from the former Soviet Union and Ethiopia.

THE PEACE PROCESS

The Gulf Crisis demonstrated the need for a comprehensive peace in the region. When the cease-fire was announced, hope was high that parties such as Israel and Syria—for the first time on the same side of a regional conflict—could be brought to the bargaining table. In July 1991, Syria surprised the world with the announcement that it would attend a regional peace conference. At a summit meeting in Moscow, U.S. President George Bush and Russian President Mikhail Gorbachev decided to host the conference jointly, and even issued invitations. A hesitant Israeli cabinet, uneasy about losing some $10 billion in additional U.S. aid, voted to attend the proposed conference provided that the PLO and residents of East Jerusalem not take part.

On October 30, 1991, the Madrid peace conference was convened, with Israel carrying on separate negotiations with Syria, Lebanon, Egypt, and a joint Jordanian-Palestinian delegation. This unprecedented gathering quickly bogged down in discussions of U.N. Resolution 242, Palestinian autonomy and rights, Jerusalem, Israeli settlements, and the PLO's role. Subsequent sessions held in Washington, D.C. did not get much further. The Palestinian representatives, including Faisal al-Husseini and Hanan Ashrawi, were in constant contact with the PLO; the charade of PLO non-involvement was wearing thin.

On June 23, 1992, an Israeli election ousted Shamir's Likud, whose West Bank settlements had attracted U.S. ire, and brought in a pragmatic Labor-led government under Yitzhak Rabin. Rabin curtailed settlement and promised Palestinian autonomy. Optimism accompanying the first round of talks under the new Israeli government, held in November 1992, was soon undermined. **Hamas,** a rejectionist-Islamist Palestinian faction which had been growing in popularity (especially in Gaza) as Palestinians became frustrated with negotiations, carried out several terrorist attacks on Israelis. In response, the Israeli government deported 415 Palestinians in December 1992, some of whom were Hamas activists and some of whom claimed no connection to the organization. The Palestinian representatives at the negotiations refused to resume talks until the deportees, trapped in the freezing no-man's-land between Israel and Lebanon, were allowed to return.

Then, almost a year later, Israel and the PLO surprised the world by announcing that representatives meeting secretly in Oslo had successfully negotiated an agreement on a framework for solving the Israeli-Palestinian conflict peacefully. The Declaration of Principles on Interim Self-Government Arrangements (the DOP— also known as the Oslo Accord) was signed on the White House lawn on September 13, 1993, with President **Bill Clinton** presiding over the ceremony. The DOP provided mutual recognition between Israel and the PLO, as well as a plan for the implementation of Palestinian autonomy in the Gaza Strip and the Jericho Area, with the autonomous areas to be expanded in stages over a five-year transitional period. The transitional period, according to the DOP, is to be followed by an agreement on final status of refugees, settlements, security arrangements, borders, foreign relations, and Jerusalem.

Israeli agreements with other Arab countries followed soon after, and throughout 1994 the world saw history being made daily.

The DOP was followed by the negotiation and signing of several other Israeli-Palestinian agreements. The first was the Gaza/Jericho Agreement which provided the details for Israeli withdrawal from these two areas and the creation of a **Palestinian Authority (PA)** headed by **Yassir Arafat** and a 24-member council. Following the implementation of the Gaza/Jericho Agreement, the two sides signed the Early Empowerment Agreement which transferred several spheres of government in the West Bank to the Palestinian Authority (PA).

In 1991, having led part of the Arab world against Iraq in the Gulf War, Egypt was invited to head the Arab League, marking the country's re-emergence at the helm of the Arab world. The Arab League is now headed by former Egyptian foreign minister Esmat Abd el-Meguid. In June 1992, Mubarak met with new Israeli Prime Minister Yitzhak Rabin, the first meeting of leaders of the two countries in six years. Egypt is also beginning to recapture its former position of power within the world arena; in 1992, **Boutros Boutros-Ghali,** a respected Egyptian diplomat involved in the Camp David negotiations, became the new U.N. Secretary-General. Cairo proudly hosted, on a stage outfitted with massive Egyptian flags, the signing of the 1994 agreement between the Palestine Liberation Organization and the Israeli government.

Israeli agreements with other Arab countries followed soon after, and throughout the second half of 1994 the world saw history being made daily. In September, Morocco and Israel established diplomatic relations. In October, Jordan and Israel ended the state of war that had existed between them since 1948. The border between Eilat and Aqaba was opened, and Israelis were allowed into Jordan for the first time. Finally, negotiations with Syria were begun, concentrating on peace between the two countries in exchange for the withdrawal of Israeli troops from the Golan Heights. Such a withdrawal is highly controversial within Israel and the Israeli Government has stated that it will place any agreement negotiated with Syria on a national referendum to be decided upon by the Israeli public.

On November 4, 1995, 25-year-old Yigal Amir, a Jewish right-wing university student, shot and killed Israel's Prime Minister Yitzhak Rabin. Rabin had just finished delivering a rousing speech in front of 100,000 Israelis at one of the largest rallies Tel Aviv had ever seen. After his oration, the crowd sang *Shir La-Shalom* (A Song for Peace). Rabin folded a paper with the lyrics and placed it in his chest pocket. The bullet, meant to derail the peace talks, pierced the lyrics; the blood-stained song sheet was read at the Prime Minister's funeral. Over one million Israelis, Arabs and Jews alike, filed by the slain leader's coffin in the days following the murder. Rabin's funeral drew over 50 world leaders to Jerusalem, including Jordan's King Hussein, Egypt's President Mubarak, and representatives from four other Arab states. Support for the peace process in both Palestinian and Israeli societies has been plagued by frustration, anxiety, and persistent mistrust. Many on both sides feel that they are getting the raw end of the deal—some Israelis argue that they are giving up their defensive territorial depth in exchange for pieces of paper that can be torn up in a moment. Some Palestinians fear that Israel will never grant them total independence and interpret the current process as a "sell-out" on the part of their leadership.

Benjamin Netanyahu, leader of the conservative Likud party, defeated Shimon Peres in a hairline victory (50.4% to 49.6%) in the May 1996 Israeli elections. Netanyahu vowed to continue the peace talks, but also assures his people that he will proceed slowly, emphasizing that Israeli security will never be compromised.

THIS YEAR'S NEWS

Over the course of the past year the peace process has corroded to the point of near collapse. Israel's building of a tunnel near a Muslim Holy site in Jerusalem caused a strong reaction from Palestinians in September 1996, when protesting led to fighting and bloodshed. Thirty-seven Palestinians and 11 Israelis died in the conflict. Palestinians voiced concerns that Israel was not serious about peace, while Israel criticized the Palestinian police force for its lack of control over demonstrations and general inflammatory behavior.

Throughout fall 1996, U.S. President Bill Clinton met with PLO leader Yassir Arafat and Prime Minister Benjamin Netanyahu of Israel to try to salvage relations between the two groups. Israel demanded increased security measures from the Palestinian Authority, and the PA denounced Israel for violating the spirit and letter of the negotiation agreements as regarding settlement and expansion in East Jerusalem and the Occupied Territory. In December, Israel announced plans to offer financial incentives to Jewish settlers in the West Bank. Arafat called the plans "a ticking bomb"; eight former U.S. foreign policy chiefs signed a disapproving letter to Netanyahu.

> **Over the course of the past year the peace process has corroded to the point of near-collapse.**

January 1997 saw the much-anticipated redeployment of troops in Hebron, but in March, Netanyahu approved a new Jewish neighborhood in the East Jerusalem area known as Jabal Abu-Ghneim to Arabs and Har Homa to Jews. Arafat and Clinton criticized the building proposal as detrimental to the peace process but Netanyahu, suffering from political setbacks caused by accusations of corruption in his government, went forward with the project. Israel's chief prosecutors decided not to charge Netanyahu with corruption in April.

Faced with growing disapproval, Netanyahu said in a joint appearance with King Hussein of Jordan on CNN television at the end of April that he would look into the way East Jerusalem Arabs had been deprived of residency rights. He offered no apology or concession on the Har Homa settlement, but said building for Arabs would also begin. Netanyahu survived a no confidence vote in Israel's Knesset, even though his own foreign minister demonstrated his lack of confidence by being absent during the vote.

Meanwhile, the Palestinian Authority imposed a death sentence for the "crime" of selling land to Jews, and carried through on their decree. Two successive murders aroused fear among Palestinians and indignation among Jews.

At the end of June, tension rose in Hebron after posters appeared depicting the prophet Muhammad as a pig. Palestinians threw rocks and homemade bombs at Israeli soldiers, who in turn fired back, injuring many in Hebron and killing a teenager in Gaza. The young Russian immigrant who had distributed the poster was put on trial, and the Israeli government officially apologized for the incident.

The Israeli-Hizbullah agreement not to attack civilian targets on the Israel-Lebanon border collapsed as Israeli shells in Lebanon killed a Palestinian woman and her son and Hizbullah fired in the response. There have since been casualties on both sides.

At the end of July, two suicide bombers killed 16 people, including themselves, in a crowded West Jerusalem market. The Israeli government proceeded to impose a security crack-down in the West Bank and Gaza Strip. Arafat offered condolences and was told to put pressure on Islamic militants. The United States government, pressed by the urgency of the situation, made a policy decision to take a more active role in the process. Amidst the scramble to rescue the peace process, Secretary of State Madeleine Albright lifted the U.S. travel ban to Lebanon. The ban was imposed in the mid-80s during the height of the hostage crisis. The lifting of the ban was seen as an important step in Lebanon's path to recovery from the 15-year civil war that ended recently. The May visit of Pope John Paul II was also a morale-booster for the country; he was welcomed by both Christians and Muslims, and called for the complete restoration of Lebanese sovereignty.

▓ Religion

RELIGION IN ANCIENT EGYPT

The people of pre-Dynastic Egypt were ruled by a bewildering array of local gods representing the cosmos, the natural elements, animals, and the life-cycle. Each independent district had its own local deity, pair of deities, or trinity, and in the early days, these gods were represented by animals. The Greeks and Romans considered these representations to be evidence of barbarism in otherwise advanced Egypt. The Greek influence certainly played no small part in the shift from animal deities to deities with human form and costume. As Egypt was united, the pharaohs found that they needed one syncretic pantheon to link disparate cults. The Heliopolian Theogony, centered near the first capital, Memphis, was a complex faith explaining the emergence of an ordered world out of chaos. The leading god, Rē-Atum, was represented by the sun. His descendants were known as the Ennead. They included Geb (Earth) and Nūt (Sky), who were worshipped as the parents of the moon, stars, humans, and younger gods, Osiris, Isis, Seth, and Nephthys. These youthful deities had been adapted from southern cults and were held dear by many Egyptians.

The most enduring cult was the **Osiris cycle,** centered at Abydos on the Upper Nile. This popular faith gave Egyptians a framework for understanding the most important things in life: sex, death, the seasons, and royal succession. According to the religion, Seth murdered his brother Osiris, a king from time immemorial, and scattered the pieces of his body throughout Egypt. His faithful sister-wife Isis found his remains all over the kingdom and erected monuments over each of the body parts; this is why there were so many temples to Osiris. Isis conceived and gave birth to Horus, who became Osiris' son and heir. Young Horus avenged Osiris and took back the crown from his usurping uncle. The pharaohs saw Horus as the ideal righteous and strong ruler, and identified themselves with him while on earth. Upon death they were identified with Osiris, the king

The Osiris cycle helped Egyptians understand the most important things in life: sex, death, the seasons, and royal succession.

of the dead. The pharaoh was thus literally a god and worshipped as such, and the religious fervor he engendered united the country. Seth was viewed as the god of foreigners, and represented the invasions that occasionally troubled Egypt (see also **Meet the Gods,** p. 189).

The first pharaohs imposed the **Memphite Theogony** over the earlier cults and adapting a new god, **Ptah,** who represented the boundary between order and chaos and was the father of the Ennead. At the same time, Horus was provided with a wife, Hathor. This pair, originally worshipped at Hierakonpolis (near modern Edfu), provided the Egyptians with a young, attractive couple to venerate. Middle and New Kingdom pharaohs installed the sun-god **Amun** (similar to the older, more low key Rē-Atum), his wife, **Mut,** and their sun, **Khonsu,** over the older gods, thus concentrating Egyptian state-religion around Thebes. All these centralizing efforts had little effect on the faith of the Egyptian masses, who neither understood nor cared much for the aristocratic gods imposed by the high-priests. They only saw the eternal order of a world ruled by the god-pharaoh and characterized by constants as the daily rising of the sun and the annual flooding of the Nile. Any change was viewed as evil, a disruption of the divinely ordained order, which, in its most complex and complete form, was venerated as **Ma'at.**

Some historians believe that in the Old Kingdom religious hierarchy, only the pharaoh could enter the afterworld. Minor royalty took to grouping their tombs around the king's, hoping that the proximity would also draw them into the next life. By the Middle Kingdom, the netherworld was open to all of the righteous, and Egyptians' central concern became life after death. By the time the New Kingdom rolled around, priests were selling funerary services to anyone who could pay. All the while, earthly existence was seen as a short interlude to be endured until the afterlife brought eternal happiness and reward to those who passed divine judgement. The divine and secular worlds were not strongly demarcated, however; the preservation of the earthly body through mummification was considered essential for the afterlife of the **Ka,** or soul, and the tomb had to be supplied with all the comforts of home.

The Pyramid Texts were spells inscribed on the walls of the royal pyramids to ensure the success of the king's or queen's journey to the afterlife. As the underworld democratization took hold, these texts were adopted by more plebeian folk and inscribed on the sides of their coffins. The New Kingdom's Book of the Dead, a collection of spells written on papyrus and put in sarcophagi, described not only how to get to the afterlife but also how to enjoy oneself once there.

The Macedonian Ptolemies, who ruled Egypt in the wake of Alexander (see **History: Ancient Egypt,** p. 46) sought to become pharaonic god-kings to their subjects. By merging Greek and Egyptian elements in the Serapis cult and building temples to the ancient gods, they achieved what Assyrian and Persian invaders before them never could—they became spiritual successors of the pharaohs. Many of the great temples of Upper Egypt date to Ptolemaic times. The conquerors, however, may have been more influenced than influencing; the mystery cults of Osiris, Isis, and Horus spread throughout the Hellenistic world and were pervasive in the later Roman Empire.

JUDAISM

Neither theologians nor historians can pinpoint a date when Judaism began. The Israelite religion has been evolving, however, for perhaps the past four millennia. According to the Bible, **Abraham** was the first to establish a covenant with God with his self-circumcision at the ripe old age of 99. This act is symbolically repeated with each generation of Jewish males, but now a ritual circumciser (the *moyel*) performs the honors, and it is gotten over with on the eighth day of life. Abraham's grandson, Jacob (a.k.a. Israel), fathered twelve sons from whom descended twelve tribes, the nation of Israel. Abraham, his son Isaac, and his grandson Jacob are believed to be buried with their wives, Sarah, Rebecca, and Leah in the Cave of the Makhpela in **Hebron.** Because Ishmael, Abraham's other son, is believed to be the ancestor of Islam, the resting place of the patriarchs and matriarchs is holy to both faiths.

The Bible says that the founding period of the Israelite nation was the generation spent wandering in the Sinai desert en route from Egypt to the Holy Land, under the leadership of Moses. It was this generation that received the Torah, the central text of Judaism, at Mt. Sinai. Historians theorize that the disparate tribes later known as the Israelites had gradually united under a national god by the third millennium BCE. This god, Yahweh, is thought to have been a young, warlike version of the older Canaanite deity, El (or Elyon, see Exodus 3:15). Some scholars believe Yahweh (God) was introduced to the highland Canaanites by Semitic tribes escaping from Egypt (see **The Ancient Levant,** p. 47), and that He was worshipped as an alternative to the lowland storm-god, Ba'al. When the Israelites formed a kingdom, worship of God was centralized in the capital, Jerusalem.

Historians estimate the present form of the **Torah** to be 2500 years old, although the Torah has been continuously interpreted and re-interpreted over the centuries in an effort to maintain its vitality and applicability. The Written Torah, (also known as the Pentateuch, or the Books of Moses), which consists of the first five books of the Bible, formed the template for the Oral Torah, a series of interpretations and teachings eventually codified in final form around 200 CE as the *Mishnah.* The *Mishnah,* along with the *Gemara,* are the basis of the Babylonian and Jerusalem *Talmuds,* finalized during the 5th century CE. The Talmud was the springboard for a new series of interpretations and teachings that continue to build upon each other. "Torah," which has come to refer to all Jewish thought and teachings, has been at the core of Jewish life through most of history.

> According to the Bible, Abraham was the first to establish a covenant with God with his self-circumcision at the ripe age of 99.

Among Jews, faith in God is assumed, and the energy of Jewish life is concentrated on observing the commandments. The Torah contains 613 *mitzvot* (commandments) including directives for ritual observances and instructions concerning moral behavior. Over the ages, rabbis have interpreted these *mitzvot* and expanded them to include countless more. This entire set of laws is called *halakha* (literally "the way"). Much of modern Jewish life revolves around the synagogue (*beit knesset* in Hebrew, *shul* in Yiddish). The synagogue plays a multi-faceted role in Jewish life; the Hebrew word means "house of assembly" and the Yiddish word means "school." The *aron ha-kodesh* (Holy Ark) houses the Torah scrolls and determines the orientation of the synagogue. Synagogues normally face toward Jerusalem; within Jerusalem, they face the Temple Mount. Above the *aron ha-kodesh,* a flickering *ner tamid* (eternal flame) usually hangs. The raised platform from which prayers are led is called the *bima.* Most orthodox synagogues are in Israel and contain a *mehitza,* or divider between men's and women's sections. Usually, the two sections have separate entrances. Men should cover their heads when entering a synagogue. Often there is a box of *kippot* (skullcaps, sing. *kippah*) by the entrance. Head coverings symbolize a reverence for God.

Worshippers wear other items as reminders of their devotion. The *talit,* or prayer shawl, has four *tzitzit,* sets of strings twisted and knotted to symbolize the commandments. On weekdays, worshippers wear *tefillin,* boxed scrolls wrapped around the arm and head with leather straps. Visitors are welcome at most synagogues during prayer services. There are three prescribed prayer times every day: in the morning (the *shaharit* service), in the afternoon (the *minha* service), and in the evening (the *ma'ariv* service). Smaller synagogues, however, do not meet for every service. On *Shabbat* and holidays there is an additional service during the day. The *Kabbalat Shabbat* service, on Friday nights, welcomes in the Sabbath. Visitors to a synagogue should dress modestly and nicer attire is in order on Shabbat or holidays. Interesting times to visit are when the Torah scroll is brought out and read: Shabbat, holidays and each Monday and Thursday. It is at these times when you might catch a *Bar Mitzvah* ceremony (*Bat Mitzvah* for girls), a coming of age ritual signifying the point at which a Jew becomes legally eligible to fulfill the *mitzvot.* Remember that photographs on *Shabbat* and holidays are highly inappropriate.

CHRISTIANITY

Christianity began in Judea among the Jewish followers of **Jesus.** The most significant sources on the life of Jesus are the **Gospels.** Scholars agree that the "synoptic gospels" of Mark, Matthew, and Luke were written in that order some time after 70 CE, drawing on an oral tradition which recorded the words of Jesus. The Gospel of John was written about 100 CE, but has roots as old as the others. These sources provide a history influenced by the experiences of the church fathers and the belief that Jesus was the **Messiah** ("anointed one").

Various historical events date the birth of Jesus, the man regarded by millions as their savior, between 4 BCE and 6 CE. According to Matthew, **Bethlehem** is the birthplace of Jesus, and Mary and Joseph moved to **Nazareth** to protect him; in Luke, Jesus' parents are only temporarily in Bethlehem, and in Mark and John, the birth is not even mentioned. The Bible says that Jesus was conceived and brought forth by Mary, a virgin, making him a product of God's creative power and free from humanity's original sin. Catholics additionally hold that Mary herself was conceived without sin: an **Immaculate Conception.**

Jesus was baptized (ritually washed) in the Jordan River by **John the Baptist,** a popular evangelist later hailed as the reincarnation of the 9th-century prophet **Elijah,** herald of the Messiah. Afterwards, Jesus preached in the Galilee, speaking passionately for the poor and the righteous, most notably in the Sermon on the Mount.

St. Paul successfully adapted the faith of Christianity to meet the spiritual needs of the largest body of converts: former pagans.

After about three years of preaching, Jesus went to Jerusalem, where the Passion, the events of his death, took place. The Gospels give slightly differing accounts, but key events in the story include Jesus throwing the money-changers out of the Temple, eating the Last Supper, being betrayed by Judas, being arrested in the Garden of Gethsemane, and being condemned to death by Pontius Pilate and the Romans at the urging of the Pharisees. On Good Friday, he carried his cross down the **Via Dolorosa,** stopping at what became known as the Stations of the Cross, until he reached the hill of Golgotha (or Calvary; now marked by the Church of the Holy Sepulchre), where he was crucified.

According to the Gospels, three days after Jesus' crucifixion, on what is now celebrated as Easter, Mary and two other women went to Jesus' tomb to anoint his body and discovered the tomb empty. An angel announced that Jesus had been resurrected; Jesus subsequently appeared to the Apostles and performed miracles. Later, on Pentecost, the Apostles were given "tongues of fire" and were directed to spread the Gospel. The **Resurrection** is the point of departure for the Christian faith, the beginning of a new age in which the faithful wait for Christ's *parousia,* or second coming.

At first, Christianity was a sect of Judaism, accepting the Hebrew Bible. But Christianity's defining tenet that Jesus was the Messiah severed it from mainstream Judaism. St. Paul (originally Saul of Tarsus), successfully adapted the faith of Christianity to meet the spiritual needs of the largest body of converts: former pagans. Paul abandoned standard Jewish practices like mandatory circumcision, further separating Christianity from Judaism. The Book of Acts documents the early Christians, and the Letters of Paul, which comprise most of the rest of the New Testament, gives advice to the early Christian communities and explains the delay of the second coming. As Christianity developed, it absorbed earlier practices. The incorporation of ancient festivals such as the winter solstice helped draw the common people to the new religion, and the incorporation of Platonic doctrines converted many intellectuals.

The Christian faith was officially legitimized by the Edict of Milan, issued by Emperor Licinius in 313 CE, which proclaimed the toleration of Christianity. In 325 CE, the Emperor Constantine made Christianity the official religion of the struggling Roman Empire. Constantine also summoned the first of seven Ecumenical Councils, held in Nicaea, to elaborate and unify the content of the faith. The Council of Nicaea came up with an explicit creed, declaring that Jesus Christ was of the same essence as the Father, and that there were three equal parts to God. This crucial doctrine of the **Trinity,** which is only implicitly supported in the Gospels, maintains that the Father, Son, and Holy Spirit are distinct persons yet all one God.

The Church was called "the body of Christ" and believed to be integral and indivisible. Nonetheless, the Christian community suffered many schisms. The **Egyptian (Coptic) Church** broke off in the 3rd century (see below), when other eastern branches (the Nestorians and Maronites are examples) began to drift apart from western Christianity. In 1054, the Great Schism, caused primarily by the inflexible Cardinal Humbert, split Christendom into the western Roman Catholic Church and the Eastern Orthodox Church. Whereas Rome upheld the universal jurisdiction and infallibility of the Pope, Orthodoxy stressed the infallibility of the church as a whole. The Spirit, according to the Orthodox, proceeds through the Father, while Roman theology dictates that the Spirit proceeds from the Father and the Son. Orthodox Christians believe that God is highly personal, that each man can find God by looking within himself. In 1517, the German monk Martin Luther sparked the Reformation, which quickly split northern Europe from Roman Catholicism, and led to the development of Protestantism. Protestantism is itself composed of many sects, which generally believe in salvation through faith rather than good works. Eastern Orthodoxy, too, is divided into multiple nationalist traditions (Greek, Russian, Armenian). Only in the 18th century did these diverse churches come to speaking terms, and only in the 20th has the ecumenical movement brought extensive cooperation.

The central part of the church service for Catholics is the mass, basically a reenactment of the last supper: the priest blesses bread and wine and they are changed to Jesus' body and blood by the Holy Spirit. The congregation receives the host just as the apostles did. When visiting churches, it is inappropriate to partake in communion if not a Catholic.

The Coptic Church

"Copt" derives from the Greek word for Egyptian, *Aiguptious,* shortened in Egyptian pronunciation to *qibt,* the Arabic word for Copt. Copts in Egypt usually have tattoos of either a domed cathedral or a tiny cross on their wrists. Of 58 million Egyptians, five to seven million are Copts, most of whom live in Cairo or Middle Egypt. Today, portions of the liturgy are still conducted in Coptic, though most of the service is in Arabic. The Copts recognize their own patriarch—spiritual authority resides in Cairo and Alexandria.

According to Coptic tradition, St. Mark introduced Christianity to Egypt in 62 CE. Mass conversions transformed Alexandria into a Christian spiritual center, but Roman persecution increased proportionately. The bloodiest days passed under Diocletian, who murdered so many Christians that the Copts date their Martyr's Calendar from 284 CE, the beginning of his reign.

In 451 CE, the Alexandrian branch of the Church declared theological and political independence from Constantinople, forming the Coptic Orthodox Church. The split derived from a dispute over the interpretation of the Trinity. While the Ecumenical Council at Chalcedon defended the definition of Christ's nature as diphysite, with the human and the divine aspects clearly differentiated, the doctrine of the new Coptic Church centered around monophysitism, which holds that Christ's nature is of such unity that the human and divine elements are fused and indivisible.

The Byzantine Emperor **Justinian** sought to restore unity by exiling Coptic clergy to isolated desert monasteries. Rebellious Copts thus welcomed the Persians as liberators when they captured Egypt in 619. Since the 7th century, the Egyptian Christian community has lived as a religious minority in an Islamic state. Relations between the Copts and the Muslims have vacillated throughout history, as the Islamic government has used Qur'anic verses and extracts from the Hadith to justify either lenient or oppressive treatment. Recently, the Copts have felt

The Byzantine Emperor Justinian sought to restore unity by exiling Coptic clergy to isolated desert monastaries.

besieged by Egypt's increasingly vocal Islamists, and acts of violence are often aimed at Coptic population centers.

Coptic Christianity served as a link between the Roman-pharaonic and Islamic eras, leaving its own mark on modern Egypt. Coptic art incorporates the influences of pharaonic and Hellenistic cultures. The Coptic cross borrows from the *ankh,* the hieroglyphic sign for "life," as well as from the crucifix on Golgotha. Embroidered tapestries and curtains displaying nymphs and centaurs descend from Greco-Roman mythology. Islamic art often borrows from the Coptic style; many of Cairo's mosques were engineered by Coptic architects, and some are converted Coptic churches. Unlike the monumental art of the pharaohs, the art of the Copts tends to preserve ancient folk media.

Coptic churches usually have one of three shapes: cruciform, circular (to represent the globe, the spread of Christianity, and the eternal nature of the Word), or ark-shaped (the Ark of the Covenant and Noah's Ark are symbols of salvation). The churches are divided into three chambers. The eastward sanctuary *(haikal)* containing the alter lies behind a curtain or *iconostasis,* a wooden screen of icons. The next chamber, the choir, is the section reserved for Copts. Behind the choir is the nave, which consists of two parts, the first of which is reserved for the *catechumens* (those who are preparing to convert). The back of the nave is for the so-called weepers, or sinners. These Christians, having willfully transgressed, were formerly made to stand at the very back of the church. Above Coptic altars hang ostrich eggs, symbolizing the Resurrection (life out of what seems lifeless). The ostrich egg, of religious importance in pre-Christian times, was preserved as a symbol of God's eternal love and care for the Church. Jill Kamil's *Coptic Egypt: History and Guide,* Barbara Watterson's *Coptic Egypt,* and Iris H. Elmasry's *Introduction to the Coptic Church* are all good introductions to the religion.

ISLAM

The Arabic word *islam* translates, in its general sense, as "submission." The basic tenet of Islam is submission to God's will. Islam has its roots in revelations received from 610 to 622 CE by Muhammad, who was informed by the Angel Gabriel of his prophetic calling. These revelations form the core of Islam, the **Qur'an** (recitation). Muslims believe the Arabic text to be perfect, immutable, and untranslatable—the words of God embodied in human language. Consequently, the Qur'an appears throughout the Muslim world—the majority of which is non-Arabic speaking—in Arabic. Muhammad is seen as the "seal of the prophets," the last of a chain of God's messengers which includes Jewish and Christian figures such as Abraham, Moses, and Jesus. The Qur'an incorporates many of the biblical traditions associated with these prophets.

Muhammad rapidly gathered followers to his evolving faith. Staunchly monotheistic Islam was met with ample opposition in polytheist Arabia, leading to persecution in Muhammad's native city of Mecca. In 622, he and his followers fled to the nearby city of Medina, where he was welcomed as mediator of a long-standing blood feud. This *Hijra* (flight, or emigration) marks the beginning of the Muslim community and of the Islamic calendar. For the next eight years, Muhammad and his community defended themselves against raids and later battled the Meccans and neighboring nomadic tribes. In 630 Mecca surrendered to the Muslims, making Muhammad the most powerful man in Arabia. After the surrender, numerous Meccans converted to the new faith voluntarily. This established the pattern for *jihad* (struggle), referring first and foremost to the spiritual struggle against one's own desires, then to the struggle to make one's own Muslim community as righteous as possible, and lastly to the struggle against outsiders wishing to harm the Muslim community. Sadly, only the last aspect is commonly known to the West.

> **Any place where Muslims pray is a mosque or "masjid," best translated as "place of prostration."**

Islam continued to grow after the Prophet's death, flourishing in the "Age of Conquest." The four Rightly Guided Caliphs *(Rashidun)* who succeeded Muhammad led wars against apostate nomadic tribes. Faith in Islam was the strength of the Arab armies, which defeated the once-mighty Persian empire by the year 640. The fourth Caliph, Muhammad's nephew and son-in-law Ali, was the catalyst for the major split in the Muslim world. Ali slowly lost power, and was murdered in 661. The *Shi'at Ali* (Partisans of Ali or Shi'a) believe Ali, as a blood relative of the Prophet, to be the only legitimate successor to Muhammad, thus separating themselves from Sunni Muslims. Contrary to popular Western perception, Shi'ism is not a creed of fanaticism, but is Islam with a sharp focus on divinely chosen leaders (or *Imams*) who are blood descendants of the Prophet through Ali and his wife, the Prophet's daughter Fatima (see **History: The Rule of the Caliphs,** p. 49).

The prophet Muhammad is not believed to be divine, but rather a human messenger of God's word. His actions, however, are sanctified because God chose him to be the recipient of revelation; several verses of the Qur'an demand obedience to the Prophet. The stories and traditions surrounding the Prophet's life have been passed on as *sunna,* and those who follow the *sunna* in addition to the teachings of the Qur'an are considered to be especially devout Muslims. The term Sunni is derived from *sunna.* The primary source for *sunna* is the *Hadith,* a written collection of sayings attributed to Muhammad. A *hadith* had to go through a rigorous verification process before it was accepted as true; the tale had to be verified by several sources, preferably those who saw the action with their own eyes, and the greatest weight was given to testimony by Muhammad's close followers and relatives.

In the 10th century, under the weight of tradition and consensus, Sunni Muslim scholars *(ulama)* proclaimed "the gates of *ijtihad* (individual judgment)"

Allahu akbar: Ash-hadu an la ilaha illa Allah. Ashadu anna Muhamadan rasul Allah.

closed; new concepts and interpretations could no longer stand on their own but had to be legitimized by tradition. This proscription notwithstanding, *ijtihad* continues today, though not on the scale of the first centuries of Islam. There have been numerous reform movements throughout the Islamic world, including the Wahhabbi movement in the Arabian peninsula, the movement of the thinker Jamal ad-Din al-Afghani in the Middle East, and Muhammad Iqbal in South Asia. There are four main schools of thought in the Islamic legal system, and the applicability of *sharia,* or Islamic law, is a subject of much strife in a number of Muslim countries, which have seen challenges to entrenched governments by movements carrying the banner of Islam.

Any place where Muslims pray is a mosque or *masjid,* best translated as "place of prostration." The *imam* (leader of prayer, not to be confused with the Shi'a leaders) gives a sermon *(khutba)* on Friday. In many areas of the Islamic world, men and women still pray in different sections of the mosque. Women must cover their hair and everyone must remove their shoes.

The **Sufis** are a mystical movement within Islam, stressing the goal of unity with God. They are organized in orders, with a clear hierarchy from master to disciple. Different orders prescribe different ways of life in order to reach Allah; some preach total asceticism, others seem almost hedonistic in their pursuit of pleasure. Sufi *sheikhs* (masters) and saints are reputed to perform miracles, and their tombs are popular pilgrimage destinations. Jalal ad-Din Rumi, the great medieval intellectual, founded the famous order of the whirling dervishes. The term "whirling dervish" derives from the joyous spinning and dancing, meant to produce a state of mind conducive to unity with Allah, at Sufi festivals. Marijuana has also been used by some of the Sufis for this purpose.

Pillars of Islam

Allahu akbar. Ash-hadu an la ilaha illa Allah. Ashadu anna Muhammadan rasul Allah. (God is great. I swear that there is no god but Allah. I swear that Muhammad is God's messenger.) These words compose the first lines of the Islamic call to prayer *(adhan),* which emanates hauntingly five times a day from live or recorded *muezzins* perched atop their minarets. The first line glorifies God *(Allah).* The next two lines form the *shahadah* (the testimony of faith), which is the first of the five pillars

ESSENTIALS

of Islam. It reflects the unity of God *(tawhid)*, and the special place of Muhammad as God's final Messenger. Any person who wishes to convert to Islam may do so by repeating these lines three times, thereby completing the **first pillar** of Islam and becoming a Muslim. Enemies of Islam often memorized the lines before going into battle, thus providing themselves with an emergency survival tactic.

The second pillar is **prayer** *(salat)*, performed five times per day, preferably following the call of the *muezzin*. However, if someone is unable to pray at that exact moment, the prayer may be made up and performed whenever possible before the next prayer time. Prayers, preceded by ablutions, begin with a declaration of intent and consist of a set cycle of prostrations. No group or leader is necessary for prayers—they constitute a personal communication with God. The person praying must face Mecca as he or she does so. The word for Friday in Arabic means "the day of gathering;" on that day, communal prayer is particularly encouraged.

The third pillar is **alms** *(zakat,* or purification). Every Muslim who can afford to is required to give one third of his or her income to the poor.

It is believed that Muhammad received the Qur'an during the month of **Ramadan.** Fasting during this holy month is the fourth pillar of Islam. Between dawn and sunset, Muslims are not permitted to smoke, have sexual intercourse, or let any food or water pass their lips; exceptions are made for women who are pregnant or menstruating,

Between dawn and sunset, Muslims are not permitted to smoke, have sexual intercourse, or let any food or water pass their lips.

people who are sick, and people who are traveling— they must make up the fast at a later date. Fasting is meant to teach Muslims to resist temptation and thereby control all their unchaste urges. In addition, by experiencing hunger they are meant to better understand the plight of the poor; and also to be more thankful for the food which Allah has provided them. Finally, Ramadan inspires a sense of community. Ideally, Muslims read the Qur'an during the daylight hours. As soon as the evening *adhan* is heard, they break the fast and begin a night of feasting, visits to friends and relatives, and revelry. In places like Cairo, the city stays up until just before dawn. In quieter areas, a neighbor may circulate to houses, banging a drum and waking people for *suhur,* a small meal eaten just before dawn in an attempt to avoid extreme hunger upon waking. During the month, offices and businesses not catering to tourists may be closed or keep shorter hours.

The last pillar, required only once in a lifetime, is **pilgrimage** *(hajj)*. Only Muslims who are financially and physically able to are required to fulfil this pillar by journeying to **Mecca** and **Medina** during the last month of the Muslim calendar, and those who are able to make the trip talk about it for the rest of their lives. While *hajj* is essentially a re-creation of the actions of the Prophet Muhammad, its effects are to unite Muslims and to stress the equal status of all people who submit to the will of *Allah,* regardless of gender, degree of wealth, race, or nationality. All pilgrims, from Gulf Princes to Cairo street-sweepers, must wrap themselves in white cloth and remove all accessories, which might indicate wealth, and all perform the same rituals. If you are traveling during *hajj,* you may experience delays and general pandemonium in airports.

As with any religion, degrees of interpretation and observance produce a wide range of practices. For more information, try *An Introduction to Islam* by Frederick Denny, *Islam: The Straight Path* by John Esposito, or *Ideals and Realities of Islam* by Seyyed H. Nasr. A sampling of Islamic texts can be found in Kenneth Cragg and Marston Speight's *Islam from Within.* If you feel inspired to study the Qur'an, you may wish to read Muhammad Pickthall's *Meaning of the Glorious Koran.*

Mosque Architecture

Several architectural features deserve special attention in mosques. There are two basic designs. The Arab style, based on Muhammad's house, has a pillared cloister around a courtyard, while the Persian style has a vaulted arch on each side. Most prominent are the towering minarets from which the chants of the *muezzin* summon the faithful to prayer five times daily. Mosques are generally rectangular with cool arcaded porches *(riwaqs)* surrounding a central open courtyard *(saha).* These usually contain a central covered fountain (sabil) for ablutions before prayer. The focus of each mosque is the qibla wall, which holds the prayer niche (mihrab) and indicates the direction of Mecca. Particularly in Mamluk mosques, the mihrab and qibla are elaborately decorated with marble inlay and Kufic inscriptions. Because some religious teachers consider representations of nature (animals, people) to be blasphemous imitations of God, abstract artwork dominates the mosques' decorations. In the Fatimid period, interlaced foliate patterns in carved stucco and plaster were popular ornamentation. Geometric patterns and elegant calligraphy appeared later, in Mamluk times. Particularly beautiful examples of work from this period are found on the pulpits (minbars) that usually stand beside the mihrab. Under the seat of the minbar, on the side, there is often an archway, allowing you to cross to the other side as you make a wish, called a "wishing door."

OTHER FAITHS

The Druze

The faith of the Druze, a staunchly independent sect of Shi'a Muslims, centers around a hierarchy of individuals who are the sole custodians of a religious doctrine hidden from the rest of the world. Many Druze consider themselves a separate ethnicity as well as a religious group, while others consider themselves Arabs. The Druze believe that the word of God is revealed only to a divinely chosen few, and that these blessed few must be followed to the ends of the earth. Wherever the Druze settle, however, they generally remain loyal to their host country. Israel has a Druze population of about 85,000, Syria 500,000, and Lebanon 300,000.

The religion was founded in 1017 by an Egyptian chieftain, Ad-Darazi, who drew upon various beliefs in the Muslim world at the time, especially Shi'a. The Druze believe that God was incarnated in human forms, the final incarnation being the Fatimid Caliph Al Hakim (996-1021, see p. 49). The Druze have suffered a history of persecution and repression for their beliefs, which may partially explain the group's refusal to discuss its religion. The late 1600s was a period of prosperity, however, and under Emir Fakhir ad-Din the Druze kingdom extended from Lebanon to Gaza to the Golan Heights. Sixteen villages were built from the Mediterranean Sea to the Jezreel Valley to guard the two major roads on which goods and armies were transported. In 1830, a Druze revolt against the Egyptian pasha was crushed, along with all but two of the 14 Druze villages in the Carmel (see **Isfiya and Daliyat Al Karmel,** p. 361). In the 1860s, Ottoman rulers encouraged the Druze to return to the Carmel.

Because the Druze will not discuss their religion, most of what Westerners know about them comes from British "explorers" who fought their way into villages and stole holy books. Many of the Druze themselves are not completely informed. As far as outsiders

The Druze have suffered a history of persecution which may partially explain the group's refusal to discuss its religion.

know, Jethro, father-in-law of Moses, is their most revered prophet. The most important holiday falls in late April. In Israel, Druze gather in the holy village of Ḥittim, near Tiberias. Devout Druze are forbidden to smoke, drink alcohol, or eat pork, but many young Druze do not adhere strictly to these prohibitions. Some Druze believe in reincarnation and speak of their past lives. Gabriel Ben-Dor's *The Druze in Israel: A Political Study,* details their ideology, lifestyle, and political situation.

The Baha'i

This movement began in Teheran in 1863, when Mirza Hussein Ali (a son of Persian nobility) turned 46, renamed himself **Baha'u'llah** ("Glory of God"), and began preaching non-violence and the unity of all religions. Baha'u'llah's arrival had been foretold in 1844 by the Persian **Siyyid Ali Muhammad** (also known as **Al Bab,** or "Gateway to God"), the first prophet of the Baha'i religion, who heralded the coming of a new religious teacher and divine messenger. Baha'u'llah was imprisoned and then exiled to

Palestine, where he continued to teach in the city of Acre (Akko). He is buried near the city. Al Bab is buried in Haifa, which is now home to a large Baha'i population.

Baha'u'llah's teachings fill over 100 volumes; his religion incorporates elements of major Eastern and Western religions. Baha'i believe in a Supreme Being, accepting Jesus, Buddha, Muhammad, and Baha'u'llah as divine prophets. The Scripture includes the Bible, the Qur'an, and the Bhagavad Gita. A central doctrine of the faith regards the Baha'i vision of the future. Instead of warning of a final Judgement Day or an end of the world (like many other religions), Baha'u'llah prophesied a "flowering of humanity," an era of peace and enlightenment to come. Before this new age can arrive, however, the world must undergo dreadful events to give civilization the impetus to reform itself. The Baha'i espouse trans-racial unity, sexual equality, global disarmament, and the creation of a world community. The rapidly growing Baha'i faith currently boasts nearly six million adherents, with two million converts worldwide in the last decade.

The Karaites

The small sect of Jews known as the Karaites dwell principally in Ashdod, Be'er Sheva, and the Tel Aviv suburb of Ramla. The community, whose existence dates to the 9th century CE, counts about 15,000 adherents today. Formed out of the political and religious turmoil following the Muslim invasion, Karaites adhere strictly to the five books of the Torah, though they reject all later Jewish traditions. They are generally cohesive, and have their own religious courts. To an outsider, however, their practices appear similar to those dictated by traditional Jewish observance.

The Samaritans

Currently, the Samaritan community is a tiny one, with roughly 550 adherents divided between Nablus on the West Bank and Holon, a suburb of Tel Aviv. Originally the residents of Samaria, Samaritans consider themselves the original Israelites, descended from the tribes of Joseph (Manasseh and Ephraim) from whom other Israelites learned monotheism. The religion is seen by non-members as an offshoot of Judaism marked by literal interpretation of the Samaritan version of the Old Testament and the exclusion of later Jewish interpretation (i.e. the *Mishnah,* the Talmud, and all books of the Hebrew Bible after Joshua) from its canon. A gradual, centuries-long separation between the two religions culminated with the destruction of the Samaritan temple on Mt. Gerizim by the Hasmonean king John Hyrcanus in 128 BCE. The mountain is still the most holy site of the Samaritan religion. Centuries of persecution by the various rulers of Palestine shrunk the community further and included thousands of deaths in a 529 CE uprising against Byzantine rule. While the Rabbinate does not recognize Samaritans as Jews, the Israeli government applies the Law of Return (granting settlement rights) to them.

EGYPT مصر

US$1=3.39 Egyptian Pounds (E£)	E£1=US$0.29
CDN$1=E£2.44	E£1=CDN$0.41
UK£1=E£5.43	E£1=UK£0.18
IR£1=E£4.99	E£1=IR£0.20
AUS$1=E£2.54	E£1=AUS$0.39
NZ$1=E£2.18	E£1=NZ$0.46
SAR1=E£0.72	E£1=SAR1.38
NIS1 (New Israeli Shekel) =E£0.96	E£1=NIS1.04
JD1 (Jordanian Dinar) =E£4.80	E£1=JD0.20

For important information on travel in general and some specifics on Egypt, see the **Essentials** section of this book. Egypt's **International Phone Code** is 20.

The Arab Republic of Egypt (Goumhouriyyat Misr El Arabiyya, or simply Misr) is a land of intense geographical contrast. The Nile Valley, source of the country's fertility, is located smack in the middle of the planet's greatest desert. This trick of northeastern African geography has been crucial to the birth and growth of one of the world's most ancient civilizations. The Nile's bounty and the hostility of the surrounding wasteland provided for both the formation of a settled society and the creation of its strong cultural and political identity. Through 5000 years and numerous foreign invasions, the foundations of Egypt's character have remained unshaken.

The tourist's Egypt has five regions. The first is the **Mediterranean Coast.** Highlights include Alexandria, Egypt's summer capital; Marsa Matrouh, home to incredible beaches; and the beautiful Siwa Oasis, a pilgrimage into the Western desert. The **Nile Valley** is the most popular region and the most tremendous in distance and sights. It is divided into Upper Egypt in the south, Middle Egypt, and Lower Egypt in the north (designated with respect to the direction of the river's flow—upstream and downstream). Lower Egypt includes the Cairo and the Nile Delta; Upper Egypt includes Luxor and Aswan. Nubia, where African and Egyptian culture merge, begins at the First Cataract of the Nile in Aswan and extends south into the Sudan. Most Nubians migrated north to Aswan and Kom Ombo or south to Sudan after Lake Nasser, a product of the High Dam, flooded much of their traditional homeland. The least explored region is the **Western Desert,** where palms shade the paradisiacal waterholes of Bahariyya, Farafra, Dakhla, Kharga, and Baris. Finally, on Egypt's **Red Sea Coast** and the **Sinai Peninsula,** snorkeling, scuba-diving, hiking, windsurfing, and spectacular scenery can revitalize even the most sight-weary traveler.

Egypt can be a budget traveler's paradise. The sights are stunning, the culture is fascinating, and bargains are a way of life. On the other hand, travel there requires plenty of time, stamina, and patience. Most travelers find that with a relaxed attitude, the difficulties of navigating the hassles are well overshadowed by the intensity and beauty of the experiences Egypt has to offer.

ONCE THERE

■ Entry

A **visa** is required to enter Egypt (see **Visas and Visa Extensions,** p. 8). Generally, all personal items brought into the country to be taken out upon departure are exempt from taxes. There is no formal declaration for personal items, but passengers may be asked to open their bags for customs officials when leaving the airport.

Upon arrival at the **Cairo International Airport** (often reminiscent of Rodin's *The Gates of Hell*), purchase a visa stamp at one of the six currency exchange booths, if you have not done so already. Visas cost around US$15. Visas can be purchased at any point of entry to Egypt; two-week Sinai-only visas can be purchased at the Israeli border. Visas purchased at the airport are good for one month but can be renewed at police stations or at passport offices in major towns if you provide one photograph, E£12, and (officially) receipts showing that at least US$200 has been changed into Egyptian currency. Reports vary on the strictness of this last rule.

After exiting customs, you will likely be approached by individuals who claim to be "tourist agents" or employees of the Ministry of Tourism. They wait for unescorted travelers and, pretending to help, set you up in their employers' hotels. Do not let anyone direct you to a hotel or even a cab; take **cabs** from the official stand, which is monitored 24 hours a day by tourist police officers wearing black berets and arm bands. Don't pay more than E£20-25 for a ride to downtown Cairo. For help navigating, see **Cairo: Orientation,** p. 90.

Minibus #27 goes to the Nile Hilton station in Cairo from the Airport's old terminal (50pt-E£1, depending on whether you sit or stand). Bus #400 runs between the airport and Tahrir Square in Cairo (24hr., 50pt). Gem Travel runs a 24-hour **shuttle bus** to downtown ($4). The counter is on the right as you exit customs.

All **trains** into Cairo stop at **Ramses Station.** Bus #59 runs from there to Tahrir Sq. Black and white **taxis** to Tahrir Sq. cost about E£2. The **Metro,** just opposite the station, will whisk you to Tahrir Sq. for 50pt. To walk (30min.), climb the pedestrian overpass and walk south on Ramses St., away from the statue of Ramses II.

Buses from the Sinai, Israel, and Jordan usually drop passengers off at **Abbasiyya Station**. Buses from Jordan usually drop you off at **Abd el-Moneim Riyadh Station**. To reach Tahrir Square from Abbasiyya station, hop into a southbound black and white cab (E£4-5) or walk left down Ramses St. as you leave the station; go beyond the overpass, and to the first bus stop on the right. From here many buses travel to Tahrir Square. From the Abd el-Moneim Riyadh Station, walk right onto Galaa St. as you exit, until you come to the Corniche el-Nil. At the Corniche take a left onto Sharia at-Tahrir, which will lead you to Tahrir Sq.

Mr. Salah Muhammed (tel./fax 298 06 50; email samo@intouch.com), a tour guide, offers a **free "VIP" 24hr. shuttle service** from the airport to downtown Cairo for *Let's Go* users who will take his tour of the Pyramids at Giza, Memphis, Saqqara, and the carpet school at Harania (special *Let's Go* price: E£23, not including entrance fees to sights; free shuttle only if you reserve ahead of time by email). For more information on Mr. Muhammed's tour, see **Pyramids at Giza**, p.132.

It used to be that the first sight to visit in Cairo was the voluminous gray building in Tahrir Sq. called **El Mugamma'**, home to **Passport Registration**. As of August 1996, however, visitors of all nationalities need only get their passport stamped upon entry—no further hassle required. For more information, see **Cairo: Practical Information,** p. 99-102.

■ Getting Around

Transport to obscure sights may not be as plentiful in summer (the off-season for tourism). Before that camel, Peugeot, or minibus spirits you off to a Nilometer or distant praying baboon statue, make sure it's up for the ride back as well. See **Cairo Transportation**, p. 93, and **Alexandria Transportation,** p. 151, for more information on surviving travel to sights.

> Road travel in Egypt is extremely hazardous. Egypt has one of the highest road casualty rates in the world. To lower your risk, avoid overcrowded buses and minivans, and avoid night travel whenever possible. If the bus driver is operating the vehicle in a reckless manner, demand to be let off immediately, and report the incident to the American Embassy. In Egypt, 44.1 people are killed in traffic accidents for every 100 million km of vehicle travel; in the U.S., the comparable rate is 1.1 persons. (Source: *Association for Safe International Road Travel.*)

Travel Restrictions It is prudent to check with the local tourism authorities or the Ministry of the Interior before venturing in private transport off the main roads in the Western Desert (especially near the Libyan and Sudanese borders), along the Suez Canal and Red Sea Coast, and in the Sinai. If you need a permit, apply at the Ministry of the Interior in Cairo at 110 Qasr el-Aini St. (tel. 354 83 00). In restricted zones, the police are entitled to confiscate your passport and hold you for questioning. If you find yourself in such a pickle, sincere apologies and professions of ignorance may put the matter to rest.

A law (seldom enforced) forbids Egyptians from traveling or even walking with foreigners without special permission. A travel agent's license, a marriage certificate proving the Egyptian and the foreigner are married, and wads of bribe money have all been used as ways to get around this restriction, but it is meant to protect you.

Trains Egypt's railway system was the first established in both the Arab world and in Africa. The first short lines were built in 1834, linking quarries in Moqattam with the Nile. Trains now serve even the smallest of towns. Schedules and signs in the train stations are never in English, but schedules can be obtained from the tourist office or, as a last resort, from ticket windows; a fellow passenger or the man on the platform can also help you out. It is not at all unusual for a train to come three hours late, and schedules and prices are in constant flux.

A good thing about trains is that they offer **student discounts** of up to 50% (but with an average of about 30%). ISIC cards are required to qualify for student rates. **Air-conditioned second-class** cars have comfy reclining seats and are a great value; shelling out more for first class gets you slightly larger seats and loud, annoying Egyptian videos. Third-class cars are sorely overcrowded and not entirely safe, so tourists are often not allowed to use them for long trips. **Second-class sleeper cars,** available on some regular trains, might be more comfortable for trips of ten hours or more but, at a cost several times that of regular second-class, are overpriced. They are also difficult to book; plan well in advance. Discounts on sleepers are less than on regular seats, and you might not get a discount at all on the luxurious **wagon-lits.** You can reserve space in a sleeper at the *wagon-lit* offices in Cairo, Luxor, Aswan, and Alexandria. Purchase other tickets at the station of departure; allow plenty of time for waiting. For a fee, a travel agent or your hotel will send someone to buy a ticket for you. Seats for Cairo-Alexandria (especially in summer) and Cairo-Upper Egypt (especially in winter) should be reserved one or two days in advance.

Round-trip reservations cannot be arranged at the point of departure. If you intend to take a sleeper, take care of return reservations as soon as you reach your destination. During the last week of Ramadan and the following week, as well as before Eid el-Adha, trains are completely booked. If you plan to travel during these periods, book your tickets at least one week in advance.

If lines are long and you're in a hurry, try boarding the train without a ticket. The conductor will usually sell one on board for an additional fee, even if the train is full. The real problem will be finding a seat or an empty space on the floor. Travelers who miss their train may be issued a ticket on the next train out—even if there are officially no seats available. To return reserved tickets, go to the stationmaster's office before the scheduled departure and your money (minus a little) will be refunded.

Buses Only large cities have intra-city bus systems. The public buses are inexpensive but often slow, crowded, and brain-meltingly hot. In some places they are your only option. Private companies include **West Delta Bus Company, East Delta Bus Company,** and **Superjet.** Regular West Delta buses are on par with public buses, but they have a deluxe branch called **Golden Arrow.** Golden Arrow and Superjet are air-conditioned and have bathrooms and refreshments on board. Unfortunately, they often show Egyptian melodramas replete with women in head scarves shrieking at unsustainable volumes. They serve the Cairo-Alexandria and Cairo-Luxor routes. East Delta Bus Company runs generally comfortable, air-conditioned buses throughout the Sinai. When you buy a ticket for one of these luxury buses, you will be assigned to a certain seat. Unlike the trains, private bus companies offer no student discount.

Taxis Another way to get from one town to another or between towns and sights is the **service taxi** (pronounced ser-VEES). We refer to them throughout the book as *service;* they are also known as *taxi bin-nafar* (particularly in Middle and Upper Egypt) and *taxi ugra.* Keep all three names in mind. They can take the form of Peugeot station-wagons and other cars, covered pick-up trucks, or minibuses, and depart from stands in the various cities and towns. In smaller towns the "stand" may be nothing more than a stretch of road. Board the vehicle and wait for it to fill up, which usually takes 15 to 30 minutes. In the off-season, it will take longer to collect tourist companions. Drivers depart when their cars are full or when everyone is tired of waiting and the passengers have agreed to split the price of a full carload. The best thing about *service* is flexibility—no schedules or incorrect timetables. You're also unlikely to be cheated because all passengers pay the same amount.

The intracity version of *service* is the **minibus,** prowling the same streets day in, day out. Flag one down and pay the bargain-basement fare once aboard. **Private taxis** are cheap and convenient in Cairo (where they are black and white) and Alexandria (black and yellow or orange). Skillfully using them will make you feel like a stud on wheels (see **Cairo Transportation,** p. 93, and **Alexandria Transportation,** p. 151).

"**Special**" is Egyptian code for **rip-off.** If this word is mentioned in your presence, calmly repeat "*La*" (No) and the words you have learned for *service. Bin-nafar* and *ugra* are particularly helpful in this situation. Within cities, avoid being ripped off by hailing a private taxi on the street instead of in front of a tourist trap. If a cabbie approaches you first, be especially wary. Either don't talk about the price before you get in and pay what is appropriate when you get out (see our city and sights sections for estimates) or settle on a suitable price before you climb in.

Hitchhiking Hitching is not common in the highly populated parts of Egypt. In recent years, the newspapers have been full of crimes perpetrated by hitchhikers along the roads between Cairo and Alexandria. Because of this, drivers may be reluctant to pick people up. Rides are reportedly easy to obtain in isolated areas, such as along the Great Desert Road, or for short jaunts in remote parts of the Nile Valley, where public transportation is difficult to find. Many drivers who pick up hitchhikers will expect money anyway, so public transportation should be used where it is available, which is almost everywhere. **Women, whether in a group or alone, should not hitchhike.** Nobody traveling alone should accept a ride in a private car. Egypt is mostly untraveled desert; never count on getting a ride before you **die of dehydration.** *Let's Go* does not recommend hitchhiking. Don't hitchhike.

Car Rental Renting a car is a useful option only in the Sinai and Oases. If you plan to drive, remember to obtain the necessary permits (see our coverage of the specific area you plan to drive in). There are few places to drop off rental cars. An **International Driver's License** is theoretically required to drive in Egypt. Your insurance may not cover you here; contact your provider and see **Driving Permits and Insurance** on page 12 for more information. Age requirements are not always strictly enforced by rental agencies. The cheapest rentals run around US$35 per day. It is often cheaper and easier to make reservations with a car rental agency before leaving your home country. Realize that your life is forfeit once you enter the melee of Egyptian motoring.

Planes **EgyptAir** serves major cities in Egypt out of Cairo International Airport. All prices listed are out of Cairo, one-way, economy class: to Luxor (1hr., US$121); Aswan (1½hr., US$167); Alexandria (45-50min., US$71); Abu Simbel (1¾hr., US$238); and Hurghada (1hr., US$131). Add an additional E£5 tax. EgyptAir's main office in the U.S. is at 720 Fifth Ave., Suite 505, New York, NY 10019 (tel. (800) 334-6787). See **Practical Information** listings for offices in specific cities. **Air Sinai,** in the courtyard of the Nile Hilton, is a charter serving the Sinai and Israel. Call (62) 44 28 31 for information. Below are one-way fares; don't expect the round-trip to be discounted. Foreigners may have to pay in U.S. dollars. Air Sinai flies from Cairo to Sharm esh-Sheikh (50min., E£543), from Hurghada to Sharm esh-Sheikh (50min., E£653), and between Cairo and Tel Aviv (40min., E£653). For more information, contact the office at 12 Qasr en-Nil St., Cairo (tel. (02) 75 06 00 or 75 07 29) or another EgyptAir office.

■ Useful Addresses

Tourist Services The **Egyptian Tourist Authority (ETA)** (see also **Tourist and Information Offices,** p. 3) has offices in most major cities. The **Tourist Police** are actually meant to assist visitors. Go to them in case of theft or if you feel you have been taken advantage of in any way. Most offices employ at least one person who speaks some English. The officers' uniforms are black in winter and white in summer, with green "Tourist Police" arm bands.

Medical Emergencies and Health Luxury hotels may have resident doctors, and other hotels can usually get someone dependable in an emergency. You can also ask your embassy for a list of recommended physicians and pharmacists, or see individual city listings. Several major hospitals in Cairo provide 24-hour service, including the **Misr International** (12 Sataya St., Finney Sq., Dokki; tel. 360 82 61 through 82 69), the **Anglo-American Hospital** (Botanical Garden St., Gezira-Zamalek; tel. 340 61 65), and the **As-Salaam International Hospital** (Corniche en-Nil, Ma'adi; tel. 363 80 50, emergency 362 33 00).

Even big-city **pharmacies** (identifiable by the snake-on-a-staff symbol or by a red crescent) do not carry American or European brand-name drugs; some Egyptian brands are, however, equally effective and reliable. They are also much, much cheaper. Before you do any major traveling, stock up on headache, diarrhea, and constipation pills. Also take along some of the electrolyte and nutrient rehydrating solution used for babies; if you get dehydrated or experience a minor sunstroke, this will help your recovery process. Egypt is a bit more relaxed about prescriptions than the U.S. or other Western countries. **Condoms** are available over the counter at city pharmacies. Ask for *kabout, tops,* or *'azil.* "Tops" is the Egyptian-made condom brand. Condoms are not available in small towns or in conservative Middle Egypt. You will also have trouble finding deodorant and tampons. Most Egyptian brands of **pads** are uncomfortable wads of cotton, though the *Always* brand appears in many towns. Pharmacists in Egypt are authorized to write prescriptions and give injections. There should be at least one pharmacy in each town, although finding a 24-hour store may prove difficult in small towns. **Dial 123 for emergencies.** (Also see **Health,** p. 17, and **Practical Information** listings for specific cities.)

■ Money Matters

Currency and Exchange Egypt's array of coins and banknotes is gradually becoming simplified as the old bills and coins pass out of circulation and into the hands of collectors. The **Egyptian Pound (E£)** (pronounced gin-EEH in Arabic) is divided into 100 **piasters (pt)** (*irsh,* plural u-ROOSH). Technically, *piasters* are divided into 10 *millims,* but the only vestige of this minuscule denomination is an extra zero to the right of the decimal point on some posted prices. **Banknotes** are color-coded and printed with Arabic on one side and English on the other; the notes come in the following denominations: E£100 (green), E£50 (red), E£20 (green), E£10 (red), E£5 (blue), E£1 (brown), 50pt (red and brown), and 25pt (blue). Bills do not vary much in size. It's best to break your large bills into smaller denominations of E£1 and below, as most people are reluctant to make change. **Coins** come in denominations of 5pt (copper-colored) and 10pt and 20pt (both silver-colored—check the Arabic numbering). Hoard them; they are useful for various piddling expenses. Shopkeepers may not bother with change below 25pt; often they will offer candy or gum instead.

Save all exchange receipts in case authorities ask for them when you are leaving the country. You are not allowed to carry more than E£20 into or out of Egypt, nor would you want to, so exchange what you think you'll use, or visit the 24-hour bank at the airport on your way out to change back what you haven't used.

Prices A brief lesson in Egyptian Arabic: After *min fadlak* (please) and *shukran* (thank you), the most important word to know is *khawaga* (kha-WA-ga), because you are one. *Khawaga* means "tourist," but is understood locally as "clueless and rich." No matter how destitute you consider yourself, you are probably wealthy by Egyptian standards. Egyptians know this. Aside from those in hotels and restaurants, most prices are not posted, which means that *khawagas* may be charged more than Egyptians. Avoid salespeople and shops near tourist hubs and look upon unsolicited offers of goods or services with grave suspicion, even if (especially if) you are told there is no charge. Agree on a price before you accept anything, and do not pay until you receive the goods. At official sites, entrance fees are set and **students get discounts of up to 50%** with proper student ID, making the purchase of an **ISIC** worthwhile. Shutterbugs are slapped with a photography/video fee, usually E£5-10. The people who work at ticket kiosks will charge you the correct fee (bring exact change), but guides who solicit your business at sights and museums should be ignored. Report serious hustlers and rip-off artists to the Tourist Police. (The **Practical Information** section in each city provides listings for Tourist Police.)

Shopping in Egypt can be an adventure. For basics, you should go where the Egyptians go and pay what the Egyptians pay; rare is the department store or pharmacy that thrives on ripping off *khawagas*. When shopping for souvenirs and native sundries, stoke your cynicism. Valuable craftwork is out there, but it's rare. Avoid souvenir shops and kiosks flanking tourist attractions. The bazaars in the cities are chaotic, but they are the best places to find great leather, woodwork, glassware, textiles, or jewelry. There are great deals everywhere on beautifully crafted silver. The key word is: **bargain.**

Tipping and Bakhsheesh Another crucial Arabic word for *khawagas* to know is *bakhsheesh,* the art of tipping. It is an ancient tradition in Arab societies and went on long before *khawagas* trampled onto the scene. Although *bakhsheesh* is different from straightforward charity, it stems from the belief that those who have should give to those who have not, particularly in return for a favor or service. There are three kinds of *bakhsheesh.* The most common is similar to **tipping**—a small reward for a small service. Baggage handlers, guards, and bathroom and parking attendants expect to receive a tip of 50pt-E£1. Do not let yourself be railroaded into forking over huge sums; if a smiling worker demands E£5, smile back and give 50pt-E£1. *Bakhsheesh* becomes most useful when used to procure special favors; almost any minor rule can be broken for *bakhsheesh.* If a custodian gives you a private tour of a mosque or lets you in long after hours, a pound or two is in order. Never expect recipients of *bakhsheesh* to make change—one more reason to carry small bills. Ignore demands for more if you feel you've been fair and only tip in exchange for a service (i.e. don't tip smiles).

The second kind of *bakhsheesh* is the giving of **alms.** Everywhere in Egypt you will encounter beggars who are willing to bestow rhetorical blessings in return for a little charity. There are also those who insist on opening a door before you can get to it or snatch your baggage from your hands and then demand *bakhsheesh.* Don't feel obligated to give money in these situations. The final form of *bakhsheesh* is simply a **bribe,** generally a bad idea. Don't try to bribe government officials. Offering *bakhsheesh* to people of rank is quite insulting.

Business Hours On Friday, the Muslim day of communal prayer, most government offices, banks, and post offices are closed. Bank hours are ordinarily Sunday to Thursday 8:30am-2pm (although some banks in big cities are open daily), with money exchange available daily 8:30am-noon and 4-8pm. Foreign banks keep longer business hours, usually Sunday to Thursday 8am-3pm. Other establishments, such as restaurants, remain open seven days a week. Store hours are ordinarily Saturday to Thursday 9am-9pm, with many stores also open Friday. Government office hours are usually 9am-2pm. Government business is best done in the morning, as workers often leave before official closing times. Archaeological sites and other points of interest are typically open 8am-5pm (4pm in winter), though in summer the most important ones are open 6am-early afternoon..

Ah, to be a khawaga

Egypt's reliance on the tourist industry has led it to apply a different set of rules to foreigners (*khawagas*) than to natives. Most foreign couples, married or not, can take a room together in a hotel. For Egyptian couples, it's not so simple. In all but the cheapest hotels, only a married couple can share a room. Borrowing your friend's wedding rings won't do, either—a marriage license is required. Tourists can also gamble, a sport forbidden to citizens. While foreign status might bring unwanted hassles and scams, it also grants a degree of freedom withheld from most Egyptians.

During the month-long holiday of **Ramadan** (Dec. 31, 1997-Jan. 16, 1998; see **Holidays,** p. 2), some restaurants close entirely, while some others open only after sundown when the daily fast is broken. The streets empty at dusk as everyone sits down to *iftar* (the breaking of the fast), after which business resumes. Shops close at about 3:30pm during Ramadan and reopen 8-11pm. Egyptians sit down for the second daily meal of Ramadan (*suhur,* pronounced su-HOOR) in the middle of the night, about 2-3am, before going to sleep. Although traveling during Ramadan can be inconvenient, the excitement of nighttime celebrations offsets daytime hassles.

■ Accommodations

Hostels Egypt's **Hostelling International (HI)** youth hostels vary in quality. Most are grungy, crowded, and tucked away in obscure corners that are difficult to find and far away from any interesting activity. Most destinations offer much nicer accommodations for only slightly more money. Keep a careful eye on your valuables and take your passport and money to bed with you. Advance reservations are usually unnecessary. A valid HI card is seldom required, but at some hostels it will save you some money. You can get an International Guest Card at Egyptian hostels for E£24. For hostel expenses, don't count on being able to use your credit card or traveler's checks. Most hostels have kitchen facilities. Write to the **Egyptian Youth Hostel Association,** 1 El Ibrahimy St., Garden City, Cairo (tel. (02) 354 0527; fax 355 03 29). Their Youth Travel Department also answers questions, helps plan tours, has maps, and sells International Guest Cards.

Hotels Egypt's hotels run the gamut from opulent new resort complexes to ramshackle dives in dingy alleys; in between is an array of clean, comfortable, inexpensive hotels. Prices depend almost solely upon competition. In towns with heavier tourist traffic, you may spend as little as E£8 per night for clean, comfortable surroundings. Lower-quality accommodations in a town with few hotels and even fewer visitors can cost anywhere from E£10-25. Prices vary considerably between high and low season. The high season in Alexandria is June to August, in the Nile Valley October to April. There is a **hotel tax** which varies by location, averaging around 21%. Unless otherwise noted, the tax is already included in the price, but breakfast is not unless listed. Cairo is an international city where credit cards, ATM cards, and traveler's checks are all helpful and readily accepted. Outside of Cairo, most credit cards are useless, although traveler's checks are still widely recognized. There are **ATMs** in towns throughout the Sinai, especially in the more heavily touristed dive centers.

Many budget hotels have private bedrooms but shared bathrooms. In most places, E£5-10 extra will secure the luxury of a private bath. Air-conditioning also increases the price. Fans are usually included in the room price, especially in the hotter regions of the country. Do not expect to find towels, cute little bars of soap, or bottles of shampoo and conditioner. Don't count on toilet paper, either. (Guess what that little squirting pipe in the toilet is for.) Some places can send your laundry out for 50pt-E£1 per piece. Many hotels will allow you to use their washing machines and kitchens, but bring your own soap. Alternatively, plugging up the sink and scrubbing it by hand has been known to get the job done.

Be careful: in the savage jungle of the tourism industry, you are like a lion cub amongst hyenas. You will start off defenseless and lost, but you can grow into a fearsome budget travel machine. The most important thing to remember is that everyone who approaches you is trying to get your money, despite what they may say. Hotel owners and their agents will lie and scheme to get you in their clutches. Beware of impostors. Don't be afraid of being **rude and nasty** should the situation demand it. There have been many cases of male hotel employees harassing female visitors, from Peeping Tom incidents to unwanted sexual advances. In general, keeping your distance will increase your chances of passing through unbothered. Make it clear early on how you will react to such a situation.

■ Keeping in Touch

Mail Airmail letters and postcards from Egypt to any destination outside the Middle East cost E£1. Most hotels sell stamps, though a 5pt surcharge may be added. The most dependable place to receive mail is at **American Express offices,** but this privi-lege is for the most part reserved for cardholders; **Poste Restante** is also available in major cities. Confusion over first and last names can be avoided by printing the last name in capital letters and underlining it, for example, Katherine <u>MODEL</u>, Poste Res-tante, City, Country. As a general rule, mail *to* Egypt is much faster than mail *from* Egypt. In either case, don't hold your breath—two or three weeks delivery time is normal. In theory, all mail leaving Egypt is opened and inspected.

For faster service that won't break the bank, seek international **Express Mail Ser-vice (EMS),** available almost everywhere. It usually takes 3-20 days to the U.S. and 3-15 days to Europe. To send packages by **Federal Express,** contact the office at 1079 Corniche en-Nil St., Garden City, Cairo (tel. (02) 357 1304; fax 357 1318). **DHL Inter-national Courier** delivers stuff door-to-door all around the world. The main office is at El Mona Towers, 16 Lebanon St., Mohandiseen, Cairo (tel. (02) 302 9801; fax (02) 302 9810).

Telephone **Long-distance** and **international calls** can be made from most govern-ment telephone offices (*maktab et-telephonat, centrale* in Alexandria), usually open 24 hours and packed to capacity in the evenings. In very small towns the process is less than a joy—your hair may turn gray before you hear Mom's voice on the line. In most cities you can make calls using brand-new, life-saving **phone cards** emblazoned with the Sphinx's stern visage (E£5, 15, 20, 30, or 40). The cards are sold at some tele-phone offices for use at bright orange phones either in the offices themselves or in train stations and other public places. Alternatively, go up to the desk and provide the number you are calling and the amount of time you want to speak. You will be sent to a booth when your call comes through and asked to hang up when your time is up. Rates are lower at night. Refuse to pay for incorrect connections. You can also call from private phones with international lines. Major hotels have good connections but can be expensive.

For AT&T **collect calls,** USADirect, or World Connect, call (02) 510 02 00 (AT&T) from anywhere in Egypt. Within Cairo, leave out the (02). If you have trouble with the connection, call a local operator and ask to be connected to AT&T or USADirect. Some ritzy hotels have USADirect phones in their lobbies; some also have UK, Can-ada, and JapanDirect. Call (02) 355 5770 for MCI WorldPhone or collect calls. Call (02) 365 3643 for CanadaDirect calls using a Bell Canada calling card. Kiwis should call (02) 365 3764 to reach their island home direct, while Brits should call (02) 365 3644 to reach theirs. These telephone numbers are in Cairo, and you will pay as if you had been talking to someone in Cairo for the duration of your call overseas. Don't try to explain the process to telephone office employees. Tell them you are calling Cairo and pay for that call. You can also call from the gray, coin-operated pay phones in most telephone offices, but you risk being unceremoniously cut off if you neglect to pump it with coins every two seconds or so. The orange phones are more conve-nient. The Cairo operator can place a collect call for you or connect you to any num-ber in the U.S. if you have that party's calling card. The **international phone code** for calling to Egypt is **20.**

Local calls can be dialed directly anywhere in Egypt (10pt for 3min. from a public phone, 50pt for 3min. from private phones in stores, restaurants, or hotels). Use the gray coin-operated payphones. Be wary of using phones in hotel rooms at all; it could cost an arm and an ear.

■ Women Travelers

Foreign women traveling alone will undoubtedly be harassed by Egyptian men. Harassment can take many forms, from a mildly sinister "hello," to frightening and potentially harmful physical contact. Western women have the reputation, transferred through movies and television, of being "free" in their behavior. Some common-sense precautions will help avoid uncomfortable situations: dress conservatively and do not visit isolated areas alone.

Some "precautions" do not necessarily mesh with common sense. For example, a 50-year-old man will have no qualms about harassing ten women; but if there is even one man in your group, the dynamic changes considerably. Also, the concept of friendship between men and women has not quite reached these shores. Many Egyptian men still think that a woman even speaking to them implies a sexual advance of some sort. They will believe the same about any non-Egyptian male friends you make. Use this to your advantage by traveling with groups of tourists in possibly dangerous areas. The best way to deal with harassment from strangers in the street is to ignore it, but repeated advances should be quelled with a loud, indignant response in front of many people. Alert the tourist police—that's why they're there. For more information, see **Safety & Security,** p. 15, and **Women and Travel,** p. 33.

LIFE AND TIMES

The burgeoning population of Egypt, 63 million strong, is composed of a broad spectrum of cultures and classes, including Christian Copts (many of whom reside in Cairo and Middle Egypt), Bedouin, and southern Egyptians claiming to be the pure and direct descendants of the Pharaohs. The majority claim Arab ancestry or mixed Arab and Egyptian blood, while the upper classes trace their heritage to Turkey. Darkskinned Nubians from southern Egypt began migrating north when their villages were flooded out of existence by the creation of Lake Nasser. The Nubians fill mostly menial jobs in today's urban centers and suffer because of racism which goes unrecognized by most Egyptians. Finally, people with Greek, Armenian, Jewish, Kurdish, and Albanian origins add spice to the mix, especially in Alexandria. But there is one important commonality that unites these ethnicities: most people consider themselves wholly Egyptian. The great majority of the lower class lives in appalling poverty, some relying on family and relatives abroad (usually in the Gulf) for support. The cheapest commodity in resource-poor Egypt is labor. Along the banks of the Nile, *fellaheen* farm the rich land as their ancestors did 5000 years ago, but Egypt must supplement these products with imported food. In this diverse but traditional society, Violent crime is uncommon, and it is usually safe to wander in large cities.

Egyptians are known throughout the Arab world for their sense of humor and love of fun. Although tourism and poverty here have made hospitality less common than in other Arab countries, you won't be in Egypt long before you are invited to tea, a meal, or a wedding. Directions and advice are freely offered, but some Egyptians so fear looking foolish that they will give incorrect directions rather than fail to offer assistance. Most hosts or helpers expect something in return.

Egypt is a conservative, patriarchal society with a strong Islamic tradition. Western mores do not apply, especially in matters of family and sex. The visibility and freedom of most Egyptian women is limited. Do not challenge traditions or mores by trying to force yourself into arguments or places in which you do not belong.

From the Western tourist's point of view, Egyptians' apparent lack of concern for time may be disconcerting. Simply accept this, slow down, and mellow out. Tempers are most likely to howl in encounters with Egypt's mind-occluding bureaucracy; don't spend more time buying train tickets and placing phone calls than exploring ancient temples. Bring books written by Cairene Nobel Laureate Naguib Mahfouz (or better yet, *Let's Go*) to read as you wait in line, and relax.

■ Government and Politics

According to its 1971 constitution, Egypt is a "democratic, socialist state," but in reality it's neither democratic nor socialist. It is more of an election-legitimated authoritarian regime, in which the president serves a six-year term and is almost inevitably reelected for additional terms. He appoints the vice president and ministers. Since the 1952 revolution, changes in the presidency have happened only when Gamal Abd en-Nasser died in 1970 and when his successor, Anwar es-Sadat, was assassinated in 1981. The legislative branch of government consists of the 444-member People's Assembly, half of whom must be workers or peasants and a whopping 30 of whom must be women. This popularly elected assembly ratifies all laws as well as the national budget. Despite the regime's ultimate authority (the assembly is very much a rubber-stamp body), and the (relatively small) internal secret police force, Egypt's government is somewhat liberal for an Arab nation.

The most significant political threat to current President Hosni Mubarak's regime comes from the Islamist parties. Mubarak's inauguration followed the assassination of Sadat by militants whose aim was to overthrow the Egyptian government and establish an Islamic republic in its place. Islamists gained parliamentary strength in the May 1984 elections for the People's Assembly. A fundamentalist group, the Muslim Brotherhood, joined with the Wafd Party, and the alliance achieved the necessary 8% minimum for parliamentary representation. Islamists were elected to university student councils, often gaining majorities and faculty support and they have now gained control over most professional syndicates as well. In attempts to quell the Islamic militants, the government acquiesced to several fundamentalist demands. Mubarak has consistently appeased Islamic moderates (the majority) in order to isolate militants, who have been targets of brutal repression. Alcohol was banned on EgyptAir flights, Dallas was taken off TV (to the chagrin of many), and an Islamic newspaper, Al-Liwa'al-Islami, was initiated. Divorce laws were also changed, allowing the state to force annulments on intellectuals declared apostate. Under pressure from Islamic fundamentalists, a law banning female genital mutilation was repealed.

The past several years have seen a rise in Islamist-generated violence, with militants based in Middle Egypt striking at the status quo via attacks on government figures and assassinations of secularist intellectuals. Civilian and tourist deaths shook Egyptian society in 1993, but massive jailings and several executions failed to stop the Islamists. The focus of their violence has recently shifted to governmental and security forces. The country as a whole remains stable but tense and under tight security controls. For more information, see the warning for traveling in Middle Egypt (p. 175). An attempt on Mubarak's life by Sudanese Islamists in July of 1995 raised tensions on Egypt's southern border, and waves of anti-Sudanese propaganda may lead to greater crises in the near future.

■ Economy

At the beginning of this century, Egypt was the richest of the Arab nations. However, the mushrooming population and a shortage of arable land have greatly inhibited its economic development. All but 4% of Egypt is desert, and the land that is fertile is overcrowded. Nonetheless, Nasser's land reforms greatly altered the economy's complexion; in 1952, 3% of the population owned more than half of the land, while today, no private citizen may own more than 50 acres.

About half of the Egyptian labor force works in the agricultural sector, growing primarily cotton, corn, rice, and grain. A growing proportion of workers is involved in manufacturing, which now accounts for as much income as does agriculture. The government employs almost all the rest of the work force in its colossal bureaucracy. As the population grows at nearly 2.4% per year, many educated Egyptians leave to find work in wealthy, neighboring oil states (there may be as many as 3 million expatriated workers). Illiteracy remains high (over 50% of the population over 10 years old), poverty is widespread, and the typical diet is inadequate.

EGYPT

To help combat these problems, Egypt's government follows whatever political wind is carrying the most money and, as a result, receives vast amounts of foreign aid. Through the 1970s, Saudi Arabia, Qatar, Kuwait, and the United Arab Emirates supplied Egypt with tens of billions of dollars in aid and, in 1977, formed the Gulf Organization for the Development of Egypt (GODE). After the Camp David Accords in 1979, Egypt received grants from the United States as well. Under the Carter Plan, the U.S., Western Europe, and Japan agreed to provide Egypt with US$12.25 billion over five years. For its support in the Gulf War, Egypt received further assistance from the West (including the forgiving of US$6.7 billion of military debt to the U.S.) and renewed aid from the Gulf states. Revenue from the Suez Canal has consistently been about US$1.5 billion per year during the last decade. The US$3.5 billion per year tourism industry doesn't hurt, either—that's a lot of *kebab*.

■ Religion and Holidays

About 94% of Egypt's population is Sunni Muslim (see **Islam,** p. 66). Most other Egyptians are Christian Orthodox of the Coptic (Egyptian) Church. Smaller religious minorities include Shi'a Muslims, Protestants, Roman Catholics, Greek Orthodox, and Jews. Government offices and banks close for Islamic holidays, but tourist facilities remain open. Though sometimes proving inconvenient for non-Muslim travelers, Ramadan can be a wonderful time to visit, especially in festive Cairo or Alexandria. For the dates of Islamic and national holidays, see the **Appendix**).

Along with the Islamic festivals, watch for the two **Sufi** rituals of **Zikr** and **Zar.** In the former, a rhythmic group dance builds in fervor, and the group members become whirling dervishes, mesmerized into a communal trance. The latter is a group dance performed by women, primarily as an exorcism rite. Both rituals are practiced on Fridays in some populous areas. The Coptic celebrations of Easter and Christmas are tranquil affairs marked by special church services.

Sham en-Nissim falls on the first Monday after Coptic Easter. Though its origins are a hodgepodge of Coptic and pharaonic influences, it has developed into a secular holiday. Egyptians traditionally spend the day at a picnic eating *fasikh,* a dried, salted fish difficult for most Western palates to appreciate.

■ Language

One of the earliest forms of writing was Egyptian **hieroglyphs** (sacred carvings). Alongside this pictorial system developed the **heiratic,** an abbreviated cursive script, which retained only the vital characteristics of the pictures. After the 22nd Dynasty, scribes changed the hieratic writing to a form known as **Enchorial** or **Demotic,** used primarily in secular contexts. The *Book of the Dead* was translated into this script. Well before the end of the Roman period in Egypt, hieroglyphs had been fully replaced by Demotic, Greek, and Latin. Egyptian no longer served as the spoken language. **Coptic,** today used only in liturgy, is a derivation of ancient Egyptian that uses Greek letters plus six letters of Demotic.

Since the Islamic conquest, the primary language of Egypt has been Arabic. Modern **Egyptian Arabic** differs greatly from classical Arabic, and the Egyptian dialect varies significantly from that used in Jordan, Syria, and other Arab nations. Even within Egypt the vernacular varies; Cairo, Lower Egypt, and Upper Egypt each have their own dialects. For more information, see the **Phrasebook,** p. 574.

■ The Arts

Throughout most of the second half of the 20th century, Egypt has had a near monopoly on the Arabic entertainment industry. Egyptian films, widely distributed and appreciated throughout the Arab world, range from emotionally wrenching, skillfully done modern dramas to comedies pitting down-and-out students against evil capitalists and bumbling police officers, with a smattering of southern Egyptians (stereotypically portrayed as idiots) thrown in for comic relief. The musicals of the 50s and 60s, still very popular, featured well-dressed young hipsters singing their hearts out and knitting their brows in consternation over the cruelty of love, the generation gap, and the difficulty of college examinations.

Mini-dramas or short-term **soap operas** are also popular. In these, women swathed in eye shadow and head scarves hung with golden coins battle insults to their reputations, pine quietly for the hard-working medical student upstairs, and thank Allah profusely when chastity and morality win out in the end. The country also boasts many **theatrical successes:** summertime brings brightly-painted billboards advertising plays patronized by Egyptians and Gulf vacationers.

LITERATURE

Most of the writings of the **ancient Egyptians,** such as the *Book of the Dead,* deal with magic and religion. The ancients dabbled in poetic love songs as well. The *Song of the Harper* advises immediate gratification in the face of transitory life. Folklore was not as often preserved in stone, but *The Tale of the Eloquent Peasant* has survived to tell of a slippery peasant and his travails.

Modern literature offers insights into the nation's culture. In 1988, Cairene novelist **Naguib Mahfouz** became the first Arab to win the Nobel Prize for literature. His *Midaq Alley* describes the life of a stifled young girl in the streets of 60s Islamic Cairo, and his classic allegory *Children of Gebelawi,* banned in Egypt, retells the stories of the Qur'an in a modern Cairo setting. *Miramar, Fountain and Tomb, Palace Walk,* and other works by Mahfouz are also readily available in translation. Yusuf Idris, a leading short-story writer, offers a witty account of modern Egyptian middle-class life in his *Cheapest Nights.* Sunallah Ibrahim's *The Smell of It,* a semi-autobiographical account of his life after release from prison, was censored in all Egyptian editions, but unabridged copies are available in the West. Master writer Taha Hussein's best-known work is his autobiography *Al Ayyam;* also worth reading is Tawfik el-Hakim's *Bird from the East.* For a range of Egyptian fiction, pick up *Arabic Short Stories,* edited by Mahmoud Manzalaoui. The Egyptian theater of the absurd is mostly composed of el-Hakim's *Fate of the Cockroach and Other Plays.* Egyptian feminist Nawal es-Saadawi, whose novels include *The Circling Song,* is controversial within Egypt and widely known among women of developing countries.

Many **non-Egyptians** have written accounts of their travels and experiences within the country. In *The Innocents Abroad,* Mark Twain describes his misadventures in Egypt and other countries. *Flaubert in Egypt* (edited by Francis Steegmuller) also tells tales of the stranger-in-a-strange-land variety. In *Maalesh: A Theatrical Tour of the Middle East,* French playwright Jean Cocteau makes insightful and humorous observations about Egypt. For an eye-opening account of early Western explorers roaming the Nile, read Alan Moorehead's *The White Nile.* The companion volume, *The Blue Nile,* includes hair-raising chapters on the French invasion of Egypt and the rise of Muhammad Ali. Michael Ondaatje's award-winning *The English Patient* contains wonderful descriptions of early desert expeditions. Another classic for travelers

---

Puff the Magic Sheesha

In Egypt, relaxation has become synonymous with the gurgling and puffing noises emanating from *ahwas* and cafes everywhere. These sounds of contentment are usually accompanied by the smell of sugary honey, apple, or rose tobacco. The instrument of pleasure, a popular smoking apparatus known in Egypt as a *sheesha* (elsewhere as an *argeileh*), 1-3 ft. in height, rainstorm plain to ornately decorated. Water vapor carries tobacco smoke through a tube and into the mouth, making each puff smooth and sweet. The *sheesha* is thought to have been introduced in Egypt by the Turks, and became fashionable among the elite during the late 17th century. For a long time *sheesha* smoking remained an upper-class pleasure, but it seems the apple- and honey-drenched puffs of smoke have ushered in a veritable national pastime.

is Olivia Manning's *Levant Trilogy,* about the wartime marriage of two British citizens who meet in Cairo during the 40s.

MUSIC

With a musical tradition probably more rich and diverse than that of any other Middle Eastern country, Egypt is the capital of the Arab music industry and a magnet for aspiring artists from all over the Arab world. Some Egyptian music falls into the larger category of Arabic music that, between the 7th and 10th centuries, was so highly esteemed by Middle Easterners that hyperprotective measures were taken against the infiltration of Western musical trends. While Western classical music is characterized by mellifluous harmonies, Arabic classical music favors simple, extended melodic lines. Usually a single instrument speaks the melody while percussion instruments chant in the background.

The type of music you will hear most often in Egypt, blaring from taxis, *ahwas,* and homes, is a slightly updated brand of traditional classical music. **Sayyid Darwish** and the legendary **Muhammad Abd el-Wahhab** began as early as the 1910s and 20s to integrate Western instrumentation and techniques into Arabic song. What resulted was a mesmerizing music with Arab melodies and repetition backed by traditional percussion instruments, with violins, other stringed instruments, and sometimes full orchestras accompanying. This type of music had its heyday in the 40s, 50s, and 60s; its popularity shows no signs of waning today.

In the 40s, 50s, and 60s, emphasis fell on strong, beautiful voices to unite the music's sometimes disparate elements, and several "greats" of Egyptian music emerged. Every Egyptian has his or her favorite singer/composer/performer. The hands-down winner, however, is **Umm Kulthum,** whose incredible, versatile voice enraptures. This woman began by singing religious music for festivals in the provinces with her brother and father, and went on to tour Europe, sing Egyptian anthems, and generally dominate the airwaves throughout the Arab World for fifty years. Her diction and mastery of the Arabic language are widely noted and respected. You will probably not leave Egypt without hearing Umm Kulthum or seeing her sunglasses-clad face on a television screen or wall mural. Others with a loyal following include Abd el-Halim Hafez and Farid Atrash; more recent favorites are Warda and Fairouz.

The 80s and 90s saw a wholesale incorporation of Western influences into Egyptian pop music. This music features danceable, often synthesized drumbeats and comes with music videos and posters of teen heartthrobs. Many of its purveyors are one-hit wonders; every summer three or four tapes will be the undeniable hits. Teen dream **Amr Diab,** however, has endured. His upbeat songs, best taken in small doses, provide sing-along and dance material at weddings, parties, and discos.

Another important part of one's introduction to Egyptian music scene is traditional folk music. Consisting mainly of drums and nasal horns, the mesmerizing music nearly compels you to sway back and forth as though in a trance. You can catch inexpensive performances in the Abd el-Wahhab theater in Alexandria. **Nubian music** is equally enthralling. In general, it eliminates the horns and focuses on slow, almost physical drumbeats and chant-like choruses. In Aswan, ask for *musiqa nubiyya.*

Stores selling tapes are plentiful and more than willing to play a tape for you before you decide whether or not to purchase it. Just mention any of the artists described above and watch the shopkeeper's face light up in recognition. Tapes cost between E£5 and E£7.

■ Food and Drink

French, Greek, Persian, and Turkish cuisines flavor Egyptian fare. Since food in Egypt often wreaks havoc upon unhabituated digestive systems, it is mistakenly reputed to be strongly spiced; the truth is that it can sometimes be rather bland. Intestines new to the scene should avoid green salads in all but the expensive restaurants and eat fruit only after it has been washed well and, preferably, peeled.

The Egyptian breakfast of choice, which also serves as a snack or cheap meal throughout the day, is *fuul* (pronounced fool), cooked fava beans slightly mushed, blended with garlic, lemon, olive oil, and salt, and eaten with bread and vegetables. What's known as falafel in Israel—chick peas and/or fava beans mashed, shaped into balls, and fried—is called *ta'miyya* in Egypt. This, too, is eaten all day, often in sandwiches. Try the larger *ta'miyya* made with peppers. *Lu'met el-qadi*, a distant cousin of pancake batter fried into golden balls and served with syrup and/or powdered sugar, is available fresh in the early mornings.

Egyptian families generally eat large lunches and lighter dinners. A meal extremely popular with children is *mulukhiyya*, a green leaf (Jew's Mallow, little-known in the West) finely chopped and cooked with chicken broth and garlic into a thick soup. It is either served over rice or with bread. Vegetable stews including okra *(bamya)*, green beans *(fasulia)*, and peas *(bazella)* are also common, cooked in tomato sauce with lamb and ladled over rice. *Biftek*, sometimes represented on restaurant menus as veal *panné*, is thinly sliced veal, breaded and fried.

Egyptian restaurants do not even come close to representing the variety of Arabic cuisine; it is rare for meals cooked at home to make their way onto restaurant menus. On a certain long strip of the Nile Valley, you might feel that all you will ever get to eat will be *kofta, kebab,* and chicken. These carnivorous joys are almost always served with tomato-less salads, bread or rice, and *tahina*, a sesame-based sauce which adds invaluable TANG! to any meal. *Kofta* is spiced ground beef wrapped around skewers and grilled; *kebab* is chunks of lamb cooked the same way. Chicken is either fried (without batter), roasted on a rotisserie, or skewered, grilled, and called *shish tawouq*. Most expensive restaurants go the European route. All manner of badly-done quiches and even *paella* have been spotted. A couple of Egyptian specialties, however, should not be missed. Stuffed pigeon *(hamam)* is a source of national pride. Fish *(samak)*, shrimp *(gambari)*, and squid are great in sea-skimming towns.

In addition to *fuul* and *ta'miyya*, several street foods offer instant gratification for rumbling bellies. *Kibdeh* (liver) sandwiches smell disgusting until you try them; ask around in Luxor and Aswan to see which stands make the best. Corn cooked over coals in the big cities taxes both your stomach and your teeth. *Shawerma* made its way from the Levant to Egypt only a few years ago; it is supposed to be sinfully fatty lamb rolled into a pita with vegetables and *tahina*, but Egyptians will slap any sort of meat into bogus French bread and call it *shawerma*. The ever-popular *kushari* is a cheap, carbo-filled, tasty meal consisting of various shapes of pasta plus rice, lentils, and fried onions in a bit of tomato sauce. Slather on the hot sauce to give your tastebuds a ride. *Fitar* are flaky, chewy, doughy delights, filled with anything and everything and eaten either as a meal or for dessert.

Other desserts include *ba'laweh* (ubiquitous all over the Mediterranean), rice pudding flavored with rose-water *(roz bel laban)*, and various Frenchified pastries and chocolates. The best dessert option is fruit. Steel-coat your stomach and indulge; it would be a shame to miss Egypt's ruby-red watermelon *(butteekh)* and unbelievable figs *(teen)*. Late summer produces the papaya-like *teen shoki* (cactus fruit), sold from wooden donkey carts by old men or young boys with leather hands. Unless you like splinters, allow them to peel it for you on the spot.

Shopping in the *souq* (market) is the cheapest alternative to restaurants, but you must select your food carefully. Bread, subsidized by the government, is available in three types: *aish baladi* (round unleavened loaves made with coarse flour), *aish shami* (similar to baladi but made with refined white flour), and *aish fino* (leavened French-style loaves). Cheese comes in two locally produced varieties: *gibna beida* (white feta cheese) and *gibna rumi* (a hard, yellow cheese with a sharp flavor). You can also get Danish-supervised feta (in year-long shelf life, no-refrigeration-needed packs—the stuff is great for long road trips or cheap breakfasts in your room) or imported cheeses at reasonable prices. *La Vache Qui Rit* (The Laughing Cow) is so

EGYPT

popular that it has been adopted as a disparaging nick-name for President Hosni Mubarak. *Zabaadi* (yogurt) comes unflavored and makes a filling side dish.

Fruit juices are a great value and a crucial re-hydrator for travelers. Small stands all over serve seasonal juices (sweet orange and mango juice abound in summer) along with perennial favorites like '*asab* (sugar cane juice, said to increase sexual prowess), *tamr hindi* (tamarind), *farawla* (strawberry), and '*er 'asous* (carob).

Egyptians are coffee and tea fiends. Egyptian tea, similar to the Western variety, is normally taken without milk and with enough sugar to make it syrupy. Though you can get Western-style coffee, Egyptians prefer *ahwa* (Arabic coffee), which comes in three degrees of sweetness: *ahwa saada* (no sugar), *ahwa mazbuta* (just right), and *sukkar ziyaada* (with a full year's harvest of sugar cane). Especially when you are in Upper Egypt, try *karkadeh,* a red drink unlike anything you've ever tasted, made by brewing hibiscus flowers and served hot or cold. Egypt brews its own beer, Stella, which costs between E£2.50 and E£6 in restaurants and bars. (Stella brewed for domestic consumption comes in green bottles; export Stella comes in brown bottles, tastes no better, but costs more. You figure it out.) Egypt also produces a selection of justifiably obscure red and white wines, sold for E£2-5 per bottle. Non-alcoholic beer (Birell and Brew) is also available.

Cairo القاهرة

> I arrived at length at Cairo, mother of cities and seat of Pharaoh the tyrant, boundless in multitude of buildings, peerless in beauty and splendor, the meeting-place of comer and goer, the halting-place of feeble and mighty, whose throngs surge as waves of the sea.
>
> —Ibn Battuta

Since the beginning of recorded history, religious and political leaders have tried to capture the glory of this one-time capital of Cheops and Muhammad Ali. The Crusaders, Napoleon, and Hitler all tried to achieve the immortality that only control of *El Qahira*—"the Conqueror"—could have assured. Today's Cairo seems to be more conquered than conqueror, weakened under the barrage of challenges brought about by its burgeoning population (estimates vary from 15 to 22 million). Expansion of Africa's largest city has lead to over-crowded neighborhoods, clogged thoroughfares, and urban pollution. Places where pharaohs and kings once lounged now teem with barking street merchants and silver-tongued con artists. But, like Athens or Rome, Cairo transcends daily life, enriched by the aura of deep-rooted history. As you walk through Cairo's streets, you walk in the eight-century-old footsteps of Salah ad-Din; stop to contemplate this, and you might not notice the cars careening toward you. Cairo's tumultuous present is only the current incarnation of Cairo's tumultuous past, and the former can be cherished just as the latter is. Amid tangled webs of unlabled streets and the dizzying calls of hawkers, Cairenes find their favorite *sheesha* halls, navigate labyrinthine bazaars, and descend on hundreds of places of worship: mosques, churches, and even a synagogue. The deep spirituality can elude newcomers, who often hear the call of the *muezzin* as just another part of the dizzying and omnipresent noise. Fortunately, strolling along the Nile after sundown or watching it flow at sunset from a riverside coffeehouse can foil even the most jaded anti-Cairene. The Nile, lifeblood of Egypt and of civilization, runs directly through the city, and it is the true conqueror, drawing millions to it and capturing their imaginations.

■ History

The strategic significance of the sandy plateau just above the Nile Delta did not escape the pharaohs of the Old Kingdom. On the western bank, the ancient capital of

---

Memory Lane

Street names in Egypt are used repeatedly in different cities. Most of these popular names have historical significance. Here is a brief sample:

26 July Street: Commemerates the non-violent coup of 1953 in which General Naguib and his Free Officers overthrew the king.

Sa'ad Zaghloul: He was the leader of the nationalist movement during World War I. In 1918, Zaghloul formally presented the British High Commissioner with a demand for complete autonomy which was automatically rejected. Eventually, he was arrested and deported to Malta.

6 October Street: The date in 1973 when President Anwar es-Sadat staged a surprise attack against Israeli forces in the Sinai, raising a great deal of popular support for him.

Salah ad-Din Street: Salah ad-Din Al-Ayyubi assumed control of Egypt in 1171, fortified Cairo, and built its Citadel. His reign was a golden age for Egypt, and he was revered as one of the great heroes of Islam—for his humility, personal courage, and brilliant military and administrative mind.

Memphis flourished as one of the world's earliest urban settlements. On the eastern bank, pharaonic remains suggest the presence of slightly older, similarly important cities, Heliopolis and Khery-Aha—an area later known as Babylon. When the upper and lower kingdoms of Egypt united around 3000 BCE, Memphis was the natural choice for a capital. Heliopolis became an important religious center around 3100 BCE. Even though the royal capital moved to Thebes and elsewhere after 2250, Memphis and Heliopolis remained important political and religious centers until the Ptolemaic period, when Heliopolis faded along with the Th.ult of the sun (see **Religion in Ancient Egypt,** p. 61). Memphis endured until the beginning of the Christian era, when massive population shifts left only two settlements: Giza on the western bank, and Babylon, an economic base for the Romans protected by its Byzantine fort, on the eastern bank.

During the first century CE, St. Mark introduced Christianity to Egypt. The Romans resisted, intent on maintaining control, and bloody wars ensued. For 600 years, the Coptic Church marked the wrists of its faithful with tattoos, and left even more enduring marks on the Cairene landscape by building the churches of Old Cairo.

The early decades of the 7th century CE found Cairo in the throes of power struggles with the Persian and Byzantine empires—Memphis and Alexandria changed hands many times. Warfare near Babylon drove many urban dwellers to the villages, leaving the city bereft and deserted by the time of the Arab conquest in 641. General Amr Ibn el-As, head of the invading Arab forces, came to Egypt with specific instructions from Caliph Omar to center the new state at Babylon, not Alexandria. Babylon had a strategically superior location, and the desert-dwelling invaders found the Mediterranean culture of Alexandria suspicious. Amr founded the outpost of Fustat (the Latin and Byzantine roots of which mean "entrenchment"), the seed of modern Cairo, on part of the plain due east of the ruins of Babylon. On the western edge of Fustat, Amr built Egypt's first mosque. Political expansion and upheavals caused the settlement to expand to the north and northeast.

In 868 the 'Abbasid governor Ibn Tulun, appointed from Baghdad, declared Egypt an independent state. He built a palatial new city around his Grand Mosque, modeling it after the elaborate metropoli of Iraq where he had been educated. When the Fatimids swept in from Tunisia in 969, they occupied the empty northern plain and built a magnificent walled city for the new caliph and his court. Legend has it that Gawhar Al-Sikelli, the Fatimid leader, set up a primitive telegraph system of bells connected by strings with which his astrologers could alert all of the workmen to begin construction at the most auspicious moment. A crow landed on the line just as Mars, the planet of war, was ascendant, and the workers began to build. Peeved but resigned, Gawhar dubbed the city El Qahira, "The Victorious." Today, three of the walled city's gates survive (Baab el-Futuh, Baab en-Nasr, and Baab Zuweila).

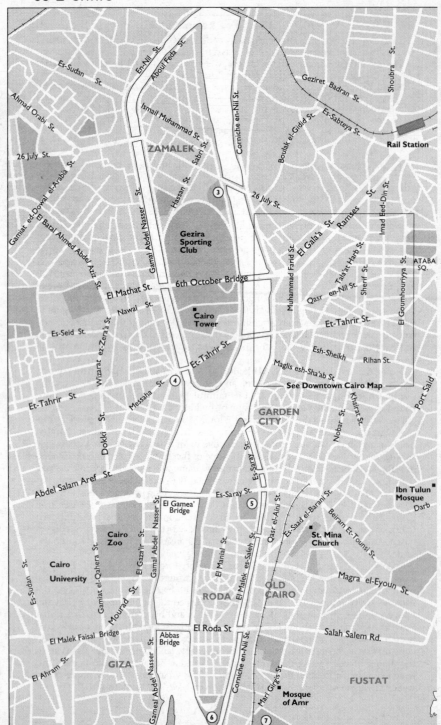

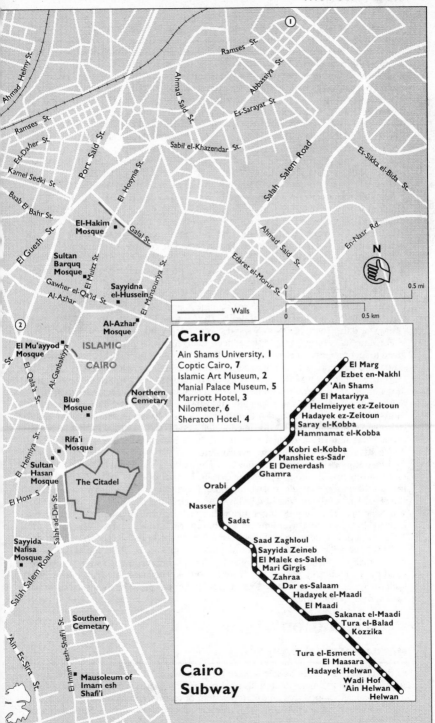

Cairo

Ain Shams University, 1
Coptic Cairo, 7
Islamic Art Museum, 2
Manial Palace Museum, 5
Marriott Hotel, 3
Nilometer, 6
Sheraton Hotel, 4

Cairo
Subway

Fustat continued to swell in size and grandeur and became known by the Semitic name for Egypt, Misr. This was Cairo's Golden Age, when, along with Damascus and Baghdad, it was a center of the most advanced culture west of China. During the 11th century, the twin cities of El Qahira and Fustat enjoyed a symbiotic relationship, and both thrived. But these two would stand together for less than a century: Fustat suffered from plague, famine, and political unrest, while El Qahira continued to grow.

The Ayyubid Kurd Salah ad-Din overthrew the Fatimids in 1171. He opened the walled enclosure of El Qahira to the populace and built another fortress, the Citadel, on the hills to the south, above the rubble of Fustat. During the short reign of the Ayyubids and the longer, more violent period of the Mamluk Sultans, the city continued to expand. Throughout the Middle Ages, it was far more populous than any city in Europe. Almost every sultan and prominent amir graced the place with a mosque, school, or hospital, usually raiding pharaonic ruins for building materials. The casing stones of the Giza Pyramids and Memphis are now strewn throughout Islamic Cairo.

Mamluk, meaning "one who is owned," was used to describe non-Muslim Turkish children who were captured and brought to Egypt as slaves. They received intense training in military arts and eventually overthrew their masters. The Bahri Mamluks (1250-1382 CE) received their name because their original barracks were on Roda Island in the Nile—*bahr* means river. The still-standing complexes of Sultan Qalaoun, Sultan Hasan, and the Mosque of Sultan Baybars date from this period. The second group of Mamluks, the Burgi (so named because *burg* means "tower," signifying the towers of the Citadel in which they lived), reigned from 1382-1517 CE. During this period, each Mamluk tried to outdo his competitors by building bigger, better mosques and complexes. Nearly every Mamluk was murdered by a rival; Qaytbay was the lone Sultan who died a natural death. The Mosque of Barquq, the buildings of El Ghouri, and the Tomb of Qaytbay stand as reminders of the Mamluk period.

The Ottoman conquest of 1516 reduced Cairo to a provincial center. Power was given to incompetent viceroys, and disorder and mutinies reigned, yet the Turks held onto Cairo for centuries. Although Napoleon successfully invaded Egypt in 1798, the Ottomans, allied with British sea forces, drove him out and appointed the Albanian Muhammad Ali to rule. The extravagant royal family built with little desire to fit Egyptian architectural styles, and it erected Turkish-style mosques and palaces. The enormous Mosque of Muhammad Ali in the Citadel is a lavish imitation of the grand mosques of Istanbul. The European-educated *khedives* (hereditary rulers) who succeeded Muhammad Ali, designed the broad, straight avenues of the New City on the new land created by the Nile's westward shift.

The educational history of the *khedives* foreshadowed a period of European influence and intrusion into Egypt. After the Suez Canal opened in 1869, the British thought Egypt too strategic to trust to "foreign" hands and took Cairo for themselves in 1882. Many of the budget hotels downtown are in the run-down remains of colonial buildings. The early 20th century witnessed the creation of a new Heliopolis, planned by aristocrat Baron Empain as a haven for Europeans. Two years after the 1952 revolution under Gamal abd en-Nasr (Nasser), the British agreed to pull out.

During the 1960s, Cairo's population reached 4 million. By 1980, it had ballooned into 14 million, and today it races toward 17 million. Population pressure has necessitated the continuous construction of new suburbs. The latest, Medinet Nasser, was built on the edges of the Eastern Desert in an attempt to preserve the precious arable land in the Nile Valley itself.

■ Orientation

METROPOLITAN CAIRO

At the center of it all is **Tahrir Square** (also known as Midan Tahrir or Liberation Square), one of the many central districts planned by British and French colonialists. It was originally hoped that an ordered system of squares connected by straight avenues would alleviate crowding. The three most important streets coming out of

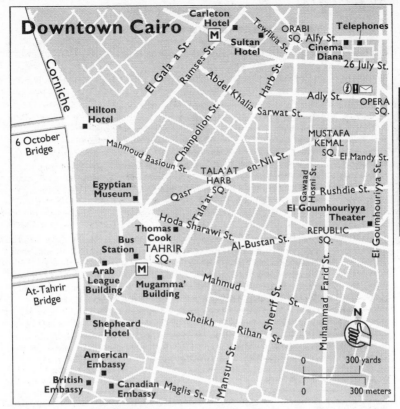

Downtown Cairo

Carleton Hotel
Sultan Hotel
ORABI SQ.
Telephones
Tewfikia St.
Alfy St.
Cinema Diana
26 July St.
El Gala a St.
Ramses St.
Abdel Khalia
Harb St.
Adly St.
OPERA SQ.
Corniche
Hilton Hotel
Sarwat St.
Champolion St.
6 October Bridge
Mahmoud Basioun St.
MUSTAFA KEMAL SQ.
El Mandy St.
TALA'AT HARB SQ.
en-Nil St.
Gawaad Hosni St.
Rushdie St.
Egyptian Museum
Qasr
Tala'at
El Goumhouriyya Theater
Hoda Sharawi St.
REPUBLIC SQ.
El Goumhouriyya St.
Thomas Cook
Al-Bustan St.
Bus Station
TAHRIR SQ.
Arab League Building
Mugamma' Building
Mahmud
Muhammad Farid St.
Sherif St.
St.
N
Shepheard Hotel
Sheikh
Rihan St.
At-Tahrir Bridge
American Embassy
Mansur St.
0   300 yards
British Embassy
Canadian Embassy
Maglis St.
0   300 meters

EGYPT

Tahrir Sq. are Qasr El 'Aini Street, Qasr en-Nil Street, and Tala'at Harb Street. **Qasr El 'Aini Street** runs south from Tahrir Sq. and ends at **Old Cairo,** the historic and spiritual center of the Copts (Egyptian Eastern Orthodox Christians), also known as **Coptic Cairo.** Just south of Tahrir Sq., sandwiched between Qasr El 'Aini St. and the Nile, foreign embassies and banks cluster along the streets of the serene **Garden City** residential area. The British government designed this district in the early 20th century as an escape from their embassy. The **American University of Cairo (AUC),** Parliament, the Ministry of Social Affairs, the Ministry of the Interior, and some of the city's most beautifully preserved 19th-century colonial mansions line Qasr El 'Aini Street. **Qasr en-Nil Street** begins in front of the Nile Hilton and continues on to **Mustafa Kamel Square.** In between lie many of Cairo's western-style stores, banks, travel agents, and American Express. Further south, the exclusive district of **Ma'adi** serves as a home for many of Cairo's expatriates. On **Tala'at Harb Street,** running east from Tahrir Sq., you'll find most of the budget hotels and eateries. Due north of Tahrir Sq. lies **Abdel el-Moneim Riyadh Square,** the starting point of **Ramses Street.** Heading northeast away from the Nile, Ramses St. traverses **Ramses Square,** next to the Cairo train station, which is also called **Ramses Station.** Further out on Ramses St. are the **Cairo Stadium,** home to intense soccer rivalries, and **Heliopolis,** a fashionable suburb where President Mubarak lives. Farther to the east are the market districts of Al Muski and Darb al-Ahmar, known together as **Islamic Cairo.**

The main bridge crossing the Nile from the Downtown area is **Tahrir Bridge,** connecting Tahrir Sq. to the southern tip of **Gezira Island** (also called Zamalek). The northern half is Cairo's ritziest residential area, **Zamalek.** South of Zamalek is its fellow Nile isle, **Roda Island,** the site of the Manial Palace Museum and the Nilometer. .

The Pros of Cons in Cairo

Although you may miss out on a wonderful personal encounter, it's safest to assume that anyone approaching you in Cairo wants something. Scams begin the moment you step off the plane and get your passport stamped. The guy with the photo-ID card on his lapel asking you if you have anything to declare probably isn't a customs official; he just wants to get you in his buddy's cab to Cairo for E£25, to have you check in at his uncle's E£100-a-night hotel, and to show you the Pyramids at inflated prices. Instead, take the shuttle or the public bus to town. Be firm and strong in your conviction to go to the hotel you have selected.

Travel agents in the downtown area have been known to add airport taxes (there is no departure tax from Cairo) and other fees to tickets. Sometimes they charge massive cancellation fees if you get fed up and decide not to book a ticket through their office. You should demand receipts for every pound you hand over and have them give you written estimates, including all taxes, for every flight you purchase, even if you're just going across the street.

These scams are just the start. Imaginative scammers think up new ones daily.

Past Tahrir Bridge on the western bank of the Nile, the Cairo Sheraton Hotel presides over the residential neighborhood of **Dokki,** home to a handful of important embassies. North of Dokki lies **Mohandiseen** (Engineer's City), built in the late 1950s by Nasser as a neighborhood for engineers. South of Dokki, past the Cairo Zoo and across the Giza Bridge, is **Giza Square. Pyramids Road,** where overpriced bars provide nightly sleazefests, begins at the square and runs to the **Pyramids of Giza.**

The major streets in Cairo are sometimes labeled in both English and Arabic, but a good **map** is helpful (the map provided by the ETA does not qualify). Maps cost E£10-E£30 and are available at the American University of Cairo or Shorouk bookstores (See **Practical Information,** p. 99). *Egypt Today* (E£9) publishes up to date street listings. Look for their *Dining Guide* and *Travel & Recreation Guide* (E£15 each).

DOWNTOWN CAIRO

Tahrir Square is the heart of Cairo. Buses depart from here for every metropolitan destination. At the north end of Tahrir St. facing the square is the sandstone **Egyptian Museum;** adjacent to it on the west side of the square is the Nile Hilton. At the southern end of the square is the massive, concave **Mugamma' Building,** headquarters of the Egyptian bureaucracy. The **American University of Cairo (AUC),** directly to the east of the Mugamma' Building across Qasr El 'Aini St., has gardens filled with English-speaking Egyptians and Arabic-speaking Americans, plus an excellent bookstore.

Tala'at Harb Street runs from the northeast side of Tahrir through Tala'at Harb Sq. **Ramses Square** to the north and **'Ataba Square** to the east (both major transportation hubs) form a rough triangle with Tala'at Harb Sq. enclosing the main business and shopping district, which is crammed with travel agents, banks, restaurants, juice stands, clothing stores, language schools, and budget hotels.

ISLAMIC CAIRO

Islamic Cairo occupies an area southwest of downtown Cairo, marked by the Citadel and **Ibn Tulun Mosque** in the south and the **Al-Azhar Mosque** and **University** in the north. Although this district was not laid out with urban planning in mind, there are a few key streets and areas, the first of which is **Salah ad-Din Square** (Midam Salah ad-Din, Midam Al-Qala'a). Both the **Sultan Hasan Mausoleum** and **Rifa'i Mosque** border this square, as does the gargantuan **Citadel. Salah Ad-Din St.** runs south to the Southern Cemetery, while **El-Qala'a St.** is a main north/south thoroughfare. Branching off of El Qala'a and heading towards **Al-Azhar** and the **Khan Al-Khalili** is **El Muizz St.,** once the main avenue of the city. Finally, Al-Azhar connects Islamic Cairo to **Ataba Square** and circumnavigates the Khan al-Khalili and Al-Azhar Mosque and University.

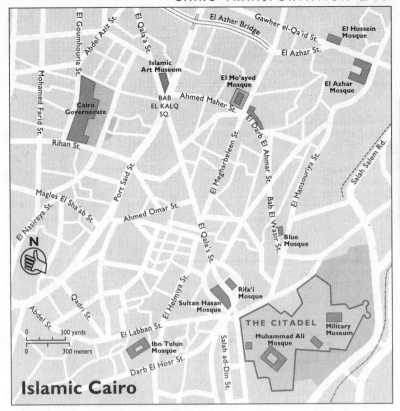

Islamic Cairo

■ Cairo Transportation

A little aggravation is good for the soul.

WALK LIKE AN EGYPTIAN

One positive aspect of Cairo's layout is that almost everything in the city is within easy walking distance of Tahrir Sq. Though it may take more time, you can see most of the sights of the downtown areas, as well as Roda and Zamalek Islands, without using mechanized transport. Islamic Cairo, a 25-minute walk, might merit other transportation, however. Many argue that walking is the only way to see the city; on foot, you will indubitably catch many fascinating glimpses of Cairo life which would go unseen from a bus or car.

Drivers expect pedestrians to look after themselves. If you imagine that crossing the street is only a real-life game of *Frogger,* you might actually have some fun doing it. It is wise to face oncoming traffic and heed the horns. A long, uninterrupted honk usually indicates that the driver is either unwilling or unable to swerve. Don't be alarmed if you are pushed or tugged by Egyptians attempting to avoid cars. Ignore traffic lights; everyone else does. Cairenes warn against being too careful when you cross a street—if you stop short or break into a run you'll upset the rhythm of the drivers speeding toward you.

METRO

The Cairo Metro system, completed in 1987, is a world apart from the rest of Cairo public transport. A joint project with the French and the Japanese, the Metro is the cleanest and fastest ticket in town. Trains run along the main line, a 40km route linking the southern industrial district of Helwan to El Marj in Heliopolis, with a number of stops downtown (look for the enormous, red "M" signs). An additional line connecting Shubra was recently added, and tracks are currently being built to Giza (should be open by publication date). Downtown stations feature TV screens with random programs, including *America's Funniest Home Videos,* cartoons, and Egyptian ads. Trains run about every six minutes (daily 5:30am-1am, in winter daily 5:30am-midnight; 50pt-E£1). Keep track of your ticket; you'll need it to exit. The stations downtown are Mubarak (Ramses Sq. and Railway Station), Orabi (Orabi St. and Ramses St.), Nasser (26 July St. and Ramses St.), Sadat (Tahrir Sq.), Sa'ad Zaghloul (Mansur St. and Ismail Abaza St.), Sayyida Zeinab (Mansur St. and Ali Ibrahim St.), El Malik es-Saleh (Salah Salem Road), and Mar Girgis (Old Cairo). Trains are often packed and sweaty during rush hour (before 9am and 2-5pm). The first compartment is always **reserved for women;** the second is reserved for women until 4pm.

TAXI

Never take the large, unmetered, colorful Peugeot taxis within the city—they charge E£2-3 for a ride around the corner, and the only advantage is their luggage rack. Avoid taxis that lurk in front of major hotels. Instead, flag the metered **black-and-white taxis** that often collect more than one group of passengers along the way.

To hail a taxi, pick a thoroughfare headed in the general direction you wish to travel, stand on the side of the street, stretch out your arm as a taxi approaches, and scream out your destination as it goes by. If the drivers are interested in your business, they'll stop and wait for you to run over to their cars. Jump in and repeat your destination. Don't be alarmed if the taxi seems to be going in the wrong direction; drivers sometimes take circuitous routes to avoid traffic-clogged main arteries.

Meters have been installed in all Cairo taxis, but drivers rarely use them, since passengers jump in and out—haggling only implies that you don't know what you owe. Cairenes simply hail a cab, hop in, and pay what they think is adequate upon arrival. *Never* ask the driver for the fare. Usually, the most comfortable way to handle the situation is to open the door as you are paying with folded bills and leave the taxi without looking to the driver for approval. Also, try to have the exact change—the last thing you want is the driver taking an "adequate" share of your E£20 bill.

Rides in the downtown area (from Ramses Sq. to Garden City or Zamalek to Islamic Cairo) should cost about E£3-4. From downtown, Mohandiseen and the Northern or Southern Cemeteries cost E£4, the Pyramids or Imbaba E£7-10, and Ma'adi and Heliopolis E£8-10. You will be expected to pay extra for additional passengers, suitcases, and waiting. A taxi to or from the airport should cost no more than E£20.

Do not expect a taxi driver to speak English, or to know the location of every address or street. Try to identify a major landmark or thoroughfare near your destination and learn to pronounce it in Arabic. Better yet, have someone at the tourist office or your hotel write out the address and directions in Arabic.

Between 6am and 4pm, **river taxis** provide a more relaxing means of transportation to Old Cairo. Boats depart every 30-40 minutes to the Nile barrages and Old Cairo (via Giza) from the corniche in front of the television building, about 750m north of Tahrir Sq. (50pt)

MICROBUS

If you manage to get on the right microbus, these 14-seaters are the best way to get to areas of Cairo not reached by Metro. They function more like buses than taxis, but differ from minibuses. Generally, they follow fixed routes to certain destinations but tend to be flexible as long as all passengers are going to the same area. Microbus stops are sometimes marked by a wooden shelter. Listen to the drivers as they yell out des-

Beep, Beep, Beeeeeeeeep

Egyptians love to use their car horns. In any city or town, day or night, the incessant honking of horns can be heard. To a visitor new to Egypt, all this noise may sound the same: the random cacophony of reckless drivers. The din *is* quite meaningful, and, with the help of this simple guide, might save you from being flattened like a pita:

City Driving
  Single, quick beep (from taxi or *service*): "Would you care for a ride?"
  Multiple quick beeps: "I am quickly bearing down on you and will soon run you over."
  Single, long beep: "I do not have enough speed to run you down, but nonetheless you are in my way. If you don't move, I will drive over you slowly."
Highway Driving
  Single, quick beep from passing vehicle: "I am passing you now by any means possible."
  Single, quick beep from vehicle being passed: "I acknowledge that you are passing me, yet I may still cut you off."
  Single, long beep (by vehicle close behind another): "You are traveling at less than the speed of sound. I will sit three inches behind your bumper until you let me pass."

tinations. It's a good idea to know the Arabic pronunciation, as drivers won't be yelling in English. From **'Ataba Sq.** microbuses go to Ramses Sq., Tahrir Sq., Northern Cemetery, Zamalek, Islamic Cairo, and Heliopolis. From **Tahrir Sq.** microbuses leave for Heliopolis, Giza Sq., Dokki, Mohandiseen, and the Pyramids. Fares run 50pt-E£1 for the luxury of not having to stand.

MINIBUS

Red-and-white or orange-and-white Mercedes minibuses operate along many of the same routes served by the far less tourist-friendly city buses. Don't confuse these with the older, privately operated multi colored taxi-vans. Although more expensive than the regular buses (50pt-E£1), the minibuses are also far more comfortable. Finding the right one may be confusing, but most Egyptians will be glad to help. The following are important minibus routes: the Mugamma' Station recently closed, and all of its minibuses moved to the Nile Hilton station. Minibus numbers appear in Arabic only:

From the Nile Hilton Station

#16 (١٦): Gala'a Bridge—Agouza.
#24 (٢٤): Ahmed Hilmi Sq.—Shubra.
#25 (٢٥): Airport.
#27 (٢٧): Masr el-Gadida—Airport (old terminal).
#30 (٣٠): Nasr City—'Abbasiyya Sq.—Ramses Sq.
#32 (٣٢): Mugamma'—Ramses Sq.—'Abbasiyya.
#35 (٣٥): 'Abbasiyya.
#49 (٤٩): Tahrir Sq.—Zamalek.
#50 (٥٠): 'Ataba Sq.—Citadel.
#52 (٥٢), **56** (٥٦): Ma'adi—Old Cairo.
#54 (٥٤): Tahrir Sq.—Rifa'i Mosque—Ibn Tulun Mosque—Citadel—S. Cemetery.
#55 (٥٥): Ma'adi via Dar es-Salaam.
#58 (٥٨): Ramses Sq.—Manial (no stop at Tahrir Sq.).
#59 (٥٩): Ramses Sq.—Tahrir Sq.
#77 (٧٧): Bulaq ad-Dakrur—Khan el-Khalili.
#84 (٨٤): 'Ataba Sq.—Tahrir Sq.—Dokki, Giza.

From 'Ataba Square

#26 (٢٦): Roxy, Tahrir Sq.—Dokki—Giza.
#48 (٤٨): Zamalek.
#57 (٥٧): Citadel.

BUS

This should be your last resort. Few foreigners actually brave the bus system; those who are so inclined, however, should pass up overcrowded vehicles so as to avoid unabashed stares, wandering hands, and unbearable heat. Sometimes the buses get so full that all you see is a tangle of mangled limbs and the sparks that fly when the bottom of the overburdened bus scrapes the road. The red-and-white and blue-and-white public buses run often and everywhere, and they're the cheapest available means of transportation (10-50pt), but have a high breakdown potential. Numbers and destinations are usually written in Arabic. Most buses run 5:30am-12:30am (during Ramadan 6:30am-6:30pm and 7:30pm-2am), with the exception of one new schedule: bus #400, with 24-hour service to the airport from Tahrir Sq. Ask someone at the station to point out the correct bus. Cairo's central local bus depot is **Abd el-Moneim Riyadh Station** to the north of the Egyptian Museum, just below the towering triangular Ramses Hilton. Several buses depart from in front of the old **Arab League Building,** to the west of the Mugamma' along Tahrir St., adjacent to the bridge. Other bus stations are at **Midan El 'Ataba ('Ataba Square),** east of the Azbekiyya Gardens (to the Citadel, the Manial Palace, Giza, and Tahrir Square), and at **Giza** (to the Pyramids, airport, and Citadel).

Outside the main stations, catching a bus is merely a matter of chasing one down and properly timing your leap, as they seldom come to a full stop. Except at a terminus, enter through the rear doors which have been torn off most buses to facilitate this practice. To disembark, pick a moment when the bus is not moving too rapidly and face the front as you jump off. If you want the bus to come to a full halt at an official bus stop, you must exit through the front door. The front of a bus is generally less crowded than the rear, so it's worth the effort to push your way forward. When traveling by bus, keep wallets and valuables securely embedded in your person. Although violent crime is rare in Cairo, a *khawaga* on a crowded bus is an irresistible opportunity for the occasional pickpocket.

From the Arab League Building
#13 (١٣): Zamalek.
#19 (١٩), **102** (١٠٢), **110** (١١٠), **166** (١٦٦), **203** (٢٠٣): Dokki.

From 'Ataba Square
#404 (٤٠٤): Citadel—Tahrir Sq.
#801 (٨٠١), **951** (٩٥١): Citadel.
#904 (٩٠٤): Mugamma' Station—Pyramids.
#930 (٩٣٠): Qanatir.

From Giza Square
#3 (٣): Pyramids.
#30 (٣٠): Ramses Station (from the pyramids).
#907 (٩٠٧): Tahrir Sq.—Airport.
#949 (٩٤٩): Airport (both terminals).

From the Abd el-Moniem Riyadh Station
#8 (٨): Tahrir Sq.—Qasr el-'Aini—Manyal—Giza—Mena House Hotel (Pyramids).
#63 (٦٣), **66** (٦٦): Al-Azhar—Khan el-Khalili.
#72 (٧٢): Sayyida Zeinab—Citadel—Mausoleum of Imam Esh-Shafi'i.
#75 (٧٥): Islamic Museum—Baab Zuweila.
#82 (٨٢), **182** (١٨٢): Imam Esh-Shafi'i Mausoleum—Southern Cemetery—Citadel.
#99 (٩٩): Agouza—Sudan St.—Lebanon Sq. (Midan Libnan).
#128 (١٢٨): 'Abbasiyya Sq.—'Ain Shams.
#173 (١٧٣), **194** (١٩٤), **609** (٦٠٩): Tahrir Sq.—Citadel.
#173 (١٧٣), **403** (٤٠٣): Citadel—Sultan Hasan.
#174 (١٧٤): Sayyida Zeinab—Ibn Tulun—Sultan Hasan—Citadel.
#400 (٤٠٠): Old Cairo Airport via Heliopolis (Midan Roxy).
#422 (٤٢٢): New Cairo Airport.

#666 (٦٦٦): El Gaili Museum.
#900 (٩٠٠): Tahrir Sq.—Qasr el-'Aini—Manial (Youth Hostel)—Cairo University—Giza—Pyramids—Holiday Inn Hotel (very crowded except early in the morning).
#923 (٩٢٣): Giza Sq.

From Ramses Station

#30 (٣٠): Pyramids.
#160 (١٦٠): Citadel—Tahrir Sq.

■ Intercity Transit

For more information on traveling around in Egypt see **Getting Around,** p. 73.

SERVICE TAXI

Service are best for short trips. From Ramses station, catch them to Alexandria (E£10-12), Suez (E£5-7), Ismailiyya (E£6), Port Said (E£9), or El Arish (E£15). You can also hire *service* to Fayyum (E£5) at Giza Square by the train station; to Alexandria (E£11) from in front of the Nile Hilton; and to Wadi Natrun from Kolali Sq. (about E£10). The Ahmed Hilmi Square bus station covers Mansura (E£9), Tanta (E£6), Zagazig (E£5), and the rest of the Delta. You'll have to hunt for taxis to the Sinai. Ask the driver for the price before starting the trip so that you don't face a nasty surprise upon arrival. *Service* are slightly cheaper than buses, and you'll get there faster.

BUS

Unfortunately, Cairo has no single bus depot. You'll have to sniff out the various points of departure. Augmenting the **public bus system,** which can be unbearably crowded, chaotic, and grimy, private operators run similar routes, sometimes at slightly higher prices. These buses are clean, air-conditioned, and often serve food and show Egyptian films. One drawback is that reservations, especially for popular destinations, must be made ahead of time, in person. Public buses running to Upper Egypt tend to be in poorer condition.

To Sinai and Israel: The **East Delta Bus Company** (tel. 83 95 83) and its subsidiary, the **South Sinai Company** (tel. 82 47 53), run buses from **Abd el-Moneim Riyadh Station,** beneath the Ramses Hilton, to: **Sharm esh-Sheikh** (6:30am, E£41; 7:30am and 1pm, E£51; 9am, 3pm, and 4pm, E£46; 9pm, E£50; and 10:30pm, E£56; 7 hr.), to **Dahab** (6:30am and 4pm, E£46; 1pm, E£56; and 11pm, E£71; 8hr.); to **Nuweiba'** (7am, E£51; and 10pm, E£56; 8hr.); and to **Taba** (7:30am, E£51; and 10pm, E£76; 9hr.). Buses to El Arish and Israel leave from **Abassiyya Station,** 5km northeast of Ramses Station at the end of Ramses St. From Tahrir or Ramses Sq. you can catch local bus #54, 710, or 728 or minibus #24 or 32. Buses used to travel from here to Tel Aviv and Jerusalem, but now only go as far as **Rafah** (8am, 9hr., E£35) or **Taba** (8am, E£45; and 11pm, E£70; 9hr.). From there, a change is necessary to continue into Israel. Reserve all of these long hauls well in advance. **Misr Travel** also sends buses from the **Cairo Sheraton** in Dokki to **Tel Aviv** and **Jerusalem** (daily 5am, 10hr., E£102, round-trip E£153; Sun., Tues. and Thurs. 3:30pm, E£119, round-trip E£170). You can buy your ticket from Misr Travel at 7 Tala'at Harb St. (tel. 393 02 01 or 59; open Sat.-Thurs. 9am-8pm) or at the Sheraton (tel. 335 54 70).

To Alexandria and North Coast: Buses leave from **Abd el-Moneim Riyadh Station,** north of the Cairo Museum and next to the Ramses Hilton, and they pass by **Giza Station,** Giza Sq. The best is the comfy and air-conditioned **Superjet** (tel. 579 71 71) to **Alexandria** (5:30am-11pm, every hr., 3hr., E£20), and **Marsa Matrouh** (7:30am, 5hr., E£36). The almost-as-good **Golden Arrow** also runs buses to **Alexandria** (5:30am-12:30am, every hr., E£20) and **Marsa Matrouh** (7:30am, 5hr., E£36). The **West Delta Bus Company** sends its mediocre buses along the same schedule but for less, as well as to **Wadi Natrun** (6am-10pm, 2hr., approx. every hr., E£24, money collected on board).

To Upper Egypt and Hurghada: The ancient green public buses are best avoided; they are dirty, crowded, and unsafe. A better choice would be **Upper Egypt Bus Co.** to **Hurghada** (9am, noon, and 3pm, 7hr., E£45.5); to **Aswan** (5pm, 13hr., E£50); or to **Luxor** (9pm, 9hr., E£48). Buses leave from **Abd el-Moneim Riyadh Station** at the base of the triangular Ramses Hilton. If these coaches are booked up, try both Golden Arrow and Superjet at the same station.

To the Western Oases: Buses leave from **Al-Azhar Station,** 45 Al-Azhar St. (tel. 390 86 35), 25m from the intersection with Port Said St. through a driveway on the south side of the street. Private companies run daily buses (some with A/C) to: **Bahariyya** (10am, 5hr., E£15); **Farafra** (Sat., Mon., and Thurs., 8am, E£30); **Dakhla** (7am and 5pm, 12hr., E£32-40); and to **Kharga** (10am, E£30; and 8pm, E£35; 12hr.). You can also catch a **service** or **minibus** to **Bahariyya** (5hr., E£11) or **Kharga through Asyut** (E£23) from Ramses Station or Sayyida Zeinab Station.

To the Eastern Delta and Canal Zone: Buses leave from **Kolali Square** (Midan El Kolali; tel. 574 28 14), a 5min. walk from Ramses Sq. (follow the elevated road to your right for 2 blocks; turn right and the station office is 50m up on the right). **East Delta Bus Company** runs every hr. 6:30am-6:30pm to **Port Said** (E£10-12), **Suez** (E£4.50-5), and **Ismailiyya** (E£5.25-6.25). Frequent service to **Mansura** (7:30am-8:30pm, E£6.30) and **Ras el-Bar** (7:30am-4:30pm, E£13). **Superjet** goes to Port Said (5:45am-5pm, every 30min., E£15) from **Ramses Station.**

To Arab countries and Turkey: Buses depart from **Abd el-Moneim Riyadh Station.** Add US$32 to all fares for ferry. East Delta Bus Co. runs buses to **Jordan** (8pm, 1 day, E£63), **Syria** (8pm, 1 day, E£113), and **Turkey** (8pm, 2 days, E£280).

TRAIN

Ticket windows at Ramses Station (Metro: Mubarak) are open daily 8am-10pm. The **tourist office** (open daily 8am-9pm), on the left as you enter the station, can write out your destination and other details in Arabic to avoid confusion. Which line you stand in depends upon whether you are reserving a seat in advance or trying to buy a ticket for the same day (often impossible). Women (and men traveling with women) can take advantage of the special **women's line** that may form at crowded times, which is much shorter and faster than the corresponding men's line. In addition, women are permitted (and expected) to push to the front of the line, head held high. Third-class travelers (not safe for unescorted women, or most anyone for that matter) can buy tickets on board the train. Students get 30% discounts on fares with an **ISIC card.**

The trains enter their berths at least half an hour before departure time. None of the train numbers or destinations are in English, but fellow travelers and the tourist police may lend a hand. Nonetheless, be prepared for yet another confusion infusion (also see specific town listings).

Tourists are expected (though not required) to ride first or second class due to security concerns. For long trips, such as to Luxor and Aswan, only two express trains are reserved for tourists. These trains depart at 7:30am and 10pm to **Luxor** (9-12hr., first class E£53, students E£37.10; second class with A/C E£33, students E£23.10) and **Aswan** (13-16hr., 1st class E£63, students E£44.10; 2nd class with A/C E£39, students E£27.30). **Sleepers** to Luxor and Aswan cost the same whacko price for both destinations (E£313 one way, no student discount available) and depart at 7:45pm. The express train makes stops in Minya, Sohag, Asyut, and Qena. Trains to **Alexandria** are comfortable, frequent, and tourist-restriction free (6am-8pm, E£17-22). Trains to **Port Said** leave daily at 8:45 and 11:30am, 2:35 and 6:35pm (3hr., 2nd class A/C E£18, no A/C E£8).

In between waiting in lines and declining offers for taxis, take a moment to admire the towering **Statue of Ramses II** in front of the train station. The statue was excavated in 1888 near the remains of the ancient city of Memphis.

PLANE

Tourists pay triple what Egyptians pay for airfare within Egypt. **EgyptAir** flies to Luxor, Sharm esh-Sheikh, Aswan, and Hurghada, while Air Sinai flies to the Sinai and

Israel. EgyptAir has offices at 6 Adly St. (tel. 391 12 56) and in the Nile Hilton (tel. 76 52 00 or 77 24 10; reservations and information 392 74 44 or 72 05). **Air Sinai** is at the Nile Hilton (tel. 76 09 48; open daily 9am-5pm).

▓ Practical Information

A reliable directory for goods and services is the *Cairo Telephone List*, published by the Ma'adi Women's Guild and available for E£20 at the American Chamber of Commerce, Marriott Hotel #1541, Zamalek (tel. 340 88 88).

Tourist Office: Egyptian Tourist Authority. Sprinkled throughout the city, the offices provide free maps and info. **Cairo International Airport** (tel. 66 74 75), at the entrance as well as next to the duty-free shops. In theory, open 24hr. **Giza** (tel. 385 02 59), in front of Mena House Hotel. Open Sat.-Thurs. 8am-5pm. **Railway Station** (tel. 76 42 14), on the left if you enter the station's main entrance. Open daily 8am-9pm. **5 Adly St.** (tel. 391 34 54), a 20min. walk from Tahrir Sq. Follow Tala'at Harb St. and turn right on Adly St. The office is 3 blocks down on your left, marked "Tourist Police." Very helpful. Open daily 8:30am-8pm.

Tourist Police: 5 Adly St. (tel. 126, 39 19 44, or 390 60 28), in the same building as the Tourist Office. Other locations at **Cairo International Airport** (tel. 247 25 84), **Giza** (tel. 385 02 59), the **Manial Palace Hotel,** and **Ramses Station.**

Student Cards: Medical Scientific Center, 103 Mathaf el-Manial St., El Manial (tel. 363 88 15). South of the Manial Palace across the street from Kentucky Fried Chicken (look for the ISIC sign). Much more comprehensive and helpful than the name implies. Provides ISIC and Go25 cards (E£25; bring a photo). Great source of information for travelers. Student volunteer staff speaks excellent English and will quote prices for sights and entertainment. The center gives out free maps and pamphlets, and organizes excursions to the Pyramids and Sufi dancing.

Thomas Cook: 17 Mahmoud Bassiouny St. (tel. 574 37 76 or 39 55 or 39 67; fax 76 27 50), ½ block west of Tala'at Harb Sq. Travel agency, money transfers, currency exchange, and cash advances on MC/Visa. Cashes traveler's checks. Come here to replace a lost MC/Visa. Open daily 8am-5pm. Other offices throughout city.

Embassies: Australia, 1191 Corniche en-Nil, Bulaq (tel. 575 04 44), World Trade Center 11-12th floors. Past the 26 July Bridge. Passports generally replaced in 3-7 working days (AUS$306 for 32-page passports, AUS$459 for 64-page passports, payable in E£ equivalent only). Immediate replacement in case of emergency. Open Sun.-Thurs. 8:30am-4:15pm, visas Sun.-Mon., Wed.-Thurs. 9:30am-noon. **Canada:,** 5 Midan es-Saraya el Kobr, Garden City (tel. 354 31 10 or 19), 3rd floor of Arab-African Bank Bldg. Passports replaced within 2 working days for E£145. Embassy open Sun.-Thurs. 8:30am-4:30pm, visas Sun.-Mon., Wed.-Thurs. 9-11am. **Ireland,** 3 Abu el-Feda St., Zamalek (tel. 340 82 64 or 85 47; fax 341 28 63), in the Abu el-Feda building. Passports replaced for E£78, new passports E£234. Consular services open Sun.-Thurs. 9am-noon. Embassy open Sun.-Thurs. 8am-3pm. **South Africa,** 21/23 Giza St., Giza (tel. 571 72 38 or 39), 18th floor. File applications for new passports here; they're then sent to South Africa for processing. The entire process takes 8 weeks. In the meantime, you are issued a 1pg. Emergency Passport good for 3 months (E£50). Consular services open Sun.-Thurs. 9am-noon. Embassy open Sun.-Thurs. 8am-4:30pm. **U.K.,** 7 Ahmed Ragheb St., Garden City (tel. 354 08 50), south of U.S. Embassy. Handles **New Zealand** affairs, too. Will replace both nationals' passports within 5 days (E£99 for 32-page passports, E£150 for 48-page passports, payable only in E£). Open Sun.-Wed. 9am-1pm. **U.S.,** 5 Latin America St., Garden City (tel. 354 82 11), 2 blocks south of Tahrir Sq. For the consulate, enter on Lazaughli St. around the block. Lost or stolen passports replaced overnight for US$65 or E£ equivalent (US$65 for a renewal). Open Sun.-Thurs. 8am-4:30pm, consulate 8am-noon. **Israel,** 6 Ibn el-Malik St., Dokki (tel. 361 03 80 or 04 58). Cross over to Dokki from Roda Island on University Bridge (El Gama'a). The street to the right of and parallel to the bridge is Ibn el-Malik. Look up at the top floors for the Israeli flag or for the security guards by the entrance who will ask to see your passport. Visas E£65 for all nationalities. Open Sun.-Thurs. 10am-12:30pm. **Jordan,** 6 El Goheina St., Dokki (tel. 348 55 66, 61 69, or 75 43, or 349 99 12), 2 blocks west of the Cairo Sheraton. Visas (photograph and letter of introduction required) free for Australians, E£42 for New Zealanders, E£86 for Britons, E£112 for Americans, E£224 for Canadians. Same-day service. Visas may be picked up noon-2pm. Open Sat.-Thurs. 9am-noon; arrive early to avoid the crowd. **Lebanon,** 5 Ahmed Nassim St., Giza (tel. 361 06 23, 04 74, or 03 92; fax 361 0463). **Syria,**18 Abd er-Rahim Sabri St., Dokki (tel. 337 70 20). Bring 2 photos for a visa (valid for one entry only; free for Canadians and Australians, E£116 for Americans). You are advised to apply for visas in your home country. Americans are often denied visas at Syrian embassies in other Arab countries. (See **Visas and Visa Extensions,** p. 8). Open Sat.-Thurs. 9am-2:30pm, visas 9am-1pm. Any evidence of having been to Israel prohibits obtaining a Syrian visa, but you can get a new passport at your country's embassy.

Passport Office: 2nd floor of the **Mugamma Building,** the massive concave gray edifice at the southern side of Tahrir Sq. Registration open Sat.-Thurs. 8am-8pm. Open for visa extensions Sat.-Thurs. 8am-1pm. Prior to Aug. 1996, a mandatory stop on all travelers' itineraries. Now, passport registration is not required; you just need to get it stamped at the border. Not as jam-packed is the second floor of the **Ministry of Economy and Foreign Trade Building,** 8 Adly St. (tel. 390 43 63), next to the EgyptAir office. Bring a passport photo for visa extensions (2-6 mo. E£14, 1 yr. E£50). Open Sat.-Thurs. 8am-1:30pm.

Currency Exchange: Banks and exchange services litter downtown. **Bank Misr** has branches at the Ramses and Nile Hiltons, Marriott, Shepherd, and other major hotels, with a main office at 151 Muhammad Farid St., downtown (tel. 391 75 71). All branches open Sat.-Thurs. 8:30am-2pm and 6-9pm. **Cairo Barclays International Bank,** 12 Sheikh Yousef Sq., Garden City (tel. 354 94 15 or 22), 3 blocks south of Tahrir Sq. along Qasr El 'Aini St., accepts traveler's checks and has worldwide money transfer services. Open Sun.-Thurs. 8:30am-2pm; during Ramadan, 10am-1pm. Foreign banks are closed Fri.-Sat., but most Egyptian banks are open Sat. Money can be wired to Egypt through **Citibank,** 4 Ahmed Pasha St., Garden City (tel. 355 18 73 or 74; open Sun.-Thurs. 8:30am-2pm). See also American Express and Thomas Cook listings.

Western Union: 1079 Corniche en-Nil, Garden City (tel. 357 13 00, 74-5, or 84-6). In the FedEx office. Worldwide money transfer. Open Sun.-Thurs. 9am-8:30pm.

ATM: Egyptian British Banks have machines that accept **Visa, Plus, Global Access,** and **Express Net** cards. Locations in Semiramis Intercontinental, Nile Hilton, Ramses Hilton, Zamalek Marriott, and Cairo Sheraton.

American Express: 15 Qasr en-Nil (tel. 574 79 91 or 92-96), off Tala'at Harb Sq., opposite EgyptAir toward Ramses St. Cashes traveler's checks. Members can have money sent and use **Client Letter Service.** Open daily 8:30am-5pm. Letter service open Sun.-Thurs. 8:30am-4pm (Ramadan 8:30am-3:30pm). Other locations: **Nile Hilton** (tel. 578 50 01-03), **Marriott Hotel** (tel. 341 01 36), **Pullman Ma'adi** (tel. 350 78 51), **Mohandiseen,** 4 Syria St. (tel. 70 79 08 or 14).

Flights, Trains, Buses, Metro, Taxis: See Transportation, p. 92.

Car Rental: For maniacs willing to risk life and limb to achieve relative freedom of mobility. **Avis** (tel. 354 86 98 or 74 00), open daily 8am-3:30pm. Branch at Cairo International Airport (tel. 291 42 66, 77, 88). Open 24hr. Join millions of middle-class Egyptians driving a Suzuki Swift for US$37. Charge for each km over 100km.

Lockers: Ground floor of Ramses Station, 30pt per day (14-day max.). Ask anyone in uniform, *"Feen al-makhzan?"* (Where are the lockers?) Open 24hr. Dubious security and many unsavory characters. Most hotels have safe deposit boxes, and many will store luggage. Be sure to get **written proof** of having stored anything.

English Bookstores: AUC Bookstore, Hill House, American University in Cairo, 113 Qasr El 'Aini St. (tel. 357 53 77). Classic novels, guidebooks, and maps. Bring your passport, you'll need it to enter the high security campus. Open Sun.-Thurs. 8:30am-4pm, Sat. 10am-3pm. AUC Press also has a bookstore at 16 Muhammad Ibn Thakeb St., Zamalek (tel. 339 70 45). **Lehnert and Landrock,** 44 Sharif St. (tel. 393 53 24). Between Adly St. and 26 July St. Also has a wide selection of guidebooks and maps. Open Mon.-Fri. 9:30am-2pm and 4-7:30pm, Sat. 9:30am-1:30pm. **Madbuli** (tel. 575 64 21), in Tala'at Harb Sq., has books on Egypt and by Naguib Mahfouz. Open daily 10am-10pm. Also at 45 El Batal Ahmed Abd el-Aziz St. (tel. 347 74

10; open 24hr.). **Shorouk Bookshop** (tel. 391 24 80), on Tala'at Harb Sq., is packed with schlock romance and whodunits. Look harder to find guidebooks, Arabic phrase books, and maps. Open daily 9am-10pm, Ramadan 10am-4pm and 8pm-12am. **Anglo-Egyptian,** 165 Muhammad Farid St. (tel. 391 43 37), has new and used books at reasonable prices. Open Mon.-Sat. 9am-1:30pm and 4:30-7:30pm.

Newspapers and Magazines: The *Egyptian Gazette* and the *Al-Ahram Weekly* (both 75pt), Egypt's two English newspapers, come out every Thursday. *Egypt Today*, a monthly magazine (E£7), is handy for current restaurant and entertainment listings. All publications are sold at **The Reader's Corner,** 33 Abd el-Khaleq Sarwat St., downtown. Open Mon.-Sat. 9:30am-7pm. Kiosks along Tala'at Harb Sq., near AUC, or at the intersection of 26 July and Hasan Sabri St., Zamalek, sell American and European periodicals.

American Cultural Center: 5 Latin America St., Garden City (tel. 354 96 01 or 76 27 04; library 355 05 32 or 357 34 12). Inside the U.S. Embassy, across from the British Embassy. If you'll be in Egypt for at least 12 months you are eligible to join. To do so, take along your passport (any nationality) and two photos. Members can borrow books and watch videos in the library. Occasional free films and lectures; call 357 33 66 for a schedule. Open Sun.-Fri. 10am-4pm; in winter Mon.-Fri. 10am-4pm.

Film Developing: Kodak, 20 Adly St. (tel. 394 22 63), opposite the synagogue. Camera batteries and film. Open Mon.-Sat. 9am-9pm. If you can't find it, Kodak signs swarm around Tala'at Harb Sq., Adly, and Alfy St. Developing a roll of 36 exposures will cost E£29.

Supermarkets: Sunny Supermarket, 11 El Aziz Osman St., Zamalek (tel. 342 11 21 or 341 20 32), next door to the Mayfair Hotel south of 26 July St. Gargantuan range of Egyptian and Western products offered, for not-quite-budget prices. Will deliver. Open daily 8am-10pm. **Seoudi Market,** 25 Midan El Missaha St., Dokki (tel. 348 84 40 or 41), also at 50 El Quds esh-Sharif St. (Jerusalem St.), Mohandiseen (tel. 344 00 37 or 346 03 91), and 15 Ahmad Hishmat St., Zamalek (tel. 341 35 86 or 340 95 96). A fully-stocked supermarket with fair prices. All open daily 10am-10pm.

Laundry: Circle Cleaning, 24 26 july St. (tel. 76 08 55), near the Supreme Court and the intersection with Tala'at Harb St. You're probably better off either doing it yourself or paying one of the maids in your hotel to do your load (50pt per piece is reasonable); the laundromat can be a mad-house. Open daily 9am-9pm.

Toilets: Most squares have public toilets; ask for *el-hammam*. These are often crowded and will offend your nostrils. If you are in the downtown area, you can always combine your budget travel and acting skills and walk confidently into one of the five-star hotels, which are sure to have plenty of toilet paper in their stalls.

Swimming Pools: Fontana Hotel (tel. 92 21 45 or 23 21), Ramses Sq., has a teal-tiled pool on its 7th-floor patio (E£15 per day). Cairo's many sporting clubs sell day passes for E£20. The best are the **Gezira Sporting Club,** (tel. 340 22 72) in front of the Marriott Hotel in Zamalek, the **Ma'adi Sporting Club,** 8 En-Nadi Sq. (tel. 350 55 04), and the **Heliopolis Sporting Club,** 17 El Merghany St. (tel. 291 48 00). Sometimes the guards insist that you enter with a club member.

Late-Night Pharmacy: Victoria Pharmacy, 90 Qasr El 'Aini St., Garden City (tel. 354 86 04). Open 24hr. **Pharmacy Mondial,** 2 Ahmed Hishmat St., Zamalek (tel. 341 11 80). Ask for Dr. Mamdouh. Open daily 9:30am-10pm. **Zarif Pharmacy,** Tala'at Harb St., next to Shorouk Bookshop.

Hospitals: Best-equipped is **As-Salaam International Hospital,** Ma'adi (tel. 363 80 50, emergency 362 33 00), Corniche en-Nil. **Anglo-American Hospital,** Gezira-Zamalek (tel. 340 61 or 62-65), on Botanical Garden St. below the Cairo Tower. **Cairo Medical Center,** Heliopolis (tel. 258 05 66, 02 17, or 10 03), Roxy Sq.

Emergency: Fire: Tel. 125 or 391 01 15. **Ambulance:** Tel. 123.

Police: Tel. 122, 126, or 303 41 22 or 51 22; central station: tel. 13.

Federal Express: 1079 Corniche en-Nil, Garden City (tel. 357 13 04). Opposite the Meridien on the east bank of the Nile. Open 24hr.

Main Post Office: 55 Sarwat St. (tel. 391 26 14). On the corner of 'Ataba Sq., under the dome. Often crowded, but blissfully empty just before the office closes. Packages require an export license from the airport; major hotels and tourist shops also provide this service. Open Sat.-Thurs. 8:30am-7pm; Ramadan 9am-3pm. **Poste Restante** located around the corner on Bidek St. Open Sat.-Thurs. 8am-6pm. **Express**

Mail (EMS) on Bidek St. across from *Poste Restante.* Open daily 24hr. Most branches in Cairo sell stamps and have EMS. One conveniently located branch is in Tahrir Sq. (tel. 575 43 13) at 13 Metitte Bash St., a small alley opposite the eastern wall of the Egyptian Museum. Open Sat.-Thurs. 9am-5pm.

Telegraph and Telex Office: 'Ataba Sq., opposite the main post office. Open 24hr. Most of the telephone offices have these services (see below) and can send **faxes.**

Faxes: You may send and receive faxes at the business office of the Ramses Hilton (fax 575 71 52 or 578 22 21). They charge according to destination for sending and E£4 per page to receive. Most of the telephone offices can send faxes.

Telephone Office: Main Office, Ramses St., 1 block north of 26 July St. Other offices in Zamalek, Airport, Ma'adi, Tahrir Sq., Adly St., and Alfy St., under the Windsor Hotel. Look for the handset sign. All open 24hr. Collect and credit card calls available at the USADirect, U.K. Direct, Canada Direct, and Japan Direct phones in the lobbies of the Ramses Hilton, Marriott, and Semiramis hotels. For a 25% surcharge, make international calls easily at the business service offices in the Meridien, Sheraton, and Nile Hilton hotels (24hr.). All major hotels have local pay phones, operated with expensive tokens (25-50pt.). **Directory Assistance:** Tel. 140. **Telephone Code:** 02.

■ Accommodations

Downtown Cairo, on and around **Tala'at Harb Street,** is littered with dozens of budget hotels and dorms occupying the upper floors of colonial buildings. If you want to splurge on one of the swankier listings, you'll be rewarded with the chilling effects of high-powered air conditioning.

When selecting your room, keep in mind that the higher up you go, the farther away you are from the noise. Moreover, breezes at higher elevations keep mosquitoes away (they get altitude sickness) and help travelers endure the hot summer months. All of the prices listed below include continental breakfast and all places have fans and 24-hour hot water unless otherwise noted. Check-out time is usually noon, although you can often negotiate an extra hour or two. Maids at each establishment will gladly take the opportunity to earn a little extra cash if you have them do your laundry (usually about 50pt per article). If you are planning on being in Cairo for a while or are here during the low season, try to bargain for a reduced rate. Single-sex groups should have no problem renting a **flat** (undesirable ones go for as low as E£200 per month, upscale ones for E£1000), but building owners often frown upon renting to mixed sex groups. The billboard at Sunny Market in Zamalek lists available apartments.

The terms "hotel" and "hostel" are more loosely defined in the Middle East than in, say, Europe. Many of the budget accommodations listed below offer dorm beds similar to those in what are usually known as "hostels." While technically called "hotels," we have grouped these budget options and Cairo's HI Youth Hostel together and ranked them starting with the best value.

BUDGET

Sultan Hotel, 4 Souq et-Tewfikia St., 1st and 5th floors (tel. 77 22 58), off Tala'at Harb St. on the market street running parallel to 26 July St. The bedrooms could use a bit of a makeover and mice make occasional cameos, but the helpful staff, perfect location, and unbeatable price compensate. Ask the staff anything about Cairo; they honestly want you to love their city. Try to get the room with the fruit market view. The 5th floor rooms are less crowded, cheaper, and breezier. Expressive paintings by talented travelers adorn the bedroom walls. Breakfast is not included, but guests may use the kitchen. Free luggage storage for up to 1 week. Dorm beds E£8; 1st-floor dorm beds E£9; doubles E£17-18.

Venice Hotel, 4 Souq et-Tewfikia, 4th floor (tel. 574 32 69), in the same building as the Sultan Hotel. Cool breezes waft into the spacious, high-ceilinged rooms of this hotel, providing a welcome respite from the heat and clamor of the street. All rooms have either balconies or windows, making up for a lack of fans. Redone hardwood floors and spotless bathrooms confound budgeteers who only pay E£10 for a dorm bed. Less English is spoken here than at the Sultan. Singles E£17; doubles E£25.

Safary Hotel, 4 Souq et-Tewfikia St., 5th floor (no phone), in the same building as the Sultan Hotel. Japanese tourists, the faithful frequenters of this relaxed hostel, cook up communal meals in the palatial kitchen and kick back in the sitting room. Chaotic dorm rooms which resemble a gypsy camp gone awry have 2-5 beds. English and Japanese spoken. Beds E£6 each.

Pensione Roma, 169 Muhammad Farid St. (tel. 391 10 88 or 13 40), 1 block south of 26 July St. and 2 blocks east of Tala'at Harb St., turn right on Adly St. then left after the synagogue; look for the hotel's green sign above the Gattegno department store. High ceilings and refurbished hardwood floors transport you to Italy. Toilet paper, towels, and soap make Roma seem like more than a budget hotel. Nothing is perfect, however. Some travelers have complained of a bed-bug problem here. The dining room serves E£10 plates of steak, potato, and veggies, along with many other menu items, and the salon area is grand. Free lockers. French, Italian, and English spoken. Singles E£12.50; doubles E£42, with bath E£46; triples E£55, with bath E£63.

Anglo-Swiss Hotel, 14 Champollion St., 6th floor (tel. 575 14 97), 2 blocks west of Tala'at Harb Sq. From Tahrir Sq., turn right on Champollion in the northeastern end of the square next to the museum. The hotel will be to your left at the intersection with Mahmoud Bassinni St. You can play a prelude on the piano in the sunny dining hall or watch some satellite TV in the lobby before retiring to quiet, clean rooms with hardwood floors and (if you play your cards right) balconies. Clean bathrooms. Flexible check-out times. Free luggage storage. Friendly staff with faltering English can fetch train and bus tickets for you (E£4 charge per ticket) or secure you an ISIC card (E£25). Singles E£25; doubles E£50, with bath E£55; triples E£60, with bath E£65. 15-25% discounts depending on duration of stay.

Youth Hostel (HI), 135 Malek Abd el-Aziz es-Saud St., Manial Roda Island (tel. 364 07 29; fax 98 41 07). Take Metro to Sayyida Zeinab. Exit to the right and walk straight to the Nile. Cross the Sayala Bridge and continue straight across Roda Island to the main channel of the Nile. Turn left just before the University (El Gama'a) bridge (with Salah ad-Din mosque to your right); the hostel is 10m away on the left. Quiet and clean, the HI houses a mixture of foreign backpackers and young Egyptians. It also features new bathrooms, a large kitchen for guests, a reasonably priced restaurant, and a comfortable lounge area. Bunk beds are crammed into spartan but clean single-sex rooms. The men's section tends to fill faster than the women's; call ahead. Non-members pay E£4 extra per night. No lockout. Curfew 11pm. Dorm beds (6 per room) E£12.60. Triples E£17.60-22.60.

Pension Select Hotel, 19 Adly St., 8th floor (tel. 393 37 07), next to the synagogue. High above the street noise, Select offers spacious 3-per-room dorm style set-ups. Rahim, the gracious, elderly proprietor, is a relief from the young whippersnappers who hassle you in the street. All dorm beds E£20. Solo travelers should resist being fooled into paying a surcharge.

Hotel Minerva, 39 Tala'at Harb St. (tel. 392 06 00 or 01 or 02), 1 block toward Tala'at Harb Sq. from 26 July St. Reception is 4 doors past the Bamboo Clothing Store on your right. A quality establishment: beautifully renovated bathrooms, vast balconies, and all-new light fixtures add a touch of elegance. Bottled water and a variety of soft drinks are for sale at the front desk. Singles E£19; doubles E£28, with bath E£33; triples E£45.

Gresham Hotel, 20 Tala'at Harb St. (tel. 575 90 43), just off Tala'at Harb Sq. Renovations have made the hardwood floors and common baths gleam. Rooms are nothing to write home about, but good quality mattresses and bureaus do the job. There is a restaurant open for lunch and dinner (entrees E£10-E£12), and the receptionists provide sound advice about tours to Islamic Cairo and the Pyramids at Giza. Single E£30, with bath E£35; doubles E£40, with bath E£50; triples E£55, with bath E£60.

Hotel Nefertiti, 39 Tala'at Harb St. (tel. 392 51 53), 2 floors above the Bamboo Clothing Store, 100m from Cinema Metro. Enter through the alleyway to the right, next to the entrance for Hotel Minerva. Ideal for groups of 2 or 3 who want a private, clean room. Rooms are a little dark and drab, but the price is right. Doubles with shower E£15; triples with shower E£21. Breakfast not included.

Hotel Viennoise, 11 Mahmoud Bassiouny St. (tel. 574 31 53; fax 575 31 36), at Champollion St., 1 block from Tahrir Sq. Look for the big yellow sign. Vast corridors and a grand lobby decorated with 19th-century European furniture do little to ameliorate fanless rooms. The manager speaks limited English. Singles E£25, with bath E£35; doubles E£35, with bath E£40; triples E£45.

Sun Hotel, 2 Tala'at Harb St., 9th floor (tel. 578 17 86); look for the sign on your right just as you leave Tahrir Sq. Brand new hotel has carpets and MTV, an overworked staff and a largely Australian clientele. The mammoth beds and peaceful 9th floor location ensure that you will sleep soundly. Bargain with the manager for lower rates if you plan to stay longer than 3 days. English, French, Italian, and Japanese are spoken. Dorm rooms E£15; singles E£25; doubles E£40; triples E£51.

Venus Hotel, 38 Ramses St., 10th floor (tel. 575 04 96), one block towards the Nile on your right. The location is perfect for those arriving by train, as other hotels are a 20-min. walk away. Unlike the 70s kitsch in the lobby, rooms are stark but attractive. Singles E£30, with bath E£40; doubles E£50, with bath E£60; triples with bath and A/C E£65; quads with bath E£70.

A BIT SWANKIER

Windsor Hotel, 19 Alfy Bey St. (tel. 591 58 10 or 52 77; fax 92 16 21; email wdoss@link.com.eg), behind Cinema Diana. Very clean, with an atmosphere of old-time colonial grandeur. The Barrel Bar, so named because all the furniture is made from retired barrels, was once the British Officers' Club. Monty Python's Michael Palin hung out at the Windsor while filming *Around the World in Eighty Days*. Excellent service. All rooms have A/C, towels, crisp sheets, and comfy beds. Singles with shower E£58, with shower and toilet E£83; doubles with shower E£80, with toilet E£106. These prices include breakfast, tax, and a 25% *Let's Go* discount. 5% credit card service charge.

Carlton Hotel, 21 26 July St. (tel. 575 50 22; fax 575 53 23), beside Cinema Rivoli, near Tala'at Harb St. and 26 July St. intersection. Metro: Nasser. Colonial lobby and hardwood floors are just the beginning. Each room has satellite TV, A/C, and a balcony with patio furniture. Dinner is served nightly on the rooftop garden, which affords a luxurious view of downtown Cairo. Manager is very helpful. Singles E£65; doubles E£75.

Berlin Hotel, 2 Hoda Shaarawi St. (tel. 395 75 02). From Tala'at Harb Sq. go one block toward Tahrir Sq. and look left. Proprietor Hisham, a young graduate of Cairo University, has helped boost this brand-new hotel to instant popularity. Elegant rooms boast full-length velvet curtains and freshly-painted walls. A neighboring fitness club offers weights, sauna, and massage at a discounted rate for hotel guests. Singles E£60; doubles E£80; triples E£90. Rates are negotiable and lower in winter.

El Malky Hotel, 4 El Hussein St. (tel. 592 88 04), next to El Hussein Mosque and Khan el-Khalili market. Situated in the heart of Islamic Cairo, El Malky gets you away from downtown. You'll get used to the *muezzin* call to prayer five times a day; Cairo's most famous mosque is next door. Singles with TV, fridge, and balcony E£40, with A/C E£50; doubles E£55, with A/C E£65.

Mayfair Hotel, 9 Aziz Osman St. (tel. 340 73 15), parallel to Hassan Sabri St., on the corner of Ibn Zinky St. 2 blocks south of 26 July St., in Zamalek. Tidy rooms (most with balconies) in the heart of Zamalek. On school days, noisy young 'uns across the street could rob you of the peace you paid for. Sip tea on the homey veranda or visit the great restaurants, pastry shops, and bars of Zamalek. Some rooms have private bath and A/C. Singles E£30-45; doubles E£40-60. 10% *Let's Go* discount.

Horris Hotel, 5 26 July St. (tel. 591 04 78, 05 47, or 08 55). Enter also from Alfy St. behind Cinema Diana. Try to get a room on the upper floors to enjoy a spectacular view of the city from the flowery balconies. Three reasonably priced restaurants (E£15 per meal) along with a barren bar and a disco on the roof. All rooms have A/C and are clean and spacious. International telephone service. Not to be confused with the Horrus Hotel. Singles E£43; doubles E£74; triples E£88.

■ Food

Cairo is a world-class city, and has the diverse restaurant line-up to prove it. If you choose to stick with the same old *fuul* and falafel (more often called *ta'miyya* in Egypt), you'll only need 40pt to fill your stomach. *Kushari,* an Egyptian specialty (with lentils, macaroni, rice, grilled onions, and tomato sauce) will only set you back about E£1.50. Wash it all down with exhilarating fruit juices, on sale anywhere you see bags of fruit hanging around a storefront. At places without waiters, pay first and then exchange your receipt for food. Hygiene might not be a priority at most food and juice stands (especially those without signs), but if you stick with the crowds you should be okay.

A clean sit-down meal is often relatively cheap by Western standards and is usually worth the investment. Even at more expensive restaurants, you can create a handsome meal out of hummus, *baba ghannoush* (grilled eggplant dip), and salad for under E£5. *Fatir,* a *fillo* dough-like flat bread with vegetables, meats, jam, or sweets piled on top and stuffed inside, is far tastier than the imitations of Italian pizza in town and, at E£5-10, usually cheaper. There are a 5% sales tax on food and a 10-12% service charge at sit-down restaurants included on the bill; a small **tip** (E£1) is still in order.

While eating local food is an essential component of the Egyptian experience, the (cleaner, faster, air-conditioned) Western alternative is always there. Fast food chains have invaded Cairo in the past few years. In the downtown area, they're lined up across from the AUC on Mahmoud St. **Pizza Hut** offers slices for E£1.90 each (home delivery 356 26 28 or 27 55). Next door, **Kentucky Fried Chicken** is a bit cheaper and more crowded, but serves buns instead of the flaky biscuits so treasured by the Colonel and his cohorts. Opposite the AUC gate is **McDonald's** (tel. 355 81 31), where a combo meal sizzles for E£8.50 (all 3 open daily 11am-midnight and offer free delivery up to 2km).

DOWNTOWN

Felfela, 15 Hoda Sharawi St. (tel. 392 27 51 or 28 33), off Tala'at Harb St., 1 block south of Tala'at Harb Sq. Consistently excellent. A favorite among Egyptians and tourists alike, this award-winning restaurant was started by an Egyptian model in 1958 and is now a chain that extends to Hurghada. The ambience is bursting with bamboo, aquariums, mosaics, and live birds. Spiced *fuul* (E£2.25-5.25) and falafel dishes (E£1.50-2.95). Full meal of *wara 'einab* (stuffed grape leaves) E£12, spaghetti E£5.50. Also delicious is *om ali,* a pastry baked with milk, honey, and raisins (E£5.75). Another entrance on Tala'at Harb St. leads to a self-service counter with cold drinks and sandwiches (40-80pt). Open daily 7:30am-12:30am.

Brazilian Coffee Shop, 38 Tala'at Harb St., at the intersection with Adly St. Look for the Miami Cinema. Air-conditioned restaurant upstairs serves real cappuccino (E£2) and espresso (E£1.75). A great place to read the morning paper. Sausage and potato dinner E£10, mixed grill dinner E£15. Open daily 6am-midnight.

Ali Hassan al-Hati, 3 Halim St. (tel. 591 60 55), between Alfy St. and 26 July St., 1 block south of the Windsor Hotel. High ceilings, crystal chandeliers, and many mirrors. Flavorful meal options change daily, but usually include *kebab, kofta,* and fish (E£9-18). Try the *fatteh* (garlic, meat or vegetables poured over crunchy baked bread and covered with a yogurt sauce, E£2-3.50). Open daily noon-11pm.

El Haty Cafeteria, 8A 26 July St. (tel. 391 88 29), in an alleyway to the south of the street. The "cafeteria" is not to be confused with the restaurant upstairs, where the average meal costs more than E£40. Marble tile and mirrors add to the welcome hygienic atmosphere. Salads E£1.50, sandwiches E£2-4, entrees E£8-17.50. The lunch special (*kofta, kebab,* oriental rice or macaroni, salad, bread, and dessert) is E£16.50. Take-out is also available; play pool at their table while you wait. Credit cards accepted. Open daily noon-midnight.

Fu Ching, 28 Tala'at Harb St. (tel. 576 61 84), in an alleyway running west from the street. Scrumptious exotic items like shark fin soup (E£6), as well as a diverse array of vegetarian options, make this Chinese restaurant a delicious escape from the usual street fare. Treat yourself to a romp in the land of non-Egyptian fare! Entrees E£10-20. They even calculate your bill on an abacus.

Estoril Restaurant, 12 Tala'at Harb St. (tel. 574 31 02), across the street from Felfela's take-away counter. This Egyptian/French restaurant is popular with locals. Dishes like Coqauvin (E£24) and chocolate mousse (E£6) seem incongruous amidst the surroundings but are tasty nonetheless. Open daily noon-4pm and 7:30-11pm.

Le Pacha, 15 Mahmoud Bassiouni St., (tel. 574 61 69). One block west of Tala'at Harb Sq. Chomp on *spaghetti bolognaise* (E£3.75) and breaded or grilled chicken fillet (E£15) in this small air-conditioned restaurant. Open daily 8am-midnight.

ZAMALEK

If you want a break from downtown Cairo, search out the tree-lined boulevards of Zamalek. All restaurants listed here are north of 26 July St. There are numerous pastry shops and bars for dessert and drinks after your meal.

Harry's Pub, Cairo Marriott Hotel, Zamalek. Wide selection of drinks; you name it, they've got it, but be prepared to pay dearly. On Mondays, Harry's serves good ol' American grub; all the hot dogs, hamburgers, and salad you can eat for E£10 (served 1-6pm). A/C and satellite TV. Open daily noon-1:30am.

Maison Thomas, 157 26 July St. (tel. 340 70 57), on your right near the base of the bridge as you come into Zamalek from Cairo. Italian deli replete with hanging salami, olives, and rounds of cheese. Salad niçoise is a refreshing E£11. Don't miss the calzone: the regular size easily feeds two people (E£17.55), and the large is a bit absurd (E£24.70). Take away, eat in, or home delivery. Open 24hr.

Bon Appetit, 2 Ismail Muhammad St. (tel. 340 43 82 or 91 08), 1 block from the Flamenco Hotel on the west side of Zamalek. Big sandwiches are highly praised by AUC students living in the hostel a few minutes away. The cleanest place in town to try a brain or a tongue sandwich (E£7.70). The mammoth chicken fillet (E£13) will keep you clucking for days. Open 9am-2am. Visa, MC, AmEx.

Hana Korean Restaurant, 21 Ma'had as-Swissry St. (tel. 340 18 46), in the En-Nil Zamalek Hotel. Take a right off of 26 July St. onto Hassan Sabri St. (also called Brazil St.). Decorated with Chinese lanterns, this air-conditioned haven is popular with in-the-know locals and expats. Don't miss the Korean BBQ *(Bulgogi)*, tender slices of beef you barbecue right at the table (E£21). The *kimchi* (pickled cabbage) fried rice (E£15) is scrumptious, and an order of egg rolls made with real egg instead of pastry is a bargain at E£9. Serves alcohol. Open daily noon-11pm.

MOHANDISEEN

Al-Omda, 6 El Gazeir St. (tel. 346 22 47), a few doors from the Atlas Hotel on Gam'at ed-Duwal St., down an unmarked staircase. This popular, clean, air-conditioned joint serves tasty pizza and stuffed grape leaves (E£8-E£15). Alongside the standard offerings of *fuul, falafel,* and *kushari* is an extensive list of chicken and hamburger sandwiches (E£2-5.25). Open 24hr.

Chili's, El-Themar St. (tel. 361 70 04), near Mustafa Mahmoud Mosque. This American Tex-Mex favorite recently opened restaurants in Heliopolis and Mohandiseen with success. The only chips 'n salsa, turkey *quesadillas,* and "wings over buffalo" in town are here! Non-alcoholic margaritas are refreshing on the small patio and E£35-50 meals will soothe a homesick stomach. Open daily 11am-1am.

Prestige Pizza, 34 Geziret al-Arab (tel. 347 0383), just east of Wadi en-Nil St. Coming from Gam'at ed-Duwal St., turn right before Al Ahli Bank. Egypt's top actors and film producers scarf down slices in the outdoor section. Generous "normal" size pizzas E£5-8, "prestige" size E£12-15. Good Egyptian lentil soup, too. Open daily noon-2am. E£2.25 cover charge. AmEx, Visa, MC.

KHAN EL-KHALILI

Coffee Shop Naguib Mahfouz, 5 El Badistante Lane (tel. 590 37 88 or 593 22 62), 2 blocks west of El Hussein Mosque. This pricey restaurant is an oasis of delectable food in the maddening bustle of the *Khan.* True to its name, it is known as the hangout of Nobel laureate Naguib Mahfouz. Every night, live music accompanies a

Lebanese meal: *kebab* (E£39), *tabbouleh* (E£6.75), fruit drinks E£4-6. Min. charge E£3.50 per person, E£1.50 music charge. Open daily 10am-2am. Visa, MC, AmEx.

Egyptian Pancakes, 7 Al-Azhar Sq. (tel. 590 86 23), 1 block from the intersection of Al-Azhar St. and Gohar el-Qa'it St. Topped with sweets (honey, coconut, or raisins) or meats (hot dog or tuna). These *fatir* (E£10-15) have nothing to do with Western pancakes; their light fluffy texture is much better. Open 24hr.

Al Gamhorya, on Al-Azhar St. 1 block east of the green pedestrian overpass at El Ghouri Mosque and Mausoleum. Look for the white marble facade with red-trimmed windows. A perfect *kushari* (E£1) stop-off. Open daily 9am-11pm.

SPLURGES

It's easy to fill up for mere piasters, but not much more can buy a pharaoh's feast.

Al Dente, 26 Bahgat Ali St., Zamalek (tel. 340 91 17). From the Western Corniche, take a right onto Anis Pasha St. Al Dente is 2 blocks ahead on your left. Chef Sa'ad, after 15 years of experience in Italy, has built a good reputation in a remarkably short time. A wide selection of pastas with 18 different sauces; the *al quattro formaggi* blends mozzarella, parmesan, Roquefort, and ricotta cheeses. Side dishes such as the *insalata al funghi* (salad of mushrooms and garlic) and *bruschette aglio e olio* (grilled baguette topped with garlic and olive oil) are equally tempting. A full meal costs around E£35. Open daily noon-2am.

Arabesque, 6 Qasr en-Nil St. (tel. 574 78 98), just off of Tahrir Sq. The exquisite entrance through an art gallery is only the beginning. Tapestries adorn white walls and tables are laid with crisp linen. Middle Eastern and Continental cuisine includes *tahina, baba ghanoush,* grilled pigeon, and Châteaubriand with bérnaise sauce (all under E£40). Open daily 12:30-3:30pm and 7:30pm to 12:30am.

Le Tabasco, 8 Amman Sq., Mohandiseen (tel. 336 55 83). Dim candlelight and soft jazz. Menu changes weekly, but the prices stay in the same range: appetizers E£10-24, pasta E£12-17, main dishes E£21-34. Recent menu selections include *cascadilla* (grilled tomato soup), frogs' legs Provençale, prawns in spicy garlic sauce, and fresh pear *crêpes.* Open daily 7pm-2am. Visa, MC, AmEx. Reservations required.

Peking, 14 Saraya el-Azbakia St. (tel. 591 23 81; free delivery), behind Cinema Diana, between Alfy and 26 July St. Romantic and lantern-lit, this is one of Cairo's most popular Chinese restaurants. Spicy calamari and spring rolls are especially yummy. Don't miss the honey-walnut Tarte Lee for dessert. Full meal with a starter, 3 dishes, and dessert will set you and a friend back E£40-45 each. Open noon-midnight. Alcohol served. AmEx, Visa, MC. Other branches in Mohandiseen (tel. 349 90 86), New Ma'adi (tel. 352 34 50), and Heliopolis (tel. 418 56 12).

■ Sights

ISLAMIC CAIRO

Cairo's medieval district is home to resplendent mosques and monuments which are touted as some of the finest Islamic architecture in the world. Unlike Damascus and Baghdad, the two other Middle Eastern capitals of the medieval Islamic world, Cairo was spared the devastation of Mongol invasions. Attacks today come not from roving warriors, but from the ever-encroaching modern world. Packed with mosques, lumbershops, metal factories, and homes, Islamic Cairo has a wrinkled, withered exterior. Beneath the Muslim city's dingy facade lies a wealth of ornate friezes, Arabesque stucco, finely-carved wooden grillwork, and vaulted and domed ceilings. Countless minarets serve as observation decks from which you can get your bearings as well as a magnificent view of the city. To get the most out of your visit, you might want to brush up on Islam before you go (see **Islam,** p. 66).

It takes at least two days to explore Islamic Cairo. We suggest spending your first day in southern Islamic Cairo starting at the Ibn Tulun Mosque and working your way to central Islamic Cairo and the Citadel. El Muizz St., Khan el-Khalili, and the northern walls can fill a second day. However, even a two-day itinerary is rushed. A set of four detailed maps of Islamic Cairo is published by SPARE (Society for the Preservation of Architectural Resources in Egypt; E£10 each). The *City Map of Cairo* (E£10) has an indexed map of Islamic Cairo. For in-depth descriptions and history, we recommend *Islamic Monuments in Cairo: A Practical Guide* by Caroline Williams. The book and most maps are available at the AUC bookstore.

Many of the important monuments charge admission (E£6-12; half-off with ISIC). At sights that don't charge, and mosques in particular, you will be expected to give *bakhsheesh*. Usually at the bigger mosques the man who "guards" your shoes while you are inside will expect compensation of some kind. Students purchasing discounted tickets should only pay 50pt-E£1 in *bakhsheesh*, rather than paying the difference between the regular ticket and the student one. Climbing the minaret is included in the ticket price. When visiting smaller monuments or trying to see the interiors of tombs, hunt down the custodian. Opening hours are estimates at best, so declare your interest to whomever is around and usually the caretaker will magically swish into being. If you confine your tour of Islamic Cairo to unlocked doors, you'll miss many of the city's treasures.

Most mosques are open from 8am to 5pm, but visitors are not welcome during prayer times. Wait a few minutes after the congregation has finished before entering. Night visits are not permitted, although some travelers rave about watching the sunset paint Cairo dusty pink from atop a minaret. Avoid visiting on Friday afternoons, when the Muslim community gathers for afternoon prayer. Certain highly venerated mosques—Sayyidna Hussein, Sayyidna Zeinab, and Sayyidna Nafisa—are believed to contain the remains of descendants of Muhammad and are officially closed to non-Muslims, although some adept in subtlety and modesty have been known to enter.

Visitors must **dress modestly** in Islamic Cairo; revealing clothing will attract a great deal of unsolicited and unfriendly attention and will prevent admission to many mosques. Residents consider shorts, miniskirts, and exposed shoulders disrespectful. It is important to wear sensible clothes that you don't mind getting a bit grungy: while Islamic Cairo is full of charm, its streets are rather filthy. Sometimes head coverings are required (these can usually be rented for a few piasters). In some mosques (such as Muhammad Ali) an entire toga is provided for free. Sensible shoes are also a must and, since you will be asked to remove your shoes altogether, socks are a good idea. Bring a plastic bag for your shoes to avoid the 50pt charged by custodians to watch your shoes while you are touring, or simply carry them with the soles facing one another. Never place the soles of your shoes on the floor of a mosque.

To get to the southern monuments, take minibus #54 or bus #72 from Tahrir Sq. Or, take the metro to Sayyidna Zeinab and then bus #501 (35pt) to Kadri St., which leads straight up to Ibn Tulun. Coming from Giza, take bus #923; from the Pyramids, #905, or share a group taxi (E£5) to "Masjid Ibn Tulun."

Ibn Tulun Mosque

The **Mosque of Ibn Tulun** is the largest, third oldest (879 CE), and most sublime of Cairo's Islamic monuments. If you stand on Kadri St., the entrance is around the left side. Once in the gate, the Gayer-Anderson Museum is to your left and the mosque's courtyard is straight ahead. The serene courtyard covers almost seven acres and has six *mihrabs* indicating the direction to Mecca. In the center of the courtyard, an ablution fountain, or *mayda'a*, added in 1296 by a Mamluk sultan, is still used for washing before prayer.

Ahmed Ibn Tulun, son of a Turkish slave, was sent to Egypt as governor of El Fustat in 868 and became governor of the entire province in 879. He declared independence from Baghdad and built a new royal city, *Qataii*, north of the original capital of El Fustat. This grand mosque is all that remains. The minaret, with its unusual external staircase, was probably built in the 13th century to resemble Ibn Tulun's original tower, which in turn was modeled after the minaret at the Great Mosque of Samarra in Iraq. A less substantiated theory explaining the unique external staircase attributes the design to the architectural period; it was built before it became clear that the *muezzin*, or prayer caller, could see impure things during his ascent to the top of the minaret. His glimpses of unveiled women relaxing in their homes or of people doing less than ascetic things in the streets led architects to build inner stairwells with hopes that the *muezzin* would have an easier time staying focused on the prayer he was about to deliver. Both the minaret and roof are accessible without having to lay out *bakhsheesh* (mosque open daily in the summer 8am-6pm, until 5pm in the winter, until 4pm in Ramadan; admission E£6, students E£3).

On the right, as you step out of the main courtyard of Ibn Tulun Mosque is the spectacular **Gayer-Anderson Museum** (see **Museums,** p. 123). Exit from the main entrance of Ibn Tulun and head left. Take a right at the intersection with Khodairi St., which eventually will turn into Saliba St.

Sabil Umm Abbas

On the left side of Saliba St., this mosque became the home of the **Life and Culture Center** in 1990 when the Ministry of Culture moved artists here from their well-known center on Roda Island. Now, tucked away in Islamic Cairo, the artists rarely get visitors and are anxious to share their passion with interested travelers. Contemporary Egyptian artists employ the techniques of their ancient predecessors. Artists specialize in textile production, batik, printing, glass blowing, and silk screening. Be sure to speak with Muhammad Reda Nasr, whose unique art combines calligraphy and nature (canvases are often made from egg shells and leaves). His subjects are meant to portray the many sides of Egypt (open Sat.-Thurs. 9am-2pm; free).

Continue north on Saliba St. between the double **Mosques of Shaykhon.** The one on the right has well-kept stained glass and a superb painting of Mecca on the far southwestern wall. Look for the guard if it's locked (free).

Exit the mosque and continue north on Saliba St., which becomes Shaykhon St. At the fork, stay left and you'll eventually see Sultan Hasan and Rifa'i Mosque on your left and the Citadel to your right through Salah ad-Din Sq.

Sultan Hasan and Rifa'i

The 19th Mamluk Sultan of Egypt, Sultan en-Nasser Hasan, busted the bank in building this *madrasa* and mausoleum in 1356 C.E. When he died, no one wanted to deal with the unfinished project, so they let it stand until it became a tourist attraction. To reach these massive edifices and the Citadel, you can either approach from the south starting at Ibn Tulun or you can take bus #173 or #194 from Tahrir or minibus #72. From 'Ataba Sq., take Muhammad Ali St., which becomes El Al'a (Citadel) St. from the southern edge of the square.

Sultan Hasan is not a mosque but a combination *madrasa* and mausoleum with an added prayer niche. Because much of it was built with exterior casing stones pilfered from the Pyramids at Giza, it was spurned by devotees of pharaonic art. The commodious interior courtyard—32m on each side—belongs to the Madrasa of Sultan Hasan and is surrounded by four enormous vaulted *iwans,* arcades off the courtyard, each of which once housed one of the four schools of judicial thought in Sunni Islam. Hundreds of *qanadeel* (decorated oil lamps) hang just above head level, to bring the mammoth building to a more human scale. Inside the southeastern *iwan,* the *mihrab* is flanked by a pair of Crusader columns. On either side of the easternmost *mihrab,* bronze doors open into the Mausoleum. Open Sat.-Thurs. 8am-6pm, Fri. 9-11am and 2-5pm; in winter 8am-5pm; during Ramadan 8am-4pm. Admission E£12, students E£6.

Directly across from the Sultan Hasan Mosque stands the enormous **Rifa'i Mosque.** Rifa'i's stupendous size and polished interior will make your neck sore as you marvel at the awe-inspiring ceiling and marble tombs. Named after Imam Ahmed ai-Rifa'i, an Egyptian spiritual leader, the mosque was completed in 1912 by Khedive Isma'il's mother, Princess Koshair Hanem. She is buried here with her son Isma'il and grandsons King Fouad and King Farouk, Egypt's last monarch. In the room next to Farouk lies the tomb of Muhammad Reza Pahlavi, the last Shah of Iran. On the other side of the mosque, look for the mosaic-decorated *mihrab* and the elegant *maballigha,* a wooden stand where the *muezzin* echoes the *imam*'s prayers. The stand is depicted on the E£10 note. Both the Rifa'i and Sultan Hasan Mosques are illuminated at night (hours and admission same as the Sultan Hasan).

Between these two mosques is a pleasant **garden** filled with children playing *futbol* and adults reading the paper. There is also a splendid bit of greenery in Salah ad-Din Square, a good spot to rest before hitting more mosques and the Citadel.

The Citadel (El Al'a)

Dominating Islamic Cairo, the lofty **Citadel** *(El Al'a)* was begun by Salah ad-Din in 1176 and has been continually expanded and modified since then, most notably by the Mamluks and Muhammad Ali. The complex contains three large mosques and four operating museums. To reach the Citadel, take bus #82, 83, or 609 from Tahrir Sq. From 'Ataba Sq., take bus #401 or minibus #50 or 55. Enter from either the northern or the southern gate. From Hasan and Rifa'i head left along the wall past the post office on your right. The road, Baab el-Gded St., dead ends at the gate to the Citadel. (Open daily 8am-6pm, in winter 8am-5pm, Ramadan 8am-4pm, closed every Fri. during prayer. Entrance locked 1hr. before closing time. Admission E£20, students E£10, including all the museums and mosques.)

As you enter from the northern gate, the **Police National Museum** is to your right. Enter to examine mounds of confiscated narcotics. Much more interesting than the museum is the spectacular view of Cairo and the Pyramids from the garden. The **Military National Museum,** a joint venture spearheaded by President Hosni Mubarak and North Korea's Kim Il Sung in 1990, has fighter jets, tanks, and missiles on display in the garden. Inside, you'll find a detailed reconstruction of the citadel complex and accounts of Egypt's war ventures.

Between these museums and the Mosque of Muhammad Ali is the **Mosque of Sultan En-Nasir,** built from 1318 to 1335 by one of the great Bahri Mamluk builders. En-Nasir made many additions to the Citadel, but this mosque was the only one to survive the renovations of Muhammad Ali. Unfortunately, the interior of the mosque was largely gutted by Ottoman Sultan Selim the Grim, who made off with its marble panels. Nonetheless, the mosque still has some impressive features: pharaonic and Coptic columns, a high wooden ceiling from India, and an olive oil-operated chandelier. Just south of the mosque lies **Yousef's Well,** built by Crusader prisoners. A water wheel, or *saqya,* worked by oxen was used to raise water during wartime.

Near the eastern end of the northern enclosure is a the small-domed first Ottoman mosque in Cairo, known as the **Mosque of Suleiman Pasha.** It was built in 1527. The mosque, also known as Sariat el-Gabal (the mountain palace), has a small prayer hall decorated with different calligraphic styles and a courtyard consisting of four *iwans*.

To reach the massive **Mosque of Muhammad Ali,** head for the thin, unadorned Turkish minarets (they look like pencils). Muhammad Ali leveled the western surface of the Citadel, filled in the famous 13th-century Mamluk palace Qasr el-Ablaq, and built his mosque on the ruins in 1830 as a reminder of Turkish domination. Modeled after the Hagia Sophia mosque in Istanbul, the edifice is more attractive from a distance. The mosque was refurbished by the Department of Antiquities during the 1980s; its silver domes and marble-and-alabaster decorations now twinkle on the Cairo skyline. While popular with tourists and postcard makers, it is hated by art historians, who consider it a third-rate copy of the great Ottoman mosques in Istanbul and an obnoxious reminder of Muhammad Ali's ego.

The mosque consists of two parts: the courtyard and the Prayer Hall. The courtyard's main attraction is not the elaborate ablution fountain in the center, but rather a nameless, 17m-deep **well** whose underground cavity is as big as the courtyard itself. Call down something polite, and the well-dwellers will echo mystical, magical music right back at you. A charming and unexpected French gingerbread clock overlooks the courtyard; King Louis Philippe of France presented the clock in 1845 in appreciation of Muhammad Ali's gift of the obelisk from Luxor Temple that now stands in the Place de la Concorde in Paris. The interior is quite impressive, especially just after prayers when the large chandelier and tiny lanterns are lit. The edifice is also known as the Alabaster Mosque because it is covered inside and out with the clearest alabaster, hauled over from Beni Suef. (One outer face remains bare; when Muhammad Ali died, so did the funding.) The Prayer Hall is lit by a huge chandelier, and 365 lanterns (symbolizing the days in a year) provide additional lighting. A die-hard Francophile, Muhammad Ali put splashes of Parisian decor across the five large domes and 15 smaller ones that tower overhead. His tomb is to the right as you enter the prayer hall. Behind the mosque is the Southern enclosure, which provides an extraordinary view of Cairo's pollution. On exceptionally clear days this vantage point can afford views of the Southern Cemetery and Old Cairo, but rarely any further.

Qasr el-Gowhara (the Diamond Palace), built in 1811 by Muhammad Ali and named after one of his wives, lies to the southwest of the Muhammad Ali Mosque. In 1974, a burglary attempt resulted in a fire that destroyed half of the palace. The surviving half consists of a large reception room where Muhammad Ali received 500 of his closest Mamluk allies and cordially slaughtered them. The elaborate wooden benches next to the wall concealed the murder weapons in hidden compartments below the seats. Also on display are a few of the gold- and silver-adorned tapestries from the Ka'ba in Mecca. Mecca presented Egypt with one of these tapestries every year until 1961. Only die-hard Muhammad Ali fans should walk over to the **Carriage (Hatour) Museum,** housing carriages of the great one's family.

Blue Mosque and Mosque of Qijmas el-Ishaqi

Coming after some of the other mosques of Islamic Cairo, the **Blue Mosque,** or Mosque of Aqsunqur, can be a bit anticlimactic. If you have the energy, however, it's worth a peek. The first street after the Hasan and Rifa'i mosques, if you proceed around the Salah ad-Din rotary in a clockwise fashion, is Baab el-Wazir St. This fascinating thoroughfare, once a main north-south artery in Islamic Cairo, plunges into the heart of the old city. Overloaded carts pulled by weary donkeys easily outnumber cars, and chickens and goats mix freely with passersby. Follow Baab el-Wazir until it breaks free of the wall at the post office on your right. The mosque is a few blocks to the north. The 14th-century edifice owes its name to the colored Syrian tiles that line the interior. The flowery tiles were added in 1652 by a Turkish governor homesick for Istanbul's grand tiled mosques. The prayer hall, to the right, has one of the oldest marble *minbars* (pulpits) in the Islamic world. The top of the minaret is a great vantage point for viewing the Citadel to the south, Khan el-Khalili to the north, and the southern end of the pastel-colored City of the Dead to the east. (Open daily 8am-6pm, in winter 8am-5pm, during Ramadan 8am-4pm. Admission E£6, students E£3.)

To reach the simple and unobtrusive **Mosque of Qijmas el-Ishaqi,** turn right as you leave the Blue Mosque and continue up the same street; its name changes to Darb el-Ahmar (Red Way) in memory of Muhammad Ali's massacre of the Mamluk generals here. The mosque's unremarkable façade gives no inkling of the serene, colorful interior light from the stained-glass windows. Under the prayer mats in the east *iwan* lies an ornate marble mosaic floor. Tip the custodian to uncover it for you. El Ishaqi was Chief of the Royal Stable and Chargé d'Affairs for the annual pilgrimage to Mecca. As you step out, notice the grillwork of the *sabil* on your right and the carved stonework of the columns. Head back to Salah ad-Din Sq. to catch a ride home. Bus #194 goes to Tahrir and a cab should run you E£4-5.

Fatimid Cairo: El Muizz Street and Al-Azhar

You can take bus #922 or minibus #77 to Al-Azhar Mosque and the Khan el-Khalili area. A taxi to this area from downtown should run you E£3-5, though it's only a 20-minute walk. Head west on Al-Azhar St. for about 200m and turn left on El Muizz lid-Din Allah, which runs north-south through the medieval city, connecting its northern and southern gates and providing a good place to begin a tour of the district. If you stand on the corner of El Muizz lid-Din Allah and Al-Azhar, Baab el-Futuh will be to the north, Baab Zuweila to the south, and Al-Azhar Mosque one block east.

Southern El Muizz Street

Today El Muizz St. is a minor thoroughfare bisected by the much larger Al-Azhar St., but during the Fatimid period, it was the main avenue of the city. At the southern corners of the intersection of Al-Azhar and El Muizz st. stand impressive Mamluk structures. The **Madrasa of Sultan El Ghouri** (1503) occupies the southwest corner. El Ghouri, the last powerful Mamluk sultan, invested so heavily in construction that the area is often called *El Ghouriyya*. In addition to the school and *wakala*, he restored the citadel and reconstructed the pilgrimage road to Mecca. His *madrasa*'s minaret was the first four-crowned minaret in Egypt. The *madrasa* was under renovation during the summer of 1997, with no estimated opening date.

Across El Muizz St. from the *madrasa* is the **Mausoleum of El Ghouri,** where **sufi dancers** enchant travelers Wednesday and Saturday nights at 9pm (see **Performing Arts,** p. 129). The **Wakala of El Ghouri** is easier to miss. From the mausoleum and mosque, head east on Al-Azhar St. then right onto Sheikh Muhammad Abduh St. At #3 (on your right) you'll see the magnificently-preserved *wakala* (built in 1505), now transformed into a center for handicrafts and folkloric arts. The structure originally served as a commercial hotel (mausoleum and *wakala* open Sat.-Thurs. 9am-9pm; admission to all 3 E£6, students E£3).

Head back to El Muizz St., walk two blocks south of Madrasa el-Ghouri past textile stores, then turn left onto Khushqadam St. just before El Fakahani Mosque (look for the signs). On the left is the 16th-century **House of Gamal ed-Din,** the most splendid surviving Ottoman mansion in Cairo. Beautiful wooden ceilings, Turkish tiles, and *mashrabiyyahs* make it an anomaly amid the grunge of the city, Gamal ed-Din is shining white and cool, with intricate tile and lattice work (open daily 9am-5pm; admission E£6, students E£3; the custodian will expect at last E£1 in *bakhsheesh*).

Farther south along El Muizz St. on the right at the corner of Ahmed Maher St. is the entrance to the **Mosque of El Mu'ayyad,** built between 1415 and 1420. Look for the two minarets towering above the Fatimid gate, a stone-carved dome, and an imposing *muqarnas* portal. The huge door may remind you of the ones at Sultan Hasan Mosque: it was stolen from there. The interior has a pleasant garden, and the *qibla riwaq* is covered by an extensively restored ceiling. At the northern end of the *qibla* wall is the mausoleum of the alcoholic Mamluk sultan, El Mu'ayyad. The second mausoleum, at the other end of the wall, is an Ottoman addition (open 8:30am-9pm; admission E£6, students E£3).

Baab Zuweila is the most impressive of the three remaining gates of Fatimid Cairo. The gate, named after the Berber tribe which helped build it, had two cylindrical towers, now replaced by the minarets of El Mu'ayyad Mosque. Egyptians also call it *Bawwabet el-Metwali* (the Gate of the Tax Collector), after the civil servant who used to wait for victims at the gate.

Across the street from Baab Zuweila and to the right stands the **Zawiya of Sultan Faraj** (built in 1408), a small rectangular structure. During the 19th century, execution by strangulation was carried out beside the railings outside. Access is difficult for non-Muslims. Opposite this structure, across the street from Baab Zuweila, stands the elegant **Mosque of Salih Talai,** built in 1160. When the mosque was erected, the street was at the level of the series of shops standing behind the iron railing. The five keel arches form a remarkable projecting portal, unique in Cairo. The courtyard opens into a small *riwaq*. The custodian (who will expect E£1 *bakhsheesh*) will show you to the roof (open 9am-5pm). Continuing south on El Muizz St., you'll enter a covered bazaar known as the **Street of Tentmakers,** followed a few blocks down by a similar covered alley called the **Street of Saddlemakers.** Turning left as you step out of Baab Zuweila, you'll find yourself on Darb el-Ahmar St. heading toward the Citadel. A right turn leads to Ahmed Maher Street, lined with the shops of carpenters, tombstone-carvers, and metalworkers. The street leads out to Baab el-Khalq Sq. on Port Said St., across from the Museum of Islamic Art.

To backtrack, head back up El Muizz St. to explore the northern sights. Al-Azhar and Khan el-Khalili are essential stops before proceeding north of the intersection of El Muizz and Al-Azhar Streets.

Al-Azhar and Khan el-Khalili

The oldest continuously operating university in the world and the foremost Islamic theological center, the **University and Mosque of Al-Azhar** stands just a few steps from the midpoint of Al Muizz St. at the end of Al-Azhar St., facing the large square. Al-Azhar University was established in 972 CE by the Shi'a Fatimids and rose to preeminence in the 15th century as a center for the study of Qur'anic law and doctrine, a position it still holds. Ever since the Ayyubids came, the emphasis has been on Sunni learning. Students are often found sitting on the plush red carpets of the *riwaq*, or arcaded aisle around the courtyard, cramming for exams. Don't be afraid to approach these learned souls and ask them to share their knowledge of Islam with you. To reach the central court, enter through the double arched gate and pass under the minaret of Qaytbay (built in 1469). Although the stucco decoration of the courtyard's façade is a reconstruction, the *mihrab* (the niche indicating the direction to Mecca) in the central aisle is original. The library, just left of the main entrance, holds over 80,000 manuscripts. For about E£1 the caretaker will allow you to climb one of the locked minarets for a fantastic view of Cairo and Khan el-Khalili below you. Check the first wooden door on your left after you enter the courtyard to see if it is unlocked before handing money to the doorman.

Around the corner from the mosque is the institute where Al-Azhar's 8000 students take classes from October and May. The theological curriculum has remained virtually unchanged since the Mamluk era; physics and medicine are more recent arrivals. Women, although allowed in the mosque, may not study at Al-Azhar. They attend a "sister school" near Abbasiyya Sq. You can still observe the traditional form of instruction: Socratic questioning with a professor seated in the center of a circle of students (open Sat.-Thurs. 7:30-9pm, Fri. 9am-noon and 2-7pm; admission E£12, students E£6). Women without head coverings must wrap up (free) at the entrance.

Across El Hussein Sq., 100m north of Al-Azhar Mosque, stands the **Sayyidna el-Hussein Mosque,** highly revered throughout the Islamic world as the resting place of the skull of Hussein, grandson of the prophet Muhammad. The head is rumored to have been transported to Cairo in a green silk bag in 1153, almost 500 years after the death of its owner in the battle of Karbala in Iraq. The present edifice was built in the 1870s by Khedive Isma'il and is distinctly Turkish in style (note the pencil-like minarets). Recent renovations did away with the mosque's unique exterior and left it looking like any other modern mosque. If you choose to enter this mosque, realize that you are in a very sacred place. Women enter around the corner into a room from which they approach the elaborate glowing trunk containing the remains of Hussein.

On *Mawlid an-Nabi* (the Birthday of the Prophet), the president of Egypt traditionally comes to pray at Sayyidna el-Hussein while boisterous festivities take place in the square. During Ramadan, this square is the best place to witness the breaking of the fast after evening prayers (about 8pm). Restaurants display their fare half an hour before prayers begin, and famished patrons stampede to the tables afterwards. After blood sugar levels return to normal, the square erupts in celebration.

Khan el-Khalili, the largest bazaar in Egypt, lies to the west of El Hussein Sq. Mamluk prince Garkas el-Khalili established the market in the 1380s. Today, the market thrives on tourists bringing back that perfect little gift for Aunt Rhodie in Tallahassee. As you meander through the *souq* you will undoubtedly be asked if you'd like to "see my perfume store" or if you would like to buy "real papyrus, no banana leaf." It can be annoying, but it can also be fun. Revel in the free-market frenzy as you pass through copperware, perfume, spice, gold and silver, or *sheesha* sections of this massive bazaar. Though the tacky souvenirs are often overpriced, the time-honored institution of bargaining still thrives. Be ferocious if you intend to strike a good deal (often a third of the starting price, if not less). However, there is a sort of unwritten consensus among *khan* shopkeepers that they will not go below certain prices. Thus, if you are allowed to walk away after making a bid, you probably won't get a better price elsewhere. Women are generally more successful bargainers than men; a male merchant does not feel that his machismo has been challenged if he lowers the price for a female. **Fishawi's** offers respite from the market bustle with flavored *sheesha* and exotic juices (see **Ahwas and Casinos,** p. 127). The farther you go from the heart of the market, the more authentic the wares become. A word of warning, though: Khan el-Khalili is a paradise for **thieves;** wallets can easily disappear while you are haggling.

Slightly less tourist-ridden is **El Muski,** the long bazaar where Egyptians shop for men's cologne, shoes, cloth, furniture, pillowcases, and food. El Muski stretches from El Muizz St. all the way to Port Said St., running parallel to and one block north of Al-Azhar St. El Muski is a convenient route between Islamic and downtown Cairo.

Northern El Muizz Street

Between Al-Azhar Mosque and Baab el-Futuh, El Muizz St. is lined with Fatimid and early Mamluk architectural attractions. This area is dubbed **Bayn el-Qasrayn,** Arabic for "between the two palaces," after the two Fatimid palaces that once stood here, and gives its name to one of Naguib Mahfouz's novels. El Gammaliya St. runs roughly parallel to El Muizz St. from Baab en-Nasr past the Mosque of el-Hussein to the square in front of Al-Azhar. To minimize mileage, you can walk from Al-Azhar up El Muizz St., through both Baab el-Futuh and Baab en-Nasr, and then return by way of El Gammaliya St. Expect to shell out a total of about E£15 if you plan to enter each of the sites listed below. If you're short on funds, this is still a wonderful way to see ancient Islamic architecture from the outside, if not from within.

A good tour starts by proceeding north on El Muizz St. from the intersection with Gohar el Qa'id St. After passing four little side streets you can see the **Tomb and Madrasa of Malik es-Salih Ayyub** on your right, its nearly square minaret gracing the heavens. The entrance is off a small alley on the right. The *madrasa* has ornate keel-arched windows and the minaret crowns a passageway. El Malik es-Salih Ayyub, the last ruler of Salah ad-Din's Ayyubid Dynasty, was the husband of Shagarat ad-Durr, an indomitable Turkish slave who became ruler of Egypt (see the **Tomb of Shagarat ad-Durr,** p. 118). The custodian has keys to the adjacent domed mosque which was recently restored by a German team.

The **Mausoleum, Madrasa,** and **Hospital of Qalawun** lie further along on El Muizz St. Mamluk sultan Qalawun sponsored the construction of these impressive edifices in 1284 before his death en route to attack the Crusader fortress in Akko (see **Akko,** p. 364). Qalawun's architects were influenced by the Crusader architecture of the Levant, hence the Romanesque windows. The three high *iwans* of the original *muristan* (mental hospital) remain. The ornate stucco work inside is original, though the undersides of the arches have been restored. To gain access to the mausoleum, hunt down the guard, purchase a ticket, and unlock the door. The exquisite wood screen separating the tomb from the rectangular forecourt dates from the original construction (complex open daily 8am-6pm; admission E£6, students E£3). Video cameras are not allowed without written permission from a tourist office; the nearest one is on Ed-darb al-Asfar St., next to Beit es-Suheimi.

Before the 14th century, Egypt was the world's center for glasswork, and stained-glass windows adorn many of Cairo's mosques. The Qalawun mausoleum offers especially dazzling glass and mosaic work. The intricately embellished tomb caused quite a controversy at the time of its construction, as Islamic doctrine (as opposed to pharaonic procedure) forbids displaying wealth at the time of burial. By the 11th century, however, the practice of building ornate tombs, especially for rulers, was not unusual, and by the 13th century, lavish burial sites had become commonplace.

Just north of Qalawun's mausoleum and tomb stands his son's, the **Mausoleum-Madrasa of En-Nasr Muhammad,** completed in 1304. En-Nasr Muhammad's 40-year reign marked the height of prosperity and stability in Mamluk Egypt. The square minaret exhibits an exceptional, intricately carved stucco surface, but almost nothing of the interior remains. The authorities like to blame the 1992 earthquake, but the custodian says it was simple neglect. You can still see the four *iwans*, but they are in bad shape (supposedly open daily 10am-6pm; free).

Next door, to the north along El Muizz St., is the **Mosque of Sultan Barquq.** Barquq, the first Circassian Mamluk sultan, seized power through a series of assassinations. His mosque was erected in 1386, a century after Qalawun's complex, and the difference in styles is striking. The inner courtyard has four *iwans,* the largest and most elaborate of which doubles as a prayer hall. Its beautiful timber roof has been restored and painted in rich hues of blue and gold. Four porphyry columns, quarried in pharaonic times from mountains near the Red Sea, support the ceiling. The round disks of marble floor are slices of Greek and Roman columns, used because Egypt has no indigenous marble (open daily 10am-7pm; admission E£6, students E£3).

El Muizz St. comes to a fork north of the Mosque of Barquq. Walk 25m down Darb Kermez St., the small side street to the right of the fork, and you'll find all that remains of **Qasr Bishtak,** a lavish palace from the 14th century that originally stood five stories high. All floors of the palace had running water, a technological achievement unmatched by Europe for another 300 years. In the center of the fork is the slim 18th-century **Sabil Kuttab of Abd er-Rahman Kathuda,** an active Qur'anic school. You should pay less than E£5 (students E£3) to see both together (open daily 8am-6pm, but may be closed sporadically).

Bear left at the fork and continue north along El Muizz St. to the next right-hand side street. On the corner stands the small but architecturally important Fatimid **Mosque of El Aqmar.** Built in 1125, this was the first Cairene mosque to have a stone-facade-and-shell motif within the keel-arched niche. *El Aqmar* means "the moons" and refers to the way the stone facade sparkles in the moonlight. The northern corner is typical of later Cairene architecture: the height of the niche is just about equal to that of a loaded camel, and it was intended to make the turn onto the side street easier for the hump-equipped creatures to negotiate.

Proceeding north from El Aqmar Mosque, turn right on Ed-Darb el-Asfar (the next sidestreet on the right) and follow the winding alley about 50m. The doorway on the left marked with a small, green plaque is the entrance to Cairo's finest old house, the 16th-century **Beit es-Suheimi.** The *sheikh* of Al-Azhar Mosque, Suheimi, built this elaborate residence for himself and his various wives. The house has carved wooden ceilings, stained-glass windows, tile mosaics, marble floors, and fountained salons. Both the mosque and the house are under renovation. Walk along the same alley, away from El Muizz St., and you'll eventually come to El Gammaliya St. Across the street is the facade of the 14th-century *khanqah* (Sufi establishment) of **Baybars el-Gashankir.** Erected in 1310, this building is the oldest surviving example of a *khanqah* in Cairo. From here, continue north on El Gammaliya St. until you pass through Baab en-Nasr; Baab el-Futuh is to the left (see below).

Northern Walls

Islamic Cairo is bordered on the north by the extensive remains of the Fatimid walls. Built in 1087, these colossal fortifications are the best surviving examples of pre-Crusader Islamic military architecture. The original walls built by Gawhar as-Sikelli in 969 had eight gates, two on each side. Three of the rampart's original gates still stand. **Baab en-Nasr** (Victory Gate), at the top of El Gammaliya St., and **Baab el-Futuh** (Conquest Gate), at the northern end of El Muizz St., in front of the El Hakim Mosque, are connected by a stretch of wall so thick it easily accommodates a tunnel; these walls once wrapped all the way around the Fatimid city to **Baab Zuweila.**

The Fatimid **Al Hakim Mosque,** just inside the walls between the two gates (entrance off El Muizz St.), was built between 990 and 1010 and remains the second largest mosque in Cairo. Al Hakim, the grandson of El Muizz, was known to his contemporaries as the "Mad Caliph." His unpredictable rages meant death to Christians, Jews, his enemies, his friends, and, on one occasion, all the dogs in Cairo. He ensured the confinement of women by forbidding cobblers to make shoes for them. He even banned the cooking of *mulukhiga,* a green vegetable eaten throughout Egypt, and renamed it *mulukiyya,* meaning royal, restricting its consumption to his family. He was assassinated soon after he announced that he was an incarnation of God. His chief theologian, Ad-Darazi, fled to Syria where he founded the Druze sect. The mosque was recently restored (amid great controversy) by the Aga Khan foundation. Rather than restoring the mosque to its original appearance, they chose to curry it up with chandeliers and a neon *mihrab,* outraging many art historians and Islamic experts (open daily 9am-6pm; E£6, students E£3).

CITIES OF THE DEAD

The Cities of the Dead teem with life if you know where to look. The areas to the northeast and south of the Citadel are home to hundreds of tombs and mausolea erected since the Mamluk era, which double as a shanty towns, home to hundreds of thousands of Cairenes. Unlike most graveyards, the Cities of the Dead have streets, house numbers (unlike the city center), and even a regular postal service. The modern residents of the medieval necropoli dwell amidst the funerary architecture, and many households have even incorporated the grave markers into their houses and yards where tombs serve as clotheslines and soccer goals. On Fridays, the grave sites swarm with visitors arriving to pay their respects to the deceased. Many of the plots are enclosed by walls, encompassing an adjoining chamber and small house where families pray for their ancestors on holy days. The Egyptian custom of picnicking at the family tomb on feast days may be an ancient holdover from pharaonic times, when the corpse was believed to require nourishment for good health in the afterlife. Visitors are not permitted in the mosques on Fridays or during prayers.

Mamluk sultans, unlike their more pious Islamic predecessors, spared no expense in the construction of their final resting places—perhaps because they knew that their dynasties would not survive. Elaborate tomb complexes with domed mausolea, mosques, and adjoining *madrasas* were erected for Cairo's rulers. Gravestones built for the families of Mamluk nobles vary widely; cenotaphs of all shapes and sizes dot the crowded thoroughfares of the royal necropoli.

The **Northern Cemetery,** northeast of the Citadel, is characterized by wide avenues and courtyards. It contains the finest monuments of the Cities of the Dead, with beautiful modern mausolea alongside structures dating from the later Mamluk period (14th-16th centuries). A visit to the Northern Cemetery can be tacked onto a tour of Islamic Cairo. Follow Al-Azhar St. due east, around the north side of Al-Azhar Mosque, over a slight hill to the six-lane Salah Salem St. Cross this automotive deathtrap and enter the cemetery 250m beyond the green overpass covered with Coca-Cola ads. Bus #176 from 'Ataba Sq. terminates just in front of the Mausoleum of Barquq. Bus #77 or 904 from Tahrir Sq. will also take you to the vicinity. The far more crowded **Southern Cemetery** houses Ayyubid mausolea and the oldest Mamluk tombs (12th-14th centuries). It's accessible by foot from Ibn Tulun, the Sultan Hasan Mosque, or the Citadel. Take bus #82 or 182 or minibus #54 from Tahrir Sq. From Ibn Tulun or Sultan Hasan, proceed east to Salah ad-Din Sq., just southeast of the Citadel, then head directly south following the southern slope of the Citadel. When you reach the traffic circle, walk under the overpass and take the right-hand fork, El Qdiriyya St., which becomes Imam esh-Shafi'i St., the main thoroughfare in the cemetery. Although most of the people here are dead and therefore harmless, the isolated areas should be **avoided at night,** especially by women.

Northern Cemetery

At the northern end of the cemetery, the imposing **Mausoleum of Barquq** (*Khanka Faraq Ibn Barquq*), easily identified by its matching pair of ornately sculpted minarets, is a good place to start your tour. Built in 1400 for Sultan Barquq by his son, this enormous family plot encompasses 5329 square meters. The *minbar* beneath the western arcade was donated by the Mamluk ruler Qaytbay. Two matching domes—the earliest stone domes in Cairo—shelter the family mausolea located in either corner. Sultan Barquq is interred below the northeast corner of the complex, and his two daughters occupy the chamber beneath the southeast dome. In the northeast corner of the complex, the second level holds the remains of a large *kuttab* (Islamic school) and numerous monastic cells that once housed Sufi mystics (mausoleum and minaret open daily 8am-6pm, 8am-5pm in winter; E£6, students E£3).

Just around the corner to the southwest, in front of the Mausoleum of Barquq, stands the **Tomb of Barsbay el-Bagasi.** Built in 1456, the tomb is decorated with an intricate geometrical design resembling a tulip, a variation on the Moroccan motif of *dari w ktaf* (cheek and shoulder). The nearby **Tomb of Amir Suleiman** was built about 90 years later; its dome is decorated with a series of zig-zag stripes. Admission to these two tombs is free but the caretaker will expect *bakhsheesh* (E£1).

The **Mosque and Mausoleum of Sultan Ashraf Barsbay** are 50m south of the Mausoleum of Barquq, along the cemetery's main thoroughfare. Originally intended as a *khanqah* (Sufi establishment), the 15th-century mosque has meticulously fashioned marble mosaic floors; lift the protective prayer mats to see the colorful tilework. Adjoining the mosque to the north is the Barsaby's Mausoleum, a domed chamber containing his and his slaves' remains, an elaborately decorated *mihrab,* and gleaming mother-of-pearl and marble mosaics (open daily 9am-sunset; free.)

Follow the same road south to reach the 15th-century **Mausoleum and Mosque of Qaytbay,** the cemetery's most celebrated structure. Approach through the open square for the best view of the facade's polychrome-striped brickwork, recognizable from the Egyptian one-pound note. Qaytbay was a Mamluk slave who rose through the ranks of the army to become leader of Egypt near the end of the 15th century. Reigning for 28 years, he became a powerful sultan and imposed order after years of anarchy. Qaytbay was not without enemies, so he watched his back. He designed the mosque with three secret doors for quick escapes. Apparently his efforts paid off—Qaytbay was the only Mamluk ruler not to be assassinated. Even in death, Qaytbay situated the prayer niche so that it would require the devotee to pray over the ruler's remains before reaching Allah. Enter the complex through the marble northern doorway, passing through a rectangular sanctuary. In the office to your left is a hole leading to a massive well beneath the mosque. The domed mausoleum, to the right, houses the marble tombs of Qaytbay and his two younger sisters. Also in the chamber are two black stones bearing footprints said to be those of the Prophet Muhammad. The 40m minaret is adored by architects for its elaborately decorated tiers (open daily 9am-9:30pm; E£6, students E£3).

Follow the main road south of the mausoleum through the **Gate of Qaytbay,** a stone archway that once guarded the entrance to the tomb complex, to reach two more monuments. When this thoroughfare intersects with a paved road, turn right and head west toward Salah Salem St. Just beyond the next main street (Sultan Ahmed St.) are the remains of the **Tomb of Umm Anuk** (1348), a ribbed dome adjoining a sweeping pointed archway. Umm Anuk was the favorite wife of Sultan En-Nasir Muhammad, and her devoted husband presented her with a correspondingly lavish tomb. He also constructed the **Tomb of Princess Tolbay** across the way for his principal wife. Muslim law required him to treat the two women equally, but the sultan apparently obeyed only the word and not the spirit of Qur'anic law.

Sultan Ahmed St. goes north to the Mausoleum of Barquq (where you can pick up the #167 bus). Heading west to the overpass leads you to Al-Azhar St.; south brings you to the Citadel.

Southern Cemetery

The Southern Cemetery's most impressive edifice is the celebrated **Mausoleum of Imam esh-Shafi'i.** The largest Islamic mortuary chamber in Egypt, the mausoleum was erected in 1211 by Salah ad-Din's brother and successor in honor of the great Imam esh-Shafi'i, founder of one of the four schools of judicial thought of Sunni Islam. Shafi'i Islam is still the dominant judicial school in Egypt and much of East Africa. In 1178, Salah ad-Din built a large monument over the grave of Imam esh-Shafi'i, which is currently housed within the 13th-century mausoleum and often crowded with Muslims offering prayers. The teak memorial shows the Imam himself, and is one of the finest surviving pieces of Ayyubid wood carving. Two mosques adjoin the tomb chamber, one dating from 1190, the other from 1763. The older mosque is closed to non-Muslims. The other, open to all, remains a vital center of worship. (open daily 6am-7pm; free, but E£1 *bakhsheesh* is appropriate).

The **Mosque of Sayyida Nafisa,** Egypt's third-holiest Islamic shrine, stands on the western edge of the Southern Cemetery not far from Es-Sultaniyya, and honors the great-great-great-granddaughter of the Prophet. One of Cairo's three congregational mosques, Sayyida Nafisa is closed to non-Muslims. To reach the mosque from the main intersection southeast of the Citadel, walk southwest on Salah Salem St. alongside the 12th-century **Wall of Salah ad-Din.** Sayyida Nafisa's tall single minaret and ornate dome can be seen to the right approaching the cemetery. After Sayyida Nafisa's death in 824, her tomb attracted droves of pilgrims. So many mausolea were erected in the immediate vicinity of her tomb that historians suspect that it was the construction of this sacred shrine that sparked the development of the Southern Cemetery.

Adjoining the Mosque of Sayyida Nafisa on the eastern side are the less-than-impressive **Tombs of Abbassid Caliphs.** At the peak of their authority, the Abbassid caliphs ruled the entire Muslim world (except Spain) from Baghdad. The last reigning caliph fled Baghdad in 1258 after invading Mongols toppled the regime. The Mamluk sultan welcomed the caliph upon his arrival in Egypt and went so far as to exalt the deposed ruler in an effort to legitimize his own sinecure. Subsequent Mamluk rulers continued to harbor a succession of caliphs, all the while preventing them from gaining any real power. Finally, the sultan in Istanbul declared himself caliph in 1517, thereby consolidating the authority of the Ottoman Sultanate. With Egypt under Ottoman rule, it was impossible for the regional government to protest the abolition of their local charade of religious authority. The Abbassid caliphs have since been deposed, but their succession continues to the present day; members of the family are still buried within the 13th-century mausoleum. Inside are wooden memorials marking the graves of the caliphs. A caretaker can unlock the gates (E£1 *bakhsheesh* accepted anytime).

From the square in front of Sayyida Nafisa, turn right along El Khalipha St. to find the **Tomb of Shagarat ad-Durr,** the last Ayyubid building to be constructed in Cairo (1250) and the burial place of a politically prominent Muslim woman. Shagarat ad-Durr (Tree of Pearls) was a slave who rose to power after marrying Es-Salih Ayyub, the final ruling member of Salah ad-Din's Ayyubid Dynasty. She concealed the sultan's death in 1249 for three months until her son returned from Mesopotamia to claim the throne. Realizing that her frail son would never muster the authority to command a following among Mamluk slave troops, the wily mother promptly engineered his murder. Proclaiming herself Queen, Shagarat ad-Durr governed Egypt alone for 80 days before marrying the leader of the Mamluk forces and engineering the succession of the Mamluk Dynasty. The renegade couple managed to consolidate power over the next several years, but their happy rule ended when the queen discovered that her new husband was considering a second marriage and had him murdered. Not to be outdone, the prospective second wife avenged the death of her lover by beating Shagarat ad-Durr to death with a pair of wooden clogs and then hurling her body from the top of the Citadel, leaving her corpse to the jackals and dogs. The remains were put together in this small tomb which fails to reflect the significance of its owner. Even so, the wall mosaics are worth the E£1 *bakhsheesh.*

If you turn left at the small market square beyond the tomb, you will reach the Mosque of Ibn Tulun. If you go straight, a right turn at the next big street will return you to the Citadel and the Mosque of Sultan Hassan.

OLD CAIRO

A day's exploration through Coptic Cairo and Fustat will confirm the image of Cairo as a meeting place of the minds; Coptic, Jewish, and Islamic monuments sit side by side here. Nine hundred years before victorious Fatimids founded the city of El Qahira, the Roman fortress town of Babylon occupied the strategic apex of the Nile Delta just 5km south of the later city site. This outpost became a thriving metropolis during the 4th century CE, and a number of churches were built within the walls of the Roman fortress. Old Cairo includes the Fustat area, a handful of beautiful Coptic churches, the excellent Coptic Museum, and the Mosque of Amr.

Located outside the walls of the Islamic city, Old Caraways also the center of Cairo's Jewish community. Although most of the Jewish population of the city left in 1949 and 1956, approximately 30 Jewish families still inhabit this quarter and worship at the ancient Ben-Ezra Synagogue. The fact that Old Cairo is outside the "Islamic City" is somewhat misleading, for it also contains the remains of the first Islamic capital of Egypt, El Fustat.

The easiest way to reach Old Cairo is to take the Metro from Tahrir Sq. towards Helwan to Mari Girgis station (50pt). Buses #92, 94, 134, or 140 also run from Tahrir Sq., stopping beside the Mosque of Amr. If you take a taxi to the outskirts of Old Cairo (E£2-3), ask to go to *Masr el-Qadima* or *Gami 'Amr*. All of the sights listed below are within walking distance of each other. Most of Cairo's Coptic churches are tucked away from the street, and the older structures have simple entrances. Though none of the churches in Coptic Cairo charge admission, all contain donation boxes. Those seeking serenity should avoid these sights on Sunday or the churches' Saint's day, when hundreds of Coptic Cairenes and their children migrate from church to church receiving blessings and pronouncing their faith (churches open daily 9:30am-5pm; masses daily 7-9am; no photography).

Coptic Cairo

Ancient Egypt inspires images of towering pyramids, hieroglyphics, mummy cases slathered in jewels, and Cleopatra. Many assume that the pharaonic era shifted directly into the Islamic age of mosques, medieval fortifications, and integration into the Arab world. But for a period beginning in 30 BCE, Hellenistic culture and then Christianity were the dominant forces in Egypt. In the first century CE, Christianity stood as a symbol of resistance against Rome, and continued to be so even after the Roman Empire adopted Christianity in the 4th century CE. Egyptian Christianity was spread by the agency of the Coptic Orthodox Church, which split off from the main body of the Christian Church in 451. Currently, some five to seven million Egyptians are Copts. Most live in Cairo or in Middle Egypt (see **The Coptic Church,** p. 65).

In front of the Mari Girgis Metro Station is the **Coptic Museum** (tel. 363 97 42 or 362 87 66), home to the world's largest and finest collection of Coptic art, texts, textiles, metalwork, and iconographic materials (see **Museums,** p. 123). If you don't have expendable pounds for the museum, you can get a pretty good idea of the Coptic tradition by visiting the area's churches for free.

In front of the museum stands Cairo's only substantial classical ruin: the imposing **Roman battlement** that originally flanked the main entrance to the **Fortress of Babylon,** built by Emperor Trajan in the first century CE. This particular bastion (the only remaining one of ten) extended over a full acre, but it only comprised a fraction of the mammoth fortress, which encompassed 60 acres. It took invading Muslims more than seven months to overpower the fortifications in the 640-641 siege. Babylon surrendered only when ordered by Patriarch Cyrus. This section of the fortress was originally part of a massive harbor quay (the fortress overlooked the Nile before the river shifted west). A flight of stairs leads down to the slime-flooded foundation. Visitors are not permitted to use the stairs at all, much less swim.

With your back to the Coptic Museum, the 3rd-century **Church of El Mu'allaqa** (also known as the Church of St. Mary and St. Dimiana), is on your left. The name translates as "the hanging" because it was once suspended 13m above the ground between two bastions of the Fortress of Babylon. It is almost impossible to discern which parts of this repeatedly restored church are new and which old. Pointed arches and colorful geometric patterns enliven the main nave; in the center, an elegant pulpit used only on Palm Sunday rests on 13 slender columns—one for Christ and each of his disciples. The conspicuous black marble symbolizes Judas. Ostrich eggs symbolizing the Resurrection hang over head. El Mu'allaqa is ark-shaped, its roof is held up by eight pillars on each side of the church, one for every member of Noah's family. Because an altar can only administer the liturgy once per day, this church contains seven. Some of these altars are set off by a cedar altar screen. The screen is inlaid with pentagons and crosses of ebony and ivory—all of which are fit together without nails, like a jigsaw puzzle. In the chapel to the right you can sometimes see a carpenter making the intricate lattice.

Among El Mu'allaqa's 110 icons is the 1000-year-old image of St. Mark made with bright, natural pigments. Notice that the tormentor standing above him is striking him with the left hand, traditionally thought of as the weaker hand. Boktor is being tortured, not mercifully killed. The most mesmerizing of the icons is that of the Virgin with her baby son. This church holds a special place in the annals of Coptic belief due to its congregation's involvement in the miracle of Mokattam Mountain: a troublesome caliph picking on the biblical claim that those of faith can move mountains, proposed an ultimatum to Pope Ibrahim Ibn ez-Zar'a and the Coptic population—prove it or die. The congregation stayed to pray in this church three days and three nights. On the third day, each Kyrie eleison (Lord have mercy), accompanied by a bow en masse, supposedly shook the earth and moved Mokattam a few inches. (Coptic Orthodox masses held at El Mu'allaqa on Wed. 7-9am, Fri. 8-11am, and Sun. 6-8:30am and 9-11am.)

On the opposite side of the Coptic Museum is the 6th-century Greek Orthodox **Church of Mari Girgis** (Church of St. George). Erected over one of the towers of the Fortress of Babylon, this church is dedicated to the Roman soldier George. You can't miss him atop his stallion, slaying a reckless dragon. The common circular layout of this church teems with worshippers intent on touching the chains which were supposedly used to torture the saint. The nunnery around the corner claims to have the same chains. If you're in town, visit on April 11th, St. George's special day (open daily 8am-12pm and 2-5pm; free).

To the left as you face the Church of St. George, a staircase on Mari Girgis St. (labeled by a yellow sign proclaiming "free entrance") descends into Old Cairo proper. The first main doorway on the left is marked with a tin plaque indicating the 14th-century **Nunnery of St. George.** Get thee there. You might witness a chain-wrapping ceremony in the chapel. Worshippers symbolically reenact the Saint's persecution and recite a prayer. With your back to the nunnery, head to the left about 50m, until you see the entrance to the **Church of Abu Serga** (St. Sergius) on your right. This 10th-century church has sunken several feet below street level. The Holy Family is believed to have rested in the church's crypt.

Leaving the Church of Abu Serga, turn right and head to the end of the alley. Just to the left lie the cavernous 5th-century **Church of St. Barbara** (pronounced bar-BAR-a) and the Fatimid-era Church of St. Cyrus and St. John. Legend holds that when the caliph discovered both Christian churches being restored, he ordered the architect to destroy one of them. Unable to choose, the architect paced back and forth between the two buildings until he died of exhaustion. Moved, the caliph allowed both to stand. The Church of St. Barbara was rebuilt in the 10th century, when the decorated aisles were added. St. Barbara was killed by her father when she attempted to convert him. Her bones rest in the tiny chapel accessible through a door to the right as you enter her church. St. Catherine's bones supposedly lie here as well (see **St. Catherine's**, p. 253). An inlaid wooden *iconostasis* from the 13th century graces the church's ornate interior. Most of the furniture is now in the Coptic Museum.

With your back to St. Barbara's, the **Ben-Ezra Synagogue** is approximately 25m to the left. The synagogue that occupied the site in pre-Christian times was demolished in the first century CE to make room for construction of the Roman fortress. Later, a Christian church was built on the site; the building was transformed into the present synagogue in the 12th century. Distinctive Sephardic ornaments and a collection of manuscripts, including 6th-century Torah scrolls are kept here. Although most of the Jewish population emigrated, about 120 Jews still live in Cairo.

Fustat

To reach Fustat, take the Metro to the Mari Girgis station. With your back to the station, head north along Mari Girgis St. for about five minutes until you see the Mosque of Amr minarets on your right. Fustat sprawls over the large area behind the mosque. If you venture out to this district in the heat of summer, bring plenty of water. Also be aware that the ground near the site is unstable in places. Avoid this area at night.

Adjoining Coptic Cairo to the north are the partially excavated remains of Fustat, one of the oldest Islamic settlements and the capital of Egypt during its first 250 years as a Muslim province. The architectural remains of Fustat are insubstantial, and a stroll through the site reveals little more than traces of cisterns, drains, cesspits, and rubbish. In the northwest corner of the site, the **Mosque of Amr,** Egypt's first mosque, has been restored for use. In addition to architectural fragments, thousands of pieces of fine Islamic pottery and imported Chinese porcelain have been discovered here; they are currently displayed at the Islamic Museum and in the new Islamic Ceramics Museum. Also behind the Mosque of Amr is the **pottery district,** where you can watch modern-day artisans at work. Kilns heave black smoke from fires fed by leather scraps and garbage. Hold your valuables close and ask before you snap a Kodak moment if you don't want to be charged E£5 by your subjects.

Fustat was the name of a garrison town that some historians maintain comes from the Latin word for entrenchment, *fossatum.* A different account of the founding of Fustat holds that the conquering general Amr sent word to the caliph in Medina that the magnificent Roman port of Alexandria would be the perfect place for the capital of Egypt. To Amr's dismay, the caliph preferred to establish his outposts along desert trade routes, which were invulnerable to the naval attacks of seafaring Christians. The disappointed general returned to Babylon to find that a white dove had nested in his tent during his absence. Interpreting this as a divine omen, Amr founded the new capital of Egypt on the site of his tent, and dubbed it *El Fustat* (City of the Tent).

Fustat remained the capital of Egypt until the Fatimids established the neighboring city of El Qahira in 969 CE. By the middle of the 12th century the Fatimid Dynasty was failing; in 1168, Crusader King Amalric of Jerusalem invaded and fought the Fatimids near Cairo. During the battle, Fustat was burned to the ground to prevent it from falling into the hands of the Crusaders. Except for the great mosque, little survived of the city; by the end of the 14th century Fustat was virtually abandoned.

Credit for the construction of Egypt's first mosque goes to Amr himself, who made many lasting contributions to the nation. During his rule, the mosque served as the seat of government, the post office, and the city's religious center. The huge, open square could accommodate nearly 12,000 worshipers—the size of Amr's army. Fustat later developed a large treasury and elaborate plumbing and sewage systems, the likes of which were not seen in Europe until the 17th century.

The present-day Mosque of Amr occupies the site of the original building of 642, and is four times the size of its predecessor. The oldest portion of the current mosque is its crumbling southeast minaret, added during the Ottoman period. The mosque's 18th-century design includes a single, spacious courtyard lined on four sides by stately white marble columns, pilfered from local Roman and Byzantine buildings during medieval times. The Mosque of Amr was renovated so extensively in the mid-80s that many tourists find it hard to believe that this is Cairo's oldest mosque (open daily 9am-5pm; E£6, students E£3).

Near the Mosque of Amr is **Deir Abu Saffein,** a complex of three 8th-century Coptic churches. Walk straight down the street directly opposite the entrance to the mosque; the wooden entrance to the churches will be about 500m ahead on your right (complex open 8am-5pm).

The main attraction is the **Church of St. Mercurius Felopatir** (or the Church of Abu Seiffein), dating from the 4th century but extensively restored during the Middle Ages. Saint Mercurius Felopatir, a Roman Christian soldier, assured his frazzled king that divine assistance would dispose of the annoying Berbers who were troubling the Empire. After a Roman victory, the king beheaded the no-longer-useful Mercurius. He is called Abu Seiffein (which means "two swords") because an angel gave him a heavenly sword to go with his military saber. The cathedral contains 14 altars, various relics of saints venerated in the Orthodox Church, several early icons, and the original, delicate ebony, ivory, and cedar *hegab* or *iconostasis,* which separates the nave of the church from its front vestibule. The elaborate gabled roof is an impressive feat of Coptic carpentry, as every piece is fitted with the next without screws or nails.

On the northern wall of the main chamber, an icon picturing St. Barsoum marks the entrance to a tiny vaulted crypt where the saint supposedly lived with a cobra for 25 years. For 50pt the *bawwab* (caretaker) will let you descend into the dusty burial chamber. Mass is celebrated in the crypt on St. Barsoum's feast day, September 10. If the caretaker is in a good mood (the E£5 it takes to lift his spirits may not be worth it), he'll take you upstairs to see the ancient, tiny Churches of St. George of Rome, St. John the Baptist, and the 144,000 Martyrs, all of which were rediscovered when the plaster was accidentally chipped away from multiple layers of icons.

Down the street is the late 4th-century **Church of St. Shenouda,** dedicated to one of the most famous Coptic saints. This chapel contains seven altars and two fine *iconostases*—one of red cedar and the other of ebony. The smallest of the three main structures at Deir Abu Saffein is the early 8th-century **Church of the Holy Virgin,** a one-room chapel crammed with rare icons, paintings, and three altars. The *odass* (liturgy) is read in these churches (Sun. 6-10am, Wed. 8am-noon, and Fri. 7-11am).

Crossing the Nile from Old Cairo towards Giza, you may want to stop at the **Nilometer,** at the southern tip of Roda Island. Designed to measure the height of the river and thereby predict the yield of the annual harvest, the structure dates from the 9th century BCE. Under Muhammad Ali's reign, it was restored, and the conical dome was added. Narrow steps descend into a paved pit well below the level of the Nile, culminating at the graduated column that marks river's height. The entrance to the Nilometer is often locked, but if you express interest, one of the local children will pester the nearby custodian (open Sat.-Thurs., 9am-4pm; E£6, students E£3). The eastern entrance is always locked—wait at the western side for assistance.

MODERN CAIRO

Cairo's sidewalks teem with thousands of people. Vendors bellow the virtues of their wares while laundry flutters from the remnants of colonial architecture. In the evenings, particularly on weekends, the latest cinematic gem lets out every two hours and hundreds of film connoisseurs flood the streets, pastry shops, and *ahwas*. An evening stroll along the **Nile** is a Cairene tradition not to be missed.

Cairo's two main islands merit short visits. Dominating **Zamalek** (also called Gezira or "the island") is the 187m **Cairo Tower (Burg El Qahira).** Early or late in the day, you can see the Pyramids, the medieval citadel, and the Delta. For E£18 you can take the elevator to the observation deck, and for another E£11 you will be allowed to use your camcorder. E£59.75 purchases soup, salad, entree, dessert, and the view at the rotating restaurant "Panorama" on the 14th floor (open daily 9am-1am).

Settled only in the last century, Zamalek was once symbolic of Cairo's colonial society; today its quiet streets house diplomats and the expatriate community. The southern third of the island is occupied by the Gezira Sporting Club, the ultimate symbol of British privilege until the 1952 Revolution and a focal point for upper class Cairene life. The one-block stretch around Hassan Sabri St. north of 26 July St. is filled with colorful shops, cafes, bars, and specialty stores. On the eastern shore of the island, near the 26 July Bridge, towers the palatial **Cairo Marriott Hotel.** Built by Khedive Isma'il to house foreign dignitaries and heads of state attending the Suez Canal opening ceremonies in 1869, the palace became a hotel in 1952 and is today considered one of the best luxury hotels in the Middle East.

On the southern tip of Roda Island stands one to Central Cairo's most noteworthy ancient monuments: the **Nilometer,** best visited when you tour Old Cairo (see **Old Cairo,** p. 122). At the northern end of the island, near the Meridien Hotel, stands the wacky Manial Palace Museum (see **Museums,** p. 123).

Walking west across the island from the palace and over the El Gama'a (University) Bridge, you'll reach a lush section of the neighborhood of **Giza.** Straight ahead, at the end of the broad boulevard, is the handsome, crowded campus of **Cairo University.** Along the boulevard to the north stretches the neglected **El Urman Garden** (Botanical Gardens), the best place in town to toss a frisbee or vegetate under a shady tree (open daily 8:30am-5pm, winter 8am-4pm; free; camera privileges 50pt). Along the full length of the boulevard to the south and facing the botanical gardens is the **Cairo**

Zoo, one of the oldest in the world. If zoos have a tendency to make you blue, this one could horrify you with downtrodden animals in dreary conditions. On the other hand, it's a great place to mingle with Egyptian families. The lax security allows you unusually close contact with the animals. Tip the zookeeper and he'll let a giraffe eat off your head. If you time the photo well, it looks like a kiss. If you're lucky, you can watch Makaka the monkey smoke a cigarette (open daily 8am-5pm, but avoid overcrowded Fridays; 20pt, 20pt extra for reptile house and "special collections").

MUSEUMS

Egyptian Museum

The **Egyptian Museum,** the world's unrivaled warehouse of pharaonic treasures, stands in Tahrir Sq. The most conspicuous displays in the museum are not always the most interesting; try not to overlook smaller, tucked-away rooms. But don't look for too long—local legend has it that if you were to spend one second at every exhibited item, it would take six months of non-stop viewing to see everything! Consider a lunch break to help clear your mental palate. Unless you choose to buy the E£100 catalog, the item to check out should be the wall map to the left of the entrance or the CD-ROM presented by the Cultural Preservation Foundation to the right.

In the small glass case opposite the entrance, behind the 3000-year-old monkey, is the **Narmer Palette,** which commemorates the unification of Upper and Lower Egypt in about 3100 BCE by King Narmer. Some believe that King Narmer was the incarnation of Menes, the mythical founder of united Egypt (see **Ancient Egypt,** p. 46). From here, the corridors and rooms leading around the central domed courtyard present a chronological sampling of pharaonic art from the Old Kingdom to the Greco-Roman period.

The unusually well-preserved paint on the **statues** of Prince Rahotep and his wife Nofret (room #32) expresses the extraordinary realism of funerary statues sculpted 47 centuries ago. Nearby stands the world's oldest colossal metal statue, depicting the warlike King Pepi I of the 4th Dynasty. The statue was fashioned by beating heated metal sheets around a wooden core.

Walking down the west corridor, the four rooms on your right each merit a few minutes. The first two feature the best of the Old Kingdom, including a diorite statue of Chephren and a wooden statue named "Sheikh el-Balad" by workers who discovered that it resembled their boss. The third room displays limestones from the Middle Kingdom. The fourth room's claim to fame is the "Egyptian Mona Lisa," an eerie painting in the left corner next to a sandstone mini-chapel from the New Kingdom. Like those of her Italian cousin, the eyes seem to follow you.

In the **Akhenaton room** at the rear of the first floor are statues of the heretical pharaoh who introduced a form of monotheism to ancient Egypt. He worshiped Aton as the sun god, the source of life; Aton was represented as a disk with rays that ended in hands which sometimes held *ankhs,* the Egyptian symbol for life (see **Ancient Egypt,** p. 46). Akhenaton-period artwork is recognizable for its distinctly realistic portraits.

Of all the collections in the museum, the cornucopia from **Tutankhamun's tomb** is the best-displayed and most popular. Originally squeezed into less than 100 cubic meters, the treasures now occupy a quarter of the **second floor.** The eastern corridor contains decorated furniture, golden statues, delicate alabaster lamps, weapons, amulets, fossilized undergarments, and other bare necessities for a King of the Underworld. Room #4, the most magnificent of all, flaunts the famous coffins and funeral masks, as well as an astounding collection of amulets, scarabs, and jewelry. One elegant mask is made with more than 4kg of solid gold inlaid with quartz and lapis lazuli. In the hallway sit the King's internal organs, each in its own gilded coffin.

When your eyes become gold-plated, head to the rooms off the corridor toward the center of the building. Room #43, off the eastern hall, holds a collection of toys, tools, weapons, and household items that reveal how people lived and artisans worked thousands of years ago. Animal rights activists will like Room #53, where mummified cats, dogs, birds, and monkeys repose in frozen honor.

Last, and probably least, the controversial mummy room is in the southeastern corner of the second floor. Former president Sadat closed the famed room in 1981 because the display offended some Islamist groups. The re-opening of the room was delayed by the mummies' continued decomposition, which left them offensive to just about everyone. Now restored and lodged in an isolated, air-conditioned, dimly lit room, the mummies might offend your budget and will not enhance your understanding of the mummification process since there are absolutely no descriptions. Consider, however, that this may be your only opportunity to stare a 5000-year-old man in the eye. You might not get your mummy's worth, and the monkey near room #53 will give you an idea of what its human uncles look like. (Admission to see the carcasses E£60, E£30 for students. Museum open daily 9am-4:30pm. Admission E£20, students E£10. Camera privileges E£10, video E£100.) For more on mummies, see **Who is That Masked Man?** p. 137.

The Coptic Museum

Located in the 19th-century Qasr ash-Shama on Mari Girgis St., the **Coptic Museum** (tel. 363 97 42 or 362 87 66) houses the world's finest collection of Coptic art, with 14,000 pieces. Halls are paved with spotless white marble and a host of elegantly carved wooden *mashrabiyya* screens cover the windows. An added attraction is the museum's location on the site of the ancient Roman fortress of Babylon. The museum, founded in 1908, is home to Coptic metalworks, frescoes, textiles, psalm books, and icons. Compare an icon of the Virgin Mary suckling the Baby Jesus and a carving of the goddess Isis suckling her son, the sun-god Horus. The museum displays a variety of architectural fragments (niches, columns, pulpits, etc.) brought from the sanctuary of St. Menas at Maryut and the monastery of St. Jeremiah at Saqqara, as well as illuminated manuscripts and numerous paintings, icons, and ivories. Don't miss the Coptic textiles (located on the second floor), which were once exported to many quarters of the world. The Library of Gnostics, next to the textiles, contains 7000 volumes of non-standard gospels (e.g., Thomas' gospel) from the 13th and 14th centuries, along with other Coptic texts from various periods. Some of these shine with intricate gold foil, while others barely remain in one piece. The ticket office sells guides for E£4.50 or you can read the English introductions on the walls of each section of the museum. Respite for the tired awaits in the building's tranquil courtyard. The museum is directly across from the Mari Girgis stop on the Metro (open daily 9am-5pm; admission E£16, students E£8; camera privileges E£10, video E£100).

Museum of Islamic Art

Easily combined into a walk through Fatimid Cairo, the **Museum of Islamic Art** (tel. 390 99 30) is housed in a massive pink building in Baab el-Khalq Sq. at the intersections of Port Said St., Muhammad Ali St., and Ahmed Maher St. The museum is the hiding place of many of the artifacts that seem to be missing from the mosques, mausoleums, and *madrasas* of Cairo. Carpets, wood carvings, metalwork, glassware, ceramics, and pottery are masterfully presented in this generally quiet and uncrowded museum. Be sure not to miss the gold-leaf Qur'ans in the calligraphy room (open Sat.-Thurs. 9am-4pm; Fri. 9am-11:30am and 1:30-4pm in winter, 9am-11pm and 2-4pm in summer. Admission E£16, students E£8).

Other Museums

Gayer-Anderson Museum (tel. 364 78 22), just in front of the Ibn Tulun mosque. Originally 2 separate buildings, these 16th- and 18th-century mansions were merged when Major Gayer-Anderson, an English art collector, arrived here in the 1930s. You may recognize some of the rooms from the James Bond flick *The Spy Who Loved Me*. Anderson filled his home with eclectic artifacts and furniture. When he left Egypt in the 1940s, he gave the mansion and its contents to the Egyptian government. A guard will lead you through the maze-like mansion to ensure protection of the priceless pieces. He may also point out secret passageways. Open daily 8am-3:30pm. Admission E£16, students E£8. Camera E£10, camcorder E£25.

The Museum of Egyptian Modern Art (tel. 341 66 65), within the Opera Complex, Zamalek. Walk over the bridge from Tahrir Sq. Tastefully exhibited Egyptian paintings and sculptures from 1922 to the present. A welcome reminder that in a city known for its ancient offerings, art is not confined to coffins. Open Tues.-Thurs. and Sat.-Sun. 10am-1pm and 5-9pm, Fri. 10am-prayer time (around 1:30). Admission E£20, students E£10. If you don't want to fork over the fee, you can still go to the Opera House's **free art gallery,** open daily 10am-1:30pm and 4:30-8:30pm.

The Manial Palace Museum (tel. 98 74 95), at the northern edge of Roda Island; the entrance is near the Cairo Youth Hostel on Sayala St., which leads to Cairo University Bridge. In a complex built by Muhammad Ali in the last century, visitors may access the "reception palace," a private mosque, a residential palace, a throne room, and a fascinating collection of Islamic art. The most intriguing artifact in King Farouk's hunting museum is right by the entrance: a beautiful table made from an elephant's ear. Open Sat.-Thurs. 9am-4pm, Fri. 9am-1pm and 2-4pm. Admission E£10, students E£5. Camera E£10, video E£175.

The Mukhtar Museum (tel. 340 25 19), after Tahrir Bridge and just before El Gala'a Bridge on Tahrir St. in Zamalek. Built by architect Ramses Wissa Wassef, this museum is devoted to the works of sculptor Mahmoud Mukhtar (1891-1934). The museum's most well-known piece is the *Awakening of Egypt.* You might recognize Mukhtar's style from his sculpture in front of the Cairo Zoo or the statue of the man with a raised hand at the base of the Tahrir Bridge. Open Tues.-Sun. 10am-1pm and 5-9pm. Admission E£1, students 50pt.

The Mahmoud Khalil Museum, 1 Kafour St. (tel. 336 23 76), in Giza, 200m from the Giza Sheraton. Contains a fantastic collection of European and Islamic art, including works by Monet, Renoir, Van Gogh, Toulouse-Lautrec, Degas, and Rubens, as well as Chinese jade carvings and Islamic pottery and tiling. Open Sat.-Thurs. 10am-5:30pm. Admission E£25, students E£10. Bring your passport as ID.

Mugamma' el-Funun Center of Arts (tel. 340 82 11), on the corner of Ma'had es-Swissry St. and 26 July Bridge, Zamalek. Formerly the residence of Aisha Fahmy, today the center has rotating exhibitions by Egyptian and foreign artists. It also houses a cinema, theater, and library. The grounds of the Center of Arts boast a somewhat out-of-control garden with decent views of the Nile and downtown Cairo. Open mid-Sept. to mid-July Sat.-Thurs. 10am-1:30pm and occasionally 6-9:30pm for important exhibitions. Free.

Museum of Islamic Ceramics, El Gezira Arts Center, 1 Sheikh Marsafy St., Zamalek, across from the Marriott Hotel. Currently closed, but houses a rare collection from the Ayyubid, Fatimid, and Mamluk eras. Expected to open in early 1998.

The Agricultural Museum (tel. 360 86 82), at the western end of the 6th October Bridge, Dokki, behind a large, attractive garden. A run-down building with more than you ever wanted to know about Egyptian agriculture. Also on display is the only remaining mummified Apis bull from the Serapium at Saqqara. Open Tues.-Sun. 9am-1:30pm. Admission 10pt.

Mohammed Nagui Museum, 9 Mahmoud el-Guindi St., Hudaek el-Haran (off the Cairo-Alexandria road). This collection of works by one of Egypt's leading contemporary artists is a trek, but worth it (you'll need to take a taxi, E£15-20). Housed in Nagui's former studio. Open Tues.-Sun. 10am-5pm. Admission E£10, students E£5.

▓ Shopping

Buying and selling in the Egyptian capital transcends mundane business—it's an intricate game of give-and-take that has evolved over centuries. No price is set in stone—bargaining is required, and successful merchants enjoy the haggle. Remember that the shopkeepers do this for a living and have the benefit of experience. Think of bargaining as a game to be savored, not a battle to be won. If you play hardball, the merchant will not lower the price—chatting will bring you more success. Theatrics, rather than stubbornness, get results. Walk away in disbelief several times. Never get too enthusiastic about the object in question. Instead, point out flaws in workmanship and design. Have a friend discourage you from your purchase—if you seem to be reluctant, the merchant will want to drop the price to interest you again. Your starting price should be half the asking price at most.

Cairo's biggest, most famous market is the **Khan el-Khalili** (see p. 113). Navigating the maze of passages and alleyways that lie within the Khan may seem like madness, but there is method in it. Most gold, copper, and antique dealers lie along Khan al-Khalili St., which changes to al-Badestane St. as it heads east. Perfumes, spices, and cloth can be found a few blocks further south, between Al-Azhar St. and al-Muski St.

In the market south of **Sayyida Zeinab,** each alley offers different wares (Metro: Sayyida Zeinab, then walk 5min. towards the high minarets of the Sayyida Mosque). Other major markets are located northeast of **'Ataba Square** and in **Bulaq** (for 'Ataba Sq. from Tahrir Sq., go eastward along Tahrir St., then up Abd el-Aziz St.; for Bulaq take bus #46). The **Souq el-Tewfikia** runs between Ramses and Tala'at Harb St., one block north of 26 July St. Produce stalls stand beside kitchen-equipment vendors, all laid out in brilliant displays. On hot summer days, hose-holding shopkeepers water the entrance to their shops to reduce heat and settle the dust.

If bargaining doesn't appeal to you, head to one of Cairo's **department stores,** monstrous consumer meccas peddling everything from refrigerators to bikini waxings. The **World Trade Center** on the corniche, north of the Ramses Hilton, is the biggest. A bit less expensive is the **El Yamama Center** (affectionately called the Yo Mama Center by expats), at 3 Dr. Taha Hussein St. in Zamalek, where you can watch music videos or sporting events on the large-screen TV in the ground floor cafe.

Papyrus

The "papyrus" sold throughout Cairo is usually banana leaf, a cheap lookalike. Real papyrus can be scrunched up and will not retain any wrinkles, while banana leaf crackles and stays crunched. To see the real stuff at correspondingly higher prices, head to **Dr. Ragab's Papyrus Factory**, a right turn off the Gala'a Bridge heading west from Tahrir Sq. Another authentic option is the **Said Delta Papyrus Centre** (tel. 512 07 47), located in Islamic Cairo. Within the Khan el-Khalili itself is **Wafik Ismail Ali,** near the Naguib Mahfouz Coffeeshop, which sells fake but surprisingly vivid "papyrus" for around E£10. Instead of searching the bowels of the bazaar for true papyrus, look at artwork and design quality—back home, nobody will be scrunching up your souvenir to test its authenticity.

Backgammon

Et-tawileh boards cost E£80-120, depending on quality and bargaining skills. Make sure the board is absolutely flat when opened and laid on a table, as occasionally they are warped or wobbly. Pieces are often made separately from the board. Check to see that they fit on the triangles, and that there are 15 of each color. You should pay less if the pieces are plastic. **Maka el-Mokarama,** 7 Adly St. (tel. 393 89 80), next to the tourist office, has quality boards without the hassles and fun of Khan el-Khalili.

Spices and Perfume

Thousands of perfume and spice stores give sections of Cairo a fragrant smell. Egyptian spices like *za'tar* are excellent and hard to come by in the West. The quality of perfumes range dramatically. Rub some on the back of your hand—if it's oily or shiny, they've added oil to the perfume to stretch the liquid weight. An ounce can go for as low as E£5. **Harraz Agricultural Seeds, Medicinal, and Medical Plants Co.,** 1 Baab el-Khalq St. sells every imaginable spice at reasonable prices (open Sat.-Thurs. 9am-9pm). If the self-proclaimed "sheikh of spice" won't cut you a good deal, **Khodr,** next door, has similar wares.

Textiles and Clothing

At the **tent-makers bazaar,** south of Baab Zuweila in Islamic Cairo, you can commission the making of a Bedouin tent (far out of a budget traveler's price range) or buy appliqué pillowcases (E£30) and bed covers (E£105). The **Nomad Gallery,** at 14 Saraya el-Gezira, 1st floor, Zamalek (tel. 341 19 17), near the Marriott, is known for its top-quality jewelry, textiles, and crafts. They're not big bargainers here, but their prices are as low as you could get them at the tent-makers bazaar (open Mon.-Sat. 10am-3pm; credit cards accepted). Without a doubt, the best places to shop for woven **rugs** are the stores along **Saqqara Rd.,** near the Pyramids, where Harania artists weave up a storm (see p. 136).

There's a crazy **second-hand clothing market** daily at the east end of 26 July Bridge. The stands hawk modern Western clothing, 60s Western clothing, and even some traditional Egyptian garb. Women tired of getting hissed at can pick up a *gallabiyya* here or splurge on a new one at the market south of El Ghouri Mosque and Khan el-Khalili on El Muizz St.

Jewelry and Metalware

Islamic Cairo is the center of the jewel trade, and prices tend to be markedly lower than in the West. Often, gold or silver jewelry can be made to order for barely more than the cost of the metal itself. There are still a number of scam artists out there, so be wary of jewelers who weigh the precious items out of sight. Make sure to shop around—there is a surprising amount of variety out there, and price shopping can save you from getting ripped off.

Plates and trays of varying sizes, engraved with intricate designs, are available throughout the *Khan* for E£15-20. You may also be able to find either copper or brass mugs, coffeepots, and ashtrays, but nothing is as old as the shopkeeper claims.

■ Entertainment

As the sun sets on the Egyptian capital, *sheesha* smoke fills the air, the corniche fills up with strollers, and the upper crust gets decked-out for discotheques and salons. *Cairo by Night,* a free weekly periodical available in hotels, describes happenings around town, and *Egypt Today,* a monthly magazine sold at newsstands, runs articles on attractions in the metropolitan area and lists foreign films, musical performances, and art exhibits.

During **Ramadan** (Dec. 31-Jan. 30), Cairenes take to the streets around Al-Azhar and Hussein Sq. and along the corniche and the bridges across the Nile. Starting at around 10pm, there are street performances, magic shows, and general shenanigans. Most cinemas have midnight screenings during this month.

AHWAS AND CASINOS

Although you'll never guess it from observing Cairo's drivers, city folk love to relax, meet with friends, and contemplate the sweet mysteries of life in the *ahwas* (coffeehouses) that dot many street corners and alleys east of the Nile. A typical *ahwa* will have gossipers in one corner, backgammon players in another, and *sheesha* smoke and Turkish coffee steam everywhere. *Sheesha* smoke is much stronger than cigarettes, but the smoke is more delicious. Foreign men and women are welcomed at all *ahwas* listed below, but not all *ahwas* in the city.

Fishawi's Khan el-Khalili (tel. 90 67 55), 4 doors down from El Hussein Hotel, just off El Hussein Sq. Since 1752, this traditional teahouse in the heart of the old bazaar has served the most famous *sheesha* in Egypt. Nicknamed "Cafe des Miroirs," Fishawi's is furnished in 19th-century European style with hammered brass tables that can barely hold two cups. Order as the locals do: a pot of mint tea, a cold *karkadeh,* and an aromatic *sheesha* (all under E£3). Open daily 24hr.

Maroush, 64 Lebanon St., Mohandiseen (tel. 645 09 72), a E£5-7 taxi ride from downtown. Skip the hoity-toity restaurant upstairs and head to the patio for a cool, laid-back *sheesha.* Open daily 8am-2am.

Bint es-Sultan, As-Sawra Sq., Mohandiseen, behind the Shooting Club (Nadi es-Sayd). This ritzy *ahwa* has breezy, outdoor tables for pleasurable idleness. Min. charge E£7 in the evening. Open daily 10am-1am.

In the evenings, middle-class Egyptian couples swarm to the cafes, called **casinos,** lining the Nile on Gezira Island. Some of these are boats permanently anchored at the edge of the water. The **Casino an-Nil,** on the west side of Tahrir Bridge, is one of the best (min. charge E£6). Dozens of others range from simple to swank. Most are jammed on Thursday nights, partially because of post-nuptial *haflahs* (parties). For real **gambling,** head for the Nile Hilton, Marriott, or Sheraton hotel. You must show your passport to enter and are not permitted to game with Egyptian currency. Don't worry—they can change E£ to US$ faster than you can lose them (min. bet US$5). Drinks are free as long as you gamble.

PASTRIES, ICE CREAM, AND COFFEE

El 'Abd, 25 Tala'at Harb St. (tel. 392 44 07), opposite the Arab Bank building. This upscale bakery provides the perfect antidote for Cairo's heat—a whopping 3-scoop ice-cream cone for E£1.50! The croissants here are the best in Cairo (E£1). Pay first, then take the token to the scooper. You can ask to try any of the pastries. Open daily 9am-11pm. Another branch is on 26 July St., 1 block east of the intersection with Tala'at Harb St.

La Poire, 18 Latin America St. (tel. 346 10 67), across the street from the British Embassy in Garden City. Come for the extensive selection of ice cream flavors (E£1.75 per scoop), but stay for the croissants, eclairs, and sticky-sweet *ba'laweh* (E£2.50). All pastries made on the premises and best enjoyed with a cup of flavorful cappuccino or espresso (E£2.25). Open daily 7am-midnight.

Simonds Coffee Shop, 26 July St., Zamalek (tel. 340 94 36), just east of the intersection with Hasan Sabri St. Italian feel lures an eclectic mix of locals and foreign emissaries. Espresso drinks, hot chocolate, lemonade (E£1.25 each), pastries (E£1.75).

Samadi, 47 El Batal Ahmed Abd el-Aziz St., Mohandiseen, off Gam'at ed-Duwal St. Most Egyptians recognize Samadi as the best pastry shop in Egypt. Crunchy, toasty, and super-sweet treats. Try their *burma.* Open daily 9am-3am.

Mandarin Koedar, 17 Shagaret ed-Durr St., Zamalek (tel. 340 50 10). Take a right off 26 July St. at the Misr Gas Station onto Shagaret ed-Durr St., then follow the crooked street for 200m. The exceptional ice cream is pricey (E£1.75 per scoop) and the pastry selection is limited, but the heavy-duty A/C and elegant interior make up for it. Open daily 9am-11pm.

Flamenco Postres, 11 Corniche Abul Feda (tel. 340 08 15, ext. 422), behind the Flamenco Hotel on the western side of Zamalek. Wonderful breads (E£8-12). Open daily 7am-11pm.

CLUBS

Cairo is oceans away from Rio, Barcelona, or Montreal. Dance clubs are fewer, tamer, and less crowded, but there is a unique scene. The clubs on **Pyramids Road** in Giza can overflow with sweaty shimmiers, and evenings often degenerate into pick-up fests. Disco balls in major hotels spin above more behaved crowds.

Jackie's Joint, Nile Hilton, Tahrir Sq. (tel. 578 04 44). As Cairo's new hot spot, "the Joint" has lines out the door most nights. To improve your chances at the door, wear something sleek, black, and non-denim, and bring a date. Minimum charge E£25. Open daily 10pm-3am.

Atlas, or **Tamango,** Atlas Zamalek Hotel, 9th floor (tel. 346 41 75). Still all the rage with the young Arab clientele of this hotel, Atlas continues to pack in Armani- and Drakkar-Noir-clad Egyptians. Students and expats file in to get down to the latest Euro and Arabic dance music. Dress is *haute*-casual. Men unaccompanied by women are turned away. Admission E£45. Open daily 10:30pm-3:30am.

Casanova Disco (tel. 341 47 46), in the El Burg Hotel, Zamalek; over the Tahrir Bridge, by the Opera House. Solo men are not admitted to this popular groovefest. Cover charge of E£30 includes a drink. Open daily 10:30pm-4:30am.

Atlantis, Shepheard Hotel, Corniche en-Nil, Garden City (tel. 355 34 00). It seems that when the Russian strip show left the Atlantis a few months ago, so did all the customers. The talented DJ spins to a nearly empty room most nights, but lots of flashing neon keeps things lively. Couples only. Admission E£45.

BARS

Cairenes aren't known for beer-guzzling, but they do have a good number of bars, considering the Islamic prohibition against alcohol. The liveliest bars are filled with non-Muslim expats. For great eats with your pint, try **Harry's Pub** (see p. 106). Most bars listed here have plentiful snackage as well.

Deals, 2 El-Maahad El-Swissri St., Zamalek (tel. 341 05 02), a right turn off 26 July St. at the base of the bridge to downtown. Cairo's younger set mingles in this tiny restaurant and bar, attracted by the low prices and eclectic decor. Fried chicken drumsticks with thick bleu cheese dressing provide a diet-busting complement to your Stella; you can also order French wine by the glass. A/C and loud rock music ensures that this popular hangout fills quickly. Open daily 4:30pm-2am.

Pub 28, 28 Shagaret ed-Durr St., Zamalek (tel. 340 92 00), kitty-corner to the Mandarin ice cream store. Take a right off 26 July St. at the Misr Gas Station; the pub's brick facade will be on your left. A top choice of expats, upper class Egyptian businessmen, and the occasional flight attendant. Steaks are juicy and big (E£24), and the club sandwich won't break your bank (E£10). Open noon-2am. Visa and AmEx.

Cairo Cellar, 22 Taha Hussein St., Zamalek (tel. 341 67 51), in the basement of the President Hotel. Head north on Shagaret ed-Durr St. off of 26 July St., until it zigzags and becomes Taha Hussein St. *Cheers*-style familiarity draws a crowd of regulars. Not as hip or accessible as Pub 28 or Deals, but attentive service makes this a worthwhile stop. Open daily noon-2am. Visa, MC, AmEx.

Odeon Palace, off Tala'at Harb St., 1 block east of Tala'at Harb Sq. A relaxing spot for insomniacs. Cheap beer, food, and *sheesha* on the roof. Open 24hr.

Taverne du Champs du Mars (tel. 578 04 44, ext. 289), in the Nile Hilton Hotel. The entire Belle Époque interior of this bar was brought from Belgium and reassembled. Parisian atmosphere and prices (Stella E£12, snacks E£20-30), but the E£15 cover charge includes a beer, and the ambience is hard to beat. Open daily 11am-1am. Visa, MC, AmEx.

Longchamp, 21 Ismail Mohammed St., Zamalek (tel. 340 23 11 or 12), on the 5th floor of the Longchamp Hotel. Turn north onto Shagarat ad-Durr from 26 July St., then left onto Ismail Mohammed St. Share Stellas (E£10-25) with a foreign businessman in this tranquil terrace bar. An old radio provides quiet musical interludes. Open daily 4pm-2am.

PERFORMING ARTS

Dance

Mausoleum of El Ghouri (tel. 510 08 23), on El Muizz St., just south of the pedestrian overpass near Al-Azhar University in Islamic Cairo. Hosts **whirling dervishes** every Wed. and Sat. night (summer 9pm, winter 8pm; be sure to arrive one hour early as the seats fill up fast). No video cameras, but flash photos allowed. In any case, it's hard to capture the beauty of the Sufi dancers on film. Free.

Balloon Theater (tel. 347 74 57 or 17 18), on En-Nil St. at the Zamalek Bridge, Agouza. Regular performances of **Rida's Troupe,** one of the best Egyptian folk dance companies in Cairo. Also hosts plays and famous Arab singers. Tickets E£10-30. Shows daily at 9:30pm.

Falafel Restaurant (tel. 77 74 44), at the Ramses Hilton. Serves an excellent but expensive *prix-fixe* dinner (E£95), including a fabulous **folk dancing** show by the Hasan Troupe. Call the Ramses Hilton for details.

Coquillage (tel. 340 61 26), at the foot of Tahrir Bridge, Zamalek, connected to the Qasr en-Nil casino. Arabic dancing and singing makes this place hop at night. People lounge in this lavish hall of stained glass and Roman columns overlooking the Nile. A dinner of spaghetti or fettucine with chicken (E£30) will dazzle your palate; the variety show will dazzle your eyes and ears. Open daily 11am-4am. Visa, MC.

Nile Maxim Cruise (tel. 340 88 88), at the Marriott Hotel in Zamalek. Glitzy Nile cruiser with chandeliers, mirrors, enormous windows, and jacked-up A/C. Superb meals cost between E£65-105, but it pays for the belly dancers, sufi dancers, and lounge lizards. 2hr. trips depart every evening at 8 and 11pm. Call to reserve a spot.

Twist and Shout

Known to Westerners as the whirling dervishes, the **Sufi** sect of Islam began in Konya, Turkey, during the mid-13th century. The origin of the word Sufi is a mystery. Some think that it's derived from the root *suf* (wool), used to describe the woolen garments worn by the first members of the sect. Another school of thought is that Sufi comes from the Greek *sophos,* meaning wisdom. The Persian word *darwish* literally means the "sill of the door"—hence, *dervish* would refer to the Sufi who is at the doorstep of Paradise or enlightenment.

The dervishes hope to cast off mundane worries and reach a higher spiritual plane through their perpetually whirling dance. The ritual is an entrancing display of color and devotion, a dizzying spin during which the dervish throws off cloak after cloak of earthly possession, eventually left with the soaring white fabric of his inner robe. Their spiritual dance likely inspired the "spinners" made famous at Grateful Dead concerts.

Music and Theater

Cairo Opera Complex (tel. 342 05 98), Opera House in Gezira, southern Zamalek. This massive new complex hosts the symphony orchestra, jazz performances, and visiting operas. Jacket and tie are required for the opera only, and travelers have been known to borrow snazzy clothing from kind hostel workers. Tickets for the small hall can be had for as little as E£2 (E£10 for the main hall). Box office open daily 9am-9pm. Check *Al Ahram* newspaper (75pt) for current performances.

Goumhouriyya Theater (tel. 342 21 53 or 21 59), at the intersection of Goumhouriyya and Abd el-Aziz St., Giza. Performances by the Arabic Music Troupe and the Cairo Symphony Orchestra, usually on Fri. evenings.

Wallace Theater (tel. 357 50 22 or 69 34), on the New Campus, Muhammad Mahmoud St. near McDonald's off Tahrir Sq. Run by the American University in Cairo (AUC). Features two plays in English per year. The AUC also hosts a variety of concerts, from jazz to chamber music, and free movie festivals at the library. Open fall-spring. Check bulletin boards on the Old Campus (near the bookstore), or call.

Cairo Puppet Theater (tel. 591 09 54 or 83 67), in Azbakia Gardens near Opera Sq. Performances in Arabic, but universally understood. Shows Wed.-Mon. at 7:30pm, Fri. and Sun. matinee at 10:30am. All tickets E£3.

British Council, 192 En-Nil St., Agouza (tel. 303 15 14), 1 block south of 26 July St. next to Balloon Theatre. Sponsors free performances by visiting British artists and groups and sometimes presents films. Call for information on upcoming events. Facilities include a large library with CD and video privileges and a traveler-oriented teaching center. Main office open Sun.-Thurs. 9am-3pm.

Egyptian Center for International Cultural Cooperation, 11 Shagarat ed-Durr St. (tel. 341 54 19), Zamalek. Free art exhibitions, lectures, tours, and performances Sept.-June.

OTHER DIVERSIONS

In the last few years, **billiards** has become the cool pursuit in Cairo, especially among the Gezira Sporting Club set. Expect to pay E£10-20 per game for pool and E£20-25 for snooker. Sunglass-clad players show off at **Alamein,** in the World Trade Center, 119 Corniche en-Nil (tel. 340 99 87), and **Versailles,** at 10 Muhammad Thakeb Pasha St. in Zamalek (tel. 341 89 80; open 10am-2am). **Aristocrat,** 15 Isma'il Muhammad, Zamalek (tel. 341 26 28), is an American University of Cairo (AUC) student haunt (open 24hr.). The pool tables at **Whiskies Pub,** 20 Gam'at ed-Duwal el-Arabiyya St., Mohandiseen (tel. 346 65 69, 41 75, or 72 30), are a stairwell away from dancing at Atlas Zamalek Hotel (open late).

At **Sacha,** 29 Ahmed Heshmat St., 7th floor, Apt. 2, Zamalek (tel. 340 61 67), in the massive building with the "TK&M" sign on the side, you can treat yourself to aromatherapy or reflexology for E£70. Hop into an aerobics class (E£10, students E£8) or use the gym for a day (E£18). This place is a popular workout spot for in-shape AUC students and Western women who realize that a run on the streets of Cairo is next to impossible (open Sat.-Thurs. 9am-9pm, Fri. 9am-4pm). **Jazzercise** is available elsewhere in Zamalek; call the Jazzercise hotline (tel. 340 33 32) for details.

For those looking to get some exercise and maybe a little something extra on the side, the **Cairo Hash House Harriers** meet year-round, two hours before sunset, for daily walks and runs in Cairo. For further information, call "Sir Clugs" (tel. 347 66 63) or check out their website at www.cairohash.com. The **Creative Dance and Fitness Center** gives classes in *tae kwon do*, gymnastics, self-defense, *kung fu*, ballet, jazz, flamenco, ballroom, and belly dancing. They've got a gym and a steam room to relax sore muscles after all that dancing. Locations are in Ma'adi (tel. 352 12 52) and Dokki (tel. 361 26 13).

Cairo has a few **cinemas** that run English-language films about four to six months behind their release in the U.S.; check the *Al-Ahram* newspaper (75pt) for listings. All of these air-conditioned theaters are packed with Egyptian hipsters on Thursday nights. Seats closer to the screen are cheaper than those in the balcony, a remnant of the British colonialist belief that people whose feet were above others' heads were of a higher class. (Films usually run at 1, 3:30, 6:30, and 9pm, with a midnight showing on Thurs. Tickets E£8-10, E£15-20 for balcony.)

Consider hiring a swallow-winged **felucca** and lazing on the river during the day or night. Most *feluccas* can accommodate up to eight people comfortably. The more passengers, the cheaper. Bargain for a good rate. *Feluccas* for hire dock just south of the Qasr en-Nil (Tahrir) Bridge on the east bank. Across the corniche (on the water) from the Meridien Hotel, shrewd negotiators can snag a boat for E£5 during the day, E£7 in the evening. A nominal tip (E£1-2) is expected at the cruise's completion. Travelers seeking multi-day cruises should see *Let's Go*'s advice on p. 178.

Hantour (horse carriages) are also enjoyable, especially on a breezy evening, and will prove that Cairo is far more than a one-horse town. Avoid those in front of major hotels, particularly in the summer when Saudi tourists inflate prices. Don't pay more than E£10 for a lengthy ride (30min.).

About 5km south of downtown in Jacob's Island in Giza is the Disney-esque **Pharaonic Village** (tel. 571 86 75), founded by former ambassador Dr. Ragab, Ph.D., who also claims to be the papyrus king of Egypt. Visitors board motorboats and chug through canals past statues of the gods and historically reconstructed scenes of ancient papyrus-making, temple-wall-painting, mummification, etc. All this is described in detail by a guide speaking the language of your choice. Disembark to view a temple, houses, and King Tut's tomb reconstructed to appear as it did when Howard Carter discovered it in 1922. The price is quite steep, but you get tons of information without having to read a thing or move too many muscles. It's only worth it if you're not going to see the real thing in Luxor (open 9am-9pm, winter 9am-5pm; E£40 per person, E£30 for groups of 10 or more; lunch E£17).

You can catch a **soccer (futbol) game** at the stadium on Ramses St., in Nasser towards the airport. Local rivals Zamalek and Ahly take on teams from further afield. Riot police seem to outnumber flag-wielding fans. Be cautious of the people next to you; if their team scores, they may set off a firecracker. If you're more interested in seeing ballistic fans than athletes, grab a bleacher seat (E£5). First- and second-class seats are E£25 and E£10 respectively. A bus runs to **Hedmet Sted** from Abd el-Moneim Riyadh Station beneath the Ramses Hilton (50pt). Games start at 3pm or 9pm—check *Al-Ahram* newspaper or ask around.

Budding thespians can either watch or perform with the **Cairo Players** (tel. 340 01 37), an amateur theater group that organizes regular productions, play readings, and drama workshops. Membership is available only to English speakers (congratulations—you've got the part!). Environmentalists can commune with the like-minded Egyptians and foreigners of the **Tree Lovers' Association** (tel. 352 93 65), dedicated to planting trees and protecting nature in Egypt.

On the **Fourth of July,** homesick American budgeteers' dreams come true at the Cairo American Primary and Secondary School, Ma'adi, where 5000 Americans consume all the hot dogs, soft drinks, and pot luck they can stuff into their pot bellies while discussing world domination. Just bring your American passport—you've already paid in taxes. Call the embassy for hours and directions.

NEAR CAIRO

■ Pyramids at Giza الاهرام

For the hundreds of thousands of tourists who flock here each year, the Pyramids *are* Ancient Egypt. The straight lines of the Pyramids contrast with the rolling dunes of the desert, arousing wonder with their angular beauty. Originally constructed to honor the pharaohs in death, these three massive stone monoliths are also monuments to generations of slaves who devoted their lives to building them. While all of the royal loot has been plundered by grave robbers, the enormous stones still tower over the desert with timeless grandeur.

Since everyone likes to see awe-inspiring monuments to human achievement, nowhere else is Egypt's ravenous tourist industry so persistent. For a solid mile leading up to the pyramids, souvenir shops, alabaster factories, and papyrus museums conspire to pawn off ancient artifacts made while-u-wait. At the foot of the Pyramids, an army of hustlers not unlike the Biblical swarm of locusts hounds you: Bedouin imposters rent camels and Arabian race horses, children peddle tourist dreck at inflated prices, and self-appointed guides approach at every turn. *La, shukran* ("no thanks") can prove useful at the Pyramids, even with the man who claims to be the mayor of Giza (he isn't). Don't let the racket deter you from spending at least a few hours exploring this seventh wonder of the ancient world.

PRACTICAL INFORMATION

To get to the Pyramids *(El Ahram)*, take either **minibus** #83 (40pt), or the faster **microbus** (50pt). Both leave from the station in front of the Nile Hilton. The last stop is often 1km from the Pyramids.

Hotel managers in Cairo can arrange a **tour.** Mr. Salah Muhammad (tel./fax 298 06 50; email samo@intouch.com) offers chauffeur-driven tours of Memphis, Saqqara, the carpet school at Harania, and the Pyramids at Giza for E£23, entrance fees excluded (leave at 9am, return exhausted at 5pm; E£5 *Let's Go* discount if you book directly with him). The exuberant Salah can get you to the Pyramids, but won't be able to tell you what they're about. If the group is big, he can procure a guide for an extra E£60 (shared by the whole group). He also offers a free 24-hour **shuttle service** from the airport to downtown Cairo for *Let's Go* users who take his tour (see **Entry**, p. 72).

The **Giza Tourist Office** (tel. 383 88 23), on Pyramids Rd., next to the police station, can't offer more than bus information and suggested prices for rides (open daily 8:30am-5pm). A **tourist police** station is adjacent to the ticket office. Rest houses next to the Cheops Pyramid and the Sphinx sell overpriced refreshments. Both have **public bathrooms,** where attendants expect tips for handing you towels.

Renting a **horse** can be fun, even though many of the overworked and underfed animals have one hoof in the glue factory. For longer rides and more reliable beasts, walk beyond the Sphinx and turn right after the Sound and Light Auditorium. You'll find a row of reputable establishments including **AA Stables** (tel. 385 05 31; open 5am-8pm) and **SA Stables** (tel. 385 06 26; open 7am-11pm). They provide professional equipment (boots, hats, etc.) for a reasonable charge. Although the tourist police post prices for an hour ride at E£12 for a horse and E£10 for a camel, the going price at these establishments is closer to E£20 for a guided trek on either. E£5-10 is a fair price without a guide (in the unlikely occasion that the owner agrees), but one should be a confident rider; some mounts only obey hieroglyphics and may gallop swiftly off into the desert, ignoring their riders' hysterical yells.

Go early to beat the crowds, or plan your trip for Friday, when most of the hagglers take the day off. Failing that, visit between the Pyramids' official closing time of 5pm and sunset, when the site is free of tourists and hustlers. You can't get inside the Pyramids or boat museum past 5pm, however. Good shoes are key if you plan on internal climbing (external climbing is no longer permitted).

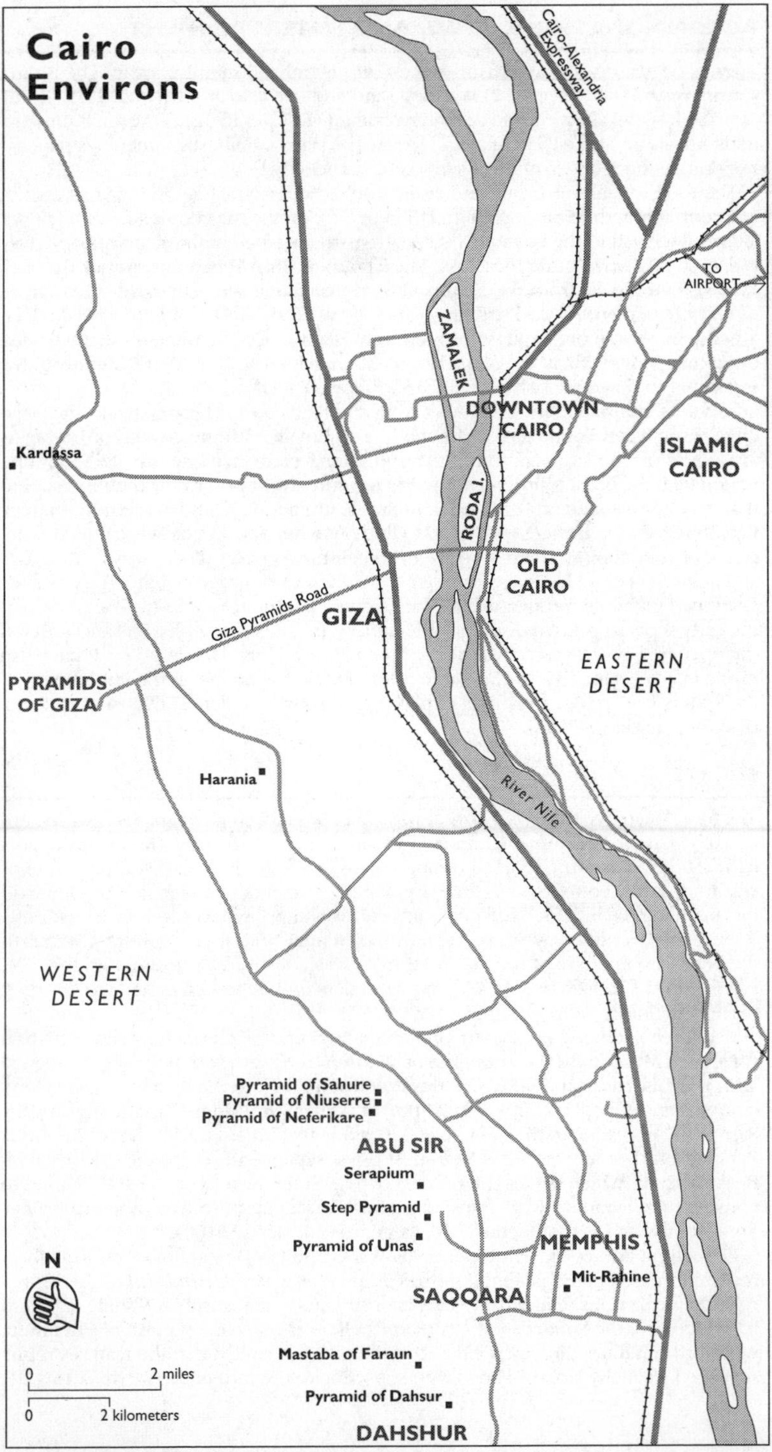

Cairo Environs

Kardassa

ZAMALEK

DOWNTOWN CAIRO

RODA I.

ISLAMIC CAIRO

OLD CAIRO

TO AIRPORT

Cairo-Alexandria Expressway

Giza Pyramids Road

GIZA

PYRAMIDS OF GIZA

EASTERN DESERT

Harania

River Nile

WESTERN DESERT

Pyramid of Sahure
Pyramid of Niuserre
Pyramid of Neferikare

ABU SIR

Serapium

Step Pyramid

Pyramid of Unas

MEMPHIS

Mit-Rahine

SAQQARA

N

Mastaba of Faraun

Pyramid of Dahsur

DAHSHUR

| 0 | 2 miles |
| 0 | 2 kilometers |

ACCOMMODATIONS, FOOD, AND ENTERTAINMENT

There's no reason to stay in Giza since Cairo is only 30 minutes away. The **Salma Campground** (tel. 384 91 52) is a nice sand and sun retreat, however. It has semi-clean toilets and showers and a small restaurant (E£7 per night). Take a left off Pyramids Rd. at the Maroutiya Canal and follow the signs. Minibuses sometimes pass by, but don't count on it. Without a car you're stranded here.

The food situation is bleak, and again, you're better off eating in Cairo if you can hold out. If not, the **Felfela Café** (tel. 383 02 34), on the Alexandria Rd. about 500m after the turn-off to the Pyramids, serves Egyptian fast-food in the same passable way it does at its myriad other locations. The **Pyramids Shishkebab Restaurant** (tel. 385 10 78), two blocks from the Sphinx Rest House along the main road has a cheap *ta'miyya/shawerma* stand and serves traditional salads, *fuul*, and *falafel* inside (E£1-4 per item, meat more expensive; open daily 10am-1am). The **Khan el-Khalili Coffee Shop** (tel. 383 68 28), at the Mena House Oberoi Hotel at the end of Pyramid St., is a sleek spot to sip coffee or mint tea (E£3.25; open 24hr).

As far as entertainment goes, it's the Pyramids or bust. There's always the over-rated, overpriced **Sound and Light** show. You can sit with the crowds of Egyptians anywhere on the site and watch the show for free. Otherwise, pay E£33 and be seated with the other tourists—not worth it if you saw or plan to see the show at Karnak (two shows nightly, 6:30 and 9:30pm in summer, 6:30 and 7:30pm in winter). Call 385 28 80 or check *Egypt Today* to find out when the Sphinx will gab in the language of your choice. The first show is in English except on Wednesdays, Thursdays and Sundays. For added surrealism, go on a different language's night. The Sphinx's chagrined expression suggests it wishes it could get the rest of its head shot off. Hit the early show to get two displays—the under-par laser show with a real-life sunset as the opener. The expensive bars at the **Mena House Hotel** (tel. 383 32 22) have live music in an elegant setting. If it's solitude you seek, the people in the stables next to the Sphinx can arrange overnight expeditions through the dunes (E£20-45, see **Practical Information,** p. 132).

SIGHTS

The three main pyramids *(haram)* at Giza were built for three pharaohs from the 4th dynasty: **Cheops** (Khufu), **Chephren** (Khafre), and **Mycerinus** (Menkaure). This father-son-grandson trio reigned during the 26th century BCE. Each of the pyramids was once attached to its own funerary complex, including a riverside pavilion and mortuary temple in which the pharaoh's cult was supposed to continue for eternity. A long, narrow causeway linked the mortuary temple with the neighboring waters of the Nile. The mummy of the deceased ruler was conveyed by boat across the Nile, carried up the causeway in a solemn procession, and deposited in its sacred resting place at the heart of the pyramid.

The three pyramids are lined up in descending order of chronology and size, from Cheops to Mycerinus. The entrances of all three face north and the bases are aligned with the four cardinal points. The ticket will admit you to the Pyramids and Sphinx complexes. (Site open daily 6:30am-8pm; in winter 7am-10pm. Pyramids open daily 8am-5pm. Admission to the complex E£20, students E£10; to the interior of the Great Pyramid E£20, students E£10.) You must buy a separate ticket for the Cheops Solar Boat Museum, which details the process by which the huge alabaster blocks used to construct the Pyramids were transported from Upper Egypt to Giza (open daily 9am-5pm; admission E£20, students E£10, camera E£10, video E£100).

Crouching below the three pyramids is the **Sphinx.** Hewn almost entirely from rock, the poised figure is 80m long and 22m tall. Known as *Abul-Hul* (father of terror), the mysterious feline man wears an inscrutable, almost sublime smile. Opinion is divided over the Sphinx's identity. Some believe the face is a portrait of Chephren, whose pyramid lies directly behind it, while others maintain that the features represent the local deity Horan. Those who subscribe to the former theory think that the

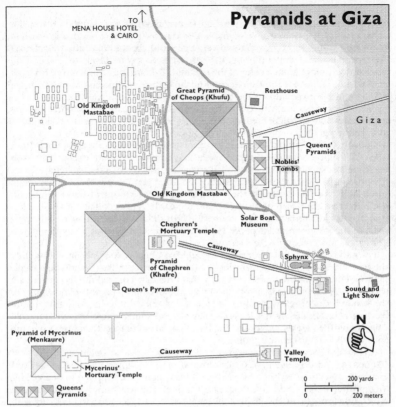

Pyramids at Giza

TO
MENA HOUSE HOTEL
& CAIRO

Old Kingdom
Mastabae

Great Pyramid
of Cheops (Khufu)

Resthouse

Causeway

Giza

Queens'
Pyramids

Nobles'
Tombs

Old Kingdom Mastabae

Solar Boat
Museum

Chephren's
Mortuary Temple

Causeway

Sphynx

Pyramid
of Chephren
(Khafre)

Queen's Pyramid

Sound and
Light Show

Pyramid of Mycerinus
(Menkaure)

Causeway

Valley
Temple

Mycerinus'
Mortuary Temple

Queens'
Pyramids

N

0   200 yards
0   200 meters

EGYPT

Sphinx emerged from a sturdy knoll facing Chephren's complex. Failing to flatten it, architects transformed it into the figure you see today. Another tale tells how Chephren, living a life of luxury, had fallen asleep by the sphinx's foot while hunting. The Sphinx spoke out and said, "I shall make thee Pharaoh if thou wilt dig me out of the sand." This theory does not sit well with archaeologists, who suggest that the body and head of the sphinx were carved at different times. They argue that these two parts of the Sphinx are not proportional to one another and that the erosion styles of the body and head are different. Whatever explanation you believe, the majesty of this work of art is indisputable. Wind and time have visibly aged the soft limestone of this noble creature. Used for target practice during the Turkish occupation, the Sphinx lost not only its nose but also its beard (the latter is now in the British Museum), and a large chip fell from its shoulder in 1988. The Sphinx is getting a nose job and a face lift to prevent the rest of his features from sliding off. The renovation process is nearly finished (they're currently refurbishing his tail end), and the stone glows with newfound cleanliness. At the foot of the Sphinx, just around the corner to the south, is the I-shaped **Valley Temple of Chephren,** discovered in 1853. Sixteen great pillars support the roof of this edifice, soaring to a height of 15m each.

The **Pyramid of Cheops,** built around 2550 BCE, is the first pyramid you'll encounter upon entering the site. It initially stood 146m high, but over the course of four and a half millennia its height has decreased by 9m. While the exact technology used in building the pyramid is still debated, it is now believed that it took 10,000 people about 11 years and 2.3 million limestone blocks to build this great monument. The total weight of Cheops is estimated at 6,000,000 tons. One story recounts that Cheops hired his daughter out as a courtesan and required each of her admirers to give her a stone for her dad's grave. Considering that this pyramid took 3¼ million cubic yards of stone, even a life of one hundred years of perfect health and romantic popularity would have provided only enough stone for the tip of the pyramid. To appreciate its mass, crawl through the narrow passageways inside that lead to the pharoah's chamber in the center of the pyramid. This arduous climb through a dank, cool passage is not for the faint-hearted or the claustrophobic and costs E£20. The highlight of this expedition is the tall, narrow gallery with 9m walls formed from 14 massive slabs of granite. The king's chamber is a large, square room containing only the cracked bottom half of the sarcophagus. Its most novel feature is the collection of 19th-century graffiti.

Outside, walk around to the southern face of the structure to see the **Solar Boat,** one of the oldest boats in existence, unearthed near the pyramid base in 1954. Now enclosed in a special climate-controlled container, this vessel most likely transported Cheops across the Nile from the "land of the living" on the east bank to his resting place in the "land of the dead"; the boat was buried close to the pharaoh so he could use it to cross the ocean of death beneath the earth. A plywood and glass structure resembling a Modernist ski lodge houses the boat today. On the east side of the pyramid are the meager remains of the **Mortuary Temple of Cheops.** Only the foundations and a few column sockets remain.

The middle member of the trio, the **Pyramid of Chephren,** is only 3m shorter than the Pyramid of Cheops. It actually looks a bit taller thanks to its position on a higher plateau. Portions of the limestone casing that originally covered the monument still sheathe its apex, making it Egypt's most splendid pyramid. Also notice the granite on the summit; Chephren wanted to add a layer of granite atop the limestone but he died too soon. Relatively spacious passageways and a finely preserved interior make Chephren's the best for exploring. The burial chamber contains Chephren's sarcophagus and more 19th-century graffiti.

Finally, the **Pyramid of Mycerinus,** comparatively small at only 62m, belongs to Cheops's grandson. Legend has it that instead of devoting his attention to his death chamber, Mycerinus lavished his energy on his daughter, attempting to become her lover. After she hanged herself due to great grief, she was buried in a golden cow which was brought into the light of the sun once a year, according to her dying wish. Outside, at the pyramid's northeast corner, lie the quarried remains of the **Mortuary Temple of Mycerinus.** The smaller pyramids surrounding the Big Three belonged to the pharaohs' wives and children. Farther away, the ruins of the unexcavated Valley Temple of Mycerinus are swathed by a blanket of sand.

■ Near Giza: Kardassa and Harania

On the road from Cairo to Giza, a turn-off to the right at the second canal before the pyramids leads to the village of **Kardassa,** where the Western Desert and the camel road to Libya commence. The village has become a popular tourist destination owing to its variety of local crafts; much of what appears in Cairo's tourist shops is made in Kardassa. The main products of the village are wool and cotton scarves, *gallabiyyas* (E£30-70), rugs, and Bedouin weavings. The shops are in a sand lot across the canal from the village. Artisans' workshops are usually in the back of the store or in side alleys off the main commercial drag. Also for sale among the scarves and rugs is a disturbing number of animals, including stuffed gazelles, jackals, and rabbits. Despite the efforts of the Egyptian Environmental Affairs Agency, this illegal but highly profitable trade continues. Tourism is beginning to rob Kardassa of its charm as well although the prices are still lower and the quality of the merchandise better than at Khan el-Khalili. Taxis from Giza Sq. to Kardassa cost E£10-15. Minibuses run to Kardassa from Giza Sq. (40pt.), as well as from the turn-off from Pyramids Rd., known as the *Mash'al* stop (35pt).

More interesting is the artists' school at **Harania,** located 200m to the right of Maroutiya Canal Rd., about 3km south of Pyramids Rd., right next to the Salome Campground. Look for signs to both. Here, young children are encouraged to

Who Is That Masked Man?

Ancient Egyptians wanted to live forever, which meant making sure their bodies were fit for the long haul of the afterlife. In pre-dynastic times, people were buried in simple pits in the sand. The heat and arid conditions dried the body out and prevented decay. As civilization advanced, efforts were made to provide for a person's comfort in the afterlife, but elaborate tombs served to speed decay, separating the corpse from the drying sands. The process of mummification was perfected during the New Kingdom era. There were several different levels of preservation that were performed before the body was wrapped in the characteristic white linen bandages. The least effective and least expensive was a simple washing and cleansing of the corpse. The next level involved filling the body's orifices with caustic, corrosive fluid, then plugging up the holes. Several days later, the plugs were removed and the putrid fluid drained. The super-deluxe preservation package required that an incision be made in the abdomen. All of the viscera save the heart and kidneys were removed (including the brain, either through the base of the skull or through a nostril) and preserved in canopic jars. These jars were amphora-shaped containers made out of alabaster, with folkloric engravings on the sides and lids. The body was then packed with natron, a natural salt found in Wadi Natrun. After 40 days, the salt was removed and ointments, spices, and oils were administered in combination with intricate patterns of wrappings. The essences reacted over time to form a black, pitch-like substance that gives mummies their names (*moumiya* is Arabic for pitch).

develop their creativity through weaving brilliantly colored carpets and making pottery. Since its inception in 1942, two generations of tapestry-weavers have studied at the school; many are still in practice as adults. Some of the most notable works are showcased in the museum at Harania, and the book *Threads of Life—A Journey Through Creativity* is available at the center. The results of this creative process are stunning but expensive (open 9am-5pm, summer 9am-6pm; E£200-2000; Visa, MC). Harania is best visited with the Salah Muhammad tour (see **Pyramids at Giza: Practical Information,** p. 132). Walking is the only non-taxi alternative to a guided tour.

■ Saqqara and Environs سقارة

Even though it is the namesake of Sokar, a Memphite god of death, Saqqara can be fun. The tombs scattered around the area are archaeologically fascinating and show the evolution of the pyramids, and there is a pleasant dearth of tourists. Unless you are with a tour, however, public transportation can be sparse and expensive. Saqqara served as the royal necropolis during the early years of the Old Kingdom (Third Dynasty, around 2600 BCE), when nearby **Memphis** was the seat of power.

ORIENTATION AND PRACTICAL INFORMATION

The easiest way to see Saqqara is to take Salah Muhammad's tour (see **Giza: Practical Information,** p. 132). If you choose to go on your own, begin your journey at the ruins of **North Saqqara.** Short of hiring a taxi, there's really no simple way to get here. Public transportation lovers can take a minibus from Giza Sq. to the village of **Abu Sir** (50pt). From here, the killer 4km walk to the entrance takes between 30 and 60 minutes, depending on your sand-speed. Walk south (to the left as you arrive) along the canal just before the village and keep following the dirt road by the canal until you reach the paved road. Turn right and it's 200m to the site entrance. You can also hire a **pick-up truck** at the canal in Abu Sir (about 50pt per person) to take a group to the site. From downtown **Cairo,** a taxi will demand at least E£20. A fun (if expensive) alternative to mechanized transport is to hire a **steed** (this is your chance to go through the desert on a horse with no name). A horse or camel costs about E£15 per hour, and you will probably have to pay for a guide (and his ride) as well. The ride to Saqqara from Giza takes about four hours, so you'll need the beasts all day.

To get to the pyramids at Abu Sir, either ride (horses and camels available at North Saqqara for around E£10 roundtrip) or walk through the burning sands (not fun, at least 1hr.). **South Saqqara** is at least 30 minutes away by foot, or rent a critter for E£10. To get to **Memphis,** take the Metro to Helwan (60pt) then take a ferry to *El Badrasheen.* Memphis is a 30 minute walk from there (once in the village, look for the microbus which occasionally passes by for the ruins; hop on for 25pt). Minibuses also run from Memphis to *El Badrasheen* (25pt) and from *El Badrasheen* to Giza (50pt). From Giza, it is possible to take either a minibus or public bus #987 back to Tahrir Sq. or Ramses Station in Cairo. It may help to have someone write your destination in Arabic to help locate your minibus.

Get a very early start—it takes time to travel around the sites at Saqqara. Summer afternoon sun can be immobilizing; be sure to bring plenty of **water,** a hat, and your own food, and make sure you're wearing **good shoes.** Though sandals will keep your feet cool, they also let sand in. Stick to real shoes—sneakers or even boots—or you'll be one unhappy camper. Lighting inside most of the tombs is poor; with your own flashlight you can avoid paying the *baksheesh* the guards will request.

All the sights are officially open 8am-5pm (8am-4pm in winter), but the guards lock up and go home a couple of hours early in low season or stay a bit longer in summer. Make the pyramids of Abu Sir your lowest priority: they're hollow inside. (Admission to North Saqqara E£20, students E£10; camera privileges E£10, video privileges E£25.) The ticket is good for all Saqqara sites; Abu Sir does not require a ticket.

SIGHTS

Saqqara consists of five archaeological finds scattered over a very large area, with nothing but sand dunes in between. The primary destination for most visitors is **North Saqqara,** site of the funerary complex and the great Step Pyramid of Djoser I. The three pyramids of **Abu Sir** lie 6km north of North Saqqara, only a few km from the tiny village of the same name. The two pyramids and the funerary complex of **South Saqqara** are about 4km south of North Saqqara. The historically significant but scanty ruins of **Memphis** are farther from the necropolis of Saqqara, located next to the Nile just south of the village of Mit-Rahine. The pyramids of **Dahshur** form the southern tip of the row, but are located on a military base and therefore require special permits which are supposedly available from the Ministry of the Interior.

North Saqqara

Saqqara's most famous site is the oldest pyramid in the world. The **Step Pyramid of Djoser-Netcherikhe** was begun around 2630 BCE by super-architect Imhotep, one of the most learned men of his time. The monument began as a simple stone *mastaba,* a low, rectangular building covering a burial shaft carved into the earth. Imhotep was not satisfied with just a simple rectangle; he modified the original structure, eventually greatly expanding it and, more importantly, stacking several layers on top of the original base. This was the first monumental tomb and the inspiration for Egypt's many subsequent architectural wonders.

Enter the Step Pyramid complex from the southeastern side of the limestone enclosure wall. The paneled barrier was designed to resemble the mud-brick work which graced the fortifications surrounding the cities and palaces of the period. Two fixed stone panels, carved to resemble a massive wooden doorway, open onto a 40-pillared colonnade **entrance.** You shouldn't be fooled by Imhotep's thirteen false entrances, now mostly dust. The walls and roof have been restored as part of a lifetime project of reconstruction undertaken by the French archaeologist Jean-Philippe Lauer. The Egyptian pillars, ridged to create the stylized effect of a bundle of papyrus stems, are probably the world's first stone columns (Imhotep, unlike the chumps before him who used mud brick, was building for eternity). This corridor culminates in the **Hypostyle Hall,** a fledgling version of the great hallways found at Karnak and Abydos.

The halls open onto the **Great South Court.** The two altars in the center, symbolizing Lower and Upper Egypt, are quite weathered. In the northern end, at the base of the Step Pyramid, lie the remains of the *mastaba* that was the seed of Djoser's tomb. In the center of the pyramid's south face is an entrance to the tomb's locked interior. To the east, past the colonnade, the **Heb-Sed Court** runs the length of one side of the courtyard. During the Archaic Period (the time prior to the First Dynasty), the pharaoh would have to prove that he was fit to rule by performing various athletic feats at the annual Sed Festival. If he failed, the flabby pharaoh would be put to death and a stronger replacement crowned. In a marvel of foresight, later pharaohs turned the Sed into a rejuvenation ceremony and did away with the ritual regicide portion of the program. The Heb-Sed Court in the funerary complex and the panels inside the pyramid that depict Djoser running a ceremonial race were meant to ensure his eternal rejuvenation.

The more substantial **House of the South** stands next door, on the eastern side of Djoser's pyramid. The inside walls are inscribed with ancient graffiti left by a starving Egyptian artist in the 12th century BCE. The messages, expressing admiration for King Djoser, were hastily splashed onto the walls with dark paint, scrawled in a late cursive style of hieroglyphics. The Lotus columns here represent Upper Egypt—hence the name House of the South. Heading north, you'll come to the **House of the North** (symbolized by the papyri columns). Nearby, directly in front of the Step Pyramid's northern face, is the most haunting spectacle at Saqqara, the **Statue of King Djoser.** The pharaoh stares out from a slanted stone hut pierced by two tiny apertures. This small structure, known as the **Sardab,** was designed to enable the spirit of the pharaoh to communicate with the outside world. The striking figure is a plaster copy of the original, now gazing, eyes askew, in the Egyptian Museum in Cairo.

On the southwestern corner of Djoser's complex, up the steps to the right of the pit and over the enclosure wall, looms the massive **Pyramid of Unis,** the last pharaoh of the 5th dynasty. You can go spelunking in the interior burial chamber of the crumbled monument—originally 44m high, now a mere 11m. Find a guard if the door is locked. Although the passage into the tomb is uncomfortably low at points, the central burial chamber is spacious. The wall carvings, known as the **Pyramid Texts,** discovered in 1881 by Thomas Cook, constitute the earliest known example of decorative hieroglyphic writing on the walls of a pharaonic tomb chamber. Carefully etched into the shiny alabaster, the well-preserved texts record hymns, prayers, and articles to protect the king and facilitate his resurrection in the afterlife. On the western edge of the main chamber sits the open basalt sarcophagus of Unis, with its lid on the ground beside it. You'll need a flashlight.

Opposite the south face of the Pyramid of Unis, an inauspicious shack covers the shaft leading to three of Egypt's deepest burial chambers, the **Persian Tombs** of Psamtik, Zenhebu, and Peleese (of the 16th dynasty). A dizzying spiral staircase drills 25m into the ground, ending in three vaulted burial chambers linked by narrow passageways. Colorful chambers make the exercise worthwhile. According to the ancient inscriptions, Zenhebu was a famous admiral and Psamtik a high-ranking doctor of the pharaoh's court. The guard will expect some *bakhsheesh;* E£1 is enough.

East of the Pyramid of Unis, a smooth, narrow causeway runs down the hill. Nearly 1km long, it linked the pyramid with a lower valley temple on the banks of the river. Strewn by the causeway's sides are the **Old Kingdom Tombs.** Here the ancient nobility attempted to ride the pharaoh's coattails into the afterlife. Over 250 *mastabas* have been excavated here, though only a few of the largest and best-preserved are open. The 6th-dynasty **Mastaba of Idut,** next to the southern enclosure wall of Djoser's funerary complex and just east of the Pyramid of Unis, has 10 chambers. Nearby are the **Mastaba of Mehu** and the **Mastaba of Queen Nebet.** South of the causeway is a pair of enormous **Boat Pits,** finely sculpted stone trenches used either to house the royal barques (as at Giza) or simply to signify them.

Southwest of the Pyramid of Unis, a 200m path leads into the desert to the unfinished **Pyramid of Sekhemkhet,** a paltry pile of rubble unearthed in 1951. The pyramid, built by Djoser's successor, was intended as a replica of its neighbor, but construction was abandoned when its walls had reached a height of 3m. The inside of the pyramid is closed to the public.

At the end of the causeway, head 300m uphill and southward to the **Monastery of St. Jeremiah.** Built in the 5th century CE, the monastery's long history of being pilfered began in 950 CE, at the hands of Arab raiders. Most recently, the Antiquities Service ransacked it, moving all decorative carvings and paintings to the Coptic Museum in Cairo and leaving a despoiled shell to be overrun by advancing sand dunes. The leftovers are best reached by car or horse; it's usually too hot to walk.

Western North Saqqara

With a car, you can return to the entrance of Djoser's mortuary complex and drive around to the western portion of North Saqqara. *Sans* vehicle, you can hike five minutes across the desert to reach the **Tomb of Akhti-Hotep and Ptah-Hotep,** halfway between the Step Pyramid and the canopied Rest House. The paved road is far more convenient, though somewhat longer. This remarkable double tomb housed the bodies of a father and son, inspectors of the priests who served the pyramids, and ministers of the treasury. The pair designed their own mortuary complex, which contains some of Saqqara's finest reliefs, showing the Hoteps on war and hunting excursions, and surrounded by musicians. The structure is accessible through a long, columned corridor, ending up in the burial chamber of Akhti-Hotep.

West of the Hoteps' tomb is a shady and expensive **Rest House** with a bathroom and a small cafeteria. Farther along the highway, where the road turns sharply to the west, an area has been cleared to reveal badly weathered **Greek statues,** known as the **Philosophers' Circle,** said to represent Homer (at the center), Pindar (to his left), Plato (to his right), and two unknowns (possibly Pythagoras and Heraclides).

The **Serapium,** a few hundred meters west of the Rest House at the terminus of the main road, was discovered in 1854. The mausoleum, a series of eerie underground tunnels with tiny lanterns, houses the **Tombs of the Apis Bulls,** where 25 sacred oxen, representing Ptah's pets, were embalmed and placed in enormous solid granite sarcophagi. Only one of the bulls was discovered (the rest had been stolen or roasted) and is now displayed in Cairo's Agricultural Museum. At the end of the tunnel you'll reach metal steps which allow you to climb into one of the gigantic coffins.

The Serapium is the legacy of a bull-worshipping cult that thrived during the New Kingdom. The sacred oxen of Ptah, the Apis bulls, were traditionally associated with Osiris and the afterlife. During the Ptolemaic period, their worship was combined with that of the Greek god Zeus, who often took the form of a bull, especially during liaisons with mortal women. The combined Zeus-Apis cult was especially strong around Alexandria. Work on the main portion of the underground complex was begun in the 7th century BCE by Psamtik I and continued through the Ptolemaic era, though much older tombs adjoin this central set of chambers. In the oldest portion of the Serapium, two large gold-plated sarcophagi and several canopic jars containing human heads were found, as well as the undisturbed footprints of the priests who had laid the sacred animals to rest more than 3000 years earlier. (This portion of the tomb is no longer accessible.) Recessed tombs flank the main corridor on both sides, each containing a sarcophagus. It's difficult to imagine these mammoth coffins being transported to the confines of the cave; their average weight is 65 tons. In the final tomb stands the largest sarcophagus, hewn from a single piece of black granite.

The **Tomb of Ti,** 300m north of the Serapium, was excavated in 1865 and has since been one of the primary sources of knowledge about both daily and ceremonial life during the 5th dynasty (25th century BCE). Serving under three pharaohs, Ti had almost as many titles as the Library of Congress: Overseer of the Pyramids and Sun Temples at Abu Sir, Superintendent of Works, Scribe of the Court, Royal Counselor, Editor, Royal Fluffer, Royal Tea Brewer, and even Lord of Secrets. Some scholars also believe he was a practitioner of a stealthy martial arts discipline similar to that of the Japanese ninjas. His rank was so lofty that he was allowed to marry a princess, Nefer-Hotep. In the tomb paintings, his children wear braided hairpieces, marking them as royal contenders for the throne. The guard will demand a tip for being there; don't be afraid to ignore him and head for the door.

Although now entirely buried in sand, an Avenue of Sphinxes once ran the full width of the site, commencing near the Tomb of Ti, running a straight course east past the Step Pyramid complex, and ending at the river's edge near the **Pyramid of Titi** (founder of the 6th dynasty). This weathered pyramid can be reached by following the east-west highway past the Rest House to the fork and then heading a short distance north. The interior of Titi's tomb has several interesting sacred inscriptions, but it's usually closed to the public. The 30 rooms comprising the magnificent **Tomb of Mereruka,** just next door to the Pyramid of Titi, are open to the public. The naturalistic portrayal of wildlife found inside the Tomb of Mereruka has enabled scientists to learn a great deal about ancient Egyptian fauna. Various species of fish can be differentiated thanks to the minutely detailed work of the artists. The tomb was built in 2340 BCE by 5th dynasty priest and high official Mereruka, and also contains the tombs of his wife, Hertwatetkhit, and his son, Meri-Teti.

Farther east is the neighboring **Tomb of Ankhma-Hor.** Though the decorations are relatively sparse, there are several representations of medical operations, including toe surgery and a circumcision. One noted Egyptologist has asserted that the 6th-dynasty tendency to depict funerary scenes indicates a growing fixation with the afterlife as the Old Kingdom went into its final decline.

South Saqqara

The most interesting funerary monument at South Saqqara is the **Tomb of Shepseskaf** (popularly known as Mastabat Far'aun), an enormous stone structure shaped like a sarcophagus and capped with a rounded lid. Although Shepseskaf, the sixth king of the 4th dynasty and son of Mycerinus (whose pyramid stands at Giza), reigned for only three or four years, his brief stint on the throne was long enough to qualify him for a grand tomb. Originally covering 7000 square meters, Mastabat Far'aun is neither a true *mastaba* nor a pyramid. Scholars see it as a transitional experiment. The interior consists of long passageways and a burial chamber containing fragments of a huge sandstone sarcophagus. Ask a guard to admit you.

Abu Sir أبو صير

The pyramids of Abu Sir are isolated in the Eastern Desert 6km north of Saqqara. No tour buses make it here; take this opportunity to escape camera-clicking clowns. The site (2.5km from the village of Abu Sir) can only be reached by foot or hoof.

The **Pyramid of Neferirkare,** the most imposing of the three main pyramids, stands tall at 68m. It once had a stone facing like its neighbors at Giza, but has suffered a similar loss of face. The exterior now resembles that of a step pyramid. Nevertheless, the Pyramid of Neferirkare is one of the best-preserved monuments in the Saqqara area. The **Pyramid of Niuserre** is the youngest of the trio, but the most dilapidated. It's possible to enter the **Pyramid of Sahure,** the northernmost member of the group, on its north face. One of the custodians at the site will show you the entrance, which is about 0.5m high and 2m long, and requires you to worm your way along the sand floor. The small chamber inside was the pharaoh's tomb. More pyramids are visible from here than from any other site in the country. If you wish to walk on to the village of Abu Sir, have the guards point out the route.

If you are traveling by animal between Abu Sir and Giza, have your guide stop off along the way at the 5th-dynasty **Sun Temple of Abu Surab,** about 1.5km north of the Pyramid of Sahure. Located on the fringe of cultivated fields, the temple was built by King Niuserre in honor of the sun god Ra. It features an impressive altar constructed from five massive blocks of alabaster. A horse or camel ride from Djoser's pyramid in North Saqqara costs E£20, but if business is slow, it may be possible to bargain to a cheaper price. Prices can sometimes be haggled to as low as E£5.

Memphis ممفيس

As late as the 13th century CE, Arab historians wrote with awe about the remnants of the Old Kingdom capital at Memphis. The city was founded 5200 years ago by the semi-legendary Menes (who was later eaten by a hippopotamus) and was the most likely seat of Snefru, Cheops, Chephren, Mycerinus, Ælvyse, and other Old Kingdom rulers. Though the brick houses of this city of 500,000 had by then melted into mud, many of the stone monuments were not destroyed until much later, when they were pilfered for construction in Cairo. Only an ancient canal (responsible for the lush vegetation) and the **museum** pieces in **Mit-Rahine** remain. Near the museum is the famous alabaster sphinx, which probably stood at the south entrance of the Temple of Ptah. Also worth seeing is the colossal 14m statue of Ramses II. The statue, displayed horizontally, is well preserved, with readable cartouches engraved on the shoulders and the waist. (Museum open daily 7:30am-5pm in summer, 7:30am-4pm in winter. Admission E£14, students E£7. Camera privileges E£5, video privileges E£25.) You might have to take a **taxi** to Memphis from Saqqara or Abu Sir. **Hitchhiking** from here is dangerous and is not recommended.

■ The Nile Delta

QANATIR

Qanatir is the most beautiful and accessible cure for the Cairo blues. Situated 16km north of Cairo, the town marks the official beginning of the Delta, where the Nile splits into the eastern (Dumyât) and western (Rashid, or Rosetta) branches. Qanatir is also the site of the **Nile barrages,** bridges that regulate the flow of water into the Delta. Turrets and arches decorate the 19th-century structures, which were built to help the Delta's cotton production. The point of land where the Nile splits is home to parks, cafes, and an arcade. Visitors can stroll or rent a bike (E£1-3 per hr.), moped (drive at your own risk), or horse to explore the barrages. Rowboats and motorboats are also available for rent. For true local flavor, visit on a Friday, when Cairenes on holiday flock to Qanatir for a breath of fresh air.

Bus #953 from Subra El Khema station in front of the Ramses Hilton runs frequently to Qanatir (45min., 40pt.). On Fridays and Sundays, a passenger **ferry** runs along the Nile from Cairo to Qanatir. The dock is located on the corniche, behind the Ramses Hilton and in front of the Television Building (9am-4:30pm, 1½ hr., E£2). It is also possible to hire a **felucca** from the same area, but the journey will take three hours, as the mast of the boat must be lowered for each bridge.

BUBASTIS

It was primarily in Lower Egypt that the Old Kingdom thrived and many looming monuments were erected in the Delta throughout the Pharaonic Period. Due to the looseness of the soil, the use of irrigation canals, and the natural fanning out of the river, almost all of the major Pharaonic sites in the Delta have been lost. Southeast of Zagazig lie the ruins of **Bubastis,** now called **Tel Basta.** The original name means "House of Basted" and refers to the feline goddess to whom the main temple was dedicated. The festivals here in honor of the cat goddess attracted over 700,000 devotees who would dance and sing, make sacrifices, and consume gluttonous quantities of food and wine. Herodotus marveled that "more wine is drunk at this feast than in the whole year beside." He described the temple as the most pleasurable to gaze upon of all of the Delta's pharaonic sites. Herodotus would roll in his grave if he could see the condition of Bubastis today, as the sanctuary looks like a scattered pile of kitty litter. Unless you have a specific interest in the site, it is not worth the trip from Cairo.

Trains run to Zagazig throughout the day (6:20am-6:30pm, every hr., 1½hr., E£6); otherwise, take a *service* taxi from Ahmed Hilni Sq. bus station (1¼hr., E£4.50). To reach Tel Basta, take a taxi from the Zagazig train station (10min.). In Zagazig, the Orabi Museum houses a small collection of local archaeological finds (open daily 9am-5pm; admission E£6, students E£3; camera privileges E£10; video privileges E£15). Take a taxi from the train station (10min.).

TANIS

One of the region's most impressive sites is ancient **Tanis**. A 3½hr. drive from Cairo, the remains of the city lie in the northeast corner of the Delta's fertile triangle, and a 10-minute walk from the dilapidated town of **San el-Hagar.** The capital of the 21st (Tanite) dynasty, Tanis was founded in the 11th century BCE by Pharaoh Smendes. Though the past 31 centuries have taken their toll on Tanis, the site is still impressive. Countless obelisks, statues, and carvings dot the site, evoking much of the city's former glory. The tombs of Smendes and other ancient notables feature impressive hieroglyphs. Though the ruins are not as amazing as *Raiders of the Lost Ark* would have you believe, there is a structure remarkably similar to the well of souls. Tanis is a very long daytrip from Cairo. Take the **train** or **bus** (from Ahmed Hilni Sq., 2½hr., E£4) to **Faqus,** which is closer than Zagazig. From there, take a *service* taxi to San el-Hagar (1hr.). Someone there will point you to the ruins. The site also includes a small museum (admission to the ruins E£16; camera privileges E£5).

■ Wadi Natrun وادى النطرون

If the dirt, noise, and hustle of Cairo has left you aggravated, Wadi Natrun's monasteries, flowering trees, cooing doves, and friendly monks will restore tranquility. For 1500 years the 50 monasteries of Wadi Natrun were the backbone of the Coptic community in Egypt. The four that stand today, forming an ill-proportioned cross in the desert landscape, are not just impressive relics; they are functional places of worship serving the spiritual needs of Egypt's Orthodox Christian population who flock here in tour buses all summer.

The first Christian monastery in Egypt was established in the Eastern Desert by St. Anthony the Great (250-355 CE). In 330 CE, one of Anthony's disciples established the monastic life-style in Wadi Natrun. More than a millennium and a half later, in the 1980s, interest in Coptic monasticism was so great that new rooms were added to accommodate the many novice ascetics arriving in the Natrun Valley.

Wadi Natrun is also home to the last surviving type of **papyrus.** Due to the high salinity of water (*wadi* = river, *natrun* = salt), it is a dwarf sub-species which does not reach over 2m. The last large papyrus, which could reach 6m, was found in the mid-19th century by a Prussian soldier in the Delta.

Orientation and Practical Information A West Delta Bus Company **bus** leaves from Abd el-Moneim Riad Sq. bus station, near the Ramses Hilton (6:30am-5pm, about every 30min. or whenever the bus fills up, 2½hr., E£3.25 collected on board). Ride past the Wadi Natrun Rest House into Wadi Natrun town; from the terminus you can take a pick-up truck to monastery **Deir Anba Bishoi** (10min., E£1). **Taxis** run from the Rest House to the monasteries; bargain fiercely. A better option might be to rely upon the kindness of pilgrims. Coptic pilgrims are often willing to pick up travelers. This is also the best way to travel between monasteries. Start your journey early if you plan to return to Cairo or Alexandria in the evening, as there are no places to stay in Wadi Natrun town. To leave Wadi Natrun, wait at the **Wadi Natrun Rest House** for *service* taxis or for buses, which go to Alexandria (*service* leave about every hr., E£4), or Cairo (E£4 for frequent *service*; buses leave about every hr. until 6pm, E£3.25). Friendly Coptic Egyptians may offer you a ride; if you play your cards right you'll be eating homemade *fuul* all the way home. As with hitchhiking, use careful judgment when accepting a ride from strangers.

Deir Anba Bishoi alone is open every day of the year; Deir es-Suryan, Deir Anba Baramus, and Deir Abu Maqar close for various feast and fast days, particularly around Christmas and Easter. With the exception of Deir Abu Maqar, the monks happily receive foreign tourists and will provide free tours of their monasteries. It is sometimes possible to arrange an overnight stay, although this is primarily a privilege of true religious pilgrims. For information on overnight stays, contact the Coptic Patriarch in Cairo at 22 Ramses St., Aboiyye (tel. 282 53 74, 284 31 59, or 285 78 89), and see the specific monastery descriptions below for details.

EGYPT

Sights As with most religious sites in the Middle East, wear modest attire when touring the monasteries; no shorts or sleeveless shirts. Remember to remove your shoes before entering a church. For more information, see **Religion,** p. 61.

Deir Anba Bishoi (the Monastery of St. Bishoi), 15km from the Rest House and 500m from Deir es-Suryan, is the most accessible of the four monasteries. With seven churches, it is also the largest. Ask for Father Sedrak, a monk who speaks excellent English and is the designated tour guide.

Dating from 381 CE, Deir Anba Bishoi's original limestone and silt construction is now covered in plaster. The Church of St. Bishoi has three *haikals,* or altar rooms, because Communion can only be offered from an altar once a day. It was rebuilt in 444 after being sacked by nomads and now contains the remains of St. Bishoi, who is still believed to perform miracles for the faithful. Monks used to sleep in the desert, coming to the church only for services, but Bedouin attacks in the 9th century prompted the construction of sleeping chambers and a protective wall. The second floor's Chapel of the Virgin Mary exhibits 1500-year-old Gothic-style arches (an Egyptian innovation brought to Europe from Byzantium by the Crusaders). Don't leave without hearing the amplified echo in the old communal dining room (monastery open daily 8am-5pm).

Deir es-Suryan (the Monastery of the Syrians, for the Syrian monks who once inhabited it), is visible 500m northwest of the Monastery of St. Bishoi and is only five minutes away on foot. Rather than following the road, walk along the monastery walls. The monastery was established in the 4th century, when a group of monks broke away from the Monastery of St. Bishoi following a theological dispute. With the resolution of the dispute in the 5th century, this alternative monastery was no longer needed by the Egyptian Copts. In the beginning of the 8th century, it was purchased by a Syrian merchant for use by monks from his homeland, the first of whom arrived at the beginning of the 9th century. The monastery was prominent throughout the 10th century, and by the 11th century it housed the largest community in Wadi Natrun. The design is modeled on Noah's Ark. Note the beautifully painted frescoes, many more of which are suspected to lie beneath the plaster walls. The monks will be quick to tell you that they have what is considered the most beautiful Annunciation fresco in the world. One of the most striking items in the church is the enormous ebony **Door of Symbols,** whose six leaves form the screen to the sanctuary in the Church of the Virgin Mary. The panels depict the seven epochs of the Christian era. The **miracle tree** supposedly sprang from the staff of a Syrian saint in the 4th century. At the back of the church is a low, dark passageway leading to the private cell of St. Bishoi. The monks will show you an iron staple and chain dangling from the ceiling and explain how St. Bishoi would fasten it to his beard, thereby maintaining a standing position lest he fall asleep during his all-night prayer vigils. Set in the floor at the western end of the church is the *lakan* (marble basin), which is used for washing the monks' feet on holy days (monastery open Sun.-Fri. 9am-6pm, Sat. 9am-3pm; summer Sun.-Fri. 9am-7pm, Sat. 9am-5pm). **Overnight stays not allowed here.**

Deir Anba Baramus (The Monastery of the Virgin Mary), the oldest monastery in the Natrun valley, is about four kilometers northwest of Deir Anba Bishoi. "Baramus" derives from the Coptic word "Romeos," or Romans, in honor of the Roman Emperor Valentinus's two sons (and ex-Deir Anba Baramus monks) Maximus and Domitius; tradition holds that a crypt under the altar holds their remains. Take a taxi from Wadi Natrun town or catch a ride from Deir Anba Bishoi. Relics of St. Moses and St. Isadore are kept in the first section of the old church. The corpse of St. Moses once shook hands with passers-by through a small aperture in his casket, but for the past 200 years, he has not been quite as cordial and the aperture has been sealed. The delightfully cool tea room provides a good place for a rest (monastery open 10am-5pm).

Deir Abu Maqar (the Monastery of St. Maccarius) lies roughly 8km southeast of Deir Anba Bishoi. Founded by St. Maccarius the Great (300-390 CE), it was the first of the Wadi Natrun monasteries. St. Maccarius remained a religious hermit throughout his life and lived in a cell connected by a tunnel to a small cave. Virtually none of the original building remains. In the beginning of the 11th century, the monastery

---

A Night with the Living Dead

The monks that inhabit the four functional monasteries live, eat, and pray together. Few are allowed to leave unless on medical or church business. Their day begins in church at 3:45am with group prayer. On Sundays, the monks of **Deir Anba Bishoi** set their alarms for 12:45am for six hours of uninterrupted prayer. Amid billows of incense, wide-eyed icons, and flickering candlelight, they sing psalms and cantillate the Coptic liturgy. The service is punctuated by entrancing triangle and cymbal music (arrive before 9am to attend). The monks are swathed in black, which indicates that they are symbolically dead—an honored status. When initiated, a new monk's former self "dies," and he leaves the world of earthly desires. The monks' black hoods symbolize the "helmet of salvation" (Ephesians 6:17), upon which 13 crosses are embroidered. The 12 crosses on the sides represent Christ's apostles and the 13th on the back symbolizes Christ Himself.

---

became the refuge of monks fleeing Muslim persecution. During the Middle Ages, the monastery was famous for its library, which remained intact until Europeans discovered the treasures in the 17th century and removed them. Visitors are not permitted without prior approval. If interested, send a letter to the monastery at P.O. Box 2780, Cairo. State the date and time of your proposed visit, and how long you wish to stay (no longer than two hours), as well as whether you would like to eat there. Overnight visits are only granted to religious groups. If you are invited, the easiest way to reach the monastery is by hiring a car at the Wadi Natrun Guest House for the 15-minute drive. The price depends entirely on your bargaining skills.

■ Fayyum الفيوم

The Fayyum Oasis is a vast agrarian settlement just over 100km from Cairo. Fayyum's 1.8 million people live in 157 small villages that dot a sandy landscape swathed with chrysanthemum and sunflower fields. Lake Qar'un to the north is a popular beach resort, and the local government is cultivating the rest of the area for tourism.

Fayyum was first developed through canal-building and irrigation by the rulers of Ancient Egypt's 12th dynasty (20th-19th centuries BCE). The Ptolemies made the area into a rich province with its capital at Crocodopolis (near the site of modern Fayyum, to the left of Alligatoropolis), the headquarters of a cult that worshipped Sebak and other reptilian deities. Roman conquerors used Crocodopolis as a vacation resort and as one of the primary granaries of the empire. The oasis was an early center of Coptic Christianity; it also sheltered a large population of exiled Jews in the 3rd century CE. Muslims believe the extensive canals to be the work of the biblical Joseph during his stay in Egypt; Bahr Yusef is named for the interpreter of dreams. Fayyum also boasts several hard-to-find Pharaonic ruins that are still under excavation and rarely visited.

ORIENTATION AND PRACTICAL INFORMATION

Fayyum is a roughly triangular area, stretching about 90km east to west. The eastern edge is bordered by the Nile. The saltwater **Lake Qar'un** separates the northwest edge of Fayyum from the sandy plateau of the Western Desert. The city of Fayyum is almost in the center and is the area's transportation hub. The main hotels and offices are located around the waterwheels in the center of town. The city runs along the **Bahr Yusef Canal,** which flows west from the Nile. At the center of town **Bahr Sinnuris** separates from Bahr Yusef at a right angle and flows north toward the farmlands. **El Goumhouriyya** and **El Huriyya Streets** run along the north and south banks of Bahr Yusef respectively. There are four groaning waterwheels next to the tourist office. The inverted pyramid dominating the eastern end of Bahr Yusef is Fayyum's newest landmark, the **Culture Palace,** housing a theater, cinema, and public library.

Tourist Office: tel. 32 52 11, ext. 177, in a small pre-fab box on El Goumhouriyya St. beside Cafeteria El Medina, 50m east of the juncture of the 2 canals. Provides a colorful but fairly useless map. Open daily 8am-3pm.

Currency Exchange: Bank of Alexandria (tel. 31 24 72), opposite the Palace Hotel on El Goumhouriyya St. Open Sun.-Thurs. 8:30am-2pm, Ramadan 10am-1:30pm. Exchange open daily 8am-2pm and 6-9pm; in winter 5-8pm.

Buses and Service: The bus station behind the youth hostel, 1km east of the tourist office, serves **Cairo** (every 30min., 6am-8pm, 2hr., E£3.75). *Service* leave from here to Giza Sq. in Cairo (E£5; faster but more dangerous). Another bus/*service* station serves **Beni Suef** and points south. Walk to the 3rd bridge over the canal west of the tourist office, turn left, and walk 1km. Don't be misled by the local bus depot past the main crossroads: the station is 200m farther down on the right.

Local Transportation: Service travel around town and to nearby locales (50pt-E£1), but the town is easily walkable. You can also hire a **hantour** (horse-drawn carriage) for about E£1 anywhere in town.

Police: tel. 123.

Post Office: 100m south of the first bridge east of the tourist office. Open Sat.-Thurs. 8am-3pm. **EMS** and **Poste Restante** available.

Telephones: On southern bank of Bahr Yusef, 2 bridges west of the tourist office. International calls available. Open 24hr. **Telephone Code:** 048.

ACCOMMODATIONS

Although Fayyum is an easy daytrip from Cairo, an overnight stay is pastoral bliss. Fayyum city has a few cheap beds, but the 40km long Lake Qar'un and heavenly Wadi el-Ruwayan are much more peaceful roosting options. The **Fayyum Youth Hostel** (ask for *"shabab"*; tel. 32 36 82) is at Hadaka, Block 7, Flat #7. With your back to the hustlers at the Cairo bus stop, turn left and walk 250m to the intersection with a five-story brick building. Take a sharp left, then a left at the green "FYH" sign 50m ahead. The hostel is the second building on the right. It is clean and budget-friendly, and has a common kitchen (dorm beds E£3). The **Palace Hotel** (tel. 32 12 22), on El Huriyya St. one block west of the tourist office under a blue English sign, has clean, breezy rooms overlooking the canal, with folded-down sheets, towel, and soap. Owner Ashraf Arafa speaks flawless English and is more helpful than the tourist office (singles E£20, with shower E£30, with A/C E£45; doubles E£35, with shower E£45, with A/C E£60; tax and continental breakfast included; lunch and dinner E£13-15).

FOOD

Kushari and falafel shops cluster around the railroad tracks. **Cafeteria El Medina** (tel. 32 20 28), in the town center, has a pleasant view of the waterwheels, outdoor seating, attentive service, and tasty spiced pigeon. Meals with rice are E£20-25. Vegetarians will be pleased with the veggies, rice, and cucumber salad at the Palace Hotel (E£7). The **Governorate Club,** on Governorate St., has the best *kebab* in town but watery *tahini*. Ask your *hantour* driver for *Nadi el-Muhafzah*. You can get full meals here for under E£10 (open until 1am). For a sugar infusion, head over to **Lebanon Pastry** (tel. 32 29 36), on El Goumhouriyya St. (3 bridges from the tourist office), which offers ice cream and Arabic sweets for 25pt-E£1 (open daily 10am-1am).

SIGHTS

Fayyum city is filled with Egyptians living tourist-free lives; the real beauty is outside the city. Visitors who weren't ossified by the Islamic architecture in Cairo should visit the Mamluk **Mosque of Qaytbay,** about 1km west of the town center, along the canal, at the very end of El Huriyya St. The mosque is named for the Mamluk Sultan El Ashraf Seif ed-Din Qaytbay, who ruled Egypt from 1468 to 1496 despite his long name. It was built by a river that once flowed here, allowing worshippers to wash before prayers. The ivory on the *mihrab* was brought all the way from Somalia. For a quick introduction to the rural life of Fayyum, head north out of town along Bahr Sinnuris. After 2km of boundless green fields, you'll reach the first of seven **water-wheels,** still used in the irrigation system. Unlike Western versions, these great wooden tires are not used to power pumps, but are pumps themselves, ingeniously using the flow of the stream to lift the water to a higher level.

■ Near Fayyum

Ain Sileen Springs, 18km northwest of town, is the most easily reached but least rewarding of the area's attractions. The road to the springs winds through fields bristling with corn, palms, fruits, and vegetables, split into perfect sections by canals. The most convenient way to get there is to take a *service* or bus from the station (35-50pt). Several restaurant-cafes provide a place to sit and imbibe as the murky streams babble by. The water, high in titanium, is supposedly good for hypertension. Drink from the springs at your own risk. The springs feed a small **swimming pool** crammed with Egyptian children. Foreigners bathing here will create a stir; foreign women will cause widespread apoplexy. A visit to the "Exhibition of Productive Families," which displays local carpet and clothing articles, will arouse less controversy. There's a **tourist office** 50m from the springs road and several small farm stands selling the sweetest **mangos** you'll ever taste. A restaurant with gorgeous views of the greenery serves *kebab* (E£10), pigeon (E£7), and salads (E£1).

Fifteen km farther north past some sunflower patches is the salt-water **Lake Qar'un,** lined with expensive hotels and day-use picnic areas on its southern shore. The beaches have a tropical feel, with toasty sand, warm, inviting, blue-green water, and palm frond *palapas* offering shade. The beaches are within daytripping range from Cairo and a quick jaunt from cheap rooms in Fayyum. The closest thing to budget lakeside accommodations is the air-conditioned **Waha Hotel** (singles E£40; doubles E£60; tax and breakfast included). In winter, the hotel rents jet skis, sailboards, and other water toys. **Tourist police** are located near the Auberge Hotel.

To reach Ain Sileen, Lake Qar'un, or any point north of Fayyum, walk north from the information stand to the railroad tracks running parallel to Bahr Yusef Canal. Turn left and walk to the fourth crossing; you'll find a "taxi" stand 300m down on your left. Pickup trucks shuttle between Fayyum, Ain Sileen (50pt), and Lake Qar'un (E£1). It will probably be necessary to change trucks at the village of **Sanhur** to reach the lake; the total price should be about the same.

Wonderful **Wadi er-Ruwayan** lake and waterfalls are an hour's drive from Lake Qar'un, along what becomes a pure desert passage. You can hire a taxi from Fayyum or Lake Qar'un to bring you here (no more than E£40 per carload), and hitching is reportedly easy (although always risky) in the winter. Sand dunes and cool cobalt waters ripple side by side, separated by no more than a few meters of greenery. If you find it hard to tear yourself away, lounge amidst camel herds at the aptly named **Paradise Safari Camp,** owned by English-speaking Muhammad Marzuk (E£17.50 per person; breakfast included). The camp, on the lake's shore, is surrounded by golden dunes ripe for exploration. Each large tent has two crisp-sheeted beds and a nightstand with a candle (there is no electricity here besides the generator, which is used solely for the refrigerator in the kitchen). The three waterfalls, a two-minute walk from the camp, plunge 3m over the mossy rocks into a clear lake (admission to park E£5, car E£5). Be sure to bring plenty of sunblock and insect repellent. A restaurant serves meals (E£15).

Far less spectacular is **Hawara Pyramid,** 9km southeast of Fayyum City, built by Amenemhat III's daughter to honor her father (19th century BCE). In order to confuse grave robbers, she had the entrance constructed at the southern side of the pyramid. This little device, however, did not prevent looters from snagging Amenemhat's body and booty. Climb to the top for an excellent view of the region. The best way to reach Hawara is to take a private (E£10-15) or collective (E£2) taxi 6km toward Hawara and then walk 3km into the desert.

Mediterranean Coast

▓ Alexandria الاسكندرية

Alexandria (*El Iskandariyya*) is the only place in Egypt where one meal can combine Greek *souvlaki*, British ale, French confection, and the serenade of a *muezzin*'s call to prayer. This cultural mingling makes Alexandria unique among Egyptian cities; Western fashions are more prevalent, the alcohol flows more freely, and French replaces English as the second language of choice.

Thousands of Cairenes descend upon Alexandria during the summer. Although Alexandria shares the dirt, crowding, and noise of Cairo, a different spirit pervades this city. Whereas summer in Cairo sears streets and patience alike, in Alexandria it gently warms vacationing Gulf Arabs, Africans, and Egyptians. During the day, hundreds of thousands splash in the Mediterranean, and at night they stroll along the corniche or fritter their time in theaters, nightclubs, cafes, and restaurants. If *El Qahira* is "The Conqueror," then *El Iskandariyya* is surely the spoils.

HISTORY

Alexander the Great wrested Egypt from the Persians in 331 BCE. After a triumphant but tasteful reception at Memphis, he set off for the **Oracle of Amun** in the distant **Siwa** Oasis to discover whether or not he was actually the offspring of divinity—he was. On the way down the seacoast he happened upon Rhakotis, a small fishing village blessed with a fine natural harbor. Instantly enamored by the spot, he ordered a city to be built there. Exhibiting a charming Ramsesian modesty, he dedicated it to himself. Then, leaving his architect Dinocrates behind to figure out the details, he left for Siwa and never came back.

Upon Alexander's death nine years later, Egypt fell into the hands of his general, **Ptolemy** Soter. Ptolemy glorified his former employer with attention to the new city. He even got carried away and hijacked Alexander's corpse—which was on its way to Siwa according to the emperor's last wishes—and interred it with great pomp under Alexandria's main square. The body, its tomb, and the whole of the Ptolemaic city are now supposedly buried somewhere underneath the downtown jungle, although Siwans claim that the great king is buried near the Siwa oasis.

Ptolemy and his descendants dedicated themselves to bringing the best of Greek civilization to Egyptian soil. The Museion, including the famous 500,000-volume library, was the greatest center of learning in the ancient world. **Euclid** invented his geometry here, while Erastosthenes estimated the circumference of the earth. To satisfy the spiritual needs of his subjects, Ptolemy gathered a committee of Egyptian and Greek theologians, who together devised a tremendously popular syncretic faith in which aspects of the Hellenic god Zeus and the Pharaonic god Apis (in the form of a bull) were fused into the new deity, Serapis. Pompey's Pillar is from a temple built for the new god by Diocletian.

With the construction of the **Lighthouse** of Pharos Island under Ptolemy II, the city became the site of one of the seven wonders of the ancient world. The immense 400 ft. tower featured multiple mirrors and a flaming beacon. Ships packed the previously unused harbor with increasing frequency, and Alexandria's trading made it the richest commercial center of its day. The city's bountiful culture inevitably solicited the attention of those pesky Romans. When Roman general Pompey's 48 BCE power grab went sour at Pharsalus, he fled to Egypt with his rival Julius Caesar in hot pursuit. There they found a 15-year-old king, Ptolemy XIV, fighting a civil war with a 20-year-old queen—his sister and wife—the enchanting Cleopatra VII. Whether you prefer Shakespeare's version or Hollywood's, the story is well-known. Ptolemy tried to charm Caesar by assassinating Pompey, but Cleopatra tried more subtle tactics: she won his favor and bore his child. After Caesar's death she and Marc Antony hooked

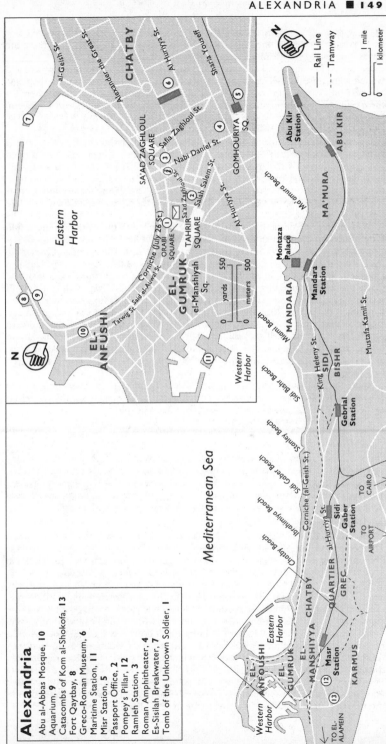

Alexandria

Abu al-Abbas Mosque, 10
Aquarium, 9
Catacombs of Kom al-Shokofa, 13
Fort Qaytbay, 8
Greco-Roman Museum, 6
Maritime Station, 11
Misr Station, 5
Passport Office, 2
Pompey's Pillar, 12
Ramleh Station, 3
Roman Amphitheater, 4
Es-Sisilah Breakwater, 7
Tomb of the Unknown Soldier, 1

EGYPT

— Rail Line
--- Tramway

0   1 mile
0   1 kilometer

Mediterranean Sea

Eastern Harbor

Western Harbor

CHAT... [partial]

up, pragmatically dreaming of ruling the known world. But it was not to be: defeated by Octavian (soon to be the Emperor Augustus Caesar) at the Battle of Actium, the lovers committed suicide rather than be paraded through Rome in chains.

Alexandria lost superpower status under Roman control as its fortunes waxed and waned with those of the Empire. Scholarly interests shifted from science to theology. The first Greek translation of the Hebrew Bible, the **Septuagint,** was written here for the expatriate Jewish population after the destruction of the Temple in Jerusalem. Many think that the translation is named for the 70 scholars who each labored in isolation and yet reputedly produced the exact same text.

Legend also teaches that St. Mark introduced Christianity here in 62 CE, founding what would become the Coptic Church. Mass third-century conversions transformed Alexandria into a Christian spiritual center, but Roman persecutions increased accordingly. The oppression reached a bloody height under **Diocletian,** who murdered so many Christians that the Copts date their calendar from the beginning of his reign, calling it the Martyr's Calendar. The basilica of the **Church of St. Mark** is visible today on Coptic Church St.

With Emperor Constantine converted, the influence of the Christians grew, and they turned on their pagan neighbors with vengeful fury. The last remnant of the Great Library was burned during anti-Roman riots in 309. The Egyptian Church differed from the Byzantine and challenged the authority of the latter by establishing a Patriarchate of its own in Alexandria. The Byzantines persecuted the schismatic Copts to such a degree that when Amr Ibn el-Ass conquered Egypt (with an army of recently Islamicized Arabs) in 640, he was received as a liberator. Alexandria fell on hard times under Arab Rule. The new capital in Cairo eclipsed Alexandria's glory, and a series of earthquakes in the 13th century finally reduced the immense lighthouse to rubble. Pharos Island itself gradually silted in and became a peninsula, attached by an hourglass-shaped isthmus. The Mamluks exiled political opponents to Alexandria, and by the time the canal from the Nile dried up, the city found itself a neglected backwater.

Napoleon Bonaparte arrived to try his luck in Egypt in 1798. After fortifying the city walls and building some forts, the French forces got spanked by Admiral Nelson in the naval battle at Abu Qir, and took to their heels in 1801.

The modern city burst forth, rejuvenated, when **Muhammad Ali** made it a port for his navy and redug the canal to the Nile. During the 19th century Alexandria became a favorite holiday spot for expatriate Europeans, wealthy Turks, and Egyptians. The entire colonial government migrated here from Cairo for the summer. After the Revolution of 1952, Alexandria endured extensive building and heavy crowding. Today, with over five million inhabitants, it is Egypt's biggest port, second-largest city, and summer capital. Perhaps the most famous history of the city, the fabulous *Alexandria: A History and Guide,* was written by one-time resident E.M. Forster.

ORIENTATION

The governorate of Alexandria stretches from Abu Qir Bay to the western harbor. The entire 28km of coastline is crowded with glistening skyscrapers and deteriorating hotels jockeying for a spot near the Mediterranean. Ancient Alexandria was built around Pharos Island (now a peninsula separating the Eastern and Western harbors), and the area still serves as the heart of the city. The downtown commercial district, called **El Manshiyya, Mahattat er-Ramleh** (Ramleh Station), or simply **El Balad** (the city), is the hub of Alexandria's transportation network, nightlife, and tourist trade. Along the curve of the eastern harbor, just west of downtown, lies **El Goumrouk,** a grandiose residential neighborhood that is home to many old mosques. Immediately southeast of El Manshiyya lies **El Attarien,** which encompasses **Misr Railway Station,** the city's main depot. South of El Manshiyya and El Attarien, the streets of **Karmouz** overflow with students, workers, and the rest of the proletariat. Here you will find Pompey's Pillar and the Catacombs of Kom esh-Shoqafa. El Anfoushi occupies the furthest tip of Pharos Island, and is home to the majestic Fort Qaytbay.

When downtown, the best way to orient yourself is **Sa'ad Zaghloul Square,** on the waterfront with a massive statue of the man himself. Four streets border the square: on the north side is the **corniche;** on the west side in front of the Cecil Hotel is **Nabi Daniel Street,** running south through downtown to the **service taxi station;** on the east side is **Safia Zaghloul Street,** the city center's principal north-south boulevard, running through downtown and ending at Misr Station; on the south side of the square heading east is **Alexander the Great Street;** and on the south side heading west to Orabi Sq. is **El Ghorfa et-Tigariyya Street.** Both Safia Zaghloul and Nabi Daniel run south up a slight hill; at the top, they intersect **Sultan Hussein Street,** and then descend to their intersections with **Al Huriyya Street.**

Bordering the southeast corner of Sa'ad Zaghloul Sq. is **Ramleh Station Square,** the main depot for the intracity tramway and a hub for intercity buses. Many municipal buses and minibuses service the busy stop in front of the square on the corniche or on the south side across from Trianon Cafe.

Heading west on Ramleh Station Sq.'s south side is **Sa'ad Zaghloul Street** (which does *not* border Sa'ad Zaghloul Sq.), a main shopping artery which runs to **Orabi Square.** The two squares serve as transportation hubs. All yellow trams out of Ramleh Station pass through here, and this is where a number of minibuses begin their journeys. The southern end is also called Tahrir Sq., and the larger area El Manshiyya Sq.

The **corniche** starts at the northern tip of El Anfoushi and winds the length of the city to reach **Montaza Palace** and **Ma'mura Beach** (a hangout for the kids), which demarcate the city's far eastern borders. Note that the corniche is also called **26 July Road** along the Eastern Harbor and **El Geish Road** between Es-Silsilah breakwater (the western promontory of the Eastern Harbor) and Montaza.

In addition to the corniche, the stretch from downtown to Ma'mura is traversed by two main arteries. The first one inland is **Alexander the Great (El-Iskandar el-Akbar) Street** which changes its name to Omar Lotfy Street in Chatby, Sidi Gaber Street as it heads past the sporting club, Ahmed Shawki Street in Roushdi, President Abdel Salam 'Aret Street from Gleem to the Victoria tram station (the end of the line), and finally Khaled Ibn al-Walid Street through Sidi Bishr until it ends at Miami (yes, Miami) Beach. The second is **Abu Qir,** also called Fouad Street or Al Huriyya Street, though officially named Gamal Abd en-Nasser Street. Lined with banks, businesses, and travel agencies, Abu Qir runs all the way to Montaza.

A map can ease the transition from bewildered tourist to street-savvy traveler. *Archeological Sites of Alexandria* (E£10) is an excellent all-purpose map available at **Al-Ma'aref Bookstore,** or in the Cecil Hotel giftshop. The Schultz American School's *Guide Book to Alexandria* (E£25), with its fold-out neighborhood maps, is great for navigating the city's tangled streets.

GETTING AROUND

Alexandria's main squares, transportation centers, and corniche all lie within walking distance of each other. A brisk half-hour walk will take you from old Pharos Island to the Shooting Club along the corniche. The rest of the city is accessible by municipal tram, bus, minibus, and private microbus or taxi. **Trams** all start from Ramleh Station and come in two colors. Blue trams head east and pass by the Sporting Club before ending at En-Nasr Station. Yellow trams head west and pass Orabi Sq. before turning north or south. They run every few minutes until midnight (sometimes until 1am; Ramadan until 2am) for only 10pt for westbound rides, 15pt for rides heading east. The middle car of every three-car tram is for women only; on two-car trams, one is marked "ladies" and the other "gentlemen." Hop on at any stop and pay on board. Find out which one to take by looking at maps in the stations or talking to Alexandria's finest. The tram is comfortable and convenient, though slow for longer runs.

City Buses

There are four main terminals—two in Sa'ad Zaghloul Sq. (on the northern corniche side and on the southern intercity bus stop side), one in Orabi Sq., and one in Misr Station. Buses run from approximately 5:30am to midnight or 1am (2am during

Ramadan) and cost 25-35pt, 50pt to outside beaches like El Agami or Montaza. Buses are marked in Arabic numerals.

From Orabi Square:
#203 (٢٠٣): to airport.
#220 (٢٢٠): to Sidi Bishr.
#231 (٢٣١): to Citadel.
#251 (٢٥١): to Abu Qir via Al-Huriyya St.
#260 (٢٦٠): to Abu Qir via the corniche.

From Ramleh Station:
#210 (٢١٠): to Maritime Station.
#221 (٢٢١): to Ma'mura.
#403 (٤٠٣): to Dakhla.
#460 (٤٦٠): to Hannoville.

Minibuses

A more appetizing alternative to the crowded city buses, these run from 5:30am to 1am (2am in Ramadan) and cost 25-50pt. Stand somewhere on the side of the street and hold up the number of fingers equal to the number of passengers in your group. If there's room inside, the driver will nod and pull over.

From Orabi Square:
#703 (٧٠٣): to the airport via Ramleh Station.
#704 (٧٠٤): to the fishing club via Ramleh Station
#727 (٧٢٧): to Abu Qir.
#736 (٧٣٦): to Ma'mura.
#779 (٧٧٩): to Mandara.

From Sa'ad Zaghloul Sq.:
#707 (٧٠٧): to the Citadel.
#725 (٧٢٥): to the Citadel via the corniche.
#735 (٧٣٥): to Montaza.
#750 (٧٥٠): to Bitash.
#760 (٧٦٠): to Hannoville.
#781 (٧٨١): to International Gardens.

From Misr Station: #728 (٧٢٨) to Montaza and Abu Qir; **#729** (٧٢٩) to Abu Qir, **#755** (٧٥٥), **765** (٧٦٥) to El Agami; **#770** (٧٧٠) to Ma'mura.
From Montaza: #719 (٧١٩) to Sa'ad Zaghloul Sq. and Qaytbay.
From Ras et-Tin: #735 (٧٣٥) to Montaza (along the corniche).

Taxis

A local taxi ride in Alexandria is marginally less death-defying than in Cairo, and a comparatively inexpensive way to avoid the slow grind of the tram and the sardine-can squalor of the city buses. Don't wait for an empty taxi: hail one going in your direction and shout your destination into the window. The meters never run, so pay as you please. No matter how big your group (3 is the maximum), you can get away with E£2 to almost anywhere, E£3 if you're feeling generous. Longer trips (Montaza or Abu Qir) enter the E£4-5 range, and past midnight E£5-7 is expected. Long trips past midnight (the length of the city to Montaza) will be E£10. There is a E£1 minimum (even for a block or two) and as a tourist you will be haggled for more.

INTERCITY TRANSIT

Alexandria lies at the junction of lush Delta farmlands, the barren Western Desert, and the Mediterranean coast. Cairo is a three-hour drive to the southeast on either of two roads. The scenic Delta road (231km) crosses both branches of the Nile and passes through the industrial city of Tanta, while the desert road (225km) nudges Wadi Natrun and passes through Giza.

Buses

Superjet Buses (tel. 421 90 92 or 422 85 66) offer A/C, snacks, drinks, bathrooms, and loud Egyptian movies. Buses and ticket booth in a space-age complex in 15 May Sq., behind the Sidi Gaber train station. Buses to Cairo every 30min. around the clock. To downtown or the airport (E£20 before 5pm; 5pm-12:30am E£25 downtown, E£31 to the airport). Daily buses to: **Marsa Matrouh** (7:15am and 4:30pm in summer only, 6hr., E£23); **Hurghada** (8pm, 12hr., E£70); and **Port Said** (6:45am, 4½hr., E£22).

West Delta Bus Company (tel. 80 96 85) has 2 types of buses. Regular buses run to destinations within Egypt and don't have A/C, while **Golden Arrow** buses are reserved for longer distances, and offer the same luxuries as Superjet. Tickets are sold from a booth at the south side of Sa'ad Zaghloul Sq., but buses depart from the same location as Superjet, behind Sidi Gaber Station. Daily buses go to: **Cairo,** stopping at Giza Sq., Tahrir Sq., and usually the airport (every hr. round the clock, 3hr., E£20); **Marsa Matrouh** (7 and 8am, 3pm, 6hr., E£15-20); **Port Said** (6am and 4:30pm, 4½hr., E£20); **Ismailiyya** (7 and 9am, 5hr., E£15); **Suez** (6:30am and 2:30pm, 4½hr., E£19); **Siwa** (7 and 11am, 8hr., E£18-35); **Hurghada** (6am, A/C, 12hr., E£55); **Tanta** (10am, noon, 4, and 6pm, 1½hr., E£10); **Mansura** (7, 9, and 11am, 3hr., E£8); **Zagazig** (8am and 2pm, 3hr., E£8); **Dumyat** (Damietta) (6:30 and 7:30am, 3hr., E£10-16); and **Mataria** (2:30pm, 3hr., E£10).

Trains

The turbo **Turbino** trains leave at 8am, 2 and 7pm (2hr.; 1st class E£22, 2nd class E£17; no student discount). The slightly slower **French line** departs at 10 and 11am, 1, 3:30, 5, and 8pm (2½hr. 1st class E£20, 2nd class E£12; 30% student discount). Trains to **Marsa Matrouh** leave at 6:45am (with A/C, E£17) and 1:30pm (no A/C, E£8.10), 6hr. A train to **Luxor** leaves at 10:10pm (11hr.; 1st class E£62, 2nd class E£37; student discounts available) and the train to **Aswan** leaves at noon (22hr. 2nd class with A/C E£40, without E£19.60).

Service Taxis

Service are cheap and comfortable. Because of all the competition from other means of transportation, however, they depart less frequently than in other cities. Shared vans or station wagons (mainly Peugeots) depart from Misr Station, in front of the main gates. *Service* go to: **Cairo** (3hr. by the desert road, E£10); **Marsa Matrouh** (3hr., E£10); **Tanta** (2hr., E£4); **Mansura** (3hr., E£4); **Abu Qir** (30min., 60pt); **Zagazig** (2hr., E£10); **Rashid** (1hr., E£3); and **Port Said** (4hr., E£10).

Planes

EgyptAir is at 19 Sa'ad Zaghloul St., just east of Ramleh Station Sq. (tel. 482 59 38; open daily 8am-8pm). Alexandria's small airport lies several km southeast of downtown. Local bus #203 and minibus #703 run between Orabi Sq. and the airport. **Lufthansa,** 6 Tala'at Harb St. (tel. 482 26 07), flies nonstop from Alexandria to Frankfurt Wednesday and Sunday at 8am (one-way E£2737, youth E£1444). **Olympic Airlines,** on Sa'ad Zaghloul St. one block east of EgyptAir (tel. 482 10 14 or 72 95; fax 482 89 01; open Mon.-Fri. 8:30am-4:30pm, Sat. 8:30am-12:30pm), flies from Alexandria to Athens (one way E£1280, youth E£702).

PRACTICAL INFORMATION

Tourist Office: Main office (tel. 484 33 80) on Nabi Daniel St., at the southwest corner of Sa'ad Zaghloul Sq. English spoken fluently. Open daily 8:30am-6pm, winter 8:30am-5pm, Ramadan 9am-4pm, holidays 8am-2pm. Branch offices at **Misr Station** (tel. 492 59 85; same hours) and the **Maritime Station** (tel. 480 34 94; open 8am-5pm and additional hours for boat arrivals), and at the **airport** (tel. 420 20 21 or 20 36). Pick up a free copy of *Alexandria by Night and Day* and *Alexandria and the Beaches.*

Tourist Police: Montaza Palace (tel. 547 33 95). Branch office upstairs from the tourist office in **Sa'ad Zaghloul Sq.** (tel. 483 33 78). Both open 24hr. Also branches in the **amphitheater** (tel. 490 62 73), **Citadel** (tel. 480 91 44), and the **Greco-Roman Museum** (tel. 482 89 12).

Passport Office: 28 Tala'at Harb St. (tel. 483 77 51). Walk west on Sa'ad Zaghloul Sq. from Ramleh Station Sq. and bear left on Falaky St. when Sa'ad Zaghloul curves toward the sea. Tala'at Harb St. is your first left. Open Sat.-Wed. 8:30am-2pm and 7-9pm, Thurs. 8:30am-1:30pm. Conduct your business in Cairo if possible.

Consulates: Ireland, 36 Khafra Abd Street, Roushdi (tel. 546 46 86). Open Sun.-Thurs. 9am-3pm. **U.K.,** 3 Mena St., Roushdi (tel. 546 70 01), off Kafr Abdou St. About 6km east of downtown, several blocks south of the corniche. Open Sun.-Thurs. 8am-1pm. **Israel,** 207 Abd es-Salem Aref St., Loran (tel. 586 38 74). Open Sun.-Thurs. 9:30am-12:30pm. **Lebanon,** 64 Liberty St. (482 65 89). For **U.S.** consular questions, contact the American Center (see Cultural Centers, below) or the U.S. Embassy in Cairo (see p. 99).

Currency Exchange: Many exchange places offer better rates than banks but will only take cash. Egyptian banks are on every other downtown corner; most are open Sat.-Thurs. 8:30am-noon or 2pm and 5-7 or 8pm. **National Bank of Egypt** in the **Cecil Hotel** in Sa'ad Zaghloul Sq. is quick (open daily 8:30am-8:30pm, Fri.-Sat. 9am-1pm and 6-8pm). **Sheraton Montaza** (tel. 548 05 50) on the corniche. Open daily 9am-11pm. The **Bank of Alexandria,** 59 Sa'ad Zaghloul St. (tel. 483 85 88 or 89). Open Sun.-Thurs. 8:30am-2pm (10am-1:30pm during Ramadan). **Bank Misr,** Safia Zaghloul St. between the Metro Cinema and Al Huriyya St. won't cash traveler's checks, but gives Visa and MC advances. Open Sun.-Thurs. 8am-2pm.

American Express: Main office at 34 El Mou'asker er-Roumani St. (tel. 541 01 77 or 17 08; fax 545 73 63), 50m south of the Pizza Hut on the corniche in Roushdi. Open Sat.-Thurs. 8:30am-5pm. Full service office, but it doesn't hold mail.

Thomas Cook: 15 Sa'ad Zaghloul Sq., P.O. Box 6 (tel. 483 51 18 or 484 78 30; fax 483 40 73). Full range of services. Open daily 8am-5pm.

Buses, Taxis, Flights: see **Getting Around,** p. 151, and **Intercity Transit,** p. 152.

Car Rental: Avis (tel. 483 71 73; fax 483 64 01), in the Cecil Hotel, on Sa'ad Zaghloul Sq. Rents a Fiat (E£127, 50pt. every km over 100). Insurance and emergency assistance are extra—but if you really want to drive in this vehicular slaughterhouse they're probably worth it. Open daily 8am-10pm.

English Bookstores: The best is **Al-Ma'aret,** 44 Sa'ad Zaghloul St. (tel. 483 33 03), another entrance on the south side of Sa'ad Zaghloul Sq. Strange selection of textbooks, translations of Arabic works, and trashy paperbacks. Open Mon.-Sat. 10am-9:30pm. **General Egyptian Book Organization,** 49 Sa'ad Zaghloul St. (tel. 482 29 25), just down the street from Al-Ma'aret. Medium-sized selection ranges from *Sweet Valley High* to *The Art of Pediatrics.* Open daily 9am-9pm.

Cultural Centers: U.S., 3 Phara'ana St. (tel. 483 60 24). Take a left on Al Huriyya St. from Safia Zaghloul St., walk 1 block past the sign for the Greco-Roman Museum, turn left and then the first right. Fine book/video library. Inquire about **teaching jobs** at the English Teaching Program. Cultural events calendar posted outside. Open Sun.-Thurs. 8:30am-4:30pm. **British Council,** 9 Ptolemies St. (tel. 482 98 90 or 481 01 99). Open Sun.-Thurs. 10am-3:30pm. Library open Sun.-Wed. 10am-7:30pm, Sat. and Thurs. 10am-4pm.

Cotton Candy Machine Rental: The roving dealership is usually stationed in Orabi Sq. Ask for the "Fluffy Ahmed" week-long special (E£32).

Pharmacy: Oxford Pharmacy, 10 Faculty of Medicine St. (tel. 483 67 20). One block south of Sa'ad Zaghloul Sq., one block east of Safia Zaghloul, at the top of the hill. No English sign—look for the big red crescent with a cross in it. Open 24hr.

Hospital: El Mowasah (tel. 481 28 85 or 88), on Al Huriyya St. in Al Haddara.

Emergency: Ambulance: tel. 123. **Tourist Police:** tel. 126. **Police:** tel. 122. If possible, contact the Tourist Police.

Post Office: All open Sat.-Thurs. 8am-3pm and do **EMS** (until 2pm) unless otherwise noted. A branch at the tram stop at **Ramleh Station Sq.** (tel. 482 07 46) and 2 on **El Ghorfa et-Tigariyya St.** (3 blocks west of Sa'ad Zaghloul Sq. and 2 blocks west of Orabi Sq.) with no **EMS,** but **Poste Restante** until 1pm (packages held at **Misr Station,** 10m south of Al Huriyya).

Telephone Office: Ramleh Station Sq. office charges E£24 for 3min. to the U.S.; minimal phone card discount. Open 24hr. Also at **Misr Station,** at the west end of Sa'ad Zaghloul St. on the corner of Sultan Hussein St. Phones require cards, but they don't sell them. Open daily 7am-midnight, and in the post office on Safia Zaghloul St. **Luxury hotels** (try the Cecil in Sa'ad Zaghloul Sq.) offer more expensive overseas connections. Rates for 3min. to: U.S./Canada E£211, U.K. E£21, Australia E£31. **Information:** tel. 125. **Telephone Code:** 03.

ACCOMMODATIONS

E.M. Forster liked Alexandria so much he wrote a book about it and named a character in *A Room with a View* after the Cecil Hotel. Steer clear of the ultra-cheap (E£10 per night) dives that line the streets running south from the corniche near Ramleh Station Sq. It's better to stay in one of the hotels listed below: all are clean, cheap, and within walking distance of the two main squares. None have fans, unless noted; most Alexandrians depend on sea breezes for air-conditioning. In summer, look for corner rooms with cross ventilation.

Streets in **El Manshiyya Sq.** bristle with budget hotels. For a beachside retreat, head out to Sidi Bishr (14km) or Montaza (18km), where the amenities balance the inconvenience of staying so far from the center of town. There is **camping** by the beach at Abu Qir for 50pt (see p. 161).

Hotel Union, 164 26 July St. (tel. 80 73 12 or 77 71), on the corniche; enter on the side street. Facing out into the Eastern Harbor, the views from the lobby and select rooms cannot be beat. Marble baths provide the perfect complement to the airy, modern rooms. Singles E£25, with bath E£32; doubles E£31, with bath E£41. TV for rooms with private bath E£3. From July-Sept., mandatory breakfast E£6. Extra beds E£10. 20% tax.

Hotel Marhaba, 10 Ahmed Orabi Sq. (tel. 480 09 57 or 95 10), on the northwest side of Orabi Sq. The former summer residence of the King of Libya. Rooms are large and breezy, and there are 3 pool tables (E£10 per hour), an international phone, and a neat coffee shop with a neon fountain. Louis XV sitting room on each floor, and all rooms have color satellite TV. Singles E£30, with bath E£36; doubles E£42, with bath E£50. Tax and rooftop breakfast buffet included.

New Capri Hotel, 23 El Mina esh-Sharaya, 8th floor (tel. 480 93 10 or 97 03). Same building as tourist office in Sa'ad Zaghloul Sq. Corner rooms offer panoramic views of the corniche and Sa'ad Zaghloul Sq. Firm beds, blue baths, and a lifeboat in the dining room. Singles E£18, with bath E£22; doubles E£24, with bath E£28.

Hotel Acropole, 27 Rue de Chambre de Commerce (tel. 480 59 80), 4th floor. Breezy, lacy TV lounge. Teeny tiny toilet smells like mothballs. Beds are lumpy and dusty, but comfy. Amazing views dictate the price. Singles E£15-20; doubles E£25-30. Breakfast included.

Sea Star Hotel, 24 Amin Fakri St. (tel. 483 17 87 or 53 43; fax 483 23 88). The wood-and-glass futuristic lobby is definitely the best thing about the Sea Star—take the temperamental elevator upstairs and you'll find the medium-sized rooms to be nothing special. International phone and fax and a funk-oozing TV lounge. Singles E£18-22.50; doubles E£25-30, depending on bath and view.

Hotel Normandy, 8 Gamal ed-Din Yassin St., 4th floor (tel. 480 68 30). Mentioned in Australian phenom Ted Simon's landmark travel narrative *Jupiter's Travels.* All rooms have 3 beds, high ceilings, and shared baths. Some have a decent view of the water. The baths are old but clean. Rooms E£30 with view, E£25 without; in winter E£25, E£20. Discounts for students, groups, or longer stays.

Hotel Gamil, 8 Gamal ed-Din Yassin St., 4th floor (tel. 481 54 58). Dedicated to students and youth. Warm, polished wood. Small doubles with big beds. E£22, no view E£17; winter E£12, E£8. Breakfast E£2. Free use of the kitchen.

Hotel Dar Mekka, 8 Gamal ed-Din Yassin St., 4th floor (tel. 480 89 40 or 78 72). Light blue molding and pseudo-antique flair make for a quaint lobby. Steamy pink-tiled bathrooms manage to stay sanitary. Some rooms have balconies with ocean views. Singles E£25; doubles E£30; triples E£50.

FOOD

Alexandria is renowned for its seafood, but it's no surprise that the cheapest, most abundant eats are at *fuul* and *ta'miyya* stands. You shouldn't have to pay more than 50pt for sandwiches around Misr Station. Ramleh Station Square now boasts three **fast food** joints: Baskin Robbins, McDonald's (tel. 483 28 79 or 02), and KFC (tel. 482 96 58). The latter two and Domino's Pizza (tel. 546 57 78) deliver.

Meat, fruits, seafood, and vegetables can be found in the *souq* in El Moasker (take any blue tram six or seven stops east and walk south). The fishmongers will cook your purchase on the spot for E£3-5. **Supermarkets** dot the area around Sa'ad Zaghloul Sq. Gastronomic voyeurs should sneak a peek into **Atelier Trianon,** where an international staff makes wonderful pastries (Rue Sharm esh-Sheikh, between Istamboul and Nazmi Boutros St.). Muhammad Ahmed's **Falafel Workshop** dishes out insight into the falafel-making process (go up Abd el-Fatlah el-Hadari St. from Ahmed's *fuul* restaurant and turn right down the first alley, to the brick building on the left); green industrial-revolution-era falafel churners spin chickpeas into a heavenly mash.

The **Asteria** liquor store sells beer, wine, and liquor seven days a week, even during Ramadan (located behind the Elite on the left). The **Venobles** has a similar selection with slightly higher prices (adjacent to the post office near the Spitfire, closed Sunday). If the Egyptian heat has made you *really* thirsty, head to the **Stella depot** behind the Cecil Hotel, where Egypt's finest brew can be bought by the case (E£106). Look for the Stella label colored door.

Muhammad Ahmed Fuul, 17 Abd el-Fattah el-Hadari St. (tel. 483 35 76), 1 block south of Sa'ad Zaghloul Sq. and 1 block west of Safia Zaghloul St. 10m up on the left; no English sign. Join Egyptian families who flock here nightly and have some of the best *fuul* of your life (falafel, *fuul,* salad, and Coke E£5). A/C. Open daily 6am-midnight, later in summer.

Restaurant Denis, 1 Ibn Bassam St. (tel. 482 10 79), 4 blocks east of Sa'ad Zaghloul Sq., adjacent to the corniche. Great budget seafood. Allow Shokri, the English-speaking owner, to lead you into the kitchen to select your prey (fish E£25-30 per kg, calamari E£20, shrimp E£80), and then enjoy it with a variety of breads, dips, and salads. Beer and wine. Open daily noon-11pm.

Elite, 43 Safia Zaghloul St. (tel. 482 35 92), 1 block north of Al Huriyya St. Breezy, stylin' artists' cafe and restaurant (since 1900), run by a friendly Greek matriarch. Filled with gallery posters and world-weary expats. The haze of smoke vibrates with a bizarre mix of music: 50s jazz and high-energy techno. Good food, slow service, and weekly postings of activities for foreigners (rice with meat E£3.50, omelette E£6.50, Stella E£5).

Taverna (tel. 482 81 89), on the southern side of Ramleh Station Sq., across from the trams, next to KFC. Amiable, French-speaking chef grills up excellent *souvlaki* (E£4.50), and standard (but tasty) pasta dishes (E£5.50-9). Good bargains at the ground-level take-away. Open daily 7:30am-2am. Also at Montaza Gardens (tel. 547 54 38); Manshiyya (tel. 80 49 07); Ekbal (tel. 586 48 02); and Ma'mura (tel. 547 18 63). Visa, AmEx.

Trianon (tel. 482 09 86), on the corner of Sa'ad Zaghloul and Ramleh Station Sq. Alexandrian lovebirds coo across coffee and cake in the salon while the upper crust dine in the art deco restaurant with piano accompaniment (entrees E£20-30). Watch the world go by from white armchairs under parasols. Moussaka Trianon E£11, Beef Burguer Le Salon E£15. For dessert try the heavy-duty *crème caramel* (E£6) or *om aly* (E£12).

Restaurant Bleck, 18 Sa'ad Zaghloul St. Walk west on Sa'ad Zaghloul until you're 2 blocks from Orabi Sq. Vegetable soups and salads E£1-4, Lebanese specialties E£4-14, fish and meat E£11-16, *osso bucco,* quail, and brain. Also serves a variety of Egyptian pastries (E£3-6). Limited menu after 7pm (mainly *kobebu,* a hearty meat and grain dish, and stuffed grape leaves). Open daily 6am-midnight,

Cafeteria Asteria, 40 Safia Zaghloul St. (tel. 482 22 93), across from the Metro Cinema. Come hang with the locals for filling, basic fare (pizza E£7-9, sandwiches E£1.20-2.40, Stella E£5.50). Open daily 8am-midnight.

Gad Restaurant, on the south side of Ramleh Station Sq., across from the trams. Gad has locations all over town. Large, zesty *ta'miyya* and *fuul* for 35pt. Greaseball *shawerma* for a few E£ more. Open daily 24hr.

Kadoura Restaurant, on the corniche about a block before the Tikka Grill sign. More good seafood. Pick your poison downstairs (several varieties of fish, crab, calamari, and sometimes even lobster) then head up the slippery spiral stairs for a great view of the ocean and the corniche crowd below. A gut-busting meal of seafood, salad, bread, and drink (enough for two) E£25. Open noon-midnight.

Tikka Grill (tel. 481 76 04), jutting into the Eastern Harbor near Abu el-Abbas Mosque, 1.5km west of Sa'ad Zaghloul Sq. An Alexandrian favorite with good service, an excellent salad bar, and a sweeping view of the corniche. The entrees are not as good as the supporting cast. Full meals cost around E£30. Alcohol served. Open daily 1pm-1am. AmEx, Visa, MC.

Coffee, Sweets, and Smokes

Sa'ad Zaghloul Square is packed to the gills with coffee and pastry shops, and ice cream parlors cool off the Ramleh Station Square. Along the corniche you'll find ritzy cafes and *sheesha* joints; cheaper, more traditional *ahwas* are found further inland.

Sultana (tel. 482 27 69), on the south side of Ramleh Station Sq., across from the trams. Fantastic ice cream (E£1.25 per scoop), fruit salad, and toppings. Rotating seasonal flavors and made-while-you-watch waffle cones. A madhouse in the evenings. Open daily 8:30am-3am, and they deliver.

Brazilian Coffee Store, in two locations: a sit-down at 20 Salah Salem St. (open daily 7am-10pm) or a stand-up at 44 Sa'ad Zaghloul St. (tel. 482 50 59; open daily 7am-midnight). Home-roasted and ground beans for hot or iced coffee (E£1, cappuccino E£1.50, ice cream 33pt per scoop, cake E£1.50).

Sofianopoulo Coffee Shop (tel. 483 15 17), on Sa'ad Zaghloul St. as it curves seaward. Classic coffee shop with huge roasters and grinders. Cappuccino (E£1.25) is the cheapest around. Tang on tap. Open 8am-10:30pm.

Cafe Baudrot, 23 Sa'ad Zaghloul St. A fine retreat from the busy street. Great vine-tressled garden in back for beer (E£5.05), coffee (E£2.05), and cakes (E£1.85).

Samadi Patisserie, adjacent to Tikka Grill in a lush patio setting, doles out generous helpings of *ba'laweh, bashouseh, kinafeh,* and other goodies. Fresh strawberry ice cream E£1.50. Open daily 10:30am-2am. Visa, MC, AmEx.

Pastroudis (tel. 492 96 09), Al Huriyya St., one block west of Safia Zaghloul. Art nouveau atmosphere. E£5 minimum charge. Open daily 8am-9pm.

Delices (tel. 482 54 60), opposite the corniche in Sa'ad Zaghloul Sq. Cosmopolitan French and Middle Eastern pastry. Pricier and posher than the competition. Ice cream E£2.25 per scoop, pastries E£5-8, coffee E£3.50. Open daily 8am-1am.

SIGHTS

Very little remains of ancient Alexandria, since the modern city was built directly atop the old. The excellent **Greco-Roman Museum,** 5 El Mathaf er-Roumani St. (tel. 482 58 20), displays the most interesting relics of ancient Alexandria and its Hellenistic civilization. The cult of Serapis is well represented; look for handsome sculptures of Zeus, Apis, and the Greek youth Harpocrates with his finger in his ear. The museum's courtyard contains an intriguing crocodile temple attributed to the cult of Phepheros, as well as a mummified crocodile and other assorted delights from Egypt's Greco-Roman past. There's also a large collection of brightly painted *tanaga* statuettes, a sort of Ptolemaic action figure. To reach the museum, walk south from the corniche along Safia Zaghloul St., turn left on Al Huriyya St., then again at the museum sign (open daily 9am-4pm, Ramadan and holidays 10am-3pm; E£8, students E£4; camera privileges (no flash) E£10, video E£150).

From the museum it's an easy meander to the three major ancient sites, all of which lie within a few km of downtown. Just northwest of Misr Station and south of Cinema

Amir is the beautifully preserved white marble **Roman Amphitheater,** the only one of its kind in Egypt. Behind the 13-tiered theater, the ruins of a Roman bath, villa, and cistern decompose. "Guides" may offer to sneak you in for a fee, but don't bother—almost everything of interest is visible from the theater. Excavations are still under-way in the bath area, and new pieces are unearthed regularly. From Sa'ad Zaghloul Sq., walk up Nabi Daniel St. past Al Huriyya St. to the next big intersection. Turn left across from a gas station and go 200m; the entrance will be on your left (open daily 9am-4pm, Ramadan 10am-3pm; E£6, students E£3).

Named by ignorant Crusaders in the Middle Ages, **Pompey's Pillar** actually dates from Diocletian's time (several centuries after Pompey), and was part of the Serapium, a religious center where the rites of the bull god were conducted. Responding to a revolt in Alexandria, Emperor Diocletian swore that he would massa-cre the rebellious people until blood stained the knees of his horse. As he entered the defeated and cowering town, his mount stumbled into a pool of blood, prematurely fulfilling his oath. The emperor spared the city and its inhabitants, and the lone pillar remains as a symbol of the people's gratitude to him and his klutzy horse. Made of pink granite from Aswan, this 25m megalith was the tallest structure in ancient Alex-andria. The ruins of the Serapium (leveled once the Roman Empire turned Christian) were excavated and the best finds were moved to the Greco-Roman museum (site open daily 9am-5pm, Ramadan 9am-3pm; E£6, students E£3). To get to the site, take bus #309 from Ramleh Station Sq. and get off on Karmouz St. when you see the pillar. Enter on the southern side of the complex. You can also take tram #16.

Just after the entrance to the pillar complex, take a right and climb the hill to reach the **Catacombs of Kom esh-Shoqafa** (Hill of Potsherds), three-tiered Roman tombs descending about 35m. The sculptures and reliefs of Egyptian gods with virile Roman bodies are a blend of Pharaonic and Roman Art. A statue of jackal-headed Anubis stands near the entrance to the innermost burial chamber. To the left (as you enter the central rotunda) is the Triclinium, a set of three benches upon which mourners could recline and dine during funerary rites (open daily 9am-4pm, during Ramadan 9am-3pm; E£12, students E£6; camera privileges E£10).

For more graves, visit the **Tombs of Chatby,** Port Said St., across from St. Mark's College. Dating from the 4th century BCE, these tombs are believed to be the oldest surviving in Alexandria. The post-mortem trinkets that once filled the two separate chambers have been taken to the Greco-Roman museum (open daily 9am-4pm; E£6, students E£3; camera privileges E£5).

The **Anfushi tombs,** just east of the Ras et-Tin Palace on Ras et-Tin St., were built for Greek occupants who had adopted Egyptian customs in the first half of the 3rd century BCE. Cut into the limestone of what was once Pharos Island, they are placed in two groups around a staircase leading into an open court and may well extend far-ther under the palace gardens (open 9am-4pm; E£12, students E£6; camera privileges E£5). Take tram #16 or minibus #735. The **Mustafa Kamal Necropolis,** located on Moaskar el-Romani in Roushdi, consists of four tombs from the 2nd century BCE dec-orated in a more Hellenic style (open daily 9am-4pm; E£12, students E£6; camera privileges E£5). To reach the Mustafa Kamal Necropolis, take tram #1, 2, or 5.

The Islamic **Fort Qaytbay** (tel. 80 91 44) was built on the ancient island of Pharos, on the foundations of the lighthouse. Silt connected the island to the mainland, leav-ing the fort at the tip of a peninsula. Built in 1480 CE by the Mamluk Sultan Ashraf Qaytbay, the citadel houses the remains of the French fleet sunk by Admiral Nelson in the battle of Abu Qir. There is a small mosque in the center of the tower—the entire fortress is aligned so that its *mihrab* faces Mecca. The fort is still classified as a mili-tary installation (open daily 9am-2pm; E£6, students E£3; camera privileges E£5). To reach the fort, take yellow tram #15 west from Ramleh Station and get off when it makes a sharp left turn, or take any of the buses going to Ras et-Tin. You'll find your-self in the middle of an open-air **fish market.** At the point where the tram turned left, you should make a right on the road between the Kuwait Airlines sign and the mosque; the fort is at the end of this road. Minibus #707 or 719 from Ramleh Station Sq. will take you to the beginning of the street.

The **Mosque of Morsi Abu el-Abbas** is Alexandria's most prominent and elaborate example of Islamic architecture. Located 1km south of the fort along the corniche, it is the city's largest mosque and a destination for worshippers. The holy Sidi Shehab ed-Din Abu el-Abbas Ibn el-Khazragi came from Andalucia just before the expulsion of the Moors to spread the teachings of the Qur'an throughout Egypt. His tomb rests in the back of the mosque. Legend professes that he rose from his tomb to catch falling bombs during World War II raids. The coffin, like the exterior of the mosque, is often bathed in a green neon glow. Although the tomb dates from the 13th century, the mosque was built by an Italian in the 20th. Women are only allowed in the back room (open daily 5am-10pm, except prayer times; dress modestly).

The **Eliahou Hannabi Synagogue,** on Rue Dr. Hussein Faladi, an alley one block south of Safia Zaghloul St. between Nabi Daniel and Rue Abd el-Fattah el-Hadari, is the modern-day center of Alexandria's ancient Jewish community (open Sun.-Fri. 8am-1pm). The gracious Joe Harari (in the *Communauté Israelite Grand Rabbinate* office to the right as you enter the courtyard) will show you around, let you look at old photographs, and tell you all about Alexandrian Jewry. Built in 1885 by Baron Jacques L. de Menasce for the then-thriving community (there was a synagogue in each neighborhood), the synagogue is a towering edifice with five aisles, stained glass clerestory windows, 28 pink Italian marble columns, dangling chandeliers, and wooden pews (check out the international assemblage of names on the brass seat markers). Most other Jewish buildings in Alexandria have been destroyed. The 1860 **Temple Menasce** in Orabi Sq. still stands but is locked and guarded; the **Temple Chaaré Tefila** on Rue Eleusis in Camp Caesar was reincarnated as a mosque and then a medical clinic, and the **Hospital Israelite Foundation de Menasce** in Sporting is now the Et-Talaba Hospital. Three Jewish cemeteries, one in Mesarita and two in Chatby, remain (the guards may let you in).

The **Coptic Orthodox Patriarchate** houses a beautiful church (founded in 67 CE and rebuilt in 1950) at 19 Elah Abad St., adorned with mosaics, stained glass, hanging ostrich eggs, and a finely painted iconostasis. The first 47 patriarchs of the Alexandrian See (regional seat of church authority), beginning with St. Mark, now lie within; their names are listed in a nook on the right side of the church. Mark's relics are in a chapel to the left of the *baikal.* Take off your shoes before you enter (open daily with services Wed. at noon and Sun. and Fri. at 8am; foreigners welcome).

The 17th-century church in the **Greek Orthodox Monastery of St. Saba** is another impressive testament to the historical importance of Christianity in Alexandria. Inside is a marble columnar table on which St. Catherine was beheaded, as well as beautiful paintings, a spectacular collection of amulets, and a gigantic bronze bell. From Sa'ad Zaghloul Sq. walk up Safia Zaghloul St. to Sultan Hussein St., make a right, then take your second left (open daily 7:30am-12:30pm and 3:30-6pm. Sun. service 8am; foreigners welcome).

Behind the governor's residence sits the architecturally intriguing **Royal Jewelry Museum,** 27 Ahmed Yehia St. (tel. 586 83 48), in Glim. It was originally the Palace of Fatima ez-Zahraa. The museum contains the gleaming baubles of the Muhammad Ali era. Most memorable are the pieces once belonging to the royal family, all of which were nationalized after the reign of King Farouk. Take tram #2 (look for the red sign) to get there (open Sat.-Thurs. 9am-4pm, Fri. 9-11:30am and 1:30-4pm; E£10, students E£5; camera privileges E£10). The **Fine Arts Museum,** 1 Menasce St. (tel. 493 66 16), in Moharram Bay contains a small but interesting collection of modern Egyptian art as well the city's public library. Exhibitions by contemporary foreign and Egyptian artists are often held here; call for details (open Sat.-Thurs. 9am-1pm and 5-8pm; free). From Misr Station walk east on Mahmoud Bey Salama St., along the southern side of the railroad tracks. The museum is on the right at the first major intersection, about 1km down. You can also take tram #2, 6, or 8.

ENTERTAINMENT

Beaches

Alexandria's most popular attraction is the waterfront—Cairenes come here by the thousands during the blazing summer months. The majority of the crowded coastline in Alexandria is lined with trash, but if the hordes haven't sent you scurrying to the Sinai, you'll be pleased to know that some sand strips are nicer than others.

The highlight of Alexandria's eastern beaches is the **Montaza Palace and Gardens** (tel. 86 00 56 or 79). Originally built in 1892, this former summer retreat of King Farouk includes 400 acres of gardens. The palace and its museum have been closed to the public, but the gardens and groves are still a favorite picnic spot for Alexandrians. The gardens can get quite crowded on weekends, especially on Fridays. Ice cream stores, Pizza Hut, Chicken Tikka, a juice stand, and a supermarket lie within the garden gates. Along the beach, you can rent pedal boats (E£15), regular boats (E£40), or jetskis (E£180) by the hour (admission to the gardens E£4; to a nicer beach in front of the Palestine Hotel E£15; on holidays, E£8).

Just east of Montaza you'll find **Ma'mura,** a favorite among Alexandria's youth (admission E£1.25). Both Montaza and Ma'mura can be reached by bus #221, 250, or 260, or by minibus #728, 736, or 770. Closer to the city center lies **San Stefano,** about halfway between Montaza and Sa'ad Zaghloul Sq. Chairs and umbrellas go for E£4-6, small changing rooms on the beach cost E£10 per day, and larger cabanas start at E£25. Take tram #1, 2, or 5 from Ramleh Station Sq. west of Alexandria—the beaches are much broader, cleaner, and far less crowded (see p. 163).

Bars, Clubs, and Discos

The days of Hellenistic hedonism are long gone. Despite its former cosmopolitan glory, nightlife in the city is a do-it-yourself affair. If you yearn for the mystery and exoticism that only sequin-clad flesh can capture, head to a **nightclub,** found in most luxury hotels. Try the Cecil (open 11:30pm-4am, E£65) or Lourantos (tel. 482 22 00; E£45; call for hours) for something close to downtown.

All of the **discos** are located in the major hotels and play a mix of Western and Arabic music. The **Ramada,** located along the corniche in Sidi Bishr, is the youngest and most happening place to shake your groove (entrance on the corniche side; open nightly 10pm-4am; E£25). The beautiful people head to the **Sheraton** to display their Rolexes as they grind (open nightly 10pm-4am, E£26). The small disco at the **Cecil Hotel** is full of day-glo Oriental decor (open nightly 8pm-2am, E£15). Many discos don't allow single men or women, and some relegate unescorted males to the bar and forbid them from dancing. These rules change constantly, but are usually relaxed for foreigners (especially wealthy foreigners). There are no cover charges, but **minimum charges** can be steep.

There are several often-empty **bars.** The coolest option around is the **Spitfire,** 7 Rue Bourse el-Hadema, two blocks up from the corniche between Sa'ad Zaghloul and Orabi Sq. (Stella E£6.50). Every inch of this expat favorite is covered in some decal or poster, and mellow Western music soothes rattled nerves (listen for Jimmy Buffet's decidedly non-Egyptian classic "Why Don't We Get Drunk and Screw?"). The **Athineos** also has a bar with a view of the corniche, although it's a bit cramped (Stella E£5). To relive WWII memories, head to **Monty's Bar,** on the second floor of the Cecil Hotel. Prints of classic paintings and occasional synthesizer music now occupy General Montgomery's former headquarters. If Monty's dim lights have got you down, head up to the **roof garden** for a fantastic view of the square and the water, but be careful where you sit—the sharp, green seats are actually cacti (Stella E£8 at both). The simple, breezy **Greek Club** attracts an older clientele and is popular with TOEFL teachers (Stella E£4.25). Take the blue trams east to El Moaskar, go south two blocks, then take a left; look for the "Micapaciatikoc" sign.

Other Diversions

Alexandrian nightlife follows a much more mellow, refined pace than that in Cairo. As the sun sets, the corniche fills with peaceful strollers, and the spacious *sheesha* parlors that line Sa'ad Zaghloul Sq. start smokin'. One of the more lively waterfront scenes can be found at Ma'mura, where a youthful crowd buzzes until well after midnight. Popular for grub and *sheesha* are the **Antazza Café** (no English sign, across from the mosque); **Minouche** (decent Italian food, E£10-20); and **Cafino** (above Antazza, open late, and has music videos).

Billiards tables, charged by the hour, are sprinkled throughout the city. You'll find the hippest table in town at **Cafino** (see above). The **Marhaba Hotel,** in Orabi Sq. (E£10, alcohol served, open late), and **Black and White,** on the left up a side street from the lively Camp Caesar *sheesha* cafes (E£15, 24hr.), have three tables each. For more highbrow entertainment, check with either the **Conservatoire de Musique d'Alexandrie,** 90 Al Hurriyya St. (tel. 483 50 86) or the **Sayed Darwish Theater,** 22 Fouad St. (tel. 482 51 06); both sponsor classical music concerts and dance recitals.

Every summer the breezy, outdoor **Muhammad Abd el-Wahab Theater,** on the corniche at Ramleh Station Sq., shows **traditional dancing.** Fir'et Rida (Rida's troupe) and El Fir'a el-Qawmiyya (the National Troupe), both featuring legendary belly dancers, perform high-energy dances representative of various areas in Egypt—including the exuberant men's cane dance from Upper Egypt (performances nightly 10:30pm; reserve tickets 1 or 2 days in advance; front-row E£10.50, cheap seats E£5; avoid the uncomfortable box seats). You may think you left the **circus** behind when you left Cairo, but the Ringling Brothers' Egyptian cousins are in Alexandria every summer (ask at the tourist office for the location of the 2 daily shows; tickets E£2-7). In September, the **Alexandria World Festival** brings theater, dancing, and other performing arts to the city. Ask at the tourist office for details.

English-language **films** are shown on nearly every corner in Alexandria. The **Amir** (tel. 492 76 93; admission E£5-15) and the **Metro** (tel. 483 04 32; admission E£5-15) are both in the downtown area. Movies are occasionally subtitled in French, and the French Cultural Center on 30 Nabi Daniel St. (tel. 492 04 84) shows films daily. The American Cultural Center does the same (see **Practical Information,** p. 153).

If the sound of thundering hooves makes your pulse race, head to the **Antoniadis Palace and Gardens** in Smouha on the wide road bordering the zoo. For over 50 years, Alexandria's working classes have gathered here on summer Sundays to watch working horses, with carriages of all kinds, race each other along this road at breakneck speed (arrive by 6pm; free). Ask at the tourist office for info on the various **sporting events** in the Alexandria Municipal Stadium.

■ Near Alexandria

ABU QIR ابو قير

The fishing village of **Abu Qir** (pronounced abu EER) lies on a peninsula 5km past Montaza and has yet to be absorbed by Alexandria's relentless expansion. The site of Nelson's 1798 naval victory over Napoleon's visions of Egyptian conquest is now a great place to sample Mediterranean seafood. You can avoid the crowds by visiting on a weekday, but people-watching on the weekends can be as good as the food. From Misr Station you can take **local bus** #251 or 260 or **minibus** #727 (every 30min., 7am-10pm, 20min., 50pt). There are also 3rd-class **trains** from Misr or Sidi Gaber Station (every 30min., 6am-10pm, 30min., 45pt), **local taxis** from downtown (15min., E£10), or **service taxis** from Misr Station (15min., E£1). Within Abu Qir, horse-drawn carriages (*hantour*) start their trots from El Bahr el-Mayyit St. (E£2-3).

To get seafood fresher than at Abu Qir's waterfront tables, you'd need to be a shark. Anglers right off the boat will cook the sea creature of your choice. **Zephyrion,** 14 Khalid Ibn al-Walid St. (tel. 560 13 19), has been an Abu Qir landmark since 1929. A full dinner at the beach pavilion, with lapping waves and lapped beer, costs about

E£40. The E£10 octopus (*kaborya*) plate is especially satisfying (open daily noon-midnight). Next door to Zephyrion is the similarly-priced **Bella Vista** (tel. 560 06 28; open daily noon-midnight). To reach either restaurant head north to the waterfront from the main mosque; they're both right on the beach.

Abu Qir Camp (tel. 560 14 24), located on El Bahr el-Mayyit St. about 500m south of the Zephyrion, supplies the only consistently available **camping** possibilities in the greater Alexandrian area (E£5, with your own tent or one of theirs).

RASHID (ROSETTA) رشيد

Rashid (Rosetta) lies on the northern edge of the Nile Delta, about 45 minutes east of Abu Qir and one hour east of Alexandria. The city serves as the western meeting point of the Nile and the Mediterranean (Dumyat is the eastern meeting point), but has received most of its notoriety from the 1799 discovery of the Rosetta Stone by Napoleon's soldiers. Dotted with provincial Ottoman mosques and houses from the 17th and 18th centuries, the port is steeped in Islamic architecture.

The **Rosetta Museum** features nothing of interest, but gives you something to do while in Rosetta (open daily 8am-4pm; E£10, students E£5; camera privileges E£10). The badly damaged 17th-century **Zaghloul Mosque** is at the end of the main street running south from the train station. For a more scenic approach, walk inland from the corniche, past the museum, and south through the **souq**. If you look past the rancid water and trash, you'll see some Arabic inscriptions, archways, and columns.

About 5km from Rosetta, the recently restored **Fort of Qaytbay** (not to be confused with the one in Alexandria) guards the strategic entrance to the Nile (open daily 9am-4pm, Ramadan 9am-3pm; E£6, students E£3). Built in 1479 by Sultan Ashraf Abu Nasr Qaytbay to serve as a first line of defense against the Ottoman Turks and the Crusaders coming from the Delta, this structure used to overlook the surrounding land; clay and silt deposits have built up around it so that the ground has risen to the level of the fort. Further fortification of the fortress by the French in 1799 required the importation of stone from Upper Egypt. A soldier noticed carvings on one of the stones, and this **Rosetta Stone** enabled Jean-François Champollion to unlock the mystery of the hieroglyphic alphabet. The stone (or a cast of it—the original resides in London) describes the coronation and numerous titles of Pharaoh Ptolemy V in three tongues: Demotic (the common language), ancient Greek (the royal language), and hieroglyphs (the holy language). (For more information, see **It's All Hieroglyphs To Me**, p. 192.) Although hieroglyphs had been indecipherable, ancient Greek was certainly not—by comparing the two translations, scholars finally had discovered a basic dictionary of hieroglyphics. Recent excavations have revealed Rashid (pharaonically named "Bulubatin") to be a site rich in ancient Egyptian history. The cheapest way to get to the fort is by green-and-white local taxi (one-way E£3-4, round-trip E£5). The romantic way to get there is to find a willing fisherman and go by boat (20min., E£5 per person round-trip). You'll see some beautiful scenery on the way.

To visit the peaceful **Mosque of Abu Mandur,** perched on the bank of the river, catch one of the southbound taxi boats at the main dock just across from the cannon in El Huriyya Sq. (round-trip E£4 per person). A nearby sandy hill offers a nice view of the countryside and an idyllic picnic spot.

West Delta Bus Co. buses run from Misr Station in Alexandria (every hr. 8am-10pm, E£2.50). The last return bus leaves at 5pm. You can catch **microbuses** from the Tikka Grill in Alexandria, one block inland from the corniche (E£3). The **train** (3rd-class only) runs from Misr Station (9 per day, 6:45am-10pm, 75pt). Trains return to Alexandria (9 per day, 5:50am-7:45pm, 60pt to Ma'mura, 70pt to downtown). **Service** to Alexandria depart somewhat infrequently (E£3-5).

WEST OF ALEXANDRIA

Construction of beach resort complexes stretches west from Alexandria as far as the eye can see, but there are still secluded spots to be found along Egypt's Mediterranean coast. These less-known areas draw a more local contingent of Egyptian families. Modesty is still the rule here; women will need to cover up. Even so, the mellow townsfolk and coastline's natural beauty can do wonders for the tired body and soul.

El Agami (20km from Alexandria) is popular with the Egyptian middle- and upper-classes and makes a convenient daytrip from Alexandria. Continuing west, you will notice that almost every inch of sand has been bought by one "vacation village" or another. Many of these cater to certain segments of Egyptian society: engineers, police, and doctors hole up in private concrete complexes near the beach. Most "villages" require a car and membership card. The plush **Aida Beach Hotel** (tel. 410 28 02), 72km from Alexandria, gives a choice of beach-use fees which fluctuate by season. The lower rate (E£8-12) includes snacks; the higher one (E£27-35, 2 person min.) includes lunch and use of a beach cabin; both include pool use. If you want to stay the night, be prepared to pay US$30-52 per person in a six-bed villa or US$37-60 in a double room (breakfast and dinner included). Day use at the **Atic Hotel** (tel. 906 07 17), 89km west of Alexandria (the domed gatehouse with red letters above it), costs E£45, but you get a beautiful beach, two pools, a playground, and lunch.

The war cemeteries of **El Alamein,** 99km from Alexandria, mark the site of Africa's fiercest and most significant World War II battles. The cheapest sandy spot in the area is the **Marina Beach Club,** 94km west of Alexandria. The E£15 day charge gets you on a beautiful beach, populated by wealthy Alexandrians zipping around on jet skis, but not into the pools. **Marsa Matrouh,** close to Libya, is a colorful resort town on a bay, featuring one of the world's most beautiful beaches. Though many coastline segments between Alexandria and Matrouh are depressingly clear of budget hotels, opportunities for free, secluded camping are virtually unlimited (simply check in with the nearest police or military office).

If you time your day right you could bask and feast at the beach, stop to visit the El Alamein memorials, and make it to Marsa Matrouh by sunset. **Microbuses** and *service taxis* cruise the Alexandria-Marsa Matrouh road all day; just flag one down (E£3.50 from Alexandria to the Atic, another E£5-8 to get to Marsa Matrouh).

■ El Agami الـﻟ.ـجمى

This haven for upper-middle class sun worshippers is close enough to Cairo and Alexandria to benefit from big city trends (Mercedes and cellular phones), but far enough to eschew the frantic pace and persistent hassle of the megalopolis. During the peak summer months, flesh bumps up against flesh in the competition for beach space, and women grow increasingly courageous in the quest to bear it all. In winter, hours shorten, prices drop, and the town quiets down.

Orientation and Practical Information El Agami is actually two towns in one—Bitash and Hannoville. When Egyptians say "El Agami" they're generally referring only to the former. In **Bitash,** villas and expensive hotels mingle with restaurants and Western-style boutiques, and American Top-40 rules the radio waves. **Hannoville,** the quieter, more practical sister city, houses a few budget hotels alongside rows of apartments. The entrances to the towns are right turns off of the highway. In both cases, cars turn onto the town's main road (Bitash St. or Hannoville St.), each lined with 2km of supermarkets, pharmacies, furniture stores, *sheesha* joints, and restaurants, before hitting the end of the road and the Mediterranean.

Minibus #760 and bus #460 (both from the south side of Sa'ad Zaghloul Sq. in Alexandria) will drop you off in front of The Costa Blanca Hotel in Hannoville. Minibus #765 and bus #465 (both from Misr Station) depart daily and stop right across the street in front of the Gad Restaurant (all routes run 6am-midnight, E£1).

Transportation between Bitash and Hannoville is cheap, but requires three **bus** transfers. From Hannoville, catch any bus heading to the T at the south end of town (25pt), and then catch another bus heading toward Alexandria, which will let you off at Bitash 2km further down (25pt). From here, it's a 2km walk to the heart of Bitash or another 25pt bus ride. Buses shuttle people around until midnight or so during the summer months. A **taxi** between Bitash and Hannoville should cost E£3-5.

The **National Bank of Egypt**, at #84 Bitash St., exchanges traveler's checks and cash (open Sun.-Thurs. 8:30am-2pm). Halfway between the beach and the road to Alexandria, **Banque Misr** (tel. 430 26 97) changes cash and does Visa and MC cash advances (open daily 8:30am-2pm). At the top of Bitash St. across from the gas station is the **bus stop,** where you can catch a summer bus to Cairo (daily 6pm, E£25). Most **pharmacies** on Bitash St. are open from 9am to 2am in the summer and from 8am to 10pm in the winter. The white facade of the **El Wah-Afaa Hospital** (tel. 435 83 18 or 85 06) is down Bitash St. at #53. At #62, the **Farouk Hospital** (tel. 433 29 25) has a 24-hour English-speaking receptionist (tel. 433 89 25 to reach the hospital's English-speaking doctor at home). The **telephone office,** on the corner of Bitash's intersection with Hanafiyya St., sells cards for its orange phonecard phones (open daily 8am-midnight).

Accommodations and Food To make the most of El Agami, sleep in Hannoville's cheaper beds and wine and dine in Bitash's more interesting restaurants. The **Costa Blanca Hotel** (tel. 430 31 12) in Hannoville recalls the Greek roots of this region with its white-washed stucco walls and spacious balconies. The throne in the courtyard surrounded by expectant chairs is probably some kind of misguided but well-intentioned tribute to Greek aesthetic design (singles E£25.50; doubles E£38; all with shower). Across the street is the **Gad Restaurant** (tel. 430 61 79), part of a chain with branches in Alexandria. Doting waitstaff does its best to communicate with non-Arabic speakers. Stuff yourself with the falafel platter (E£4), or just point at the Arabic menu and hope for the best (open daily 10am-midnight). There are no budget accommodations in Bitash, but if you can't bear to be away from the excitement, the **Agami Palace Hotel** (tel. 433 03 86; fax 430 93 64) on the beach has doubles (US$55), as well as breakfast and a variety of activities (billiards, swimming, dancing, etc.).

The culinary epicenter of Bitash is where the main road forks into Bitash St. and El Asal St., about 150m before the beach. Bitash is growing rapidly, and its restaurants with it. One new establishment is **El Omda** on El Asal St. The specialty here is meat, and lots of it. **La Poire** on El Asal St. recently opened a new branch just past the fast food strip, where it serves excellent *shawerma*, chicken, and roast beef sandwiches (all E£4). **Kentucky Fried Chicken, Pizza Hut,** and **Baskin Robbins** lurk 100m further down El Asal St., while **McDonald's** flaunts its golden arches on Bitash St. about 50m from the fork. For dessert, **La Dolce Vita,** on Bitash St. past McDonald's on the right, scoops up excellent Italian-style gelato.

Entertainment The cleanest and hippest **beach** (and the most liberal on Egypt's Med coast) is the **Fardous (Paradise) Beach** in Bitash. Belly buttons and biceps abound. Turn left onto Hanafiyya St. from Bitash St. at the telephone office and go straight until you reach the private beach. The guards are loathe to let any non-members catch the rays, but with a healthy dose of butt-smooching you might get in. It's worth it, especially when it's packed and hopping on Fridays. At the end of El Asal St. on the beach, **Fireball** is an air-conditioned **disco** that has recently become *the* hip place to work it out on hot summer nights. Two other dance spots are **Felfela,** which serves Egyptian food and has a billiard room and a pool (at night women must be 16 and men 21; open 1pm-4am), and **Michael's,** a pricey, open-air beachside French restaurant. If you can get the bouncer to like you, **Andrea,** on Armed Forces St., is a cool bar for cocktail-sipping. Another in place to see and be seen is **Magic Billiards,** down the street from the telephone office, one of Bitash's many 24-hour billiard rooms.

■ El Alamein   العلمين

El Alamein is too distant from the water to attract many tourists, but there was a time when it was infinitely less quiet, less out-of-the-way, and certainly less empty. In November 1942, the Allied forces, commanded by British Field Marshal Sir Bernard Montgomery, halted the advance of the Nazi Afrika Korps here. The Nazis thought of El Alamein as the gateway to Alexandria and the key to controlling the continent. The Allied victory here marked the beginning of the end for the Axis Powers in North Africa and crushed the mystique surrounding the "Desert Fox," German Field Marshal Erwin Rommel, whose force of Panzer tanks had previously seemed invincible. Nearly 10,000 soldiers lost their lives at El Alamein, and 70,000 were wounded.

On the east side of town lies the **British War Cemetery,** the burial place of 7367 men, 815 of whose headstones bear only the inscription "Known Unto God." Ringed by purple flowers and set against the seemingly interminable desert, the excruciatingly tidy rows are a dramatic memorial. Maintained by the British War Graves Commission, the cemetery is free and almost always open.

The **War Museum** at the west side of the village is near the bus stop and main square. It contains displays of weaponry and military garb and descriptions of Rommel, Montgomery, and other participants in the battle. A map bedecked with hundreds of tiny red and green bulbs recreates the changing landscape of the North African campaign (open daily 8am-6pm; winter and Ramadan 9am-3pm; closed Fri. 1-2pm; admission E£5, with camera E£10, with video E£25; 50% student discount on entry and photography rates). The less-frequently visited **German** and **Italian Cemeteries** (8km and 12km west of town, respectively) are perched on a petite peninsula overlooking the sea. Without a private car or hired taxi, it is difficult to get directly to these monuments. Microbuses along the Alexandria-Matrouh road will let passengers off two km from the monuments—lucky travelers may be able to convince *service* drivers to give them a door-to-tomb ride. Whichever way you travel, make sure you're armed with lots of water.

Non-air-conditioned West Delta **buses** traveling between Matrouh and Alexandria or Cairo can drop you off at El Alamein. During the summer you can usually flag down a **service taxi** or **minibus** heading to Alexandria (1hr., E£5) or Marsa Matrouh (2hr., E£5-8). During the winter, prospects are bleak and more expensive. A hired taxi is E£100, whether doing a round-trip from Alexandria or a cross-desert run.

■ Marsa Matrouh   مـرسى مطروح

Fanning out from a bay of purest cobalt blue, this resort city is too often neglected by foreign travelers and used only as a springboard to Siwa. During the summer months, Egyptian families pack the mold-and-pour concrete villas and bathe along the 5km crescent of white, sandy, near-perfect beaches. Marsa Matrouh's natural harbor has served travelers, merchants, and soldiers from Alexander the Great to Rommel. Now the majority of sea vessels in Matrouh are rented by the hour, and officers on holiday are the only major military presence in town.

ORIENTATION AND PRACTICAL INFORMATION

You need to know only two streets to find your way around Marsa Matrouh: the lively **corniche,** which stretches the length of the bay, and busy **Alexandria Street,** which runs perpendicular to the corniche, beginning at the Marsa Matrouh Governorate and heading inland to the train station and hill 1km south of town. Most of the hotels and government offices are clustered along the corniche and the streets running parallel to it. From the corniche inland, the most important of these are **Galaa, Tahrir** (sometimes referred to as Gamal Abd en-Nasser), **Goul Gamal,** and **Allam Er-Rum.** Parallel to Alexandria St. to the east are **Port Said Street** and **Zaher Galal Street.** Parallel to Alexandria St. and three blocks to the west lies **Shokri el-Kowatiy Street,** where you can catch buses, minibuses, and *service.*

Your **feet** will serve you well in Marsa Matrouh—a cross-town stroll should take no more than 15 minutes. Because Marsa Matrouh is only 215km from **Libya,** there is a noticeable military presence in the surrounding areas. It is wise to carry your **passport** with you outside of town and on the more obscure beaches. There may be a passport check on the road into town.

Tourist Office: Egyptian Tourist Authority, tel. 93 18 41, on the corniche 1 block west of Alexandria St., behind the Governorate building. Kind, English-speaking staff and A/C. Ask for the helpful map booklet *Alexandria and Marsa Matrouh,* which lists a few hotels and restaurants. Open daily 8am-8pm, in winter 8am-6pm.

Tourist Police: tel. 93 55 75, next door to the Tourist Office. Little English spoken, but the staff at the Tourist Office or one of the Superjet ticket sellers can help you communicate in a crisis. Open 24hr.

Passport Office: tel. 93 53 51, 1 block north and ½ block east of the train station, just off Alexandria St. Open Sat.-Thurs. 9am-2pm for visa extensions.

Currency Exchange: The National Bank of Egypt, 3 blocks west of Alexandria St. on Galla St. Open daily 8:30am-2pm and 6-9pm. **Cairo Bank** (tel 93 49 08), Port Said St., 1 block east of Alexandria St. Open daily 9am-2pm and 6-9pm. Both change cash and traveler's checks.

Flights: EgyptAir (tel. 93 43 98), on Galaa St., 3½ blocks west of Alexandria St. Flies to and from **Cairo** (Thurs., Fri., and Sun., leaves Cairo at 9am, leaves Matrouh at 10:30am, 1hr., US$115). Office open June-Sept. Tues.-Sun. 9am-2pm and 6-9pm. There are no flights during off-season months.

Trains: tel. 93 39 36, 1 block east of the southern end of Alexandria St., about 750m from the corniche. To **Alexandria** (7am and 3:45pm; 6hr.; 3rd class E£4, 2nd class with no A/C E£8; 50% student discount).

Buses: West Delta's non A/C buses leave the depot 3 blocks west of the southern end of Alexandria St. To: **Alexandria** (7, 11am and 1, 2, 3, 5, 8pm; 5hr.; E£11); **Cairo** (daily 7:30am, 7hr., E£25); and **Siwa** (daily 7am and 1pm, 5hr., E£7; 4pm, 5hr., E£10). **Golden Arrow** runs A/C buses to **Alexandria** (9am and 4pm, E£20; 3pm, E£23; 3hr.) and **Cairo** (8:30am and 2:30, 3:30, 4:30pm; 5hr.; E£35). A/C **Superjet** buses (tel. 93 47 87) also go to **Alexandria** (2:30pm, 3hr., E£23) and **Cairo** (11am and 3, 4pm; 5hr.; E£36). Book ahead for Cairo buses, especially during the summer. Both Golden Arrow and Superjet buses depart from their respective ticket booths in front of the tourist office one block west of Alexandria St. A/C bus services are either drastically or totally cut back in the off season (Nov.-May).

Service taxis: Opposite the West Delta bus station. *Service* to **Alexandria** (E£10) and **Cairo** (E£20). Infrequent service to **Siwa** (E£10).

Local taxis: Pick-up truck taxis to 'Agiba and Cleopatra beaches, E£2 one way. The same service to Rommel Beach is approximately 50pt.

Bike rental: On Galaa St., 1 block west of Alexandria St. E£2 per hour, E£10 per day; bargain for long-term rental.

Photo supplies: Film and batteries can be purchased at the Kodak booth around the corner from the West Delta and Superjet ticket booths. Open daily 9am-1am.

Pharmacy: El Farghaly Pharmacy, at the corner of Alexandria St. and Allam er-Rum St., 3 blocks south of the corniche. Open daily 8am-midnight.

Hospital: Military Hospital (tel. 93 52 86), on Galaa St. 3 blocks west of Alexandria St. Facilities aren't impeccable—if possible seek treatment in Alexandria or Cairo.

Emergency: Police: tel. 93 33 76; emergency 122, on the 1st street south of the corniche, 2 blocks east of Alexandria St. Not much English spoken. **Ambulance:** tel. 123 or 93 43 70. Open 24hr.

Post Office: tel. 93 23 67, 2 blocks east of Alexandria St. and 1 block south of the corniche. No Poste Restante. Open Sat.-Thurs. 8:30am-3pm.

Telephones: Opposite the post office; crowded and unreliable for international calls. Sells phone cards for its phonecard-accepting phones. Open 24hr. **Hotel Riviera Palace** on Alexandria St. has a more expensive but more dependable telephone and fax service. Open daily 9am-10pm. **Information:** tel. 10. **Telephone Code:** 03.

Marsa Matrouh

Marsa Matrouh Governorate, **4**
Passport Office, **1**
Romel Museum, **3**
Taxi Station, **2**
Tourist Bus to Alexandria, **5**
Youth Hostel, **A**

Mediterranean Sea

EGYPT

B E A C H

④

⑥ ⑤ ⓘ

← TO SIWA

A

El Magaul St.

El Matar St.

El Galaa St.

Alexandria St.

Zahar Galal St.

El Galaa St.

El Mina El Kadima St.

Anwar El Sadat St.

El Tahrir St.

Shoukri El Kouwatli St.

Libya St.

Omar El Mokhtar St.

Port Said St.

Goul Gamal St.

Alam El Roum St.

El Kadi St.

El Madrasa El Thanawiya St.

El Madrasa El Thanawiya St.

Alexandria St.

Zahar Galal St.

Hafiz Abdel Aziz St.

Abdala Issa St.

③

②

✛

N

Train Station

ACCOMMODATIONS

Marsa Matrouh sees the bulk of its tourist action during July and August, but high season technically lasts from mid-May to mid-September. Winter months are typically dull (with the exception of a quick spurt of Egyptian vacationers during Ramadan); fish boats replace frolicking swimmers in the bay. Mid- to late September is the ideal time to visit, when crowds have headed back to Cairo and the weather is still idyllic. During the off-season, upscale hotels along the corniche offer surprisingly low rates. No matter what time of year it is, there are always rooms available in the budget hotels on and near Alexandria St. Because few foreigners frequent these places, many have no English signs or English speakers—**sign language** may be in order. Ask at the tourist office for recommendations. Men with small budgets and open minds can rent a bed in a crowded room for E£2-3 but should guard their belongings.

Groups of two or more might consider taking one of the many flats in town. **Hotel Awam** (tel. 93 23 63) to the west of Alexandria St., on the corniche near the Mosque of Awam, has two-bedroom flats for up to six people with living room, bathroom, and kitchen for E£50. Couples can relax at **Marine Fouad** on Rommel's Peninsula where a wonderful new room with bath, porch overlooking the sea, and three meals a day is E£120 for two (open June-Sept.). Reserve by calling Mr. and Mrs. Boray in Cairo at (02) 241 02 94. **Camping** in town is permitted on the beach in front of the Semiramis Hotel, free of charge. If you would like to pitch a tent farther out, contact the Egyptian Tourist Authority so they can let the tourist police know.

Reem Hotel (tel. 93 36 05), on the corniche. The best deal in town, with luxurious rooms right across from the beach. Private baths, year-round hot water, and full breakfast make the prices seem absurdly low. Singles E£35; doubles E£50.

Ghazala Hotel (tel. 93 35 19), Allam er-Rum St., in a 3-story white building 4 store-fronts east of Alexandria St., 6 blocks from the corniche (around the corner from El Farghaly pharmacy). When this hotel opened 25 years ago, Suleiman Morsi charged backpackers 50pt a room. Although the price has risen since then, the affability remains. Well-kept rooms, but the hot water in the dank common bathrooms is turned off during summer. Don't expect any cross-cultural exchange here—Egyptians and foreigners are housed on different floors. Singles E£7.50; doubles E£15.

Hotel Hamada (tel. 93 33 00), on the corner of Tahrir and Alexandria St. Cushioned mattresses and bare-bones rooms await. Each floor has a large common room with shared refrigerator, stove, and bath. Learn to love the call of the *muezzin*—there's a mosque just down the street. Singles, doubles, and triples E£10 per bed.

Arafat Hotel (tel. 93 36 06), east of Alexandria St. on Tahrir St., next to the Qahwa Auberge. Spotless rooms, sheets, and baths, and luxurious hot water year-round, but costs a bit more. Singles E£20; doubles E£35; triples E£60; quads E£72.

Hotel Ageba, Alexandria St. (tel. 93 23 34), about 2 blocks before the hill rises out of town. Big apartment-block building with 200 clean, cheap rooms, some with balconies. Get a room facing north on the inside of the building—you'll get the ocean breeze, not the honking truckers. No hot water in summer, but maybe a few roaches. Singles, doubles, and triples with shower E£10 per person.

Haidy Park Hotel, 3 blocks west of Alexandria St. on Galaa St. No phones or showers, but it's clean and you can't argue with the price. Singles E£3; doubles E£6.

FOOD

The cheapest way to eat in Marsa Matrouh is to shop at the local markets on the roads east of Alexandria St. Seafood restaurants, groceries, and pseudo-French bakeries congregate along Alexandria St. itself. There are several pizza spots along the corniche, and the usual falafel, *shawerma,* and ice cream stands.

Pizza Gaby, just past the Negresco Hotel at the westernmost end of the corniche. The hefty menu includes a variety of tasty pizzas (E£8-12), grilled meats (E£16-30), and Middle Eastern salads (E£3). Overlooking the sea, this air-conditioned haven provides the perfect spot to contemplate the sunset. Open daily 10am-midnight.

Kushari, 4 blocks west of Alexandria St. (look for the picture of the waiter holding a bowl of pipin' hot yellow stuff). Biggest, baddest *kushari* this side of the Sahara. Huge servings. Open daily 6am-midnight.

Samara Fish Restaurant, 2 storefronts east of Alexandria St. on Goul Gamal St., 2 blocks south of the corniche. This small restaurant serves up the catch of the day with bread, rice, and salad for E£15-23. Open daily 8am-1am, in winter 8am-9pm.

Panayotis Greek Restaurant (tel. 93 24 74), on the west side of Alexandria St., 2 blocks south of the corniche. Join the hungry cats outside in your quest for food at the oldest restaurant in Marsa Matrouh. Simple menu offers a stellar fish dinner (E£13), calamari (E£15), and Stella (E£4.75). Open daily 8am-1am.

New Alexandria Tourist Restaurant (tel. 93 23 15), on Alexandria St., 2 blocks south of the corniche. The "new" in the name hints at the recent renovations; now A/C and an ocean of chrome aim to please. The full fish platter (E£15) is a budget eater's dream. Open daily 9am-midnight with 24hr. take-out.

Restaurant Sharisard (tel. 93 31 61), on the corner of Alexandria and Galla St., across from Panayotis. Good *fuul*, falafel, *shawerma*, and other Egyptian favorites for E£1-2. Open daily 6am-2am.

SIGHTS, SAND, AND ENTERTAINMENT

Marsa Matrouh's glorious **beaches** are its *raison d'être*. However, the 5km of white sand that rims the crescent-shaped bay is closed after sunset, and soldiers patrol the coast nightly to deter drug trafficking. As in Alexandria, some women here swim fully clothed, and as in all of Egypt (except the Sinai), bikinis or revealing one-pieces could start a riot. **Rommel Beach,** where one-pieces are acceptable, and secluded spots at 'Agiba (see below) are good places for tanning. The **Beau Site Hotel** (on the far west end of the corniche), though somewhat overrun by frolicking Egyptian children, has a private beach which is cleaner and more liberal than most others. There is no charge for non-guests, but they politely encourage you to rent an umbrella (E£10 per day), a chair (E£3 per day), or a sea kayak (E£7 per hr.).

East of the port, the shoreline arches into a peninsula that faces the town from across the bay. This stretch of land, called **Rommel's Isle,** can be reached by donkey cart (E£1), bike (E£10 per day), boat (E£7), or pick-up truck taxi (50pt). The dull **Rommel Museum,** 3km east of town on the peninsula, is built into the caves that Rommel used as his headquarters during the North African campaign (open daily 10am-4pm in summer, closed in winter; E£1). On the ocean side of the isle, an old **U-boat** juts out of the water, now a rusting wreck. You can rent a surf kayak to paddle out to it: head toward the red buoy on your left. The sub lies parallel to the beach 20m toward the mosque from the buoy, but you'll need a mask to see it clearly.

To the west of the main beach, the **Beach of Love** (Shatii el-Gharaam) fondles the western horn of the bay and is easily reachable by foot or kayak. Inconsiderate visitors have recently begun to spoil the sand while enjoying the sun, and heaps of litter float out daily. Fourteen kilometers farther west you'll encounter more wind, less trash, and the tantalizing **Cleopatra's Beach,** on the far right-hand side of a small cove called **Cleopatra's Bath.** Legend has it that the queen and Marc Antony would come here to bathe—as the waves crashed into the cove, the water would shoot towards the heavens and cascade back down on the lovers' entangled bodies. **Obaiyid Beach,** 18km from Marsa Matrouh, fills up with frolicking families who stay at their corporation's tents along the shore, but the water is peaceful and shallow. The farthest and most spectacular spot of all is **'Agiba,** about 24km from Marsa Matrouh. 'Agiba (meaning "miracle") is an inlet in a series of rocky cliffs interrupted by caves. 'Agiba's beach can be crowded, but it is possible and to find a private spot below the cliffs and spend the day swimming off the rocks. Bring your own **food**—there is only a soft-drink stand. Along the way, hidden in the sand near Umm Araham village, are the ruins of the tiny **Temple to Ramses II.**

To reach these beaches take a shared **taxi** or **minibus** from the bus station (E£2-3 per person to 'Agiba), a shared **pick-up truck** from the stand on the corner 300m north of the main bus station (E£1.50 to 'Agiba), or the open-sided *tuf-tuf* bus (E£1.25 to Cleopatra or 'Agiba). The bus shuttles to and from the bus station when there are enough passengers (usually every hr. 9am-4:30pm; summer only).

At night, conversation in *awhas* and strolls along the corniche replace bars and discos as the favored forms of entertainment. Bars in the Rady and Beau Site Hotels serve over-priced drinks. One hundred meters west of the end of the corniche (across from the armed services hotel compound) stands a raised outdoor patio which, during summer, often hosts energetic live music in a breezy, friendly setting. The corniche and Alexandria St. offer fine cafe and *sheesha* opportunities.

■ Siwa Oasis واحة سيوة

Surrounded by 300km of barren desert wasteland, the very existence of this oasis and town seems improbable, if not impossible. With its own language, dress, and customs, Siwa is quite different from the rest of Egypt. In 331 BCE, Alexander the Great made a long pilgrimage to Siwa to visit the Oracle of Amun. Today's paved road follows the same path, but buses zoom across the sand dunes in a mere four hours. Siwa's isolation has made it legendary—the ancients told tales of the strange cities and mysterious kingdoms in the desert. The fickle twists of weather, however, defeated most attempts to find the truth—in 525 BCE a desert sandstorm blew the entire Persian army to smithereens.

In 1984, the Egyptian government completed the road connecting Siwa to Marsa Matrouh, and the town experienced drastic changes. Cairo integrated the oasis into the national economy, leading to better-stocked stores, universal education, two new quarries, and more diversified agricultural production. Arabic replaced Siwi, the local Berber dialect, as the language of instruction. Today, younger Siwan women don Egyptian fashions, and *The Bold and the Beautiful* is gradually replacing Grandma's stories of Siwan folklore. Nonetheless, the 300 km of barren desert isolating Siwa preserves many elements of the oasis's unique culture. Siwi, not Arabic, is spoken at home and on the street, and the few married women who venture into town cover themselves from head to toe in their blue *tarfudit* veil. Inside the home, the matron wears an *agabir* (a loose dress, often bright yellow or red) which was part of her dowry. Older women still sport the traditional Siwan costume, with intricately braided hairdos and heavy silver jewelry around the neck, arms, and head.

The tourism industry has made inroads into Siwa: Italian investment has opened a new water-bottling plant, tour buses arrive from Cairo daily, and there's even Nintendo™ for the kids. Still, these changes have yet to dent the overwhelming hospitality and staunch conservatism of the Siwans. The residents of this village mandate that women cover arms and legs, and "alcohol and affection are forbidden in public."

Ahmed Fakhry's *Siwa Oasis* (E£35), available at the AUC Bookstore in Cairo and several shops in Siwa itself, is a richly detailed 200-page tome. Local tourist guru Mr. Mahdi keeps a copy on hand in the tourist office and will let you borrow it.

ORIENTATION

Siwa Oasis lies in a desert depression about 300km southwest of Marsa Matrouh. Its western edge comes within 50km of the closed Libyan border. The depression stretches for 82km west to east, and between three and 30km north to south. Most visitors concern themselves only with the **town of Siwa** and the nearby villages.

Siwa's **climate** is similar to that of other oases and Aswan. Winter is pleasantly warm, with cool nights which necessitate sweaters. Summer is brutally hot, and air-conditioning is but a mirage, except in the tourist office. Eleven thousand people live in the town; 4000 more Siwans and a few hundred Bedouin live in villages scattered elsewhere in the oasis.

The most practical way to reach Siwa is by bus from Marsa Matrouh or Alexandria, but groups with a car full of courage can travel the 420km stretch of the rough road from Bahariyya. For more information, see the **Siwa-Bahariyya Road,** p. 174.

The paved road from Marsa Matrouh passes the **Arous el-Waha Hotel** and the bright white tourist office at the northern edge of town and continues 200m into the center of town, ending at the **King Fouad (Sidi Suleiman) Mosque** and the town **market.** The eerie geometry of the ruined houses of **ancient Siwa** rise just south of the market on a rock acropolis. Streets have unmarked Siwi names, but most establishments hand out maps as advertisements. The best one can be picked up free at the tourist office.

PRACTICAL INFORMATION

Tourist Information Office: tel. 61 30, in the new white building across from the Arous el-Waha Government Hotel. Knowledgeable Mahdi Muhammad Ali Hweity, sociologist, fluent English-speaker, and native Siwan, arranges sight-seeing expeditions and provides maps and other invaluable information. Open Sat.-Thurs. 8am-2pm, Fri. 6-8pm, and possibly in the late evenings during winter.

Buses: West Delta Bus Co. goes to Siwa from Marsa Matrouh daily (7am and 4pm, 5hr., E£7; 1pm, E£10). From Alexandria's Misr Station, there is 1 non-A/C bus daily

(7am, 10hr., E£13.50) and one A/C bus (11am, 9hr., E£25; winter service unpredictable). Buses run from Siwa to **Marsa Matrouh** at 7am and 2pm (4hr., E£7); the 7am bus continues on to Alexandria (total 8hr., E£13.50). An A/C bus makes the trip as well (daily 10am; 4hr., E£10 to Matrouh; 8hr., E£25 to Alexandria).

Local Bus: Crawls west from Siwa near the big mosque to the village of El Maraqi, making a 60km loop and breaking down often along the way (round-trip E£2). There are usually 2 per day (7am and 3pm), but only the tourist office knows for sure.

Bike Rental: Several establishments in the market square (E£1 per hr., E£5 per day). Hotels will also rent.

English Bookstore: Hassan's Handicrafts and English Bookshop, next to the telephone office. Sells a few English AUC books on Egyptian history and culture (including Fakhry's *Siwa Oasis*). Open in the evenings after Mr. Hweity finishes up at the tourist office. The store is named for his son, Hassan.

Pharmacy: Yousef's Pharmacy, on the road leading south from the town center towards the Cleopatra Hotel. Wide selection, good English, and A/C. Open summer daily 9am-2pm and 6pm-midnight, winter 9am-noon.

Hospital: Go south 1km from the town square and take a right at the first four-story building on your left. Open daily 24hr.

Police: tel. 60 08. Located in the same building as the post office. Open 24hr.

Post Office: Across the street from Arous el-Waha Hotel in the northwestern part of town. Open Sat.-Thurs. 8am-2pm.

Telephone Office: Behind the Arous el-Waha Hotel. Only call from Siwa if absolutely necessary—the connections are horrible. Open 24hr. **Telephone Code:** 03.

ACCOMMODATIONS

Most of the crash pads in Siwa are in or near the town center. During summer months, lack of business insures that you get your pick of the line-up. In winter months, however, especially around Christmas, New Year's, and Ramadan, the entire town is filled to the gills. If you know the dates you are heading to Siwa well in advance, consider writing a letter to the tourist office to reserve a spot.

Palm Tree Hotel (tel. 63 04), 20m down a side road from the market square. Clean, comfortable doubles with fans and balconies. Some have private baths, although the common baths are large and spotless. Shady garden in back with wicker furniture and split date palm benches. Rooms overlooking the garden are the choicest. Laundry service. Bike rental. E£5.50 per bed, E£6.50 with bath.

Yousef Hotel, in the center of town. Balconies have a view of Siwa and beyond. Clean rooms; top floor has all new rooms, some with bath. E£5 per bed.

Cleopatra Hotel (tel. 61 48), south of the town square on the main road past the Shali fortress. A new, comfortable, and somewhat pricier establishment, with spacious balconies, great views, and immaculate bathrooms. Fans available in summer. Dorm beds (3 to a room, no fan or balcony) E£5; back-view doubles E£12, with bath E£16; front-view doubles E£15, with bath E£20.

El Medina Hotel, next to Yousef Hotel in the town center. Owned by the same folks as the Palm Tree, but understandably cheaper. The cluttered lobby, squatter toilets, and well-used rooms without fans set you back only E£3.50 per night.

Badwi Hotel, south of town on the same road to Cleopatra Hotel. Take a right at the first large 4-story building. A bit of a hike from the center of town, but the brand new rooms and sturdy beds are great. Men and women are lodged in separate quarters. Single or double E£8.

Amun Hotel, at Dakrur Mountain, 4km east of town (take a *caretta* for 20min. or ride a bike until your butt is sore). If Siwa isn't off the beaten track enough, consider staying here. The view of the palms and salt lakes are pristine, but only worth it if the other hotels are full. Doubles E£8.

Free **camping** in shelters is available on **Dakrur Mountain,** 4km south of town, and at **Bir Wahed (Well #1),** 12km south (see p. 174). Bring your sleeping bag and insect repellent. Check with Mr. Hweity at the tourist office before pitching your tent.

FOOD

Several restaurants line the two market squares and are generally open from 8 or 10am to midnight or 1am. In summertime the menus shrink. Standard offerings include macaroni, chicken, couscous, omelettes, and *shakshuka* (a mixture of meat, eggs, and sauce) for E£1-5. For breakfast try pancakes with banana, honey, and yogurt (E£2.50). Siwan eateries are pretty much indistinguishable from one another, but some tried and true places are **Lekany,** on the northeastern corner of town, and **Abdou's Restaurant** further west. The latter serves excellent couscous and mint tea. Local **stores** are well stocked with canned goods, cold soda, mineral water, and (in season) fresh and dried dates and figs.

Because Siwans tend to be more reserved than residents of most Egyptian towns, the traveler will be lucky to receive an **invitation** to eat or stay with a local family. Invitations are usually offered by children, but sometimes by men. At dinner, your hosts may want to sell you homemade handicrafts, or they may simply want to talk. Women will be invited much more readily than men. As always, exercise caution before accepting hospitality—solo women should decline invitations from single Siwan men.

SIGHTS

Surrounded by gashes of black rock, waves of sand, and piercing blue desert sky, Siwa is Egypt's most beautiful oasis. From atop the ruins of the crumbling medieval fortress-town of **Shali** (which simply means "town" in Siwi), the quiet streets of Siwa town wind through a cluster of mud houses and luxuriant palm gardens. Shali's encircling wall once protected the Siwans from marauding Berbers and Bedouin. Houses within the walls were cramped, and the stagnant, sweltering air did little to facilitate breathing. To make matters worse, twice a century, **apocalyptic rains** wash away all buildings on the acropolis. It's not surprising that Siwans gradually moved from their mountaintop abodes to the more spacious homes at the base. The flight began when **Muhammad Ali** conquered Siwa in 1820. By 1900 the ancient city had become a virtual ghost town. Wandering among the haunting skeletons of these ancient abodes, you will find inhabitants in random dwellings and old men turning corners on their way to unknown business. The most recent rains, in 1985, washed away much of Shali and most of the Siwan mud-dwellings, but due to the increased number of concrete buildings, the devastation was not total. The rains were enough to motivate one Canadian ambassador, however. Fearing the washing away of history, he raised funds to construct the permanent **Traditional Siwan House,** just down the road from the tourist office and opposite the Mosque of King Foad. The house serves as a museum of traditional Siwan garb, silver jewelry, and children's toys. Abu Bakr, the knowledgable English-speaking guide, will gladly show you around and chat about soccer (open Sat.-Thurs. 9am-noon, ask at the tourist office for other hours; E£1.50).

A second acropolis, **Gabal el-Mawta** (Hill of the Dead) rises 1km to the northeast of ancient Siwa (free). The hill is home to several Ptolemaic-era tombs that were robbed and reused by Romans. Many of these tombs were discovered during World War II when Siwan families crammed into caves seeking shelter from Italian bombs. The scattered human bones and mummy wrappings that litter the sight belonged to the Romans, as do the niches that maul the ancient frescoes. A custodian is on hand to unlock the tombs daily from 9am to 1pm but it is best to confirm the custodian's whereabouts with Mr. Hweity at the tourist office. The **Tomb of the Crocodile** has been closed. The steep ascent to the top of the hill is rewarded with an exhilarating Kodak moment, although one needn't climb to the summit to enter the tombs. The **Tomb of Si-Amun** is covered with a beautifully painted ceiling which depicts the six stages of the sun's journey across the sky. Marred murals on the walls show the Hellenized portrayal of the bearded nobleman Si-Amun, his sons worshiping Egyptian deities. The size of this elaborate resting place indicates the Si-Amun was probably a wealthy land-owner or merchant. The **Tomb of Niperpathot,** the oldest tomb in Siwa, housed the body of a nobleman of the 26th Dynasty. The **Tomb of Mesu-Isis** is

5m to the east of Si-Amun and has ancient frescoes depicting the gods Isis and Osiris. E£2 *bakhsheesh* is appropriate but not necessary.

Like Siwa town, the village of **Aghurmi**, 3km to the east, rests peacefully at the foot of a formerly inhabited acropolis. To get there, rent a bike from town or hail a *caretta* (E£10 per load) and rattle off through the palm groves. A 13th-century gate made of palm logs graces the entrance to the acropolis. Pass a sturdy old mud **mosque** and you'll see, perched dramatically atop a cliff, the well-preserved **Oracle of Amun,** where Alexander came to consult the renowned priests of Amun. You'll have to go through the same steps that he did to reach the oracle: pass through the stone temple's simple gateway into the outer court, then cross the inner court to reach the center. Greek and Roman historians recorded the mystical rituals needed to invoke an answer from the oracle. Priests carried a sacred boat containing the image of Amun as women sang and danced in procession. The oracle is said to have confirmed suspicion that Alexander was a god-king, proclaiming him the "son of Amun." Alexander also asked the oracle a question in private, but what that was will never be known. The secret died with him, fewer than ten years after his visit. The Oracle of Amun is thought to date from the 26th Dynasty (c. 660 BCE). It became widely celebrated in later dynasties and was well known to the ancient Greeks, who constructed many shrines to Amun in their own country. Twentieth-century visitors enjoy unrestricted access to the entire Aghurmi acropolis—no guards, no fees, but alas, no answer-spewing oracle. Or so they would have you believe...

One kilometer southeast of Aghurmi lie the emaciated remains of the **Temple of Amun.** Beyond the temple, about 2km south on the same road, lies the cool and mossy **Pool of Cleopatra.** Like many of the approximately 200 natural springs in Siwa, it has been encircled with a stone basin, with an irrigation duct running out one end. Although the pool is mostly frequented by men, fully clothed women should also feel comfortable swimming here (as comfortable as swimming fully clothed can be) and may enter the enclosure next to the spring. If you visit these sights at sunrise or in the late evening, you may be the only person there. Continue another 1km east to **Dakrur Mountain,** where nearly 1000 rheumatics congregate each summer for ten-day stints in the **hammam ramel** (sand baths). The procedure, which sounds like a Siwan torture method, is as follows: under the supervision of a specialist, the "bather" is buried in sand from the neck down, while the head is protected from the sun's heat. These sand saunas have been popular for 300 years. In 1975, a Danish man, looking for a cure for his ailing daughter, came to Siwa. After a two-week treatment, his young child was able to walk again. You can try the bath for E£25 (includ-

---

Siwi Made Simple

Most Siwan children's first language is Siwi, a Berber dialect incomprehensible to the rest of Egypt. As the children grow up, parents and schools make sure they speak Arabic so that they can get along when not in Siwa. Siwi is unwritten and at times sounds almost Scandinavian. The possible permutations of the following words should keep you occupied until the donkeys come home:

meshi	*yes*	gaf lahk	*I go*
oula	*no*	ehk sehk	*I want*
aman	*water*	shiek	*you*
aksoom	*meat*	oushi	*give me*
azumur	*olives*	tene	*dates*
ihkseik teswi aman		*I want to drink water.*	
tanta elhal ineik		*How are you?*	
tanta wook		*What is this?*	
betin lsmetinik		*What is your name?*	
sewil dede		*Speak with me.*	

ing room and board), but be forewarned that you'll sweat like a demon, and your pores will dilate to the size of donuts.

Behind Dakrur Mountain, perfectly rounded sand dunes make for an interesting walk. Every October at the full moon, Siwans gather for a huge feast at the rocks of **Dakrur.** A "chief of the feast" oversees the distribution of food to small groups spread over the plain. Each family contributes money for the purchase of meat and all donate 10 pieces of bread. Community problems are arbitrated by the head honchos. No one may begin to eat until the chief climbs to the top of the rock and hollers *"Bismallah!"* (in the name of God). Tourists are invited to attend. Contact the tourist office for the exact date of this and other harvest time (fall) festivities.

All of Siwa is idyllic, but the best place to watch the late afternoon sun dip into the endless sands is the breathtaking **Pool of Fatnas,** 4km west of town. Accessible by a small causeway, the Fatnas Pool is slightly smaller than the Cleopatra Pool but not as frequented by the locals. From the far western point of the adjoining garden, you can see across a glistening salt lake to a limitless sea of sand. The road west to **El Maraqi,** which traverses a low desert pass, is lined with craggy yellow buttes honeycombed with caves and Roman tombs. The assemblage of villages which make up El Maraqi lie in their own lush oasis, virtually severed from the rest of Siwa by the clenching fingers of the desert. Gruesome sights await 9km from Siwa at the recently discovered tombs of **Deheyba.** Human skulls, thigh bones, and feet are strewn amidst the sand and sea fossils after a rather careless excavation a year and a half ago. A full mummy used to lie unprotected in one of the numbered tombs (there are 100 total), but even more careless tourists have forced the closure of the display. Further west is the **White Mountain** and the village of **El Jari.** On the southern side of the mountain are over 110 tombs and a fabulous view of Fatnas, the Sea of Sands, and Siwa. You can take a refreshing dip in the salt lake here before heading back to town. If you are on a tour sponsored by Mr. Hweity at the tourist office, you'll continue west to some of the springs, the other villages of El Maraqi, and the supposed **Tomb of Alexander** (closed to the public in the summer of 1997). A half-day trip is a bargain at E£15 per head. If you rent a bike, Deheyba and the White Mountain make a fabulous day trip, but be sure to bring ample water and sunscreen. **Campers** can ask for special permission to sleep in these parts and then take the bus back to Siwa the next morning.

Bir Wahad (Well #1), 12km south of Siwa and surrounded by lush vegetation, sports hot water clean enough for bathing. There are a number of Siwans who can take you for around E£45. Inquire at the tourist office to find out who has the best package. If you spend the night, bring a blanket from your hotel—it gets cold in the desert, even in mid-July. About 6km from Siwa and only 1km off the main road, a fabulous stretch of water erupts amidst sand dunes (known as the **fish farm**). It's accessible by bike, although you'll have to walk the 1km from the road into the dunes.

While in Siwa, you can shop for exquisite **handicrafts,** including intricately embroidered clothing, veils, and *margunahs* (large decorated baskets that weave elegance into every Siwan household). Several stores have sprung up around the town square: **Siwa Original Handicraft,** to the left of Abdou Restaurant, and **Hassan's Handicrafts,** next to the phone office. Bargaining in craft shops can be difficult because the women set the prices and aren't around to haggle. Many crafts are changing to accommodate tourist demands—the baskets and shawls are most authentic. Precocious children will also likely drag you into a private home to view their family's selection of handiwork.

■ Moving On: The Siwa-Bahariyya Road

The eight-hour crossing from Siwa to Bahariyya is an arduous undertaking. In winter, truckloads leave every few days to make the cross-desert run, but in summer it's even harder to round up the 7-10 people that make the trip affordable. One year ago, Ahmed and his protege Abdullah Addas were the only ones doing this trek; now there are six different services to choose from. Mr. Hweity at the tourist office can help you pick the one best suited to your needs. Expect to pay E£500-600. It is imperative that anyone making the journey does so in a **4x4**—the road is not suitable for

Greased Lightning

Not long ago, Siwans ran a smuggling operation, secretly carrying goods from Libya into Egypt on donkeys. The nighttime treks would proceed perfectly until the beast, unaware of the clandestine nature of the mission, would bray, alerting the Border patrol officials and spoiling the whole kit 'n caboodle. Siwans wracked their brains to figure out a way to pacify the carriers. An ingenious plan was developed: someone (somehow) discovered that if the asses' asses were greased, the brutes were unable to create the force needed to let air out of their mouths. A team of French scientists is currently conducting further research on this exciting discovery.

cars. Also, make sure to bring plenty of **water** (5 bottles per person) and several spare tires. If you can manage to relax, you'll experience dark yellow sunsets and a burning white moon not visible from the oases.

Abu Shrouf, 40km east of Siwa towards Bahariyya, is cooler, deeper, and cleaner than any of Siwa's pools. Local legend has it that Abu Shrouf is the only place in the oasis with female donkeys. If a male donkey escapes from Siwa, the first place they look is Abu Shrouf. If a Siwan man has a pleasant night with his wife, he tells his buds "Last night I went to Abu Shrouf!" You too can visit it with the Mahdi Hweity tour, or by car from Siwa (about E£25 for a full load, round-trip).

Nile Valley وادى النيل

How doth the little crocodile
Improve his shining tail
And pour the waters of the Nile
On every Golden Scale.

—Lewis Carroll

Originating at the equatorial high water marks of Lake Victoria and Lake Taru, the Nile winds its way north through Uganda, Ethiopia, and the Sudan, pouring into Lake Nasser and Egypt, where its banks are home to 95% of the country's millions.

Before the construction of the Aswan High Dam in the 1971, the Nile overflowed its banks every year, depositing the rich silt that made the valley the most fertile region in the world. This yearly inundation was the most important time of the year for ancient Egyptians, and the reason that much ancient religion focused on the river's cycles. Today, the length of the Valley is still full of temples and monuments.

The region between Cairo and Luxor is known as **Middle Egypt,** home to the majority of the country's Copts. Akhenaton built his capital at Tel el-Amarna; further south stand the quietly impressive temples at Abydos and Dendera. Travel in this area is dangerous (see **warning** below).

As of summer 1997, the Egyptian and U.S. governments strongly discourage any surface travel through **Middle Egypt.** Political instability and the rise in extremist activity have made the area unsafe for tourists. There is a massive police and military presence in the area, making visits unpleasant as well as ill-advised. *Let's Go* heeded the warnings of the U.S. State Department and Egyptian Ministry of Tourism and did not send a researcher to sights or cities between Beni Suef and Luxor this year. The temple at Abydos is closed to the public, as are many other sites.

Luxor marks the northern boundary of **Upper Egypt,** stretching all the way upstream (south) to Lake Nasser and the Sudanese border (formerly Lower Nubia). There are busloads of sights in Upper Egypt, and trainloads of tourists flock to see the maze of ancient architecture on Luxor's west bank and the imposing temples at Edfu and Abu Simbel.

In the summertime, when the weather is hot, temperatures average over 45°C, frequently breaking 50°C. This is rather warm, but the complete lack of humidity makes it possible to continue most essential biological processes even as the sand turns to glass. Scalding heat makes summer the low season for tourism. Hoteliers, guides, and others of their ilk are desperate, so bargain hard. If you don't like the heat, plan to do most of your touring between 6 and 11am; if you don't like the crowds, shoot for high noon. In November through May, prices increase as the temperature drops.

GETTING AROUND IN THE VALLEY

By Land

Traveling by **service taxi** is the most efficient, cheap, and convenient option for shuttling between the river towns at almost any time of day. However, the Egyptian police insist that tourists travel at certain times with police convoys. *Service* drivers may refuse to take you, fearing that they may have to turn back. Out of Aswan or Luxor, the only option may be the public bus. You'll also need nerves of steel to cope with the insanity of the drivers. Prices below are one way.

> **From Luxor to:** Esna (1hr., E£2), Edfu (1½hr., E£4), Kom Ombo (2-3hr., E£7), Aswan (3-4hr., E£7).
> **From Aswan to:** Kom Ombo (45min.-1hr., E£1.25), Edfu (2½hr., E£3), Esna (2-3hr., E£5).
> **From Kom Ombo to:** Edfu (1hr., E£2), Daraw (15min., 25pt).
> **From Esna to:** Edfu (1hr., E£2).

Buses are often cheaper than *service*, though not by much. They run more frequently, but are horribly slow, hot, and unreliable. Most stop running at 6pm. Buses are best for transport out of Luxor or Aswan, where you can reserve the air-conditioned buses by going to the station a day or two in advance. In the smaller towns between, you may not find an empty seat, and schedule reliability plummets.

> **From Luxor to:** Esna (1½hr., E£5), Edfu (2hr., E£10), Kom Ombo (3hr., E£10), Aswan (5hr., E£14). Buses depart from near the Luxor Museum.
> **From Aswan to:** Daraw (1hr., E£1), Kom Ombo (1hr., E£2), Edfu (2hr., E£3), Esna (3½hr., E£4), Luxor (4hr., E£6.50).

Trains are a hassle for short trips. For the entire Luxor-Aswan haul, however, the trains with first- or second-class air-conditioned compartments are great. (From Aswan to all points north at 5:30am and 6pm; 5hr. to Luxor, E£10-20. Southbound from Luxor at 6:30am and 4:30pm; 5hr. to Aswan, E£11-14. Northbound from Luxor at 11:30am and 11:30pm.) Authorities discourage tourists from taking third-class trains.

By Water

Nile Cruiser

Tough times for tourism in Egypt have opened up an option for the budget traveler on a binge: the **Nile Cruiser.** You can book a cabin on triple-decker, pool-topped cruise ships and slip from Luxor to Aswan or vice versa (one way is 2 nights) hobnobbing with French tourists. Travel agents can book for you at a mark-up (US$45-50 per night) or you can go to the dock yourself and chat with the boat receptionist about open cabins (as low as US$35 a night). The air-conditioned, two-room suites have TVs and showers, and all meals are included. Drinks are extra, and extra pricey. A *kalish* will cart you to the temple and back at each stop. Several travel agents dot the corniche south of the Winter Palace in Luxor (Eastmar, Misr Travel). In Aswan, agencies can be found near the corniche tourist office. If you find a bargain, you'll enjoy two days of pure bliss: sitting by the pool sunning yourself, watching the palms and desert float by, getting interrupted only to be fed three times a day.

EGYPT

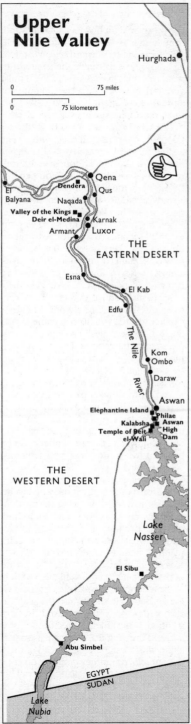

Felucca

For those on tight budgets but still wanting the semi-pharaonic experience of drifting from temple to temple on the Nile, a **felucca** cruise is a slow-paced way to absorb the Egyptian countryside and regain sanity after days in overcrowded *service.* To ensure an enjoyable experience, be aware of the inherent **risks** in *felucca* travel. We don't want to sound like killjoys, but you must be on guard *at all times,* from the moment you start shopping for a captain until you reach your final destination. Police records and hotel comment books are filled with tales of watery woe: druggings, beatings, theft, rape, harassment, and even death.

The word *felucca* means boat; the typical Nile-cruising variety sleeps up to eight people, has a single tall mast with a characteristically angled boom, and is piloted by an English-speaking Arab or Nubian Egyptian. When not traveling with friends, gather a group of like-minded tourists (aim for a group of six) in hotel lobbies or the many restaurants along the Nile. You can also ask at the tourist office (a good resource throughout the *felucca* planning process). As a last resort, you can join a group already assembled by a captain. Be sure to meet these people beforehand, or you may find yourself in a horrifying Middle Eastern version of MTV's *Real World.*

Starting from the moment you step off the train in Aswan, you will be approached every 28 seconds by a *felucca* captain or, more often, a middleman sent out to round up suckers. Every hotel manager and every man in the local *ahwa* has his favorite *felucca* captain (from whom he receives a commission), so the word on the street is almost useless. You should go down to the river yourself, meet and talk with several captains, inspect several boats, and take a list of potential candidates to the tourist office to make sure they aren't pirates or perverts. Ask to see comment books and talk to fellow travelers. Be skeptical of any cute nicknames the captain uses; an honest captain will tell you his real name if asked. Also be wary of captains who speak little English. These typically younger captains often lack the experience necessary to handle sailing emergencies. There have been several capsizings in recent years caused by high winds and inept sailors. You are better off with a gnarled, **crusty old man** who speaks English well (if a bit colorfully) than with some punk who is just learning the ropes. Don't book *felucca* trips through commission-charging hotels.

You'll probably embark from Aswan, the *felucca* capital. Most trips last two days and end in Edfu. If you'd like to spend more time on the river, be persistent and have a group to back you; captains would rather stay close to home (it takes them longer to return to Aswan against the current). Be sure you have arranged the final destination, and that it is clearly understood by the captain. Unscrupulous boatsmen have been known to drop their passengers off 40km from a town, claiming that it was "close enough."

Purveying provisions has become an opportunity for a scam (it's the sailor's loophole for making up the money he lost in giving you that "special price"). Many a traveler has arrived at his or her destination either sick from low-quality food or hungry from low rations. Others embark to find that the captain has only bought one bottle of water per person, per day. You have two options: shop with the captain and choose what you want to eat yourself (a time-consuming process), or review the planned menu carefully, insisting on adding whatever's on your wish list, and asking to see it all before you set out. For greater leisure, choosing a captain who takes care of the cooking himself is highly recommended. An extra-special captain who cooks Nubian dishes in the *felucca* or arranges to stop at his village for a home-cooked meal is a godsend. He should also bring at least two cartons of bottled water; make sure it is aboard before you depart and check that the tabs are sealed, lest it be tap water. In addition, bring at least three bottles of water per person per day for drinking, cooking, and brewing tea. You can also ask for a big jerry can of tap water to be brought along which can be used instead of the Nile for washing dishes and faces.

Your *felucca* journey could be one of the most relaxing and enjoyable parts of your trip to Egypt, but be vigilant: keep all belongings well-secured. Sleep with passports, money, airline tickets, and traveler's checks adhered to your flesh (theft of money-belts is common). Most *feluccas* have compartments in front that lock, but their safety is suspect. Groups of women should not embark unless they see the trip as a singles cruise with their captain. The unfortunate fact is that most Egyptian men either respect or fear men far more than women. The law prohibits any Egyptians, apart from the captain and his minimal crew (often just a young boy who helps him) from traveling with foreigners. Some *felucca* parties like to party; there is a growing drug scene on many Nile trips. Be careful: Egyptian law is harsh and entrapment is common.

Officially, members of a six- to eight-person group leaving Aswan should pay E£25 each to Kom Ombo (1 day, 1 night), E£45 to Edfu (3 days, 2 nights), E£50 to Esna (4 days, 3 nights), and E£60 to Luxor (5 days, 4 nights). Most captains add to this E£5 per day for food and water, and a E£5 registration fee. Prices don't vary much from captain to captain; the most important variable is the vibe you get.

For registration in Aswan, the captain will ask for your passport and the E£5. Brush up on the relaxation skills you will need for the trip by letting him do the paperwork for you, but have an assembled group ready, or the captain may keep your passports as collateral until he can corral other passengers.

Finally, although there are many dangers inherent in a *felucca* cruise, there are also many honest, reputable captains out there and that a trip by *felucca* should ease your worries, not aggravate them. Have fun, but be careful.

■ Luxor الاقصر

> *And so sepulch'red in such pomp dost lie,*
> *That kings for such a tomb would wish to die.*
>
> —John Milton

This ancient capital of Upper and Lower Egypt still humbles visitors three millennia after the height of its power. The city is built on the site of *Ta Ipet* (known by its Greek name, Thebes), and flexed its influential muscles during the five-century rule of the New Kingdom (18th-20th Dynasties, 1550-1070 BCE).

Egypt's ancient history is felt more here than anywhere else in the Nile Valley. The sandstone columns and mysterious tombs attract droves of tourists all year. Unfortunately, the tourism industry has spawned a society of ruthless hoteliers, greedy guides, and cunning cabdrivers. If somebody says the word "free," walk away—nothing is free in Luxor. A few pounds a day can buy decent accommodations, tasty food, and access to unforgettable sights. The sights of Middle Egypt were once convenient day trips from Luxor, but travel to the north is currently discouraged by the government. Points south (Esna, Edfu) are safe and rewarding destinations.

ORIENTATION

Luxor lies on the eastern bank of the Nile, 670km upstream from Cairo and 220km downstream from Aswan. Surrounded by a heavily cultivated floodplain, the city is an agricultural area (with a *souq* on Tuesdays). Archaeologically, the city can be divided into three sectors: Luxor City, the village of Karnak a few kilometers north, and Thebes on the west bank. Although there are only a few street signs, finding your way around Luxor is easy as long as you know the main thoroughfares. **El Mahatta Street** (Station St.) runs perpendicular to the Nile and connects the **bus stop** and **train station**, 750m inland on the eastern edge of Luxor. Exit the train station at a 45° angle to your left and you will eventually reach **Television Street,** where signs advertising the many budget hotels and pensions in town begin to appear. **En-Nil Street** (the corniche) runs along the river, turning into Khalid ibn al-Walid St. past the **Novotel.** The bus stop is on **El Karnak Street,** running parallel to En-Nil St. slightly inland. **Luxor Temple** is on the corniche at the center of town, and **Karnak Temple** is 3km further northeast one block inland from the corniche.

You can easily get around Luxor by foot, but if you'd rather ride, **kalishes** (carriages) line the Nile. A ride is good for easy transport of baggage or a pleasant trip out to Karnak Temple (E£5). The cheapest transportation in the city is by **minibus** (25pt). The most common route is El Karnak St. to El Mahatta St. to Television St.

PRACTICAL INFORMATION

Tourist Office: (tel. 37 22 15 or 32 94), in the **tourist bazaar** next to the New Winter Palace Hotel. Open daily (including Ramadan) 8am-8pm. Branches at the **train station** (tel. 37 02 59; open 8am-8pm) and in the **airport** (tel. 37 23 06). Low on free and useful literature, but the office in the tourist bazaar has handy bus and train schedules with price listings.

Tourist Police: (tel. 37 66 20), in the **tourist bazaar** on En-Nil St. and at the **train station** (tel. 37 38 45). Both open 24hr. It's best to deliver complaints in person, though English-speakers are few.

Passport Office: tel. 38 08 85, Khalid Ibn Al-Walid St. 1km south of the Novotel, near the Isis Hotel. Extend visas in the foreigners' office. Open Sat.-Thurs. 8:30am-2pm and 5-9pm, Fri. 10am-2pm; visa business Sat.-Thurs. 10am-2pm; during Ramadan 10am-2pm and 8-10pm.

Currency Exchange: Most luxury hotels change money 8am-10pm for a commission. Try **Bank Exchange** on El Karnak St., across from the bus stop. Open 8am-2pm and 5-8pm. **National Bank of Egypt**, En-Nil St., 50m south of Old Winter Palace Hotel. Open daily 9am-10pm. There is an **ATM** machine outside **Banque Misr**, south of the *service*/bus stand: Visa, MC, Plus, AmEx, and Cirrus.

American Express: En-Nil St. (tel. 37 83 33), in the Old Winter Palace Hotel, south of Luxor Temple. Holds mail, sells traveler's cheques, and wires and exchanges money and checks. Open daily 8am-7pm.

Thomas Cook: Winter Palace Hotel (tel. 38 21 96; fax 38 65 02). Books cruises and tours, and changes money. Open daily 8am-8pm.

Flights: Airport 5km northeast of town (no bus; taxi E£10). Served by **EgyptAir** (tel. 38 05 80), next to the Old Winter Palace. Flights to: Cairo (4-5 per day, 1hr., E£417); Aswan (3 per day, E£189); Sharm esh-Sheikh (3 per week, E£413). More flights to all destinations in winter.

Trains: Station is at the head of El Mahatta St. (Station St.), 750m inland from Luxor Temple (tel. 37 20 18). Looks like a temple itself. **Lockers** 90pt per day. For security, tourists often restricted to 2 express trains to Cairo (11:30am and 11:30pm, 8-12hr., A/C 2nd class E£22-31, 1st class E£31-51). Trains to Aswan (6:30am and 4:30pm, 4-5hr., A/C 2nd class E£11-13, students E£7-9) are less comfortable than *service* or *feluccas*. You can pay a walk-on fee but it's safer to reserve a seat. Cairo trains are especially crowded. Reserve sleeper cars 3 days in advance.

Buses: Station at El Karnak and El Mahatta St., by the mosque behind the Luxor Temple. To: Cairo (2:30 and 4:30pm, 7pm with A/C; 11-12hr.; E£35, with A/C E£50); Esna (on the hr. 6am-10pm, 1hr., E£5); Edfu (1½hr., E£10); Kom Ombo (3hr., E£10); Aswan (4½hr., E£14); and Hurghada (6:30am, 3hr., E£8; 11:30am, E£10; 2:30 and 7:30pm E£16). Hours and rates change frequently.

Service Taxis: Off El Karnak St., 1 block inland from the Luxor Museum. Early morning and late afternoon *service* leave whenever they fill up, about every 15min. Some *service* drivers may refuse to take you for fear of being turned back for carrying tourists without a police convoy. This is especially true when entering or leaving Aswan and Luxor. Prices here are one-way. To: **Qena** (1hr., E£2); **Esna** (1hr., E£2); **Edfu** (2hr., E£4); **Kom Ombo** (2½hr., E£7); and **Aswan** (3-4hr., E£7). Less frequent departures from a station on the west bank where the local ferry docks.

Bike Rental: El Mahatta St. and Television St., or ask at your hotel (E£5-7 per day). **Motorbikes** at the Sherif Hotel on Television St. (E£50-60 per day; no helmets).

Swimming Pools: A small but pleasant pool at the **Luxor Wena Hotel** charges E£10, including billiards and backgammon; the **Norotel** charges E£15. The smallish new **Emilio** on Yousef Hassan, **Karnak** behind the Hilton, and **St. Joseph** on Khalid Ibn Walid St. are bargains at E£8-10. The **Shady** has a summer deal of E£15 for their mediocre lunch buffet and pool use.

English Bookstore: Aboudi Bookstore has 3 locations in the tourist bazaar complex on El Nil St. Dozens of good but costly Egyptology books, countless sappy

EGYPT

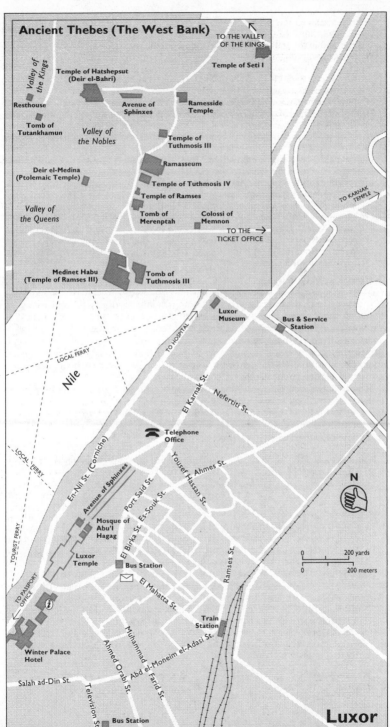

Ancient Thebes (The West Bank)

TO THE VALLEY OF THE KINGS

Temple of Seti I

Valley of the Kings

Temple of Hatshepsut (Deir el-Bahri)

Resthouse

Avenue of Sphinxes

Ramesside Temple

Tomb of Tutankhamun

Valley of the Nobles

Temple of Tuthmosis III

Ramasseum

Deir el-Medina (Ptolemaic Temple)

Temple of Tuthmosis IV

Temple of Ramses

Valley of the Queens

Tomb of Merenptah

Colossi of Memnon

TO THE TICKET OFFICE →

Medinet Habu (Temple of Ramses III)

Tomb of Tuthmosis III

Luxor Museum

Bus & Service Station

TO KARNAK TEMPLE

LOCAL FERRY

Nile

TO HOSPITAL

El Karnak St.

Nefertiti St.

LOCAL FERRY

En-Nil St. (Corniche)

Telephone Office

Yousef Hassan St.

Ahmes St.

Avenue of Sphinxes

Port Said St.

N

TOURIST FERRY

Mosque of Abu'l Hagag

El Birka St.

Es-Souk St.

Ramses St.

0   200 yards
0   200 meters

Luxor Temple

Bus Station

TO PASSPORT OFFICE

El Mahatta St.

i

Train Station

Winter Palace Hotel

Muhammad Farid St.

Abd el-Moneim el-Adasi St.

Salah ad-Din St.

Ahmed Orabi St.

Television St.

Bus Station

Luxor

romances, and a few serious novels in English, French, and German. Swap 2 used paperbacks for 1 of theirs. Open Sat.-Thurs. 8am-10pm. Kiosks in front of tourist bazaar and in the train station sell foreign periodicals.

Pharmacy: 24hr. duty rotates—try asking a hotel employee. **Rania Pharmacy,** at the north end of Television St. is well-stocked with Egyptian medication and basic toiletries. Open 8am-11pm. **El Manshia,** on Abd el-Moneim el-Adasi St., has mostly medication. Open daily 8am-11:30pm.

Hospital: Luxor General Hospital (tel. 37 20 25), En-Nil St. north of the museum.

Emergency: Medical: tel. 123. **Police:** tel. 37 23 50, off El Karnak St. about 200m north of Luxor Temple.

Post Office: Poste Restante and **Express Mail** (until noon) on El Mahatta St., 100m east of Luxor Temple. They will try to "tax" you 50pt for each piece of Poste Restante mail. This is for "confirmation," they say. Get angry, wave your mail around and say "No taxation without representation!" hoping they will decide you are crazy and let you go. Other branches near the tourist office and in the train station. Open Sun.-Thurs. 8am-2pm. Train station branch open 8am-noon and 2-8pm.

Telephones: Central Telephone Office, off El Karnak St. to the west, just north of the tourist bazaars. Open 24hr. Other offices are on En-Nil St. in front of the Old Winter Palace Hotel (cheapest **fax services** in the city here) and in the train station (open 9am-9:30pm). Hotels may charge twice as much as telephone offices. Send **telegrams** from the main post office or telephone offices. **Directory Assistance:** tel. 16. **Telephone Code:** 095.

ACCOMMODATIONS

If you come to Luxor by train, you will disembark into a writhing mass of arms waving hotel cards. Some agents are legit, others are not. Often people masquerade as employees of the popular hotels in town, then lead you elsewhere. The hotels are a short walk from the train station and easy to find. Women traveling alone can bet on sexual advances from young employees of smaller hotels. If a refusal doesn't do the trick, complain to the manager or the tourist police. All travelers should carry valuables on their persons at all times.

Most budget hotels cluster around Television St. and Salah ad-Din Sq. Competition is fierce, so you don't have to settle for their first offer. A roof or terrace mattress may be available for E£3-4. Listed accommodations all have 24hr. hot water, fans, and free use of washers and kitchens, unless otherwise noted. Most provide information, maps, and organized tours (sometimes scams).

Fontana Hotel (tel. 38 06 63), the first left turn after the bus garage on Television St. Train and bus schedules posted on the walls make the lobby resemble a major transit hub. Clean rooms and huge tiled bathrooms. Towels and toilet paper included. Singles with fan E£6, with A/C E£8; doubles with private bath and A/C E£15; small triples with bath and A/C E£20. Breakfast included. Prices E£10 higher in winter.

Everest Hotel, En-Nozha St. (tel. 37 00 17), off Television St. This hotel and its helpful staff have established a good reputation in their first few years. All rooms have A/C and modern bathrooms. Tiled floors and new paint. Bargaining is expected. Hassle-free information about tours. Singles E£15; doubles E£25; triples E£30; quads E£40. Towels and breakfast included.

Oasis Hotel, Muhammad Farid St. (tel. 38 16 99). From the train station, go left down Abd el-Moneim el-Adasi St., and take a 2nd left at the juice stand. Clean, spacious rooms, with a sitting room on every floor. Sometimes pushy about tours. Small roof garden with a limited view. Doubles with A/C and bath E£18, with fan E£12; triple with A/C and bath E£21. Breakfast included.

Pyramids Hotel, Yousef Hassan St. (tel. 37 32 43). From the train station, take a right down Ramses St. and turn left at the end—it's 200m down on the right. Spacious, carpeted rooms with baths and A/C. In the winter, the roof garden is a nice place to down a Stella (E£5). Manager Ziggy goes out of his way to please and entertain. With *Let's Go* discount, singles E£16; doubles E£20; triples E£24.

Sherif Hotel, Badr St. (tel. 37 07 57). First right off Television St. Bob Marley's image, music, and habits thrive in this new, friendly establishment. Some rooms have pot-ted plants and balconies, although the vistas of downtown Luxor are hardly epiphanic. Relax on the aging couches in the small, dim lobby. Singles E£5, with A/C E£10; doubles E£12, with A/C and private bath E£15.

Happy Land (tel. 37 18 28), on El Qamar St. Take the 2nd right before the bus station off Television St. onto El Madina St., go 100m, then take another right. Clean rooms, but no singles with A/C. Singles with fan E£10; doubles with A/C and bath E£20. Prices 25% higher in winter.

Moon Valley Hotel, Ash-Shams St. (tel. 37 57 10). Make first right off Television St., slanting onto Al Medina-Amanaw St. It's 6 blocks down on the right. Clean lobby with sumptuous sofas. The owner likes to introduce himself as Michael Jackson. Singles with A/C E£10, with fan E£8; doubles with A/C E£25, with fan E£20.

Arabesque Hotel, Muhammad Farid St. (tel. 37 12 99), behind the Luxor Temple. A bit more than the rest, but classier. Spotless rooms, some with an incredible Nile view. Roof garden and swimming pool have a view of all Luxor. Rooms have A/C and TV. Singles E£50; doubles E£60. Prices double in winter. Breakfast E£6. Visa and MC with 4% commission.

Grand Hotel, Muhammed Farid St. (tel. 38 29 05). From the train station, go left down Abd el-Moneim el-Adasi St., take the 2nd left at the juice stand, then take the 3rd right. Although cheap, quiet, and relatively clean, it doesn't quite live up to its name. No A/C, all bathrooms outside. Singles E£7; doubles E£13. Cheaper deals can be arranged. Breakfast included.

Accommodations on the West Bank (Ancient Thebes)

It is generally more convenient to sleep on the East Bank in Luxor proper, but the west bank offers quiet surroundings and the chance to roll out of bed and into the Theban necropolis at the opening bell. Unfortunately, you don't get quite as much for your money. Call ahead before lugging your bags across the river. A taxi from the ferry docks (E£5) is the only practical way to get to hotels. For information on crossing the Nile, see **Getting There,** p. 188. The **Pharoah's Hotel** (tel. 31 07 02), near the Medinet Habu temple on an unpaved road, is this area's best hotel with carpeted, air-conditioned rooms and a flowery garden with ping pong. When business is slow, prices may skyrocket; insist that you know better. (Singles E£25, E£30 in winter; doubles E£50, with bath E£60; E£5-10 more in winter. Breakfast included.)

FOOD

Luxor may be an archaeologist's paradise, but it is purgatory for the frugal gourmet. Learn to love the three k's of Egyptian cuisine: *kafta, kebab,* and *kushari.* All three are sold in stands along El Mahatta St. or near Salah ad-Din Sq. Two *kushari* houses stand out from the pack: **Sayyida Zeinab** (on Television St.) and **Sayyida Nafisa** (on Yousef Hassan St.). *Ta'miyya* (falafel) and *fuul* stands are everywhere.

Fresh produce and bread are sold in the *souq* parallel to El Karnak St. beyond the tourist shops. Juice and fruit stands crowd Salah ad-Din Sq. Most budget restaurants serve an array of unimpressive pizzas and pastas, notably the tourist haven of **Amoun Restaurant** on El Karnak St. The coffee shop in the New Winter palace has a bargain all-you-can-eat dessert buffet for E£14. There are **liquor stores** on Ramses St. directly to the right if you're walking out of the train station and on El Mahatta St. Pension managers can procure beer for you (less than E£5.50). A few **supermarkets** at the southern end of Television St. sell staple food, toothbrushes, *Always* pads, yogurt, juice boxes, and toilet paper (large water E£1.50).

A big drawback to staying on the **west bank** is its lack of decent, cheap restaurants. **Tutankhamun** and **Africa** next to the ferry landing offer the usual chicken and *kebab* dinners for E£15-20. Most hotels have restaurants, but they're often closed and the quality is inconsistent, especially when business is slow.

El Houda, on Television St., 100m past the bus garage. Travelers gush about the friendly staff and tasty meals. Excellent, hearty pizza starts at E£6. The *escalope* is enormous and well-prepared (E£9). *Shish tawouq* E£6 or ¼-chicken E£4.50. A/C. Open daily 10am-midnight.

Abu-Haggar (tel. 37 63 06), on the street linking the train station and Television St. An upper-crust Egyptian restaurant recommended by locals. Escape the dirt and grime of the outside world and dine surrounded by beautiful marble. No A/C. *Kafta* E£6.50, chicken E£7, veggies E£2.50. Open daily noon-4am.

Restaurant Khased Khear (tel. 38 45 80), on El Mahatta, 1 block from the train station. A/C and an outdoor kitchen (manned by 3 chefs, they'll have you know) keep this tiny, 2-level restaurant cool. The specialty is *kebab* (beef or lamb entrees average E£9). Take-out available. Open daily 10am-2am.

Sultana Restaurant (tel. 32 54 50), on Television St. 1 block past Mish Mash. This hip new cafe serves gigantic pizzas loaded with garlic. Listen to Arabic pop music while enjoying hummus (E£1.75), sandwiches (including Club and Roast beef), and the usual Egyptian dishes. Open daily 9am-1am.

Ali Baba Café, on Port Said St. next to the Luxor Wena Hotel. A spiral staircase takes you to this shaded roof garden near the temple. Good Egyptian food at reasonable prices. Pizza, pastas E£10. *Sheesha* E£1. Open daily 11am-11pm.

The Classic Restaurant (tel. 38 17 07), Khalid Ibn el-Walid St. Look for the blinking yellow sign near the passport office. A bit pricey, but a welcome break from Egyptian food (although that's also on the menu). Hosts of foreigners enjoy a wide range of European dishes (E£35 for grilled shrimp) and polished, professional service. Fantastic bread with meals. Open daily 6-10:45pm. MC, Visa, AmEx.

Pink Panda (tel. 37 27 50), on Khaled Ibn El Walid St. in the Isis Hotel. If you have a craving for Chinese (or Egypt's version of it), you'll have to pay dearly (meat dishes E£30-40, veggie dishes E£18-20). Waiters buzz about in red coats and black bowties attending to your every need. You can even get a martini. Open daily noon-3pm and 6-11pm. Visa, MC.

SIGHTS IN LUXOR

Luxor has two big temples and a museum. Luxor Temple, the smaller of the temples, stands in the heart of the city adjacent to the Nile. Going north along the corniche, the small but excellent Luxor Museum of Ancient Egyptian Art houses sculptures unearthed at Karnak and elsewhere. Karnak Temple, the Godzilla of pharaonic architecture, sprawls just a few kilometers further north. Karnak Temple is best seen early in the morning before the sun is high, while the museum might best be seen in the afternoon.

Luxor Temple

Although Karnak gets the glory, Luxor Temple is grand in its own right, and more comprehensible to the visitor than the more northerly temple. Most of Luxor Temple, built by Amenhotep III on top of a Middle Kingdom site, dates from around 1380 BCE. Significant portions were erected by famous pharaohs from Ramses II to Tutankhamun, each striving to make his mark. Luxor Temple was meant to serve as a Love Nest for the Gods. Once a year, during the Opet festival, the statues of Amun and his consort Mut would be taken from Karnak temple and loaded onto a ceremonial sacred boat. Amidst much rejoicing and drinking of beer, the happy couple was carried on the shoulders of priests to the Luxor Temple, where they spent 24 days and nights together in the sanctuary. During this time, the moon god Khonsu was conceived, completing the Theban triad.

Later work on the temple was done by Ramses II, who built the enormous **First Pylon,** nearly 24m tall and 65m wide. The pylon is inscribed with images of Ramses II smiting the Hittites. In front of the pylon stand three of the originally six **Colossi of Ramses II,** two seated and one standing. There is a solitary red granite obelisk flanking the doorway; its twin was given to France in 1819 and now graces the Place de la Concorde in Paris.

The granite statues of the **Court of Ramses II,** past the pylon, originally portrayed Amenhotep, but were altered when ancient Egypt's favorite egomaniac assumed the throne. Continue through the court's papyrus columns to the **Colonnade of Amenhotep III**, where the columns have open lotus crowns. The walls of the colonnade were inscribed with scenes from the festival of Opet by Tutankhamun. From here, proceed into the **Court of Amenhotep III.** Beyond this court rises the hypostyle hall, or antechamber, and its 32 gigantic columns. Latin inscriptions to Julius Caesar adorn an altar in a room to the left of the pillared hall. Alexander appears in pharaonic attire before Amun and other deities in some bas-reliefs in the **Sanctuary of Alexander the Great** at the end of the corridor. Fertility god Min receives disproportionate attention in the sanctuary. The Romans used the whole temple as a *castrum* (military camp) in the 4th century CE. The excavation of the temple remains incomplete, as the Mosque of Abul-Haggag, added by the Fatimids in 1077 CE, prevents work on the left-hand gallery. The mosque, towering 20m overhead, is still in use today and serves as a startling reminder of the depth of sand and rubble cleared by archaeologists.

The temple and its well-groomed lawns are a comfortable retreat, especially at night. As of summer 1997, an extensive surveying project is underway to monitor water levels and restore the temple by removing material from earlier conservation attempts. The lights go on at 7pm year-round. Enter on En-Nil St., 400m north of the New Winter Palace (open daily 6am-10pm; in winter 6am-9pm; during Ramadan 6am-6:30pm and 8-11pm; admission E£20, students E£10; half-price after 7pm.)

Luxor Museum

Unlike the heaps of objects squeezed into Cairo's Egyptian Museum, Luxor's curators have provided visitors with multilingual descriptions, including the site and probable date of each subject. The Luxor Museum has arguably the best, most edifying collection of antiquities in Egypt—testament to the fact that less is sometimes more. The museum is thoughtfully arranged with the help of the Brooklyn Museum of New York. Key features include the relatively unscathed statue of Tutmose III (1498-1436 BCE) found at Karnak, and a sphinx with the face of King Tutankhamun (1350-1336 BCE). The gallery also includes smaller artifacts—drinking vessels, precious jewelry, bronze statuettes, and Alexandrian period coins from the second century CE.

The **New Hall** was built to display the cache of 16 marble and granite statues found in the 1980s beneath Luxor Temple. Of the royalty, handsome Amenhotep III (1405-1367 BCE) in red granite is the most striking. The museum is a 15min. walk north of the Luxor Temple on the corniche (open daily 9am-1pm; additional hours 5-10pm in the summer, 4-9pm in the winter; wheelchair accessible; E£30, students E£15).

Karnak Temple

Karnak Temple is overwhelming in its intricacy and proportions. Every major period in Egypt's ancient history since the collapse of the Middle Kingdom is represented in the additions to this complex of shrines dedicated to Amun and his family. Karnak represented the power of the Theban ruler and the importance of the cult of Amun. It was also the center of power for Amun's high priest, whose powers often exceeded those of the pharaoh.

The Karnak complex covers over five acres of land and is difficult to cover thoroughly. If you seek more than a general impression of the place, a guided tour is useful (latching onto one is easy). The **sound and light show** is another way of exploring the temple (English shows Mon. 7:45pm, Tues. 10:15pm, Wed.-Sun. at 9pm during the summer. Winter performances Mon. 6pm, Tues. 9pm, Wed.-Sun. 7:30pm. Admission E£33.) The entire 3km route between the temples of Luxor and Karnak was once connected by the sacred **Avenue of the Sphinxes,** built by Queen Hatshepsut. Ramses II took the liberty of adding a small statuette of himself to each sphinx. The final stretch of the avenue remains complete with two rows of sphinxes at the northern end of El Karnak St. by the **Temple of Khonsu,** to the right of the main entry to Karnak Temple.

Enter Karnak Temple from the west with the Nile at your back and pass through the **Avenue of the Rams,** another double-rowed boulevard of creatures (lions' bodies with rams' heads) dedicated to Ramses II. The curly-horned ram was one of Amun's sacred animals. The temple is a hodge-podge of additions and alterations spanning millennia, but because of the traditionalism of pharaonic architecture, the different pieces comprise a harmonious whole. The Karnak complex expands outward from

---

Get Down and Dig It

An archaeologist's work is never done, especially in Luxor. Although it would appear that most of the treasures of the old tombs and temples have been whisked away, archaeologists are still concerned with what they can learn through excavation (finding a little treasure is also nice). The Department of Antiquities oversees and conducts many of the ongoing projects in Egypt, from the restoration of the Ramesseum to current digs at the Karnak Temple and the Valley of the Kings. One of the most promising recent finds is the discovery of a large, 107-room (and counting) tomb being excavated by a team from the American University of Cairo. The name of Ramses II has been identified four times, giving rise to speculation that this tomb could be the final resting place of the great pharaoh's many sons. Entry into the tomb has been hampered by falling rocks (it is completely off limits to the public). Other avenues of research include remote sensing, which detects irregularities beneath the surface without costly digging, and excavation within the city of Luxor itself.

---

the center, where you will find most of the oldest treasures. The further you proceed from the entrance, the farther back in time you go. The temple is oriented along two axes; a primary east-west axis that follows the path of the sun god Amun and a secondary axis proceeding north-south to Luxor Temple.

The first and largest pylon was never completed and probably dates from the 25th dynasty. The **Great Court,** the single largest individual element of the temple complex, dates from around the same time. Chambers on the left are dedicated to the Theban triad of Amun, Mut, and Khonsu. They were built during the 29th dynasty. On the right is a temple built under Ramses III and lined with 20 7m-tall statues of himself. The three chapels behind the temple's inner court are also dedicated to the Theban Triad. An open papyrus column in the center of the Great Court is all that's left of the pavilion of the Ethiopian king Taharq of the 25th dynasty (689-664 BCE).

Pass through the recycled second pylon (Ramses II made it with blocks from one of Akhenaton's temples) into the **Great Hypostyle Hall.** With 12 central columns and 122 subsidiary columns, it's one of the pinnacles of pharaonic architecture. The central colonnade (1375 BCE) is the oldest part of the hall; other additions are by Ramses II. Emerging from the forest of sandstone, find the 30m-high pink granite **Obelisk of Queen Hatshepsut,** the tallest obelisk in Egypt, in front of the fourth pylon. Hatshepsut, who considered herself a female king, brought the stones from Aswan and inlaid them with bushels of gold. Every centimeter of the ceiling, walls, and columns is carved with inscriptions. Note the depictions of the fertility god Min doing what he does best. Passing through the rubble of the fifth pylon and the granite sixth pylon, enter the **Hall of Records,** containing two elegantly proportioned granite pillars, one decorated with carvings of the lotus of Upper Egypt, the other with the papyrus of Lower Egypt. The **Sanctuary of the Sacred Boats,** behind the hall, was added by Alexander the Great's brother Philip, around 300 BCE.

Straight ahead, the **Festival Hall of Thutmosis III** dominates the eastern edge of the Karnak complex. Built to commemorate the pharaoh's victories in the mysterious north, it contains carvings of strange plants and animals brought back from his campaigns. The star-studded ceiling survives intact, supported by 52 tapering pillars. Some of the bases were actually whittled down to make room for large processions. In the 6th century CE, the hall was converted into a church; frescoes of haloed saints still adorn the interior walls and column shafts. Beyond a low wall to the east, the **Gate of Nectanebo** marks an early entrance to the complex. South of the Festival Hall, the limpid waters of the **Sacred Lake** sizzle in the heat. Every morning, priests purified themselves in the holy waters of this rectangular pool before performing ceremonies within the temple. Note the large scarab beetle on the southwestern corner of the lake—it is said that if you run around the scarab in a clockwise direction three times, you will soon be pregnant.

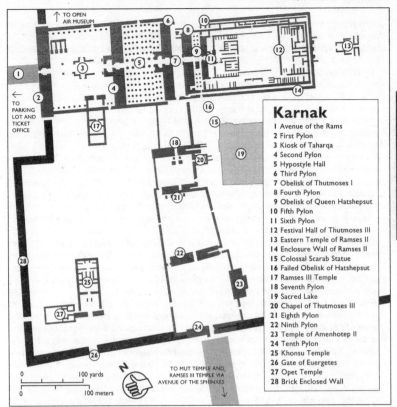

Karnak

1 Avenue of the Rams
2 First Pylon
3 Kiosk of Taharqa
4 Second Pylon
5 Hypostyle Hall
6 Third Pylon
7 Obelisk of Thutmoses I
8 Fourth Pylon
9 Obelisk of Queen Hatshepsut
10 Fifth Pylon
11 Sixth Pylon
12 Festival Hall of Thutmoses III
13 Eastern Temple of Ramses II
14 Enclosure Wall of Ramses II
15 Colossal Scarab Statue
16 Failed Obelisk of Hatshepsut
17 Ramses III Temple
18 Seventh Pylon
19 Sacred Lake
20 Chapel of Thutmoses III
21 Eighth Pylon
22 Ninth Pylon
23 Temple of Amenhotep II
24 Tenth Pylon
25 Khonsu Temple
26 Gate of Euergetes
27 Opet Temple
28 Brick Enclosed Wall

The **Karnak Open Air Museum** is to the north of the great court; look for a small sign and return toward the entrance. The museum is comprised of three excavated chapels and a motley collection of well-labeled wall fragments. The **Red Chapel** of Queen Hatshepsut is displayed in long rows of blocks, along with the Middle Kingdom **Alabaster Chapel.** The later has white walls streaked with brown, a welcome relief from the acres of sandstone.

It takes a long time to see the temple, so bring water and come early in the day. There are hideously overpriced refreshments available near the sacred lake. Jill Kamil's *Luxor* is an excellent guide to the complex (E£30-40). You can reach the temple by bike, foot, or *kalish* (E£5-10). Local minibuses run between Karnak Temple and the train station (25pt). Ask first to make sure the driver is going as far as the temple (temple open daily 6am-5pm; winter 6am-4pm; admission E£20, students E£10; includes open-air museum).

SIGHTS ON THE WEST BANK (ANCIENT THEBES)

When they weren't preoccupied with empire-building and invader-expelling, the rulers of Thebes busied themselves by preparing for eternity. As followers of the sun god Amun, the elite of the New Kingdom aspired to tombs on the west bank, where the sun sets and the afterlife commences. Pharaonic obsession with the afterlife made the necropolis of Thebes into what is quite possibly the world's most well-endowed graveyard. Over millennia, robbers and archaeologists have nabbed much of the treasure, but the site still features an unparalleled collection of Egyptian funerary art.

Security was key for the New Kingdom rulers. Earlier pharaohs had been too convinced of the inviolability of their sacred tombs. Thieves had mastered the delicate art of pyramid pilfering at Memphis, making off with many of the afterlife amenities thought to make the second go-round a little easier for expired royalty. A radical change in burial practices was in order. The pharaohs of Thebes would not have their treasure rest anywhere but beside their mummified remains.

To conceal the location, contents, and design of the tombs, the work was done in utmost secrecy by a team of laborers who dwelt within the necropolis itself. Perfecting techniques of tomb construction, decoration, and mummification, this community of 300 artisans devoted itself to the City of the Dead over the course of generations, passing expertise down through its families. The remains of Deir el-Medina (the Workers' Walled City) have been thoroughly excavated and are among the most complete town remains in Egypt. Tomb design reflected the new emphasis on secrecy. Instead of a single ostentatious pyramid, there were pairs of funerary monuments: an underground grave, lavishly outfitted with the articles demanded by the hectic afterlife and sequestered in an obscure recess of the desert, and a grandiose mortuary temple where the monarch could be worshiped for eternity. Architects incorporated dead-end passages, fake sarcophagi, hidden doorways, and deep shafts to foil the most cunning robbers. Once a stiff pharaoh was safely stowed, workers immediately began to construct the tomb destined for his successor.

One region in particular seemed ideal for entombment: a narrow, winding valley walled on three sides by jagged limestone cliffs and approachable by a single rocky footpath. This isolated canyon, known as the **Valley of the Kings,** became the burial place of New Kingdom pharaohs. Although it looked promising on papyrus, it failed to deter hoodlums, and few of the tombs escaped vandalism.

Queens, favored consorts, and select offspring were accorded ceremonial burial with full honors and security precautions in a separate corner of the west bank, the **Valley of the Queens** (which is constantly under renovation). Esteemed members of the Theban aristocracy also practiced elaborate burial customs, and several of the resulting **Tombs of the Nobles** rival royal burial chambers in craft and design. Last but not least, the **Valley of the Artisans** has two very impressive tombs of pharaonic artists. Over 400 tombs molder in the necropolis, but only a handful are accessible.

In addition to tombs, the west bank hosts massive mortuary temples. Most imposing are the **Temple of Hatshepsut** in Deir el-Bahri and **Medinet Habu** near the Valley of the Queens. The ruins of the **Ramesseum,** though shattered, still merit a visit.

Getting There

The first step is crossing the river. The cheapest way is a **local ferry.** One docks directly in front of Luxor Temple (E£1, bicycles 25pt extra), the other docks just north of the Novotel (E£1, bikes free). **Tourist ferries** are faster and more frequent (E£2, no bikes allowed). One docks about 300m north of Luxor Temple, the other in front of the Winter Palace Hotel, 200m south of the temple. Both tourist ferries shuttle you to the ticket kiosk and operate daily 6am-5pm; local ferries run later. During the summer, the local ferry may be your only option. The local ferry does not dock at the ticket office. **Private motorboats** can take you across for E£5-10 per boat. From the local ferry landing, it is a 1km walk north to the ticket kiosk, then 3km to the Colossi of Memnon.

There are several options for exploring the west bank. **Bicycles** are cheap (E£3-5) and allow for individual freedom and a chance to view the surrounding scenery of green fields abutting sandy dunes. There are a few serious hills (nearly unbearable in summer). You can rent bikes in Luxor or by the local ferry landing.

Hiring a **taxi** is more expensive (E£30-40 for the morning after bargaining), but allows you to cover the most ground. Hordes of drivers wait at both ferry landings. You can hire a taxi in Luxor, but the car ferry is slow and erratic. When bargaining, ignore any nonsense about government rates and per person charges.

Mark Twain wrote that riding a **donkey** in Egypt "was a fresh, new, exhilarating sensation worth a hundred worn and threadbare pleasures." The novelty of donkey travel (which has a way of wearing off quickly) and the fantastic views afforded by the trail as it climbs its way up and around to the Valley of the Kings has led to a burgeoning burro-borrow market. Through your hotel, you can arrange an excursion

Meet the Gods

The endless tombs and awe-inspiring temples that line the Nile have enticed archaeologists and historians for centuries. But unless you've done your homework, the complicated hieroglyphic sagas can be baffling. Although the many depictions of immortal god-figures may suggest otherwise, the ancient Egyptians were technically monotheistic. They recognized the existence of one Supreme Being; the other gods were merely intermediaries. The most widely known of these lesser gods are the jet-setting couple Isis and Osiris.

Osiris: a.k.a "the Good God." Often shown with green skin. He was the King of Thebes in 4200BCE. As a god, he presided over the judgement of souls. When someone died, the heart of the deceased was placed on a scale, counterbalanced by a feather symbolizing the goddess **Maat.** If the heart was not weighed down with wrongdoing, the soul could join Osiris in the afterlife. Otherwise, it was eaten by a beast with the head of a crocodile and the body of a hippo; nobody liked that.

Isis: The wife of Osiris, and the goddess of love and beauty. After Osiris was dismembered by his gentle brother **Seth** and his body scattered throughout Egypt, Isis searched for the pieces. She reassembled his bod, except for his penis, which had been eaten by a fish. Osiris was revived by Isis's love, and he, not having a penis, impregnated her with the gleam in his eye. She gave birth to Horus, symbolized by the falcon.

Horus: The consort of Hathor. He was raised in a papyrus swamp where he plotted his revenge against the evil god Seth.

which includes donkey (with guide) and ferry ride (E£30-40). Larger groups get lower prices. Or, do away with middlemen and hire your own animal in the village of Gezira just inland from the ferry or at the local ferry dock. This allows you more leeway with your itinerary—tours usually take you only to the Valley of the Kings, the Temple of Hatshepsut (Deir el-Bahri), the Ramesseum, and the Colossi of Memnon.

If you have time and stamina, the best way to see the sights on the west bank is to **walk** to them. All of the sights (except for the Valley of the Kings) are within a 3km radius of the Colossi of Memnon, which is an easy 3km from the ticket office. A good strategy is to buy your tickets and start walking to the sights. Once you are on the main road (1km from the ticket office) you can catch a covered pick-up truck to the Colossi of Memnon (25pt). Trucks heading toward the Nile end at the local ferry landing. Naturally, there are no *service* taxis near the ticket office, only "special" taxis. Special taxis from the ticket office to the Colossi of Memnon can be as little as E£5, more in the summer. The Valley of the Kings is 8km by paved road, but the better route follows the donkey trail up and over the **Jabal al-Qurn** (Hill of the Horn). The peak was once sacred to the goddess Mirtseger, "she who loves silence." You don't have to go to the top of the hill to cross into the Valley of the Kings, but the view is well worth the extra effort. Walking in the middle of the day lets you have the sights to yourself, but you must be extremely **cautious** in the unforgiving sun and heat.

Guided tours in air-conditioned coaches with English-speaking guides can be arranged through the various corniche travel agents (E£70-100 per person, including admission; Isis Travel and Misr Travel on the corniche are good places to start). All hotels can book a tour for you. Most tours visit the Valley of the Kings, the Valley of the Queens, the Colossi of Memnon, and Temple of Hatshepsut. Invariably you will find yourself standing in an alabaster or papyrus shop that was secretly part of the itinerary. The larger your group, the better your bargaining leverage. A final option is to rent a **motorbike.** Many hotels, the Everest and Sherif included, rent bikes for E£50-60 a day. Helmets and leather are nowhere to be found.

Valley of the Kings وادى الملوك

The Valley of the Kings lies 5km from the Nile but there's no direct path. There are two possible routes to the beginning of the Valley road: past the Colossi of Memnon, then 3km northeast past the sites of the necropolis to the beginning of the Valley road, turn right (northeast) at the canal (follow the signs) and go 2km along the canal, then turn west by the Abul Kasem Hotel and go 1.5km to the base of the Valley road. The well-paved, gently sloping road winds for 5km into desolate mountain valleys. The Valley of the Kings itself, no more than 400m long and 200m wide, can easily be toured on foot using the clearly marked, well-groomed gravel paths. Over 64 known and numbered tombs honeycomb the valley; the numbering is in the order of discovery. Most of them are not open to the public, but the best-known tombs are almost always accessible. Every few months the open tombs are rotated to minimize wear and tear as well as to add a little variety.

The west bank's most renowned tourist attraction, the **Tomb of Tutankhamun (#62),** stands directly in front of the Rest House in the middle of the valley. It requires a special ticket (E£40, students E£20). The real treasures are at the museum in Cairo and the interior of this small tomb may not be worth the extra ticket. If you plan to see it, visit it first or you'll probably be disappointed after seeing the others.

Tutankhamun's mummy was encased in the innermost of four snugly nested, superbly decorated cases, three of which can be seen in the Egyptian Museum. Fortunately, the raiding Egyptologists left behind the outermost case, a gilded wood extravagance luxuriating in rich jewels, along with Tut's exquisitely carved sarcophagus. The interior walls of the burial chamber, perfectly preserved, depict colorful scenes from the *Book of the Dead.* The only pharaonic tomb to evade grave robbers, Tut's treasure box was discovered in 1922 by archaeologist Howard Carter. The king's priceless belongings have toured the world several times and now reside permanently in the Egyptian Museum in Cairo. Egyptologists had expected that the tomb would contain little of interest because the pharaoh reigned only two years before he died. Carter ignored professional censure, toiling for six seasons in the Valley of the Kings. After more than 200,000 tons of rubble had been moved, Carter's patron reluctantly decided to abort the project. Before admitting failure, Carter explored one more possibility: a site in front of the tomb of Ramses VI, in an area covered with workers' huts. Confounding the critics, he chanced upon an ancient doorway beneath the shanties. The tomb had been opened by robbers, but the luckless thieves had apparently been caught in the act by necropolis guards, because the treasures had been hastily stacked and the entrance resealed. Three mummies were found in the tomb, including that of the boy-king himself.

The 12th-century BCE **Tomb of Ramses IX (#6),** on your left once you enter the valley, features fantastic ceiling murals of gold figures manifesting their *joie de mourir* against a deep blue background. To the right of the entrance the pharaoh is shown offering a gazelle to Amun-Re. Farther on the right the reliefs show him making offerings to the God of Justice (the guy with the balance) and to Osiris, god of resurrection. Through 136 negative confessions (I never lied, I never spent time in a Turkish prison…), he is seeking to enter the heavens. Directly opposite these reliefs, Ramses is playing the same game with Horus to gain safe passage through the two lakes of fire. A long corridor descends to an anteroom covered with protective demons, serpents, and wild beasts. Beyond, a pit in the burial chamber once held Ramses IX's sarcophagus. The ceiling of the chamber was not smoothed and the text appears in a short band form because Ramses IX died before his tomb was ready. Most of the painting was done during the 70 days needed for mummification.

The tomb of his grandfather, **Ramses IV (#2),** the first one on the right was used as a Byzantine church. The well-preserved wall decorations contain excerpts from the *Book of the Dead* and *Book of Fates.* On both sides of the tomb, 365 small statues of the Pharaoh's guardian spirit were believed to facilitate his resurrection every night of the year when Amun-Re crossed to the west bank. A technicolor ceiling and huge, cartouche-shaped sarcophagus make this one of the best tombs in the valley.

The most dramatically situated burial site in the necropolis is the cliffside **Tomb of Thutmosis III (#34),** reached by a long, steep staircase that ascends a precipitous ravine squeezed between towering limestone cliffs. This location provides the ultimate example of 18th dynasty pharaohs' attempts to hide their tombs. Thutmosis III's is built in a fault, where it became naturally concealed by debris left from flash floods.

This strategy was short-lived because it, like so many others, failed to deceive grave robbers. Thutmosis III, Hatshepsut's stepson and rival, was a great military leader (although freakishly short). His conquests reached as far as the fourth cataract of the Nile to the south, Crete and Cyprus to the north, and the Euphrates to the east. His grave is decorated with unusual heiratic (short-hand hieroglyphic) text and strangely beautiful stick-figure representations of Khnum and other gods. The novel cartouche-shaped burial chamber still contains his red granite sarcophagus (don't tip the guard for showing you that it's empty). To get to the tomb, follow the dirt road that begins next to the Tomb of Ramses III leading southwest up the hill.

Named the "Tomb of the Harp Players" after two musicians depicted plucking away in one of its interior chambers, the **Tomb of Ramses III (#11)** boasts a vividly colorful portrayal of ancient races on the left side of the penultimate chamber. Luck-less Ramses III was killed in a palace plot, burgled post-mortem, and as a final insult, kidnapped and shipped in his magnificent sarcophagus to the Louvre.

The steep entrance next to the Tomb of Seti I descends into the **Tomb of Ramses I (#16),** a single burial chamber dominated by Ramses' pink granite sarcophagus. The tomb walls, some of the most vivid in the valley, are painted with scenes of Ramses (founder of the 19th dynasty) hobnobbing with the gods. The first corridor is the shortest in the valley, a consequence of Ramses' brief rule (1320-1318 BCE).

The **Tomb of Meneptah-Siptah (#18)** includes some very nice ceilings painted with vultures and ram-headed falcons (19th dynasty, 13th century BCE). The rough-hewn burial chamber has suffered a good deal of damage, but the large red granite sarcophagus (carved with images of crocodiles and cobras) is still intact.

Three other tombs are worth a visit. The **Tomb of Seti I (#17),** the valley's longest tomb, honors the great 19th-dynasty military leader. The **Tomb of Ramses VI (#9)** is the third largest tomb in the Valley after Ramses II and Seti I. This crypt is known for its ceiling depictions of winged cobras, decapitated enemies, and elongated ladies with stars on their bellies. The **Tomb of Amenhotep II (#35)** is inscribed with the entire text of the Book of the Dead and still contains a beautiful red sarcophagus.

There is a **Rest House** near the entrance to the necropolis featuring overpriced water and warm juice. **Public toilets** are also available (open daily 6am-5pm in summer, 8am-4pm in winter).

Mortuary Temples

The pharaohs may have hid their tombs beneath a valley, but they didn't want the living world to forget about them. In addition to the spectacular rock-hewn tombs, the west bank is peppered with **mortuary temples,** mammoth structures honoring the royal stiffs. Though overshadowed by Luxor's Karnak Temple in scale and importance, the West Theban temples of Hatshepsut (Deir el-Bahri), Ramses III (Medinat Habu), Ramses II (Ramesseum), and Seti I are still stupefying.

The following temples, all accessible from a road that runs parallel to the Nile, are described from south to north. From the ferry docks, head inland 3km past the Colossi of Memnon until you come to an intersection. A road to the left leads to Medi-net Habu, 500m to the southwest.

All that remains of the largest mortuary temple, that of Amenhotep III, are the **Colossi of Memnon,** a pair of towering statues seated in magnificent isolation on the northern side of the entrance road to the necropolis (free admission). Looking over the plain from a height of 20m, these figures of Amenhotep were Thebes' greatest tourist attraction during the Roman era. At night, an eerie whistling sound emanated from the statues, which the Romans interpreted as the voice of Memnon, mythical son of the goddess of dawn, Aurora, who wailed in anticipation of his mother's rays. The sound, according to scientists, was actually produced by grains of sand splitting off from the statues as the rocks contracted in the cool night air. Unfortunately, the Colossi ceased to sing after repairs during the reign of Antoninus Pius..

It's All Hieroglyphs to Me

Hieroglyphic writing was used in instances of special religious significance, such as inscriptions on a temple wall, or spells designed to speed a pharaoh to a happy afterlife. They also served an ornamental purpose and are frequently inscribed with remarkable artistic skill. Since the inscriptions are in part decorative, they are often written in mirror-image pairs; in such cases, the writings are read from different directions. To tell which direction is the beginning, look for a human character; the direction the person or god is facing is usually the beginning. Before the discovery of the **Rosetta Stone** (p. 162), the most popular theory was that each glyph represented an idea. Elaborate, fanciful, and utterly incorrect translations were made from many papyri and inscriptions. The Rosetta Stone provided the revolutionary insight that each glyph stood for an individual sound, rather than a complex meaning. The stone became the key to the long forgotten script because of its trilingual engraving—Greek, demotic, and hieroglyphic. The hieroglyphic alphabet uses combinations of sounds to represent words, much like the English alphabet. To provide more exact syntax, the hieroglyphic alphabet also includes characters that impart the meaning to the sounds and resolve the problem of homonyms.

Medinet Habu

To the left at the end of the road after the Colossi stands **Medinet Habu**, a series of well-preserved edifices constructed in several stages. The most impressive structure in the complex is the **Mortuary Temple of Ramses III,** decorated with reliefs of the pharaoh's numerous successful military campaigns, including his victories over the mysterious "Sea Peoples," who dangle by their hair from his fist. The temple is warrior-themed throughout; the main pylon, also known as the Royal Pavilion, resembles a military fortress rather than a temple. A relief explains the importance of securing houses of worship so that peace and order could then spread elsewhere. Other reliefs show prisoners being put to death. On the back of the main pylon are piles of conquered hands and tongues. Beyond the gate are two relief-rich courts. In the second court on the left side is a window opening supported by statues of human heads. This "window of appearances" was used for royal speeches and was meant to show the king standing on the heads of his vanquished enemies. Relatively few tourists visit the site; a tranquil hour is enough to take it in

The Ramesseum

Farther north, beyond the student ticket office, is the **Mortuary Temple of Ramses II,** or the **Ramesseum.** The same pharaoh who had Abu Simbel tailor-made to his specifications built the Ramesseum to house another mammoth exercise in narcissism. The 1000-ton, 17m **Colossus of Ramses II** (the forefingers alone are over 1m long) was transported in one piece from the pharaoh's granite quarries in Aswan to Thebes. Even shattered, the remnants (including head, upper arms, and one foot) are imposing. This colossus originally overlooked the passageway leading into the second court. A tour of the Ramesseum won't exceed half an hour.

The Temple of Hatshepsut (Deir el-Bahri)

Just north of the Ramesseum, a paved road leaves the main north-south thoroughfare and heads northwest, winding around to the **Temple of Hatshepsut.** If you are on foot, you can save some time by cutting through the village on the left side of the road (before it splits). Located in the center of the necropolis, the temple is 500m north of the Tombs of the Nobles. Hatshepsut's masterpiece rises in three broad, columned terraces from the desert floor against a backdrop of sheer limestone cliffs. The Temple's ancient Egyptian name, Djeser Djesern, means "most splendid of all."

After the death of her husband Thutmosis II, Hatshepsut became the ruler of the kingdom, the only woman to assume the title of Pharaoh. Her temple, currently under excavation by a team of Polish archaeologists, has been skillfully restored with modern materials. No images of Hatshepsut remain intact; after her death, the great Thutmosis III, who had to wait 20 years in her shadow before coming into his own as Pharaoh (she refused to marry him), defaced virtually all of them. Men.

Walk from the lower court up a wide ramp to the central court. The colonnaded back wall contains, from left to right, the Shrine of Hathor, the Colonnade of the Expedition of Punt, the Birth Colonnade, and Shrine to Anubis. The Punt reliefs show Egyptian expeditions to that land (today's Somalia), and the exchange of goods (trees, animals, etc.) with the locals. The Birth Colonnade details Hatshepsut's birth and childhood. Another huge ramp leads to the upper court with a rock-cut sanctuary. Badly ruined, and sadly defaced by Christians who used the temple as a Coptic monastery in the 7th century, this court is closed to the public.

Temple of Seti I

You'll have a fair amount of trouble getting here and there's not that much to see. From the Temple of Hatshepsut return to the main road, turn north, and follow it to the end. Turn right to visit what remains of the **Mortuary Temple of Seti I,** father of Ramses II, a warrior who enlarged the Egyptian empire to include the island of Cyprus and parts of Mesopotamia. Seti was also one of the first men to wear earrings—archaeologists could tell this from his well-preserved mummy-lobes. Although the booty from his successful campaigns has been stolen, the relief work, among the finest executed in ancient Egypt, remains.

Valley of the Artisans (Deir el-Medina)

To reach the plentiful though visually uninspiring remains of the **Workers' Walled City,** go past the Colossi of Memnon and follow the small road west. About 60m down the road stands the small temple of **Deir el-Medina** (Monastery of the Town), an elegant shrine dating from the Ptolemaic era. Dedicated to Hathor, the goddess of love, and Maat, the representation of divine order (see **Religion in Ancient Egypt,** p. 61), the temple was named during Christian times when monks constructed a monastery next door. The Workers' Walled City was the only inhabited area on the west bank necropolis during the New Kingdom. Since the workers and artists knew the whereabouts of the tombs they were digging and were using precious, expensive materials, their movements were strictly controlled and observed and they lived in isolation (the entire walled city was roofed over). Many of the workers were killed when construction was completed. A typical house consisted of a kitchen, a living room, and one bedroom. Some had stairways for access to the rooftops, a welcome relief from the heat and smell below.

Several **Tombs of Artisans** can also be found here. The accessible ones are in such excellent condition that it is hard to believe they were painted so many centuries ago. Unlike the formal decorations dictated by priests on the walls of royal tombs, these tombs contain very creative drawings of the afterlife that can be considered a form of free-hand art. Perhaps it's the exceptionally long painting time that led to the imposing relief—some spent almost 30 years building their tombs. They could only work on their own tombs on the single rest day of the ancient ten-day week. Two amazing tombs are open to the public—the **Tomb of Sen-nedjen,** artist of Ramses III, and **Tomb of Inherku,** "deputy master of the two Egypts in Truth Square;" in short: head artist of Ramses IV. One admission ticket includes the Temple of Deir el-Medina, the two tombs, and the Workers' Walled City.

Tombs of the Nobles

A few hundred meters southeast of the Temple of Hatshepsut is the west bank's sardine-packed burial site, more than 400 Tombs of the Nobles. The area is divided into four regions: the Tombs of Rekhmire and Sennofer; the Tombs of Ramose, Userhet the Scribe, and Khaemhut; the Tombs of Nakht and Mena; and the Asasif Tombs. You must buy a separate ticket for each. The first two groups provide the most punch for your tomb-going pound. Many villagers will volunteer their services, but a guide is unnecessary. Maps are available in bookstores on the East Bank.

EGYPT

Throughout the New Kingdom, Theban aristocrats had *de facto* control over much of the pharaoh's empire and served as advisors. The pharaoh often remained ignorant of the most crucial political developments while members of the elite fought amongst themselves for control of the kingdom. Some aristocrats affected pharaonic status by amply providing themselves with luxuries for the afterlife and devising well-hidden underground tombs. Unlike the divine pharaoh who would assuredly live among the gods after his death, Theban aristocrats needed more assurance that a comfortable existence awaited them in the afterlife. Accordingly, every facet of their earthly lives was carefully recorded on the walls of their tombs, leaving the decoration more naturalistic and mundane than the reliefs found in pharaonic tombs. Because the limestone in this portion of the necropolis was inferior, artisans could not carve in relief; instead they painted murals on a whitewashed stone surface. These tombs are architecturally simpler than those of the Pharaohs; they all start with a terrace leading to a decorated vestibule followed by a corridor.

Tombs of Ramose, Userhet, and Khaemhut

The **Tomb of Ramose (#55)** was built during the reign of the heretic king Akhenaton (Amenhotep IV). Ramose was Governor of Thebes and Vizier under Amenhotep and Akhenaton, and was one of the first converts to Akhenaton's new god, the Aton.

In the columned first chamber, all of Egypt pays obeisance to Aton, a blood-red disk emitting shafts of light which end in small hands holding *ankhs* and other religious symbols. On the wall through which you enter, the images carved in unpainted relief reflect the traditional, stylized tastes of the Old Kingdom, with scenes of Ramose and his family making offerings and Egyptians cheering Ramose's conversion to the Aton cult. In contrast, the wall to the left as you enter displays the strangely distorted figures and realistic composition typical of Akhenaton's reign. The tomb was never completed and a lot of the carvings were left unpainted since Ramose abandoned this tomb and chose to build a bigger one in the monotheistic necropolis of Tel el-Amarna, near Minya. An interesting theory about Akhenaton is supported in these images. The sun-disc Aton looks startlingly like a flying saucer. The oblong heads and elongated arms resemble modern representations of **space aliens.** Hmmm. The guard will offer to show you the dull, dark burial chamber, perhaps not worth the *bakhsheesh*.

Continue up from the depression containing the Tomb of Ramose to the **Tomb of Userhet the Scribe (#56),** a few meters to the south. Although an early Christian monk who made his home within the chamber destroyed most of the female figures adorning the walls, the tomb's decor retains a certain blithe spirit because of the unusual pink tones of the interior frescos. Userhet, Amenhotep II's royal scribe (around 1408 BCE), had his resting place painted with every-day scenes: on the right-hand wall of the first chamber, men wait their turn in line for the local barber, while hunting and duck-offering scenes cover the wall of the entrance.

Next is the less-than-impressive **Tomb of Khaemhut (#57),** another of Amenhotep's scribes. The only thing worth seeing are the statues of the scribe and his wife.

Tomb of Nakht

Slightly north of the Tomb of Ramose, a trail leads off the main road and winds east a short distance to the **Tomb of Nakht (#52).** The first chamber contains a reconstruction of an exquisite statue of Nakht, scribe of the royal granaries under Thutmosis IV (the original was lost at sea on its way to the U.S. during World War I). Also in the first chamber are photographs of some of the other removed contents and a series of well-labeled diagrams explaining the images within the second chamber. The most famous image from the Tombs of the Nobles, three musicians playing the flute, harp, and lute, is on the left wall; Nakht's wife was a singer.

Tombs of Rekhmire and Sennofer

The westernmost tomb belongs to Rekhmire, a governor of Thebes who advised Thutmosis III and prided himself on his administrative genius. A historian's delight, the **Tomb of Rekhmire (#100)** is comprised of biographical narratives depicting the

Mummies in the Night

In the late 1870s, members of the Antiquities Service noticed a large number of New Kingdom funerary objects appearing on the European black market. Charles Wilbur, a wealthy American antiquer, was enlisted to go undercover and identify the source of the treasures. By making clear that he would pay high prices for authentic pieces, Wilbur was eventually led to Luxor. Across the river in the town of Qurna, he was shown a piece that had come from a recently opened royal burial. Wilbur secretly telegraphed Gaston Maspero, the Director General of the Antiquities Service, who rushed to Luxor and began intense questioning of all involved. Several weeks later, Muhammad Abd er-Rasul, the head of the most prominent antiquities-dealing family in Luxor, confessed that his family had found a tomb near the Mortuary Temple of Hapshetsut. Archaeologists were quickly summoned, and found the deep shaft burial containing the mummies of the New Kingdom's greatest kings: Thutmosis III, Amosis (founder of the New Kingdom, and the legendary Ramses II, among many others. The Abd er-Rasul family had kept the shaft a secret for ten years, quietly selling their stash. The Antiquities Service, aware of the security risk that a public disclosure would cause, employed hundreds of men to load the hushed mummies onto ships. The bodies were hurried down the Nile at top speed and now reside in the Egyptian Museum.

full range of activities Rekhmire oversaw. This tomb is perhaps the most absorbing of all the tombs in the Theban necropolis.

In the first chamber, tax evaders are tried by Rekhmire, who sits with a set of rolled papyrus texts strewn at the foot of his judgment throne; the presence of the papyrus suggests that written law existed as early as 1500 BCE. On the inner, left-hand wall, a procession of tribute-paying expeditions arrives from Crete (top), Syria (middle), and the African Kingdoms of Punt and Nubia (bottom). Making contributions to the pharaonic menagerie, Nubian representatives offer a giraffe, assorted monkeys, a tiger, and an elephant tusk. Other scenes show Egyptians drinking themselves into a stupor during what was known as the "Festival of the Valley." The niche at the top of the rear wall was intended to contain a statue of Rekhmire himself.

Trek 50m up the hill to the west of Rekhmire's tomb to reach the **Tomb of Sennofer (#96).** This impressively vivid tombt is known as "Tomb of the Vines," after the filigree grapevine crawling all over the ceiling. The delightful lattice of purple and green simulates a shady arbor for Sennofer, overseer of the royal gardens of Amun under Amenhotep II. The plan of the tomb is as unusual as its decor: a curving wall leads into the first room, which in turn leads straight back into the pillared burial chamber. The big, wet eyes of **Hathor the love-cow** follow you around the tomb from the tops of the columns. The superb condition and remarkable expressiveness of the paintings of this small tomb make it worth the detour.

Asasif Tombs

Southwest of the Temple of Hatshepsut lies **Asasif,** a current archaeological hot spot. Asasif became the most popular aristocratic burial area during the 25th and 26th dynasties (about the 7th century BCE), though the **Tomb of Kheruef (#192),** the finest portion of the necropolis, was constructed 700 years earlier. Enter the burial site through an outer courtyard containing other tombs, where a series of well-wrought reliefs stands against a protecting wall. Note the provocative ceremonial dance featuring a chorus line of women, a jumping bird, a noisy monkey, flutists, and drummers to the left of the doorway. On the right, pharaonic heartthrob Amenhotep III is surrounded by 16 swooning princesses.

As you enter the **Tomb of Kiki (#409),** about 10m to the north of Kheruef, the gods Thoth and Anubis discuss the readings of a giant scale. The burial chamber remains unfinished, leaving a series of faceless figures outlined in red. To get to the **Tomb of Nefer-hotep (#48),** walk 100m east along the dirt path from Kiki, then turn right (south) and walk 20m to the tomb, immediately in front of a village house. Most of the seated stone figures within the tomb are fairly intact.

Valley of the Queens وادى الملكات

During the later years of the New Kingdom, a special burial area was chosen for the wives and children of the pharaohs. Traditionally, the pharaoh's closest relatives were buried beside the monarch, but this arrangement changed during the reign of Ramses I (14th century BCE), when princes, consorts, and wives were buried in the Valley of the Queens. Directly west of the Colossi of Memnon at the end of the main road, the Valley of the Queens contains fewer than 30 royal tombs. Check at the ticket kiosks to find out which are currently open.

The **Tomb of Amonherkhepeshef (#55)** is richly bedecked with bas-relief carvings: Ramses III introduces his nine-year-old son to each of the major deities and Amonherkhepeshef wears the groomed topknot of a pharaonic prince. The colored scenes of deities and farmers fill entire walls—a rare sight in Theban tombs. The small sarcophagus that held the prince's mummy stands in the rear burial chamber. A desiccated fetus lies curled in a small glass display next to the sarcophagus. A flashlight is helpful in the burial chamber. The extremely pricey **Tomb of Queen Nefertari (#66)** is open to the first 150 people who can afford a ticket (E£100, students E£50). Touted as Egypt's finest tomb, the vivid tones are genuinely startling. It took seven winters, US$6 million, and the world-renowned expertise of the Getty Institute to preserve and restore this masterpiece. The reliefs in the first chamber include the goddess Hathor leading Nefertari by the hand, thousands of hieroglyphs, and a scarab-faced goddess. A sea-green and starry ceiling canopies the stairs down to the queen's burial chamber. Four columns in the burial chamber portray Osiris in his green-skinned glory, along with the cow-goddess Hathor. The tomb was monitored for a few years to ensure its stability, before being opened to the public. You'll have ten minutes to absorb what you can, so stay alert.

ENTERTAINMENT

This ain't no Cairo or Alexandria. For true Luxorious diversion, fritter away afternoons aboard a **felucca** on the Nile. **Banana Island** is a popular destination; two miles upriver, it's a small peninsula studded with palms and fruit trees. Overpriced souvenir stands detract from an otherwise rustic experience. *Feluccas* are prohibited from sailing after sunset (round-trip 2-3hr.; E£10 per person for groups over 4). The family that owns the island charges E£3.50 admission.

You will probably be invited to a wedding party while in Luxor (or at least asked to get liquor at the duty free store "for my sister's wedding tomorrow"). Think twice before disrupting a wedding party—often "invitees" are expected to pay admission.

The **Mercure (a.k.a. ETAP) Hotel**, on the corniche, is the most happening **discotheque** in Luxor. There is a E£20 minimum charge, but nobody pays attention to it during the summer. Every night at 11:30pm, the music changes from Top 40 dance remixes to drum machine and synthesizer Arabic music and the belly dancing starts. An older crowd joins the youngsters for the nightly display of undulating flesh (Stella E£9; open nightly 10pm-2am). Most popular with local swingers is **Disco on Le Lotus** at the Novotel (intersection of Salah ad-Din and the corniche), on a boat docked behind the hotel (open 10pm-2am; E£20 minimum). The **Ultimate Night Spot**, where American and European music reverberates late into the night (drinks E£12). You can make requests or bring in your own music.

Quieter options are **billiards** at the **Mercure** (E£5 per game) or **backgammon** and **foosball** at the downstairs **Novopub** in the Novotel (drinks E£12). The **New Winter Palace Hotel** has a breezy terrace and a live band (drinks E£15), and the **Pyramid Hotel** has a relaxing roof garden in winter (drinks and food E£5).

Ahwas are filled with Egyptians smoking *sheesha,* drinking coffee, and playing dominoes and backgammon until the wee hours. Foreigners are usually welcome, but solo women may attract unwanted comments. The **Tikkya**, on Television St., is comfortable and friendlier than the other shops. If you have money you don't need, you can lose it at the Hilton **casino** (open 8pm-1am, foreign currency only). Finally, you can check out the Luxor Museum or Temple by night, or witness the infotainment spectacular of the Karnak **sound and light show** (see **Karnak Temple**, p. 185).

■ Near Luxor: Dendera

The **Temple of Hathor** at Dendera is one of the few sights in Middle Egypt that has remained accessible throughout the fundamentalist uprising. A visit is only recommended for die-hard temple fans. The smoothest way to see the temple is by boat from Luxor, emptying wallets at E£150 per person for a day cruise including lunch (book with a travel agent on the corniche). Another option is to hire a taxi with a group of people; ask your hotel for help in corralling other passengers. The trip should cost between E£120-150, depending on your bargaining skills and the vehicle. You'll have to travel at specific police convoy times, usually 7am, but check with the Tourist Office or your hotel for current convoy times. Once there, you'll be surrounded by police who will rush you through your visit. For your trouble, you'll get to see a temple without the crowds of Karnak or Luxor. The temple is smaller and not as old, but still an impressive display of ancient devotion to the gods.

The **Temple of Hathor** only dates from the first century BCE, although worship of Hathor is much older. The late Ptolemies and the Romans found it politically expedient to associate themselves with the benevolent goddess. Hathor is depicted as cow-headed or with cow's ears, or shown wearing a crown of two horns cradling the sun disk. Because her specialty was love, Hathor, the "Golden One," was identified by the Greeks as Aphrodite. During an annual festival, a statue of Hathor was carried in a sacred procession down the Nile to meet Horus of Edfu.

Eighteen columns are topped by cow heads in the **Great Hypostyle Hall.** In the temple's inner sanctum, wall paintings portray the embalmer's art, while the ceiling is decorated with pictures of the goddess Nut. The second hypostyle hall, also called the **Hall of Appearances,** gives way to the **Hall of Offerings,** where the daily rites were performed. In the kiosk in the southwest corner of the roof, priests performed the ceremony of "touching the disk," in which the soul of the sun god Ra appeared in the form of light. If you look to the right you will notice a gently sloping staircase which leads up to the roof.

The **Hall of the Ennead** immediately precedes the inner sanctuary. The chamber on the left is the wardrobe; opposite it, a doorway leads through a small treasury into the **Court of the New Year** where sacrifices were performed during the New Year festival. On the ceiling of the colorful portico, Nut gives birth to the sun, whose rays shine upon the head of Hathor. The **Mysterious Corridor** surrounds the **Sanctuary** on three sides, and 11 chapels, each with a distinct religious function, open off of it. A small chamber known as the **Throne of Ra** sits behind the northernmost of the three doorways behind the sanctuary. A minuscule opening in its floor leads to the crypt, a subterranean hallway embellished with reliefs, some of inlaid alabaster. Many rooms on the upper floors carry ceiling paintings of Nut swallowing the sun at sundown and giving birth to it at dawn. On the roof of the temple, near the edge, is graffiti left by French soldiers in 1799. During the summer, bats inhabit the secluded portions of the temple; a flashlight comes in handy (admission E£12, students E£6).

■ Between Luxor and Aswan

Along the 228km stretch of the Nile from Luxor to Aswan you'll pass the drowsy rural towns of Esna (58km south), Edfu (50km south of Esna), and Kom Ombo (100km past Edfu). Bright green corn and date palm fields line the riverbank and quickly give way to lifeless desert. The area is dotted with hamlets of mud-brick houses clustered together on the cliff face at the desert's edge. Going by river is the sweetest of joys. The area is an enchanting mixture of older Arab *fellaheen* communities and Nubian villages created by those whose homes are now submerged by Lake Nasser. Each of the major towns is graced by an outstanding Ptolemaic temple.

Whether you go by *service,* bus, train, or *felucca,* each of these towns is worth a stop. They also make excellent daytrips: Esna and Edfu from Luxor; Edfu, Kom Ombo and the camel market at Daraw from Aswan. By boat, the entire Luxor-Aswan route takes three to five days, including stops in Esna, Edfu, and Kom Ombo.

ESNA اسنا

Quiet, provincial Esna snoozes on the western bank of the Nile 55km south of Luxor. It boasts blue waters, a turn-of-the-century British barrage, and the remains of a Roman-era temple sitting in the middle of town. From Esna, a small highway ambles along the bank to West Thebes. As always, expect to be bombarded by *kalish* drivers and others wanting to be your "friend."

Esna has only a few main streets important to tourists. The highway and rail lines are on the eastern side of the river, connected to the town by a bridge. The **train station** lies to the east of town on the other side of the Nile. The **bus** and **service** stations are at the town's western edge, down the street just south of the telephone office (E£1 to temple). You can take a **kalish** from either station to the temple (don't pay more than E£1.50-2 for a ride anywhere in town), or walk (2km). Once you have crossed to the west bank of the Nile, you will, appropriately enough, be on **Nile Street.** Following it south, you will find the **telephone and telegraph office,** 50m to the right (tel. 40 05 12; open 24hr.; international calls). Nile St. then veers slightly west and crosses a canal to the **police station** (tel. 40 08 89; open 24hr.). From here it saunters 20m to **El Malak Pharmacy,** then cuts sharply left and then right to follow the river. From the river it's about 300m south to the **Bank of Alexandria** (tel. 40 05 26; open Sun.-Thurs. 8:30am-2pm, 6-9pm for exchange; in winter 5-8pm; during Ramadan 10am-1:30pm). There is no post office in Esna, but there are several red **postal boxes** past the mosque on Nile St. Another 100m brings you to the temple **ticket booth.** (Open summer 6am-6:30pm, winter 6am-5:30pm. Admission E£8, students E£4. Don't buy tickets from hawkers in the bazaar.) At the ticket booth, Nile St. is met by **Souq Street,** a 200m stretch of tourist bazaars which runs up to the temple, passing the non-English speaking **tourist police** (tel. 40 06 86) on the left. Esna is delighted to have a **hospital** (tel. 40 07 09; for **ambulance** dial 502). Esna's **telephone code** is 095.

There is little to keep you beyond a temple visit, but if you must stay, the worn out **Hotel El Haramen** (tel. 40 03 40) is perhaps not the world's cleanest establishment. The hotel is one kilometer south (through the *souq*) of the temple's eastern wall (pass to the right of the white wall enclosing a gray concrete building, and walk another 100m). There are no signs along the way (singles E£5, none with bath; doubles E£10, with bath E£15; triples E£15, with bath E£20; quads E£20, with bath E£25). The *souq* can provide *ta'miyya, fuul,* and produce.

Khnum was a ram-headed creator god worshipped in the area of the first cataract before and after Egypt's unification. This local deity, who reputedly molded the first human being on a potter's wheel, had his sanctuary on Aswan's Elephantine Island. The cataract was an important regional center for the area south of Luxor, and the pharaohs of the 18th dynasty, seeking stronger popular support, dedicated this temple to the local deity. Although the **Temple of Khnum** was begun in the 18th dynasty, it is largely a Roman creation and was in many ways a feeble imitation of inherited technical and artistic achievements. Archaeologists discovered the elaborate hallway in excellent condition. Today the temple is an astounding spectacle lying in a pit, surrounded by the *souq* and the everyday bustle of modern life.

The Romans, attempting to decorate the temple in a pharaonic manner, carved a procession of stiff, oddly deformed figures marching solemnly across the walls. The ceiling designs are among the more interesting aspects in the temple. Faint blue and red hues on the tops of the 24 columns hint at the interior's former brilliance (open daily 6am-6:30pm; in winter 6am-5:30pm; admission E£8, students E£4).

Just to the north of the turn off to the temple, a **barrage** (a series of gates that can be raised or lowered to control water flow), completed in 1908, stretches across the river. Upgraded and restored in the 1940s to meet increased demand, the old barrage has nevertheless been made obsolete by a new one (financed with Italian help) 1km to the north. The government hopes that the new barrage will help reclaim some 300,000 *feddans* of land.

EL KAB

If you have time and energy to spare while traveling between Esna and Edfu, either by the main highway or by *felucca*, consider a stop at **El Kab**, 20km north of Edfu and 3km south of the village of **El Mahamid**. The government has only recently opened El Kab for tourism, and the site has yet to become overrun; if you manage to get to El Kab, you will probably have the site to yourself. The downside is that if you want to visit the temples, which lie at 2.5 and 4km from the roadside tombs and city wall, you'll have to walk. Bring several bottles of water (there's not a leaf of shade). If you come by *felucca*, your captain might not know where El Kab is; give him the distances indicated here and be on the lookout for the Roman wall on the east bank of the Nile. From Edfu, the cheapest way to El Kab is a one-way *service* (75pt), although some will say that *service* don't go there. The best time to leave is early morning, before the sun is high. To get back to Edfu, travelers can hail a pick-up taxi.

The religious center of El Kab was dedicated to the vulture-goddess Nekhbet, protector of the pharaohs and lady of the mouth of the desert. The remains are interesting, but not on the order of Edfu or Valley of the Kings. The escarpment by the road is pocked with a number of tombs. The four most important ones date from 1570-1320 BCE. They have locked gates and a stairway; a guard will let you in. The most well-preserved is the **Tomb of the Paheri**. A multi-talented royal servant, Paheri was chief priest, royal tutor to Prince Wadjmose (son of Pharaoh Thutmosis I), and scribe of the accounts of corn. This tomb features brightly colored illustrations of long lines of seated lotus-sniffers, Egyptians cultivating crops, fishing, shipping, and making wine, and an impressive assortment of international 19th-century graffiti and a statue of happy Paheri flanked by two female figures. **The Tomb of Setau** belongs to the powerful high priest of Amun under Ramses III through IX (20th dynasty). The **Tomb of Aahmes** is the resting place of a warship captain who suppressed a rebellion in Upper Egypt and led 18th dynasty forces under Amenhotep I and Thutmosis I in Nubia and Syria. Both tombs are poorly preserved. The **Tomb of Renini,** superintendent of priests under Amenhotep I, contains a geometrically painted ceiling and two big eyes which look out from either side of a broken central statue.

Two and a half km along an unpaved but passable track brings you to the tiny **Chapel of Thoth** (1320-1200 BCE), built by the high priest of El Kab for Ramses II and dedicated to Nekhbet, Thoth (Wisdom), and Horus. The much larger **Ptolemaic Temple** built under Ptolemies IX through XI has an impressive ramped entryway leading to a forecourt with a few nice broken capitals and a chamber with ceiling paintings and inscriptions. Wake up the guard in the shack across the road to open the locked gates; he'll then ride with you another 1.5km to the small **Temple of Amenophis III** with well-preserved colored paintings and carvings of Nekhbet herself coiffed with a swinging 60s *That Girl* bob. Caravans going to and coming from gold mines deeper in the desert once stopped here for prayer (site open daily 8am-5pm; E£10, students E£5).

GEBEL ES-SILSILAH

The quarries at **Gebel es-Silsilah** are a fascinating bonus prize for *felucca* travelers who succeed in persuading their captain to stop here. Although a ramp and stairs have been built down to the water's edge in anticipation of Nile cruiser stops, the site is not yet officially open, but *bakhsheesh* to the guard and a promise to be quick should win access. The sandstone quarries were in use from the New Kingdom (1500 BCE) up to the Ptolemaic (and possibly the Roman) period. There are quarries on both sides of the Nile, but boats only dock on the west bank. A guard can unlock a well-preserved **temple** constructed under the anti-Aten Pharaoh Horemheb, a general under Tutankhamun who seized the throne during power struggles after Tut's death. The forecourt has well-preserved relief scenes. From the temple, a 200m path leads south along a bluff 15m above the Nile, ending in the cavernous belly of the quarry. Huge blocks of sandstone were cut from the cliff, loaded onto boats, and

EGYPT

transported along the Nile to construction sites; notice the boat and ostrich graffiti etched into the wall's face. A scramble to the top of the cliff yields a fine Nile view.

EDFU ادفو

Edfu is a tiny town with a big temple. Like many temple towns in the Valley, there is a good deal of hustling going on, but here the psychological warfare waged by *kalish* drivers and bazaar hawkers is a bit calmer. A few blocks beyond the town's central square, oblivious to 2000 years of change, stands a stunningly well-preserved Temple of Horus. The intricacy of this temple rivals the serenity of Kalabsha and even the awesome scale of Abu Simbel, making it one of Upper Egypt's most spectacular sights. If you can time your visit to avoid the tourist flood, exploring the dark, eerie chambers and towering columns can be quite a thrill.

Orientation and Practical Information Edfu lies 50km south of Esna on the west bank of the Nile, roughly halfway between Luxor (112km south) and Aswan (121km north). The Edfu bridge, with the **train station** on its eastern end and the **service taxi station** near its western end, crosses the Nile at the northern edge of town. Trains run north and south until 9 or 10pm, as do *service*. Local **pick-up trucks** (E£1), *kalishes* (E£2-3), or **private taxis** (E£3-5) can take you from either station to the temple. The bus station is 50m north of Temple Sq. (a right turn off El Maglis St.). Buses run north and south hourly until 6pm (at the latest). Another 200m down on your right is the **Bank of Cairo** (tel. 70 36 97; open summer Sun.-Thurs. 8:30am-2pm and 6-9pm; winter 8:30am-2pm and 5-8pm). Across the street from the bank is the **Ezzat Pharmacy** (tel. 70 38 60; open Mon.-Sat. 7:30am-11pm). One hundred meters from Temple Sq. is a tourist bazaar, the **tourist police** (tel. 70 01 34; open 7am-5pm), and the temple. The **post office** is on Tahrir St., on the right side 50m south of Temple Sq. (open Sat.-Thurs. 8am-2:30pm). From the bridge, the riverfront road runs 100m south to the **telephone office** (tel. 70 17 77; open 24hr.) and another 200m to **El Maglis Street,** which links the Nile with Temple Sq. The telegraph office, located on the south side of Temple Sq., can help with calling card calls (E£1.10 per 3min. for the call to Cairo). Edfu's **telephone code** is 089.

Accommodations and Food The cleanest budget hotel in town is the **El Madina Hotel** (tel. 70 13 26), just off Temple Sq. (singles with breakfast E£25, less without bath; doubles E£30; triples E£40; settle on a price before staying). The **Semi-Ramis Hotel** is near the bank (E£3 per bed makes it popular). The **New Egypt Restaurant,** off Temple Sq., serves rice, vegetables, salad, and either meat or half a chicken for E£7. Edfu's **produce souq** (open Sat.-Thurs. 8am-9pm) is to the left on Goumhouriyya St. To the right is a *ta'miyya, fuul,* and tea stand market.

Sights The Temple of Horus took over 200 years to construct and was not completed until 57 BCE, making it one of the last great Egyptian monuments. The Ptolemies designed this temple and the one at Dendera, dedicated to Horus's wife Hathor, as a matched set. Like Dendera and many other locations in the Valley, Edfu has been the site of a temple since at least New Kingdom times, the current building being just the most recent incarnation. Several important religious festivals dealing with the life of Horus were celebrated at Edfu. During the annual "Union with the Solar Disk," Horus's earthly form was brought to the roof of the temple to be rejuvenated by the rays of the sun. Another important ritual was the "Festival of the Happy Reunion," in which the god's icon was removed from the temple in a ceremonial boat and taken to Dendera to bring Hathor home to Edfu for some postmortem cavorting. There is a polished black granite shrine in the inner sanctuary that once held the icon statue of Horus. In a chamber behind the sanctuary, there is a modern reconstruction of the ceremonial boat used to carry the statue during festivals.

Enter the temple through the 12 gigantic columns of the **Great Hypostyle Hall** and proceed to the second Hypostyle Hall, outfitted with a similar arrangement of smaller pillars. Doorways on either side lead to the **ambulatory,** a narrow exterior passageway running between the temple and its protective wall. The temple is honey-combed with smaller passageways that enabled the priests to walk around the entire complex without crossing in front of the sanctuary or speaking to one another. The doorway on the right side of the second hall leads to a side chapel with an amazing ceiling depiction of the sky goddess Nut reaching around the Zodiac. Sadly, most of the reliefs have been thoroughly defaced, although some isolated rooms remain largely untouched (bring a **flashlight**). The grounds surrounding the temple are scattered with broken ceramics, the legacy of careless "archaeology."

Outside the temple, directly in front of the main entrance pylon, is a well-preserved Roman *mammisis* (birthhouse), where the birth of Horus was reenacted annually with appropriate hoopla. Copts later defaced the images of the growing god on the columns of the *mammisis*. Note the images of **pot-bellied pygmies,** brought to court for the royalty's entertainment, atop of the exterior side columns (site open daily 7am-6pm; winter 7am-4pm; E£20, students E£10).

KOM OMBO كوم أمبو

Forty-five kilometers north of Aswan on the east bank of the Nile stands Kom Ombo, the site of an Egyptian temple as renowned for its location as for its unique construction and design. Unlike many of the temples in Upper Egypt, Kom Ombo is still situated in its original spot along the banks of the Nile, giving virtually the same visual impression today as during Ptolemaic times.

Orientation and Practical Information Kom Ombo town Highway runs north-south, paralleling the nearby train tracks. **Port Said Street** runs north-south and lies 150m east of the tracks (away from the Nile). Three hundred meters west of the tracks is **26 July Street,** which runs north-south. **Goumhouriyya Street** runs east-west on a slight diagonal, intersecting all the others and heading down to the Nile. A footbridge crosses the railroad tracks 100m south of Goumhouriyya Street and opens onto the main **souq** street, also called **Nabin Monsur Street.**

The **train station** is on the east side of the tracks between Goumhouriyya St. and the footbridge. Trains run north and south, usually twice daily, in the morning and evening. Ask at the station well in advance and be prepared to wait. If the ticket office is closed (it probably will be), don't fret—the conductor will sell you a ticket on the train. The **bus station** is on 26 July Street, 150m south of Goumhouriyya St. The **service taxi station** is on the northern edge of the intersection of 26 July and Goumhouriyya St. (to: Aswan E£1.50, Daraw 25pt, Edfu E£2). There is also a small *service* stand on the Cairo-Aswan highway 50m south of Goumhouriyya St. Covered **pick-up trucks** run between the center of town and the river, about 1km north of the temple (E£1 round trip). **Private taxis** cost E£3-5 each way. If you're coming from Aswan by *service* or bus, ask to be let off at the well-marked turn-off to the "tembel" 2km south of town. From the turn-off, walk 1.5km along the lonesome road to the temple site. The **Bank of Alexandria** is down a small alley behind the mosque on the Cairo-Aswan highway, on the left side coming from the highway (open daily 8am-2pm and 6-9pm).

The **El Fateh Pharmacy** is 100m south of Goumhouriyya St. on the Cairo-Aswan highway. The **police station** (tel. 50 00 23) sits 200m south of Goumhouriyya St. on Port Said St. The **post office** is on the corner of Port Said St. and Nabin Monsur St. at the south end of town (open Sun.-Thurs. 8am-2pm).

Accommodations and Food The **Cleopatra Hotel** (tel. 50 03 25), just off 26 July St. near the *service* stand, has rooms with fans, towels, and toilet paper in the shared bathroom (singles E£10.50; doubles E£18; triples and quads E£24). For food, the **Venus Cafeteria and Restaurant,** on the Nile halfway between the temple and the taxi stop, serves limp feta sandwiches, overpriced soda, and ice cream with raisins and coconut (all E£2), in a pleasant patio setting (open daily 24hr.). Produce, *fuul* vendors, and tea shops can be found in the **souq.**

Sights Although a temple has stood here since the time of the Middle Kingdom, the current edifice dates back only to 150 BCE. The older portions of the **Temple of Kom Ombo** now rest at the Louvre and at the Egyptian Museum in Cairo. After the decline of paganism and the Roman Empire, the rising waters of the river left the temple almost completely buried in silt. In later years the portion above ground was used as a quarry for neighboring edifices; as a result, the side walls have vanished.

The temple, uniquely, was dedicated to two gods and is therefore rigorously symmetrical throughout. Double halls and double colonnades lead to double doorways which open onto double chambers and double sanctuaries. The two-fold temple was dedicated to the deity duo of Sobek, the crocodile god who was locally important due to the many crocs lurking in the Nile near Kom Ombo, and Horus the elder, avenger of Osiris and the source of the pharaohs' divine power. The temple's dualism is evident throughout the site, but is especially clear in the columns of the hypostyle hall. Designs on the right columns feature razor-toothed **Sobek,** while those on the left depict bird-beaked **Horus.** The ceiling of the adjoining vestibule is strikingly well-preserved; bright blue and black images of Horus hover protectively over the chamber. The temple interior contains the remains of the Hall of Offerings and the inner sanctuary homes of Sobek and Horus. Ask the guard to show you the reliefs of **Cleopatra II and VII.**

Adjoining the north edge of the temple are the Roman water supply tanks and, to the west, the remains of a Roman *mammisis.* The now-putrescent well is rumored to have crawled with crocodiles in days gone by. Cleopatra's bubble bath is also supposedly nearby. The **Chapel of Hathor,** to your right as you enter the compound, houses a graphic collection of crocodile mummies unearthed near the road leading to the site (open daily 7am-6pm, winter until 4:30pm; E£10, students E£5).

Near Kom Ombo: Daraw دراو

Sudanese merchants, Bishari tribespeople, and Egyptian *fellaheen* convene in Daraw (de-RAU) every Tuesday morning for a **camel market.** The Bishari, Saharan nomads with their own language and culture, purchase camels for the equivalent of E£200, march for one month through the desert to Daraw, and resell the humped beasts at a 500% profit. Look for the occasional businessman in full traditional dress: flowing pants, fighting sword and dagger, and a cloak draped over the shoulders. Typically, a Sudanese camel-owner will pay a Sudanese or Bishari shepherd to drive his camels north to Egypt. The owner then flies up to oversee the selling. The going rate for a big male camel is E£1200-1500, a saving of E£1000 over prices in Cairo.

Tuesday is the only summer market day; in winter, camels are sometimes sold on Sundays and Mondays. The camel market is adjoined by a **fruit and vegetable market** and a **livestock market** where farmers sell cattle, water buffalo, sheep, and goats. The animals are hauled in by truck or occasionally toted on the merchants' shoulders. On market day, impromptu shaded *fuul* and tea stands offer refreshment to merchants, buyers, and gawkers. The market runs from 7am to 2pm but slows down after about 11am. A good strategy is to rise very early in Aswan, visit the camel market, and move on to see the temple at Kom Ombo. To reach the market from the stations, walk 300m down the main street toward the Nile. You'll pass *ta'miyya* and juice shops on your left and the **hospital** on your right. When you reach a dead end, bear right for 20m, then left; just follow everyone else. You'll know you've arrived when you see 200 people smacking the heinies of bound, groaning camels to display their vigor. If you're gliding by on a *felucca,* have the captain stop at the Daraw ferry landing and a covered pick-up truck will take you to the market.

Service taxis careen to Daraw from Kom Ombo, 8km to the north (10min.), and Aswan, 37km to the south (1hr.). Some trains and buses running between Luxor and Aswan stop in Daraw. The **taxi stand, bus station,** and **train station** all lie along the main highway. Thirty meters north of the main shopping street that runs down to the market is a **telephone office** (domestic calls only).

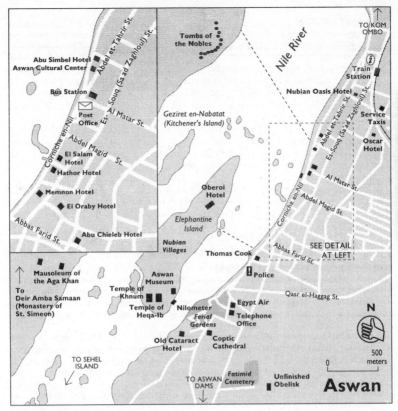

■ Aswan أسوان

Aswan is the southernmost city in Egypt, a trading center where the Middle East overlaps with Africa and Upper Egypt gives way to Lower Nubia. The Soviet-designed High Dam, an engineering miracle when it was completed in 1971, created nearby Lake Nasser (the world's largest reservoir) and boosted Egypt's agricultural and energy potential. The dam also flooded most of Nubia, forcing massive migrations to Egypt and Sudan. Although the High Dam has calmed the river's destructive powers, it also traps nutrient-rich silt in the reservoir. How this will affect the environment in the future remains to be seen (see also **The Dams and Quarries,** p. 210).

The fertile corridor nourished by the Nile is very narrow this far south—so much so that the desert nearly reaches the banks themselves. Summer temperatures average over 40°C, though they dip to a chilly 35°C in winter. The river also harbors a thriving *felucca* industry, with nearly 300 Aswani boat captains preying on a growing number of tourists. The otherwise pleasant corniche is a hunting ground for these men and their young helpers (for more on *felucca*s, see **Getting Around,** p. 73).

Summer, when temperatures are high and tourists are few, is the best time to experience a *felucca* trip. Nile water here is clean enough to swim (though not to drink). In the winter the city becomes a resort, but foreigners are welcomed in any season; restaurants, hotels, and shops are accommodating when there's money to be made.

The large Nubian community that was compelled to migrate when the Dam was built now thrives in Aswan, giving the city a uniquely African flavor. The gentle charm of the Nubians and the cool breeze along the corniche mellow the heat and coax travelers into extending their visits.

ORIENTATION

You're rarely more than two blocks from the river in Aswan. The northern half of the city lies along three long avenues parallel to the Nile. The riverfront **Corniche en-Nil** is the most picturesque, featuring several hotels, shops, banks, floating restaurants, and docks. Two blocks inland, the market-lined **Sa'ad Zaghloul Street** features everything from watermelons to water pipes. Also called Es-Souq Street, it begins at the train station at the northeast corner of town and runs south 2km to Abbas Farid St. In the southern half of town, the corniche continues for another 1km and ends at the **Ferial Gardens.** The northern grid pattern falls apart at the central market. South of the *souq*, inland streets form a labyrinth of alleys. Sandwiched between the corniche and the market street, **Abtal at-Tahrir Street** begins at the youth hostel in the north and culminates in a small cluster of tourist bazaars, resuming as a narrow lane farther south.

After haggling, a horse-drawn **kalish** should cost E£5 for a short ride, E£10 for a more extended tour. **Taxis,** everywhere along the corniche, shouldn't be more than E£5 for all city travel. Walking is a pleasant option, especially in the evenings.

Aswan is a convenient base for exploring the southernmost parts of Egypt; plan on four days if you want to see the sights and stay sane. You can also take *felucca* trips to Kom Ombo, Edfu, and Luxor (see **Getting Around,** p. 176).

PRACTICAL INFORMATION

Tourist Office: tel. 31 28 11. This beige box on the right as you exit the train station is a good first stop in Aswan. Shukri Sa'ad can give you info on anything and everything, including what you should pay for a *felucca* and how best to see Abu Simbel. Open daily 9am-3pm and 6-8pm.

Tourist Police: tel. 31 43 93, above the corniche tourist office. Open daily 9am-3pm and 8pm-1am. **24hr. branch** (tel. 30 31 63) on the south side of train station.

Passport Office: tel. 31 22 38, Corniche en-Nil, in the police building on the 3rd floor. Will register passports and extend visas. Open Sat.-Thurs. 8am-2pm.

Currency Exchange: Banque Misr, 103 Corniche en-Nil (tel. 31 66 92, 93, or 95; fax 31 66 94). Visa and MC advances. Open Sun.-Thurs. 8:30am-2pm. The **ATM** next to Banque Misr on the corniche takes Visa, MC, Plus, and Cirrus cards. **National Bank of Egypt** (tel. 31 20 13), on Corniche next to the Memnon Hotel. Visa advances and accepts Eurocheques. Open daily 8am-2pm and 6-9pm.

American Express: tel./fax 30 29 09, at the southernmost end of the corniche in the lobby of the Old Cataract Hotel. Exchange and banking services and holds mail for cardholders. Open daily 9am-5pm.

Thomas Cook: tel. 30 40 11 or 68 39; fax 30 62 09, on the corniche just north of the police building. Travel and financial services. Open daily 8am-8pm.

Airport: tel. 48 03 20, 23km south of town near the High Dam. E£15-20 1-way by taxi. Served by **EgyptAir** (tel. 31 50 00; fax 31 50 05), on Corniche en-Nil, at the southern end near the Ferial Gardens. (Open daily 8am-8pm). Another EgyptAir office at the airport (tel 48 03 07), but you can't buy tickets there. 4 flights daily to Cairo, 8 in winter (E£573 one-way). Daily flights to Abu Simbel leave 3 times per day (E£508 round-trip). **Airport Police:** tel. 48 03 07.

Trains: tel. 31 47 54, at the northern end of Sa'ad Zaghloul St. 1st and 2nd class A/C trains depart for **points north** at 5:30am and 6pm. Luxor is 5hr. away, Cairo 15hr. The tourist office can give the most current fares (roughly E£20 to Luxor, E£63 to Cairo). Frequent trains run south to the **High Dam** (9 daily, 30min., 50pt.). There are often student discounts on trains.

Buses: tel. 30 32 25, on Abtal at-Tahrir St. behind the Abu Simbel Hotel. 10 buses per day to: **Kom Ombo** (1hr., E£2); **Daraw** (45min., E£1.50); **Edfu** (2hr., E£4); and **Luxor** (4hr., E£6.50). Buses to **Qena** (5:30am, 11:30am, and 12:30pm, 5hr., E£8.50); **Asyut** (7am, 8hr., E£25); **Hurghada** (8am, 7hr., E£18; 3:30pm with A/C, E£35); **Cairo** (3:30pm, 10hr., E£55); **Suez** (7am, 3:30 and 5pm, 12hr., E£35); and **Abu Simbel** (8am and 3pm, 4hr., E£26 round-trip; returns to Aswan at 6:30am and 2pm). Also service to the **Old Dam;** ask at the tourist office.

Ferries: Get to **Elephantine Island** from Esh-Shatii Restaurant on the southern end of the corniche, or across from the EgyptAir office even farther south (every 15-20min. 6am-6pm, E£1). Float to the western bank tombs and villages in a **Seti Tours** ferry, opposite the corniche tourist office (every 20min. 6am-6pm, E£1).

Taxis: In summer, taxis run infrequently within Aswan and Luxor. More dependable between the 2 cities, but those leaving from Aswan are extremely unreliable. Taxis leave from the covered station 1km south of the train station, east of the tracks and next to a large underpass (roughly 4am-6pm, leaving every 15-30min. depending on demand. Taxis to Aswan environs and south wait in the square at the base of Et-Tabia Mosque (Aswan's main mosque, perched on a hill and illuminated at night). To: **Daraw** or **Kom Ombo** (40min., E£1.50); **Edfu** (1¼hr., E£3); **Esna** (2-3hrs., E£6); **Luxor** (3hrs., E£8); Qena (4hrs., E£9); and Khazan/Old Dam (75pt).

Bike Rental: 3 locations: on Abtal et-Tahrir St. next to the Poste Restante office; near the train station on es-Souq St. and farther down es-Souq St. next to the Nubian Oasis Hotel. E£5 per day or E£1 per hr. in summer if you can stand the heat. Prices may double in winter. The youth hostel (on Abtal et-Tahrir St.) occasionally organizes winter bike tours.

Photo Developing: Photo Sabry (tel. 30 64 52), on Corniche en-Nil just north of Egypt-Air. 36 color exposures (4x6) for E£35. Open Sat.-Thurs. 9am-2:30pm and 6:30-11:30pm. A smaller office located across from the Nubian Oasis Hotel. Both will supposedly have your film ready in an hour.

Bookstore: Islamic Books, next to the Abu Simbel Hotel, sells translations of Islamic works into English, French, and German. Photocopy machine in store. Large hotels usually have small bookstores, which carry European newspapers.

Laundromat: Most hotels do laundry for 50pt-E£1 per garment. Several also offer do-it-yourself laundry for free. Laundry service and dry-cleaning shop under the Nubian Oasis Hotel. Open Sat.-Thurs. 8am-2pm.

Swimming Pools: The nicest hotels have the nicest pools. The **New Cataract Hotel** (E£35, including up to that amount in food and drink), and the **Oberoi Hotel** (E£25) are fancy and expensive options. At E£5, the **Hathor Hotel** rooftop pool is cheap, but sometimes low on water (diving can be painful).

Pharmacy: El-Nile Pharmacy (tel. 30 26 74), on the corniche across from the Isis gateway. Open daily 7am-midnight. Other pharmacies line the corniche and *souq*.

Hospital: German Evangelical Mission Hospital (tel. 30 21 76), on the southern end of the corniche. Open 24hr. Every hotel reception can provide the name of a **doctor.** These private offices are usually very modern. The **Government Hospital** (tel. 32 28 55 or 24 19) on Qasr el-Hagga St. is nothing less than a last resort.

Emergency: Medical: tel. 123. **Police:** tel. 122.

Post Office: Corniche en-Nil, toward the northern end of town. Offers **EMS** and **telegraph** services. Open Sat.-Thurs. 8am-2pm. For occasional **Poste Restante,** walk south from the main post office and turn left down Salah ad-Din St. then immediately left again. It's in the yellow and black building known locally as the Old Post Office; requests for Poste Restante may meet with confusion, but persistence helps. Open Sun.-Thurs. 8am-2pm.

Telephones: Telephone office (tel. 31 38 69), 2 doors south of EgyptAir. Open daily 24hr. **Fax** service available 8am-2pm and 6-9pm, E£30 for 3min. to the U.S. International lines are also available in most hotels and at the **Business Center** (tel. 30 39 15), open daily 8am-11pm. **Information:** tel. 16. In 1997, numbers beginning with 32 changed to 30. **Telephone Code:** 097.

ACCOMMODATIONS

Prices rise in winter and decline in summer; rates listed are approximate. All listed hotels have laundry service and breakfast unless otherwise stated, but none dance the credit card tango. Be sure to ask for applicable student and group discounts.

Nubian Oasis Hotel, 234 Sa'ad Zaghloul St. (tel. 31 21 23 or 26; fax 31 21 24). Take a left out of the train station and walk 5min. Tidy but run down. Staff can be pushy about *felucca* trips. Big TV lounge, A/C in all rooms, clean bathrooms, and more *felucca* paintings than you can shake an oar at. Singles E£15; doubles E£25; triples E£35. Prices are slightly lower without bath. Entrees at the restaurant average E£8.

El Salam Hotel, 101 Corniche en-Nil (tel. 30 36 49). Beautiful, wrap-around balconies, tasteful decorations, and gigantic, pristine tiled bathrooms distinguish El Salam from the competition. All rooms have bath and A/C. Singles E£27-31; doubles E£40-50; triples E£50-62. Group discounts available.

Memnon Hotel, Corniche en-Nil (tel. 30 04 83), entrance on the street parallel to the corniche, behind the National Bank of Egypt. A homey 30-room, Nile-view throwback to the early 60s. TV lounge has American cowboy movies in the evening with Arabic subtitles. Rooms have A/C and private bath. Singles E£25; doubles E£40, without view E£35; triples E£60; suites E£60. Lunch E£10, dinner E£12. Student discounts.

Hathor Hotel, Corniche en-Nil (tel. 31 45 80; fax 30 34 62), right in the middle. New ceramic floor and wood furniture give the Hathor a relatively sophisticated air. Sometimes there's water in the tiny rooftop pool. All rooms have bath and A/C. Singles E£25; doubles E£45-50; triples E£55-60. Rooms are 25% cheaper without a view. International phone line. Lunch E£10, dinner E£12.

New Abu Simbel Hotel (tel. 30 60 96; fax 30 20 10), a few blocks north of the train station on Atlas St. in a large, modern stucco building. Garden patio, high-ceilinged lobby, and spacious, spotless A/C rooms. TV for E£3 extra. Singles E£25; doubles E£35; triples E£45. Student discounts.

El Oraby Hotel, El Mahkama el-Qadima St. (tel./fax 31 75 78). From the corniche, walk up Salah ad-Din St. to Es-Souq St., turn right, go 300m and take a left at the Khan el-Khali Center. It's 75m up, with an outstretched ibis over the doorway. Wood-paneled interior, hammocks and ping-pong on the roof garden, and an informational library room. Doubles E£20; triples E£30, E£18 without A/C.

Aswan Youth Hostel (HI), 96 Abtal et-Tahrir St. (tel. 30 22 35), 2 blocks from the train station. Reminiscent of a warehouse in both size and cleanliness. Caustic pink and green color scheme, worn-out mattresses, and loud, inefficient fans. Great price, though: E£8 with bath, E£5 without. Breakfast not included.

There is a **campground** 2km south of town adjacent to the unfinished obelisk, but very few travelers camp in Aswan, and as a result the grounds are neglected and lonely. Contact the tourist office before planning a stay. The campground is inconvenient without motorized transport; expect to pay at least E£3-4 for a taxi into town.

FOOD

Fruit, vegetables, bread, and pigeon, not to mention falafel, liver sandwiches, and *kushari,* are available in Aswan's **souq.** Beware of *ta'miyya* vendors, who sometimes use the same oil for many days. The highest concentration of vendors is at the southern end of Es-Souq St. where it intersects Es-Sayyida Nafisa. **Vegetarians** may find that their choices in restaurants are limited to a few rice dishes. The vegetable markets lie to the north. A large **vegetable souq** is tucked away near the train station, on the northeast edge of Es-Souq St. For a full range of options come in the morning, but there are always street vendors selling produce.

At the other extreme, you can swing out on huge buffets and gourmet Arab and continental cuisine at the luxury hotels. The Oberoi offers an elegant E£22 **breakfast buffet** (6-10:30am) in their stunning cupola-covered ballroom restaurant.

Sayyida Nafisa, just off Es-Souq St., 1.5km south of the train station. As you approach, the ground in the *souq* turns rosy red from colored wood shavings. Named after a relative of Muhammed, this restaurant's reputation precedes it. Popular with locals and visitors. Better-than-average Egyptian food E£7-10. Refreshing juices E£1.50. Open noon-11pm.

El Masry, El Matar St. (tel. 30 25 76). Go south from the train station and turn left on El Matar St. Since 1954, shiny marble and an extensive menu have attracted throngs to this elegant and extremely clean establishment. Main courses E£10-15.

Darwish Restaurant, Sa'ad Zaghloul St., 2 blocks from the train station. Hospital white and hospital clean. Flashing neon sign announces some of the best pigeon in Aswan (E£8 fried). All meals come with vegetables, soup, rice, and salad (full meal E£20-25). Open daily 11am-1am.

Hamam Restaurant, Corniche en-Nil. Mirrors and *felucca* murals decorate this cafeteria. Rice with your choice of meats (E£8-15). Beware of the recycled soda bottles filled with "spicy ketchup." Open daily 24hr.

Floating Restaurants

This is the true heart of the Aswan restaurant scene. Popular with Egyptians as well as tourists, these aquatic eateries offer decent meals and the perfect setting for watching the sun go down over the desert hills of the west bank. All serve basically the same array of meat dishes (E£4-12) and salads, dips, drinks, and desserts (E£1-4), with slightly differing quality and atmosphere. They are listed below from south to north; just look for the blinking lights.

Aswan Panorama (tel. 30 61 69). The best of floating cuisine; the Panorama could moonlight as an ethnographic museum. The delicious food and fruit trees amongst the tables make it well worth the walk down the corniche. Try the Bedouin coffee served on coals (flavored with cardamom, cinnamon, and cloves, filtered with dried grass). No seating after 9pm.

Monalisa. You'll know you've arrived when you see her smile amid the Mediterranean decor. The Monalisa Cocktail is truly divine and the spaghetti locally popular.

EMY's. Lonely neon letters top the only actual boat among the floating restaurants. Sit on the top level of the barge to sway gently as you chew (and chew and chew) your *kebab.* An above average selection of meatless dishes. They serve breakfast (E£3) and beer (E£5). 20% student discount.

Aswan Moon Restaurant. Made popular by its convenient location at the north end of the corniche. Earns the Las Vegas Award for most blinking lights. Decorated platform hosts Nubian musicians and *felucca* chiefs chatting up tourists. Service can be slow, but what's the hurry?

SIGHTS

On the west bank of the Nile, directly across from the city, the wind-swept sand piles into dunes with pronounced edges and sweeping contours, in sharp contrast to the lush palms by the water. Along the desert horizon, a mausoleum, a monastery, and cliffside tombs blend in with the blowing sands. In the middle of the river floats a cluster of islets where the remainder of the city's official attractions can be found. The largest of these, **Elephantine Island,** hosts the **Aswan Archaeological Museum,** admission to which covers the museum, adjacent ruins, and the Nilometer. The museum's collection is miniscule; highlights include a few gilt sarcophagi and a mutilated skull (open 8am-4pm; E£12, students E£6).

Carved into a rock to the left of the museum's entrance is a **Nilometer.** Built during the Pharaonic era and renovated by the Romans, the long stairway-shaft was used to measure the depth of the Nile. In ancient times nothing was of greater practical significance than the Nilometer's oracle. Its reports could predict a bountiful harvest or hunger and misery. The ancient econometric device was also used to set pharaonic taxes based on projected agricultural output.

Aswan grew from Elephantine Island much as Paris grew from Île de la Cité. The remains of the ancient settlement have been excavated on the southeast corner of the island, directly behind the museum. You will find here the **Temple of Khnum** and the modest **Temple of Heqa-Ib** (particularly attractive when viewed from the Nile), in addition to a small Ptolemaic temple dedicated to Alexander II. The temple of Heqa-Ib is currently being excavated by German archaeologists. The central section of the island has several Nubian villages where you'll find friendly residents, adoring youngsters, and brightly-painted homes. Be modest in your dress and behavior. Less spoiled villages are found at the northern end of the west bank, reachable by local ferry (see ferries, p. 204) The Oberoi Hotel and adjacent construction sites dominate the northern half of the island. The hotel is surrounded by a tall *cordon sanitaire;* to reach the inner sanctum take one of their silly-looking ferries from the launching point at the center of the corniche.

Behind Elephantine Island and not visible from central Aswan, **Geziret en-Nabatat** ("Island of the Plants," or **Kitchener's Island**) is a lovely botanical garden where African and Asian tropical plants flourish and a variety of exotic and flamboyant birds congregate. Bilingual tree plaques provide the names of plant species. To reach the island, you can hire a *felucca* to combine an island visit with stops along the west bank and Elephantine Island (a full afternoon rental at E£10 per hr.). It is also possible to hire a rowboat from the west side of Elephantine Island (about E£3 for 1-2 passengers only). Make sure boats wait for you or come back to pick you up by withholding payment until the end of the trip (open daily 7am-6pm; E£5).

The most placid attraction on the west bank of the Nile is the **Mausoleum of the Aga Khan,** a short climb from where the *felucca* docks. Aga Khans, the hereditary titles of the *imams* of the Isma'ili Muslims, are believed to be direct descendants of Muhammad and the inheritors of his spiritual responsibilities of guidance. They used to rule from Pakistan (where their followers were once known as the *Assassins*), but political shifts sent them westward. Aswan became the favorite winter retreat of **Sultan Muhammad Shah Al-Husaini,** Aga Khan III (1877-1957), the 48th *imam* of the Isma'ilis. Upon his death, the Begum (the Aga Khan's wife) oversaw the construction of the mausoleum. While the edifice sports an imposing fortress-like exterior, the interior, modeled after the Fatimid tombs of Cairo, has the quiet simplicity of a peace palace. Opposite the entrance stands a marble sarcophagus inscribed with passages from the Qur'an. A *bakhsheesh*-free zone with commanding views up and down the Nile, the mausoleum is a calm respite from the jostle of central Aswan (open Tues.-Sun. 9am-4pm; free; remember to take off your shoes).

A short 1km walk across the dunes from the mausoleum stands **Deir Amba Samaan** (Monastery of St. Simeon), isolated and majestic. Built in the 6th and 7th centuries CE and abandoned in the 13th, the monastery is on a terrace carved into the steep hills and visible from the mausoleum. With 6m turreted walls, the monastery looks more like a fort than a religious sanctuary. The original walls of the complex stood 10m high and enclosed a community of 300 monks. Upstairs, the monks' cells and their stone beds (with Bible and *gallabiyya* wall slots) are currently occupied by bats. The monastery also had a church and accommodations sufficient for several hundred pilgrims and their camels. There are remnants of the baptismal fount and drain pipe, well-preserved paintings of Mary and Joseph, and Communion wine-making facilities in St. Simeon's chamber. Simeon's chamber has a slot in the roof for a piece of rope he slipped around his neck to keep him awake and on his feet during all-night prayer vigils (monastery open Tues.-Sun. 7am-4pm; E£12, students E£6).

To get there, follow the paved path that starts in front of the Mausoleum of the Aga Khan (15-20min.) or hire a camel near the *felucca* stop (E£10 per camel for 2 people). Women do not need to cling tightly to the camel driver, despite his concerns for safety, nor should the driver need to grab his passengers' legs to ensure stability. If you feel at all uncomfortable, forget the beasts and their camels.

The **Tombs of the Nobles** lie farther north along the west bank of the Nile, incised into the face of desert cliffs and impressively illuminated at night. These tombs of governors and dignitaries date from the 23rd- to the 18th-centuries BCE. Four millennia of decay and pilfering have severely damaged most of the tombs. The bright color and detail of the reliefs in the **Tomb of Sarenput II,** however, merit the easy trip across the Nile. Note the sacrificial stone slab with a blood drainage spout. The mummy shuffled to Cairo, but there are plenty of bones in the corner. The interconnected 6th-dynasty **Tombs of Nikhu and Sabni,** father and son, have depictions of donkeys, water buffalo, fish, and birds. The cheapest way to visit the tombs is to take the ferry from the corniche, across the small park from the tourist office (E£1). Once across, walk uphill to the office on the left (open daily 7am-4pm; E£12, students E£6; photo permission E£10).

For a taste of Egypt not found north of Aswan, visit a **Nubian village.** You may even be invited to join the celebrations and ululations of a wedding ceremony; the Nubians consider it a mark of honor to have guests from far-flung villages attend their nuptial festivities. Nubian weddings traditionally involve 15 days of partying, but the demands of modern life have trimmed the celebration down to three or four. Nubians may feel slighted if you reject their offers of hospitality, so be diplomatic in declining. The large Nubian houses, made of Nile mud, consist of six rooms around a courtyard; each cluster of rooms has its own dome or cylindrical roof. The brightly painted huts belong to families that have completed the *hajj,* or pilgrimage to Mecca. When the High Dam threatened to destroy this traditional style, architect-genius Hasan Fathy stopped by and whipped up these reconstructed and relocated villages, vaulting Nubian architecture into the international limelight.

The ferry to the west bank tombs (E£1) can bring you to **Gharb Aswan,** a series of Nubian villages less frequented by tourists than those of Elephantine Island. From the ferry dock catch a pick-up truck north to the villages (about E£1). Whether or not you make it to a village, a E£6 tape of rhythmic Nubian music from the Aswan *souq* is sure to bring a smile to your face and a snap to your step.

To reach the sights on the west bank of the Nile, it's easiest to hire a *felucca.* The official rate for *felucca* transport in the vicinity of Aswan is E£10 per hour regardless of the number of passengers, but it'll take some negotiation. A complete tour of Elephantine Island, Geziret en-Nabatat, the Aga Khan's Mausoleum, St. Simeon's Monastery, and the northern tombs goes for E£30 per group. A cheap alternative is to hire a rowboat or motorboat to the west bank (E£2-3), then trek from sight to sight on foot. Transport back to the corniche or Elephantine Island, either by ferry (E£1) or rowboat (E£8) is easy, as long as you don't get stranded late in the day when the boatmen have you at their mercy.

SHOPPING AND ENTERTAINMENT

"Nightclubs" in Aswan feature a group of drummers and tambourinists with a loud organ player and a male singer/M.C., plus the miraculous gyrations of a sequin-clad belly dancer enticing the men into tossing bills. **Beware the belly.** Check out the scene at **Salah ad-Din Restaurant** on the water or at the **Ramses Hotel** in town. There are often cover charges or minimums for discos and nightclubs, but they change frequently (usually E£5-10 cover or 2-drink minimum). The **Oberoi** has a **piano bar** where you can even sit down and play (drinks E£10-35), and a little disco with a pounding dance mix. The **New Cataract** has a **pub** and disco (open 7pm-2am, E£15 minimum for disco), and the comfortable Pullman **bar** in the **Old Cataract** has no minimum. For more subdued enjoyment, try the **pool and snooker** tables at the **Basma Hotel,** on the corniche, south past the Kalabsha Hotel (E£5-15 cover), next to EMY's restaurant.

If you seek more than the ubiquitous alphabetical hieroglyphics t-shirt, peruse Es-Sayyida Nafisa St. for western-style garments made to order. Tailors will cut your garment with lightning speed while you watch (pants E£10-25, shorts and simple shirts E£10-15, shirts with collars and buttons E£25-35). For Egyptian clothing, there are numerous *gallabiyya* and *koftan* merchants in the *souq.* If you have the time, you can go to one of the government shops on the corniche (Benzion is a large one), buy high-quality government cloth at posted government prices, then have your garments made to order by one of the many tailors on Sa'ad Zaghloul St.

In winter, the **Aswan Cultural Center,** on Corniche en-Nil across from the Rowing Club, features Nubian dancing and handicrafts (open Sat.-Thurs. 9-11pm; E£5). There are also many cafes where you can join locals for a cup of tea, a puff of *sheesha,* or a hard-core game of dominoes. And let's not forget the Philae Temple's **sound and light show** (see **Philae,** p. 212).

For a taste of the good life, walk south along the corniche and around the Ferial Gardens to the elegant **Pullman Cataract Hotel** (the Old and New Cataract Hotels are within a single compound). Walking through the gorgeous gardens, pool, and outdoor terrace cafe that overlook the river, it's easy to see why the film version of Agatha Christie's *Death on the Nile* was done here (drinks E£15 and up, no shorts on the terrace after 3pm). Spontaneous *futbol* games occasionally spring up around the stadium in the northern part of town. For more structured and expensive exertion, report to Oberoi's health spa (tel. 30 34 55) for relaxing and rejuvenating treatments and exercises (priced individually from US$3-20).

■ South of Aswan

Aswan proper may lack antiquities, but the 15km stretch of the Nile upstream of Aswan will blow your mind. The region of the **first cataract** includes two dams, two temples, and most of an obelisk. The **Old Dam,** 5km south of Aswan, was built by the British in 1902, only to be dwarfed by the Soviet-designed **High Dam** 10km upstream. On an island in the lake between the two, the lovingly-preserved **Philae Temple** proclaims the glory of Isis. Beyond the west end of the High Dam, the desolate **Temple of Kalabsha** sinks peacefully into the desert on the banks of Lake Nasser. The red granite and alabaster that fed pharaonic monument building was taken from quarries just south of Aswan. Here you'll find the **Unfinished Obelisk** in all its almost-glory. All sights are easily reachable from Aswan.

Getting Around

An excellent road follows the Nile from Aswan to Khazan, a village near the Old Dam, providing access to both the Dam and the motorboat launch to Philae Temple. The route to Khazan is served by *service* (50pt-E£1, depart from *service* stand) and by public bus (25pt-E£1). Both run frequently until about 9:30pm. Frequent trains run to the High Dam, leaving you at the station on the eastern end of the dam. Vehicles and pedestrians are not allowed to cross the dam after 6pm.

Many hotels offer combination trips to Abu Simbel and the other antiquities in the area. The "short" trip that just visits Abu Simbel and the High Dam costs E£25. You can see everything in one day by taking epic trip to Abu Simbel, both Dams, Philae, Kalabsha, and the 'Unfinished Obelisk (E£35). A more relaxed itinerary runs as follows: Abu Simbel and the quarries in one day, the High Dam and Kalabsha on another, then the Philae temple at night.

THE DAMS AND QUARRIES

The best-known attraction in the area is modern Egypt's great monument, the **High Dam (Es-Sidd el-Ali),** completed in 1971. The dam is more interesting intellectually than visually; those visualizing a sheer wall with a bulging lake behind it will be disappointed. The High Dam lacks the aesthetic magnificence of ancient Egypt's colossi, but it could teach them a thing or two about size: 1km thick at the base, 3.6km long, and 111m high, the dam contains more than 17 times the material used in the Great Pyramid of Cheops. The construction of the dam created **Lake Nasser,** the world's largest artificial lake, and covered all of Lower Nubia in waters as deep as 200m. Thousands of Sudanese and Nubians were forced to relocate. Ancient Nubia's archaeological treasures were threatened; the Egyptian government sent out an international plea for help and many countries responded, individually and under an ambitious UNESCO plan. The long-term environmental effects of the massive project have not been studied. A rise in the Sahara's water table has been noticed as far away as Algeria, and archaeologists suspect that this effect has damaged the necropolis at Luxor and the base of Giza's Sphinx. Another danger of the dam is the possibility of sabotage. Should the dam be destroyed, the Noah-proportioned flood would wipe out all but 2% of Egypt's population.

On the brighter side, the dam's 12 turbines doubled Egypt's electrical output. Agricultural productivity has been greatly enhanced, and the acreage of Egypt's arable soil has been increased by 30%. The dam enabled Egypt to enjoy a healthy water supply during the drought of the past decade, and in August 1988 it saved Egypt from the floods suffered by Sudan when the Nile overflowed after heavy rains.

The High Dam has had significant international repercussions as well. Plans for the construction were unveiled after World War II, when it became apparent that Egypt had achieved maximum agricultural output and could no longer feed its rapidly increasing population. When the United States reneged on offers to provide loans for the High Dam project in 1956, President Nasser ordered the nationalization of the **Suez Canal** as a means of generating the necessary hard currency. This triggered the **Suez Crisis,** in which France, Britain, and Israel invaded Egypt. The Soviet Union decided to provide the necessary loans and technology, and work began on the dam in 1960. Despite over a decade of cooperation on the dam's construction, Egypt severed its Soviet relations and turned to the United States shortly after its completion, which accompanied Anwar Sadat's rise to power.

On the east bank (near the train station), just before the dam, the **Visitor's Pavilion** features plaques and sculptures blending Soviet socialist-realist motifs with Egyptian figures and symbols (open daily 7am-5pm; free). Plans for the construction of the dam—written in Russian and Arabic—include a map and some technical drawings. At the center of the pavilion is a dusty 15m model of the High Dam and its environs, minus the water. It also includes pictures and diagrams of Abu Simbel's relocation. The domed pavilion is well off the road from the dam and most taxis will not stop at it unless you insist; ask for the *mekat* (model).

To cross the dam you must pay E£5. The soldiers at the eastern end won't let you walk across but will stop passing vehicles and make them give you a ride. At the other end is the towering Soviet-Egyptian friendship monument, perhaps premature given the alacrity with which the Egyptians spurned their Soviet benefactors once the dam was complete. A stylized lotus blossom, the monument looks eerily like an ICBM silo springing into action. Due to the rise in terrorist activity, you are supposed to secure police permission to go to the top, either in Aswan or in the large yellow gift shop west of the monument (open 7am-2pm). Some have been known to illegally *bakhsheesh* their way to the top if the dam authorities are closed (E£1-2).

The **Old Dam** is 10km to the north. Built by the Brits between 1898 and 1902, the dam supplied most of Egypt's power for years. The Old Dam can be reached by taking *service* or a temperamental public bus from the Aswan corniche to Khazan (see **Getting Around,** p. 210). The fertile area known as the **First Cataract** is one of the most idyllic spots in the Aswan area. The view of what is left of these rapid waters, churning around rocky outcrops to the north from the Old Dam, gives some idea of the peril of early Nile expeditions, when ships were hauled past this dangerous spot with ropes. In the picturesque village of **Khazan,** 90-year-old British villas, now Britless, are nestled peacefully within walled gardens.

Just below the waters of the First Cataract, **Sehel Island,** boasting a hospitable Nubian village, scanty ruins, and a variety of inscriptions ranging from the 4th dynasty to the Ptolemaic period, attracts very few tourists. This island makes a nice destination for longer *felucca* rides out of Aswan (a 3-hour tour...a 3-hour tour).

Taxi drivers returning to Aswan from the High Dam or Philae might agree to stop at the Fatimid Tombs, the adjacent Unfinished Obelisk, and the nearby granite quarries. These sites are all near the camping area, 300m east of the main road at a turn-off 1km south of Aswan and are all easily within walking or *kalish* (E£5-7) range. The **Fatimid Tombs** are typical early Islamic shrines: squat, square stone buildings with crescents on their roofs. They are easily spotted across the street from the Obelisk. The tombs have been more or less abandoned; it can be spooky wandering around the dark cemetery, empty except for ghosts. The **Unfinished Obelisk** was abandoned at its site because of a flaw in the granite; it was to have soared to a whopping 41.7m on a base 4.2m on each side. In its unadorned, supine state, the obelisk looks—well, unfinished. But it reflects the mammoth effort that went into its creation. Notice the channels along each side with curved indentations just big enough for a man to sit in and pound away with a diarite ball (diarite is harder than granite). The earthbound side of the massive shaft would have been cut free either with copper or bronze chisels, or by pounding passages with diarite balls, inserting wooden beams and flooding the channels so that the expanding wood would break the remaining stone. The adjacent **granite quarries** supplied most of ancient Egypt with the hard pink or black granite and porphyry that was favored for temple and monument building. Alabaster quarries lie farther west (obelisk and quarries open daily 7am-6pm, but the guard often leaves early; E£10, students E£5.)

PHILAE فيلة

Called by one of Napoleon's soldiers "the pearl of Egypt," the beautiful temple of Isis at Philae has attracted visitors since classical times, drawing the pious and the curious. The completion of the Old Dam by the British in 1902 partially submerged the temples only a few years after their resurrection as a popular tourist destination. Victorian vandals gathered around the pillars and chipped their names into the protruding columns. The graffiti now marks the earlier water level. Archaeologists feared the waters would eventually undermine the foundations of the temples and hasten their collapse. The construction of the High Dam would have utterly destroyed Philae were it not for the efforts of UNESCO and the Egyptian Antiquities Department. Between 1972 and 1980, the entire complex of temples was transferred from Philae Island to higher ground on nearby Agilkia Island. In 1980, the new site of the ancient temples reopened to tourism.

You can visit Philae most easily by **taxi** as part of an itinerary including other sights, or you can take a **bus** to the Old Dam from the Aswan corniche; get off when it stops at the checkpoint on the east end of the dam. A **service** to Khazan is faster (see **service,** p. 204). Tell the driver to let you off at the Old Dam (Es-Sidd el-Qadeem). From the checkpoint, walk south along the shore to the concrete boat dock (about 2km). After paying for admission, you must hire a **motorboat** to reach the island at the official rate of E£20 per boat roundtrip. Find a few travelers to share the expense of the boat (it could be a long wait in the summer). The captain will try to con you into paying more, so be firm. If there are serious problems, complain at the tourist office in town. The boat captain is obligated to wait for you as you tour the site, so there is no need to rush (open daily 7am-4pm; E£20, students E£10).

The well-preserved **Temple of Isis,** the last bastion of ancient Egyptian religion, dominates the island's northern edge. Isis was the mother of nature, protector of humans, goddess of purity and sexuality, and sister-wife of the legendary hero Osiris (see **Religion in Ancient Egypt,** p. 61). Her cult following continued long after the establishment of Christianity, fizzling out only in the 6th century during the reign of Justinian, who successfully replaced her with Mary. Nearly all the structures on Philae date from the Ptolemaic and Roman eras, when Egyptian artistic quality was in decline—hence the inferior quality of the decorative relief work. Nile waters may have damaged their intrinsic beauty, but the temple remains an impressive edifice.

From the landing at the southern tip of the island, climb the short slope up to the temple complex past Philae's oldest structure, the **Portico of Nectanebo.** The paved portico once formed the vestibule of a temple. The arrangement of Philae's courtyards corresponds to the status of the people allowed in each: the outermost courtyard was for commoners, while each successive inner courtyard was reserved for increasingly important people—the innermost for High Priests. The larger edifice has been washed away, but the eastern side of the colonnade remains. Ptolemy, Isis, and Horus are depicted on the **first pylon,** which rises 18m on either side of the temple's main entrance. Note the channels cut into the face of the pylon on either side of the doorway where brightly painted square-cut cedar flagpoles once stood. Through this entrance is the **central court,** on the western edge of which reclines a Roman *mammisis* (birthhouse) devoted to Horus, its elegant columns emblazoned with the head of the cow-goddess Hathor, his consort. The walls depict the falcon god in the marshes of his birth. On the temple wall opposite the *mammisis*, Horus is shown being transported in a boat on the shoulders of servants en route to visit another member of the divine family. To the north is the slightly off-center **second pylon,** marking the way to the temple's inner sanctum. The *pronaos* (vestibule) was converted into a church by early Christians, who inscribed Byzantine crosses on the chamber walls and added a small altar. Farther north is the *naos,* the temple's innermost sanctuary. With a little *bakhsheesh* you can climb to the roof of the temple, or enter a trap door on the interior right side leading to an inscribed crypt. Outside the temple, at left-rear, is a **Nilometer** with a stairwell and the grooves used to measure the depths of the water. The stairwell is directly across from a French inscription from Napoleon's expedition. Because Egyptian gods liked to make house calls, outside the temple (to the right) is **Trajan's Kiosk,** the beautiful columned open air garage (called **pharaoh's bed** by the Victorians), which housed the bark of whatever god (or its icon) came to visit Isis. In true Egyptian temple style, Philae has a **sound and light show** (English performances Mon.-Tues. 9:30pm, Wed. and Fri.-Sat. 8pm; in winter Mon.-Tues. 7:30pm, Wed., Fri.-Sat. 6pm).

KALABSHA كلبشة

The enormous **Temple of Kalabsha,** dramatically situated above the placid waters of Lake Nasser, is one of the most striking pharaonic ruins in the Aswan area. Dedicated to the Nubian god Mandulis (who was renowned for his hundreds of wives and legions of children), the temple was begun by Amenhotep II, continued during the reign of Augustus, and used as a church during the Christian era. In 1962-63, the West German government paid to have the entire temple dismantled and transported in 13,000 pieces from its Nasser-flooded home to the present site, 50km north of the original. Many Egyptologists consider well-preserved Kalabsha to be second only to the treasures of Abu Simbel.

Somewhat difficult to reach and poorly publicized, the temple allows its visitors a chance to explore in relative peace and quiet. The temple is just south of the High Dam on the western bank, about 2km past the military checkpoint. The cheapest way to reach Kalabsha is to take the **train** to the east end of the dam, ride to the west end (you will have to pay the E£5 dam fee), then walk to the boat landing for the temple (from the western checkpoint, continue straight ahead for 100m, then veer left through the shipyard, following the curve of the water). A **taxi** from Aswan is less of a hassle but more expensive. Try bargaining down to E£25-30, even less for large groups. The High Dam closes to traffic at 6pm. No matter what other forms of transport you take, you will have to walk the last 1km through all manner of decrepit ships and fishing boats. Bring lots of water, cover your head, and watch your step. To cross the water to the temple, you can get a rowboat (E£10 per load, which holds no more than 2-3 people) or a larger motorboat (E£20 for a load of 10 or so).

Pick your way through more nautical refuse to an immense causeway of dressed stone that leads from the water to the temple's main entrance. The first pylon is off-center from both the causeway and the inner gateways of the temple itself. A carving of St. George and Coptic inscriptions survive from early Christian times. The grand forecourt between the pylon and the vestibule is surrounded by 14 columns, each with a unique capital. This is one of the only temples in Egypt where you can legally get to the top: take the stairs to the roof from a small room just beyond the vestibule for a commanding view of the entire site.

Because the temple faces east, light flows into the **Holy of Holies** (innermost chamber) only in the early morning. Bring a flashlight at other times, and be prepared for bats. A passageway leads north through the vestibule to an inner encircling wall; around the wall to the south is a well-preserved **Nilometer.** Extraordinary carvings of Mandulis, Isis, Horus, and Osiris cover the outside walls.

Outside the huge fortress-like wall, the remains of a small **shrine** are visible to the southeast; the present structure is largely a reconstructed facade. The Nubian reliefs include pre-dynastic elephants, a large giraffe, and gazelles. The double-image technique, characteristic of Nubian art, is used to portray motion in some of the drawings. Carcasses of enormous desiccated fish are surrealistically scattered amongst the sand, as are lonesome disembodied stone heads. Slightly to the southwest of Kalabsha Temple are ruins of the **Temple of Kertassi.** Two Hathor columns remain, as well as four columns with elaborate floral capitals and a lone monolithic architrave.

A stone pathway leads up the hill behind and to the right of the Temple of Kertassi to the **Rock Temple, Beit el-Wali** (House of the Holy Man), rescued from the encroaching waters of Lake Nasser with the aid of the U.S. government. Ask the guard to let you in. One of many Nubian temples constructed by Ramses II, it features typically humble scenes of Ramses conquering foreigners, Ramses receiving prisoners, and a particularly understated scene of Ramses storming a castle half his size. Like a miniature Abu Simbel, this cave-temple was hewn from solid rock. Examine the bas-relief scenes closely: political and social history are portrayed in everything from graphic chariot battles to household squabbles over whose turn it is to walk the camel (open daily 7am-5pm; E£12, students E£6).

ABU SIMBEL أبو سمبل

The grandeur of the pharaonic monuments reaches its peak at Egypt's southernmost tip. Four 22m-tall statues of Ramses II, carved out of a single slab of rock, greet the sunrise over Lake Nasser from the Great Temple of Abu Simbel. Ramses II had this grand sanctuary and the nearby Temple of Hathor built more than 3200 years ago to impress the Nubians with the power and glory of Egyptian rule; Abu Simbel still serves its purpose, leaving no visitor unmoved. For a sneak preview of the site, look at the back of the Egyptian one pound note.

Orientation and Practical Information Abu Simbel, 50km from the Sudanese border, is a long 297km south of Aswan. Due to political tensions, the **Sudanese border** is not passable and should not be approached by tourists for any reason. Two **buses** come here from Aswan (8am and 5pm, E£10, E£26 roundtrip); the morning bus gives you an ample 2½ hours to explore the temple. Buy your ticket at the Aswan bus station a day in advance; buy the return ticket on the way back. Neither bus has air conditioning.

The tourist office and most hotels in Aswan arrange **minibus trips** to Abu Simbel. The trips generally cost E£25-35, and sometimes include the other sights south of Aswan (entrance fees not included). Arranged tours generally leave at 4am and return in Aswan by 2pm; overzealous authorities insist that tourist groups travel in a police convoy. You'll be miserable if your minibus doesn't have air-conditioning, since blowing sands may preclude opening the windows for much of the trip, but it is both expensive and difficult to find. A private taxi, arranged independently, could save money if you have a group of seven. A Peugeot with air-conditioning and desperate driver could be as little as E£20 per person; make sure the car is also up to it.

Several **flights** wing it between Aswan and Abu Simbel. Frequency depends on demand, but there are generally two or three daily. EgyptAir provides shuttle service from the airport to the temple; after a whirlwind tour, you'll be driven back for the return flight (normal price E£508, but watch for frequent special fares; 50% off for one-way, but it's too far to walk back).

Sights The **Great Temple of Abu Simbel** is Ramses II's masterpiece. This temple is supposedly dedicated to the god Ra-Hurakhti, but as in all of Ramses' monuments, the focus is clearly on the great pharaoh himself. As you proceed through the temple, the artwork depicts Ramses first as a great king, then as a servant of the gods, next as a companion of the gods, and finally, in the inner sanctuary, as a card-carrying deity. The entrance is guarded by 3½ 20m-tall statues of the king wearing the Old and New Kingdom versions of the crowns of Upper and Lower Egypt. An earthquake in 27 BCE crumbled the upper portion of one of the Colossi. Modern engineers were unable to reconstruct the figure (and there were debates about whether they should—if it's been broken for 2000 years, don't fix it), so they left it in its faceless state. There are (much) smaller statues of mother Taya, wife Nefertari, and some of the kids, along with rows of praying **baboons.** Ancient Egyptians admired the baboon's habit of warming themselves in the sun's morning rays; they thought the beasts quite pious to pray to the sun god every dawn.

Farther into the temple are antechambers that once stored objects of worship; the walls show Ramses making sacrifices to the gods. In the inner sanctum, four seated statues facing the entrance depict Ramses and the gods Ra-Hurakhti, Amun, and Ptah. Originally encased in gold, the statues now wait with divine patience for February 22 and October 22, when the first rays of the sun reach 100m into the temple to bathe all except Ptah in light. February 21 was Ramses's birthday and October 21 his coronation date, but when the temple was moved, the timing of these natural feats shifted by one day. They just don't build temples like they used to. A door to the right of the

Cut and Paste

As the water level of Lake Nasser rose in the mid-60s, Egypt realized it would lose a large piece of its heritage. Help was sought from the United Nations and individual governments that funded a US$36 million relocation effort. The international concern was not entirely selfless; any country that assisted could claim half of the antiquities it helped to rescue and receive special archaeological concessions for future research. As a result, the Temple of Dendur is now enclosed in New York's Metropolitan Museum of Art, Debed Temple can be found in Madrid, and El Lessiya is claimed by Turin.

The first tentative plan was to raise each temple, removing the surrounding mountain and encasing the structures in protective concrete boxes. The boxes would be slowly jacked up, and a thick concrete base built beneath them. Another possibility was to build a second small dam around the temples to keep the water at bay. Both of these schemes were too expensive.

To the chagrin of Egyptologists, the cheapest method was chosen—cutting the temple into pieces. The mountain had to be cut away, a job that would endanger the sandstone statues below. Bulldozers covered the facade of Abu Simbel with sand, and the mound of sand was penetrated with a steel tunnel so that rescue workers could set up supportive steel bars inside. It took months to saw the temple apart and move the 3000 pieces to higher ground. When it was reassembled, hollow concrete domes were engineered to support the new artificial mountain.

large temple's facade will lead into the concrete dome that supports the new and improved mountain.

The smaller **Temple of Hathor** next door was built for Ramses II's favorite wife Nefertari, and dedicated to the young goddess Hathor. Six 10m statues of King Ramses and Queen Nefertari (as the goddess) adorn the facade. Along with the temple of Hatshepsut in West Thebes, this is one of the only temples in Egypt dedicated to a woman. Ramses is everywhere; scenes on the walls depict his coronation with the god Horus placing the crowns of Egypt on his head. The temple was constructed in the typical three-room style; the first chamber was open to the public, the second chamber to nobles and priests, and the inner sanctuary only to the pharaoh and the high priest (site open 6am-5pm; admission to both temples E£36, students E£19.50; flash photographers will be escorted out).

Western Desert Oases

Scattered across the expanse of Egypt's Western Desert, the oases dot the sea of sand and rock like a green archipelago. Hot and cold springs irrigate groves of dates, oranges, and mangoes, fields of watermelons, cucumbers, and corn, and even rice paddies. Bedouin and Egyptian *fellaheen* (peasants) who dwell beside the robust fields greet strangers with comforting hospitality, but getting around is more difficult than along the Nile. While there is at least (and sometimes only) one reasonably comfortable place to stay in each oasis, tourist facilities are minimal and meals are simple. But for those of sound body and free spirit, the oasis circuit can be one of the most impressive journeys in Egypt.

The Western Desert, known as the Libyan Desert until World War II, is the largest in the world, covering two-thirds of Egypt's area but supporting only 1% of the country's population. It is one of the driest areas on earth and boasts some of the highest temperatures on record. The series of oases sprinkled throughout—**Bahariyya, Farafra, Dakhla,** and **Kharga**—marks the trail of a prehistoric branch of the Nile. Each oasis sits in a depression surrounded by an escarpment, the top of which marks the usual level of the desert floor. Because the depressions are at or near sea level, subterranean water is accessible. A flow of water originating with the rains of equatorial Africa replenishes the wells and springs annually. This water takes thousands of years to journey north through underground fissures. Kharga, Dakhla, Farafra, and Bahariyya have sweeter and more plentiful water than their northerly cousin Siwa, where the water becomes highly saline before emptying into the Mediterranean Sea.

The fortunes of those living in the oases have ebbed and flowed with the water supply. Dinosaurs romped at Bahariyya oasis during the Cretaceous period, but by the end of the last Ice Age (around 8000 BCE) the depressions had taken their present form and the dry desert climate had set in. The hunter-gatherers and later farmers of the region, who had once enjoyed a milder climate with rain and lakes, high-tailed it to the oasis depressions, where water was still available.

The Romans, with their waterwheels and aqueducts, were able to tap deeper water and push back the desert. Today, there are as many as 400 *Ain Romani*, the ancient wells drilled by the Egyptians and Romans, in each oasis. The population grew and prospered for 300 years, but over-irrigation and abandonment of fallow farming eventually hindered productivity. The oases slipped into a slow decline that lasted until 1958, when the government found considerable stores of water below the desert floor, accessible with new drilling techniques. The government's **New Valley Project** was designed to fully exploit this underground water for the promotion of agriculture and habitation in the desert, and a massive relocation of landless peasants from the Delta to the New Valley was begun. Unfortunately, experts now disagree as to whether the underground water is replenished by seepage or is just a finite supply left over from 6000 to 12,000 years ago which may run out in a few hundred years. Government attention has meant radical change for citizens of the oases, as new roads and other recently introduced conveniences usher in Western culture.

October through April is the best time to visit the oases, which are similar in clime to their latitudinal sisters on the Nile (Bahariyya is like Minya, Kharga like Luxor). It is not unusual for summer temperatures, especially at Dakhla or Kharga, to reach 52°C (126°F). Even at night, summer temperatures persist into the upper 20s (low 80s F)—and you won't find air-conditioning anywhere, except Kharga (which makes it a good first or last stop, depending on whether you like your sweet dessert before or after your harsh desert). In any case, finding accommodations is easy in summer.

GETTING AROUND

Daily **buses** run from the Al-Azhar bus station in Cairo to the oases. Inexpensive buses also run from Asyut to Kharga and Dakhla (see **warning**, p. 175). Between the various oases, bus travel requires a little more flexibility and patience than in the rest of Egypt. Published schedules are rough guesses, and bus officials, townies, and passers-by all peddle wildly contradictory and inaccurate departure times. Ask as many people as possible, follow the consensus, arrive early, and bring your thumbs for twiddling. Your best information will come from the local tourist offices and bus officials. Kharga is served twice weekly by EgyptAir **flights** (reservations and info 392 74 44) from Cairo and Luxor. **Service taxis** travel to Bahariyya from Cairo, and to Kharga from Asyut, and can sometimes offer a faster and more comfortable journey—check out what the vehicle looks like and how many people will be stuffed in (see the individual chapters on the oases, Cairo, and Asyut for detailed transportation information). *Service* between all oases are affordable and often quicker than buses. Some people **hitchhike** from one oasis to the next, but they often have to wait a day or so for a ride, especially between Farafra and Dakhla. Military checkpoints outside each oasis are the most promising spots to find a ride. In the heat and isolation, hitchers run a real risk—Let's Go strongly discourages hitchhiking.

Car rental is a convenient and comfortable, though expensive, option for desert travel. A giant loop along the Great Desert Road and the Lower Nile Valley in either direction beginning in Cairo is about 1700km (over 1000 miles). Any car must be in top condition and fully outfitted for intense desert travel in order to survive the long, hot, poorly maintained roads. Four-wheel-drive is highly recommended. Another option is a caravan (trailer); renting one can solve a lot of problems, including those of transporting food, water, and extra gas, and finding a comfortable place to sleep.

A number of caveats are in order concerning **desert driving.** It is always a long way between gas stations. While every oasis has at least one fuel pump, it is essential to buy jerry cans and fill them with enough gas to cover the vast distances between towns. A caravan guzzles huge quantities of fuel; bring enough extra to fill an entire tank. Several containers of potable water are also vital in case you get stranded. Foreigners are (probably wisely) prohibited from leaving the main road. Try to drive in the cool of the morning or in late afternoon, but never drive at night—the chances of getting lost on unlit roads increases exponentially and hidden potholes are especially lethal. Don't pull a *Lawrence of Arabia:* never, ever drive in a **sandstorm.** If you do get caught in one, stop, turn the car's rear to the wind, and wait.

SOME TIPS

Where to Sleep
The best alternative to staying in hotels in the oases is **camping.** Most fertile land belongs to farmers who will usually permit you to pitch your tent. The ideal spot is just outside the main town of an oasis, where you can usually find a small pool of water (ask the locals for the *bir,* or spring) and the sound of silence. The desert itself may be more comfortable, as cool temperatures and breezes carry away the mosquitoes and the sand makes a soft mattress, but sleeping on the dunes can be dangerous. You might be sharing the desert expanse with ticks, wasps, scorpions, cheetahs, fennec foxes, mice, rats, and tiny hedgehogs that roll into spiky balls when frightened. There are also seven kinds of poisonous **snakes** in Egypt, including lethal vipers. They rest under rocks and sand, coming out to drink at night. If you see snake tracks going in one direction, calmly go in the other. Common sense, a first aid kit, and a snake bite kit are recommended. If you prefer mosquito bites to reptile venom, each oasis has at least one bearable and cheap **hotel** or **rest house.**

Oasis groundwater tastes much better than that of the other Egyptian municipalities; if you want to risk the local grog-o-the-earth, this is a safer place than the cities. Then again, is it really worth ruining the rest of your trip? The main towns of all the oases have restaurants and market places where you can fill up on **food,** but don't expect variety or refinement. The best meals are at people's homes—with a winning smile and a little luck you can taste for yourself.

Women Travelers
Women should follow certain guidelines when swimming in oasis springs. In isolated springs unfrequented by locals, female travelers are not likely to be bothered. The same goes for pools cordoned off and connected to tourist rest houses. Women should not, however, enter pools where men are already bathing. Sometimes there is a separate pool where women may bathe, provided they wear a *gallabiyya* (loose-fitting robes). Local women bathe separately from men, often in the evening.

Women traveling without men should not embark on overnight desert excursions unless pre-arranged by a tourist officer. Even then, care and common sense are required. Lone women heading for the oases should be prepared to deal with harassment. For more information, see **Women and Travel,** page 33.

Taxes, Tourism, and Trust
The requirement for foreigners to obtain permission to visit the oases was lifted in 1985-86. Despite what out-of-date sources may tell you, you need only flash a **passport** at the numerous military checkpoints. In Dakhla, Kharga, or Farafra, you will be asked to pay a E£4.50 **tourism development tax** by a tourist officer or by an employee of your hotel. Keep the **receipt** as proof or you may have to pay again.

The beauty of the Western Desert, with its traditional village lifestyle, stunning landscapes, and low prices, has been attracting an increasing number of visitors. With them comes the slowly creeping disease that the smell of tourist money inevitably brings. In each oasis you will find those whose English is good, whose knowledge of the area is fair, and whose sense of capitalism is extraordinary. They are often friendly and helpful, but the assistance has a bloated price tag trailing behind. For the best information, head for the New Valley's **tourist officers.** In Kharga, the extraordinarily competent and friendly Ibrahim M. Hassan; in Dakhla, the punctilious and knowledgable Omar Ahmed; and in Farafra, the authoritative and entertaining Muhammad Ra'afat all speak excellent English and will answer your questions and arrange for fairly-priced guides and transportation. Without them, you are at the mercy of the wolves. Any assistance you receive from a tourist officer should be *free* of charge.

■ Bahariyya الواحات البحرية

This small oasis is historically significant as a stopover for caravans traveling between the Nile Valley and the rest of North Africa. It lies about 330km south of Cairo and is linked by a decently paved road which leads past the Pyramids of Giza and southwest across the desert to **Bawiti,** a four- or five-hour car trip. Since pharaonic times, the arrival of merchants and their heavily-laden camels was a major event in Bahariyya; for many centuries, pilgrims on their way to Mecca would join traders on the trans-desert trek and enjoy an enthusiastic welcome from Bahariyya's faithful. Nowadays, the only "pilgrims" in Bahariyya are the caravans of rip-roaring European adventurers gallivanting through the oasis in Land Rovers.

Because of its relative proximity to Cairo, Bahariyya attracts many foreign visitors who crave a few days in the desert. The constant traveler traffic has created an atmosphere far more commercial and cutthroat than that of the other oases. Bahariyyan men badger tourists with offers of safari trips and desert picnics, while kids chant a *"mumkin pen, mumkin camera"* mantra.

Bahariyya's ancient ruins are scanty and largely inaccessible. The nearby gardens, springs, and desert offer some relief, but not enough to make anyone stay longer than necessary. Conveniences like food stores, a market, coffee shops, and three gas stations make the oasis a viable (and unavoidable) stop for those heading to Farafra.

ORIENTATION AND PRACTICAL INFORMATION

All services in Bawiti are on or just off a 500m stretch of the main road.

Tourist Office: First floor of the government compound. The green and red sign is on your right as you walk into town from the Cairo end. Staffed by city council member Muhammad Abd el-Qader. Open daily 8am-2pm. After 2pm, look for Mr. Abd el-Qader in the Paradise Hotel.

Currency Exchange: Bank el-Watani is next to the post office. Exchanges cash only. Open Sun.-Thurs. 8am-2pm.

Buses: The **bus ticket and reservation office** is in a green shed next to the telephone office. Open 8-11am and roughly 9-11pm. Buses from Cairo to Bahariyya leave from Al-Azhar station daily 10am and 3pm; also Sun., Wed., and Fri. 8am (5hr., E£12.50). All 8am buses continue to **Farafra** after taking a short break at the coffee shop in Bahariyya (Mon., Thurs., and Sat. 2pm, 3hr., E£10). Get there early to secure a seat. Buses to **Cairo** daily (7am, 5pm, and 1am, 5hr., E£12.50).

Minibuses: Minibuses run daily from Bahariyya to **Cairo** (6:30am and 4pm, 5hr., E£11). Returns to **Bahariyya** from Sayyida Zeinab bus station in Cairo.

Gas Stations: One behind the police station, 2 more on the main road as you head out of town toward Cairo.

Police: Across the street from the telephone building. They speak no English and have no phone on which to speak no English. Stick with the tourist office.

Post Office: Two buildings down from the government compound as you move toward Farafra. Limited services. Open Sat.-Thurs. 8:30am-3pm.

Telephones: In a driveway 10m off the main road, on the side of a building beside the government compound. No direct international calls but can connect with an international operator. Within town dial 1404; the operator will connect you. 3min. to Cairo E£1. Open 8am-midnight. **Telephone Code:** 10.

ACCOMMODATIONS AND FOOD

Ahmad's Safari Camp is 4km south from the center of town. The massive grapevine-covered veranda, clean common bathrooms, good food, and free rides to and from town sweeten the fanless rooms, lack of hot water, and isolation (bare-bones hut E£5 per person; concrete cabana with breakfast E£10 per person; deluxe, white-domed gazebo with shower, fan, and breakfast E£40). The government-run **Paradise Hotel** is across from the telephone office on the main drag. There is a small but pleasant garden with patio furniture, and basic rooms are cleaner and nicer than the cabanas at Ahmad's. Abdul Abdelrhim will be proud to show you around his hometown. The shared bathrooms are rather grimy (shared room E£3.50 per person, E£5 with breakfast). Standing with your back to the city council building and the tourist office, head down the street in front of you to the white-domed **Hotel Alpenblick,** 250m past the "cheapest shop in town" sign. Rooms here are a bit nicer than other options in Bawiti but you don't quite get your money's worth. Rooms have carpets, fan, and not-too-spectacular bathrooms (singles E£20; doubles E£35, with bath E£46m; triples E£53, with bath E£69; breakfast included). **Saleh's Campground** at Bir Ghaba spring is 18km from town. The folks at Alpenblick may give you a ride. A concrete slab in a straw hut costs E£5 per person and is removed from the hassles of Bahariyya. Bring food, water, plenty of insect repellent, and a flashlight.

There are only a few "restaurants" in Bawiti. Bayoumi's **Popular Restaurant** is next to the government compound across from the police station, just off the main road to Cairo. Ask in advance about prices (full meal E£8, Stella E£5). You might also try the kitchen at the **Alpenblick.** The **Paradise** restaurant, **Restaurant Rashed,** and **El Gahsh** all offer standard meals for E£6. El Gahsh serves morning *fuul* and falafel.

SIGHTS

As you leave metropolitan Cairo you'll pass just north of the Pyramids of Giza. Beyond lies **October 6th City,** one of Egypt's new planned cities designed to accommodate some of the country's expanding population. On the approach to Bahariyya, the entire landscape lurches into a deep shade of red—vast deposits of iron are quarried in an immense **iron mine** just off the highway 40km before Bawiti.

Nature is Bahariyya's real attraction, but two museums in Bawiti are also be worth a visit. Friendly and talented local artist Mahmoud Eed creates and stocks his **Oasis Heritage Museum** (900m out of the town center on the left as you head towards Cairo; free) with clay figurines, creating dioramas that depict traditional oasis life. 400m back towards town, up a dirt drive on the opposite side of the road, is the government **Antiquities Museum.** This is where they hoard all the great stuff from the surrounding ruins. It is closed to the public, but you can ask at the tourist office to arrange a free visit. There is also a painted, subterranean pharaonic **tomb** that you might be able to see if you can find the Inspector of Antiquities who has the key.

Bir el-Ramla (2km out of Bawiti along a village track parallel to the road to Cairo) features a 45°C hot spring. The walk here passes apricot and date gardens. Men can bathe here in shorts, but women must be fully clothed and may only swim later at night. **Bir el-Mattar's** cold (25°C), slightly sulphurous water pours out of a viaduct into a small cement pool. The government operates a spartan camp here for E£5 per hut. Taxis to this popular site (8km southeast of Bawiti) cost E£10 round-trip. Men bathe here by day, women by night. The "road" (really a desert track—drivers beware) to Bir el-Mattar continues southeast through the desert to **Bir el-Ghaba,** 17km from Bawiti, with both a hot and cold spring in another sumptuous oasis landscape. Men and women can swim in this deserted spot (taxi E£25 round-trip). Much less appealing but closer is **Bir el-Ghilis,** a steamy, pump-activated spring only 2.5km out of the town center. Nine km from town stands a large natural pyramid, sometimes called **Pyramid Mountain,** surrounded and topped by dunes. Closer to town (about 2.5km from Bawiti on the track heading to Bir el-Mattar) sits **Black Mountain** (called **Gabal El Engeliz,** or English Mountain, by the locals), a flat-topped hill with ruined fortifications from the British occupation.

Ruined chapels, tombs, and temples from the 26th dynasty cluster **El Qasr,** Bawiti's western sibling and the capital of Bahariyya in pharaonic times. Inquire at the tourist office to obtain **permission** to visit these locked sights.

All of the hotel managers run tours of the area. For no more than E£10 a head with six people (less if you are a larger group), you should be able to visit all the nearby springs, sights, and viewpoints. You can hire a taxi through the tourist office, or on your own (full day about E£40 per car).

THE ROAD TO FARAFRA

The road from Bawiti to Farafra oasis (183km) runs past spectacular canyons, wind-blown mesas, and rugged desertscape, and the brand-new **paving** makes it the Autobahn of Egypt's oases. The precipitous eastern and western escarpments of the Bahariyyan depression meet at a point about 60km south of Bawiti. The road winds through this pass and onto a brief plateau, then plummets into the Farafra depression.

The fabulous terrain between the oases is marred only by the outrageous prices demanded by Bahariyyans who offer desert tours. It is cheaper to go on such tours from Farafra, especially to the White Desert. All points except El Wadi Oasis can be reached by regular car, but dune-cruising in a 4x4 is more fun. For overnight tours including food, a **pick-up truck taxi** should not exceed E£60-80, a more comfortable **Peugeot** E£70-90, and a **4x4** E£150-175. Summer is the cheapest time to go, but the hardest time to find riding partners. Jeep jockeys will probably start the bidding at E£800 for a trip to Farafra. Depending on the supply and demand curves of the week, they have been known to get at least that much. Bargain hard.

Leaving Bawiti, the scenery is stunning as you pass through the **Black Desert** with its dark mesas and crumbly flats peppered with tufts of dry desert grass. The idyllic oasis village of **El Hayiz** (E£50 per truckload as a daytrip from Bawiti) lies 5km off the main road to Farafra, 40km from Bawiti. Gardens, a spring, and a simple village lifestyle make this a nice spot to camp overnight; you can even eat fresh watermelon or apricots for breakfast. Between El Hayiz and Farafra lie dunes and flats, punctuated occasionally by mesas. **Crystal Mountain** (really just a rise by the roadside with some quartz deposits) rises about 100km from Bawiti. Further along is **Al Sillim Pass,** affording a view of the escarpment cascading into the distance of the desert. The palm trees and small, desolate spring of empty **El Wadi Oasis** (the only place you'll need a 4x4 to reach) lie about 140km from Bawiti. The oasis is striking amidst towering dunes and the grazing gazelles. About 45km outside Farafra, the black buttes suddenly give way to the **White Desert,** where spooky fungoid rock formations stand stark white in daytime, glow shades of bashful fuchsia by dusk, and turn orange by dawn. Leaving the White Desert at the main road there is a cold spring.

If you want to arrange a **tour** from Bahariyya, Muhammad Abd el-Qader (at the tourist office or Paradise Hotel), Yehi Kandil, or Badry Mahcpool (at the Popular Restaurant) are all helpful. Ahmad's Safari Camp also offers tours. From Farafra, you can organize an overnight to the desert with Muhammad Ra'afat (see p. 220). If you can't put together a posse, you can still see this interesting area from the window of the public bus (sit on the left side for the best views).

■ Farafra واحة الفـرافـرة

Although it is only one of the 26 provinces in Egypt, Farafra claims an impressive 16% of the land, with its borders caressing Libya and Sudan. Two years ago, the area was home to a mere 5,000 people, but immigration has swelled the population to over 12,000. Province president Muhammad Ra'afat Amin has spearheaded the campaign to provide government funding for land reclamation through a massive irrigation effort—an effort that has done little to increase tourism in the area. The 3,000 people who live in the sleepy main city still use donkey carts and bicycles despite new roads and a new gas station. Farafra is a great place to plan a trip to the nearby White Desert, 40km to the north.

Orientation and Practical Information The bus and all *service* taxis arrive and depart from the cafe on the Bahariyya-Dakhla road. Heading back toward Bahariyya, you'll pass the **police station** and the **post office with telephone service** (open Sun.-Thurs. 8am-2pm; telephone available daily 8am-midnight) before you arrive at **city hall's** white arches marked with colorful murals (open Sun.-Thurs. 8am-2pm). Here, meet the knowledgeable Muhammad Ra'afat Amin who is helpful in organizing whatever excursions you may desire. If he's not in the office, you can ask someone to take you to his massive hilltop house 2km from town (E£2 is a fair price).

Buses depart in front of the cafe to **Bahariyya** (Mon., Wed., and Sat., 6am, 3hr., E£10), continuing on to **Cairo** (8hr., E£25). There's also a daily commercial bus to Cairo—check times with Muhammad Ra'afat Amin at City Hall the night before. Buses from Cairo leave Al-Azhar Station (Mon., Thurs., and Sat. 8am, 8hr., E£25) and stop in Bahariyya along the way. **Minibuses** and **service taxis** are the best way to get to **Dakhla** (early morning is best; ask around the night before to secure a seat, 5hr., E£15). There is also supposedly a night bus (2:30am, 5hr., E£15). If you're considering **hitchhiking,** reconsider—it can be deadly (see **Getting Around,** p. 216).

Accommodations and Food You can count the hotels in Farafra on one very small finger. The government-run **Tourist Rest House,** 1.5km from the bus stop (or ask to be let off here), looks like an abandoned building. With grimy bathrooms and the tell-tale signs of used sheets, it is overpriced (E£9.50 per bed). In summer, the E£8 meal may migrate with the chef. **Camping** in the nearby desert or at **Bir Sitta** (6km from town) might make for a more organic experience but be sure to temper it with plenty of insect repellent. Also check your shoes and pants before getting dressed—scorpions and huge biting ants thrive in these parts. Always let Muhammad Ra'afat Amin know your travel plans. Clustered around the bus station are several **restaurants** which make omelettes (E£1), macaroni (E£2), and full meals with meat (E£5).

Sights In town, the **Art Museum,** a unique project by local artist Badr, displays expressive sculptures and paintings which depict life in Farafra. Mounted local wildlife and an exhibit of Farafran artifacts round out the collection. The museum, in the mud-brick building with the decorated facade, is near the city hall about 100m to the northwest behind a school. Many of Badr's murals also adorn the outside walls of local houses. The hot **Bir Sitta** (Well #6), 6km west of town, is an idyllic spot to swim and camp (transportation about E£5 per carload). Sometime in the next two years a 150-person vacation village will spring up next to Bir Sitta, most likely squeezing this area out of the budget traveler's range. The **White Desert** (40km from Farafra) offers overnight camping opportunities and breathtaking views. An average overnight trip in a 4x4 from Farafra should be about E£300 per carload; you'll visit both **Wadi Henis** and **Karaween,** whose springs and gazelles are marvelous. Once again, contact Muhammad Ra'afat to help you plan your trip. For more information on desert trips, see **The Road to Farafra,** p. 220.

THE ROAD TO DAKHLA

In 1997, most of the 310km road from Farafra to Dakhla was repaved in sticky, black asphalt. Be careful where you drive—shifting dunes have obscured the southern part of this road for years, making travel between Dakhla and Farafra an unpredictable undertaking. The road is now kept partially clear, but sees little traffic. Buses and taxis make the journey without much ado, save for the occasional swerve to avoid a mischievous sand dune.

Ten kilometers south of Farafra is a tiny, uninhabited oasis officially considered part of the town. Although the villagers take care to cultivate the land there and an occasional farmer wanders across the road, the spot is deserted and quiet—the best place in the area to pitch a tent. Still farther down the road toward Dakhla, about 35km from Farafra, is the diminutive, sparsely inhabited **Oasis of Sheikh Merzuq,** where a sulphur spring with a viaduct carries water into a coed concrete pool. The locals will show you the way to an ancient **Roman well,** where fresh water spurts from a deep spring. These watering holes can only be reached via private transport.

■ Dakhla الواحات الداخلة

Dakhla's fields, rice paddies, and fruit orchards stubbornly hold out against the harsh desert. In two places, the desert does consume the greenery, segmenting Dakhla into three separate oases. Regardless, 75,000 Dakhlans are the clear victors in the struggles against the dunes. Basking in government attention, the people of Dakhla have reclaimed this recalcitrant wasteland, planting peanuts and rice and gradually introduced more fragile crops which expand in variety each year. The New Valley Project may have rendered the urban center of Kharga unappealing to visitors, but in Dakhla something of the opposite has occurred. Here the oasians beam under broad-brimmed straw hats and share their infectious enthusiasm with visitors. In this "pink oasis"—so named because of the pink cliffs jabbing the horizon—visitors will be closer to the traditional life of the oases than anywhere else in the New Valley.

ORIENTATION AND PRACTICAL INFORMATION

Farthest from Cairo of the oases, Dakhla bubbles 310km from Farafra and 200km from Kharga. The center and capital of the oasis is **Mut** (pronounced "moot"), named for the Egyptian goddess married to Amun. **West Mawhub,** 80km west of Mut, and **Tineida,** 45km east of Mut, are smaller repositories of green which mark the oasis's edges. Cultivated regions dot the main, well-paved highway. The three most appealing and historic towns are **El Qasr,** 32km west of Mut and **Balaat** and **Bashendi,** 35 and 40km east of Mut.

Mut has two focal points: **Tahrir Sq.,** at the intersection of New Valley St. and the Kharga-Farafra Highway (running southeast-northwest), and **New Mosque Sq.,** 1km south along New Valley Street.

Tourist Information Office: There are two offices. The new (tel. 94 16 86 or 15 85) is 750m away from Tahrir Sq. on the road to Farafra, across the street from Abu Muhammad Restaurant in a building shared with the Egyptian Tourist Authority. The old office (tel. 94 04 07) is across from the mosque in New Mosque Sq. in the same building as the Tourist Rest House. The knowledgeable Omar Ahmed speaks English and will help arrange transportation. If he's not in, feel free to reach him at home (tel. 94 07 82). Both offices open Sun.-Thurs. 8am-2pm and 8-11pm.

Currency Exchange: Misr Bank (tel. 94 00 63), in Tahrir Sq. near the police station. Changes traveler's checks and cash. Open Sun.-Thurs. 8am-2pm and 6-9pm, sporadically open Sat. 8am-2pm for changing money.

Buses and Service: Mut Station (tel. 94 15 38), located in New Mosque Sq. **Local buses** go to **Balaat** and **Bashendi** (8:30am, 2, and 4pm; 50pt; return to Mut 1hr. later) and **El Qasr** (10:30am and 2pm, 50pt; return to Mut 2hr. later). These buses are not very reliable. It is best to take a service taxi early in the morning. To **Cairo** (6am, 5pm (A/C), and 7pm (A/C); 13hr., E£28 and E£37, reservations should be made a day in advance); **Kharga** (8:30am, 2pm, 4pm; 3hr., E£7); and **Asyut** (8:30am, 2pm, 4pm; 6hr., E£17). Cairo-bound buses go to both cities. Bus schedules change frequently; ask the tourist office for updates. **Service taxis** and **minibuses** go to **Kharga** (E£7) and **Farafra** (6am or whenever one fills up, 5hr., E£15).

Taxis: Special sight-seeing **tours** E£40 for 1 day, E£8-10 for a trip to eastern or western Dakhla. Ask in New Mosque Sq. Covered pick-up trucks shuttle frequently between Tahrir Sq. and El Qasr and between the hospital stand and **Balaat** and **Bashendi** (75pt- E£1 one way) and El Qasr (E£1). The early bird catches the truck.

Bicycle Rental: Nasser's Hotel (E£5 per day), **Abu Muhammad's Restaurant** (E£5), and the **Gardens Hotel** (E£7), less if you rent for a few hours or half-day.

Gas Station: The outskirts of eastern Mut, on the Kharga Hwy. (on your left as you leave town). Open 24hr.

Pharmacies: There are 3 pharmacies on New Mosque St. Most are open daily 8am-2pm and occasionally at night.

Hospitals: The main hospital (tel. 94 15 55 or 13 32) is 1km from Tahrir Sq. towards Kharga. Smaller hospitals in each village.

Emergency: Ambulance: tel. 94 13 33. **Police:** tel. 94 15 00, in Tahrir Sq.

Post Office: One in New Mosque Sq., another on El Ganeim St., around the corner from the telephone office. Both open Sun.-Thurs. 8am-2pm.

Telephones: From New Mosque Sq., walk east along 23 July St. to Anwar Restaurant, then veer left toward the red and white tower about 30m ahead on your left. Calls within Egypt only. Open 24hr. For **international service,** go to the Mebarez Hotel. **Telephone Code:** 092.

ACCOMMODATIONS

If you're visiting during the winter months, consider staying in one of the hotels on the outskirts of town—transport into town will be easier than during summer months and the quiet, retreat-like atmosphere is more relaxing. In summer, though, these fanless hotels are deathly.

Gardens Hotel (tel. 94 15 77), 20m down a dirt road from Anwar's Desert Paradise Restaurant, has patio furniture, a pleasant garden, and friendly management. Clean, breezy rooms with fans, or a desert-sky rooftop bed. Singles E£10, with bath E£12; doubles E£12, with bath E£16. Breakfast E£2.

El Qasr Tourist Rest House, next to the road to the old village. Big double beds with fans, outside baths (E£5 per person). Transportation in summer to Mut may be a problem. The *ahwa* downstairs has sandwiches and backgammon.

Tourist Rest House (tel. 94 04 07), in the same building as the Tourist Office in New Mosque Sq. The bedrooms are marginally clean, but the bathrooms are less so. Cold showers only. E£4.35 per person.

Mebarez (tel. 94 15 24), on the edge of town, 800m from Tahrir Sq. on the road to Farafra. This 4-story mustard-yellow building is more upscale than the Gardens. Handles large tour groups from Europe in winter. Will place international phone calls. Rooms are carpeted, with balconies and fans. Singles E£28, with A/C and bath E£34; doubles E£42, with bath and A/C E£48. Breakfast included.

Hot Springs Rest House (tel. 94 15 30), 3km out of town on the road to Farafra. This is the government's Art Deco incarnation of a rejuvenating spa, between rice paddies and sand dunes. Two large, circular pools are replenished with "curative," orange, 42°C water from the nearby hot spring. Swimming is free for non-residents who pay the tourism development tax. With no fans, rooms may be too hot in the summer. Double rooms with bath E£12 per bed, E£17 with breakfast; separate villa with garden and quiet back porch E£5 per bed.

Nasser's Hotel, 5km out of town on the road to Kharga on the edge of a traditional farming village. To get to the hotel, find Nasser at Hamdy Restaurant (which he runs with his brother), 100m before the Mebarez Hotel on the road to Farafra. Surrounded by fields replete with waterwheels, water buffalo, and goats. Very isolated, with basic facilities, shared bathrooms, and a kitchen. Nasser speaks English and will arrange day or overnight trips by car, camel, donkey, or motorcycle to out-of-the-way villages, springs, and dunes. No singles. E£5 per person.

FOOD

Dakhla has the best food in the oases (everything's relative). **Hamdy Restaurant,** just before the Mebarez Hotel, serves chicken or meat meals (E£10). The cook worked in the kitchen of an American petroleum company in Saudi Arabia, so he can whip up pancakes and other tourist delights. Give him a little warning before coming with a large group in the summer. Around the corner from the Garden Hotel is **Anwar's Desert Paradise Restaurant** (full meal E£7.50, beans and rice E£3). Along the highway, **Shehaab,** just west of New Valley St., is a local favorite (full meal E£5). **Abu Muhammad's Restaurant,** across from the new tourist office, serves the same food as other places for nearly double the price. The comment book is an amusing read. Be sure to confirm the price of any meal before you dig in.

SIGHTS

Strolling near the New Mosque Sq., you'll stumble upon the future site of the **tourist village** designed by Hassan Fathy (it was started nearly a decade ago). The arched ceilings provide natural air conditioning, and the mud-brick walls contribute to both atmospheric and aesthetic coolness. Past the Gardens Hotel into the residential area, you'll find the Old Village, the ruins of old mud brick houses crowded along narrow alleys. Much less exciting is the **Dakhla Ethnographic Museum** (tel. 94 13 11), which exhibits a reconstruction of a typical Dakhlan family dwelling. Expressive clay figurines, created by Mabruk, an artist from the Kharga oasis, recreate scenes of village life. The museum is two blocks past Anwar's restaurant to the left of the fork. Arrange a visit through the tourist office or by calling Ibrahim Kamel Abdallah (tel. 94 17 69), the museum's curator, at the Ministry of Culture office on New Valley St. near the cinema (admission E£2).

Mut points you to the rewarding outlying villages (for transport options, see **Practical Information,** p. 222). In the cooler months, biking to some spots becomes feasible. Be sure to rent one with strong tires and brakes, and bring camels of water.

Western Dakhla

Traveling west from Mut for 6km will bring you to the small Bedouin village of **El Douhous.** The road then splits for 25km before joining up again. The left fork takes you to the distinctly medieval village of **Kalamoun,** the capital of Dakhla in Mamluk times. In the Islamic era, Kalamoun was an administrative center; its inhabitants today claim Turkish and Mamluk ancestry. The town's name has two possible translations: "Amun's pens" (*kalam* means pen), for the scribes who lived here, or "Amun's citadel" (*qala'a* means fortress). Like most oasis towns, Kalamoun's panoramic hilltop perch offered both military and climactic defense. Near the center lies an Ayyubid mosque which can be reached by winding through the maze of narrow passages and traditional mud brick houses. Leaving the town and continuing on the road for 5km you reach **El Gedida,** or "new town," so named because it's only 300 years old. The nascent village is well known for its **arabesque factory** which, in cooperation with Ain Shams University and the German Embassy, makes decorated woodwork with palm tree branches (open Sat.-Thurs. 8am-2pm; free). For more delicious handiwork, sample the town's sweet harvests: apricots (May), mangoes (late July), and dates (Oct.). Three km further down the road is **Mushiya,** whose gardens boast old, broken waterwheels. Six kilometers more bring you to the ruins of a yet-to-be-excavated Roman village, **Amheida.** You rejoin the main road 8km farther down.

Joining the main road and traveling west (to the left) for 3km will bring you to the **Mousawaka Tombs,** which can only be seen from the outside until renovation repairs the ceilings. Ask Omar Ahmed at the Tourist Office for updates. Two kilometers farther along the main road from the Mousawaka turn-off is a dirt road which twists and turns around a small village passing three large Roman remains before leading up to a ridge from which the Roman temple of **Deir el-Haggar** is can be seen. The temple is a 1.5km dirt track trek. Dedicated to the Theban triad of Mut, Amun, and Khonsu, it was built in the first century BCE during the reign of Nero and added to by his immediate successors (open daily 8am-5pm; E£20, students E£10).

Heading back towards town about 3km past the junction with the loop road, or 32km from Mut on the northern fork, is the village of **El Qasr,** probably the most edifying daytrip from Dakhla. This charming contemporary town was built in and around the substantial remains of Dakhla's medieval Islamic capital. A model of comfortable architecture, its mud buildings remain cool in summer and warm in winter. The **old village** of El Qasr lies 400m to the north of the main road through the new village. At the western edge of town on the main road is a large map of the village. Within the old village, arrows direct you to the sights.

The **Minaret of Nasr ed-Din** is the only extant part of an 11th-century Ayyubid mosque. A 19th-century mosque surrounds the old tower. Down the gnarled alleys north of the minaret is **Qasr Madrasa,** an intact two-story mud-brick building that is thought to have been either an Ayyubid schoolhouse or the entertainment hall of an Ottoman palace; villagers later used the building as a courtroom. Many of the doorways of the old village are adorned with ornate wooden lintels that reveal the name of the owner, builder, and carpenter as well as the date of construction. The bits of a pharaonic arch and a Roman doorway hint at El Qasr's pre-Islamic past. On the southern fringes of the old town you can see a waterwheel and functioning **pottery works**, where the villagers churn out everything from ashtrays to chamberpots. On the main road, at the turnoff to the old village, is the **El Qasr Tourist Rest House,** serving simple meals of cheese and omelettes in summer and a more complete menu in winter (full meal E£6). Cold drinks and ice cream are also available. Also in the small town are a market, 30m from the hotel on the same side of the road, and a **telephone office** (open 24hr.) and **medical clinic** on the opposite side, 50m toward Mut.

Heading back to Mut, 4km east of El Qasr, is the turn-off for **Bir el-Gabal,** or "tourism wells." The hot spring is connected to the main highway by a 6km road which passes a little farming settlement. Travelers who are dropped off by a pick-up or public bus will have to walk or hitch a ride with some workers from the nearby quarry (as always, *Let's Go* does not recommend hitchhiking). At the end of the asphalt road you'll see a small rise on the left with a dilapidated mud house; go left and follow the palm frond fence. You'll arrive at a paradisiacal pool overhung by two palms (that frothy orange gunk around the edges is just oxidized iron). Another 12km along the main road (16km from Mut), you can stop for a back-pounding water massage at the spring just past **Budkhulu.** Lukewarm water pours forcefully out of a pipe into a large concrete pool. The spring lies 30m down a wide dirt track, by the side of the road between the village and a long row of eucalyptus trees.

You can do this entire loop by hiring a pickup for a day (E£40) or by leapfrogging on the pickup truck taxis which circle the sites daily.

Eastern Dakhla

Two historic villages on the eastern side of Mut may restore your faith in rural living. In the crowded old section of Islamic **Balaat** (population 5000), long, dark passageways burst into a courtyard with palm fronds and grape vines. These ceilinged pathways were a defense tactic—during invasions, the bad guys' camels and horses could not fit through the alleys. This village has the reputation of being the cleanest in the area, perhaps because its roads are strewn with bright orange sand a few times each day. Ask to be shown the mayor's house with its assembly courtyard, speech balcony, and ornate wrought iron lamps and bedframes.

The unguarded red-brick tombs of **Ed-Daba,** where Dakhla's pharaonic governors were buried during the 6th dynasty, are behind the village, just northeast of the main road. First walk 1km east from the official bus stop to a building with white stone columns; from there, walk 750m straight into the desert. The ongoing work of a team of French archaeologists has revealed several bizarre inverted step pyramids (open daily 8am-6pm; E£20, E£10 with ISIC).

Bashendi is 5km farther east, 40km from Mut. Though less picturesque than Balaat, its ruins reward the trip. The village stands on top of a recently discovered temple and various Roman-era tombs. The large stone **Tomb of Ketenus** contains six rooms, including one decorated with scenes of a 2nd-century Roman owner mingling with the gods Min and Seth. Arrows point the way, but the key is held by a villager whom locals will look for upon request (E£16, students E£8). Next door, the prominent **Tomb of Bashendi,** the base of which is a Roman foundation but whose domed roof is distinctly Islamic, commemorates the village's beloved namesake; you might join locals who decorate the inside of the holy man's tomb with *henna* in hopes of finding missing objects. If the guard isn't around to open the tombs, a villager may do the honors. There are also a number of hot and cold springs to which locals can direct you, though village leaders would rather lead you to the Bashendi **carpet works,** where local youths are trained to weave.

The **road to Kharga,** with views of sphinx-shaped mountains and natural pyramids, should only take about two hours. The rest house at the midway point has *sheesha*, tea, and *samsa* biscuits. Crescent-shaped sand dunes creep across the road just outside Kharga, necessitating occasional detours.

■ Kharga الخارجة

Egypt's most effective attempt at a desert boomtown is the city of Kharga, capital of the New Valley Province (El Wadi El Gideed) and the most accessible and developed of all the Western Desert oases. Little is known about Kharga in early pharaonic times, although it must have been agriculturally sound—its hieroglyphic name is *hibis*, or "plow." It became prosperous during Roman times due to its proximity to trade routes, including **Darb El Arba'een** (the forty days road), the important slave trade route beginning in Sudan's Darfur Province and ending in Asyut, which thrived until 1884 when the rise of the Dervish empire closed the Egyptian-Sudanese border. Beginning in the 4th century, Kharga became a large Christian settlement and a center for monasticism where major figures, including Bishop Nastorius, former Patriarch of Constantinople, were exiled by religious and political rivals. The oasis's Australia-like function as a distant exile continued into the 20th century; Nasser banished Mustafa Amin, founder of *Al-Akhbar*, Egypt's largest circulating daily, to Kharga after the 1952 revolution. When the New Valley Project was begun in earnest in the early 1980s, the town again prospered. The greater Kharga population is now in six figures. Modern Kharga, with its cookie-cutter apartments and wide, empty streets, is a largely lifeless and boring town by Egyptian standards, but the ruins on its periphery are astounding. Welcome relief from Kharga's New Town can be found in the narrow alleyways of the Old Town. Locally-made ceramics, carpets, and souvenir beef entrails are available in the *souq*, which begins at Showla Sq.

ORIENTATION

Of all the oases in Egypt's Western Desert, Kharga lies closest to the Nile Valley, 240km from Asyut. The greenery begins about 20km north of the town of Kharga. A newly paved road heads south from Kharga, skirting dunes and small oases on the way to **Bulaq** (15km south), **Baris** (90km south), and smaller settlements between.

Gamal Abdel Nasser St. runs north-south and is intersected in the middle by **En-Nada St.** (which heads west to Dakhla) where you'll find the **Misr Bank,** the police and fire stations, and the cinema. At the northernmost end of Gamel Abdel Nasser St., you'll find the **tourist office** and rest house before the road heads off to the ruins and then on to Asyut. The southern end of Gamal Abdel Nasser St. intersects **En-Nabawi el-Mohandis St.,** which runs east-west. This street curves slightly northeast to **Showla Sq.,** where you'll find the *service* taxi and minibus station, the *souq,* and the old town. Convenient covered-truck taxis scurry along Nabawi St. from Showla Sq., turn up Nasser St., and head for the tourist office at the northern end (10pt.).

PRACTICAL INFORMATION

Tourist Office: tel. 90 12 05 or 06, at the northern end of Nasser St. in the Modernist building with the ecru concrete canopy. Mr. Ibrahim Hassan, trained in Egyptology, is committed to making your stay in Kharga as pleasant as possible. Mohsen Al Moneam is also very helpful. Open Sun.-Thurs. 8:30am-2pm and daily 8pm-midnight. Over 2km from the bus station, so grab a pick-up taxi (10pt).

Tourist Police: tel. 90 13 67, next to the tourist office. Open 24hr.

Passport Office: tel. 90 10 96, facing tourist office. Open Sat.-Thurs. 8am-2pm.

Currency Exchange: Misr Bank, opposite Cinema Hibis, corner of Nasser St. and En-Nada St. Changes traveler's checks and cash and will do Visa cash advances. Open Sun.-Thurs. 8:30am-2pm, and 6-9pm in summer, 5-8pm in winter. **Cairo Bank** (tel. 90 15 51 or 35 55; fax 90 42 22), 100m east of the 1st traffic circle. Exchanges traveler's checks. Open Sun.-Thurs. 8:30am-2pm.

Flights: EgyptAir (tel. 90 16 95), 2 blocks north of Misr Bank intersection on Nasser St. Airport turn-off is 3km north of town on Asyut Rd., then another 2km southeast. On Sun. and Wed. to **Cairo** via **Luxor** (6:30am) and back to Cairo (8:50am). Cairo to Kharga E£450, Luxor to Kharga E£350, no flights from Kharga to Luxor. Minibus or shared taxi from Showla Sq. E£5.

Buses: Intercity buses arrive and depart from Showla Sq. To: **Cairo** (6am, 10am, 9pm, 10:30pm; 12hr., E£37); **Asyut** (4 per day, 4hr., E£6); **Dakhla** (7am, noon (from Assyut), 4pm, and 3am (from Cairo); 3hr., E£7). **Local buses** to: **Baris** (7am, noon, and 2:30p;, 3hr., E£1.60); **Dush** (from Baris: 6 and 11am, 3hr., E£7). Bus schedules in the oases change frequently; check with the tourist office for updates.

Service Taxis and Minibuses: Catch them in Showla Sq. Fairly frequent service to **Asyut** (3½hr., E£9) where you can transfer to a Peugeot for **Cairo** (5½hr., E£15). Occasionally to **Dakhla** (E£8). "Special" (unshared) to Dakhla, E£56. Irregular service to **Baris** (E£1-2), or hire one for the day (E£50).

Pharmacy: El Mhaba Pharmacy, 1 block east of Showla Sq. on En-Nabawi St. Open daily 8am-2pm and 6pm-midnight.

Hospital: Main branch (tel. 122 or 90 15 02), off Nasser St. north of En-Nabawy St. intersection. Open 24hr.

Emergency: Ambulance: tel. 123. **Police:** tel. 122 or 90 10 44. Opposite Misr Bank. **Fire:** tel. 180. Next to the police station.

Post Office: Main office off Nasser St. behind Cinema Hibis has **EMS.** A smaller branch is in Old Kharga's Showla Sq. Both open Sat.-Thurs. 8am-2pm.

Telephones: Opposite the main post office. 90pt for 3min. to Cairo. Open 24hr. Dodgy international service. Branch in Shoqla Sq. open 8am-midnight. **Telephone Code:** 092.

ACCOMMODATIONS AND FOOD

In summer, splurge for a room with a fan or you'll drown in a pool of hot sweat.

Hotel El Dar El Beada (tel. 90 17 17), in Showla Sq. Small but brand-new with a homey lobby. Drinks available for 50pt. E£10 per person with bath and fan, E£8 without bath. No breakfast.

Waha Hotel (tel. 90 03 93). Towers over En-Nabawi St. just east of Nasser St. Kharga's cheap spot. Near groceries and restaurants, and a 15min. walk from Showla Sq. Floors and walls bear reminders of former clients, but the linen and bathrooms are clean. No hot water in common bathrooms. Singles E£6; with hot water, bath and fan E£15; doubles E£12-20; bare necessity triples E£13.50.

El Goumhoureah Rest House, 70m down the street directly across from the tourist office in a rose-colored stucco building. Lounge, garden, and upstairs rooms with fan or A/C. Take the taxi to town for dinner and water. Singles E£12, with or without A/C; doubles E£8 per bed.

Tourist Office Rest House, adjacent to the tourist office on Nasser St. Ideal for groups of 4 or more; villas have living rooms with TV, kitchens with stoves and fridges, and bedrooms with A/C. Large chalets for up to 9 people E£97; smaller versions for 4 E£35; a few single beds in summer E£20.

Hamad Allah Hotel (tel. 90 06 38), just off En-Nada St., 1 block from the telecom tower. The better value of the 2 upscale options (the other being the Kharga Hotel near the tourist office). Large sitting rooms on each floor give a VIP waiting room feel. Clean doubles with refrigerator, A/C, TV, bath, and towels. One person E£53, 2 people E£75; includes breakfast. Lunch E£15, dinner E£17.

Khargan cuisine is adequate at best, though fairly good rotisserie chicken seems to be a specialty (whole bird E£8, half E£4). Plan to subsist on chicken; vegetarians must do with beans and rice. A restaurant at the entrance to the *souq* street offers *fuul* and falafel (50pt) for breakfast. If you're staying in the northern end of town, either go shopping in the evening or take a taxi into Showla Sq. for breakfast. **Restaurant** (no other English name) in Showla Sq. offers the usual Egyptian favorites: chicken, *kebab,* and *kafta* (E£2-5). A calm cafe beneath the Waha Hotel offers cheap, standard Egyptian lunches and dinners (E£1-7).

SIGHTS

In addition to the antiquities, a few other Kharga spots are of interest. A little more than 500m south of Nawaby St. down Nasser St. is the **Pottery and Carpet Factory** where local handicrafts are made and sold (Sun.-Thurs. 8am-2pm). Another 300m down Nasser St. is the **date factory,** where 200 women at conveyor belts take plucked, washed, steamed, dried, and sorted dates and stuff them with peanuts and other goodies (Aug.-Feb., Sat.-Thurs. 8am-1:30pm, free). 200m past the date factory is the **duck farm** where thousands of them quack placidly on a pond. The *pièce de resistance* of the New Valley's tourism drive is the sparkling new **Museum of Alwady el-Gadid,** housing a massive collection of artifacts collected from the New Valley oases and a few pieces from the Cairo Museum. A large variety of pharaonic and Islamic artifacts, from wooden sarcophagi and sandstone sphinxes to mascara jars and Roman coins (open daily 8am-5pm; E£20, E£10 with ISIC).

Kharga's important ruins cluster at the northern end of town. A shared covered taxi will take you as far as the tourist office (possibly farther for E£1), within walking distance of the sites. The **Temple of Hibis,** 2km north of the Hotel El Kharga and close to the road on the left, was begun in 588 BCE by Apnias of the 26th dynasty and completed by Darius I in 522 BCE, making it one of only two Persian-built Egyptian temples (the other was also in Kharga). Although dedicated to the Theban triad of Amun, Mut, and Khonsu, the temple is distinguished by its depictions of Persians and the god of the Oases, Seth (blue body, falcon head). First-century Roman inscriptions discuss legal issues including women's rights (covered with wooden scaffolding during the summer of 1997, the site will soon be open daily 8am-6pm; E£16, students E£8). Across the road to the southeast, the **Temple of Nadura,** built in the 2nd century BCE during the reign of Roman Emperor Antonius, crowns a knoll. Little of it stands today, but the site provides an exemplary view of the oasis.

The spooky 263 above-ground tombs (also called chapels) of the Christian **Necropolis of El Bagawat** stand at the desert's edge, 500m past the Temple of Hibis on the road to Asyut. From the 3rd to 8th centuries CE, a sizable Christian community, including many hermits and some of the religion's first monks, inhabited Kharga. Most fled or were exiled during the divisive 4th and 5th centuries, when Constantinople attempted to force the Melkite doctrine (stating that Jesus was not always of the same essence as the Father) on Egypt. Egypt's Christians resisted, and clung to their original Monophysite position. The Egyptian view had been put forth by Athanasios, a Khargan exile, at the first great Christian Council at Nicea in 325. The necropolis is visible from the road, and an asphalt road leads to the ticket booth. If you go up the hill along the marked path, you'll come to the **Chapel of Exodus.** Inside, the ceiling mural depicts the pharaoh's Roman-looking army chasing the Jews as they flee from Egypt. Other scenes show Adam and Eve and *ankh*-like crosses. In front of the Chapel of Exodus are the interconnected frescoed chapels #23-35, the resting place of members of a local wealthy family. The interior frescoes of biblical scenes in the **Chapel of Peace** (#80) exemplify Coptic painting of the early Alexandrian style. Greek inscriptions identify Adam and Eve, Noah's Ark, and the Virgin Mary. Atop the cemetery's central hill are the remains of a 4th-century mud-brick basilica (open Apr.-Sept. 8am-6pm, Oct.-Mar. 8am-5pm.; E£20, students E£10).

THE ROAD TO BARIS

If you've come all the way to Kharga, don't miss the road along the old 40-day camel trail south to Baris. This legendary caravan route extended from the western Sudan all the way to the Egyptian Nile Valley and trafficked more slaves than any other land route in the world.

Vast sandscapes are all that thrive between Kharga and **Khwita Temple,** 17km to the south. The impressive 10m walls of the temple-*cum*-fortress command a hill 2km east of the road. Dedicated to Amun, Mut, and Khonsu, and built by Darius I with later Ptolemaic additions, the temple served as the center of a thriving community famous in pharaonic times for its grape production. This site was later used to garrison troops for guarding the caravan route; today, remnants of the fortress surround the temple itself (open 8am-6pm, 5pm in summer; E£16, students E£8). At the 25km mark you'll come across the shaded, dirty **Nasser Wells.** Farther on, the better-developed **Bulaq Wells** offer a simple government **rest house** (beds E£5, meals E£8-12) and hot springs. **Zayan Temple,** dedicated to Amun, is 5km east of Nasser Wells near the village of Araf, on a road that loops around from the north of Khwita Temple to a point north of Bulaq. Originally built in the Ptolemaic era, it was restored by the Romans who used the site to build a fortress of which there are still remains (open 8am-5pm, until 6pm in winter; E£16, students E£8).

The secluded village of **Baris** (the sign at the edge of the town ironically reads "Paris") is 90km south of Kharga and infernally hot in summer (over 50°C). Merchants make a 40-day camel trek from here to the border of Chad to purchase an ingredient used in local soap. It is estimated that each expedition brings the merchant E£20,000 in profit. Think twice before going into business for yourself, however, since only one family in town is privy to the location of vital water wells along the way. There is a government **rest house** north of town, but no sign to mark it; look for the yellow, gray, and red buildings, in a row perpendicular to the highway, about 500m north of the "Paris" sign. You can arrange your stay through the tourist office in Kharga or get the groundskeeper to let you in (beds E£5). **Tourist officer** Mr. Farkhat is available in Baris Thurs.-Sun.; during the rest of the week he can be found in Kharga. If you walk down the central street, perpendicular to the main road, old Baris will be on your right, the gardens straight ahead. Half a dozen small **kiosks** sell soda, mineral water, and canned goods. The blue structure resembling a doghouse sells *kebab, fuul,* and falafel every day except Friday.

An abandoned public housing complex designed by modern Egyptian architect Hassan Fathy (using cooling properties of traditional oasis architecture) stands 300m northwest of the rest house. Construction was halted during the 1967 war with Israel and never resumed; the government wisely decided that villagers would not want to live in buildings resembling tombs. Americans seem to mind less—Fathy built a similar complex in New Mexico.

A recently paved road leads 23km southeast to the **Dush Temple.** The building has an abundance of heat and a shortage of visitors during the summer, but there's more to it than meets the eye. Originally built for the worship of Serapis and Isis, the temple dates back to the Roman emperors Trajan and Hadrian. Around the temple the sand is slowly parting to reveal a church, pottery shards, and a well with clay pipes that lead to an underground city. It seems that Dush, a prosperous settlement, was abandoned when the wells ran dry.

The easiest way to get to these sights is to hire a **pickup taxi** for a day from Kharga (E£50-60). Plenty of shared taxis go from Kharga as far as Bulaq (50pt). Catch them at the southern end of Nasser St. Each day, three **buses** go to **Baris** (7am, noon, and 2:30pm; 3hr., E£1.70) and three return (6 and 11am, 3hr., E£1.70). The 7:30pm Baris bus continues on to **Dush,** where the driver lives (3½hr. from Kharga; E£2) and doesn't return until the next morning (6am). Baris pickup taxi drivers will make a special round trip to Dush for E£20 (waiting included), but are sometimes hard to find. Instead of tackling Baris in a day (your road time will total 7hr.), consider doing an overnight. For transportation to Zayan Temple, hop on a pickup or public bus headed for Baris and have the driver drop you off on the way. To return to Kharga or continue on to Baris, walk the 1km to Bulaq and catch a pickup taxi, or wait by the road (bring lots of water). **Hitchhiking** is difficult and dangerous.

You may want to take the **road from Baris to Luxor** to avoid going to Asyut (see **warning** on p. 175)—it's passable and paved all the way, but rough in spots. There is no public transportation, towns, gas stations, or rest stops, but it is an impressive desert drive. During the winter you might be able to find a group to make the E£300 "special" taxi affordable; consult the tourist office and ask around Shoqla Sq., but don't hold your breath in summer. The road pulls its way up the escarpment to rejoin the normal level of the desert and winds through an old dry river valley before penetrating the lush green fields at the Nile's edge.

The 240km road to **Asyut** passes miles of monotonous desert, punctuated only by telephones lines. After several hours, you'll land in the rock quarries, and concrete factories that dot the post-apocalyptic world of Asyut. The **Al Obbur Rest House,** also called the **112km resthouse,** serving water and refreshments, is located halfway to Asyut. The Egyptian government and *Let's Go* strongly discourage tourists from passing through Asyut. If you dare, you can use Asyut as a quick transfer before heading north to Cairo or south to Luxor.

Suez Canal قناة السويس

The strategically located Suez Canal is a miracle of 19th-century engineering based on an 18th-century idea. Napoleon Bonaparte considered digging a canal between the Mediterranean and the Red Sea but feared that the waters of the Red Sea were higher than those of the Mediterranean.Years later, another Frenchman, Ferdinand de Lesseps, came up with a similar plan and persuaded Said Pasha, the *khedive* of Egypt, to begin construction. Excavation started on April 25, 1859 and took ten years to complete. On August 18, 1869 the canal was opened in a grand ceremony attended by over 6000 dignitaries.

Spanning 195km and reaching a maximum depth of 15m, the canal connects Port Said on the Mediterranean to Suez on the Red Sea. Because it allowed for rapid travel from Europe to the Indian Ocean, the canal became a crucial element of the infrastructure of the British Empire. Nasser nationalized the canal in 1956, precipitating a British-French-Israeli invasion (see **The Suez Crisis and the Rise of Pan-Arabism,** p. 53). During the 1967 War against Israel, Nasser blocked the canal with sunken ships. It remained closed through the 1973 War, and was reopened in 1975.

▓ Port Said بورسعيد

Founded in 1860, Port Said (Bor Sa'id) became Africa's gateway to the Mediterranean upon completion of the Suez Canal. Tourist brochures justifiably speak of the European atmosphere of Port Said, a claim that is well-deserved. The city's wide, tree-lined streets and sidewalks make Port Said feel worlds away from the rest of Egypt; you might be in Tel Aviv, Sorrento, or Perth.

Since 1976, when it was declared a tax-free zone, Port Said has developed into a shopping resort for Egyptians cashing in on duty-free deals. The town is saturated with clothing stores containing fashions unseen since the 1970s. Port Said comes alive at night, when the town takes to the streets to window shop, talk, or enjoy the cool breeze and twinkling lights of the canal.

ORIENTATION AND PRACTICAL INFORMATION

By road, Port Said is 343km east of Alexandria and 220km northeast of Cairo. The town is surrounded by water on three sides: the Mediterranean to the north, the Suez Canal to the east, and Lake Manzala to the south. The point at which the canal meets the Mediterranean is Port Said's northeastern corner. **Corniche Street** runs along the sea, and **Palestine Street** follows the edge of the canal. **Goumhouriyya Street** runs parallel to Palestine St. two blocks inland. Another important thoroughfare, **23 July Street,** runs parallel to Corniche St. three blocks inland.

Tourist Office: 5 Palestine St. (tel. 23 52 89), 2 blocks from the southern end of the street. Provides a very good map of the city, but staff speaks little English. Open Sat.-Thurs. 9am-2pm and 4-8pm.

Tourist Police: tel. 22 80 75, 5th floor of the abandoned Post building on Goumhouriyya St. Most tourist police speak very little English.

Currency Exchange: Small offices abound. The most convenient is **Thomas Cook,** 43 Goumhouriyya St. (tel. 33 62 60; fax 23 61 11). Open daily 9am-6pm. **Bank of Alexandria** (tel. 33 87 40), on the corner of Goumhouriyya and El Gabart St. Open 8:30am-2pm and 6-9pm, in winter 5-9pm. **ATM:** Bank Misr on Goumhouriyya St., the block north of Babel St.

American Express Office: Menatours, 18 Goumhouriyya St. (tel. 23 33 76). AmEx services for both card and non-card holders. Will hold mail. Open Sat.-Thurs. 9am-7pm. Closed Fridays.

Trains: Go to the southwest end of Goumhouriyya St. and turn right onto Mustafa Kamel St. The jam-packed station is .5km down, on your left; trains go to **Cairo** (5

EGYPT

Suez Canal

Port Fouad

FERRY TO PORT FOUAD CITY

Mediterranean Sea

← TO DOMIETTA

Port Said Stadium

El Amin St.

23 July St.

Old Corniche Rd.

New Corniche Rd.

Saad Zaghloul Garden

Safia Zaghloul St.

Saad Zaghloul St.

El Nahda St.

Oraby St.

Ferial Garden

Mohammed St.

El-Gomhoriyya St.

Palestine St.

Mahmoud St.

Ramses St.

Hafiz Ibrahim St.

Saleh Salim St.

Salah ad-Din St.

Mustafa Kemal St.

TO CAIRO

Port Said

Beach, 1
El Salam Mosque, 13
Memorial Monument, 4
Military Museum, 3
Palace Gardens, 8
Port Said National Museum, 7
Post Office, 6

Superjet (Buses to Cairo), 11
Telephone Exchange, 9
Tourist Office, 10
Train Station, 12
West Delta Bus Company, 5
Youth Hostel, 2

per day, 4½hr., 2nd class E£6, with A/C E£14); to **Ismailiyya** (5 per day, 1¾hr., 2nd class E£2, with A/C E£6. To reach **Suez,** change at Ismailiyya.

Buses: The **West Delta Bus Company** (tel. 22 68 83) depot is located on Salah ad-Din St., on the northern side of Ferial Gardens, 2 blocks west of Goumhouriyya St. Daily buses to **Cairo** (6am-7pm every hr., E£10-15), **Alexandria** (2:30 and 4:30pm, E£20), **Ismailiyya** (6am-7pm every hr., 1½hr., E£4), and **Suez** (6am, 10am, 1pm, and 4pm, E£9). The **Superjet** bus depot is next to the train station on Mostafa Kamel St., with buses to **Cairo** (7am-7pm, 11 per day, E£15, 3hr.) and to **Alexandria** (daily 4:30pm, 4hr., E£22.).

Service Taxis: Near the train station and the Superjet depot (ask for *taxi ugra*). Run to and from Port Said.

Bicycles: A great way to get around the city. Can be rented on the south side of Hafiz Ibrahim St., between Palestine and Goumhouriyya St. (E£3 per hour).

Pharmacy: Hussein Pharmacy (tel. 33 98 88; fax 33 97 77), on Goumhouriyya St., the block south of Muhammed Mahmoud St. Open 9am-1am. Many other pharmacies line Goumhouriyya St.

Hospitals: El-Delauram Hospital (tel. 22 36 95) is Port Said's best hospital for tourists. The **Et-Tadaman Hospital** (tel. 22 17 90) is the 2nd choice.

Emergencies: Ambulance: tel. 180. **Police:** tel. 122.

Post Office: Southeast corner of the Ferial Gardens. Walk 3 blocks along the canal from the tourist office on Palestine St. Take a left on Muhammad Mahmoud St. and continue to its intersection with El Geish St. For **Poste Restante,** walk south from the post office, take the first left, then walk 30m. Open Sat.-Thurs. 8am-5pm.

Telephones: tel. 22 01 66; fax 325 705, 2 blocks north of the tourist office on Palestine St. Phone cards available for E£15, E£20, and E£30. Direct international dialing (to the U.S., E£24 every 3min.). Fax to U.S. or Europe E£13.65 per page, receiving E£6 per page (open 24hr.). The 4-star **Sosnet Hotel,** at the northwest end of Goumhouriyya St., will connect you to a long-distance operator for an appalling E£2 for 3min., not including call's charge. **Telephone Code:** 048.

ACCOMMODATIONS

Most accommodations in town are either on or just off of Goumhouriyya St. Super-cheap hotels are hard to come by, but there are many midrange and luxury hotels.

Akri Palace Hotel, 24 Goumhouriyya St. (tel. 22 10 13), 2 blocks from the southern end of Goumhouriyya St. Owned by the friendly, Greek Nicolandis brothers. Charming, well-worn rooms have high ceilings, wood floors, sinks, desks, and dressers. Huge balcony doors provide a nice breeze. Singles E£13; doubles E£21; triples E£25. Private bath E£10-13 extra.

Hotel de la Poste, 42 Goumhouriyya St. (tel. 22 96 55 or 99 94). Deserves both of its 2 stars. Clean, well-lit rooms with luxurious private baths, A/C, TV, fan, and fridge. Singles E£24, streetside E£18; doubles E£31, streetside E£25.

Qasr el-Baron Hotel, 2 Deghla St. (tel. 23 23 00), on the corner of Ramses and El Disla St. Comfy rooms with big beds. Red and brown color scheme transports you to the 70s. Most rooms have TV, fridge, phone, and A/C. Groups of 4 can get a 5-room suite. Singles E£33; doubles E£47; triples E£57; quads E£110.

Youth Hostel (HI), Muhammad el-Sayed Sirhan St. (tel. 22 87 02), opposite the stadium. A 20min. walk or E£1.5 taxi ride from the town center. Near the beach amid a number of upscale yet reasonably priced restaurants. Modern and sterile. Dorm beds E£8.70 (6 per room); triples E£14.50 with bath. Breakfast included.

FOOD

Although seafood is the main fare, most restaurants provide options from both land and sea. Dirt-cheap meals are hard to come by, but the extra pounds are well-spent.

Popeye Restaurant (tel. 23 94 94), on the corner of Gourmhouriyya and Safia Zaghoul St. Lively modern restaurant offering all kinds of food. Try the brown rice with shrimp (E£5) and a banana split. Sit on their large, covered patio and watch Gourmhouriyya St. Open 8am-1am.

Pizza Ninja (tel. 23 97 11), at the north end of Goumhouriyya St., near the beach. Excellent Italian-American food, burgers, sandwiches, and salads. The best pizza this side of the canal (E£8 and up). Owner Muhammed learned the art of pizza making in Boston. Open 11am-2am. Free hotel and home delivery.

Haman, on a side street just off Goumhouriyya. With Galal on your left, take a right on the small street by the gas station. Haman will be a few feet forward on your right; yellow and red florescent sign in Arabic. The people standing outside drinking mugs of cloudy beer with a small head aren't patrons of a drive-through Stella bar; they're chugging fresh-pressed sugar cane juice. Sip the 50pt mugsfull into the early morning. Also serves lemonade and fruit juice. Open 8am-1am.

Crystal Restaurant (tel. 33 39 61), on Atef el-Sadat St. near the Youth Hostel. Clean and cheerful. Despite the Christmas and New Year's decorations hanging from the ceiling, Crystal serves good food all year round. Soup, seafood (starting at E£20), and chicken, all with huge salads, will satisfy the hungriest beachgoer. Open 10am-4am. AmEx, Visa, MC. 20% off with GO25 card.

Galal Restaurant, 60 El Goumhouriyya St. (tel. 22 96 68). Standard Egyptian food at reasonable prices. Everything from plain rice to stuffed pigeon (E£8). Seafood dishes for E£15, rice and lentils for E£4; make the most of your money by sitting outside. Ignore or befriend the large plastic crustaceans above your table. Open daily 7am-2am; closed during Ramadan. Visa.

Reana, across the street from the Akri Palace, upstairs from Cecil's. Reminiscent of London or New York, impeccably clean Reana offers slightly expensive Asian food. Chicken (E£18 and up), seafood (E£22 and up), and vegetarian platter (E£13-15) served with cold beer. Open Mon.-Sat. 10am-1:30am, Sun. 5pm-1:30am.

SIGHTS

The **Port Said National Museum,** at the north end of Palestine St., houses an impressive collection of Egyptian historical artifacts ranging from delicate bone needles from the Islamic period to Khedive Ismail's horse carriage, which paraded in the canal's inauguration. It's cool and usually empty, perfect for casual browsing (open Sat.-Thurs. 9am-5pm, Fri. 9am-noon and 2-5pm; Ramadan 8:30am-1pm. Admission E£12, students E£6, camera privileges E£10). Port Said's **Military Museum** (tel. 22 46 57), west of the obelisk on July 23 St., has dioramas of pharaonic and Islamic battles but concentrates on Egyptian victories in the 1973 Arab-Israeli War (open Sat.-Thurs. 9am-2pm and 6-10pm; admission E£2). In front of the museum, the not-so-clean **beach** extends east to the canal. Beach chairs and umbrellas can be rented for E£5, and showers are located every 100m along the beach. If the words "duty-free" make your wallet tremble with anticipation, there's always the **shopping** melee on El Togary, El Nahda, and El Goumhouriyya St.

■ Ismailiyya الاسماعيلية

Once known as Timsah Village, Ismailiyya was named after Ismail, the last independent *khedive* of Egypt. Situated halfway between Port Said and Suez, Ismailiyya is considered the capital of the Suez Canal District. This tiny, tranquil town of tree-lined boulevards is home to a tremendous canal trade and over 50,000 people. Since it sustained heavy damage during the Arab-Israeli Wars of 1967 and 1973, Ismailiyya has been completely rebuilt. Today, one may wander through the quiet streets, relax in sprawling gardens, or swim at the nearby beaches. With few tourist attractions, Ismailiyya remains relatively free of foreigners.

ORIENTATION AND PRACTICAL INFORMATION

Midway along the Suez Canal, Ismailiyya is linked by road and the Ismailiyya Canal to the Delta, and by highway and railroad to Cairo (140km) and Alexandria (280km). While you can't see the canal from the center of town, Ismailiyya's two main streets, **Sultan Hussein Street** and **Goumhouriyya Street,** run roughly parallel to the waterway. **Orabi Square** is in between the two streets, three blocks north of Sala Saleem

St., which forms the town's southern border. Restaurants and shops line Sultan Hussein St.; most offer the free Port Said, Ismailiyya, Suez, & Sinai (PISS) guide, which has an old but useful map of the city. The main bus station is on the busier Goumhouriyya St. **Mallaha Park** stretches along Salah Salem St.

Currency Exchange: The **Bank of Alexandria** is on the eastern side of Orabi Sq. next to Travel Misr. Open Sun.-Thurs. 8:30am-2pm and 6-9pm. An **ATM** is located 3 blocks up the first street on your left. Visa, MC, Cirrus, Plus.

Trains: To **Cairo** (5 per day, 1st class E£11, 2nd class with A/C E£11).

Buses: The station in Orabi Sq. runs buses to **Cairo** (6:30am-6pm every hr., 2hr., E£5-6) and **Alexandria** (2 per day, 4½hr., E£14-17). The **East Delta Bus Company,** in the main bus station on Goumhouriyya St., services **El Arish** (5 per day, 4hr., E£7) and **Port Said** (8 per day until 6pm, 1½hr., E£4) and **Suez** (frequently until 6pm, 1½hr., E£3).

Service taxis: Opposite the bus station, with frequent and fast service to **Cairo** (E£5), **Port Said** (E£3.50), **El Arish** (E£8), and **Suez** (E£3.50). *Service* are faster than the train but hotter and not as safe.

Pharmacy: Ismailiyya Pharmacy, 24 Sultan Hussein St. (tel. 22 93 19). Open daily 9am-5pm and 6:30-11:30pm.

Hospital: 2 private clinics, **Elsafa Hospital** (tel. 22 29 20) and **Karin Hospital** (tel. 22 75 59), serve the area. **University Hospital** (tel. 22 13 95 or 96), on the circular road, also has a good reputation.

Emergency: Ambulance: tel. 123. **Police:** tel. 13. Station is 1 block west of the Governorate Building on Salah Salem St., along the water.

Post Office: In Orabi Sq. Open Sat.-Thurs. 7:30am-6pm; closed holidays.

Telephones: 24hr. office in Orabi Sq. **Telephone Code:** 064.

ACCOMMODATIONS

Ismailiyya Youth Hostel (HI), Omhara Rd. (tel. 32 28 50; fax 33 14 29). Far from the center of town (a 3km hike or a E£1.50-2 taxi ride), but otherwise a great choice. Lake Timsah provides a wonderful setting for this new, spotless 266-room youth hostel. The large patio, sandy beach, volleyball court, and comfy common room make it a backpacker's dream resort. Curfew 11pm. 6-bed dorm E£12.60; doubles E£22.60; triples E£17.60. All but the 6-bed room have private bath. Breakfast included, lunch or dinner E£5. Nonmembers E£1 extra.

Nefertari Hotel, 41 Sultan Hussein St. (tel. 32 28 22), 3 blocks north of Bank Misr. Its Miami Vice decor wins the best-colored hotel award. Bright purple exterior and stairwell. Comfy pale green rooms with A/C and private bath. Each floor has a sitting area and fridge. Singles E£36; doubles E£42; triples E£45.

New Palace Hotel (tel. 32 63 27 or 32 77 61), next to the Bank of Alexandria in Orabi Sq. Small rooms with carpeted floors and high ceilings. TV, A/C, or phone E£5 each. Most rooms have private bath. Singles E£35; doubles E£60; triples E£75. Breakfast E£5.

Isis Hotel (tel. 22 78 21). The cheapest of the budget hotels with a central location. Small rooms with tile floors and pea-green walls. The price is right: singles E£10, with bath E£15; doubles E£15, E£25; triples with bath E£30; quads with bath E£40. Simple breakfast E£4.

FOOD, SIGHTS, AND ENTERTAINMENT

Vendors line the streets with cheap Egyptian fare, but for excellent seafood, try Ismailiyya's sit-down venues. **Nefertiti's,** (tel. 22 04 94), on Sultan Hussein St. south of the Nefertari Hotel, has a cozy, romantic atmosphere. Huge portions of seafood (E£9 and up) and meat (E£15) satisfy the hungriest carnivore. Beer and wine are available (open noon-11pm). **George's Restaurant,** next door to Nefertiti's on Sultan Hussein St. has 47 years of experience to justify the higher prices. Fish, meat, and pasta meals run E£10-30. The owner recommends the fried calamari; if nothing else, pull up a stool at the fully stocked bar. For pizza, pasta, and garlic bread, stop by **Pizza Inn** (tel. 34 08 45) at 41 Goumhouriyya St. Let the A/C cool you down while you munch a 3-cheese pizza (small E£5.75; open daily 10am-2am; free delivery). The **King Edward Restaurant** (tel. 32 54 51), is at 171 Tahrir St. off Sultan Hussein St., one block south of the Nefertari Hotel. Clean, cool, and quiet, King Ed prides itself on its seafood (E£5-45). The rice with curry is excellent; or, try your luck and order "craps" if you don't have them already. For dessert, **Groppi's Supermarket** (tel. 32 82 28), across from Nefertiti's, serves tempting pastries (E£1.25) and a great selection of candy (open Sat.-Thurs. 9:30am-9:30pm; closed Sun. and the 1st half of Ramadan).

The **Ismailiyya Regional Museum,** near the canal at the northern end of town on Salah Salem St., has pharaonic, Islamic, and Roman collections (open Wed.-Mon. 9am-3pm; admission E£3, students E£1.50). Near the museum, the **Garden of the Stelae** contains sphinxes from the age of Ramses II. Inquire at the museum entrance for permission to visit. **Mallaha Park** is worth a frolic with 210 hectares of rare flowers, trees, and palms. **Lake Timsah** (crocodile lake—just a name, not a warning) and the **El Marrz Lakes** are nearby for sunning. **Cinema Royal,** next to the Nefertari Hotel on Sultan Hussein St., shows American and Arabic action films at around 5pm.

■ Suez السويس

Suez (Es-Suweis) is located at the junction of the Red Sea and the Suez Canal. While it may not be the most attractive or exciting of Egypt's cities, Suez is not as bad as most claim it to be. Its residents are friendly and helpful, and Port Tawfik provides an excellent place to watch the canal at work. Nearby **'Ain Sukhna** is quite beautiful; its proximity to Cairo provides a convenient sun-swim-snorkel option. Most travelers pass through Suez en route from Cairo to the Sinai by way of the **Ahmed Hamoli Tunnel** (running under the canal 17km north of town), or on their way south along the Red Sea Coast. Others stay a few days looking for passage on a boat at the Yacht Club.

Orientation and Practical Information El Geish St. runs east-west through the center of Suez, from the **bus station** and across the canal to **Port Tawfik,** where the **tourist office** (tel. 33 11 41 or 33 11 42) is located at the easternmost end of town (open 8am-8pm). The **tourist police** (tel. 33 11 40) share the building. The tourist office provides the somewhat helpful **PISS** guide (Port Said, Ismailiyya, Suez, Sinai) along with a Suez map. For transport within the city, exit the bus station and go behind the row of food stands. **Minibus** drivers will be yelling out their destinations. To travel to and from Port Tawfik, simply flag down a minibus on El Geish. The **Bank of Alexandria,** near the bus station on El Geish, **exchanges currency** (in winter daily 8am-2pm and 5-8pm, in summer 8am-2pm and 6-9pm). If exchanging traveler's checks, be sure to bring the check's invoice. **American Express** services are available for all travelers at **Menatours** (tel. 22 88 21), next to the tourist office in Port Tawfik. The **El Salam Pharmacy** (tel. 22 03 92), at 364 El Geish St. four blocks east of the bus station, is open daily 9am-2am. The **post office** (with **Poste Restante**) is on Hoda Sharawi St., one block north of and parallel to El Geish St. (open Sat.-Thurs. 8am-3pm). Another branch is next door to the tourist office in Port Tawfik (same hours). The **telecommunications office** is about three blocks south of El Geish on the corner of Shohada'a and Sa'ad Zaghloul St. (open 24hr.). The **telephone code** is 062.

Buses shuttle from Suez to: **Cairo** (every 30min. 6am-5pm, every hr. 5-8pm; 2hr.; E£6.50); **Ismailiyya** (every 30min. 6am-4pm, 1¼hr., E£4); **Alexandria** (7am and 2:30pm, 5hr., E£22); **Port Said** (6 per day, last bus 3:30pm, 2½hr., E£9); **Hurghada** (over the Red Sea Highway, 8 per day, last bus 10pm, 6hr., E£22); and **'Ain Sukhna** (6:30am, 10am, and 2pm; 1hr.; E£1.75). Tickets to Hurghada and Alexandria should be reserved a few days in advance. **Service taxis** travel these routes (except for Alexandria) at similar prices (Cairo E£5, Port Said E£7, Ismailiyya E£3, Hurghada E£20). They usually depart more frequently than buses, but don't expect A/C. Six **trains** per day rattle along to **Cairo** (E£1-3) and **Ismailiyya** (90pt), but the coaches are hot and uncomfortable.

Suez is the main launching ground for forays into the **Sinai. Buses** run daily to: **Sharm esh-Sheikh** (7, 11am, and 1:30 and 3pm, 6hr., E£18); **St. Catherine's** (2pm,

6hr., E£18); **Dahab** (11am, 7hr., E£22); **Nuweiba'** (3pm, 4hr., E£25); and **Taba** (3pm, 6hr., E£21). **Uyoun Mussa, Ras Sudr and Hamman Far'aun** can usually be reached on the Sharm el-Sheikh bus—inquire at the ticket office. *Service* drivers charge by the trip, so the more people in the van the less you will pay. Taxis to the Sinai are generally prohibitively expensive. Buses or service are better options.

Accommodations and Food The **Star Hotel,** 17 Bank Misr St. (tel. 22 87 37), has large, clean rooms, all equipped with turbo fans. They will even make your bed in the morning (singles E£14, with bath E£17; doubles E£14, with bath E£21; triples E£21). The **Misr Palace,** 2 Sa'ad Zaghloul St. (tel. 22 30 13), is around the corner from the Star, six blocks east of the bus station. Long, dark, empty hallways lead to clean rooms with private baths. Many rooms have a closed-in balcony bigger than the room itself (singles E£20; doubles E£36; triples E£55; breakfast included). To get to the **Hotel Medina** (tel. 22 40 56), walk three blocks up Tahrir St., take a right, and walk to the next street. The hotel is on the left. Rooms are functional and decently priced (singles E£12, with bath E£15; doubles E£20, with bath E£25). If your budget is extra tight, the **Hotel Haramee** (23 00 51) is six blocks north on Tehrir St., which is seven blocks north of the bus station. Take a right at the "Hotel" sign. Rooms have stained walls and well-used sheets (singles E£6; doubles E£6; triples and quads E£6-10).

Suez's lack of tourist attractions is offset by its excellent restaurants. The impeccably clean **Seaside Restaurant,** 23 Sa'ad Zaghloul St. (tel. 22 32 54), is six blocks east of the bus station and five blocks south. It boasts an upstairs terrace, A/C, and excellent food. Salads and pasta cost E£3 and meat or fish cost E£10-15. Takeout is available 24 hours. For top-notch custom-made pizza rolled, tossed, and cooked before your very eyes, try **El Eltakia** on El Geish St. Look for the small shop with a pizza oven out front, almost opposite Sa'ad Zaghloul St. Pizzas from E£5; open Sat.-Thurs. 1-5pm, Fri. 1-5pm and 7:30pm-1am. Across El Geish St., **Mahmoud Rawash Restaurant** cooks great Egyptian food at great Egyptian prices (falafel E£2.50, *fuul* and pita E£2.50). Take the first right off El Geish St. heading east after Sa'ad Zaghloul St. The restaurant is the second on your right (open daily 7am-1am).

Sights and Entertainment The only monuments in Suez itself are three American-made tanks on the corniche, captured from Israel in 1973. The beach at **'Ain Sukhna** (Hot Spring), 60km south along the Red Sea, rivals those of the Sinai. **Buses** run there early in the day (6:30 and 10am, and 2pm, 1hr., E£2) and return around 1½ hours later (last return bus to Suez around 3:30pm, sometimes earlier). **Service** also run down the coast from Suez to 'Ain Sukhna. The hot spring (35°C), originating in the Ataka Mountains, empties out onto a gorgeous sandy beach, and is a perfect place for swimming or just lying on the sand. Get off the bus when you see the large sign for the **'Ain Sukhna Hotel** (tel. 32 84 88). From the road, walk through the main gate and follow signs for the reception. Day-trippers can pay the E£15 day-use fee for chairs and umbrellas and enjoy the crystal clear water from anywhere on the beach. The mouth of the hot spring is also available for prolonged soaks. The hotel offers an expensive but incredible fish, salad, and hummus meal for E£26. Bring your own food, as there are no other options. Entertainment in Suez can be found at **Ninja Games,** on the corner of Tahrir and Hoda Shaarawi St. This pool hall and video arcade is open daily 10am-2am. Suez occasionally attracts travelers hoping to hop on a private boat that is traversing the canal. This can be an exciting and rewarding way to travel, as Suez attracts yachts en route to all four corners of the globe, but this is nothing more than aquatic hitchhiking. From the moment you set foot on board, your life is entirely in the captain's hands. You should be absolutely comfortable with the boat and its crew before accepting a lift, and remember that the nicest captain on land can turn into Captain Hook on the sea. Two places in Suez are good starting points for aspiring seafarers: the **Suez Yacht and Rowing Club,** in Port Tawfik, and **Prince of the Red Sea Co.,** in Port Tawfik near the post office. Inquire at these two spots about the current yacht situation in Suez. Generally, boats are sailing north to the Mediterranean in the summer, and south in the winter. Experience with boats is extremely helpful for yacht seekers.

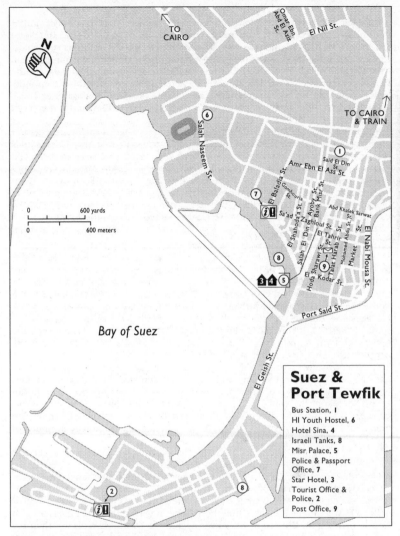

Suez & Port Tewfik

Bus Station, 1
HI Youth Hostel, 6
Hotel Sina, 4
Israeli Tanks, 8
Misr Palace, 5
Police & Passport
Office, 7
Star Hotel, 3
Tourist Office &
Police, 2
Post Office, 9

Red Sea Coast

▨ Monasteries of St. Paul and St. Anthony

The isolated monasteries of St. Paul and St. Anthony lie 30km apart (82km by road) near the Red Sea. These centers of faith, dating from the early Christian monastic tradition, are inhabited by monks whose austere lifestyle differs remarkably little from that of 16 centuries ago. Reaching the monasteries is a serious endeavor without a car, however. A group of seven can hire a taxi from Suez or Hurghada. In Suez, if you deal directly with a taxi driver you should pay E£150-200 for both sites. The easiest way to reach the monasteries is on an organized tour from Hurghada. Most travel agencies organize trips, ranging in price from S£50-100 per person for groups of 4-6.

Another way to reach the monasteries is to join a church expedition. For further information in Cairo, contact the monasteries' administration office (tel. (02) 90 60 25) or the YMCA, 27 El Goumhouriyya St. (tel. (02) 91 73 60). The former sends a car to the monasteries every week. Note that you must have a letter of recommendation from the administration office in Cairo if you plan to stay overnight at either of the two monasteries (tel. 90 02 18), although the monks may overlook this if their monastery doesn't already have many guests. Only men can stay at St. Anthony's; St. Paul's accommodates both men and women. The monks provide food and water (both monasteries are open 9am-5pm).

St. Anthony's is the more interesting of the two monasteries and also the harder one to reach. If you attempt to get there by public transportation, the closest stop is **Ras Za'frana,** about 33km east of St. Anthony's (Deir Anba Anton). From there, you might be able to catch a ride with a Christian family. The closest stop to St. Paul's from a Hurghada-bound bus is by the St. Bola sign. The monastery lies a sweaty 12km walk from the road, but a pilgrim driving by might give you a lift. The best time to hitch is Sunday. Although pilgrims tend to be friendly and catching a ride relatively easy, hitchhiking, especially in the desert, is an inherently risky proposition.

ST. ANTHONY'S MONASTERY

St. Anthony, raised in the Nile Valley, scorned worldly concerns and retreated into the Eastern Desert where he became the first famous ascetic of the Christian Church. Anthony's dramatic move reflected the restlessness that overtook some Christians in the 4th century CE when Constantine made Christianity the official religion of the Roman Empire. This was a disturbing development for many who felt that the church had gained worldly security and wealth at the expense of its spiritual focus. In Egypt, some of these Christians, mostly educated middle-class men, sought to escape the secular world by retreating to the desert where they could pray in solitude and render their lives unto God, rather than Caesar.

St. Anthony suffered paradoxically; his desert hermitages became popular pilgrimage sites, and crowds of the pious and the curious deprived the recluse of precious penitent isolation. Icons of Antonius adorn the walls of many Coptic churches in Egypt. Soon after the saint's death, his disciple St. Athanasius told the story of his choice of poverty and hardship, his wild battles with demons, and his wise counsel to monks and layfolk. Athanasius' *Life of Anthony* became the prototype for much of later Christian hagiography.

A few years after St. Anthony's death, his followers settled at the present site and established the first Christian monastery. The Monastery of St. Anthony served as a refuge for some of the monks of Wadi Natrun when their own sanctuaries were attacked by Bedouin in the 6th century. During the 7th and 8th centuries the monastery was occupied by Melkite monks, and in the 11th it was pillaged by the army of Nasr ed-Dawla. About 100 years after the sacking, it was restored and transferred to Coptic hands. The **Church of St. Anthony** and the southern walls are the only remains predating the 16th-century construction of the present monastery.

With ancient frescoes embellishing each of their sections, Anthony's church and its small chapel are the most impressive parts of the monastery. East of the Church of St. Anthony, the **Church of the Apostles** contains three haikals. During Lent, the monks cantellate the liturgy in the 18th-century Church of St. Mark. As in the Wadi Natrun monasteries, the Chapel of St. Michael is on the top floor of the keep. The impressive library contains more than 1700 manuscripts.

The major religious attraction in the vicinity of the church is the **Cave of St. Anthony,** where the ascetic himself is said to have lived. The vista from the cave, 276m above the Red Sea, rewards the 1½ hours of hoofing and huffing. The best time to climb the mountain is when the sun is relatively low, before 6am or after 4pm. Try to return before dark (or light) and remember to bring oceans of water. St. Anthony's has a small snack shop (soda and cookies) and a gift shop. Donations are requested.

St. Anthony and St. Paul

St. Anthony and St. Paul actually met and became friends towards the end of St. Paul's life. God wanted to reveal the holiness of St. Paul and led St. Anthony to his cave. As the two conversed, St. Paul's crow dropped a *whole* loaf of bread for them. St. Paul, realizing that he was talking to another holy man, told St. Anthony that he was nearing death and asked, as one final request, to wear the robe of Pope Athanasius. St. Anthony immediately departed to fetch the garment. On his return he had a vision of angels carrying St. Paul's soul to heaven. He arrived at the cave to find St. Paul dead. While pondering what to do with the body, two lions descended from the mountain and dug a grave. St. Anthony wrapped St. Paul in the papal robe and buried him. He then carried St. Paul's palm leaf garment back to Athanasius, who sported it every Christmas, Epiphany, and Easter.

ST. PAUL'S MONASTERY

St. Paul (not the disciple) was born into an affluent Alexandrian family in the 3rd century CE. When his father died, he left his estate to young Paul and his brother. This caused instantaneous squabbling between the two and, when the family had heard enough, they were sent off to see a judge. Not on speaking terms, the two young men took separate routes. Paul happened to pass the funeral service of a wealthy man and, for some unexplained reason, was profoundly affected (why he wasn't so moved at his father's funeral no one knows). Like St. Anthony, St. Paul cast off all worldly concerns and, guided by an angel, headed for the hills. He lived in a cave near Mt. Nemra and made his garments from palm leaves and branches. Legend has it his strict ascetic diet of one half loaf of bread per day was dropped to him by a crow; water came from a secret source high in the mountains (which still exists today). These divine provisions enabled St. Paul to live alone for over 80 years.

The original monastery was built on the cave site not too long after St. Paul's death—probably before 400 CE. St. Paul's has been attacked by Bedouin throughout its history, most notably in 1484 when the churches were burned, the library destroyed, and all of the monks killed. Bedouin occupied the monastery for 80 years. After they left, Coptic Patriarch Gabriel VII sent replacement monks to rebuild the churches, but the buildings were destroyed again a hundred years later.

Finally, at the end of the 16th century, Coptic Patriarch Ioannis had monks from St. Anthony's reconstruct and inhabit St. Paul's. These monks were the wisest yet: they built a five-story tower with a drawbridge leading to the fourth story. The first two floors of the tower were for food and water storage and allowed the monks to endure sieges of up to three months.

The monastery was most recently renovated in 1974 but, aside from the electrical generators and guesthouse, it is the same as it has been for centuries. The most impressive part of the monastery is the **Church of St. Paul,** built in the cave where the famed hermit dwelled. Many of the church's 4th- and 7th-century frescoes have somehow survived. Ostrich eggs symbolizing the Resurrection hang from the roof. You can fill your Baraka bottles with holy water coming from the same secret source St. Paul was believed to have lived on.

The monks at both monasteries live much the way they have for centuries, rising early and praying for four hours every morning. They warmly welcome visitors, most in excellent English, and are happy to answer questions. While it's possible to visit one of the monasteries in a few hours, spending the night is interesting.

■ Hurghada الغردقة

Since the early 1980s, when peace with Israel opened Egypt to foreign investors and tourists, scores of resorts have sprung from the sands of Hurghada (pronounced El Erdaha). This frenzy of development has made Hurghada one of the fastest-growing towns in the country. The growth shows no sign of slowing down, and ambitious developers hope that soon the entire 500km between Hurghada and the Sudanese border will be littered with holiday villages. Hurghada offers aquatic splendors, along with a slew of budget accommodations and backpacker-friendly amenities. Luxury yachts and Rolex watches can be spotted on outlying beaches, but *Let's Go*ers occupy the downtown area.

Unfortunately, the beauty of the coastline has been marred by overzealous developers without zoning restrictions. Some oil has been spotted on the public beaches (perhaps oozing from slick shop owners), and streets are lined with shops selling shiny conchs and marine corpses (dried out, stuffed with newspaper, and shellacked). Snorkelers and divers alike have taken a terrible toll on the reefs surrounding the city. Since there are no land attractions to speak of, once the reefs go, so will Hurghada's appeal. "Save the Red Sea" posters are now ubiquitous and strict penalties are supposedly being enforced. Unless drastic changes occur, most experienced divers estimate that within 10-15 years, the tourist boom will move south. Buying shells or coral in the stores is not only a blow to the reefs, but a waste of money—your souvenirs may be confiscated at the airport and you risk serious fines.

Hurghada is oriented more towards getting you in the water than letting you lie beside it. The only clean beaches are private and costly, and dive shops aggressively recruit customers. Better beaches lie farther south and in the Sinai.

ORIENTATION

Paved highways link Hurghada with population centers, but the town itself is remote. 70km north of Luxor in the Nile Valley, it's a barren, mountainous 160km to Port Safaga on the Red Sea coast, and another 50km of coastline north to Hurghada. Suez lies 410km north at the far end of the Gulf of Suez, with Cairo another 130km west.

Hurghada is a typical coastal town, growing along the coast and not very wide inland. Downtown Hurghada (known as **Dahar**) lies 2km north of the **harbor** of **Saqala,** the original fishing town out of which Hurghada grew. Buses and *service* arrive in Dahar, where budget hotels and restaurants await. Saqala has a more authentic Egyptian flavor, with plenty of dive shops and cafes but few budget hotels. South of Saqala, the five-star resorts preside over private beaches.

En-Nasr Road, the main thoroughfare, begins inland from the coastal road and connects the town and harbor. Almost everything you need, from the passport office in the north to the bus station in the south, lies along a 2km stretch of this street. Smaller streets to the east of En-Nasr Rd. contain the budget hotels, restaurants, tourist bazaars, and the **souq,** all separated from the sea by a sandy mound posing as El Afish "mountain."

PRACTICAL INFORMATION

Tourist Office: tel. 54 65 13, 100m before the Mosque at the northern end of En-Nasr Rd., in a shack next to the Ritz Hotel. Well-intentioned but unhelpful advice. Provides mediocre magazine and map. Open Sat.-Thurs. 8am-2pm.

Tourist Police: tel. 54 67 65, Tahrir Sq. in the tourist office shack. Open 24hr.

Currency Exchange: National Bank of Egypt, on En-Nasr Rd., 500m north of the bus station. Open Sun.-Thurs. 9am-2pm and 6-9pm. Nearby **Banque Misr** has an **ATM** (Visa, MC, Plus, Cirrus). Open daily 8:30am-2pm and 3-9pm.

American Express: tel. 54 74 64, on En-Nasr Rd. across from the bus station and slightly north; look for the large "Xerox" sign. Open Sat.-Thurs. 9am-3pm and 6-11pm. Doesn't seem to offer any AmEx services, but employees might drive you to the bank to cash traveler's checks.

Thomas Cook: tel. 44 33 38, on Sheraton St. in Saqala, just south of El Saqala Square. Exchange and helpful travel agency services. Open daily 9am-2pm and 6-9pm.

Passport Office: tel. 44 67 27, on En-Nasr Rd. behind the Red Sea Security Dept. building at the northern edge of town, 2km from the bus station. Provides visa extensions. Open Sat.-Thurs. 8am-2pm.

Airport: tel. 44 28 31 or 37 94, 15km south of town, about 1½km inland. Served by **EgyptAir,** with flights to **Cairo** (daily 8:45am and 7:15pm, E£450) and **Sharm El-**

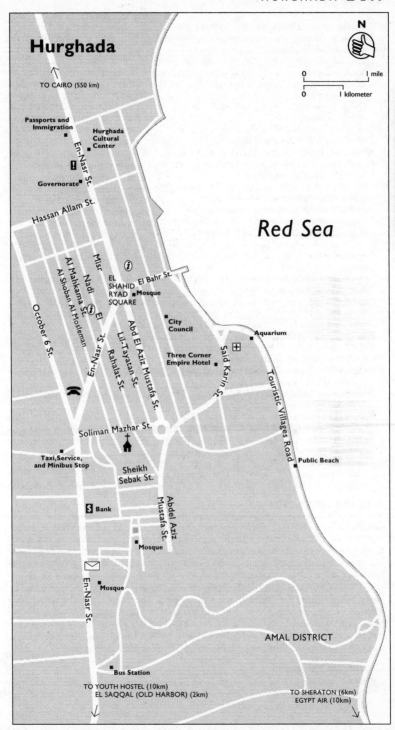

EGYPT

Hurghada

TO CAIRO (550 km)

Passports and
Immigration

Hurghada
Cultural
Center

En-Nasr St.

Governorate

Hassan Allam St.

Red Sea

Misr

Nadi

Al Mahkama St.

Al Shoban Al Mosleman

October 6 St.

En-Nasr St.

El

EL
SHAHID
RYAD
SQUARE

El Bahr St.

Mosque

City
Council

Three Corner
Empire Hotel

Aquarium

Said Karin St.

Touristic Villages Road

Abd El Aziz Mustafa St.

Lil-Tayatan St.

Rahalat St.

Soliman Mazhar St.

Taxi, Service,
and Minibus Stop

Public Beach

Sheikh
Sebak St.

Bank

Abdel Aziz
Mustafa St.

Mosque

Mosque

En-Nasr St.

AMAL DISTRICT

Bus Station

TO YOUTH HOSTEL (10km)
EL SAQQAL (OLD HARBOR) (2km)

TO SHERATON (6km)
EGYPT AIR (10km)

N

0   1 mile
0   1 kilometer

Sheikh (twice a week, E£328). Tickets can be booked through **Karnak Travel** (tel. 54 78 93) across from the mosque on northern En-Nasr Rd. Open daily 9am-9pm. Book flights in advance.

Buses: Upper Egypt Bus Co., En-Nasr Rd., 300m from the southern end of town. Book seats at least 1 day in advance. Standing room may be available at the last minute. Buses to: **Cairo** (9 per day, 6hr., E£35-45); **Suez** (13 per day, 5hr., E£14-16); **Alexandria** (7pm, 10hr., E£37); **Luxor** (noon and 5pm, E£9) or Luxor via **Qena** (7am, 8am, 11pm, E£9; see **warning** on p. 175 regarding travel to Middle Egypt); **Aswan** (4pm and 11pm, E£18). **Superjet Bus Co.,** 50m off En-Nasr, just south of the Mosque at the northern end of town. Buses to **Cairo** (2:30pm and 6pm, E£45) and **Alexandria** (2:30pm, E£70). Book at least 2 days ahead.

Minibuses: Run from downtown through Saqala and south to the resorts (E£1), and vice versa. The best place to catch one is on En Nasr Rd. or the coastal road.

Service Taxis: Off En-Nasr Rd., besides the rotary just south of the phone office. Prices are per car; form a group. To: **Cairo** (5hr., E£500); **Suez** (4hr., E£300); and **Qena** (2hr., E£200; see **warning** on p. 175 regarding travel to Middle Egypt).

Ferries: To Sharm esh-Sheikh from the "New" Harbor (Sun., Tues., Thurs. 9:30am, 6-7hr., E£100). Reserve at least 1 day in advance through a hotel manager, the ferry office in the harbor (tel. 54 69 01) or a travel agent. Keep warm clothes accessible. Soda, tea, and cheese sandwiches sold on board (E£1-3).

English Books: There is a small **bookshop** on En-Nasr Rd. across from the post office. **Aboudi Books,** across from Peanuts Bar, has romance novels and Egypt guides. Open daily 10am-1pm and 5pm-midnight. Visa, MC. Books and newspapers available in most five-star resorts.

Laundry: Most hotels will send your clothes out (E£1-3 per piece). Quality varies. **Stop Shop** (tel. 54 75 28), past the bus station, at the southern end of En-Nasr, offers overnight service (shirt E£2.65). Open daily 7am-11pm.

Pharmacy: Dr. Montaser Rand (tel. 54 48 90), on Abd el-Aziz Mustafa behind Sherry Hand Restaurant and **Mary's Pharmacy** (tel. 54 84 60), on En-Nasr Rd. just south of Bank Misr. Both open daily 9am-1am.

Hospital: The best is **General Hospital of Hurghada** (tel. 54 67 40), on Said Karin St. 200m east of Peanut's Bar.

Emergency: Ambulance: tel. 54 64 90 or 54 67 40. **Police:** tel. 122, on En-Nasr Rd. at a bend in the road 900m north of the bus station.

Federal Express: tel. 44 27 71; fax 44 27 72, on Sheraton St., ½km south of El Saqala Square. Expensive but reliable worldwide express mail. Open Sat.-Thurs. 8am-5pm.

Post Office: En-Nasr Rd., 300m north of the bus station on the right. **Poste Restante, EMS,** and orange international phones. Open Sat.-Thurs. 8am-2pm.

Telephones: En-Nasr Rd., on the left after the road turns at the police station. Open 24hr. **Faxes** (tel./fax 54 88 45) in a hut across from phone office. Open Sat.-Thurs. 8am-2pm and 8-10pm). 1 page fax to U.S./Europe E£14-20. **Telephone Code:** 065.

ACCOMMODATIONS

Hurghada is a piaster-pincher's paradise. You may have to fight off hotel-hawkers insisting you come with them (particularly at the ferry dock) but budget accommodations are plentiful and comfortable. As always, see a room and fix a price before resting bags and body. The hotels near the beach have magnificent views, but the sea air has made some of the managers a little salty with their guests; watch out for spontaneous price inflation. Many of the cheaper hotels work with diving centers and get hefty commissions for the customers they bring. This either means that you'll be strongly encouraged to dive or snorkel or that you cannot stay in the hotel unless you book a trip with them. If you plan to dive or snorkel, check the hotel's prices before taking a room—it is far more convenient to book through your own hotel than through another establishment. All hotels listed below have ceiling fans.

Closest to the beach

Oscar Hotel (tel. 44 84 13), on the coastal road opposite the public beach. Huge rooms with futon beds and the best ocean view in town. Guests relax on the enormous roof. Singles E£12, with bath E£15; doubles E£25, E£30; triples E£32, E£35.

Hotel California (tel. 54 91 01). Friendly owner Abdul is justifiably proud of his hotel. Wall murals and cozy rooms, some with sea views. Singles E£10, with bath E£15; doubles E£20, E£25; triples E£25; sleep on the roof for E£5.

Sea Waves (tel. 54 50 71), across from the public beach behind Sea Oasis Dive Center. Clean rooms, shiny floors; kitchen use. Free local transport for guests. Singles E£10, with bath E£15; doubles E£20, E£25; triples E£25, E£30. Breakfast included.

Luxor Palace (tel. 54 92 60), past the huge 3 Corners Empire Hotel on the right. Ask for an upstairs room with a balcony. Doubles E£15; triples E£25. Breakfast included. Kitchen and washing machine available. May push diving on guests.

Alaska Hotel (tel. 54 84 13), directly opposite the 3 Corners Empire Hotel on Said Karin/General Hospital St. Beware of the "free" taxi from the beach—it's not so free. Clean rooms, constant water. Singles E£10; doubles E£20; E£5 extra for private bath. Breakfast included; E£2.50 off if you don't eat.

Downtown

Happy House Hotel (tel. 44 75 07), on Mosque St. behind the post office. A true home away from home. Owner Ahmed will go out of his way to help you—he's also quite a disco dancer. Great location near both the downtown area and the beach. Clean doubles and triples E£7.50 per person. Free use of fridge and kitchen.

Sunshine House (tel./fax 54 51 13), almost directly across from the bus station. Friendly and knowledgeable Hassan can arrange snorkeling trips (E£40, 10% student discount) and night parties on Geftun Island. Clean separate-sex bathrooms in the hall. The dining room becomes a hangout in the late afternoon. Large 3-bed dorm room E£5 per person; doubles E£15. Breakfast E£2.50.

Shakespeare Hotel (tel. 44 62 56), at the intersection of Abd el Aziz Mustafa St. and Said Karin/General Hospital St. Family atmosphere. Comfortable lounges and fridges on every floor. Clean, inviting rooms, small garden, and lovely pink private bathrooms. Doubles E£35; triples E£45. A/C E£6 extra.

St. George's (tel. 54 82 46), 1½ blocks behind Banque Misr, off En-Nasr St. Charming rooms, fantastic bathrooms, friendly owner. Singles E£20; doubles E£30; triples E£40. E£5 extra for private bath.

Gobal Hotel (tel. 44 66 47), on the corner of Abd el-Aziz Mustafa and Sheikh Sebak St. Clean but stuffy rooms with portable fans and bidets. Free use of beach and pool at Sand Beach. Singles E£15; doubles E£25; triples E£35. Breakfast included.

FOOD

Hurghada's restaurants can keep even the hungriest traveler happy. Most specialize in pasta, fish, and meat, though inexpensive Egyptian food can be found both in Dahar's *souq* and Saqala.

Felfela (tel. 44 24 10), south of Saqala on Sheraton Road, 10min. from Dahar by minibus. This installment of the national chain has the best view in town. Meals to suit every budget and an outside terrace you'll never want to leave. Vegetarian-friendly. *Fuul* (E£2-4), salads (E£2-5), meats (E£12-24). Open daily 9am-12:30am.

Norhan Restaurant, on Said Karin/General Hospital St., between Peanuts Bar and the Shakespeare Hotel. Look for the cheerful green and white awning. Norhan grows its own fresh basil in flowerpots beside the tables—the pungent *spaghetti basilicum* (E£4.75) is delicious. The owner/chef is particularly proud of his fresh tomato soup. Ten varieties of spaghetti (E£6-12). Open daily 10am-12:30am.

Bella Riviera, on Abd el-Aziz Mustafa St., south of the Shakespeare Hotel. One of Hurghada's best deals. Amuse yourself by watching the waiters scamper in and out of the secret door in the wall. Some Egyptian dishes aren't on the menu. Cheap drinks, lasagna (E£3), salads (E£1.25-2.50), and pizzas (E£5-8). A/C.

Pizzeria Tarbosh, Abd el Aziz Mustafa St., after the Shakespeare Hotel. Owner Muhammed loves travelers so much that he'll give you 30% off if you flash this book. Good, cheap eats. 25 types of pizza (E£6.50-15), salads (E£1.75), meat (E£8).

Red Sea Restaurant, in 2 locations: on Said Karin/General Hospital St. and on En-Nasr Rd. A bit pricey, but excellent seafood, pizza, and Lionel Richie tunes. Entrees E£15. Open daily 10am-1am.

EGYPT

Young Kang, by the Gobal Hotel. Solid Chinese food. Huge menu, generous portions (noodles E£8-15.50, chicken E£11.50-15.50, seafood E£17.50-20). Visa, MC.

Zeko's, across from Happy House Hotel. Eat your fill of *fuul* and falafel. Popular with the locals—hence the cheap, non-tourist prices.

Geisum, behind the Geisum Hotel on the beach. Burgers (E£7), *kebab* (E£14), and pasta. Hopefully the large tourists in small bathing suits won't ruin your appetite.

Samos Greek Tavern, Sheraton Rd. (tel. 44 34 84), in Saqala across from the Omar Inn. A little taste of Greece, but only a little—it's mostly meat and fish (E£14 and up). Open daily 10am-12:30am.

Del Mare, on En-Nasr Rd., between the post office and banks. Tasty fish sandwiches (E£2.50-3) and hot dogs.

Omar Khayyan, on En-Nasr Rd., 100m north of the banks. Booze-to-go: Stella (E£5), wine (E£25), gin or vodka (E£55).

SUNKEN SIGHTS

Hurghada's attractions are silent and submerged. Red Sea creatures flabbergast with their array of colors, shapes, and sizes. Buck-toothed trigger fish, iridescent parrot fish, rays with blue polka dots, sea cucumbers, giant clams, and a million others star in this briny show. The shimmering, variegated blues of Hurghada's waters have been spared the terrors of oil exploration (for the moment anyway), and the shifting colors will woo even the sternest terranean (see **Sinai: Underwater Adventures,** p. 248, for important information on snorkeling and scuba diving).

There are a few reefs you can reach without a boat, including one near the Sheraton, but to reach Hurghada's most brilliant aquatic scenery you must take a barge. Hotels offer an all-day trip to **Geftun Island,** usually including two one-hour snorkeling stops near the island and a fish meal prepared on board. Most hotels advertise the trip at E£40, though some charge E£30-35; you may be able to bargain as low as E£25. Some Geftun-bound boats are as crammed as cattle cars and stop only once for snorkeling. Snorkeling from a dive-boat might give you access to better underwater sights but is a little more expensive. The best (and least crowded) reefs are north of Hurghada. The northern waters aren't shielded by islands like the southern ones, so calm weather is a must to go there.

To save money, a group can make independent arrangements with a boat owner—perhaps a fisherman in Saqala—or with one of the sea-trip offices around town. One possibility is to go to Geftun and see different reefs; or, organize an overnight trip (E£60-90 per person, including meals). Excursions to other locales can be less crowded and cheaper. For information, talk to Sayad of **Sunshine Dive Center** (tel. 54 51 13) on En-Nasr Rd., between the post office and bus station, Muhammad of **Red Sea Wonderland,** next to Happy House Hotel, or Jackie of **Sea Oasis Dive Center,** opposite the public beach. Rent your own snorkeling gear (E£10-15 per day for mask, snorkel, and fins) at any office in town. GO25 cards might give you discounts.

While Hurghada may have some of the best **scuba diving** in Egypt, it also has some of the worst dive shops. Sloppy boat handling and careless driving make many dive shops active contributors in the destruction of Hurghada's marine life. Worse still, some shops can be negligent when it comes to their customers **safety**—you wouldn't even want to dive into a **bathtub** with them. Choose your dive shop carefully, and be sure to check your instructor's or guide's certification and experience. Shops that are members of HEPCA, a marine protection organization, are often more environmentally conscious underwater. One well-established and professional (and hence expensive) dive center is **Subex,** in between the Luxor and California Hotels. They offer open water dive certification for US$445; most smaller centers charge $250 for the same. Choose carefully—save your life before your money.

There are a variety of **beaches** to choose from. Public beaches next to the Geisum Hotel and the port in Saqala are the smelliest and most packed. Women will undoubtedly feel uncomfortable here if they choose to bare anything more than toes. Head to the hotels for more liberal bathing fashions. Just north of the public beach downtown, the **Shedwan, Three Corners,** and **Sand Beach Hotel** all open their beaches and pools to non-guests for E£15. **Geisum** charges E£10. A skilled charmer may be able to bypass the fee. Another option is **Shellghada Beach** just before the Sheraton, where E£10 buys a day on their soft sand and use of showers. The **Sheraton** has one of the nicest beaches and will let in for E£11. These beaches can be reached by minibus (E£1 from Saqala) or taxi (E£5-10).

Landlubbers rejoice! Hurghada's underwater splendor can now be enjoyed without even getting your feet wet. Aspiring Captains Nemo can go a couple of leagues under in the **Sinbad Submarine** (tel. 44 46 88). US$50 will buy a seat aboard a real 44-person sub for a one-hour undersea voyage. Reservations can be made at any luxury hotel or over the phone. View some of the same fish from the safety of the **Hurghada Aquarium.** Reminiscent of a pet store, the aquarium houses a variety of fish in small tanks (open 9am-10pm; E£5).

DRUNKEN NIGHTS

Just like the reefs, Hurghada's active nightlife attracts creatures of all shapes and sizes. The bars in town are supplemented by the resorts, which all have pubs, bars, or nightclubs where you can dance like an Egyptian. **Peanuts Bar,** on Said Karin/General Hospital St. in downtown Hurghada, fills up every night. **Scruples** pub and steak house, on En-Nasr Rd. near the center of town, buzzes and pops with neon lights and beer. Rack up a game of **pool** or jive to "world famous" Daoud and his soft-rock cover band at **The Pub,** the Sonesta's hopping joint. The best party in town is on Tuesday night, when people head to **Cha-Cha's** disco for a little boogie wonderland, but be forewarned: the E£30 minimum charge won't cover the cost of two drinks. When the Soviet Union collapsed, it seems as though there was a mass exodus of **slavic dancers** to Hurghada. You can catch the craze, which consists of 4-5 scantily clad Russian women performing everything from the hula to the macarena, at the Hilton (Tues. nights at midnight) and nightly at the Said Beach Hotel. Egyptian dancing can be seen every night in the **Bedouin Tent** (nothing to do with real Bedouin) at the Sinbad Resort. For a E£20 minimum charge, you can sit in the tent all night with brew and *sheesha.* If you've got the money, visit the Ebb Tide **Bowling Center** across the street from the Sinbad Resort, just north of the Sonesta (E£25 per game).

Sinai السيناء

The Sinai is the collision point of two continents, an enormous tectonic summit where the two land masses continue applying pressure to the steep peaks soaring above the Gulf of Aqaba coast. The sandy shelf where mountains meet sea is broad enough to accommodate a highway and a handful of small towns. The rest of the dry, rough landscape is inhabited only by Bedouin. The greatest profusion of life in the region is in the warm waters of the upper Gulf of Aqaba, where a carnival of brilliant coral and fish thrive just offshore.

Travel in the Sinai is unquestionably easier than in the rest of Egypt. Women can comfortably wear shorts and sleeveless shirts in most places, and professional con-artists are rare. You'll never be the only *khawaga* in a restaurant or on a Sinai bus. Although many Bedouin have given up their camels for Camaros, there are still places in the Sinai where travelers can experience their nomadic lifestyle.

HISTORY

The Sinai has had a surprisingly long history of war. Pharaohs' troops trampled the broad plains of the northern Sinai on the march to Syria and Canaan, and marauding, Egypt-bound Hyksos, Assyrians, Persians, Greeks, Arabs, and Turks all trod the same ground. In 1903, the British drew the borders of the Sinai from Rafah to Eilat in an attempt to keep Turkey and Germany a safe distance from the Suez Canal. After the 1948 Arab-Israeli War, this border became the armistice line between Israel and

Egypt. Israel captured all of the Sinai in the 1956 Suez War, but returned it due to intense American and Soviet pressure as well as a United Nations promise to keep the Straits of Tiran (formerly under Egyptian blockade) open to Israeli shipping. In 1967, Israel recaptured the Sinai four days into the Six-Day War. This time Israel refused to return the Sinai and held on to the territory, building a defensive line along the Suez Canal, paving roads, and settling civilians in several places along the Red Sea and Mediterranean coasts. Suddenly, the Sinai was easily accessible to tourists. The new development altered the lives of many Bedouin, who began to give camel tours and help out in hotels. For the first time they had large amounts of cash, and some began to abandon their traditional nomadic lifestyle.

In the 1973 War, Egyptian forces crossed the canal in a surprise offensive to recapture the Sinai. The Egyptian army rapidly broke through the Israeli Bar-Lev defense line, but later Israeli counterattacks recaptured most of the peninsula. Israel retained the Sinai until the land was returned to Egypt in two stages under the terms of the 1979 Camp David accords: the first half in 1979, the second in 1982. U.N. troops stationed in the Sinai monitor the treaty, most visibly at the MFO base in Sharm esh-Sheikh (see **War and Peace: 1970-1981,** p. 56).

GETTING AROUND

The Sinai's major destinations all lie on the Gulf of Aqaba Coast. Towns are located on the single coastal highway, so all you really need to know about getting around is which side of the road to wait on (mountain-side cars go south, beach-side cars go north). The noble machines of the **East Delta Bus Company,** battered cruelly by the rocks, ruts, and dust of Sinai roads, heroically tread the scorched highway. With towns few and far between, separated by mountain passes, it's no surprise that schedules reflect a seldom realized administrator's fantasy. At Sinai bus stations, patience becomes more than a virtue.

A reasonably priced and convenient alternative to buses is the **service taxi.** Weathered old Peugeot 504s piloted by Bedouin cabbies are ubiquitous. You can hop in with other passengers, or negotiate first with a driver and wait while he recruits more travelers to your destination. Women should try not to ride alone with a driver. *Service* are comparable in price to the bus under ideal circumstances, but only with a full load of seven. You'll get to where you're going a lot faster, but this speed has its perils. Traffic laws do not apply; the laws of physics, however bent, are the bottom line here. Prices will drop immediately before the arrival of a bus, then skyrocket after the bus has departed.

This just in: **Hitchhiking** is not recommended, though some find it handy. Keep in mind that you're in the desert, it's dry, and you're a fragile mammal with serious water requirements. Women should *never* hitch alone; all should be wary.

PRACTICAL INFORMATION

A number of **regulations** govern travelers to the Sinai. Unguided travel is restricted to main roads and settlements, but you can visit parts of the desert interior with a Bedouin guide. Sleeping on the beach is prohibited in some areas (notably Na'ama Bay), and the police often harass sleeping backpackers. Since these areas are not always marked, ask around before settling down for the night. Nude sunbathing is illegal, as is the oft-hawked marijuana. You cannot bring a rented car or any four-wheel drive vehicle into the Sinai from Israel.

Prices are higher in the Sinai than elsewhere in Egypt. If you're coming from the Nile Valley, change money before arriving in the Sinai. Food is cheapest at Dahab, and most expensive around Na'ama Bay. Beware the **bottled water black market—** before you pay for Baraka, be sure that the plastic seal is intact (small 75pt, large E£1.50).

Budget **accommodations** are simple, but cheap and abundant. Sheets are not usually provided. In winter, warm clothes and a sleeping bag are advisable. Toilet paper and tampons are now widely obtainable, but it can't hurt to bring your own supply.

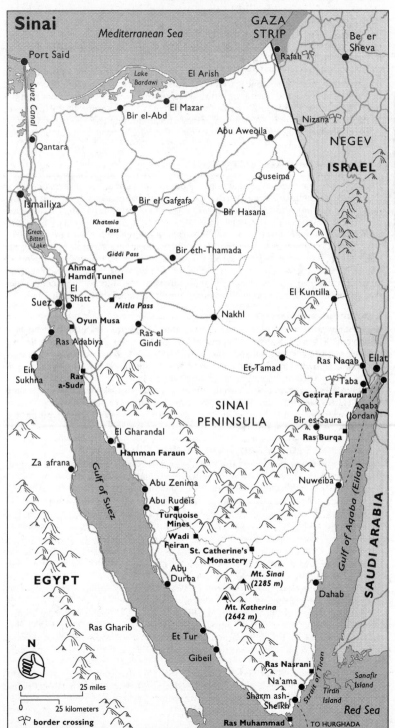

Sinai

Mediterranean Sea

GAZA STRIP

Port Said

Lake Bardawi

El Arish

Rafah

Be'er Sheva

El Mazar

Bir el-Abd

Abu Aweqila

Nizana

NEGEV

Qantara

Suez Canal

Quseima

ISRAEL

Ismailiya

Bir el Gafgafa

Bir Hasana

Khatmia Pass

Great Bitter Lake

Giddi Pass

Bir eth-Thamada

Ahmad Hamdi Tunnel

El Shatt

El Kuntilla

Suez

Mitla Pass

Nakhl

Oyun Musa

Ras el Gindi

Ras Adabiya

Et-Tamad

Ras Naqab

Eilat

Ein Sukhna

Ras a-Sudr

Taba

Gezirat Faraun

Aqaba (Jordan)

SINAI PENINSULA

Bir es-Saura

El Gharandal

Ras Burqa

Hamman Faraun

Za'afrana

Gulf of Suez

Abu Zenima

Nuweiba

Abu Rudeis

Turquoise Mines

Wadi Feiran

Gulf of Aqaba (Eilat)

SAUDI ARABIA

St. Catherine's Monastery

EGYPT

Abu Durba

Mt. Sinai (2285 m)

Mt. Katherina (2642 m)

Dahab

Ras Gharib

Et Tur

Gibeil

Ras Nasrani

N

Na'ama

Sharm ash-Sheikh

Strait of Tiran

Tiran Island

Sanafir Island

Red Sea

0   25 miles

0   25 kilometers

Ras Muhammad

TO HURGHADA

border crossing

EGYPT

Weather in the Sinai can be as extreme and erratic as a stoned monkey. In summer, the mercury bubbles up to 50°C (122°F). Nights are cool in the mountains, but on the coast it's always hot—drink about a bathtub of bottled water every day. Winter is dramatically different—St. Catherine's may see snow or ice. Spring and early summer is **bug season** in the Sinai. Dahab is periodically clouded by mosquitoes and flies with the munchies. Some travelers rig mosquito nets; others claim that sleeping by the beach keeps the bugs away. In summer no one wears or carries much, and it only takes a few days before most travelers begin to reexamine conventions of hygiene and appearance. "Washing" begins to mean nothing more than the first two syllables of a western democracy's capital city. The **telephone code** for all of the Sinai is 062.

UNDERWATER ADVENTURES

Without question, the Red Sea has some of the greatest coral reefs and marine life in the world. All coral reefs from Dahab south to Ras Muhammad are under the jurisdiction of the Ras Muhammad National Park; regulations forbid removing or damaging any material, living or dead, animal, plant, or shell, from the sea. The park is fighting a difficult battle with developers hungry to exploit the region for tourism.

You can do your part to preserve the reefs by observing a simple rule: look but don't touch. Ras Muhammad, like most James Bond movies, has underwater police who will chase you out of the water if they see you breaking this rule. Even accidentally bumping the coral can damage it (and damage you), so try to be graceful underwater. For more information, see **Ras Muhammad National Park,** p. 264.

Equipment and Courses

Snorkeling gear can be rented all over, but **dive shops** are concentrated mainly in Dahab and Sharm esh-Sheikh. You must be certified to rent equipment; most five-day courses provide certification and cost around US$300. Dahab and Na'ama Bay have decompression chambers, but the newest one is in Sharm esh-Sheikh. If you're certified but rusty, you can take a check-out dive for US$35.

Beginning divers should be certain their instructors speaks their language flawlessly. (Little misunderstandings can have big significance underwater: "Tanks!" "You're welcome.") Also be sure the that instructor is certified to teach your particular course, whether it's PADI, CMAS, or NAUII—ask to see his or her card. Some

---

Ten million ways to die. Choose one.

Hidden among the crevices in the reef are creatures capable of inflicting serious injury or death. If you see something that looks like an aquatic pin cushion, it's probably a **sea urchin** or **blowfish,** both of which should be touched only as sushi. Avoid the feathery **lionfish** as well—its harmless-looking spines can deliver a paralyzing sting. The well-named **fire coral** can bloat a leg to mammoth proportions, leaving welts the size of croquet balls. The **stonefish** is camouflaged flawlessly to resemble a mossy lump of coral or rock—step on one, then puff up and die in a few hours. Reach into a hole and a 2m-long **moray eel** will lock its jaws onto your hand. The list is long—before plunging in, ask at any diving shop for a look at one of the cards that pictorially identifies these nautical nasties.

When snorkeling, try to enter the water in a sandy area to avoid damaging underwater plants and animals. If you have no choice but to enter where sea creatures and coral may be dwelling, be sure to wear foot protection. **Sharks** are attracted by blood, so never enter the water with an open wound or if menstruating. Panicking and thrashing tends to excite sharks—if you see one, calmly climb out of the water and casually share the news. Most sharks, however, are not aggressive and wouldn't (even if they could) give you the time of day; most marine animals get aggressive only if *you* have done something threatening or irritating. If you see an animal getting defensive, simply back away slowly, keeping an eye on it at all times.

clubs are active in protecting the reefs, participating in annual clean-up dives, and making sure their operations have minimal impact on the marine ecosystems. The size of the club is also an important factor: larger centers often have more scheduled dives and more extensive facilities, but smaller ones will give you personal treatment and will usually run a course for just one or two people rather than wait for six to sign up. Reputation, quality of equipment, and safety records are important. Ask lots of people, preferably divers.

■ El Arish

El Arish is the capital of the North Sinai Governorate. Once an important stopover on what was perhaps the oldest military route in history, the small north Sinai town of El Arish has since settled down to a more peaceful pursuit: the beach. The sand here is inviting and spotted with palm trees. El Arish is also far less crowded than its more popular cousin, the South Sinai, and its waterfront is cleaner than any other spot along Egypt's Mediterranean coast.

Orientation and Practical Information There are only two roads to know in El Arish: **Fouad Zekry St.,** which runs along the beach, and **Tahrir St.,** perpendicular to Fouad Zekry. The ETA **tourist office,** on Fouad Zekry St. (tel. 34 10 16), is just off the beach (open daily 9am-2pm). Coming from the downtown/Tahrir St. area, bear left at the intersection with Fouad Zekry—the tourist office will be on your right. The exuberant **tourist police** (open 24hr.) share the same building. There are several banks along Tahrir St., including the **National Bank of Egypt** and **Banque Misr** (both open Sun.-Thurs., 9am-2:30pm), where you can exchange traveler's checks, cash, or get a cash advance with a credit card.

The **bus station** is at the far south end of Tahrir St., about 2km from the beach. Buses run daily to: **Cairo** (7am, 4 and 5pm; 5hr.; E£25); **Rafah** (7:15 and 10am; 45min.; E£2); and **Ismailiyya** (1:30, 2, and 3pm; 3hr.; E£8.50). Right next door are the **service taxis,** which charge E£12 to Cairo and E£7 to Ismailiyya. Getting around the downtown area by foot is not a challenge, but a walk to the beach is a bit far. Consider taking either a microbus or a *tut-tut* bus (frequent service, 25pt) or one of the brightly colored Mercedes **taxis.** There are scores of **pharmacies** in the downtown area (generally open 8am-1am). The **Government Hospital** (open 24hr.) is located on el-Geish St. The **police station** is located on the northern end of Tahrir Square, but you're better off paying a visit to the tourist police. The **post office** (open Sat.-Thurs. 8:30am-2:30pm) is two blocks north and two blocks west of Tahrir Square, and the **telephone office** (open 24hr.) is right across the street.

Accommodations and Food Most of El Arish's beachfront hotels are reasonably priced. The **Green Land Beach Hotel** (tel. 34 06 01), on Fouad Zekry St., offers double or triple rooms with fan, fridge, TV, balcony, hot water shower, and breakfast for only E£30. The **Moon Light Hotel** (tel. 34 13 62) is further down, past the tourist office. The hallways are a bit dark, moonlight or no, but the pink rooms are like a cheerful vision of the dawn, and there's a waterfront patio with a superb view of the sunset (singles E£20; doubles E£35; both without shower). The airy **El Salam Hotel** (tel. 34 12 19), is located on Tahrir St., just off the square. The paint is peeling in the drab, no-frills rooms, but the price is right. Ask to be away from the street (singles E£6.50; doubles E£15.50; triples E£21.75; all with shower).

Food in El Arish consists mostly of standard Arabic fare, with the exception of **Maxim's** (tel. 34 28 50), on the beach about 75m east of the tourist office. Hearty owner Sammy serves guests a feast of fresh-grilled mullet, french fries, green salad, *tahina*, and bread for E£25. The only other option along the beach is **Sindebad** (tel. 35 39 02), which has grilled meats, chicken, or fish for E£7-20, and sandwiches for E£2. In town, the best budget meal award goes to **Aziz** (tel. 34 03 45), located next to El Salam Hotel on Tahrir St., which has a variety of grilled foods (E£7-10) and side

---

Smell that Sea Air

El Arish first sprang to prominence during the 13th century BCE when the Pharaoh, Seti I, planned a military course that passed directly through its borders. Later dubbed the "Via Maris," this route became exceedingly important—90% of subsequent invasions in the area used the path. El Arish's status as a military crossroads lured many different people to the small town over the years: there are records of a substantial number of Greeks, Persians, Jews, and Romans who lived and died here. It was the Romans who most likely gave the town its name, calling it "Laris" after the deity Lars. But it was undoubtedly the Egyptian ruler Actisanes (7th century BCE) who provides us with the most interesting etymological lore. This feared authority fell into the practice of sending his captured enemies to a penal colony in El Arish and cutting off their noses as a means of prisoner identification. Thus during the Ptolemaic Period (332-31 BCE) El Arish was known as "Rhinocolura"—the city of severed noses.

---

dishes of rice or noodles (E£3). Across the street is the **Sabri Restaurant,** which serves excellent falafel (E£2).

Sights and Entertainment Activity in El Arish revolves around the Mediterranean. The entire length of the **beach** is pristine, and, except for brief sections in front of the Semiramis and Egoth Oberoi Hotels, there is no difference between public and private. There are a few interesting **Bedouin craft stores** at the north end of Tahrir St. Every Thursday, Tahrir Square comes alive when local Bedouin trade silver, garments, and camel accessories at the weekly **souq.** A few km east of town on the road to Rafah is the **Sinai Heritage Museum,** which details traditional Bedouin life on the peninsula (open Sat.-Thurs. 9:30am-2pm; admission E£2, E£5 for camera, E£25 for video). At night, the entire town comes to Tahrir Square to socialize and smoke *sheesha* in a genial community atmosphere. Less people and more drinks lurk in the **bars** of the Semiramis and the Egoth Oberoi, but they are expensive (Stella E£12).

■ Western Sinai

The Sinai Peninsula's west coast doesn't compare in beauty to the Gulf of Aqaba side. The Gulf of Suez is a much shallower body of water with neither reefs nor rugged peaks hugging the beaches. The Suez coast is dotted with oil rigs and flame-belching smokestacks. If you see this area out the window of the Cairo to Sharm el-Sheikh bus, you have seen enough. Then again, truckloads of Western tourists avoid the Western Sinai, leaving its few attractions unpopulated.

Moses buffs everywhere will be enthralled by **Uyoun Mussa,** 15km south of Suez, where Moses devised an early water purification system with the help of a tree branch. Today there are several circular wells, some of which you can swim in, but it's pretty boring unless you're Moses. Daily buses from Suez can drop you off, but finding a ride back could be dangerously unreliable. If you're set on going, the best option is to hire a taxi from Suez (E£40-50). Be sure to insist on seeing the wells; your taxi driver may deny their existence!

For the advanced seeker of obscure places, **Ras el-Gindi** is a spot 50km inland from Ras el-Sudr that features the ruins of Salah ad-Din's 800-year-old fortress known as **Qal'at el-Gundi,** "the Fortress of the Soldier." If you take the bus to Sudr, you'll have to hire a taxi for E£80-100, so get a group together. Taxis can be found at the petrol station after the turnoff for Sudr. The ruins stand impressively on top of a small mountain (about a 1hr. climb). Bring gallons of water, a camera, and a solid pair of hiking shoes. Be careful, as the path drops off considerably on either side: one misstep and you'll wind up next to your sleeping taxi driver below. Getting back to Suez can be tough; be sure you know the (alleged) bus schedule, and prepare to be stranded. Farther south on the coast you can steep in the **Far'aun Hot Springs,** just off the main highway 80km south of Suez, where you'll also find a nice beach. Though the hot springs and beach are attractive, their location makes reaching them more trouble than it's worth; the beach at 'Ain Sukhna is infinitely more convenient. If you've got your heart set on Far'aun, your best bet is to hire a taxi from Suez (E£100).

More logistical challenges await those who try to get to **Sarabit el-Khadim.** You'll have to rent or hire a four-wheel-drive vehicle and most likely get permission from the military to venture into the desert. Sarabit el-Khadim is the site of an ancient temple, extending over 200m of desert. During the 12th dynasty (c.1900 BCE), a small chapel was dedicated to the goddesses Sodpu and Hathor, "Mistress of Turquoise." Later, in the 18th dynasty, the temple was elongated and expanded. Ramses VI (c.1100 BCE) was the last pharaoh to visit the temple. The stones of the ruins are decorated with religious spells and accounts of mining expeditions. Around the temple are ancient turquoise mines waiting to be explored. This adventure, should you choose to undertake it, takes about three days (two for traveling, one for exploring). The best place to start is the Suez tourist office (see p. 235). They can inform you of the latest regulations regarding travel to this seldom visited site.

■ Mount Sinai

And Mount Sinai was wrapped in smoke, because the Lord descended upon it in fire; and the smoke of it went up like the smoke of a kiln, and the whole mountain quaked greatly.

—Exodus 19:18

The Holy Peak of Mt. Sinai, or, as some locals call it, Mt. Moses (Gabal Mussa), stands 2285m above sea level. The Bible describes a mountain engulfed in fire and smoke that Moses ascended to receive the Ten Commandments while the Israelites built a golden calf at its base. Mount Sinai is one of only two places in the Old Testament where God revealed himself to the people, making the desolate peak sacred for both Christians and Muslims (Jews have not universally identified the modern Mt. Sinai with the promontory made famous in the Bible). In the Book of Exodus, God warned the people, "Take heed that you do not go up into the mountain or touch the border of it; whoever touches the mountain shall be put to death" (Exodus 19:12). This prohibition has long been forgotten—busloads of tourists climb the peak each day. God should have included an 11th commandment: "Give a hoot, don't pollute!" Many climbers leave trash on the trail and on the peak. Despite the Baraka bottles and the crowded summit, the view from the top is as inspiring as it must have been ages ago.

The hike to the top is challenging but certainly not impossible. You should leave all but the bare essentials behind. The monks of **St. Catherine's** will allow you to leave your bags in a room for E£2 per piece. The **Steps of Repentance,** the shorter of the two paths up (about 2hr.), is the more difficult route. It is said that the 3750 steps were built by a single monk in order to fulfill his pledge of penitence. The monk cut corners here and there (who could blame him?) and made many of the steps the height of two or three mortal ones. The steps are treacherous by night; if you arrive after dark they will be difficult to follow even with a flashlight. Save them for the descent in the morning.

The other route, a **camel path** carved in the 19th century (at night about 2½hr. by toed foot, 1½hr. by cloven), begins directly behind the monastery. Camel rides up the mountain usually cost E£30 during peak hours, but if you can stand the sun and the heat, you can get a ride up in the middle of the day for the low price of E£10. Unfortunately, the camels are not always available when you need them—you may arrive at the dispatch area and find only dung.

To find either path, walk up the hill to the monastery, bear left at the fork, and continue to the back of the monastery structure. The path continues for 100m or so, until you reach a graphic sign at a fork in the path indicating "camel" or "steps." One juncture that usually confuses hikers is almost at the top, when the camel path intersects with the steps, soon after passing through the camel path's narrow, steeply walled

---

Holy Mt. Serbal?

In some religious circles, the debate still rages over whether Mt. Sinai is actually the site where Moses received the Ten Commandments. Though most believe that Mt. Sinai is the mountain referred to in the Bible, there are those who maintain that the actual site is Mt. Serbal, twenty miles to the west of Mt. Sinai. According to most biblical scholars, however, the Mt. Serbalists are fighting a losing battle. The Bible mentions three characteristics of the mountain in question: it is surrounded by a vast plain, the summit is visible to all below, and it is accessible to all who surround it. All three describe Sinai, none Serbal. Furthermore, it is doubtful that the Israelites would have chosen to camp for a year in the valley beneath Mt. Serbal, which is the site of fierce floods, little drinking water, and hordes of mosquitoes. Besides, nobody wants to tell 18 generations of pilgrims that they've been climbing the wrong mountain.

---

stone corridor. Turn left to reach the summit. The camel path stops here. Riders will have to get off their high humps and huff up the rest of the way.

If you turn right at the juncture about two-thirds of the way up, you'll arrive at a 500-year-old cypress tree dominating the depressional plain known as **Elijah's Hollow.** Here the prophet Elijah is said to have heard the voice of God after fleeing the wrath of Jezebel (I Kings 19:8-18; see also **Muhraqa,** p. 362). Two small chapels now occupy the site, one dedicated to Elijah and the other to his successor Elisha. Moses supposedly hid in the cave below when he first came face to face with God: "while my glory passes by, I will put you in a cleft of the rock, and I will cover you with my hand until I have passed by" (Exodus 33:22). The chapel is almost always unattended and closed in the afternoons, but is usually open immediately after sunrise for one to two hours. You can still see the watering hole used by the prophet.

Most people choose to begin their climb (via the camel path) around 2am. You can enjoy the cool night and catch the sunrise at the top. The modern invention of the flashlight takes on a mystical quality here. Pilgrims, Bedouin, and grungy travelers are briefly united as the separate beams of lights form a trail slowly zigzagging up the mountain. Unfortunately, the unity and charm is lost once the anonymous lights become dreaded crowds at the top.

An excellent option is to hike when it's still light, watch the sunset, and sleep on the summit. Socialites can stake out a spot directly on the summit platform by the tea and refreshment stands; this becomes a zoo station in the early morning hours. You can find a secluded spot by carefully picking your way through boulders and human feces down the sloping shoulder to the west. Walk about 40m until you cross a ravine; the small summit ahead has several campsites protected by stone windbreaks. Don't try this at night; **cliffs** loom on every side. You can beat the crowds by sleeping in Elijah's Hollow or climbing at mid-day (not recommended in summer).

Overnighters should bring ample food, and everyone should bring enough water for the ascent (2-3 bottles). The cheapest place to buy food and water is in the supermarkets in the town of St. Catherine's. The monastery **rest house** also sells snacks and water at reasonable prices. There are refreshment stands on the way up, but prices increase with altitude. A stand on the summit sells tea (E£2), water (E£4), and various snacks (E£3-5). If you plan to spend the night on the mountain, bring a **sleeping bag** and warm clothes. Even in the summer, it's often 8-10°C at night and the breeze makes it feel much colder. Those without the necessary gear can rent blankets (E£2.50) and mattresses (E£5) at the top. There are also "toilets" at the summit (holes in the ground with little privacy and many flies). Hikers should bring a warm change of clothing—sweaty shirts quickly turn to frozen shirts. You don't need a guide. Neither men nor women should hike alone, especially at night—should you injure yourself, you don't want to be like Moses and sleep alone in a cave.

■ Saint Catherine's

The region's rich history of monasticism started in the 3rd century CE when Christian hermits, attracted by the tradition designating the valley below as the site of the **Burning Bush,** migrated here in a quest for holiness and freedom from Roman persecution. Living in complete poverty and isolation (except on holy days, when they gathered at the Burning Bush), these hermits often fell victim to harsh weather and raiding nomads. In 313 CE **Constantine the Great** officially recognized Christianity, and soon after the monastery was founded by Constantine's mother, Empress Helena. The first permanent structure was erected in 330, when Helena built a small church and a tower at the site of the Burning Bush. Around 530 CE, **Emperor Justinian** ordered a splendid basilica within a walled fortress to be constructed on the top of Mt. Sinai. When Stephanos, Justinian's trusted architect, found the mountain's peak too narrow, he built the **Church of the Transformation** next to St. Eleni's chapel instead. The peeved emperor ordered Stephanos's execution, but the builder lived out his days in the safety of the monastery and achieved sainthood. His bones are in the ossuary. The monastery has thrived for the ensuing 1400 years, continually protected by the rulers of the day (including Muhammad and Napoleon). As a tribute to the monks' tradition of hospitality to Christians and Muslims alike, it has never been conquered.

Today, pilgrims and curious tourists of all faiths visit St. Catherine's throughout the year. Though much of the monastery is closed to the public, its beautiful architecture, nestled amidst the surrounding mountains insures an unforgettable visit. The monastery is closed Fridays, Sundays, and frequent holidays (see **Sights,** below).

ORIENTATION AND PRACTICAL INFORMATION

Saint Catherine's monastery is hidden away, at an elevation of about 1600m, in the mountainous interior of the southern Sinai. Excellent roads run west to the Gulf of Suez and east to the Gulf of Aqaba, both about 100km away. Tiny St. Catherine's town lies about 3km east of the monastery.

If you're going straight to St. Catherine's, ask the driver to let you off on the road to the monastery. From there, the monastery is a 20-minutes walk. Otherwise you'll be deposited in the town, which, despite its size, boasts a number of modern conveniences. The **bus station** is at the main square (it's not a "station" per se, but a point in space where the bus is assumed to stop). On one side of the square is an arcade with a **Bank Misr** which exchanges money or traveler's checks and where you can withdraw cash on your Visa card (open Sun.-Thurs. 8:30am-2pm and 6-9pm, Fri. 9-11:30am and 6-9pm, Sat. 10am-1:30pm and 6-9pm). The **tourist police** (open 24hr.) and a **hospital** (tel. 47 03 68; 24hr.) are opposite the bus station. Within a stone's throw of the mosque are the **post office** (open 8am-3pm) and the 24-hour **telecommunications office** with **telegraph** and **international phone** service. The **police station** (tel. 47 03 13) is farther up the hill.

Buses frequently skip one, even two, days at St. Catherine's. Prepare to be stranded if you are not willing to pay the price of a *service.* That said, buses are supposed to leave daily for **Cairo** (11:30am, 9hr., E£35), **Suez** (11:30am–Cairo bus, 6hr., E£25), and **Sharm el-Sheikh** (1pm, 3hr., E£18) via **Dahab** (1½hr., E£10). **Taxis** are always available, but the price is entirely dependant on both the number of people and the bus schedule. Popular destinations are Dahab (E£90 per car) Sharm el-Sheikh (E£200 per car) and Cairo (E£275-300). Lone women should generally avoid them. Taxis hover around the central square during daylight hours; ask at the market if you don't see any. Intimidate the driver by growling or hissing while you bargain.

ACCOMMODATIONS AND FOOD

The cheapest and most popular choice in the area is free **camping** on Mt. Sinai's cool peak. The nearest budget alternative is the monastery's **youth hostel** (tel. 47 03 43). To get there, turn right at the fork just before the monastery. The clean but cramped rooms are within earshot of the monks. The location alone is worth the price (7-8 person dorm bed E£35; 3-4 person dorm bed E£40). Dinner and breakfast are included, and lunch is free if you stay two nights. Reservations are recommended if you are arriving after 11pm or in August or April.

A cheaper option, though farther from the monastery, is the **Alfairoz Hotel** (tel. 47 04 46). To reach the Alfairoz, walk out of town towards the monastery and take your first left. The hotel, surrounding a giant sandy lot, is a five-minute walk away and has an incredible view of the surrounding mountains. For E£5 you can pitch your tent in the sand courtyard, or for E£12 you can join the other sardines in the 10 person dorm room. There are also rooms with private baths available (singles E£50; doubles E£60; triple/quad E£70). The **Green Lodge Camp** (tel. 47 00 80) is 10km east of the monastery. After climbing Mt. Sinai, you can lounge in their pillowed courtyard, where they have nightly fires in winter. A free ride to and from camp is often available; check in their office two doors away from the post office (2 person tents for E£11; dorm bed in 5-person room E£21; breakfast E£5; lunch or dinner E£12).

Gift shops, supermarkets, and **restaurants** serving spaghetti or rice and chicken (E£5-8; open 8am-11pm) surround the bus station. The restaurants are virtually identical, offering hearty food with a side order of flies. Some of them will even cook food you've purchased from a supermarket. Opposite the mosque is a traditional brick-oven **bakery,** where the price of pita is constantly negotiable.

SIGHTS

Saint Catherine's Monastery is believed to be the oldest example of unrestored Byzantine architecture in the world. Once the hoppin' home of hundreds of monks, the monastery's population has dwindled to a handful. The remaining monks, members of one of the strictest orders, never eat meat or drink wine, and wake up at 4am each morning when the bell of the **Church of the Transfiguration** is rung 33 times.

If you see one of the monks wearing boots and spurs, don't be surprised; one of the order hails originally from Texas, U.S.A. Both St. Helena and Justinian dedicated their structures to the Virgin Mary, since Christian tradition asserts that the Burning Bush foreshadowed the Annunciation. The main church became known as the "Church of the Transfiguration," owing to its spectacular almond-shaped mosaic depiction of this event in Jesus' life. The complex was named St. Catherine's Monastery after the body of the martyred Alexandrian evangelist was miraculously found on top of Gabal Katerina, to the south. About to be tortured on a wheel of knives for converting members of the Roman emperor's family, Catherine was miraculously saved by a malfunction in the wheel. Unfortunately, they slit her throat anyway. Her body showed up centuries later on top of the isolated mountain. In the 7th century, Muhammad dictated along document granting protection to the monastery and exempting it from taxes; a copy of this document still hangs in the icon gallery, near a similar letter penned by Napoleon in 1798.

The monastery possesses many treasures, including over 2000 exquisite 5th-century **icons.** The icons with brushed gold halos have a near holographic effect—an artistic style unique to the Sinai. Just as impressive is the monastery's **library,** which contains over 8000 books and manuscripts. So precious is the collection that it is said to be second only to the Vatican library in terms of both numbers and value of the texts. The monastery is currently working on copying its world-renowned collection onto microfiche so it will be accessible to scholars everywhere. It's an expensive project, but they're receiving Princely support from Charles.

Unfortunately, only the central nave of the Church of the Transfiguration is open to the public. On tiptoe you can see mosaics of a barefoot Moses in the **Chapel of the Burning Bush,** behind the altar. Should you manage to visit the icons back there, you'll have to remove your shoes, as the roots of the sacred shrub extend under the floor. Such privileges are only accorded to true pilgrims, who are traditionally allowed to ask God for one favor. The monks themselves, with the help of the local Gabaliyya Bedouin (descended from Byzantine slaves), built a **mosque** within the fortress walls to convince advancing Ottoman armies that the complex was partly Mus-

The Manna Mystery

"The quails came up and covered the camp: and in the morning…when the dew that lay was gone up, behold upon the face of the wilderness there lay a small round thing, as small as the hoar frost on the ground. And when the children of Israel saw it, they said one to another, it is manna…" (Exodus 16:13-15).

The quails and manna mentioned in the Bible have mystified people for years. In *The Bible as History,* Werner Keller recounts the findings of botanists and environmentalists who discovered that Biblical quails are the same birds that Bedouin eat today. The birds migrate from Africa to Europe and often stop in the Sinai to gather energy for their next flight. Worn out from their journey, they can be caught by hand. The curious manna has nothing to do with birds—the sweet seed-like food which fueled the children of Israel is actually a secretion from an insect that invades Tamarind trees. The Bedouin still collect manna, a tasty addition to their diet.

lim. The gruesome **ossuary,** a separate building outside the walls, houses the remains of former monks (bishops have special niches in the wall—the skeleton in black vestments is Stephano's). A **gift shop** sells books on the monastery's history for E£8 (modest dress required to tour the complex; free).

Entering the monastery may pose a challenge (open Mon.-Thurs. and Sat. 9am-noon; closed on all Orthodox holidays—in 1998: Jan. 6, 7, 14, 19, March 2, 3, 4, April 7, 16, 18, 20, June 8, Aug. 19, Nov. 14, and Dec. 8). For information call the monastery's Cairo office (18 Midan el Daher, 11271 Cairo; tel. 48 28 513; fax 48 25 806). A good plan is to spend the night on the mountaintop, watch the sunrise, then hike down at 7am and reach the monastery just as the doors are opened (by doing this you'll also avoid the crowds). To get to the monastery from the access road, continue straight past the tourist police for about five minutes until you get to a fork in the road, then bear left and continue until the monastery is on your right. To reach Mt. Sinai's trail head, continue past the monastery to the rocky path behind it.

■ Exploring the High Sinai

If the climb up Mt. Sinai is too tame, the path too littered with Baraka bottles, and the top too crowded and touristy, there is an escape. You are, after all, in the heart of a desert that extends for 60,000 sq. km and surrounded by a natural world vastly different from the tour bus pasture known as St. Catherine's. *Wadis,* shrouded in misty heat, lead in every direction, snaking their way through and around mountain ranges, lush oases, and Bedouin homesteads. Many of the more appealing sites, such as the oases, are as yet untouched by the wear and tear of tourism.

These hikes are not easy, but you can tell your guide what pace you wish to go and he will accommodate. You should also consider the weather—spring and fall are nicest. In summer you may spend a lot of the day resting in the shade with the Bedouin until the sun calms down, and in winter you'll freeze. The nights are more constant: they're very cold year-round. You may be able to rent blankets from the Bedouin, but don't count on it; bring warm sleeping bags. The area has yet to be declared a National Park, but it should be treated as such anyway.

To venture into of any of the mountains besides Gabal Mussa (Mt. Sinai), you must be accompanied by a Bedouin guide and you must have a regular **Egyptian tourist visa**—the Sinai only visa won't do. **Sheikh Moussa** (tel. 47 04 57), the head of Mountain Tours, has a monopoly on all the mountains, and every trip must be arranged through him. You are required by law to leave your passport with Mr. Moussa; he will notify the army of your whereabouts. To get to his office in St. Catherine's town, walk uphill from the town square and past the petrol station. Take your first right and walk for three minutes; Mr. Moussa will most likely be lounging outside.

The Sheikh will procure both a guide and a permit for you. The price is E£80 per day, regardless of the number of people. The ideal group is three to five people, though Moussa will accommodate groups of any size. Extra camels can be rented to haul your gear around (E£40 per day), and surplus gear can be stored in Sheikh Moussa's house. You'll leave for your hike within an hour of arriving at Sheikh Moussa's, making just one stop at the supermarket in town to buy food (E£30 per person per day). Buying food with your guide guarantees these extra cheap prices. There is a wide range of desert landscapes to choose from: mountain springs, pools, secret gardens, or apricot and berry trees. You and your guide will camp with the Bedouin, so be prepared for long nights by the fire, smoking "Bedouin tobacco," drinking tea, and learning a great deal about a little-known culture.

Tell Sheikh Mussa what you want to see and at what pace you'd like to travel, and he'll come up with a tailor-made itinerary. The following are some possibilities:

Gabal Banat: A mountain north of the town of St. Catherine overlooking a vast desert landscape. 2 days.

Gabal Bab: From this peak you can see west all the way to the Gulf of Suez. 2 days.

Gabal Katherina: The highest mountain in Egypt (2642m). The path to the top is more difficult, secluded, and beautiful than Mt. Sinai's highway. A chapel replenishes you with shade at the summit. 6km south of Mt. Sinai. 11hr. roundtrip.

Gabal Abbas Pasha: A rock with a ruined palace and excellent views. 2 days.

Gulat el-Agrod: A deep, crystal clear mountain pool for swimming in the shade of overhanging trees. You can dive off of the surrounding rocks. 3 days.

Wadi Talla: There are two, a big one and a small one. Go to the big one for some swimming in spring-fed pools. 3 days.

Wadi Nogra: A rocky valley with a natural dam (Nogra Dam). The water trickles off moss-covered boulders to form a natural shower. By the time you get there, you'll need it. 3 days.

Sheikh Owat: A picturesque oasis with a few tall palm trees, a deep well, and a lot of goats. 3 days.

Farsh Romana: A good campground equipped with showers! On the way to Gabal Banat. 2 days.

Wadi Feiran: An amazingly lush oasis 50km west of St. Catherine's Monastery; Islamic tradition holds that Hagar fled there when banished from Abraham and Sarah's camp. Today there is a nunnery in the center of the valley. The best way to get here is by taxi from St. Catherine's (E£70 roundtrip). Although buses to and from Cairo pass by, the schedules are unpredictable, and you might get stranded.

You'll feel like an ancient Israelite who has been wandering for 40 years as you climb mountains and see for miles, like a Bedouin as you descend into walled gardens and sleep outside stone huts, and like a pack animal as your bag turns your legs into noodles. Your trip will be a lot more enjoyable if you remember to bring a few **necessities:** a solid pair of hiking shoes or sneakers (no sandals), a warm sleeping bag, lip balm, sunscreen, bug spray, a flashlight, a good pair of socks, a basic first aid kit, toilet paper, matches, plastic bags (to take your trash out of the desert), a swimsuit, a hat, water purification tablets (some tourists drink from the mountain springs every year with no problem, but considering the number of animals in the area, you should purify), and a few pounds for the Bedouin who will offer you their undying hospitality. Sheik Moussa will provide all the necessary cooking equipment. Note that a onenight trip costs as much as a two-day trip, a two-night trip, three days, etc.

Organized tours can be arranged in Israel through **SPNI. Neot Ha-Kikar,** an Israeli travel outfit, specializes in Sinai tours (offices in Tel Aviv, Jerusalem, and Eilat), with trips beginning in Eilat and Cairo (6-day high range circuit US$360). No matter where in Israel you book your tour, you'll eventually end up at Sheikh Mussa's office. You'll save a lot of money by starting there, too.

■ Sharm el-Sheikh شرم الشيخ

No one comes to Sharm el-Sheikh for the sights, though with the dozens of wrecking balls, cranes, and half-finished buildings, there is ample opportunity to see ruins.

Sharm, like the rest of the Sinai coast, is in the middle of a building boom. Sharm el-Sheikh and Na'ama Bay are often called twin resorts, but they are far from identical. Na'ama got the good looks and good-looking travelers, Sharm got the big boats and big buildings. Wealthy Italian and German vacationers fill the four- and five-star hotels, but most backpackers head elsewhere. There is no beach, and the tiny bay is crammed with dive boats attracted by the calmness of the water. Those in search of excitement should head north to Na'ama.

Practical Information Sharm el-Sheikh is a transportation hub. The **ferry** to Hurghada leaves here three times weekly (Mon., Wed., and Sat. 11am; 7hr.; one-way E£100) from the port just south of Sharm-el-Sheikh. From the Sharm Marina, keep walking around the harbor and over the hill at the southern end. Book tickets a day ahead, either through a hotel or at Thomas Cook (tel. 60 18 08), 50m south of the Pigeon Huurc Hotel. **Buses** leave daily for **Cairo** (7:30, 10:30am, 1, 2:30, 6:30, 10, 11pm, and midnight; 7hr., E£45-65); **Suez** (7, 9, and 10am; E£20); **Taba** (9am, 3hr., E£15); **Nuweiba'** (9am, 2hr., E£12); **St. Catherine's** (7:30am, 2½hr., E£20); and **Dahab** (6:30, 9am, 2:30, 5pm, midnight; 1½hr., E£8-10). Most buses leave from behind the Mobil station between Na'ama and Sharm el-Sheikh, though some leave from Sharm itself—check ahead of time to be certain. An **Egypt Air** office (tel. 60 10 56) is south of the bus station.

At the top of the hill, next to the post office, are two banks for **currency exchange.** The **Bank of Alexandria** allows money withdrawal with MC/Visa (open 8:30am-2pm, 6-9pm, in winter 5-8pm). Or try the **National Bank of Egypt** (open Sat.-Thurs. 8:30am-noon and 6-9pm). The **tourist police** (tel. 60 03 11; open 24hr.) and **police station** (60 04 15) are 300m from the banks. **Diving World Dive Club** (tel. 60 01 66) is across from the yacht jetty. The **Pharmacy Sharm-el-Sheikh** is in the same complex as the post office (tel.60 03 88; open 9am-1am). The **Pharmacy Nadaa** is at the bottom of the hill, in the shopping center across from the Barcude Hotel (open 9am-2am). The **post office** (tel. 60 05 18), with **Poste Restante** and **EMS,** is at the top of the hill and to the right (open Sat.-Thurs. 8am-2pm). The **Hyperbaric Medical Center** (tel. 60 09 22 or 3; **ambulance** 60 05 54) is reliable. The **telephone office** (tel. 60 04 00; open 24hr.) is 300m from the banks, near the tourist police. Sharm el-Sheikh's **telephone code** is 062.

Accommodations If there is room at Na'ama Bay there is absolutely no reason to stay in Sharm. If you must, the cheapest place is the **Youth Hostel,** at the top of the hill and to the left (from the bus station, follow the signs for the Cliff Top Hotel). Beds in a high school atmosphere cost E£18.60 (E£19.60 for non-members; breakfast included). Gates close at 11pm, and 10pm in winter. Another option is the **El Kheima Hotel** (tel./fax 60 01 66), next to the Diving World Dive Club. Be sure to tell them that you *only* want bed and breakfast, or they'll charge double and include dinner (bungalow singles E£45; doubles E£61 with portable fans; breakfast included). A last resort is **Safetyland** (tel. 60 03 59; fax 60 03 73), located at the bottom of the hill, at the intersection of the road leading to Na'ama Bay and the road leading to the Sharm bus station. They have stuffy thatched bungalows situated in a what looks like a construction site (reception open 24hr.; open tent sites E£16 per person; singles E£43; doubles E£66; breakfast included).

■ Near Sharm el-Sheikh: Ras Muhammad

Sticking out into the Red Sea at the tip of the Sinai peninsula, **Ras Muhammad National Park** is the most famous dive site in Egypt and arguably the most spectacular in the world. The tiny neck of land is bordered on the west by the Gulf of Suez and on the east by the Gulf of Aqaba (park open daily 8am-5pm, strict closing time; US$5 per person, US$5 per car).

Above sea level, the park is brown, rocky, and apparently lifeless, but below the surface, life flourishes in vivid splendor. Deep red and purple fans gently wave while brilliant yellow, turquoise and orange fish wander in the warm, clear current. The waters of Ras Muhammad contain over 1000 species of fish. Many species are unique to the Red Sea, and one species of shrimp is found only within the boundaries of the park. In the 80s, it became clear that tourist and fishing traffic was destroying the underwater treasures of Ras Muhammad; the Egyptian government established this park in 1983. The underwater habitat is very fragile and most of it is closed to the public. In a good year, coral may grow only 1cm. It is against Egyptian law to remove any material, living or dead, from the park. Picking up coral may hurt you as well as the environment—the creatures are surprisingly sharp (for underwater warnings, see **10 Million Ways to Die,** p. 248). Diving, snorkeling, and swimming are only permitted in specified areas, mostly around the very tip of the peninsula.

The park is accessible by boat and taxi (E£100), although you'll have a lengthy surface swim to get to the wall reef. On rough days, snorkeling at Ras Muhammad can be difficult. The park is beyond the jurisdiction of a Sinai-only visa, so you need your **passport** and a full **Egyptian tourist visa** to go there. Dive shops run trips to the park, and you may not need a full visa if you stick to their boats and hotels. Camping is permitted in designated sites—check with the park visitor center for details. Further information on the park is available from its Sharm El-Sheikh **info office** (tel. 60 05 59) and from the Cairo branch (tel. 34 06 777).

■ Na'ama Bay

One of the diving meccas of the world, this hamlet of five-star resorts is the center of Egypt's anti-backpacker sentiment. If you look nice and clean (and act like you own the place) you can freely roam the waterfront shops and hotels. But as soon as you don your most recently purchased apparel from Dahab or strap on your backpack, you invite stares along the promenade and may be barred from certain areas. Most of the beach is owned by five-star hotels—as you stroll along the promenade, you'll cross from Hilton land to Marriott country. Nevertheless, many budget travelers flock here each year. They are drawn by the world-class diving and snorkeling and the nightlife, which is perhaps the most active in the Sinai. It is sometimes possible to get a **job** at a hotel or dive center. The pay is not very high, but it's enough for food and entertainment (if you work for a hotel, you usually get free accommodations; if you work at a dive club, you get free diving lessons or courses). Knowledge of Arabic is not necessary but French and Italian are helpful.

PRACTICAL INFORMATION

Na'ama Bay is a long strip of hotels on the water side of the highway (the town's only street). Between the beach and hotels is a promenade, where most of the restaurants, bars, and diving clubs are located. The **bus stop** is officially in front of the Marina Sharm Hotel, but the bus will drop you off at any hotel along the road. Southbound open sided minibuses (E£1) and taxis (E£10) go to Sharm el-Sheikh.

The **tourist police** (tel. 60 05 54) are located just north of the Helman Hotel. The **National Bank of Egypt** has branches in the Marina Sharm, Gazala, Mövenpick, and Hilton Hotels, and will exchange money (open 8:30am-2pm and 6-9pm). In the shopping center south of the Mövenpick there is an **ATM** outside the **Bank Misr** (follow the sign for "Chims Chimere Restaurant"). Much of the town shuts down between 3 and 7pm. The **Lifeline Clinic** (tel.60 08 06) has American and German trained doctors, including Dr. Taher who can be reached in an **emergency** at the Hilton, room 2012 (tel. 60 02 66 or 02 71); or call an **ambulance** (tel. 60 04 25). The **Iowa Pharmacy** is in the bazaar south of the Mövenpick. The **post office** is in Sharm el-Sheikh, but most hotels will deliver mail for you. Na'ama's **telephone code** is 062.

ACCOMMODATIONS AND FOOD

Pigeon House, at the northern end of the bay (tel. 60 09 96; fax 60 09 95), is the only relatively cheap place to roost in Na'ama. Nest in one of their thatched huts with fans (singles E£38; doubles E£56; breakfast buffet included) or their rooms (singles E£65; doubles E£85; breakfast included). Pigeon House also has a happening courtyard— *the* place for a Stella or *sheesha.* **Shark's Bay Camp** is 4km north of town. This Bedouin camp overlooks a quiet bay and has a breath-taking view of Tiran island, an excellent restaurant, and their own dive club. However, the cost of a taxi to Na'ama (E£20 one way) makes Shark's Bay a very expensive choice. They offer clean bunga-lows (singles E£50-60; doubles E£65-75, triples E£90-100).

Food in Na'ama Bay is of high quality, at least along the main hotel strip, so you can relax the dietary caution that applies to the rest of the Sinai. **Tam Tam Oriental Cor-ner,** on Ghazala Hotel beach (bordering Hilton Beach), is the cheapest place in town (open noon-12:30am). For E£6.50 you can get an enormous bowl of *kushari.* A good variety of salads all cost E£2.50. **Pigeon House** hotel serves excellent pork, meat, and fish. Spaghetti Napolitain E£6.50, *kebab* E£19. **Viva Pizza,** opposite the Red Sea Div-ing College in Kanabesh beach (not to be confused with the pricey Viva Restaurant) serves a variety of tasty pizzas for E£15-22 (open noon-midnight).

SIGHTS AND ENTERTAINMENT

Na'ama Bay itself has no spectacular reefs, but veritable coral reefs lie just outside the bay to the north and south. Dive centers have maps of the reefscape; pick one up and put on your flippers. The closest sites are **Near Gardens** to the north and **Sodfa** to the south; both are moderate walks down the beach. Farther along are **Tower, Turtle Bay, Paradise,** and **Fiasco.** Ask at a dive center which sites are accessible by land— some can prove tricky to get in and out of.

Those in the know swear that boat-based snorkeling is the best. For US$15-25 you can spend a day on a boat and dive in spectacular water. Arrange trips through the dive clubs. The legendary reefs of **Tiran Island** are distant and accessible by boat only. **Ras Nasrani** and **Ras Umm Sidd** are also good sites, and a little closer to town. Inquire at the club what kind of dive is planned; drift dives can prove problematical for surface snorkelers.

You can probably find over a dozen **diving centers** in Na'ama Bay. Prices are fairly standard (five-day PADI course US$280-300, certification US$30). Introductory dives are US$40-45, full gear rental US$50, and a full day (2 dives) US$50. The friendly **Camel Dive Club** (tel. 60 07 00; fax 60 06 01), across from Cataract Resort has been around since 1986. By winter 1997 they will have completed extensive new facilities, including a new pool and both dormitory and private accommodations. They wel-come handicapped divers: their new pool will be equipped with a wheelchair ramp. **Red Sea Diving College** (tel. 60 01 45; fax 60 01 44), next to Kanabesh Hotel, offers PADI instruction and has plush accommodation for its divers. **Oonas Dive Club** (tel. 60 05 81; fax 60 05 82) at the northern end of the bay, boasts much better after-hours camaraderie than the other centers. There are many other safe and reputable diving clubs, with new ones emerging all the time. All centers accept major credit cards, even when they're wet.

Water activities are not restricted to diving. **Sun-n-Fun** booths at the Hilton and Aquamarine beaches have **windsurfing** (E£40 per hr., lessons E£55 per hr.), **water-skiing** (E£40 per 15min.), **jet skiing** (1-person jet E£60 per 15min., 2-person E£70), and **sailboating** (E£40 per hr., E£55 for a lesson). There are even **glass bottom boats** (every hr. 10am-4pm, E£25 per person, E£55 for the big *Discovery*). There is even **free fun** to be had at the **public beach** just south of Gafy Land Hotel.

Landlubbers can strap on some plaid pants and tee off at the Hilton for a game of **minigolf** (E£10 per game, E£55 deposit on clubs). **Horseback riding** is available across from the Nosotel Hotel for £50 per hour. **ATV trips** are available across from the Novetel and next to the Pigeon House. Most leave before sunset ($35 per hour). A good daytrip is to **Nabq,** a gorgeous, untouristed wildlife reserve on the coast 20km north of Na'ama Bay. The region of Nabq is over 500 sq. km, but the most notable site is a strip of coastline where the largest mangrove forest in the Sinai flourishes, attract-ing herons, ospreys, foxes, and hard-to-spot gazelles. The mangroves sprout in a few feet of warm clear water with a sandy bottom, making Nabq an ideal swim and relaxation spot. The problem of maintaining traditional Bedouin lifestyles in the modern world is being actively addressed in Nabq: a Bedouin "reservation" attempts to preserve the culture, and openly welcomes visitors. Almost all hotels organize trips to Nabq. Be warned that wandering off the path in the park is extremely dangerous: there are still a number of **landmines** in the area.

More popular than Nabq is **Wadi Kid,** a deep, fertile canyon 40km north of Na'ama Bay, where you can hike among rock formations and fruit trees. Most hotels affiliate with a **tour** company that goes once a week. The Mövenpick Hotel recreation center organizes a half day trip to both Nabq and Wadi Kid for US$30.

Nights in Na'ama are most often spent tossing back Stellas and swapping diving stories. One of the best places to do this is the **Pigeon House.** The courtyard starts to fill around 5pm; the stella flows and the *sheesha* smoke billows until 12:30am or so. Slip on your eye patch and head for the **Pirate's Bar,** a popular watering hole in the Hilton. With cutlasses and rigging hanging from the wall, the bar attracts a mix of burly MFO troops, ridiculously tan diving instructors, and stylish Europeans. They serve free bar munchies, Stella (E£8) and import draught beer (E£18-20). The staff of **Oona's Dive Club** is hoping to restore their bar to its former glory by '98. The popular **disco** changes weekly—ask around if you're feeling the fever.

■ Dahab دهب

Dahab is one of those places, like Kathmandu or Amsterdam, that has grown larger than life in the minds of travelers. For most, it conjures up images of glossy-eyed, tie-dyed hippies lounging on the shore and blissfully asphyxiating themselves in blue clouds of marijuana smoke. While this scene is still a significant part of the Dahab experience, Dahabitants no longer think of Jamaica with the reverence that Mecca inspires in the rest of the Arab world. The hippies are slowly becoming outnumbered by cleaner-cut travelers and dive instructors. Dope is still available, but you may also meet those who don't know pot from the thing on their stove. Clean eateries serving good food dot the beach, providing tasty alternatives to Dahab's notorious but colorful restaurants. "Bedouin" camps are the cheapest, most social places to stay, but travelers seeking more comfort can choose from a number of more expensive, middle-range hotels with air-conditioning and a family atmosphere in the southern end of the village. Dahab die-hards of yesteryear may lament it's relative cleanliness, but the town is becoming more like paradise, not less—today's Dahab can be all things to all people. Dahab has not lost the eclectic spirit and laid back atmosphere that has drawn millions to its shores. It's still a great place to kill a day, or ten.

ORIENTATION AND PRACTICAL INFORMATION

Dahab city is of almost no significance to the budget traveler, who only glimpses it between climbing off the bus and getting into a taxi headed for the Bedouin village—the "real" Dahab as far as tourists are concerned. Use the city for exchanging money at the **National Bank of Egypt** (open daily 8:30am-2pm and 6-9pm; winter 9am-1pm and 5-8pm). There is also a **post office** with **Poste Restante** (open Sat.-Thurs. 8am-3pm), **supermarket** (open daily 8am-10pm), **police station** (tel. 64 02 15) and **telephone office** where you can make calls within Egypt or through Cairo to an international operator (open 24hr.). In the Bedouin Village there are a few supermarkets which have phones connecting to Cairo and a **Banque de Cairo** where you can draw money with a credit card (open Sat.-Thurs. 9am-2pm and 6-9pm, Fri. 9am-noon and 6-9pm; MC/Visa). Above the Ghazala supermarket at the village's southern end is the **Dahab Polyclinic** (tel. 64 01 04, open 24hr.).

Buses leave daily from the city for **Cairo** (8am, noon, 9:30pm; 7hr., E£45-71); **Suez** (8:15am, 5hr., E£21); **Taba** (10:30am, noon, 3hr., E£12); **Nuweiba'** (10:30am, 6:30pm, 1½hr., E£10); **Sharm el-Sheikh** (8, 8:30, and 10am, noon, 2:30, 5:30, and 9:30pm, 1hr., E£8); and **St. Catherine's** (9:30am, 1hr., E£9). If you get a group together, you can convince a driver to go to any destination. These *service taxis* end up being more expensive, but the rides are much faster because the cars are more reliable than the ramshackle buses. From the bus stop you can take a **taxi** to the village; it should cost E£5 for a car, less for a crowded pickup.

ACCOMMODATIONS AND FOOD

There are over 50 **camps** in the Bedouin village, and the number grows weekly. Dahab camps are an unfortunate bastardization of the thatched beach hut; someone came up with the brilliant idea of casting the huts in concrete, and connecting them in rows around a central courtyard—creating what amounts to bare cells with minimal ventilation. Rooms with just a mattress are cheap—most cost E£5-10. Only very plush rooms should be more expensive. Rooms with private bath will cost you more: E£10-30. The huts mostly serve as storage space for your stuff while you lounge outside in one of the restaurants. The camps are many, and an untrained observer might say they all look the same; one can, however, detect subtle variations that distinguish one from the other. Towards the southern end of town there are a few more upscale hotels. The **Penguin Camp** is a five-minute walk along the beach south of town, with a beautiful location on the beach and a comfy hammock. The **Auski Camp** is near the Sphinx Hotel. Friendly owner keeps the rooms spic and span and smelling fresh. **Muhammad Ali Camp** is clean, cheap, and right in the middle of the action. For those looking to get away from the scene and willing to pay for it, the **Jasmine Pension and Restaurant** at the southern end offers quiet, clean, luxurious rooms and snorkeling. Rabia, the owner/chef, will whip up delicious, gourmet meals to order (E£7-15) while you watch the day pass from the comfortable lounge (doubles E£35-50, all with bath, some with sea views and balcony).

The combination of intense heat during the day and no ventilation at night has a funny effect: the rooms get hot. Travelers have been known to approach this problem in three ways: (1) take all their clothes off, throw the covers on the floor, and sweat profusely in bed; (2) put all their clothes on, walk with the sheets into the shower, drench everything, then go to sleep wet; or (3) take the room key and a sheet and go to sleep in the "million-star hotel" outside, braving mosquitoes. Don't be too concerned about losing sleep at night—you'll make it up during the day.

Food, like sleep, is an important part of the ritual of Dahab living, and is intermingled with it: travelers snooze in the outside restaurants before, during, and after their meals. Continual complaints about the quality of many of the restaurants have precipitated the opening of a number of new, clean restaurants. **Cafe Juz** is new to Dahab, and already one of the town's favorites. Sandy, the Kiwi chef, cooks up absolutely amazing (and mostly vegetarian) meals for under E£15. Juz is so popular that dinner orders need to be placed in the afternoon. **Club Red Restaurant,** behind Club Red Diving Center, serves up the tasty creations of John, their Scottish chef. His Sunday dinner has become the talk of the town. **The Dolphin Coffee Shop,** north of Dolphin Camp, turns out top notch Indian fare for under E£15. Stop in for a bite of tandoori chicken and a chat with owners Katy and Hassan. **Tota** is rumored to have the best pizza in town and (importantly) a liquor license. There are numerous supermarkets around, the best of which is the **Ghazala Market** at the southern end of town.

SIGHTS AND ENTERTAINMENT

The **Bedouin village** is no longer really that. It's so loaded with tourists that the Bedouin themselves have moved north to 'Aslah. These days, the bay is lined with restaurants, camps, and gift shops that peddle the famous "Dahab pants" (E£15) and the kind of colorful backpack (E£5-15) that is now commonly sighted in places like Nepal or Thailand. Meanwhile, camels and horses trot up and down the beach road carrying Dutch women or pink-hued Brits (per 30min.: camels E£5, horses E£10). Pillowed courtyards hug the beach; it's quite a sight at night when cheerfully illuminated by electric lights and Baraka Bottle lanterns (an innovative use for these pesky petroleum products which will someday bury the entire town).

Dahab sports two well-known dive sites: **Canyon** and **Blue Hole.** The latter is an 80m deep hole about 15m out from the shore that swallows several divers each year. The dive involves a traverse through a passage at a depth of 60m; experienced divers say this is just plain nuts, and they're right. There's plenty of excellent diving that's less death-defying, and several dive clubs to help you get started. The best clubs are all in the village. **Fantasea** (tel. 64 04 83; fax 64 00 43; email: fdc@intouch.com), at the northern end, offers everything from open water to assistant instructor courses. **Nesima Diving Center** (tel. 64 03 20 or 21; fax 64 03 21), at the southern end, has a friendly staff who teach a number of specialty courses. **Club Red** (tel. 64 03 80), also at the southern end, has nice facilities and hotel rooms (singles US$10; doubles US$18). Prices are comparable to Na'ama Bay (5-day PADI certification course US$280-300, two guided dives with full gear US$50-55, introductory dive US$40-45; credit cards accepted). Fantasea has the lowest prices for individual dives. The **snorkeling** is excellent as well; enter the blue at either end of the bay where you see waves breaking on the reefs (just be sure to wear shoes or flippers, because if the sea urchins don't get you, the coral will). Trips to Blue Hole and Canyon are arranged every morning by most camps, and you can rent snorkel gear at camps or on the beach (E£5). Make sure the gear fits, the mask is intact, and the snorkel works before paying. Paddleboats are available for rental near the northern part of the village (E£15 per hr.; use them to truck to some of the more secluded spots).

Other popular excursions are by jeep to the **Colored Canyon** (E£50 per person for a group of 6), by camel or truck to the brackish oasis of **Wadi Gnay** (E£30 per person), or a one-day camel trip to **Nabq** (E£35-50). Hamed the Lobster Man runs **Crazy Camel Camp** and organizes jeep and camel safaris. He also takes people on night **lobster hunting** trips that culminate in lobster feasts on the beach. A great way to explore the Sinai is with Ehab of **Emba Safaris** (tel. 64 04 47), next to Pizzeria Trattoria. Ehab runs dive trips and land safaris (US$40-45 per person, per day). His goal is to educate people about the Bedouin lifestyle, and his trips are as fun as they are educational. If you want to go anywhere, ask around the Bedouin community. They know these hills better than anyone, and will often be happy to organize a trip.

In order to get an alcohol license in the Sinai, an establishment must first possess a building license (obliging the owner to keep his building above certain standards) and pay a property tax. Thus, there are only five sources of booze in Dahab: the restaurant at the Nesima Dive Club, the Crazy House Restaurant, Tota, the Sphinx Hotel, Green Valley, and Neptune Billiards. This lack of liquor is one of the reasons Dahab grew notorious for its **dope scene.** Though it is far less noticeable, dope is still available for those who want it. If you do choose to smoke, be careful. Possession of drugs is illegal in Egypt, and Egyptian jails rate low on the Michelin system. Dealers may win an all-expenses-paid trip to the hereafter via firing squad.

Dahab veterans will be sorry to hear that the Black Prince Disco has closed. The Helma Hotel, 20km north of town, has opened up the **Zanzibar Disco.** There is a free shuttle from town around midnight, and on a good night the disco can draw quite a crowd. Pool sharks can rack up a game at Neptune Billiards, where E£10 will buy you an hour on the table (open 10am-2am).

Betrayal of the Bedouin

The recent explosion of resorts and dive centers along the Red Sea has introduced a sticky issue: whose land is the Sinai? Political control of the desert peninsula has been juggled back and forth between Egypt and Israel, but the only group with a history of habitation in the Sinai identifies with neither. Generations of Bedouin have lived in the Sinai long before any hotels were built here. According to Egyptian law, developers need only pay money to the Egyptian government before beginning to build. In reality, companies must also cut a deal with the local Bedouin tribe. A hotel in bad standing with the Bedouin faces serious trouble. Although the hotels and tourist services provide jobs and increase the standard of living for many Bedouin, the development has irreversibly altered their nomadic lifestyle. Some Bedouin now live on government land reserves like **Nabq,** near Na'ama Bay, which are reminiscent of the Native American reservations in the United States.

■ Nuweiba' نويبع

One of Sinai's natural oases, Nuweiba' lies at the mouth of an enormous *wadi*. For about 10 months of the year the *wadi* is filled with drifting sand, but in winter, a sudden, rampaging wall of water 3m high may charge down its banks to the sea. Nuweiba' resembles a younger version of Dahab: a town with no inherent appeal or style, fortunate enough to have a cheap, carefree Bedouin camp and a magnificent beach. Dolphin beach, just south of the port, is the home of a friendly dolphin and her new baby, who like to swim with visitors.

PRACTICAL INFORMATION

Nuweiba', named after the Bedouin tribe whose territory reaches to Taba, is divided into Nuweiba' Port and Nuweiba' City, 10km to the north. **Ferries** leave for Aqaba from the port (for more information, see **Going To Jordan,** p. 264). The bus stop is in front of the Helman Hotel. Buses leave daily for **Cairo** (3pm, 7hr., E£55); **Sharm el-Sheikh** (2½hr., E£10) via **Dahab** (7am, 4pm, 1½hr., E£7); and **Taba** (6am and noon, 1hr., E£7). Travellers to St. Catherine's should switch buses in Dahab. Next to the Helnan, there is a **National Bank** (open 8:30am-noon and 6-8pm, currency exchange only) and **tourist police** (tel. 50 02 31). To get to **Tarabin,** either walk north along the beach (30min.), or take a taxi (E£10 per load). At the Hilton Hotel, there is a Bank de Cairo (open Sat.-Thurs. 9:30am-1pm and 6:30-9pm, Fri. 9:30-11:30am, and 6:30-9pm. Ramadan 10:30am-1pm and 8-11pm). They allow you to withdraw money on credit. There is another branch in the port. Most stores are in one of two commercial centers aptly named the "new" and the "old." The new center is closest to the Helman. Both centers have supermarkets and food stores, but the old center keeps longer hours. A **newsstand** in the old center has English Egyptian newspapers, international telephone service, and bus schedule info. The old center also houses the **pharmacy** (open 24hr.). Farther north, past the communications antenna are the **telephone office** (open 24hr.), a **post office** with **Poste Restante** and **EMS** (open 8am-2pm), the **hospital** (tel. 50 03 03; open 24hr.) and the **police station** (tel. 50 24 24; open 24hr.) Higher quality Israeli health care is just over the border.

ACCOMMODATIONS AND FOOD

The **El Waha Village** (tel. 50 04 21, fax 50 04 21), located ½km south of the Helman, offers garden shed style bungalows (singles E£25; doubles E£35; triples E£45) and large tents with mattresses (E£10 per person). Breakfast costs E£8.50. Nuweiba' city has one road, on which everything you need lies north of El Waha village at the Helman. **Dr. Shishkebab** and **Ali Baba,** in the old commercial center, offer sandwiches (E£3-4), meat entrees (E£8-10), and vegetarian dishes (E£6). **El Suezi Restaurant,** in the center, will showcase their collection of frozen fish (E£10-20).

SIGHTS AND SAFARIS

Nuweiba's most rewarding sight is **Dolphin Beach.** The story behind the beach is a tale straight out of *Flipper:* one of the Bedouin is a deaf and mute man named Abdallah. While fishing off Nuweiba', Abdallah befriended two dolphins who would always swim with his boat. One day, the male dolphin became caught in a net and was mistaken for a shark by soldiers who shot him. Horrified, both Abdallah and the female dolphin rushed to their dying friends. In grief, the female dolphin lay crying in the water while Abdallah stroked her. From that day on, she has not left the vicinity of the beach, where visitors swim with her every day. It seems that Abdallah is not her only admirer, however. In the spring of 1997, Abdallah's dolphin became the mother of a bouncing baby dolphin. Both mother and child entertain visitors everyday with smiles that would make any dentist proud. Dolphin Beach is a 20-minute walk south of Nuweiba' Port, or a E£5 taxi ride. Tell your driver "dolphin"—everybody understands. The beach is open until 6pm. Bedouin will charge you E£10 to swim, and another E£10 for mask, snorkel, and fins.

EGYPT

Like all Sinai coast towns, Nuweiba' is surrounded by beautiful coral reefs, but unlike the reefs in Dahab, Na'ama Bay, or Sharm esh-Sheikh, these Nuweiba' spots are not teeming with dive clubs. There are only two dive clubs in town. **The Aqua-Sport Dive Club** (tel. 52 03 27), in the Hilton Hotel, opened in 1996 and offers PADI open water training and certification for US$307. Two suited dives with full equipment and transport cost US$65. **Diving Camp Nuweiba'** (tel. 50 04 03, ask for the dive center; fax 50 02 25), in the Helman Hotel, caters to a mostly German clientele. Open water training costs US$330, while two dives cost US$60 with jeep transport, US$65 with boat. Call ahead if you want English instruction.

The attractions in Nuweiba' are not limited to the waters. The town is an excellent starting point for **camel** or **jeep safaris** to remarkable desert terrain. Some of the more popular trips are as follows: the **Colored Canyon,** a *wadi* with cliffs of beautifully patterned sandstone, is the best-known destination, 30km from Nuweiba' (4hr. jeep tour); **Ain Umm Ahmed** is a frequently-visited desert oasis which can be reached by jeep (2 days); **Ain Furtuga,** only 10km out of town (camel range) is another popular oasis; **Ain Khoudra** and **Bayar al-Sabreyer** are both oases in the spectacular **Wadi Khoudra** (1-day jeep trip) on the road to St. Catherine's (within 2-day camel range of Nuweiba'). Two places to ask about these trips are: **Explore Sinai** (tel. 50 01 41; tel./ fax 50 01 40), in the new commercial center (open 9am-4pm and 7:30-11pm), and Moonland Camp in Tarabin. Moonland Camp is the cheaper of the two, offering colored Canyon Trips for E£50 per person. You may be able to save E£10-15 per day by dealing directly with a guide. Look for one at Tarabin if none approach you. Bedouin guides here are generally trustworthy and safe.

Technically, you need permission just to step off the highway in the Sinai. Desert trips require a permit, achieved by some mysterious passport fermentation process at your friendly neighborhood police station. Your guide will take care of it for you. Tour prices always include food, but often exclude water. The price of bottled water rises dramatically during the safari, so be sure to start off with a large supply.

GOING TO JORDAN

To go to **Aqaba** from Nuweiba', you can take a **ferry** from the port. Unfortunately nobody, not even the ferry workers, knows what time it leaves. The regular ferry leaves sometime around noon and also between 4 and 5:30pm. It costs US$32 and theoretically takes 3½ hours. There is also a **speedboat** that leaves around 11:30am and again between 3:30 and 4:30pm. The trip takes an hour and costs US$42, but the extra US$10 is well worth it. To be sure of catching the boat, show up 1½ hours before the earliest possible departure time to deal with customs and ticketing. Jordanian **visas** can be obtained on board (Australia free, Canada JD31, Ireland JD5, New Zealand JD4, South Africa free, U.K. JD23, U.S. JD15). There is no Egyptian departure tax. Nuweiba' **buses** will drop you off at the port. Taxis from Nuweiba' city or Tarabin to the port cost E£15-20. Buses from Cairo to the ferry can be overcrowded with Egyptians bound for jobs in Jordan, Saudi Arabia, and the Gulf states.

▓ Northern Gulf Coast

The 70km stretch between Nuweiba' and Taba is undoubtedly the most magnificent part of the Sinai: the mountains come right down to the beach, the reefs and sand turn the water a magnificent shade of turquoise, and the mountains of Saudi Arabia tower in the distance. Unfortunately the view will soon be ruined by the five-star hotels that are popping up like weeds along this beautiful coast. The coastline is dotted with camps, which are accessible by bus or service from Taba or Nuweiba'. Drivers may not know the names of some camps: keep your eyes peeled for the signs or you'll go right past. The camps follow a standard layout: a number of huts and a central lounge and restaurant. Most huts do not have electricity—bring a flashlight. It's quiet out here; the days are spent reading and swimming and the nights bring backgammon, stargazing, and **hanky-panky.**

TARABIN طربين

Tarabin is a miniature Dahab. Camps, restaurants, and supermarkets line the beach, but on a far smaller scale than its southern counterpart. There is only one road, and the main strip can be walked to the end in five minutes. Unlike Dahab, there is actually a beach and the water is warm and clean. Tarabin is rumored to be the source of much of Egypt's dope. It is widely available, but, as usual, risky.

There is little difference in the quality of the huts at most of the camps. Most charge E£5-10 and have their own Bedouin-style restaurant. Muhammad, who runs the **Carmina Camp** at the southern end of town, will make you feel right at home in one of their many huts. The **Moon Land Camp,** run by Mossallam Farrag, offers guided **camel, jeep,** and **trekking tours. Mondial Restaurant,** in the center of town, makes a great cheese omelette for E£7. Also see coverage of Nuweiba' (p. 263) for more info.

FARTHER NORTH

A number of beautiful, but more expensive, camps lie 10-15km north of Nuweiba'. **Magana Beach,** a Bedouin camp near colorful rock formations, has reefs and a restaurant. Huts cost E£15-20 for doubles, E£10 a piece for triples. **Devil's Head** (Ras Shaytan), is named for a rock formation 3km north of Megaine. There are four camps at Devil's Head—the southernmost, **Moon Land,** being the most simple and secluded (bamboo hut singles E£20; doubles E£40; triples E£50). Moving north, the second and fourth camps offer more huts (singles E£20; doubles E£30; triples E£45). Bargain at all three camps. There is a rumor that some of the camps occasionally let people sleep on the beach for free. Nearby **Bawaki** is only for the wealthy, but does have a few non-A/C sheds for US$20, and you'll be able to use their pool.

Between Basata and Taba is a remote and beautiful spot called **The Fjord,** where a small inlet cuts into the steep hills. The **Salima Restaurant and Camp** (tel. 53 01 30) is right off the highway on a small ledge overlooking the sleepy bay. There are a few rooms crammed between the restaurant and the rock slope behind it (E£30 per person), or you can camp on the beach.

Basata بساطة

"Basata" means "simplicity" in Arabic. Indeed, this super-environmentally-conscious camp (about midway between Nuweiba' and Taba) is unlike any other you will find in Sinai. Designed to minimize its impact on Sinai's environment, Basata is a beautiful place that you can enjoy without pangs of ecological guilt. Glass, metal, and plastic are all recycled. Water is desalinated and electricity generated on site. Organic trash is used as livestock feed. A vegetarian (E£18) or fish (E£24) meal is cooked every evening, though you can save money by cooking for yourself. The fully stocked kitchen functions on trust: take what you want and write down what you take, but beware the prices. The atmosphere at Basata is family-oriented, with nightly communal dinners, a comfy common area with games and books, and lots of rules: no public nudity, no drugs or alcohol, no sleeping in the common area, and no dirty dishes (camping E£15, bamboo huts E£25 per person). All prices are subject to a 10% tax.

The camp is run by German-educated Sherif Ghamrawy (tel. 50 04 81). Sherif organizes **camel** and **jeep tours** (camel tours E£75 per day; jeep tours E£55-60). **Snorkeling** equipment (E£15) is also available. Due to recent publicity, Basata has gotten quite popular. Huts often sell out, but the beach is almost always available except when European/Egyptian/Israeli holidays overlap.

Pharaoh's Island جزيرة فرعون

Pharaoh's Island (Jezirat Fara'un; Israelis call it Coral Island), 8km south of Taba, is a rocky outcrop just offshore which holds the extensively renovated ruins of a Crusader castle built around 1115. Salah ad-Din took the fortress in 1171 but abandoned it in 1183 after European counterattacks. The ruins have a few neat towers and passageways and a large water cistern. A boat ferries visitors to the island (E£14 or JD20 from Aqaba), where you must then buy another ticket to tour the castle (E£20, stu-

EGYPT

dents E£10). Unless you're a real castle buff, or plan on snorkeling, you're better off staying on shore (the view of Sinai from the castle is shamefully ruined by the five-star Salah ad-Din Hotel, and the view of the castle is best from the mainland). Pharaoh's Island is a popular excursion from Eilat, Aqaba, and Taba. The complex coral reef formations off the northeastern tip of the island are great for diving, and snorkeling. Bring your own food, as food on the island is overpriced and often unavailable.

GOING TO ISRAEL

To go to Israel from Egypt you must cross from **Taba** to **Eilat.** You will be issued a free visa at the border, the length of which is entirely determined by the border guards' mood and your appearance (min. 1 week, max. 3 months). You will have to pay a E£2 exit tax if you have traveled beyond the Sinai. The walk through the stations shouldn't take more than an hour. You will automatically get an Israeli stamp in your passport unless you request to get it on a separate sheet. If you plan on traveling to Syria or Lebanon, get it on a separate paper—you will not be allowed to enter these countries if there is an Israeli visa in your passport. You can get rid of your extra Egyptian pounds at the Israeli snack bar. The border is open 24 hours.

See specific Sinai towns for information on transportation to Taba. Bus #15 runs every 15 minutes from the border checkpoint to Eilat daily until about 11pm except on Fridays, when the last bus is at 5:30pm (NIS3.20). Rented cars are not allowed to cross in either direction.

ISRAEL ישראל

US$1=3.52 New Israeli Shekels (NIS)	NIS1=US$0.28
CDN$1=NIS2.53	NIS1=CDN$0.40
UK£1=NIS5.63	NIS1=UK£0.18
IR£1=NIS5.18	NIS1=IR£0.19
AUS$1=NIS2.64	NIS1=AUS$0.38
NZ$1=NIS2.26	NIS1=NZ$0.44
SAR1=NIS0.75	NIS1=SAR1.33
E£1 (Egyptian Pound) =NIS1.04	NIS1=E£0.96
JD1 (Jordanian Dinar) =NIS4.98	NIS1=JD0.20

> For important information on travel in general and some specifics on Israel, see the **Essentials** section of this book. Israel's **international phone code** is 972.

At age 50, Israel still lives with a constant personality conflict between the secularism of its modern cities and the reverence inspired by religion and deep history. This tension spawns myriad reactions: pensive philosophers and enterprising capitalists share the streets with patriotic Zionists and live-for-the-moment disco-goers. Israel has been controversial since its inception. From persecution culminating in the Holocaust, Jews of all cultures and backgrounds came together to make a brand new kind of state and remake themselves, sometimes at the expense of indigenous Palestinian Arabs. With the country's identity in constant flux, all Israelis have their own vision of what Israel should be. To give one eloquent example, Amos Oz, Israel's leading novelist, sees his fellow Israelis as "a warm-hearted, hot-tempered Mediterranean people that is gradually learning, through great suffering and in a tumult of sound and fury, to find release both from the bloodcurdling nightmares of the past and from delusions of grandeur, both ancient and modern." Of course, many Israelis see Oz as a stuck-up intellectual, and will tell you at length about how *they* see their country—there is no lack of impassioned political or apolitical opinions. But talk with Israelis about their bewildering national situation for long enough, and they will eventually smile or shrug and say, *"Yihiyeh tov"* (It'll be OK).

ONCE THERE

▓ Entry

Security upon arrival in Israel is fairly relaxed (less so for visitors of Arab origin), especially compared to the scrutiny your luggage will receive at Ben-Gurion Airport upon your departure. Normally you can take the "Green Channel" to exit the airport. Most items can be brought in duty-free as long as you intend to carry them out when you depart. Take the "Red Channel" if you need to declare articles. Duty must be paid on large quantities of perfume, alcohol, and cigarettes. You will also need to take the "Red Channel" if you bring in new-looking computer, video, or diving equipment, but duties will be refunded upon your exit from the country.

There is a **Government Tourist Information Office (GTIO)** in the arrival hall at Ben-Gurion (tel. (03) 971 14 85). **Egged buses** run regularly to major cities (#475 to Tel Aviv). **Sherut (shared) taxis** run regularly from the airport to Jerusalem (NIS32).

■ Getting Around

Buses   Buses are the most popular and convenient means of travel. Except for the **Dan Company** (tel. (03) 639 44 44) in Tel Aviv and the **Arab buses** serving the West Bank, Galilee, and Gaza, the **Egged Bus Cooperative** (tel. (03) 537 55 55) has a monopoly on intercity and most intracity buses in Israel. The modern, air-conditioned buses are either direct *(yashar),* express, or local *(me'asef).* Students with ISIC receive a 10% discount on all fares; be sure to show your ID first to the ticket seller, then to the driver, then to the ticket inspector. Buses are sometimes crowded, especially on Saturday nights after *Shabbat* and during morning and afternoon rush hours. You can shove your way into and out of the bus, as long as you preface each push with the word *slipa,* as Israelis do.

Most bus stations have printed schedules, often in English. Egged has intercity **information lines** in the major cities (tel. (03) 537 55 55 in Tel Aviv, (04) 854 95 55 in Haifa, (02) 530 45 55 in Jerusalem). For information on local lines, call the area's central bus station. Signs in stations direct you to buy your ticket at the ticket window. This is only really necessary for highly-traveled long-distance routes; otherwise, buy the ticket from the driver. You can buy a *kartis* from any bus driver (NIS32); this gives you 11 local rides for the price of ten. Most local bus rides cost NIS3.30. Buses between cities usually leave from the central bus station *(tahanat merkazit).* If you buy roundtrip tickets rather than one-way, you will usually get a 10% discount.

Taxis   Israeli companies offer both private and less expensive **sherut** (shared) taxis. Regular private taxi rides are called special (pronounced "spatial"). City taxis operating as special must have meters *(moneh);* make the driver turn it on. Offers of special but unspecified "discount" rates (translation: no meter and an exorbitant fare) should be adamantly refused. If you know the route and can estimate a decent price, you can get a better rate by setting the price before you enter the taxi.

Sherut taxis hold up to seven people. Certain companies operate sherut taxis seven days a week from offices in each city. Intercity sherut operate on loose schedules, departing when they fill up; on Saturdays, they often whiz along the streets in search of passengers. Intracity sherut never follow a schedule and cruise the streets daily. Most routes have set fares comparable to bus prices; ask for quotes at tourist offices or from the nearest Israeli. Always settle on a price before you depart.

Cars   More Israelis die in **automobile accidents** than from any other cause. Widespread public transportation makes cars generally unnecessary; but some places (especially the Golan) are most easily reached by a little coupe of your own. The legal driving age is 17, but most agencies will only rent to credit-card holders aged 21 years or older (a few will rent to 18-year-olds). An American license works just as well as an International Driver's License. Roads are usually well-marked, and maps are available at all tourist offices. Israelis drive on the right. Rentals usually run about US$55-70 per day with a 250km daily limit. There is often a discount for rentals of three days or more. Prices in shekels are considerably higher in some cases, and deals arranged beforehand from overseas are often *much* cheaper. See **Practical Information** in each city for agency addresses.

Trains   Rail service in Israel is useful only for travel along the northern coast. The circuitous Tel Aviv-Jerusalem line is slower than highway travel but considerably more scenic. Like buses, trains screech to a halt during *Shabbat.* Avoid traveling on Friday afternoons when the trains are most crowded. Train fares are slightly cheaper than bus fares. Students with an ISIC receive a 50% discount.

Hitchhiking   The incidence of sexual harassment and assault has increased dramatically in recent years. License plates carry meaning; yellow are Israeli, black with a ⴶ are army, red are police, blue or gray are occupied territories, and white are diplomatic. Those who hitch in the Negev or Golan (where sometimes the only option

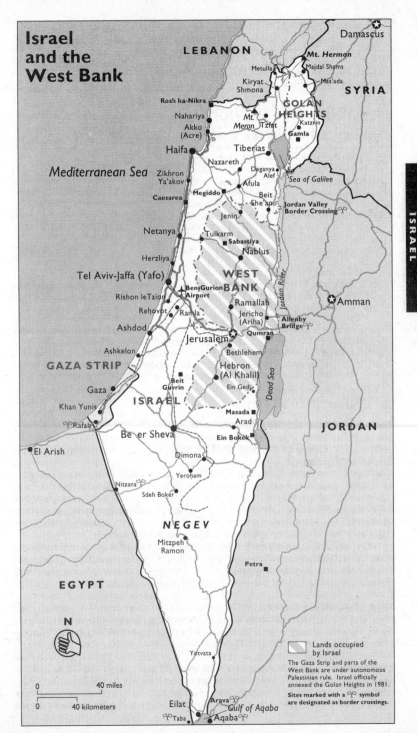

Israel
and the
West Bank

LEBANON

Damascus

Mt. Hermon

Metulla

Majdal Shams

Kiryat
Shmona

Mas'ada

SYRIA

Rosh ha-Nikra

Nahariya

GOLAN
HEIGHTS

Akko
(Acre)

Mt.
Meron

Tzfat

Katzrin

Gamla

Haifa

Tiberias

Nazareth

Mediterranean Sea

Zikhron
Ya'akov

Deganya
Alef

Sea of Galilee

Afula

Caesarea

Megiddo

Beit
She'an

Jordan Valley
Border Crossing

Jenin

Netanya

Tulkarm

Sabastiya

Herzliya

Nablus

Tel Aviv-Jaffa (Yafo)

WEST
BANK

Ben Gurion
Airport

Rishon leTzion

Ramallah

Amman

Reḥovot

Ramla

Jericho
(Ariha)

Allenby
Bridge

Ashdod

Jerusalem

Qumran

Ashkelon

Bethlehem

GAZA STRIP

Hebron
(Al Khalil)

Gaza

ISRAEL

Beit
Guvrin

Ein Gedi

Dead Sea

Khan Yunis

Rafah

Masada

Arad

JORDAN

Be er Sheva

Ein Bokek

El Arish

Dimona

Yeroham

Nitzana

Sdeh Boker

NEGEV

Mitzpeh
Ramon

Petra

EGYPT

N

Lands occupied
by Israel

The Gaza Strip and parts of the
West Bank are under autonomous
Palestinian rule. Israel officially
annexed the Golan Heights in 1981.

Sites marked with a ♌ symbol
are designated as border crossings.

0   40 miles

0   40 kilometers

Yotvata

Eilat

Arava

Gulf of Aqaba

Taba

Aqaba

ISRAEL

is a military vehicle) run the risk of getting a ride that doesn't go all the way to their destination; in which case you will be stranded. Hitchers flag cars by pointing to the far side of the road with the index finger. Those who stick out their thumb will get nothing but rude looks—the thumbs up sign means something very different in the Middle East. **Let's Go does not recommend hitchhiking.** *Tremping,* as it is called, is not what it used to be in Israel.

■ Useful Addresses

TOURIST AND TRAVEL SERVICES

Israel Ministry of Tourism: 24 King George St., Jerusalem 94262 (tel. (02) 675 48 11). Maps, transportation schedules, and information on current events. Arranges for foreigners to spend an evening with Israeli families (the *Meet the Israelis* program). They also have a complaint department for troubled tourists. Jerusalem-specific queries are handled by the GTIO (see **Practical Information,** p. 286).

Israel Youth Hostels Association (A.N.A.): 1 Shazar St., P.O. Box 6001, Jerusalem 91009 (tel. (02) 655 84 00; fax 655 84 30). Operates 31 hostels. Organizes tours for groups and individual packages to Israel, Sinai, Jordan, and Egypt.

National Parks Authority: 4 Rav Aluf M. Makleff St., P.O. Box 7028, Tel Aviv 61070 (tel. (03) 576 68 88; fax 691 02 62). Material on parks and historical sites. Also sells an NIS49 ticket for admission to all sites, good for 14 days.

Society for the Protection of Nature in Israel (Ha-Ḥevra LeHaganat Ha-Teva, SPNI): Tel Aviv (main office), 4 Ha-Shfela St. (tel. (03) 638 86 77); other offices in major cities. In the **U.S.,** ASPNI, 28 Arrandale Ave., Great Neck, NY 11024 (tel. (212) 398-6750; fax (212) 398-1665). Call (800) 323-0035 for reservations and nature trails brochure. Organizes hikes, sight-seeing tours in English, and camping trips. Dues US$25 per year (tax deductible; includes discounts on trips).

Israel Student Travel Association (ISSTA): Jerusalem, 31 Ha-Nevi'im St. (tel. (02) 625 72 57); **Tel Aviv,** 109 Ben-Yehuda St. (tel. (03) 521 05 55); **Haifa,** 2 Balfour St. (tel. (04) 867 02 22 or 832 67 39). Information on tours, flights, student IDs.

■ Money Matters

Currency and Exchange   The primary unit of currency is the **new Israeli shekel (NIS).** Notes come in denominations of NIS200, NIS100, NIS50, NIS20, and NIS10; coins come in NIS10, NIS5, NIS1, NIS0.50, 10 agorot, and 5 agorot. There are 100 agorot in a shekel.

Money can be exchanged at any bank or authorized hotel; always bring your passport. Hotel rates of exchange are usually slightly worse than those in banks. A maximum of US$500 worth of shekels can be reconverted at banks. To change more than US$500 (up to US$5000), show a receipt verifying your original conversion into shekels. Banks are generally open Sun., Tues., and Thurs. 8:30am-12:30pm and 4-5:30pm, Mon. and Wed. 8:30am-12:30pm, Fri. and holidays 8:30am-noon.

ATMs are abundant in Israel; **Bank Ha-Poalim** ATMs take **bank cards** affiliated with *Cirrus* and often *Plus* networks for free, but your home bank may charge you. Inquire before you go. See **Essentials,** p. 12, for important money information. **Credit cards** are widely accepted, but only at relatively upscale places.

Use of Foreign Currency   Many services and shops accept Australian, Canadian, and U.S. dollars and British pounds in addition to shekels. If you pay in foreign currency, your change will come back in shekels and you will be exempt from the domestic **Value Added Tax (VAT)** on goods and services (17%). Many shops include VAT in listed prices in shekels, so you may have to insist that 17% be removed from your charge if you pay in foreign currency. VAT refunds can also be obtained if you present receipts from your purchases at any export bank upon your departure. There are limitations to this refund; purchases must be made at stores bearing the proper logos, must be worth at least US$50, must be wrapped in a plastic bag that will remain closed for the duration of your trip, must be on your person (not packed), and must have been manufactured in Israel. And you thought you were getting something for nothing. The *Customs Guide for the Reimbursement of VAT to Tourists* is available at the airport. The refund will be in the currency you used; if the bank cannot scrape together enough, it will be mailed to your home address. Eurocheques may be written in shekels and counted as foreign currency for discounts.

You may bring an unlimited amount of currency, foreign or shekels, into the country. Upon departure you are permitted to take up to US$100 cash. Anything over this must be accompanied by receipts to prove that it was brought into the country. Exchange all your shekels before leaving Israel.

Tipping A 10% tip is expected in restaurants, bars, and hotels, unless a service charge is already included in the bill. Taxi drivers will happily accept tips, but they are not expected.

Business Hours Business hours in Israel are difficult to pinpoint. Because of the variety of religions, different shops close on different days. Most Jewish shops and offices are closed for *Shabbat* from early Friday afternoon until Sunday; some stores reopen after sundown on Saturday. Typical shopping hours are Sunday through Thursday from 8am to 7pm and Friday from 8am to 2pm. A few establishments close between 1 and 4pm. Shopping malls are open until 9-10pm. Muslim-owned establishments close on Fridays, while Christian businesses close on Sundays. **Entertainment** spots are usually open every day, with extended hours on weekends. Bars begin to fill up around midnight. **Public transportation,** including Egged and Dan bus lines, also shuts down for *Shabbat* throughout the country, though some lines still run in Haifa. Don't expect to catch a bus after 2pm on Friday. Arab buses and taxis, however, do continue to run (at increased prices) on *Shabbat.*

Businesses close down on major Jewish holidays, keeping Friday hours the day before. During *Sukkot* and *Pesaḥ*, shops close for the first and last days and are open until early afternoon during intermediate days. In Arab areas, some restaurants close for the entire month of Ramadan (for more information, see **When to Go,** p. 2).

■ Accommodations

Hostels Although often crowded in summer, Israel's **Hostelling International (HI)** youth hostels are usually clean and close to historic sites and scenic areas. Most HI hostels accept reservations and have no age limit. There are many excellent unofficial hostels and pensions in Israel, which are generally less expensive than HI hostels. Most dorm rooms and bathrooms in Israeli hostels are coed. **Guard your valuables.** All accommodations are required by law to have safes for use free of charge; many also have lockers, for a minimal fee.

Hotels Hotel accommodations are usually too costly for the budget traveler. There are some reasonably priced one- and two-star hotels in the larger cities; a few have singles for approximately US$25-30 and doubles for US$35-40. Prices can often be bargained down substantially when business is slow. Ask at the tourist office for booklets *Israel: A Youth and Student Adventure* and *Israel Tourist Hotels.*

Camping Israel's campsites usually provide electricity, sanitary facilities, public telephones, first aid, a restaurant or store, a night guard, and on-site or nearby swimming areas. In July and August most sites charge NIS10-20 per night for adults.

Don't crash in areas not officially designated for camping. Certain stretches of beach are off-limits for security reasons, and others are full of thieves (Haifa, Tel Aviv, and Eilat). **Women should not camp alone.** Always heed mine field warning signs.

Alternative Accommodations If you plan to sleep in Nazareth, Jerusalem, Jaffa, Tiberias, or on Mount Tabor, consider staying in a **Christian hospice.** They are officially designed to provide reasonably-priced room and board for Christian pilgrims, but most listed in this book welcome tourists as well. Bed and breakfast costs US$18-25 per person at most places. Though austere, the hospices are conveniently located in important religious centers and are usually quiet, comfortable, and impeccable; most also serve cheap, filling meals. But accommodations are limited, and sometimes difficult to obtain in the tourist season. For a list of hospices write to the Ministry of Tourism, c/o Nancy Shelaz, Pilgrimage Promotion Committee, 23 Hillel St., Jerusalem P.O. Box 1018 91009 (tel. (02) 623 73 11 or 79 62; fax 625 86 70).

In some cities it is possible to rent a room in a **private home.** The GTIO and some private travel agencies can arrange accommodations. Consider finding a place on your own; prices should be no more than what you would pay at a hostel. But exercise caution, as quality varies greatly. Hometours International, Inc., P.O. Box 11503, Knoxville, TN 37939 (tel. (800) 367-4668 or (423) 690-8484), helps travelers find short-term **apartment rentals** in Jerusalem, Tel Aviv, and Netanya from the United States. They also have **bed-and-breakfast, kibbutz,** and **moshav** locations throughout Israel (fee US$50, half of which goes towards rent).

Some kibbutzim offer accommodations at **Kibbutz Hotels.** Most are expensive and have three-star ratings from the Ministry of Tourism. For information, contact them at 90 Ben-Yehuda St., Tel Aviv 63437 (tel. (03) 524 6161). Try **ISSTA** for cheap package deals on accommodations.

■ Keeping in Touch

Post offices are usually open Sunday through Tuesday and Thursday 8am-12:30pm and 3:30-6pm, Wednesday 8am-2pm, Friday 8am-1pm, and are closed Saturdays and holidays. In the larger cities some offices may keep longer hours. Mail from North America to Israel can take up to two weeks; mail sent from Israel to North America is considerably faster. On the street, yellow mailboxes are for mail within the same city, red mailboxes are for all other mail. Most post offices offer international **Express Mail Service (EMS),** which supposedly takes three days (reality: 4 at least).

Travelers have two means of receiving mail: **Poste Restante** (*doar shamur*) and American Express Client Letter Service (see **Essentials: Keeping in Touch,** p. 43, for more information). You can send a **telegram** from a post office or hotel. **Fax** is available in many post offices around the country.

Telephone   **Public telephones** are everywhere. Older telephones devour *asimonim* (tokens) for local calls (NIS0.50; avoid calling long distance direct from an old pay phone—making a connection may take hours and bucketfuls of *asimonim*). Far more common are the beige-colored telephones (marked with yellow signs) that operate with **Telecards** (20 units NIS10.50, 50 units NIS23, 120 units NIS52—buy them at the post office). Telecards are good for long distance and international calls (roughly NIS5.90 per min. to the U.S.). International rates drop by up to 50% late at night and on Saturday and Sunday.

Bezek, Israel's phone company, has offices with metered phones for international calls in Tel Aviv and Jerusalem. It may be more economical to call overseas from there, because they charge only for the time you were on the phone; phone cards must be purchased with a fixed set of units and you may be left with extra units at the end of the call. Nonetheless, there's nothing you can do at a telephone office that you can't do from a pay phone. English telephone directories are available at hotels and main post offices, or dial 144 for the **operator** or **information.**

Toll-free direct-dial numbers (toll-free numbers begin with 177) are the easiest way to make overseas calls; you dial an overseas operator who places your collect or calling-card call. The following toll-free numbers (preceded by 177) are for **AT&T:** (177) 100 27 27 (USADirect, WorldConnect, or collect calls), 440 27 27 (BT Direct, for the U.K.), 105 27 27 (Canada Direct), 353 27 27 (Ireland Direct), 640 27 27 (New Zealand), and 270 27 27 (South Africa). For **MCI** World Phone, dial (177) 150 27 27.

For **direct international calling,** dial 00, then the country code, area code, and telephone number. For collect, person-to-person, and credit card calls dial 188 for an **overseas operator.** The same number works for **international directory assistance.** Israel's **international phone code** is 972.

LIFE AND TIMES

■ Government and Politics

Israel is a parliamentary democracy. There is no written constitution; instead, a series of Basic Laws form the constitutional framework for legislation. The Israeli parliament is called the Knesset. Israelis do not directly elect individual candidates for seats in the Knesset; instead they vote for political parties, eleven of which are represented in the present Knesset. The percentage of the popular vote received by a given party is then converted to a proportion of the 120 seats of the Knesset, provided that the party receives at least 1.5% of the national vote. In the past, the head of the party receiving a plurality of votes would form a government, over which he or she would preside as Prime Minister. Under this system, it was generally necessary for the Prime Minister's party to form a coalition with one or more smaller parties, so that at least 61 Knesset members supported the government and could thus defeat a vote of no confidence by the parliamentary opposition. This political necessity tended to give small parties political power beyond their numbers, an oft-criticized aspect of the electoral system.

Public dissatisfaction with the system prompted legislative revision in 1992. As of 1996, Israelis elect their prime minister directly, in addition to voting for a parliamentary party. Intended to bolster the stability of the government by reducing the leverage of smaller parties, the current system enables the directly elected prime minister to claim a national mandate irrespective of party politics in the Knesset. A vote of no confidence in the prime minister by a majority of the Knesset must be immediately followed by new elections for both the premiership and the entire Knesset.

The two major parties are **Labor** (*Avoda*, sometimes still referred to as *Ma'arakh*, or Alignment) and **Likud.** Labor's roots are in old-style Labor Zionism, while the Likud still carries the banner of Revisionist Zionism. The critical issue separating left and right in Israeli politics is the question of territorial compromise in exchange for peace (see **The Peace Process,** p. 58).

■ Economy

Poor in natural resources, stymied by socialist inefficiencies, and carrying the burdens of large defense expenditures and Jewish refugee absorption, Israel for years relied upon substantial financial assistance from diaspora Jewish communities and foreign governments (especially the U.S.). Throughout the last few years, however, the country has begun to reap the fruits of extensive privatization, free trade with the U.S. and the European Community, and the development of a high-tech export-oriented economy. Israel is currently in the midst of an unprecedented economic boom, with steady growth of about 5% per year and a GNP of US$70 billion. The country's main industries are chemicals, diamond cutting and polishing, textiles, high-tech (especially bio-medical and computer) products, and military hardware. Israel is also a leader in desert agriculture and plant genetics. The high inflation rates of the past have given way to a new stability of currency; the new Israeli shekel (NIS) has held steady against the dollar for the past five years.

The peace process has led to further economic optimism. Increased international confidence in the stability of the area has led to a surge of foreign investment and an upgrading of Israel's international credit rating. Israeli businesses are also developing profitable relationships with foreign companies that previously feared the Arab boycott. Finally, trade between Israel and its Arab neighbors is growing and the possibilities for large-scale regional economic cooperation, should real peace ensue, are enormous. Plans are already in the works for major economic projects such as integrated power-grids, road networks, and shared ports to be undertaken jointly by Israel and neighboring Arab states.

In addition, the immigration over the past few years of approximately 500,000 Jews from the former USSR has flooded Israel with highly educated workers and professionals. While it took time for the economy to accommodate so many skilled individuals (horror stories abound of scientists forced to sweep streets), the net result has been a tremendous economic boom. With Israeli incomes rising and Palestinians increasingly prevented from entering Israel to work, Israel has begun importing tens of thousands of workers from Asia and Eastern Europe to work the menial jobs Israelis no longer want. Israel's newfound prosperity and the current trends of the U.S. government to concentrate on domestic issues have led many to predict that the large American foreign aid traditionally received (US$3 billion per year plus loan guarantees) will be significantly reduced in coming years.

■ Kibbutzim and Moshavim

Three percent of the Israeli population lives on **kibbutzim** (plural of kibbutz), somewhat socialist rural societies where production is controlled by members. The kibbutzim of today hardly resemble the fiercely ideological pioneer agricultural settlements that began 80 years ago. These days, most rely more on industry than on agriculture. In addition, the passion for austerity is subsiding; kibbutzniks now demand the same luxuries enjoyed by other Israelis (i.e. larger living quarters, TVs and VCRs, trips to Disney World, Bart Simpson rhinestone jackets). Many kibbutz children now live with their parents in nuclear family homes, whereas just a decade or two ago nearly all lived in separate dormitories and saw their parents only at certain times.

Today's kibbutzim face mounting problems. Labor shortages are becoming common as two-thirds of younger members leave the settlements to test their skills elsewhere. In addition, debt is a daunting threat; kibbutzim collectively owe over US$4 billion, more than US$31,000 per kibbutznik.

Moshavim (plural of *moshav*), another type of rural settlement, provide roughly 40% of Israel's food. Members of a *moshav* typically harvest their own piece of land, though marketing is often done collectively; some have a crop that all members help cultivate. Recently, many *moshavim* near big cities have gone suburban—their members commute to the city.

■ Religion and Ethnicity

Freedom of religion is safeguarded by the state; in 1967, the Law for the Protection of Holy Places was passed after Israel annexed Jerusalem's sacred sites. **Jews** make up 88% of the population (4,400,000), **Muslims** 10% (500,000); the remaining 2% (100,000) includes Christians and Druze. Each community operates its own religious courts, funded by the Ministry of Religion, and controls its own holy sites. Every religion's days of rest are guaranteed by law.

The vast majority of Israeli **Jews** are secular; only about 15% are Orthodox or Ultra-Orthodox (though in Jerusalem it might appear otherwise). The religious establishment is quite powerful; the electoral system has helped Jewish religious parties to wield disproportionate power. Much to the aggravation of many secular Israelis, Rabbinical courts have a state monopoly on matrimonial issues.

Israeli Jews are divided along ethnic lines: **Sephardi** Jews (many of pre-1492 Spanish origins) come from Arab or other Mediterranean countries; **Ashkenazi** Jews have northern or eastern European origins. The rift in Israeli society is deep and wide, and goes back to the 1950s, when Sephardi Jews from Morocco and Iraq were brought to an already established, Ashkenazi-dominated state. While Sephardim compose more than 50% of the Jewish population in Israel, Ashkenazim still fill most of the power positions in government, economy, the military, and academia, while Sephardim are the vast majority among the poor.

After Mecca and Medina, the most important **Muslim** holy site is in Jerusalem—the Al Aqsa Mosque. Muslim *hadith* tells of Muhammad's journey from Mecca to Al Aqsa (The Farthest) and up through the Seven Heavens to meet with God.

Many **Christian** sects are represented in Israel, including the Armenian Orthodox, Abyssinian, Anglican, Coptic, Greek Orthodox, Roman Catholic, and Syrian Orthodox. Most are Arab by language and origin.

Israel's **Druze** population is divided between the Galilee and the Golan Heights. Those in the Galilee remain loyal to Israel and serve in the army, while those in the Golan long to return to Syria. Druze generally live in separate villages and have their own communal institutions. (See **Religion,** p. 61 for more details.)

■ Language

The contemporary Hebrew language was created from biblical Hebrew by **Eliezer Ben-Yehuda,** who compiled the first modern dictionary in the 1920s. In a surprisingly short period, the revived biblical dialect matured into a full-fledged language, spanning from colloquial speech to poetry. While a Semitic language (like Arabic) in structure, modern Hebrew contains elements of European languages; many words for which no equivalent biblical concept exists have been lifted almost as-is. Most Israelis speak English, and signs are usually written in English (and sometimes Russian) as well as Hebrew and Arabic, the official languages of Israel.

The **appendix** of this book contains a list of useful Hebrew words and phrases.

■ The Arts

LITERATURE

The compilation of the biblical narrative was followed by the age of the *Mishnah* (200 BCE-700 CE), when *halakha* (laws derived from the Bible) and *agada* (elaboration on the Bible) were compiled. This age also saw the growth of the *piyyut* (liturgical poem). In the Middle Ages, Jewish poetry included *Megillat Antiohus* and *Megillat Hanuka,* while narrative prose focused on demonological legends.

The revival of Hebrew as a secular language in the 18th century brought a drastic shift in Hebrew literature. Josef Perl and Isaac Erter parodied Hasidic works in their writings. In Czarist Russia, Abraham Mapu wrote *The Hypocrite,* the first novel to portray modern Jewish social life in a fictional context. The generations that followed moved toward realism, often employing Yiddish, a more versatile language.

At the turn of the 20th century, Hebrew was revived for literature by Joseph Brenner, whose hallmark character was the tragic, uprooted settler. His works are remarkable not only for their influence on subsequent generations of Israeli writers, but also for their pessimistic depictions of social interaction between Jews and Arabs. In the 1920s and 1930s Nobel Laureate **Shmuel Yosef (Shai) Agnon** confronted the breakdown of cultural cohesion among modern Jews in *A Guest for the Night, The Bridal Canopy,* and *Twenty-One Stories.*

Just before the creation of the State of Israel, a group of native Hebrew authors rose to prominence. Their style, characterized by concern for the landscape and the moment, is exemplified in S. Yizhar's *Efrayim Returns to Alfalfa.* Beginning in the late 1950s, writers such as Amos Oz and A. B. Yehoshua began to experiment with psychological realism, allegory, and symbolism. In the 1960s, new skepticism surfaced in Israeli literature. David Shahar has been called the Proust of Hebrew literature for his *The Palace of Shattered Vessels,* set in Jerusalem in the 1930s and 40s. Ya'akov Shabtai's *Past Continuous,* about Tel Aviv in the 1970s, is perhaps the best

Israeli novel of the decade. A stunning, though initially confusing, must-read is *Arabesques,* by Anton Shammas, an Arab Israeli writing in Hebrew. On the poetry front, a read through the gripping work of Yehuda Amichai will ensure that you never look at Jerusalem stone in the same way again. Most major Israeli works have been translated into English.

An increasingly prominent genre of Israeli literature focuses on the Israeli-Palestinian conflict by way of fiction, nonfiction, or some combination thereof. Oz's *In the Land of Israel* is a series of interviews with native Israelis and West Bank Palestinians that documents the wide range of political sentiment; his *A Perfect Peace* is a semi-allegorical account of kibbutz life just before the Six-Day War. David Grossman's *Yellow Wind* tells of one Israeli Jew's journey to the West Bank just prior to the *intifada,* while his *Sleeping on a Wire* explores the precarious predicament of Israeli Arabs. For informative accounts written from the Palestinian perspective, check out *The West Bank Story* by Rafik Halabi, an Israeli Druze television reporter, and Fawaz Turki's autobiographical *The Disinherited.* To wipe your tears, pick up Ze'ev Chafetz's *Heroes and Hustlers, Hard Hats and Holy Men,* a hilarious satire of Israeli society and politics.

Israel's short but tumultuous history has inspired a number of historical novels. Consider trying Ḥayim Potok's *Wanderings,* James Michener's *The Source,* and Leon Uris' *Exodus.* For a more sober textbook history of the land read Barbara Tuchman's *Bible and Sword,* which chronicles Palestine from the Bronze Age to the Balfour Declaration of 1917. The elegant works of Solomon Grayzel also give historical background. The dense but provocative *The Arabs in Israel,* by Sabri Jiryis, describes just that. Serious academic types should pick up Nadav Safran's hefty *Israel: The Embattled Ally* or Conor Cruise O'Brien's lighter *The Siege.*

The Israeli **press** is far livelier than the Western norm; politics are taken seriously and opinions expressed vociferously. The liberal *Ha'Aretz* is the most respected daily; *Ma'ariv* leans just right of center. *Yediot Aḥronot* is more tabloid-esque and therefore more widely read. *The Jerusalem Post,* the only English-language daily, tilts to the right, while the bi-weekly English-language *Jerusalem Report* has high-quality reporting and analysis and dovish editors. The *Post* reprints *The New York Times* "Week in Review" section each Monday.

MUSIC

Music became organized after World War I, when Jews in Palestine assembled chamber groups, a symphony orchestra, an opera company, and a choral society. During the 1930s, with the rise of Nazism in Europe, Jewish musicians fled to Israel. This influx spurred the formation of several music groups. Today seasonal music activities from October into July are held in such varied settings as the historic Crusader Castle at Akko and the modern, 3000-seat Mann Auditorium in Tel Aviv.

Israeli **popular music** started emerging from its folk-chant origins (often echoing Russian folk melodies) in the late 1960s. Since the 70s, Israel has been catching up with international music fashions; local bands momentarily lingered on punk, reggae, heavy metal, grunge, and even rap. **MTV** now keeps Israeli youth abreast of the goings-on in London and Seattle, and they expect nothing less of their own local acts. Tel Aviv is the unequivocal hub of the cutting-edge music scene in Israel, though performances occur throughout the country. If faced with the opportunity to see a concert atop **Masada,** grab it.

The most popular performers in Israel play music that's somewhere in between kick-butt rock and a more mellow, acoustic sound. Some native classics still on the performance circuit are David Broza, Shlomo Artzi, Achinoam Nini, Yehudit Ravitz, and Gidi Gov. In many places you can hear simple Middle Eastern-style music, heavy on synthesizers and drum machines, blasting from car stereos and boomboxes: this is *muzika mizraḥit* ("oriental music"), very popular with Sephardic Jews (if you're interested, pick up a recording of Avihu Medina's *mizraḥi* tunes).

■ Food and Drink

Some Israelis' diets are affected by *kashrut* (meaning proper or properly prepared), the Jewish dietary laws. Observant Jews will not eat or shop in a place that carries non-kosher goods; consequently, to keep kosher clientele coming, the big supermarket chains in Israel carry only kosher products, and many restaurants (and most hotels) serve only kosher food. Still, observance of *kashrut* is hardly the norm in Israel—many restaurants, particularly in Haifa and Tel Aviv, are avidly *non*-kosher.

The typical Israeli eats a large breakfast, returns home for a big mid-day dinner, and has a light, late supper. Because of the poor quality and high cost of beef and lamb, Israelis rely largely on chicken, dairy, and vegetable products. Popular items in the Israeli diet include **hummus** (mashed chick-peas, garlic, lemon, and *taḥina*); "salad", a finely chopped mix of tomatoes and cucumbers, garnished with oil and vinegar; *gvina levana,* soft white cheese; *schnitzel,* breaded and fried chicken breast; *chips* (french fries); and a variety of sweet dairy snacks.

Israel's most popular **street food** is a Mid-Eastern staple: falafel are deep-fried ground chick-pea balls served in pita bread with vegetables and *taḥina* sauce. Other common pita-fillers are hummus and *shawerma* (chunks of roast turkey, sometimes posing as lamb). Falafel, hummus, and *shawerma* stands always have a colorful selection of salads and toppings such as *ḥarif,* a red-hot sauce. *Burekas* (filo dough folded over a cheese, potato, spinach, or meat filling) come in different shapes and are available at pastry and some fast-food shops. Pizza also abounds. On hot summer days, street vendors sell what look like hand grenades. Not to worry—these are *sabras* (a prickly cactus fruit), and the inside is edible, although the seeds give some indigestion. (*Sabra* is also a term for a native-born Israeli; both the fruit and the people are said to be thorny on the outside, sweet on the inside.)

The variety of ethnic cuisines in Israel is impressive; **restaurants** run the gamut from Chinese to French to Moroccan to American to Yemenite. Many restaurants serve typical Middle Eastern food. In Yemenite restaurants, *malawaḥ,* thin fried dough usually dipped in a watery tomato sauce, is a cheap specialty. Restaurants serving Eastern European Jewish food are few and very expensive; go to New York.

Preparing your own food is cheap, especially in summer, when fresh fruits and vegetables are available in every outdoor *shuk* (market). You can buy groceries inexpensively at local *shuks,* at the neighborhood *makolet* (small grocery store), or in supermarkets. Israeli bread is tasty and cheap; on Thursdays and Fridays, stores sell fresh loaves of *ḥallah,* egg bread sprinkled with sesame or poppy seeds. Supermarket refrigerators sport a huge selection of dairy products, from low-fat yogurts (try Prikef) to cream-topped chocolate snacks (try Milki). In the deli section you can get food-to-go by the gram, including cookies, miniature *burekas,* and other pastries, as well as an assortment of salads, pickles, and olives.

Two Israeli **beers** are the decent, deep-amber Goldstar and the lesser Maccabee lager. Goldstar is a common draft beer; Maccabee comes in bottles only. Other brews commonly available on tap are Carlsberg, Tuborg, and Heineken. Supermarkets carry a small selection of liquor; note that Nesher "black beer" is a sweet, non-alcoholic malt brew. The official drinking age (not strictly enforced) is 18.

In Arab restaurants, if you ask for **coffee** with no specifications, you'll get a small cup of strong, sweet, Arabic coffee, sometimes referred to as *turki* (Turkish). If you want something resembling American coffee, ask in Hebrew for *ḥafukh* (mixed with milk) or *filter*. Instant coffee *(nes)* is also popular. "Black" *(shaḥor)* or "mud" *(botz)* coffee is Turkish coffee brewed in a cup; watch out for the sediment.

Jerusalem ירושלים القدس

There are men with hearts of stone,
and there are stones with hearts of men.

-Rav Kook

When the sun sets over the Judean hills, Jerusalem's white stone turns gold and peace seems to be within the city's grasp. The domes, spires, and minarets of three faiths' places of worship rise over crenelated walls in quiet harmony. But Jerusalem is not always as serene as its evening breeze and rooftop view. The blindingly white stone, a requirement on all of Jerusalem's buildings, is indelibly, if invisibly, stained with the blood of centuries.

In this city where religion and the freedom to practice it are inextricably tied to daily life, the magnificent spirituality that defines Jerusalem can itself become a burden. As Israeli poet Yehuda Amihai commented, the "air over Jerusalem is saturated with prayers and dreams, like the air over industrial cities. It's hard to breathe."

Spiritual over-saturation doesn't hinder Jerusalem's magnetic attraction; it heightens it. Jews, from ultra-Orthodox to secular, Palestinians, both Christian and Muslim, Armenians, Mormon missionaries, pilgrims and tourists from every continent, fanatics, mystics, and raving lunatics all come and bring their spiritual baggage with them. Jerusalem is timeless and on the verge of history. It is the modern capital for ancient peoples and a headline grabber for age-old disputes. The time warp is most evident on a city bus, where black robes, habits, and *kafias* mingle with halter-tops and baseball caps. All go about their daily business along the city's eternal streets.

■ History

Biblical Times, the Greeks, and the Romans

During Jerusalem's 5000 years, 18 conquerors have presided over the city. Archaeological findings indicate that Jerusalem (Jebus, then) was a Canaanite settlement for 2000-3000 years before King David's conquest around 1000 BCE (II Samuel 5). David established Jerusalem as the capital of the Israelite kingdom; his son Solomon extended the city's boundaries northward to include the present-day Temple Mount. Solomon built the First Temple on the Mount, where sacrificial observances were to be centralized and the Ark of the Covenant was kept.

The Israelite kingdom split shortly after Solomon's death in 933 BCE. The tribes of the northern Kingdom of Israel created their own capital, while those of the south retained Jerusalem as the center of the Kingdom of Judah. Over three prosperous centuries, Judah's citizens developed Judaism and the Jewish identity. Then, in 596 BCE, a Babylonian army led by King Nebuchadnezzar besieged the city and forced its capitulation. The Babylonians kidnapped the aristocracy and kept Jerusalem disarmed and powerless. When Zedekiah instigated a rebellion ten years later, a wrathful King Nebuchadnezzar ordered the exile of the Jews to Babylon and the burning of Jerusalem's finest buildings, including the Temple. In 539 BCE, though, the Babylonians succumbed to Cyrus of Persia who permitted the Jews to return from exile (2 Chronicles 36). Reconstruction commenced soon thereafter, and in 515 BCE the Second Temple was rededicated (Ezra 6:15).

Jerusalem enjoyed more than a century of undisturbed revival under the Persians until Alexander the Great swept through the city in 332 BCE. Hellenization was soon embraced by much of the educated population. After a century and a half of Hellenic rule and a brief spell of Egyptian Ptolemaic control, the Seleucid Empire took Jerusalem (198 BCE). King Antiochus IV forbade all Jewish practices, including *Shabbat* observance, circumcision, and the reading of the Torah. When he installed the cult of Zeus in the Temple, non-Hellenized Jews revolted. The rebels, led by Judas Maccabeus, were successful. In 164 BCE, the temple was resanctified and the priestly hierarchy assumed control of the city. The resulting Hasmonean dynasty zealously ruled the area's Jews for the next century.

Roman general Pompey seized control of Jerusalem in 64 BCE, ushering in six and a half centuries of Roman rule. The Romans installed Herod the Great, child of a Jewish father and Samaritan mother, to reign over what they called the Kingdom of Judea. While occupying the throne (37-4 BCE), Herod commanded the reconstruction of the temple and the creation of the well-known and partially extant Western Wall to better support the enlarged Temple Mount. In 6 CE the Romans bequeathed the governance of the province to a series of procurators, the most famous of whom was Pontius Pilate. Sixty years later, the Jews revolted against Rome. The Roman commander Titus crushed the revolt after four years, destroying the temple, razing the city, and casting many Jews into slavery or exile; life in the Diaspora had begun. After the Bar Kokhba Revolt (a second Jewish revolt named for its leader) ended in 135 CE, the city was destroyed once again by Emperor Hadrian and Jerusalem was declared off limits to the Jews.

That very year Hadrian built a new city over Jerusalem, Aelia Capitolina, to serve as a Roman colony. The pattern of the present-day Old City corresponds to the plan of Hadrian's city: divided into quarters by two major roads (the Cardo and Decumanus) and oriented north to south. You can see the remains of the Cardo in the Old City's Jewish Quarter. When Roman Emperor Constantine adopted and legalized Christianity in 331 CE, his mother Eleni visited the Holy Land in order to identify and consecrate Christian sites. Subsequent Byzantine rulers devoted their energies to the construction of basilicas and churches for the glorification and celebration of the city's Christian heritage.

Muslim Rule and the Crusades

Following a brief period of Persian rule in the early 7th century, Muslim caliph Omar, one of the *Rashidun* (Rightly Guided Caliphs), conquered Aelia in 638. The Temple Mount was cleansed and hallowed anew as a center of Muslim worship. In 691 his successors completed the Dome of the Rock (see p. 297). Under the tolerant Muslim rule, Jews were allowed to return to the city.

In the 10th century Jerusalem fell into Egyptian hands. The Fatimid despots destroyed all synagogues and churches (the "mad caliph" Al Hakim sacked the Holy Sepulchre), and passed on their policy of persecuting non-Muslims to their successors, the Seljuk Turks. Their rumored closing of pilgrimage routes enraged Western Christians and added fuel to the fire of the Crusades, culminating in the Christian capture of Jerusalem in 1099. With cries of *"Deus vult"* (God wills it), the Crusaders mercilessly slaughtered Jerusalem's Muslim and Jewish inhabitants. The Crusader Kingdom of Jerusalem lasted almost 90 years. During this time, churches were built or rebuilt; hospices, hospitals, and monastic orders were founded; and non-Christian sites of worship were desecrated. In 1187 Salah ad-Din expelled the Crusaders, and both Muslims and Jews once again began to resettle the city. Jerusalem became a thriving center for Muslim scholarship from the 13th to the 15th century under the Mamluks.

Ottoman Rule and European Influence

In 1516 Jerusalem capitulated to the Ottoman Turks, the city's rulers for the next 400 years. In 1537 Ottoman emperor Suleiman the Magnificent set out to rebuild the city walls, a task that took four years. The planners deviated from the older design, leaving Mount Zion and King David's tomb beyond the walls (see **The Walls and the Citadel,** p. 296). This negligence infuriated Suleiman, who had the architects' heads put beyond the walls, too. In later centuries, many foreign countries began demanding extra-territorial rights for their citizens living under Turkish rule. The world political climate forced the Ottoman sultan to issue the 1856 "Edict of Toleration" for all religions. The small, deeply religious Jewish and Christian communities in Jerusalem still needed charity from abroad to make ends meet, but the trickle of immigrants coming from Europe and Russia increased to a steady flow.

Jerusalem

Arab Bus Station, **38**
Bank of Israel, **3**
Bible Lands Museum, **8**
Binyanei Ha-Uma, **2**
Central Bus Station, **1**
Church of the Holy
 Sepulchre, **37**
Cinematheque, **29**
City of David, **34**
David's Tomb/Cenacle, **32**
Dome of the Rock, **36**
Dormition Abbey, **33**
El Al Office, **44**
Ethiopian Church, **19**
Garden Tomb, **39**
Gethsemane, **41**
Great Synagogue, **16**

GTIO, **18**
Hebrew Univ. Givat Ram
 Campus, **6**
Histadrut Bldg., **43**
Islamic Art Institute, **13**
Israel Museum, **9**
Italian Synagogue, **45**
Jason's Tomb, **12**
Jerusalem Theater, **15**
Jewish Agency, **17**
King David Hotel, **26**
Knesset, **10**
Mamilla Pool, **24**
Monastery of the Cross, **11**
Natural Science Museum, **30**
Police District HQ, **22**
President's Residence, **14**
Prime Minister's Office, **5**

Rockefeller Museum, **40**
Russian Cathedral, **23**
Sultan's Pool, **28**
Supreme Court, **4**
Train Station, **31**
Ticho House, **20**
U.S. Consulate, **42**
University Stadium, **7**
Western Wall, **35**
Windmill, **27**
YMCA, **25**
Zion Square, **21**

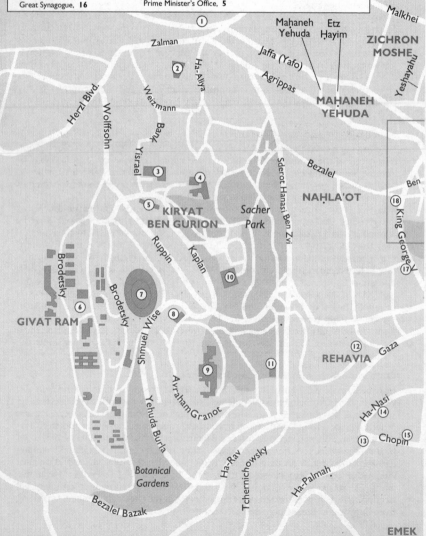

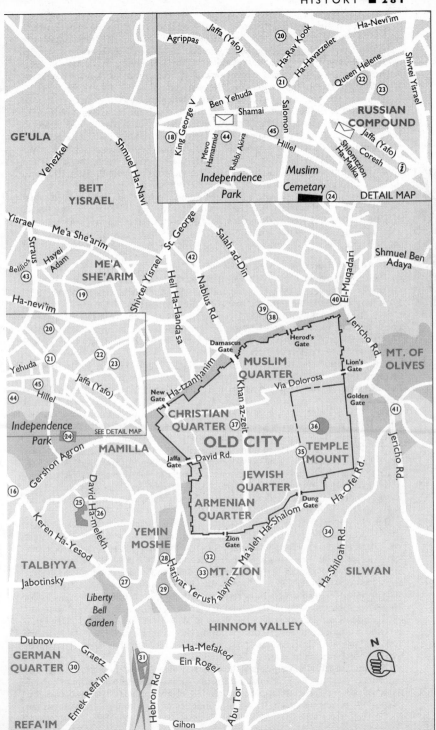

Sir Moses Montefiore, a British Jew, took several trips to Palestine between 1827 and 1874, sponsoring Jewish settlements outside the city walls. These areas soon expanded into bustling neighborhoods, the foundations of West Jerusalem. Heavier Western influence and the increasing influx of European immigrants led to the designation of Jerusalem as an independent *sanjak* (Ottoman province) in 1889, with its own *pasha* (governor) appointed directly from Istanbul.

Ottoman rule over Jerusalem ended in 1917, when the city fell without resistance to the British army. Both Jews and Arabs came to resent the increasing influence of the British in Jerusalem. During World War I, Britain made separate declarations to both Zionists and Arab nationalists, implying that each would eventually gain sole sovereignty over the city. In the end, though, the British kept Palestine for themselves as a League of Nations Mandate. Under British rule, tension between the Jewish and Arab communities heightened, bursting into violent confrontations in 1929 and 1933, and virtual civil war between 1936 and 1939.

The uneasy World War II truce between Arabs and Jews quickly dissolved when the war ended, and violence ravaged Palestine for the next three years. The British announced that they were no longer capable of governing the country. They solicited a settlement from the newly formed United Nations, which resolved to split Palestine into separate Jewish and Arab states, leaving Jerusalem an international city.

1948 to the Present

In the war that followed the 1948 British evacuation, West Jerusalem and the Jewish Quarter were besieged by the Arabs, who blocked the single road out of the city. West Jerusalem held out until the first cease-fire, but the Jewish Quarter of the Old City capitulated to the Jordanian Arab Legion after extensive and exhaustive house-to-house fighting. Jordan demolished the ancient Quarter and dynamited synagogues. The Jordanian-ruled and Israeli sectors of the city were separated by a buffer zone. This division lasted nearly two decades.

When the 1967 (Six-Day) War broke out, Israel requested that Jordan not get involved; King Hussein attacked West Jerusalem nonetheless. In the course of the Six-Day War Israel captured East Jerusalem, the Old City, and the West Bank from the Jordanians; on June 29 that year Israel declared the newly unified Jerusalem its "eternal capital." The walls separating the Israeli and Arab sectors were torn down, and life under Israeli rule began for Jerusalem's Arabs.

The 25 years following the Six-Day War saw large scale construction outside the Old City. Land owned by Palestinians who had fled during the war was taken over by Israel. Vast new Israeli housing developments were built north and south of the city, assuring a Jewish presence in areas previously under Jordanian rule. The old campus of the Hebrew University on Mt. Scopus, maintained as a military post since 1948, was expanded. Intensive gardening projects blossomed throughout the city including verdant parks that now encircle the Old City.

The 1987 outbreak of the *intifada* (uprising) of Palestinians protesting Israeli occupation had some effect on Jerusalem, though demonstrations were more common in West Bank towns. The Palestinians made it clear that they still regarded East Jerusalem as a part of the West Bank and the future capital of their desired Palestinian State. Meanwhile, violent clashes between the Israeli army and stone-throwing Palestinians, as well as occasional stabbings of Jews in the Old City, turned East Jerusalem and the Old City into alien territory for most residents of West Jerusalem and other Israelis visiting town. Matters were made worse in October 1990 when fighting broke out between Jews and Palestinians at the Western Wall. Israeli police killed 17 Palestinians and wounded almost 150 others during the ensuing crackdown. In February 1996, the militant Palestinian group Hamas brought bloodshed to West Jerusalem in two bus bombings killing dozens of commuters.

The future of Jerusalem is perhaps the most sensitive issue of the current Israeli-Palestinian negotiations. Israel adamantly refuses to discuss withdrawing from its capital, while Palestinians fervently oppose abandoning claims to their most important city. Despite the recent terrorism, Jerusalem continues to draw tourists from across the world, including Jordan, whose citizens are now permitted to visit their ancient neighbor following the peace treaty.

■ Orientation

Known as **Yerushalayim** in Hebrew and **Al Quds** (the holy) in Arabic, the Israeli capital is a sprawling city, most of which was only developed in the last 50 years of Jerusalem's three-millennia history.

West Jerusalem denotes the Jewish parts of Jerusalem, from French Hill in the northeast and East Talpiyot in the southeast, to Kiryat Menaḥem in the southwest and Ramot in the northwest. West Jerusalem's main street is **Jaffa Road** (Derekh Yafo), running from the central bus station (at the end of the Jerusalem-Tel Aviv highway) to the Old City's **Jaffa Gate.** Midway between the two, **Zion Square** (Kikkar Tzion) sits at the corner of Jaffa Road and the **Ben Yehuda midraḥov,** and forms one corner of Jerusalem's triangular downtown area. **King George Street** (Ha-Melekh George) forms the third leg of the triangle and meets Ben Yehuda at the end of the popular *midraḥov* (pedestrian zone). **Salomon Street,** running south from Zion Square, is a food-lover's fantasy, and **Queen Helene Ha-Malka Street,** off Jaffa Road, leads to the heart of the **Russian Compound's** pub scene.

Jerusalem's most important historical and religious sites are concentrated within the walls of the **Old City,** still divided into the four quadrants laid out by the Romans in 135 CE. To get from the city center to the Old City, take Jaffa Rd. past the post office to Jaffa Gate. Here you can follow the promenade along the ancient walls to most of the seven other gates. The main road in the Old City is the roof-covered **David Street,** an extension of which, **Baab as-Silsilah Street** (Gate of the Chain), runs just up to the Western Wall. The **Armenian Quarter** is to the right as you enter through Jaffa Gate and is directly accessible via **Zion Gate.** Left of Jaffa Gate is the **Christian Quarter,** which can also be reached directly from the **New Gate. Damascus Gate** provides direct entry into the heavily populated **Muslim Quarter.** To get there from Jaffa Gate, turn left onto **Khan az-Zeit** from David Rd. and it will be on the right. A right turn off David Rd. onto **Ha-Yehudim Street** leads to the **Jewish Quarter,** which is directly accessible via **Dung Gate.**

The old Green Line separating Jordan from Israel pre-1967 runs along Derekh Ha-Shalom (Peace Rd.), and is still a good general demarcation between Palestinian and Jewish areas of Jerusalem. **East Jerusalem** is the name normally given to the Palestinian parts of Jerusalem, and sometimes includes the Old City. East Jerusalem is immediately to the north and east of the Old City. **Suleiman Street,** in front of Damascus Gate, and **Salah ad-Din Street,** which runs out from Herod's Gate, are the main roads in central East Jerusalem. The latter is full of offices and stores. Two Arab bus stations serve the area; the larger one is located on Suleiman St. between Nablus Rd. (Derekh Shekhem) and Salah ad-Din St. The other station, on Nablus Rd., serves routes northward. **Ha-Nevi'im Street** (Musrada in Arabic), converges with Nablus Rd. at Damascus Gate, and has many dry goods stores and hostels. Central East Jerusalem is the financial and cultural hub of the Arab community.

> Tensions sometimes make East Jerusalem and parts of the Old City unfriendly to Israelis and Jewish foreigners. Jewish travelers should make their tourist status as pronounced as possible. Wearing *kippot* is a bad idea in Arab parts of town.

■ Transportation

GETTING AROUND TOWN

Most distances in Jerusalem make for reasonable, pleasant walks, as long as you can take the heat and the hills. You can reach any section of the city by bus from the **central bus station** (tel. 530 45 55) on Jaffa Rd., west of city center (NIS3.90 per ride; a

ISRAEL

NIS39 *kartisiya* buys 11 rides, 20 for those under 18). For more information see **Getting Around,** p. 268. Egged buses stop along the road outside the station entrance, and in front of **Binyanei Ha-Umma Convention Center** (across the street from the station through the underpass). Arab buses run every day; Egged service stops at about 4:30pm on Fridays, and resumes after sunset on Saturday. With a knack for figuring out bus routes, you can visit sights quickly and cheaply.

#1 (from Binyanei Ha'Umma): To Mea She'arim, Dung Gate, Western Wall.

#4A: To Emek Refa'im, Liberty Bell Park, Ramat Eshkol, Mt. Scopus.

#5, 6, 8, 13, 18, 20, 21: To West Jerusalem center; get off at the intersection of Jaffa Rd. and King George St. #5, 8, and 21 go to the train station.

#9: To the Knesset and the Israel Museum, Mt. Scopus, West Jerusalem center, and Hebrew University at Givat Ram.

#13, 21, 23: Down Jaffa Rd., to Jaffa Gate by the Old City.

#27: West Jerusalem center, Damascus Gate, and East Jerusalem (not on Sat. night)

#99, the Jerusalem Circular Line: From Jaffa Gate or central bus station, passes 34 major tourist sights. In summer, Sun.-Thurs. (every hr. 9am-5pm; Fri. every hr. 9am-1pm. Runs less frequently in winter. One loop NIS18.

Taxis are widely available as well: try **Jerusalem Taxi,** 4 Ha-Histadrut St. (tel. 625 52 33), near the junction of King George and Ben-Yehuda St. (open Thurs.-Sun. 6am-11:30pm, Fri. 6am-1hr. before *Shabbat,* Sat. sunset-11:30pm); and **Taxi Israel,** 11 Ha-Histadrut (tel. 562 52 33-36).

GETTING OUT OF TOWN

By Train

Trains depart from **Remez Sq.** (station tel. 673 37 64), southwest of the Old City, just south of Liberty Bell park. To get to the station from downtown, take bus #21 or 48. Trains to **Tel Aviv** (2:55pm, 2hr., NIS15, students NIS12) and **Haifa** (2:55pm, 3hr., NIS29, students NIS22) are slower than buses but a bit cheaper and more scenic.

By Bus

Egged Central Bus Station has posted destinations, fares and information windows, but not much English is spoken. Flash your ISIC card for a 10% discount, and keep your passport handy for drivers to inspect. Buses run to:

Tel Aviv: Central Station, #405 direct (every 5-20min., Sun.-Thurs. 5:50am-midnight, Fri. 5:50am-5pm, Sat. sundown-midnight; NIS16); **Arlozorov terminal,** #480 direct (every 15-20min., 6am-10pm).

Haifa, #940 direct (roughly every 30min., Sun.-Thurs. 6:30am-7:15pm, Fri. 7:30am-3½hrs. before sundown, Sat. sundown-10pm; NIS34).

Ben-Gurion Airport, #945 or 947 (Sun.-Thurs. every 15-40min. 6am-7:30pm, Fri. 7:30am-4:30pm, Sat. sundown-11pm; NIS18).

Eilat, #444 (Sun.-Thurs. every 2-3hrs., 7am-5pm; Fri. every 2-2½hrs., 7am-2pm, less frequently in winter; NIS53; round-trip NIS96.40; book in advance).

Be'er Sheva, #446 direct (every 30min.-1hr., Sun.-Thurs. 6am-8:30pm, Fri. 6am-4:30pm, Sat. sundown-10:30pm) or #470 (runs irregularly—check schedule; 6:20am-6:15pm, Fri. 10am-3pm); both buses NIS27.

Two bus stations serve the **West Bank. Suleiman St. Station,** in East Jerusalem between Herod's and Damascus Gates, serves routes south while **Nablus Rd. Station** serves points north. See **West Bank: Getting Around,** p. 439, for routes and prices and **West Bank: Coming and Going,** p. 438, for information on travel to the West Bank from Israel.

By Taxi

Jerusalem is served by two main **Intercity Sherut Taxi** companies. **Ha Bira** (tel. 625 45 55), at the corner of Ha-Ravkook St. and Jaffa Rd. (near Zion Sq.) goes to **Tel Aviv**

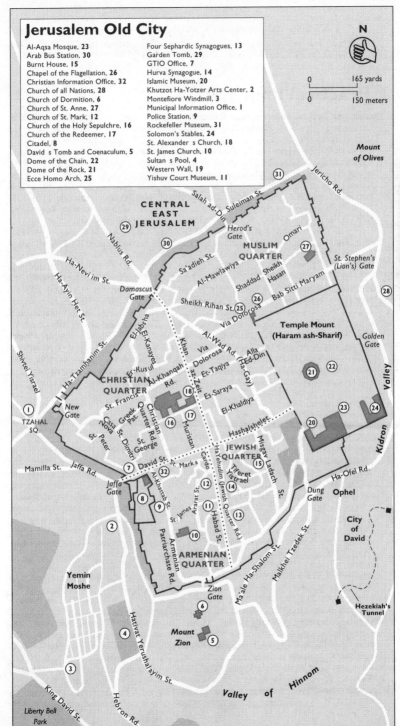

Jerusalem Old City

Al-Aqsa Mosque, 23
Arab Bus Station, 30
Burnt House, 15
Chapel of the Flagellation, 26
Christian Information Office, 32
Church of all Nations, 28
Church of Dormition, 6
Church of St. Anne, 27
Church of St. Mark, 12
Church of the Holy Sepulchre, 16
Church of the Redeemer, 17
Citadel, 8
David's Tomb and Coenaculum, 5
Dome of the Chain, 22
Dome of the Rock, 21
Ecce Homo Arch, 25

Four Sephardic Synagogues, 13
Garden Tomb, 29
GTIO Office, 7
Hurva Synagogue, 14
Islamic Museum, 20
Khutzot Ha-Yotzer Arts Center, 2
Montefiore Windmill, 3
Municipal Information Office, 1
Police Station, 9
Rockefeller Museum, 31
Solomon's Stables, 24
St. Alexander's Church, 18
St. James Church, 10
Sultan's Pool, 4
Western Wall, 19
Yishuv Court Museum, 11

N

0   165 yards
0   150 meters

ISRAEL

Mount of Olives

CENTRAL EAST JERUSALEM

Jericho Rd.

Salah ad-Din St.
Suleiman St.

Herod's Gate
Omari

MUSLIM QUARTER

St. Stephen's (Lion's) Gate

Nablus Rd.

Ha-Nevi'im St.

Ha-Ayin Het St.

Sa'adieh St.

Al-Mawlawiya

Shaddad Sheikh Hasan

Damascus Gate

Sheikh Rihan St.

Bab Sitti Maryam

Via Dolorosa

Temple Mount (Haram ash-Sharif)

Golden Gate

El-Jabsha
El-Kanayes

Khan az-Zeit

Al-Wad Rd.
Via Dolorosa
Alla (El-Din)
Et-Taqiya

Golden Gate

Shivtei Yisrael

Ha-Tzamhanim St.

Er-Rusul

Al-Khanqah Rd.

Es-Saraya

Valley

CHRISTIAN QUARTER

St. Francis
Casa Nova
Greek Pat.
St. Dimitri

Christian Quarter Rd.
St. George

Muristan Rd.

El-Khaldiya

Hashalshelet

Misgav Ladach St.

Kidron

New Gate

TZAHAL SQ.

Mamilla St.

Jaffa Rd.

David St.

St. Marks

JEWISH QUARTER

Yitzhak

HaYehudim (Jewish Quarter Rd.)

Tiferet Yisrael

Ha-Ofel Rd.

Jaffa Gate

Al-Khatab St.

Ararat St.

St. James St.

Habad St.

Dung Gate

Ophel

Yemin Moshe

Armenian Patriarchate Rd.

ARMENIAN QUARTER

Zion Gate

Ma'ale Ha-Shalom St.

Malkhei Tzedek St.

City of David

Hezekiah's Tunnel

Mount Zion

Hativat Yerushalayim St.

King David St.

Hebron Rd.

Valley of Hinnom

Liberty Bell Park

(daily 6am-11pm; NIS15, students NIS14; *Shabbat* NIS25). It has fixed rates and service on *Shabbat* while the rest of the city slumbers. *Sherut* taxis also leave from the central bus station to points through Israel. Split among a group they can be as cheap as buses. **Nesher,** 21 King George St. (tel. 625 72 27 or 623 12 31), provides door-to-door service to the airport (open 24hr.; NIS35; reserve 1 day ahead).

■ Practical Information

Municipal Tourist Information Office (MTIO): 17 Jaffa Rd. (tel. 625 88 44), at Tzahal Sq. Open Sun.-Thurs. 9am-3:30pm, Fri. 9am-noon. Another branch inside Jaffa Gate in the Old City (tel. 628 04 57 or 03 82). Open Mon.-Thurs. 8:30am-5:45pm, Fri. 8am-1pm. Both offices offer pamphlets and maps, but neither have **Carta's Map** (NIS29), the best of the city, available at Steimatsky's and other stores.

Tours: Every Saturday at 10am the municipality sponsors a free **Shabbat Walking Tour** (info tel. 625 88 44) in Hebrew and English. Meet at 32 Jaffa Rd. at the entrance to the Russian Compound, near Zion Sq. *This Week in Jerusalem* lists itineraries (also posted at the MTIO office at 17 Jaffa Rd.). **Zion Walking Tours** (tel. 628 78 66 or 671 35 43) offers 3hr. tours (not of the Gilligan variety) of the Old City. Buy tickets inside Jaffa Gate, across from the Citadel (US$10, students US$9). Zion's 3½-hr. tour includes rooftops and the Western Wall tunnel (US$14, students US$13). Other routes (Mt. of Olives, the Southern Wall excavations) US$17-18, students US$16-17. **Archaeological Seminars Ltd.** (tel. 627 35 15) offers guided tunnel and ramparts walks as well as tours of the Jewish Quarter, the City of David, Mt. Zion, and other areas. (3hr. tour at 9:30am US$16; 2hr. tour at 2pm US$14). Reserve in advance. Meet at 34 Ḥabad St. above the Cardo 15min. beforehand. Guided walking tours are available through the **King George, Ben Yehuda,** and other hostels in the area for NIS15 or US$5. **Society for the Protection of Nature in Israel (SPNI),** 13 Helena Ha-Malka St. (tel. 625 76 82), organizes tours throughout Israel and the Sinai. Tours range from 1-day explorations of Jerusalem (US$46) to 7-day Grand Sinai tours (US$380). In July and Aug. they give 3hr. Jerusalem tours along unusual routes (NIS25-37). Some *Shabbat* tours free. Reserve in advance. Open Sun, Mon., Wed. 9am-3:45pm, Tues. 9am-4:45pm, Thurs. 9am-5:45pm, Fri. 9am-12:30pm.

Budget Travel: Mazada Tours, 9 Koresh St. (tel. 623 57 77), at the corner of Shlomo Ha-Melekh. Runs guided trips to Jordan (2-4 days, US$269-425) and Egypt (3-8 days, US$179-333), and transportation service to Amman and Cairo. Open Sun.-Thurs. 9am-6pm, Fri. 8am-1pm. **Budget Travel Consultants,** 3 Ben Sira St., (tel. 623 39 90), just off Hillel St. Offers 1-4 day trips to Jordan (US$149-459) and 4-10 day jaunts to Egypt (US$150-600). Open Sun.-Thurs. 9:30am-5:30pm, Fri. 9am-1pm. **Neot Ha-Kikar,** 5 Shlomzion Ha-Malka St. (tel. 623 62 62). Similar trips and prices, and specializes in Sinai tours (US$55 for 1 day). Open Sun.-Thurs. 9am-5pm, Fri. 9am-12:30pm. **ISSTA,** 31 Ha-Nevi'im St. (tel. 625 27 99). ISIC cards NIS35; bring proof of student status and a photo. Student discounts on flights to Europe and Cairo, car rentals, and Eurail Passes. Lines can be long. Open Sun.-Tues. and Thurs. 9am-6pm, Wed. and Fri. 9am-1pm. Also on Mt. Scopus Hebrew University campus (tel. 582 61 16) in the Goldsmith Building and at Givat Ram campus (tel. 651 87 80); both open Sun.-Thurs. 8:30am-4pm. Call toll free for flight info and ticketing (1(77) 622 23 33).

Consulates: U.S., 27 Nablus Rd. (tel. 628 24 52), in East Jerusalem. Open Mon.-Fri. 8am-noon; answers phone calls 2-4pm. Closes for Israeli and U.S. holidays. **U.K.,** 19 Nashashibi St. (tel. 582 82 81), in East Jerusalem near Sheikh Jarrah. Open Mon.-Fri. 8am-noon. Other countries have consulates in Tel Aviv.

Currency Exchange: Changepoint, 33 Jaffa Rd. (tel. 625 55 72) with another location at 2 Ben Yehuda. Generally better rates than banks and charges no commission. Zion Sq. has a few options: the **Kent** competes with **Bank Ha-Poalim** (tel. 620 70 70), which is open Sun., Tues., and Thurs. 8:30am-12:30pm and 4-6pm, Mon. and Wed. 8:30am-12:30pm, Fri. 8:30am-noon. **Bank Leumi,** 21 Jaffa Rd. (tel. 620 15 11), next to the main post office, is open Sun.-Thurs. 8:30am-1:30pm, Fri. 8:30am-noon. Their **Foreign Resident and Tourist Center,** 16 King George St., (tel. 620 76 76), has same hours. The air-conditioned **post office** exchanges cash.

American Express: 40 Jaffa Rd. (tel. 623 17 10; fax 623 15 20). Full service office with traveler's check cashing, purchasing, and replacement for cardholders. Mail held, but not packages. If you lose your traveler's checks, call 24hr. toll-free (177) 440 86 94. Open Sun.-Thurs. 9am-5pm, Fri. 9am-1pm.

Flights: El Al information (tel. (03) 972 33 44). Bags for morning flights can be checked in and inspected the night before at #7 Kanfey HaNesharim, 1st floor, (tel. 624 67 25 or 26) on the corner of Jaffa Rd. near the central bus station.

Car Rental: Superdrive, 10 King David St. (tel. 625 08 43), rents to drivers 18 and older. Complete insurance coverage. Credit card required. US$75 per day, US$70 for two days. July-Aug. US$85 per day, US$75 for two days. Open Sun.-Thurs. 8am-5 or 6pm, Fri. 8am-1:30pm. **Thrifty,** 8 King David St. (tel. 625 08 33). Min. age 21. High season US$69 per day, low season US$60 per day. Open Sun.-Thurs. 8am-6pm, Fri. 8am-2pm.

English Books: Sefer ve-Sefel, 2 Ya'avetz St. (tel. 624 82 37), near the corner of 49 Jaffa Rd.; 3rd door on the right and up the stairs. Jerusalem's best place for books and browsing. Huge inventory. Enjoy your purchase in the pleasant balcony cafe. Open Sun.-Thurs. 8am-8pm, Fri. 8am-2:30pm. **Yalkut Books—New and Used,** 8 Aliash St. (tel. 625 70 58), in Kikkar Rejwan, upstairs from the Lev Yerushalayim Hotel. Good selection of fiction paperbacks. Open Sun.-Thurs. 8am-7pm, Fri. 8am-1:30pm. **Steimatzky,** 7 Ben-Yehuda St. (tel. 625 36 54), on the *midraḥov;* other locations as well. Great for maps, magazines, and travel and gift books. Open Sun.-Thurs. 8:30am-9pm, Fri. 8:30am-7pm, Sat. sunset-11pm. **Dani Books,** 57 Jaffa St. (tel. 623 12 03). Varied selection and special "6 books for NIS10" rack. Sun.-Thurs. 9am-7pm, Fri. 9am-2pm. The **SPNI Bookstore** (see **Tours,** p. 286) often has the lowest prices on guidebooks and maps. **Hebrew Union College,** 13 King David St. (tel. 620 33 33), has an air-conditioned **library** with an extensive collection of Jerusalem lore (open Sun.-Thurs. 8:30am-5pm).

Religious Centers: Christian Information Center, P.O. Box 14308 (tel. 627 26 92; fax 628 64 17), inside Jaffa Gate and to the right, just past the Citadel. Genuinely friendly staff sells books and provides maps and detailed lists of Christian services, hospices, and sites in Jerusalem. Open Mon.-Sat. 8:30am-1pm. **Franciscan Pilgrims Office,** P.O. Box 186 (tel. 627 26 97), in the same building as the Christian Information Center. Makes reservations for mass at all Franciscan sanctuaries. Talk to the priest here about going to Christmas midnight mass in Bethlehem. Want to prove you've been to the Holy Land? Pilgrimage certificates available (US$3). Open Mon.-Fri. 9am-noon and 3:30-5:30pm, Sat. 9am-noon. **Jewish Student Information Center,** 5 Beit El (tel. 628 26 34, after-hours (052) 86 77 95; fax (06) 28 83 38), in the Jewish Quarter across from the Ḥurva Arch. The roving info center is known as Jeff Seidel. If he doesn't find you first, he's often at Mt. Scopus, the Wall, or Ben Yehuda. Offers *Shabbat* hospitality, Jewish classes, and Old City tours. Primarily geared for those just beginning to explore their Jewish roots. Free *Shabbat* meals with religious families (ask Jeff when to meet at the Wall). While some travelers have wonderful experiences here, others find the JSIC too preachy. Open Sun.-Thurs. 9am-5pm, Fri. 9am-noon.

Lesbian Organization: KLAF (tel. 625 12 71) welcomes guests and tourists to its periodic parties and outings.

Ticket Agencies: Bimot, 8 Shammai St. (tel. 624 08 96), and **Kla'im,** 12 Shammai St. (tel. 625 68 69). Often have discount tickets for students and tourists for concerts, shows, and sporting events throughout Israel. Both open Sun.-Thurs. 9am-7pm, Fri. 9am-1pm. **Ben Na'im,** 38 Jaffa Rd. (tel. 625 40 08) is primarily for sporting events. Open Sun.-Thurs. 8:30am-2pm and 3-7pm, Fri. 8:30am-1pm.

Laundry: Baka Washmatic, 35 Emek Refa'im St. (tel. 563 18 78). Take bus #4, 14, 18, or 24, get off at Emek Refa'im post office, cross the street, and continue for ½ block. Open Sun.-Thurs. 8am-7pm, Fri. 8am-2pm. 10kg wash, dry, and fold NIS55; 7kg NIS37. 20% *Let's Go* discount. **Ha-Merkaz Laundry,** 11 Kakal St. (tel. 566 42 46), just off Usishkin St. Open Sun.-Thurs. 8am-1pm and 3-7pm, Fri. 8am-1pm. 5kg wash and dry NIS43. **Laundry Place,** 12 Shammai St. (tel. 25 77 14). Do your own laundry (NIS9 for 7kg; dry NIS3 per 10min.) while watching MTV. Drinks and video games available. Detergent NIS3. Open Sun.-Thurs. 8am-midnight. Fri. 8am-5pm.

Swimming Pools: Jerusalem Swimming Pool, Emek Refa'im St. (tel. 563 20 92), open Mon.-Fri. 6am-6pm (NIS35, students NIS30). Bus #4 or 18. Get *Shabbat* tickets in advance. **Beit Zayit** (tel. 534 62 34). Take bus #151 (10 per day) from central station to the last stop. NIS22, children NIS17; Fri. and Sat. NIS27. Open daily 9am-7pm and some evenings.

Camping Supplies: The most extensive stock of camping gear is at **Orcha Camping,** 12 Yoel Solomon (tel. 624 06 55). Affiliated with SPNI. Open Sun.-Thurs. 8:30am-7pm, Fri. 8:30am-3pm. **Steve's Packs,** 11 Ben Hillel (tel. 534 83 02) on the *midraḥov,* has lots of them. **Jerusalem Camping,** 14 Ben Hillel (tel. 625 11 40) off the *midraḥov.* Open Sun.-Thurs. 8:30am-8:30pm, Fri. 8:30am-3:30pm, Sat. after *shabbat*-midnight.

Help Lines: Rape Crisis Center (tel. 625 55 58). Open 24hr., will accompany you to the police and explain procedures. **Mental Health Hotline** (tel. 561 03 03), also called **Eran,** assists tourists. Open 8am-11pm. **Alcoholics Anonymous** (tel. 563 50 62). **Na'an** offers advice to mentally disturbed teens (tel. (177) 022-3011). Open Sun.-Thurs 5-8pm.

Services for the Disabled: Yad Sarah Organization, 43 Ha-Nevi'im St. (tel. 624 42 42). Free loans of medical equipment. Look for a big blue ex-train. They can meet you at the airport. Open Sun.-Thurs. 9am-7pm, Fri. 9am-noon.

Pharmacy: Superpharm, 5 Burla St. (tel. 678 41 39 or 679 59 33), near Hebrew University Givat Ram campus; bus #17. Open Sun.-Thurs. 8:30am-midnight, Fri. 8:30am-3pm, Sat. 9pm-midnight. Also at 3 Ha-Histadrut (tel. 624 62 49 or 45), between Ben-Yehuda and King George St. Open Sun.-Thurs. 8:30am-11pm, Fri. 8:30am-3pm, Sat. sundown-11pm. **Alba Pharmacy,** 7 Ben-Yehuda St. (tel. 625 77 85) and 42 Jaffa St. (625 37 03). Open Sun.-Thurs. 8am-7pm, Fri. 8am-2pm. No 24-hr. pharmacies, but two are on rotating duty nightly and on *Shabbat.* Schedules and phone numbers available on pharmacy doors and in newspapers.

Medical Emergency: tel. 101. **Magen David Adom First Aid:** (tel. 652 31 33), next to the central bus station. Will see any medical problem (NIS180); treatment may cost more. Open 24hr. Hospital emergency rooms are much more expensive. Newspapers list hospitals on duty for emergencies. **Blue Cross-Blue Shield** members may be eligible for medical coverage at Hadassah Ein Kerem and Mt. Scopus hospitals (tel. 677 60 29 for info).

Police: tel. 100 for emergencies. Located in the Russian Compound (tel. 539 11 11), off Jaffa Rd. in West Jerusalem. Has a tourist desk (tel. 539 12 54 or 63). There is also an Old City branch, inside Jaffa Gate on the right (tel. 622 62 22).

Internet Access: Strudel Internet Cafe and Wine Bar, 11 Monbaz St., Russian Compound (tel. 623 21 01; fax 622 14 45; email strudel@inter.net.il). **Email, web, photoscans, telnet** services are the cheapest in town. Happy hour 7-9pm (15min. Internet time and a beer for NIS10). Open Mon-Fri. 10am-late, Sat. 3pm-late. MC, Visa. **Surfer's Paradise,** 4 Durst Rishonim (tel. 623 69 34). Pay higher prices for prime location. Quiche NIS12, internet access NIS8 for 15min, NIS15 for 30min. Kosher. Open Sun.-Thurs. 8am-11pm, Fri. 7:30am-4pm.

Central Post Office: 23 Jaffa Rd. (tel. 629 08 98). Open Sun.-Thurs. 7am-7pm, Fri. 7am-noon. **Poste Restante, Western Union, telegram,** and **fax** services available. For telegrams, dial 171 (24hr.). **Branch post offices** throughout the city.

Telephones: Solan Communications, 2 Luntz St. (tel. 625 89 08; fax 625 88 79), off Ben-Yehuda St., on the *midraḥov.* Fax and telegram services, private booths for reduced-price local and international calls (cheaper than with telecard), and cellular phone rentals. **Information:** tel. 144. **Telephone Code:** 02.

■ Accommodations

WEST JERUSALEM

Accommodations in West Jerusalem are generally roomier, cleaner, safer, comfier, and more conveniently located than their old city counterparts. They are correspondingly more expensive, and what they boast by way of amenities they lack in rustic charm. Hostels here are better for club-goers; many have no curfew, and some are located directly above the action. You may not have to pay the 17%VAT if you pay in your home currency. Accommodations in private houses are a second choice. Locals may approach you at the bus station, but be aware that their places may not be licensed and therefore not subject to government inspection. Women should be especially cautious, even if approached by a female.

Jerusalem Inn Guest House, 6 Ha-Histadrut St. (tel. 625 12 94; fax 625 12 97), off Ben Yehuda St. 1 block before King George St. Bus #14, 17, 31, or 32 from the central station. Friendly, clean, and in the middle of town. A lounge/reception area outfitted with cable TV is a relaxing spot for a drink (NIS2-4). Mostly young, English-speaking guests. Strict no-visitors policy and locked front door. Communal refrigerator and small, shared baths. Crowded, clean rooms have ceiling fans and 24hr. heating in winter. No smoking. Check-in before 11:30pm. Check-out 10:30am. Midnight curfew, but keys given for NIS20 deposit. Limited number of dorm beds US$12; singles US$26-36; doubles US$46-52; group rooms US$16 per person. 10% cheaper in winter. US$2 breakfast available 8am-noon.

Jerusalem Inn Hotel, 7 Horkanos St., (tel. 625 27 57) just off Heleni Ha-Malka. Bus #6, 18, or 21 from the central bus station. Myriad amenities include cable TV, phones, voicemail, ceiling fans, balconies, and full bath in every room. Quiet, classy oasis in the middle of a happening neighborhood. Extra money well-spent on airy, cool rooms and comfortable mattresses. Reception 8am-midnight. Check-out 10:30am. No curfew. Singles US$40; doubles US$58-68; triples US$66-69; 6-person rooms US$133. Cheaper in off-season. Reserve in advance with credit card.

Hotel Noga, 4 Bezalel St. (tel. 625 45 90 until 1pm, 566 18 88 after; ask for Mr. or Mrs. Kristal). Near corner of Shmuel Ha-Nagid St. Feels like your own private apartment; managers leave at night. 10 bright, airy rooms on 3 floors, each with a kitchen (free tea and coffee). 2 spotless balconies overlook the Bezalel Art Institute. Free luggage storage; heated in winter. Mr. Kristal loans tennis rackets and balls for free. Parking in back. Min. 2-night stay, special price for extended stays. Singles US$28; doubles US$35; triples US$45; quads US$55. Reserve in advance.

Ben Yehuda Hostel, 23 Ben Yehuda St. (tel. 624 80 21 or 625 71 25; fax 625 30 32). No earlybirds here. Perched precariously above the notorious Underground (see **Dancing,** p. 316), the party rocks all night long. Drinks NIS2-4. Lockers NIS5. Laundry NIS20. 24hr. check-in. Check-out 10am; Sat. checkout can be extended until after *Shabbat* for small fee. No lockout. No curfew. Dorm beds (6-8 per room) NIS30/US$8; doubles NIS109/US$32; triples NIS132/US$39; quads NIS163/US$48.

Beit Shmuel Guest House (HI), 6 Shammai St. (tel. 620 34 73 until 5pm), near the King David Hotel. Part of the Beit Shmuel Center for Progressive Judaism complex; enter through the Safdie-designed Hebrew Union College. Antiseptic, safe, remarkably hotel-like. Lounges, courtyard, gardens, coffee shop, Fri. night concerts (guests receive 10% discount), all on the premises. Wheelchair accessible. Elevator, A/C, heat in winter. 24hr. reception. Check-in 3-11pm. Check-out 9am. No curfew. Dorm beds (6 per room) US$20; singles US$40.50; doubles US$59 (non-members US$29, US$70, and US$76). Breakfast included. Oct.-April prices drop US$8-10.

Davidka Hostel (HI), 67 Ha-Nevi'im St. (tel. 538 45 55; fax 538 87 90). Bus #27, 35, 36, or 39 from central bus station. Super-hostel with 250 beds in clean, relatively safe, A/C rooms, each with no more personality than a gray blob. Watch out for the hordes of high schoolers who think that gray blobs are the coolest! No curfew or lockout. Free safe. 24hr. reception. Check-out 10am. Cafeteria serves munchies from 8am-midnight. Dorm beds US$19; singles US$39; doubles US$56. Nonmembers add US$1.50 per person. Negotiable surcharge for check-out in evening. Breakfast included. Reservations recommended. Visa, MC.

Beit Bernstein Youth Hostel (HI), 1 Keren Ha-Yesod St. (tel. 625 82 86), at the corner of Agron St., tucked behind a synagogue. Bus #7, 8, 9, 14, 31, or 32 from the central bus station. Clean rooms, TV lounge, and a great garden in the back await those who can keep the midnight curfew. Often filled with teen tour groups during the summer. Reception open 9am-noon and 2pm-midnight. Check-in 2pm. Check-out 9:30am. Dorm beds (single-sex floors, 4-7 per room, heated in winter) NIS50 (US$14). Breakfast included.

ISRAEL

OLD CITY

Most of Jerusalem's cheapest hostels—from quiet sanctuaries to hang-from-the-rafters hangouts—are located in the Old City. Benefits of staying here include great views from rooftops and balconies, proximity to major sights, and free wake-up calls from *muezzins*. Conditions vary within a given hostel; a fellow traveler may be sleeping on a piece of foam while you get a heavenly feather puff. Bargain if business seems slow. Lodgings cluster near Jaffa and Damascus Gates. Most have "flexible curfews" (managers will let you in late if you inform them ahead of time and if the night guard stays awake). Some Old City hostels are also sources of temporary (1-2 nights) and not so temporary (11-12 months) employment; some travelers have been known to come for a week and stay for a year, working a few hours a day to pay for their stay. Don't leave luggage unattended in hotel rooms if you can avoid it. All hostels have safes for your valuables. In most places, you can pay in either U.S. dollars or shekels.

> Be extremely cautious in the empty streets of the Old City after dark. Those staying in the Muslim Quarter should avoid walking alone and should make their tourist status pronounced. Only the busiest streets in the Old City are lit at night, so you should learn your way back to your hostel during the day.

Near Jaffa Gate

Walk down Jaffa Rd. or Agron St. to the end, or take bus #13, 19, 20, 21, 23, 30, or 99.

Citadel Youth Hostel, 20 St. Mark's Rd. (tel. 627 43 75). Take the first alleyway on the right off David St. and go up the stairs that curve left past Michael's Cafe; the hostel is on your right. Super tidy rooms with high, stone walls and vaulted ceilings. Rooftop solarium has beds and a classic view, but gets hot some days. Atrium sitting area, TV room, and common kitchen. 24hr. check-in. Check-out 11am. Flexible midnight curfew. Max. stay 2 weeks. Eye-popping low prices: dorm beds NIS20, students NIS15; private rooms NIS60-90. 20% *Let's Go* discount.

Lutheran Youth Hostel, 7 St. Mark's Rd. (tel. 628 21 20), after the Citadel Hostel on your right. Luxuriously calm, with a courtyard, lush gardens, and a kitchen and dining hall worthy of the Last Supper. Women's basement dorm room has 40 beds. Men's room (above ground) has 20 beds. Check-in noon. Check-out 9am. Lockout 9am-noon. 10:30pm curfew. Free lockers. Dorm beds NIS24; singles NIS130; doubles NIS230. Guests must be under 35.

Petra Hostel (tel. 628 66 18), the first hostel on your left on David St. just before you enter the *souq*. Spartan accommodations attract Jerusalem's hard-core backpackers. Watch the sunset with them from the roof, beer in hand. Hot water available at selected times. 24hr. check-in. Check-out 10am. No curfew; knock after 11pm. Roof beds NIS15; dorm beds NIS20; singles NIS60; private rooms NIS70-100.

New Swedish Hostel, 29 David St. (tel. 626 41 24 or 627 78 55), straight into the *souq* on the left. Hopping with travelers. Spotless modern bathrooms and showers, kitchen, TV lounge, and free tea. Lockers NIS3 for as long as you stay. Coed and single-sex accommodations. Check-in until 3am. Check-out 11am. Curfew 3am. Dorm beds NIS13; private rooms NIS45-50.

Lark Hotel, 4 Latin Patriarchate Rd. (tel. 628 36 20), the first left from Jaffa Gate. Spotless rooms with showers. Small 2nd-floor balcony and sitting space overlooks quiet street. 1st-floor Armenian restaurant run by same friendly people. Open 6:30am-11pm, but keys available. Check-out anytime. Singles, doubles, and triples about US$22 per person; prices flexible. Continental breakfast included.

Jaffa Gate Youth Hostel (tel. 627 64 02), off the Jaffa Gate square area, across from the entrance to the Tower of David. Long dorm room walls are painted to look like stone. Homey TV lounge, common kitchen and outdoor eating area. Guests have schlepped their packs all over the world. Check-out noon. Curfew 1am. Dorm beds NIS25 (students NIS20); private rooms with bath NIS125-150, off-season NIS70-110.

Near Damascus Gate

Reach Damascus Gate by walking to the end of Ha-Nevi'im St. or by taking a left from Jaffa St. onto Ha-Tzanḥanim St. from the city center. Buses #1, 13, 23, and 37 go here. Hostels here are cheaper and livelier, but the area is less safe after dark.

Armenian Hospice, 36 Via Dolorosa (tel. 626 08 80), a left off Al-Wad Rd. Lavish wood furnishings, gleaming tile floors, and possibly the thickest mattresses in town. Gold linens make the place feel like a palace. New TVs and phones in every room. Sparkling bathrooms have hair dryers. 24hr. reception. No curfew or lock-out. Check-out noon. Central heating in winter. Dorm beds US$12; singles US$50; doubles US$60; triples US$66. The old section is not as palatial or expensive: clean, sunny building has dorm beds (US$12) and private rooms (US$30-35). Visa, MC.

Austrian Hospice, 37 Via Dolorosa, P.O. Box 19600 (tel. 627 46 36), on the corner of Al Wad Rd. Lush grounds and spotless tiled rooms. Feels like the setting for a Von Trapp family reunion. German library, private chapel, and glorious roof view. Dark, tightly packed basement dorms. Wheelchair accessible. *Wiener Kaffeehaus* inside (open daily 9am-10pm) serves Austrian cakes (NIS7) and drinks (NIS4-7). Check-in 10pm. Check-out 10am. Strict 10pm curfew. Dorm beds US$12; singles US$44; doubles US$68; triples US$96. Breakfast included. 3-course meals US$9 for guests. Reservations recommended.

El Hashimi Hotel and Hostel, 73 Khan az-Zeit (tel. 628 44 10). Take the right fork from Damascus Gate. Brand new, sunny 3-story hostel has glowing white walls and floors, and incredible views of the Dome of the Rock. Squeaky clean bathrooms, sturdy beds. Kitchen facilities, with free tea and coffee, and TV room. Laundry NIS20 per load. Single-sex dorm rooms available. Heat in winter. 24hr. reception. Check-out 10:30am. Curfew 3am. Roof beds NIS10. Dorm beds NIS15; singles NIS50; doubles NIS90. Accepts and exchanges traveler's checks.

Ecce Homo Convent, Eastern Via Dolorosa, P.O. Box 19056 (tel. 627 72 92). Turn left onto Via Dolorosa from Al Wad Rd. Look for the "Notre Dame de Sion" sign down the road on a door on the left. The sisters provide blissful refuge and a tran-scendental view of Jerusalem. Kitchen and study areas. Reception open daily 6:30am-11pm. Check-out 10am. Curfew 11pm. Dorm beds (women only) US$8; coed dorms (10-12 beds per room) US$16; singles US$31. Breakfast included. Lunch or dinner US$10. Guests go free to the Ecce Homo excavations below.

Tabasco Hostel, 8 Akabat Tekreh (tel. 628 34 61), just off Khan az-Zeit Rd. A huge, clean, dirt cheap hostel with rows of beds. Bedouin-style Tea Room serves beer (NIS8) and snacks (NIS5-10), but no Tabasco. Hot showers. Management runs cheap daytrips to Masada and Jericho. No lockout or curfew. Check-in 24hr. Checkout 11am. Dorm beds NIS16; roof mattress NIS12; private rooms NIS70.

Al-Ahram Hostel, 64 Al Wad Rd. (tel. 628 09 26). Enter Damascus Gate and bear left onto Al Wad Rd. at the fork. Opposite 3rd station of Via Dolorosa. Midnight cur-few, but keys may be procured. Check-out 10am. Free safe. Roof beds NIS10. Dorm beds (4-7 per room, co-ed and single sex) NIS15; private rooms with showers NIS70; triples NIS90. Higher prices in winter. Free luggage storage.

Black Horse Hostel, 28 Aqabat Darwish St. (tel. 628 03 28), off Via Dolorosa. Crowded, cavernous hostel. Bedouin tent-style sitting room/bar. Heated in winter. Happy hour 7-8:30pm (2 beers NIS10). Phone and fax service, kitchen, TV, and video. Check-in 7:30am-1:30am. Check-out 10am. Curfew 1:30am. No lockout. The alley can be dark and isolated at night. Dorm beds NIS15, with ISIC NIS13; singles/ doubles NIS50-70. Breakfast NIS10; Sat.-night courtyard barbecues NIS15.

Jewish Quarter

The Old City Youth Hostel (HI), 2 Ararat St. (tel. 628 86 11). Walk down David St. into the market and follow the signs: a right onto St. Mark's Rd., a right again across from the Lutheran Hostel, and up the narrow street with half-arches; it's behind the iron gate. Renovated hospital with high ceilings, sparkling-clean rooms, and com-mon bathrooms. Sometimes crowded with teenage tour groups and soldiers on leave. No smoking, TV, or radio on *Shabbat*. Check-in 5pm-9pm. Check-out 9am. Lockout 10am-5pm. Flexible 11pm curfew. Dorm rooms US$15; singles US$20; doubles US$30-40; triples US$45-60. Kosher breakfast included.

EAST JERUSALEM

East Jerusalem, radically different from the Western part of the city, can be a hotbed of tension. Feel out the situation before you decide to stay here. In quiet times, this can be a great place to experience the Palestinian lifestyle. Travelers, especially women, should not walk alone at night. Visibly Jewish travelers (particularly men in *kippot*) should stay away. Several hostels line Ha-Nevi'im St., which intersects Suleiman St. and Nablus Rd. across from Damascus Gate.

Faisal Youth Hostel and Crusader Cafe, 4 Ha-Nevi'im St. (tel. 627 24 92). Pleasant and relaxing atmosphere with crowded bunks, TV, large kitchen, and several cats. Manager Hudson, from Maryland, refers to his gorgeous balcony as "Jerusalem's best box seat." Check-out 11am. 24hr. guard. Washing machine use NIS10. Single-sex dorm beds NIS16; private rooms NIS60.

Cairo Youth Hostel, 21 Nablus Rd. (tel. 627 72 16). Laid-back hostel on East Jerusalem's major street (last stop on bus #27). "No long term residence" policy keeps atmosphere dynamic. Clean, with large sitting area, never-ending roof, high ceilings, and a sunny kitchen and balcony. Heat in winter. Free luggage storage. Curfew 1:30am. Check-out 11am. Dorm beds NIS15; private rooms (1-4 people) NIS60.

Palm Hostel, 6 Ha-Nevi'im St. (tel. 627 31 89). Recent conversion into a "Christian believers hostel" makes the Palm fairly staid. You can play checkers, smoke, or catch several videos a day in the upper common room. Family-friendly, but not gay- or lesbian-friendly. Solar heating system brings you 24hr. hot water. Heated in winter. Check-out 10am. Dorm beds NIS16; private rooms NIS70. Storage NIS3.

LONGER STAYS

If you'll be in Jerusalem for over two months, consider renting an **apartment.** During July and August college students go on vacation and many rent out their flats. A single room in a shared apartment will cost at least US$250-400 per month. The best source of information is the classified section of the local weekly *Kol Ha-Ir.* If you find someone to translate, you can submit a free ad requesting an apartment. A more thorough but expensive option is the **She'al Service,** 21 King George St. (tel. 625 69 19), which grants one month's access to its voluminous listings in English for NIS140 (open Sun.-Thurs. 8:30am-7pm, Fri. 8:30am-1pm). The **Ma'agar Meida,** 5 Dorot Rishonim (tel. 625 37 28), on the *midraḥov,* offers an identical service (open Sun.-Thurs. 8am-8pm, Fri. 9am-1:30pm). The bulletin boards at Hebrew University and upstairs at the Israel Center on the corner of Strauss and Ha-Nevi'im St. may be helpful. There is another bulletin board at Tmol Shilshom restaurant off Naḥalat Shiva Rd. The "Bed and Breakfast" listings at the GTIO are a reliable source.

■ Food

The *Jerusalem Post* "Good Food Guide" and *Jerusalem Menus* magazine are distributed at hotels and tourist offices, and include listings of international cuisines.

OLD CITY

Cheap Middle Eastern food stands and restaurants lurk behind the unsavory aroma of the Old City markets. Most places are buried deep within the narrow alleys, but a few huddle close to the gates. Price usually increases with convenience, but not necessarily with quality. The chicken restaurants at **Khan az-Zeit** (look for the huge rotisseries and follow the smell) are popular with locals. The market also drips with sugary shops selling honey-drenched Arab pastries for NIS8-12 per 0.5kg. You'll find loads of fresh veggies in and around Damascus Gate. Street vendors sell fresh, large, soft sesame *ka'ak* throughout the *souq;* ask for *za'tar* to go with it and dip away. It should cost NIS1.5-2, but you'll see clueless camera carriers paying thrice that. Jerusalem's only Roman restaurant, the **Culinaria** (tel. 626 41 55), in the Jewish Quarter Cardo, can provide a genuine *Old* City experience. The waiters will wrap you in togas and bring you plate after plate of chicken, fish, salad, and pita and olive oil. Unfortunately, inflation has not been kind over the last 2000 years—dinners are now NIS100 per person and lunches NIS60 (open Sun.-Fri. noon-3:30pm, dinner by reservation only).

Abu Shanab Pizza, 35 Latin Patrichate Rd. (tel. 626 07 52), the first left from Jaffa Gate. The best food, ambiance, and service in the Old City. Candlelight gleams off the stone walls and intimate tables. Cherished crusty pizzas (NIS6-20) and easygoing waitstaff. Happy hour 6-7pm (2 beers NIS8), featuring a different "Star Cocktail" for each astrological sign. Live jazz weekly. Open Mon-Sat. 10am-11pm.

Jerusalem Star Restaurant, 32 Al Wad Rd. (tel. 628 71 75). Full *kebab,* pita, salad, *baklava,* and coffee meal NIS25. Friendly staff and cool dark interior. Beer NIS7. Open daily 9am-10pm.

Abu Shukri, 63 Al Wad Rd. (tel. 627 15 38), 200m from Damascus Gate, on the left when the Via Dolorosa turns to the right. Given thumbs up by the Israeli press. Falafel platters NIS8. Open daily 8am-4 or 5pm.

The Coffee Shop (tel. 626 40 90), near Jaffa Gate, next to the Christ Church Hospice. Ivy stenciling, Jerusalem-tiled tables, and a no smoking rule make this A/C hall the most pristine restaurant in the Old City. All-you-can-eat soup and salad (NIS21), sandwiches (NIS9-10). Open Tues.-Sun. 11am-6:30pm.

Bakery Muhammad Ali (a.k.a. **The Green Door**), 5 Aqabat Sheikh Rihan (tel. 627 61 71), left off Damascus Gate Rd. The room has few tables and is often empty, but Abu and son bake good, inexpensive pizza (NIS5) in their stone oven. Free tea and coffee. Open daily 7am-midnight.

The Armenian Tavern, 79 Armenian Orthodox Patriarchate Rd. (tel. 627 38 54), through Jaffa Gate and to your right. Armenian music echoes in the mosaic-floored underground room that serves up all sorts of tasty Armenian edibles. And did we mention that it's Armenian? Sandwiches (NIS10-12), salads (NIS6-23), and meat dishes (NIS35-40). Special Fri. night dinners. Open daily 11am-11pm. Visa, MC.

Quarter Cafe (tel. 628 77 70), above the corner of Tiferet Yisrael and Ha-Sho'arim St., Jewish Quarter (look for the sign). Epic view from roof and balcony tables warrant a cake or salad stop (NIS8-15). Full lunches are overpriced (NIS35-45). Open Sun.-Thurs. 9am-6:30pm, Fri. 9am-4pm. Kosher.

EAST JERUSALEM

East Jerusalem is crawling with vendors selling falafel, spicy *kebab,* rolls, and ears of corn, all for less than NIS4. Follow the smoke, smells, and solicitations to the corner of Suleiman and Nablus. **Nasser Eddin Bros.** on Suleiman St. across from Damascus Gate and to the right, just past the bus station, stocks Arabic delights (open daily 8am-7pm). Boxes along Suleiman St. overflow with the cheapest produce in the city (1kg zucchini NIS2-3). Salah ad-Din, Az-Zahra, and Suleiman Streets have it all, from bustling rotisserie and falafel places to quieter haunts with extensive and expensive menus. **Al Amin** (tel. 628 83 34), at 14 Ha-Nevi'im, is a sweet-smelling 24-hour bakery with delicious egg pizza *(ras el bed)* for NIS5.

Kan Zaman (tel. 628 32 82), on the patio of the Jerusalem Hotel on Nablus Rd. The height of East Jerusalem chic. Delicate tables shaded by vines. Vegetarian dishes (NIS14-15), meat and fish meals (NIS20-29), sandwiches (NIS10-15), and salads (NIS10-15). Sat. night Lebanese buffet (NIS50 after 8pm). Live classical Arabic music Thurs. and Sat. nights. Open daily 11am-11pm.

Sultan Suleiman's Lounge (tel. 627 24 16), 2nd floor of Pilgrim's Palace Hotel on Suleiman Rd. near Herod's Cafe. Sit in cool, rose marble comfort overlooking the crowds below. Overpriced entrees, but tasty sandwiches and omelettes (NIS8-13). Beautiful view of the Old City walls at sunset. Open daily 8am-midnight.

Al Quds Restaurant, 23 Suleiman St. (tel. 627 20 52). The semicircle English sign is hard to see, so keep your eyes peeled. You might feel like a roasted chicken as you walk through the hot smoky aisle past the rows of rotisseries, but there is a light at the end of the tunnel: clean white tables and a delicious feast for a mere NIS12-14. *Shawerma, shish kebab,* or chicken platter (includes salad, fries, and pita) NIS15. Open daily 8am-midnight.

ISRAEL

Al Ayed, 4 Ha-Nevi'im St., across from Damascus Gate. Delicious falafel in pita (NIS2.50) or *shawerma* (NIS6). Open Sun.-Fri. 8am-6pm.

WEST JERUSALEM

West Jerusalem's restaurant scene reflects the cosmopolitan, international makeup of its growing population. Dining here spans a full spectrum of price ranges, from fancy French to fried falafel and from sushi to *shawerma*. Restaurant-goers have the choice of cool stone terraces or crowded tables on the *midraḥov*.

For the cheapest of the fresh and the freshest of the cheap head for **Maḥaneh Yehuda,** the raucous open-air market between Jaffa Rd. and Agrippas St., to the west of the city center. Elbow your way past bag-laden fellow shoppers to the fruit and vegetable stands, pita bakeries, and sumptuous displays of pastries that line the alleys. There's a small grocery store *(makolet)* with rock-bottom prices at almost every corner. You can get 10 loaves of pita here for NIS3 or less; 1kg tomatoes goes for the same price. The Yemenite section (follow the alleys east from Maḥaneh Yehuda St.) is the cheapest for produce, and the stands along Etz Ha-Ḥayim St. sell the best *halva* at NIS6 per 0.5kg. **Mispar Eḥad** (Number One) sells excellent hummus and salads for NIS4.5 per ¼kg; from Agrippas St., take your first right into the *shuk,* climb some stairs, and look to your right. **Marzipan** (tel. 623 26 18), at 44 Agrippas St., sells *rugelaḥ* to die for—eat a kilo (NIS12) and you just might. *Me'orav* ("assortment"), a mix of inner parts grilled with onions and packed in pita pockets, is an area specialty. The choicest innards are on **Agrippas Street.** A small portion (*mana ketana*) is plenty, but sharing a large one is a better deal. *Shishlik* (cubes of grilled meat) and *kebab* are never far behind. On the corner of Agrippas and the uncovered *shuk* street, falafel is good and cheap (NIS5, *esh tanoor* NIS6).

The best hours to visit are at closing time (Sat.-Thurs. 7-8pm, Fri. 1-2hr. before sundown) when merchants lower their prices shekel by shekel to sell off the day's goods. Friday morning prices are the highest, but they plummet in the afternoon, when thousands scramble through the alleys in a frantic effort to stock up for *Shabbat.* **Supermarkets** include **Co-Op,** in the basement of Ha-Mashbir department store at the intersection of King George and Ben-Yehuda St. (tel. 625 78 30; open Sun.-Thurs. 8am-7:30pm and Fri. 8am-2:30pm), and **Supersol** on the corner of Agron and Keren Ha-Yesod St. (tel. 676 09 56; open Sun.-Thurs. 7am-midnight, Fri. 7am-3pm, Sat. sundown-midnight).

Pepperoni's, 4 Rabbi Akiva St. (tel. 625 78 29). By far the best Italian restaurant in Jerusalem. A full lunch including fresh baked bread, 12 types of salads and antipasti, sausage, drink, and main course is NIS33. The shebang minus the main course is NIS24. Prices go up for dinner (NIS45-60). At **Foccaccia,** the airy patio out front, the namesake dish is filling. Open daily noon-midnight. Visa, MC, AmEx.

Village Green, 10 Ben Yehuda St. (tel. 625 20 07 or 14 64), and 1 Bezalel St. Scrumptious made-from-scratch vegetarian food served up cafeteria style. Soups (NIS13) and pastas (NIS16-22) served with all the whole wheat bread, tahini, and dressings you can eat. A hungry budget traveler's dream. Open Sun.-Thurs. 11am-10pm, Fri. 11am-3pm. Visa, MC, AmEx. Kosher.

The Yemenite Step, 10 Yoel Salomon St. (tel. 624 04 77). Grand stone building with high ceilings and outdoor seating. Try the heavenly *malawaḥ,* their specialty (NIS11, with filling NIS32 and up). Open Sun.-Thurs. noon-12:30am, Fri. noon-4pm, Sat. after *Shabbat*-12:30am. Kosher.

Bali-Baguette, 31 Jaffa Rd. (tel. 625 67 15), near Rivlin St. Scrumptious foot-long baguettes stuffed with meats and salads (NIS9) prove that it's possible for both your stomach and your wallet to be full. Friendly owner takes photos of travelers and pastes them on the walls. Open Sun.-Thurs. 9am-4am, Fri. 9am-5pm. Kosher.

Fat Danny's Diner, 3 Yoel Salomon (tel. 625 19 18). American 50s style food stop with jukebox and Norman Rockwell prints. Burgers (NIS21-25), shakes (NIS16), and fried chicken with French fries (NIS29). Eggs, hash browns, veggies, and coffee (free refills) NIS19-23. An order of pancakes or waffles NIS19. Open daily 24hr. Visa, MC, AmEx.

Bonkers, 41 Jaffa St. (tel. 672 15 01) in Zion Sq., and King George St. near Agrippas St. The end of an era of kvetching over the dearth of real American bagels in the Jewish state. Little space to sit. Bagels NIS2, topped with cream cheese NIS6, with tuna and cheese NIS8. Open 24hr., but closed on *Shabbat*. Kosher.

The Seventh Place, 37 Hillel St. (Beit Agron building), 2nd floor (tel. 625 44 95). Excellent vegetarian Indian food. Main dishes (NIS17-29), appetizers (NIS10-12). Free live music: Sat.-Sun. American folk; Tues. gypsy; Wed. jazz; Thurs. Israeli folk. Open Sun.-Thurs. 9am-1am, Fri. 8am-4pm, Sat. sundown-2am. Visa, MC, AmEx.

Me Ta'amei Ha-Muḥan, 119 Jaffa Rd. (tel. 623 29 59), in the heart of the Maḥaneh Yehuda market district. This small restaurant's name means "tasty and ready." Well-balanced cafeteria-style meals: main dish with two sides NIS25. Choose from lovingly-made goulash, chicken, veggies, mashed potatoes, or *kugel*. Side dishes NIS5. Open Sun.-Thurs. 10am-10pm, Fri. 10am-4:30pm. Eat in or take-out. Glatt Kosher.

Steakiat Ḥatzot, 123 Agrippas St. (tel. 624 40 14), almost at the corner of Bet Ya'aqov St. Sign only in Hebrew. Uniquely spiced meats lure athletes, politicians, and actors to the "Midnight Steakhouse," an Israeli legend past the *shuk*. Me'orav (mixed grill), liver, *kebab, shishlik,* or chicken grilled to your liking in a pita (NIS20-26), or on a plate with salad, fries, pita, and dip (NIS33-45). Hummus NIS10. Huge portions. Open Sun.-Thurs. 10am-1am, Sat. sundown-1am.

Mama Mia's, 38 King George St. (tel. 624 080), behind parking lot. A great place to splurge if you feel like a treat. Crisp, white interior with stucco ceilings and green trim. Peaceful patio. romantic table for two on a small balcony, and a separate non-smoking room. Delicious fettuccine made fresh daily NIS25-36, pizza NIS32-40, and great homemade ravioli NIS27-36. Business lunch NIS35. Open Sun.-Thurs. noon-11pm, Fri. noon-3pm, Sat. sundown-11pm. Visa, MC, AmEx. Kosher.

Alumah, 8 Ya'avetz St. (tel. 625 50 14), off Jaffa Rd. between King George St. and Zion Sq. Quiet, spacious stone veranda; botanical interior. Everything is made from scratch. Specializes in stone-ground, yeast-less whole wheat, sourdough, and rye bread. The quiche here is as organic and delicious as they come (NIS23). Main dishes NIS18-29, all served with bread and raw vegetables. Open Sun.-Thurs. 10am-11pm, Fri. 10am-2pm. Visa, MC. Glatt kosher.

Cheap Quickies

There is nothing like the quest for cheap **falafel** to unite natives and tourists. West Jerusalem teems with small, crowded stands and sit-downs for pizza, **shawerma,** ice cream, and fruit juice. Creating the ultimate falafel or shawerma is an art all its own, and many stops on King George St. between Jaffa Rd. and Ben-Yehuda or in Maḥaneh Yehuda come close to perfecting it.

Melekh Ha-Falafel ve Ha-Shawerma (tel. 625 85 16), on the corner of King George and Agrippas. Savory falafel (NIS6) and *esh tanoor* (in *lafa* bread, NIS7).

Ta'ami, 3 Shammai St. (tel. 625 36 44). Favorite hummus den, notorious for urging folks to finish up and get out. Open Sun.-Thurs. 9:30am-6pm, Fri. 9:30am-noon.

Apple Pizza, 13 Dorot Rishonim St. (tel. 623 15 17), off Ben-Yehuda. Serves thin-crust "Big Apple" pizza baked to the tune of rock classics for an expensive NIS6.50 per slice (whole pie NIS49). Open Sun.-Thurs. 10:30am-midnight, Fri. 10:30am-4pm, Sat. 8:30pm-midnight. Kosher.

The **Merkaz Ha-Pa'amon** shopping center, on King George and the *midraḥov,* has an **Angel's Pizza** (tel. 623 31 05; NIS5-5.50 per slice). The long-awaited, much-debated, non-kosher **McDonald's** (tel. 624 93 52), on 4 Shammai St., near the *midraḥov,* doles out Big Macs for NIS10.90. This may signal the decline of Israel's own **Burger Ranch,** 18 King George St. (tel. 623 37 66), near Hamashbir department store, where a Ranchburger goes for NIS11.90.

The best place for **ice cream** is **Katzefet** (tel. 625 37 22), on the *midraḥov* at the corner of Ben-Yehuda and Luntz St. (ice cream NIS4). Their specialty is frozen yogurt (pronounced *frrrozen*) blended with your choice of fresh fruits, nuts, or chocolates (small with 3 flavors NIS7). **Ben and Jerry's,** at 5 Hillel St. (tel. 624 27 67), just off King George St., scoops its signature stuff for NIS8.90 for an order of two scoops. Several stands near the Ben Yehuda-King George intersection concoct fresh **juice** on the spot. Choose among mango, fig, peach, watermelon, and many others (regular size NIS2.50-4, medium NIS4.50-7; orange juice NIS5.50).

■ Sights

OLD CITY

If you take a shovel, pick any spot in the Old City and dig, you'll probably be face to face with ancient marvels in no time. Excavations under the Old City have uncovered over 20 distinct layers of civilization. There's something about this tiny plot of land that makes it holy, not only for Jews, Christians, and Muslims, but to dozens of ancient religious groups as well. Before beginning a tour, it's helpful to get an idea of what the city looked like in ages past. The **Holyland Hotel** in West Jerusalem (tel. 643 77 77) has an excellent knee-high model of Jerusalem circa 66 CE, towards the end of the Second Temple Period. Take bus #21 from downtown (open daily 8am-10pm; NIS15, NIS12 with ISIC). The entire Old City is only about one square km; a walking tour is a great way to get to know it (see **Tours,** p. 286).

The Walls and the Citadel

The present walls of the Old City were built by Suleiman the Magnificent in 1542. The city had been without walls since 1219, when Al Muazzan tore them down to prevent the Crusaders from seizing a fortified city. There are eight gates, some of which have three names: Christian/Latin, Jewish/Hebrew, and Muslim/Arabic (the most commonly used names are listed here). **Golden Gate,** blocked by Muslim graves, has been sealed since the 1600s. It is thought to lie over the Closed Gate of the First Temple, the entrance through which the Messiah will purportedly pass (Ezekiel 44:1-3). Of the other seven gates, **Jaffa Gate** is the most convenient from West Jerusalem and is the traditional entrance for pilgrims; there has been a gate here since 135 CE. (Some people don't give Jaffa Gate the respect it deserves. Gustave Flaubert recalled: "We enter through Jaffa Gate and I let a fart escape as I cross the threshold very involuntarily. I was even annoyed at bottom by this Voltaireanism of my anus." No doubt his companions were, too.) Going clockwise from Jaffa Gate is **New Gate,** opened in 1889 to facilitate access to the Christian Quarter. **Damascus Gate** serves East Jerusalem. **Herod's Gate** stands to the east of Damascus Gate. **St. Stephen's Gate** (or Lion's Gate), is the beginning of the Via Dolorosa. **Dung Gate,** first mentioned in 445 BCE by Neḥemiah, opens near the Western Wall and was given its name in medieval times because dumping dung here was considered an especially worthy act. **Zion Gate** connects the Armenian Quarter with Mt. Zion.

The walls embrace a circumference of 4km. You can walk the entire circuit except the parts by the Temple Mount and the Citadel. This **ramparts walk** provides an unsurpassed view of the Old City and an idea of the wall's military importance through the centuries. Tickets to the ramparts are sold at the Citadel and Damascus and Jaffa Gates (tel. 625 44 03 or 04). They are good for unlimited admission for two days after the purchase, three days if purchased on a Friday (walls open Sat.-Thurs. 9am-4pm, Fri. 9am-2pm; admission NIS9, students NIS5). The Citadel divides the walk into two sections; from Jaffa Gate, you can walk in either direction. To go to the Christian and Muslim Quarters, ascend the rampart on the left as you enter the gate. For the Armenian and Jewish Quarters, enter the Citadel parking lot and follow the building around to the left.

To ascend the ramparts from **Damascus Gate,** you must go down the steps to the right before you cross the bridge, walk under the gate, and continue through the ancient carriageway to the left of the plaza. The level of the carriageways on either side corresponds to the middle Roman period in the 2nd century CE. At the rampart entrance you can visit the **Roman Square Museum,** set among the excavations from Aelia Capitolina (as the city was known in 200 CE). The museum displays a copy of the 6th-century **Madaba map** from Madaba, Jordan; the map is the earliest known blueprint of the city's layout. The huge centipede that seems to crawl from Damascus Gate at the northern tip to Dung Gate at the southern is actually a two-dimensional rendition of the **Cardo,** the main thoroughfare; its "feet" are the Roman columns lining the street. The map has aided archaeologists in concluding that the Cardo recently unearthed in the Jewish Quarter is not part of the Roman original, but a Byzantine addition. Scholars have also discovered a plaza at the gate's entrance with a statue of Hadrian mounted on a huge column. This explains the Arabic name for Damascus Gate: *Baab al-Amud* (Gate of the Column). The plaza has been partially uncovered, but the black column is missing; you'll have to settle for the hologram on display (open Sat.-Thurs. 9am-4pm, Fri. 9am-2pm; admission NIS4, students NIS2).

Another place to dig the history of the Old City is the **Citadel** complex just inside Jaffa Gate and to the right. The **Tower of David,** sometimes called the Citadel (*Migdal David* in Hebrew), resembles a Lego caricature of overlapping Hasmonean, Herodian, Roman, Byzantine, Muslim, Mamluk, and Ottoman ruins, but nothing from David's era (during his reign, this was outside the city and unsettled). The tower provides a superb vantage point for surveying the Holy City. Winding through the rooms of the fortress, the high-tech, information-packed **Museum of the History of Jerusalem** tells the story of the city in Hebrew, Arabic, and English through videos, holograms, and talking models. (Open in summer Sun.-Thurs. 9am-5pm, Fri.-Sat. 9am-2pm, winter Sun.-Thurs. 10am-4pm, Fri.-Sat. 10am-2pm. Admission NIS20, students NIS15, children NIS10; price includes guided tour in English Sun.-Fri. 11am.) At night, there's a 45-minute English **sound and light show.** Booming voices tell the history of Jerusalem as splotches of light are tossed around a few stone walls (April-Oct. Mon. and Wed. 9:30pm, Sat. 9pm. Admission NIS22, students NIS16, children NIS11; combined tickets with museum entrance NIS38, students NIS27, children NIS19.) In spring and summer, you can play the Citadel's game of **Murder Mystery**—a full costumed cast helps you find the culprit Saturday evenings at 10pm (mystery game NIS26, students and children NIS22; combined light show and murder mystery NIS35, students and children NIS30).

Temple Mount, Dome of the Rock, and Western Wall

The **Temple Mount** (Al Haram ash-Sharif in Arabic, Har Ha-Bayit in Hebrew), a 35-acre area in the southeastern corner of the Old City, is one of the most venerated religious sites in the world. A seeming spiritual magnet, the hill is central today to Judaism and Islam and served as a holy site for at least 10 ancient religions. The Temple Mount is traditionally identified with the biblical Mt. Moriah, where God asked Abraham to sacrifice his son Isaac (Genesis 22:2). The First Temple was built here by King Solomon in the middle of the 10th century BCE (2 Chronicles 3:1), and destroyed by Nebuchadnezzar in 587 BCE, when the Jews were led into captivity (I Kings 5-8; II Kings 24-25). The Second Temple was built in 516 BCE, after the Jews' return from exile (Ezra 3-7). In 20 BCE, King Herod rebuilt the temple and enlarged the Mount, reinforcing it with four retaining walls. Parts of the southern, eastern, and western retaining walls still stand. Religious scholars believe that the Holy of Holies, the most sacred and important spot on the Temple where only the High Priest was allowed to enter once a year, was closest to what is now the **Western Wall,** making this wall the holiest approachable site in Judaism. Observant Jews will not ascend the Mount because of the possibility that they will walk on the Holy of Holies, off limits until the Messiah arrives.

The Second Temple is remembered by Christians as the backdrop to the Passion of Christ. Like the First Temple, it lasted only a few hundred years. In the fourth year of the Jewish Revolt (70 CE), Roman legions sacked Jerusalem and razed the second Temple. Hadrian built a temple to Jupiter over the site, but the Byzantines destroyed it and used the platform as a municipal sewage facility (giving nearby Dung Gate its name). After Caliph Omar conquered Jerusalem in 638 (just six years after Muhammad's death) he ascended the Mount and began the clean-up himself, personally removing an armful of brown gook. The Umayyad Caliphs built the two Arab shrines that still dominate the Temple Mount: the silver-domed **Al Aqsa Mosque** (built in

ISRAEL

715 and rebuilt several times after earthquakes), and the magnificent **Dome of the Rock** (built in 691). A stunning display of mosaics and metallic domes, the complex is the third-holiest Muslim site, after the Ka'ba in Mecca and the Mosque of the Prophet in Medina. According to Muslim tradition, this is the point to which God took Muhammad on his mystical Night Journey *(miraj)* from the Holy Mosque at Mecca to the outer Mosque (*al aqsa* means "the farthest") and then on to heaven (17:17). The Dome of the Rock surrounds what Muslims believe was Abraham's makeshift altar where he almost sacrificed Ishmael, his son by Sarah's maid Hagar (not Isaac, as Christians and Jews believe).

Although the dome was once of solid gold, it was eventually melted down to pay the caliphs' debts. The domes of the mosques and shrines were plated with lusterless lead until the structures received aluminum caps during the restoration work done from 1958 to 1964. The golden hue of the Dome of the Rock was previously achieved with an aluminum-bronze alloy, but in 1993 it was re-coated with new metal plates faced with a thin coating of 24-karat gold, leaving it more brilliant than ever. Many of the tiles covering the walls of the Dome of the Rock were affixed during the reign of Suleiman the Magnificent, who had the city walls built in the 16th century. Scrutiny will distinguish these from the ceramic tiles added in the 1950s and 60s and paid for with Jordanian King Hussein's private funds.

Next to the Dome of the Rock is the much smaller **Dome of the Chain,** the exact center of Al Haram ash-Sharif, where Muslims believe a chain once hung from heaven which could be grasped only by the righteous. Between the two shrines flows a *sabil* (fountain) called **Al Kas,** where Muslims perform ablutions before prayer. Built in 709 CE, the fountain is connected to underground cisterns capable of holding 10 million gallons. The arches on the Temple Mount, according to Muslim legend, will be used to hang scales to weigh people's good and bad deeds. The **Islamic Museum,** by the ramp entrance beside the Western Wall, is filled with fantastic relics such as crescent-topped spires that once crowned older domes, and elaborately decorated Qur'ans.

Al Haram ash-Sharif and the museum are open Saturday through Thursday 8am-12:30pm and 1:30pm-3:30pm. All hours are subject to change during Ramadan and other Islamic holidays, although the Mount is usually open 8am-10:30am. The entrance to the mount is just right of the Western Wall, up the ramp. It is also accessible through a tunnel-like marketplace—follow Al Wad Rd. to the end and go up the stairs to the left (tickets sold at a booth between Al Aqsa and the museum until 3pm; admission NIS30, students NIS20). The Mount is sometimes closed without notice, and you might inexplicably be denied entrance. Remember that the area is highly sensitive—incidents in the past have resulted in violence. Any conspicuous action, no matter how innocent, may get you ejected. Modest dress is required, although hare krishna-like gowns are provided for those who need them. Be aware that many sections considered **off-limits** by the police are not marked as such, including the walls around Al Aqsa, the area through the door to the south between Al Aqsa and the museum, and the Muslim cemetery

The 18m tall **Western Wall** (Ha-Kotel Ha-Ma'aravi in Hebrew) is part of the retaining wall of the Temple Mount, built about 20 BCE, and was the largest section of the Temple area that remained standing after its destruction in 70 CE. The Wailing Wall, a dated moniker, refers to Jewish worshipers who visited the wall in centuries past to mourn the destruction of the Temple. Today's visitors, Jewish or otherwise, often see the Wall as a direct connection with God, and tuck written prayers into its crannies. Don't expect your scribble to wait there for the Messiah: all notes are periodically removed from the overburdened wall and buried, in accordance with Jewish Law. An innovative service from Bezek (the telephone company) lets you fax in urgent messages to be deposited in the crevices (fax 561 22 22). The Wall can be reached by foot from Dung Gate, the Jewish Quarter, Baab as-Silsilah St., or Al Wad Rd. About 3m off the ground, a gray line indicates the surface level before 1967. Nearly 20m of Herodian wall still lies underground. You can identify the Herodian stones by .their carved frames, or dressing; the smaller stones that lie above were added by Byzantines, Arabs, and Turks.

Tour of Duty

One of the most competitive professions in Israel is the tour guide. All tour guides must complete a two-year course and receive a government license. Each year, over 500 (and some years as many as 1000) applicants hope to get into tour guide school, but the ruthless admissions committee takes only a lucky 45. After two years of intense training in religion, archaeology, geology, botany, zoology, folklore, and history, about half of the admitted class receives the coveted license. To even be considered for tour guide school, applicants must speak at least two foreign languages fluently, but many candidates speak three or four. Once licensed, guides must complete annual recertification courses, where they are kept up to date on new sights and archaeological discoveries. Israel's licensed tour guides are respected throughout the country.

Pre-1948 photos show Orthodox Jews praying at the wall in a crowded alley; after the 1967 War, the present plaza was built, and Israeli paratroopers are sworn here to recall the Wall's capture. The Ministry of Religion has decreed that all rules applying to Orthodox synagogues also apply to the Wall. Men must cover their heads (paper *kippot* are in a box by the entrance) and women must cover their legs (wraps can be borrowed from the Holy Sites Authority). The prayer areas for men and women are separated by a screen with the Torah scrolls kept on the men's side, along with recently excavated sections of the Wall. **Wilson's Arch** (named for the English archaeologist who discovered it), located inside a large, arched room to the left of the Wall, was once part of a bridge that spanned Cheesemakers' Valley, allowing Jewish priests to cross from their Upper City homes to the Temple. A peek down the two illuminated shafts in the floor of this room gives a sense of the wall's original height (women may not enter). The wall continues from here through closed tunnels for over 500m. Women and groups can enter the passageways through an archway to the south, near the telephones. Underneath the Western Wall is an underground passage where Jewish radicals hid explosives in the early 1980s in a plot to destroy the Dome of the Rock. To get into the passage, call the **Western Wall Heritage Foundation** (tel. 627 13 33). English tours are held irregularly (NIS10). **Archaeological Seminars** and **Zion Walking Tours** both visit the tunnels as part of their walking tours (see **Tours,** p. 286).

At the far end of the Wall plaza (near the bathrooms), halfway up the stairs, is the **Holocaust Memorial Hall.** The sculpture and room inside are designed by Agam, designer of the Dizengoff fountain in Tel Aviv. His steel tree contains 1200 brilliant lights, and the ceiling and floor tiles are in triangles that can be arranged into stars of David (open Sun.-Thurs. 11am-4pm; free).

On Fridays, Yeshivat Ha-Kotel organizes dancing to usher in *Shabbat.* The festivities start before sundown and go until late. Half a dozen Bar Mitzvahs occur at the Wall simultaneously on Monday and Thursday mornings. These ceremonies mark the coming of age of Jewish boys. Photography is appropriate at these occasions, unlike on *Shabbat* or holidays. On other nights, the Wall is brightly lit, the air cool, and the atmosphere reflective and quiet.

The excavations at the southern wall of the Temple Mount are known as the **Ophel** (tel. 625 44 03), though "Ophel" technically refers to the hill just outside the southern wall, where the City of David is located (open Sun.-Fri. 7am-7pm; admission NIS9, students NIS4.50; English tours daily 9am, NIS25, children NIS15). Scholars have uncovered 22 layers from 12 periods of the city's history. A tunnel brings you outside the city walls to the foot of the steps leading to the Temple Mount. **Archaeological Seminars** runs an excellent walking tour of the area (see **Tours,** p. 286).

Jewish Quarter

The Jewish Quarter is in the southeast quadrant of the Old City, the site of the posh Upper City during the Second Temple era. The quarter extends from Ha-Shalshelet St. (Baab as-Silsilah) in the north to the city's southern wall, and from Ararat St. in the west to the Western Wall in the east. Reach the quarter by climbing the stairs diagonally across from the Western Wall. From Jaffa Gate, either head down David St. and turn right at the sign for the Cardo Maximus or turn right past the Citadel onto Armenian Orthodox Patriarch Rd. and make the first left onto St. James Rd. Jews settled here when they returned to Jerusalem in the 15th century. The Jewish community grew from 2000 in 1800 to 11,000 in 1865, when settlement began outside the walls. Today, about 650 families live in the Jewish Quarter.

Much of the Jewish Quarter was damaged in the 1948 War and after two decades of Jordanian rule the Quarter lay in ruins. The Israelis annexed the Old City after the 1967 War and immediately began extensive restoration of the neighborhood. City planners made archaeological discoveries with every lift of the shovel, and have managed to gracefully integrate the ancient remains into the new neighborhood. Today the gentrified Jewish Quarter is an upper-middle-class neighborhood, with an almost exclusively Orthodox Jewish (and largely American) population.

If you follow St. James Rd. from the Jaffa Gate until it becomes Or Ḥayim Rd., you'll see the **Yishuv Court Museum** at 6 Or Ḥayim St. (tel. 628 46 36), on your right. The small exhibition depicts life in the Jewish Quarter before 1948. Sephardic and Ashkenazi-style guest rooms are furnished with period artifacts. A highlight of the collection is a display of wooden Torah cases (open Sun.-Thurs. 9am-2pm; admission NIS8, students NIS6). The synagogue may be entered free of charge.

If you continue down Or Ḥayim St. pass Ḥabad St. and descend a staircase, you'll see remains of the **Cardo,** Jerusalem's main thoroughfare during Roman and Byzantine times. A large part of the Cardo has been excavated alongside Jewish Quarter Rd. (make a left at the bottom of the stairs). The uncovered section is built over a Byzantine extension of Emperor Hadrian's Cardo Maximus, which ran from Damascus Gate to about as far south as David St. Archaeologists suspect that Justinian constructed the addition so that the Cardo would extend as far as the Nea Church (beneath Yeshivat Ha-Kotel). Sheltered by the Cardo's vaulted roof are expensive gift shops and art galleries. Near the entrance to the Cardo, you can climb down to an excavated section of the Hasmonean city walls and remains of buildings from the First Temple period. Farther along the Cardo is an enlarged mosaic reproduction of the Madaba map, the 6th-century plan of Jerusalem discovered in Jordan. The Cardo is open and illuminated until 11pm. The enormous remaining pillars denote its original monumental proportions. Between the expensive Cardo shops is the **One Last Day Museum** (in the same building as the Cardo Culinaria), which recounts with photographs the fall of the Jewish Quarter in 1948 (open Sun.-Thurs. 9am-5pm, Fri. 9am-1pm; admission NIS5, students NIS4).

The **Broad Wall,** near the post office on Plugat Ha-Kotel Rd. off Jewish Quarter Rd., is the remains of the Israelite wall that encircled the City of David, the Temple Mount, and the Upper City. The wall was built by King Hezekiah in the 7th century BCE and, along with his famous tunnel, formed part of the city's defenses (see **City of David,** p. 306). The small chunk of wall is over 4m thick—much broader than the current Ottoman fortifications. Continue left on Plugat Ha-Kotel and turn right onto Shonei Ha-Laḥot St. to find the **Israelite Tower,** part of the same defense system as the broad wall. You can descend beneath the tower to see the remains of two older defensive towers which were important bastions for the first wall built in the north of the city. Maps indicate how the city walls have changed over the centuries (open Sun.-Thurs. 9am-5pm., Fri. 9am-1pm; admission NIS4, students NIS3). Across the street is the **First Temple Period Model** (tel. 628 62 88). Admission includes a 30-minute film presentation which explains the history in detail. Call for a schedule of presentations in English (open Sun.-Thurs. 9am-4pm, Fri. 9am-1pm; admission NIS8, students NIS6).

Across Jewish Quarter Rd. and on the left from the southern end of the Cardo, a single stone arch soars above the ruins of the **Ḥurva Synagogue.** Built in 1700 by followers of Rabbi Yehuda the Ḥasid, the synagogue was destroyed by Muslims when the Ashkenazi community could no longer afford to uphold its place of worship. It was then that the synagogue earned its name (*ḥurva* means "ruin"). This proved an ominous title; in 1856 the building was restored as the National Ashkenazic Synagogue, only to be destroyed once again during the 1948 War. In 1967, renovators opted to rebuild only the single arch as a reminder of the destruction. The **Ramban Synagogue** next door was named for Rabbi Moshe Ben-Naḥman, also known as Naḥmanides ("Ramban" is an acronym for his name). Inside is a letter written by the rabbi describing Jerusalem's Jewish community in 1267, the year he arrived from Spain. During a period of nearly four centuries (1599-1967), Jews were forbidden to worship here, and the building had stints as a store, butter factory, and mosque. Today it is open for morning and evening prayers.

From the main plaza area near the Ḥurva Synagogue, Ha-Kara'im St. (heading east from the telephones) leads to the **Herodian Quarter** (tel. 628 34 48), an excavation of three mansions built for the Second Temple's high priests *(kohanim)*. The posh houses contain mosaics, several ritual baths *(mikvaot),* and fine pottery (open Sun.-Thurs. 9am-5pm, Fri. 9am-1pm; admission NIS12, students NIS10; combined ticket to Burnt House and Herodian Quarter NIS14, students NIS12).

Also near the Ḥurva Synagogue, the **Four Sephardic Synagogues** are down Mishmerot Ha-Kehuna St., near the parking lot. The synagogue of Rabbi Yoḥanan Ben-Zakkai, the Prophet Elijah Synagogue, the Central Synagogue, and the Istanbuli Synagogue (tel. 628 05 92) were built by Mediterranean Jews starting in the 16th century in accordance with a local law that prohibited the construction of synagogues taller than the surrounding houses. To attain a semblance of loftiness, these synagogues were built in large chambers deep underground. The current renovated structures date from 1835. The synagogues remain the spiritual center of Jerusalem's Sephardic community, with religious services held here twice a day. A Portuguese *minyan* gathers in the Istanbuli room. A small exhibition features photographs of the synagogues pre-destruction and pre-renovation (open Sun.-Mon. and Wed.-Thurs. 9:30am-4pm, Tues. and Fri. 9:30am-12:30pm; admission NIS6, students NIS3).

Ha-Karaim St. leads directly to the **Tiferet Yisrael Synagogue.** From the plaza, you can reach the synagogue by walking down Tiferet Yisrael St. and taking the stairs on the right. The synagogue showcases old photographs that depict the house of worship's heyday. Built by Ḥasidic Jews during the 19th century, the synagogue was captured and destroyed by Jordan in 1948. The **Karaite Synagogue** next door was established by this divergent sect of Judaism, and is now the center of the Karaite community in Jerusalem (see **Other Sects,** p. 69).

Farther east on Tiferet Yisrael Rd. smolders the **Burnt House** (tel. 628 72 11), the remains of the dwelling of a priest's family from the Second Temple era. In 70 CE, the fourth year of the Jewish Revolt, the Romans destroyed the Second Temple and broke into Jerusalem's Upper City, burning its buildings and killing its inhabitants. The excavation of the Burnt House provided direct evidence of the destruction of the Upper City. Near a stairwell the grisly bones of a severed arm reach for a carbonized spear. Sound and light shows are set inside the Burnt House, re-creating the events of its destruction (virtual fire, of course). Reservations are recommended for English presentations (open Sun.-Thurs. 9am-5pm; admission NIS6, students NIS5).

In the shadow of the Burnt House is the **Third Temple Museum,** on Ladakh St. off Tiferet Yisrael Rd. The folks here are actively hoping to rebuild the Jewish High Temple, and plan to relocate the Dome of the Rock (Muslim worshipers are not amused). The museum is filled with modern-built instruments to be used in the anticipated Third Temple. As much as possible, the objects are built to the ancient specifications as written in the Talmud.

Armenian Quarter

The Armenian Quarter, in the southwestern part of the Old City near Mt. Zion, is home to Jerusalem's small Armenian Christian population. Aramaic, the ancient language of the Levant, is spoken both during services and in casual conversation at the **Syrian Orthodox Convent** on Ararat St. The Syrian Church believes this to be the site of St. Mark's house and the Last Supper, while most other Christians recognize the Cenacle on Mt. Zion as that hallowed place. To reach the convent, enter Jaffa

ISRAEL

Gate and walk beside the Citadel onto Armenian Patriarchate Rd. Turn left onto St. James Rd. and left again onto Ararat St. A vivid mosaic marks the door to the convent, on the right after a sharp turn in the road. Visit during the afternoon, and ring the bell if the door is closed. The **Armenian Compound,** down Armenian Patriarchate Rd. past St. James Rd., is a city within a city, home to about 1000 Armenians and a slew of sites closed to tourists.

Farther down Armenian Patriarchate Rd. on the left is the entrance to the **Mardigian Museum,** chronicling the history of Armenia from the beginnings of its Christianization in 46 CE to the Turkish genocide of one and a half million Armenians in 1915. The ornate religious artifacts and grand courtyard are worth the NIS5 (students NIS3) admission fee (open Mon.-Sat. 10am-4pm).

Next to the museum, the **St. James Cathedral** is open for services for a half-hour each day. Look for the carved lintel reading "Convent Armenian St. Jacques" on your left as you come from Jaffa Gate. The original structure was built during the 5th century CE, Armenia's golden age, to honor two St. Jameses. The first martyr, St. James the Greater, was beheaded in 44 CE by Herod Agrippas. His head, supposedly delivered to Mary on the wings of angels, rests under the gilded altar. St. James the Lesser, entombed in a northern chapel, was the first bishop of Jerusalem, but was run out of town by Jews who disliked his version of Judaism. Persians destroyed the cathedral in the 7th century, Armenians rebuilt it in the 11th century, and Crusaders enlarged it in the 12th. Armenians make the tiled street signs for the entire Old City and cover the church with beautifully decorated tiles. Chandeliers, hanging lamps, and censers lighten the colorful space. Pilgrims left votive crosses in the courtyard before the entrance—the oldest cross dates from the 12th century. Enter the cathedral from Armenian Patriarchate Rd., just past St. James St. (open for services daily 3-3:30pm).

Christian Quarter and Via Dolorosa

In the northwest corner of the Old City, the Christian Quarter surrounds the Church of the Holy Sepulchre, the site traditionally believed to be the place of Jesus' crucifixion, burial, and resurrection. The alleyways of the Quarter pass small churches and chapels of various denominations, and the streets bustle with pilgrims, nuns, monks, and merchants peddling rosaries and holy water.

The **Via Dolorosa** (Path of Sorrow) is the route that a cross-bearing Jesus followed from the site of his condemnation (the Praetorium) to the site of his crucifixion and grave (the Calvary). Each event on His walk now has a chapel commemorating it; together these chapels comprise the 14 Stations of the Cross. The present route was mapped out during the Crusader period and spans the Muslim and Christian Quarters. Modern New Testament scholars have suggested alternate routes based on more recent archaeological and historical reconstructions.

One bone of contention involves the beginning point of Jesus' final walk as a mortal. It is generally agreed that Jesus was brought before Pontius Pilate, the Roman procurator, for judgment. Normally, Roman governors resided and fulfilled their duties in the palace of Herod the Great, south of Jaffa Gate and the Citadel area. But on feast days such as Passover, the day of Jesus' condemnation, the governor and his soldiers presumably based themselves at Antonia's fortress (also built by Herod) to be closer to the Temple Mount. Reflecting this holiday relocation, the **Tower of Antonia,** near St. Stephen's (Lion's) Gate, is considered by most to be the First Station. Nevertheless, you may see small groups, notably the Catholic Dominican Order, setting out from Jaffa Gate. The placement of the last five stations inside the Church of the Holy Sepulchre contradicts an alternative hypothesis that the crucifixion took place at the skull-shaped Garden Tomb.

To begin the walk that Jesus and millions of tourists and pilgrims have taken, start at **St. Stephen's Gate.** If you are coming from Damascus or Jaffa Gates, you'll have to walk along part of the Via Dolorosa to get to your starting point and may be tempted to see the stations out of order. Waiting and following the traditional sequence will provide you with a more fulfilling and rewarding experience. On Fridays at 3pm

(July-Aug. 4pm), you can walk the Via Dolorosa with a procession of pilgrims lead by Franciscan monks starting at Al Omariyyeh College.

Starting at St. Stephen's Gate, you will first see the **Church of St. Anne** on your right. Commemorating the birthplace of Jesus' mother Mary, the church is one of the best preserved pieces of Crusader architecture in Israel. The church survived the Islamic period intact because Salah ad-Din used it as a Muslim theological school, hence the Arabic inscription on the tympanum above the doors. Tradition is layers deep here: the simple, solemn, citadel-like structure stands over the ruins of a 5th-century basilica that is itself believed to cover a 2nd- or 3rd-century chapel. The church is tilted to one side, symbolizing the crucifixion.

Within the grounds of the church is the **Pool of Bethesda.** Crowds of the infirm used to wait beside the pool for an angel to disturb its waters; the first person in after the angel would supposedly be cured. Jesus also healed a sick man here (John 5:2-9). Also worth noting are the remains of a Byzantine cistern and a Crusader chapel façade (church and grounds open Mon.-Sat. 8am-noon and 2-6pm, winter Mon.-Sat. 8am-noon and 2-5pm; admission NIS5, students NIS3).

Two hundred meters west of St. Stephen's Gate, a blue ramp leads to the courtyard of the **Al Omariyyeh College,** one site identified as the **first station,** where Jesus was condemned. Opposite the school from the Via Dolorosa, enter the Franciscan monastery; to your left is the **Condemnation Chapel,** the **second station,** where Jesus was sentenced to crucifixion. On the right is the **Chapel of Flagellation,** where he was first flogged by Roman soldiers. A crown of thorns adorns the dome (open daily 8am-11:45am and 4-6pm; winter 8am-11:45am and 1-5pm).

Continuing along the Via Dolorosa, pass beneath the **Ecce Homo Arch,** where Pilate looked down upon a Jesus clad in crown of thorns and cried, "Behold the Man." The arch is actually part of the triumphal arch that commemorates Emperor Hadrian's suppression of the Bar Kokhba revolt in the 2nd century (open Mon.-Sat. 8:30am-12:30pm and 2-4pm; admission NIS5, students NIS3). Adjacent lies the **Convent of the Sisters of Zion,** beneath which excavations have cleared a large chamber thought by some to be the judgment hall, making it an alternative first station. The convent is closed to the public, but the excavations are not. To get to them, walk down the Via Dolorosa from the second station and turn right on Aqabat ar-Rahbat St. Knock on the brown door on your left (open Mon.-Sat. 8:30am-12:30pm and 2-4:30pm; admission NIS3.50).

Although the following stations—the destinations of countless pilgrims—are all marked, they are nonetheless difficult to spot. At the **third station,** to the left on Al Wad Rd., Jesus fell to his knees for the first time. A small Polish chapel inside a blue gate marks the spot; a small relief above the entrance depicts Jesus kneeling beneath the cross. At the **fourth station,** a few meters farther on the left, just beyond the Armenian Orthodox Patriarchate, a small chapel commemorates the spot where Jesus saw his mother (look for the light blue iron doors). Turn right on Via Dolorosa to reach the **fifth station,** where Simon the Cyrene volunteered to carry Jesus' cross (look for the nearby brown door with the Roman numeral V). Fifty meters farther, the remains of a small column designate the **sixth station** (marked with a "VI"), where Veronica wiped Jesus' face with her handkerchief. The mark of his face was left on the cloth, now on display at the Greek Orthodox Patriarchate on the street of the same name. Look for and face a pair of doors, one green and one dark brown. Stations three through six are all on your left.

The **seventh station,** at the intersection with Khan az-Zeit, marks Jesus' second fall—precipitated by the sudden steepness of the road. In the first century, a gate to the countryside opened here, and tradition holds that notices of Jesus' condemnation were posted on it. Crossing Khan az-Zeit, ascend Aqabat al-Khanqa and look beyond the Greek Orthodox Convent for the stone and Latin cross that mark the **eighth station.** Here Jesus turned to the women who mourned him, saying "Daughters of Jerusalem, do not weep for me, weep rather for yourselves and for your children" (Luke 23:28). Backtrack to Khan az-Zeit, take a right, walk for about 50m through the market, ascend the wide stone stairway on the right, and continue through a winding passageway to the Coptic Church. The remains of a column in its door mark the **ninth station,** where Jesus fell a third time. Again retrace your steps to the main street and continue up until the next right, which should lead you out from under the covered marketplace and to the entrance of the Church of the Holy Sepulchre, where the Via Dolorosa ends.

The **Church of the Holy Sepulchre** marks Golgotha, also called Calvary, the site of the Crucifixion. The location was first determined by Eleni, mother of the Emperor Constantine, during her pilgrimage in 326 CE. Eleni thought that Hadrian had erected a pagan temple to Venus and Jupiter on the site in order to divert Christians from their faith. As Jerusalem's first archaeologist, she sponsored excavations and uncovered the tomb of Joseph of Arimathea and three crosses, which she surmised had been hastily left there after the crucifixion as the Sabbath approached. Constantine built a small church over the site in 335, which was later destroyed by the Persians in 614, rebuilt, and destroyed again (this time by the Turks) in 1009. Part of the original church's foundations buttress the present Crusader structure, built in 1149. When the present building was erected, its architects decided to unite all the oratories, chapels, and other sanctuaries that had cropped up around the site under one monumental cross. By 1852, tremendous religious conflicts had developed within the Holy Sepulchre over such issues as who had the right to clean the doorstep. The uninterested Ottoman rulers divided the church among the Franciscan order, the Greek Orthodox, Armenian Orthodox, Coptic, Syrian, and Ethiopian churches. The first three are the major shareholders, entitled to hold Masses and processions and to burn incense in their shrines and chapels.

One of the most revered buildings on earth, the church is also somewhat decrepit. The bickering among the various denominations lends the structure some of its interest, but has also kept the building in shambles, marred by perpetual construction. The effects of major fires in 1808 and 1949 and an earthquake in 1927 demanded a level of cooperation and a pooling of resources that could not be mustered. Restoration work in any part of the basilica implies ownership, making each sect hesitant to assist and eager to hinder the others. The result is that little, if anything, is ever accomplished. In 1935 the church was in such a precarious state that the colonialists desperately propped it up with girders and wooden reinforcement. Since 1960, partial cooperation has allowed the supportive scaffolding to be gradually removed. To this day, however, the question of who gets to change a given light bulb can rage into a month-long controversy.

The church's entrance faces the slab on which Jesus was supposedly anointed before he was buried. To continue along the stations, go up the stairs to the right just after the entrance. The chapel at the top is divided into two naves: the right one belongs to the Franciscans, the left to the Greek Orthodox. At the entrance to the Franciscan Chapel is the **tenth station,** where Jesus was stripped of his clothes, and at the far end is the **eleventh,** where he was nailed to the cross. The **twelfth station,** to the left in the Greek chapel, is the unmistakable site of the Crucifixion: a life-size Jesus, clad in a metal loincloth, hangs among oil lamps, flowers, and enormous candles. Between the eleventh and twelfth stations is the **thirteenth,** where Mary received Jesus' body. The station is marked by an odd statue of Mary adorned with jewels, a silver dagger stuck into her breast.

Jesus' tomb on the ground floor is the **fourteenth** (and final) **station.** The **Holy Sepulchre,** in the center of the rotunda, is a large marble structure flanked by huge candles. The first chamber in the tomb, the Chapel of the Angel, is dedicated to the angel who announced Jesus' resurrection to Mary Magdalene. A tiny entrance leads from the chapel into the sepulchre itself, an equally tiny chamber lit by scores of candles and guarded by priests. The walls of the tomb have been covered, but if you're lucky, the priest in charge will show you a small section of the original wall hidden behind a picture of the Virgin Mary. The raised marble slab in the sepulchre covers the rock on which Jesus' body was laid. Nudging the back of the Holy Sepulchre is the tiny Coptic Chapel. To the right of the Sepulchre, the **Chapel of Mary Magdalene** recalls the place where Jesus appeared to her after his resurrection.

The rest of the church is a dark labyrinth of small chapels through which priests, pilgrims, and chatty tourists wander. Because a denomination's ability to hang anything on the church's walls also indicates ownership, the building houses only religious paintings and spindly oil lamps. Near the eastern end, steps lead down to two cavernous chapels commemorating the discovery of the true cross. In a small chapel on the ground floor just below Calvary, a fissure runs through the rock, supposedly caused by the earthquake following Jesus' death. According to legend, Adam (of Adam and Eve fame) was buried beneath Calvary, allowing Jesus' blood to drip through this cleft and anoint him. (Church open daily 5am-8pm; winter 4am-7pm. Men and women must cover their knees.)

St. Alexander's Church, a block east of the Church of the Holy Sepulchre on Via Dolorosa, houses the Russian mission-in-exile. Prayers for Czar Alexander III are held Thursdays at 7am (open Mon.-Sat. 9am-1pm and 3-5pm; admission NIS1.50; ring bell). Across the street is the **Lutheran Church of the Redeemer** (tel. 627 61 11); enter on Muristan St. and climb a seemingly endless narrow spiral staircase to the bell tower to see an amazing view along with your vertigo. (Open Mon.-Sat. 9am-1pm and 1:30-5pm. English service Sun. 9am. Admission NIS2, students NIS1.50.) The **Greek Orthodox Patriarchate Museum** (tel. 627 11 96), on the street of the same name, is a more recent addition to the Christian Quarter. Under the Patriarch Benedictos Papadopoulos, the scattered liturgical riches, gifts of pilgrims, and early printings of the Patriarchate's 19th-century press are arranged in a spacious, reconstructed Crusader building (open Tues.-Fri. 9am-1pm and 3-5pm, Sat. 9am-1pm; admission NIS3).

Take a left from the Russian mission, another onto Khan az-Zeit St., and walk up the stairs to the left to reach the **Ethiopian Monastery** (near the 9th station), over part of the Church of the Holy Sepulchre and open all day. The Ethiopians possess no part of the church itself, so they have become squatters on the roof. The modest compound is comprised of white buildings with green doors. Walk around and follow the "Please Watch Up Your Head" signs to the small but super-spiritual church.

Muslim Quarter (Excluding Via Dolorosa)

The Muslim Quarter, with architecture from the Ayyubid and Mamluk periods, is the largest and most heavily populated quarter in the Old City, but also the least known. Inquire at the GTIO or with individual tour groups about tours in the area. Self-appointed tour guides of varying quality linger around Jaffa Gate; agree on a price before setting out. Don't pay more than NIS10 for a trip around the Quarter.

During the day, the main streets are crowded with tourists and merchants. At night, the quarter becomes dark, isolated, and possibly dangerous. The stretch of **Baab as-Silsilah Street** extending to the Temple Mount is partly founded on the ancient Mamluk causeway which crossed the Tyropoeon Valley, linking the upper city to the temple platform. Mamluk architecture lines the street, but blends into the bustle. There are sites to see here, but not to enter. At the beginning of the street stands the **Khan as-Sultan** (or Al Wakala), a remarkably preserved Crusader-period *caravanserai* which provided lodging for merchants and their donkeys. Just past Misgav Ladakh St. (farther down the street on the right) is the **Tashtamuriya Building,** formerly an Islamic college, housing the tomb of its namesake (d. 1384). The multitude of Mamluk public institutions can be attributed to their system of succession, which prevented them from passing their wealth on to their children; constructing public institutions was the best way to preserve their legacy.

Continuing down Baab as-Silsilah to its intersection with Western Wall St. (Ha-Kotel), you'll arrive at the **Kilaniya Mausoleum,** with its characteristic Mamluk stalactite half-dome; the **Turba Turkan Khatun** (Tomb of Lady Turkan) is at #149. At the end of Baab as-Silsilah, on your right and often surrounded by tour guides in training, is the **Tankiziya Building,** built by a Mamluk slave who worked his way up to become governor of Damascus in 1312, and then back down to imprisonment and execution in Alexandria 30 years later. This venerated structure, on the site of the original seat of the Sanhedrin, is currently controlled by Israelis due to its proximity to the Western Wall and Temple Mount.

NEAR THE OLD CITY

Mount Zion

Rising outside the city walls opposite Zion Gate and the Armenian Quarter, Mt. Zion (Har Tzion) has long been considered the site of the Tomb of David, the Last Supper, and the descent of the Holy Spirit at Pentecost. The name Zion, which is also applied to Israel as a whole, is derived from the Jebusite fortress called Zion, first seized by King David when he conquered the eastern territory. During the siege of the Jewish Quarter in 1948, the area around **Zion Gate** was the scene of some of the fiercest fighting in Jerusalem; bombshell pock marks remain. To reach the mount, you can take Egged buses #1 or 38, which run between Jaffa Gate and Mt. Zion (#1 goes through Me'a She'arim to the central bus station, #38 goes to the center of town). On foot, you should exit the Old City through Zion Gate, turn left, and follow the wall around, forking right at the convent. At the next fork, take a left.

A stairway through the grey door on your left leads to the bare **Coenaculum (Cenacle),** identified by most as the site of the Last Supper. Its no-frills appearance is due in part to a law from the British Mandate forbidding any changes, including decorations, to be made to the church. This attempt to avoid sectarian disputes came into effect three centuries after the building was used as a mosque. As a result, the mosque's *mihrab* is still visible in the southern wall (open 8:30am-5pm).

To enter **David's Tomb,** exit the grey door and turn right. Above the turquoise, velvet-draped cave tomb, silver crowns mark the years since the creation of the State of Israel. Archaeologists doubt the authenticity of the site, because it is written that kings and only kings were buried within the city, and Mt. Zion was never encompassed by David's walls (tomb open Sat.-Thurs. 8am-6pm, Fri. 8am-2pm; winter Sun.-Thurs. 8am-5pm, Fri. 8am-1pm; free.)

The **Palombo Museum** (Beit Palombo, tel. 673 66 40), across the street and to the left, displays works by the sculptor who crafted the gate to the Knesset and contributed works to Yad Va-Shem (open by appointment; free).

The huge, fortress-like **Basilica of the Dormition Abbey** (tel. 671 99 27) lies off the right fork of the road leading to the Cenacle, on a site that has harbored many memorials. The present edifice, commemorating the death of the Virgin Mary, was completed in 1910. Parts of the precariously situated basilica were damaged during battles in 1948 and 1967 and never repaired. The ground floor is inlaid with zodiac symbols, and the crypt contains a figurine of the Virgin (open Mon.-Sat. 8am-noon and 12:30-6pm, Sun. 10am-noon and 12:30-6pm; free).

The City of David and the Kidron Valley

Archaeologists still wonder about the origins of Biblical Jerusalem. The **City of David** stands on the spot where the Israelite capital reputedly began, though only recently have the pieces of the puzzle begun to fit together. Archaeologists have confirmed that the ridge of Ophel—south of the Temple Mount and outside the city walls—is the site of Jebus, the original Canaanite city captured by King David.

Excavations of the earliest Canaanite walls indicate that the Jebusites were confined to an area of about eight acres. The size and location of the city, above the Kidron Valley, were chosen so that the inhabitants would have access to the nearby water source (the Gihon Spring) and at the same time remain high enough on the ridge to ensure adequate defense. In times of peace, townspeople passed through a "water gate" to bring water into the city. For continued supply during times of siege, a shaft enabled them to have access to water without leaving the walls. This shaft played an important part in David's strategy for taking Jebus (II Samuel 5:8): his soldier Joab simply climbed its walls. In 1867, Warren confirmed this biblical account when he discovered the long, sleek shaft that now bears his name. In the 1960s, Kathleen Kenyon located the Jebusite city walls which date from 1800 BCE and lie just above the Gihon Spring.

Later, King Hezekiah devised a system to prevent David's strategy from being turned against the Israelites: he built a 500m-long tunnel to bring the Gihon waters into the city walls and store them in a pool, hiding the entrance of the spring and keeping invaders such as the Assyrians from finding water when they camped outside the wall. In 1880, a few years after the tunnel was excavated, a local boy discovered an inscription carved by Hezekiah's engineers describing the jubilant moment when the north and south construction crews met underground. The original inscription is in Istanbul, but a copy is on display at the Israel Museum (see p. 310).

You can slosh through **Hezekiah's Tunnel** with a flashlight or a candle, but you probably shouldn't do it alone. The water is about 0.75m high, and wading through it takes about 30 minutes. There are two ways to tackle the tunnel; both will get you wet. You can start at the Gihon Spring source on Shiloah Way, which branches to the right from Jericho Rd. as you approach the Kidron Valley from the bottom of the Mount of Olives. The tunnel ends at the Pool of Shiloah (Silwan in Arabic, Silo'am in Hebrew). Alternatively, you can start from the Pool of Shiloah, only a short walk from Dung Gate. Walk left from the gate and make a right onto Ma'alot Ir David St. After the small playground on your left, turn left into the alleyway; the entrance is on your left. If it is shut, follow the road around the hill until it loops back around to the other entrance (open 8:30am-4:30pm; admission NIS3).

Several organizations offer tours; check at the tourist office for schedules. Recent years have witnessed increasing tension in this much-disputed area. Orthodox Jewish nationalists have attempted to establish a Jewish presence in the midst of Arab **Silwan;** Arab homes were quietly purchased and their residents evicted in a dramatic, middle-of-the-night maneuver. A Jewish bastion, guarded by barbed wire, is perched precariously and conspicuously in the center of this Arab neighborhood; unaware tourists may find themselves walking into a potentially dangerous situation. As always, read newspapers and consult tourist offices before exploring.

About 100m past the entrance to the City of David is a small museum with photos of the most recent excavations. A spiral staircase leads down to **Warren's Shaft** (tel. 628 81 41). With a flashlight, you'll be able to see the entire length of the walls that Joab scaled (open Sun.-Thurs. 9am-5pm, Fri. 9am-1pm; admission NIS7).

To see excavations in progress, walk out of Dung Gate, turn left, and walk downhill to the City of David entrance, on your right just past the UNRWA office. The excavations in this part of the Ophel, called **Section G,** were halted in 1981 when a group of Orthodox Jews protested that the area might have once been the Jewish cemetery mentioned in the diaries of several medieval pilgrims. After considerable political and sometimes violent ballyhoo, the Supreme Court of Israel ruled that the site should be closed. As a compromise the Israeli government promised that digging would continue only under rabbinic supervision. No bones have been found.

Four tombs are located down Shiloah Way, in the **Kidron Valley.** The first is **Absalom's Pillar,** allegedly the tomb of David's favored but feisty son (II Samuel 15-18). Behind it and to the left is the **Tomb of Jehosaphat.** A dirt path on the left leads to the impressive rock-hewn **Tomb of B'nei Hezir** and the **Tomb of Zechariah.**

The Mount of Olives

The bone-dry slopes of the **Mount of Olives** (Har Ha-Zeitim in Hebrew) to the east of the Old City are dotted with churches marking the sites of Jesus' triumphant entry into Jerusalem, his teaching, his agony and betrayal in Gethsemane, and his ascension to heaven. That the Mount of Olives has three gardens of Gethsemane and two points of Ascension may cast doubt on the precision of the locations, but nothing can detract from the splendor. Jews believe that the Messiah will arrive in Jerusalem from the Mount of Olives. Tradition holds that the thousands of people buried here will be the first to be resurrected upon his arrival.

The best way to visit all the important churches, tombs, gardens, and observation points is to take a cab to the top (NIS15-20) and walk down on the winding road that passes through the hill's sights. This is most enjoyable in the morning, when the sun shines at your back and permits sparkling views of the Old City. Most churches are closed on Sundays and from about noon to 3pm.

The **Chapel of Christ's Ascension** is the geographical apex of noteworthy sites, if not the aesthetic peak. Built in 392, this was the first church erected to commemorate the event. Towards the end of the 11th century, the Crusaders adorned the Chapel with columns and arches, and in the late 12th century Salah ad-Din fortified the chapel with walls and added a domed roof. Inside there's a sacred footprint, unidentifiable after generations of non-sacred treadings of relic-happy pilgrims. (Open 8am-5pm; ask for a guard in the mosque courtyard if it's closed. Admission NIS2).

Descending from the chapel and turning left, the next important stop is the **Church of the Pater Noster** (Latin for "Our Father"). When St. Eleni founded the church in the 4th century she named it the Church of the Disciples; it is also referred to as the **Church of the Eleona** (Greek for "olive grove"). This was the site of the grotto where Jesus revealed the "inscrutable mysteries" to his disciples—foretelling the destruction of Jerusalem and his Second Coming. The church commemorates the first recitation of the Lord's Prayer. Polyglots can read the prayer in 77 languages (including Old Frisian) on the tiled walls. In the midst of the translations is the tomb of the Princesse de la Tour d'Auvergne, the woman who worked here for 17 years (1857-74) and financed the excavations and renovations. The Lord's Prayer was her favorite, and she was determined to uncover the long-lost grotto where it was originally taught (tel. 689 49 04; open Mon.-Sat. 8:30-11:45am and 3-4:45pm).

For a monumental view of the Old City, stop by the observation promenade outside the nearby **Seven Arches Hotel.** To the north, the bell tower of the **Augusta Victoria Hospital** on Mt. Scopus marks the highest point in Jerusalem (903m above sea level).

Down from the Seven Arches, a gate on the left leads to two tunnels, traditionally identified as the **Tombs of the Prophets** Malachi, Haggai, and the wily Zechariah. Archaeological evidence, however, suggests that the graves are far too recent—probably dating from the 4th century CE (open Sun.-Fri. 8am-3pm). The orange sign with black Hebrew lettering marks the **Common Grave** of those who died defending the Jewish Quarter in 1948. Next to the Common Grave lies the **National Cemetery,** and farther down the path sprawls the immense **Jewish Graveyard,** the largest Jewish cemetery in the world.

Continuing on the path you'll reach the **Sanctuary of Dominus Flevit** ("the Lord wept"), erected in 1955 to mark the spot where Jesus wept for Jerusalem. During the construction, supervised by the renowned Italian architect Antonio Barluzzi, several unrelated ruins were unearthed (open daily 8am-noon and 2:30-5pm). Farther down the road on the right stands the **Russian Church of Mary Magdalene,** with seven golden onion domes (tel. 628 43 71). Czar Alexander III built the church in 1885 in the lavish 17th-century Muscovite style and dedicated it to his mother, the Empress Maria Alexandrovna. The crypt houses the body of a Russian grand duchess, smuggled to Jerusalem via Beijing after her death in the Russian Revolution. Now a convent, the church basks in the aura of the sacred shrines that surround it, and even claims a part of the Garden of Gethsemane (ordinarily open Tues. and Thurs. 10-noon, but call to make sure; free).

Near the bottom of the path, the **Church of All Nations** (Basilica of the Agony) faces west toward the Old City. Enter through the gate to the Garden of Gethsemane, below the Church of Mary Magdalene. The garden is where Jesus purportedly spent his last night in prayer and was betrayed by Judas (Mark 14:32-42). Although the site has been venerated since the 4th century, the present building, also designed by Barluzzi, was built with international contributions after World War I. Inside, mosaics depict Jesus' last days, including the proverbial kiss of death. The building's facade portrays Jesus bringing peace to all nations (open Apr.-Oct. 8am-noon and 2:30-6pm, Nov.-March 2:30-5pm). The nearby **Tomb of the Virgin Mary** and **Cave of Gethsemane** are the last stops on the path (both open 8am-noon and 2:30-5pm).

North of the Old City

Midway between Damascus and Herod's Gates, **Solomon's Quarries** plunge into the city's bowels and provide refuge from the midday heat. Many believe that it was in these cool caves, extending about 250m beneath the Old City, that workers quarried limestone for the building of ancient Jerusalem in the time of the First Temple. They used an Ancient Egyptian technique to remove blocks of stone from the cave walls: wooden planks were set in crevices and soaked with water, and the expanding planks wedged the stone apart. Legend has it that Zedekiah, Judah's last king, fled the city through a passage to Solomon's quarries when King Nebuchadnezzar of Babylonia invaded in 587 BCE. The sign for the quarries reads "Zedekiah's Cave" (open Sat.-Thurs. 9am-4pm, Fri. 9am-2pm; admission NIS5, students NIS2.50).

Farther east on Suleiman St., near the northeastern corner of the city walls, a driveway leads to the **Rockefeller Archaeological Museum** (tel. 628 22 51), one of the best in the country. The museum records the region's history, beginning with the remains of the 100,000-year-old Mt. Carmel Man, and chronicles the cultural impact of imperialism. Check out the impressive, intricately carved wood panels from the 9th-century Al Aqsa Mosque. The museum was designed in the 1920s by British architect Austen S. B. Harrison in his inimitable Orientalist-Gothic style (open Sun.-Thurs. 10am-5pm, Fri.-Sat. 10am-2pm; admission NIS20, students NIS12). Take Egged bus #1, 27, or 23.)

A short distance up Nablus Rd. on Schick St., a sign points toward the **Garden Tomb,** noticed first by Otto Thenius in 1860. The garden is a candidate for Golgotha, the site of Christ's crucifixion. The hill does indeed resemble a skull, and some claim that a nearby tomb is that of Joseph of Arimathea, who placed Jesus' body in his own tomb after the crucifixion (open Mon.-Sat. 8am-12:15pm and 2:30-5:15pm. English service Sun. 9am). As you continue along Nablus Rd., stop at the lovely, seldom-visited **St. George's Cathedral.** The cathedral houses modest collections of Palestinian embroidery and pottery.

Following Salah ad-Din St. up to Nablus Rd., you'll find a Tombeau des Rois **(Tomb of the Kings)** sign on your right just before the intersection. Judean kings were thought to be buried here, but evidence shows that the tomb was in fact built in 45 CE by the Mesopotamian Queen Helena for her family. Bring a candle or flashlight (open Mon.-Sat. 8am-12:30pm and 2-5pm; admission NIS10, students NIS5).

WEST JERUSALEM

West Jerusalem is known for the eateries, dance clubs, and sandal stores of the pedestrian *midraḥov*. The ever-popular *midraḥov* does provide welcome entertainment for tourists, but explorations of West Jerusalem's subtler side—its elegant neighborhoods, well-kept parks, and impressive museums—are often much more rewarding. Since a few Jews moved outside the protective walls of the Old City in the 1860s, West Jerusalem has flourished, though sometimes at the expense of other communities. By municipal law, all new buildings must be cased with off-white Jerusalem stone, creating a harmony between uninspired developments, ritzy architectural displays, and the ancient buildings of the Old City.

Near Zion Square (City Center)

Zion Square (Kikkar Tzion), at the eastern end of the *midraḥov,* is the center of West Jerusalem and one of the few places in the city that is lively at all hours. **Ticho House,** 7 Ha-Rav Kook St. (tel. 624 50 68), near Zion Sq. about two blocks up the hill, displays watercolors and drawings, including many Jerusalem scenes, by artist Anna Ticho. She lived here with her husband, whose collection of *menorahs* is also on display. The well-groomed building, gardens, and restaurant make for a relaxing mid-city respite (see **Food,** p. 292). (Museum open Sun.-Fri. 10am-5pm; free. A small library shows a videotape of Anna Ticho's life and work upon request.)

The northern end of Ha-Rav Kook Street spills out onto Ha-Nevi'im Street, across from which opens the quiet, stone-wall-lined Ethiopia Street. Houses here are arranged with alternating front and back walled-in gardens. At the end of the street on the right is the handsome **Ethiopian Church,** built at the turn of the century. Directly across from the entrance to the Church, at #11, is the one-time home of Hebrew language founder **Ben Yehuda,** but the building is now closed.

Me'a She'arim ("Hundredfold," an invocation of plenty), just north of Ethiopia St., is one of the few remaining Jewish *shtetl* communities that used to flourish in pre-Holocaust Eastern Europe. Several thousand Ultra-Orthodox Jews live here, preserving traditional habits, dress, customs, and beliefs with painstaking (and somewhat frightening) diligence. Me'a She'arim's relatively few extremists are vocal and receive a good deal of publicity. The Neturei Karta (City Keepers), the most extreme sect of the Satmar Ḥasidim, oppose the Israeli state, arguing that Jewish law prohibits the legitimate existence of a Jewish country until the coming of the Messiah. While many other Ultra-Orthodox Jews hold similar views, Neturei Karta once went so far as to ask Yassir Arafat to accept them as a minority in the future Palestinian state. If your newfound grasp of Hebrew lets you down here, it may because you're hearing Yiddish, spoken by some residents who consider Hebrew too holy for daily use.

Signs in the area read, "Daughters of Israel! The Torah requires you to dress modestly," and then proceed to explain exactly what this means. Whether you're Jewish or not, take this warning seriously if you don't wish to offend (and face the wrath and saliva of angry *ḥasidim*). Women should wear below-the-knee skirts and past-the-elbow shirts, men below-the-knee pants. Always ask before taking photographs.

Me'a She'arim is probably the cheapest place in the world for Jewish books and religious items. Bargaining is the rule; try stores on the eastern end of Me'a She'arim St. The neighborhood also has some of the city's best **bakeries,** most of which are open all night on Thursdays, baking *ḥallah* and cake for the Sabbath. The one at 15 Rabbenu Gershom St. (off Yeḥezkil St.) has great *burekas* and chocolate rolls.

Naḥla'ot and **Zikhron Yosef,** neighborhoods just south of the Maḥaneh Yehuda market, are also crowded and predominantly religious. Residents are mostly Jews from Yemen, Iran, Turkey, and Morocco, and, increasingly, artists and students in search of cheap housing. The narrow, winding alleys and tiny courtyards are festooned with laundry and lined with barber shops, blacksmiths, and sandal-makers.

The modern **Great Synagogue of Jerusalem,** 58 King George St. (tel. 623 11 74), across from the Sheraton Plaza, is enormous and ornate, but not terribly inspiring (open Sun.-Fri. 9am-1pm). Consider a stop at the **Wolfson Museum** next door, on the fourth floor of the Hekhal Shlomo building. The museum exhibits Jewish religious and ceremonial objects. Note the texts painted on eggshells and the Algerian Torah decorations (museum open Sun.-Thurs. 9am-1pm, Fri. 9am-2pm; admission NIS2). Also close to the city center is the **Italian Synagogue** and its **Nahon Museum of Italian Art,** 27 Hillel St. (tel. 624 16 10). Browse through the impressive collection of items including pieces from the Conegliano Veneto Synagogue dating from 1701 (open Sun.-Thurs. 10am-1pm, Wed. also 4-7pm; NIS4).

The **Underground Prisoners Museum** (tel. 623 31 66) inside the Russian Compound off Jaffa Rd. commemorates the work of Israel's underground movement in the pre-1948 struggle against British rule. Originally erected by Russian pilgrims, the hall was converted during the British Mandate into Jerusalem's main prison and now serves as a small but powerful exhibit. Enter through Cheshin St., just off Jaffa Rd. where it splits with Shlomzion Ha-Malka St. Follow the green Museum signs (open Sun.-Thurs. 8am-4pm; NIS6, students NIS3).

Giv'at Ram

The **Israel Museum** (tel. 670 88 11 or 73) is the largest and most comprehensive museum in Israel. With extensive collections of antiquities, sculptures, ancient and modern art, books, the legendary Dead Sea Scrolls, and a even children's section, the museum has nearly as many facets as the country itself.

Rock and rust enthusiasts should go straight to the **archaeology** section—30,000 years of human habitation in the Fertile Crescent are summarized with an extensive collection of tools and weapons. Guided English tours are given on Monday and Thursday at 2pm. Straight ahead from the bottom of the steps is the **ethnography** exhibit, tracing the important events of the Jewish life cycle. Guided tours of the Judaica and ethnography galleries are given on Sunday and Wednesday at 2pm.

The museum boasts a fabulous collection of **art,** including the largest display of Israeli art in the world. There is a fairly large Impressionist and Post-Impressionist collection, and even a few period rooms (including a spectacular French Rococo *salon* donated by the Rothschilds). The **Weisbord Pavilion,** directly across from the ticket building, houses a few Rodin sculptures and early modern paintings, and rotates contemporary art exhibitions. The **Billy Rose Sculpture Garden** displays some incredibly stationary masterworks by Henry Moore, Auguste Rodin, and Pablo Picasso. Pick up a schedule of evening outdoor concerts at the museum, and try to visit on a Tuesday night when the garden is illuminated.

The museum's biggest attraction is the **Shrine of the Book,** which displays the Dead Sea Scrolls. The building's white dome and black walls are supposed to symbolize the struggle between the Sons of Light and Dark, an important theme to the Qumran sect, and was designed to resemble the covers of the pots in which the scrolls lay hidden for 2000 years in the **Caves of Qumran** near the Dead Sea. Although the roof is shaped to resemble one of the airtight containers in which the scrolls were found, when the fountains are on it looks more like a Hershey Kiss taking a shower. Dating from the 2nd century BCE to 70 CE and belonging to an apocalyptic, monastic sect called the Essenes, some of the scrolls contain versions of the Hebrew Bible almost identical to the books that passed through the hands of countless Jewish scribes. On the bottom level of the museum is a collection of letters and relics that pre-date the destruction of the Second Temple and have been crucial to scholars studying the late first to early second century CE (guided tours in English Sun.-Mon. and Wed.-Thurs. 1:30pm, Tues. 3pm, and Fri. 12:45pm).

To get to the museum, take bus #9, 17, or 24. From the ticket building, walk along a shrub-lined path and up the steps to the main building. There is also a free bus for disabled or elderly visitors and their escorts running every 10 minutes all day, except from 1-1:30pm. At the booth in the lobby you'll find museum maps, information on current exhibits, and schedules for special events, lectures, and tours; specific pamphlets are NIS1 each. (Open Sun.-Mon. and Wed.-Thurs. 10am-5pm, Tues. 4-10pm, Fri. 10am-2pm. The Shrine is open the same hours except on Tues., when it's open 10am-10pm. English museum tours Sun.-Mon. and Wed.-Fri. 11am, Tues. 4:30pm. Admission to museum and Shrine NIS26, students NIS20. Fee includes admission to Rockefeller Museum. Repeat visit within 2 weeks NIS13. NIS115 annual student membership allows unlimited entrance to the Israel and Rockefeller Museums.)

Although the Israel Museum overwhelms with its sheer magnitude, the new **Bible Lands Museum** (tel. 561 10 66) across the street is artfully arranged and much more manageable. The ancient pottery, jewelry, seals, and figurines comprise the private collection of Dr. Elie Borowski, an eager Canadian antiquities collector. An interactive computer program beckons you in with flashy graphics and catchy music, and teaches you everything you could possibly want to know about cylindrical stamps and seals (open Sun.-Tues. and Thurs. 9:30am-5:30pm, Wed. 9:30am-9:30pm, Fri. 9:30am-2pm, and Sat. 11am-3pm; English tour Sun.-Fri. 10:15am, Wed. also 5:30pm; NIS20, students and children NIS12).

At the **Knesset,** discover why Israeli schoolteachers compare excessively rowdy pupils to parliament members. Israel's Parliament is located on Eliezer Kaplan St. It's directly across the street from the Israel Museum, but you'll have to walk around the block to the entrance. You must have your **passport,** and you may be subjected to a body search (open sessions Mon., Tues., or Thurs. after 4pm and Wed. after 11am; call to make sure that the Knesset is in session). Free tours (Sun. and Thurs. every 30min. in 1 of 10 languages, 8:30am-2:30pm) include an explanation of the structure of the Israeli government and a look at the Chagall tapestry and mosaics that adorn the building. Take bus #9 or 24 (tel. 675 34 20 or 16 for information).

The **Wohl Rose Garden** next to the Knesset is a sublime picnic spot. A path leads from here to the gorgeous new seat of the **Israeli Supreme Court,** completed in late 1992. The designers (Karmi & Assoc.) combine Modernist architecture with themes from ancient Jerusalem building traditions. Sit in on a trial—it's like Court TV, only live and in Hebrew (open Sun.-Thurs. 8:30am-2:30pm; movie in English at noon).

ISRAEL

Across Rupin Rd. from the government center is the Giv'at Ram campus of **Hebrew University.** At the engaging **Bloomfield Science Museum** (tel. 561 81 28), kids will leap at the chance to interact with live phenomena like gravity (open Mon. and Wed.-Thurs. 10am-6pm, Tues. 10am-8pm, Fri. 10am-1pm, Sat. 10am-3pm; NIS16, students and children NIS12). Another Giv'at Ram sight worth looking into is the **Ardon Window** in the **National Library** (tel. 658 50 27). One of the largest stained-glass windows in the world, it depicts Jewish mystical symbols in rich, dark colors (open summer Sun.-Thurs. 9am-6pm, winter until 7pm, Fri. 9am-1pm; free).

South of Zion Square

South of Independence Park lie some of Israel's most elegant and affluent residential areas. **Reḥavia,** the area trisected by Azza Rd. and Ramban St., was founded in the 1920s and became the refuge for the many German Jews fleeing Nazi persecution in the 30s. For years, it was famous as a *Deutsch* high-culture enclave, where dark wood libraries were lined with Goethe and Schiller and Mozart grooved on the gramophone. Little of the German flavor remains today, but the legacy lives on in the many International Style houses, designed in the best tradition of German Modernism. Flowery hedges fill the spaces between the well-kept stone-dressed buildings, making a walk around the neighborhood's lush streets a verdant pleasure.

In the middle of Reḥavia on Alfassi St. is **Jason's Tomb** (near #12, the sign says "Rock Cut Tomb"), built around 100 BCE as the burial site of a wealthy Hasmonean-era Jewish family. Pottery found at the site indicates that three generations were buried there, while charcoal drawings on the plastered porch wall depict ships, suggesting that one of the deceased was involved in naval excursions. The pyramid topping the tomb is a reconstruction. Further east past Azza Rd. is the **Prime Minister's official residence,** in the guarded house at the corner of Balfour and Smolenskin St. Next door on Balfour St. is the **Schocken Library,** designed by renowned architect Erich Mendelssohn who resided in Jerusalem in the late 1930s (he lived in the windmill on Ramban St. near Kikkar Tzarfat, now a ritzy shopping complex).

Farther south are the neighborhoods of **Talbiyya** (Komemiyut) and **Qatamon** (Gonen), still known by the names they had before their Arab inhabitants were dispossessed in 1948. The ornate villas (one of which was the home of renowned cultural theorist Edward Said) have become favorites of Hebrew University faculty and, more recently, well-to-do professionals. The official residence of the Israeli President is on Ha-Nassi (President) St., and the plush **Jerusalem Theater** is on the other side of the block, on the corner of Chopin and Marcus Rd.

Around the corner from Ha-Nassi St. is the **Mayer Institute for Islamic Art,** 2 Ha-Palmaḥ St. (tel. 566 12 91), displaying a significant collection of miniatures, paintings, and artifacts from the Islamic world. Take bus #15 from the center of town (open Sun.-Mon. and Wed.-Thurs. 10am-5pm, Tues. 4-8pm, Fri.-Sat. 10am-2pm; NIS12, students NIS8, under 18 NIS6; free on Sat.)

On the other end of Jabotinsky St. is **King David Street.** 300m up the street toward the city center, the **YMCA,** built in 1933, has an imposing bell tower offering fine views of the whole city (open Mon.-Sat. 8:30am-6pm, NIS2). Directly across the street, the historic **King David Hotel** retains an aura of old-world luxury, making it a favorite accommodation for international celebrities. The King David served as the British Headquarters and was bombed by Jewish underground forces during the 1948 War. Heading along King David St. toward the center of town you'll find **Hebrew Union College,** the American Reform Movement's outpost in Israel. Check out their **Skirball Museum,** 13 King David St. (tel. 620 33 33), showcasing an excellent exhibit of relics from three ancient cities: Laish, Gezer, and Aroer (open Sun.-Thurs. 10am-4pm, Sat. 10am-2pm; free). Down the other side of King David St., at the intersection with Keren Hayesod and Jabotinsky St., is the sprawling, green haven of **Liberty Bell Park** (Gan Ha-Pa'amon). An amphitheater, basketball courts, climbable sculptures, and a Liberty Bell replica grace the lawns. On Saturday nights, the park hops with folk-dancing festivities (take bus #14, 18, or 21 from the center).

Cross the street to get to the restored neighborhood of **Yemin Moshe**. It was here that Sir Moses Montefiore, a British Jew, first managed to convince a handful of residents from the Old City's overcrowded Jewish Quarter to spend occasional nights outside the city walls, thus founding West Jerusalem. To strengthen the settlers' confidence, Montefiore built **Mishkenot Sha'ananim** (Tranquil Settlement), a small compound with crenelated walls resembling those of the Old City. The original buildings, now housing an exclusive municipal guest house and a pricey French restaurant, are located at the bottom of the hill. Montefiore also erected his famous stone windmill, now containing a tiny museum (open Sun.-Thurs. 9am-4pm, Fri. 9am-1pm; free). Yemin Moshe is now an artists' colony with galleries crammed between picturesque alleyways. The now-dry **Sultan's Pool** sits in the valley below. Named after Suleiman the Magnificent, renovator of this Second-Temple reservoir in the 16th century, the pool figures prominently in Palestinian novelist Jabra Ibrahim Jabra's *The Ship*. Today the Sultan's Pool is most famous for its open-air concerts.

If you walk farther south on King David St., turn right at the gas station, and bear right onto Emek Refa'im St., you'll reach the **German Colony**, a leafy neighborhood of somber European houses and spacious Arab villas. To the southeast, the **Haas Promenade**, on the road to Armon Ha-Natziv, is a hillside park and promenade with great views of the Old City and the Dead Sea, perfect for gazing or grazing. The dusk experience alone is worth the trip (take bus #8, 44, 48, or 99).

North of Zion Square

Bus #2 from the city center to Ha-Sanhedrin St. (off Yam Suf St.) takes you to a park carpeted with pebbles and pine needles, and the **Tombs of the Sanhedrin**. Composed of esteemed male sages and leaders, the Sanhedrin was the high court of ancient times; it ruled on legal matters and even reviewed Jesus' case. Separate burial areas were designated for the members (open Sun.-Fri. 9am-sunset; free).

The **Tourjeman Post**, 4 Ḥeil Ha-Handasa St. (Highway #1) (tel. 628 12 78), recounts Jerusalem's history from its division in 1948 to its reunification in 1967. The building withstood severe shelling during the 1948 War and became an Israeli command post from 1948 to 1967, when the Jordanian border was just across the street. To reach the building, walk northwest up the wide new road springing from Ha-Zanḥanim St.; the museum will be on your left, just before the intersection with Shivtei Yisrael St. (bus #11 or 27; open Sun.-Thurs. 9am-5pm).

Before the Six-Day War, **Ammunition Hill** (Giv'at Ha-Taḥmoshet; tel. 582 84 42) was Jordan's most fortified position in the city and commanded much of northern Jerusalem. Taken by Israeli troops in a bloody battle, the hill now serves as a memorial to the Israeli soldiers who died in the Six-Day War. The somber, architecturally striking museum is housed in a reconstructed bunker and gives an account of the 1967 battle. Buses #4, 9, 25, 28, and 45 let you off at the foot of the hill (open summer Sun.-Thurs. 8am-6pm, Fri. 8am-2pm; winter Sun.-Thurs. 9am-5pm, Fri. 9am-1pm; NIS8, students and children NIS4).

After 1948, the **Hebrew University of Jerusalem** had to relocate from **Mt. Scopus** (Har Ha-Tzofim), where it was founded in 1925, to the new campus in **Giv'at Ram**. From 1948 to 1967, Mt. Scopus was a garrisoned Israeli enclave in Jordanian territory. Every week for 19 years, U.N. supplies were flown in to relieve the community; every week seven Israeli soldiers were let in, and seven were let out. After 1967, all but the natural and physical sciences departments moved back to the original campus. Massive reconstruction was funded largely by international donors, whose names emblazon the libraries, promenades, and pebbles that comprise modern Mt. Scopus. Free guided tours depart from the Bronfman Reception Center in the Sherman Administration Building (Sun.-Thurs. 11am). Pick up a map from the Reception Center to stroll around Israel's top university on your own. You can browse through the bookstore, library, computer labs, and botanical gardens. For a fabulous view of Jerusalem, head to the overlook point, outside the university gates along the south side of the campus. The **Hecht Synagogue** in the Humanities building, overlooking the Old City, is also worth a visit; enter via the Sherman Building. The university's gorgeous **amphitheater** faces the **West Bank.**

Southwest of Zion Square

Yad Va-Shem, meaning "a memorial and a name" (tel. 675 16 11), is the largest of Israel's Holocaust museums. Don't plan to do too much right after your visit; the museum's several buildings deserve some time and take an emotional toll. It's best to start at the **historical museum,** which traces the origins of the Holocaust through photographs, documents, and relics. The exhibit ends with a simple, powerful memorial: symbolic tombs showing the number of Jews who were killed in each country, and a tiny shoe that belonged to one of the Holocaust's younger victims. **The Hall of Names** (closes 15min. before museum) contains an agonizingly long list of all known Holocaust victims. Visitors may fill out a Page of Testimony, recording the name and circumstances of death of family members killed by the Nazis. **The Hall Of Remembrance** houses a *ner tamid* (eternal fire) to memorialize the Holocaust's victims, with the name of each concentration camp engraved into the floor. The nearby **art museum** displays drawings and paintings composed by Jews in the ghettos and concentration camps; in the museum and on its grounds are a number of evocative works by sculptor Elsa Pollock. By far the most haunting part of Yad Va-Shem is the stirring **Children's Memorial,** where mirrors are positioned to create the illusion of an infinite sea of candles, while a recorded voice recites the names and ages of young victims. The **Valley of the Communities** is an enormous labyrinthine memorial dedicated to the destroyed villages of Europe. Carved in stone are the names of *shtetls* that are no more; surviving family members wander around in search of their former towns. To get to Yad Va-Shem, take bus #13, 17, 18, 20, 23, or 27 and get off at the huge, orange arch just past Mt. Herzl. Turn around and take a left on Ein Kerem St., then follow the signs down Ha-Zikaron St. for about ten minutes (open Sun.-Thurs. 9am-5pm, Fri. 9am-2pm; free guided English tour of Yad Va-shem Sun. 10am and 2pm, Wed.-Fri. 10am).

You'll see signs near the bus stop for **Mount Herzl** (Har Herzl), where Theodore Herzl, the founder of modern political Zionism, is buried. The **Herzl Museum** (tel. 651 11 08) encapsulates the energy of the man, a newspaper correspondent who made the most prominent modern articulations of Zionism and lobbied for the creation of a Jewish state until his death in 1904. For more detailed information on his life, see **Zionism,** p. 51 (open Sun.-Thurs. 9am-6:30pm, Fri. 9am-1pm; NIS2, students NIS1). Ze'ev Jabotinsky, Levi Eshkol, Golda Meir, and Yitzhak Rabin are also buried here. Nearby is the **Israeli Military Cemetery,** the resting place of fallen soldiers. The Military Cemetery is two bus stops before Mount Herzl, but you should go to the Herzl Museum first to get a walking map.

The scenic **Jerusalem Forest** and the pastoral village of **Ein Kerem,** just west of Mt. Herzl, are perfect for picnics and short hikes. You can get to the village by taking city bus #17 or 17a from the central bus station or Zion Square (runs every 20-30min.). Formerly an Arab village, tiny Ein Kerem (fountain of vines) is the traditionally professed birthplace of **John the Baptist.** The tranquil streets of this thriving artists' colony are now lined with charming studios and craftshops.

The **Church of St. John** (tel. 641 36 39), with its soaring clock tower, marks the spot where John was born. The church displays several paintings, including the *Decapitation of Saint John* (open April-Sept. daily 6am-noon and 2:30-6pm; Oct.-March 8am-noon and 2:30-5pm; Italian Mass celebrated Sun. at 8:15am; modest dress; free). In the church's **Grotto of the Nativity** there is a lovely Byzantine mosaic of pheasants—the symbol of the Eucharist. Ask the guardian for a key.

Across the valley, down Ma'ayan St. from St. John's gate, the **Church of the Visitation** (tel. 641 72 91) recalls Mary's visit to Elizabeth and contains a rock behind which the infant St. John hid when the Romans came to kill babies. The newer Upper Chapel depicts the glorification of Mary (open April-Sept. daily 8-11:45am and 2:30-6pm, Oct.-March 8-11:45am and 2:30-5pm). The pink tower belongs to the **Russian Monastery** (tel. 625 25 65 or 641 28 87), which you can visit by appointment only.

The synagogue at the **Hadassah Medical Center** (tel. 677 62 71), near Ein Kerem (not to be confused with Hadassah Hospital on Mt. Scopus), houses the **Chagall Windows,** depicting the 12 tribes of Israel in abstract stained-glass designs based on Genesis 49 and Deuteronomy 33. Chagall donated the windows to the hospital in 1962. When four of the windows were damaged in the 1967 War, Chagall was sent an urgent cable. He replied, "You worry about the war, I'll worry about my windows." Two years later he installed four replacements. Three of the windows still contain bullet holes. (Free tours Sun.-Thurs. every hr. on the half-hr. 8:30am-12:30pm and 2:30pm, Fri. every hr. 9:30-11:30am. Synagogue open Sun.-Thurs. 8am-1:15pm and 2-3:45pm, Fri. 8am-noon. Admission NIS9, students with ID NIS4.50.)

In the hospital's Tannenbaum Center, you can get a ride to the **Jerusalem Forest** (ask for Pinchas), and participate in the **Jewish National Fund's tree-planting program** (trees US$10 each, call 670 74 33 or 563 96 50 for information). A nice place for lunch is **Pundak Einheram,** at 13 Ha Ma'ayan St. The pasta and views are both enchanting (open daily 11pm-late).

▓ Entertainment

Tel-Avivians hate to admit it, but Jerusalem nightlife is no longer joke-worthy. Once the city's conservative majority is safely tucked into bed, the bar and club scene comes to life, peaking Thursday to Saturday nights. Cultural events, from lunchtime chamber music to the early summer **Israel Festival,** long a source of Jerusalem pride, add to Jerusalem's blossoming arts scene. The best info is in *Kol Ha-Ir,* a Hebrew weekly. The entertainment section of Friday's *Jerusalem Post* and the MTIO will also help. In June, look out for **Student Day** at Hebrew University, with trips during the day and fireworks at night.

BARS

In the **Russian Compound** (Migrash Ha-Russim), two blocks east of Zion Sq., neon beer signs glow through the crisp night air, luring liquor lovers like moths. After midnight, stylish bars in old stone buildings fill to capacity (and overflow into the street) with a young, hip crowd. It's not hard to choose a haunt that suits your mood: they're all concentrated around one block. The **Yoel Solomon** area offers some nice escapes from this crazy scene, and it's only five minutes away.

Shanty, 4 Naḥalat Shiva St. (tel. 624 34 34), between Yoel Solomon and Rivlin St. Take the first left on Yoel Solomon from Zion Sq., then turn left. An Israeli enclave in a tourist domain; ensures an absence of teens by carding harder. Single women have been known to sit for hours without losing their faith in human decency. Hot cinnamon spiced wine NIS14, beer NIS10-15, salads NIS24. Open Sun.-Thurs. 7:30pm or 3am, Fri. 9pm-3am, Sat. 8:30pm-3am or 4am. Kitchen closes at 11pm.

Biankiny, 25 Hillel St. (tel. 623 21 19), at the corner of Biankiny. If the comfy cushioned divans don't relax you, the honey and apple flavored tobaccos will. *Argeileh* (NIS17) and mint tea (NIS7); also try their divine *yoadiho* (hot milk and Irish cream, NIS16). *Caravanserai* meets rave in their funky UV room. Open daily 24hr.

Glasnost, 15 Heleni Ha-Malka St. (tel. 625 69 54), off Zion Sq., in the Russian Compound. Spins jazz, funk, and rock; live bands play salsa (Mon. 11pm) and reggae (Tues. 11pm). The cardinal rule of Jerusalem bar-hopping: judge not by the beer, but by the olives. Glasnost does both well. Sit indoors or outside on an airy, music-filled patio. Beer NIS10-18, daiquiris NIS20, hard liquor NIS15-30. Also serves spaghetti, chicken wings, burgers, and cakes (NIS12-35). Open 7pm-whenever.

Mike's Place, 14 Hokanos St., on your way to the Russian Compound. Israeli and expat crowd digs live blues and rock, Tues.-Sat. No cover. Cheap pints of Guiness (NIS15). Goldstar NIS10, whiskey NIS14. Happy hour 7-8pm with 2 beers for the price of 1. Open daily 7pm until you hear "mooo's."

Cannabis, 11 Mounbar St. (623 36 35). Enter to the left, up the stairs behind the bright yellow Tom's Pub sign—look for the gigantic hemp murals. Spacious bar and balcony. Try the watermelon and vodka (NIS25) but no herbal goods. 10% off with ISIC. Open daily 8pm-as late as it takes.

The Rock, 11 Yoel Salomon (tel. 629 51 70). Sidewalk seating with unsurpassed population density as drinkers shuttle between the Underground and the Arizona. Beer NIS8-14. Happy hour Sun.-Thurs. 5-9pm. Open Sun.-Thurs. 5pm-2 or 3am, Sat. nightfall-3 or 4am. Kosher.

Sergey (tel. 625 85 11), Heleni Ha-Malka St., at the corner of Mounbaz St., next to Glasnost. Packed with an intellectual twenty-something crowd—angst-ridden Bezalel Art Institute students so hip they don't even wear black. Sun. is blues night. Italian food. Beer NIS10-16, mixed drinks NIS14 and up. Open 8pm-3 or 4am.

CAFES

Tmol Shilshom, 5 Yoel Solomon St. (tel. 623 27 58). Tucked behind the street up a staircase. This gay-owned bookstore-cafe is poet Yehuda Amiḥai's favorite. He and other local greats give readings here while aspiring writers scrawl over coffee and tea (NIS5.50-14). Open-mike poetry and live music jams twice weekly (Mon. jazz and Tues. folk). Curries, baked potatoes, and salads NIS19-25. All-you-can-eat breakfast buffet Fri. morning NIS25. Open Sun.-Thurs. 8:30am-1:30am, Fri. 8:30am-3pm, Sat. 8:30pm-1:30am. Kosher.

Cafe Ta'amon, 27 King George St. (tel. 625 49 77), at the corner of Hillel St. A legendary hole in the wall where older Israeli writers and intellectuals mingle with vodka lovers. Owner Mordekhai Kop's IOUs book is a veritable *Who's Who in Israel.* Coffee, tea, sandwiches, pastries NIS5. Beer NIS8-10. Fri. (1-5pm) is *cholent* day, when regulars come for the traditional Jewish meat and potato stew (NIS15). Open Sun.-Thurs. 6:30am-2am, Fri. 6:30am-5pm, Sat. sundown-2am.

Caffit, 35 Emek Refaim St. (tel. 635 284). Draws the post 20-something crowd to green umbrellas on a large patio. Usually a wait to get in. Cakes and pies (NIS14.50-20) and a large selection of coffee drinks (NIS7-10); ornately garnished veggie meals NIS17-28. Open Sun.-Thurs. 7:30am-2am, Fri. 7:30-sundown, Sat. after *Shabbat*-2am. Visa, MC, AmEx.

Aroma, 18 Hillel St. (tel. 625 53 65), at the corner of Rav Akiva. Hip espresso bar with good coffee and light meals. Coffee and croissant combo NIS12. Coffee drinks NIS5-6; cheaper to take out. Open daily 24hr.

Ha-Mizraka Tea House, 12 Yoel Salomon St. (tel. 625 52 22). Serves 24 kinds of tea (NIS10 per pot, NIS4 more with rum) and assorted snacks in a candle-lit, cushion-clad cave. Open Sun.-Thurs. 7pm-2am, Fri. 9pm-3pm, Sat. sundown-2am.

DANCING

The **Underground,** 8 Yoel Salomon St. (tel. 625 19 18), is the dance club everyone hates but goes to anyway, with a bar and a Batcave-like disco downstairs. Wall-to-wall funky fluorescent graffiti and sweaty dancers shed layers of clothing as the hours turn wee. From 7:50 to 8:10pm, all the beer you can drink for NIS5. It's free to enter the rock music bar room, but to get into the techno lair you'll have to buy a drink (NIS15 and up). The **Arizona,** 37 Jaffa Rd., has a similar policy. This dance inferno is a mite smaller and cheesier, and features a Western-theme bar. The disco is the Underground's twin; in fact, they are separated by one thin wall. Both feature testosterone-heavy, confident clientele who grind atop picnic tables. Both are open 7:30pm-4am.

Larger clubs are in Jerusalem's southern industrial neighborhood, **Talpiot,** down Hebron Rd., and include **Umman 17, Archaeus, Campus,** and **Incognito.** The cover charges range from NIS40-45 for Friday and Saturday nights (open 9pm-5am).

For a night of bacchanalian revelry, visit the unique **Mo'adon Canaan** at 8 Ta'asiya St. (tel. 673 56 33 or 57 21; a NIS20 cab ride). NIS35 buys carafes of all the wine you can drink as you jive to Israeli folk-turned-rock music: you may even start banging a tambourine and dancing on tables with a wild horde of Israelis and tourists. NIS66 also buys a multi-course meat dinner (open Tues., Thurs., and Sat. 9:30pm-1:30am; reservations strongly recommended).

There are many options for folk dancing in Jerusalem. The **International Cultural Center for Youth** (ICCY), 12a Emek Refa'im St. (tel. 566 41 44), has dancing on Tuesdays at 8pm (take bus #4 or 18; NIS12). The **House for Hebrew Youth** (Beit Ha-

No'ar), 105 Ha-Rav Herzog St. (tel. 678 94 41), holds folk-dancing classes (Wed.-Thurs. 8pm; bus #19, NIS12). The **Liberty Bell Gardens** hosts a freer setting for post-*Shabbat* gyrations. Dances are taught to aspiring Astaires of all ages.

PERFORMING ARTS AND FILM

The **Jerusalem Symphony** (tel. 561 14 98 after 4pm) performs frequently at the Jerusalem Theater on David Marcus and Chopin St. (NIS80-100; students up to 50% off; season runs Sept.-June), and the **Israel Philharmonic Orchestra** (tel. 625 24 81) plays at Binyanei Ha-Umma. Plays, dances, and concerts are held at the Israel Museum (tel. 563 62 31). **Asaf's Cave** (tel. 671 68 41), in the Mount Zion Cultural Center near David's Tomb, stars the Diaspora Yeshiva Band; bid *Shabbat* good-bye here weekly at 9pm (in winter 8pm) with Hasidic dancing and English, Hebrew, and Yiddish music—a unique Jerusalem experience (cover NIS12; call to make sure there is a performance). Friday nights at 10:30pm, popular Israeli singers perform at **Beit Shmuel,** 6 Shammai St. (tel. 620 34 56; NIS30-60; reservations recommended). Seize any opportunity to attend a performance at **Sultan's Pool** (Brekhat Ha-Sultan), open in summer only (see p. 313). Tickets for American or British rock stars start at NIS80.

The **Palestinian National Theater** (Al Hakawati), on Nablus St. (tel. 628 09 57), near the American Colony Hotel, has survived through years of Israeli occupation and IDF raids. They stage plays and musicals, many of which are political; English synopses are provided. Walk up Nablus Rd. and take the first right after the intersection with Salah ad-Din St. The theater is 100m farther on the right, at the end of a short driveway. Locals greet visitors cordially (NIS15; call to inquire about performances).

Built by Ottoman Turks in the 1880s as a caravan stop, the **Khan** (tel. 671 82 81), across from the railway station in Remez Sq., contains an intimate theater, restaurant, art gallery, and a cafe featuring Hebrew stand-up comedy, jazz (Tues. 10:30pm) and classical music concerts (NIS10-30). It's rarely frequented by tourists, but the concerts and plays, mostly in Hebrew, are critically acclaimed (Egged buses #7, 8, 21, 30, and 48, and Arab buses #21 and 22 pass by the railway station).

At the **Jerusalem Cinematheque** on Hebron Rd. in the Hinnom Valley (tel. 672 41 31), southwest of the Old City walls (bus #4, 4a, 7, 8, 14, 18, 21, or 48), two screens show several films every evening (Sun.-Thurs. 5-9:30pm, Fri. 2, 10pm, and midnight, Sat. 11am, 4, 8, and 10pm. Tickets NIS23; call to find out about Fri. night "movie marathons"). The annual **Israeli Film Festival** brings international films to Jerusalem and introduces local creations in the first part of July. Pick up a free book of listings (also in English) at the Cinematheque, or read the Friday supplement of the *Post.* For some films you'll need to buy tickets well in advance.

■ Shopping

Budget shopping in Jerusalem can be fun if you keep your wits about you. Often the deal of the century is found after relentless comparison shopping or by bargaining until you're blue in the face (for bargaining tips, see **Old City Markets,** below, and **Cairo: Shopping,** p. 125). It's best to pay in foreign currency to avoid the VAT. Otherwise, be sure to get a refund form to be redeemed at the airport.

Jewelry

You can buy jewelry everywhere in Jerusalem—in Arab *souqs,* on the *midraḥov* Ben Yehuda, from street vendors, or from fine shops in hotels. **Eilat stone,** a green or turquoise semi-precious stone from the hills around Eilat, is a common element in rings, necklaces, earrings, and pendants. **Baltinester,** 40 Jaffa Rd. (tel. 625 66 46 or 624 40 78) has caseloads of jewelry in all price and quality ranges. Jewelry can be inscribed in two to six days (14K gold nameplate US$30-90; open Sun.-Thurs. 9am-7pm, Fri. 9am-2pm; credit cards accepted). Booths of cheap jewelry abound at **The Pit,** an open-air market at the end of Yoel Solomon St. Merchants set up shop in the afternoons and evenings. On Friday, they start at 10am and end before *Shabbat.* On Saturday, they hawk from nightfall until late.

Ceramics and Woodwork

Israel is home to many accomplished artisans. Often pieces are made from olive-wood, Jerusalem stone, and other native materials. **Jerusalem Pottery,** along Via Dolorosa between Al Wad St. and Khan az-Zeit St., has beautiful handpainted ceramic tiles, cups, and containers. The Armenian owners paint the tiles that mark Old City streets. Their work appears throughout the *souq,* but the biggest selection is at their own store. Custom ceramic nameplates take ten days to make and are worth the wait (NIS15 and up). At **Kakadu** (tel. 625 64 12) on Rivlin St., Reut and Aaron Shaher hand-design beautiful pinewood trays, notebook covers, and other gift items (open Sun.-Thurs. 9am-11pm, Fri. 9am-4pm; credit cards accepted). Owner Neḥemiah hand-carves all the wood himself at **Almaz Olive Wood Shop,** 26 Me'a She'arim (tel. 682 47 15). Boxes (NIS22), clocks (NIS53), bookstands (NIS30), and other items can be personally engraved (open Sun.-Thurs. 10am-8pm, Fri. 10am-3pm).

Judaica

If you're looking for *menorot, mezuzot, kippot,* or other ritual items, you've come to the right city. The *Talmud* says that it is not enough to fulfill the commandments; one must beautify the ritual with pieces of art. As a result, making ceremonial objects has been an outlet for talented Jewish artists. Items are often crafted in precious metals and sold in jewelry stores. Rows of inexpensive Judaica shops crowd the streets of **Me'a She'arim.** Nearer the city center, **Yermiyahu's,** 3 Yanai St. (tel. 661 00 58), off Shlomzion Ha-Malka just before it intersects with Shlomo Ha-Melekh, sells very nice *kippot* and *tallitot* at bargain prices (open Sun.-Thurs. 8am-7pm, Fri. 8am-1pm). **Chen Eilat,** 11 Me'a She'arim (tel. 637 01 28), has a huge selection of *ḥallah* covers (NIS20-100), candles (NIS20-40), and other things Jewish (open Sun.-Thurs. 9:30am-7:30pm, Fri. 9:30am-2:30pm; credit cards accepted).

Music

Pop songs in Israel can tackle subjects as heady as life in the army, the religious-secular conflict, and coping with terrorism. Lyrical folk songs by Naomi Shemmer and others have become second anthems to the young state, and capture the worries and hopes of Israel better than a thousand pictures. **Derekh Ha-Ozen Music,** 23 Ben Yehuda (tel. 625 50 77), at the corner of King George (other location at 4 Luntz St. near the *midraḥov*), is the best and cheapest place to listen to and shop for Israeli music. The knowledgeable staff can help you find any type of Israeli, Jewish, or Ḥasidic music. Feel free to listen to any recording in the store. Ask a clerk and they'll gladly unwrap the cellophane and set you up at a listening station, without pressuring you to buy a thing (open Sun.-Thurs. 9am-9:45pm, Fri. 9am-4pm, Sat. after *Shabbat*-midnight; CDs NIS59, tapes NIS39).

Old City Markets

The minute you cross the threshold of Jaffa Gate, marketeers begin shoving their wares in your face. **David Street** plunges into the heart of the Old City, and, along with **Baab as-Silsilah Street,** is the central artery of the bustling *souq.* Palestinian craftwork is beautiful, such as Hebron-style wine glasses, mother-of-pearl inlaid boxes, ceramic tiles, and spherical Jerusalem candles. Other items (cheap t-shirts and plastic-mold Domes of the Rock) aren't. If you cannot throw out enough t-shirts to fit an *argeileh* into your pack, settle for a short but powerful smoke (NIS1-2) at an *ahwa*. Women should make sure the *ahwa* is not exclusively male. The honey tobacco is especially delicious. At several local haunts inside Damascus Gate, you can rent an *argeileh* for NIS5, and they'll keep refilling the coals until your lungs say stop.

Do not buy from the first air-conditioned wonderland you enter. Often, the exact same wares are sold from closet-like alcoves for a lot less. There's a lot of supply in this market—remember the rules of **economics** and use them to your advantage. A good rule of thumb is to begin bidding at half of the quoted price. Walk away and you will probably be called back. Beware of your own body language—fumbling for a wallet while insisting on a lower price speaks volumes to wily salesmen. And there's no backing off—you must be prepared to pay any price you offer.

Halfway down David St. on the left, two cavernous rooms house a **produce market** called *Souq Aftimos*. **Al Wad Road** connects the Western Wall area to Damascus Gate. A right off Al Wad onto **Via Dolorosa** leads to an array of small ceramics shops. Shops between **Christian Quarter Road** and the Church of the Holy Sepulchre have the largest selection of rosaries, crosses, and other Christian items. The **Khan az-Zeit** market extends north from David St. to Damascus Gate. Actual Old City-folk shop here and along Al Wad Rd. There aren't many gifts, but there are cartloads of cheap shoes, clothing, sewing products, jewelry, lingerie, spices, and kitchenwares.

Much decorative masonry in the *souq*—stone set within stone over entries and passageways—is characteristic of Mamluk architecture. Paintings of the Dome of the Rock and the Ka'ba shrine of Mecca adorn doorways. A painting of the latter signifies that a member of the family has been on the *hajj*, the Islamic pilgrimage to Mecca and Medina. Women should dress modestly for a more heckling-free shopping excursion.

BETWEEN JERUSALEM AND TEL AVIV

■ Abu Ghosh אבו גוש أبو غوش

Thirteen kilometers west of Jerusalem lies the Arab village of **Abu Ghosh.** One of many shared sacred sites in the region, Abu Ghosh is revered by Christians and Jews alike as an early site of the Ark of the Covenant, which King David later moved to Jerusalem. In the 18th century, Sheikh Abu Ghosh required pilgrims to pay a toll here as they traveled to the Holy City; the town was the last of a series of caravan stops en route to Jerusalem. Historically, the Arabs of the village have always had good relations with neighboring Jewish settlements, even during the 1948 War. The town now has a Jewish mayor. To get to Abu Ghosh, take Egged bus #185 or 186 (every 30min., 20min., NIS8.5), which leaves from the central bus station. *Sherut* traveling between Jerusalem and Tel Aviv will stop at the exit, 2km from Abu Ghosh.

The **Bet Meir Youth Hostel (HI)** (tel. (02) 534 26 91; fax 534 20 98) is situated within a religious community about 20km west of Jerusalem. On bus #186 from Jerusalem (NIS11.50, 40min.), continue past Abu Ghosh to arrive at Bet Meir. Enter the *moshav*, take the first left and after about 200m, go down the road on your right. Follow the signs for Ramot Shapira. At the bottom of the hill lies a large complex housing 40 guest rooms and behind it a number of "cottages" containing dorm rooms. The cozy guest rooms have up to four beds, wall-to-wall carpeting, and A/C (US$22, US$21 for students with a three-person minimum). Those staying in the dorms must be content with fans (US$18.50, US$17.50 for students). Both alternatives have attached shower and toilet, and breakfast is included. Young teens gobble up rooms—call ahead and ask for English-speaking Asher (reception open 8am-4pm; no lockout or curfew; HI members receive 10% discount).

There are many **restaurants** to curb your midday hunger on the road between the village's two churches. Join the hordes from Jerusalem at the **Caravan Inn Restaurant** (tel. (02) 342 744 or 333 573). Although the meat dishes are a little pricey (*shishlik* for NIS39), you can get a plate of hummus for NIS8 and enjoy the breezy terrace with amazing views of Abu Gosh and the hills of Jerusalem (credit cards accepted).

Notre Dame de l'Arche d'Alliance (Our Lady of the Ark of the Covenant; tel. (02) 342 818), at the top of the hill, was built on the site of the Ark's ancient holding place. The current church was built in the 1920s on the ruins of a demolished Byzantine church; fragments of the old mosaic floors remain (open daily 8:30-11:30am and 2:30-6pm, but you can usually enter at any reasonable hour).

Below the sacred hill, in a beautiful garden, stands the magnificently preserved **Crusader Church of the Resurection,** built in 1142 and acquired by the French government in 1873. Excavations beneath the church have uncovered remains dating back to Neolithic times. The church lies below the main road; head for the minaret of the attached mosque and look for a door in the wall on your right (open Mon.-Wed. and Fri.-Sat. 8:30-11am and 2:30-5:30pm; free).

The stalagmite and stalactite cave of **Avshalom** (the **Soreq Cave**) contains spectacular speleological splendors. Discovered less than thirty years ago when a routine blast at a nearby quarry exposed a view into the cave, this site has been transformed into a major tourist attraction. The artificial lighting and paved pathways may disappoint adventurous spelunkers but can't detract from the natural majesty. The cave is 19km southwest of Jerusalem, 7km from the village of Nes Harim. Stalwart hikers can take bus #184 (every 1-2hrs., NIS10.50) to Nes Harim and walk from there. Otherwise try hiring a taxi from Nes Harim (open Sat.-Thurs. 8:30am-3:45pm, Fri. 8:30am-12:45pm). Admission (NIS13, children NIS7) includes a slide show and guided tour (tel. 991 11 17). Photography and solo wanderings are permitted on Fridays only.

■ Latrun לטרון

Latrun lies about halfway between Jerusalem and Tel Aviv and has three attractions. The **Latrun Monastery** (tel. (08) 922 00 65 or 925 51 80; fax 925 50 84) was founded by the French Trappist Order (belonging to the great monastic family of St. Benedict) as a center for contemplation and reflection. Famous for its wine, the monastery is built on a hillside granting it beautiful views of the surrounding area (particularly the biblical sites of Emmaus, Agalon, Bethoron, and others). An inspiring church and peaceful gardens sit beside the monastery (both open Mon.-Sat. 8am-noon and 3:30pm-5pm). On Saturdays, a short film explaining the life of a monk is screened. The shop near the main gate offers a wide selection of wines and spirits (open Mon.-Sat. 8am-1pm and 2pm-6pm). The paved road opposite the Paz filling station leads to the monastery; continue 600m until you see an uphill road on your left (the entrance is marked by an orange sign reading "Monastery Latroun").

If the march to the monastery has you in a military mood, head back towards the filling station and check out the **Armored Corps Museum** (tel. (08) 925 52 68), a heaven on earth for anyone enchanted by the sight of tanks. The museum contains over 120 armored battle vehicles. There is also an exhibit of stamps about armed forces from all over the world and a complete reconstruction of the tank planned by Leonardo da Vinci over 500 years ago. (Open Sun.-Thurs. 8:30am-4:30pm, Fri. 8:30am-12:30pm, Sat. 9am-4pm; hours may vary in the winter. Admission NIS15, children NIS9, senior citizens NIS8. Group rates available.)

On the other side of the Tel-Aviv-Jerusalem highway is the **Emmaus (Nicopolis) Church,** where Jesus was said to have appeared to two of his disciples after his resurrection (Mark 16:12-13, Luke 24:13-31); it is now the French Prehistorical Research Center. Another 100m along the road is the entrance to the **Canada Park**, a beautifully forested area with water holes and the remains of an amphitheater. The best (and virtually only) option for a snack and a cool drink in Latrun is **Ganei Ayalon** (tel. (08) 925 51 84), which has seating in a green and yellow tent behind the Paz Station.

Latrun can be reached by bus #404, 425, or 433, from either Jerusalem (30min., NIS15) or Ramla (20min., NIS12.20). Service is every 30 minutes. Make sure you tell the driver in advance that you want to stop in Latrun (and remind him a few more times along the way).

Tel Aviv-Jaffa תל אביב–יפו

Tel Aviv's mayor writes that "life here never stops and has therefore earned itself the expression 'The City That Never Takes A Break'." Although apparently not quite as active as "The City That Never Sleeps," Tel Aviv shares more in common with New York and other Western metropolitan areas than just a suspiciously similar nickname. Although the city does sustain some clustered religious communities, the most conspicuous Tel Avivans are the city's exuberant youth—tapping away on keyboards in internet cafes, shopping for combat boots and navel rings in trendy Sheinkin Street boutiques, and bronzing en masse on the beach on Shabbat. Tel Aviv and Jerusalem, though only 45 minutes apart, are virtual opposites: Jerusalem thrives on the past, Tel Aviv lives for the moment; Jerusalem is sacred, Tel Aviv proudly secular. Ever since the 1940s and 1950s when cutting-edge authors and poets clustered in Dizengoff Street's intimate cafes, Tel Aviv has dedicated itself to taking Israeli culture in new directions. The moisture that hangs in the air soaks out orthodoxy; most Tel Aviv establishments stay open Friday nights.

Today an integral part of Tel Aviv, Jaffa (Yafo, or "beautiful," in Hebrew; Yafa in Arabic) has one of the oldest functioning harbors in the world. Once the busiest port in the region, Jaffa harbors small fishing boats since the rise of modern shipping centers in Haifa and Ashdod. Starting in the 1960s, Israel undertook a massive renovation project, restoring and cleaning many of Jaffa's convents, mosques, alleyways, and Crusader walls. The result may be a little too sterile, with restaurants and galleries catering mostly to tourists and generally avoided by locals. Still, the winding alleys and stunning seaviews of Old Jaffa provide a classically Middle Eastern antidote to the postmodern hubbub of Tel Aviv.

■ History

Tel Aviv's long history begins with Jonah and the whale. According to the Bible, the recalcitrant prophet Jonah shirked his divine calling and fled to Jaffa to catch a boat to Tarshish. When a tempest threatened to destroy his ship, Jonah, knowing the Lord had created the storm, asked the crew to hurl him overboard. The sea calmed, but an enormous serpent-fish swallowed the prophet. After three days and nights, Jonah repented and the fish spewed him onto dry land.

The earliest archaeological finds in Jaffa date from the 18th century BCE. In 1468 BCE, the Egyptians conquered Jaffa by hiding soldiers in human-sized clay jars that were brought into the city market. King David conquered the city in about 1000 BCE, and under Solomon it became the main port of Judea, a position it maintained until the development of Caesarea under King Herod. During the 12th century, Jaffa was captured by the First Crusaders, Salah ad-Din, Richard the Lionheart, the Muslims, and then Louis IX. Louis built magnificent walls and towers, parts of which remain today. In 1267 the Mamluks overpowered the city, and Jaffa remained an important Arab stronghold until 1948.

Jewish immigrants began to settle in Jaffa as early as 1820; at that time the Palestinian town of Yafa served as the area's major port. Later in the century there were enough Jews to create the first two exclusively Jewish neighborhoods just to the north: Neveh Tzedek in 1887 and Neveh Shalom in 1891. As the Jewish population in Jaffa continued to increase, settlers decided to found a new suburb in this area. On April 11, 1909, they parceled out the land they had acquired north of Jaffa, naming the area Ahuzat Bayit (Housing Estate). One year later, the suburb was renamed Tel Aviv (Spring Hill) after the imaginary town Theodore Herzl had envisioned in his turn-of-the-century utopian novel *Altneuland* (Old-New-Land). Appealing to more bourgeois Jewish immigrants from Eastern Europe, the new town quickly developed in the 1920s and 1930s, becoming the largest Jewish town in Palestine.

The increased settlement of the area did not happen without protest. In 1929, 1936, and 1939, Jaffa was the scene of anti-Zionist riots. In the 1948 war, many of the Palestinians in Jaffa and its surrounding villages were forcibly displaced. Some of the villages were then razed; no trace of them remains beyond the memories of their former inhabitants. Jaffa was officially incorporated into the Tel Aviv municipality in 1949 and remains a mixed Jewish-Arab neighborhood today.

Despite most Tel Avivians' lack of strong religious beliefs today, the city itself is very political; Tel Aviv acts as the home of Israel's foreign embassies and financial institutions. For a brief period in the winter of 1991, Tel Aviv was the focus of world attention (via CNN) as a target for Saddam Hussein's SCUD missiles during the Gulf Crisis. The Middle East peace process has taken its toll since then; in the past two years, Hamas bombings have claimed a number of lives in the city. It was here in November 1995 that Yigal Amir, a Jewish student, fired the fatal bullet that killed Prime Minister Yitzhak Rabin. The assassination cast a shadow over all of Israel, but no place felt it more acutely than Tel Aviv.

■ Orientation

Located in the center of Israel's Mediterranean coastline, Tel Aviv is 63km northwest of Jerusalem (50min. bus ride) and 95km (1¼hr.) south of Haifa. The two main points of entry into Tel Aviv are **Ben-Gurion Airport** at Lod and the **New Central Bus Station.** Frequent bus service from the airport is supplemented by the vans that warring hostels send to lure potential customers.

Much of Tel Aviv's seemingly haphazard street layout was actually carefully planned, following the 19th-century English "garden suburb" scheme. House numbers generally increase from the sea eastward and from the more modest southern part of the city up to the wealthier north. The street signs are in English as well as Hebrew and announce the range of building numbers for that block.

Almost all hotels, restaurants, and places of interest are in the rectangle marked by the beach to the west, the **Ayalon Highway** to the east, the **Yarkon River** to the north, and **Salameh Rd.** to the south. Running along the beach beginning around Gordon St. and extending south to the Charles Clore Park is the **Tayelet** (Promenade), lined with chairs, gazebos, and inviting cafes. **Ha-Yarkon St.** runs parallel to the beach behind the first row of buildings facing the sea. The next major north-south artery, **Ben-Yehuda St.,** runs one block east of Ha-Yarkon and is lined with travel agencies and more affordable restaurants. Intersecting Ben-Yehuda to the south is **Allenby St.,** home to plentiful *shawerma* shops and a handful of bars and clubs. Parallel to Ben-Yehuda, **Dizengoff St.** is loaded with Tel Aviv's trendy cafes, chic bars, and *haute couture*. At its heart is Kikkar Disengoff, an elevated plaza surrounded by a bevy of mall-style shops and a cineplex. **Ibn Gvirol Street,** with its shaded arcades, runs from the Yarkon River in the north until it turns into Yehuda Ha-Levi St. in the center; halfway is the vast **Kikkar Yitzḥak Rabin** (formerly Kikkar Malkhei Yisrael), in front of City Hall. **Namir Rd.** (which also goes by its old name, **Haifa Rd.**) is a major thoroughfare farther east; the **central train station,** which has service to all major cities, is at the intersection of Haifa Rd. and **Arlozorov St.,** which runs east-west.

Kikkar Magen David (at the corners of Allenby, King George, and Sheinkin) is the starting point of **Shuk Ha-Carmel** to the southwest, the *midraḥov* (pedestrian mall) of **Naḥalat Binyamin** to the south, and the hip **Sheinkin St.** to the east. Northwest of the *shuk* are the winding alleyways of **Kerem Ha-Temanim** (the Yemenite Quarter). The crumbling (but gradually gentrifying) neighborhood of **Neveh Tzedek,** with the beautiful **Kikkar Suzanne Delal,** lies just south of Shuk Ha-Carmel and Naḥalat Binyamin. **Jaffa** and its waterfront lie further south, outside the downtown area.

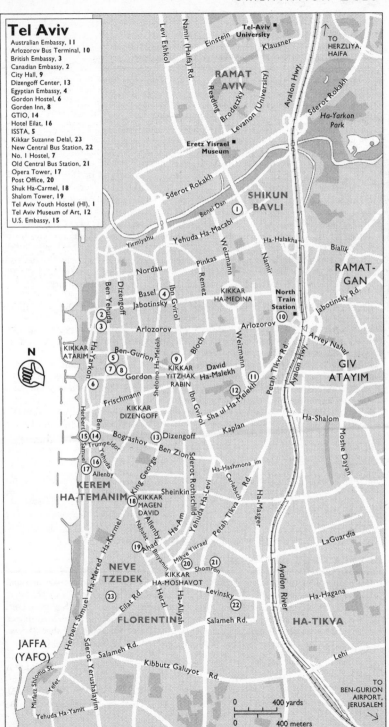

Tel Aviv

Australian Embassy, 11
Arlozorov Bus Terminal, 10
British Embassy, 3
Canadian Embassy, 2
City Hall, 9
Dizengoff Center, 13
Egyptian Embassy, 4
Gordon Hostel, 6
Gorden Inn, 8
GTIO, 14
Hotel Eilat, 16
ISSTA, 5
Kikkar Suzanne Delal, 23
New Central Bus Station, 22
No. 1 Hostel, 7
Old Central Bus Station, 21
Opera Tower, 17
Post Office, 20
Shuk Ha-Carmel, 18
Shalom Tower, 19
Tel Aviv Youth Hostel (HI), 1
Tel Aviv Museum of Art, 12
U.S. Embassy, 15

ISRAEL

■ Transportation

GETTING AROUND TOWN

Tel Aviv is mostly manageable by foot. On a hot August afternoon, though, a NIS3.90 bus ride may seem like the deal of the century. Buses in Tel Aviv are frequent, air-conditioned, and comfortable; take them to sights north of the Yarkon, in the Ramat Aviv area, or in Jaffa, which are beyond walking distance from the city center.

Opened in August 1993, the **New Central Bus Station** on Livinsky St. stands next to its grungy, now minimally used, predecessor. The new station transcends being a mere transportation hub. Over 3000 entrances, exits, and ramps open onto the six (soon to be seven) stories of its air-conditioned interior, which houses music stores, banks, a McDonald's, and even buses. Information booths on the third, fourth, and sixth floors are supplemented by scores of electronic bulletin boards which list intercity bus schedules in both English and Hebrew. Telephones and pay-to-pee restrooms (NIS1) abound, and **baggage check** rooms let you shed your load for NIS5 per item per day (bag check open Sun.-Thurs. 7am-11pm, Fri. and holiday eves 7am-3pm).

Buses within Tel Aviv are operated by **Dan** (tel. 639 44 44). Generally, **city buses** run Sunday-Thursday 5am-12:15am, Friday 5am-5pm, and Saturday 8:15pm-12:15am, but some stop running earlier. Buses do not run on *Shabbat.* For extended stays, consider buying Dan's **monthly bus pass** (NIS122). Dan's office is located at 39 Sha'ul Ha-Melekh (tel. 695 55 55). These six routes are the most important for tourists:

#4: From the New Central bus station (4th floor), runs parallel to the coastline up Allenby and Ben-Yehuda St. and back. Every 5min.

#5: From the New Central bus station (4th floor), runs north along Rothschild Blvd. and Dizengoff St. to Dizengoff Ctr., then turns around at Nordau and Yehuda Ha-Maccabee. Every 5min.

#10: Runs from city hall to Jaffa along Ben-Yehuda St. Every 15-20min.

#25: Runs between Tel Aviv University and Bat Yam via Haifa Rd., Yehuda Ha-Maccabee, Ibn Gvirol, King Solomon, King George, Allenby, Shuk Ha-Carmel, and Jaffa. Every 15-20min.

#27: From the New Central bus station (1st floor), runs along Petah Tikva Rd. and to Haifa Rd., the train station, Tel Aviv University, the *kenyon* (shopping mall) in Ramat Gan, and back. Every 10-15min.

#46: From the New Central bus station (1st floor) to Jaffa and back. Every 8-10min., every 15min. at night.

Minibuses operating as **sherut taxis** run along the routes of buses #4 and 5, and are numbered accordingly. At NIS3, they're cheaper than the bus and will stop for you anywhere along the route. Late at night and on *Shabbat* minibuses operate with less frequency and at a 25% higher fare. There's a **private taxi** stand at Allenby St. and Simḥat Beit Ha-Shoeva, but you can hail a cab anywhere. Taxis also queue up by Migdal Shalom. You can call a taxi anytime (tel. 524 90 90 or 527 19 99).

GETTING OUT OF TOWN

Intercity buses are operated by Egged (info. tel. 537 55 55). The **Arlozorov terminal,** on Arlozorov St. across from Haifa Rd., has connections to major cities. To: **Jerusalem** (#480 direct; every 15min., Sun.-Thurs. 6am-10pm, Fri. 6am-4pm, Sat. 8:30pm-11pm, 50 min., NIS16.50); **Haifa** (#980 direct; Sun.-Thurs. 6am-8:30pm, Fri. 6am-4pm, Sat. 8:30pm-10pm, every 20min., 1¼hr., NIS16.50); **Be'er Sheva** (#380 direct; Sun.-Thurs., 6am-8pm, Fri. 6am-4pm, Sat. 8:30-10:30pm, every 30min., 1 hr., NIS16.50).

The **New Central Bus Station** has intercity departures on the sixth floor. To: **Jerusalem** (#405 direct; Sun.-Thurs. 5:40am-11:30pm, Fri. 5:40am-5:30pm, Sat. sundown-midnight, every 10-15min., NIS16.50, students NIS14.85); **Haifa** (#900 direct; Sun.-Thurs. 5:45am-9pm, Fri. 5:45am-4pm, Sat. sundown-10pm, every 10-20min., NIS21, students NIS18.90. Late-night #901 express; Sun.-Thurs. 9-11pm, every 20min.,

NIS21, students NIS18.90); **Be'er Sheva** (#370 direct; Sun.-Thurs. 5:45am-9pm, Fri. 5:45am-4:40pm, Sat. sundown-11pm, every 15-20min., NIS21, students NIS18.90).

The central **train station** is on Arlozorov St. across from Haifa Rd. (info tel. 693 75 15; open 6am-9pm). Several air-conditioned trains go to Haifa, Netanya, and Nahariya. Trains to Jerusalem leave at 10am (1hr., NIS17, students NIS13). Trains to Haifa leave every hour from 5:50am-10pm (1hr., NIS18, students 14.50). To get to Arlozorov, take bus #10, 18, 20, 32, 61, or 62. There's an **intercity taxi** stand on Allenby Rd. at Ha-Moshavot Sq.

▓ Practical Information

Tourist Information Office: (tel. 639 56 60), in the New Central Bus Station on the 6th floor, near platform 630. From the city center, take bus #4 or 5 south. Maps of Tel Aviv and other cities and information on accommodations, food, shopping, tours, and cultural events. Can book hotel and tour reservations. Open Sun.-Thurs. 9am-5pm, Fri. 9am-1pm.

Tours: SPNI, 3 Ha-Shfela St. (tel. 638 86 74), between Petah Tikva Rd. and Ha-Sharon St. Their highly qualified English-speaking guides lead the best 1-12 day tours, year round. Day tours US$48-51. Open Sun.-Thurs. 8am-5pm, Fri. 8-11am. **Egged Tours,** 59 Ben-Yehuda St. (tel. 527 12 12). Not as uniformly spectacular as SPNI. Guided tours around Israel and to the Sinai (½ day tour of Tel Aviv US$25, full-day tour of Jerusalem US$57). **United Tours,** 113 Ha-Yarkon St. (tel. 693 34 12). Also offers tours around the country with multilingual guides (day tours US$57-71, 10% student discount with ISIC if booked directly from their office).

Budget Travel: ISSTA, 128 Ben-Yehuda St. (tel. 521 05 55), on the corner of Ben-Gurion St. For ISICs, bring a photo, a current student ID, and NIS35; for Youth Hostel cards bring a photo and NIS30. Open Sun.-Thurs. 9am-7pm, Fri. 9am-1pm. **Mona Tours,** 45 Ben-Yehuda St. (tel. 523 09 20), specializes in student and charter rates. ISIC not always required if you are under 28. Open Sun.-Thurs. 9am-6pm, Fri. 9am-1pm. Both take credit cards.

Consulates: Australia, 37 Sha'ul Ha-Melekh Blvd., Europe House, 4th fl. (tel. 695 04 51). Open Mon.-Thurs. 8am-noon. **Canada,** 7 Ḥavakuk St. (tel. 546 58 10), north of Nordau St. Open Mon.-Fri. 8am-noon. **South Africa,** Top Tower, Dizengoff Ctr., 16th fl. (tel. 525 25 66). Open Mon.-Fri. 9-11am and Wed. 2-3pm. **U.K.** (also serves travelers from **New Zealand**), 1 Ben-Yehuda St., Migdalor Building, 6th fl. (tel. 510 01 66 for passports, 510 04 97 for visas). Open Mon.-Fri. 8-11:30am for visas, 8am-1pm for passports. **U.S.,** 71 Ha-Yarkon St. (tel. 519 75 75). Open Mon.-Fri. 8-11am and Wed. 2-3:30pm for passports; Mon.-Thurs. 8-10am for visas. **Egypt,** 54 Basel St. (tel. 546 41 51 or 52), just off Ibn Gvirol. Open Sun.-Thurs. 9-11am. For a visa, bring your passport, photo, and NIS60 (U.S. citizens NIS40)—be sure to say if you are going beyond the Sinai, or you'll automatically get a "Sinai Only" visa. **Jordan,** 14 Aba Hillel (tel. 751 77 22), in Ramat Gan. If crossing to Jordan through Allenby Bridge, you must get your visa beforehand. Open Mon.-Fri. 9am-1pm.

Currency Exchange: The best rates (no commission) are at **Change Point,** 94 Ha-Yarkon St. (tel. 524 55 05) or 70 Ben-Yehuda St. (tel. 527 28 58; both open 9am-10pm). **Change Spot,** 140 Dizengoff St. (tel. 524 33 93), also offers no-commission exchange. Open 9am-9pm. Most **banks** are open Sun., Tues., and Thurs. 8:30am-12:30pm and 4-5:30pm, Mon., Wed., Fri., and holiday eves morning only. Main bank offices: **Bank Ha-Poalim,** 104 Ha-Yarkon St. (tel. 520 06 12); **Israel Discount,** 27 Yehuda Ha-Levi St. (tel. 514 55 55); **Bank Leumi,** 130 Ben-Yehuda St. (tel. 520 37 37). Branches throughout the city and suburbs. Bank Ha-Poalim **ATMs** are compatible with most cards from abroad.

American Express: 112 Ha-Yarkon St. (tel. 524 22 11), near the Sheraton. Mail held for cardholders, but no packages. If you've lost your AmEx traveler's checks, call their toll-free 24hr. line (tel. 177 440 86 94). Changes traveler's checks at bank rates, but without commission. Cardholders can buy traveler's checks with personal checks (1% service charge; bring your passport). 3% charge to buy traveler's checks with cash. Open Sun.-Thurs. 9am-5pm, Fri. 9am-1pm.

Airport: Ben-Gurion Airport, 22km southeast of Tel Aviv in Lod (tel. 973 11 22 for recorded information in English about flights on all airlines). Egged bus #475 to the airport leaves from the 6th fl. of the New Central Bus Station (Sun.-Thurs. 5:20am-11:35pm and Fri. 5:20am-5:30pm, every 20min., NIS7). United Tours shuttle #222 (tel. 693 34 04) stops near several hotels on Ha-Yarkon St. (Sun.-Fri. 4am-midnight and Sat. 1pm-midnight, buses every hr., NIS13.40). Taxis from the airport to Tel Aviv run at a fixed tariff (about NIS48, each piece of luggage NIS2; 25% surcharge on evenings and *Shabbat*).

Ferries: Caspi, 1 Ben-Yehuda St. (tel. 517 57 49), Migdalor Bldg., facing the street. Boats to: Cyprus (Sun., Thurs. 8pm, arrive next morning 7am; US$58, in winter $47); Rhodes (Sun., Thurs. 8pm, 2 days travel; US$101, in winter $81); Piraeus (3 days travel; US$106, return US$85, summer US$96.) Port tax additional US$22. **Mano Passenger Lines, Ltd.,** 97 Ben-Yehuda St. (tel. 522 46 11). Books tickets on ships to Cyprus. Boats leave from Haifa (Sun. 8pm; cabins only; US$65, return US$110; lower in winter). Port tax additional US$25 each way. Open Sun.-Thurs. 9am-7pm, Fri. 9am-2pm; winter Sun.-Thurs. 9am-5pm, Fri. 9am-1pm. Both ferry lines take credit cards.

Car Rental: Sharet Rent-a-Car (tel. 522 20 55), US$50-60 per day depending on the season. Weekly discounts. Jeep rental. Min. age 21. **I. Gindy Ltd. Rent-a-Car** (tel. 527 83 44). US$50 (summer US$60) per day. Weekly rental nets big discounts and unlimited mileage. Min. age 21. **Avis** (tel. 527 17 52), manual transmission US$52 per day, min. age 23; automatic US$65 per day, min. age 26. **Budget** (tel. 523 15 51), US$85-95, min. age 23. **Rent-a-Reliable-Car** (tel. 524 97 94), manual transmission US$63 per day; automatic US$83. Min. age 25, but drivers 21-24 allowed with a US$70 per day surcharge.

Shopping Hours: In general, 8:30am-1pm and 3-7pm, but many places stay open until 10pm, especially those in shopping malls. Most stores stay open late on Thurs. night, and almost all close Fri. by 2pm.

English Bookstores: The Book Boutique, 190 Dizengoff St. The best place for used English-language books in Tel Aviv. A vast selection of texts: from historical novels to westerns to erotica, plus free lemonade for thirsty bibliophiles. Buys books, too. Open Sun.-Thurs. 10am-7pm, Fri. 10am-3pm. **Katzman Gallery Books,** 152 Dizengoff (tel. 523 52 43). A fabulous selection of magazines, comics, and cheap used books, which they'll buy back afterwards. Open Sun.-Thurs. 10am-2pm and usually 5-8pm, Fri. 8am-3pm. **Modan Prosa Bookstore,** 162 Dizengoff St., (tel. 523 54 77). A small but good selection of English fiction and nonfiction. Open Sun.-Thurs. 9am-8pm, Fri. 9am-3pm. Visa, MC. **Steimatzky** has many stores, including 107 Allenby Rd., 109 Dizengoff St., the Opera Tower at 1 Allenby Rd., Kikkar Ha-Medina, and the new Central Bus Station.

Library: British Council Library, 140 Ha-Yarkon St. (tel. 522 21 94). A peaceful, A/C haven with English-language books, newspapers, videocassettes, and magazines, open to the public. Open Mon.-Thurs. 10am-1pm and 4-7pm, Fri. 10am-1pm.

Camping Supplies: LaMetayel, Dizengoff Center, Gate 3 or 5 (tel. 528 68 94), near the Lev Cinema. The largest camping store in the area, with books, maps, information, and a full range of equipment. The place to meet young Israelis gearing up for their post-military grand tour. Open Sun.-Thurs. 9:30am-8pm, Fri. 9:30am-2pm. **Maslool Travelers' Equipment and Information Center,** 36 Ben-Yehuda St. (tel. 528 84 18). Gives discounts for those who show *Let's Go*; buys used equipment. Open Mon.-Thurs. 8:30am-7:30pm, Fri. 8:30am-3pm.

Film Developing: Fotofilm, 84 Allenby St. (tel. 517 12 41). 1hr. developing, lenses, film, video supplies—anything you and your camera could possibly want. Open Sun.-Thurs. 9am-7pm, Fri. 9am-2pm. **Clarni,** 154 Dizengoff St. (tel. 523 09 90). 1hr. developing, film supplies. Open Sun.-Thurs. 8am-7pm, Fri. 8am-2pm.

Ticket Agencies: Rococo, 93 Dizengoff St. (tel. 524 88 24 or 522 36 63). Open Sun.-Thurs. 9am-7pm, Fri. 9am-2pm. **Hadran,** 90 Ibn Gvirol St. (tel. 524 87 87), north of Kikkar Yitzhak Rabin. **Castel,** 150 Ibn Gvirol St. (tel. 604 76 78 or 47 25). **Le'an,** 101 Dizengoff St. (tel. 524 73 73). All sell tickets for concerts, plays, sporting events, and other performances. Discount student tickets available.

Laundry: Self-service laundromats abound on most streets, and hostels and hotels often have their own laundry services. **Nikita,** 98 Ben-Yehuda St., has coin-operated machines. NIS10 washes 7kg. NIS1 dries clothes for 4min. Detergent NIS2.

Bu'ot, 49 Sheinkin St. (tel. 524 26 54 and 629 20 94) will pick up, clean, and drop off up to 6kg of laundry for NIS 28.

Help Lines: Alcoholics' Anonymous (522 52 55). **Rape Crisis** (tel. 685 00 41), 24hr. **Drug Counseling** (tel. 546 35 87), Sun.-Thurs. 8:30am-7pm. All speak English.

Pharmacy: Ben-Yehuda Pharmacy, 142 Ben-Yehuda St. (tel. 522 35 35). Open Sun.-Thurs. 8am-3am, Fri. 8am-4pm. **Superpharm** (tel. 620 37 98 or 07 95) in Dizengoff Center (and other locations) has a larger selection. No 24hr. pharmacies in Tel Aviv, but 2 pharmacies are always on duty for night and *Shabbat* calls. Schedules and phone numbers on pharmacy doors and in newspapers.

Emergency: Police: tel. 100. **Fire:** tel. 102. **First Aid:** tel. 101.

Post Office: 7 Mikveh Yisrael St. (tel. 564 36 51), 2 blocks east of the south end of Allenby St. **Post Restante** (tel. 564 36 60; open Sun.-Thurs. 7am-10pm); **fax, telegram,** and **telex** services (Sun.-Thurs. 8am-6pm, Fri. 8am-noon). Other branches throughout the city. Main office open Sun.-Thurs. 7am-6pm, Fri. 7am-noon.

Telephones: Solan Communications, 13 Frishman St. (tel. 522 94 24; fax 522 94 49). Private booths for international calls. Local calls 10% cheaper than a regular telecard. Provides telecards, international calling cards, fax services daily 24hr. **Change Spot,** 140 Dizengoff St. (tel. 524 33 93; fax 524 36 66). Discounted international calls. Open Sun.-Thurs. 9am-11pm, Fri. 9am-2pm. **Telephone Code:** 03.

Accommodations

Most hostels are on or around Ben-Yehuda St. and Ha-Yarkon St., with some just off Allenby Rd. or Dizengoff St. When choosing, keep in mind that drunken revelry and honking horns downtown may continue late into the night. Hostels fill quickly, especially in summer, so make reservations and arrive on the early side. If all beds are taken, a rooftop mattress can be heavenly, especially on summer nights. Prices drop by about 10% in the off-season; paying in foreign currency will generally save you the 17% VAT (see **Money Matters,** p. 270), and most places offer cheaper weekly rates. All places listed take credit cards unless otherwise noted. Sleeping on the beach is illegal and dangerous. Theft and sexual assault, especially against women traveling alone, are not uncommon.

Gordon Inn Guest House, 17 Gordon St. (tel. 523 82 39), just off Ben Yehuda St., 5min. from the beach and Dizengoff Ctr. The best value near the city center. If the daytime fans and nighttime A/C don't keep you cool, the trendy new bar/cafe will. Single-sex or coed rooms. No curfew or lockout. Lockers NIS5. Credit card reservation requested but not required. Dorm beds US$16; singles with bath US$44; doubles with bath $US56. Prices rise in high season. Breakfast included.

Tel Aviv Youth Hostel/Guest House (HI), 36 B'nei Dan St. (tel. 544 17 48 or 546 07 19; fax 544 10 30), near Ha-Yarkon St. Take bus #5, 24, or 25 to Weizmann or Ha-Yarkon. Spotless and organized, this hostel is a long haul from the beach action. All rooms have A/C and private bath. Check-out Sun.-Fri. 10am, Sat. noon. No lockout or curfew. Dorm rooms US$15; roomier guest house lodgings (4 beds per room) US$19; singles US$34.50; doubles US$49. Small surcharge for nonmembers. Full breakfast included. Lunch and dinner also available in the spacious dining room. Lockers NIS5 for 1 day or more.

The Wandering Dog, 3 Yordei Hasira St. (tel. 546 63 63). Take the #4 bus to the last stop on Dizengoff St. Yordei Hasira will be on the left. "The Dog" made its impressive debut in July 1996. The friendly clientele parties on the rooftop lounge, which has a fantastic panoramic view of the sea and features cable TV, a pool table, a pair of hammocks, comfy couches, and a sauna. Yes, a sauna. Add your artwork to the hallway murals on your way out. Co-ed and single-sex dorm beds with shared, spotless bath NIS28. Breakfast included. Free safe. Lockers NIS5 per day. Wash and dry NIS20. Discounted weekly and monthly rates.

Dizengoff Square Hostel, 11 Dizengoff Sq. (tel. 522 51 84; fax 522 51 81), next to the Chen cinema. A fresh coat of colorful paint and groovy furnishings make this the best decorated hostel in Tel Aviv, and A/C makes it the coolest. Personable staff knows residents' names and the night manager is the patron saint of travelers. Popular with the long-term crowd. 24hr reception. Check-out 10:30am. Lockout

10:30am-2:30pm. No curfew. Beds in a rooftop bungalow with shared bath NIS27; coed and single-sex dorm beds (6-11 per room) NIS31; doubles US$39-49, NIS115-145. Breakfast included. Free safe. Lockers NIS8. Wash and dry NIS6 each.

Hotel Nes Ziona, 10 Nes Tziona St. (tel. 510 34 04; fax 510 60 84), just off Ben-Yehuda St. This clean, quiet hotel is a pleasant escape from the grunge of the backpacking world. Some rooms have balconies, all have private bath and blissful A/C, although cheaper rooms without bath are sometimes available. 24hr. reception. Check-out noon. No lockout or curfew. Singles US$35, NIS130; doubles US$40, NIS150. Call ahead, reservations requested.

No. 1 Hostel, 84 Ben-Yehuda St., 4th floor (tel. 523 78 07). The Gordon Inn's beachier blue and yellow twin, just 2 blocks from the shore. Sunny reception lounge has a skyline view, cable TV, foosball table, and new cappucino machine. 24hr. reception. Check-out by 10:30am. Lockout 11am-2pm. No curfew. Kitchen closes at 11pm. Co-ed and single-sex dorm beds (4-8 per room) NIS33; private single/double NIS117. No private baths. Breakfast included. Free safe deposit for documents. Lockers NIS3 per day. Wash and dry NIS8.

Old Yafo Hostel, 8 Olei Tzion St. (tel. 682 23 70; fax 682 23 16, email reservations ojhostel@shani.net), 3 blocks south of the clock tower (bus fare from airport reimbursed with receipt). Enter in the back. Located in the middle of Jaffa's *Shuk Ha-Pishpeshim* (flea market), this hostel is famed for converting day-trippers into residents and piping music into the bathrooms to enhance ambience. Check-out noon. No lockout or curfew, but lights off at 11pm. Hippie crowd drinks Dutch beer (NIS3.50) and sleeps on the roof (NIS22) or in bungalows (NIS28). Co-ed and single-sex dorm beds (10 per room) NIS28; singles NIS60; doubles NIS90. The "royal room" for NIS160 gets you a spacious suite with A/C, kitchenette, shower, and a big-screen TV with cable. Computer lets you eat and sleep on credit and gives an itemized bill. Free use of kitchen and safe. Storage NIS1.

Gordon Hostel, 2 Gordon St. (tel. 522 98 70; fax 523 74 19), on the corner of Ha-Yarkon St. Great location near the beach, with several rooms overlooking the sea. Reasonably clean, although the bathrooms could use a makeover. Lovely rooftop bar; new cafe downstairs under construction at presstime. Arranges cheap flights and tours. Arrive early to get a room. 24hr. reception Check-out 10:30am. Lockout 11am-2pm, some rooms 10am-2pm. No curfew. Coed and single-sex dorm beds (6-8 per room) NIS30. Free safe. Laundry service NIS10.

The Office, 57 Allenby St. (tel 528 99 84). The friendly, relaxed clientele enjoy funky wall art and in-house beer. 24hr. reception. Lockout 11am-2pm. Dorm beds NIS25 (4-10 beds per single-sex or co-ed room); rooftop bungalows NIS25. Lockers NIS5 per day, free safe.

The Mograby Hostel, 30 Allenby St. (tel 510 24 43). A long-term crowd of blissed-out day-laborers chills in the rooftop tents (NIS22) of this centrally located hostel. 24hr. reception. Dorms NIS27; singles NIS80;doubles NIS90. Free lockers in rooms.

Hotel Joseph, 57 Allenby St. (tel. 525 70 70). Friendly staff, simple lodgings. Dorm beds in coed and singles-sex rooms NIS25, all with fan. Cash only.

Beit Immanuel Hostel, 8 Auerbach St. (tel. 682 14 59; fax 682 98 17), corner of 10 Eilat St. In the newly renovated part of Old Yafo, this Christian hospice is immaculate. 11pm curfew ensures that guests are as pristine as the hostel's interior. Psalms adorn the walls. Secluded garden has tables and a small playground. Great for families. Reception 7am-11pm. Check-out 10am. No lockout. No smoking. Bed in a single-sex dorm (10-13 beds) NIS39; singles NIS95-115; doubles NIS165-195. Dinner NIS27 (*Shabbat* NIS39). Laundry NIS15. Cash only.

Hotel Eilat, 59 Ha-Yarkon St. (tel. 510 24 53 or 517 53 68). Great location with clean, simple rooms. Beware the local partyers from the Down South Pub downstairs. All rooms have A/C and private bath; some have impressive oceanviews. 24hr. reception. No curfew or lockout. Singles US$48, NIS150; doubles (with phone and cable TV) US$60, NIS200; triples US$80, NIS225; quads US$80, NIS250.

Sea & Sun Hostel, 62 Ha-Yarkon St. (tel./fax 517 33 13 or 73), on the corner of Nes Tziona. A stumble away from the beach and nighttime hotspots. Spacious balcony with TV room. Large rooms with simple furnishings and cable TV. 24hr. reception. Check-out 11am. Lockout 11am-2pm. No curfew. Coed dorm rooms (4-18 beds) NIS30; doubles NIS140.

▨ Food

Tel Aviv is at its most cosmopolitan come mealtime. Restaurants range from Tex-Mex to southeast Asian, from falafel and hummus to French *haute-cuisine*. After a brain-melting day at the beach, however, fast food and frozen yogurt might sound just as good. You'll have plenty of time to make up your mind—almost all restaurants stay open until midnight or later, on weeknights and weekends alike.

For quick, cheap belly-fillers, head for the self-service eateries on Ben-Yehuda St. Sandwiches and burgers with a side of chips go for under NIS8, and most places let you "customize" your falafel with various toppings. The trick for serious penny-pinchers is to find a place selling falafel by the pita; you can keep refilling it until your stomach hits the ground. The eateries near Shuk Ha-Carmel and along Bezalel St. off Allenby and Ha-Melekh George stay open the latest (usually until 1:30am).

Kerem Ha-Temanim (the Yemenite Quarter), between Shuk Ha-Carmel and the beach, boasts moderately priced Yemeni spicy fried-dough foods, often stuffed with meat, among its small red-roofed houses and narrow streets. **Shechunat Ha-Tikva,** in Tel Aviv's southeastern-most quarter, is renowned for its lamb, chicken, and beef skewers, often accompanied by cheap beer. Israelis flock from nearby cities to have *kebab* or *la'afa* here. Take bus #15, 16, or 41 to Ha-Tikva—it's too far and unsafe to walk.

The maze of narrow streets surrounding the **Jaffa Clock Tower** is peppered with cheap falafel stands, *al-ha'esh* (barbecued) meat establishments, and sweets vendors. More romantic is the beautifully renovated **Old Jaffa,** where you can eat among gardens overlooking the Mediterranean (but beware of priceless menus). In **Jaffa Port,** just south of the renovated old city off Pasteur St., picturesque waterfront restaurants offer seafood so fresh you can almost see the gills moving (daily catch entrees NIS30).

Back in town, **Dizengoff Square** and the stretch of **Dizengoff Street** just north of the Square are lined with pizza parlors, blintz joints, and hot dog stands, where crowds of tourists and throngs of young Israelis gorge themselves amidst exhaust-spitting vehicles. The northern end of the street, around Yirmeyahu Street, which runs between Dizengoff and Ben-Yehuda just before they intersect, has another agglomeration of restaurants. They tend to be better (and pricier) than those around the Square, and you're less likely to choke on bus fumes if dining *al fresco*. Fast-food yearnings can be quelled at **McDavid's** (43 Frischmann St., off Dizengoff) or **Subway** (130 Dizengoff St.), where a six inch sub goes for NIS5.30-10 (open daily until midnight). **Domino's** delivers medium-sized pizzas for NIS22 (NIS4 per topping; call 527 23 30 for northern locations, 562 77 70 for southern locations and after midnight).

Reluctant spenders should shop at the large, outdoor **Shuk Ha-Carmel.** Most of the produce stands are at the southwest end of the market, on and near Ha-Carmel St. To catch prices at their lowest (and crowds at their loudest), shop an hour or two before the beginning of *Shabbat*. **Supermarkets** can be found throughout town. **Supersol,** 79 Ben-Yehuda St. near Gordon St., may be the most convenient (open Sun.-Tues. 7am-midnight, Wed.-Thurs. 24hr., Sat. after sundown); other Supersol branches are on the corner of Arlozorov and Yehoshua Ben-Nun and on Ibn Gvirol and Nordau. **Co-op** has branches right in Dizengoff Sq. (open daily 7am-8pm), in the basement of the Ha-Mashbir department store in Dizengoff Center, and on Ibn Gvirol St. near the junction of Sha'ul Ha-Melekh. **Keep hydrated** while about-towning, but be sure to watch prices: a Kinley mango drink on Dizengoff costs NIS5-6, while the same money at a supermarket nets you a 1.5L bottle of mineral water or cola.

There are several good ice cream places in Tel Aviv. **Dr. Lek,** in the Opera Tower, just up from the Jaffa clock tower on the main road heading north to the Promenade, has excellent ice cream, but sorbets are their specialty (try the cinnamon cheesecake). **Ben and Jerry's** sells the usual rich concoctions all over Tel Aviv, with creameries at the north end of the promenade, below the Ramada Continental Hotel and at 93 and 284 Dizengoff St. The superb **Glida Be'er Sheva,** on the corner of Dizengoff and Nordau, has the biggest and most inventive ice cream selection in town. Most ice cream places scoop until 1am. Prices run NIS6.50-8.70 for two scoops.

The restaurants listed here take credit cards unless otherwise noted.

Alexander's, 81 Yehuda HaMaccabee St. (tel. 605 89 10). A lively destination for a stylish adventure in *gourmandisme*. Mouthwatering menu of Mediterranean favorites, including sandwiches on fresh *Ciabatta* bread with grilled vegetables (NIS23-24), innovative salads (NIS33-38), and decadent desserts (NIS12-25). Open Sun.-Thurs. 7am-1am, Fri.-Sat. 7:30am-3am.

Thai House Restaurant, 8 Bograshov St. (tel. 517 85 68). With its colorful batik tablecloths, plentiful plants, and photographs depicting life in Thailand, this restaurant brings a delicately spiced taste of the Far East to the Middle East. Entrees range from NIS15-48. The menu features a wide selection of vegetarian dishes, including the ubiquitous *pad Thai* (NIS18). Top it all off with a fried banana in mango sauce (NIS10). Open daily noon-midnight.

Yotvata B'Ir, 78 Herbert Samuel St. (tel. 510 79 84), off the *tayelet*. Kibbutz Yotvata, renowned producers of dairy goods, ventures into the city with this well-lit oasis of fresh veggies, cheeses, and fruits. Menu features salads large enough to feed a small family (NIS33-42), pasta dishes (NIS37-42), and blintzes (NIS37-39) to swoon for—try the raisin and sweet cheese. Pitchers of fresh juice in every imaginable flavor are a specialty (NIS10.50). Open daily 7:30am-4am.

Shipudi Itzik Hagadol/Big Itzik's Skewers, 3 Raziel St. in Jaffa (tel. 518 48 02). Sign in Hebrew only. Hungry locals meet, greet, and eat skewered meat at this clean, friendly establishment. Plentiful mini-salads and a huge round of *la'afe* precede Iztik's sizzling specialty *kebabs* (NIS11-25); herbivores can get heavenly hummus (NIS9). Open Sat.-Thurs. noon-2am. Kosher.

Dr. Shakshuka, 3 Beit Eshel, corner of Yefet St., Jaffa (tel. 682 28 42). Scrumptious Libyan food in the heart of Old Jaffa. Eponymous dish is the *shakshuka*—a mouthwatering tomato and egg concoction (NIS15). Couscous (the real thing) with meat (NIS38) or veggies (NIS22) so big you'll want to share it with a friend. Open Sun.-Thurs. 9am-1am, Fri. 9am-sundown, Sat. sundown-2am.

Dizengoff 99, address same (tel. 527 48 08), close to the heart of the city. This friendly blue- and yellow-bedecked Italian bistro serves up scrumptious *gnocchi* and ravioli (NIS25-33), as well as tasty, fresh pizzas (NIS24-34). Lengthy, luscious dessert menu. Open Sun.-Thurs. 8am-2am, Fri.-Sat. 8am-4am.

Said Abou Elafia and Sons, 1 block behind the Jaffa Clock Tower. Popularly known as "Aboulafia," this bakery is so famous that its name is used by Israelis to denote all stuffed-pita foods. Wade through the crowds to taste fresh sesame-covered *bagelah*, *samuza* stuffed with thyme and potatoes, and pizza-like pastries, all for NIS2.50-8. Take-out only. Open 24hr. Cash only.

Pelican, 92 Ben-Yehuda St. (tel. 524 94 74). Unconventional salads (NIS29), pasta (NIS25-42), and cakes (NIS10-15) served fast and fresh. Arrive in the early hours and try the Israeli breakfast of eggs, cheese, vegetables, bread, and coffee or juice (NIS19). Open Sun.-Fri. 7am-12:30am, Sat. 11am-12:30am.

Café Nordau, 145 Ben-Yehuda St. (tel. 524 01 34), on the corner of Arlozorov. Good food, generous portions, lively setting. Largely, but not exclusively, gay clientele; sells *Maga'im* (the gay newspaper) and provides current info on gay life and hot spots. Full meals NIS30-40. Open Sun.-Fri. 8am-2am, Sat. 10am-2am.

Ilana Goor Museum Café, 4 Mazal Dagim St. (tel. 683 76 76). The trendiest place to grab a bite in Jaffa. Situated in the heart of the artists' colony, the rooftop cafe overlooks Jaffa Port. Feast on delicious salads (NIS6) and quiche (NIS24) or simply take in the artsy ambience with a frothy cappuccino (NIS6.50-8). Don't miss the great museum downstairs (see **Jaffa,** p. 336). Open Sun.-Mon., Wed., Sat. 10am-10pm, Tues., Thurs. 10am-2pm, Fri. 10am-4pm.

Dalas Restaurant, 68 Etzel St. (tel. 687 43 49), in the southeastern Ha-Tikva neighborhood. The combination of wall-paintings of Southfork Ranch and outstanding Yemenite food is positively surreal. In one of Tel Aviv's poorer sections, accessible by bus #15 or 16. Hummus (NIS10), delicious Iraqi pita (thick, fluffy, pocket-less, NIS1.50), and *kebab* (NIS12-15 per skewer) attracts many locals. Every cow part is served including bone marrow, testicles, spleen, and udder. Open Sun.-Thurs. 11:30am-3am, Fri. 11am-1hr. before sundown, Sat. 8:30pm-2am. Kosher.

Café Kazze, 19 Sheinkin St. (tel. 629 37 56). Israeli stars sometimes dine at this trendy cafe. Eat in sunny, airy rooms or on the garden patio in back. Fast, friendly service, large portions. Vegetarian *couscous* (NIS26) and shepherd's salad with goat cheese (NIS28) are popular. Open Sun.-Thurs. 8:30am-12:30am, Fri. 8:30am-4:30pm, Sat. 8:30am-8pm. Kosher.

A Taste of Life, 60 Ben-Yehuda St. (tel. 620 31 51). An immaculate vegan paradise staffed by members of the Black Hebrew community, a group whose dietary laws prohibit both milk and meat. (See also **Dimona,** p. 421.) Creative (and nutritious) alternatives, many with tofu or seitan. Veggie hot dogs (NIS16), steaks (NIS33), and *shawerma* (NIS16) are all quite tasty. Non-dairy ice cream (NIS4) and other non-dairy, no-egg desserts sold as well. Open Sun.-Thurs. 9am-11pm, Fri. 9am-3pm, Sat. after sundown-midnight. Kosher. No credit cards.

Mon Jardin, 186 Ben-Yehuda St. (tel. 523 1792). Recently remodeled Romanian grill. Stuffed vine leaves NIS10, *mousaka* or *tzorba* soup NIS17, and Romanian *kebab*s and chicken; full meals NIS26-60. Fancy-schmancy atmosphere. Open daily noon-midnight.

▓ Sights

There's more to do in Tel Aviv than there is to see. The best-known attraction in Tel Aviv is its graceful **Promenade** along the beach, where lovers stroll, vendors sell, and folk dancers strut their stuff. Nearby, at the intersection of Allenby and Ha-Yarkon, stands the Miami Vice-esque **Opera Tower.** The interior features a magnificent atrium, with statues overlooking both a fountain and Israel's first **Tower Records** store. For a more down-and-dirty shopping experience, famed **Shuk Ha-Carmel** (Carmel Market) is located at the intersection of Allenby Rd. and Ha-Melekh George St. Waving polyester undergarments and red plastic sandals, vendors bellow their products' virtues. Farther south, toward the parking lot, you can buy fresh fruit and vegetables at the lowest prices in the city. Huge mounds of plucked chickens make for a fowl sight. One block south of the shuk lies Nahalat Binyamin and Ramban Street *midrahov,* which transforms into a street fair on Tuesdays and Fridays. From 10am-4pm (weather permitting) local artists and craftspeople sell jewelry, pottery, original paintings, Judaica, and bizarre candelabras. The winding cobblestone street is full of musicians and mimes.

If pushy passers-by make you lose your sanity, rise above it. You can look down on the chaos of the market and the entire city from the tranquil **rooftop observatory** (tel. 517 73 04) in nearby **Migdal Shalom.** At 1 Herzl St. and Ahad Ha-Am St., this 40-story tower was the tallest structure in the Middle East until its recent eclipse by the slightly taller (including antennae) communication tower in the military base near the Tel Aviv Museum. The observatory offers panoramic views of Tel Aviv and environs (open Sun.-Fri. 10am-6:30pm, Sat. 11am-4pm; admission NIS13, students NIS9).

Kikkar Yitzhak Rabin is past Dizengoff Center at the end of King George St. Formerly Kikkar Malkhei Yisrael (Kings of Israel Square), the Square was renamed in 1995 in memory of Prime Minister Yitzhak Rabin. On November 4, 1995, Rabin was assassinated by Yigal Amir, a Jewish student, during a crowded peace rally. The Square has since drawn mourners who have left photos, candles, flowers, and poetry.

The **Great Synagogue,** at 110 Allenby St. (tel. 560 49 05 or 560 40 66), stands just east of the Shalom Tower. Completed in 1926 and renovated in 1970, this huge, domed building showcases arches and stained glass windows from synagogues around the world. (Open Sun.-Fri. 8am-9pm, Sat. 8-11am. Saturday prayer open to the public; head coverings and modest dress are required.)

More architecturally inspiring are Tel Aviv's **historic neighborhoods. Neveh Tzedek,** just west of the intersection of Herzl and Ahad Ha-Am streets, is the oldest Jewish neighborhood outside of Jaffa and one of the few Tel Aviv neighborhoods with a 100-year-old history. The area is being gradually renovated to accommodate local yuppies who are attracted to the Mediterranean-village charm of its narrow streets and stone architecture. The **Suzanne Delal Center** (tel. 510 56 56) is in the heart of Neveh Tzedek at 5 Yekhieli St., near Amzalag and Heloukhe St. A hot spot for theater and dance, the newly renovated buildings and courtyard amphitheater of this performing arts center are worth a peek even if you skip the performances (see also **Performing Arts,** p.336). Happily unrenovated is **Kerem Ha-Temanim** (the Yemenite Quarter), northwest of Allenby and Ha-Melekh George, near Shuk Ha-Carmel. This area maintains its village-like appearance despite the relentless sky-scraping all around it.

Tel Aviv University remains Ramat Aviv's star attraction, and is home of the superb **Beit Ha-Tfutzot** (see **Museums,** p. 332). Take bus #6, 7, 13, 24, 25, or 27 to get there. Directly behind Beit Ha-Tfutzot from Gate 2 is the vast central lawn, flanked by pleasant Modernist buildings. Facing the sea, the first building on your right is the Central Library. From here you can go straight down the gently sloping path to the glitzy new main gate complex on Levanon St. The **University Gallery** is in the pink pavilion right next to the gate. The grim concrete building across the street houses the university dorms—most students prefer to live off-campus. There is life, however, on campus, at least in the daylight hours during the school year. Ask people to direct you to the Gilman or Law cafeterias for a peek at the chic student scene, or stop by the more upscale (but not necessarily better in quality) **Einstein Cafe.**

West of Namir (Haifa) Rd. (bus #25) is the **Sportek,** a collection of sports fields, and a miniature-golf course. Tel Avivians crowd the park just across the river from Sportek as well as the nearby Gan Ha-Yehoshua. To arrive at Gan Ha-Yehoshua from the city center, take bus #47 or 48 from King George, or 21 from Dizengoff St. Barbecue some *kebab* and play some *matkot* (paddleball); you'll fit right in.

Baby rhinos frolic at the **Zoological Center** in Ramat Gan (tel. 631 21 81). Take bus #30, 35, or 43 to get there. This combination drive-through safari park and zoo features 250 acres of African game in a natural habitat. You can walk within one meter of tigers or stare over a *wadi* at gorillas and Syrian bears. Bring a picnic or have lunch at the moderately priced restaurant. Those without a car can ride the park's own vehicles through the habitat. Pedestrian tours offered as well. (Open Sun.-Thurs. 9am-4pm, Fri. 9am-1pm. Admission NIS38, children NIS33.) Continue beastwatching across the street at the massive **Ramat Gan National Park** (open dawn-dusk; free).

■ Museums

The **Eretz Yisrael Museum,** 2 Lebanon St. (tel. 641 52 44) in Ramat Aviv (the northernmost part of the city) is a large complex composed of eight pavilion museums built around an archaeological site. One admission ticket (NIS25, students NIS15) is good for access to all eight pavilions and the Eretz Yisrael Library, containing over 30,000 books and periodicals. The most famous attraction in the complex is the **Glass Museum,** with one of the finest collections of glassware in the world. Across the patio, the **Kadman Numismatic Museum** traces the history of the region through ancient coins. The **Ceramics Pavilion** has an extensive collection of Arabic pottery, especially the Gaza and Acre styles. The **Nehushtan Pavilion** holds the discoveries of the excavations of the ancient copper industries at Timna, better known as King Solomon's Mines. Across the entrance area past the grassy amphitheater is the **Man and His Work Center,** an exhibition of Arab and other folk crafts and techniques. To the southeast, still in the museum complex, are the **Tel Qasila Excavations,** which have revealed a 12th-century BCE Philistine port city and ruins dating from around 1000 BCE. The area at the top of the hill contains the remains of three separate Philistine temples built one on top of another. Down the hill to the south are scattered remains of the residential and industrial quarter of the Philistine town. A useful free guide is available in the small **Tel Qasila Pavilion** (open Sun.-Thurs. 9am-2pm) to the east, which displays artifacts found at the site. Past the Philistine town is the **Folklore Pavilion,** with Jewish religious art, ceremonial objects, and ethnic clothing. The Eretz Yisrael complex also houses the **Alphabet Museum,** the **Lasky Planetarium** (admission NIS15; shows in Hebrew only), and the **Museum of Science and Technology.** Take any bus (#24, 29, 45, 74, or 86) to the Ramat Aviv Hotel from the central bus station. (Complex open Sun.-Tues., Thurs. 9am-2pm, Wed. 9am-7pm, Sat. 10am-2pm.)

Also in Ramat Aviv is **Beit Ha-Tfutzot (The Diaspora Museum)** on the Tel Aviv University Campus (tel. 646 20 20). This outstanding museum chronicles the history of Jewish life outside the land of Israel from the Babylonian exile (596 BCE) to present-day diaspora communities. A display of synagogue models shows how Jews incorporated local architectural ideas in building their houses of worship: they resemble Italian villas, American ranches, and Chinese pagodas. Short films and multi-media displays throughout the museum highlight Jewish life, from the ethos of the *yeshiva* to the evolution of Yiddish theater (all displays in both Hebrew and English). The museum also has a **Genealogy Department** that can trace Jewish family trees back dozens of generations. (Museum open Sun.-Tues. and Thurs. 10am-4pm, Wed. 10am-6pm, Fri. 9am-1pm. Admission NIS22, students and seniors citizens NIS16.)

Uptown, the **Tel Aviv Museum of Art,** 27 Sha'ul Ha-Melekh Blvd. (tel. 695 73 61), has split-level galleries and a sizable collection of Israeli and international modern art. The handsome lobby boasts a Lichtenstein (look back as you enter), and the museum itself runs the gamut from Impressionism (Renoit, Corot, and Pissaro) to Surrealism (including works by de Chirico and Magritte) to cutting-edge multi-media installations by more recent artists. Rotating thematic exhibits are exceptionally well-curated and range in subject matter from "Music in Art" to "Stage Design." An English program listing exhibits and events is available in the ticket booth, or check the Friday *Jerusalem Post.* Take bus #7, 9, 18, 28, or 70. (Open Sun.-Mon. and Wed.-Thurs. 10am-6pm, Tues. 10am-10pm, Fri.-Sat. 10am-2pm. Admission NIS25, students and seniors NIS18.)

Just north of the *shuk*, off Allenby St., lies Bialik St., named after Ḥayim Naḥman Bialik, Israel's national poet. His recently restored home, now the **Beit Bialik Museum,** 22 Bialik St. (tel. 525 45 30) is maintained almost exactly as it was when he died; it is a fine example of 1920s Tel Aviv architecture. Bialik's manuscripts, photographs, articles, letters, and 94 books (with translations in 28 languages) are on display. An English brochure is available, but the absence of English translations on the display cases makes this museum opaque for non-Hebrew speakers. (Open Sun.-Thurs. 9am-4:45pm, Sat. 11am-1:45pm. July-Aug closed Sat.; free.) At 38 Ha-Melekh George St., the Likud party headquarters, is the new **Etzel Irgun Tzva'i Le'umi Museum** (National Military Organization); (tel. 528 40 01 or 525 13 87). It traces the pre-1948 history of late Israeli prime minister Menaḥem Begin's military movement (open Sun.-Thurs. 8:30am-4pm; admission NIS5, students NIS2). A second Etzel Museum with large models depicting the 1947-48 history is found in a half-stone, half-glass building along the Promenade between Tel Aviv and Jaffa on the #25 bus line (open Sun.-Thurs. 8:30am-4pm; admission NIS5, students NIS2). The **Jabotinsky Institute** (tel. 528 73 20), in the same building, has works written by and about Ze'ev Jabotinsky, father of right-wing Zionism (open Sun.-Thurs. 8am-4pm; free).

One block south of the Great Synagogue, the **Hagana Museum,** 23 Rothschild Blvd. (tel. 560 86 24), traces the history of the Israeli Defense Force (IDF). Movies glorify the Yom Kippur War and the Hagana's efforts to break the British blockade of ships carrying World War II refugees to Palestine (open Sun.-Thurs. 8am-4pm, Fri. 8am-2pm; admission NIS6, students and children NIS3).

Nearer to the shore, you can visit the **David Ben-Gurion House,** at 17 Ben-Gurion Ave. (tel. 522 10 10). Ogle at an exciting exhibition of books, pictures, and mementos of Israel's first prime minister, including letters from Ben-Gurion to John F. Kennedy, Winston Churchill, Charles de Gaulle, and other world leaders. In the **Hillel Cohen Lecture Hall** next door you can invade the man's privacy even further, as you examine Ben-Gurion's passports and one of his salary slips (house and lecture hall open Sun. and Tues.-Thurs. 8am-3pm, Mon. 8am-5pm, Fri. 8am-1pm; free).

▓ Entertainment

Though most travelers prefer to fry by day and suck down Goldstar by night, the appetite of the Israeli jet set cannot be sated by mere beaches and brew. The Promenade and Sheinken St. are lined with jazzy cafes, and there is no shortage of sweaty discothèques, highbrow concert halls, and world-class theater.

BEACHES

The Hebrew word for beach is ḥof. Familiarize yourself with the flag language of the beach as well: black means swimming is forbidden, red means swimming is dangerous, white means swim on. Most beaches have lifeguards on duty until 4pm.

The beaches within the city are sandy, clean, and free, and all have relatively sanitary showers, toilets, and changing rooms. The beaches are (from north to south) Sheraton, Hilton (behind those hotels), Gordon, Frischmann (at the ends of those streets), and the Jerusalem beach at the end of Allenby Rd. (the last three are almost one continuous beach). The southern coastline, with fewer amenities and no luxury hotels, tends to be quieter during the day. The **Sheraton beach** is also quite peaceful, populated by children and their grandparents. **Gordon** is packed with tourists and people trying to pick them up, while the **Hilton beach** swarms with surfers and those trying to pick *them* up. A marina near Kikkar Atarim rents sailboats and surfboards. Beware *matkot* (paddleball) players who'll trample you to continue a volley. Skip past the over-priced refreshment stands; Ben-Yehuda St., with cheap food and drink, is never more than a two-minute walk from the beach. All of Tel Aviv's beaches are rife with theft; if possible, lock your valuables up before you hit the sands.

CAFES AND PROMENADES

The Mediterranean art of laid-back people-watching can be perfected in Tel Aviv's streets and cafes. The wide sidewalks of **Dizengoff Street** are the most crowded showcase in town. The northern parts of the street, lined with many high-concept, high-priced boutiques, are great for a relaxed evening stroll. **Dizengoff Square** hosts an ever-changing scene, from retirees feeding pigeons in the midday sun to late-night punks cluttering the overpass stairs. The revolving, multicolored, fire-spitting **fountain,** designed by the illustrious Israeli artist Agam (he did the Dan Hotel coloring, too), crowns the square with an unsurpassed celebration of municipal kitsch. The tunes come from the fountain itself, orchestrating its own hourly multi-media show to music ranging from Ravel's *Bolero* to Israeli folk songs.

Sheinken Street is also designed for crowd-gazing, if the kind of crowd you want to watch wears silver platform shoes and sheer half-shirts revealing multiple belly-button rings. For the quintessential Sheinken experience, park yourself in the **Tamar Cafe,** 57 Sheinken St. (tel. 685 23 76), immortalized in a song by the Israeli pop trio Mango ("Living on Sheinken/drinking coffee at the Tamar Cafe/my dream is to make a short film"). The Tamar is a diner-like haven crammed with locals (open Sun.-Thurs. 7am-8pm, Fri. 7am-7pm). Hipper-than-thou former Sheinken devotees have recently relocated to **Basel Street** (just south of Nordau, between Dizengoff St. and Ibn Guirol St.), which has sprouted its own crop of chi-chi cafes.

There's always the **Promenade,** where cafes stretch below the end of Gordon St. **Ha-Ḥof Ha-Ma'aravi** (the Western Beach), at the northern end of the Charles Clore Park, rocks every Thursday night with Brazilian music and swarms of Israeli youth.

DISCOS AND LIVE MUSIC

Tel Aviv's dance scene is always on the move; the *only* club one year may be empty the next and a hardware store after that. Patron demographics are no more stable. Current bastions of the pubescent may have been collegiate havens in their prime. Most of Tel Aviv's discos open at 10pm, but no one arrives before midnight. Thursday, Friday, and Saturday are the nights to go. Expect to pay at least NIS15 cover.

The Dolphinarium, a sprawling club on the beach near the southern end of the Itayelet, features house parties with body-numbing bass on Thursdays and Brazilian *salsa* and *samba* on Fridays and Saturdays. Late-night weekenders have been known to catch spontaneous *capoeira* competitions. **Allenby 58** (at that very address) is famous for its theme nights. Past themes have included zoo night, when dancers dress like animals, and banana night, when the teeming crowd goes Chiquita yellow (opens after midnight). To groove under the stars with Israelis and tourists alike, shimmy at **Shanbo,** 33 Lillienblum St. (tel. 517 44 08; cover NIS15-25). **KU** (koo), 117 Salameh Rd., not far from Herzl St., are specialists in "Happy House" soul and funk (cover NIS25; beer NIS8; open Tues. and Fri.-Sat. midnight-6am). For deafening reggae of all varieties, slide over to **Soweto,** 6 Frischmann St. (tel. 524 08 25), at the corner of Ha-Yarkon (cover Mon.-Wed. NIS10, Thurs.-Sat. NIS15). The **Colosseum** (tel. 527 11 77), at Atarim Sq., attracts a huge crowd of tourists and Israelis unabashedly trying to pick them up. The cover is generally NIS15-20 for men, free for women. Drinks are cheap and the first three are free. On Saturdays, men pay NIS25 to enter, and women still get in free. Get the picture?

Tel Aviv is the headquarters for young Israeli rock bands. **Cat Blue** (pronounced "Baloo"), 10 Ben Avigdor St. (tel. 562 03 10), features live performances. When the music is good (which is the norm) the crowd takes to dancing on the tables. Nearby, **Echoes,** 14 Twersky St., features alternative rock bands (open Thurs.-Sat. nights only). The basement of **Camelot,** 16 Shalom Aleichem St. (tel. 528 53 33), echoes with blues and R&B (cover NIS10-25), while the upstairs pub stays mellower. Reserve tickets before going to **Logos** (tel. 516 11 76), off Naḥalat Binyamin St. on Shefer St., which features rock and blues performances nightly at 11pm; the cover varies with the band's fame. An upstairs cafe shows the downstairs concerts on TV screens and occasionally hosts milder acts of its own. Two amphitheaters at **Ha-Yarkon Park** also have concerts. *Ha-Ir,* a weekly Hebrew magazine, has a section called "Akhbar Ha-Ir," with comprehensive listings.

BARS

A recent influx of day-laborers who have taken up semi-permanent residence in Tel Aviv has made bar-hopping more common than pricey clubbing among travelers. An exhausting day of dishwashing or cement-slinging deserves an evening of icy Carlsberg in good company. Most bars get crowded around midnight, and seats are scarce after 1am (especially Thursday through Saturday). Bars abound on **Ha-Yarkon St.** and around hostel-heavy **Allenby Rd.** The **Hard Rock Cafe** in Dizengoff Ctr. (tel. 525 13 36) is open Sun.-Thurs. noon-12:30am, Fri. noon-3am, Sat. noon-1am, and features a young crowd, Israeli rock paraphernalia, and a suit worn by Elvis. Israelis frequent **Ha-Arba'a St.,** off Carlebach and Ibn Gvirol, near the Tel Aviv Cinemathèque, which is in the midst of a six-pub competition for hot-spot status. Pick your poison:

Mulligans, 109 Ha-Yarkon St. A big hit with the working crowd, this bar sports a shamrock-covered interior with pool tables and picnic-style seating. The real draw is the Turkish patio, where customers gaze beachward from Oriental cushions and suck on *argeileh* pipes. Carlsberg NIS7, draught Tuborg NIS8.

The Embassy, 22 Allenby St. Where else can you get sloshed and shoot some pool while doing your laundry? Toss NIS10 in the washing machine and NIS5 in the dryer and join the laid-back crowd for a brew (Tuborg NIS10) or a heavy meal (toasts and pastas NIS14). In summer, open 24hr.; in winter, from 10am until the last socks have been washed.

M.A.S.H. (More Alcohol Served Here), 275 Dizengoff (tel. 605 10 07). A trek to the north; take bus #4. Tourists and Israelis alike slam drinks to music from the 60s to the 90s. Good burgers (NIS19), local beer (NIS9), and imported beer (NIS11-18). Open daily 10pm-5am. During 5-8pm happy hour, drinks are 25% off.

The Buzz Stop, 80 Herbert Samuel (tel. 510 08 69), on the beach. A boisterous crowd of tourists on a mission: inebriation.

The Church, 58 Ha-Yarkon St. Heavy tables, loud music, and a raucous crowd that spills onto the bar's steps and sidewalk. Carlsberg NIS7.

Lola, 54 Allenby St. (tel. 517 37 88). A favorite Israeli student hangout. Old German newspapers on the walls and faux marble tables. 11 kinds of tequila (NIS17-24), Goldstar (NIS9), fresh-baked baguettes, and Addams Family pinball.

The Office, 57 Allenby (tel. 528 99 84), nestled by the reception area of a hostel (see **Accommodations,** p. 328). Trippy backpackers relax with pints of Guiness (NIS13).

Ha-Shoftim, 39 Ibn Gvirol St., on the corner of Ha-Shoftim. Attracts 30-somethings with its outdoor seating, dark interior, and blues/jazz. Open nightly 7pm-3am.

Ha-Misba'a, 344 Dizengoff St. (tel. 604 23 60). Wilder and more expensive. Live music (often Israeli folk) every night at midnight; arrive at 11 to get a seat. When all are sufficiently ripped, people dance on chairs and sing along. The crowd stays until the musicians collapse. Open daily 10pm-5am. Cover NIS40-50.

PERFORMING ARTS

There are plenty of things to do in Tel Aviv that won't get you sunburnt or smashed: nightly opera, ballet, jazz, classical music, and dance performances. There are also more than 40 **movie theaters** showing American and Israeli flicks. Check the *Jerusalem Post* for English listings for the **Tel Aviv Cinémathèque,** 2 Sprinzak St., at the corner of Carlebach St.

The **Suzanne Delal Center,** 5 Yehiely St., in Neveh Tzedek has indoor and outdoor dance, theater, and musical performances, to name a few. Call 510 56 56 for a schedule. Take bus #8, 10, 25, or 61 from downtown or # 40 or 46 from the central bus station. The center is best known as the home of the Inbal (tel. 517 37 11) and Bat Sheva (tel. 517 14 71) dance companies, both of which perform contemporary ethnic dances. Inbal's performances are NIS40-50; tickets to the Bat Sheva shows are NIS45-60. Your passport will get you a 20% tourist discount (box office open daily 9am-5pm; Visa and Diners Club accepted). **Beit Lessin,** 34 Weizmann St. (tel. 694 11 11), has live jazz acts (NIS25). The **Tel Aviv Cameri Theater,** 101 Dizengoff St. (tel. 523 33 35), at the corner of Frischmann St., offers simultaneous-translation earphones during performances for NIS5 (tickets NIS65-90).

For the most detailed information on performance schedules and other activities in the Tel Aviv area, see *Tel Aviv Today, Events in Tel Aviv,* and *This Week in Tel Aviv,* all free at the tourist information office and major hotels.

■ Jaffa (Yafo) יפו يافا

An Israeli folk song describes Jaffa (*Yafo* in Hebrew) as possessing a "mysterious and unknown" element which allows its atmosphere "to seep like wine into the blood." Jaffa's stone houses and winding streets do intoxicate. Next to Tel Aviv's skyscraper hotels and glass storefronts, historical Jaffa is a breath of fresh Mediterranean air.

The **Jaffa Clock Tower,** completed in 1906, stands by the entrance to Jaffa from Tel Aviv and is a useful marker for all other destinations in the city. A free **tour** of Old Jaffa by the Tourism Association begins here (Wed. 9:30am, line up at 9). Bus #46 from the new central bus station will plunk you right in front of the clock tower. To get to the **Old City** of Jaffa, make a right a bit south of the clock tower, and head towards the sea. The main road becomes the **Mifratz Shlomo Promenade,** with unbelievable views of Tel Aviv's action-packed coast and skyline. Along the promenade, you'll find the **Museum of Antiquities of Tel Aviv-Jaffa** (tel. 682 53 75), containing artifacts from nearby sites in the old city and a comprehensive collection of coins found in Jaffa. (Admission NIS10, students NIS5; open Sun., Mon., Thurs. 9am-2pm; Tues. and Wed. 9am-7pm, Sat. 10am-2pm.) Up the Promenade sits **Kikkar Kedumim,** Jaffa's commercial, historical, and tourist center, and site of outdoor summer concerts. Following signs to the Visitor's Center, head down the stairs to take a peek at archaeological excavations from 2300-year-old Tel Yafo featuring Roman remains (open Sun.-Thurs. 9am-11pm, Fri. 9am-2pm, Sat. 10am-11pm; free). Near Kikkar Kedumim, the colorful Greek Orthodox **Church of St. Michael** and the Catholic **Monastery of St. Peter** (visiting hours March-Sept. daily 8-11:45am and 3-6pm; Oct.-Feb. 8-11:45am and 3-5pm) are worth a brief tour. **Andromeda's Rock,** site of Perseus's rescue of the Greek princess, is visible from the lighthouse to the south.

Down the stairs from Kikkar Kedumim is the cluster of museums, restaurants and galleries that make up Jaffa's touristy artists' colony. The 20th century hits Old Jaffa in the form of the playfully modern **Ilana Goor Museum** (tel. 683 76 76), on Mazal Dagim St. established in September 1995. This artist's home-turned-museum, once an

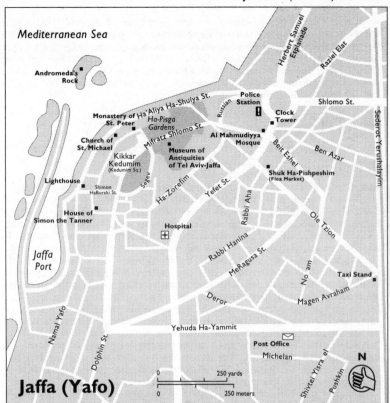

Jaffa (Yafo)

Mediterranean Sea

Andromeda's Rock

Monastery of St. Peter

Church of St. Michael

Lighthouse

House of Simon the Tanner

Jaffa Port

Kikkar Kedumim (Kedumim Sq.)

Shimon HaBurski St.

Ha-Pisga Gardens

Museum of Antiquities of Tel Aviv-Jaffa

Hospital

Police Station

Clock Tower

Al Mahmudiyya Mosque

Shuk Ha-Pishpeshim (Flea Market)

Shlomo St.

Post Office

Michelan

N

0   250 yards
0   250 meters

ISRAEL

Ottoman soap factory, then a shelter for pilgrims, and later the city's first Jewish hostel, now houses Goor's art. Her work, casually displayed, includes furniture, jewelry, and sculpture made mostly of metal and leather. The museum encourages visitors to "please touch" the artist's creations, and the bookshelf in Goor's sitting room is worth a browse, too—a sign on the wall simply asks that visitors return texts to the shelf after use. (Admission NIS15, students NIS12; open Sun., Mon., Wed., Sat. 10am-10pm, Tues., Thurs. 10am-2pm, Fri. 10am-4pm.) On the top floor is an absolutely incredible café overlooking Jaffa port (see **Food,** p. 277). Another spot worth a browse is the **Frank Meisler Gallery,** 25 Mazal Arie St. (tel. 681 35 02), home of kitschy, interactive sculptures made of gold, silver, bronze, and pewter. His pieces come with hefty price tags, but are fun to look at. Check out the human figurines whose stomachs open up to expose what "they're really made of"—usually sexy women and lascivious goodies. His work is often commissioned by Israeli heads of state to be presented on official visits.

A wooden footbridge from Kikkar Kedumim leads to the grassy **Ha-Pisga Gardens,** containing a small, modern amphitheater as well as a tiny excavation of an 18th-century BCE Hyksos town and a later Egyptian city. A white, ladder-like sculpture dominates one hill in the gardens; its three sections depict the fall of Jericho, the binding of Isaac, and Jacob's dream. Down Mifratz Shlomo, towards the clock tower, is the minaret of the **Al Mahmudiyya Mosque,** an enormous structure erected in 1812 into which only Muslims can enter.

Jaffa's large **Shuk Ha-Pishpeshim** (Flea Market) is one of the livelier markets in Israel, with covered rows of overflowing stalls offering dust-covered Middle Eastern knick-knacks, modern hand-dyed clothing, Persian carpets, leather goods, and brassware. A vast selection of enormous *argeilehs* (waterpipes) is also available. Bargaining is a given. You should begin by offering half the asking price or less. To reach the flea market from the clock tower, continue one block south on Yefet St. and turn left. The *shuk* is squeezed between Olei Tzion and Beit Eshel St. and is closed on Saturdays. The **Jaffa Port,** just south of Ha-Aliya Ha-Shuiya St., is still an active fishermen's wharf. The fishermen usually mend their nets in the afternoon, leave for sea at nightfall, and return in the early morning with their fresh catch.

NEAR TEL AVIV

■ Rishon Le Zion ראשון לציון

Rishon Le Zion (First to Zion) was the first modern Jewish settlement in Palestine. In "Rishon," as the city is nicknamed, the Jewish National Fund was created, the Israeli flag was first flown, and the world's first national Hebrew school opened its doors. Rishon has exploded with immigrants in recent years; speedily built concrete apartment buildings testify to the population growth. The **Rishon Le Zion Museum,** 2-4 Aḥad Ha'Am St. (tel. (03) 964 16 21 or 968 24 35), at Rothschild St. across from the Great Synagogue, traces the history of the town from the early pioneers to the present. This small museum displays the tools of the early settlers, and various memorabilia and photographs follow up with a sound and light show in the old **Village Well,** further down Rothschild St. (Museum open Sun. and Tues.-Thurs. 9am-2pm, Mon. 9am-1pm and 4-8pm; admission to museum and well NIS8. Free tours and admission 10am-2pm on the 1st Sat. of every month. Advance reservations required for Sat. tours and to ensure an English-speaking guide.)

Pioneer's Way is marked by a yellow line painted along Rishon's pavement, and directs you to 18 of the town's historic sites, each marked with a plaque. Pick up a guide at the museum. Starting at the end of the Rothschild Street **pedestrian thoroughfare,** the yellow streak leads down Ha-Carmel St., where you will pass Israel's largest **winery,** 25 Ha-Carmel St. (tel. (03) 964 20 21 or 965 36 62), built by Baron Edmond de Rothschild in 1887 and still used today to produce Carmel Mizraḥi wine. One-hour tours of the winery feature an audio-visual presentation, an explanation of a remarkable life-size mural by German painter Gershom Schwarze, a tasting, and a souvenir bottle. (Admission NIS12, seniors and students NIS10; tours at 9am, 11am, 1pm, and 3pm. To book a tour with an English-speaking guide, call Sun.-Thurs. 8am-4pm.) Across the street from the winery, you can buy liquor at wholesale prices at **Sokolik** (tel. (03) 964 13 43; open Sun.-Wed. 6am-2:30pm, Thurs. 6am-5pm, Fri. 6am-3pm). They card, so those under 18 are out of luck.

For an inexpensive bite, join Rishonians at the **Madari Kiosk,** the only hole-in-the-wall falafel joint that switches locations during the day. The owners can't bear to part with either spot, so they begin their day at the corner of Rothschild St. and Mohliever St., where the street begins after the *midraḥov.* After 1pm, they move further up Rothschild St., behind a bus stop on the left. Both locations are unmarked, but come lunchtime you can't miss the line (falafel NIS8). You can also sit down at **The Well,** 19 Rothschild St. (tel. 966 81 03), which offers a varied menu. Most main courses go for NIS25-35, including fish, pasta, pizza, and meat dishes. During the day the restaurant is usually empty, but by night you'll need some luck to snag a table. Open daily 9am-1am.

The Rishon Le Zion **bus station** is on Herzl St. Buses #200, 201, 371, and 301 from Tel Aviv stop in Rishon and continue on to Reḥovot (every 15-30min., NIS6.10); you can come here from Reḥovot for the same price. With your back to the bus station, walk two blocks onto Rothschild St. to find the museum, the well, and other sites.

■ Reḥovot רחובות

Reḥovot, a somewhat secluded town, is known primarily for its world-famous **Weizmann Institute of Science.** The institute is named for Israel's first president, Dr. Ḥayim Weizmann, a research chemist who, during World War I, discovered an innovative way to produce acetone, the smelly fluid that proved essential to England's military effort (as well as nail polish removal). Weizmann's discovery, combined with his formidable character and convictions, helped persuade Lord Balfour to issue the 1917 Balfour Declaration favoring the establishment of a Jewish national homeland.

In the southeast corner of the institute stands the **Weizmann House** (tel. (08) 934 20 28), an elegant example of early International Style and Israel's first presidential residence. It is home to the **Weizmann Archives,** which holds the scientist-statesman's papers. The house and archives are closed for renovation; the house is scheduled to reopen sometime in the next two years. When the renovations are finished tourists will not be allowed to look at the Archives. The main gate to the Weizmann Institute is at the north end of Herzl St., a 30-minute walk north from Manchester Sq., and a 20-minute walk south from the central **bus station,** where buses #200 (express) and 201 make the 20km trip from Tel Aviv every 15 minutes (NIS9). Many inter-city buses also have stops near the Institute's white stone entrance.

The Institute's scientific staff conducts research in all of the natural sciences. Projects include research on cancer, immunology, aging, and the environment. Pick up maps and brochures at the **Visitors Section** (tel. (08) 934 37 49), in the Wix Library Building, the first building on the right from the main gate (enter through the second door; open Sun.-Thurs. 9:30am-12:30pm, 1pm-3:30pm). The city's main avenue, Herzl St., is lined with falafel shops and self-service restaurants (falafel NIS9-10). For authentic, spicy Yemeni dishes, head south along Herzl St. several blocks from the bus station to the **Sha'arayim** neighborhood and its wealth of restaurants. A word of **warning,** though: Don't spend your last shekel on falafel or ice cream here, because it is hard to get currency exchanged without commission.

■ Ramla רמלה

Founded in 716 by the formidable Umayyad Caliph Suleiman ibn Abd el-Malik, Ramla is the only town in Israel that was established and developed by Arabs. Until the arrival of the Crusaders in the 11th century, Ramla was the capital of Palestine, known for its magnificent palaces and mosques. After the 1948 war, the Arab majority was forced to flee. Today the community is predominantly composed of Jewish immigrants and a minority of Christian Arabs. Ramla's vibrant *shuk* is worth a visit, not to mention its many places of worship.

Among the main sights are the **Great Mosque** (formerly the Crusader Cathedral of St. John) and the **Church and Hospice of St. Nicodemus and St. Joseph Arimathea.** The Great Mosque is hard to miss because of the white minaret which rises majestically above the mosque. For NIS2, the guard will let you into the mosque to peek at the medieval vaulted arches (open Sun.-Thurs. 8am-1pm). The church, on the corner of Bialik and Herzl, is a large stone complex built in the 1500s but renovated in 1902. Ring the bell and ask the monk to show you around. Further north on Danny Moss St. is the majestic **Tower of Forty Martyrs** (a.k.a. the **White Tower**).

Ramla's lively *shuk* attracts Israelis from neighboring towns who come here to wander among endless stalls of clothing, toys, and cheap food. The *shuk* is open every day but is especially lively on Thursdays. It is located on Ze'ev Z'abutinski, which is closed to traffic until 7pm.Locals lunch in the shady, palm-lined park by the corner of Herzl and Ze'ev Zabutinski St. For a more ordered culinary experience, head to the **Chalil Restaurant,** 6 Kehilat Detroit (tel. (08) 922 22 84), where owner Nader serves up simple but tasty treats (hummus NIS9, *kebab* NIS17; open daily 6am-8pm; all credit cards accepted).

From Tel Aviv, take **bus** #455, 450, or 245 (every 30min., 30min., NIS7).

ISRAEL

■ Ashdod

The modern port of Ashdod draws new immigrants and commerce, but the city's cultural profile has faded drastically since it served as one of the five ancient religious centers for the Philistines. Just outside Ashdod's central bus station is the **Merkaz Ha'Ir,** where Domino's and McDonald's compete for the attention of the largely Russian-speaking population. A stroll down Shavei Tzion St. leads to the beach. Dominated by the mother of Ashdod malls, the **Kenyon,** the beach itself is remarkably clean and mostly deserted on weekdays. A boardwalk and the marina are in the works.

History lives on at the small but well-kept **Corine Maman Ashdod Museum,** 16 Keren Ha-Yesod St., with its multimedia exhibit on the world of the Philistines (open Sun.-Tues. 9am-1pm and 5-7pm, Thurs. 9am-noon, Sat. 10:30am-1:30pm). Ashdod is reachable from Tel Aviv by **bus** #312 or 314 (every 20min., 45min., NIS11.50).

SOUTH OF TEL AVIV

■ Ashkelon אשקלון

Ashkelon was first settled in the 3rd millennium BCE and then conquered by the Philistines, the Israelites, the Greeks, the Romans, the Crusaders, and the Muslims. Under the Philistines, the city grew into an important port and caravan stop along the Via Maris, a famous trade route connecting Egypt and Syria. One of the Philistines' five great cities, it was known for its anti-Israelite sentiment. It is believed that Herod the Great was born here, a possible explanation for the many elaborate buildings that were constructed during Roman times.

Known for its sandy beaches and seaside national park, Ashkelon attracts both Israeli sun-seekers and archaeologists. Development and investment have produced a multitude of resorts, making access to Ashkelon's sparkling shore rather pricey. The wealth of the city lies in the ruins, the real gems in its synthetic crown of shopping malls, cineplexes, and housing projects.

ORIENTATION AND PRACTICAL INFORMATION

Ashkelon is 56km down the coast from Tel Aviv. **Afridar,** the new commercial neighborhood, contains the **bus station,** the museum, and **Zephania Square. Migdal** to the east is much older. Narrower streets, a *midrahov,* and a *shuk* make the neighborhood more charming. Afridar fronts **Bar Kokhba Beach.** To the south is the more popular **Delila Beach,** and further south, along the sea, is the **National Park.**

Tourist Office: (tel. 677 10 55 or 13 61), in the City Hall behind the bus station: walk down the alleyway between the concrete block wall and the Giron Mall to Ha-Gvurah St., make a left, and continue halfway down to the shopping center. Hebrew sign, flags flying by the entrance. Standard supply of maps and schedules. Open Sun.-Tues. and Thurs. 8am-1pm and 4-7pm, Wed. and Fri. 8am-1pm.

Currency Exchange: Bank Ha-Poalim, just past the tourist office. **ATMs** accept NYCE and Cirrus. The post office in Migdal has good rates with no commission.

Buses: Central bus station (tel. 675 02 21) located on Ben-Gurion St., about a 25min. walk from the beach. Information booth supplemented by an electronic bulletin board that flashes in Hebrew and English. Buses to **Tel Aviv** (#300 or 311 until 10:40pm, every 15-30min., 1hr., NIS15.50, students NIS16.20); **Jerusalem** (#437 until 7:15pm, every 30min.-1hr., 1-1½hr., NIS21, students NIS18); **Be'er Sheva** (#363 or 364 until 10pm, every 40min.-1hr., NIS20, students NIS18.50).

Public Transportation: Local bus #5 goes to Zephania Sq. in the heart of the Afridar neighborhood and to the *midrahov* in the Migdal area, stopping in between at the central bus station. Bus #6 (also bus #13 in July-Aug.) goes to the National Park, the beaches, and Migdal once every hour.

Taxis: *Sherut* to **Tel Aviv** (NIS15), try **Moniot Ha-Merkaz** (tel. 673 30 77), across from the central bus station; also call them for a cab around town.

Pharmacy: Super-Pharm (tel. 671 14 31 or 21), next to the bus station in the Kenyon Giron (a shopping mall). Open Sun.-Thurs. 8:30am-11pm, Fri. 8:30am-3pm, Sat. 10am-midnight.

Emergency: First aid: 101 or 672 33 33. **Fire:** 102. **Police:** (tel. 100 or 677 14 440), at the corner of Ha-Nassi and Eli Cohen St.

Post Office: Central branch at 18 Herzl St. in Migdal open Sun.-Tues. and Thurs. 8am-12:30pm and 4-6:30pm, Wed. 8am-1pm, Fri. 8am-12:30pm; **Poste Restante** open Sun.-Wed. 8am-12:30pm and 4-6:30pm, Thurs. 8am-1pm, Fri. 8am-12:30pm.

Telephone code: 07.

CAMPING AND FOOD

There are no youth hostels or pensions in Ashkelon; Tel Aviv is a 45min.-1hr. bus ride, making this an easy daytrip. **Camping** is available at **Park Leumi Ashkelon** (Ashkelon National Park). Those with tents can settle on one of the grassy areas for free,. There are no showers. Entrance to the park is free if you go on foot (NIS10 by car). The snack bar and two beach-side restaurants in the park itself are convenient and relatively inexpensive (steak, *shishlik,* or hamburger on a pita NIS8-12). Camping on the beach adjacent to the city is dangerous and not recommended.

The highest concentration of affordable eateries is on and off the Herzl St. *midrahov* in Migdal. Air-conditioned **Nitzahon,** 30 Herzl St. (tel. 675 12 00), on the last block of the *midrahov,* has the town's best selection of steaks, *me'orav* (mixed grill), *kebab,* and stuffed cabbage for NIS14-20 per plate. A few doors down, at **Sandwich Tunisien** (the sign in Hebrew goes by a different title: Shawerma Shel Ha-Hakham—the wise man's *shawerma*) on 31 Herzl St., Tunisian Amos Sidbon serves traditional sandwiches outside on the *midrahov.* For NIS10, you'll get a symphony of tuna, capers, salads, potatoes, hot peppers, spicy *harisa,* lemon, and olives in a baguette. Well-endowed falafel is NIS5. A cheap and lively **outdoor shuk** has everything for sale; from the *midrahov* take Ha-Kerem St. towards David Remez St.; it is between the two and is open Mon. 6am-1pm, Wed. 6am-9pm, Thurs. 5:30am-9pm.

In Afridar, there are a number of outdoor, locally frequented, inexpensive restaurants on the corner of Ha-Nasi St. and Zephania at the Afridar Center, with *schnitzel,* hamburger, *kebab* for NIS12-15. **Delila Beach** showcases the city's collection of fish restaurants (meals NIS22-58). The **Ship Restaurant** (tel. 673 02 94), housed in a large boat, serves grilled fish, meat, and oriental food under the stars in a quasi-romantic Mediterranean setting. You can pick up supplies for your own romantic beachside meal at the **Hypercol Supermarket** (tel. 671 14 22), in the Kenyon Giron shopping mall right next to the bus station (open Sun.-Tues. 8am-10pm, Wed.-Thurs. 8am-midnight, Fri. 8am-3pm, Sat. after *Shabbat*-midnight).

SIGHTS AND ENTERTAINMENT

Ashkelon National Park (tel. 673 64 44) is on the waterfront. Buses #6 (year round) and 13 (July and Aug. only) go to a path leading to the park's entrance, but they run infrequently. The walk from the central bus station takes three to five minutes and offers enticing peeks at the sea. From the station, take a right onto Ben-Gurion Blvd. and follow it around the curve to the T junction; turn left onto the road to the park. The park was built on the site of 4000-year-old Canaanite remains buried beneath ruins of Philistine, Greek, Roman, Byzantine, Crusader, and Muslim cities. Free **maps** are available at the main entrance. (Open Sun.-Thurs. 7am-7pm, Fri. 7am-9pm, Sat. 7am-7pm. Closed in winter except non-raining Sat.; free, NIS10 with car.)

Between the well-maintained lawns tower the remains of a once-thriving Philistine city. A Roman colonnade and a series of Hellenistic and Roman columns, capitals, and statues, including two magnificent statues of Nike, the winged goddess of victory, grace the park's center. Coming through the main gate, you will see the **Bouleute-**

rion, the Council House Square when Ashkelon was an autonomous city-state under Severius in the 3rd century CE. The sunken courtyard-like area on the right is actually the inside of a Herodian assembly hall. There is also an Italian marble statue of the goddess Isis with her god-child Horus, sculpted between 200 BCE and 100 CE. Behind the Bouleuterion lies an **amphitheater.**

Along the southern edge of the park are segments of wall from the 12th-century Crusader city. Most peculiar is the assembly of Roman columns sticking out of the ancient Byzantine sea wall on the beach. Originally these massive marble columns were used to support the walls, which were destroyed in 1191 by Salah ad-Din. Richard Lionheart partly restored them in 1192, as did Richard Cornwall in 1240, only to have them finally demolished by the Sultan Baybars in 1270.

Ashkelon's coast has four beaches where swimming is permitted; **Delila Beach** is the best of the bunch. While other beaches often fly the daunting black flag, the breakers at Delila permit you to swim without fear of being whisked away by the undertow. Shady canopies and snack bars give relief to sun-scorched bathers. Also appealing is the nighttime revelry on Delila Beach, where Richard Marx and the Beach Boys croon to a sandy, happy crowd. For fun in the water—*sans* sand—there's the **Ashkeluna water park** (tel. 673 99 70) near Delila Beach and the road to the National Park. Israelis from Be'er Sheva to Yavneh flock to Ashkelon's cheesiest attraction, which boasts water slides, aerobics sessions, and games with prizes (open daily 9am-4pm; closes an hour early Sat. May-June; NIS25-35).

Of relative interest in Ashkelon is **Kikkar Ha-Atzma'ut** (Independence Sq.), one block behind the Migdal stop on buses #4, 5, 6, or 7. Once a caravan rest stop, this dilapidated intersection was the site of the first reading of Israel's Declaration of Independence in 1948. The **Ashkelon Museum,** in the square, traces the history of Ashkelon from Roman times to the present. A few minutes is adequate for both sights (open Sun.-Thurs. 9am-1pm and 4-6pm, Fri. 9am-1pm, Sat. 10am-1pm; free).

■ Near Ashkelon

YAD MORDEKHAI יד מרדכי

From May 19th to 24th, 1948, the 165 members of Kibbutz Yad Mordekhai withstood an attack by an Egyptian battalion of 2500. A model of the battle comes with soldiers, tanks, weapons, and a recorded explanation. The famous **museum** (tel. (07) 672 05 29) also illustrates the story of the Warsaw ghetto resistance movement (museum and battlefield open daily 8am-4pm; admission NIS8, students and seniors NIS6). Buses #36 and #365 will take you to the Mordekhai junction, but not directly to the kibbutz, and they only run every few hours. If you get stuck in the late afternoon, go back to the bus stop on the highway and try flagging a passing bus from Rafah.

KIRYAT GAT AND BEIT GUVRIN קרית גת ובית גוברין

About 22km east of Ashkelon, **Kiryat Gat** is easily accessible by **bus** from Tel Aviv (#369, every 30-45min., NIS15.30), Jerusalem (#446, every 30-45min., NIS18.50), and Ashkelon (#25, every 30min., NIS10.50). This small industrial town is the capital of the **Lakhish** region, a network of 30 villages established in 1954, and the launching pad for exploration of several sites at **Beit Guvrin.** It's best to go by car or **taxi** from Kiryat Gat (NIS50); getting to and from Beit Guvrin by **bus** requires advance planning. Bus #11 from Kiryat Gat goes directly to Kibbutz Beit Guvrin. (Sun.-Thurs. 8:05am and 5:10pm, Fri. 8:05am and 2:15pm, NIS 7.30; return from Beit Guvrin at 8:25am and 5:30pm, Fri. 8:25am and 2:30pm. You'll have to catch one of the morning buses if you don't want to spend the night.) Bring plenty of portable shade (a hat or white scarf, sunglasses, and sunscreen) and at least 1.5L of water. Taxis run from **Tel Aviv's central bus station** to Beit Guvrin, Tel Maresha, and Tel Lakhish.

Beit Guvrin was a flourishing Jewish metropolis in the fourth and third centuries BCE and in the years between the destruction of the Second Temple and the Bar Kokhba Revolt (132-135 CE). The Arab village of Beit Jibrin stood nearby until the

1948 War, when its inhabitants were evacuated; since 1949, the modern **kibbutz** of Beit Guvrin has stood on its ruins. **Beit Guvrin National Park,** encompassing the ruins of Maresha and Beit Guvrin, is one of Israel's hidden gems. Its complex caves and magnificent views make this site unforgettable. The biblical city of **Maresha** was one of the cities of Judah fortified by Rehoboam (Joshua 16:44). The area was settled by Edomites after the destruction of the First Temple, Sidonians during the 4th century BCE, and eventually Greeks, who converted the area into a bustling economic center. Before the turn of the first century BCE the Hasmonean king John Hyrcanus I perpetrated one of the relatively few historical instances in which Jews forced conversion upon others. Many angry Hellenes left the city, and in the year 40 BCE, the Parthian army destroyed it. Even if you ache at the sight of ruins, the unbelievable 360° view from Tel Maresha makes the trip worth your time. On a clear day, you can see Tel Aviv and the Mediterranean to the west, and the Jordanian hills and the Dead Sea to the east. The ruins in the lower city, near the *tel*, are also worth the hot and hefty walk. Most impressive are the Hellenistic houses with maze-like series of cisterns underneath them. There are also two spooky Sidonian burial caves. The park is located just off Rte. 35, near Kibbutz Beit Guvrin, across from the gas station. (Open Sun.-Thurs. 8am-5pm, Fri. 8am-4pm; winter Sun.-Thurs. 8am-4pm, Fri. 8am-4pm; admission NIS16, students NIS12, children NIS7.)

The Beit Guvrin region is characterized by some 800 **bell-shaped caves,** hidden among the cacti and fig trees. Most of the caves were carved by Greeks, Byzantines, and others as they quarried for limestone. The shape of the caves is a product of the quarrying technique, in which a narrow hole dug in the crust of the earth was widened at greater depths. Once dug, the caves were used for storage, penning animals, and water collection, and later became sanctuaries for hermits and monks. Saint John and others came here seeking solitude, and often carved crosses and altars into the walls. The saintly Sylvester Stallone was here for the filming of *Rambo III.* The site is well-tended with marked trails and some facilities.

Mediterranean Coast

The stretch of coastline north of Tel Aviv is home to most of Israel's population and agricultural output. Beaches along the shore are crowded with Israeli vacationers and dotted with Roman ruins. When pioneers arrived in the beginning of the 20th century, they drained the swamps of the coastal plain, clearing the path for the modern, industrial state.

▨ Herzliya הרצליה

Named after Theodore Herzl, Herzliya and its affluent western suburb Herzliya Pituah are only 15km outside of Tel Aviv. Herzliya Pituah is home to beautiful beaches, luxury hotels, and foreigners who tan and schmooze for a living. Neither it nor Herzliya, however, has any cheap accommodations; they are best visited as a day trip or afternoon jaunt from Tel Aviv. **Buses** #501 (every 30min., 1hr., NIS6.10) and 502 (every 30min., 40min., NIS6.10) run from Tel Aviv.

Herzliya's cultural hub is the **Yad Labarim Memorial Center,** which can be reached by walking two blocks south from the bus station on Ben-Gurion St. until it intersects with Ha-Banim St. The Center houses the diminutive and avant-garde **Herzliya Museum of Art** (tel. (09) 955 1011 or 950 2301; open Sun.-Thurs. 4pm-8pm, Fri.-Sat. 10am-2pm; free) and the **Center for Analysis of Propaganda in International Media** (tel. (09) 950 0762), where tourists are generously encouraged to sample the wares (call for lecture schedules). An outdoor amphitheater attached to the building overlooks the museum's modern **Sculpture Garden** and is the setting of concerts by the **Herzliya Chamber Orchestra.**

Zionist history buffs may enjoy the **Beit Rishonim** (First Settlers' House) **Founders Museum.** From the central bus station, walk north along Ben-Gurion St., turn left on Sokolov St., and then right on Ha-Nadiv St. (the museum is between 8 and 10 Ha-Nagiv St.). Beit Rishonim features an idyllic garden full of mothers and baby carriages, and a life-like statue of Herzl leaning against his second-floor balcony. The museum reconstructs the story of Herzliya from its days as a colony in 1924 via computerized presentations as well as furnishings and tools from the early settlement period. (Open Sun. and Thurs.-Fri. 8:30am-12:30pm, Mon. 8:30am-12:30pm and 4-6:30pm. Admission NIS7, students NIS3.50.)

The attraction of **Herzliya Pituah** is the gorgeous, sparklingly clean shore, and accordingly most of the large beaches charge admission (NIS5-15). City buses #13 and 29 go to **Nof Yam** and **Sidna Ali Beaches,** which are happily free of both tourists and fees. Ask the driver to let you off at Sidna Ali, then follow the road up the hill and go through the gate in the fence. Notice the prominent **Sidna Ali Mosque** to your right; you may be able to enter if you are modestly dressed and it is not prayer-time.

At the beach, informed travelers search out Herzliya Pituah's most unique attraction, an inhabited sand castle known as the **Hermit's House.** This fantastical residence built into the side of a cliff by "hermit" **Nissim Kakhalon** is a must-see for anyone to whom "arts and crafts" is not incompatible with Surrealism. Kakhalon claims, "I put my ass in this house!" In other words, he spent 25 years turning other people's garbage (tires, toys, tiles, etc.) into this hallucinogenic maze of winding tunnels, flower-strewn antechambers, and plush gardens. What's even more impressive is that everything in the artful interior is absolutely functional, from the bathroom ceiling made entirely of Maccabee Beer bottles to the loveseat with a mirrored mosaic on one side and a huge sculpted stone face on the other. Even the manure from the family of goats Kakhalon keeps on the premises is used to grow fragrant basil. The more respectful and demonstratively appreciative you are, the grander the tour "the caveman" will give you. This hermit is quite friendly, after all, and more showman than recluse.

A better choice than Kakhalon's tiny cafe for a quick bite is the **falafel stand** at 10 Ben-Gurion St., diagonally across from the central bus station. Tuvya, an Egyptian expat who can charm you in English, French, Arabic, or Hebrew, serves deliciously fresh falafel (NIS7) and a variety of salads. Ask about the bridal pictures on the wall.

■ Netanya נתניה

Founded in the 1920s as an agricultural center, Netanya has grown into a popular beach resort full of affluent retirees who don't know a plow from a cow. This Miami-on-the-Med's bridge club, orchestra, and social scene cater to wealthy tourists whether they're from Amarillo, Texas or Amman, Jordan. A growing variety of activities and businesses are making an effort to attract young people and budget travelers; there are even a few Israelis (someone has to run the information office). Located between Haifa and Tel Aviv, Netanya tends towards Tel Aviv in both location and ethos and is a convenient base for exploring the sites between these two cities. Netanya is valued for its beautiful beaches as well; stunning Mediterranean surf is less crowded than in Tel Aviv and more accessible than other, smaller towns.

ORIENTATION AND PRACTICAL INFORMATION

To get to the center of the action from the central bus station (tel. 833 70 52), push your way through neon-lit snack stands to Binyamin Blvd. (which turns into Weizmann Blvd. farther north) and walk one block north to **Herzl St.,** the town's main shopping area. Turning left on Herzl, you'll get to Dizengoff St. and arrive at the **midraḥov** (pedestrian zone), lined with expensive outdoor cafes, *shawerma* stands, and dairy restaurants. On the other side of the *midraḥov* (past King David St.) is **Ha-Atzma'ut Sq.** (Independence Sq.). Behind the square is **Ha-Melech Park,** where palm trees provide welcome shade for a picnic or a game of chess. The park also has an outdoor amphitheater. From the park, stairs lead down to the beach and the well-kept promenade continues to the north.

Tourist Office: (tel. 882 72 86). Located in a small, strangely shaped brick building in the southwest corner of Ha-Atzma'ut Sq., next to the beach stairs. City maps, bus schedules, and events schedules. Open Sun.-Thurs. 8:30am-7pm, Fri. 9am-noon.

Currency Exchange: Change Point (tel. 884 49 66; fax 884 49 04), at the north side of Ha-Atzma'ut Sq., changes money with no commission. Open Sun.-Thurs. 9am-7pm, Fri. 9am-1pm. **Bank Hapoalim** and **Bank Leumi** also flank the square. Both open Sun.-Fri. 8:30am-12:30pm and Sun., Tues., and Thurs. 4pm-5:30pm.

Buses: The central bus station is at 3 Binyamin Blvd. (tel. 833 70 52). Buses #600, 601, and 602 run to **Tel Aviv** (approx. every 10min., 30min., NIS10.50). Bus #945 runs to **Haifa** (every 30min., 45min., NIS18.60). From **Jerusalem** take bus #947 (every 30min., 1½hr., NIS28.20). Schedules are displayed on the electronic timetable board facing the information booth.

Taxis: The main services include **Ha-Shahar** (tel. 861 44 44), **Ha-Sheron** (tel. 882 23 23), **Hen** (tel. 833 33 33), and **Netanya** (tel. 834 44 43).

Car rental: Hertz (tel. 882 88 90), **Avis** (tel. 833 16 19), and **Eldan** (tel. 861 69 82) have offices at Ha'Atzma'ut Sq.

Pharmacies: Air-conditioned **Centerpharm**, 1 King David St. (tel. 884 15 31), stays open the latest (Sun.-Thurs. 8am-midnight, Fri. 8am-5pm). At least one pharmacy is always open for emergencies; the roster is posted on each door.

Hospital: The main hospital is **Laniado Hospital** (tel. 860 46 66).

Emergency: Magen David Adom first aid: tel. 101, or 862 33 33 or 35. **Police:** tel. 100 or 860 44 44 **Fire:** tel. 102.

Post Office: The branch at 59 Herzl St. (tel. 862 15 77) offers **Poste Restante.** Another branch is located at 2 Herzl St. (tel. 862 77 97). Open Sun.-Tues. and Thurs. 8am-12:30pm and 3:30-6pm, Wed. 8am-1:30pm, Fri. 8am-noon.

Telephones: Solan, 8 Ha-Atzma'ut Sq. (tel. 862 21 31). Private booths for discount international calls; fax and telegrams. Open daily 24hr. **Telephone Code:** 09.

ACCOMMODATIONS AND FOOD

Almost all hotels in Netanya are expensive, but many lower their prices by 10-15% from November to February. The **Atzma'uth Hostel** (tel. 882 25 62 or 862 13 15), at the corner of Ha-Atzma'ut Sq. and Usishkin St., is the only youth hostel in town. Occupying the third and fourth floors of an elevator-equipped building, this three-year-old hostel still sparkles. Each room has A/C, fridge, and private bath, and all guests receive freshly laundered linens and towels. The friendly, multilingual staff will let you leave your bags during day trips. There's a TV lounge and free safe for valuables. (Check-out 11am. No lockout. No curfew. Dorm beds US$10; singles US$20; doubles US$30.) The **Orit Hotel,** 21 Ḥen Blvd. (tel./fax 861 68 18), off Jabotinsky St. south of Ha-Atzma'ut Sq., is the next-cheapest option. The Swedish management keeps scrupulously clean rooms, a pleasant common room, a small library (in a variety of languages), and a communal fridge. Rooms have newly renovated private baths, fans, and balconies. A quiet rule is enforced after 11:30pm, and no smoking is allowed. (Reception open 7am-9pm, till 11pm in summer. Check-out 10am. No curfew. Singles US$30; doubles US$45; each additional bed US$18. Reduced rates for kibbutzniks. Breakfast included.) The most popular areas for **beach-sleeping** are near the 24-hour cafes. As always, camping on the beach is unsafe, especially for solo women.

Cheap food *is* available in Netanya. In **Ha-Atzma'ut Square,** pizza goes for about NIS7 and *malawah* for NIS10. Closer to the central bus station, the prices go down. **Sha'ar Ha-Gai Street** is lined with falafel stands and self-service restaurants which will stuff just about anything into a pita (falafel NIS6, *shawerma* NIS9, *schnitzel* NIS10). **Binyamin Blvd.,** at the end of Sha'ar Ha-Gai, has two 24hr. bakeries, where *burekas* go for NIS3-4 and sweet pastries for NIS1-3: **Hatachana** bakery at 11 Benyamin Blvd., and **Bel-Vil** bakery, at 4 Binyamin Blvd. (tel. 862 59 33). Before picnicking on the grass or sand, stock up at the **Nitza supermarket** (tel. 862 82 16), 8 Nitza Blvd. (off King David St.). For fresh fruits and vegetables, shop at the **open market** on

ISRAEL

Zangwill St., 2 blocks east of Weizmann Blvd. near the center of town (open Sun.-Thurs. 7am-6:30pm, Fri. 7am-2pm). From Ha'Atzma'ut Sq., take King David St. past King Solomon's Hotel to Nitza Blvd. The **Kenion Ha-Sharon mall,** located at the intersection of Petach Tikva Rd. and Herzl, has a **Co-op** supermarket.

For a more satisfying (and expensive) experience, consider some of Netanya's mid-range restaurants. The **Mini Golf Restaurant and Pub,** 21 Nitza Blvd. (tel. 861 77 35), is perched on the edge of a cliff overlooking the sea. The atmosphere is relaxing and romantic, with separate milk and meat areas. The grilled dishes (most NIS22-32) are excellent, and the stuffed vegetables (NIS12-30) will turn even the most bloodthirsty carnivore into a veggie (open Sun.-Thurs. 11am-3am, Fri. 11am-7pm, Sat. 8:30pm-3am). **Apropo** (tel. 862 44 82) is conveniently located between the amphitheater and the stairs to the beach. Sample from the new Thai menu (NIS29-39) while sea-gazing through the restaurant's glass walls. Pastas (NIS33-35) and toasts (NIS31-38) are served in large portions (open Sun.-Thurs. 9am-midnight, Fri. 9am-5pm, Sat. 6pm-midnight). **Patisserie Antverpia,** 1 Eliyahu Krause St. (tel. 833 53 90), one block south of Herzl St. off Smilansky St., serves fresh ḥallah and luscious cream pastries at slightly lower prices than its tourist-district counterparts. Sandwiches cost NIS10, hearty breakfasts NIS16 (open Sun.-Thurs. 7:30am-9pm, Fri. 7:30am-3pm). Credit cards accepted at Mini Golf and Apropo; Antverpia accepts only cash or checks.

SIGHTS AND ENTERTAINMENT

Netanya's **beaches**—11km of them—are all free; the northernmost are least crowded. You can go **horseback riding** along the beach, although at NIS30 per 30 minutes your wallet may tire before your thighs. For information, call Cactus Ranch Horseback Riding (tel. 865 12 39) or take bus #7 to the intersection of Itamar Ben-Avi St. and Jabotinsky St. and ask them in person (open daily 11am-7pm).

The Netanya municipality organizes various forms of **free entertainment** almost every night during the summer and often during the winter. The tourist information office has complete listings of concerts, movies, and a host of other activities. During the summer, you can watch the sun set over the Mediterranean while listening to classical music in the **Ha-Melekh Park Amphitheater** (Sun.-Thurs. 6-8pm). There is a performance of Israeli and American 60s songs in the lobby of the Park Hotel every Friday (info. tel. 862 33 44). Talented Russian musicians play classical music at 11 Ha-Atzma'ut Sq. (Mon. noon-1pm). If you'd rather see karats than hear clarinets, there are several diamond centers which give free guided tours of their premises: **National Diamond Center** at 90 Herzl St. (tel. 862 47 70) and **Orco Jewelry** at 11 Raziel St. (tel. 882 90 70; both are usually open Sun.-Thurs. 8am-7pm, but call ahead to be sure).

The favorite spot come pub time is **Uri's Pub,** 26 Dizengoff St. (tel. 882 87 31). Coming from Ha-Atzma'ut Sq., take a right at the eastern end of the *midraḥov*. In summer, everyone gathers outside in the garden. At press time, Uri's had just come under new management and was anticipating major menu changes, a shift in focus towards slightly older clientele, and possibly a new name. Customers will still be able to enjoy occasional jam sessions, movie nights, and Wednesday barbecues (domestic beers NIS9, large Heineken draft NIS13; open 9am until the crowd goes home).

■ Near Netanya

The beautiful **Poleg Nature Reserve,** about 8km south of Netanya, begins where the Poleg River meets the sea. The walk upstream leads past flowering plants and eucalyptus trees planted during the last century to dry up the swamps that once covered the Plain of Sharon. A few kilometers south, near **Kibbutz Ga'ash,** seaside cliffs reach 60m, forming a beautiful backdrop for one of Israel's loveliest and least crowded beaches. Take Egged bus #601 or 604 (5:30am-10:30pm, every 30min., from Netanya NIS5.50, from Tel Aviv NIS9.40); ask to be let off at Ga'ash or Naḥal Poleg. Just before the main kibbutz gate turn left and continue south for about 200m along the unpaved road. Head west along the field until you reach a small dirt "parking lot" (about 1½km). A path that begins at the southwest corner of the parking lot leads to the beach, or you can follow the jeeps that continue along the unpaved roads several kilometers north to one of Israel's favorite **nude beaches.** You can also explore the **Naḥal Alexander Nature Reserve** along the banks of the Alexander River, only 1km north of the youth hostel (see below).

The quiet **Emek Ḥefer Youth Hostel (HI)** (tel. (09) 866 60 32) is located 6km north of Netanya, only a short walk from free beaches. Take bus #642 from Tel Aviv (NIS14), #29 or 706 from Netanya (NIS 7.30), or #921 from Haifa (NIS18.50), and get off at Tzomet Bet Yanai at Kfar Vitkin. Walk north on the eastern mile of the highway until you see a path leading to an open gate with flags on either side. The reception building is through the parking lot (closed 2-5pm). Some of the utilitarian dorm rooms are in concrete bungalows, some in small bomb-shelterish huts. Most are equipped with a private bath, refrigerator, fan, and lockers. Some have A/C; all have access to the basketball court (no lockout or curfew; dorm beds (4-8 per room) US$17; nonmembers US$18.50; breakfast included; lunch US$8; dinner US$6). **Ḥanout Shohar Supermarket** (open Sat. 9am-8pm, Sun.-Thurs. 8am-8pm, Fri. 8am-5pm, winter until 4pm) and the **Original Israeli Pancake House** (open 24hr.; pancakes NIS15-32, Mexican menu NIS12-25; alcohol served) are great if you don't want to eat all your meals at the hostel.

▓ Caesarea קיסריה

At the end of the first century BCE, Herod the Great built Caesarea (Kay-SAHR-ya in Hebrew) on the site of a small Phoenician anchorage. Caesarea was a planned city, with a network of crisscrossing streets, a temple, a theater, an amphitheater, markets, and residential quarters. Built in only 12 years, this city transformed rapidly into a great commercial center and became the headquarters of the Roman government in Palestine. Excavations began in 1873 by the Palestine Exploration Fund and have unearthed the Roman theater and amphitheater, Byzantine mosaics, aqueducts, a Crusader city, and an extremely sophisticated 2000-year-old harbor. Caesarea's multi-layered ruins constitute one of Israel's finest archaeological sites.

Not far from the ancient ruins, a growing residential community boasts some of the most beautiful villas in Israel. Add to this the Dan Caesarea (a five-star hotel) and the country's only golf course and it's not hard to see why Caesarea has become a popular choice for Israel's *nouveau riche*. Although the town's Roman townhouses are set apart from the modern ones, touristy cafes and gift shops have managed to nestle themselves among the antique buildings. Bus service to Caesarea is infrequent.

HISTORY

Phoenician travelers of the 4th century BCE established a small town and harbor called Strato's Tower on the main trading route between Phoenicia (present-day Lebanon and coastal Syria) and Egypt. The town and surrounding coastal strip were soon captured by Greeks and later fell into the hands of **Augustus Caesar,** who granted it to **Herod the Great,** vassal king of Judea. Because of its strategic location and access to the harbor, Herod transformed Strato's Tower into one of the eastern Roman Empire's great cities, renaming it "Caesarea" in honor of the emperor. Construction began in 22 BCE and within 12 years the city had a theater, a hippodrome for chariot racing, aqueducts carrying fresh water from the north, and a harbor capable of accommodating 300 ships. In 6 CE, Caesarea became the capital of the Roman province of Judea, and it remained the seat of Roman power in the area until the fall of the Empire. **Pontius Pilate,** the Roman prefect of Caesarea from 26 to 36 CE, ordered the crucifixion of Jesus. The first evidence of Pilate's existence outside the accounts of the Gospels and the historian Josephus was uncovered here in 1961.

In 66 CE, fighting between Jews and Romans in Caesarea sparked the six-year Jewish Rebellion (the Great Revolt), which resulted in the destruction of Jerusalem's Second Temple in 70 CE. The Romans celebrated Jerusalem's fall by slaughtering thousands of Jews in Caesarea's amphitheater. Sixty years later, ten Jewish sages, among them the famous **Rabbi Akiva,** were tortured to death in the arena as punishment for their participation in the Bar Kokhba revolt, a second Jewish uprising against Rome. Caesarea later became a center of Jewish and Christian scholarship.

During the Crusades, Caesarea changed hands four times before finally falling to **King Louis IX** of France. Saint Louis strengthened and expanded the city's fortifications in 1254, building the massive ramparts, battlements, and moat, all of which are still in excellent condition. Despite Louis' efforts, Caesarea was conquered and destroyed in 1275 by the Sultan Baybars. The city remained uninhabited until 1878 when the Muslim Boshnaqs (Bosnians) resettled it in 1878. Caesarea's population was driven out a final time in the 1948 War, but within decades Caesarea began to thrive once again—this time as a tourist site and resort for wealthy Israelis.

ORIENTATION

Getting to Caesarea is by no means simple. The only practical way is via Ḥadera, the nearest town. Be warned that while buses to Ḥadera are plentiful (#852 from Tel Aviv, 40min., NIS12; #706 from Netanya, 20min., NIS8.30; #921 (1 hr.) or 941 (30 min.) from Haifa, NIS14.50, and #945 from Jerusalem, NIS27.50, 1[hr., the only bus to or from the ruins is #76 from Ḥadera (30min., NIS7.30), which travels several times per day in each direction. Call ahead to avoid a wait in Ḥadera's central bus station in the heat. While it is possible to get a taxi from the station in Ḥadera for NIS25, you won't find one for the ride back from the ruins unless you arrange in advance, which will cost NIS30 each way. An intercity Egged bus goes to the Caesarea exit along the old Ḥadera-Haifa road, an unrewarding 3km west of the ruins (ask the driver for Tzomet Or Akiva and watch carefully). Caesaria's **telephone code** is 06.

ACCOMMODATIONS AND FOOD

There are two options for budget accommodations around Caesarea. Just south of the Roman theater is the friendly, quiet **Kibbutz Sdot Yam.** To get to the reception office, enter the kibbutz's main gate near the Roman theater (the last stop on bus #76), pass the tile factory and bus stop, and bear right at the fork in the road. Follow the signposts to the "Kef Yam" office building at the top of the hill. 16 private apartments (all have A/C, private baths, refrigerators, TVs, and telephones) are ideal for families or for three to four person groups (singles US$68; doubles US$104; additional people US$39 each; in winter singles US$47, doubles US$63, additional people US$23 each). For independent travelers, there are 6-7 bed dorm rooms with showers and toilets in the hall (US$21 per person, US$17 in winter). An additional US$7 (US$3 in winter) gets you a bed in a five-bed dorm room with a private shower and toilet. All rooms are equipped with A/C, and washing machines are available. Call in advance (tel. 636 44 70 or 44; fax 636 22 11. Open daily 7am-7pm, winter 7am-4pm).

Next to the southern end of the kibbutz, near the beach, is the cheaper and more touristed **Caesarea Sports Center** (tel. 636 43 94 or 13 73 or 41 29; fax 636 15 79). Go through Kibbutz Sdot Yam, head toward the beach, turn left at the "T," and walk past the Hannah Senesh House; the Center is just beyond the big brown building. There are two buildings with guest rooms; the Beit Gil Building has 40 rooms with A/C and private baths (4-5 bed dorm rooms NIS155-205). The hostel building has no A/C and baths are shared by five rooms, but the prices are a bit lower (4-5 bed dorm rooms NIS110-140). Prices are highest in August, and rates jump NIS10-20 for Saturday stays. Full board is included in all dorm prices. *Let's Go* readers can negotiate with owner Shimshon for use of the sports facilities (yachting, basketball, volleyball, and training center) and for possible discounted bus fares.

Many visitors to Caesarea unroll their sleeping bags on the beach, but camping in some places, such as Hofshonit Beach, is forbidden. Restaurant prices in Caesarea are as high as the Crusader walls, though places like **Charly's Cafe Restaurant** and the **Citadel Restaurant** have great views. The **Sdot Yam Cafeteria** in the kibbutz offers all-you-can-eat breakfast (NIS23), lunch (NIS34), and dinner (NIS23). It serves standard but tasty kibbutz food—*litsitsot*, salads, mashed potatoes, etc. The best food deal is at Sdot Yam's **mini-market** (in the lower level of the dining hall building). Fresh produce and other cheap staples make a good picnic on the beach.

SIGHTS

Caesarea's sights include a Roman city and an ancient port. Though the Roman city is not fully excavated, most of the site is well marked; relics include the main road and several statues. The granaries and residences are Arab remains, and the walls and churches date from the Crusader period. Don't be surprised to find pieces of a marble column used as street pavement—medieval contractors frequently re-used Roman remains when erecting cities. The harbor and beaches of Caesarea are also of major archaeological significance. Extending along the ancient city is Herod's now-semi-submerged port which incorporated the first breakwater in the Eastern Mediterranean. A constant stream of international archaeologists and volunteers continue to excavate both the dry ground and underwater areas of Caesarea.

The enormous, restored **Roman Theater** is a 500m stroll south of the Roman city (tel. 636 13 58). Reopened in 1961, this 3500-seat structure has hosted Eric Clapton, the Bolshoi Ballet, and the New Israeli Opera. Admission (NIS16, seniors and students NIS7) covers both the city and the Roman Theater; the other sites are free. You can purchase tickets and get a free map at either site (both open daily 8am-6pm, winter 8am-4pm, Fri. and holidays eves until 5pm). By visiting the Roman city after hours, you can avoid the entrance fee and watch a Mediterranean sunset. The catch is that you won't be able to get into the theater.

Although most of the ruins are within the Crusader walls, a number of interesting Roman remnants lie outside the site proper. Behind the cafe, across from the entrance to the Crusader city, is an excavated **Byzantine street** and Caesarea's most famous find: colossal **Roman statues** from the 2nd century CE. The two headless figures, one of red porphyry, the other of white marble, were discovered accidentally by kibbutzniks ploughing fields. A one-km walk north along either the water or the road that runs along the Crusader walls leads to Caesarea's beach and the well-preserved **Roman aqueduct.** The most recent excavations have uncovered another Herodian amphitheater (at press time it was inaccessible to the public).

The intensely blue cool water is inviting, but swimming within the walls of the city costs NIS20. Unless you wish to go snorkeling in the ancient harbor, the free public beach behind the aqueduct is a better place to swim. Diving in the harbor is an expensive but rewarding experience at the **Caesarea Diving Center** (tel. 636 17 87; fax 636 03 11). Full scuba equipment is NIS150 per day.

About one km along the main road running east from the theater stands an archway leading to the ruins of the **Roman Hippodrome,** now overgrown with banana and orange groves cultivated by nearby Kibbutz Sdot Yam. In its heyday, the 352m by 68m racetrack could hold 20,000 spectators. Most of the relics unearthed, including coins and inscriptions, have been put on display at the **Sdot Yam Museum of Caesarea Antiquities** (tel. 636 43 67), located within the kibbutz. Ask the curator to show you around the museum's three rooms, which contain Jewish, Christian, and Muslim artifacts, 3500-year-old Egyptian urns, and Roman discoveries. Next to the museum is the **Beit Hannah Senesh,** built in honor of a Sdot Yam parachutist who died while trying to save Jews from the Nazis during World War II. (Both open Sat.-Thurs. 10am-4pm, Fri. and holiday eves 10am-2pm. Admission to the memorial's museum and film NIS8, students and seniors NIS6.) The **Kef Yam Office** in the kibbutz offers glass-bottomed boat tours of the ancient harbor (NIS28, students NIS27). You *must* call ahead for reservations (tel. 636 44 44).

■ Near Caesarea

Just outside Moshav Beit Ḥananya, on the old coastal road between Caesarea and Ma'agan Mikha'el, are two well-preserved **Roman aqueducts,** believed to have carried water from the Shuni springs northeast of present-day Binyamina down to the ancient city of Caesarea. North of the *moshav*, excavations are in progress at **Tel Mevoraḥ,** where several important Roman artifacts have been unearthed. Two of the marble sarcophagi discovered in the ruins of a Roman mausoleum are on display in the Rockefeller Museum in Jerusalem.

Kibbutz Ma'agan Mikha'el is one of the largest and loveliest kibbutzim in Israel. Take bus #921 from Haifa (NIS12, 1hr.) or Tel-Aviv (NIS15½, 1½hr.) and get off at the Ma'agan Mikha'el intersection. The huge industrial plant at the entrance belies the cultivated fields and acres of neat, rectangular fish ponds set between the coastal road and the sea. Part of the kibbutz is a wildlife preserve with an aviary and a small museum displaying archaeological finds from the fields.

The gorgeous **beach** at **Dor** (tel. 634 09 22) is protected by four small, rocky islands, each a bird sanctuary, explorable at low tide (beach open 7am-6pm, NIS10 entrance fee). Take bus #921 from either Haifa (NIS9.60, 30min.) or Tel Aviv (NIS19.20, 2hr.), and get off at the Kibbutz Dor intersection; it's a 3km walk to the beach. The **Tel Dor** archaeological site is on the hill at the far northern end of the beach; you'll need shoes to traverse the rusty-wire-and-sand road. Though the site was probably founded in the 15th century BCE and was part of King David's empire, most of the important remains at Dor date from the Greek and Roman periods. The site includes temples dedicated to Zeus and Astarte, as well as the ruins of a Byzantine church.

Next to the beach, within the boundaries of **Kibbutz Nachsholim,** is the **Center of Nautical and Regional Archaeology (CONRAD)** (tel. 639 09 50), also known as **Hamizgaga Museum.** The unique stone edifice was formerly a glass factory built by Baron Edmond de Rothschild. Today it serves as a repository and display for objects found at Tel Dor and for underwater archaeological finds retrieved by the center's diving team. A special exhibition traces the history of the building (open Sun.-Thurs. 8:30am-2pm, Fri. 8:30am-1pm, Sat. and holidays 10:30am-3pm; admission NIS8, NIS6 for students and seniors).

Nearby, next to **Kibbutz Ein Karmel,** is the **Naḥal Me'arot Nature Reserve** (tel. (04) 984 17 50 or 22), with prehistoric caves inhabited some two hundred thousand years ago. Experienced guides explain the significance of the nearby caves and can suggest or lead longer hikes in the surrounding area. Admission (open 8am-4pm, NIS13; under 18, NIS7) includes a film inside one of the caves which recreates the life of prehistoric man. Bus #421 goes to the site (from Haifa: 20min., NIS9.60; from Tel Aviv: 2 hr., NIS20.40); get off at Ein Carmel Junction. Walk a few minutes south along the road until you see a sign indicating the Nature Reserve. A few hundred meters east of the main road is the entrance to the caves.

■ Zikhron Ya'akov זיכרון יעקב

Zikhron Ya'akov (Zikhron for short) was established in 1882 on swamplands drained with the generous financial assistance of Baron Edmond de Rothschild. The town's name means "Jacob's Memorial" (for the Baron's father) and is known today for the libations produced from surrounding vineyards.

Bus #872 from Tel Aviv (1½hr., NIS19.20) and 202 from Haifa (35min., NIS14.50) will take you to the small **central bus station.** There are **no return buses** to Haifa between 3:15pm and 5:45pm. The white building behind the station is the **tourist office** (tel. 639 88 92; tel./fax 639 88 11), which offers maps, brochures, and information about city events (open Sun.-Thurs. 8:30am-1pm, Fri. 8:30am-noon). Zikhron's **telephone code** is 06. To the right of the central bus station, two blocks past the concrete arches, is the newly-renovated, cobblestone **Ha-Meyasdim St.,** with old-fashioned decorative lamp posts on both sides. Along this picturesque strip are a number of pricey restaurants. The only real budget food option is a packed lunch or a "meal" of ice cream and chips from one of the souvenir kiosks on HaMeyasdim St.

Just outside the city limits lies **Ramat Ha-Nadiv,** the Rothschild Family Tomb and Gardens. *Sherut* taxis on their way to Binyamina will drop you off at the side road leading to the estate for a mere NIS2.50. The remaining 15- to 20-minute walk features inspiring views of the valley below. The rock-hewn crypt containing the remains of Edmond de Rothschild and his wife is modest relative to the Baron's wealth. More impressive is the greenery. The rose garden, palm garden, cascade garden, fragrance garden, and small amphitheater are all separated by masterfully landscaped meadows (open Sun.-Thurs. 6:30am-4pm, Fri. 6:30am-2pm, Sat. 8am-4pm; crypt closed on Sat. and holidays; free).

Zikhron Ya'akov is best known for the **Carmel-Mizraḥi Winery** (tel. 634 12 41), founded 100 years ago by the Baron himself. The winery now produces a significant share of Israel's domestic wine as well as a large stock for export. The one-hour tour of the winery includes a look at the old wine cellars, an audio-visual presentation, wine tasting, and a souvenir bottle. It's best to visit during the harvest season (Aug.-Oct.). From the central bus station turn right onto Ha-Meyasdim St. Continue downhill for a few blocks and turn right onto Ha-Nadiv St. where the cobblestone ends. The winery is at the bottom of the hill (open Sun.-Thurs. 9am-3pm., Fri. 9am-noon; NIS12, students NIS10, children NIS9; call ahead for tours in English). The winery also hosts **wild wine and cheese parties,** usually accompanied by an Israeli singer. You *must* call in advance (tel. 639 78 83; NIS60-65).

Other sites of interest in Zikhron Ya'akov include the beautiful **Ohel Ya'akov Synagogue** which was erected in 1886 (situated on the junction of Ha-Meyasdim St. and Ha-Nadiv St.), and the **Beit Daniel Music Center** (tel. 639 90 01) which hosts a chamber music festival every year on *Pesaḥ* and *Sukkot*. The **Baron's Winery** (tel. 638 04 34) is located down the hill from the entrance to the Baron's Tomb in Ramat Ha-Nadiv. The smaller winery also gives tours and wine tastings for NIS10 (open Sun.-Thurs. 8am-4pm); Carmel-Mizraḥi is worth the extra NIS2.

■ Haifa חיפה حيفا

Haifa is a prosperous city built on the steep, forested slopes of Mt. Carmel. Though it boasts the country's largest port, two of Israel's eleven universities, and the most diverse topography in the state, Haifa does not compete with Tel Aviv or Jerusalem for tourists. Budget accommodations are sparse, the seafront distant, and the museums less than spectacular. The city has recently embarked on the "Haifa 2000" project to transform its coastal beaches into a Riviera-esque strip, but for the moment Haifa's most powerful and memorable points of attraction are its thickly forested neighborhoods and striking vistas.

Since the prophet Elijah fled from the wrath of King Ahab to the caves of Mt. Carmel (I Kings 18-19), Haifa has continued to harbor religious minorities. Crusaders built the first of several monasteries above **Elijah's Cave,** which eventually gave shelter to the wandering (but now settled) Carmelite Order of monks. **German Templars,** who established Haifa's German colony, and **Baha'is,** whose world headquarters are in Haifa, have also found homes here. During the 1930s, waves of European Jews seeking refuge from Nazism poured onto the beaches of Haifa. In the 1948 War, Haifa was the first territory secured by Jewish forces.

While Haifa contains a small Orthodox Jewish community, the prevailing tenor of the city is decidedly secular. Haifa's population of a quarter million includes a sizable Arab minority, but there is little tension; in fact, supporters of the Israel-Palestinian peace accords often cite Haifa as the paradigm for peaceful Jewish-Arab co-existence.

ORIENTATION

Haifa, Israel's principal port and a hub for ferry transport, lies on a small peninsula on the Mediterranean coast, about 100km south of Lebanon and due west of the Sea of Galilee. Built into the northern slopes of the Carmel mountain, the city is divided into three terraces. In this vertically oriented town, social stratification is more than just a metaphor; the rich really do live on the top, the poor at the bottom. The **Ha-Ir** area, aptly named "downtown," is at the foot of the mountain. The **central bus station** is adjoined to the **train station** on this level, at the intersection of **Derekh Yafo** (Jaffa Rd.) and **Rothschild Blvd.** Follow Jaffa Rd. to the west to find yourself in the Old City area across from the **Haifa Port. Beaches** lie along the peninsula's northern coast, near the bus and train stations. **Ben-Gurion Blvd.,** perpendicular to Jaffa Rd., runs uphill and intersects **Ha-Geffen St.** at the first of the Baha'i gardens.

The middle terrace is the **Hadar** district, home to businesses, cafes, bakeries, and bazaar stands. Its main street is **Herzl Street,** along which several staircases make for easier climbing up and down the mountain. **Ha-Halutz Street,** parallel to Herzl but one street down (i.e., north, or toward the port), contains too many falafel stands to count. Buses from this street go to the central bus station rather than up the mountain. The street parallel to and above Herzl is the **Nordau Midrahov** (pedestrian zone), bordered on the west by **Balfour Street** and on the east by **Arlozorov Street.**

The highest area is known as **Carmel Center,** characterized by posh homes, five-star hotels, restaurants, and discos. This district is traversed by **Ha-Nassi Boulevard** and **Yefeh Nof Street,** both of which run west to east past all the major hotels. Follow either of these streets to the Dan Panorama Hotel and go one block up to reach **Gan Ha-Eim** (Mother's Park), which has a peaceful **promenade** and a panoramic view of the lower city and the port area. From Carmel Center, Moriya Street takes you to **Ahuza**—a previously bare intersection, now graced with stylish cafes, restaurants, and a large shopping center, Merkaz Horev.

TRANSPORTATION

The **central bus station,** like the city itself, has three tiers. Buses bound for other cities leave from the first floor, Haifa city buses are on the second, and both inter- and intra-city buses arrive on the third. All urban rides are NIS3.90. For longer stays, a *cartisiya* (NIS39 for 20 trips) can save money.

On weekdays, buses run from 5:30am to midnight. On Fridays, they stop at 5:30pm; on Saturdays, they begin running at 9:30am and run less frequently than on weekdays. **Saturday buses** do *not* run from the central bus station but from the Hadar area, many from Daniel St. The following are some helpful tourist routes: **Downtown (Ha-Ir),** #17 and 41; **Hadar,** #21, 24, 28, and 37; and **Carmel Center,** #21, 28, and 37. **Bus #3** goes to all three districts and then the central bus station.

Haifa's main mode of transportation is the **Carmelit subway** system, running from the downtown area to Carmel Center. Though this subway has only one line, its six stops are great for conquering the distance between **Kikkar Paris** and **Gan Ha-Eim** in less than six minutes. Ascending the hill, the subway also stops at Solel Boneh, Ha-Nevi'im (Hadar), Masada, and Golomb. Yellow pavilions indicate entrances. Trains run every 6-7 min. (open Sun.-Thurs. 6am-10pm, Fri. 6:30am-3pm, Sat. 15min. after sundown-midnight; NIS3.90 per ride, 10-ride pass NIS 35.10).

A more scenic alternative for getting from bottom to top and back is to take the **Rakbal cable cars** (tel. 833 59 70 or 00 09). Colloquially known as "the Carmel's Eggs" for their spherical shape, the cable cars run down the Carmel's northwestern slope, shuttling between the orange-and-turquoise **Yotvata B'Ir** dairy restaurant on the Bat Galim Promenade and the **Stella Maris monastery** area at the mountain's peak. To reach the bottom station, walk west on Ha-Hagana Blvd. from the central bus station for five minutes. There is a small walkway underneath the elevated train tracks on the right. From the tracks, walk one block down Rahaf St. and turn left onto Ha-Aliya Ha-Shniya St. The restaurant is several blocks down. You can also take bus #42 to its last stop. The view from the car is striking but the trip is short and the pre-recorded explanation (in English or Hebrew) is rushed and uninformative (open Sun.-Thurs., Sat. 10am-5:45pm, Fri. 9am-1:45pm, NIS13, round-trip NIS19).

PRACTICAL INFORMATION

Tourist Information Office: 18 Herzl St. (tel. 866 65 21 or 22 or 864 36 16; fax 862 20 75), in Hadar. Take bus #10 or 12 from the port area or #21 or 28 from the central bus station to **Beit Ha-Kranot.** Maps, train schedules, and an incredible CD-ROM computer that prints information in Hebrew or English. Ask for the bimonthly *Events in Haifa* booklet. Open Sun.-Thurs. 8:30am-5pm, Fri. 8:30am-1pm. A smaller office is conveniently located on the lowest level of the **Egged Central Bus Station** (tel. 851 22 08). Open Sun.-Thurs. 9:30am-5pm, Fri. 9:30am-2pm. Other offices at **City Hall** in Hadar, 14 Hassan Shuki St. (tel. 835 62 00). Open

Haifa

Bahai Shrine, 11
Carmel Youth Hostel, 18
Carmelite Monastery, 2
Central Bus Station, 4
Central Post Office, 8
Central Train Station, 5
City Hall, 9
Dagon Grain Silos, 6
Elijah's Cave, 1
Gan ha Em Park, 15
GTIO, 12
Haifa Auditorium, 16
Haifa Museum, 10
Haifa Theater, 14
Maritime Museum, 3
Merkaz Horev, 17
Old Technion, 13
Plumer Train Station, 7

ISRAEL

Sun.-Thurs. 8am-1pm. And in **Carmel,** 106 Ha-Nassi Blvd. (tel. 837 40 10). Open Sun.-Thurs. 8am-7pm, Fri. 8am-1pm; winter Sun.-Thurs. 8am-6pm, Fri. 8am-1pm.

Tours: Society for the Protection of Nature in Israel (SPNI): 18 Hillel St. (tel. 866 41 35, 36, or 59; fax 866 58 25). Ask about hiking trips into the Carmel Mountains. Most day tours on a bus cost between NIS80-150 (English tours more expensive). Open Mon. and Wed. 9am-3:45pm, Tues. and Fri. 9am-12:30pm, Sun. 9am-5pm.

Budget Travel: ISSTA, 2 Balfour St. (tel. 866 91 39 or 867 02 22). ISICs and HI memberships NIS30. Student rates on plane and ferry tickets. Open Sun.-Tues. and Thurs. 9am-6pm, Wed. and Fri. 8:30am-1pm. Another location at **Technion** (tel. 832 67 39; fax 832 67 41), in the Student Building. Open Sun.-Thurs. 9am-3:30pm, Fri. (summer only) 9-11:30am.

American Consulate: 12 Yerushalayim St. (tel. 867 06 15; fax 867 57 57), in Hadar. Call Sun.-Thurs. 9am-1pm (consular services by appointment only). In emergency, call (03) 519 73 72.

Currency Exchange: Barclays Discount, 65 Ha-Atzma'ut St. (tel. 852 22 91); **Ha-Poalim,** 5 Ha-Palyam Blvd. (tel. 868 15 74); **Israel Discount,** 47 Ha-Atzma'ut St. (tel. 854 61 11); **Leumi,** 21 Yafo St. (tel. 854 71 11), in the new Ha-Meginim Tower (other branches throughout the city). Open Sun., Tues., and Thurs. 8:30am-12:30pm and 4-6pm; Mon., Wed., and Fri. 8:30am-noon. No-commission services cluster around Palmer Sq. by the port, including **Change Spot,** 78 Ha-Atzmaut Rd. (tel. 862 11 32), on the corner of Natan St. Open Sun.-Thurs. 8:30am-5:30pm, Fri. 8:30am-1:30pm. Slightly less savory **Money Net,** 3 Khayat, is nearby. It's easy to exchange money in Haifa's **black market,** but also easy to get ripped off.

American Express: Meditrad Ltd., 2 Khayat Sq., P.O. Box 1266 (tel. 864 22 66 or 58 35; fax 864 22 67). Entrance in alleyway next to Steimatzky off Ha-Atzma'ut St., opposite Sha'ar Palmer St. **Client Letter Service** available. Open Sun.-Thurs. 8:30am-5pm, Fri. 8:30am-1pm.

Trains: Station in Bat Galim (tel. 830 31 33 for Hebrew-only schedule and prices), connected by tunnels to the central bus station. Trains to: **Tel Aviv** (NIS15); **Netanya** (NIS14); **Nahariya** (NIS9); and **Akko** (NIS7.0). To get to Jerusalem you'll have to change stations, so you're better off taking the bus. Trains are generally the best choice when traveling north. 20% discount with ISIC. The TIO has schedules.

Buses: Central Bus Station (tel. 854 95 55 for intercity lines, 854 91 31 for city lines) is on Jaffa Rd. at the corner of Rothschild Blvd. **Baggage storage** on lower level open Sun.-Thurs. 8am-4:30pm, Fri. 8am-12:30pm; NIS7 per item. A **lost and found** also operates from here. Buses #251, 270, 271, and 272 go to **Akko** and **Nahariya** (Sun.-Thurs. 5:15am-11:30pm, Fri. 5:15am-5:20pm, Sat. 4:25pm-midnight; every 15-20min.; Akko 30min., NIS9.40; Nahariya 40min., NIS11.50). Buses #900 (direct) and 901 (express) go to **Tel Aviv's** central bus station (every 20min.; Sun.-Thurs. 5:30am-11pm, Fri. 5:30am-5pm, Sat. 8:10-11pm; 1½hr., NIS20.50). Buses #940, 945, and 947 go to **Jerusalem** (every 30-45min.; Sun.-Thurs. 6:15am-8pm, Fri. 7:30am-3:20pm, Sat. after 8:30pm; 2½hr., NIS34). Buses #331, 332, 341, and 431 go to **Nazareth** (every 30min., 5:30am-8:40pm, 40min., NIS14.90). #430 and 431 go to **Tiberias** (every 30-40min., 5:30am-8pm, 1½hr., NIS20.50). To **Ben-Gurion Airport,** take either #945 or 947 (2hr., NIS25).

Ferries: Terminal next to the train station. Ferries to Cyprus, Crete, and mainland Greece leave Sun. and Thurs. 8pm (you need to be there 3:30-6pm for security check) and Fri. 7pm for Cyprus only (be there by 1pm for security check; the port closes by 1pm, so you won't be able to enter later). South Africans need visas to enter both countries. Tickets at **Caspi Travel,** 76 Ha-Atzma'ut St. (tel. 867 44 44; open Sun.-Thurs. 8am-6pm, Fri. 8am-1pm); **Mano,** 2 Sha'ar Palmer St. (tel. 866 77 22; open Sun.-Thurs. 8am-6:30pm, Fri. 8am-noon); and **Dolphin,** 104 Ha-Atzma'ut St. (tel. 852 39 53; open Sun.-Thurs. 8am-6pm, Fri. 8am-1pm). Ferry tickets also available through ISSTA, which may be more convenient.

Taxis: Most taxis leave from Eliyahu St. in Paris Sq. near the Carmelit stop. For "special" taxis call **Kavei Ha-Galil** (tel. 866 44 44 or 45; home pick-up). To **Akko** (NIS60), **Nahariya** (NIS76), or **Lod** (NIS200). **Amal's Sherut Service** (tel. 866 23 24) will take you from 6 Ha-Ḥalutz St. in Hadar to **Tel Aviv** (NIS18) and to **Ben-Gurion Airport** (NIS42). Other taxi services include **Carmel Ahuza** (tel. 838 27 27) and **Merkaz Mitzye** (tel. 866 25 25).

Car Rental: Avis, 7 Ben-Gurion Blvd. (tel. 851 30 50); **Budget,** 46 Ha-Histadrut Blvd. (tel. 842 28 32); **Hertz,** 90 Ha-Atzma'ut St. (tel. 853 12 34); **Reliable,** 33 Ha-Histadrut Blvd. (tel. 842 40 04); **Eldan,** 12 Ha-Histadrut Blvd. (tel. 842 11 14). All open Sun.-Thurs. 8am-6pm, Fri. 8am-2pm. Most require minimum age of 23; Hertz and Eldan rent to 21-year-olds with double insurance payments.

Shopping Hours: Most shops open Sun.-Thurs. 8:30am-1:30pm and 4-7pm, Fri. 8:30am-2pm, Sat. 8-11pm. Department stores and malls usually open 8:30am-7pm.

English Bookstores: Beverly's Books, 18 Herzl St. (tel. 866 48 10), 2nd floor of Beit Ha-Kranot. Buys and exchanges used books. Open Sun.-Tues. and Thurs.-Fri. 9am-1pm, call to see if open (usually Wed. 4-6pm). **Studio 5,** 5 Ha-Yam St., in Merkaz Ha-Carmel district, sells used English books. Open Sun.-Mon. and Wed.-Thurs. 9am-1pm and 4-7pm, Tues. and Fri. 9am-1pm. **Steimatzky** has branches downtown, in Hadar, in Carmel Center, and in the bus station. All open Sun.-Thurs. 8:30am-7pm, Fri. 8:30am-2pm.

Ticket Offices: Haifa boasts an array of plays, musicals and concerts. **Haifa,** 11 Baerwald St. (tel. 866 22 44), open Sun.-Wed. 9am-1pm and 4-7pm, Thurs. 9am-1pm; **Garber,** 129 Ha-Nassi Blvd. (tel. 838 47 77), open Sun.-Thurs. 9am-1pm and 4-7pm, Fri. 9am-2pm; and **Nova,** 15 Nordau St. (tel. 866 52 72), open Sun.-Mon. and Wed.-Thurs. 10am-1pm and 4-6:30pm, Tues. 10am-1pm, Fri. 10am-1:30pm.

Swimming Pools: Maccabee Pool, 19 Bikurim St. (tel. 838 83 41), in central Carmel. Heated and covered in winter. Open Sun., Tues., and Thurs. 6am-2pm and 4-10pm, Mon. and Wed. 6am-2pm and 6:30-10pm, Fri. 6am-2pm and 4-6pm. Admission NIS30. The **Dan Panorama Hotel,** 207 Ha-Nassi Blvd., has a pool open to the public daily 8am-5pm. Admission weekdays NIS25, Sat. NIS33. The **Technion Pool** (tel. 823 59 44 or 829 33 00) has a 50m pool and a sauna in addition to a few smaller pools, but the only way in is with a hefty 12-visit pass (NIS350, students NIS250). Open Sun.-Thurs. 6am-8pm, Fri. 6am-6pm.

Hospitals: Rambam, Bat Galin (tel. 854 31 11); **Benei Zion (Rothschild),** 47 Golomb St. (tel. 835 93 59); **Carmel,** 7 Michal St. (tel. 825 02 11); **Haifa Medical Center (HMC),** 15 Horev St. (tel. 830 52 22).

Pharmacies: Shomron, 44 Yafo St. (tel. 852 41 71), downtown; open Sun.-Thurs. 7am-4pm, Fri. 7am-2pm. **Ha-Halutz,** 12 Ha-Halutz St. (tel. 866 29 62), in Hadar; open Sun.-Thurs. 8am-1pm and 4-7pm, Fri. 8am-1pm. **Merkaz,** 130 Ha-Nassi Blvd. (tel. 838 19 79), in Carmel Center; open Sun.-Thurs. 8am-7pm, Fri. 8am-2pm.

Emergency: First Aid: 6 Yitzhak Sadeh St. (tel. 101). **Emotional First Aid** (tel. 867 22 22), open 24hr. English spoken. **Police:** 28 Yafo Rd. (tel. 100). **Fire:** tel. 102.

Post Office: (tel. 864 09 17). Shabtai Levi and Ha-Nevi'im St. in Hadar. Open Sun.-Thurs. 8am-7pm, Fri. 8am-1:30pm. Other branches at 152 Jaffa Rd. on corner of Sha'ar Palmer; 19 Ha-Palyam Blvd. near port; 63 Herzl St. in Hadar; and 7 Wedgewood Blvd. in Carmel. Most branches open Sun.-Thurs. 7am-7pm, Fri. 7am-noon. **Poste Restante** at Ha-Palyam branch only (tel. 830 41 58).

Telephone Code: 04.

ACCOMMODATIONS

Slim pickings. Haifa is short on budget hotels, and its youth hostels and campsites, while close to the sea, are far from the city center. The Hadar district is a good place to stay in town, but it's not terribly cheap. Christian hospices offer immaculate premises and decent prices, but their strictly enforced curfews eliminate any chance of enjoying Haifa's nightlife.

Carmel Youth Hostel (HI) (tel. 853 19 44; fax 853 25 16), 4km south of the city at Hof Ha-Carmel (Carmel beach). Beautiful view of the Mediterranean, but far from the center of town. Bus #30 *alef* goes past the hostel; ask the driver to stop. Buses #43, 44, and 45 run more frequently but drop you off on the main road; ask to be dropped off at the Sports and Recreation Center. Cross Ha-Hagana St. toward the gas station on Flieman St. and turn left just past it. Follow the road as it curves uphill and to the right. A new guest house should be completed by early 1998. Dorm beds (6 per room, no A/C) US$16.50/NIS58. Beds in a room with A/C, toilet, and showers US$18/NIS67. Under 18, US$15 (US$16 with A/C). 10% discount for

HI members. Breakfast included; lunch and dinner US$8/NIS29 each, under 18 US$7; Sat. US$9.50, under 18 US$8.50. Lockers NIS5 per day. If you arrive before 7am or after 11pm, call ahead to make sure a key will be left at reception.

Saint Charles Hospice, 105 Jaffa Rd. (tel. 855 37 05), 2 blocks off Ben-Gurion St.; look for the green gate. Primarily a convent, but welcomes tourists. Newly renovated, large rooms with high ceilings and single beds. Terrace overlooking garden with a view of the Carmel slopes. Kitchen facilities. Check-out 9am. Lockout and curfew 10pm (strictly enforced). Dorm beds (3-4 per room) US$18; singles US$27; doubles US$48. Bath in the hall. Breakfast included.

Bethel Hostel, 40 Ha-Geffen St. (tel. 852 11 10), west of Ben-Gurion St. Take bus #22 from central bus station to Ben-Gurion St. near Ha-Geffen, or walk 15-20min. up Rothschild Blvd., following the curve to the left onto Ha-Baron Hirsch, which becomes Ha-Geffen. Originally an orphanage founded by an ex-rabbi, this sparklingly clean hostel is now run by volunteers who distribute Christian religious pamphlets (*Knowing God Personally, The Homosexual Struggle*). New arrivals may leave bags in locked storage and return in the evening to register. Check-in Sat.-Thurs. 5-10pm, Fri. 4-9pm. Strict 11pm curfew, lockout 9am-5pm. Dorm beds (8-12 per single-sex room) US$12 or NIS41, all with fans. Bath in hall. On weekends in summer, snack bar open for breakfast (cornflakes NIS3.50). Free *Shabbat* dinner Fri. No smoking. Under 35 only; under 18 must be accompanied by an adult.

Nesher Hotel, 53 Herzl St. (tel. 862 06 44; fax 862 73 05), near Ḥayim St. intersection, above Mercantile Discount Bank. Simple hotel in the heart of Hadar, with 15 rooms, a small roof balcony, and a TV lounge. Reception open 8am-midnight. Check-out noon. Curfew midnight. Some rooms have A/C, others have fans. Most rooms have private showers (no toilets) but all cost the same. Singles US$27; doubles US$45; triples US$55; quads US$65. Breakfast included.

Eden Hotel, 8 Shmaryahu-Levin St. (tel. 866 48 16 or 85 93), on the corner of Ha-Ḥalutz St. Basic hotel with a TV lounge, mostly German tourists. 20 rooms, most with A/C, toilet, and showers. Reception 24hr. Check-out by 1pm. Get a room with a view of Carmel. Singles US$30; doubles (one double bed) US$45; triples US$50.

Talpiyot, 61 Herzl St. (tel. 867 37 53), where Arlozorov branches off. No frills and on a busy street. Nice sea breeze, helpful owner. TV lounge with balcony. Fans in all rooms; some have private bath for the same price. 24hr. reception. Check-out 11am. No curfew or lockout. Singles NIS120; doubles NIS150; triples NIS180.

Aliya Hotel, Ha-Ḥalutz St. (tel. 862 39 18), up the side steps. Plain, but located in the heart of Hadar, near the open-air market. 24hr. reception. Check-out noon. No lockout or curfew. Singles NIS80; doubles NIS120; triples NIS150; quads NIS160; quints NIS200.

FOOD

Downtown, follow **Yafo St.** from the central bus station toward the port and you'll walk past a dozen different *shawerma* and falafel shops. Allenby Street, between Ha-Tzionut St. and Ben-Gurion Blvd., is crammed with cheap Arabic food restaurants. In Hadar, the quantity of Middle Eastern fast food along Ha-Ḥalutz St. has prompted locals to call it **"Falafel St."** Nevi'im St., a few blocks away, is progressing along the same trend. The **Nordau Midraḥov** (pedestrian section) is dotted with slightly more expensive open-air cafes. In Carmel Center you'll find plenty of cafes along Ha-Nassi Blvd. and Yefeh Nof St. The area around the Gan Ha-Eim Carmelit stop is especially packed, with a McDonald's and several popular cafes. Sweet teeth can be indulged on the lower, even-numbered end of Herzl Street, where the heady fragrance of fresh *burekas* and *baklava* wafts from a strip of bakeries.

There is an inexpensive **fruit and vegetable market** just west of the Kikkar Paris station between Naḥum and Nathan St. Walking east on Nathan, the shop at #777 sells cow spleen at NIS13; you'll go nuts over the **ox testicles** at a mere NIS7. Another **shuk** lies one block down from Ha-Ḥalutz St. Haifans come here for clothes, groceries, and wine. The best deals are toward the center of the market.

Downtown

Iraqi Shishkebab, 59 Ben-Gurion St. (tel. 852 75 76), corner of Ha-Geffen St. *Shish-lik, kebab, sambusa,* and other Middle Eastern dishes attract locals. Two skewers and salad in pita NIS19.50, meat pastries NIS6. Open Sun.-Thurs. 12:30-11:30pm.

Avraham, King of Falafel, 34 Allenby St. (tel. 852 50 29), at Ha-Tzionut St. Sign in Hebrew only, but look for the yellow crowns and Pepsi cans next to the name. Haifans crowd around this 52-year-old falafel stand, a local favorite and probably the oldest in the Holy Land. Falafel NIS8, NIS7 for students. Everything you could want in a salad bar. Open daily 7am-midnight, Sat. sundown-midnight.

Jacko, 12 Ha-Dekalim St. (tel. 866 88 13), near the Kikkar Paris Carmelit station and past the *shuk.* Owner is a former fisherman who still gets fresh seafood daily. Excellent calamari, sea bass, and sesame-seed shrimp. Entrees NIS20-40. Open Sun.-Fri. noon-11pm, Sat. noon-6pm.

Taiwan, 59 Ben-Gurion St. (tel. 852 00 88 or 853 20 82). Next to the Iraqi Shishke-bab. If there is a machine somewhere that cranks out generic Chinese restaurants, Taiwan is definitely one of its products. Over-the-top red and pink decor, soft muzak, and sweet Szechuan standards. Meat dishes NIS35-50, vegetarian slightly cheaper. Open daily noon-3pm and 7pm-midnight. Credit cards accepted.

Ma'ayan Ha-Bira, 4 Nathanson St. (tel. 862 31 93). The "Beer Fountain" (as the name reads in Hebrew) serves its namesake on tap (NIS9 for 0.5L), but this unpretentious diner's claim to fame is its excellent home-smoked meats. Spareribs or hot pastrami NIS24. Open Sun.-Fri. 9am-5pm. Credit cards accepted.

Zahava, 28 Yafo Rd. (tel. 866 60 20). Homemade meals NIS23-25. Main meat dishes (*schnitzels, kebabs,* etc.) come with salads, bread, and either chips, rice, or veg-gies. Massive plates of couscous served on Mon., Thurs., and sometimes Tues. Open Sun.-Thurs. 7am-5pm. Kosher.

Abu Hani Falafel, 6 Eliyah St., straight ahead as you exit the Carmelit subway. Locals swear by the taste and freshness of Abu Hani's amazingly cheap chow. Falafel NIS6, *shawerma* NIS10.

Hadar

Tzimzhonit Hayim, 30 Herzl St. (tel. 867 46 67). A vegetarian restaurant founded in the 1930s. Offers tasty Eastern European favorites including *kreplach* at NIS8, sweet or savory blintzes at NIS10-12, salad from NIS8 and fish from NIS9. Portions are small but come with hearty bread. Open Sun.-Thurs. 9am-8pm, Fri. 9am-1pm.

Kosher Veta'im, 40 Herzl St. (tel. 864 59 76), near Hayim St. Elbow your way into this self-service kosher restaurant crowded with hungry locals. Large portions of *schnitzel* or beef with sides for NIS14. Soups, salads, and desserts for NIS4. Comfy and clean dining area. Open Sun.-Thurs. 10am-6pm, Fri. 10am-3pm.

Hamber, 61 Herzl St. (tel. 866 67 39), on the corner of Arlozorov St. Standard cafe, specializing in kosher meat with salads at NIS18. Open Sun.-Thurs. 8am-7pm, Fri. 8am-3:30pm.

Beneinu, 49 Hillel St. (tel. 852 41 55). No sign; look for the canvas awning and earth-toned facade. *Beneinu* means "between us" in Hebrew, and this predominately gay cafe/bar is as intimate as its name implies. Relaxed and chatty during the day, lively and sophisticated at night. The quiche is tasty (NIS22), and served with a fresh salad and a hunk of creamy cheese. Beer NIS10-14. Open Sun.-Thurs. 10am-12:30am, Fri. 10am-6pm, Sat. 6:30pm-1:30am. Reserve in advance for parties of 4 or more. Credit cards accepted.

Carmel Center

Casa Italiana, 119 Ha-Nassi Blvd. (tel. 838 13 36), next to McDonald's. Homey place run by the same family for 30 years. A favorite among Knesset members and celeb-rities—just ask to see the guest books. Pasta from NIS22.90, homemade minestrone NIS11.90, pizza NIS19.90. Open Sat.-Thurs. 5-11pm. Credit cards accepted.

Middle East Food Restaurant, 115 Ha-Nassi Blvd. (tel. 838 76 47). Mouth-watering *shishlik* and *shawerma* (NIS12) lure American and British sailors, who leave graf-fiti, hats, photos, and the very shirts off their backs here. Find out when the next ship is coming in and join the raucous crowds for beer (NIS9) and shots (NIS10).

ISRAEL

Jackie's Place, 1 Wedgewood Blvd. (tel. 838 26 86). Homemade kosher cuisine with self-service and friendly staff. Nothing special but good, cheap food (no small find for Carmel Center). Meat sandwiches NIS10, hot meals with two side dishes NIS15. Also soups and salads; takeout available. Open Sun.-Thurs. 7am-7pm, Fri. 7am-4pm. Kosher. Credit cards accepted.

WALKS

Haifa's triple-tiered design makes it an unlikely locale for extended travel on foot. However, taking a bus to the top of Carmel and working one's way down through the city is a feasible (albeit circuitous) way of seeing each district's varied attractions. For more in-depth explorations of the heart of Haifa, the tourist offices provide a map criss-crossed with four **walking tours,** each of which is supposedly 1000 steps. On Saturdays, the **Haifa Municipal Tourist Office** gives free, guided versions of the tours (2[hr.; meet at 10am at corner of Yefeh Nof and Sha'ar Ha-Levanon St. and dress modestly for stops at Baha'i holy places).

Beautiful flora and fauna can be found on a stroll through the quiet, shrub-lined walkways of **Gan Ha-Eim** (Mother's Park). The **Municipal Zoo** in Gan Ha-Eim (tel. 837 23 90 or 28 86), across from the Carmelit steps, houses a moderate number of beasts from the Levant and beyond (open Sun.-Thurs. 8am-6pm, Fri. 8am-2pm, Sat. 9am-5pm; NIS20, students NIS18). The zoo also contains three mediocre museums (see **Museums,** p. 359). Wildlife without fencing or bars can be found at **Mount Carmel National Park,** the biggest park in Israel (15min. by bus #24, 37, or 192 from Gan Ha-eim). An **SPNI nature trail** begins in Gan Ha-Eim to the right of the shell-shaped stage. Following the blue signs will lead you on a two kilometer foray around the zoo, through tangled greenery into a *wadi* in lower Carmel (buses #3 or 5 will get you back uptown).

SIGHTS

Various lookouts throughout the city provide breathtaking panoramic views. Most accessible is the breezy **Louis Promenade** on Yefeh Nof St. in Carmel Center, which commands stunning views of the Upper Galilee, Lebanon, and even snowy Mt. Hermon on clear days. The **observatory** (open Sun.-Thurs. 8am-4pm) on the 30th floor of Haifa University's **Eshkol Tower** is nestled farther up in the clouds and, accordingly, offers broader but hazier views. The tower itself crowns the vast, flat main building which serves as the center of student activities. After hours, go all the way to the edge of the huge slab at the foot of the tower (above the bus stops) for less commanding views of the city below. The rest of the concrete campus is hardly remarkable, but it boasts a larger percentage of Arab students than any of Israel's other universities (free student-guided tours Sun.-Thurs. 10am-noon, starting from the main building). Buses #24, 37, and 31 run to the university.

University buffs can also check out the **Technion,** Israel's internationally acclaimed institute of technology. In the mid-80s, the last department (architecture) moved out of Technion's original building off Balfour St. (now the site of the Museum of Science; see **Museums,** p. 360) and nestled into its current location on the wooded slope below Haifa University. The **Coler Visitors Center** (tel. 832 06 68 or 64) has English-language newsletters and computerized displays describing the institution's history from its inception in 1913 to the present (open Sun.-Thurs. 8am-3:30pm; free). Take bus #17 from downtown, #31 from Carmel Center, or #19 from the central bus station or Herzl St. to Kiryat Ha-Technion.

Despite Haifa's mostly modern, secular attitude, the city boasts some beautiful religious sites whose significance long predates the establishment of the State of Israel. Haifa's main attraction is the golden-domed **Baha'i Temple** (tel. 835 83 58), halfway up Mt. Carmel on Ha-Tzionut Ave. New landscaping scheduled for completion in a few years has left a bald patch on the slope. A large section remains intact, however, and is open to visitors. The shrine commemorates the Persian Sayyid Ali Muhammad (Al Bab), the first Baha'i prophet, and was built on the exact spot where Baha'u'llah, the religion's founder, pitched his tent following his exile from Persia to Akko (see **Religion,** p. 61). Al Bab's bones, brought to Haifa in 1809, now rest next to the shrine. Modest dress is required. To reach the temple, take bus #22 from the central bus station or bus #23, 25, 26, or 32 from Ha-Nevi'im and Herzl St. For a stunning view of the entire grounds, stand at the intersection of Ben Gurion and Ha-Geffen St. and look up; the stairs are closed until the landscaping is completed (open 9am-noon, but call in advance to make sure; gardens open daily 8am-5pm; free). Other Baha'i buildings are scattered around the grounds, but are not open to the public. The marble **Universal House of Justice** is the center of international Baha'i operations. Near the shrine, opposite 135 Ha-Tzion St., is a non-Baha'i **sculpture garden** with striking bronzes by Ursula Malbin (open 24hr.; free).

Buses #25, 26, and 31 climb Mt. Carmel to the monastery of the **Carmelite Order,** which stands on a promontory over Haifa Bay (get off at the Seminar Gordon stop). A more expensive and scenic way to get to the monastery is via the Rakbal cable car (see **Transportation,** p. 352). A Latin monk named Berthold founded the order in 1150. Napoleon's siege of Akko in 1799 forced the Discalced ("barefoot") Carmelite Order to move to their current location. The monks currently live in a relatively new church and monastery complex called **Stella Maris** (Star of the Sea; tel. 833 77 58), built in 1836 on the ruins of an ancient Byzantine chapel and a medieval Greek church. The church's dome is crowned by paintings of Elijah flying in his chariot of fire, King David plucking his harp, and scenes of the Holy Family. An exquisite statuette of the Virgin Mary (with whom the order is associated) cradling the baby Jesus stands inside. Knees and shoulders must be covered (open daily 8:30am-1:30pm and 3-6pm). Inside the Carmelite monastery is a small museum containing fragments of former Mt. Carmel cloisters dating from the Byzantine and Crusader periods which look just like pint-size rocks to the untrained eye (hours same as the monastery; free). Because of the Carmelites' affinity for Elijah (St. Elias), the Feast of St. Elias (July 20) is a great time to visit. In the days preceding the Feast, Christian Arabs set up booths with food and games, and a carnival atmosphere takes over the complex.

Just across from the monastery entrance, an inconspicuous trail leads to the shrine at **Elijah's Cave,** 230 Allenby St. (tel. 852 74 30). Three of the world's major faiths revere these sacred grounds. According to the Bible, the caves at the base of Mount Carmel sheltered Elijah from the wrath of King Ahab and Queen Jezebel, who were more than a bit peeved at the prophet's drastic attempt to win the hearts of northern Israelites from Ba'al in the 9th century BCE (I Kings 18). Muslims revere Elijah as Al-Khadar, the "green prophet" of the same-colored mountains; Jews believe he will return as the harbinger of the Messiah; and Christians hold that the caves safeguarded the Holy Family upon their return from Egypt. Adherents of each religion now pray quietly in the dim light. Modest dress is required. If you don't want to part with your pocket change, decline offers to be blessed by religious (and not so religious) worshippers. On *Shabbat,* bus #45 runs to Edmund Fley St. near the Carmelite Monastery above the cave. Approaching from below, the stairs leading to the cave's entrance are just across the street from the naval museum (cave open daily 8am-5:45pm; free).

MUSEUMS

Haifa is no Tel Aviv when it comes to museums, but there are several worth visiting. The **Haifa Museum** is composed of three separately located buildings, with each on a different level of the city. (All 3 open Sun.-Mon. and Wed.-Thurs. 10am-5pm, Tue. 4pm-8pm, Fri. and holidays 10am-1pm, Sat. 10am-2pm. Admission for all 3 NIS15, children 5-18 years old and students NIS12, seniors NIS7.50.) Three mediocre museums within the municipal zoo, the **Biological Museum,** the **Natural History Museum,** and the **M. Stekelis Museum of Prehistory,** merit a quick look only if you're already in the zoo. (All open Sun.-Thurs. 8am-3pm, Fri. 8am-1pm, Sat. 10am-2pm. Admission to zoo includes Biological Museum; others NIS3 each.)

Museum of Art, 26 Shabtai Levi St. (tel. 852 32 55), in the Hadar district; bus #10, 12, 21, or 28. Exhibiting works from all over the world, this branch of the Haifa

Museum prides itself on its collection of 20th-century graphics and contemporary Israeli paintings, sculptures, crafts, and photography.

Tikotin Museum of Japanese Art, 89 Ha-Nassi Blvd (tel. 838 35 54, 837 44 97), in Carmel Center between the Nof Hotel and the Dan Carmel Hotel; bus #21-23, 27, 30 or 31. In keeping with the Japanese tradition of displaying beautiful objects in harmony with the season, this branch of the Haifa Museum changes exhibits frequently. *Shoji*, sliding partitions made of wood and paper, soften the sunlight and make for delightful browsing.

National Maritime Museum, 198 Allenby Rd. (tel. 853 66 22), right opposite Elijah's Cave. The lowest branch of the Haifa Museum (in altitude, not quality); bus #3, 5, or 43-45. The exhibits span 5000 years and 11 different types of maritime history. The sections with the most appeal to the average landlubber are the intricately detailed ship models, the marine mythology collection (including beautiful statuettes of Eros and other deities), and the Department of Marine Ethnology.

Clandestine Immigration and Naval Museum, 204 Allenby Rd. (tel. 853 62 49), next to the National Maritime Museum and opposite the lower cable car station; bus #43 or 44. This well-researched museum is devoted to *Ha-Apala*, the story of the immigrants who were smuggled into Palestine during the British Mandate. Impressive displays on Jewish underground movements and a recreation of a Cyprus deportation camp sit alongside a somewhat incongruous exhibit of weapons, medals, and other Israeli Navy memorabilia. Perched atop the museum is the *Af-Al-Pi-Khen* (In Spite Of Everything), an old immigrant ship. Open Sun.-Thurs. 8:30am-4pm. NIS6, NIS3 for students or children.

Mané Katz Art Museum, 89 Yefeh Nof St. (tel. 838 34 82), in the heart of Carmel Center just behind Panorama Center. Displays sculptures and canvases by Mané Katz, a member of the Paris group of Jewish Expressionists that included Modigliani, Chagall, and Cremegne. Open Sun.-Mon. and Wed.-Thurs. 10am-4pm, Tues. 2-6pm, Fri. 10am-1pm, Sat. 10am-2pm. Free.

Reuben and Edith Hecht Museum (tel. 825 77 73 or 824 05 77), in the main building of Haifa University. Houses an exhibit called *The People of Israel in the Land of Israel,* a magnificent collection of archaeological finds from the university excavations. The small art wing contains some Impressionist paintings and a few others from the Jewish School of Paris. Call ahead for tour info. Open Sun.-Thurs. 10am-4pm, Fri. 10am-1pm, Sat. 10am-2pm. Free.

National Museum of Science, Planning, and Technology, on Balfour St. uphill from Herzl St., marked by a red-and-white sign. Bus #12, 21, 28, or 37. Housed in the old Technion building, this small museum boasts over 200 hands-on stations demonstrating various advances in technological history, from telecommunications to architecture. The Youth Wing's labs are ideal for children aged 7-12 (and for older visitors who wish they had paid more attention in high school physics). Open Sun-Mon. and Wed.-Thurs. 9am-5pm, Tues. 9am-7pm, Sat. 10am-3pm. Admission NIS20, students NIS10.

ENTERTAINMENT

Haifa is a great place to sun-worship without the meat-market atmosphere of Tel-Aviv's seaside scene. Although free beaches sprawl all along the northern coast, the best lie just outside of the city in **Dor** and **Atlit,** both accessible by bus #921. Within Haifa, **Hof Ha-Carmel** and **Hof Dado** are most pleasant (bus #44 or 45). **Hof Bat Galim,** near the central bus station, is packed on the weekends and a popular surf site on weekdays. Visitors can get in on the action at the **Shefahit Windsurfing Center** in the small white building next to the cable car station, where sailboards are rented by the hour and snorkeling and scuba gear by the day.

When asked about the city's sparse entertainment, Haifa's first mayor pointed to the city's factories and said, "There is our nightlife." Although today's Haifa is not exactly a bastion of Bacchanalia, times have changed since that sobering statement. The **Haifa Blues Festival,** held at the port, will be in full effect at the end of July 1998. Ray Charles once performed at this annual mob scene, but the main events are more often pop than blues (tickets NIS150 per night). **Downtown** hosts the most popular dance floors. Discos cluster around the Ha-Azmaut St. area, most notably **Amsterdam,** which hosts a raging party every Monday night after 11pm. **Maximus** trips out on weekends with techno, trance, and ambient tunes. Dancers who need a relaxing break from rump-shaking stop in nearby **Babzula,** a Dahab-style hangout with a pillow strewn floor and a selection of *argeileh* pipes. Alternatively, **The Jazz Café,** in an alley on the left side of Ha-Yam St. (near the corner of Ha-Nassi Blvd.), provides a classy musical interlude in Carmel Center, which is generally a good place to start your evening. The following list of clubs and pubs, most in Carmel Center, should start you off on the right foot.

Bear Pub, 135 Ha-Nassi Blvd. Arrive before 11:30pm or it may be too crowded to partake of the Bear's enormous bar and tasty menu (most salads and sandwiches NIS22-26; watch for the occasional *crème brulée* special).

Little Haifa, 4 Sha'ar Ha-Levanon St., between Ha-Nassi and Yefeh Nof St. The oldest pub in the area, with a raucous decibel level to match its age. Open from 8:30pm until the last customer passes out.

Camel Café, down the coast on the Ḥof Ha-Carmel. Almost every customer has a delicious fruit shake and a navel ring.

Rosencrantz, in the theater building on Joseph St. A must-see, popular with the easygoing, 20-something set. Shines on weekends, when it hosts small plays and excellent live music.

Ha-Olan Hazeh, off the Nordau Midraḥov in Hadar, near Hayim St. Locals and tourists alike cram shoulder-to-shoulder on weekends and chill out with cocktails and yummy toasts on laid-back weeknights. Open 2pm-2am.

Greg's, off Ha-Nassi Blvd. Ex-New Yorker Greg serves pricey but delicious cups of joe and steaming variations thereof. A great place to stumble when your knees start knocking after a long night.

■ Near Haifa

ISFIYA & DALIYAT AL KARMEL עוספיה ודלית אל-כרמל

Isfiya and Daliyat Al Karmel are all that remain of 14 Druze villages that once prospered on the Carmel. In 1830, a rebellion against the Egyptian *pasha* was crushed and the villages were destroyed. Thirty years later, the Turks welcomed Druze back to Isfiya and Daliyat, hoping that the towns would serve as buffers against Bedouin marauders and Christian missionaries. Today, some 17,000 Druze make their homes here. Religious Druze elders are recognizable by their thick mustaches, baggy pants, and flowing white headdresses. Observant Druze women wear dark robes and white shawls despite the sweltering sun (for more information see **Religion,** p. 61). A large portion of the population is secular. Unlike those residing in the Golan Heights, the Druze of the Carmel acknowledge their Israeli citizenship and send their sons to the army. The Druze are also known for being extremely congenial, even while engaging in the usually less-than-charming process of bargaining.

Isfiya and Daliyat, once picturesque mountain villages, are now blemished with concrete houses. Tourists flock to **Daliyat al-Karmel** to shop in the small bazaar on the main road. The bazaar is busiest on Saturdays, but weekdays are more conducive to low prices and conversation with locals. The recent increase in tourism has raised the kitsch factor in most of the bazaar. With rare exception, each store sells the same selection of enamel pottery, water pipes, jewelry, and wall hangings, and much of the merchandise is actually imported from India or made in Gaza. Wheat stalk baskets are one of the few items still made locally. In a back room of the bazaar's **Mifqash Ha-Akhim Restaurant** is the **Druze Heritage House** (tel. (04) 839 32 42 or 31 69; admission NIS7), filled with artifacts and explanations of all things Druze. Ask the restaurant owner to let you take a peek. The house will also host a group of 30 or more for a lecture about the Druze people followed by tea and baklava (NIS15). Call ahead to ask Sheikh Fadel Nasser ad-Din if you can join.

ISRAEL

The Zionist and Christian mystic **Sir Lawrence Oliphant** was one of few outsiders close to the Druze sect. In the late 19th century, he and his wife lived in Daliyat for five years, helping the Druze build their homes. Since 1980, the Israeli Defense Ministry has been restoring Oliphant's house on the outskirts of town. It is now a memorial to the scores of Druze soldiers killed in Israel's wars. Although street names are not used, anyone can direct you to **Beit Oliphant,** the stone building next to the dome. Sir Lawrence sheltered Arab and Jewish insurgents against the British in a cave between the sculpture garden in the rear and the main house. Oliphant's secretary, the Hebrew poet **Naftali Hertz Imber,** later wrote the words to "Ha-Tikva" (The Hope), Israel's national anthem, at this site. The memorial is less than spectacular, but it is dear to Daliyat's Druze.

Four kilometers from Daliyat Al Karmel is the site where Elijah massacred 450 priests of Ba'al (1 Kings 18:40), a god that had been enjoying new popularity because of a harsh drought. **Muhraqa,** the Arabic name, refers to the burnt sacrifice that the prophet offered God on an altar here. Pleased with the Israelites' renewed faith, God sent rain clouds that relieved the land's drought. The Carmelites later interpreted the clouds as symbols of the Virgin Mary, to whom their order is devoted. In 1886 they built a small **monastery** here. A short flight of stairs leads to the roof and magnificent views; on a clear day you may even catch sight of snow-capped Mt. Ḥermon (monastery open Mon.-Sat. 8am-1:30pm and 2:30-5pm, Sun. 8am-1:30pm; admission to the rooftop viewing area NIS1). There is no bus service to the monastery; you'll have to call a taxi (NIS10-12). If you're walking from Daliyat (not advisable), bear left at the only fork along the way or you'll head toward Elyakim.

Although Daliyat is by far the more touristed—and interesting—of the Druze villages, a visit to **Isfiya** might provide a more authentic glimpse of Druze life. Isfiya's only accommodation/attraction is the excellent **Stella Carmel Hospice** (tel. (04) 839 16 92; fax 839 02 33), run by the Anglican Church and open to all. A converted Arab villa, the hospice has a small, quiet library and a lounge filled with antique Persian rugs. Ask the bus driver to let you off on the main road just outside Isfiya. The hospice is marked by a small, tree-shaded sign and is located up the hill on the right side of the road opposite the PAZ gas station. There's an annex of double rooms with private baths, but unmarried couples may not share the same room. The hospice fills up, so call ahead (flexible check-out 10am, curfew 10:30pm; dorm rooms outside main house US$12; bed in 2-bed room in main house US$22.50; annex beds US$28). The hospice organizes occasional **walking tours** to the site for pilgrims. The most eventful day at Muhraqa is the Feast of St. Elias (Elijah) on July 20, when Christian Arabs celebrate in the park surrounding the monastery.

The Druze villages can be visited as a day trip from Haifa. Bus #192 (30min., NIS11.50) leaves infrequently from the central bus station, stopping first in Isfiya and then continuing along the main road to Daliyat. You can also catch a *sherut* on Eliyahu Ha-Navi St. off Ha-Atzma'ut St. (NIS8 to Isfiya, NIS11 to Daliyat) and wait by the Egged bus stop to get one back. The last bus leaves Daliyat at 2:10pm, but *sherut* taxis run and stores stay open until about 8pm.

Riding along the mountain road to the Druze villages might get your hiking hormones flowing, and rightfully so: the ridges and forests of the **Carmel mountains** spread dramatically into the Yizre'el valley to the southeast and the Mediterranean to the west. SPNI carries detailed trail maps, but ideal picnic spots are often just a few steps from the main road (see **Practical Information,** p. 352).

BEIT SHE'ARIM בית שערים

Nineteen centuries ago, Beit She'arim was the center of Jewish life, and the subterranean graveyard housing the rich and famous of ancient Israel proves it. Following the Romans' destruction of Jerusalem in 70 CE, Judaism's hub shifted to the Galilee, and Beit She'arim became a prominent Jewish city. Once it served as the gathering place for the Sanhedrin, recognized by the Roman Empire in the 2nd century CE as the Supreme Rabbinical Council and judicial authority over all of the world's Jews. Two hundred years later, when Jews were barred from Jerusalem's Mount of Olives cemetery, Beit She'arim became the site of a sacred Jewish burial ground. Since 1936, archaeologists have unearthed a labyrinth of some 20 caves whose walls are lined with dozens of intricately adorned sarcophagi. According to inscriptions found on the sarcophagi, many of the buried were brought from as far away as Sidon, Tyre, Babylon, or southern Arabia. Rabbi Yehuda Ha-Nassi, patriarch of the Sanhedrin, compiled the *Mishnah* in Beit She'arim (see also **Literature,** p. 275) and is among those buried in the catacombs. Two of these fascinating caves are usually open to the public, but Rabbi Yehuda's tomb has been closed due to the proliferation of graffiti. Bring your Indiana Jones bullwhip and a cool hat as you explore the dark passages and half-opened sarcophagi. One of the caves has a small museum with a display of artifacts found at Beit She'arim.

Buses don't run directly to the park; the closest you can get is the access road. Many buses from Haifa go near Beit She'arim, but bus #301 (every 20min., 20min., NIS9.50) is the most convenient. Ask the driver to let you off at the Beit She'arim archaeological site, not the *moshav*. From the bus stop, turn right and head down Izrael St. Turn right at the fork after a 20-minute walk and pass the unimpressive ruins of an ancient synagogue and olive press. The steep road uphill on the left leads to a statue of Alexander Zaid, an early Jewish settler, and the foundations of an ancient basilica. Continue down the road to reach the entrance to the catacombs (site tel. (04) 983 16 43; open Sat.-Thurs. 8am-5pm, Fri. 8am-4pm; closes 1hr. earlier in winter; NIS12, students NIS9).

EIN HOD עין הוד

Ein Hod's perch upon the western slopes of Mt. Carmel, 14km south of Haifa, must be conducive to artistic inspiration. Within tiny, scenic Ein Hod (meaning "Spring of Grandeur" or "Spring of Garden Rows"), artists create everything from needle crafts to abstract paintings. Bronze statues grace backyards, mobiles swing between trees, and stone figures recline lazily against fences.

Ein Hod has been a place to escape the drudgery of the work world ever since its establishment as a resort town for weary Crusaders stationed in nearby **Atlit.** Ein Hod's Arab inhabitants fled their homes in the face of Israeli military threats during the war of 1948. In 1953, the deserted village was transformed into an artists' colony by Marcel Janco, one of the founding fathers of the Dadaist artistic movement.

Workshops in glass blowing, pottery, and other crafts are offered on Saturdays, but no buses run at that time, and only residents can park their cars in the village (visitors can park in the lot up the hill). Groups can call to arrange workshops (tel. (04) 984 27 02; ask for Mara), and solo travelers can easily find one by following the signs around town. The **Main Artists' Gallery** (free), the largest gallery in Israel, displays the work of resident artists (currently numbering 150). Exhibits change every three months. The **Janco-Dada Museum** (tel. (04) 984 23 50) features shows by contemporary Israeli Dadaist artists, a permanent display of Janco's work, and a film explaining the Dada movement's origins (NIS8, students NIS4). The Main Gallery, the museum, and the **Art and Wear Gallery** (free) form the nucleus of town (all three open Sat.-Thurs. 9:30am-5pm, Fri. 9:30am-4pm). In summer, Friday evening concerts ranging from rock to classical music are held at the small amphitheater (tel. (04) 984 20 29 or check local newspapers for listings). No transportation is available after the shows. The **Ein Hod Restaurant** (tel. (04) 984 20 16), has a classy interior and a breezy terrace. Most main courses are around NIS25-35 (open Sat.-Thurs. 10am-midnight, Fri. 10am-2am).

To get to Ein Hod, take bus #921 from Haifa, which heads south along the old Haifa-Hadera road (20min., NIS8.30). From the Ein Hod junction where the bus lets you off, the town is a 2km walk (20min. uphill, excellent view). To get to the center of town, turn right at the colorful sign and then right again at the fork.

■ Akko (Acre) عكا עכו

The Old City of Akko, surrounded on three sides by the Mediterranean, gazes across the bay at Haifa's crowded skyline, but the city's stone fortresses, winding alleyways, and underground Crusader city lend it a character far removed from its modern coastal neighbor. Dominated by the emerald-domed 18th-century **Mosque of Al-Jazzar,** Akko (Akka in Arabic, historically written "Acre" in English) feels mesmerizingly ancient. Visitors can stroll through the fragrant maze of the *souq* or escape to the city's South Promenade and tilt back a Tuborg in a breezy little cafe while watching small fishing boats scuttle by.

Each contending army that washed over Akko left behind tell-tale architectural jetsam. The Canaanite city-state of Akko is first mentioned in Egyptian documents dating as early as the 19th century BCE. Akko was conquered by Egyptians, Persians, Greeks, Romans, Umayyads, and finally Crusaders, who came to the city in 1104 on their campaign to recapture the Holy Land for Christianity. After losing control of Jerusalem in 1187, they retreated to Akko, transforming it into the greatest port of their empire and a world-class showpiece of culture and architecture. The Mamluks ended Crusader rule in 1291, and almost 500 years later the Druze prince Fakhr ad-Din rebuilt the city. The Muslims couldn't disassemble the Crusader network of tunnels and basements, and opted to leave the subterranean labyrinth for wide-eyed tourists, building their city directly over it. Fakhr ad-Din's work was continued by Tahir al-Omar, who was murdered and succeeded in 1775 by Ahmed Jazzar, an Ottoman *pasha* of Bosnian extraction. Napoleon later claimed that had Akko fallen to him, "the world would have been mine." Unfortunately for him, his 1799 siege failed. After a stint under the Egyptian Ibrahim Pasha (1833-1840), control of Akko returned to the Ottomans. When the British captured the port in 1918, it was a predominantly Arab town of 8000. Members of Zionist groups employing terrorist tactics against the British were held captive in the Citadel during World War II.

One of the best ways of getting to know a city is to talk to its inhabitants, and Akko is no exception. Many locals are more than happy to share thoughts on their home and their lives. However, women traveling alone are strongly advised to be cautious of the many would-be guides in the Old City. While some of these men genuinely want to be helpful, many can cause a highly uncomfortable situation. All solo travelers are advised to avoid the alleys of Old Akko after dark; stick to the well-lit, crowded Promenade for a safer stroll.

ORIENTATION AND PRACTICAL INFORMATION

In New Akko, Ben-Ami and Herzl St. run from the central bus station to **Hayim Weizmann St.,** which continues on to the old city. **Ha-Atzma'ut St.** is the new city's major thoroughfare, home to the main post office and city hall. Once in Old Akko, visitors will likely be dismayed by the lack of street signs—locals and monuments make the best navigational tools. **Ha-Hagana St.** runs down the entire western side of the peninsula while **Al-Jazzar** and **Salah al-Din St.** extend in opposite directions from the end of Weizmann in the old city's northern region. The coast of the Pisan Harbor to the south is lined by touristy restaurants, a pleasant **promenade,** and sitting areas with great bay views.

Municipal Tourist Information Office (MTIO) (tel. 991 17 64), inside the Crusader City entrance on Al-Jazzar St. and across from the mosque. Sells a great map (NIS3), but Akko is small enough that wandering and relying on others' directions is seldom disastrous. Open summer Sun.-Thurs. 8am-6pm, winter 8am-4pm.

Currency Exchange: Mercantile Discount Bank, corner of Al-Jazzar and Weizmann St. Open Sun., Tues., and Thurs. 8:30am-1pm and 4-5:30pm, Mon. and Wed. 8:30am-1pm, Fri. 8:30am-noon. **Bank Leumi,** on Ben-Ami St. near Weizmann St. Don't bother standing in the "change" line on the first floor; foreign currency exchange is actually done upstairs. Open Sun., Tues., and Thurs. 8:30am-12:30pm

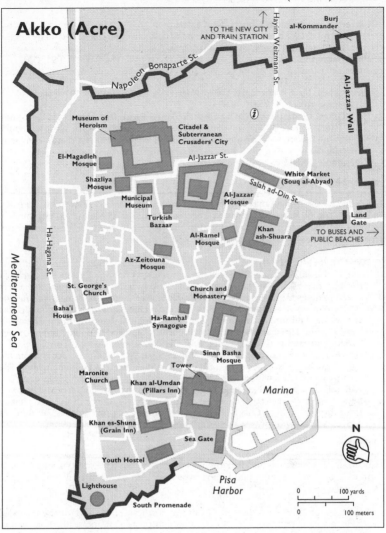

Akko (Acre)

TO THE NEW CITY AND TRAIN STATION

Hayim Weizmann St.

Burj al-Kommander

Napoleon Bonaparte St.

Al-Jazzar Wall

Museum of Heroism

Citadel & Subterranean Crusaders' City

El-Magadleh Mosque

Al-Jazzar St.

Shazliya Mosque

White Market (Souq al-Abyad)

Salah ad-Din St.

Municipal Museum

Al-Jazzar Mosque

Turkish Bazaar

Khan ash-Shuara

Al-Ramel Mosque

Ha-Hagana St.

Az-Zeitouna Mosque

Land Gate

TO BUSES AND PUBLIC BEACHES

Mediterranean Sea

St. George's Church

Church and Monastery

Baha'i House

Ha-Ramḥal Synagogue

Sinan Basha Mosque

Tower

Maronite Church

Marina

Khan al-Umdan (Pillars Inn)

Khan es-Shuna (Grain Inn)

Sea Gate

N

Youth Hostel

Lighthouse

Pisa Harbor

South Promenade

0   100 yards
0   100 meters

ISRAEL

and 4-6pm, Mon. and Wed. 8:30am-12:30pm, Fri. 8:30am-noon. Banks outside the Old City have **ATMs.**

Trains: Often the best way to get to Haifa, especially during rush hour. The station (tel. 991 23 50) is on David Remez St. across from the central bus station. To: **Haifa** (25min., NIS7.50); **Nahariya** (10min., NIS4.50); and **Tel Aviv** (2hr., NIS22). Trains run 6am-7pm every 1-2hr.

Buses: The **central bus station** (tel. 854 95 55 for information) is on Ha-Arba'a Rd. in the new city. Buses #262 and 272 (express) go to **Haifa** (45min., NIS11.50; #251 is local); bus #272 to **Nahariya** (20min., NIS5.20; #271 is local). Buses from platform #16, near the Egged restaurant, run the short distance to the **old city** (stops running at 3:30pm).

Sherut Taxis: Off Ha-Arba'a St., across from the bus station (to **Haifa,** NIS8).

Taxis: Akko Tzafon (tel. 991 66 66) or **Ariyeh** (tel. 991 33 69).

Library: Canada-Akko Library, 13 Weizmann St. (tel. 991 08 60), near the old city. Delightful A/C reading room with multilingual collection, including many English books. Open Sun.-Thurs. 9-noon and 3-7pm.

Pharmacy: At the corner of Ben-Ami and Weizmann St., **Merkaz** (tel. 991 47 02) is a true drugstore, while **Akko** (tel. 991 20 21) is more cosmetics-oriented. Both open Sun.-Thurs. 8am-1pm and 4-7pm, Fri. 8am-1pm.

Emergency: First Aid: Magen David Adom (tel. 101 or 991 23 33). **Police:** 16 Ha-Hagana St. (tel. 100 or 991 98 88).

Post Office: Central branch at 11 Ha-Atzma'ut St. **Poste Restante** open Mon.-Tues. and Thurs. 8am-12:30pm and 4-6pm, Wed. and Fri. 8am-12:30pm. Another branch in the entrance to the Crusader city next to the MTIO. Open Sun.-Thurs. 8am-3pm, Fri. 8am-noon.

Telephone Code: 04.

ACCOMMODATIONS

All of the following accommodations have heating for Akko's chilly winter. There are additional unofficial and unregulated hostels or rooms for rent in the old city, but you should get the tourist office's opinion of the place before making a decision you might regret. Beach camping is forbidden and dangerous.

Akko Youth Hostel (HI) (tel./fax 991 19 82), around the corner from the lighthouse within the old city walls. To reach the lighthouse at the tip of the peninsula, walk through the market or follow Ha-Hagana St. down the coast. A peaceful, clean haven minutes from the market and the water. The large, airy lounge with marble pillars, clusters of wicker easy chairs, and lazy ceiling fans will make you feel like you've stepped into *Casablanca*. Reception open 6:30am-10:30pm. Check-out 9am. Curfew 10:30pm. Bed in 6-8-bed dorm room US$12, nonmembers US$13. Includes kosher breakfast. Lockers NIS5. Cash or traveler's checks only.

Paul's Hostel and Souvenir Shop (tel. 991 28 57 or 981 76 86), just across from the lighthouse at the southern end of Ha-Hagana St. under a large blue awning. The only place in Akko with a real backpacker feel to it. Rooms are clean and cozy with adjacent bath and kitchen. Either Paul Elias or his brother Jerry will give you keys to the building's back entrance and the safe. 24hr. check-in and free pick-up from the bus station. Check-out noon. No curfew. Dorm beds NIS20; doubles NIS80, NIS100 with private bath. Cash only. Shop open daily 9am-9pm.

FOOD

Cheap, fresh vegetables and fish are available in the **souq**, as are dozens of exotic spices. Food stands and small **supermarkets** can be found on Ben-Ami and Yehoshafat St.

Said's, about 5min. into the *souq* from the northern end. Look for the crowded room on your right with soccer trophies and posters on the walls. Rumored to have the best hummus in Israel. NIS10 buys 3 piping hot pitas, a plate of vegetables, and a deep dish of creamy hummus doused in olive oil. Open 7am until the food runs out, usually around 2pm.

Al-Nawrus Restaurant (tel. 991 55 57), past the lighthouse on Ha-Hagana St. A bit pricey, but worth it for the spectacular sunset and the company of friendly owner Hetty and her sons. Locals and tourists come here for excellent seafood and carda-mom-scented Arabic coffee. *Argeileh* smokers puff away into the night in the cushioned, carpeted tent next door. Fish entrees from NIS35, breakfast NIS15. Open daily 11am until 2 or 3am. Credit cards accepted.

The Lighthouse Restaurant (tel. 991 76 40), under its namesake near the HI hostel. Intimate tables overlooking the water. *Kebab* or *shishlik* NIS25, hummus NIS10. Hostel patrons receive 10% discount. Open daily 1pm-2am. Credit cards accepted.

Café Tuscana (tel. 981 60 27), upstairs from the Pisan harbor. Ice cream and drinks served with a sweet view of the sea and Old Akko. Open daily 8:30am-midnight.

SIGHTS

The battlements and dungeons of **Old Akko** leave no doubt that this city was wrought with ancient conflicts. To reach the old city from the bus station by foot, walk down Ben-Ami St. to Weizmann St. and turn left. The entrance to the old city is just past Eli Cohen Park on the left. The entrance to the **Mosque of Al-Jazzar** is a short walk to your right, on Al-Jazzar St. The third-largest mosque in Israel, it dominates the city with its green dome and sleek minaret. Ahmed al-Jazzar ordered its construction in 1781 on what is believed to have been the site of San Croce, the original Christian cathedral of Akko. Inside is an attractive courtyard with Roman columns taken from Caesarea. The western end of the courtyard rests upon the cellar of a Crusader fortress. The surrounding structures are lodgings for students of the Qur'an and mosque personnel. The tower was destroyed by an earthquake in 1927, but promptly restored; the rest of the complex is in magnificent condition.

Inside, in the green cage on the marble stand, is a shrine containing a hair from the beard of the prophet Muhammad. Prayers are conducted five times per day, and you may be asked to wait if you arrive during a prayer session. Modest dress is required; scarves are available for those not already covered. To the right of the mosque is a small building containing the sarcophagi of Al-Jazzar and son; you can peek through the barred windows at the marble boxes, now covered with soil and green plants. Al-Jazzar turned the buried Crusader cathedral into an underground water reservoir, filled by rainfall. The recently renovated reservoir is accessible through a door and underground stairway at the left end of the mosque. Look for the small green sign and red arrows. Guides offer tours of varying quality (open daily 8am-12:30pm, 1:15-4:15pm, and 4:45-6:30pm; admission NIS3).

A restored white stone gate, the entrance to the subterranean **Crusader City** (tel. 991 17 64) stands across from the mosque on Al-Jazzar St. When first discovered, the rooms were thought to have been built underground, but archaeologists have since determined that Al-Jazzar simply built his city on top of once above-land buildings. Because excavations were halted for fear that the Arab town above might collapse, most of the Crusader City remains buried; only the area originally known as the "Hospitaller's Quarter" is open. Detailed explanations at every stop of the way are provided by the so-called "Easy Guide"—a hand held tape recorder, available free with the presentation of your ticket. In the entrance halls, three enormous pillars stand amidst a variety of architectural styles. Decorations with images of flowers or human forms are Crusader work, while the more abstract embellishments and the Arabic calligraphy are from the Ottomans. The 12th-century halls were probably part of a medical complex where the Hospitaller Order treated pilgrims. The arches project directly from the floor, indicating that the current floor is about 4m above the original level. The barrels and girders are modern additions used to support the original walls. From the courtyard beyond the entrance hall, you can see fortifications built by Fakhr ad-Din and Tahir al-Omar. The Ottoman gate on the left (above an earlier Crusader gate) is the entrance to the Hospitaller's fort. Turning right from here will bring you to the center of the original Crusader complex.

The passageway from the Hospitaller's fort to the **Refectory** or **Crypt of St. John** has been closed since 1990 for fear that the roof will collapse. To reach the crypt, leave the Crusader City the way you came in, turn right, and follow the signs to the crypt entrance; look for the black-and-white "crypte" sign on a metal door. The most magnificent and famous of the buried rooms, it once housed Crusader feasts. Next to the third column in the crypt is a staircase connected to a long underground passageway which in turn leads to six adjacent rooms and a central courtyard. The passageway may have been dug by the Crusaders as a hiding place in case of attack, or possibly as an elaborate sewage system. It was restored by Al-Jazzar to serve as a means of escape if Napoleon gained entrance to the city walls. The complex of arched rooms at the other end of the tunnel was used as a hospital for wounded knights. The Turks later turned the rooms into a post office, and they are now the home of a flock of **pigeons** whose eerie cooing echoes over visitor's heads. (Crusader

City open Sun.-Thurs. 8:30am-6:30pm, Fri. 8:30am-3:30pm, Sat. 9am-6pm; winter Sun.-Thurs. 8:30am-5pm, Fri. 8:30am-2pm, Sat. 9am-5pm. Admission NIS11, students NIS10.) Around the corner from the Crusader City is the **Okashi Museum,** named after late Akko resident Avshalom Okashi, a painter known for richly textured abstract paintings. The museum houses many of his great works. (Open Sun.-Thurs. 8:30am-4:30pm, Fri. 8:30am-2pm, Sat. 9am-4:30pm. Admission NIS5, students NIS4; ticket for both Okashi Museum and Crusader City NIS15, students NIS14.)

The adjacent **Municipal Museum** (really a Turkish bath that operated until 1947) is accessible through the metal door opposite the crypt entrance or the one opposite the main entrance around the corner. Its rooms are appropriately named "hot," "cold," and "lukewarm." From the entrance to the Municipal Museum, a right turn will bring you to the *souq,* a tumultuous avenue of butchers, grocers, bakers, and copper, brass, and leather vendors. Food stands along the *souq* offer *kebab,* falafel, and sandwiches (market active 7am-7pm). Near the market crouch several ancient inns (*caravanserai, khanat* in Arabic). The most impressive is **Khan al-Umdan** (Inn of Pillars), just past the Isnan Pasha Mosque and the fishing port. Al-Jazzar built this *khan* for Ottoman merchants at the end of the 18th century. The lower stories of the courts served as rented storerooms for merchants, while the upper galleries served as boarding rooms. The *khan*'s slender, square clock tower, erected in 1906 to celebrate the jubilee of the Ottoman Sultan Abdulhamit, is marked with the Turkish half-moon and star.

In the northern part of the old city, the commanding **Citadel** adjoins the Crusader City on Ha-Hagana St., opposite the sea wall. This stronghold, used by the British as their central prison, now houses the **Museum of Heroism** (tel. 991 82 64, 82 65, or 82 66), a monument to Zionist guerilla organizations. The citadel was built in the late 1700s on 13th-century Crusader foundations and was used as an **Ottoman prison.** The most famous inmate during Ottoman rule was Baha'u'llah, founder of the Baha'i faith, who was imprisoned on the second floor in 1868. During the British Mandate, the prison housed about 560 inmates under the guard of about half as many British soldiers. Members of the Etzel, Hagana, and Lehi, including Ze'ev Jabotinsky, were imprisoned here for violent anti-British activities. Nine members of the resistance were sentenced to death by hanging between 1938 and 1947. The **Gallows Room** displays the noose in place along with photographs of the nine fighters. On May 4, 1947, Etzel members staged a prison break that freed 41 or their peers and enabled the escape of 214 Arab prisoners (later depicted in the movie *Exodus,* shot on location). In summer 1997, the following areas of the museum were **closed** due to excavations in the Crusader City below the Citadel: the main courtyard, the southern wing where the breakout was staged, and the eastern wing where large groups of resistance fighters were held. To reach the museum, follow the stone stairs down to the lower garden, then the metal stairs up and around the side of the prison (admission NIS6, students NIS3). Across the street from the museum looms **Burj al-Kuraim** (Fortress of the Vineyards), often referred to as the British Fortress despite its Crusader and Ottoman construction.

A stroll along the Old City's perimeter yields an interesting look at Akko's means of seaside defense. Akko's security in recent centuries has relied upon the **Al-Jazzar Wall,** running along the northern and eastern sides of the city and surrounded by a sea water moat. The best place from which to view the wall, which originally ran the length of the harbor, is **Burj al-Kommander** (Commander's Fortress), an enormous Crusader bastion at the northeastern corner. To enter the watchtower, climb the steps beginning where Weizmann St. meets the wall. The **Tower of the Flies,** the site of the original lighthouse and at one time connected to the walls, solemnly broods in the middle of the bay. Its fortifications were toppled by a devastating earthquake in 1837. At the eastern corner near the shoreline yawns the so-called **Land Gate,** once the only entrance to the city.

ENTERTAINMENT

Twice a year, Akko plays host to major performing arts events. Excellent acoustics in the Crusader City's halls make them the perfect location for the **Haifa Symphony Orchestra** in July and the acclaimed **Israel Fringe Theater Festival** each fall. The four-day dramatic extravaganza occurs during the Jewish festival of *Sukkot* (Oct. 5-11 in 1998) and attracts small theater troupes from all over the country. Only a few of the performances are in English (check with the tourist office). During *Sukkot*, there are also prolific street performers.

Summer visitors can make a splash at the **Akko Marina** near Khan al-Umdar, where **Ramy's Diving Center** (fax 34 06 06) rents diving equipment (PADI, NAVI, and CMAS affiliated). Diving tours (US$75) explore a 30m deep Italian submarine from World War II. The **Princess of Akko** (tel. 050 50 37) gives 25-minute boat rides from the marina to the sea walls (NIS10, students NIS8), but will not depart until filled.

A relaxed *argeileh* puff by the sea is the local choice for nightlife. There is a **pool hall** tucked away between the end of the *souq* and Khan al-Umdar (travelers report fair play). Plans are underway for a cluster of new pubs on the waterfront.

■ Near Akko

Loḥamei Ha-Geta'ot ("Fighters of the Ghettos"), a kibbutz founded by survivors of concentration camps and the Warsaw Ghetto uprising, lies outside Akko toward Nahariya. The **Ghetto Fighters' House** (tel. 995 80 80; fax 995 80 07) examines Jewish life in Eastern Europe before, during, and after the Holocaust. The exhibit starts with displays on pre-war *shtetl* life and Zionist youth movements and continues with explicit chronicles of the Warsaw Ghetto and concentration camp atrocities. The recently constructed **Yad La-Yeled** in an adjoining building is a memorial to the million and a half children who perished in the Holocaust. The exhibition (winding up an inscripted 4-story tower) recounts the lost lives with audio-visual displays and stories collected from diaries, letters, and testimonies (open Sun.-Thurs. 9am-6pm, Fri. 9am-1pm, Sat. 10am-5pm; winter Sun.-Thurs. 9am-4pm, Fri. 9am-1pm, Sat. 10am-5pm; free, but donation requested). The museum complex also features a quiet, air-conditioned library where any visitor can research Jewish history; many Holocaust reference books are in English. To reach the kibbutz, take bus #271 (runs daily from Akko and Nahariya, 20min., NIS5.50).

The **Roman aqueduct** just outside the museum to the south is remarkably well preserved, largely because it's not Roman. Al-Jazzar had it built in 1780 to carry water 15km from the Kabri springs to Akko. You'll have great views of the aqueduct from the bus between Akko and Nahariya.

The **Baha'i Gardens** (tel. 981 15 69), 2km south of the kibbutz, bloom in a riveting mix of Occidental and Oriental styles. The gardens, planted from 1952 to 1956, hold the villa and **shrine of Baha'u'llah,** the prophet and founder of the Baha'i faith (shrine open Mon. and Fri.-Sun. 9am-noon; gardens open daily 9am-4pm; free). The gate on the main road is for Baha'is; all others should get off the bus just north of the gate at the yellow "traffic signal ahead" sign. Walk east 500m past the military base and enter at the small gate on the right. The gardens are on the main Akko-Nahariya road, via bus #271 (10min. from Akko). For a challenging daytrip, consider the 1km hike through **Naḥal Shagur** (also called **Naḥal Beit Ha-Kerem**), a tributary of the Ḥilazon River east of Akko, which divides the Upper and Lower Galilee.

■ Nahariya נהריה

Nahariya is literally a one-horse town—hang around Jabotinsky St. long enough, and you'll see the tired beast hauling tourists around in a white buggy from morning until night. Although not particularly thrilling, the sunny, sleepy town can provide a welcome respite from the clamor of Israel's more crowded cities and beaches. The many buses leaving Nahariya make it a convenient base for sights on the northern coast and western Galilee. Unfortunately, accommodations are more expensive than those in nearby Akko.

ORIENTATION AND PRACTICAL INFORMATION

Nahariya is the northernmost town on Israel's coast. Nearly everything you'll need is on **Ha-Ga'aton Blvd.** To reach the beaches, walk a few blocks west and stop when you get wet.

Municipal Tourist Information Office: MTIO (tel. 987 98 00), Ha-Ga'aton Blvd., on the ground floor of the Municipality Building. From the bus station, walk west on Ha-Ga'aton; the MTIO is in the large white building at the end of the plaza past Herzl St. Open Sun.-Thurs. 8am-1pm and 4-7pm, Fri. 8am-1pm.

Currency Exchange: Mercantile Discount Bank (tel. 992 46 11) and **Bank Leumi,** (tel. 992 56 31), both on Ha-Ga'aton Blvd. Both open Sun., Tues., and Thurs. 8:30am-12:30pm and 4-6pm, Mon. and Wed. 8:30am-12:30pm, Fri. 8:30am-noon.

Trains: Station at 1 Ha-Ga'aton Blvd. (tel. 856 44 46). Trains think they can to: **Akko** (15min., NIS4.50); **Haifa** (40min., NIS9); and **Tel Aviv** (2¼hr., NIS23.50). Connections to **Jerusalem** and elsewhere. Trains depart Sun.-Fri. at 5:50, 7:40, 9:40, 10:35, 11:35am, 3:10, 4:40, 5:50, and 6:30pm.

Buses: Station at 3 Ha-Ga'aton Blvd. (tel. 854 95 55). Buses #272 (express), 270, and 271 depart for Nahariya from both Haifa (45min., NIS11.50) and Akko (20min., NIS6.10). Buses #20 (2:30pm) and 22 (9:10 and 11:30am) go to **Rosh Ha-Nikra** (15min., NIS7.30). Buses from platform #5 run often to **Akhziv** (6:30am-9:15pm, 10min., NIS6.10). Bus #44 goes to **Peki'in** (45min., NIS14.50).

English Bookstore: Doron Books, 32 Ha-Ga'aton Blvd. (tel. 992 10 79). Open Sun.-Mon. and Wed.-Thurs. 8:30am-1pm and 4-7pm, Tues. 8am-1pm, Fri. 8am-2pm.

Emergency: First aid: tel. 101 or 982 33 33. **Hospital:** tel. 985 05 05, Ben-Tzvi St. **Police:** 5 Ben-Tzvi St., (tel. 100 or 992 03 44).

Pharmacy: Szabo Pharmacy, 3 Ha-Ga'aton Blvd. (tel. 992 04 54 or 11 97), in front of the bus station. Open Sun.-Thurs. 8am-1:30pm and 4-7:30pm, Fri. 8am-2:30pm.

Post Office: 40 Ha-Ga'aton Blvd. (tel. 992 01 80), has **Poste Restante** and **international calls.** Open Sun.-Tues. and Thurs. 8am-12:30pm and 3:30-6pm, Wed. 8am-1:30pm, Fri. 8am-noon.

Telephone Code: 04.

ACCOMMODATIONS AND FOOD

In summer, rooms are sometimes available in private homes. "Rooms to Rent" signs are common on Jabotinsky St.; head west on Ha-Ga'aton to the post office and turn right (NIS60 or more; polite bargaining may help). The MTIO keeps a list of rooms, but not a list of prices. **Motel Arieli,** 1 Jabotinsky St. (tel. 992 10 76), next to Ha-Ga'aton and the beach, offers neat, air-conditioned rooms in either bungalows or a main building (reception open 24hr.; check-out 10am; 2-bed bungalow NIS100; all other doubles NIS180). The **Kalman Hotel (HI),** 27 Jabotinsky St. (tel. 992 03 55; fax 992 65 39), one block from the beach, is spotless and spacious, with air-conditioning, TVs, and private baths. Owner Miron Teichner gives out coupons for the beach and restaurants, and shows off the signatures of big-shots who've stayed here, including Ezer Weizmann, Shimon Peres, and Sophia Loren. The Kalman's enormous Israeli breakfast (included) deserves its own 15 minutes of fame, so here it is (no curfew; *Let's Go* readers can rent singles for US$30; doubles US$55; triples US$75). **Beit Gabiazda,** 12 Jabotinsky St. (tel. 992 10 49), has air-conditioning and private baths, a TV lounge, and a kitchen (doubles NIS150; prices go up July-Aug. and down when you bargain). For cheap beds, head south to **Akko.** Nahariya is only a few kilometers from Lebanon, and camping on the beach is strictly forbidden.

The restaurant-cafes and falafel stands lining Ha-Ga'aton Blvd. peddle familiar Middle Eastern food. Nahariya's beaches and gardens make beautiful, lush picnic grounds; shop at the **Co-op Tzafon supermarket** (tel. 992 72 10), on the corner of Ha-Ga'aton Blvd. and Herzl St., or at fruit and vegetable stores on Herzl St. between Ha-Ga'aton Blvd. and Ha-Meyasdim St. A Moroccan bakery across from the Hod theater on Herzl St. (side entry, no sign) sells several dozen varieties of cookies (NIS10-15 per kg). Established when Nahariya was a six-year-old farm town, **Penguin Cafe,** on Ha-Ga'aton Blvd. near Jabotinsky St., attracts a trendy young crowd (Italian dishes NIS25-31, omelettes NIS19-27, blintzes NIS28). **Lachmi,** a few meters closer to the bus station, serves similar food at similar prices in slightly classier environs.

ENTERTAINMENT AND SIGHTS

Nahariya slowly roasts visitors along its sandy strip. The main beach, **Galei Galil,** has a breakwater, a lifeguard, and lots of sand, but you'll be hard pressed to see any of it on Saturdays. The beach is a right turn off the end of Ha-Ga'aton Blvd. (Open July-Aug. 8am-6pm; Sept.-June 8am-5pm; free. Admission to the nearby **indoor pool** NIS17, students NIS11. Pool open Sun.-Thurs. 6am-3pm and 7-10pm, Fri. 6am-3pm, Sat. 6am-4pm and 6-10pm.) Another free beach, south of Galei Galil, has neither a lifeguard nor a breakwater. Local youth surf here and learn to develop the nerves they'll need as functioning Israeli drivers.

The **Hod Cinema** (tel. 992 05 02), on Herzl St. across from the market, often shows movies in English, as does the **Hekhal Ha-Tarbout** (tel. 992 79 35), on Ha'Atzma'ut Rd. The latest movies play closer to Haifa.

Nahariyan nightlife is quiet, although some weekend revelers manage to make noise late into the night. A local favorite is **BK Pub,** across from the bus station on Ha-Ga'aton (enter from the side at the intersection with Ha'Atzma'ut St.). Pubs **Makom Batayelet** and **Mull Hayam** (turn left where Ha-Ga'aton meets the sand) are right on the ocean. The **Carlton Hotel disco,** also on Ha-Ga'aton Blvd., is for dancers with cash (opens Fri. 10pm and some other weekdays; NIS50). All ages participate in fun **folk dancing** at the amphitheater, on the corner of Balfour St. and Ha-Ga'aton Blvd. (late May-early Oct. Tues. and Sat. nights 7:30-9:30pm).

The dull but archaeologically important remains of a 4000-year-old **Canaanite Temple** dedicated to Asherah (the goddess of fertility) were discovered in 1947 on a hill next to the shore (a 20min. walk south on the beach). The **Nahariya Municipal Museum,** in the Municipality Building near the bus terminal, has exhibits on art, archaeology, malacology (the study of seashells), history, and Central European Jewry (open Sun.-Wed. 10am-noon and 4-6pm, Thurs. 10am-noon; free). An ornate mosaic floor is all that remains of a 4th-century **Byzantine church** (tel. 987 98 63) on Bielefeld St. near the Katzenelson School. Call ahead to visit for free.

■ Near Nahariya

AKHZIV אכזיב

Like Nahariya, Akhziv's claim to fame is its sunny shoreline. The **Akhziv beach** (tel. (04) 982 82 01), which begins 4km north of Nahariya, is popular and has a full range of amenities (open 8am-7pm; NIS12). Two roads lead to the beach: a paved one along the coast and an unpaved, noncoastal road where buses stop. Every July a **Reggae Festival** stirs it up on the beach; call for details.

The heart of the area is the **Akhziv National Park** (tel. (04) 982 32 63), with sprawling lawns and a sheltered beach forming two beautiful lagoons, equipped with showers, and changing rooms, all built on the site of an 8th-century BCE Phoenician port town (open April-Sept. Mon.-Thurs. 8am-4pm, July-Aug. until 6pm, Fri. and Sun. 8am-7pm, Sat. 7am-7pm; NIS16, students NIS8). Bordering the park on its southern side is a **Club Med,** a self-proclaimed "vacation unlike any other"; to the north is **Akhzibland,** a self-proclaimed independent state. Akhzibland was founded in 1952 by the eccentric **Eli Avivi,** who leased the land from an unamused Israeli government. An eye-catching figure in flowing robes, Avivi is unforgettable—especially when kvetchy customs officials try to figure out the "Akhzibland" stamp on your passport. **Eli's Museum** (tel. (04) 982 32 50), housed in a deteriorated but striking Arab mansion, exhibits the benevolent dictator's extensive and esoteric collection of mostly

Phoenician implements, statue fragments, and maps (open 24hr.). Beds in one of Eli's breezy **guest rooms** above the museum cost NIS100, and sleeping in the dingy **camping area** costs NIS50 (beach admission included), but the prices are entirely negotiable and may be waived if you get on Eli's good side or help him with menial chores (such as landscaping, cleaning, or passing legislation). If you decide to stay at Akhzibland, be prepared for storytime in the evening; Eli's got a lot to say, since he's 184 years old.

Across the road is the **Akhziv Diving Center** (tel. (04) 982 36 71), where you can rent snorkeling equipment for NIS25. Call ahead to check on sea conditions. The center runs jeep and sailing excursions as well. About 300m north by the "Field School West Galilee" sign, the **SPNI Field School** (tel. 982 37 62; fax 982 30 15) leads walks around the area (mostly for children; open 8am-4pm). The facility also rents private rooms, often filled with youth groups. (Check-in 2pm; check-out 9am. Dorms NIS33; singles NIS160; doubles NIS210; extra child NIS37. Meat dinners NIS24, lunch NIS34.) All **buses** from platform #5 in Nahariya (buses #22-25, 28) go to the SPNI, hostel, beach, and campground (2 per hr., 10min., NIS6.10). *Sherut* run between Akhziv and Nahariya as well and should not charge more than NIS5.

ROSH HA-NIKRA ראש הנקרה

The spectacular white chalk cliffs and grottos of Rosh Ha-Nikra occupy the northernmost point on Israel's coastline. Rosh Ha-Nikra's caves, sculpted by millennia of lashing waves, nearly make one forget the mountain of barbed wire and the Uzi-toting soldiers who guard the tense Lebanese border only a few steps from the parking lot. The British enlarged the natural chalk grottos when they dug a tunnel through the cliffs during World War II, which they intended to be a train route between Haifa and Beirut. The nearby kibbutz, smelling the chance for a new tourist trap, blasted additional tunnels through the rock to improve access to the sea caves, topped the cliffs with an observation point and cafeteria, and connected the highway to the caves with a cable car. Don't expect arduous spelunking here; a pleasant walk through the grottos is at most a half-hour event. The worse the weather, though, the better the show at Rosh Ha-Nikra—waves pound the gaping caverns, forming powerful whirlpools and echoing thunderously through the slippery tunnels. Arrive early or be caught in a throng of youth and tour groups in the afternoon. (Site tel. 985 71 09. Cable car runs April-June and Sept. Sat.-Thurs. 8:30am-6pm, Fri. 8:30am-4pm; July-Aug. Sat.-Thurs. 8:30am-11pm, Fri. 8:30am-4pm; Oct.-March Sat.-Fri. 8:30am-4pm. The "Peace Train" runs every 30min. Admission NIS27, students NIS18; includes admission to the "Peace Train" and to the audio-visual presentation.)

If the grottos seem incomplete without drunk locals dancing to live folk music as the waves roll in, you're in luck: Friday night from 10pm to 2am is coffeehouse time at Rosh Ha-Nikra. The mostly thirty-something crowd shells out a whopping NIS49 for entrance (not including drinks).

Near Rosh Ha-Nikra is the new, spotless **Shlomi Youth Hostel and Guest House (HI)** (tel. (04) 980 89 75 or 91 61; fax 980 91 63), with air-conditioned rooms and private baths. (Reception open 8am-9pm. Check-in 2pm. Check-out 10am. No curfew or lockout. Doubles NIS28; NIS73 per extra person up to 2. Non-members pay NIS4 more. Breakfast included, dinner NIS35, weekends NIS42. Wheelchair accessible.)

Bus #22 from platform 5 in Nahariya leaves for Rosh Ha-Nikra (9:30,11:30am, returns at 11:40am). Bus #20 leaves platform 5 at 2:30pm and leaves Rosh Ha-Nikra at 4pm (both NIS7.30). Buses #22 and 23 leave from the Rosh Ha-Nikra junction (9:20 and 11:40am, return 6:15pm). Bus #25 (8:15pm) runs from Goren Park on the hill opposite Montfort. A *sherut* taxi from Nahariya will take you to the junction (NIS5).

MONTFORT AND NAHAL KEZIV מונטפורת ונחל כזיב

The Crusader castle of Montfort rewards a challenging hike with splendid scenery and ruins. The windswept fortification dramatically overlooks the western Galilee's steep Keziv Valley. The main structure was built by the Knights Templar early in the

12th century and partially destroyed by Salah ad-Din in 1187. Enlarged by the Hospitaller Knights in 1230, the fortress was called Starkenburg or Montfort ("strong mountain" in German or French). Among the remains of the fortress complex are the impressive 18m tower and 20m main hall.

Frequent buses (#40, 41, 44, and 45) leave Nahariya for the Christian Arab village of **Mi'ilya** (20min., NIS8). From the stop, turn left onto the steep road toward Mi'ilya, climbing it for about 30 minutes. At the wooden sign for Montfort, the road veers right to Hilla. Continue straight and follow the red-and-white markers down the rocky path to the castle (another 30min.). The set of stone steps on the right is an alternate path to the ruins. The original trail turns to the right shortly, then travels across a small bridge and up the rocks to the castle. The site is currently under renovation and officially closed, but visitors have been known to prowl around.

A rewarding (and challenging) way to visit is to take a longer hike, saving the castle for last. The four-hour hiking loop with spectacular views begins at the lookout point on the road to Hilla (coming from Mi'ilya, turn right at the wooden sign), descends into the Naḥal Keziv valley, then circles back up to Montfort. Follow black-and-white or blue-and-white markers down into the valley, green-and-white while along the river, and red-and-white up to the castle and back to Mi'ilya.

Several other trails branch off the loop. Following the river away from Montfort, green-and-white markers lead to the **Ein Tamir** and **Ein Ziv** springs. Ascending the slope opposite Montfort lands you in **Goren Park** (follow red-and-white markers), from which you can enjoy a perfect view of the castle complex (amazing at sunset). Bus #25 (8:15pm only) goes from the park to the Shlomi Youth Hostel (see p. 372).

Just north of Montfort is the **Naḥal Betzet Nature Reserve,** another fabulous stomping ground for hikers. The blue-and-white trail follows the river upstream. To get to the enormous **Bow Cave,** a natural arch whose top affords dramatic views of the forested Galilean hills, take the red-and-white-marked trail which begins 2km from Montfort, along the road to Kibbutz Adamit.

The Keziv River extends to the Akhziv coastline (near the SPNI field school) from deep into the Galilee. Serious hikers use the trail as the first or last leg of a three-day **Yam L'Yam** (Sea to Shining Sea—Mediterranean to Galilee) trek. SPNI, with a field school in Akhziv, is an invaluable resource for planning any hike.

YEḤI'AM (JUDIN) FORTRESS מבצר יחיעם

Built in the 12th century by the Templars, **Yeḥi'am (Judin) Fortress** (tel. (04) 985 60 04) was inherited by the Teutonic Knights and destroyed by Sultan Baybars in 1265. Tahir al-Omar's restoration efforts, 500 years later, draw tourists today. Kibbutz Yeḥi'am was established in 1946 by a group that settled in the deserted castle; the fortress is still within the kibbutz grounds, the source of its new Hebrew name. Views of the western Galilee from the well-preserved tower are amazing (open Sun.-Thurs. 8am-5pm, Fri. and holidays 8am-4pm; NIS7, students NIS5.25). Buses #39 and 42 run from Nahariya and stop at the fortress (3-4 buses per day, 20min., NIS7.60). Surrounding the fort are several defense posts left over from the 1948 War of Independence, when the kibbutz was an important Galilee holdout.

At the far right-hand side of the castle's parking lot, a wooden post marks the entrance to the **Naḥal Yeḥi'am Nature Reserve,** home of a sweet and easy one-hour hike. Enter through the green door, follow the green-and-white markers, and descend into the brilliantly verdant Yeḥi'am Forest. When the trail turns into a road, follow it straight for about 30 minutes. The beautiful houses built into the surrounding hills are part of **Klil,** a village founded by Israeli environmentalists. Turn right at the first fork then turn right again a short distance later onto the two-way road. From here on, it's all paved walking (3km), but the road passes through a picturesque landscape of orchards and pastures. When you reach the Jatt Junction (on the main Tzfat-Kabri road), stay on the same side of the street to catch a *sherut* back to Nahariya (NIS5).

PEKI'IN (BKE'AH) פקיעין بقيعة

Peki'in (Bke'ah in Arabic) is where Rabbi Shimon Bar-Yohai and his son, Eliezer, fled after Roman decree banned the study of Torah. For 12 years, this erudite duo hid in a small hillside cave and, sustained by a nearby spring and a generous carob tree, delved into their illicit book of learning. It was during this period, some Jews say, that Bar-Yohai composed the *Zohar,* the central text of Kabbala (Jewish mysticism). According to popular legend, years of mystical immersion elevated Bar-Yohai to such a high level of holiness that when he emerged from hiding, his gaze started **angry fires** in the fields of those less worthy.

In its present state, the cave does not live up to the vivid legend surrounding it. Bus #44 (7-8 per day, 50min., NIS14.50) makes the round-trip to Peki'in from Nahariya and will let you off just above the cave if you ask the driver. Be sure to get off at Peki'in Ha'Atika (Old Peki'in), not Peki'in Ha-Hadasha (New Peki'in). At the blue and white sign, turn right and descend the stairs. When you reach a large bush with houses behind it, turn right and walk between the two large rocks. The cave is a tiny hole about 3m away.

Peki'in is the only city in Israel claiming continuous Jewish occupation since the Second Temple period. The Jewish presence perpetuates in the form of an old lady and an 18th-century synagogue with Temple-era stones built into the wall. To visit the synagogue, continue down the staircase near the cave, then veer right until you reach Kikkar Ha-Ma'ayan ("Spring Square") with its oddly-shaped pool. Follow the street at the far right of the square, turn left at the first intersection, and take this curving road down to the synagogue's white gate on the right. If the gate is closed, knock on the white door with a blue star, around the corner and upstairs. A small donation is requested.

Galilee הגליל الجليل

When the ancient Israelites described their country as flowing with milk and honey, they must have been picturing the Galilee. This lush region, bordering the West Bank to the south, the Golan to the east, Lebanon to the north, and the Mediterranean coast to the west, is sliced by rivers and carpeted with rolling, green hills. The Galilee is an ancient province of the Israelite kingdom, called *Ha-Galil* (the district) in Hebrew. Jesus grew up in Nazareth, he performed his first miracle at Cana, his apostles lived in Capernaum, and he gave his famous sermon atop the Mount of Beatitudes. Ever since Israel captured the strategic Golan Heights (see p. 400) in 1967 , putting the Galilee out of range of Syrian rockets, the region has blossomed into a tourist mecca. Busloads of pilgrims descend a massive metal staircase into the Jordan River at the site where John is believed to have baptized Jesus, banana boats and booze cruises skim over the Sea of Galilee to deposit passengers upon the bustling Tiberias promenade, and hikers crowd the trails of the Upper Galilee where Crusader fortresses keep their tired watch over forested valleys. Meanwhile, the ancient synagogues of Tzfat and churches of Nazareth continue to attract the faithful.

■ Nazareth נצרת الناصرة

A vibrant center of Arab life in the Galilee, Nazareth (An-Nassra in Arabic, Natzrat in Hebrew) is a far cry from the Christmas card picture of pastoral churches, quiet convents, and grazing sheep. Nazareth is indeed dear to Christian pilgrims as the setting of Jesus's younger years and the traditional home of Mary and Joseph, but it is also an engrossingly gritty town. While devotees worship in dimly lit back-alley churches, drivers swerve maniacally to avoid running down pedestrians on the main road, and crowds clamor in the business district. Nazareth's population is about half Christian and half Muslim. For the most part, Nazarean Arabs are content to be Israeli citizens,

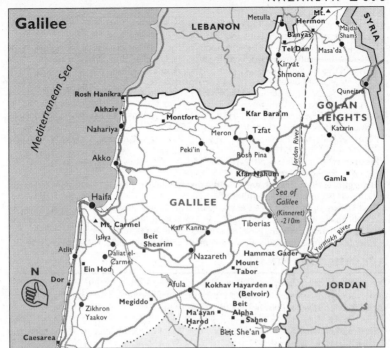

but life here is worlds away from the beaches of Haifa and Tel Aviv. Visitors (especially women) should dress modestly to avoid risking harassment on the streets and difficulty entering churches.

ORIENTATION AND PRACTICAL INFORMATION

Nazareth is 40km southeast of Haifa and 30km southwest of Tiberias, on a hill north of the Jezreel Valley. All the Christian sights are located in the old **Arab Town. Natzrat Illit** (Upper Nazareth), the new, Jewish section of town, is of little interest to tourists. The Arab town's main road, **Paul VI St.**, crosses east of the places of interest. Its intersection with **Casa Nova St.** is the busiest part of town. Up the hill from Casa Nova St., interspersed with churches, is the market area. Continue up the hill towards Salesian St. to reach the higher quality accommodations and panoramic views. Obtain a **map** of the city from the GTIO, as few of the winding streets have signs, and many that do have only numbers instead of names. Nazareth's Christian community shuts down on Sundays, but most establishments are open on *Shabbat.*

> **Tourist Office: Government Tourist Information Office (GTIO)** (tel. 657 30 03 or 05 55; fax 657 30 78), Casa Nova St., near the intersection with Paul VI St. Knowledgeable staff distributes brochures and map. Open Mon.-Fri. 8:30am-5pm, Sat. 8:30am-2pm.
>
> **Currency Exchange: Change Spot Nazareth,** in a jewelry store on Paul VI St., south of Casa Nova St. Charges no commission and lets you avoid bank hassles. Open Mon.-Sat. 8:30am-8:15pm. **Bank Ha-Poalim,** Paul VI St. (tel. 657 09 23), to the right of the Mashbir department store. Open Mon.-Tues. and Thurs. 8:30am-12:30pm and 4-6pm, Sun. and Wed. 8:30am-12:30pm, Fri. 8:30am-noon.
>
> **Buses:** The central "bus station" consists of a few stops on Paul VI St., near Bank Ha-Poalim and the Basilica. **Egged** (info tel. (04) 854 95 55) is on Paul VI St. across from the bank (open Sun.-Fri. 6am-6:30pm) Bus #431 from Haifa (every 20-60min., 30-35min., NIS14.30) continues to **Tiberias** (30min., NIS14.30). Buses #355, 357, 823, and 824 run to **Afula** (about every 20min., 20min., NIS7.30). Buses #823, 824,

and 826 go to **Megiddo** (NIS9.40; watch for the *tel* as drivers fly by it) and then continue to **Tel Aviv** (1½hrs., NIS29).

Baggage storage: The taxi stand north of the GTIO, near the Mazzawi souvenir stand will usually store your bags for NIS5 each. Open Mon.-Sat. 6am-10pm.

Taxis: Ma'ayan, Paul VI St. (tel. 655 51 05), **Abu Elassel** (tel. 655 47 45), **Galil** (tel. 655 55 36), and **Saiegh** (tel. 657 11 76). *Sherut* (tel. 657 11 40), on a side street off Paul VI St. near bus station. **Haifa** NIS13, **Tiberias** NIS15, **Tel Aviv** NIS30. *Sherut* on *Shabbat* to Tel Aviv only.

Car Rental: Europcar (tel. 655 41 29) and **Hertz** (tel. 657 53 13). Min. age 24. Both charge $58-60 per day. Credit card required.

Pharmacy: Farah Pharmacy (tel. 655 40 18), next to Egged info. Open Mon.-Tues. and Thurs.-Fri. 9am-1pm and 4-6:30pm, Wed. and Sat. 8am-2pm.

Hospitals: Nazareth Hospital (tel. 657 15 01 or 02), **Holy Family Hospital** (tel. 657 45 35), **French Hospital** (tel. 657 45 30-33).

Emergency: First Aid (Magen David Adom): tel. 101. **Police:** tel. 100 or 657 44 44. Limited English. **Fire:** tel. 102.

Post Office (tel. 656 18 43). Central branch on Paul VI St. two blocks west of Mary's Well. **Poste Restante** at far right window. Open Mon.-Tues. and Thurs.-Fri. 8am-12:30pm and 3:30-6pm, Wed. 8am-1:30pm, Sat. 8am-noon.

Telephones: International calls can be made at the post office. **Telephone Code:** 06.

ACCOMMODATIONS

During Christian holidays, you'll need divine intervention to find a room here. At other times, hospices are crowded but often have a bed to spare. Call ahead—there are very few budget accommodations in Nazareth.

Sisters of Nazareth, P.O. Box 274 (tel. 655 43 04 or 65 09; fax 646 07 41), near the Basilica; walking uphill, take a left off Casa Nova St. after the Casa Nova Hospice; it will be on the right. A pristine dormitory with a beautiful courtyard and superb facilities—kitchen, dining room, and living room. Beneath the convent are impressive excavations from the first century CE, including a tomb sealed by a stone; ask one of the sisters to take you down. Check-in 4pm, but you can leave your pack if you arrive earlier. Flexible 10am check-out and inflexible 9pm curfew. Dorm beds NIS24. Private rooms from US$18 per person, US$21 with breakfast.

Casa Nova Pilgrim's House (tel. 645 66 60; fax 657 96 30), across from the Basilica. More expensive and often full of Italian pilgrims. Check-in 2pm; check-out 9am; curfew 11pm. Doubles and triples US$25 per person; private singles US$35. Breakfast and one other meal included, US$5 more for full board.

St. Gabriel Monastery Hotel, P.O. Box 2448, Salesian St. (tel. 656 73 49, 657 21 33; fax 655 40 71). This brand new hotel with a panoramic view of the city is housed in a white stone, red roofed monastery with its own church and bell tower. Rooms have TV, telephone, and bathroom. Singles US$70; doubles US$80. Student discount makes for a NIS160 single (you may have to fight for it). Breakfast included.

FOOD

Nazareth's cuisine is not known for diversity. Falafel stands and Middle Eastern sweet shops freckle the downtown area. The crowded **Mahroum's Café** on Casa Nova St. serves fresh pastries (NIS35 per kg or NIS3-5 per piece). **Food Markets** line Paul VI St. where the buses stop. The center of town is littered with identical "Oriental" restaurants—NIS11-12 gets you hummus or *shawerma*, and chicken dishes go for twice that. Hours are generally 7am-9pm, but many places close around 4pm on Sunday. The ominously named **Tourist Restaurant,** on Paul VI St. near its intersection with Casa Nova, serves up meat or veggie baguettes for a tasty NIS12.

SIGHTS

Nazareth is synonymous with churches, and none is more prominent than the **Basilica of the Annunciation,** dominating downtown with its great faceted lantern tower. Completed in 1969, the basilica sits over the site believed to be Mary's home, where

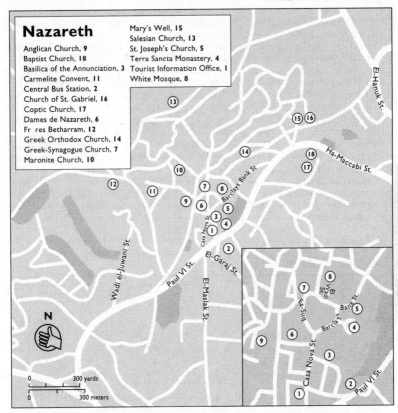

Nazareth

Anglican Church, 9
Baptist Church, 18
Basilica of the Annunciation, 3
Carmelite Convent, 11
Central Bus Station, 2
Church of St. Gabriel, 16
Coptic Church, 17
Dames de Nazareth, 6
Frères Betharram, 12
Greek Orthodox Church, 14
Greek-Synagogue Church, 7
Maronite Church, 10

Mary's Well, 15
Salesian Church, 13
St. Joseph's Church, 5
Terra Sancta Monastery, 4
Tourist Information Office, 1
White Mosque, 8

ISRAEL

the archangel Gabriel heralded the birth of Jesus. Beyond the huge, bronze doors depicting the life of Jesus, the modern basilica smothers some ancient ruins. On the ground floor, services take place before the **Grotto of the Annunciation**, on the remains of churches dating back to 356 CE. A gallery overlooking the Biblical site is lined with a series of international artistic interpretations of the Annunciation. Excavations of ancient Nazareth lie in a garden underneath the plaza, accessible from the upper floor of the church. Ask one of the Franciscan monks to show you around. To get to the Basilica, walk north from the GTIO; it's on your right. (Open Mon.-Sat. 8:30-11:45am and 2-5:30pm, Sun. and feasts 2-5:30pm; winter Mon.-Sat. 9-11:45am and 2-4:30pm, Sun. and feasts 2-4:30pm. Exposed **knees** not allowed.)

Across the plaza stands **St. Joseph's Church,** built over the cave thought to be Joseph's house. The present structure, constructed in 1914, incorporates remnants of a Byzantine church. Inside, stairs descend to caves that once stored grain and oil. Although this is usually referred to as **Joseph's workshop,** evidence suggests that these caves have been used since the late Stone Age. The **Greek-Catholic Synagogue Church** in the center of the Arab market is the site of the synagogue where young Jesus is believed to have preached. To get there, enter the *souq* from Casa Nova St., bear left at the first fork, then take the first right. The entrance will be on your right, at the yellow gate. An 18th-century **Maronite Church** is up the street past the Synagogue Church. Take the first left, and continue up the alleyway with the (thankfully) former sewage channel running down the middle (the church is officially closed, but you might get lucky on Sunday morning).

For an extraordinary view of Nazareth's rooftops and the Galilean hills, take bus #13 to the **Salesian Church** (or scale the 250-plus stairs to the top). The 20-minute ascent through Nazareth's old stone alleyways allows you to see a side of the village that is far more endearing than the chaos of Paul VI St. below. Hopefully, the cool, majestic sanctuary will be open, but the view merits the climb even if it's not.

Paul VI St. goes uphill from the buses to a circle-shaped building with a water faucet at an ugly traffic intersection-park known as Mary's Well. Many believe that the well's water miraculously heals; pity it doesn't heal its surroundings. Left and uphill from the well is the **Orthodox Church of the Archangel Gabriel,** standing over the town's ancient water source. The original church was erected in 356 CE over the spring where Mary drew water and where the Greek Orthodox believe Gabriel appeared. The present church, built in 1750, has elaborate Byzantine-style paintings and decorations. Ancient tiles adorn the entrance in the well area. (All churches in Nazareth claim to be open 8:30-11:45am and 2-5:30pm; winter 9-11:45am and 2-4:30pm; but many close in the afternoon. Sun. mornings are reserved for services. Modest dress required at all times.)

Nazareth's **souq** (open Mon.-Tues. and Thurs.-Fri. 9am-5pm, Wed. and Sat. 9am-2pm), best reached via Casa Nova St., is the place to buy olive wood camels and Bart Simpson underwear. The market area is best avoided at night, when drug addicts lurk in its dark alleyways.

■ Near Nazareth

MOUNT TABOR הר תבור

Mount Tabor (Har Tavor in Hebrew), the traditional site of Christ's Transfiguration, has become a standard stop on pilgrimage tours. The 588m-high hilltop is shared by Franciscan and Greek Orthodox monks. The **Basilica of the Transfiguration,** built in 1924, sits atop a 6th-century CE Byzantine church marking the spot where Jesus spoke with Elijah and Moses and was transfigured in the presence of apostles Peter, James, and John (Luke 9:28-36). The **Church of Elijah** nearby, built atop the **Cave of Melkhizedek,** can be entered from the outside through a small iron door. The limestone fortification, once an Arab fortress called **Al Adil,** dates from 1211. Mt. Tabor is also the site where the prophetess Deborah led the Israelites to victory over Sisera's army (Judges 4-5). (Churches open April-Sept. Sun.-Thurs. 8am-noon and 2:30-6pm; Oct.-March 8am-noon and 2-5pm. Modest dress required; no visitors during services.) Take bus #357 from the Egged information office in Nazareth (4 per day, returns 45min. later, 40min., NIS10.40). Finding a *sherut* to Nazareth from the mountain is difficult if not impossible; a driver might agree to take you to Afula for NIS10. Buses #823 and 824 leave Afula for Nazareth Illit (every 45-60min., 20min., NIS7.30). From the base of Mt. Tabor, it's a steep 3km walk up a long and winding road. If there's space, taxis taking Nazareth-based tour groups may drive an individual traveler for US$6 round-trip. To join a tour, inquire at the GTIO (tel. 672 0878).

At the foot of the mountain, in the village of Shibli, is the **Galilee Bedouin Heritage Center** (tel. (06) 676 78 75). The center has a museum honoring traditional Bedouin lifestyle. Those without a passion for things Bedouin may soon regret the NIS10 entrance fee (open Sat.-Thurs. 9am-5pm, NIS8 for students).

ZIPPORI צפורי

About 6.5km northwest of Nazareth, excavations at Zippori (Sepphoris) are uncovering a rich legacy from the Judeo-Christian, Roman, and Byzantine periods. The town was the seat of the Sanhedrin in the 3rd century CE, as well as one of the places where Rabbi Yehuda Ha-Nassi gathered the most learned rabbinic scholars to compile the *Mishnah.* Extensive finds include the remains of a 4000-seat Roman amphitheater, exquisite mosaics, a crusader fortress, and a synagogue. The synagogue is closed for repairs and renovations until early spring 1998. Zippori's most famous offering is the enigmatic mosaic of a gently smiling woman, now dubbed the "Mona Lisa of the Galilee." Within the crusader citadel are a variety of multimedia programs that present the history of the city and an exhibit of archaeological finds. One km east of the main excavations is an ancient reservoir, once part of the area's water supply system, now a vast dry shell that's fun to explore (site tel. (06) 656 82 72 or 73; open Sat.-Thurs. 8am-4pm, Fri. 8am-3pm; closes 1hr. earlier in winter; NIS14, students NIS10.50).

Direct buses pose a scheduling problem: #16 leaves Nazareth daily at 1:10pm with no return (NIS6.10). Frequent buses (#343) pass the junction about 3km south of the site (NIS5.30). Inquire at the GTIO about *sherut* taxis to the site.

TEL MEGIDDO (ARMAGEDDON)

Bible fans and heavy metal gurus have heard of Armageddon, but few realize that the demonic battleground for the End of Days (Revelations 16:16) is actually "Har Megiddo" (Mt. Megiddo), an ancient *tel* located just southeast of Haifa. Excavations of the site have uncovered an astounding 20 layers of ruins, ranging in time from the late Chalcolithic Age (c. 3500 BCE) to the 5th century BCE.

The vision of Megiddo as an apocalyptic gathering place is derived from the city's central location. Commanding the crossroads between several ancient trading routes that linked Egypt to Syria and Mesopotamia, the fortress town was the site of many fierce battles. Megiddo was razed and rebuilt by numerous civilizations, including Canaanites, Hyksos, Egyptians, Assyrians, and Israelites. The most impressive remains include a Canaanite temple dedicated to Astarte (20th century BCE), chariot stables and a palace from Solomon's time (10th century BCE), a public grain silo built during the reign of the Israelite king Jeroboam II (8th century BCE), and a man-made tunnel engineered to allow access to water during a siege. Some of the ruins have been reconstructed, and excavations are still underway.

Before negotiating the *tel,* check out the **museum** (tel. (06) 652 21 05) at the site's entrance. It explains some of Megiddo's layers, displays a model of Solomon's chariot city, and shows a video in Hebrew and English. Three gift shops have each set up camp in strategic locations around the site; they wage their own capitalistic pitched battle daily.

From the observation point atop the *tel,* you can look out over the **Jezreel Valley** *(Emek Yizre'el),* mostly swamp until 1920 when it was drained by Jewish immigrants. The lone mountain in the distance is Mt. Tabor; also visible are the Gilboa range and the hills of Nazareth.

The water tunnel terminates outside the ruins, so make sure it's your last stop at the site. When you exit, turn right and walk 500m back to the museum entrance and main road (open Sat.-Thurs. 8am-4pm, Fri. 8am-3pm; closes 1hr. earlier in winter; NIS16, students NIS12). Bus #823 runs between Nazareth and Tel Aviv, and stops at Megiddo (approx. 1 per hr.; NIS20 to Tel Aviv, NIS13 to Nazareth). Stay alert; drivers sometimes whiz by the *tel* and may charge you in advance for the return trip.

▓ Tiberias טבריה طبرية

Since the Golan Heights became part of Israel in 1967, Tiberias (T'verya in Hebrew) has become a splashing ground rivaling the waterfront hot spots of Netanya and Eilat. Although it is an ideal touring base for the Galilee and the Golan, its position 200m below sea level guarantees a hot, humid, and mosquito-ridden July and August.

Tiberias's history spans two millennia. Built in 18 CE by Herod Antipas, puppet King of Judea and tetrarch of Galilee, the city was named for the Roman Emperor Tiberius. Despite the Romans' attempt to bring in settlers, most Jews, including Jesus, refused to enter the town because it was built on the site of older Jewish graves. In the 2nd century CE, Rabbi Shimon Bar-Yohai declared the town pure, and it soon became the seat of the Sanhedrin and the religious center of the Jews. The *Talmud* was edited here, and its editors now rest in hillside tombs above the city.

During subsequent conquests by the Persians (614CE) and Arabs (636CE), Jews from Tiberias packed up and moved to Babylon and Jerusalem. In 1247 Tiberias was destroyed by the Mamluk and remained deserted until the beginning of Ottoman rule in 1517. Fifty-four years later, Sultan Suleiman the Magnificent handed the town over to a Jewish refugee from Spain who set up a Jewish state under the sovereignty of the

Ottomans and his mother-in-law. Their unsuccessful city fell into decay until Bedouin Sheikh Taher al-Omar rebuilt the city and its citadel in 1738 and settled Jews there. In 1837 Tiberias was devastated by an earthquake that rocked all of northern Palestine, but it was soon rebuilt. The city's 1940 population of 12,000 was evenly divided between Jews and Arabs. Since the 1948 war, the population of Tiberias has remained more or less entirely Jewish.

ORIENTATION AND PRACTICAL INFORMATION

Tiberias has three tiers: the **old city** by the water, the **new city** (Kiryat Shmuel) up the hill (bus #5), and **uptown** at the top of the hill (bus #7, 8, or 9). Although there aren't many ruins, most tourists never leave the old city. Boozing, boating, and beaching all take place in this area. **Ha-Galil Street** (the main thoroughfare in Tiberias) and **Ha-Banim Street** run parallel to the water; **Ha-Yarden Street** runs perpendicular to them to the north. The smaller **Ha-Yarkon** and **Ha-Kishon** streets intersect Ha-Galil and Ha-Banim to the south. The *midraḥov* (pedestrian mall) runs from Ha-Galil to the promenade.

Tourist Office: Government Tourist Information Office (GTIO) (tel. 672 56 66; fax 672 44 89), on Ha-Banim St. in the Archaeological Park next to the Jordan River and Moriah Plaza hotels. Free maps, brochures, and an Info-screen computer. Open Sun.-Thurs. 8:30am-4pm, Fri. 8:30am-noon.

Currency Exchange: Money Net Ltd. (tel. 672 40 48) changes foreign currency with no commission at the *midraḥov* on the second floor, close to Ha-Banim St. Open daily 9am-9pm. **Bank Ha-Poalim,** Ha-Banim St. (tel. 679 84 11), between Ha-Yarden and Ha-Yarkon, has a 24hr. **ATM. Bank Leumi** (tel. 672 71 11), on the corner of Ha-Yarden and Ha-Banim, has a 24hr. **money-changing machine.** The **post office** on Ha-Yarden exchanges with no commission.

Buses: tel. 679 10 80 or 81; info. (04) 854 95 55, on Ha-Yarden St. To **Jerusalem:** bus #961, 963, or 964 (every 30-45min., 6am-7pm, last Fri. bus around 3pm, 2½hr., NIS35). To **Tel Aviv:** bus #836 (direct), 840 (express), 830, 832, or 841 (at least every hr., 5:30am-8:30pm, last direct bus on Fri. around 3pm, 2hr., NIS29). To **Haifa:** bus #430, 431 or 434 (every 20-45min., about 5:30am-8pm, last direct on Fri. around 4:30pm, 1hr., NIS20).

Taxis: *Sherut* and private cabs wait in front of the bus station (last Fri. car 3:30pm). **Tiberias Taxi** (tel. 672 04 44). **Aviv** (tel. 672 00 98), on Al Hadef St. next to the gas station around the corner from the Ha-Yarden post office, has regular service to Tel Aviv only (NIS30). No *Shabbat* service. Call the night before.

Car Rental: All of the following are on Ha-Banim St.: **Reliable** (tel. 672 34 64 or 41 12), **City Car** (tel. 674 27 66; sometimes waives the age requirement), **Autorent** (tel. 672 56 88), **Eldan** (tel. 672 03 85 or 679 18 22), **Hertz** (tel. 672 39 39), and **Budget** (tel. 672 08 64 or 34 96). Get cars here for trips to the Golan.

Bicycles: Hostel Aviv and Maman Hostel are well-stocked. 18-speed mountain bike for NIS40, return on night of rental. See **Accommodations** for addresses.

English Bookstore: Steimatzky, 3 Ha-Galil St. (tel. 679 12 88). Magazines, pamphlets, greeting cards, and *Let's Go*s. Open Sun.-Mon. and Wed.-Thurs. 8am-1pm and 4:30-7:30pm (winter 4-7pm), Tues. 8am-1pm, Fri. 8am-2pm.

Laundromat: Panorama (tel. 672 43 24), south of Ha-Kishon St. and across from the city wall remnants on Ha-Galil St. Wash, dry, and fold 7kg for NIS35. Open Sun.-Mon. and Wed.-Thurs. 8am-6pm, Tues. and Fri. 8am-2pm.

Pharmacy: Schwartz Pharmacy (tel. 672 09 94), on Ha-Galil St. opposite the park. Open Sun.-Thurs. 8am-8pm. **Netanel Pharmacy** (tel. 679 06 13), on the corner of Bibas and Ha-Yarkon St. Open Sun.-Thurs. 8am-8pm, Fri. 8am-3pm.

Emergency: tel. 101. **First Aid (Magen David Adom):** tel. 679 01 11, corner of Ha-Banim and Ha-Kishon St. Open 24hr. **Police:** tel. 100 or 679 24 44. **Fire:** tel. 102.

Post Office: Central office with **Poste Restante** on Ha-Yarden St. (tel. 672 00 19). Take a right onto Ha-Yarden St. as you exit the bus station; the office is on the left just before Al Hadef St. Open Sun.-Tues. and Thurs. 8am-12:30pm and 3:30-6pm, Wed. 8am-1:30pm, Fri. 8am-12:30pm. Branch office in **Kiryat Shmuel** (tel. 672 08 94), on the corner of Bialik and Ehrlich St.

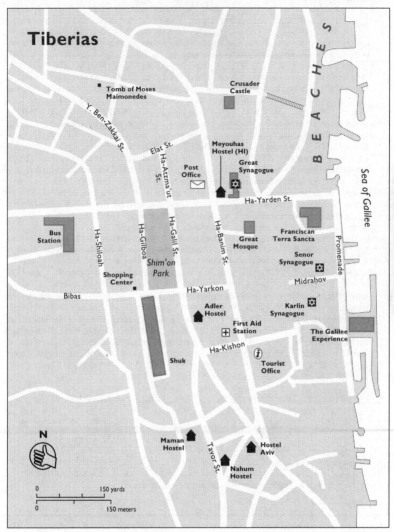

Tiberias

Tomb of Moses Maimonedes
Crusader Castle
Y. Ben-Zakkai St.
Elat St.
Ha-Atzma'ut St.
Meyouhas Hostel (HI)
Post Office
Great Synagogue
Ha-Yarden St.
BEACHES
Sea of Galilee
Bus Station
Ha-Shiloah
Ha-Gilboa
Ha-Galil St.
Shim'on Park
Ha-Banim St.
Great Mosque
Franciscan Terra Sancta
Senor Synagogue
Midrahov
Promenade
Shopping Center
Bibas
Ha-Yarkon
Adler Hostel
First Aid Station
Karlin Synagogue
The Galilee Experience
Shuk
Ha-Kishon
Tourist Office
N
Maman Hostel
Tavor St.
Nahum Hostel
Hostel Aviv
0   150 yards
0   150 meters

ISRAEL

Telephones: Solan Express (tel. 672 64 70), on the *midrahov*. Fax and A/C phone booths; charges 10% less per unit than public phones. Open 24hr. **Telephone Code:** 06.

ACCOMMODATIONS

Competition is fierce in Tiberias; the second you step off the bus, hoteliers rush to woo you. Prices rise between July and September, and reservations are recommended. The Jewish holidays of Pesah, Rosh Ha-Shana, and Sukkot are mob scenes. Some hostels will arrange Golan tours. None of the hostels have lockouts. Accommodations take credit cards unless otherwise noted.

Meyouhas Hostel (HI) (tel. 672 17 75 or 679 03 50; fax 672 03 72), at the corner of Ha-Banim and Ha-Yarden, in a beautiful 1862 building made of local black basalt rock. Clean and airy, with TV room, balcony, A/C, and 24hr. reception. Check-in

2pm, check-out 10am. No curfew. Dorm beds (4-6 per room) US$15.50, nonmembers US$16.50; singles US$34; doubles US$48; triples US$61.50; quads US$76; quints US$85. Nonmembers add US$1.50. Breakfast included. Lockers NIS4. Reservations recommended; members have priority.

Maman Hostel (tel. 679 29 86), on Atzmon St. From Ha-Yarden St., turn south on Ha-Galil, then bear right on Tavor St. and turn right at the first intersection—look for the red-and-white sign. Easygoing atmosphere, clean baths, pool, kitchen, and A/C. Reception open 7am-midnight. No curfew. Dorm beds (4-8 per room) July-Aug. NIS30, Sept.-June NIS25; private rooms July-Aug. NIS120, Sept.-June NIS80.

Hostel Aviv (tel./fax 672 35 10), on Ha-Galil St., 1 block south of intersection of Ha-Galil and Ha-Banim St. All rooms have fridge and A/C, many have balconies. Kitchen, TV room, and bar. Clean, lively backpacker atmosphere with super owners. Golan tours are US$32 for a day in a 14-person truck. 24hr. reception. Check-out 10am. Dorm beds (4-7 per room) NIS25, low season NIS20; doubles NIS60, low season NIS50; with private bath NIS90, low season NIS80. Lockers NIS5.

Minilon Hostel, 8 Achiva (tel. 679 04 34), turn right at the Panorama Hotel. Run by the same friendly folk as the Hostel Aviv. Large rooms have fridge, A/C, shower, toilet, and cable TV. Peaceful atmosphere. 24hr reception. Doubles July-Aug. NIS100, Sept.-June NIS80. Ask for kitchen facilities at no extra charge.

Hostel Adler (tel. 672 00 31), on Ha-Galil St. Central location, with A/C, TV room, bar, and kitchen. 24hr. reception. Flexible check-out 11am. Dorm beds (3-4 per room) NIS25; doubles with bath NIS80. Cash only.

Hostel Galil (tel. 671 67 10), at the intersection of Ha-Galil and Tavor St. Clean A/C rooms, some with balconies or private baths. Kitchen and cable TV; separate men's and women's toilets and bath. Reception 8am-11pm; checkout 9am. Rooms for up to five people NIS100-120. Cash only. Free coffee and tea.

Naḥum Hostel (tel. 672 15 05). From Ha-Yarden St. turn south on Ha-Galil, then right on Tavor St. Relaxed, with clean rooms, most with private bath. Downstairs rooms are dim but have kitchenette. Rooms with A/C available, but in the summer you're just as likely to get stuck with a portable fan and a view of the backlot. Lively rooftop bar with MTV and breezy Galilee views. Reception open 8am-11pm. Dorm beds (6-7 per room) NIS30; doubles NIS140. Cash only.

Camping is a good way to escape the city heat. Before you throw down your sleeping bag, check out the MTIO/SPNI information booth (tel. 675 20 56) at Tzemaḥ on the southern tip of the lake (open summer 9am-5pm; take bus #18, 21, 22, 24, 26, or 28). Their free map shows the 25 lakeside campgrounds interspersed among the private beaches (NIS40 per car; free for car-less campers). You provide the food, water, and insect repellent, and the government kicks in with jiffy johns and trash bins. Take the Ein Gev bus from Tiberias and get off when you see a site, or walk south along the coast. Be wary of **theft.** Women should never camp alone.

FOOD

For a town of its size, Tiberias boasts a surprisingly varied culinary landscape. The **shuk,** in a square block starting at Ha-Yarden St. and going south, sells cheap, high-quality produce every day except *Shabbat.* Pick up a light meal at one of the street's many **falafel** stands, running from Ha-Banim St. toward the bus station. Grilleries near the *midraḥov* serve *shishlik* with salad and pita for about NIS12, and waterfront seafood restaurants offer idyllic settings if you can block out the jet skiers and plastic bottle flotillas. A dinner of St. Peter's fish, a Sea of Galilee specialty, costs about NIS35-40. Ha-Galil and Ha-Banim and the squares in between burgeon with culinary possibility. Check out the cheap Thai stirfry (NIS15) and more upscale Mexican restaurants around the *midraḥov* and down HaGalil St. Two inexpensive Ha-Galil establishments are **Stekiat Aḥim Elfassi,** near Ha-Kishon St., where a barbecued feast goes for NIS8, and kosher **Weizmann's Pizza,** where a slice is NIS4. There is a **Co-op supermarket** in the Great Mosque Plaza across from Meyouhas Hostel with super variety and super prices (open Sun.-Fri. 7am-8pm).

Maman Restaurant (tel. 672 11 26), corner of Ha-Galil and Bibas St. Crammed with Israeli regulars. Hummus or *tahina* (NIS10), or *shishlik*, chips, and salad (NIS20). A/C. Kosher. Open Sun.-Thurs. 11am-11pm, Fri. 11am-sundown.

Panda, 32 Hamisgad Sq. (tel. 679 02 21), behind Big Ben on the left up the short flight of stairs. Their business lunch (NIS32) provides the hungry-budget-traveler-disguised-as-business-person with egg roll, soup, main course, and fried rice. Best service this side of the Great Wall complemented by surreal Chinese techno music. Open daily noon-midnight; lunch special until 3pm.

Little Tiberias (tel. 679 21 48 or 28 06), on Ha-Kishon St. Excellent French and Italian cuisine and seafood in a cozy retreat from *midrahov* mayhem. Filet steak (NIS55), lasagna (NIS28), salads (NIS10). Open daily noon-2am. MC, Visa, AmEx.

Guy Restaurant (tel. 672 30 36 or 19 73), on Ha-Galil St. south of Ha-Kishon St. Cool, quiet, kosher Moroccan kitchen. Stuffed vegetables (NIS7-9) and various salads. Specialties include 7 types of eggplant and fried, meat-filled "cigars" (NIS3). Open Sun.-Thurs. noon-11pm, Fri noon-sundown, Sat. after dark.

El Gaucho, 19 Ha-Banim St. (tel. 672 41 71), next to the *midrahov*. Sumptuous Argentinian grill. Between noon and 5pm, get a meal for NIS39. Large chef's salad NIS26. Open Sun.-Thurs. noon-midnight, Fri. noon-6pm, Sat. 7pm-midnight.

Coffee Show (tel. 672 12 72), on the *midrahov* opposite Big Ben. Excellent coffee (NIS9-12). Pastries brought in daily from Tel Aviv. Spectacular dessert (NIS15) and great service. 10% off with ISIC. Open daily 8am-3am. MC, Visa.

SIGHTS

All that's left of the **old city,** shaken by earthquakes and conquerors, is a few wall fragments which litter the modern town. The **Tomb of Moses Maimonides,** on Ben-Zakkai St., commemorates the controversial but hugely influential 13th-century rabbi and philosopher whose works synthesized neo-Aristotelian-Arab philosophy with Judaism. According to legend, an unguided camel carried his coffin to Tiberias. To reach the tomb, take Ha-Yarden St. east (toward the water) and turn left on Ben-Zakkai St. The tomb is two blocks up on the right. You'll see a red fence and black pillars; the white half-cylinder with Hebrew writing is the actual tomb. Ask for the tomb of "Rambam," the rabbi's Hebrew acronym (Rabbi Moshe Ben-Maimon). The **Tomb of Rabbi Akiva** is on the hillside above the Galilee (take bus #4 and ask for directions). Believers gather to have their illnesses cured at the hillside tomb of Akiva's student, **Rabbi Meir Ba'al Ha-Nes,** above the hot springs (tombs open Sun.-Thurs. 8am-7pm, Fri. 8am-2pm; modest dress required).

On the promenade next to the Caesar Hotel stands the **Franciscan Terra Sancta Church,** (tel. 672 05 16), also known as St. Peter's, built in the 12th century to commemorate St. Peter's role in the growth of Christianity. The apse behind the altar is arched like the bow of a boat, in honor of his pre-apostolic fishing career. In the courtyard is a statue of the Virgin Mary created by Polish troops who lived in the church from 1942 to 1945 (open daily 8-11:45am and 2-5pm).

Farther south is a blue-and-red marina, home to shops and the **Galilee Experience** (tel. 672 36 20), a 36-minute must-see film on the past 4000 years in the Galilee emphasizing the life of Jesus and the formation of Israel. Composed of almost 2000 slides and 27 slide projectors, this is an informative way to escape the midday heat (shown every hr. 8am-10pm except during *Shabbat;* US$8/NIS27, students US$6/NIS21; screened in 13 languages).

Cool kids can kick back in the slimy waters of the world's earliest known **hot mineral springs.** One legend maintains that the springs were formed in the Great Flood when the earth's insides boiled. Another holds that demons heat the water under standing orders from King Solomon. Cleanse body and wallet (NIS45, Sat. NIS50). Admission includes pools, sauna, jacuzzi, and beach. A massage is NIS92 (Sat. NIS102) and a private mineral bath NIS72 (Sat. NIS82). The older building, **Tiberias Hot Springs** (tel. 679 19 67), has single-sex baths with very hot water (open Sun.-Fri. July-Aug. 7am-4pm, Sept.-June 7am-2pm). The newer building, **Tiberias Hot Springs Spa** (tel. 679 19 67), serves those seeking less scalding rejuvenation (open Sun.-Mon. and Wed. 8am-8pm, Tues. and Thurs. 8am-11pm, Fri. 8am-6pm, Sat. 8:30am-8pm). The springs are 3km south of town on the coastal road; bus #5 (every 20min.) runs from the central bus station and Ha-Galil St.

The small **Lehmann museum** (tel. 672 52 87) displays Tiberias's hot spring history. Walk out the museum's back door to reach the ruins of the **Hammat Synagogues,** six ancient buildings constructed on top of one another. The four upper synagogues were used from the 6th to the 8th centuries CE. Below these ruins are the remains of Roman spas, still releasing scalding water. The jewel of the exhibit is a mosaic floor that was once part of three separate synagogues (museum and synagogues open Sun.-Thurs. 8am-5pm, Fri. 8am-4pm; NIS7, students NIS5.50).

Karnei Ḥittim (the Horns of Ḥittim) is where Salah ad-Din defeated the Crusaders in 1187. From this mountain peak, you can see Jordan to the east, the Mediterranean to the west, and Tzfat to the north. Take bus #42 and ask the driver where to get off. The walk to the top of the hill takes about 50 minutes, but the view will leave you more breathless than the climb (open 8am-5pm).

ENTERTAINMENT

For many **beaches** on the Galilee, you'll have to bring your own sand—otherwise, bring sandals for walking over the sizzling black rocks. Beaches in the city and the immediate vicinity are owned by hotels that charge hefty fees in exchange for changing rooms, showers, boat rentals, and food. The beaches farther north are located along Gedud Barak Rd., off Ha-Yarden.

Lido Kinneret (tel. 679 05 64), just off Ha-Yarden St., charges NIS15 for admission and more for waterskiing (NIS115 for 15min.; open daily 8am-10pm). Just north, the somewhat dilapidated **Nelson Beach** (NIS15) has two-person kayaks or four to five-person paddle boats (NIS50 per hr.), water skiing (NIS90 for 15min., discount for group of four), and the only speed-boat-drawn **inflatable banana** on the Galilee (NIS30 for 15min.; open 24hr.). In the summertime, these beaches have rock concerts and camping (NIS10). Further north are the meticulously tended **Quiet Beach** (tel. 679 01 25; open 8am-6pm; NIS25) and **Blue Beach** (tel. 672 01 05; open 8:30am-6pm; NIS16, Sat. NIS20). A 15-minute walk or a short ride on bus #5 south of Tiberias brings you to the **Municipal Beach** (tel. 672 07 09; open 9am-5:45pm, Fri. 9am-4:45pm; NIS10). Next to it is the **Holiday Inn Beach** (tel. 679 28 90; open 8:30am-5pm; NIS15). Look for the bridge connecting hotel and lakefront. A **religious beach** on Gedud Barak Rd. (entrance opposite the Church of Scotland Guest House) is open to women Sunday, Tuesday, and Thursday, and men Monday, Wednesday, and Friday 8am-5pm. To avoid the hefty admission prices of most beaches, you can circle the old city walls at the southern end of the promenade and walk 200m along the dirt path through the field to a small **free beach.**

Nightlife in Tiberias centers on the *midraḥov* and promenade area. In summer, street musicians, popcorn vendors, and the occasional palm-reader set up shop here. Israelis dance on outdoor tables to live, cutlass-brandishing rock (Tues.-Wed. and Sat. 10 or 11pm) at **La Pirate Pub,** at the corner of the *midraḥov* and the promenade (0.5L beer NIS11-17; open daily 5pm-4am). **Big Ben,** toward the promenade end of the *midraḥov,* is less rowdy, despite being filled with young, drunk Brits giving each other the time of day (0.25L of beer NIS13). At the northern end of the promenade is a bar known locally as **The Coconut,** with occasional live music (open daily 10pm-4am). Continuing the fruit theme is nearby **Papaya,** with its long bar and excellent music—a hip spot in the past. **Amstel,** at the northern end of the marina, is chock full of Israeli youth (you can't miss the crowds) drinking the namesake beer. If you'd rather nurse your hangover than start another one, head to **Makom Baḥutz** (tel. 672 26 68), around the corner from the north end of the promenade. Their frozen yogurt with fresh fruit mix-ins (NIS10 for 3 toppings) and outdoor screenings of Israeli comedies or music videos make for a relaxed evening on the town.

Get out your white polyester duds and thigh highs for Lido Kinneret Beach and Kinneret Sailing's nightly **disco cruises** (departing nightly 8-11pm depending on the number of people amassed; NIS15). Overindulgence on powerboats may lead to power-boots—landlubbers should stick to La Pirate.

A tangle of waterslides swishes one km south of Tiberias at **Luna Gai Beach** (tel. 679 07 90; open daily 9am-5pm; admission NIS45). Walk or take bus #5 from the central bus station or Ha-Galil St. The mother of all water parks is **Luna Gai,** operated by Moshav Ramot on the eastern shore. This **aquataganza** has bumper boats! slides! pools! waterfalls! an inner tube ride! all that *and* an excellent beach! (tel. 673 17 50; open daily 9:30am-6pm; admission a wallet-drenching NIS55.)

The **Sea of Galilee Festival** brings international folk troupes to Tiberias during the second week of July. Check at the GTIO for information on this and other area fests, including Ein Gev's **Passover Music Festival** and Tzemaḥ's **Tu b'Av Love Fest** (mid-August), where happy young Israelis gather for some love, sweat, and rock 'n' roll.

■ Near Tiberias: Beit She'an בית שאן

Beit She'an, one of the finest archaeological sites in the country, is a Sephardi development town containing a vast complex of mostly Roman and Byzantine ruins. Excavations on **Tel al-Husn,** the main archaeological mound, have already revealed some 20 layers of settlements dating back as far as the 5th millennium BCE. Of particular interest is the **Roman theater,** one of the largest extant Roman constructions in Israel. Built in 200 CE by Emperor Septimius Severus, the theater accommodated 7000 riotous spectators in its three tiers of semi-circular seating.

The remains of other grand structures branching off from the theater include colonnaded Roman streets, a Byzantine bathhouse, and a Roman temple to Dionysus. Climb to the top of the *tel* to get your bearings. To the southeast are the remnants of a 2nd-century CE **Roman amphitheater,** used for gladiatorial spectacles, and a 4th-century CE Byzantine residential quarter. North of the *tel* is the **Monastery of the Noble Lady Maria,** founded in 567 CE and abandoned after the Persian invasion of 614. The monastery has a mosaic depicting the months of the year. A much earlier period of Egyptian control left the ruins of the **Ashtaroth Temple,** built by Ramses III for his Canaanite allies. Beit She'an can be fully explored in about an hour. To get to the site from the Beit She'an bus stop, turn left at the main street, right after Bank Leumi, and then follow the paved road (site tel. (06) 658 71 89; open Sat.-Thurs. 8am-5pm, Fri. 8am-4pm; closes 1hr. earlier in winter; NIS16). Buses #412 and 415 leave Afula for Beit She'an (every 20min., 35min., NIS9.40). From Tiberias, take bus #434, 961, 963, or 964 (50min., NIS17). Beit She'an's newest attraction is the **border crossing facility** into Jordan (take bus #16 from town, 8:15 and 9:20am and 2:15pm). This tiny bridge, built by Ottomans, is one of Israel's busiest crossings. Allow a half day to cross, especially on Thursday and Sunday. For more information on **border crossings into Jordan,** see page 436.

Near Beit She'an: The Road to Afula

Along the road from Beit She'an to Afula (buses #412 and 415 travel there) are several sights of natural and historical interest. To get to Afula from Nazareth take bus #355, 357, 823, or 824 (every hr., 20min., NIS7.30).

Within Kibbutz Hefziba is the 6th-century CE **Beit Alpha Synagogue** (tel. (06) 653 20 04), whose highlight is a magnificently preserved mosaic of a zodiac wheel surrounding the sun god Helios (identified with the prophet Elijah), reflecting the Hellenic influence on the area. (Open Sat.-Thurs. 8am-5pm, Fri. 8am-4pm; closes 1hr. earlier in winter. Admission NIS7, students NIS5.25.) Take bus #412, 415, or 417 from either Afula (30min., NIS8) or Beit She'an (20min., NIS5.20). Don't be misled by the sign for Kibbutz Beit Alpha (1km closer to Beit She'an).

Gan Ha-Shlosha (tel. (06) 658 62 19), also known as **Saḥne,** 1km west of Beit Alpha, is worth an afternoon excursion. Its waterfalls and crystal-clear swimming holes are refreshing in both summer and winter (at a constant 28°C). The springs have been popular since Roman times; the covered pool and waterslides haven't (open daily 8am-6pm; NIS21). Brave souls leap into the pools from the rocky ridges above. Watch out for theft on overcrowded weekends. Bus #412 and 415 from Afula (NIS8) or Beit She'an (NIS4.70) go to Saḥne. A 10-minute walk along the road behind the park leads to the **Museum of Regional and Mediterranean Archaeology** (tel. (06) 644 80 45), a collection of Hellenistic and Islamic art and pottery gathered from a local Canaanite temple, an Israelite community, and a Roman colony. You can't miss the Greek columns scattered around the entrance (open Sun.-Thurs. 8am-2pm, Sat. and holidays 10am-2pm; park admission required to see the museum). Opposite the museum, across the bridge, is the recently opened **Tel-Amal Stockade and Tower.** Critical in defending Israel in its formative years, the first stockade and tower settlement was set up here in 1936. The reconstructed tower offers wonderful views of the surrounding area. There is also an English and Hebrew audio-visual presentation (open Sun.-Thurs. 10am-2pm).

Three km from Afula is the **Ma'ayan Harod National Park,** named after the Harod spring which flows out of Mt. Gilboa. This is the site where Gideon's men were chosen to fight the Midionites. Above the spring are the graves of Yehoshua Hankin (who purchased the land for the Jewish National Fund) and his wife Olga. Close by is a brass monument commemorating those who gave their lives in the struggle for independence. The hordes of Israeli schoolchildren who visit the park are not interested in any of this; they come for the large, icy **swimming pool.** After a perusal of the yawn-inspiring sights, you may understand why (park open daily 8am-4pm; NIS20).

An even better reason to visit the park is the neighboring **Ma'ayan Harod Youth Hostel (HI)** (tel/fax (06) 653 16 60). Bus #35 from Afula (11:45am and 6:15pm) will take you directly to the hostel; bus #415 (express), 402, 405, and 412 go to the access road, 1km away. Just before the entrance to the national park, take a left (the green sign for the hostel is obscured by tree branches). All cabins have air conditioning and attached bathrooms. The reception has maps of the area, and the hostel is a great base to start hikes to surrounding sights. Guests get a 50% discount at the national park. You can pay in foreign currency, which saves you the tax (dorm beds NIS52; singles NIS116; doubles NIS150; reception open 8am-noon and 4-7pm, Fri. until 2pm; check–out 10am; US$1.50 HI discount; call ahead July-Aug.).

▪ Near Tiberias: The Sea of Galilee (Lake Kinneret)

GETTING AROUND

All the sights on the Sea of Galilee are in some way accessible by **bus** from Tiberias, but, believe it or not, renting a **mountain bike** is the more convenient and scenic way to go (try **Hostel Aviv,** p. 382). A complete circuit of the lake takes four to five hours, plus the time you spend at the sights. As you peddle along, there are two creatures to watch out for: the furry little hyrax (a close relative of the elephant) and the screeching, careening Israeli driver (a close relative of the crash test dummy). Spring is the best time for biking; the hills are unbearable in summer. The **Lido Kinneret Sailing Co.** (tel. 672 15 38) operates a **ferry** between Lido Beach and Ginnosar (NIS15 oneway; no extra charge for bikes). An excellent, albeit expensive, way to explore the northern coast of the Galilee is on **horseback.** For information on guided tours, horse rentals, and lessons, write to: **Vered Ha-Galil,** Korazim, or call (06) 693 57 85. To rent a trusty mount, take bus #459, 541, 841, or 963 from Tiberias and get off at Korazim junction, in front of Vered Ha-Galil. Several kibbutzim and *moshavim* also offer horseback riding; check at the Tiberias GTIO. The region's **telephone code** is 06.

SIGHTS ON THE SHORE

Thirty minutes southeast of Tiberias, the hot baths of **Hammat Gader** (Al Himma in Arabic; tel. 675 10 39) lie in former Syrian territory. In Roman times the town, combined with its other (Jordanian) half on the western side of the Yarmuk River, formed part of the Decapolis (see **The Ancient Levant,** p. 47). The more interesting remains are in Jordan (see **Umm Qeis,** p. 510), but Roman ruins here, including a small pool that was reserved for lepers, have been partially reconstructed. At the southwest corner of the complex is the hottest spring in the area—so hot (51°C) that the Jews call it *Ma'ayan Ha-Gehinom* (Hell's Pool) and the Arabs *Ain Maqla* (Frying Pool). The

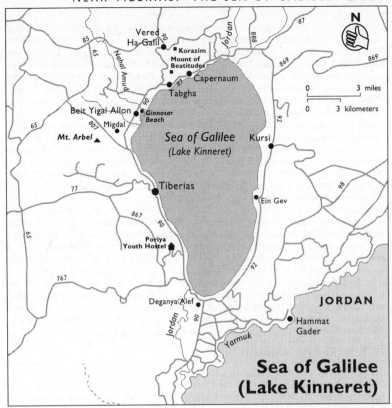

Sea of Galilee
(Lake Kinneret)

hot pool is crowded with families; the leper pool isn't. There is also an area for slathering on black mud that purportedly cures skin ailments. Just west of the Roman baths are the ruins of a 5th-century **synagogue.**

Ḥammat Gader boasts an **alligator park,** where hundreds of large, somnolent gators sun themselves and slog through murky water. The first generation was imported from Florida, but the reserve now raises its young in a hothouse at the entrance to the ponds. There is also a trampoline play area, a reptile house, and kitschy alligator and parrot shows throughout the day. (Open Mon.-Sat. 6:15am-11pm, Sun. 6:15am-4:30pm. Admission NIS32-40 depending on time of day. Slink in for NIS20 6:15-7am.) **Bus** #24 leaves from Tiberias at 8:45 and 10:30am, returning at noon and 3pm (Fri. bus returns at noon and 1pm).

Near the spot where the Jordan River flows out of the Sea of Galilee, about 8km south of Tiberias and west of Ḥammat Gader, is **Deganya Alef,** Israel's first kibbutz and birthplace of General Moshe Dayan. The kibbutz was founded by Russians in 1909 and now manufactures diamond tools. At the entrance is a Syrian tank, a testimony to the 1948 War of Independence, when the Syrians were repelled from the kibbutz.

Did you ever wonder why every kibbutz and podunk town in Israel insists on having at least two museums? Wonder some more at nearby **Beit Gordon** (tel. 675 00 40). One is on Galilee archaeology, the other on natural history—stuffed animal carcasses abound (open Sun.-Thurs. 9am-3:30pm, Fri. 9am-noon, Sat. 9:30am-noon; NIS8). Deganya's frightening uniformity leads easily to misdirection. Take a right after the tennis courts and ambulances and ask for directions. Next to Beit Gordon is the **SPNI Kinorot Field School** (open Sun.-Thurs. 8am-3:30pm., Fri. 9am-1pm) with guides for hire and maps for sale. The best **hikes** in the area are the trails at **Mt. Arbel** and **Naḥal Amud,** both to the northwest of the Sea of Galilee. Naḥal Amud flows from the lake far out into the Galilee. Serious backpackers use the trail as either the first or last leg of a three-day **Yam L'Yam hike** (Sea to Shining Sea—Galilee to Mediterranean; see Montfort and Naḥal Keziv, p. 372). Hiring a guide is strongly recommended, and consulting maps, compasses, and the SPNI are a must. The Naḥal Amud trail is also a small component of the **Israel Trail,** which stretches all the way from Metulla to Eilat. From Tiberias, buses #23, 24, 26, and 29 pass through town.

The low water level of the Galilee in 1985-86 had one serendipitous effect—the discovery of an **ancient boat** under a segment of newly exposed lake bed off the beach of Kibbutz Ginnosar. Its wooden frame, turned to mush after centuries of marinating in mud, was encased in a fiberglass brace and hauled to shore. The boat, dating from 100 BCE to 100 CE, has been restored to near-pristine condition. Noting its age, some Christians have dubbed it "the Jesus boat." While it *is* a fishing boat, even of the sort the apostles might have used, archaeologists suspect it was sunk in a great sea battle (described by Josephus) between the Romans and Jews (boat and 20min. film NIS9, students NIS6). It rests right next to the new **Yigal Allon Center** (tel. 672 29 05) in an airtight glass tank, where it will undergo nine more years of cosmetic repair. The center is named after a central figure in the establishment of the state of Israel. It contains several exhibitions on its four floors: models and photographs of different settlements, a chance to reenact several military engagements (ranging from the Bar Kochba Revolt to the six-day war), and a multitude of audio-visual presentations (open Sat.-Thurs. 9am-5pm, Fri. 9am-1pm, Sat. 8:30am-4pm; admission NIS13, students NIS11). Next door is shady green **Ginnosar Beach** (tel. 679 21 61; open 9am-6pm; NIS20, students NIS15; paddle boats NIS40 per hr., kayaks NIS30). To get there, take **bus** #50-52 (20min., NIS5.50) from Tiberias to Beit Yigal Allon.

NEW TESTAMENT SIGHTS

According to the New Testament, Jesus walked on the waters of the Sea of Galilee. Four of the most significant stories in Christian history are set in the steep hills of its northern coast. Modest dress is required for entrance to these sights—no shorts or bare shoulders.

Migdal, the birthplace of Mary Magdalene, lies north of Tiberias, halfway to Capernaum. Though an important town when the Crusaders built a church here in the 12th century, today it is an agricultural community, founded in 1910, with a tiny, white-domed shrine. Buses #50-52 run to Migdal from Tiberias (10min.).

In **Tabgha,** 2km southwest of Capernaum along the coastal road, the **Church of the Primacy of St. Peter** (tel. 672 47 67) marks the site of the miracle of the loaves and fishes and the spot where Jesus made Peter "Shepherd of his People." According to the Book of John, Peter led the apostles on a fishing expedition 100m offshore from Tabgha. A man on shore called to them to throw their nets over the starboard side and assured them of a catch. When the nets hit the water, a swarm of fish swam in. Peter jumped off the boat and swam to shore, where he found the man, whom he now realized was Jesus, preparing a meal for the Twelve. This was the third time that Jesus revealed himself to the disciples after the Resurrection. When the others sailed in, Jesus asked Peter, "do you love me?" When Peter replied that he did, Jesus told him to "tend my sheep" and to "follow me." (John 21:15-19). The Church of the Primacy is built around a rock said to be the table of this feast. The first church at this spot was built in the 4th century, destroyed in 614 CE, and rebuilt with black basalt by the Franciscans in 1933. On the seaward side of the church are the steps where Jesus called out his instructions; on the shoreline are the "thrones of the Apostles," a series of six double- or heart-shaped column bases built by early Christians (open Sun.-Thurs. 8am-noon and 2-5pm).

Just west of the Church of the Primacy along the northern coast of the sea lies the **Church of the Multiplication of the Loaves and Fishes.** A mosaic inside relates how Jesus fed 5000 pilgrims with five loaves and two small fish (Matthew 15:29-39). A section of the mosaic has been removed to reveal the original 4th-century foundations (open Mon.-Sat. 8:30am-5pm, Sun. 10am-5pm, modest dress required). Around the right side of the church, past the "private" sign and up the stairs, is a small **hospice** (tel. 672 10 61; doubles with A/C NIS50 per person; some with showers and toilets). Take bus #459, 541, 841, or 963, and get off at the Tabgha Junction.

On the **Mount of Beatitudes,** overlooking sea, field, and town, Jesus gave his Sermon on the Mount (Matthew 5). A church funded by Benito Mussolini stands on the Mount, its octagonal shape recalling the eight beatitudes. To reach the Mount, take bus #459, 541, or 963 from Tiberias; get off at the second stop after the bus turns uphill away from the lake. From here, a sign points the way to the church, 1km along a side road (open daily 8am-noon and 2:30-5pm).

From the Mount, the ancient town of **Capernaum** (Kfar Naḥum in Hebrew, Tel Num in Arabic) is 3km down to the coastal road and marked by a white signpost. Jesus healed Simon's mother-in-law and the Roman Centurion's servant here (Luke 4:31-37 and 7:1-10), and Peter was born here. A modern church arches over the ruins of a 5th-century octagonal church, marking the site believed to have held Peter's house. Nearby, the ruins of a synagogue, perched in the middle of the old town, contain Corinthian columns and friezes dating from the 4th century CE. Since Capernaum did not participate in the Jewish revolts against the Romans of the first and 2nd centuries CE, it survived unscathed (open daily 8:30am-4:15pm; NIS2). Buses #459, 541, 841, and 963 from Tiberias pass the Capernaum junction about once an hour on the way north to Kiryat Shmona and Tzfat. Get off before the bus turns up the Mount and walk 3km along the shore.

Four kilometers north of the Sea of Galilee and 2km east of the Tiberias-Rosh Pina road, you will find the ruins of the Jewish town of **Korazim** (tel. 693 49 82), one of the unrepentant towns chastised by Jesus (Matthew 11:21). The white sign leads to the modern town; follow the orange sign to the site. There you'll find a synagogue dating from the Talmudic period (3rd-4th centuries CE). The bare, rolling landscape is strewn with the dark basalt rubble of what were once streets and dwellings. The remains suggest a basic village layout characteristic of the time: housing quarters centered around a paved courtyard, and a synagogue with some detailed ornamental pediments and a reconstructed interior cornice (open Sun.-Thurs. 8am-5pm, Fri. 8am-4pm; closes 1hr. earlier in winter; NIS12, students NIS9). Take bus #459, 841, or 963.

On the eastern side of the lake, 7km north of Ein Gev, lie the ruins of **Kursi** (Gergessa or Gerasa), a Christian settlement dating from early Byzantine times (5th-6th centuries CE). According to the New Testament, it was at Kursi that Jesus exorcised several demons from a man's body and caused the demons to possess a grazing herd of pigs; the pigs raced into the sea and drowned. Jesus' feat came to be known as the "Miracle of the Swine" (Luke 8:26-31, Matthew 8:23-34). The site is popular with Christian pilgrims and has impressive remains of a large monastery and a small chapel—both reconstructed, both with mosaic floors (site tel. 673 19 83; open Sat.-Thurs. 8am-5pm, Fri. 8am-4pm; closes 1hr. earlier in winter; NIS7, students NIS5.25). Buses #15, 17-19, 21, and 22 run from Tiberias to Kursi (30min., NIS9.70).

Perched above the Sea of Galilee is the **Poriya Youth Hostel (HI)** (tel. (06) 675 00 50; fax 675 16 28), on Rte. 7677 opposite Barniki Beach. The hostel has a great view, but only athletes will make it up the 3km from the main road. (Check-in 2pm; check-out 10am. Bed with A/C and private shower US$30; dorms without either US$18; wooden cabins US$33; US$1.50 discount for members. Credit cards accepted.)

▓ Tzfat (Safed) צפת صفد

The mystical city of Tzfat will enrapture anyone who's ever had a profound thought (or faked one). Built upon Mt. Kenaan, Tzfat is a city of mesmerizing beauty and tranquility, where the difference between history and myth is slight and each street corner has its own odd set of legends. Jewish traditions are taken seriously in Tzfat. The Talmud translates the town's name as "vantage point" because of the city's panoramic view of the Galilean hills, but others claim that the name derives from the root for "anticipation." Many in Tzfat await the arrival of the Messiah, whom they believe will pass through on His way from Mt. Meron to Jerusalem. The modern-day mystics of Tzfat may dress in uniformly black garb, but they come from diverse backgrounds: some are descendants of old *shtetl* rabbis, others are *baalei t'shuva* (literally, "masters of return"), who came to Ḥasidic Judaism after living much of their lives as agnostic real-estate agents or Buddhist backpackers.

Tzfat hasn't always been a bastion of Jewish spirituality. Its Crusader-built castle was captured by Salah ad-Din in 1158, then lost in 1240 to the Mamluk Sultan Baybars. It wasn't until the Middle Ages (most notably after the Spanish Inquisition) that many Jews arrived in Tzfat, seeking refuge in the relatively tolerant Ottoman Empire. Rabbi Isaac Luria, often called by the acronym Ha-Ari, established Tzfat as the center of Kabbalistic mysticism in the 16th century, and his work (combined with worsening conditions in Eastern Europe) brought Ḥasidic Jews from Poland in 1778. However, the city's population soon dwindled after it was pillaged by the Druze in 1837. New settlements began in the second half of the 19th century and triggered violent Arab protests. By 1948, 12,000 Arabs lived in uneasy coexistence with 1700 Jews. In May 1948, Israeli Palmaḥ troops defeated the Iraqi and Syrian forces entrenched in Mt. Meron. Tzfat's native Arab population fled with their armies. The evacuated homes now house an artists' colony.

Today, tourists of all denominations come to enjoy Tzfat's unique character and its crisp, sweet air, which sages call its characteristic "element." Of course, it is possible to get too much of Tzfat's atmosphere: in 1777, a rabbi who had trekked to Tzfat all the way from Europe ultimately packed up and left for Tiberias, complaining that the angels had kept him up at night. Modern-day hostels don't provide refunds for angel-infested accommodations.

ORIENTATION AND PRACTICAL INFORMATION

Tzfat is arranged in circular terraces descending from the castle ruins at the town center. **Jerusalem (Yerushalayim) Street,** behind the central bus station, follows the lines of what was once the castle's moat and makes a complete circle around **Gan Ha-Metzuda** (Park of the Citadel). **Ha-Palmaḥ Street** begins off Jerusalem St. near the central bus station and crosses the main street via a stone bridge.

The city could be divided into three districts: the **Park Area,** at the top of the mountain (ringed by Jerusalem St.), the **Artists' Quarter,** southwest and down the hill, and the **Synagogue Quarter** (Old City), immediately to the north of the Artists' Quarter on the other side of Ma'alot Oleh Ha-Gardom St. The **midrahov** (pedestrian mall) is the strip of Jerusalem St. running southwest of the Park Area, up the hill from the Artists' and Synagogue Quarters.

Government Tourist Information Office (GTIO): tel. 692 09 61 or 62. The 1st office on the right, on the 1st floor of the Wolfson Auditorium on Ha-Palmaḥ St. From Jerusalem St., take a right on Aliyah Bet St., and walk until you reach the plaza at the top; the auditorium is on the left. Free map and propagandous brochures about Tzfat, the Galilee, and Messianic Judaism. Open Sun.-Fri. 9am-2:30pm.

Currency Exchange: Several **banks** on Jerusalem St. Most open Sun., Tues., and Thurs. 8:30am-12:30pm and 4-6pm, Mon. and Wed. 8:30am-12:30pm, and Fri. 8:30am-noon.

Buses: Central Bus Station, Ha-Atzma'ut Sq. (tel. 692 11 22). Bus #459 runs between **Tiberias** and Tzfat (every hr. until 7pm, NIS14.50). #361 and 362 go to and from **Haifa** through **Akko** (every 20min.; last bus Sun.-Thurs. 8:45pm, Fri. 5pm, 1st Sat. bus 9:10pm.; 45min.; NIS25). Bus #846 to **Tel Aviv** (5:15am and 5:35pm, 2½hr., NIS40). Buses #501 and #511 to **Kiryat Shemona** (every hr. until 7pm, 45min., NIS15). #964 direct to **Jerusalem** on Fri. (12:30pm, 2½hr., NIS40).

Taxis: Kenaan Taxis (tel. 697 07 07), near bus station. *Sherut* to Tiberias, Rosh Pina.

Laundry: Dry Cleaning, 38 Jerusalem St. (tel. 697 38 77), with a large sign. NIS10 per kg. Open Sun.-Mon., Wed.-Thurs. 8:30am-2pm and 4-7pm, Tues. and Fri. 8:30am-2pm.

Pharmacy: Golan Pharmacy (tel. 692 04 72), just opposite the Municipality building on Jerusalem St. **Canaan Pharmacy** (tel. 697 24 40), under the Ha-Palmaḥ Bridge. Both open Sun.-Thurs. 8:30am-1pm and 4-7pm, Fri. 8:30am-1pm.

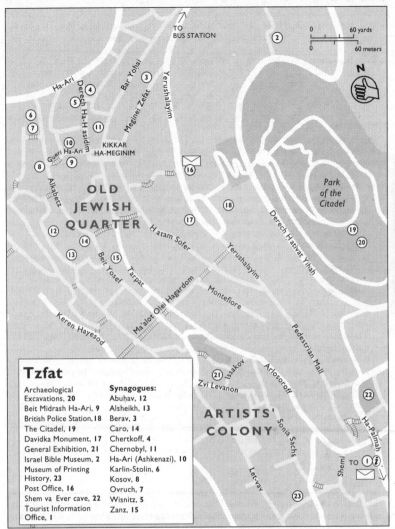

Tzfat

Archaeological Excavations, **20**	**Synagogues:**
Beit Midrash Ha-Ari, **9**	Abuḥav, **12**
British Police Station, **18**	Alsheikh, **13**
The Citadel, **19**	Berav, **3**
Davidka Monument, **17**	Caro, **14**
General Exhibition, **21**	Chertkoff, **4**
Israel Bible Museum, **2**	Chernobyl, **11**
Museum of Printing History, **23**	Ha-Ari (Ashkenazi), **10**
	Karlin-Stolin, **6**
Post Office, **16**	Kosov, **8**
Shem va Ever cave, **22**	Ovruch, **7**
Tourist Information Office, **1**	Wisnitz, **5**
	Zanz, **15**

Emergency: First Aid (Magen David Adom): tel. 101 in emergencies, otherwise 692 03 33; next to the central bus station. **Police:** tel. 100 in emergencies, otherwise 692 04 44 or 697 24 44.

Central Post Office: Ha-Palmaḥ St. (tel. 692 04 05), next to a radar dish visible from the corner with Aliya Bet; includes **Poste Restante.** Open Sun.-Tues. and Thurs. 8am-12:30pm and 3:30-6pm, Wed. 8am-1:30pm, Fri. 8am-noon. A more convenient branch on Jerusalem St. near the GTIO has similar hours.

Telephone Code: 06.

ACCOMMODATIONS

Tzfat's **youth hostel** is well equipped and only a short ride or 20-minute walk from the bus station. Other options, primarily in high season, are the inexpensive **guest rooms** and flats provided by town residents. The best way to find a rental is to walk around Jerusalem St. and the old city looking for "*ḥaderim l'haskir*" (rooms to let) signs. Always inspect your potential quarters before paying (blankets are a plus for Tzfat's chilly nights, even in summer), and bargain if you think the price is high.

Beit Binyamin (HI) (tel. 692 10 86; fax 697 35 14), near the Amal Trade School in South Tzfat. Take bus #6 or 7. Exceptionally clean, recently renovated rooms have private baths, refrigerators, and bounteous closet space. Pleasant gardens and a TV lounge. Check-in anytime, check-out 9am, no curfew or lockout. Dorm beds (4-6 per room) US$18.50; singles US$40.50; doubles US$59. US$1.50 discount for members. Breakfast included. Prices expected to rise by spring 1998. Wheelchair accessible. Takes credit cards.

Beit Lifshitz (tel. 697 47 10), on Ha-Palmaḥ St. near the bridge, in the alley down the stairs from the "Ruth-Rimon Inn" sign and through a green door. Very simple furnishing, but large rooms have fridges and cluster around a cozy, shaded garden. Communal kitchen. 24hr. check-in, no curfew or check-out. Dorm beds NIS25.

Hadar Hotel (tel. 692 00 68), on Ridbaz St. Ridbaz is an alley off Jerusalem St.; take a right coming from the bus station and look for the sign on the left side of Ridbaz. Homey atmosphere with helpful staff. Rooms have bath and balcony; some have A/C. Rooftop lounge has a great view of the city. Check-out 11am, ring the bell after the midnight curfew. Singles NIS80; doubles NIS170. Winter prices NIS20 less.

Ascent Institute of Tzfat, 2 Ha-Ari St. (tel. 692 13 64 or 697 14 07; fax 692 19 42; e-mail ascent@act.com.co.il). The first right off Jerusalem St. from the bus station. Jews only. Run by Lubavitch Ḥasidim, many of whom are cheerful, New-Agey American expats. *Shabbat* guests get free dinner and lunch with local Ḥasidic families. Evening services held outside on the patio with spectacular sunset view. NIS10 rebate for each class you attend on Jewish texts and traditions. Reactions from secular Jews may range from personal revelation to annoyance. Reception open Sun.-Thurs. 9am-1pm and 4-8:30pm, Fri. 9am-4pm. Check-out 11am. Flexible 11:30pm curfew. Beds in clean, airy dorm rooms (4-8 beds each) NIS50. Credit cards accepted.

Shoshana's Hostel (tel. 697 39 39), across the alley from Beit Lifshitz . Simple but clean, with newly renovated kitchen facilities. Flexible 9am check-out and midnight curfew. Dorm beds NIS30; singles or doubles NIS80 per person.

Galilee Getaways, 8 Korchak St. (tel. 050 46 27 06), in the Artists' Colony near the Howard Johnson. Possibly the best deal on an apartment rental in Tzfat, this double-occupancy flat on the 2nd floor of an old Arab house has a full kitchen with mosaic floors and a balcony with a spectacular view of Lebanon to the north, Mt. Meron to the west, and Tiberias to the south. US$60 per night. Call or email Moshe Goldstein (goldsteinm@jazo.org.il) to make reservations; summer visitors should plan well in advance.

FOOD

The stretch of Jerusalem St. north of the bridge to #48 is lined with falafel joints and fairly expensive restaurants. Many establishments close on *Shabbat*—shop before Friday afternoon. A fruit and vegetable **market** is held Wednesdays 6am-2pm next to the bus station. There are **supermarkets** throughout town, including a **HyperKol** on the *midraḥov* (open Sun.-Thurs. 9am-8pm, Fri. 7am-2pm).

Ha-Mifgash Restaurant, 75 Jerusalem St. (tel. 692 05 10 or 697 47 34), opposite the small observation point and park, serves great kosher food in a homey cavern. Chicken soup connoisseurs must try Ha-Mifgash's golden, velvety brew (NIS10). *Shishlik* NIS35, spicy hot dogs NIS25, Hungarian goulash NIS10. Open Sun.-Fri. noon-11pm. Credit cards accepted.

Café Baghdad (tel. 697 40 65), halfway up the *midraḥov*. Plenty of time to enjoy the spectacular view of Tzfat from this outdoor cafe while you wait for the spectacularly slow staff to bring your meal. Tasty salads NIS22-30, pizza NIS22-30, pancakes NIS12-22. Open Sun.-Thurs. 8am-2am, Sat. from sundown. Credit cards accepted.

Rafi's Laffa, 88 Jerusalem St. (no English sign; tel. 692 14 96). This tiny grill 2 doors west of the bridge serves up delicious *me'orav* (mixed grill) in pita (NIS11) or as a large *laffa* sandwich (NIS14). Falafel and omelettes NIS7.

Pinati (tel. 692 08 55), toward the end of the *midraḥov* on the left. Elvis stands in for the Messiah here. The walls are plastered with memorabilia from the swivel-hipped one's tumultuous life, but you won't find peanut butter and banana sandwiches on the menu. Soups NIS10-14, stuffed vegetables NIS18, meat meals NIS30-40 including side dishes. Open Sun.-Thurs. 9:30am-midnight, Fri. 9:30am-1pm, Sat. sundown-midnight. Kosher.

Pizza Phone (tel. 692 27 27), at the top of the *midraḥov* shopping center. Spectacular views; often more packed than your El-Al flight. Spaghetti NIS20-26, omelettes NIS20, decent pizza NIS28-32. Open Sun.-Thurs. 8am-1:30am, Fri. 8am-4pm, Sat. sundown-1:30am. Takes credit cards.

California Falafel, 92 Jerusalem St., next to Ha-Palmaḥ bridge. Great falafel despite its dubious name; restaurant consistently filled with American tourists. Falafel NIS10, *shawerma* NIS11. Open Mon.-Thurs. 9am-11pm, Fri. 9am-3pm. Kosher.

SIGHTS

The best—and inevitably, the only—way to see Tzfat is to get lost in its circuitous sidestreets. Fortunately, there are a few **tour guides** on hand to inject some order into the chaos of navigating the city. **Aviva Minoff** (tel. 692 09 01; mobile tel. (050) 640 91 87) gives entertaining tours starting from the Municipal Building or the Rimon Inn Hotel (Mon.-Thurs. 10am, Fri. 10:30am, 2hr.). **Yisrael Shalem** (tel. 697 18 70) leads tours on demand (2hr., call ahead, dress modestly), and his helpful book *Six Self-Guided Tours to Tzfat* (NIS15) is available at Greenbaum's Books on the *midraḥov*. Call **Moshe Goldstein** (tel. 050 46 27 06) in advance, and he will tailor the tour to suit your needs. He can expound on a variety of topics, from Galilee's flora and fauna to local religious history.

The 12th-century Crusader fortress that once controlled the main route to Damascus now lays scattered in meager ruins in **Gan Ha-Metzuda,** a wooded park good for picnics. There's also a monument to the Israelis who died here during the 1948 War. The **Davidka Monument** near the GTIO memorializes the weapon responsible for the Palmaḥ's victory in Tzfat—the duds that were launched made a noise so frightening that the Arab forces feared an atomic attack and fled town.

The **Israel Bible Museum** (tel. 699 99 72), just north of the park and up the steep stone stairway, displays art by Phillip Ratner, a modern American artist whose work depicting biblical scenes and public personalities is also in permanent collections at the Statue of Liberty, the White House, and the U.S. Supreme Court (open June-Sept. Sun.-Thurs. 10am-4pm, Fri. 10am-1pm; Oct.-May Sun.-Thurs. 10am-2pm; free). The **Shem va'Ever Cave** is believed to be the burial site of Noah's son Shem and grandson Ever. The cave is near the top of Ha-Palmaḥ bridge at the intersection of Jerusalem and Arlozorov St. If the shrine around the cave is locked, knock at the small, domed synagogue nearby. English signs can direct you down the hill to the **General Exhibition** (tel. 692 00 87), which displays work by local artists in the town's former mosque, empty of worshippers since the 1948 War (open Sun.-Thurs. 9am-6pm, Fri. 9am-2pm, Sat. 10am-2pm). On the way, you can take a detour off Arlozorov St. into the **Artists' Quarter** and wander through the alleys and galleries just south of the Jerusalem-Arlozorov intersection. The quality of the art varies, but a keen eye might lead you to a few real jewels. One locally popular medium is **microcalligraphy,** creating pictures out of verses from traditional Jewish texts (most shops open 10am-1pm and 4-7pm).

Navigating the gnarled **Synagogue Quarter** *(kiryat batei ha-knesset)*, also called the Old City *(ha-ir ha-atika)*, is a matter of luck. Note landmarks carefully, but when you get lost (and you will get lost), enjoy it: it's a nice place to wander. Each of the tiny synagogues described below are still used. The **Chernobyl Synagogue** was founded by Jews from that tragic Ukrainian town. Some here believe the reactor was built over Jewish graves and that it melted down on the anniversary of the death of the chief rabbi buried beneath it. The **Chertkoff Synagogue's** chief rabbi predicted in 1840 that the messianic redemption would begin when 600,000 Jews inhabited the Land of Israel. It's almost 50 years late.

The **Caro** and **Ha-Ari (Ashkenazi) Synagogues** are the most famous in Tzfat. To reach the Caro Synagogue, take Ma'alot Oleh Ha-Gardom St. off Jerusalem St. and turn right onto Beit Yosef St. Ask to see the old books and Torah scrolls. It was here that Yosef Caro, chief rabbi of Tzfat and author of the vast *Shulḥan Arukh* ("The Set Table," a standard guide to daily life according to Jewish law), studied and taught in the 16th century. In the basement lives the angel with whom he used to confer. To reach Ha-Ari Synagogue, follow Beit Yosef until it becomes Alkabetz St., take a right up a stairway marked with stained glass Stars of David, and continue under the stone arch. The synagogue will be to your right on Najara St. Rabbi **Isaac Luria,** the famous mystic and founder of Lurianic *Kabbalah,* led congregants outside to welcome the *Sabbath* at this site. He is most famous for penning the *Kabbalay Shabbat,* an arrangement of prayers in preparation for the Sabbath; Alkabetz, his student, wrote the now-standard liturgical hymn *Lekha Dodi.* The lion at the top of the ornately decorated Ark was originally painted with the face of Moses, but some of the features have been rubbed off by those who deemed the hybrid beast blasphemous. Around the corner from Ha-Ari Synagogue is **Safed Candles** (tel. 692 10 93), a Ḥasidic factory producing intricate, colorful beeswax candles (starting at NIS9) and figurines. A **Sephardic Ha-Ari Synagogue** lies farther down the hill near the cemetery. Just downhill from the Caro Synagogue, off Abuhav St., stand the **Abuhav** and **Alsheiḥ Synagogues.** Take a left off Beit Yosef St. onto Alsheiḥ St. and make a sharp right; both buildings will be to your right. Abuhav's ark contains a Torah written by its namesake, Rabbi Issac Abuhav (1433-1493). Only Caro, Ha-Ari, and Abuhav are open to the public; dress modestly and don't take pictures on *Shabbat.*

Stenciled onto many of the Old City's buildings is a funny-looking Hebrew sentence that reads נ נח נחמ נחמן מאומן, or "Na-Naḥ-Naḥma-Naḥman from Uman." The words refer to the late Naḥman of Breslev, leader of the Breslever Ḥasidic sect, whose followers chant his name in this fashion to bring good fortune. The lucky charm can be spotted throughout the Galilee.

Three adjoining **cemeteries** sprawl on the western outskirts of the old city off Ha-Ari St. Follow the steps all the way down, past the new stone buildings on the left. The small building on the left when the path turns into the cemetery is Ha-Ari men's *mikveh,* or ritual bath. This *mikveh* was the bathing place of Ha-Ari himself, and its vibes have attracted the interest of mystics the world over, including the Dalai Lama. The local rabbinical court has ruled that women may not enter the *mikveh's* icy waters, but renegade females have been known to take a dip in the wee hours of the late night or early morning. Getting a male friend to guard the door, though, is a must.

The oldest cemetery contains the 17th-century graves of the most famous Tzfat Kabbalists as well as a domed tomb built by the Karaites of Damascus to mark the grave of the prophet Hosea. Legend has it that hidden under this same hill lie Hannah and her seven sons, whose martyrdom at the hands of the Syrians is recorded in the Book of Maccabees. This cemetery is the domain of an eighth-generation Tzfat resident named Mordekhai Shebabo, who left his position as a pedicurist to single-handedly restore the graves. Every visible grave is the result of this man's efforts.

ENTERTAINMENT

Shabbat in Tzfat brings tranquility, introspection, and not much else. For those in need, there are two pools which can chlorinate mysticism away. To get to the **Blue Valley Swimming Pool and Leisure Center** (tel. 692 02 17), walk down Ha-Atzma'ut Rd. from the bus station and turn left. The turn-off is 100m farther on the left (open July-Aug. Sat.-Thurs. 8am-7pm, Fri. 8am-6pm; women only Tues. and Thurs. 1-5pm; men only Sun. and Fri. 1-5pm; NIS17, students NIS10). The other pool (tel. 697 42 94), in the industrial district of south Tzfat, is heated, has a sauna and ping-pong, and is open year-round (open Sun.-Thurs. noon-9pm, Fri. 11am-5pm, Sat. 10am-5pm; women only Mon. 6-8:30pm; men only Wed. 6-8:30pm; NIS17, students NIS10). To get there, take bus #6 or 7.

Having a wild night in Tzfat takes some creative thinking. The only real pub in town is **Rafi's Bar,** on the third floor of the *midraḥov's* underground mall, where laid-back locals partake of a cozy atmosphere, good beer (NIS12 for .5L), and a dubious list of "cocktails." Occasional karaoke livens things up (open daily 8pm-2am).

If you are traveling with friends, a late-night walk through the old cemetery can be a beautifully surreal experience. Stars twinkle with the cemetery's *yahrzeit* (memorial) candles, and Ḥasidim pass by on their way to Ha-Ari's grave late into the night. The nearby *mikveh* is open 24 hours; nocturnal bathers are greeted by the echoes of their own voices and the icy trickle of spring water flowing from the wall (see **Sights,** above; women technically prohibited).

Travelers planning a visit to Tzfat well in advance should consider arriving in time for the annual **Klezmer festival** in mid-July, a three-night extravaganza during which the city sways to the strains of everything from old-world Yiddish tunes to modern Ḥasidic rock. Outdoor concerts are plentiful and free, as is the spontaneous dancing that seems to erupt in front of each stage.

■ Near Tzfat

MERON AND MT. MERON הר מירון

For two days every spring, the tranquil hillside surrounding Rabbi Shimon Bar-Yoḥai's tomb at Meron is transformed into the scene of a frenzied religious carnival. The 2nd-century Talmudic scholar **Bar-Yoḥai** is believed by some to have authored the *Zohar,* the central work of the Kabbala (Jewish mysticism). Thousands of Jews converge upon the town to commemorate the date of his death (the holiday of **Lag Ba'Omer,** May 4 in 1998). The square outside the tomb becomes a Ḥasidic mosh-pit as crowds dance, shove, and chant Bar-Yoḥai's name. Tzfat's Ḥasidim make their way to the tomb carrying an ancient Torah scroll from the Bana'a Synagogue in the Spanish Quarter, and makeshift shops lining the hill sell a wide assortment of rabbinic and messianic paraphernalia. Contact Tzfat's GTIO for details on the festival; see page 374 for more on Bar-Yoḥai.

Near the tomb are the ruins of an aesthetically unimpressive but historically noteworthy synagogue dating from the 3rd century CE, when Meron was important in the booming olive oil trade. From Bar-Yoḥai's grave, go past the *yeshiva* and follow the uphill path to your left. The **lintel,** an engraved stone slab that once decorated the entrance of the synagogue, is virtually all that's left of the edifice. Legend has it that this lintel's fall will herald the coming of the Messiah. The Israeli Department of Antiquities has nervously buttressed the artifact with reinforced concrete, but every Lag Ba'Omer, pious Jews from Tzfat enthusiastically dance and stomp in an effort to accelerate their salvation.

Just west of the village is **Har Meron** (Mt. Meron), the highest mountain in the Galilee (1208m). A good trail affords tremendous vistas of Tzfat and the surrounding countryside—on clear days you can see Lebanon and Syria to the north, the Mediterranean to the west, and the Galilee to the southeast. It's possible to ascend the mountain from the village of Meron, but a more convenient option is to take bus #43 from Tzfat to Kibbutz Sasa, northwest of the mountain (departs 6:45am, 12:30 and 5pm; returns 7:50am, 1:50 and 6:05pm; NIS9.40). In summer, catch the early bus to avoid the midday heat. From the kibbutz, continue 1km to the turn-off on the left, then walk 1km and turn right for the SPNI field school. Their **information office** (tel. (06) 698 00 23) offers a trail map (NIS50) and some advice. To reach the trail, walk down the road from the field school turn-off until you pass an army base on the right and a small parking lot on the left. The **trail** begins in the back of the lot and is indicated by stone and striped black-and-white trail markers. A one-hour walk brings you to the summit, peppered with red-and-white markers. Stay on the trail skirting the summit, as the very top of the mountain is the site of an army radar installation. Twenty minutes farther along the path you'll approach a picnic site and a traffic circle on a road; make a left and follow it for 20m to where the trail begins again. A long, easy descent, again marked with the black-and-white-and-red-all-over blazes, ends on a dirt road just above the village of Meron. Return to Tzfat either by retracing your steps to the kibbutz or by catching bus #361, 362, or 501 from the village of Meron (every 20min., first bus around 6am, last bus around 8pm; NIS7.30).

Another option is a gorgeous, thickly-wooded 3½-hour **hike** beginning in the Tzfat cemeteries, continuing up a rocky *wadi,* and emerging by the road to Bar-Yoḥia's tomb. The trail is marked first by green-and-white, then by black-and-white markers, but it's worth getting more specific directions from SPNI; the Ascent Institute (see p. p. 392) also has a good map on file.

ALMA CAVE מערת עלמה

Legend has it that the maze-like tunnels of Alma Cave form an underground bridge between the holy cities of Tzfat and Jerusalem and contain the corpses of 900,000 "righteous men." There is no guarantee that a day-trip to the Alma Cave will land you at the Dome of the Rock or yield encounters with long-deceased rabbis, but if you would like to try your hand at the fine art of spelunking and are not daunted by mud, sweat, and claustrophobic conditions, the Alma Cave is a tailor-made adventure.

Do not bring large packs into the cave; they will not fit through some of the tighter spots. Bring one strong, reliable **flashlight** per person, and prepare to become saturated with mud. Alma Cave should only be tried by those who feel they can remain up to 108m beneath the earth for several hours without **freaking out.** It is safest to go during daylight hours with a group of at least three people.

The cave is situated between the Circassian-Muslim village of Reḥania and the Tripolian-Jewish Alma. **Bus** #45 leaves Tzfat for Alma and Reḥania (NIS9.40) at 1:15, 4, and 6:30pm, and departs for Tzfat at 6:15 and 9:15am, and 1:45, 4:30, and 7pm. By car, drive north along the Tzfat-Meron highway, and continue past the Zeition Junction to Reḥania. Across the street from Reḥania village's entrance are several dirt paths heading in the direction of the cave. Some of them are fenced off, but don't despair. Stay close to Alma (to your left), and steer away from the hilly, tree-lined area to your right. The walk is about 1.5km and runs through fields of thorny shrubs (wear shoes and pants). The cave itself looks like a large boulder with a crack in the middle. Climb (or slide) down the hole, keeping to the right. At a depth of approximately 60m (one-half to three-quarters of the way down), you should see two phallic rocks near the right-hand wall. Behind that lies a small hole leading to the "inner chambers" of the cave. There are markers indicating the correct path: white for the way in, red for the way out. When you reach a large room with a ridge and a steep slope, be sure to veer to your far right along the ridge instead of continuing down the slope. Near the end of the trail, the rocks become slippery and the caverns filled with technicolor, dripping **stalagmites** and **stalagtites.** (Which are which? Impress your friends by reminding them that stalagtites are the ones above—they grip "tight" to the ceiling—hanging like a "T.") Getting out of the cave is a true physical challenge, involving steep climbs and tricky maneuvers.

TEL ḤAZOR

The *tel* at Ḥazor is the largest archaeological mound in northern Israel. Excavations (still underway) have revealed 21 layers of settlements at the site, the oldest dating from the third millennium BCE. Like Megiddo overlooking the Jezreel Valley, Ḥazor was once a fortified city situated on the main trading route that linked Egypt to Syria and Mesopotamia. In the Bible, Ḥazor is termed "the head of all those (northern Canaanite) kingdoms" (Joshua 11:10). Ferocious Joshua, after winning a battle against a north Canaanite alliance at the Merom River, sacked Ḥazor, and, following God's command, slaughtered the entire population. Ḥazor was rebuilt and expanded by Kings Solomon (10th century BCE) and Ahab (9th century BCE) and was finally laid to waste by Assyria's Tiglath-Pileser III during his army's march through the Galilee (732 BCE). At the *tel's* northern foot lies a vast lower city, still underground and currently closed to the public. The most impressive of the *tel's* ruins is the 38m-deep tunnel, engineered during Ahab's reign to bring water into the city in case of a siege; a spiral staircase lets you descend into the gaping pit.

Buses #501 and 511 from Tzfat (35min., NIS10.50) and all buses that run between Rosh Pina and Kiryat Shmona stop near the site. Don't get off at the sleepy town of Ḥazor Ha-Gelilit; rather, continue north to **Kibbutz Ayelet Ha-Shaḥor.** The kibbutz houses a small museum (tel. (06) 693 48 55) displaying Canaanite and Israelite artifacts and explaining some of the *tel's* layers. From there, the site's entrance is a 250m walk back up the road (museum and site tel. (06) 693 72 90; open Sat.-Thurs. 8am-5pm, Fri. and holidays 8am-4pm; admission for both NIS11, students NIS9).

ROSH PINA ראש פינה

There is little to do in Rosh Pina but leave. Located on the slopes of Mt. Kenaan, Rosh Pina ("cornerstone" in Hebrew) was the Galilee's first *moshav.* Because many buses heading north pass through, the town serves as a gateway to the Upper Galilee and Golan. **Buses** #401, 459, 461, 501, and 511 go to **Tzfat** (NIS8.30), and #480, 500, 842, 845, and 909 go to **Kiryat Shmona** (NIS10.50). Travelers who find themselves stranded in Rosh Pina will have a tough time finding cheap lodgings, since the **Nature Friends Youth Hostel** (tel. (06) 693 70 86; fax 693 43 12) is reserved for soldiers during the week. However, the public may partake of the hostel's tidy, air-conditioned dorm beds from Thursday night to Saturday night (NIS97, children NIS54). Before bursting into tears and embarking on a two-hour hike to the nearest civilization (Tzfat), consider taking a brief stroll up the street from the hostel to the tranquil **Rothschild Garden,** a beautifully maintained park with shady poplars, bubbling fountains, cedar benches, and dozens of varieties of roses lining its terraces. At the top of the garden is a large stone building formerly belonging to the Baron; it now houses two restaurants whose potential for romantic *gourmandisme* may be worth the hefty prices.

▨ Kiryat Shmona קרית שמונה

Kiryat Shmona ("Town of Eight") commemorates Yosef Trumpeldor and seven others who were murdered in nearby Tel Ḥai in 1920. Situated on top of the ruins of the Arab village Al Khalsa (destroyed in the 1948 War), the city was given its new name in 1949. By virtue of its location on the Ḥula plain near the Lebanese border, Kiryat Shmona was the target of numerous bombings and terrorist attacks until Israel invaded Lebanon in 1982, and it has been subject to shelling by Iranian-backed Hizbullah as recently as August 1997. The town thus graduated from its grim name to an even grimmer nickname: Kiryat Katyusha, referring to the type of rockets used.

Although it is the transportation and administrative center of the Upper Galilee, the city is little more than a pit-stop for most tourists. The **central bus station** (tel. 694 07 40 or 41, info (04) 854 95 55) is on Tel Ḥai Blvd. (the main road). Buses #840, 841, and 963 run frequently between **Tiberias** and Kiryat Shmona (NIS18). To reach **Tel Aviv,** take bus #840, 841, 842, or 845 (NIS40). **Rosh Pina** is serviced by buses #480, 500, 842, 845, and 969 (30min., NIS10.50). Buses #501 and 511 go to **Tzfat** (every hr. until 7pm, 45min., NIS15). For a **taxi,** call Moniot Ha-Tzafon (tel. 699 23 33). For **first aid (Magen David Adom),** dial 101 or 694 43 34; for **police,** dial 100 or 694 34 44. The **post office** is south of the bus station and has **international telephone** and **Poste Restante** services (tel. 694 02 20; open Sun., Tues., and Thurs. 8am-12:30pm and 3:30-6pm, Wed. 8am-1:30pm, Fri. 8am-noon). Kiryat Shmona's **telephone code** is 06.

The nearest cheap accommodations are at the youth hostel in **Rosh Pina.** Falafel and *shawerma* stands sizzle around the intersection of Tel Ḥai Blvd. and Tchernihovsky St., and cafes and small restaurants can be found one block towards the north or south of the bus station. There is a **Co-op Tzafon supermarket** in the shopping complex just south of the bus station. On Thursday mornings an open-air *shuk* opens up at Tel Ḥai St., just north of the bus station.

■ Near Kiryat Shmona

TEL ḤAI תל חי

Tel Ḥai sits three km north of Kiryat Shmona, on a promontory overlooking the Ḥula Valley. Established in 1918 as a military outpost after the withdrawal of British forces from the Upper Galilee, the town has become a symbol of Israel's early pioneer movement and the struggle for the narrow mountain range west of the Ḥula Valley region, known as "the finger of the Galilee."

Tel Ḥai was the site of the first armed conflict between Jews and Arabs within the current borders of the State of Israel. In 1920, a group of Arabs gathered around the settlements of Tel Ḥai, Kfar Giladi, and Metulla (then part of French-administered Syria and Lebanon) and accused the Jewish settlers of protecting French soldiers who had been charged with encroachment on Arab lands. Yosef Trumpeldor, the leader of Tel Ḥai, allowed four Arabs inside the settlement to search for the French agents. Once inside, the Arabs killed Trumpeldor and seven others. The six men and two women were buried in nearby Kfar Giladi. Trumpeldor's alleged last words—"No matter, it is good to die for our country"—for years epitomized Zionist convictions. The site offers a spectacular view of the Galilee and the Golan Heights, and an audio-visual program tells the story in seven languages.

A monument to Trumpeldor stands on the compound's outskirts. The original watchtower and stockade settlement has been reconstructed as a small **museum** (tel. (06) 695 13 33) tastefully displaying farming tools (open Sun.-Thurs. 8am-4pm, Fri. 8am-1pm, Sat. 8:30am-2pm; NIS12, students NIS8). The recently opened **Museum of Photography** (tel. (06) 695 07 69), in the industrial park on the right side of the road, has a small display of modern Israeli photographs (open Sun.-Thurs. 8am-4pm, Sat. 10am-5pm; admission to the park NIS12, students NIS10). There is a collection of antique cars in the building next to the photography exhibit.

Up a hill to the left of the main road is the **military cemetery** containing the graves of the Tel Ḥai Eight. A statue of a roaring lion faces the mountains to the east. Fifty meters farther, inside the gates of Kibbutz Kfar Giladi, is **Beit Ha-Shomer** (House of the Guardian; tel. (06) 694 15 65), an IDF museum documenting the history of early Galilee defense and the exploits of Jewish regiments in the British Army during World War I (open Sun.-Thurs. 8am-3pm, Fri. 8am-noon, Sat. 9am-1pm; NIS6, students NIS3). **Buses** #20 and 21 from Kiryat Shmona go to Tel Ḥai (8 per day, NIS3.90). There are no accommodations in Tel Ḥai.

KFAR BLUM כפר בלום

Kibbutz Kfar Blum, southeast of Kiryat Shmona, has two unrelated attractions: classical music and kayaking. The **Upper Galilee Chamber Music Days** feature a week-long series of concerts in July. Tickets (NIS20-30 per concert) sell out rapidly, but you can listen in on daytime rehearsals (call (06) 694 85 28 for details). A 6km **kayaking** trip (tel. (06) 694 87 55) on the Jordan River costs NIS85 for two people and lasts about an hour; longer rides cost NIS140. Inner tube rides (NIS30) are a relaxing way to wet your bottom. Consult the *Galilee Guide,* available at the GTIO, for information on adventures in the region's gushing streams. Unfortunately, the streams tend to gush less during the summer, rendering some adventures less than thrilling. Buses #29 or 30 run five times per day from Kiryat Shmona (NIS5).

NATURE RESERVES OF THE ḤULA VALLEY

The five reserves of the Ḥula Valley showcase Israel's forested north, giving hikers the chance to discover ice-cold streams and migrating birds. A **combined ticket** (NIS26) gets you into Ḥula, Ḥorshat Tal, Tel Dan, Gamla, and Naḥal Ḥermon, and is available at all five reserves.

In between Rosh Pina and Kiryat Shmona, the **Ḥula Nature Reserve** (tel. (06) 693 70 69) harbors what is left of the wildlife that once flourished in the swamplands of the Ḥula Valley before it was drained by Israel for agricultural use in the 1950s. The 775-acre reserve has dense cypress groves and open fields; a 1.5km trail circles through papyrus thickets, swamps, and reeds, the creeping ground of turtles, mongeese, waterbuffalo, and other critters. The **visitor's center** rents binoculars for bird enthusiasts (NIS7), and has a display and a 15-minute film about the area. Arrive early to see the most wildlife and to avoid crowded family-time in the forest (open Sat.-Thurs. 8am-4pm, Fri. and holiday eves 8am-3pm; admission NIS15). **Buses** #501, 511, 840, and 841 (NIS10.50) leave Kiryat Shmona frequently and will take you to a junction 2.5km from the entrance to the reserve.

Huge hundred-year-old oak trees stand in the **Ḥorshat Tal Nature Reserve** (tel. (06) 694 23 60). According to a Muslim legend, the trees, which grow nowhere else in Israel, sprang into being because of the 10 warriors of Muhammad who once rested here. Finding no shade and not a single hitching post for their horses, they pounded their staffs into the earth to fasten their mounts. Overnight the sticks sprouted, and the holy men found themselves in a thick forest. The trees now tower over a grassy park which is crammed with picnicking families on Saturdays. The large, ice-cold **swimming pool** (actually the Dan River ingeniously diverted) is especially enticing in season. (Park open Sat.-Thurs. 8am-5pm, Fri. 8am-5pm; closes 1hr. earlier in winter; NIS21, children NIS12.) Next to the park is the **Ḥorshat Tal Camping Ground** (tel. (06) 694 23 60), on the banks of the Dan River. Sites next to the stream come with the soothing sound of gushing water (tent sites NIS25 per person; 4-person bungalows NIS140; prices rise 50% on *Shabbat* and holidays). From Kiryat Shmona, bus # 36 travels to Ḥorshat Tal infrequently (NIS6.10).

Near Kibbutz Dan to the northeast of Ḥorshat Tal is the Ḥula Valley's most thickly forested nature reserve, **Tel Dan** (tel. (06) 695 15 79). Several short, easy walking loops follow the fast-flowing Dan River, a tributary of the Jordan. The 45-minute circle trail is mostly paved for **wheelchair access;** the 1½-hour trail is rockier. Ongoing excavations at the *tel* have revealed the ancient Canaanite city of Laish, conquered and settled by the Israelite tribe of Dan around 1200BCE. The most interesting remains lie in the Cultic site, where King Jeroboam Ben-Nebat of the breakaway Kingdom of Israel placed a golden calf to rival Judah's Jerusalem (I Kings 12:28-29). Stick your head into one of the metal columns near the cultic site and feast your eyes on a miniature hologram of the ancient sacrificial scene. (Reserve open Sat.-Thurs. 8am-4pm, Fri. 8am-3pm; visitors may stay 1hr. after closing time. Admission NIS15, children NIS8. Ticket gives you a 25% discount at the Beit Usishkin Museum.)

In 1983, a remarkable find was made at Tel Dan: a broken stele, inscribed with the words "House of David" in 9th-century BCE Aramaic. Some call it shattered earth; Biblical history scholars call it earth-shattering—it was the first known reference to the biblical King David outside the Good Book itself. A replica of the stele and other finds from the *tel* are on display in the **Beit Usishkin Museum,** a gray stone building on the way to Tel Dan. (Take a left at the wooden sign. Open Sun.-Thurs. 8:30am-4:30pm, Fri. 8:30am-3:30pm, Sat. 9:30am-4:30pm. Admission NIS9, students NIS7.50. Ticket gives you a 25% discount at the Tel Dan Reserve.) To reach the reserve, take **bus** #26 or 36 (NIS5) from Kiryat Shmona to Kibbutz Dan, continue up the main road, and turn left at the sign.

The Golan's **Naḥal Ḥermon Nature Reserve,** with its hugely popular **Banyas Waterfall,** is just a few kilometers east (see p. 404). The SPNI's **Ḥermon Field School** (tel. (06) 694 10 91) is in Kibbutz Senir, off the Banyas -Tel Dan road.

METULLA מטולה

Metulla, 9km north of Kiryat Shmona, is Israel's largest village on the Lebanese border. The city's main attraction is **Ha-Gader Ha-Tova (The Good Fence),** an opening in the border barrier between Lebanon and Israel through which Lebanese Christians and Druze are allowed to pass through to obtain free medical services, visit relatives, and work in Israel. Israel began passing aid and supplies through this point to Lebanese Christians in 1971, and in June 1976 the Good Fence was officially opened. It remained open even during the war in Lebanon. From the observation point you can see some Maronite Christian villages across the border; on the farthest hill to the right (northwest) is the Crusader fortress of Beaufort, which was fortified by the PLO and used as a base for shelling Israel. A shop to the left of the fence sells Lebanese Pounds. Representatives of the U.N. get a discount at the snack bar (careful—they card hard).

Israelis head to Metulla's new **Canada Centre** (tel. (06) 695 03 70 or 71), one of the top sports facilities in Israel and home to its only genuine ice-skating rink. The hefty admission fee (NIS32, students NIS25) includes skate rental plus use of two pools, dry and wet saunas, a jacuzzi, and a fitness room. Squash courts are NIS10 per hour, basketball NIS5 per hour, and ping-pong NIS5 per 45 minutes. There are also a privately owned restaurant, massage service, and shooting range on the premises (open daily 10am-10pm; credit cards accepted).

Bus #20 runs between Kiryat Shmona and Metulla (8 per day, NIS5.60). There are two **pensions** in Metulla, both along Ha-Rishonim, the main road, but no budget accommodations. If you stay in town, expect to pay at least NIS90 per person.

South of Metulla, the cool mountain air is moistened with mist from the 18m **Tanur Waterfall** in the **Iyun Nature Reserve.** The dense mist creates the illusion of billowing smoke and gives the waterfall its name: *tanur* means "oven." The torrent, magnificent in the snow-melting season, slows to a trickle after June. There are two other falls deeper in the reserve: Mill Falls cascades 21m down a broad wall to the widening cauldron at its base, and Cascade Falls is topped by a small dam used by the British during World War II to draw water for their camps. The Iyun reserve is accessible directly by bus #20 or 21 from Kiryat Shmona; ask for the turn-off to the waterfall *(mapal)*. From there, it's a three-minute walk to the park (open Sat.-Thurs. 8am-5pm, Fri. 8am-4pm; NIS6, children NIS3.50).

Golan Heights רמת הגולן

The Golan Heights offer visitors a relatively cool climate, breathtaking views, noteworthy archaeological sites, and dozens of streams and waterfalls. This formerly volcanic plateau overlooking the Jordan Valley is sparsely-traveled except in spring, when busloads of loud Israeli teenagers on school-sponsored outings pack the normally serene trails.

The first recorded mention of the Golan is the Biblical "Golan in Basham," a city established by Moses as a refuge for Israelites guilty of manslaughter (Deut. 4:43). The Golan was an important holdout in the Jewish Revolt of 66-73 CE, and one its promontories sheltered the city of Gamla, called the Masada of the north (see **Gamla,** p. 402). In the next two centuries, the Golan became a center of the Jewish population, as evidenced by excavations of ancient synagogues. As time passed, however, the Golan became little more than a backwater Syrian province until Turkish officials planted Circassian settlers there to block the activity of Bedouin highwaymen in the 1880s.

Recent history has cast the Golan Heights back into the jaws of political controversy. Throughout the 50s and 60s, Israeli towns in the Galilee were assailed by artillery fire from Syrian gunposts atop the Heights. Israel captured the Golan in the 1967 Six Day War, but was pushed back by Syria's surprise attack in the 1973 war. Israeli forces quickly recovered and launched a counter-attack, capturing even more territory. As part of the 1974 disengagement accord, Israel returned both the newly conquered territory and part of the land captured in 1967. Israel officially annexed the remaining 768 square-km territory in 1981, arousing international protest. Today, Jewish settlements are scattered among Druze villages, rusting tanks, live minefields, and destroyed bunkers.

The future status of the Golan is currently under negotiation. Syria claims that the land was seized unfairly and demands its return. Israeli officials had always invoked the issue of security in their refusal to budge from the Heights until the Rabin and

Peres administrations announced their willingness to cede all or part of the Golan in exchange for peace and Syrian recognition of Israel. The reality is that whoever commands the elevated plateau enjoys strategic views of Damascus and all northern Israel. Netanyahu's 1996 election was viewed by many as an indication of the Israeli public's opposition to a withdrawal from the Golan. Bitter anti-government protests and the popular bumper-sticker "the nation is with the Golan" attest to many Israelis' unwillingness to compromise with the same Syrian regime that fought Israel in two successive wars. The Golan is dear to Israelis as a major source of water and as the home of ski slopes, apple orchards, wineries, and cattle pastures. Many of the Golan's 15,000 Druze, on the other hand, strongly identify with Syria and long to see their relatives across the border.

GETTING AROUND

> The Golan Heights still contain active **land mine fields.** Stay on paved roads, and avoid fenced-off areas whether or not you see the yellow-and-red warning signs.

When wandering the Golan in the summer, you'll need a hat and buckets of water. Winter, on the other hand, is cold, damp, foggy, and often snowy. The best time to visit the Golan is spring, when the heat is bearable and when cellophane flowers of yellow and green tower over your head. The best way to see the Golan is to **rent a car** in Tiberias. If you don't plan to hike, you can hit the major sights in two days. Don't be afraid to lean on your horn; in the Golan, passing other cars is as common as passing breathtaking views.

Some sights in the Golan are accessible by **Egged bus,** but infrequent service along remote roads necessitates careful planning. Double-check all schedules, and anticipate walking. Buses to sights near the Galilee generally leave from Tiberias; the Upper Galilee, Ḥula Valley, and northern Golan are served by buses from Kiryat Shmona and Tzfat. Traveling by bus makes it nearly impossible to get to Gamla and many hiking trails. Relatively few cars traverse the Golan, and hitchhiking is inadvisable. If you decide to set out on your own, take a good map, several bottles of water, and at least a day's worth of food.

Organized **tours** are faster, more convenient, and sometimes less expensive than other forms of transportation, but may go by faster than you like. **Egged** offers professionally guided full-day tours of the region from Tiberias (tel. (06) 679 10 80; March-Oct. Tues., Thurs., and Sat.; Nov.-Feb. Thurs.; US$37); Tel Aviv (tel. (03) 527 12 12; April-Oct. Sun. and Thurs.; Oct.-May, Thurs.; US$59); and Haifa (tel. (04) 854 94 86; April-Oct., Thurs.; US$55); there's a 10% discount for ISIC members. There are also private guides based in Tiberias. **Igal** (tel. (06) 672 45 74) attracts a young backpacker crowd and gives tours that combine sight-seeing with light hiking (NIS120). **Moshe Cohen** (tel. (06) 672 16 08) makes military history-oriented rounds in a taxi (NIS120). **Max Ballhorn** (tel. (06) 679 35 88) gives Egged-style tours. Three-day **SPNI** hiking and camping trips visit some hard-to-reach spots and, in summer, could include kayaking down the Jordan River. All give tours in English.

Moshav Ramot (tel. (06) 673 23 17), on the eastern bank of the Sea of Galilee, runs guided **jeep trips** (2hr. trip for 7 people NIS490). A tourist with a valid driver's license can rent a rugged, one-person *tractorium* (all-terrain vehicles; NIS120 for 1hr.) **Shevil-Golan** (tel. (06) 679 76 71), at Zeelon Beach near Moshav Ramot, runs jeep and *tractoronim* trips at similar prices. The Golan's **telephone code** is 06.

■ Katzrin קצרין

The town of Katzrin is another one of those administrative and municipal centers that seem so common in northern Israel, and an ideal base from which to explore the area. Katzrin enjoys a high standard of living for a young settlement, but its economic growth has slowed with the possibility of an Israeli withdrawal from the Golan.

Practical Information Buses #55-57 go to Katzrin from **Rosh Pina** (25min., NIS10.50). From **Tiberias,** reach Katzrin by bus #15, 16, or 19 (4 per day, first bus around noon, 45min., NIS18). Buses also run indirectly from **Kiryat Shmona** to Katzrin (NIS18.80). **Moniot Ha-Golan** (tel. 696 11 11) has a special NIS60 **taxi** fare to Rosh Pina. The town center has a **Bank Leumi** (open Sun., Tues., and Thurs. 8:30am-12:30pm and 4-6pm, Mon. and Wed. 8:30am-12:30pm, Fri. 8:30am-noon). A **mall** with a **CoOp-Tzafon Supermarket** (open Sun.-Thurs. 8am-6pm, Fri. 8am-3pm) contains the **post office** (open Sun.-Tues. and Thurs. 8am-12:30pm and 3:30-6pm, Wed. 8am-1:30pm, Fri. 8am-noon).

Sights Those wishing to hike in the Golan should visit the **SPNI Golan Field School** (tel. 696 12 34), on Zavitan St., off Daliyot St. (the main road). They sell maps (NIS50) and patiently explain the region's trail options (open Sun.-Thurs. 8am-7pm, Fri. 8am-2pm). Five hundred meters east along Zavitan St. is a **campground** (tel. 696 16 57 or 37 53). Pleasant bungalows (4-6 beds) cost NIS140 each, and tent sites are NIS15 per person. Registration is purportedly open 24-hours; ask for the manager at the field school if no one is there. The field school will also give suggestions for **housing** with families in the region.

The tiny **Golan Archaeological Museum** (tel. 696 24 12 or 13 50), in the north part of town at the opposite end of Daliyot St. from the field school, has an excellent, bilingual exhibit displaying artifacts from ancient synagogues and houses, including 6200 coins, some dating back to the New Stone Age. It shows a 20-minute film on the Great Revolt battle in Gamla (open Sun.-Thurs. 8am-5pm, Fri. 8am-3pm, Sat. 10am-4pm; NIS13, students NIS7.50). The ticket includes admission to **Ancient Katzrin Park,** located just outside modern Katzrin (2km southeast along the road heading for Gamla), where excavations have unearthed a richly ornamented synagogue in use from the 4th to 8th centuries CE. Two reconstructed houses with furnishings based on finds from the excavations give a sense of daily life in the Talmudic village. If you find the Talmudic village too sobering, the **Golan Heights Winery** (tel. 696 20 01) produces the Yarden, Gamla, and Golan labels and provides a tour that includes a video explanation, a souvenir glass, and tastings of the grapey bliss (open Sun.-Thurs. 8am-4pm and Fri. 8am-1pm; last tour about an hour before closing time; tour NIS11, children NIS6). There's a public **pool** next to the Archaeological Museum (tel. 696 16 55; open daily 9am-5:45pm; admission NIS20, students NIS15).

Dolls to Meet for Peace Negotiations

When your friends were setting up Ken and Barbie on blind dates, were you busy re-enacting the Yom Kippur War with a battalion of G.I. Joes? If so, the **Katzrin Doll Museum** (tel. 696 29 82) is the place for you. A bizarre monument to model personhood, the museum features rows of glass cases in which woolly-headed dolls, all wearing looks of blank astonishment, recreate famous scenes from Jewish and Israeli history. The doll pogrom is especially eerie, but you're sure to dig the Ḥasidic doll dancers with tiny Coke bottles glued to their heads in the *Fiddler on the Roof* wedding scene. A separate children's room displays tamer scenes from the likes of *Peter Pan* and *Alice in Wonderland* (open Sun.-Thurs. 9am-5pm, Fri. 9am-2pm; NIS12, students NIS8, under 13 NIS5).

■ Near Katzrin: Gamla גמלא

For years the lost city of Gamla was nothing more than a legend from the pages of *The Jewish War* by first-century Jewish historian Josephus Flavius (Book IV, Ch. 1). After the Six Day War, archaeologists scoured the region for a spot corresponding to ancient descriptions. Archaeologist Shmaryahu Gutman, working with a copy of *The Jewish War* in hand, finally uncovered the site. The film at Katzrin's archaeological museum (see above) is a great introduction before your visit.

In 67 CE, the Romans laid siege to a religious hilltop fortress packed with 9000 Jewish refugees. After many months, Romans on the nearby hills stormed down the corridor of land leading to the town. When the legion penetrated Gamla's walls, hordes of Jews fled up the ridge. The Romans followed, and on the steep trails beyond the town's confines, the Jews turned and killed their pursuers. Weeks later, a second attack proved too much for the Jews, who hurled themselves over the ridge's steep rock face. Two women survived to tell the tale. (Some archaeologists take issue with Josephus's proclivity for over-dramatization and claim that Gamla's inhabitants were pushed over the cliff in the mayhem of battle.)

A road leading up to ruins should be completed by January 1998. **Bus** #22 (running 6am-4pm) will drop you near the site. Otherwise, get a ride from Katzrin and walk 1km to the ridge overlooking the ruins; the descent to the ruins along the Roman route takes about 20 minutes. You'll need about two hours at the site. (Site tel. 676 20 40. Open Sat.-Thurs. 8am-6pm, Fri. 8am-5pm; closes 1hr. earlier in the winter. Admission NIS13, combo ticket including Gamla and four nearby nature reserves NIS27.)

If you continue along the red-and-white trail past the ruins, you'll reach a lookout point over the magnificent **Mapal Gamla,** the Golan's highest waterfall. As you hike, keep an eye toward the sky to catch a glimpse of soaring black **Egyptian eagles** that frequent this area.

■ Golan Hikes

Those who wish to hike in the Golan should purchase the 1:50,000 trail map on sale at SPNI offices (NIS44). It is also advisable to consult the field school in Katzrin for up-to-date advice and information. Beware of **land mines** (see **warning,** p. 401). For more detailed directions and alternative trail options in the Golan, check out a copy of Joel Roskin's *A Guide to Hiking in Israel,* on sale at Steimatzky bookstores (NIS39). It's not safe to drink water from Golan streams. Bus service to the trails, when it exists, is very irregular; call Egged and plan carefully.

For the most exciting and challenging hiking in the Golan, head to the **Ya'ar Yehudiya Nature Reserve** southeast of Katzrin. Most trails begin in **Ḥenion Yehudiya** (tel. 696 28 17), accesible by bus from Katzrin. To get to the Ḥenion by car, drive north along the lake from Tiberias, head east towards Katzrin, pass the Yehudiya Junction, and continue along Rte. 87 until you see the orange sign marking the site. The Ḥenion is equipped with a parking lot, bathroom facilities, telephones, and a SPNI information desk. Bags can be stored for NIS10 per locker, and **camping** is NIS10 per person. (Reserve open Sat.-Thurs. 7am-5pm, Fri. and holidays 7am-4pm; leave no later than 1hr. after closing time. Admission NIS16 per car, free for those without a car—you've suffered enough.)

The most popular part of the reserve is the action-packed **Naḥal Yehudiya** trail, consisting of two parts, an upper and a lower. To reach both of these aptly named trails, follow the red-and-white markers past the old Syrian houses and into the valley. Upon completion of the **upper trail** (3hr.), ascend the green-and-white trail to return to the Ḥenion; to complete the **lower trail** (4hr.), continue along the red-and-white trail, which finishes with an extremely difficult climb and a 1.5km walk along the road. Both sections are full of enticing waterfalls and pools, some of which you must swim across to complete your hike (bring a bathing suit and plastic bags to protect food and valuables). Jumping off the 9m cliff at the second waterfall is possibly dangerous, definitely forbidden, and almost universally done by trail trekkers.

The reserve is also home to the slightly drier but equally beautiful **Naḥal Zavitan,** with a number of trail options: one begins near the field school in Katzrin and several start at Ḥenion Yehudiya. The **Upper Zavitan** is good for all seasons; the more difficult **Lower Zavitan** should be avoided in the winter due to occasional flash floods; the **Black Canyon** can only be negotiated by rapelling. The spring at **Ein Netef** contains the only drinkable water in the reserve; from here, follow the red-and-white blazes to the spectacular **Brekhat Ha-Meshushim** (Hexagon Pool), where hundreds of hexagonal rock columns skirt the water's edge. The trail ends 7km down the road from the Ḥenion.

Southeast of the Zavitan and Yehudiya Rivers is **Naḥal El-Al** (no relation to Israel's major airline). In winter and spring, there is enough water here to swim beneath the falls. Bus #18 leaves Tiberias for El-Al (3 per day), and buses #18 or 19 return to Tiberias from Avnei-Eitan (4 per day). Start at Kibbutz El-Al, follow the red and white trail to **Mapal Ha-Lavan** (white waterfall), continue on to **Mapal Ha-Shaḥor** (black waterfall), and finish outside of Kibbutz Avnei Eitan (total hiking time about 5hr.).

Head to **Zaki** for a viewless but extremely refreshing hike just south of the Yehudiya Junction. Zaki is best visited in August or September, when sweltering heat makes cool water a godsend and overhanging grapes are ripe. Hike in the stream following the green-and-white trail for 3km; when you reach a pipe, get out of the water on the left side and return by way of a dirt path.

■ Northern Golan

BANYAS AND NIMROD'S FORTRESS בניס וקלעת נמרוד

The Banyas springs in the Naḥal Ḥermon Nature Reserve have witnessed an odd religious mix: Jesus chose his first disciple here, Muslims built a shrine to the prophet Elijah (Nabi Khadar) in the adjacent hill, and an ancient sanctuary dedicated to Greek God Pan remains carved into the cliffside. Because of its ancient association with Pan, the area became known as *Paneas* (Pan's Place), which was rendered in 'P'-less Arabic as Banyas. The town of Banyas itself was settled by the Arabs in the 7th century and ruled by Crusaders until 1165. It remained an Arab village until the 1967 War. Families and other visitors now flock to the reserve for afternoons of light hiking and swimming.

Banyas (tel. 695 02 72) lies only a few minutes down the road from Dan and Ḥorshat Tal in the Upper Galilee. Although it is the most popular site in the Upper Galilee-Golan area, public transportation is woefully inadequate. During the winter, **bus #14** from Kiryat Shmona to Neveh Ativ passes by (NIS9.30), leaving and returning once a day. Bus #55 travels from Kiryat Shmona through the Golan by way of Banyas twice per day, but the last bus back to Kiryat Shmona is at noon. If you want to spend the afternoon at the park, walk 5km west to Kibbutz Dan; the last bus (#35 or 36) leaves the kibbutz around 7:30pm (park open Sat.-Thurs. 8am-5pm, Fri. 8am-3pm; admission NIS15; combo ticket to 5 area reserves NIS26).

An easy 45- to 60-minute hike from the park entrance leads to the **Banyas waterfall** (Mapal Banyas), the largest falls in the region. Across the stream that transverses the park, a wooden sign marks the beginning of a path to the waterfall. All subsequent signs are in Hebrew, but there are only two forks. Go right at the flour mill/Druze pita bakery. Farther along the path, three paths intersect in a clearing by an ice-cold pool—the middle and right-hand paths lead to the waterfall.

Nimrod's Fortress (Qal'at Nemrud) stands 1.5km northeast of Banyas on an isolated hill. According to the biblical table of Noah's descendants, Nimrod was "the first on earth to be a mighty man" (Genesis 10:8). Legend holds that, besides fashioning sandals and building the Tower of Babel, he erected this gigantic fortress high enough to shoot arrows up to God. A plaque above one gate reads in Arabic: "God gave him the power to build this castle with his own strength." Historians, who just love poking holes in myths, say the fortress was actually built by the Muslims and originally named Qal'at Subeiba. Either way, the view from the top of the fortress is unrivaled anywhere in the Upper Galilee or Golan. The one-hour, uphill approach to the castle leads to a clear view into the tiny Druze village of Ein Qinya; the trail begins just off bus route #55 between Kiryat Shmona and Katzrin—the road leading to the castle is directly across from the bus stop. Bus #14 from Kiryat Shmona to Neveh Ativ also passes by here. The castle is also accessible by a footpath from Banyas beginning directly above the springs. This shadeless walk takes about 45 minutes each way (fortress open daily 8am-5pm; NIS12, ages 5-18 NIS6).

MAAS'ADA AND MAJDAL SHAMS مسعدة و مجدل شمس

The Druze of these two villages at the foot of Mt. Ḥermon differ from the Galilee's Druze in one major respect: most have remained loyal to Syria and many refuse to accept Israeli citizenship. In 1982, they staged a protest against Israeli rule, and the IDF was sent in to restore control. Since then, the villages have been quiet.

Maas'ada (pronounced MA-sa-da; if you say ma-SA-da, you are referring to the fortress in the Negev) and Majdal Shams are unprepared for tourism—there's absolutely nothing touristy to do. The emphasis here is more on tradition than on commercialism. Women are swathed in black and men wear black *shirwal* (low-hanging baggy pants), which date from Ottoman times.

Maas'ada is located at the foot of Mt. Ḥermon, at the intersection of the roads leading south to Katzrin and west to Kiryat Shmona. Maas'ada's farmers cultivate the valley and terrace the low-lying ridges around the mountain. Two kilometers down the road is the locally famous lake **Birket Ram.** The perfectly round body of water is something of a geological peculiarity formed by underground water-bearing strata. You'll know you've reached the lake when you see the parking lot of the excellent, two-story **Birket Ram Restaurant** (tel. 698 16 38). Their specialty is "Lamb in the Oven" (NIS40). Standard *shishlik* (NIS38) and liver (NIS30) are also available (open daily 8am-7pm). From the restaurant's roof you'll see a postcard-worthy view of a Druze mosque beneath sometimes snowy Mt. Ḥermon. A small **hut** in the parking lot sells delicious Druze pita with *labaneh* and *za'tar* (NIS8). A lakefront swimming and picnic area costs NIS5 (free for restaurant patrons).

Majdal Shams (Arabic for "tower of the sun") is the largest town in the Golan (pop. 8000), and a 5km walk along a quiet road through a pleasant valley. The town abuts the border with Syria; an Israeli lookout tower looming above the village sees eye-to-eye with its Syrian counterpart on the opposite peak, while a white UN base spans the neutral valley in between. Because the electric-fence border is closed and pocked with land mines, the lookout area on the outskirts of town has become the site of a sad but fascinating daily ritual. Majdal's Druze line up on the hillside (aptly dubbed *Givat Ha-Tza'akot* or "Shouting Mountain"). Armed with bullhorns, they make small-talk with their relatives on the Syrian side. The best time to witness this is on Friday and Saturday afternoons.

Two kilometers past Majdal Shams is **Moshav Neveh Ativ** (tel. 698 13 33), founded after the Golan was captured by Israel. The *moshav* has developed an expensive resort village to take advantage of the ski slopes on southern **Mount Ḥermon,** 10km away. Bus #55 travels from the *moshav* to the villages (2 per day, NIS8.80). It's also possible to take a *sherut* from Maas'ada to Kiryat Shmona in the late afternoon for the same price. The road from Maas'ada to Kiryat Shmona is scenic, running west along a gorge and past the hilltop village of Ein Qinya and Nimrod's Fortress.

About 5km before the border with Syria are two kibbutzim, **Merom Golan** and **Ein Zivan.** These were the first Israeli settlements in the Golan, founded a few months after the Six Day War. From the observation point you can see the destroyed Syrian city of **Quneitreh,** a border town-turned tourist attraction (see p. 531).

Kosher Hot Dogs

Israel may not have Colorado's reputation as a skier's mecca, but its sole ski resort, Mt. Ḥermon, offers slopes that even frequenters of Vail would find enticing. The snow-capped peak rarely gets bitter cold, and in good seasons the trails are blanketed with meters of the white stuff. The mountain straddles the Syrian border, and towers over 2800m (although the top of the cable car is actually much lower). Skiing on the Ḥermon can be challenging; there are no trees, and steep dips in the wide expanses are easy to miss. Beginners should not fret, however— gentle runs descend from the top of each lift. On clear days, skiers can see the Galilee stretch out beneath them. On cloudy days, the mountain seems to jut out of a sea of vapor. Call (06) 698 13 37 or (03) 565 60 40 (year-round) for ski conditions and lodging information.

ISRAEL

The Negev הנגב

The Negev Desert covers just over half of Israel's territory. Long the domain of Bedouin, archaeologists, and visionaries like David Ben-Gurion, the Negev is entering mainstream Israeli life as towns and kibbutzim fulfill the Biblical prophecy of making the desert bloom. New technologies such as drip irrigation and hydroponics are turning scorched red earth into banana and citrus groves, and new waves of immigrants are turning backwater desert settlements into boom towns. Be'er Sheva, the capital of the region, is the fastest growing city in Israel. As highrises and McDonald's spring up in Israel's cities, purists escape to the Negev's less populated parts: the craters and valleys of the desert are lined with miles of trails, and remote villages are becoming a haven for meditators.

Tourism in the Negev once revolved around two areas: the colorful beaches of Eilat and the mineral-rich waters of the Dead Sea. In recent years, the Negev Tourism Development Administration has sought to introduce travelers to the beauty of the harsh desert landscape. Their free pamphlet, *Sculpted Wilderness,* is available at tourist offices and offers a comprehensive introduction to the various regions of the Negev. Although tourism has skyrocketed, these 12,000 sq. km of desert have become no less forgiving. Temperatures soar at midday—those caught without a hat and water will see vultures circling overhead in a matter of minutes. Desert outfitters recommend that hikers bring one liter of water for every hour in the sun.

It's possible to tour the desert on vinyl Egged seats, but buses in the Negev are steamy and infrequent. Organized **tours** are a cooler option. The bus tour organized by the **Ben Yehuda Hostel** (tel. (02) 624 80 21) in Jerusalem gives a one-day overview of the desert and hits all the major sights, including sunrise on Masada and lunch in Jericho (12hr., NIS65). Hostel-run tours don't include sites admission. **SPNI** arranges excellent hiking tours around the Dead Sea. All-day Thursday tours are US$65, and two-day Friday-Saturday tours are US$189, including transportation, food, and lodging when applicable (Jerusalem office tel. (02) 625 23 57, Ein Gedi field school tel. (07) 658 42 88). A more exciting (though expensive) option to see the Negev is on a **jeep tour** (see Desert Shade, p. 427).

THE DEAD SEA ים המלח

How low can you go? At almost 394m below sea level, this is about it—the Dead Sea is the lowest point on the surface of the planet. If that doesn't sound momentous, wait until you drive in from Be'er Sheva or Jerusalem, pass a "sea level" signpost, and then round a bend to see entire mountain ranges whose peaks are below. The morbid moniker was coined by Christian pilgrims astonished by the apparent absence of any form of life in the sea's waters, but kill-joy scientists have recently discovered microorganisms in the lake. Its Hebrew name, Yam Ha-Melaḥ ("The Sea of Salt"), is more to the point: the lake has a salt concentration eight times that of ocean water. It is this high concentration of minerals that attracts tourists to the bitter, oily waters—the dissolved minerals make the water so dense that even fish would have to walk.

The Dead Sea is really a large lake, 65km long, 18km wide, and 400m deep. It's part of the Great Rift Valley that extends from southern Africa to Turkey and is filled with water from floods and underground streams in the surrounding desert. There is no outlet for the lake's water, but the intense sun used to evaporate just enough to keep the water level constant. Recent Israeli and Jordanian water diversion projects have caused the Dead Sea to shrink—so much so that a sand bar has emerged, cutting off the southern tip of the lake.

For many visitors, the Dead Sea is good for a quick dip, getting the famous reading-a-magazine picture, and then a much-needed shower. For others, the Dead Sea is **therapy.** According to a few scientists and all resort owners, concentrations of bro-

TO GAZA
AND TEL AVIV
232
34

GAZA
STRIP
242
234
25
241

Khan
Yunis
Rafah
Rafah
Crossing
232

4

Hazerim

Beer Sheva

222

Nevatim

Tel Arad

Arad

TO HEBRON
AND JERUSALEM

WEST BANK

Ein
Gedi

Dead
Sea

Masada

Ein
Bokek

Salt
Pan

Neve Zohar

Dead Sea
Works

Dimona

Mamshit

Yeruham

Ha-Makhtesh
Ha-Gadol

Ha-Makhtesh
Ha-Katan

Nizana
Crossing

Nizana

211

204

206

224

40

31

25

90

60

31

40

Sdeh Boker
Midreshet Ben Gurion

Ein Avdat

Avdat

171

Mitzpe
Ramon

Makhtesh
Ramon

40

13

90

Petra

EGYPT

10

ISRAEL

JORDAN

Wadi Araba Highway

12

Yotvata

Ḥai Bar Wildlife
Preserve

Timna
Park

90

TO SUEZ

Netafim
Crossing

Taba
Crossing

Eilat

TO DAHAB

Taba

Arava
Crossing

Aqaba
Crossing

Aqaba

The Negev

⚔ Border Crossing

N

0   10 miles

0   10 kilometers

mine, magnesium, and iodine 10 to 20 times higher than in the ocean can reduce skin allergies, stimulate glandular functions, and soothe the nervous system. Dead Sea mud is supposed to do wonders for the skin—those terrifying dark brown creatures by the shore are actually people caked in it.

PRACTICAL INFORMATION

Caution: this water is powerful stuff. When it's good, it may cure arthritis, but when it's bad, it's very bad. If Dead Sea water gets into your eyes, you're in for several minutes of painful blindness. Rinse your eyes immediately in the fresh-water showers found on all beaches. Don't shave the morning before you go swimming; the water will sear minor scrapes you didn't even know you had. Free public beaches are at **Ein Gedi** (located in the central Dead Sea area), **Ein Bokek** (about 40km south of Ein Gedi), and at **Ḥamei Zohar** (4km south of Ein Bokek, near the Moriah Hotel). Since you'll probably want to wash off as soon as you get out of the water, stick to these beaches, all with public showers. Ḥamei Zohar has a section of beach where men and women are separated—making both the religious and shy nudists quite happy. All are accessible by bus. Thermal baths, spas, and mud-baths are run out of hotels in and around Ein Bokek and have separate bus stops.

The Dead Sea does not have an ordinary desert climate—instead of being harsh and dry, it's harsh and humid. The sticky air, especially in the summer, makes high temperatures barely tolerable. The air has a 10% higher oxygen concentration, but exertion is sane only in the early morning. The steamroom-like weather has been known to dehydrate people simply waiting at a shaded bus stop. Standard desert rules apply: keep your head covered and take a water bottle wherever you go. Don't assume that shower and faucet water is safe to drink—most Dead Sea locations have special faucets marked "Drinking Water."

Only a few Egged lines travel the Dead Sea coast. Waits often last 45 to 90 minutes, so check schedules (under **Practical Information** for each site) and plan ahead. Buses #444 and 486 from Jerusalem to Eilat stop at Qumran, Ein Feshka, Ein Gedi, Masada, and Neveh Zohar. Bus #487, also from Jerusalem, runs only to Qumran, Ein Feshka, and Ein Gedi. Bus #385 makes about four trips per day (Sun.-Fri.) between Ein Gedi and Be'er Sheva via Arad, Ein Bokek, and Masada. Note that reservations for seats on the Eilat bus from Jerusalem cannot be made at Ein Gedi or Masada. Your chances of getting an unreserved seat are better at the height of the tourist season, since Egged often runs two buses at a time to accommodate the crowds.

Each of the region's attractions can be seen in a few hours or a half-day at most. Infrequent bus connections, the isolation of the sights, and the fact that some attractions can only be reached via long hikes from the main road make **renting a car** an excellent idea. Most companies offer a daily rental rate of US$50-60. Driving in the Dead Sea region provides spectacular vistas, but be careful—steep, windy roads mean nothing to speed-demon Israeli drivers. The best place to rent is Jerusalem, since cutthroat competition drives prices down (see **Practical Information,** p. 286). If you want to rent a car in the Dead Sea area, Rent-A-Reliable-Car (tel. 658 44 52) or Hertz (tel. 658 44 33), located in Ein Bokek, can get you rolling.

There are two **telephone codes** for the Dead Sea region: 02 for the northern part (Qumran and Ein Feshka), and 07 for Ein Gedi and points south, including Ein Bokek.

QUMRAN قمران קומרן

In 1947, a young Bedouin looking for a wayward sheep threw a rock into a cliffside cave and heard something break. Upon further inspection, he found a collection of earthenware jars containing 2000-year-old parchment manuscripts. These famed **Dead Sea Scrolls** are an important source for understanding the development of the Hebrew Bible. The largest, now displayed in the Shrine of the Book at the Israel Museum in Jerusalem, was a 7m-long ancient Hebrew text of the Book of Isaiah. Encouraged by the discovery, French archaeologists searched the caves and excavated the foot of the cliffs. By 1956 they had found the village of the sect that wrote the Dead Sea Scrolls, as well as additional scrolls.

Archaeological evidence suggests that the site was settled as long ago as the 8th century BCE, re-inhabited in the 2nd century BCE, temporarily abandoned during the reign of Herod following an earthquake, and completely deserted after the Roman defeat of the Jewish revolt in 70 CE. Historians conclude that the authors of the scrolls were the **Essenes,** a Jewish sect whose members, disillusioned by the corruption and Hellenization of fellow Jerusalemites, sought refuge in the sands. The strict and devout Essenes believed that a great struggle would ensue between the Sons of Light (themselves and the angels) and the Sons of Darkness (everyone else). Excavations at Masada suggest that the members of the Qumran sect joined with the Jews there in the struggle against the Romans.

Look for the cisterns and channels that were used for storage and transport of water in the arid climate. The **watchtower** provides a panoramic view of the site. The **scriptorium,** the chamber in which the scrolls were probably written, is still equipped with desks and inkstands. In the **honey press,** dates (rather than bees) were used to produce the sticky substance. The ruins are clearly marked, and a map of the site is posted just past the entrance. A short climb brings you to the **caves** themselves which are now empty and uninteresting. If you have a backpack, the staff at the reception booth will store it for no charge.

To see the ruins, take bus #421, 444, 486, or 487 from either Ein Gedi (NIS16) or Jerusalem (NIS18). When you get off the bus, cross the road to a steep hill with a road winding around its top. Don't panic—it's only a 100m hike, and the ruins are right around the bend. Make your way past the **boutique** selling the usual tourist crap (open daily 8am-5pm), then through the adjoining clean, air-conditioned, self-service **cafeteria** (sandwiches NIS12, salad bar NIS17, hot lunch NIS28). To your right are **public bathrooms,** and across from them is the entrance to the site. The ticket counter (tel. 994 22 35) has brochures describing the history and layout of the ruins (open Sat.-Thurs. 8am-6pm; winter 8am-4pm; NIS12, students NIS9, children NIS6).

Near Qumran: Ein Feshka فشكى عين פשקה עין

Relief from the heat is nearby: take any southbound bus (i.e. towards Masada, Ein Gedi, and Eilat) 3km to the salt- and fresh-water bathing spot at Ein Feshka (also called Enot Zukim; tel. 994 23 55), where springs wind through the *wadi's* reeds and tumble into small pools. Ein Feshka is the only Dead Sea resort with fresh-water ponds adjacent to the swimming area. Ninety-five percent of the bathers are West Bank residents; until several years ago, the place was popular with Jewish Israelis, who are now uncomfortable traveling via Jericho. There are many more men than women, and the females who do show up don't show much. Still, the welcoming management notes that travelers may dress as they like (admission NIS20). There are showers, changing rooms, bathrooms, and drinking water. The beach has a lifeguard (in case you don't float) and plenty of gray **Dead Sea Mud** (open daily 8am-5pm).

Seven kilometers north of Qumran is **Attraction Water Park** (tel. 994 23 91) in Kalya Beach (bus #421, 444, 486, or 487 will take you, but be sure to cross the road from the ruins or you'll end up in Eilat). There are water slides, games, outdoor aerobics, and Saturday performances (NIS55; open daily March-Oct. 9am-5pm).

▨ Ein Gedi עין גדי

After a hot morning on Masada or a muggy bus ride from Jerusalem, the only thing better than drinking cold water is sitting in it. Ein Gedi's verdant **nature reserve** is endowed with cascading waterfalls, wildlife, and shade. Hyenas, wolves, and the elusive leopard all call the reserve home; also keep your eyes open for the camouflaged ibex, the shy fox, and the endearing hyrax. Ein Gedi has a long history of providing shelter. David fled to this oasis to escape the wrath of King Saul (1 Samuel 24), and it was here that he forsook the choice opportunity to slay his pursuing father-in-law, who was easy prey while relieving himself in a cave. During the second Jewish revolt

(132-5 CE), rebel leader Simon Bar-Kokhba sought refuge here. His hiding place, the Letter Cave, can be visited about 6km southwest of the main settlement.

PRACTICAL INFORMATION

From Ein Gedi, bus #421 or 444 (7 per day) will take you to Jerusalem (NIS25, students NIS22.50). Get bus schedules from the Central Bus Station in Jerusalem. Bus #384 or 385 (5 per day) goes to Be'er Sheva (NIS29.50, students NIS26.60) via Arad (NIS21, students NIS18.50). Bus #486 (4 per day) runs to Masada (NIS11) and to the hotels at Ein Bokek (NIS15.50, students NIS11.50). Bus #444 goes to Eilat (6 per day; NIS46, students NIS40). There are three **bus stops** in Ein Gedi: the northernmost one is where you get off for the nature reserve, the youth hostel, and the SPNI field school. Farther south is the Ein Gedi Beach stop, where you'll find the beach, campgrounds, a mini-market, a restaurant, a gas station, and a first-aid station. Get off at the southernmost stop for the thermal baths and spas.

ACCOMMODATIONS AND FOOD

Nights in Ein Gedi can be as hot as the days—think twice about sleeping without air-conditioning. Rooms in the **Beit Sara Youth Hostel (HI)** (tel. 658 41 65), just uphill from the Naḥal David entrance to the reserve, are nicely decorated and have air-conditioning and private baths. The outdoor terrace and **bar** (open nightly 6-11pm) overlook the Dead Sea. (Office open 7am-8pm. Flexible lockout 9am-4pm. Check-in 4-7pm. Check-out 9am. No curfew. Dorm beds (8 per room) US$15/NIS60; singles US$34.50/NIS125; doubles US$49/NIS176. Each additional person US$16/NIS56. Nonmembers add US$1.50/NIS4.) A 10-minute walk from the hostel along the uphill road will bring you to the **SPNI Field School** (tel. 658 42 88; take bus #384 or 385 from Be'er Sheva or #486 or 487 from Jerusalem). The staff gives advice on hiking, distributes trail maps, and runs its own air-conditioned hostel. The dorms are often crowded with Israeli school field trips, so reservations are a good idea. The hostel also has a public kitchen, a tiny museum, a snake collection, a fantastic observation point, and a 15-minute audiovisual show about desert flora and fauna (NIS6). (Office open Sun.-Thurs. 8am-5pm. No lockout. Check-in 3-8pm during the week. Check-out 9am. Gates locked at 10pm. Dorm beds NIS64; doubles NIS245. Dinner NIS43 during the week, NIS49 on weekends. Breakfast included.) Farther south, at the Ein Gedi Beach bus stop, **Ein Gedi Holiday Resort** (tel. 658 44 44; fax 658 44 55) is just behind and to the right of the gas station. Bring your own sleeping bag or tent and get bathroom facilities and a spot of dirt for NIS25. The campground also offers slightly cramped, air-conditioned **caravans** with kitchenettes, private baths, and cushioned benches. (Lockers NIS6 (every time you open it). Singles US$64/NIS225; doubles US$71/NIS245. Each additional adult US$20/NIS65. 4-adult and 2-child max. Visa, MC.)

Quick snacks are available near the entrances to the nature reserve. **Kiosk Ein Gedi** has beer (NIS8) and lots of other goodies (open 8am-5pm). At the beach bus stop, **Pundak Ein Gedi** (tel. 659 47 61) might be worth the steeper prices. This kosher restaurant switches from milk to meat between breakfast and lunch. Yogurt and omelettes are served until about 11am, when meat lunches (NIS25) become available (open daily 8am-6pm, last hot meal order taken 5pm).

SIGHTS

Of the two entrances to the **Ein Gedi Nature Reserve** (tel. 658 42 85; fax 658 45 17), only the Naḥal David entrance, just inland from the youth hostel, is accessible by bus. Trail maps, information and lockers (NIS2) are available here. Well-placed railings provide support in steep areas, so hiking is not too difficult aside from the heat. Dead Sea temperatures can make even inhaling strenuous, so get going when they open the gates (8am). Always bring at least two 1.5L bottles of water (you can fill up at the faucets just outside the gate).

An enjoyable 15-minute hike takes you up to **Naḥal David** (David's Stream), a slender pillar of water dropping into a shallow pool. The best part of the hike is an invigorating swim in the delightfully cold water. Twenty meters below the waterfall, another trail climbs up the cliffside to **Shulamit Spring.** From the spring, continue up the cliff to **Dodim Cave** (Lover's Cave), a splendidly cool, mossy niche at the top of the fall (1hr. walk). Proceeding left from the spring will lead you to the fenced-in remains of what was once a **Chalcolithic Temple,** used 3000 years ago as a regional sanctuary. From the Temple, either retrace your steps or take the steeply descending path to **Ein Gedi Spring** (5min.). From Ein Gedi Spring a roundabout path runs to Shulamit Spring, near the base of the waterfall at Naḥal David.

A fairly difficult climb along **Naḥal Arugot,** which begins in the parking lot of the Naḥal Arugot Rd. about 3km in from Rte. 90, leads to a hidden waterfall—don't forget your swimsuit. It's a good hour walk from the road (look for the sign), but if you follow the stream you can't get lost. A beautiful deep blue pool rewards the exertion. The reserve is open daily 8am-3pm, but you can exit until 4pm; you may not start hikes to Dodim Cave and beyond after 1:30pm. There is no eating or smoking in the reserve (admission NIS15, under 18 NIS8).

Ein Gedi has a free **public beach,** where oversized umbrellas and picnic tables speckle the rocky sand. You can store your stuff here for NIS5. The water is more reminiscent of the nearby Mediterranean than the fluorescent green shores of Ein Bokek. Take a left from the entrance and walk north for ten minutes to find vats of the famous **Dead Sea mud** as well as more freshwater springs.

Between the entrances to the reserve and to Naḥal Arugot on Highway 90 lies the **Ein Gedi National Antiquities Park,** an excavated Jewish settlement dating from 200-500CE which includes a renovated **synagogue** with beautifully restored mosaics (open Sun.-Thurs. 8am-5pm, Fri. 8am-1pm; NIS10, students NIS8).

▨ **Masada** מצדה

"Masada shall not fall again," swear members of the armored division of the **Israel Defense Forces** each year at this site. Jewish Zealots' tenacious defense of Masada has been fashioned into a symbol of modern Israel, with some controversy about the metaphor's implications. Regardless of its political significance, tourists from all over the world flock to this major pilgrimage site to catch the spectacular view of the Dead Sea, experience the impressive ruins, and share in the conflicting emotions of tragedy and triumph often evoked by the tales of martyrdom.

The huge fortress (*Metzada*) was built as a refuge from marauding Greeks and Syrians by the Jewish High Priest Jonathan Maccabeus around 150 BCE, and was expanded to 610m by 220m a few decades later by John Hyrcanus I. In 40 CE, King Herod fled to Masada to avoid being massacred by Parthian-backed Hasmoneans. Masada was used once again in 66 CE, when the Judeans rebelled against Roman occupation; a small band of rebels, the original Zealots, captured the outpost. When the Romans gradually crushed the revolt, taking Jerusalem in 70 CE and destroying the Second Temple, Masada was the last holdout in all of Israel. With years' worth of food, water, and military supplies stashed behind its two defensive walls, Masada was ideally suited for resistance. The 967 men, women, and children held off thousands of Roman legionnaires through a five-month siege. The Romans, frustrated at first, called in their best engineers to construct a wall and camps in a ring around the mount. They ultimately built an enormous stone and gravel ramp up the side of the cliff, using Jewish slaves as laborers in order to prevent the Zealots from shooting them down as the ramp was built.

When the defenders realized that the Romans would break through the wall the next morning, the community leaders decided that it would be better to die, as their leader said, "unenslaved by [their] enemies, and leave this world as free men in company with [their] wives and children" rather than be captured by the Romans. Each family burned its possessions and joined in the communal suicide plan. The Jews placed stores of wheat and water in the citadel's courtyard to prove to the Romans that they did not perish from hunger. The following morning, when the Romans burst in, they encountered a deathly silence. The only survivors, two women and five children, told the story of the martyrs of Masada. The story was recorded by Josephus Flavius, a Jewish-Roman general and chronicler. Flavius, a controversial figure in his own right, never actually visited Masada, but spoke extensively with the two adult survivors, later describing them to be "of exceptional intelligence for women." He constructed his history based on their accounts; archaeologists have yet to unearth the Zealots' remains and other corroboratory artifacts.

TRANSPORTATION

Masada lies 20km south of Ein Gedi, a few kilometers inland from the Arad-Be'er Sheva road. **Bus** #421, 444, or 486 will take you to **Jerusalem** (8 per day; NIS31.50, students NIS28.40); #444 goes to **Eilat** (4 per day, last bus on Fri. 3:15pm; NIS45, students N IS40); and #384 or 385 will take you to **Be'er Sheva** (5 per day; NIS29.50, students NIS26) via **Arad** (NIS18.50, students NIS16.70). Jerusalem-bound buses stop at Ein Gedi, and buses to Be'er Sheva and Eilat travel via **Ein Bokek** (NIS11.50).

ACCOMMODATIONS AND FOOD

The **Taylor Youth Hostel (HI)** (tel. 658 43 49; fax 658 46 50), straight ahead and to the left of the bus stop, is surrounded by grass and shady trees. Each impeccable room has air-conditioning and a private bath. A TV lounge and barbecue area are available for guests. (Office open Sun.-Fri. 8am-1pm and 3-7pm, Sat. 4-7pm. Check-in 4-7pm. Check-out 9am, Sat. 10am. Dorm beds (6-8 per room) US$15/NIS60; singles US$36/NIS129; doubles US$52/NIS182. Extra person US$15/NIS60. Non-members add US$1.50/NIS4 per person. Breakfast included. Limited lockers NIS5.) A concrete pavilion in front of the hostel accommodates **campers** for free. Nearby restrooms are functional but paperless.

The food situation at Masada is dismal. The Zealots had the right idea—bring a few years' supply with you. The hostel serves kosher meat dinners (NIS34), but only when enough guests are around (usually during July and August). All other eating establishments are open from 8am to 5pm.

The glossy Masada boutique camouflages a self-service restaurant—ogle T-shirts, shot glasses, and Dead Sea facial packs before munching on a Greek salad (NIS20) or sandwich (NIS15). The citrus stand on the patio sells freshly squeezed orange and grapefruit juice (NIS10). By the entrance to the cable car, another snack bar sells sandwiches (NIS10) and ice cream (NIS7-9).

SIGHTS

There are three ways to conquer the mountain: by cable car or by either of two foot paths. The more popular, scenic, and difficult of the two is the original **Snake Path,** named for its tortuous bends. The hike takes about 45 minutes. If you start early enough (gates open at 4:30am), you'll see the sun slowly rising over the Dead Sea 450m below—one of the most dramatic experiences in Israel. The **Roman Ramp** is the easier of the two paths and starts on Arad Rd. on the west side of the mountain. The starting point of this 30-minute hike is not accessible by public transportation, and the walk around the base to the Roman Ramp is extremely arduous and time-consuming. If you hike down the Ramp and walk around the city to the east side, stick to the SPNI trail; don't descend on the incline with the water pipe. Admission is paid at the top of the summit (NIS15, students NIS11). Early-morning climbers may be able to avoid the charge. It's best to start hiking well before the afternoon, both to avoid the heat and to leave enough time for exploring. Drinking water is available only at the summit, so begin your ascent loaded with liquid.

There is a **cable car** that stops near the top of Snake Path. It runs 8am-5pm (winter until 3pm), on Friday 8am-3pm (winter until 2pm), leaving every half-hour or when 40 passengers have assembled for the three-minute ascent (round-trip including admission NIS45, students NIS29; one-way NIS34, students NIS23). Popular options are to hike up in the early morning and then take the cable car down when it gets

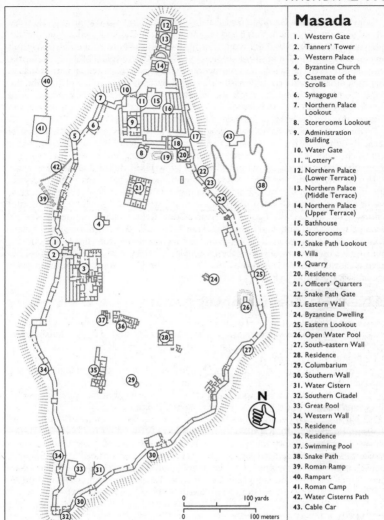

Masada

1. Western Gate
2. Tanners' Tower
3. Western Palace
4. Byzantine Church
5. Casemate of the Scrolls
6. Synagogue
7. Northern Palace Lookout
8. Storerooms Lookout
9. Administration Building
10. Water Gate
11. "Lottery"
12. Northern Palace (Lower Terrace)
13. Northern Palace (Middle Terrace)
14. Northern Palace (Upper Terrace)
15. Bathhouse
16. Storerooms
17. Snake Path Lookout
18. Villa
19. Quarry
20. Residence
21. Officers' Quarters
22. Snake Path Gate
23. Eastern Wall
24. Byzantine Dwelling
25. Eastern Lookout
26. Open Water Pool
27. South-eastern Wall
28. Residence
29. Columbarium
30. Southern Wall
31. Water Cistern
32. Southern Citadel
33. Great Pool
34. Western Wall
35. Residence
36. Residence
37. Swimming Pool
38. Snake Path
39. Roman Ramp
40. Rampart
41. Roman Camp
42. Water Cisterns Path
43. Cable Car

ISRAEL

0   100 yards
0   100 meters

hot, or to take the cable car up in the afternoon and hike down when the sun is less fierce. The site officially closes at 5pm.

The ruins at Masada were unearthed in 1963 by a team of archaeologists headed by Yigael Yadin. About one-third of the ruins you see are actually reconstructed—a black line indicates the extent of the original findings. Directly in front of the entrance to the site stands a large sign with a **map** of the ruins outlining several walking tours. From the entrance, the Northern Palace, Herod's own private pad, is up and to the right. Across the site is the Western Palace, and the Southern Citadel is down to the left at the far end of the mountaintop.

The **central public bath,** the centerpiece of the **Northern Palace,** is well preserved. The palace's lower terrace has painted frescoes and intact capitals on fluted columns, suggesting the splendor Herod enjoyed even on a remote desert butte. In the bathhouse of the lowest section, the skeletons of a man, woman, and child were found, along with a *tallit* (prayer shawl).

From the top of the Herodian palace stairs, you can skirt your way around the western edge of the mountain. You'll soon come across the **Zealots' synagogue,** the oldest synagogue in Israel and the world. Scrolls were found here containing texts from several books of the Torah (most are now on display at the **Israel Museum** in Jerusalem; see p. 310). The scrolls and discoveries such as a *mikveh* (ritual bath) indicate that the community followed Jewish strictures despite mountainous isolation and the siege. Continuing along the edge, the **Western Palace** houses a bakery and more splendid Herodian wall decorations. Next to the palace you'll find the **Byzantine Chapel,** built by Christian monks who once occupied Masada.

Farther south are stone stairs descending into a hole. Descend into the large **cistern:** it's part of the reservoir system that allowed the defenders to store an eight-year supply of water. By draining rainfall from the surrounding mountains into Masada's reservoirs, the entire cistern would fill within a few hours on the annual day of rain.

The Masada **sound and light show** lights up the fortress like a Las Vegas marquee. Shows are in Hebrew, but simultaneous-translation earphones (NIS12) are available for English, French, German, Russian, and Spanish (shows April-Aug., Tues. and Thurs. 9pm; Sept.-Oct., Tues. and Thurs. 7pm; tickets NIS30, students NIS25). Arrange round-trip transportation from Arad MTIO (tel. 695 81 44 or 59 33) before 1pm the day of the show (NIS35). You can't see the show from the Masada hostel, because it's on the wrong side of the mountain. You can, however, watch the show from a campsite for NIS12 (show ticket, campground, and summit admission package NIS45, students NIS40).

■ Near Masada: Ein Bokek עין בוקק

Ein Bokek is home to hordes of luxury hotels, two shopping centers, and racks upon racks of postcards. In summer, the beach is tourist-infested, a bright, aquamarine, spectacle. All buses passing through Masada (5km away) also stop here. The new Solarium on the southern end of the beach is drawing hordes of customers who wish to be crisped with care (sun treatment NIS28). For a Dead Sea challenge, try lifting *both* your legs at least 5 inches out of the briny waters at the same time.

Menus in Ein Bokek are both uninspired and expensive, but two restaurants give discounts for flashing this book: **Hordus Beach Restaurant** (tel. 658 46 36) has a salad bar for NIS18 (main dishes NIS30-35, desserts NIS7; open Sat.-Thurs. 8am-7:30pm, Fri. 8am-5pm). **Kapulsky** (tel. 658 43 82) is the other option (main dishes NIS35-60, open daily 8am-midnight). You're probably better off sticking to the **minimarket** in the white mall, to your left as you get off the bus, or head for the **Sandpit,** housed in the Solarium, which has beer (NIS5, daily 3-5pm). The grassy **Tamar Garden,** opposite Hotel Lot, is a prime picnic spot. **Tamar Taxi** (tel. 658 43 92 or 93; open daily 7:30am-9pm) can get you to Masada (NIS60) or Ein Gedi (NIS85).

CENTRAL NEGEV

■ Be'er Sheva באר שבע

While it is an important administrative and commercial center, the capital of the Negev is not heavily touristed. Because of this, Be'er Shevites approach visitors with disarming curiosity and friendliness. True to its origins as a caravan crossroads, the city houses a cosmopolitan international community: one that is developing so quickly you can see the pre-fab apartments rise before your eyes. Be'er Sheva's most infamous attraction is still its lively Thursday morning **Bedouin market.**

Be'er Sheva means both "well of the oath" and "well of seven" in Hebrew, and the Bible (Genesis 21:25-31) supports both etymologies. The Arabic name, Bir As-Sabe', also means "well of seven." As the story goes, Abimelekh's servants seized a well that Abraham claimed to have dug. The dispute ended with a covenant in which Abraham

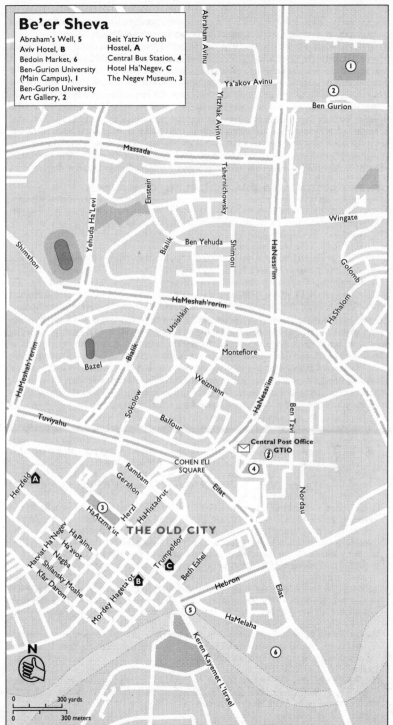

Be'er Sheva

Abraham's Well, **5**
Aviv Hotel, **B**
Bedoin Market, **6**
Ben-Gurion University
(Main Campus), **1**
Ben-Gurion University
Art Gallery, **2**

Beit Yatziv Youth
Hostel, **A**
Central Bus Station, **4**
Hotel Ha'Negev, **C**
The Negev Museum, **3**

ISRAEL

offered seven ewes to Abimelekh in exchange for recognition as the well's rightful owner. You can still see what many claim is **Abraham's well** today.

The Ottomans proclaimed modern Be'er Sheva a city in 1906 upon establishing a seat of government, a mosque, a school, and the governor's residence. They hoped that the city would function as a political, commercial, and administrative center for Negev Bedouin, who continue to dwell in tents beyond the pubs and discotheques of the city center. The precise pathwork of the old city's streets offers tastes and glimpses of immigrant communities from Morocco, Syria, Russia, Argentina, and Ethiopia, as well as the largest Albanian Jewish community in the world. Today, Be'er Sheva's 150,000 residents are doing their best to make tens of thousands of newly arrived, frost-bitten Russians feel at home in the middle of the desert, and to welcome streams of Ethiopian newcomers into its sand and concrete grasp. The city lacks affordable accommodations but serves as a base for short forays into the Negev.

ORIENTATION AND PRACTICAL INFORMATION

The city's **central bus station** is located on **Eilat Street,** across the road from **Kenyon Ha-Negev** (a shopping mall), itself a good landmark from which to orient yourself. The bus station is divided into two sections: one for the red, intercity Egged buses, and the other for the blue, independently-run municipal lines.

West of the central bus station, across Eilat St., lies the **Muslim Cemetery,** and just west of that is the **old city** area, a neat grid designed by Ottoman-commissioned German engineers. Most attractions are concentrated here, and major renovations are making the area less grimy. The main east-west streets start with the northernmost **Herzl Street.** Parallel to it is **Ha-Histadrut Street,** followed by **He-Halutz Street, Mordei Ha-Geta'ot Street,** and **Trumpeldor Street** farther south. The main north-south avenues begin with **Keren Kayemet LeYisrael Street** (**Kakal** or **KKL** for short), which is the town's newly fountained pedestrian section. One block west is **Ha-Atzma'ut Street** (on which you can see the tower of the Negev Museum), and then **Hadassa Street.** The old city streets are reassuringly close together, so miscounting blocks or making a wrong turn isn't disastrous. **Ha-Nesi'im Boulevard,** which meets Eilat St. at Kenyon Ha-Negev, will take you north to **Ben Gurion University,** and ultimately to Tel Aviv and Jerusalem.

Currency Exchange: Bank Ha-Poalim, 40 Ha-Atzma'ut St. (tel. 629 26 62), corner of He-Halutz St. Open Mon. and Wed. 8:30am-12:30pm, Sun., Tues., and Thurs. 8:30am-12:30pm and 4-6pm, Fri. 8:30am-noon. Its **ATM** accepts all major bank cards. For emergency banking call 649 29 49. **Bank Leumi** (tel. 623 92 22), just past the post office on Ha-Nesi'im Blvd. Open Sun., Tues., and Thurs. 8:30am-12:30pm and 4-6pm, Mon. and Wed. 8:30am-12:30pm, Fri. 8:30am-noon. Its **ATM** accepts Visa and Diner's Club.

Local Buses: Central bus station (tel. 627 73 81 or 82) between Ha-Nesi'im Blvd. and Eilat St. Buses #2, 3, 7-9, 11, 12, 18, 21, or 22 all go to the *shuk* and the old city (5:20am-11pm), and #13 follows Ha-Atzma'ut St. to the Negev Museum and the youth hostel (5:20am-11pm, every 20min.). All local rides NIS2.50.

Intercity Buses: Connections from central bus station on red **Egged** buses (tel. 629 43 11). To **Tel Aviv:** #370 direct to new central bus station or #380 direct to Arlozorov Terminal (both run 5:30am-8pm, every 20-30min., 1¼hr., NIS21, students NIS18). To **Jerusalem:** #470 direct (7-9am and 3-5pm, every hr., 1½hr.) or #446 express (6am-8pm, every 30min.-1hr. NIS27.50, students NIS24.80). To **Eilat:** #394 express (7:50am-1:45pm, every 1-1½hr., 3hr.), and #392, 393, 395, and 397 (all local with irregular schedules), NIS45, students NIS40.50.

Sherut Taxis: Moniot Ayal (tel. 623 30 33 or 53 33), in a booth next to the central bus station. *Sherut* to Jerusalem, Eilat, and Tel Aviv; 10% cheaper than buses, but you will have to wait for them to fill up.

Taxis: tel. 642 22 22 or 627 55 55.

Car Rental: Hertz, 5a Ben-Tzvi St. (tel. 627 27 68), across from the central bus station. Open Sun.-Thurs. 8am-6pm, Fri. 8am-3pm; min. age 21. **Avis** (tel. 627 177), across Ben-Tzvi St. from Hertz. Min. age 23.

English Bookstore: Mini Book. (tel. 644 33 69) in the passageway between Hadas-sah and Ha-Histadrut St., opposite Israel Discount Bank. Extensive selection of used books. Open Sun.-Mon. and Wed.-Thurs. 8:30am-1pm and 4-7pm, Tues. and Fri. 8:30am-1:30pm. The *kenyon* across from the bus station has a **Steimatzky,** omi-nously called "Arms Center."

Camping Supplies: Reta (tel. 623 35 77), in the *kenyon.* Open Sun.-Thurs. 9:30am-9pm, Fri. 9:30am-2pm, Sat. 9-11pm.

Pharmacies: Pharmline, 34 Herzl St. (tel. 628 06 35), across from the police station. Open Sun.-Thurs. 8am-2pm and 4-8pm, Fri. 8am-2pm. **Super Pharm** (tel. 628 13 71), in the *kenyon.* Open Sun.-Thurs. 9am-midnight, Fri. 8:30am-5pm, Sat. 10am-midnight. Phone numbers of emergency night workers posted on door.

Hospital: Soroka Hospital, Ha-Nesi'im Blvd. (tel. 640 01 11). Take bus #4 or 7 and tell the driver to let you off at the new emergency room.

Emergency: First Aid: Magen David Adom, 40 Bialik St. (tel. 627 83 33; **emer-gency** tel. 101). **Police:** 30 Herzl St. (tel. 646 27 44; **emergency** tel. 100), at the corner of KKL St.

Post Office: (tel. 629 58 32). At the corner of Ha-Nesi'im Blvd. and Ben-Tzvi St., diag-onally across from the bus station. This modern main branch has **Poste Restante, Western Union,** and **EMS** services, international calling, and also exchanges trav-eler's checks with no commission. Smaller branches on **Hadassa Street** and in the **City Hall** building. All branches open Sun.-Tues. and Thurs. 8am-12:30pm and 4-6:30pm, Wed. 8am-1pm, Fri. 8am-12:30pm. **Telephone Code:** 07.

ACCOMMODATIONS

If you can afford to stay here, Be'er Sheva is an excellent base for exploring the Negev. If not, arrive early to see everything of interest in the city before moving on to wallet-friendly hostels elsewhere.

Beit Yatziv Youth Hostel (HI), 79 Ha-Atzma'ut St. (tel. 627 74 44), 4 blocks from the old city (take bus #13). This well-kept, no-bunks hostel has its own pool (NIS18 for guests). Clean rooms have private bath, closet, A/C, and table. Check-in after 3pm. Check-out 9am. No lockout or curfew. Dorms (4 beds per room) NIS76. Next-door **Guest House** has singles (NIS146), doubles (NIS202), and triples (NIS267). Nonmembers add NIS4-6 each. Full Israeli breakfast included. Dinner NIS30-37. Credit cards accepted.

Aviv Hotel, 48 Mordei Ha-Geta'ot St. (tel. 627 80 59 or 82 58), off KKL St. Bulgarian owners Berta and Shlomo run a tidy 22-roomer with embroidered hangings, pic-tures of produce on the walls, and comfy sofas in the common room. Rooms have ancient but functioning private baths, A/C, TVs, and some balconies. 24hr. recep-tion. Singles NIS90; doubles NIS120. Croissant-and-coffee breakfast included.

FOOD

Lined with falafel, *shawerma,* pizza, and sandwich stands, the pedestrian section on **Keren Kayemet LeYisrael Street** is the best place for affordable eats. For an Ameri-can food fix, head to the food court on the lower floor of Kenyon Ha-Negev across from the bus station. **Kenny Rogers Roasters** serves chicken sandwiches for NIS16, and **Subway** subs are NIS6-16. For fast food diversity, get a full meal at **China Town** for NIS20-22. There's also a Pizza Hut, Burger Ranch, Kapulsky, and Burger King on the ground floor. (Most restaurants in the *kenyon* open Sun.-Thurs. 9am-midnight, Fri. 9am-1am, Sat. 10am-10pm.) A **Hypershuk supermarket** also inhabits the mall. The cheapest place to buy drinks and fresh produce is the **shuk,** located just south of the central bus station and easily identifiable by its arched metal rooftops. The Thurs-day **Bedouin market** also has cheap foodstuffs. This is the city that spawned **Glida Be'er Sheva,** 50 Hadassah St., the ice cream sensation that's sweeping the nation. A waffle cone with five luscious scoops is NIS11. The octogenarian in the rocking chair behind the counter is the sole proprietress of the secret recipe for her ice cream (open Sun.-Thurs. 9am-1am, Fri. 9am-9pm, Sat. 10am-2am). An additional branch is in the *kenyon.* The listings below are all in the old city area.

Panorama (tel. 623 52 49), at the corner of Ha'Histadrut St. and KKL, on the 2nd floor. Francophone owner serves kosher vegetarian pizzas, blintzes, and pasta (NIS20-25). For those not inclined to order beer (NIS7) or vodka (NIS8), there are pyramids of oranges, limes, and lichees at the juice stand downstairs (NIS7). A nice place to watch the *midrahov* meander by.

Bulgarian Restaurant, 112 KKL St. (tel. 623 85 04). Claims to be the oldest restaurant in Be'er Sheva. *Kebab, schnitzel,* and *goulash* (NIS25-40 each) have been served here since 1949. The affable proprietor will discuss your choices with you in French. Bavarian custard or chocolate mousse (NIS8); calf's foot jelly (NIS9). Mmmm. Open Sun.-Thurs. 9am-11pm, Sat. 10:30am-7:30pm.

Beit Ha-Ful, 15 Ha-Histadrut St. (tel. 623 42 53), on the corner with Smilansky St. Egyptian bean concoction in a pita with salads (NIS9) or in a bowl, with classy garnishings (NIS22). *Shawerma* in pita (NIS12). Eat *al fresco* or in an A/C dining room. Open Sun.-Fri. 8am-11pm.

Bis Lekal Kis, 98 Mordei Ha-Geta'ot St. (tel. 627 81 89). Between Hadassah and Ha'azmaut St.; look for a blue sign marked simply "Restaurant" and a pink painted rose. Generous kosher meat or fish portions (NIS15-25) in an A/C room. Hummus NIS3. Open Sun.-Thurs 10am-4pm, Fri. 10am-3pm.

Apropo, (tel. 623 67 11). At the corner of Herzl St. and KKL St. This air-conditioned, pricey chain offers variety: Thai dishes NIS30-40, omelettes NIS23-28, pasta NIS28-31, and salads NIS24-31. Over 30 enchanting desserts (NIS15-30). Open Sun.-Fri. 8am-1am, Sat. noon-1am. Credit cards accepted.

Restaurant Ilie, 21 Herzl St. (tel. 627 86 85). This Romanian haven serves *Tshorba* soup (NIS12), and broiled brains (NIS30). Great service. Open Sun.-Thurs. 6pm-midnight.

SIGHTS

Be'er Sheva's most exciting attraction is its Thursday **Bedouin Market,** established in 1905. The market is nirvana for *chatchke* lovers and bargain hunters. Amidst the clamor of screaming vendors you'll find cheap Bedouin food and excellent garments. Years ago, the Bedouin hawked camels and sheep—now they've added snow globes and t-shirts to the much-ballyhooed wares. The market is located on the south side of the city, at the intersection of Eilat and Hevron St. Trading begins early in the morning and goes all day. Many Bedouin here speak English and may compliment your beautiful eyes while charging six times the going rate for olive wood camels. Israelis and other non-Bedouins try their hand at peddling as well.

The scope of this market puts even Jaffa's *shuk ha-pishpeshim* to shame. Hundreds of Bedouin, both the semi-settled from Be'er Sheva and the nomads from deep in the desert, gather in the area to sell sheep, goats, clothes, cloth, jewelry, ceramics, spices, and digital watches. The northern part of the market features heaps of clothing. Most is junk; sift and ye shall find. As you head farther south, the quantity of rusty cans, scraps of paper, and dust increases, the smell of goat dung becomes stronger, and you can buy live rabbits, chickens, doves, or even parakeets. The southernmost part of the market houses the real gems: beaten copperware, Bedouin robes, fabrics, rugs, and ceramic items.

At the corner of Hebron and Keren Kayemet LeYisrael St. is the disputed site of **Abraham's Well.** The well dates back to at least the 12th century CE, and many believe that it was the original well of Abraham. One such firm believer is the notoriously friendly Shosh, who has taken it upon herself to spruce up the site. Ask her about the history of the well and the donkey-powered wooden cogwheel system for bringing up water, a design which dates back to biblical times (open Sun.-Thurs. 8:30am-4pm, Fri. 8:30am-1pm; free).

The last of Be'er Sheva's showpieces, the **Negev Museum,** 60 Ha-Atzma'ut St., is housed in an old Turkish mosque and chronicles 5000 years of the region's history (currently closed for structural renovations but expected to reopen sometime in 1998). The square building adjacent to the museum with the graceful front arches is the **Governor's House** (tel. 628 02 56). Built by the Turks in 1906, the building was named Be'er Sheva's City Hall in 1949. Diagonally facing the house on Azmaut St. is another Turkish building, which was used as a boarding school for Bedouin children during the British mandate and then as Red Crescent hospital during WWI. Both buildings are now part of the Negev Museum, housing changing exhibitions, Israeli art, and artifacts from various periods of Negev history (open Sun.-Thurs. 10am-4pm, Fri.-Sat. 10am-1pm; admission NIS5, students NIS3).

The modern campus of **Ben-Gurion University,** founded in 1969, lies in the far northeastern corner of the city (bus #4 leaves from the central bus station every 15min.). Near the dorms at 50 Arlozorov St. is the Taubel Community Center, which houses the **Ethiopian Jewish Handicrafts Workshop** (tel. 623 05 20 or 649 22 88). Here, you can watch demonstrations of traditional methods of creating pottery, figurines, embroidery, and gourd decorations. The crafts are for sale, but not at budget prices (open Mon.-Tues. and Thurs. 8:30am-12:30pm; free entrance).

Five kilometers northeast of the city are the ruins at **Tel Be'er Sheva,** recently upgraded to a national park. One pile of unearthed rubble is a 2nd-century Roman fortress, another an 8th-century BCE house, and a third one a 12th-century BCE well. Detailed brochures and site maps are available at an information booth facing the entrance to the park. Take Rte. 60 out of the city, then make a right at the set of lights just past the gas stations. (A taxi costs NIS20-25 each way.) Buses # 51, 52, 55, and 57 run by the site and cost NIS5.50. Solo women should not accept offers of personal tours of the site (park open Sun.-Thurs. 8am-5pm, Fri. 8am-4pm; admission NIS7). Next to the ruins is a **visitor's center** with a cafeteria and an expensive restaurant. Fashionable Israelis flock to conduct their marriages in trendy Bedouin style at nearby marriage hall **Hoalé Kidar,** complete with coffee, low couches, and *argeileh* (just like Egyptian *sheesha,* water pipes smoked with flavored tobacco).

Several kilometers north of the *tel,* the fascinating **Joe Alon Bedouin Museum** (tel. 991 33 22 or 85 97) is on the outskirts of Kibbutz Lahav. Take bus #367 or 369 to the Lahav junction (NIS11.5). By car, head north on Rte. 40 to Tel Aviv; make a right at the Devir-Lahav turnoff, and make a right again 8km later at the fork in the road. The museum is 1km up, in the Lahav forest. It showcases all facets of the nomads' lives, including traditional tools, embroidery, and customary desert garb. There's also an audiovisual presentation describing their culture and famous hospitality (open Sun.-Thurs. 9am-4pm, Fri. 9am-2pm, Sat. 9am-4pm; admission NIS12, students NIS10).

ENTERTAINMENT

Be'er Sheva has a lively nightlife that is both eclectic and convenient, centered around Trumpeldor and Smilansky St. Most of the bars open at 8 or 9pm, but remain quiet until about 11pm, when an almost exclusively Israeli crowd starts pouring in. Each pub has its trademark atmosphere: if you feel like a Flintstone, head for the cozy cave comfort of **The Hole;** for Bedouin-style divans, tapestry, and *argeileh,* visit **Psicodali;** if you can read lips over blaring Europop, catch a flick at the **Cinema Pub.** They all give you plenty to look at while you wait for your beer (NIS12) or hummus'n'chips (NIS17). **Punchline** offers live Israeli bands also. All pubs are open nightly 8pm-3am to party hounds 18 and older and charge no cover. The hottest hot spot is the **Forum,** Kiryat Yehudit 232 (tel. 627 76 72 or 78), in an industrial neighborhood. Thursdays and Fridays are disco and rock nights (NIS20-30), and live bands jam on Saturdays (NIS50). Soldiers and Negev locals flock here (open 11pm-4am). A cab from the old city costs NIS12-15. You can nurse your hangover at one of the mellow **coffeehouses** on Herzl St.

For fun that won't leave your ears ringing, try one of Be'er Sheva's **movie theaters,** four of which are in Kenyon Ha-Negev, or dive into the **swimming pool** at the Beit Yatziv Youth Hostel, 79 Ha-Atzma'ut St. (open Mon.-Sat. 8:30am-5pm, Sun. 10:30am-5pm; admission NIS23, *Shabbat* NIS24, NIS18 for hostel guests).

■ Near Be'er Sheva

ARAD עֲרָד

Arad's biggest tourist draw is its cool, dry, pollen-free air. That says a lot about this desert outpost. If you're not an asthmatic, you may be happier at the hostels on the Dead Sea or in Be'er Sheva. In its favor, Arad is a peaceful settlement, exemplifying the new Negev boom town. Only 40 years ago, Arad was nothing but a barren plateau; now it's a barren plateau with an air-conditioned mall and two pubs. Arad is also your one-stop box office for tickets to the **Masada Sound and Light Show** (see **Entertainment and Sights,** below).

Practical Information To get to the **Municipal Tourist Information Office** (tel. 995 93 33; fax 995 50 52), cross Yehuda Street from the bus station, turn left, make a right after the grocery store, walk through the pedestrian mall to its end, and look left. Make reservations for organized tours and other attractions, since there are **no sights in Arad** proper. The office can also provide you with free maps (open Sun.-Tues. 8am-7pm, Wed. 8am-4pm, Fri. 8:30am-noon).

Buses leave from the **central bus station** (4 plastic-encased benches and a parking lot) on Yehuda St., but are few and far between. Bus #389 goes to **Tel Aviv** (Sun.-Thurs. 6, 8:30am, and 2pm, last bus Fri. 1:30pm, Sat. 5 and 9pm; NIS31.50, students NIS28.40). To **Be'er Sheva,** take bus #388 (every 30-60min., 5:40am-9:30pm, NIS15) or #384 (9:30, 11:30am, 2, and 5pm, NIS15). Buses #384 and 385 (express) depart to **Ein Bokek** (NIS15), **Masada** (NIS18.50, students NIS16.70), and **Ein Gedi** (NIS21, students NIS18.90). The express leaves at 9:30am, 11:30am, 2pm, and 5pm; last Fri. bus 2pm. There is **no direct service** to Eilat or Jerusalem.

Everything you'll ever need in Arad is either next to the bus station or near the **Kenyon Arad,** a mall behind the *midraḥov.* There are several **ATM**-equipped **banks** in the pedestrian mall (all open Sun., Tues., and Thurs. 8:30am-12:30pm and 4-6pm, Mon. and Wed. 8:30am-12:30pm, Fri. 8:30am-noon). There's a **SuperPharm pharmacy** (tel. 997 16 21) in the Kenyon Arad (open Sun.-Thurs. 9am-10pm, Fri. 9am-3pm, Sat. 11am-11pm; call here for **emergencies**). The **police station** (tel. 995 70 44 or 081; dial 100 for emergencies) is right next to the bus station. Its neighbor on the other side is **Magen David Adom First Aid** (tel. 995 72 22; dial 101 for emergencies). The main **post office** branch (tel. 995 70 88) is in the commercial center across from the bus station. Here you can make **international phone calls,** use **EMS,** and receive **Poste Restante** (open Sun.-Tues. and Thurs. 8am-12:30pm and 4-6:30pm, Wed. 8am-1pm, Fri. 8am-12:30pm). Arad's **telephone code** is 07.

Accommodations and Food The **Blau-Weiss Youth Hostel (HI)** (tel. 995 71 50), on Atad St. is a four-minute walk from the bus station. Turn right on Yehuda St., take the first right onto Palmaḥ St., pass the soccer field on your left, then take the first left onto Atad St. and follow the signs. Named after the Zionist youth movement in Germany from which the Israeli youth hostels originated, this 200-bed complex has duplex and individual huts among small gardens and paths. Rooms are whistle-clean with private baths and killer air conditioning. The hostel has a kosher dining room and a cable TV room. The facilities are relaxing and often uncrowded. (Check-in 4-8pm. Check-out 10am. Reception open 7:30am-1:30pm, 4-7:30pm. Dorm beds US$16.50/NIS76; singles US$36/NIS130; doubles US$52/NIS192; triples US$64.50/NIS264. HI members subtract NIS4/$1.50 each. Breakfast included. MC, Visa.)

The most outstanding feature of Arad's culinary landscape is the absence of a falafel shop. The outdoor cafes in the *midraḥov* serve Hungarian, American, or Italian fare, and the food court in the mall offers cheap fast food (most places open daily until midnight). **Apropo** (in the Kenyon Arad) dishes out pasta, salads, and Thai food (NIS26-35); diners often swoon at live piano accompaniment. The **Burger Ranch** in the mall sells the usual (Ranchburgers NIS11.80). There's a **Supersol supermarket** (tel. 995 80 40) next to the visitor's center (open Sun.-Thurs. 7am-8pm, Fri. 7am-

2pm) and a **CoOp** (tel. 995 51 03) across from the bus station (open Sun.-Wed. 7:30am-7:30pm, Thurs. 7:30am-8pm, Fri. 7:30am-2pm).

Entertainment and Sights The **MTIO** will arrange transportation for the **Masada Sound and Light Show** (see **Masada**, p. 411) or to **Sussiya**, a 1400-year-old Hebrew city, with an impressive synagogue and a system of escape caves and tunnels. The MTIO can also provide reservations and directions if you would rather make the 22 km drive on your own. For **jeep tours**, contact Allan Levine (tel. 997 12 35; mobile phone (050) 284 301; fax 997 14 23). These wind-in-your-hair tours will make you love the desert (half-day NIS120, full-day NIS180 including food). The desert tours are a great way to see hard-to-reach areas while avoiding waits for infrequent buses. Allan also offers night tours, with wine and music performed by your host (5hr., NIS130), and a jeep tour/Masada Sound and Light Show combo (NIS210). Tell Allan *Let's Go* sent you and you'll get a 10% discount. **The Arad Visitor's Center** (tel. 995 44 09; fax 995 58 66), is across from the tourist office on Ben Yair St. The **GTIO computer** inside gives you detailed lists and pictures of the entire country (monthly-updated entries on accommodations, food, and tours). **Nature Reserve Authority** staffers can give advice on hiking. The detailed topographical trail maps for hiking in the Negev or Dead Sea area are all in Hebrew, but you can ask them to pen in the English names. The center includes a small museum and offers two audiovisual presentations about the desert region complete with a mock flood (open Sat.-Thurs. 9am-5pm and Fri. 9am-2:30pm).

Ancient Arad **(Tel Arad)** is situated about 10km west of the modern town. Arad was an early Bronze Age Canaanite city, destroyed about 2700 BCE and never rebuilt. Later, in King Solomon's era, an **Israelite fortress** was built on a nearby hill; the fortress includes a cult sanctuary whose design is unique to the southern (Judahite) kingdom (open Sat.-Thurs. 8am-4pm, Fri. 8am-3pm; NIS7, students NIS4). Take bus #388 and tell the bus driver to let you off at Tel Arad. The site is a 1.5km walk from there.

When night falls, everyone gathers at **Muza** (Tipsy), a pair of pubs in the Artists' Quarter on Yehuda Street, a ten-minute walk from the bus station or the hostel. Chug beer (NIS8) and munch olives (free) at the mellow picnic benches outside or in the raucous booths within. On *Shabbat,* this may be the only place to find a good hot dish (mushroom and cheese toast, *kebab,* falafel platters NIS18-25).

The annual **Hebrew Music Festival** (Festival Arad) is usually held in mid-July. At press time organizers were unsure about the date or content of the 1998 festival.

DIMONA דימונה

This tiny desert town near the Dead Sea holds the unlikeliest of communities—Chicagoans. The **Hebrew Israelite Community,** referred to as the Black Hebrews' Village by non-members, is a unique sect of English-speaking immigrants who trace their historical roots to ancient Israel. The community believes that the ancestors of black slaves in antebellum America lived in Israel until they were forced to migrate to Western Africa after the Roman onslaught in 70 CE. The group's vanguard returned to the Holy Land in 1969 under the leadership of spiritual guide Ben-Ami Ben Israel (formerly Ben-Ami Carter). The journey was prompted, says Ben Israel, by a vision he received and was preceded by a brief stint in Liberia. The Israeli government at first refused to grant them citizenship unless they converted to Judaism, but the Black Hebrews insisted that they were already Jews. The government and the sect came to an agreement in 1990 on a multi-step process for normalizing the community's legal status.

To get to the Hebrew Israelites from Dimona's central bus station, turn left on Herzl St., pass the tall red monument to the right and continue straight for about 10 minutes. The village is on the left as you pass a school, through the green hedges. You'll feel like one of the popular kids in junior high as villagers stop to greet you with *"Shalom, boker tov."* The community of 37 settlers who came in 1969, plus 47 who arrived in 1970, has blossomed into an 1100-person village with its own school, musical groups, and an Academy for the Performing and Fine Arts. About 600 other members of the group live in smaller communities elsewhere in Israel. The community makes its own magnificent clothes, jewelry, and food (their religious beliefs require them to wear only pure natural fabrics and prohibit them from eating any animal parts or products, white sugar, or white flour). Though you're welcome to wander through the village on your own, community leaders prefer that you call ahead (tel. (07) 655 54 00) so that they will be able to arrange a tour and take you to their **Toflé** clothing store and **Boutique Africa,** where US$35 will buy you a pair of their woven Eco-shoes. Leave them an imprint of your foot, and they will custom design a pair that you can pick up in about a week. Their **restaurant** is a godsend for protein-starved **vegans,** who can take the opportunity to stock up on scrambled tofu sandwiches (NIS6). The boutiques and restaurant keep irregular hours—drop by and they will probably magically open up. If you'd like to stay, the village has a three-room **guest house** (rooms US$20, breakfast and dinner included, call ahead). Around the second week of August, the Hebrew Israelites host the two-day **Naisik Ha-Shalom Music Festival** which highlights community entertainment and hosts Israeli bands. Daytime carnival activities are free, and nighttime concerts are almost so (tickets NIS10 and under—most way under). Singing groups from Dimona tour the country when they're not performing at home. Their music is unique—traditional Jewish texts set to a gospel beat.

Dimona's other claim to fame lies in the mysterious factory a few kilometers to the east. Any tour guide will tell you that the ominous barbed wire fences and signs forbidding photography are hiding a not-so-secret **nuclear power plant.** Officially, the place produces film, but officially, the U.S. military isn't hiding **alien ships** in New Mexico.

Buses #48 and 56 go to Be'er Sheva (every 15-20min., 35min., NIS11.5); #375, 393, and 394 go to Tel Aviv (NIS29.20, students NIS26.60); #393 and 394 go to Eilat (6am-8pm, every hr.; NIS45, students NIS40.50).

MAMSHIT ממשית

The grace of Mamshit's sunbleached sandstone steps belies the effort and ingenuity required by the Nabateans to raise a city in the simmering desert heat. Located just outside modern-day Dimona, Mamshit attests to the Nabateans' ability to prosper in an unforgiving environment—archaeologists have even discovered regal villas with courts and balconies. The Nabateans settled for nothing but the best, using only the most finely-dressed stone to build elaborate archways and columns. Even the view is majestic—the city is perched above **Ha-Makhtesh Ha-Gadol** ("The Big Crater"). Romans and later Byzantines inhabited the city. When Muslims conquered the area in 636 CE, the city was abandoned (crater open 8am-5pm; admission NIS7, youth NIS4; maps NIS10). A restaurant atop the ruins with breathtaking views in all directions offers a three-course Nabatean meal for NIS88.

Buses running between Be'er Sheva and the Dead Sea will stop 1km outside Mamshit, along the main highway. By car, the drive through **Ha-Makhtesh Ha-Gadol** is smashingly beautiful. Head south on the road just east of Mamshit (Rte. 206). After driving roughly 15km, hang a right onto Rte. 225 heading toward Yeroḥam. To view Mamshit from a camel's back with a Bedouin guide, contact the Mamshit Camel Ranch (tel. 665 10 54 or 40 12) to reserve a ride (1hr. NIS30, 2hr. NIS 40). Bedouin tea, coffee, and overnight stays are also available.

■ Sdeh Boker שדה בוקר

To make the Negev prosper "as a blessing to the state of Israel": the motto on the gateway of the *Midreshet* (Institute) of Sdeh Boker was David Ben-Gurion's dream and is this town's reality. Settled amidst endless desert, Sdeh Boker is named for the mountain behind it. Arabs call this mountain "Jabal Baqara" (Mt. Cow), which eventually changed to the Hebrew "Har Boker" (Cowboy Mt.). The **kibbutz,** established in 1952, produces olives, kiwis, and other fruit, as well as wheat, corn, and livestock, (though few cows). The institute researches methods to make the desert productive.

David Ben-Gurion, Israel's first prime minister, considered settlement in the Negev a top priority. When experts advised that developing the Negev was a waste of time and money, Ben-Gurion insisted on searching for unconventional methods of "making the desert bloom," asking, "If the Nabateans could do it, why can't we?" He was so moved by the young pioneers building fledgling Sdeh Boker on a 1953 visit that he decided, at the age of 67, to resign from office and settle here. Now the area is steeped in Ben-Gurion tributes, sights, and memorabilia. Those less enamored by B.G. will find Sdeh Boker a base for desert exploration in the nearby **Ein Avdat Natural Reserve.** There are a tremendous number of hikes in this area traversing jagged desert cliffs, natural springs, canyons, and monk caves.

PRACTICAL INFORMATION

The only public transportation to or from Sdeh Boker is Egged **bus #60,** running between Be'er Sheva and Mitzpeh Ramon (every 1-1½hr. until 9-10pm; NIS17, students NIS14.30). The bus makes three stops: at the gate of Kibbutz Sdeh Boker, at Ben-Gurion's Hut, and at the Ben-Gurion Institute (*Midreshet* Sdeh Boker). The stops are several kilometers from each other. To reach the center of the settlement, stop at the institute gate. Turn left at the end of the main entry road. The first right takes you to a **post office** (open Sun.-Mon., Wed.-Thurs. 8:30am-noon, 1-2pm; Tues. 8:30am-noon; Fri. 8:30-10:30am). The **Ein Avdat Nature Reserve** and Ben Gurion's grave are best reached from the Institute stop. Sdeh Boker's **telephone code** is 07.

To find the **SPNI Field School** (tel. 653 28 28 or 20 16; fax 656 27 31), make a right at the end of the main entry road and then a left at the large parking lot. The incredibly knowledgeable and helpful staff answers questions about hiking routes and desert flora and fauna and offers free maps of nearby trails. You can leave your bags here during day hikes (open Sun.-Thurs. 8am-5:30pm, Fri. 8am-1pm and 5-7pm).

ACCOMMODATIONS AND FOOD

The **SPNI Hostel** (tel. 653 28 28 or 20 16; fax 656 27 31), on the canyon's edge, has spotless, modern rooms with air-conditioning, private baths, and incredible views of the Zin Canyon. The six-bed dorm rooms, Sdeh Boker's only budget lodgings, are reserved for students (NIS33 per person with free use of common kitchen). Call ahead—this is a popular rest spot for Israeli regiments and the dorms may be crowded. Camping is permitted for free at designated locations within the Zin Valley; contact the **SPNI Field School** (same number as the hostel) for information about facilities and transportation. The field school also runs the **Hamburg Guest House** next door; rooms are clean, spacious, and bank-breaking (singles NIS185; doubles NIS249; weekends, singles NIS205; doubles NIS265). Both accommodations include discount use of the community swimming pool.

Food pickings are slim. The **Sdeh Boker Inn** (tel. 656 03 79), next door to Ben-Gurion's Hut, serves cafeteria-style meals (NIS15-25; open daily 8am-3pm). The **supermarket** near the post office offers standard loaves of bread (NIS4) and fresh fruit, as well as a whole aisle of instant soups and frozen pizzas (NIS16; open Sun.-Thurs. 8am-7pm, Fri. 8am-2pm; Visa). The **cafeteria** on the other side of the post office serves hamburgers, falafel, and milkshakes (NIS10-20), as well as fabulous cheese toast (open Sun.-Fri. 8am-12pm; Visa).

Tie Me Up, Tie Me Down (Just Don't Steal Me)

Many trees in the Negev and Sinai have cloth sacks tied to the branches. As the nomadic Bedouin wander around the desert, they often tie their non-essential belongings to trees rather than schlep them around in the heat. Sometimes they'll even leave valuables tied high in the branches, but theft is extremely rare. It's an unspoken rule of desert life never to touch a tree-bound bundle.

SIGHTS AND HIKES

Although many tourists are attracted to Sdeh Boker because of its Ben-Gurion memorials, B.G. himself was attracted to the kibbutz because of its majestic setting. The best way to appreciate this setting is to try some of the blow-your-mind hikes in the area. The **Ein Avdat Nature Reserve** (tel. 655 56 84), in the Zin Canyon, showcases the Negev at its most spectacular. Although the reserve has two entrances, the upper one, with no trailheads, is primarily a lookout point. You can get brochures and rough maps at either gate, but the SPNI office has the best detailed maps. Contacting SPNI is generally a good idea before heading out. Call ahead to ensure that a guide will be around. To get to the lower entrance, go to the Ben-Gurion Institute gate (*Midreshet* Ben-Gurion) and follow the road to your right (45-50min.). From the lower entrance, you can hike to **Ein Avdat** (the lower pools) in 15 minutes. To do the full hike to the upper gate, plan for 45-60 minutes. If you don't have a car waiting for you at the end of the hike, you'll either need to make a big U-turn (turn around before climbing the ladders since it's not permitted to descend them) or extend your hike a few hours by walking along the rim of the canyon once you reach the top. Among the highlights of the various trails are a **waterfall,** fresh water **pools, hermit caves,** and the remains of a **Byzantine fortress.** Feel free to wander off the trail and explore oasis plant and animal life (reserve open daily May-Sept. 8am-4pm, Oct.-April 8am-3pm; NIS10, students NIS7.50).

There are other gorgeous, secluded hikes in the area that don't require an entrance fee, but good maps and plenty of water are necessities, as these off-the-beaten-track adventures are much less trafficked. The **Havarim/Karakash Wadi** is a magnificent three-hour hike which passes an inviting pond and waterfall. The trailhead is off the main road between Be'er Sheva and Eilat about 1km south of *Midreshet* Ben Gurion. An orange sign says "Havarim Water Cistern." Follow the blue trail signs, which will take you down to Ein Avdat. At night, when there's a full moon, this hike is spectacular. Other fun hikes lead to **Ein Zik** (5-6hr.), where there's great swimming at an oasis surrounded by palm trees, and **Ein Akev** (3-4hr., camping permitted). Maps for all area hikes are free at the SPNI office. With advance notification, guides for groups (five and above) may be hired for a day (NIS300 for full day walking tour).

Back at the Ben-Gurion Institute, a walk along the canyon rim leads to the beautifully-landscaped **Ben-Gurion Tombs** overlooking the big chief's beloved Negev. In 1992, former Soviet premier Mikhail Gorbachev lay a wreath at Ben-Gurion's grave and praised the success of his style of socialism. Behind the tombs, there is a **sound and light show** about Ben-Gurion's life (tel. 653 27 17). The show is only offered to large tour groups, but individuals are sometimes allowed to crash; call ahead.

The **Ben-Gurion Institute** itself is worth a visit. Scientists and university students work year-round at the busy institute; their findings on desert irrigation and development are applied not only to the Negev, but to Africa and much of the world. The nearby **Research Center for Solar Energy** is a pioneer in the field. Those black panels and metal contraptions you see on every Israeli rooftop are solar-powered water heaters, required for households by Israeli law. The center gives tours by appointment (tel. 655 50 57; admission NIS5; open daily 9am-5pm). The institute's **Desert Sculpture Museum** displays art created from natural desert materials.

Two and a half kilometers down the road and one bus stop in the direction of Be'er Sheva, you can see **Ben-Gurion's Hut** (tel. 656 03 20 or 655 84 44), only slightly larger than the residences of his kibbutz neighbors, furnished as he left it. Family pictures, lists of medications, and copied-down Biblical passages the secular leader found meaningful give the visitor an insight into the man behind the legend (open Sun.-Thurs. 8:30am-3:30pm, Fri. 8:30am-2pm, Sat. and holidays 9am-2:30pm; free).

■ Near Sdeh Boker

AVDAT עבדת

The magnificently preserved ruins of a 4th-century BCE **Nabatean city** are perched upon a hill 11km south of Sdeh Boker. Avdat once thrived as a pit stop for caravans along the spice route from the Far East (via Petra) to Gaza that continued on to Europe. Nabateans used their strategic perch at Avdat to spy on caravans as far away as present-day Mitzpeh Ramon or Sdeh Boker. The Romans captured the city in 106 CE and it continued to flourish, reaching its economic peak during the Byzantine period. Most of the visible ruins date from this time. Seventh-century Islamic marauders renovated the Roman baths but not much else. The most important Nabatean remains are a handsome esplanade on top of the hill, a winding staircase that led to a Nabatean temple, and a potter's workshop, all dating from the first century CE. When the Nabateans converted to Christianity around 300 CE, the temple became a church. The best of the 6th-century Byzantine remains include a 20 ft.-high wall, a street, a monastery, two churches, and a baptistry. In this century, the site was resurrected on celluloid in the movie version of *Jesus Christ Superstar*.

Drinking water and bathrooms are across from the ticket booth. **Bus** #60 (Sun.-Thurs. until 9-10pm, every 1-1½ hr.; Fri. every 2hr.; 35min.) runs from Be'er Sheva to Sdeh Boker, stopping in Avdat. Make it clear to the driver that you want to go to the archaeological site and not Ein Avdat (the oasis). Near the bus stop is a **gas station** and **restaurant** with **cheap food** (falafel or *shawerma* NIS8, juice NIS4). Bring water for the 20-minute uphill hike to the ruins (tel. 655 09 54 or 658 63 91); open daily 8am-5pm; NIS16, students NIS12). The small grove just below the ruins is irrigated using ancient Nabatean water techniques and is staffed by rotating volunteers. An Avdat/Ein Avdat combination ticket is also available for NIS19.

▓ Mitzpeh Ramon מצפה רמון

Mitzpeh Ramon sits on the rim of **Makhtesh Ramon** (Ramon Crater), the most gargantuan and impressive of the Negev's four craters. Weighing in at 400m deep, 9km wide, and 40km long, Ramon is the largest natural crater in the world. In the 1920s and 30s, Makhtesh Ramon was not on any British map. The young Israeli government came upon the crater while exploring the potential of the Negev. Until a direct route to Eilat was built from the Dead Sea in the 1970s, what is now known as "Mitzpeh Ramon" (Ramon Observation Point) was the central stop-off for those heading south. Today, the crater is a national park, with well-marked trails leading through mazes of stunning geological phenomena and breathtaking cliff views.

The fascinating rock formations in the crater are millions of years old, the vegetation spans four distinct climatic zones, and evidence of human life in the area predates written history. Uphill treks wind towards phenomenal views of the desert expanse, passing bizarre insects and wildlife along the way. Around each curve of the sandy paths lie unexpected shapes and colors not normally associated with nature. Remember that the crater sinks in the middle of a desert. Bring one liter of **water** per person per hour. Afterwards, an evening on the rim comes with a free, all-natural, spectacular light show.

Practical Information From Mitzpeh Ramon, **bus** #60 runs to Be'er Sheva (every 1-1½hr., 6am-9:30pm, NIS21, students NIS17.90). Bus #391 runs to Tel Aviv (one per week, Sun. 6:30am, NIS35). Bus #392 comes through on its way from Be'er Sheva to Eilat and back; it will pick you up if there are empty seats (8:20am, 10am, noon, 4:45pm, 7:30pm; NIS33, students NIS28). Drivers are instructed to take 10-minute breaks if they feel drowsy on long desert treks, so don't panic if your bus is 10 to 40 minutes late. The very last bus stop (on Eilat St.) is closest to the town. Take a right from the bus stop and a left on Ben Gurion St. (look for the strange fountain) to get to the town's commercial center, near a **Bank Ha-Poalim** branch (tel. 658 80 86;

open Sun., Tues., and Thurs. 8:30am-noon and 4-6pm, Mon. 8:30am-12:30pm, Fri. 8:30am-noon). In an adjoining building is a **post office** with **Western Union, fax** and **telegram** services, **EMS,** and **Poste Restante** (tel. 658 84 16; open Sun.-Tues. and Thurs. 8am-12:30pm and 4-6:30pm, Wed. 8am-1pm, Fri. 8am-12:30pm). Further down Ben Gurion on the left is the **municipal pool** with a sauna and water slide (open June-Sept., Sun.-Fri. 10am-6pm, Sat. 9am-6pm; NIS32; children NIS12).

From the bus stop, take a left up Eilat Street and follow the signs to the youth hostel, visitors center, Bio-Ramon (see **Food and Entertainment,** below), and breathtaking promenade. The **Mitzpeh Pharmacy** (get the to youth hostel and take a right) is small but adequate (open Sun.-Thurs. 8am-1pm, and 3-6:30pm, Fri. 8am-1pm). Mitzpeh's **telephone code** is 07.

Accommodations On the canyon's rim, across from the visitor's center, you'll find the **Mitzpeh Ramon Youth Hostel (HI)** (tel. 658 84 43; fax 658 80 74). The spacious rooms lack air-conditioning, but you don't really need it. Rooms are crisp and clean, with private baths. There's a huge lounge, a TV-room, and a snack bar. (Reception open 7am-11pm. No lockout or curfew. Check-out 9:30am. Dorm beds (6 per room) NIS60; singles NIS129; doubles NIS182. Each additional person NIS60. Nonmembers add NIS4. Breakfast included. Visa, MC.) The **SPNI Field School** (tel. 658 86 15) is a bit isolated but charges less than the hostel and has a trail leading down into the crater. Take bus #60 to Camel Observation Point and walk 10 minutes to the right along the cliffside trail until you see the tall antennas. All rooms have air-conditioning and private baths, and guests may use the full kitchen. (Check-in Sun.-Thurs. 8am-6pm, Fri. 8-12pm, Sat. arrange in advance. Check-out 8am. Dorm beds (6 per room) NIS57 for students only; singles NIS219; doubles NIS245; each additional adult NIS85. Call ahead. Breakfast included. Dinner NIS49; lunch NIS43. Kiosk open 8-10am and 5-10pm for snacks and drinks. Visa, MC.)

Staking out a campsite in the middle of the crater is forbidden. Though campers have been known to do it, they run the risk of being awakened by an angry ranger or an even angrier **Asiatic wild ass.** The only **campground** within the *makhtesh* is the **Be'erot Camping Site,** 16km from Mitzpeh. Head down the main road until you see two orange signs pointing toward the campsite—it's a one-hour walk from the road. Shade, toilets (no showers), and picnic tables are free, and a night on a mattress in a Bedouin tent costs NIS14.50. The kiosk has cold drinks, ice cream (NIS3-4), and firewood. The other official campground is along the main road in Mitzpeh, by the gas station north of the visitors center. Follow the path towards the crater and you'll come upon a series of Bedouin-inspired, traveler-adapted tents run by Desert Shade. The place has a relaxed atmosphere conducive to music and yoga interludes. (Beds with sheets in tiny cabins NIS50. Toilets and showers on site. Breakfast included; vegetarian and Bedouin meals NIS30-40.)

For a new age desert experience there's **Succah in the Desert** (tel. 658 62 80), 7km outside town (accessible by foot or car only). The premises, a haven for artists and hard-core meditators, consist of seven *sukkot,* beautiful structures made of stones and dried palm leaves. The interiors, rich with tapestries and rugs, incorporate desert features like rock platforms for sleeping or sitting. (*Sukkot* NIS75-100 per night. Weekend rates for couples, including breakfast and dinner, NIS300 and up. Vegetarian dinners NIS30.)

Food and Entertainment The talented Esther cooks up a storm at **Hamakhtesh Restaurant,** 2 Naḥal Tzihor St. (tel. 658 84 90), one block down from the Youth Hostel. *Kebab, shishlik,* steak, and *schnitzel* (regular and veggie) go for NIS34 and come with pita, six salads, and rice or fries (open Sun.-Thurs. 9am-10pm, Sat. sundown-11pm; kosher). **Ha-Tzukit Restaurant,** near the visitor's center, has air-conditioning, a stunning view, and often a family of ibex lazing outside (sandwiches NIS7, vegetarian meals NIS22, hot meat lunch NIS28; open Sun.-Fri. 9am-5pm). **Hanna's Restaurant** (tel. 658 81 58) is connected to the Eilat St. gas station, between the commercial and visitor's centers. Sandwiches (NIS7-9) and meals (NIS25-30) are better than the unsavory location might suggest (open Sun.-Thurs. 5:30am-8pm, Fri. 5:30am-4pm; kosher). Before hiking, stock up on granola and tuna at the **Shekem supermarket** next to the post office (open Sun.-Thurs. 8am-1pm and 4-7pm, Fri. 8am-2pm).

You may not find anything to do at night in Mitzpeh Ramon, but you will find a lot of people searching at **Pub Ha-Ḥaveet**, Mitzpeh Ramon's happening night spot, in the commercial center next door to Bank Ha-Poalim. Dim lights, American rock, Iron Maiden posters, and great salads (NIS22; try the Mitzpai) attract soldiers, backpackers, and local youth (18 or older; beer NIS8; open daily noon-late).

There are two **promenades** on the rim of the crater, one behind the campgrounds near the gas station and the other behind the youth hostel. **Desert Sculpture gardens** in both areas display esoteric statuary inspired by the terrain. **Desert Archery** (tel. 658 72 74), a golf-based bow and arrow game (*sans* grass), sprawls on a 50-acre course 500m west of the city center. Individuals are welcome, but it's more fun in pairs or groups (equipment, explanation, and limitless playing time NIS22; call ahead). **Bio-Ramon** (tel. 658 87 55), just downhill from the visitors center, houses desert insects, scorpions, spiders, snakes, and lovable rodents (open Sun.-Thurs. 8am-3pm, Fri. 8am-1pm., and Sat. 9am-4pm; NIS6, children NIS5).

Hikes The *makhtesh* (erosion crater) is a geological phenomenon unique to Israel, with colorful rock formations and unusual wildlife. Trailheads for the most interesting hikes are outside of town, but there are two beautiful trails originating from Mitzpeh. Although the trails are well marked, a pre-hike stop at the visitors center for maps and terrain info is a prudent idea. You may also want to leave your planned route and expected length of trip with the field school, youth hostel, or visitor's center. While hiking, keep a fix on the Eilat road; it's the place to go if you get caught in the dark. To get to far-flung trailheads, take bus #392 to Eilat, which follows the main highway through the crater. Hitchers say that thumbing it is easy. Southbound drivers take off from the visitors center parking lot.

There are two hiking resources in Mitzpeh Ramon: the first is the **Park Ramon Visitor's Center** (tel. 658 86 91; fax 658 86 20), housed in the round building with the flat top. Nature Reserve Authority staffers will help plan hikes and provide a fabulous English map of the Negev and the crater. The audio-visual museum and the rooftop observatory will add to your appreciation of the hikes (open Sun.-Thurs. 9am-5pm, Fri. 9am-4pm, Sat. 9am-5pm; NIS16, children NIS10). The gift shop across the plaza sells detailed topographical maps (NIS15), and other books and pamphlets about the crater and the Negev. The second resource is the **SPNI Field School** (tel. 658 61 01, 86 15, or 86 16), near the edge of the crater 500m southwest of Camel Observation Point (for directions see **Accommodations,** above). They are equipped with maps and literature about hiking in the region, and occasionally offer organized tours; call ahead to find out if one will be happening when you're in town. If you're planning an unguided expedition, leave your route description and estimated trip duration at the field school before you leave—they have an on-site rescue team and direct communication with army units in the area (open Sun.-Thurs. 8am-6pm, Fri. 8am-noon).

Desert Shade (tel. 658 62 29 or (03) 575 68 85; fax 658 62 08) leads excellent tours by jeep, foot, bike, and camel (4hr. sunset tour NIS120; 2hr. morning jeep tour NIS90; 1hr. camel ride NIS30; 2-day camel ride/hike along the Nabatean Spice Route US$147). To get to Desert Shade, take bus #60 or 392 towards Be'er Sheva. It's a 15-minute walk past the gas station on the main road just outside town.

Short Hikes from Mitzpeh

An excellent three-hour hike begins from the end of the promenade, near the mini amphitheater. Green trail markers lead to **Ha-Minsarah** (the Carpentry), where piles of prism-like rock, configured and baked by volcanic heat, resemble carpenter's supplies. A turn-off point marked in red will lead you on a five-hour day-hike through the crater. The fossil-friendly **Ammonite Wall** lies along this trail. Another short hike follows the blue trail markers from the SPNI school, and eventually joins the green trail loop (3-5hr.). It's a short jaunt up the green trail to the rim, or you can extend your hike and complete the green loop's tour of the Carpentry.

Har Ardon/Ein Saharonim Hike

This hike is long (7hr. from the campsite and back); you may want to split it into two day-trips, especially during the summer. From the campsite and back, each of the two parts takes about four to five hours.

To climb **Har Ardon** (Mt. Ardon), take a left out of the Be'erot campsite and follow the signs. A steep climb up the mountain (blue trail) ends with an incredible view and a tricky descent (black trail). Along the trail, you'll pass through the crimson sand and hills of the **Red Valley.** After passing the black hill of **Givat Harut,** either take a right back to the campsite, or turn left and follow the black markings into Wadi Ardon.

Along the colorful borders of **Wadi Ardon** jut several **dikes,** or intrusions of volcanic material. You'll first pass a pair of chunky intrusions, one big and one small, known as the father and son dikes. To continue on, take the right (red) path at the next fork. Soon you'll arrive at a three-way crossroad. The blue path points towards **Parsat Nekarot** (the Nekarot Horseshoe) which includes **Sha'ar Ramon** (the Ramon Gate), where water exits the crater. The rocky river bed is flanked by soaring cliffs and cave-like enclaves which make excellent shady stops.

From Parsat Nekarot, follow the blue markings to **Ein Saharonim.** The vegetation lasts all year, but the water evanesces to mere puddles during the summer. The remains of a Nabatean *caravanserai* stand at the end of the spring on the right. To return to the campsite or main road, take a left here, in the direction of Naḥal Gevanim and the Oil Road, and ascend the hill. Upon reaching the Oil Road, a left turn and a right turn soon thereafter will take you back to the main road. A right turn at the Oil Road will lead you back to the campsite.

Har Saharonim

Along the southern edge of the crater rises Har Saharonim (literally, Mountain of the Crescent-Shaped Ornaments). From the summit, you can see the Govai Mountains and the desert expanse to the southeast and the crater to the northwest. Start the climb from the western side, closest to the main road. From the campsite, walk south on the Oil Road on the black trail. Shortly after the Naḥal Gevanim turn-off, you'll see a steep incline. When you reach the top, turn left at the green markers. The descent from Har Saharonim leads you by Ein Saharonim, from where you can follow the blue path through Parsat Nekarot or head back to the road, as in the previous route.

■ Eilat אילת

Eilat has two goals—to get you tan and to make you poor. The city is soaked with the sweat of rowdy Israelis, international backpackers, and European tourists; the air is abuzz with jet skis and cell phones. Some swear by Eilat's sun, coral, and nightlife, while others see the city as a huge tourist trap attached to a nice beach. In between the cocktails and Coppertone, stick your head underwater and you may notice some of the most spectacular underwater life the world's seas have to offer.

The Israelites lost the port of Eloth at what is now Eilat in the 8th century BCE. The Egyptian Ptolemies, the Nabateans, the Romans, the Crusaders, Salah ad-Din, more Crusaders, the Mamluks, the Ottomans, the British, and finally the Israelis have been through here—but nobody comes for history. The oldest thing you'll see in Eilat is an unbuttoned polyester shirt in one of the discos.

The busiest times of the year are Passover (April 11-17 in 1998) and *Sukkot* (Oct. 5-11 in 1998), when nearly 100,000 Israelis descend upon the city. Don't fool yourself into thinking that this is a good time to visit. True, there are more parties and crowded pubs, but hostels and restaurants charge double their normal rates, petty theft runs rampant, and every inch of beach crawls with human flesh.

Proprietors at resorts, hostels, cafes, discos, and bars are often looking to employ newcomers. Jobs with hotels and hostels often include lodging, and should offer a pittance as well. Unfortunately, most work is under the table (illegal), with long hours and miserable wages (usually about US$400 per month). In the marina on the gate leading to the boats there are lists of tourist boats looking for workers. The pay is low but you get free room, board, and social life.

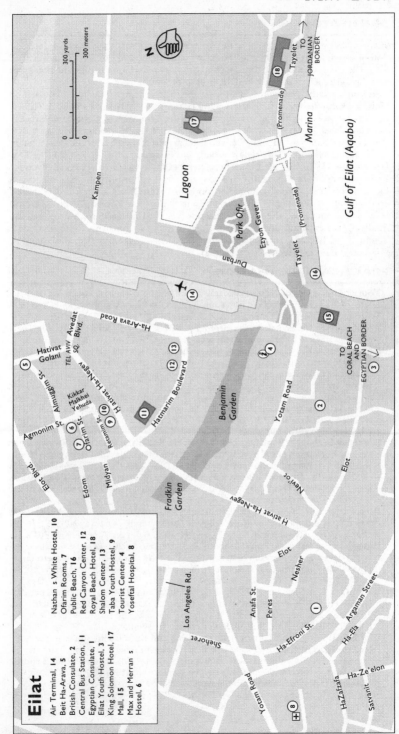

ISRAEL

Gulf of Eilat (Aqaba)

Eilat

Air Terminal, 14
Beit Ha-Arava, 5
British Consulate, 2
Central Bus Station, 11
Egyptian Consulate, 1
Eilat Youth Hostel, 3
King Solomon Hotel, 17
Mall, 15
Max and Merran s
Hostel, 6

Nathan s White Hostel, 10
Ofarim Rooms, 7
Public Beach, 16
Red Canyon Center, 12
Royal Beach Hotel, 18
Shalom Center, 13
Taba Youth Hostel, 9
Tourist Center, 4
Yoseftal Hospital, 8

ORIENTATON

Eilat is a 5km strip of coastline on the Negev's sandy bottom, the precarious intersection of Israel, Jordan, Egypt, and Saudi Arabia; at night you can see the lights of all four. The city is divided into three sections: the town itself on the hills, the hotel area and Lagoon Beach to the east, and the port to the south.

As you leave the central bus station via the main entrance, you'll find yourself on **Hatmarim Boulevard,** which crosses the center of the city from southeast (downhill) to northwest (uphill). Across the street is the **Commercial Center,** with restaurants and cafes. If you stay on the bus station side of Ha-Tmarim and head downhill, you'll immediately pass the **Red Canyon Center,** resembling a futuristic Bedouin tent and housing the **post office, supermarket,** and **cinema.** Farther downhill is the **Shalom Center.** Ha-Tmarim Blvd. ends here, perpendicular to **Ha-Arava Road.** If you follow Ha-Arava Rd. to the right, you'll pass the main entrance to the Eilat **airport.** A block later, to the right of the intersection with **Yotam Road,** a three-level conglomeration of cheap restaurants and shops calls itself the **New Tourist Center.** Ha-Arava leads to Dolphin Reef, the Coral Beach reserve, the Underwater Observatory, and finally Taba Beach and the **Egyptian Border.** Bus #15 runs this route (every 15-20min., NIS2.10-3.20). Turning left at the intersection of Ha-Arava Rd. and Yotam St. will lead you to the **beaches** at the lagoon.

PRACTICAL INFORMATION

Tourist Office: tel. 637 21 11; fax 632 58 67, at the corner of Yotam Rd. and Ha-Arava Rd. Friendly, excellent info source. Maps, brochures, and coupons. Will help find accommodations. Open Oct.-March Sun.-Thurs. 8am-6pm, Fri. 8am-2pm; April-Sept. Sun.-Thurs. 8am-8pm, Fri. 8am-2pm. **SPNI:** (tel. 637 20 21), opposite Coral Beach. Maps and information about local hiking. Open Sun.-Fri. 8am-8pm.

Consulates: U.K. (tel. 637 23 44), above the New Tourist Center (next to the Adi Hotel). **Egypt,** 68 Ha-Efroni St. (tel. 637 68 82). From the bus station, turn right on Hatmarim Blvd. Take your first left onto Hativat Ha-Negev. Continue 900m until Sderot Argaman St., where you take a right. Take the first right after that and look for the flag. Open Sun.-Thurs. 9am-noon. Fill out and submit your visa application in the morning, pick it up the same day at 1pm. Visas must be paid for in NIS (U.S. NIS50; South Africans free; all others NIS70); bring a passport photo. Sinai-only visas available at the border.

Currency Exchange: Bank Leumi and **Bank Ha-Poalim,** across from the central bus station. Both open Sun.-Fri. 8:30am-noon. Bank Ha-Poalim also open Sun., Tues., and Thurs. 4:30-6pm; Bank Leumi open Sun., Tues., and Thurs. 5-6:30pm. Holidays use Fri. hours. The **post office** exchanges traveler's checks with no commission. There are 24hr. **ATMs** (Visa, MC, Plus, Cirrus) outside Bank Ha-Poalim, next to the post office, and in the marina.

Airport: tel. 636 38 38, corner of Hatmarim Blvd. and Ha-Arava Rd. **Arkia Airlines** (tel. 637 31 42) flies to and from **Tel Aviv** (every 30min., one-way NIS257), **Jerusalem** (2-3 per day; one-way NIS257), and **Haifa** (2-6 per day; one-way NIS301).

Buses: Central bus station on Hatmarim Blvd. (tel. 636 51 20). Reserve tickets at station 2 days ahead (4 days in high season). Bus #444 takes you to **Jerusalem** (Sun.-Thurs. 7am-5pm, 4 per day; Fri. 7am-1pm, 3 per day; Sat. 4pm, 4½hr.; NIS52); #394 to **Tel Aviv** (Sun.-Thurs. 4am-1am, 10-11 per day; Fri. 5am-2pm, 7 per day; Sat. 1pm-1am, 7 per day; 5hr.; NIS56); #991 to **Haifa** (Sun. 8:30am-11:30pm, 3 per day; Mon.-Wed. 2:30 and 11:30pm; Thurs. 8:30am, 2:30, and 11:30pm; Fri. 8:30am; Sat. 2:30 and 11:30pm; 6hr.; NIS59). If full, you can take the bus to Be'er Sheva and transfer. ISIC discounts. Bus schedules change frequently.

City Buses: Bus #15 runs down Hatmarim Blvd. and Ha-Arava Rd., through the hotel area, and past the HI hostel and Coral Beach to **Egypt** (every 20-30min., Sun.-Thurs. 7am-9pm, Fri. 7am-4:30pm, Sat. 9am-9pm; NIS2.10-3.50). Buses #1 and 2 shuttle between the town and hotel area (every 30min. Sun.-Thurs. 6:15am-8:45pm, Fri. 6:40am-4:15pm, Sat. every 2hr. 10am-6pm, NIS3).

Taxis: Arava (tel. 637 41 41), **King Solomon** (tel. 633 24 24), and **Ha-Melekh Shlomo** (tel. 633 24 24). City rides NIS5, to observatory NIS20, to border NIS25-30. Taxi sharing is common. In winter *sherut* run along the #1, 2, and 15 bus routes.

Car Rental: Hertz (tel. 637 66 82), in Red Canyon Center; **Budget** (tel. 637 41 24), in Shalom Center, and **Avis** (tel. 637 31 64), next to the tourist office. Unlimited mileage US$35-40 per day. Limited use starts at US$10 plus US$0.25 per km. Insurance starts at US$12 per day. US$12 extra per day in high season. Minimum age at Hertz is 21. You can't take rentals into Egypt.

Bike Rental: Eilat Sports (tel. 631 57 20), in the Marina. Rental only in winter. US$15 per day. Open daily 9:30am-7pm. **Red Sea Sports** (tel. 633 0866) in the marina. US$20 per day.

Scooter Rental: Doobie Scooter (tel. 633 65 57), in the Dalia Hotel. Four hours NIS60-75, 1 day NIS100-125.

Camping Equipment: The National Center for Hiking Equipment (tel. 634 11 12), on the bottom floor of the mall at the corner of Yotam and Ha'arava Rd. Good selection of pricey gear.

Laundromat: Kuiskal (tel. 637 48 38) at the Razin Center, on the corner of Hatmarim and Edom St. Open Sat.-Thurs. 9am-9pm, Fri. 9am-2pm. NIS36 for 6kg full service, NIS25 for self-service. Open Sun.-Fri. 7am-8pm. Hostel services are cheaper.

Pharmacy: Super-Pharm (tel. 632 69 40). Best selection in town. Open Sun.-Thurs. 9am-midnight, Fri. 9am-5pm, Sat. 11am-midnight. **Eilat Pharmacy,** 25 Eilat St. (tel. 637 50 02). Open Sun.-Thurs. 8:15am-1:15pm and 4:15-8:50pm, Fri. 8:15am-2pm. **Michlin Pharmacy** (tel. 37 24 34) Rechter Center, next to Bank Leumi. Open Sun.-Thurs. 8am-9pm, Fri. 8am-3pm.

Hospital: Yoseftal Hospital (tel. 635 80 11), on Yotam Rd.

Emergency: First Aid: Ha-Tmarim Blvd. (tel. 101 for emergencies, otherwise 637 23 33). **Magen David Adom** first aid stations are located on some beaches. **Police:** Avdat Blvd. (tel. 100 for emergencies, 633 24 44 to chat), at the eastern end of Ḥativat Ha-Negev. "Lost and found" for packs stolen from the beach. **Fire:** tel. 102.

Post Office: (tel. 637 23 02), in the Red Canyon Center. **Traveler's check cashing, Western Union, Poste Restante.** Open Sun.-Tues., Thurs. 8am-12:30pm and 4-6:30pm, Wed. 8am-1pm, Fri. and holidays 8am-3pm.

Telephones: Starcom Gold (tel. 632 65 27; fax 632 64 94), at the New Tourist Center, main floor. Cheaper than the post office or public phones. Offers phone, fax (NIS13), and voicemail. Open Mon.-Sat. 11:30am-midnight, Sun. 7:30pm-midnight. **Telephone Code:** 07.

ACCOMMODATIONS

Finding a cheap room in Eilat is easy. Finding a safe, comfortable, and convenient cheap room is another story. As soon as you arrive at the bus station you'll be harassed by a gaggle of apartment hawkers. Yell "*Lo,*" give them the look of death, and walk away. Don't get into a cab with a stranger or commit to a room before you see it. Most hostels are located less than three blocks from the bus station—walk up the hill on Ha-Tmarim and take a right on Retaim. The atmosphere of a smaller hostel can add tremendously to your enjoyment of Eilat. Some of the bigger hostels are unfriendly and have been known to put out backpackers in favor of large groups or have you switch rooms in the middle of the night. The tourist office can assist if hostels are full. Vague pricing is easily deciphered; the low prices apply during winter, the high ones in summer. Prices change—always bargain.

Max and Merran's Hostel, 111/1 Agmonim St. (tel. 637 13 33 or 632 60 64). Welshwoman Pamela, cats Wookie Monster and Squeak, and dogs Lady and Buffalo Bill are gracious and welcoming hosts. The hostel has the best atmosphere in town. Comfy common area with lots of videos. No curfew, visitors, or alcohol. Check-out 10am. Bunk beds NIS20-25 year-round, or put up your own tent in the yard for NIS18. Free and safe luggage storage.

Ofarim Rooms, 116/2 Ofarim St. (tel. 376 289). Spotless dorms (5-6 beds) with attached baths. Fun and friendly atmosphere, with an outdoor TV lounge and pay phone for guests. Kitchen facilities until midnight. No lockout or curfew. Dorm beds NIS30-40; doubles NIS80-100. Safe NIS5 per day. 6kg laundry NIS15.

Villa Kibel (tel./fax 637 69 11, cell phone (050) 345 366; email bcs@isracom.co.il). Great upscale choice. Russell and Michelle offer fully furnished apartment-style rooms with TV, mini-fridge, fresh linen, and cooking facilities. All within 1km of the beach; some have an ocean view. 2 rooms are wheelchair accessible. Can accommodate large groups. Prices negotiable, especially for longer stays. Russell will pick you up from the bus station. Prices US$50-98 per night.

Eilat Youth Hostel (HI) (tel. 637 23 58 or 00 88; fax 637 58 35), on Ha-Arava Rd., 1 block from the New Tourist Center. Over 400 beds, a hotel-like lounge, balconies, and a discotheque (open for groups). Sterile atmosphere and lots of vacationing teens. A/C dorms (7 beds per room) US$17-18; singles US$40.50; doubles US$39. Nonmembers add US$1.50. Breakfast included. Lockers US$1.50. Refrigerators US$7, TV rental US$7, laundry US$8 for 6kg. Extra meals US$8.

Corinne Hostel (tel. 637 14 72), on Retamin just off Ha-Tmarim. Large, clean, A/C dorm rooms with private bath. Billiards/game room. No curfew or lockout. Dorm beds NIS20 and up; 2-person cabins NIS80-100 and up.

Nathan's White House Hostel, 131/1 Retamim St. (tel. 637 65 72). Go all the way down to the corner for nearly presidential accommodations. A house with simple, clean, patriotic rooms. Friendly staff sells beer. Kitchen, TV, and video. Check-out 9am. No curfew. Dorm beds (4-8 per room) NIS25; doubles NIS100-180.

Beit Ha-Arava, 106 Almogim St. (tel. 637 10 52), at the corner of Ḥativat Golani. From the bus station, go right onto Ḥativat Ha-Negev, walk 2 blocks to the end, and turn left. Veranda, kitchen, jukebox-foosball diner, and a beautiful view. Clean rooms with A/C and 6 beds max. 24hr. guard. Mixture of young Israelis and backpackers. No curfew or lockout. Outdoor tent mattress NIS20-30; dorm beds NIS25-40; doubles with bath NIS80-160. Breakfast NIS7-10. Lockers NIS4. Laundry NIS15 per load.

Spring Hostel (tel. 637 46 60; fax 637 15 43), next door to Max and Merron's Hostel. The fanciest of the hostels, but without the camaraderie. Clean rooms with A/C. 6-bed dorms NIS25; doubles NIS120-160; quads NIS80-180. Breakfast included.

There are two **camping** options in Eilat: expensive and legal, or free and illegal. During July and August, hundreds of people happen not to see the "No Camping" signs on the public beach or in the park; year after year, many are victims of theft. Aside from burglars and sexual harassers, there are also **rats** at these camps, who love biting ears and other appendages.

Caroline Camping (tel. 637 19 11 or 11 15), at the municipal campground opposite Coral Beach. Take bus #15. The campground offers a snack bar and scorching sun in summer. Tiny, pod-like huts with A/C for NIS60 per person. Pitch your own tent for NIS33. Refrigerator NIS10. Breakfast included.

Mamshit Camping (tel. 637 44 11; fax 637 52 06), next to SPNI field school, across from Coral Beach Reserve. Take bus #15. Excellent snorkeling and skin-frying. Huge, well-kept grounds with friendly management. NIS14 with your own tent. Bungalow beds (8 per room) NIS24. 1- or 2-person bungalows NIS98.

FOOD

Many falafel stands, pizzerias, and sandwich vendors stand and vend on Ha-Tmarim St. near the bus station and by the hostels near Retamim St. Burger lovers rejoice: **McDonald's** is in the waterfront mall, and **Burger King** shares the tourist office building. A mixed bag of bars on **Almogim** serves cheap food.

Since many accommodations in Eilat provide cooking facilities, backpackers can eat inexpensively by purchasing food at the **supermarket** at Eilat St. and Ha-Tmarim Blvd. (look for the blue and white squares on the building; open Sun.-Thurs. 7:30am-10pm, Fri. 7:30am-2pm). Closer to the center of town is **SuperKolbo Supermarket** in the Rekhter Commercial Center (open Sat.-Thurs. 7am-midnight, Fri. 7am-9pm) and the **Shekem Supermarket** in the Red Canyon Center (open Sun.-Thurs. 8:30am-midnight, Fri. 8:30am-2:30pm). There are three yummy bakeries on Ha-Tmarim north of the bus station.

Hard Luck Cafe, 15 Almogin (tel. 637 27 88), next to the Peace Cafe. Beer and wonderfully greasy pub food, but no rock memorabilia. Carnivores can devour the mixed grill and chips, but veggies are out of luck. Kitchen open until midnight.

Hummus Assli. Walk up Hatmarim, cross Eilot; first restaurant on your left. The best hummus in town—4 varieties (NIS12-16) and chips. Dine in or take away. Open Sun.-Thurs. 10am-2am, Fri. closes early, Sat. 8:30pm-2am.

Cafe Festival (tel. 637 49 22), outside the Shalom Center. Pricier, but you get what you pay for. Coastal-water mist-sprayers keep you cool. Great variety of salads NIS15-20. Try the meat and potato cigars with hummus (NIS21). Open Sun.-Fri. 24hr., Sat. open at 5pm.

Jackness (tel. 632 56 47), in the Moore center. A little far from the center of town but convenient if you're taking a trip to the Egyptian consulate next door. Family-run place serving large, meaty home-cooked meals (NIS24). Open Sun.-Thurs. 10am-5pm, Fri. 10am-3pm.

Mandy's (tel. 637 22 38), in the Coral Reef next to Aqua Sport. The oldest and most say the best Chinese restaurant in town. Simple bamboo interior. Large selection of meat and vegetarian dishes. Entrees NIS20-32. Open Sun.-Fri. noon-3pm and 6:30pm-midnight, Sat. noon-midnight. Visa, MC, AmEx.

Fisherman House (tel. 637 98 30), across from Aqua Sport, Coral Beach. Belly-busting cafeteria-style restaurant serving all-you-can-eat buffet of fish and meat, salads, rice, and hummus for NIS29. Open daily noon-11pm.

Toast and Rock, 100m north of bus station on Hatmarim. Eat toasted baguettes with your choice of fillings (NIS11-13) and rock on. Very tasty and filling. Open Sun.-Thurs. 24hr., Fri. until 5pm.

SUNKEN SIGHTS

Eilat's brilliant underwater world is filled with marine creatures beyond your imagination, from blubberfish to emperorfish, frolicking in a psychedelic coral paradise. For information on snorkeling and diving see **Underwater Adventures,** p. 248. Snorkeling and diving are easiest and cheapest near **Coral Beach Nature Reserve** (tel. 637 68 29). Five water trails marked by buoys go through the reef, and a bridge into the water protects coral and human feet from each other. Take bus #15 from the central bus station toward the sea (beach open Sat.-Thurs. 9am-6pm, Fri. 9am-5pm; enter until 5pm; NIS15, children NIS8, seniors NIS12, 5-day pass NIS51; coin-op lockers NIS5). Coral beach is the most crowded Red Sea reef.

Aqua Sport, (tel. 633 44 04, P.O. Box 300, Eilat 88102), next to Coral Beach, rents equipment (mask US$3.50, fins US$3.50, snorkel US$2.50, all 3 US$8, sailboards US$18 per hr.) and conducts introductory dives (US$42). A five-day diving course costs US$275. They also run daily dive trips to Sinai for US$79 per day. **Classes** can be arranged in advance; call or write Aqua Sport. **Eilat Sports,** at the Bridge House in the Marina (tel. 634 09 20; fax 634 09 23), runs cruises to Egypt (Gaziret Faraun or Pharaoh's Island) for US$49. Trips leave at 10am and return at 4pm; passports must be given at least one day in advance (snorkeling equipment and open buffet included in price. 10% discount for *Let's Go* users. See **Pharaoh's Island,** p. 265).

Red Sea Sports Club (tel. 637 65 69), across the street from Aqua Sport, at the King Solomon Hotel, offers PADI open-water courses for US$275 and dives with dolphins for US$56. Their office on North Beach near the lagoon offers windsurfing (US$18 per hr.), water-skiing (US$27 per 15min.), and parasailing (US$35 for 10min.). They also arrange **horseback riding** lessons at Texas Ranch (tel. 637 66 63), across the street (1hr. US$25, 2hr. US$35, 4hr. US$50). Upstairs, the **Photo Shop** (tel. 637 31 45, ext. 272) rents underwater cameras (US$20-30 per day) and video cameras (US$110 per day). For those joining late in the paragraph, Coral Beach is the most trafficked reef territory in the Red Sea. Head to the Sinai for privacy.

The **Galaxy** (tel. 631 63 60) is one of the city's many glass-bottomed boats (1½hr., NIS50). The **Jules Verne Explorer** (tel. 637 77 02) may not venture 20,000 leagues down, but full glass walls make it a true underwater observatory (2hr. cruise to the Japanese Gardens US$18). Both can be found at the Marina.

See the fishies without getting wet at the **Coral World Underwater Observatory and Aquarium** (tel. 637 66 66). It features shark and turtle tanks and an underwater observation room. Though interesting, it is best for those who won't be snorkeling (NIS49, children NIS34; open Sat.-Thurs. 8:30am-5pm, Fri. and holiday eves 8:30am-3pm). Live a life of ease beneath the sea of green in the **Yellow Submarine** (tel. 637 66 66), which goes 60m below the surface. The dim light results in different breeds of fish and, some say, poor visibility (NIS204, children NIS116, for observatory and submarine). **Dolphin Reef** (tel. 637 59 35), beyond the port on the #15 bus, exploits the dolphin craze with dolphin shows (every 2hr., 10am-4pm), nature films, and dolphin-watching docks. For NIS168 (children NIS161) you can snorkel with fenced-in Flipper and friends (open daily 9am-5pm; NIS29, children NIS22).

Some say that the best Eilat wildlife is not in the clubs nor the sea, but in the air. Avid **birdwatchers** flock to the salt ponds north of the lagoon mid-February through May and mid-September through November, when over 30 species fly by on their way to or from Africa. The **International Birdwatching Center (IBC),** P.O. Box 774, Eilat 88106 (tel. 637 42 76), in the Commercial Center, runs walking tours (US$5) and jeep tours (US$50). There's a birdwatching festival in March. Call or write the IBC for more information (open roughly Sun.-Thurs. 9am-1pm and 5-7pm, Fri. 9am-1pm). Pretend you're a bird at the **Airodium** (tel. 633 16 76), behind the Riviera Hotel. An air-vent contraption suspends you for an expensive but fun 10 minutes (NIS120).

DRUNKEN NIGHTS

Eilat's nightlife offers a little bit of everything. You can swill beer with hard-core backpackers, dance with greased-up Israelis, or hobnob with affluent yuppies. Most bars open at lunchtime, though drinking often starts earlier. Nightclubs open at 10:30 or 11pm, get going around midnight, and don't close until 5 or 6am. The discos are expensive (NIS25-30) and centered in the lagoon area; shorts and sandals are a bad idea. The free and mellow **Promenade** along the water offers Israel's best people-watching. Street vendors sell cheap jewelry and five-minute portraits, and Israeli studs try in vain to pick up female tourists. People start arriving at about 9:30pm and stay until it's time to go to a pub.

Bars

Hard Luck Cafe, 15 Almogim St., next to the Peace Cafe. Its proximity to the hostels has made the Hard Luck *the* place for travelers, both transient and resident, to eat, drink, and compare how broke they are. Single women might appreciate a companion (male or female). Carlsberg NIS5. Open daily 3pm until whenever.

Hemingway's, next to the New Caesar Hotel, on the east side of the lagoon. The traveler crowd often spills out into the street. Offers loud rock and reggae and NIS7 pints. Wed. and Sat. (subject to change) offer NIS5 pints. Open daily 8pm-4am.

Yacht Pub, on the marina by King Solomon's Wharf. Huge, with a fancy wooden bar. Upscale Israeli clientele and upscale prices. Live entertainment at 11pm changes every few nights. Popular Israeli folk singers or relaxing funk/soul bands. ½L Carlsberg NIS9.50, huge 1L NIS17. Open daily 10pm-3am (or later).

The Underground, in the New Tourist Center. Cheap brew and grub: spaghetti or eggs and beans (NIS9), pint of Carlsberg (NIS7), pitcher (NIS24). Daily videos. Open daily noon-6am.

Dolphin Reef (tel. 637 42 92), at the water park. Clean, classy, and expensive. Ocean view and breezes. Dance in the sand Mon. and Thurs. nights 10pm-4am. Microbrews (the cups are small) NIS8. Open until 12:30am on non-dance nights.

Peace Cafe, 13 Almogim St. A mix of backpackers, locals, and resident travelers swill beer and tell tales. The seediest of all the bars listed. Music videos by day, movies by night. Carlsberg NIS5. Open daily 9am-2am.

The Crocodile Pub, heading north on Hatmarim, take a left on Elot St. and walk past the Hard Rock and pharmacy. Small bar, friendly atmosphere, cold beer. Special deals on food and drink. Open daily 6pm until late.

Tropicana, in the Shalom Center. Friendly hole in the wall with black lights and a big bar. Nightly happy hour and occasional striptease. Open daily 4:30pm-late.

Clubs

King's Disco, at the Princess Hotel right before Taba Beach (take a cab). Hefty NIS40 cover, but you pay for what's regarded as the best disco in Eilat. For those who really want to dance.

Platinum, at the King Solomon Hotel. Ultra-modern, reflection-maximizing atmosphere with laser show. Mixes disco, pop, and new wave. Energetic bartenders and strong drinks. NIS30 cover (Fri. NIS65) includes 1 drink. Beer NIS12, drinks NIS22. Open daily 11:30pm until empty.

A LITTLE CULTURE

The tourist office has information on events at the **Phillip Murray Cultural Center** (tel. 637 22 57) on Ḥativat Ha-Negev near the bus station. The jazz, classical, rock, film, and theater seasons run September-May. The center also has a television, a reading room, and rotating art exhibits (open daily 8am-8pm). Kids of all ages like **Luna Park** (tel. 631 50 49), in front of the Queen of Sheba Hotel. Bumper cars and pirate ships cost a plank-walking NIS10; kiddie thrills are NIS5 (open Mon.-Sat. 6pm-midnight). The week-long **Hebrew Rock Music Festival,** one week prior to Passover on Eilat Beach, and the end-of-August **Red Sea Jazz festival,** with ten daily performances on four stages, are both popular annual events. Ask the tourist office for information.

GOING TO EGYPT

Crossing from Eilat to Taba takes a while and costs a few pounds. Be sure that your passport is valid for at least another three months and that your Israeli visa is valid (at least for the day you'll be traveling). If you want to go outside the Sinai, you'll need to get a **visa** at the Egyptian consulate (see **Practical Information,** p. 430). The border is open 24 hours a day and is closed only on Yom Kippur and 'Eid al-Adha.

The border-crossing process unfolds in an orderly way, but involves a surprisingly long hike. Allow one to two hours for the entire process, though it can take longer on a busy day. Keep your passport handy after you disembark from the bus (#15 from Eilat); you'll have to show it frequently as you go through the 2km obstacle course to the bus depot on the other side. The 13 exciting steps: (1) Bus drop-off. (2) Little Taba snack bar ("last beer before Sinai"). (3) Passport pre-check. (4) Passport control booth (pay NIS51.70 exit tax). (5) Israeli last passport check (they automatically stamp your passport at this point unless you ask them not to). (6) Stroll through no-man's-land. (7) Egyptian passport control (fill out entry form, get stamp). (8) Egyptian security (X-ray machine). (9) Post-border passport check. (10) 1km hike. (11) Customs, hidden on the left-hand side of the street. Don't pass it by without declaring *everything* that's of any importance that you're bringing with you into the Sinai, or the strict Egyptian border authorities won't let you leave with it. (12) Show passport and pay US$6/E£18 Egyptian border tax. The Taba Hilton is the best place to **change money.** It is open 24 hours and charges no commission for foreign currency converted to Egyptian pounds. (13) Welcome to Egypt! The bus station is a 10-minute walk from the border—you do not need to take a taxi.

If you plan on staying only in the Sinai for 14 days or fewer, you can get a **Sinai-only visa** stamped into your passport on the Egyptian side of the border. This visa limits travel to the Gulf of Aqaba coast as far south as Sharm esh-Sheikh (but not the area around Sharm esh-Sheikh, including Ras Muhammad; see **Sharm esh-Sheikh,** p. 256) and to St. Catherine's monastery and Mt. Sinai (but not sites in the vicinity of St. Catherine's). Unlike ordinary one-month Egyptian visas, the Sinai-only visa has no grace period; you'll pay a hefty fine if you overextend your stay.

From Taba there are buses to: **Cairo** (2pm, 7hr., E£70); **Nuweiba** (3pm, 1-1½hr., E£12); **Dahab** (3pm, 2-2½hr., E£15-17); and **Sharm el Sheikh** (3pm, 3-4hr., E£25). There is rumored to be a 9:30am bus to **St. Catherine's,** but don't count on it; in fact, all bus schedules should be taken lightly. There are always taxis hanging out waiting to take people to Dahab, Cairo, Nuweiba, or anywhere. You could have a long wait until they fill up, but you shouldn't pay too much more than the bus fare. After the last bus, however, you are at their mercy.

GOING TO JORDAN

To cross from Eilat to Aqaba, everyone must pay a NIS51.70 exit tax. Jordanian visas can be obtained at the border; prices vary greatly according to nationality (U.S. JD15, Canada JD31, U.K. JD23, Australia free, Ireland JD5, New Zealand JD4, South Africa free). Visas are valid up to one month. The process is easy and should take less than an hour. Changing money at the border is costly. Take a taxi to the border (NIS10-12). Taxis from the border to Aqaba cost JD4-5—there are no buses. (Border open Sun.-Thurs. 6:30am-10pm, Fri.-Sat. 8am-8pm; closed Yom Kippur and 'Eid al-Adha.)

■ Near Eilat

The beauty of the red granite mountains towering over Eilat matches that of the coral reefs thriving beneath. The **SPNI Field School** (tel. 637 20 21), across from Coral Beach (bus #15), is an essential stop for independent hikers. It sells trail maps (NIS54) and provides good advice on hikes (open Sun.-Fri. 8am-8pm). Many of the sites are accessible by northbound bus #393, 394, or 397. Buses fill up fast during high season and on Sundays and Fridays—make reservations at the central bus station two days in advance.

The hike to **Mt. Tzfaḥot** is convenient and provides great views. The green-and-white trail begins at the left end of the fence separating the highway from the field school complex. The climb to the summit takes 45 minutes. From here, the blue trail heads north, ending at the Club Inn Hotel near Aqua Sport beach. The round-trip takes about two hours and makes a good evening outing. If you wander too far on paths leading south, you may end up in Egypt.

The most exciting terrain accessible from Eilat is to the north. Some good destinations are **Ein Netafim, Mt. Shlomo**, and **Ha-Kanyon Ha-Adom** (Red Canyon). The bus driver will know when to let you off. From Red Canyon, you can hike to the lookout above **Moon Valley**, a pocked canyon in Egypt, and to the unusual **Amram's Pillars**. These hikes are not advisable in summer; October through April is the best hiking season. Before attempting any of these hikes, consult the SPNI. **Nature's Way** (P.O. Box 6121, Eilat; tel. 637 06 48) conducts guided "ecology hikes" from three hours to four days long. Prices range from US$20 to US$392 and include food and transport. They can be found next to the Birdwatching Center in the Commercial Center across from the bus station. Hikes are conducted October to April; advance reservations (3 weeks for long tours, 2 days for day trips) are required.

Jeep tours are another popular way of exploring the region. There are countless safari companies: **Egged Tours** (tel. 637 31 48) in the bus station, **Johnny Tours** (tel. 631 62 15), in the Marine Bridge House, and **Red Sea Sports** (tel. 633 08 66), also in the Bridge House. Half-day tours cost US$20-40. **Camel Ranch** (tel. 637 00 22), inland from Coral beach, offers half-day camel excursions.

Timna National Park (tel. 635 62 15; fax 637 25 42) is another hiking destination. The Timna copper mines, remarkably well preserved in the southeast corner of the park, were in mint condition 6000 years ago. Some people believe the Israelites passed through here on their way out of Egypt. Today you can find remains of workers' camps and cisterns dating from the 11th century BCE scattered amidst the whir of modern mining. The sandstone **King Solomon's Pillars** dominate the desert at a height of 50m near the 14th-century BCE Egyptian Temple of Hathor. The park's lake offers **camping** facilities (including showers) and a restaurant on its artificially created shores. **Timna Express** (tel. 637 47 41; fax 627 25 42) runs daily excursions to Timna and the neighboring kibbutz for US$36 (children US$28), including lunch. You could also head to the park yourself, as most buses that go to Tel Aviv or Jerusalem will let you off at the sign for Alipaz (don't get off at the Timna Mines signpost). The entrance is 2km away, which is, however, too far to walk in summer (park open daily 7:30am-sunset; NIS10, ages 5-18 NIS4.50).

Seeing Spots

The graceful and majestic leopard, mentioned eight times in the Bible, disappeared from the Negev about 100 years ago. In an effort to replenish desert wildlife, the Israeli government designated three quarters of the Negev as nature reserves, and the ferocious spotted cat has returned to its old home. Wildlife experts say that the leopard's presence proves that a full desert food chain is alive and kicking.

Most northbound buses will take you to the **Ḥai Bar Biblical Nature Reserve**, a wildlife park designed to repopulate animals indigenous in Biblical times, many of which have become rare in the region. The reserve has an impressive predator center, where 11 native predators can be seen in their habitats. There is also a nocturnal room, where nighttime animalia can be viewed. The bulk of the preserve is a game park, home to ostriches, wild asses, antelopes, addaxes, and oryxes (open daily 8:30am-3:30pm; NIS26, children NIS15). Those without cars will only be able to see the predator center and nocturnal room (NIS15, children NIS8). The center is a 20-minute walk (very hot in summer) from the bus stop.

The entrance to Ḥai Bar is opposite the entrance to Kibbutz Samir, 5km south of Yotvata. At Kibbutz Yotvata, the **Ye'elim Desert Holiday Village** (tel. 637 43 62; check-in 3pm) has tent space for NIS40. A **swimming pool** is free for guests. The **visitor's center** (tel. 637 60 18), opposite the kibbutz, provides information and a film about Negev ecology (open daily 8am-3pm; NIS5 for the film, free with ticket to Ḥai Bar). You can munch on Yotvata's famous cheese and yogurt at the **cafeteria**.

WEST BANK الضفة الغربية

> The West Bank and Gaza have seen considerable conflict between Palestinian residents and Israeli settlers and security forces in the recent past. Be aware of the current situation in each town you plan to visit before you go. Carry your passport at all times. The **international phone code** is the same as Israel's, 972.

West Bank residents live with a culture and struggle distinct from any other in the Middle East. For the first time in history, the Palestinian flag flies over many towns in this Occupied Territory, but the process by which self-rule was established has been long and arduous. The struggle is far from over and the outcome is unpredictable—inhabitants' careworn faces reflect the hardship of this constant uncertainty. Extremists on both sides attempt to destabilize daily life in an effort to derail the peace process, but well-informed travelers will have no problem visiting the area and befriending locals. Tourists may be invited into Palestinian homes, where hot spiced tea and muddily delicious coffee are accompanied by discussions of the *intifada* and occupation. Modest dress will make both men and women's experiences more enjoyable. The Israeli settlements are generally less accessible to tourists than the Palestinian towns, but visits can be arranged through the Jerusalem MTIO (see p. 416). The West Bank's rich history rivals its immediate political significance; Jacob built a chapel in Beitin, Joshua leveled Jericho, and Jesus was born in Bethlehem.

ONCE THERE

■ Coming and Going

> The Palestinians, Jordanians, and Israelis are still trying to figure this one out for themselves. Much of the information here is changeable, although in summer 1997 border crossings were smooth for many travelers of different nationalities.

With a private car, you can visit the West Bank from Israel; expect numerous Israeli checkpoints, and bring your passport along. Most public transportation connections are from Jerusalem. If you check with the Israeli GTIO before going, you'll probably get a standard governmental fright warning, which you should consider seriously, although some may find it heavy-handed and decide to go anyway.

The King Hussein/Allenby Bridge, open from 8am to 5pm every day except Saturday, is the only direct crossing point between Jordan and the West Bank. Everything remains unpredictable; get thorough, up-to-date information from your embassy or consulate before trying to cross. At press time, buses and *service* frequently left Amman's Abdali Station for the bridge. Public transportation goes to the first checkpoint. Shuttle buses take travelers to the next (see **Amman: Practical Information,** p. 472). Be prepared to pay JD5 to Jordanian customs officers upon leaving and reentering Jordan; for groups, the fee is usually waived. Another JD1.500 is collected on a special bus traversing the bridge. The Israeli side does not collect money. You may pay for transportation in the West Bank with Jordanian dinars.

To get to Jordan from the West Bank, you'll need a Jordanian visa, obtainable in Tel Aviv, at the border crossings between Eilat and Aqaba, and at the Sheikh Hussein Bridge near Beit She'an (see **Tel Aviv: Practical Information,** p. 325 and **Eilat: Practical Information,** p. 430). You can also get the visa before leaving your home coun-

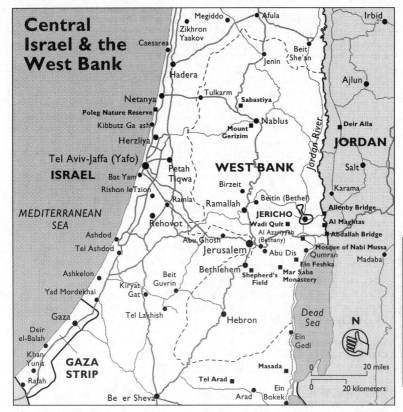

Central Israel & the West Bank

Megiddo • Afula
Zikhron Yaakov • Irbid
Caesarea
Jenin • Beit She'an
Hadera
Netanya • Tulkarm • Sabastiya
Poleg Nature Reserve
Kibbutz Ga ash • Nablus
Herzliya • Mount Gerizim
Tel Aviv-Jaffa (Yafo) • Ajlun
ISRAEL • Bat Yam • Petah Tiqwa
Rishon leTzion • WEST BANK
Ramla • Birzeit
Ramallah • Beitin (Bethel)
MEDITERRANEAN SEA
Rehovot • JERICHO
Ashdod • Wadi Qult
Tel Ashdod • Abu Ghosh
Al Azariyeh (Bethany)
Jerusalem • Abu Dis
Ashkelon • Bethlehem
Yad Mordekhai • Shepherd's Field • Mar Saba Monastery
Kiryat Gat • Beit Guvrin
Gaza • Tel Lakhish • Hebron
Deir el-Balah
Khan Yunis • GAZA STRIP
Rafah
Be er Sheva • Arad • Ein Bokek • Masada • Tel Arad • Ein Gedi • Dead Sea
JORDAN • Deir Alla • Salt • Karama • Allenby Bridge • Al Maghtas • Abdallah Bridge • Mosque of Nabi Mussa • Qumran • Madaba • Ein Feshka
Jordan River
N
0   20 miles
0   20 kilometers

WEST BANK

try from a Jordanian embassy or consulate (see p. 8). Start early in the morning. Board a *service* taxi bound for the Bridge. Make sure your *service* goes all the way to the border—some are authorized to go only as far as a checkpoint on the outskirts of town. No private vehicles are permitted to cross the bridge. At the bridge, your passport and belongings will be inspected. Once on the Jordanian side, you can catch a *service* to Amman.

■ Getting Around

The West Bank is crisscrossed by a relatively reliable and cheap network of buses and shared taxis *(service)*. Air-conditioned private taxis are readily available, but are substantially more expensive.

A system of colored **license plates** differentiates vehicles. Those registered in Israel, West Jerusalem, and Jewish settlements have yellow plates. Blue plates signify Arab cars from the Occupied Territories, and green plates belong to Arab taxis and buses. Others are white (UN or diplomatic), red (police), and black (army). It's probably safer to travel with blue plates, but many Arab-owned cars that are registered in Israel proper (thus with yellow plates) travel hassle-free in the West Bank.

East Jerusalem is the transportation hub for the West Bank, but a 1992 closure made it impossible for local Palestinians to use Jerusalem as a transit terminal. As a result, some lines were re-routed to Ramallah, and *service* from Jerusalem to places such as Nablus became less frequent.

Taxis *Service* taxis are the most convenient mode of West Bank transportation. Although slightly more expensive than Arab buses, they are faster, more reliable, and more frequent. If you get lost or disoriented, consult the drivers; they are knowledgeable in matters ranging from politics to the location of obscure ruins. Private taxis are more expensive but more practical for remote areas. Drivers will take you to the site, and (for a few extra shekels) wait while you admire it.

Buses Both Arab and Egged buses service the West Bank. Arab buses leave from two bus stations in East Jerusalem: the Suleiman St. Station between Herod's and Damascus Gates, for points south; and the Nablus Rd. Station, for points north. You can catch Egged buses at the West Jerusalem central bus station on Jaffa Rd. Egged buses cost more and often take you only to the outskirts of Palestinian towns. Take Egged to the Jewish settlements.

Arab bus schedules to the West Bank are unpredictable; the intervals listed here are approximate. Transportation to Nablus is especially erratic. Buses may also pick people up from the side of the road. Arab buses have light blue stripes on the sides (except for the Ramallah bus, which is red), while Egged buses are red and white.

From the Suleiman St. Station

#22: to Bethlehem (every 15min., NIS2.50).
#36: to Bethany (every hr., NIS2).
#36: to Abu Dees and Bethany (every hr., NIS2).

From the Nablus Rd. Station

#18: to Ramallah (every 30min., NIS3).
#23: to Nablus (Tamini Bus Co., every 1½hr., NIS6).

■ Money Matters

The **new Israeli shekel (NIS)** is the currency most frequently used, although **Jordanian dinars (JD)** and **U.S. dollars (US$)** are also accepted sometimes. Expect prices to increase by a significant margin if you try to pay for your purchase in anything other than shekels. Although Palestinians take Israeli currency, they often don't like to speak Hebrew. English, Arabic, or Klingon are better options.

■ Keeping in Touch

The **postal service** in the West Bank is, for now at least, a part of the Israeli mail system (refer to **Israel: Keeping in Touch,** p. 272). All major towns in the West Bank have at least one post office with **Poste Restante.** Letters should be addressed, for example, "<u>SHEPPARD</u>, Bede, Main Post Office, Town, West Bank, via Israel" (see p. 43). The Palestinian Authority in Jericho has its own postal system, with Palestinian stamps that are currently only good for sending letters between Jericho and Gaza.

The **telephone** system is also part of the Israeli telephone network. All services, including collect and calling-card calls, are available from any private or public telephone. Beige public telephones, operated by **telecards,** are conveniently located in most post offices, where you can also purchase the cards. Relevant area codes are (02) for Bethlehem, Ramallah, and the South, and (09) for Nablus and the North.

For now, direct calls to some Arab countries from the West Bank or vice-versa are officially impossible. Exceptions to this rule are Jordan, Egypt, and Morocco; more countries should soon become accessible. The international phone code for the West Bank is the same as that of Israel (972).

LIFE AND TIMES

■ Political History

If it's the truth you seek, talking about West Bank politics will most probably leave you disappointed and confused—there are just too many opinions. The problem is that no one wants to talk about anything else, and it's usually difficult to remove personal ideologies and emotional attachments from such a controversial discussion.

Historically, the West Bank represents the most complex facet of the Arab-Israeli conflict because of its relevance to three major groups: Israelis, Palestinian Arabs, and Jordanians. Jews lived in the West Bank long before the 1967 and even the 1948 wars. For the most part Jews were drawn to the holy city of **Hebron,** but in 1829 they fled town after Arab riots claimed 80 Jewish lives. Palestinian Arabs form the region's largest indigenous group and have resided throughout Israel and the West Bank for hundreds of years. Over 70% of the Jordanian population is of Palestinian origin.

The political division now called the West Bank was created in the 1948 Arab-Israeli War, when Jordan conquered the territory to its west (the "west bank" of the Jordan River). Jordanian **King Abdallah** angered most Palestinians by annexing the region rather than creating a separate state as the U.N. Partition Plan had stipulated. The Jordanian government subsequently did little to develop the West Bank and discriminated against its Palestinian residents. Their situation, however, was better than that of the Egyptian-occupied Gaza Strip's Palestinians, since the fertile West Bank was economically vital to Jordan.

In the 1967 Six Day War, the West Bank was one of several territories captured by Israeli forces. Rather than officially annex the area (excluding East Jerusalem, which was annexed), Israel placed it under military administration. Arab mayors and police kept their offices, Jordanian school curriculums continued to be taught, public welfare programs and National Social Security payments were instituted, and Israeli medical treatment was provided.

But Israeli occupation was not all benevolent. Palestinians suffered curfews, mass arrests, and demolition of homes in retaliation for the actions of one family member. There was no freedom of assembly—Palestinians could not have weddings, gatherings, or meetings without a permit from the Israeli authorities, which could be denied for a variety of reasons. Flying the Palestinian flag was illegal. In addition, the infrastructure, schools, and public works of the West Bank were neglected in comparison with those of towns in Israel proper. The Palestinians' own attempts at establishing institutions or some form of economic independence were likewise thwarted. **Birzeit University** was denied a building permit for years and shut down frequently. Cottage industries such as pickling, baking, and embroidery attained some success, but were often unceremoniously closed.

Israeli settlements in the West Bank were, and continue to be, a source of constant controversy. Some 160,000 Israeli Jews have settled in the West Bank since its seizure in 1967. Launched by Labor governments eager to establish an Israeli presence in areas of strategic importance such as the Jordan Valley, the settlement project has been an ideological cornerstone of right-wing Likud governments since 1977. The settlements are motivated not only by strategic considerations, but also by the desire to attain rule over *Eretz Yisrael* (the land of Israel), an area including Israel, the West Bank, the Gaza Strip, and a bit beyond. Often strategically situated on hilltops overlooking Palestinian towns, many settlements resemble military installations more than housing developments. They are surrounded by barbed wire and guarded by Israeli soldiers. Most Ireali settlers conspicuously carry guns; Palestinians may not bear arms.

In December 1987, the Palestinians of the occupied territories began the **intifada.** A traffic accident in the Gaza Strip provided the spark; two decades of occupation, economic stagnation, and increasing Israeli settlement activity erupted in stone-throwing and other violence, chanting, the unfurling of the Palestinian flag, and expressions of nationalism. Forms of resistance also included nonpayment of taxes, general strikes, and resignations from government service. The young Palestinians of the West Bank (many leaders of the *intifada* were not past their teenage years) set up underground "popular committees" which organized strikes, demonstrations, and funerals, and made sure that everyone had enough to eat. Many did time in Israeli jails, but often used this time for further education and planning. A new generation of Palestinians—those who knew nothing but Israeli occupation—had abruptly upstaged their elders, including the PLO, with a widespread resistance movement.

The *intifada* led to major changes in the nature of the Palestinian-Israeli conflict. The populist nature of the uprising and the televised suppression by the Israeli army managed to draw far more international attention and sympathy than decades of PLO terrorism; the Palestinian problem was reinstated as the focal point of the Arab-Israeli dispute. Some American Jewish groups and Israeli liberals expressed dismay at the sometimes brutal tactics of the Israeli army, and indicated to Israeli politicians that continued occupation of the territories might make them reconsider their financial and political support. After about six years of continued struggle, many Palestinians were worn out. Palestinians suspected of collaboration were dragged from their homes in the middle of the night, sometimes assaulted and even killed. The *intifada* had stopped making headlines by the time the **Gulf Crisis** began in 1991. In contrast to most Arab governments in the region, who joined a U.S.-led coalition opposing Saddam Hussein, the PLO, along with most Palestinians, supported Iraq. Some Palestinians cheered from rooftops when Iraq's SCUD missiles landed on Tel Aviv. Saudi Arabia and other oil-rich Gulf states, whose financial support had been trickling through the PLO into the territories, suspended their aid.

In the aftermath of the Gulf War, Middle Eastern governments became convinced that it was high time for a regional peace conference. After the historic Madrid conference in October 1991, negotiations between the Palestinians (in a joint Jordanian-Palestinian delegation) and the Israelis took place from 1991 to 1994 in Washington, D.C. The first Israeli delegation to the peace talks, headed by hard-line Likud prime minister Yitzhak Shamir, offered little with which to bargain. But the subsequent center-left government, formed after the June 1992 elections, brought a significant change to Israeli policy toward Palestinians and the occupied territories. Late Prime Minister Yitzhak Rabin froze all settlement activity, and pushed to promote the peace process with a special emphasis on the Israeli-Palestinian negotiations.

The talks raised polarizing debates on both sides. In Israel, many have felt that to turn the West Bank over to the Palestinians (and thereby expose the narrow coastal strip that houses three-fourths of Israel's population to hostile neighbors) would be tantamount to guiding a knife to their own throats. Other Israelis have argued that until Israel makes peace with its neighbors, terrorism and war will continue to claim countless young lives. On the Palestinian side, moderates such as negotiators Faisal al-Husseini and Hanan Ashrawi favor a compromise with Israel, but are challenged by Islamist **Hamas,** which was gaining popularity when the talks began. Hamas advocates continuing armed struggle and cannot envision a Palestinian state peacefully existing alongside Israel. For more information, see **The Peace Process,** p. 58.

At the peace talks in Washington, the different delegations took turns not showing up, storming out in protest, showing up late, and leaving in a huff when the other party arrived later. It took secret negotiations in Oslo (baby-sat by the Norwegian Foreign Minister) between representatives of the PLO and the Israeli government to rescue the ailing Washington talks and to lay the groundwork for Palestinian self-rule. The Oslo negotiations drafted the Declaration of Principles on Interim Self-Rule Arrangements (the DOP or Oslo Accord). The Oslo Accord provided for mutual recognition of Israel and the PLO, commitment by the parties to seek a non-violent settlement of their disputes, and successive stages of negotiations which would gradually transfer power to an autonomous Palestinian government over a five-year transitional period. This period is to be followed by an agreement on final status issues such as Jerusalem, refugees, settlements, security arrangements, borders, and foreign affairs.

The Oslo agreement and the more detailed Cairo agreement, signed in May 1994 and calling for Israeli withdrawal from the Gaza strip and the Jericho area of the West Bank, were implemented in mid-1994. Much of the PLO leadership relocated from Tunisia to Gaza, where they established the Palestinian National Authority (PNA), more commonly referred to as the **Palestinian Authority (PA).** In subsequent negotiations with Israel, some control over the remainder of the West Bank, excluding Israeli settlements and military outposts, was transferred to the PA. By the summer of 1995, the PA had complete control in Jericho and Gaza (except for a small number of settlements in Gaza), with Israeli powers essentially limited to foreign affairs and external security. The PA also had powers over taxation, education, social welfare, health, and tourism in the rest of the West Bank, excluding settlements and military outposts. A new round of intense negotiations during the summer led to the drafting of an interim agreement for the re-deployment of Israeli Defense Force units from Palestinian towns, the transfer of direct control over those areas to the PA, and the establishment of an elected Palestinian parliament. All IDF personnel in Arab cities would supposedly be moved to four army bases in unpopulated areas. Palestinian security forces would then be responsible for policing the territory.

After Prime Minister Rabin's assassination (see **The Peace Process,** p. 58), the May 29, 1996 Israeli election brought right-wing Likud party leader Benjamin Netanyahu to power with 50.4 percent of the vote. Netanyahu's criticisms of the Middle East peace process led many analysts to question its future under a Netanyahu government. 1996 saw the redeployment of troops in Hebron, but stepping up of settlement in East Jerusalem and elsewhere in the Occupied Territories. Disputes over Israeli settlement policy and extremist actions on both sides stalled peace negotiations almost to a standstill. The United States government decided in August 1997 to take a more active role in the peace process, fearing that it would fall apart all together. The future status of the West Bank is uncertain until Netanyahu and Arafat can come to an agreement (it could be a while).

■ Economy

The economy of the West Bank has been dependent on the Israeli economy since the 1967 occupation. Crises in Israel's economy were felt even more sharply in the West Bank because Palestinians were the first to be laid off from jobs in times of hardship. Many West Bank Palestinians continue to work in Israel with no health insurance, job security, or workers' rights.

The West Bank economy was a major battleground of the *intifada.* Palestinians boycotted Israeli products in an attempt to rid themselves of crippling economic dependence, and the Israeli government imposed economic sanctions on the Palestinian community as a form of punishment and as a way of extending domination. The Palestinian Authority has inherited this devastated economy, with an undeveloped and outdated infrastructure. The Israeli government continues to use its economic advantage to leverage control in the Occupied Territories; after two suicide bombers killed 13 other people and wounded 150 in a crowded market in West Jerusalem in summer 1997, Israel withheld a large sum of money, mostly wages, to emphasize its demand for increased security.

■ Literature

Much recent Palestinian literature is concerned with the agony of foreign occupation and exile. Ghassan Kanafani, perhaps the greatest contemporary Palestinian fiction writer, recreates the desperation and aimlessness of the refugee in his short stories *All That Remains: Palestine's Children,* and *Men in the Sun and Other Palestinian Stories,* which portrays the struggle through adult eyes. Palestinians' attachment to the land is depicted in the wonderful poetry of Mahmoud Darwish, and the longing for a homeland in the poems of Fouzi al-Asmar, collected in *The Wind-Driven Reed and Other Poems.* Jabra Ibrahim Jabra's novel *The Ship* is engrossing. Israeli Arab Anton

Shammas' *Arabesques* describes Palestinian identity crises; Fawaz Turki's autobiographical tomes discuss life in exile. The works of Sahar Khalifeh, Liyana Badr, Raymonda Tawil, and Samih al-Qassem are all noteworthy; most of these authors and others are translated in Salma Khadra Jayyusi's behemoth *Modern Palestinian Literature.*

Bethlehem بيت لحم בית לחם

Bethlehem (Beit Lahm in Arabic, Beit Leḥem in Hebrew) was the Biblical setting for Rachel's death, the love between Ruth and Boaz, and the discovery of the lyrical shepherd David, future king of Israel. The pastoral birth of Jesus really put Bethlehem on the pilgrimage map. Today, Biblical resonances are obscured behind fleets of tour buses and souvenir stands. Even as you try to peel off the layers of commercialism in your mind's eye, you will be suffocated by exhaust, blinded by flash bulbs, and drowned in floods of postcard-buying devout.

In 1995, Bethlehem celebrated Christmas for the first time under Palestinian rule. The changing of the guard has breathed new life into this small town; the mood is generally upbeat and optimistic, and the people friendly. Townsfolk whose business is tourism generally speak English. The best time to visit is during a Christian holiday (see **Appendix** for dates). Christmas in Bethlehem is especially unforgettable—make reservations generations in advance.

PRACTICAL INFORMATION

Religious sights center around **Manger Square,** across from the Basilica of the Nativity. **Najajreh** and **Star Street** are home to the town's shopping district and open-air **market** and lead into the Square. Bethlehem is 8km south of Jerusalem.

Tourist Office: PNA Ministry of Tourism (tel. 674 15 81), above the Al Andalus Hotel in Manger Sq. Gives out the free PNA town map, details about special events during Christmas and Easter, and transportation information. They also provide a list of accommodations. Open Mon.-Fri. 8am-3pm, Sat. 8am-1pm.

Currency Exchange: Cairo Amman Bank (tel. 674 49 71), in Manger Sq. Open Sun.-Thurs. 8:30am-12:30pm.

Buses: Bus station on Manger St., 50m northwest of Manger Sq., down the hill towards Jerusalem. Check with Bethlehem's tourist office to see if buses are running. Quite often they are not, due to border closings. **Take service instead.** To **Jerusalem:** #22 and 23 (from Hebron), #47 (from Beit Sahur), and #60 (from Obediyya), 30min., NIS1.50, last bus back about 5-6pm. From Jerusalem, buses depart at Damascus or Jaffa Gate. The Hebron bus stops only at Rachel's Tomb and at the intersection with Paul VI St., 3km west of Manger Sq.

Minibuses: Deheisheh (#1) from Manger St. behind the police station, heads north to Rachel's Tomb, then south to the Deheisheh refugee camp via the road to Hebron (every 15-20min. 6am-6pm, NIS1). Another goes to Beit Sahur (NIS1).

Taxis: Service taxis run from Jaffa or Damascus Gate in Jerusalem to the Bethlehem city center until about 7pm (NIS2.50). To get to Manger Sq., take another local taxi (NIS1). To get back to **Jerusalem,** get in a local cab (all rides NIS1) and either tell the driver you want to go to Jerusalem, whereby he'll drop you off at the appropriate spot to pick up a Jerusalem-going taxi, or ask to go to Rachel's Tomb (Dareekh Raha'il). From there it's easy to flag down Jerusalem-bound taxis. **Private (special) taxis** will take you to surrounding areas; negotiate a price before the journey.

Police Station: tel. 674 49 03, in Manger Sq. Helpful and conscientious.

Post Office: tel. 674 26 68, beside the tourist office in Manger Sq. Open Sun.-Tues., Thurs., and Sat. 8am-2:30pm.

Telephone Code: 02.

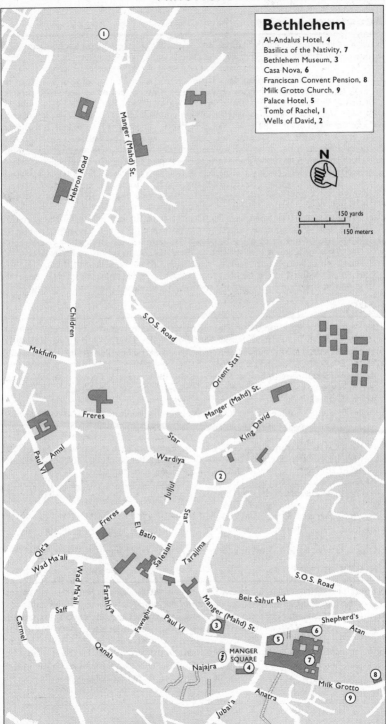

Bethlehem

Al-Andalus Hotel, 4
Basilica of the Nativity, 7
Bethlehem Museum, 3
Casa Nova, 6
Franciscan Convent Pension, 8
Milk Grotto Church, 9
Palace Hotel, 5
Tomb of Rachel, 1
Wells of David, 2

N

0   150 yards
0   150 meters

WEST BANK

ACCOMMODATIONS

While Bethlehem's accommodations are expensive, the few extra shekels provides serene comfort foreign to Jerusalem's packed hostels.

Franciscan Convent Pension, Milk Grotto St. (tel. 674 24 41), on your left past the Milk Grotto. Welcoming nuns rent sparkling, flower- and Bible- bedecked rooms. Curfew 9pm, 8:30pm in winter. Private rooms US$11 per person, ISIC holders US$8. Breakfast US$4. Rooms with shower and breakfast US$20.

Casa Nova (tel. 674 39 81 or 82; fax 674 35 40), off Manger Sq., tucked in a corner to the left of the Basilica entrance. Marble floor and stained-glass lobby windows greet a serious pilgrim crowd. Caters primarily to seminary students or groups in which at least 3 members can recite the Synoptic Gospels, but even agnostics are welcome. Modern rooms and plenty of hot water; heated in winter. Check-out 8am. Bed and breakfast US$20; half board US$25; full board US$30; US$10 extra to convert your double room into a single. 5% service charge. Reservations recommended. To stay during Christmas, reserve up to 1 yr. in advance.

Al-Andalus Hotel (tel. 674 13 48; fax 674 22 80), in Manger Sq., upstairs next to the Bank Leumi. If the door is bolted, just knock, or track down the owner at one of the shops downstairs or at Al-Andalus Restaurant around the corner to the right (10% discount if you stay at the hotel). Clean, adequate rooms with 70s decor. TV lounge. Check-out 11am. Singles with bath US$25. Doubles with bath US$46. Breakfast included in the dining room upstairs. Prices subject to change, depending on the season and mood of the owner. Bargain down the winter price hikes.

FOOD

There's fuel for your church-hopping excursions at cheap stands in Manger Sq. and on Manger St. in the form of falafel and *shawerma*. Tourists are charged slightly higher prices than locals, but bargaining helps. Many places offer student discounts.

As-Sabil Restaurant (tel. 674 27 98), in the Palace Hotel. Five-course European menu US$12, with soup, salad, pasta, meat, and dessert. Call ahead.

Al Quds Restaurant (tel. 674 10 58), off Manger St., on the right up the tiny street next to the post office. Draws locals with heavenly hummus (NIS5) and *shawerma* (NIS7 in pita). *Kabab* or half-chicken with hummus and salads (NIS17), and cheap sheep's liver (NIS15 for two 250g portions). Open daily 7am-8pm or 9pm.

Al Andalus Restaurant (tel./fax 674 35 19). Caters to large tour groups. Affordable meals are cleverly disguised as "snacks." Hot dogs, hamburgers, and cheeseburgers (NIS12-20) come with salad and fries. Open daily 8am-midnight.

Al-Atlal Restaurant (tel. 674 11 04), 1 block from Manger Sq. on Milk Grotto St. Provides neo-Crusader arches and needed respite from the hordes. *Shishlik* or *kabab* NIS22, hummus or *labaneh* NIS5.

Granada Bar and Restaurant (tel. 674 43 00), on the same side of Manger Sq. as Bank Leumi. Shaded outdoor tables with an unobstructed view of the square. *Shawerma* platter NIS8, falafel NIS5.

Quick, Lunch, Sandwiches, next door to Granada (quick lunch sandwiches NIS7).

SIGHTS

A church masquerading as a fortress, the massive **Basilica of the Nativity,** on Manger Sq., is the oldest continuously used church in the world. It's come a long way in the past 16 centuries. A far cry from any previous incarnation as a reflective, quiet sanctuary, today's church bursts with pilgrims and tourists. Under the supervision of his mother Helena, Constantine the Great erected the first basilica in 326 CE over the site of Jesus' birth. It was destroyed in the Samaritan uprising of 525 CE, then rebuilt by Justinian. During the 614 CE Persian invasion, virtually every Christian shrine in the Holy Land was demolished, with the exception of this basilica, reputedly spared because it contained a mosaic of the three (Persian) wise men which had special anti-artillery powers. Tancred, the brat of the First Crusade, claimed Bethlehem as a fief and extensively renovated the church. After the Crusaders kingdom fell, the church again lapsed into disrepair. By the 15th century it had become undeniably decrepit, but its importance as a holy shrine never waned. For this reason, during the ensuing centuries, struggle for its control among Roman Catholic, Greek, and Armenian Christians repeatedly led to bloodshed. In the 1840s the church was restored to its former dignity, but squabbles between the various sects over the division of the edifice continue. Established in 1751 and finalized 100 years later, an elaborate system of worship schedules has harmonized the competing claims of the different groups, but the confusion resulting from the Greek Orthodox Church's rejection of summer daylight savings time demonstrates the teetering balance of this arrangement.

Though it has an impressive history, the Basilica of the Nativity is not particularly attractive. The main entrance and windows were blocked up as a safety precaution during medieval times, rendering the facade markedly awkward. To enter you must assume the position and step through the narrow **Door of Humility**—a remnant of the days when Christians wanted to prevent Muslims from entering on horseback.

Fragments of beautiful mosaic floors are all that remain of Constantine's original church. View them beneath the huge wooden trap doors in the center of the marble Crusader floor. The four rows of reddish limestone Corinthian columns and the mosaic atoms along the walls date from Justinian's reconstruction. The oak ceiling was a gift from England's King Edward IV, and the handsome icons adorning the altar were bequeathed in 1764 by the Russian royal family.

The **Grotto of the Nativity** is in an underground sanctuary beneath the church. As you enter the womb-like space, notice the crosses etched into the columns on both sides of the doorway—religious graffiti from centuries of pilgrims. A star bearing the Latin inscription: *Hic De Virgine Maria Jesus Christus Natus Est* ("Here, of the Virgin Mary, Jesus Christ was born") marks the spot. The fourteen points represent the fourteen stations of the Via Dolorosa—and thus the end of Christ's life is poetically married to its beginning. The star, added by Catholics in 1717, was removed by Greeks in 1847 and restored by the Turkish government in 1853. Quarrels over the star supposedly contributed to the outbreak of the Crimean War. (Basilica complex open daily 6am-8pm; in winter 7am-5pm. Free, although donations are encouraged. Modest dress required. For further information call 674 24 25.)

Simple and airy, the adjoining **St. Catherine's Church** (tel. 674 24 25), built by the Franciscans in 1881, is a welcome contrast to the grim interior of the basilica. Use the separate entrance to the north of the basilica, or face the altar in the basilica and pass through one of the doorways in the wall on your left. Saint Catherine's broadcasts a **midnight Mass** to a worldwide audience every Christmas Eve. Superbly detailed wood carvings of the 14 Stations of the Cross line the walls. The first room, the **Chapel of St. Joseph,** commemorates the carpenter's vision of an angel who advised him to flee with his family to Egypt to avoid Herod's wrath. .The burial cave of children slaughtered by King Herod (Matthew 2:6) lies below the altar and through the grille in the **Chapel of the Innocents.** Beyond the altar, a narrow hallway leads to the Grotto of the Nativity. The way is blocked by a thick wood door pierced by a peephole. During times of greater hostility between Christian sects, this glimpse was as close as Catholics could get to the Greek Orthodox shrine. To the right of the altar, a

O Little Town of Bethlehem

Christmas in Bethlehem explodes with pilgrims and tourists, none of whom could say "how still we see thee lie." On Christmas, the town becomes a huge rollicking festival. Now that Palestinians have autonomy in the village, Yuletide has become a national celebration. Pilgrims won't find solitude, but they will find merriment. Falafel stands play tapes of *Jingle Bells* and *White Christmas*, red-robed Santa Clauses smile in the streets, and strings of colored lights adorn storefronts and church facades. Getting a ticket to midnight Mass isn't easy, but the service is broadcast on TVs throughout Manger Sq. The tourist office has a list of Christmas activities. For Mass tickets, consult the the Franciscan Pilgrims Office in Jerusalem (see p. 287).

series of rooms contain the tombs of St. Jerome, St. Paula, and St. Paula's daughter Eustochia. These lead to the spartan cell where St. Jerome produced the **Vulgate,** the 4th-century translation of the Hebrew Bible into Latin.

The Franciscan Fathers conduct a solemn procession to the basilica and underground chapels every day. To join in the 20 minutes of Gregorian cantillation and Latin prayer, arrive at St. Catherine's by noon (St. Catherine's and the tomb of St. Jerome both open daily 5:30am-noon and 2-8pm).

A five-minute walk from the Basilica of the Nativity down Milk Grotto St. leads to the **Milk Grotto Church** (tel. 674 24 25). The cellar here is thought to be the cave in which the Holy Family hid, and more importantly a spot where Mary breast-fed baby Jesus, when fleeing from Herod into Egypt. The cave and church take their names from the original milky white color of the rocks, which have now either been blackened by candle smoke or been painted blue. According to legend, some of Mary's milk fell while she was nursing the infant Jesus, whitewashing the rocks forever (well, almost forever). Male visitors may be slightly discomfited amid the women who come here to pray for fertility (open daily 8-11:30am and 2-5pm). If it's locked, ring the bell and wait for a monk to admit you.

About 500m north of Manger Sq. along Star St., the three unremarkable **Wells of David** (tel. 674 24 77; open daily 8am-noon and 2-5pm) squat in the parking lot of the King David Cinema. Thirsty David, while battling the Philistines, was brought water from the enemy's well. He in turn offered it as a sacrifice to God (2 Samuel 23:13-17). From Star St., turn right onto King David St.

The **Tomb of Rachel** (Kever Raḥel; tel. 678 75 07) is a sacred site for Jews, a spot where synagogues have been built and destroyed throughout history. On one side are fervently praying Hasidic men, and on the other weeping Yemeni women. The illustrious Rachel died in Bethlehem while giving birth to Benjamin (Genesis 35:19-20), and she became a timeless symbol of maternal devotion and suffering. Despite Rachel's misfortune, the tomb is revered as the place to pray for a child or a safe delivery. Men should don a paper *kippah* (head covering), available at the entrance.

While the IDF has left Bethlehem, the Israeli government has announced that it plans to retain control over the Tomb of Rachel, and that a special access road will link the tomb to Jerusalem, bypassing Bethlehem. The PA insists that the tomb is the property of the Islamic *Waqf,* though it intends to allow free access for Jewish worshipers. At press time, the tomb was undergoing "renovations" under the barbed wire of the vigilant IDF; the date of completion is unknown. The tomb is on the northern edge of town on the road to Jerusalem, at the intersection of Manger St. and Hebron Rd. (open Sun.-Thurs. 8am-5pm, Fri. 8am-1pm). All buses between Jerusalem and Bethlehem or Hebron pass the tomb; minibus #1 also swings by. It's a 20-minute walk from the Basilica.

Bethlehem means "House of Meat" in Arabic (*Beit Lahm*) and "House of Bread" in Hebrew (*Beit Leḥem*). The sprawling **market** which clings to the town's steep streets lives up to both names; it's up the stairs from Paul VI St. across from the Syrian Church, about two blocks west of Manger Sq. A few blocks down Star St. from the market and toward the basilica is the **Bethlehem Museum** (tel. 674 25 89), exhibiting Palestinian crafts, traditional costumes, and a 19th-century Palestinian home (open Mon.-Sat. 9am-noon and 3-5pm; NIS3).

■ Near Bethlehem

AL AZARIYYEH (BETHANY) العزرية

A relatively prosperous Palestinian village, Bethany was the home of Lazarus and his sisters Mary and Martha. A **Franciscan Church** (tel. 674 92 91), built in 1954, marks a spot where Jesus supposedly slept. The church features several impressive mosaics, including one of the resurrection of Lazarus and another of the Last Supper. Three earlier shrines, the earliest from the 4th century CE, have been excavated nearby. South of the church lie the remains of a vast abbey built in 1143 by Queen Melisende of Jerusalem. (Open daily March-Oct. 9-11:30am and 2-6pm; Nov.-Feb. 9-11:30am and 2-5pm. Ssmall donations appreciated.)

Bethany is home to the first-century **Tomb of Lazarus.** When the Crusaders arrived, they built a church over Lazarus's tomb, a monastery over Mary and Martha's house, and a tower over Simon the Leper's abode (Simon was another resident of Bethany cured by Jesus). In the 16th century, Muslims erected a mosque over the shrine, and in the following century Christians dug another entrance to the tomb so they too could worship there. Head for the red domes of the **Greek Orthodox Church** above the tomb (the Franciscan Church is just downhill). As you approach the tomb, a person will come from across the street to show you the light switch (on the right as you enter) and ask for a donation (NIS2 is appropriate; tomb open daily 8am-7pm). Ten minutes farther along the main road, the **Greek Orthodox Convent** (silver dome) shelters the boulder upon which Jesus sat while awaiting Martha (ring the bell to see the rock).

To reach Bethany from Jerusalem (4km), take a *service* from Herod's Gate (both NIS2), and get off in the town (look for the silver-domed church on your left). There are two #36 buses, one of which stops at Abu Dees first. Women should dress modestly and travel in groups.

SHEPHERD'S FIELD

Beyond the Arab village of Beit Sahur on the eastern edge of Bethlehem is the **Field of Ruth,** believed to be the setting for the biblical Book of Ruth. The name of the village in Hebrew is "House of the Shepherds," and Christian tradition holds that this is **Shepherd's Field,** where those tending their flocks were greeted by the angel who pronounced the birth of Jesus (Luke 2:9-11). Take bus #47 (NIS1) from the stop behind the police station in Manger Sq., get off at Beit Sahur, and walk 20 minutes to the site. Otherwise, you can follow the signs and walk the 1.5km from Bethlehem. A cab should cost NIS15. A sign encouraging you to turn left leads to an alternate **Franciscan Shepherd's Field,** which includes a little chapel, a monastery, and an excavated Byzantine church (open daily 8-11:30am and 2-5pm). Across the street, you will see a building with a red dome. Take a right and walk in the direction of the site claimed by the Greek Patriarchate (tel. 647 31 35). Here you'll find the remains of a Byzantine **basilica,** thrice destroyed and repaired in the 5th, 6th, and 7th centuries. The **Holy Cave** (325 CE) features mosaic crosses on the floor. In the **baptistry** you can view 1300-year-old bones belonging to victims of the Persian invasion. The newest addition to the field is the red-dome-topped Byzantine-style church, opened in 1989 but still under construction. Inside are colorful frescoes of starving local saints and a Greek imported marble floor. Six monks affiliated with Mar Saba live in Saint Sawa's Monastery (open daily 8am-12:30pm and 2-5pm).

MAR SABA MONASTERY

The remarkable Mar Saba Monastery stands isolated from nearby traffic. Carved into the walls of a remote canyon, the extensive monastery complex stands above the sewer-esque Kidron River. The monastery was built opposite the cave, marked by a cross, where St. Saba began his ascetic life in 478 CE. The bones of St. Saba are on display in the main church. Women are strictly forbidden to enter and can only view the chapels and buildings from a nearby tower; men must wear long pants and sleeves. To get inside, pull the chain on the large blue door. Once inside, you'll be given a five-minute tour in English by one of the monks (ask for Father Lucas—he's from California). The monks occasionally ignore the doorbell on Sundays and late afternoons; try to arrive early. (Open daily 7-11am and 1:30-6pm; in winter until 5pm. Free, but a donation is expected.) You need to hire a private taxi from Bethlehem to get here (16km; about NIS76 round-trip, including waiting time).

HERODION

Eleven kilometers east of Bethlehem, the curious flat-topped hill of Herodion arrests the eye with its startling silhouette. Built by the eponymous Herod as a summer palace, Herodion boasts a unique circular design—its round buildings were surrounded by round towers. Herod's trademark swimming pools and bathhouses have all been carefully dug up, and Nathan the caretaker can answer questions (site open daily 8am-5pm; NIS16, with ISIC NIS12). A round-trip private taxi ride from Jerusalem should cost NIS50 (NIS30 from Bethlehem), including waiting time. At press time, no buses served Herodion.

■ Jericho أريحا

The first city to fly the Palestinian flag and the headquarters of the Palestinian Authority, Jericho vibrates with ground-breaking activity. Streets strewn with banners, flags, and portraits of Yassir Arafat convey a feeling of pride and optimism. Settled 10,000 years ago, Jericho is believed to be the world's oldest city. Excavations are extensive, but the ruins themselves aren't that spectacular (after all, the walls are famous for having tumbled down). After Joshua destroyed the city with a blow of his trumpet (Joshua 2-6), Jericho remained in shambles for centuries. The oasis town made a reluctant comeback under the Romans, Crusaders, and Mamluks, but it never became anything more than a sleepy palm grove village in the desert. The population skyrocketed after 1967, when thousands of Palestinian refugees fled here from Israel. After it gained autonomy, the refugee camps were proudly replaced by apartment buildings and the standard of living drastically improved.

ORIENTATION AND PRACTICAL INFORMATION

Forty kilometers east of Jerusalem, Jericho is on the road to Amman, at the junction of the highway to the Galilee. For information on crossing to **Jordan,** see p. 438. The quickest and most reliable way to get to Jericho is by *service* taxi. Often, travelers will have to take a *service* to **Bethany** and switch there to get to Jericho (NIS2 to Bethany, NIS6 to Jericho from Bethany). They leave from East Jerusalem, at the parking lot across from Damascus Gate, and drop off at the central square in front of Jericho's municipality building. There is no schedule—*service* leave when full. Inquire at East Jerusalem's Arab bus station about bus #28. It used to run to Jericho and, depending on demand and the border crossing situation, may do so in the future. To return to Jerusalem, catch a taxi heading to Abu Dees (NIS5). From there switch into a taxi with a yellow license plate and go to Damascus Gate (NIS2). (See **West Bank: Coming and Going,** p. 438.)

> **Tourist Information Office:** Run by the PA and located in the old city (tel. 992 29 35). Free map. All services also available in the Municipality building in the town center. Open Sat.-Thurs. 7:30am-2pm.
>
> **Currency Exchange: Cairo Amman Bank** (tel. 992 36 27; fax 992 35 80), in the main square. Open Sat.-Wed. 8am-11:30pm and 4-6pm, Thurs. 8:30-11:30am.
>
> **Car Rental: Orabi Rent-a-car** (tel. 992 32 30), on Jerusalem Rd., across from the Pension. Starts at US$30 per day—but the blue license plates might not be the best thing to have while touring Israel.
>
> **Bike Rental:** A great way to see the sights in Jericho. **Zahi Abu Samman's Bicycle Shop** (tel. 992 36 25), in the central square east of the municipality building, rents functional, balloon-tire bombers (NIS3 per hr.). Open Sat.-Thurs. 7am-11pm, Fri. 7am-1pm. Bring lots of water and bike on the left side of the road.
>
> **Pharmacy: Arabi** (tel. 992 23 25), Ein as-Sultan St., by Hisham's Palace Hotel. Open Sat.-Thurs. 8am-10pm.
>
> **Red Cross:** tel. 992 28 48, on Ein as-Sultan St. across from Hisham's Palace Hotel. Open Mon.-Tues. and Thurs. 8am-2pm.
>
> **Hospital: Jericho Government Hospital** (tel. 992 24 06 or 25 73), on Al Quds St. near the square.

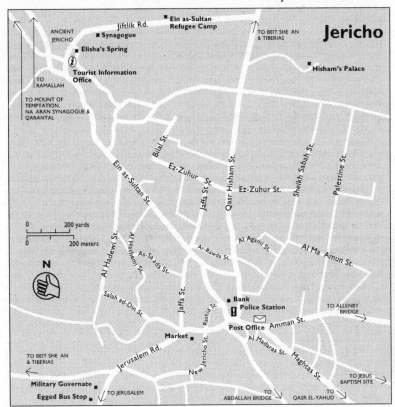

ANCIENT
JERICHO

Jiftlik Rd.

■ Synagogue

■ Ein as-Sultan
Refugee Camp

■ Elisha's Spring

ⓘ

Tourist Information
Office

TO
RAMALLAH

TO MOUNT OF
TEMPTATION,
NA ARAN SYNAGOGUE &
QARANTAL

Bilal St.

Ez-Zuhur St.

Ein as-Sultan St.

Jaffa St.

Qasr Hisham St.

Ez-Zuhur St.

Sheikh Sabah St.

Palestine St.

0   200 yards
0   200 meters

N

Al Hadewi St.

Al Hashemi St.

As-Sa'ada St.

Ar-Rawda St.

Al Agami St.

Al Ma Amun St.

Salah ad-Din St.

Jaffa St.

Rashid St.

■ Bank
■ Police Station

Post Office

Amman St.

TO ALLENBY
BRIDGE

Market ■

New Jericho St.

Jerusalem Rd.

Al Madaras St.

Maghtas St.

TO BEIT SHE AN
& TIBERIAS

TO JESUS
BAPTISM SITE

Military Governate ■

Egged Bus Stop ■

TO JERUSALEM

TO
ABDALLAH BRIDGE

TO
QASR EL-YAHUD

WEST BANK

Police: tel. 992 25 21. Next to the bank.

Post Office: tel. 992 25 74' fax 992 36 09. Down Amman St. from the police station. You can buy beautiful Palestinian National Authority (PNA) **stamps** starting at 10ag. For the time being, they're only good for West Bank- and Gaza-bound mail but they make great souvenirs. Open Sat.-Thurs. 8am-2:30pm.

Telephone Code: 02.

ACCOMMODATIONS AND FOOD

As of now, travelers have three options, and budget travelers have two. Run by kind Ibrahim, **New Jericho Pension** (tel. 992 22 15) is located across from the New Jericho mosque on Jerusalem Rd., close to the city center. Rooms have carved wooden beds with spring mattresses; the roomy common area has a TV and a radio (flexible check-out and prices: singles US$13-15; doubles US$20; triples US$30). **Hisham's Palace Hotel** (tel. 992 21 56), close to the city center on Ein as-Sultan St., doesn't have the newest facilities in town. Despite a nice outdoor porch, this is a definite second to New Jericho. The rooms have balconies, fans, and extremely bright lights (check-out noon; curfew midnight; singles NIS40, with bath NIS100; doubles NIS80).

There is such a thing as a free lunch in the West Bank; locals who befriend you may well bring you home to dine on chicken while groups of kids look on curiously. If not, many cheap n' tasty restaurants cluster around the city center, serving the usual falafel, *shawerma, kabab, shishlik,* and chicken. Most places have Arabic signs with a simple English name, "Restaurant." Falafel should be about NIS2, *shawerma* NIS5. For a pricier, all-you-can-eat experience, head to the **Maxim Restaurant,** down Ein as-Sultan St. They offer great selection of salads (NIS16) and meats (NIS24), and let you eat until you *are* the hummus (open daily 7am-midnight).

SIGHTS

Jericho's most popular sights, Hisham's Palace and ancient Jericho, lie on the out-skirts of town. It's best to visit **Hisham's Palace** (tel. 992 25 22) first, since a cluster of restaurants and a cooling spring near the ancient city can provide a pleasant rest stop after your tour. To reach the palace, follow the signs along Qasr Hisham St. and head north 3km from the eastern side of Jericho's main square. Coming from ancient Jeri-cho, head east on Jiftlik Rd., past the Synagogue and the **Ein as-Sultan refugee camp.** After 1.5km, turn right on the road back to Jericho; the turn-off to Hisham's Palace appears almost immediately on your left.

Begun in 724 CE and completed in 743, Hisham's Palace was ravaged only four years later by an earthquake. Known as Khirbet al-Mafjar in Arabic, the palace was designed for the Umayyad Caliph Hisham as a winter retreat from Damascus. The extensive ruins here are a jaw-dropping example of early Islamic architecture. The window in the courtyard, the site's most renowned feature, is in the shape of the six-pointed Umayyad star. A beautifully preserved mosaic depicts a sinister tableau in which foxes lick their chops as they watch naive gazelles frolic in the shade of the Tree of Life (open daily 8am-5pm; NIS8, NIS6 for students with ISIC).

To get to ancient Jericho from the city center, follow Ein as-Sultan St. to its end. From Hisham's Palace 2km away, turn right onto the road that runs past the Palace, then take a left at the end. Follow the "Tel Jericho" signs. On the way is the **6th-cen-tury synagogue**, featuring an expansive mosaic floor, a *menorah*, a *shofar* (ram's horn), a *lulav* (palm branch), and the inscription *Shalom al Yisrael*: peace be upon Israel. As part of extensive preliminary agreements, the PA promised to watch over this synagogue, still a functioning *yeshiva*. A little past the synagogue towards Ancient Jericho, **Elisha's Spring** is on the left. Papayas, grapes, oranges, bananas, and mint thrive behind the spring. The old city is across the street.

Ancient Jericho (info. tel. 992 29 09), thought to be the oldest city in the world (as opposed to Damascus, the oldest continually inhabited city), is now a heap of ruined walls. Called **Tel as-Sultan**, the mound contains layer upon layer of garbage from ancient (and modern) cities. The oldest fortifications, 12m down, are 7000 years old. Some of the finds date from the early Neolithic period, leading archaeologists to sus-pect that Jericho was inhabited as early as the eighth millennium BCE. A limited amount of excavation has exposed many levels of ancient walls, some of them 3.5m thick and 5.5m high. Your imagination will have to substitute for visible splendor at this site, which is distinctly unphotogenic save for its great view (open daily 8am-5pm; NIS8, students NIS6 with ISIC).

An imposing Greek Orthodox **monastery** stands on the edge of a cliff among the mountains west of Jericho; the peak is believed to be the New Testament's Mount of Temptation. The complex of buildings stands before a grotto, said to be the spot where Jesus fasted for 40 days and 40 nights after his baptism (Matthew 4:1-11). Six Greek monks now live in the monastery, built in 1895. They can point out the rock where Jesus was tempted by the devil and served by angels. The summit of the moun-tain, named **Qarantal** after the Latin word for "forty," is also a pedestal for the Macca-bean **Castle of Dok**, beside which lie the remains of a 4th-century Christian chapel (monastery open daily 9am-2pm and 3-5pm; modest dress required).

Taxis will take you on a loop of the sights for about NIS30-50; agree in advance. One-way fare to the Old City is NIS5.

■ Near Jericho

The road from Jerusalem to Jericho slices through harsh desert landscape. About 8km from Jericho, the 13th-century **Mosque of Nabi Mussa** stands on a hill in a sea of sand, a short distance from the road. This spot is revered throughout the Muslim world as the grave of the prophet Moses, and many Muslims yearn to be buried by his side. Islamic tradition holds that God carried the bones of the prophet here for the faithful to come and pay their respects. The tomb is said to have special powers—run your hands over the velvet cloth of Mussa's Tomb while making a wish and see for yourself. Across from the tomb, stairs lead upwards into a minaret with incredible views of the surrounding Judean desert. Ask the souvenir-selling boys to let you in if the door is wired shut. The only way to visit is by car or taxi (a taxi from Jericho shouldn't cost more than NIS40).

WADI QELT

Threading 28km between imperious limestone cliffs and undulating ridges of bone-white chalk, the three fresh-water springs of Wadi Qelt nourish wildlife and lush greenery. A string of murders, presumably political, have taken place here in the past several years, and the advice at press time was a resounding "Why risk it?" Inquire at the MTIO or SPNI to determine the relative safety of hiking in the area. SPNI offers one-day tours focusing on both natural and artificial attractions in the *wadi* (US$48). The pace may be slower than you'd like, but hiking with a group is much safer.

The most interesting and accessible section of the *wadi* extends from the spring of **Ein Qelt,** past the 6th-century St. George's Monastery, and down into Jericho, 10km east. The trek takes about four hours. The best place to start is at the turn-off from the Jerusalem-Jericho highway about 9km west of Jericho, marked by the orange sign for "St. George's Monastery." Egged bus #173 (6 per day, 7am-10pm, NIS11) goes from the bus stop across from the central bus station in Jerusalem to the Mitzpeh Jericho turn-off. Another possibility is to take a *service* from East Jerusalem to Jericho (NIS8) and catch a cab from there. The trip from Jerusalem takes about an hour. If you're driving, it's possible to skip the hike and follow signs most of the way to St. George's.

St. George's Monastery dates from the 5th or 6th century CE. The floor of St. George's Church is decorated with Byzantine mosaics; look for the likeness of a two-headed eagle, the Byzantine symbol of power. The neighboring St. John's Church houses a spooky collection of skulls and bones of monks who were slaughtered when the Persians swept through the valley in 614 CE. The Greek Orthodox monks who maintain the monastery can refill your canteen for the rest of the journey into Jericho. (Open summer Mon.-Sat. 8am-1pm and 3-5pm; winter 8am-1pm and 3-4pm. Modest dress required, modest donation desired.)

On the way to Jericho from St. George's, the ruins of **Tel Abu Alayia** are on your right. The palaces here, used by the Hasmoneans and later by King Herod, have decorated walls, nearby bath houses, and pools.

■ Ramallah رام الله

Perched 900m above sea level, Ramallah is famous for its cool, pleasant mountain air. Before 1967, the then-prosperous town was known as the "Bride of Palestine," a summer haven for Arabs from Jordan, Lebanon, and the Gulf region. With vacationers long gone, Ramallah and nearby Birzeit University assumed a leading role in the *intifada*. When expansion of Palestinian self-rule finally comes about, Ramallah will replace Gaza as the administrative hub of the Palestinian Authority during the interim period. It already houses several important Palestinian Authority offices, including the Ministries of Transportation and Education. Ramallah's prominence has also led to the building of new roads, the cleaning up of *intifada* graffiti, and the restoration of the town's traditional character.

Orientation and Practical Information Palestinians in Ramallah live up to the cliché about Arab hospitality. Visibly confused tourists are often surrounded by people offering countless solutions—the absence of street signs will put you in this position faster than you think. Use the opportunity to strike up a conversation and gain insight into the Palestinian perspective on the latest events. The town is among the least conservative in the West Bank; women can go in pants and a t-shirt. Due to its location 16km north of Jerusalem, Ramallah has become a transportation hub. You can go from here to most West Bank towns by direct **service.** From Jerusalem, take a *service* (20min., NIS2.50) from outside Damascus Gate, or **Arab bus #18** from the station on Nablus Rd., just north of Damascus Gate (40min., NIS1.50). Buses to Jerusalem leave from Jaffa Rd. in Ramallah, just off **Manara Square,** the main traffic circle. The last bus leaves around 5pm, the last *service* around 6pm. Most of the town is accessible from Manara Square, where the *service* stop, and which also serves as a central meeting point for Ramallah's streets.

Currency exchange places can be found on nearly every street and in Manara Sq. Cash may be withdrawn with a MasterCard at the **Jordan National Bank,** a ten-minute walk down the road to Jerusalem. The **police station** is on An-Nahda St., and you can buy beautiful Palestinian stamps (good for personal collecting and for sending letters to Gaza) at the **post office,** off of Main St. The **Ramallah General Hospital** (tel. 995 65 61 or 62) may be more accessible than Ramallah's **pharmacies,** which close either before or at 8pm.

Accommodations and Food The construction industry in Ramallah is doing well, and building contractors are not the only beneficiaries—travelers to the town will be pleased with all the hotels available. One of the best deals is the **Al-Wihdeh Hotel,** 26 Main St. (tel. 995 64 52), which provides accommodations with TV, telephone, and private bathroom in the center of town for NIS80-150. Just off Main St., **Angelo's** flings pizza into the air and onto the plates of plucky budget travelers (NIS17-40); their garlic bread is a local favorite. The **Miami Pension Hotel** (tel. 995 68 08), on Jaffa St., sports an attached Italian restaurant with a fairly good selection of vegetarian meals (come for the spaghetti, stay for singles NIS120; doubles NIS150). If the Miami Pension Restaurant is more Milan than Miami, then **Flamingo's,** off of Main St., has eclectic menu that brings a taste of Mexico to Ramallah. Joining expats Goldstein and Sandomirsky in their love for *chimichangas* (NIS32) and *chili con carne* (NIS8) will make you yearn to travel with their recent masterwork, *Let's Go: Mexico 1998.* Flamingo's restaurant and bar serves up *fattoush* (NIS10) and fried chicken (NIS22) with equal ease. Snack on peanuts from the bar's large oil drum, and add your shells to the floor while you soak up the neon and the MTV. As always, the cheapest eats can be found on the streets—good falafel, *shawerma,* and an excellent variety of Arabic sweets abound. For a real treat, stop by **Rukab's Ice Cream,** 22 Main St., which is to ice cream what *Let's Go* is to travel guides (it's good).

Sights and Entertainment The **Palestinian Folklore Museum** (tel. 995 41 23 or 68 76), in Al-Bireh, seeks to "revive Palestinian folklore and preserve it from theft or loss," and exhibits traditional costumes, handicrafts, and a two rooms of a Palestinian house with a minimum of the expected propoganda. The **M. Sayem Gallery,** on the third street on the right off Radio Blvd., displays Palestinian artwork in its space underneath the Ministry of Culture offices. The **As-Siraj Theatre** (tel. 995 70 37) and the **Ashtar Theatre** (tel. 82 72 18 or 51 22 85) produce performing arts and dance irregularly—call or ask around town for details. Ramallah and Birzeit University have recently gone **web crazy.** The site at http://www.birzeit.edu/ramallah offers information on Ramallah's present and past, including an online travel guide, and links to many of the establishments listed above.

■ Near Ramallah

BEITIN (BETHEL) بيتين

Beitin (Bethel), 5km northeast of Ramallah on the road to Nablus, is thought to be the place where Jacob lay down to sleep and dreamed of a ladder ascending to heaven traversed by angels. Upon awakening, Jacob built an altar and named the spot Beit-El, "House of God" (Genesis 28:12-19).

Until the agreement on Palestinian self-rule, Beitin was the headquarters of the Israeli civilian administration that governed the West Bank. The administration center itself is of no interest to tourists, but a visit to the nearby Jewish settlement of Beit-El may be worthwhile. Surrounded by barbed wire and guarded by army patrols, the settlement provides a glimpse into the life of a West Bank Jewish settlement. Most of the working population commutes to Jerusalem, but there are also a few cottage industries, including a workshop that manufactures *tefillin* (phylacteries). To get here from Ramallah you can walk, take a taxi, or ride the bus going to Nablus.

BIRZEIT بيرزيت

Twelve kilometers northwest of Ramallah is the largest and most important university in the West Bank. **Birzeit University**'s 2500 students have a history of vocal opposition to the Israeli occupation; throughout the occupation, the university was often shut down by the Israeli army. In the first years of the *intifada*, Israeli authorities closed it altogether; it wasn't reopened until April 1992. No buses reach Birzeit. To get here from outside Ramallah, take a **service** and ask the driver to let you off at Birzeit taxi in Ramallah (on Radio Blvd., just off Manara Sq.)—the taxi ride from there to Birzeit is NIS2. The old campus is next to the taxi office; the new campus lies 2km out of town on the road back to Ramallah.

Today, Birzeit remains a vital presence. The university takes pride in its history and its strong leadership position in the West Bank, and has even developed an internet training program and an extensive **web site** (http://www.birzeit.edu). The web site offers a wealth of information about Birzeit and includes an online travel guide to Ramallah (see above). Foreign students can study at the university through their Palestinian and Arab Studies (PAS) Program (for details, see **Alternatives to Tourism,** p. 32). Travelers can attend some of Birzeit's artistic performances, which have recently included an international troupe of flamenco dancers and a Mormon orchestra.

▓ Nablus نابلس

Beautiful, serene mountains surround the town of Nablus, founded by Titus near the site of Biblical Shekhem in 72 CE as the "New City" of Flavia Neapolis. Enjoy the serenity if you can; the city is not called *Jabal an-Nar* (Hill of Fire in Arabic) for nothing. Home to some of Palestine's oldest and wealthiest families, Nablus has a tradition of impassioned resistance to foreign occupation. Its citizens fought the Turks, the British, and the Jordanians, and were wholly consumed by the *intifada*. Now that the city is at last under Palestinian rule, its residents are zealously proud. Nablus is the largest city in the West Bank (not counting East Jerusalem), an industrial center, and home to the West Bank's second-largest university, An-Najah. Besides its predominantly Muslim population, Nablus is home to 500 Samaritan Jews, about two-thirds of the world's total Samaritan population (see **Other Faiths,** p. 70).

Nablus is a very conservative town; dress modestly. After introductions, it is not uncommon for Palestinians to invite you to their homes. Perhaps the most rewarding way to spend your time in this industrial hub is to accept the residents' hospitality.

Nablus lies 63km north of Jerusalem, 46km north of Ramallah, and 50km south of Nazareth. Take one of the **Tamini Co. buses** from Nablus Rd. in Jerusalem (irregular schedule, 1½-2hr., NIS7). **Service taxis** to and from Jerusalem are a safer bet; you will be dropped off in the center of town, after changing cars in Ramallah.

From the center of Nablus, wander south past a pleasant fresh fruit market (next to Nablus circle) and into the crowded streets and passageways of the **market,** overflowing with Nablus merchants, Palestinian customers, and tea-sipping onlookers. Try a piece of the famous, extraordinarily-rich *kinafeh nablusiyya.* Nablus churns out countless tray-fulls of this cheese concoction, which is topped with sweet orange flakes and syrup. Although you'll feel more comfortable if you're with a guide, stopping to chat and swap stories often dissipates awkwardness.

Throughout the market you'll continue to see the smiling image of **Zafer Masri,** Nablus's Palestinian former mayor. A wreathed monument next to the municipality building marks the spot where he was slain in the winter of 1986. Many hold that his assassins were Palestinians who resented his alleged chumminess with Israeli leadership; the killing still haunts Nablusians.

To the east, 3km from the town center, lie two famous but unspectacular pilgrimage sites. **Jacob's Well,** now enclosed within a subterranean Greek Orthodox shrine, is believed to date from the time when Jacob bought the surrounding land to pitch his tents (Genesis 33:18-19). A few hundred meters north of the well lies the **Tomb of Joseph.** According to the Book of Joshua, the bones of Joseph were carried out of Egypt and buried in Shekhem (Joshua 24:32). (No shorts or bare shoulders permitted; *service* run to both sites regularly from the town center.)

■ Near Nablus

MOUNT GERIZIM

This tree-covered slope southeast of Nablus features a terrific view of the Shomron Valley. Since the 4th century BCE, it has been the holy mountain of the Samaritans, who revere it as the spot where Abraham prepared to sacrifice his son Isaac and where the original Ten Commandments are buried. The Samaritans, an Israelite sect who were excommunicated in Biblical times, are distinguished by their literal interpretation of certain scriptures (see **Other Faiths,** p. 69). The Samaritan observance of Passover includes the sacrifice of sheep atop Mt. Gerizim. Tourist **buses** from Jerusalem and Tel Aviv bring visitors to witness the bloody rite. The hike up the mountain is arduous, but taxis make the climb for about NIS20.

SABASTIYA سبستية

An array of Israelite, Hellenistic, and Roman ruins crowd an unassuming hill 11km northwest of Nablus. The strategic peak on which the ruins lie was first settled by Omri, King of Israel, in the 9th century BCE as the city of **Shomron** (Samaria), and served as the capital of the Israelite kingdom until the Assyrian invasion of the 8th century BCE. Under Herod, the city was made into the showpiece of the Holy Land to win the favor of the Roman Emperor.

The ruins are just above the present-day Arab village of **Sabastiya.** Unfortunately, most of the ancient splendor is long gone. At the top of the hill lie the remnants of Israelite and Hellenistic walls, a Roman acropolis, and the bases of columns built for the **Temple of Augustus.** Watch your step—the narrow 1.5km path encircling the ruins is treacherous. *Service* taxis to Sabastiya are available from Nablus.

WEST BANK

JORDAN الأردن

US$1=0.71 Jordanian Dinar (JD)	JD1=US$1.41
CDN$1=JD0.51	JD1=CDN$1.96
UK£1=JD1.13	JD1=UK£0.88
IR£1=JD1.04	JD1=IR£0.99
AUS$1=JD0.53	JD1=AUS$1.89
NZ$1=JD0.46	JD1=NZ$2.18
SAR1=JD0.15	JD1=SAR6.62
E£1 (Egyptian Pound) =JD.21	JD1=E£4.80
NIS1 (New Israeli Shekel) =JD0.20	JD1=NIS4.99
S£100 (Syrian Pounds) =JD1.7	JD1=S£59.10

> For important information on travel in general and some specifics on Jordan, see the **Essentials** section of this book. Jordan's **international phone code** is 962.

Take it from **King Hussein**: "Jordan is a beautiful country: wild, with limitless deserts where the Bedouin roam, but the mountains of the north are clothed in green forests, and where the Jordan River flows it is fertile and warm in winter. Jordan has a strange, haunting beauty and a sense of timelessness. Dotted with the ruins of empires once great, it is the last resort of yesterday in the world of tomorrow."

The **Hashemite Kingdom of Jordan** is where John the Baptist baptized Jesus in the Jordan River, and where desert trade routes flourished during the Roman Empire. Later a neglected chunk of the Ottoman *vilayet* of Syria, modern Jordan (*Al Urdun*) was created by the stroke of a British pen; former Prime Minister Kamel Abu Jaber wrote of the event, "now a giant mixing machine called the West has thrown us together, and here we are loving it and hating it, constantly adjusting and readjusting..." The kingdom today finds itself sandwiched between some of the rougher players in a rough neighborhood: Saudi Arabia, Israel, Syria, and Iraq. There are internal troubles too; the memory of Black September 1970, a brutal suppression by Jordanian authorities of Palestinian political activity, has not disappeared. The more recent trauma of the Gulf War, in which Jordan supported Saddam Hussein, brought a slew of immigrants from the Gulf and Iraq. The 1994 peace treaty with Israel, signed by King Hussein and Israeli Prime Minister Yitzhak Rabin, has placed Jordan in a more favorable light in the West.

In addition to engrossing, hospitable people, Jordan has another bonus for the plucky budget traveler. Until recently, even the most awe-inspiring sight was relatively undiscovered. Despite growth in tourism over the past few years, most of the country and its sites of interest are uncommercialized (with the exception of **Petra**). Jordan is not a land of shrink-wrapped, for-tourists'-eyes-only sights and experiences. The Bedouin at **Wadi Rum** are genuine; close your eyes there and you could be in any century.

ONCE THERE

■ Entry

Upon arrival at **Queen Alia International Airport,** you will be welcomed by passport control, where visas can be purchased on the spot. Visas for American citizens, valid for one month but renewable at any police station, cost JD16 (for more information, see **Amman: Airport,** p. 472). A **Housing Bank** and a **Jordan Bank** (ask the customs officials to point them out) in the airport lobby will satisfy your every pecuniary desire. A 24-hour bus runs to Abdali Station every 30 minutes (JD1). Taxis to Amman are priced at a fixed JD10 (two pieces of luggage free, each additional piece 200fils).

■ Getting Around

Most visitors to Jordan stay long enough to see the major sites at Petra and Jerash, which is not long enough to master the transportation system. Organized **bus tours** and private **taxis** can cost JD4 to JD50 per day. The country has a train system, but only for freight. The only reliable long-distance bus company, **JETT,** has a limited number of routes. **Shared taxis** (called *service* and pronounced "ser-VEES") and **minibuses** shuttle between all cities, towns, and villages, although intercity *service* are not as common as they once were. Hitchhiking is a common practice among Jordanians. *Let's Go,* however, does not recommend hitchhiking.

Taxis Private taxis, useful mainly in Amman (where you may have to wait a long time for an empty one), are yellow and conveniently have "taxi" written on them. Jordanian taxi drivers take their horns seriously, their fares a little less so, and the law not in the least; insist that the driver use the meter. The starting fare is 150fils. Drivers may also charge extra (illegally) for large amounts of baggage. Women should always sit in the back seat, whether or not there are other passengers. Men, on the other hand, should always sit in the front seat when alone. It's considered rude to give exact change; drivers expect you to round up from the meter fare.

    Service are shared taxis, usually white or gray Mercedes with a white sign written in Arabic on their roofs (أجرة). The front doors have the route and number on them (again in Arabic numerals only). *Service* can be hailed en route. Payment takes place whenever the rider feels like it, traditionally just as the cab is negotiating an insanely sharp curve on two wheels. Travel within downtown Amman is generally easier on foot, but *service* are invaluable for interdistrict travel. There are specific *service* routes in Amman and between the central transport terminals in the larger cities. Within Amman, *service* cost 70 to 120fils; a ride from Amman to Aqaba goes for JD4. *Service* rarely run after 7pm, and the long-distance ones may make only two or three trips per day. Schedules are unpredictable—*service* leave when the car fills up. If you get into one alone and want to leave before it's full, you'll have to pay for the empty seats. (For routes and rates, see specific towns.)

Buses Public buses supplement the *service* taxis in Amman. The crown prince has a government-granted monopoly on intercity bus service, so the **Jordan Express Tourist Transport (JETT)** is your only bus option. However sparse, these buses cover the most popular routes, and private minibuses travel to more remote areas. Regular service on JETT buses includes daily trips from Amman to Aqaba, Petra, Ma'an, the King Hussein/Allenby Bridge, Damascus, and Cairo via Aqaba and the Sinai. (For details on schedules and stations, see **Practical Information,** p. 471) JETT (info. tel. (06) 664 146) also sponsors tours to Jerash, Madaba, Petra, Ajlun, and the Desert Castles. The **Arabella** (tel. (06) 638 110) and **Hijazi** (tel. (06) 651 341) bus companies travel to Jerash and Irbid. **Minibuses** are also used for intercity transport.

    Bus fares are slightly lower than *service* rates, but buses are slower and their routes are sometimes confusing. The JETT luxury coaches cost about 20% more than regular buses and they are air-conditioned. Those running from Amman to Aqaba come with hosts, professional wrestling videos, and highly dramatic Egyptian movies. Do note, however, that you will be charged for each and every bottle of Pepsi you drink, regardless of how generous the attendant seems when handing you one. They ensure that you will drink at least one by forbidding carry-on food and drink. The buses depart more or less on schedule, and booking ahead is often necessary. Most towns have one main terminal shared by intercity buses and *service*; Amman and Irbid have several. In Amman, most buses follow the pattern of *service*, with traffic to the north leaving from Abdali Station and buses to the south leaving from Wahdat Station. However, there are minibuses to Salt and Madaba which depart from both stations.

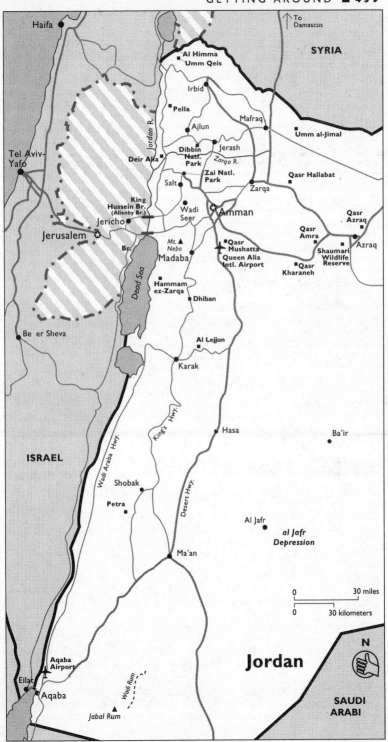

SYRIA

To Damascus

Haifa

Al Himma
Umm Qeis

Irbid

Pella

Mafraq

Umm al-Jimal

Ajlun

Jordan R.

Dibbin
Natl.
Park

Jerash

Deir Alla

Zarqa R.

Qasr Hallabat

Tel Aviv-
Yafo

Salt

Zai Natl.
Park

Zarqa

King
Hussein Br.
(Allenby Br.)

Wadi
Seer

Amman

Qasr
Azraq

Jericho

Mt.
Nebo

Qasr
Mushatta

Qasr
Amra

Azraq

Jerusalem

Br.

Queen Alia
Intl. Airport

Shaumari
Wildlife
Reserve

Madaba

Dead Sea

Hammam
ez-Zarqa

Qasr
Kharaneh

Dhiban

Be er Sheva

Al Lejjun

Karak

JORDAN

Hasa

Ba'ir

ISRAEL

King's Hwy.

Wadi Araba Hwy.

Shobak

Petra

Desert Hwy.

Al Jafr

al Jafr
Depression

Ma'an

0   30 miles
0   30 kilometers

Aqaba
Airport

Jordan

N

Eilat

Aqaba

Wadi Rum

Jabal Rum

SAUDI
ARABI

Cars Some of Jordan's greatest attractions are not served by the public transportation system. For groups of four to six, renting a car can be an affordable and efficient way to reach less accessible sights. With a car, for example, the round-trip excursion to Azraq and the Desert Castles can be done in eight to twelve hours. The astoundingly beautiful Kings' Highway route, barely served by other modes of transportation, can be seen from a private car in another full day. Some rental agencies will even let you pick a car up in one city and drop it off in another; ask around.

If you can't split the costs, car rental in Jordan will break your budget. Most rental agencies charge JD25-35 per day, including insurance, plus 45-55fils per km. Unlimited mileage deals are cheaper (JD20-25 per day), but you must rent the car for at least a week. (For details, see **Amman** and **Aqaba: Practical Information,** p. 471 and p. 500.) Always ask whether the car has a fire extinguisher—no joke. Desert heat and police regulations require them. The four-wheel drive cars that companies encourage are unnecessary except to reach Qasr at-Touba, south of Azraq, and Wadi Rum, where a light four-wheeler is absolutely necessary to get off the beaten path. Ordinary cars will be adequate everywhere else.

Gas costs about 250fils per liter. The law requires seatbelts to be worn (JD5 fine for naughtiness), and speeding tickets can reach an exorbitant JD50. Many rental companies require an International Driver's License but many do not, so call ahead to ask (see **Driving Permits and Insurance,** p. 12). **Road accidents** should be reported to the traffic police (tel. (06) 896 390); for an **ambulance** call 193.

Hitchhiking *Service* and minibuses are cheap enough to make hitching unnecessary. In remote areas such as along the King's Highway, *service* and minibuses are less frequent. For those feckless die-hards who insist on hitching, rides between small towns are reportedly easy to come by. Even short waits in the sun can be dangerous, so if you want to hitch, bring lots of water and cover your head.

Those who try hitchhiking within a city (Amman, Irbid, Jerash, Ajlun) will be pestered by empty taxis' horns as they careen by. The steady stream of trucks serving the port facilities in the south of the country offers hitching opportunities; many drivers are eager for company on their long trans-Jordan hauls. To flag down an approaching vehicle, travelers stick their arms out with their palms facing the ground. *Let's Go* does not recommend hitchhiking. and hitching along the Wadi Araba highway is forbidden to all.

■ Money Matters

Currency and Exchange The **Jordanian dinar (JD)** is a decimal currency, divided into 1000fils. Prices are always labeled in fils, but the usual spoken practice is to call 10fils a *piaster* (pt). Thus, 500fils will be written as 500fils, but referred to as 50pt. A *piaster* is also called a *qirsh*. Bills come in denominations of JD100, 50, 20, 10, 5, 1, and 500fils. Coins are silver for 250fils, 100, 50, and 25, and copper for 10 and 5. (Two separate, nonidentical mints are currently in circulation; remember that the 100fils piece is equal to the 10-*qirsh* piece). Prices are usually written in Arabic numerals, not in standard Western form, although the currency itself is marked with Western-friendly numbers. For help with Arabic numerals, see the handy-dandy **Language Glossary,** p. 574. It is useful to carry small denominations because people may be reluctant to make change.

Currency exchange is easy to find in the larger cities, but more difficult elsewhere. Bank exchange hours are regularly 8:30am to 12:30pm, with some banks opening from 4 to 5:30pm as well. Branches of the national **Housing Bank** (Bank al-Iskan) are the best bets outside Amman; there are also exchange offices located in many of the *souqs*. Queen Alia International Airport has exchange facilities for incoming passengers. A passport is required to change traveler's checks. Credit cards are only accepted in expensive hotels. **ATMs** in Jordan work only for local bank cards.

Tipping A tip of 10% is expected in restaurants, unless "service included" appears on the menu. Servers at fancier establishments expect a little something even if service is "included." Taxi drivers do not expect tips, but will round off fares to their advantage. Members of large sight-seeing groups tip the bus driver about 500fils. A small tip (500fils) to room cleaners and porters in hotels is appropriate.

Business Hours Most stores and offices are open from 8 or 9am until 1pm, take a siesta, and then reopen around 3 or 4pm. In the larger cities, the stores may remain open all afternoon. On an especially hot summer day anywhere in Jordan, stores may close early. In Amman, retail stores usually close around 8 or 9pm. In posh areas such as Abdoun, stores stay open as late as 11pm. Banks and government offices retain only a skeleton crew in the afternoon; if you care about getting something done, do it in the morning. Government offices open Sat.-Thurs. 8am-2pm (in practice, usually 1:30); during Ramadan 9:30am-2:30pm.

■ Accommodations

Though the Jordanian government has gone to great lengths to establish adequate, regulated accommodations for tourists, budget travelers have been left out for the most part. Regulated tourist hotels charge prices as high as Jordan's mid-summer temperatures. Jordan has no Hostelling International hostels.

Hotels Bargaining is difficult, but hotel owners may be more flexible in the off-season winter months. Fall and spring are the busiest times throughout Jordan, though sunny Aqaba sees the most activity during the winter and spring seasons. Single women may feel uncomfortable at some of the cheaper hotels and may, on occasion, not be admitted. Jordanian law bars unmarried couples from sharing a room; for foreign travelers, a "don't ask, don't tell" policy seems to be the norm. Hotels in Jordan are inspected annually and rated by the government according to a five-star system. The Ministry of Tourism provides a comprehensive list of classified hotels and their prices (available at the Ministry's Public Relations Office in Amman; see **Amman Practical Information,** p. 471), although the list has few low-cost options. Most budget hotels do not abide by government prices; "official" prices are listed in Arabic and cheaper ones in English.

Most hotels add a 10% service charge; ask whether it's included in the quoted price. If business is slow, use this surcharge as a bargaining chip. Some of the cheaper places charge an extra 500fils for a hot shower. Many have modern toilets, though several still use the old fashioned hole-in-the-ground technology. Hotel owners may ask to hold your passport for the length of your stay, but they will usually return it after a night if you need to change money.

Camping Camping is an option at government-approved sites, although facilities are virtually nonexistent. Approved areas include the beach north of Aqaba, Dibbin National Park, and the Dana Wildlands Campsite. Contact the Royal Society for the Conservation of Nature, P.O. Box 6354, Amman 11183 (tel. (06) 837 931 or 932; fax 847 411). Camping is allowed next to most of the government **Rest Houses** (free or JD1-2 per person per night, plus 10% tax). You'll need a light sleeping bag or blanket for the cool summer nights, and winter evenings can bring freezing temperatures.

You can spend a night with the Bedouin, whom you'll find on the outskirts of most towns and scattered around the desert. Tea, Arabic coffee, and meals are always included in an invitation, although showers and toilets are rare. While the Bedouin won't accept money, a pack of cigarettes is always appreciated.

■ Keeping in Touch

Poste Restante operates at the downtown post office in Amman and in the larger cities. **American Express** offices, located in Amman and Aqaba, also hold mail. **Post-**

age stamps may be purchased from 7am to 7pm at the downtown post office in Amman and during regular business hours at other post offices. An **air mail letter** to North America costs 400fils, an aerogramme or postcard is 300fils; the cost to Europe is 300fils and 150fils, respectively. Mail from Jordan to North America and Europe takes one to two weeks if you're lucky; some letters never make it. International **Express Mail Service (EMS)** is available in major post offices. Several international express delivery services operate in Amman, including **DHL** (tel. (06) 818 351), **FedEx** (tel. (06) 618 730), and **TNT** (tel. (06) 659 414). **Packages** may be sent from any post office. Some parcels, incoming or outgoing, may be opened; don't seal packages before you go to the post office to mail them.

Although the **telephone system** was revamped several years ago, international lines are often overloaded, especially around holidays. The rare pay phones are particularly erratic and require 50fils whether or not your call goes through. If you ask shop owners where to find a pay phone, they will probably invite you to use theirs as long as the call is local. Be sure to inquire about surcharges before using hotel phones.

No collect calls can be made from Jordan. U.S. **calling cards** will connect you to the U.S. from a private phone *only*. **International calls** can be made in Amman from the telephone center downtown (see **Practical Information**, p. 471). Three minutes to North America will cost about JD6.600. International calls can be made at luxury hotels as well, where service will be faster but even more expensive. If you can find one, use a private phone and reimburse the owner. You can dial directly to the U.S., Europe, and Australia (JD1.830-2.200 per min.; 30% cheaper 10pm-8am; for all international calls, dial 00 and international code). For an **international operator,** dial 0132. For information on local codes and other **information,** dial 121.

Telegrams can be sent to North America (220fils per word) from larger post offices, the telephone office, and some hotels.

■ Dress and Etiquette

Jordan is predominantly Muslim and socially conservative, making modest dress a necessity. Though you will not be arrested, inappropriate dress will not only alienate you from the people you have come to meet, but also will encourage stares, comments, and even groping from strangers. Modesty is required of both men and women. Do not wear shorts. Shirts that cover the shoulders and upper arms and ankle-length skirts or pants are appropriate. Women must cover their heads in mosques. Sandals that expose feet are acceptable. The exception to these rules is hedonistic Aqaba, where both men and women can wear shorts. You're also allowed a little more freedom if you're going out at night or to the pool in Amman. Looking foreign gives extra leeway in these two towns, but not much; women risk greater harassment, higher prices from offended merchants, and even butt-pinching if they wear shorts in the crowded streets of downtown Amman.

Jordanians have a very strong hospitality ethic. Bedouin invitations to coffee or tea should be strongly considered, as declining an invitation is often interpreted as a direct insult. On the other hand, women should never accept an invitation from a single man. If you choose to reject an offer for whatever reason, simply be calm and firm, and repeat yourself until the point sinks in. Most people are unlikely to take no for an answer, at least on the first try. Unlike in most Western countries, however, it is important to keep in mind that most people who offer to help you, feed you, or take you somewhere are probably not con artists; they often represent the best of a culture that is serious about kindness to visitors.

LIFE AND TIMES

■ Government and Politics

After about ten minutes in Jordan, you'll notice pictures of a handsome bald man with a smooth smile everywhere you look. Refrain from jokes, because he's the king and you are in his kingdom. Jordan is the fiefdom of Hussein bin Talal. The kingdom was a 1921 gift from Britain to the Hashemite royal family, who proudly trace their lineage directly to the Prophet Muhammad (see **Introduction to the Region**, p. 46).

King Hussein has ruled since 1953. He divorced his first two queens, the gracious Dina and Muna (a Briton who changed her name from Antoinette Gardiner); his third, Alia (a Palestinian), died in a plane crash. The current queen, Noor (née Lisa Halaby), is an Arab-American Princeton University graduate. Hussein's brother, Crown Prince Hassan, serves as advisor and heir to the throne. Educated in Britain, King Hussein is generally considered moderate; but, as Palestinians will tell you, remembering their 25,000 dead from Black September, he can be brutal if his throne is at stake (see **The PLO and Jordan,** p. 55). Above all, he is a brilliant politician; these skills have kept him alive. (Luck has also been a factor; the same bullets that killed his grandfather, King Abdallah, bounced off a medal on the young Hussein's chest.)

A meeting between King Hussein and Yitzhak Rabin in August 1994 opened the border between Aqaba and Eilat and led to the end of Jordan's 46-year-old policy of non-recognition of Israel. Much of Jordan's population is of Palestinian descent, and some Palestinians have very successfully integrated themselves into Jordanian society; others live in refugee camps and harbor the dream of returning home to Palestine. In the summer of 1988, King Hussein cut all ties with the West Bank, allowing the Jordanian government to focus its efforts on economic problems.

King Hussein's rule is a constant balancing act in the face of such pressures. He has accommodated and integrated his Palestinian subjects over the years, opening his cabinet to them as well as to the Bedouin who are the bedrock of the monarchy's support. When refugees from the 1948 and 1967 wars flooded out of Palestine, Jordan was the only Arab country that offered them full citizenship. This was true again after the Gulf War, when Kuwait expelled almost all of its Palestinian community as punishment for Arafat's support of Saddam Hussein. The King, with open arms, met the first plane-full at Amman's airport. The conservative Hashemites have faced opposition from pan-Arabists, Nasserists, Palestinian nationalists, and, most recently, the Muslim Brotherhood. An attempt at democratic reform didn't turn out as the monarchy had hoped; in Jordan's first general elections in 22 years, held in November 1989, Islamists won almost half the seats in parliament. Regardless, reform has continued. In September 1992, King Hussein approved a law permitting political parties, which had been banned in 1957. Jordan's first multi-party election since 1954 took place in November 1993. A new one-person, one-vote policy weakened the Islamists; and the first woman ever was elected to Parliament. Municipal elections in summer 1995 showed a further shift towards the center in Jordanian political attitudes, and five women were elected to various municipal councils, including the first female mayor. However, the King's sudden and quick signing of a peace treaty with Rabin and his over-eagerness to normalize relations with Israel have alienated him from some of his traditional supporters. On the international level, a tide of pan-Arabism and defiance in the face of Western power-mongering led many Jordanians, including King Hussein, to support Saddam Hussein in the Gulf War (1991). But the weakening of Iraq since the war and the peace treaty with Israel have allowed the ever-flexible monarchy to reintegrate with the West.

■ Economy

Unlike its Arab neighbors, Jordan has neither oil reserves nor abundant natural resources. The country remains dependent upon Arab and American financial aid to augment its income, one source of which is the export of phosphates and pre-season vegetables grown in the Jordan Valley. Remittances from Palestinian and Jordanian workers in the Gulf states traditionally constituted Jordan's main source of income; but after the Gulf War about 320,000 of them (mostly from Kuwait) returned to Jordan to scramble for jobs in Amman.

Back when the Iran-Iraq War broke out in 1980, Iraq became a major importer of Jordanian goods and services, and the Jordanian economy boomed. In the late 1980s, when Iraq began threatening not to pay its war debts, Jordanian exporters were left with a heap of worthless Iraqi IOUs. In April 1989, following steep government-imposed price hikes on gasoline and other goods, Jordanians took to the streets in protest until King Hussein fired then Prime Minister Zaid Rifa'i and, more importantly, instituted democratic reforms. Stability returned, and a 1991 growth rate of 1% was actually a step up from 1989 and 1990.

The aftermath of the 1990-91 Gulf War dealt a devastating blow to the economy, bringing a 1990 annual per capita income of US$2000 down to US$1400 today. Jordan's refusal to join the US-led anti-Iraq coalition of states cost the country dearly, spurring the United States, along with Saudi Arabia and the other Gulf countries, to suspend most aid to Jordan. In addition, the Palestinian and Jordanian workers in the Gulf were largely replaced by Egyptians, whose government the Saudis found to be more politically correct. Among the returnees, unemployment is at 80%. Unemployment in the general population has hit an alarming 30%.

The August 1994 Washington Declaration signed by King Hussein and Yitzhak Rabin of Israel put an end to the state of war between the two countries and reactivated the money flow from Washington and Amman. US$220 million wiped out some Jordanian debt, and an additional US$350 million is expected. England followed suit, relieving Jordan of a smaller debt. Unfortunately, this has had no real effect on the current state of the economy. Jordan hadn't been paying its debts anyway; what the economy needs is income. An increase in Israeli and Western tourism to Jordan, especially to Petra, may be able to supply part of the much-needed boost.

■ Festivals and Holidays

The **appendix** lists the dates of Islamic and Jordanian national holidays. For the Christian community, the **Easter Celebrations** (all congregations follow the Eastern Calendar for Palm and Easter Sundays) are the most spectacular of the year. **Christmas** is a smaller feast, especially for the Coptic and Abyssinian Churches, which celebrate the holiday during the second week of January rather than on December 25.

The two-week **Jerash Festival** is held every year during July or August. Amid brilliantly illuminated Roman ruins and inside ancient amphitheaters, visitors witness performances by international artists. For more information, contact the **Jerash Festival Office,** P.O. Box 910 582, Amman (tel. (06) 675 199 or 686 197).

■ Language

The official language of the Hashemite Kingdom of Jordan is Arabic. However, the spoken Arabic dialect differs from classical Arabic and varies from that used in Egypt, the Gulf States, and North Africa. Minor differences in pronunciation separate the dialects of Jordanians, Palestinians, Lebanese, and Syrians; see the **Language Glossary** for more on Arabic (p. 575).

Due to decades of British colonial rule, English is Jordan's second language, taught at both public and private schools. Almost all Jordanians have a knowledge of the language; many speak it quite well. Most signs are written in both Arabic and English, and Jordan Television's second channel broadcasts subtitled British and American programs after 8:30pm. French is spoken occasionally as a third language.

■ The Arts

LITERATURE

The Arabic language is shared by 21 nations, and Arabic literature from these countries is the proud heritage of the whole of the Arab world. The Jordanian region itself has a long tradition of prose: the oldest example of a Semitic script, the **Mesha Stele,** was found in Karak. Unfortunately, few Jordanian works are translated into other languages and thus remain inaccessible to most foreigners.

Among English travel accounts, C.M. Doughty's *Arabia Deserta* and Wilfred Thesiger's more recent *Arabian Sands* are powerful adventure stories inspired by a romanticized version of Bedouin lifestyle. T.E. Lawrence's *Seven Pillars of Wisdom* contains vivid descriptions of the battles fought and the territory explored during the Arab Revolt of 1916; even if you don't reach Wadi Rum in the Jordanian desert, you might want to see David Lean's magnificent *Lawrence of Arabia* on the big screen. Gertrude Bell, one of the first female Western travelers in the region, writes of her journeys through Jordan and Syria in *The Desert and the Sown*. King Abdallah's two-volume *Memoirs* and King Hussein's *Uneasy Lies the Head* are self-serving but dispel once and for all the myth that it's good to be king. The Arab Legion chief of the 1940s and 50s, John Bagot Glubb (Glubb Pasha), wrote *A Soldier With the Arabs* and several books based on his life. A little less adventurous but more erudite is Jonathan Raban's *Arabia: A Journey through the Labyrinth.*

The archaeologically and historically inclined can consult G.L. Harding's *Antiquities of Jordan* and Julian Huxley's *From an Antique Land.* Ian Browning's *Petra* is wonderfully comprehensive. Finally, Agatha Christie's *Argument with Death* is a light introduction to the mesmerizing power of Petra.

VISUAL ARTS

Both the Jordanian government and private groups are taking measures to promote and foster the arts. Like that of other countries of the Arab world, Jordanian art is an expression of Arab and often Muslim identity. But contemporary artists have many Western tendencies and use visual art as an outlet for personal as well as cultural expression. Modernity is eroding the traditional Islamic reluctance to portray human beings. Jordan's architecture, painting, and sculpture have all developed substantially in this century. Amman has witnessed the opening of many new **art galleries,** featuring contemporary as well as traditional media. The most impressive is **Darat al-Funeu** on Jabal al-Weibdeh (open Sat.-Thurs. 9am-1:30pm and 3:30pm-6:30pm).

When it comes to folk art, Jordanians do abide by tradition. Techniques developed over centuries make for skillful weavers of wool and goat-hair rugs and tapestries. Leather handicrafts, pottery, ceramics, and coral curios also belong to the family of mastered Jordanian folk art. Painters often display their work in galleries in Amman. Nature, Bedouin life, and longing for Palestine are all common subjects. It is wood-carving, though, that is the Jordanian specialty. Artists can do beautiful carvings of your name right on the street, for an appropriate fee. You will find most of these crafts sold proudly on the streets of Jordan.

POPULAR AND FOLK CULTURE

Homesick Yankees who aren't sticklers for highbrow culture can look for Bart Simpson to brighten their day or *The Bold and the Beautiful* to remind them of those weekday afternoons in front of the TV. These and other popular American and British shows appear on Jordanian television with Arabic subtitles. More authentic Jordanian programming includes music videos and disco dance extravaganzas. Much of the pop music in Jordan is Egyptian; listen for traditional Arabic themes under the cacophony of not-quite-Western sounds. Jordanians do, however, have their own traditional expressions of pop culture, most notably a strong oral tradition of stories, songs, and ballads. Villages often have their own songs commemorating births, circumcisions, weddings, funerals, and planting. Several Cossack dances, including a sword dance that has to be seen to be believed, are popular in Jordan, as is *dabkeh,* a dance performed to the resonating rhythm of feet pounding on the floor. Eavesdrop on weddings in some neighborhoods for a taste of traditional folk music and for the women's salutatory shouts followed by ululation, or *zaghroutah* (sounds like *ha-WEEE-ha*).

■ Food and Drink

Jordanian cuisine has evolved through centuries of Bedouin and Palestinian cooking. The national dish, *mensaf,* ideally consists of eight to ten kilograms of rice on a large tray, topped with pine nuts, an entire lamb or goat, and a tangy yogurt-based sauce. The Bedouin serve the head of the lamb on top, reserving the prize delicacies—eyes and tongue—for speechless and visually jaded guests. Traditionally eaten from a communal dish while standing, the right hand is used to ball the rice, and the flat bread to pull off chunks of meat and dip them into the warm *jamid* sauce.

Most other dishes include the main ingredients of *mensaf.* Traditional dinners are served between 2-3pm. Popular dinners include *musakhan*—chicken baked with olive oil and onions and a delicious spice called *summaq,* served on bread—and *mahshi,* a tray of vine leaves, squash, or eggplant stuffed with mincemeat, rice, and onions. *Mezze,* loosely translated as "appetizers," encompasses a wide range of savory dishes including hummus with olive oil, *mutabbal* (an eggplant dip also known as baba ghanoush), *labaneh* (thickened yogurt), cucumbers (*khyar*), tomatoes (*banadoorah*), and pickles. Supper is usually smaller. A combination of hummus, cheese, honey, jam, bread, and sometimes *fuul* form a standard breakfast. A staple is *za'tar,* thyme mixed with sesame seeds and spices and eaten either with bread dipped into olive oil and then into the mix, or pizza-style (*mana'eesh*).

At restaurants, if the menu is in English, you can't afford the food. *Kebab* is skewered lamb, *shish tawouq* chicken, and *kofta* grilled ground beef with parsley and spices. Hummus and falafel are cheap, as is *shawerma,* delicious sandwiches made of lamb (or chicken, a more recent innovation) sliced into Arabic bread with *summaq,* tahini sauce, vegetables, and sometimes pickles. Many deli-like places sell *mu'ajjanat,* dough wrapped around or topped with either spinach (*sabanekh*), lamb (in which case it's called *sfeeha*), cheese, or *za'tar* and olive oil. Fresh *ka'ik,* a bread ring with sesame seeds, is a street favorite, as is corn-on-the-cob. With *ka'ik* you will be given *za'tar* in a piece of newspaper for dipping

As in the rest of the region, desserts are heavenly but overwhelmingly sweet—take them in small doses. Desserts include *ba'laweh, kinafeh* (made of soft cheese and shredded wheat, baked, soaked in syrup, and garnished with pistachios), *basbouseh* (wheat and syrup baked to moist goodness), pistachio nougat from candy stores, and ice cream (*booza*). Mango, pistachio, and *mastika* are the best flavors. Some places advertise milk shakes, which are nearly always simply flavored milk. Exceptions include the Beefy Cafe and McDonald's in Amman. Some new *gelato* stores have opened up as well, especially in the Shmeisani area of Amman and in Aqaba.

Water in Amman is piped in from Azraq oasis and the Euphrates River in Iraq. Although certainly potable, it is hardly pure. Bottled water (300fils, more at restaurants and tourist haunts) or iodine tablets, like extra molars, are signs of wisdom. Jordan is a clean country; even salads should be safe to eat.

Coffee and tea are important expressions of Jordanian hospitality, and tourists are likely to be offered refreshment many times a day. If a hot drink doesn't tickle your fancy, ask for *barid* (Arabic for "cold"). Jordanians drink tremendous amounts of tea (*shay*), almost always made with mint (*na'na'*). You may never take milk in your tea again. Stereotypes hold that hicks (*fellaheen,* farmers) drink theirs syrupy sweet; restaurants will assume you are one unless you prove your gentility by asking for *sukkar*

Sugar and Spice and All Things Nice

Jordan is known as a crossroads of Syrian and Palestinian cuisines. Recipes for sweets like *burma* and *balorieh* were guarded secrets in immigrant kitchens until the **Jabri** and **Habiba** patisserie chains introduced them to mainstream Jordanian life around 1950. Jabri brought Damascene *ba'laweh*, while Habiba hooked the country on *kinafeh* from Nablus. Almost half a century later, the Jordanian sweet tooth can only be satisfied by the honey-coated filo dough and nuts that have become an inseparable part of the country's traditions.

---

aleel (not too much sugar). A cup of Arabic coffee *(qahwa)*, a thick, black, bittersweet brew, is espresso-strength. Avoid the silt in the bottom of the cup.

Because most Muslims agree that drinking **alcohol** is prohibited by Islam, imbibing in Jordan is subject to some restrictions and conventions. It is illegal to possess alcohol in public unless at a place licensed for liquor. Drinking and driving, or even having alcohol in the car, would be a big mistake. Nonetheless, many Jordanians drink, and with no enforced drinking age, anyone who looks older than 16 may buy at a liquor store (usually owned by Christians; bottles of vodka run JD10). Amstel, locally-brewed under license, is the most popular alcoholic drink (600fils). Imports are also available. *'Araq* is a popular anise-seed hard alcohol (similar to the Greek *Ouzo* and Turkish *Raki*) that is mixed with water until a cloudy white suspension results. Liquor is very expensive, especially at bars and restaurants, where a mixed drink may cost JD3.500-6. Beer at bars costs JD1.700-4.

Amman عمان

Amman's automobiles, careening with dangerous speed along the city's seven hills, leave visitors agape in Jordan's capital. Horns honk incessantly, but are overwhelmed five times a day by the beautiful call to prayer echoing from the minarets which grace the skyline. When the sun goes down and the lights go up, Amman's jasmine-scented streets are the perfect setting for lazy summertime strolls.

The Ammonite capital in biblical times and later the Greco-Roman city of Philadelphia, modern Amman was a mere village in the decades preceding 1948. Following the Arab-Israeli wars of 1948 and 1967, many Palestinian refugees ended up in Amman, which soon boomed. Palestinians now form about 70% of Jordan's population, but sometimes experience discrimination at the hands of the Jordanian ruling minority. Some Palestinians are highly successful doctors, businesspeople, bankers, and politicians, while others still live in Amman's huge refugee camps. Egyptian and Southeast Asian workers are also part of the city's population. Amman's nearly bursting seams were further expanded by the arrival of immigrants from Iraq and Kuwait following the 1991 Gulf War. The pre-1948 population of 6000 has exploded to well over a million inhabitants today, roughly one third of Jordan's total population.

Amman's central location makes it the country's principal transportation hub and the base for exploring Jordan's other sights. Its entertainment, government services, and reasonable hotel prices are typical of a cosmopolitan capital city, but Amman's charm resists such generic classifications. Don't feel disdain for travelers returning to suburban five-star hotels. Pity them: it is the people of downtown Amman that are the city's most valuable treasure. The "welcomes" you hear are quite sincere; chances are, they will lead to a cup of tea, a conversation, and experiences you'll never forget.

■ Orientation

Take advantage of Amman's summits to get a perspective on this roller coaster city. Rocky **Jabal al-Qala'a** (Citadel Hill), where the Archaeological Museum sits amidst unearthed remains of Roman and Umayyad palaces, temples, and hilltop fortifications, provides a panoramic view of winding streets, tall buildings, mosques, and ruins, all of which will serve as useful landmarks.

Any round object dropped to the ground will roll into Amman's downtown district, **Al Balad,** which is neatly framed by the seven hills. This is the best location from which to orient yourself in Jordan's biggest city.

Downtown Amman has three major landmarks: the **Al Husseini Mosque,** the **Roman Amphitheater,** and (believe it or not) the **post office**—because everyone knows where it is. With your back to the mosque, the city's focal point, you will be facing up **King Faisal St.,** which leads northwest to the post office and numerous budget hotels. Turn right, and you will be looking up **Hashemi St.,** which leads to the Roman Amphitheater. To the left will be the city's **main market.** If you walk up King Faisal St. towards the post office, the **gold market** will be on your right-hand side. Walk up Hashemi St. past the Roman Amphitheater and you will reach the **clock tower** and the recently built piazza.

Amman's eight **numbered traffic circles** follow a line leading westward out of town and through **Jabal Amman.** Beyond Third Circle, Amman's diplomatic center and home of most foreign embassies, traffic circles have been replaced by busy intersections. Although the city is earnestly attempting to rename these intersections "squares," each is still fondly called a "circle," or *duwwar*. From Seventh Circle, traffic heads south to Queen Alia International Airport and the Desert Highway (Aqaba 335km), to the Kings' Highway via Madaba (35km; Karak 125km; Petra 260km), and via Na'ur to the Dead Sea and the border of Israel (90km). From Eighth Circle, you can continue west to Wadi Seer, or head north to Jerash (50km).

Following King Hussein St. northwest from the city center brings you to **Jabal al-Weibdeh,** a tree-lined middle-class neighborhood perched on a hill. In this neighborhood, the **JETT** and **Abdali Bus Stations** are the third right turn off King Hussein St.—the first right after the road flattens out. The blue dome and octagonal minaret of the Jabal's enormous **King Abdallah Mosque** are visible from all surrounding heights.

To the north of the city lies **Jabal Hussein,** a largely residential district dominated by the Housing Bank complex (*mujamma' bank al-iskan*), an overgrown Love Boat next to the Forte Grand Hotel. This area is bordered to the northwest by the Ministry of Interior Circle (*duwwar ad-Dakhiliyyeh*) and the modern suburb of **Shmeisani,** complete with luxury hotels and American-style fast food restaurants. To the south of the city, in the direction of the airport, rises **Jabal al-Ashrafiyyeh.** Its ornate **Abu Darwish Mosque** can be seen above the **Wahdat Bus Station** and the Wahdat Palestinian refugee camp. While the Jordan Valley fertilizes the land to the north and west of Amman, the city recedes into desert in the south and east.

The government has installed some street signs in downtown Amman—most have English translations. Although most people know King Faisal and Hashemi St., other inquiries on street names are likely to produce blank stares. Directions usually run something like: "to the right of the third falafel stand; stop and say hello to Nabil for me, he owns the place; then take a left in front of the mosque with the green dome." Many street signs are in English and street names are listed on maps, but in general, successful navigation of Amman depends on knowing Amman's landmarks. In addition to remembering the Al Husseini Mosque, the Roman Amphitheater, and the Wahdat and Abdali bus stations, try to find out what number circle your destination is near, and you'll have an easier time finding your way. Lastly, don't hesitate to ask locals for assistance—they will be glad to help you out. Sometimes an entire neighborhood will rally together to get you where you're going—before you know it, Omar's uncle's sister's friend who owes him a favor is driving you around the city.

■ Transportation

WITHIN AMMAN

To reach locations within the city or to find the departure point for buses and *service,* ask a downtown shopkeeper. At a minimum, you'll be pointed in the right direction;

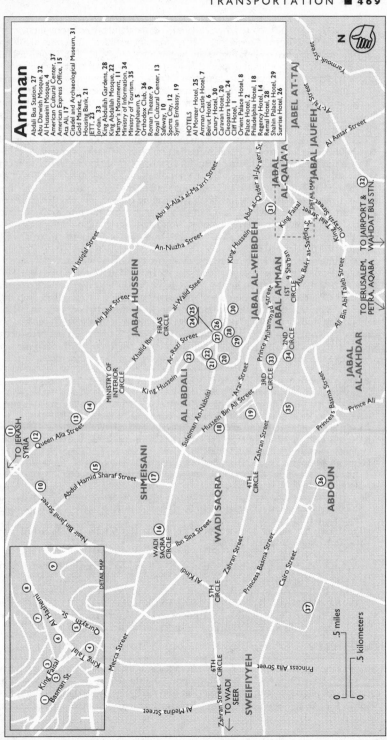

Amman

Abdali Bus Station, 27
Abu Darwish Mosque, 32
Al Husseini Mosque, 4
American Cultural Center, 37
American Express Office, 15
Ata Ali, 17
Citadel and Archaeological Museum, 31
Gold Market, 3
Housing Bank, 21
JETT, 23
Jordan, 33
King Abdullah Gardens, 28
King Abdullah Mosque, 22
Martyr's Monument, 11
Ministry of Information, 34
Ministry of Tourism, 35
Nymphaeum, 5
Orthodox Club, 36
Roman Theater, 9
Royal Cultural Center, 13
Safeway, 10
Sports City, 12
Syrian Embassy, 19

HOTELS
Al Monzer Hotel, 25
Amman Castle Hotel, 7
Beirut Hotel, 6
Canary Hotel, 30
Caravan Hotel, 20
Cleopatra Hotel, 24
Cliff Hotel, 1
Orient Palace Hotel, 8
Palace Hotel, 2
Philadelphia Hotel, 18
Regan Hotel, 14
Remal Hotel, 28
Shahin Palace Hotel, 29
Sunrise Hotel, 26

JORDAN

quite possibly you'll be escorted there, invited to dinner, and offered permanent lodging. You can flag buses and *service* anywhere along their routes, but *service* are often full (they take five passengers) from the beginning to the end of their prescribed courses. Public transportation stops at 8 or 9pm, and a couple of hours earlier on Fridays; after that, walking is a great alternative for those with strong legs. Metered **taxis** prowl the streets in search of fares until 11pm, after which time drivers expect about double the daytime fare. At night, bargain before getting into the taxi. Pay around 500fils to go from downtown to Third Circle or from Third to Sixth Circle, 350fils from downtown to Abdali. A taxi between the two bus/*service* stations should cost 800fils. The trip along Jabal Amman from First to Eighth Circle should cost no more than 800fils; check to make sure the meter is running (see **Getting Around,** p. 458.)

Buses traveling within Amman cost about 100fils; it's a little more if you're heading for the suburbs. Flag any bus traveling in your direction and ask the driver if it stops where you want to go, or find out at any bus station. Pay your fare after the ride has begun. Drivers and their assistants don't like making change, so carry 100fil pieces with you. Most buses have the name of their destination written in Arabic on the front, sides, or both. Some have numbers, but since buses going on different routes may display the same number, what worked one time may not the next. Asking around is the best way to find a bus.

Although it may cost a few more fils, transportation by **service** or yellow taxi is much easier on the nerves. *Service* routes are clearer and more comprehensive. Perhaps the best thing about traveling by *service* is the opportunity they provide to meet Jordanians. *Service* are numbered and the names of their routes are listed on the doors in Arabic. All routes within the city originate downtown, where you can ask for help finding stops. You would do best to mention major destinations or well-known landmarks. Stopping a *service* en route may be difficult—many drive at breakneck speed, so try to make yourself visible without stepping in front of it. To stop the *service,* stick out your arm, palm down. Below are some popular *service* routes.

#1 (١): Travels on Jabal Amman between Center City and Third Circle, passing First and Second Circles (70fils).

#2 (٢): Starts on Basman St. (look for the Basman Theater) and travels on Jabal Amman to Malik Abd Ribiya St. between Second and Third Circles (70fils).

#3 (٣): Starts on Kureisha St. and travels on Jabal Amman to Fourth Circle (90fils).

#4 (٤): Runs from Basman St. to Al Amaneh Circle and gardens, passing near all points of interest on Jabal al-Weibdeh (70fils).

(Not numbered): Leaves from bottom of Omar al-Khayyam St. (opposite Cliff Hotel), travels up Jabal al-Weibdeh to Queen Alia Institute, just uphill from Abdali Station (70fils).

#6 (٦): Starts on Malik Ghazi St. (better known as Cinema al-Hussein St.), then travels along King Faisal and King Hussein St. to Jamal Abd an-Nasser Circle, passing Abdali and JETT Stations (80fils).

#7 (٧): Starts by Cinema al-Hussein St. and runs past Abdali Station to Shmeisani near the Ambassador Hotel and the Gallery Alia (70fils).

Service and minibuses to Wahdat Station start at Kureisha St. (also called Sakfi Seil) near Petra Bank and pass near Abu Darwish Mosque on Jabal Ashrafiyyeh. *Service* directly to Wahdat Station from Abdali cost 120fils. Another route starts at Shabsough St. near the gold market downtown, passing Abdali Station and Jabal Hussein to the Ministry of Interior Circle (80fils). Some prices will be slightly more or less than those listed, but *service* drivers rarely cheat you—prices are generally standard.

INTERCITY

Buses to the north central and northwestern parts of the country, including the Jordan Valley, leave from **Abdali Bus Station** on King Hussein St. on Jabal al-Weibdeh. Destinations include Jerash, Ajlun, Irbid, Salt, and the King Hussein/Allenby Bridge, as well as Damascus. **Hashemi Street Station,** near the Roman amphitheater, launches traffic to the northeast, including Zarqa, Mafraq, and points east of Irbid. Traffic to and from the south is based at **Wahdat Station,** several km from downtown Amman between the Abu Darwish Mosque and the Wahdat Refugee Camp. Buses from here go to Madaba, Karak, Ma'an, Wadi Musa, and Aqaba. The **JETT** bus station, serving major towns in Jordan, Syria, and Iraq, is on King Hussein St., up the road from Abdali Bus Station (see **Practical Information,** below). It is wise to book bus tickets at least one day in advance. Intercity *service* leave from the same stations as buses, and go to the same regions. Fares tend to be 40-50% more expensive than comparable bus fares. All prices, bus and *service* alike, are government-regulated.

To go to Syria from Jordan you will need a **Syrian visa;** don't rely on the Syrian Embassy in Amman to issue visas, as it almost certainly won't. Apply for a Syrian visa from the embassy nearest you *well* in advance of leaving your home country. Buses run often between Amman and Damascus. Unfortunately, you can't make round-trip reservations from either city. Definitely make reservations for the return trip to Jordan as soon as you arrive in Damascus, or vice versa. The road between the two capitals is heavily traveled on weekends (Thurs.-Sat.)—border-crossing on these days has been known to take as long as three hours. Luckily, the process at the border is not difficult as long as you have a visa.

■ Practical Information

Ministry of Tourism: P.O. Box 224 (tel. 642 311; fax 648 465). From 3rd Circle on Jabal Amman, walk down Zahran St., to the left of the Ministry of Information. Distributes free maps, hotel price lists, and lovely color brochures. Open Sat.-Thurs. 8am-2pm.

Embassies: Australia, 4th Circle on Jabal Amman (tel. 673 246; fax 673 263), between the 4th and 5th Circles opposite the imposing Kuwaiti embassy. Helpful with foreign visas. Open Sun.-Thurs. 9am-3pm, for visas Mon. and Wed. 9am-noon. **Canada,** Shmeisani (tel. 666 124; fax 689 227), in near the Petra Bank. Open Sun.-Thurs. 9am-4:30pm, until 11am for visas. **U.K.,** Behind the Orthodox Club on Damascus St. (tel. 823 100; fax 813 759) in Abdoun. Instead of turning right to the U.S. embassy, continue on the road until you reach the Orthodox Club (the walled-in playground with the red jungle-gym protruding above the walls). Make a right, then two quick lefts. Consular division open Sun.-Thurs. 8:30am-noon. **U.S.,** In Abdoun (tel. 820 101; visa info. 813 293; fax 820 101). Heading north on Jabal Amman (Zahran St.), make a left at the 5th Circle and continue until the 1st intersection. Make a left on Cairo St.; take the 3rd right. The fortress-like complex is 500m down that road and can't be missed. Consular division open Sun.-Thurs. 9am-4pm, for visas 9am-noon. **Egypt,** Jabal Amman (tel. 605 203; fax 604 082), between 4th and 5th Circles. Take a right by the Japanese embassy and continue about 100m down the road. Embassy is on the left. Bring a photo and JD12 before noon, pick up visa on the same afternoon. Open Sat.-Thurs. 9:30am-3pm, until noon for visas. **Israel,** Rabia (tel. 552 4680), near the Chinese embassy. Visas JD13. Open Sun.-Thurs. 8am-4pm. **Lebanon,** 2nd Circle, Jabal Amman (tel. 641 381 or 751; fax 647 818). **Syria,** Jabal Amman (tel. 641 076; fax 651 945), up from 3rd Circle toward the reflecting building. Take a left at the intersection and head up the hill. Look for the Syrian flag (red, white, and black stripes with two green stars). In theory, a visa costs JD24 for Americans and JD38 for British nationals, but virtually nobody gets to the privileged paying stage. You must have a Jordanian entry stamp on your passport and no evidence of visits to the West Bank or Israel for any chance. Embassy open (for visa info) Sun.-Thurs. 9-11am.

Currency Exchange: Banking hours are ordinarily Sat.-Wed. 8:30am-12:30pm and 4-5:30pm, Thurs. 8:30am-12:30pm, some are closed on Friday. Many authorized **money changers,** found downtown between the Al Husseini Mosque and the post office, are open daily, usually late into the evening. They offer roughly the same exchange rates as banks, but will not leech a bank's commission. Bring your passport. The **Cairo Amman Bank** (tel. 639 321), on Shabsough St., can give you a **cash advance** on your MC/Visa.

American Express: International Traders, P.O. Box 408 (tel. 607 014; fax 669 905), on Abdul Hamid Sharaf St. in Shmeisani, past the Safeway supermarket and opposite the Ambassador Hotel. Holds mail and can obtain visas when cardholders purchase plane tickets. Open Sat.-Thurs. 8am-6pm.

Airport: Queen Alia International Airport (tel. (08) 530 70), 35km south of Amman. Buses connect Abdali Bus Station and the airport (24hr., every 30min, 40min., JD1). A private taxi to the airport will cost JD10. There is no *service* to the airport. Bank (open 24hr.) and tourist office (open 9am-2pm) are in the airport. Jordanian visas, good for 1 month, are available at the airport upon arrival (JD15), and are renewable at any police station. There is a JD10 exit fee when leaving Jordan by air (JD4 if by land, JD6 if by sea).

Intercity Buses: JETT (tel. 664 146; fax 605 005) runs A/C buses. To: **King Hussein/Allenby Bridge** (daily 6:30am, 1hr., JD6); **Petra** (daily 6:30am, 3hr., JD8.500, round-trip tour including guide, horse, and lunch JD26.500); **Aqaba** (5 per day, 4hr., JD4); **Damascus** (7am, 4-5hr. depending on border crossing, visa req., JD4.500); **Cairo** (Sat., Mon., Tue., Thurs., 7:30am, 20-24hr., JD48 includes luggage); and **Baghdad** (daily 2pm, 15hr., JD6 plus JD4 departure tax, visa req.). Reserve 2 days in advance. Office open daily 6am-8pm. **Other buses** depart from either the Abdali or Wahdat bus stations, depending on direction. Fares to: **Jerash** 270fils, **Ajlun** 450fils, **Irbid** 820fils, **Salt** 200fils, **King Hussein/Allenby Bridge** JD1.500. For more information, see **Transportation,** p. 468.

Intercity Service Taxis: From **Abdali Station,** fares to: **Jerash** 470fils, **Ajlun** 750fils, **Irbid** 880fils, **Salt** 350fils, and **King Hussein/Allenby Bridge** JD1.500. From **Wahdat Station,** fares to: **Madaba** 350fils, **Karak** down the King's Highway JD1.500, and **Ma'an** via the newer Desert Highway JD3.500; at Ma'an you can transfer for service to **Wadi Musa** (Petra) and **Aqaba** (500fils and JD1.500, respectively). Government price regulations are not always observed.

Car Rental: Local agencies have fewer restrictions, although a growing market has attracted big names like **Avis** (tel. 699 420; fax 819 779) and **Budget** (tel. 698 131; fax 673 312). **Reliable** (tel. 819 676) in Abdoun has brand new cars for JD23-35 per day, and boasts a 24hr. breakdown service. **Firas,** at 1st Circle, offers unlimited mileage economy cars starting at JD15 (min. age 23). Valid driver's license and passport required. Reserve in advance during the summer and high season.

English Bookstores: Al 'Ulama Bookshop (tel. 636 192), 50m uphill from the post office. History books, travel guides, dictionaries, and a couple of American news magazines. Fax available. Open Sun.-Thurs. 8am-7pm. **University Bookstore** (tel. 636 339), on Jabal al-Weibdeh near Khalaf Circle. Fiction as well as books about Jordan. Open 8:30am-7:30pm. **Istiqlal Library** is located around the corner from the Turino Hotel in Sweyfiyyeh. The English-speaking staff of this giant, air-conditioned book superstore is very helpful. Credit cards accepted. Open Sat.-Thurs. 8:30am-1:30pm and 3:30-7:30pm. The **Habib Bookshop** (tel. 642 835) across the street from Citibank at 3rd Circle sells English newspapers, magazines, and trashy novels, and stocks random necessities like razors, batteries, and glue sticks. Photocopier available. Open Mon.-Thurs. 7am-7pm, Sun. 7am-1pm. Most supermarkets also sell English newspapers and magazines.

Local Press: *Your Guide to Amman,* published monthly and available free at larger hotels, bookstores, and travel agencies, is full of helpful info. *The Jordan Times* (150fils), a daily newspaper with excellent coverage of the Middle East and Africa, lists useful telephone numbers, all-night pharmacies, and cultural events in Amman. *Jordan Today,* published monthly and available at larger hotels, has invaluable information on tourism, culture, and entertainment. The *International Herald Tribune* arrives after 3pm 1 day late at newsstands. The weekly *Jerusalem Star* (350fils) lists cultural events and all the piddling details from the lives of the royals. *The New York Times* is sometimes available 1 day late at the gift shop in the Marriott and Inter-Continental Hotels.

Radio: Those who crave an English-speaking voice can tune in to the **BBC** on 1323AM and the **Voice of America** at night on 1260AM. 96.3FM plays familiar Top 40 from 6am-2am. For the sleepless jetlagged, 88.0 and 99.0FM have 24hr. Arabic-speaking DJs spinning records from French rap to classical Arabic music.

Archaeological Resources: Department of Antiquities (tel. 644 336; fax 615 848). From 3rd Circle walk down Hussein Bin Ali St. to the mirrored-glass Ailco building, then up the street diagonally on the left. This is the national headquarters for research on digs. They have a library and distribute books and detailed maps highlighting archaeological sites. Open Sat.-Thurs. 8am-2pm. **Friends of Archaeology,** P.O. Box 2440, Jabal Amman (tel. 696 683; fax 696 682). Facing west, take a left at 4th Circle. Turn right, left, and left again, and the center will be on your right. This private local organization sponsors weekly field trips to sites. Most are for members only, but it may be possible to join a trip for a fee. Office open Sun.-Fri. 8:30am-3:30pm.

Cultural Centers: American Cultural Center: Abdoun (tel. 820 101; fax 813 759), inside the American Embassy Complex. Free American films every Sun. and Thurs., cable TV, and lectures by scholars and politicians visiting Jordan. Open to the public. Topics include Arab/American relations and Middle Eastern studies. The library has American magazines and newspapers, comfy couches, a video library, and a good selection of books, mostly non-fiction. Center and library open Sun.-Thurs. 9am-5pm. **British Council:** Rainbow St. (tel. 636 148). Facing uphill at 1st Circle, go left. The BC is past the Saudi Embassy on the right hand side. Sponsors films, lectures, and various other activities. Library (with A/C) open Sat.-Mon. 10am-6:30pm, Tues.-Wed. 10am-8pm, Thurs. 10am-1:30pm.

Laundry: Dry Clean (tel. 641 955), Jabal Amman, across the street from the Ministry of Tourism. 500fils for shirts and 750fils for pants. **Al-Jami'a Laundry** (tel. 847 857), on your first right heading away from the city past the main gate of Jordan University, is a do-it-yourself joint (wash and dry JD2). If you don't mind getting wet, washing by hand is a great option. The summer air is so dry that clothes will be ready in several hours. Some hotels will provide you with soap and a bucket.

Pharmacies: The *Jordan Times* and *Your Guide to Amman* list all-night pharmacies and doctors, both rotating weekly. There is a pharmacy almost every block downtown. The **Rawhi Pharmacy** (tel. 644 454) near the Intercontinental Hotel has an excellent English-speaking staff. **Jacob's Pharmacy** (tel. 644 945) in 3rd Circle, will close at midnight for the duration of the construction on 3rd Circle. Normal 24hr. service will resume when construction is finished (supposedly by Sept. 1997). Other pharmacies are usually open Sat.-Thurs. 8am-7pm. For non-prescription medicine, try the **Safeway,** on the edge of Nasir Bin Jamil St., near the northwestern edge of Shmeisani (open daily 24hr.).

Emergency: Anywhere in Jordan, call 192 for **police,** 193 for an **ambulance.** In case of **traffic accidents** in Amman, call 896 390.

Hospitals: The *Jordan Times, Star,* and *Your Guide to Amman* list doctors and hospitals. Some good ones include: **Hussein Medical Center,** Mecca St. (tel. 813 832), and **Shmeisani Hospital,** Shmeisani (tel. 607 431).

Post Office: tel. 121 for inquiries. At the base of Prince Muhammad St., where it joins King Faisal St. downtown. Stamps and **Poste Restante.** Open Sat.-Thurs. 8am-7pm, Fri. 8am-1pm. Cables and **faxes** can be sent from this office. **EMS** (tel. 688 190) is on Lifta St., a dead end behind Qawar Arthroscopy Center. From downtown, go up King Hussein St. past the Abdali and JETT bus stations. Take a right on Bir al-Sab'a St. and look left. Open daily 8am-8pm, holidays 8am-2pm.

Telephone Office: Exit to your left from the post office on Prince Muhammad St. and take the very first left onto frighteningly steep Omar al-Khayyam St. across from the Cliff Hotel. The telephone office is a pulse-quickening, sweat-inspiring 200m on the left. The sign is in Arabic, but you'll see the phones through 30m of windows. Open daily 7:30am-11pm. 3min. to the U.S. costs JD6.600, Great Britain JD5.500, 30% cheaper after 10pm. Pay at the desk after your call. Overseas calls can be made from any post office, from most hotels at any time for a surcharge, or from private homes. Note that you cannot **call collect** or with a **calling card** in Jordan unless it is from a **private phone.** Overseas calls can be paid in cash only. For more polite service and a better connection than at the telephone office, go to **Ziad Khalifeh's telephone office** (tel. 688 063), just downhill from the government one (look for the phone picture on the sign). Fax and photocopy services available. Open Sun.-Thurs. 9am-8pm. **Directory assistance** (in Arabic): tel. 121 or 640 444. **Telephone Code:** 06.

■ Accommodations

Most budget backpackers can be found **downtown,** which is overgrown with small, seedy hotels and is conveniently located near the main post office, telephone office, a large market, and many affordable restaurants. Every block has three or four cheapies and every alley has at least one; look carefully before committing.

Many clean and reputable (but more expensive) hotels are located near the **Abdali Bus Station** in Jabal al-Weibdeh. This area is close to the city center and convenient for transport out of Amman. Just beyond Jabal al-Weibdeh lies the opulent **Shmeisani** district, with a few reasonably priced accommodations worth the hunt.

In the off-season (non-summer months) and for longer stays, most hotel owners will give you a deal; don't be afraid to bargain with a smile. All rooms have private baths unless otherwise noted, and rooms near Abdali Station have phones. Many hotels near Abdali Station also take credit cards, while other hotels accept cash only.

Be aware that sometimes hotel managers pay cab drivers to bring tourists to their hotels. These drivers may go so far as to say that the hotel you ask for is bad, full, or shut down; they may even pretend that they don't know where it is. Be insistent, or, if you feel that you can easily find another cab, simply ask the driver to let you out.

DOWNTOWN/AL HUSSEINI MOSQUE AREA

Cliff Hotel, King Faisal St. (tel. 624 273), at the top of the street across from the post office at the base of King Hussein St., on the 3rd floor. The most popular traveler's spot in Amman. Manager Abu Suleiman calls it "the United Nations headquarters of the Middle East." Better than the Ministry of Tourism for honest information and directions and unbeatable for Arabic lessons and a little TLC. Offers tours at cheap rates to nearby sights, a great option for single travelers. Beds are sometimes left in poor condition. "Terrace" mattress JD2; singles JD6; doubles JD8. Hot showers 500fils. Reception sells bottled water and other conveniences. Reserve in advance.

Farah Hotel, King Hussein St. (tel. 651 443 or 438; fax 651 437). Just uphill from where King Hussein St. meets King Faisal St., marked by red signs with yellow writing. A worthy competitor of the Cliff, newly painted rooms have lockers and each floor has a shared fridge and 2 immaculate bathrooms with free showers. Shared rooms JD3.500 per person (negotiable for larger groups); singles JD7.

Palace Hotel, King Faisal St. (tel. 624 327; fax 650 602), 1½ blocks from Al Husseini Mosque. Look up for the red and blue "HOTEL" signs. Entrance in the alley on the left. The hotel features Roman pillar decor and a large dining/TV room with an indoor fountain and patio overlooking the city center. Rooms have telephones, but no fan. Common bathrooms are spic and span. Razors, chips, and other necessities for sale in the lobby. Singles JD7; doubles JD13; triples JD15.

Beirut Hotel, Al Hashemi St. (tel. 638 986; fax 650 916), between Al Husseini Mosque and the Roman amphitheater. Walking from the mosque, look for the blue sign with white English letters on the left side of the street. Small, cell-like yellow rooms with high windows are rather dark but clean. Private telephones and common bath. Can't beat the center-of-everything location. Singles JD5; doubles JD8; triples JD15.

Amman Castle Hotel, Shabsuq St. (tel./fax 642 766), 1½ blocks up an inclined avenue that runs directly into the Roman amphitheater. Look for "HOTEL" spelled out in red letters on a yellow background. Proprietors don't speak any English, but small rooms are comfortable and clean. Few foreigners. Not all rooms have bath. Third floor has a common kitchen. Singles JD5; doubles JD8; triples JD10.

Orient Prince Hotel, Al Hashemi St. (tel. 656 590; fax 656 472). On the left, a bit beyond the theater but before the piazza's clock tower. Look for a big green sign with yellow lettering. Entrance in an alley by the camera shop. Theater views are nice and make the dusty rooms, with their brown fur bedspreads, more appealing. Singles JD8; doubles JD10; triples JD15.

NEAR ABDALI STATION

Canary Hotel, Karmaly St., P.O. Box 9062 (tel. 638 353; tel./fax 654 353), on Jabal al-Weibdeh near Terra Sancta College. Facing downhill from Abdali Station, walk

1½ blocks along the right side of King Hussein St. When the main road forks down-hill to the left, continue straight on Al Ba'oniyah St. Take your first right on Karamaly St. and try to survive the final 1½-block climb. Khaleel Twal, a member of the friendliest family in Amman, will welcome you into his vine-entwined courtyard and comfy pastel-hued TV room. Special *Let's Go* rates with breakfast included: Singles JD15; doubles JD20; triples JD24. Reserve a few days in advance in summer. Lunch and dinner available.

Caravan Hotel, Al Ma'moun St., P.O. Box 9062 (tel. 661 195 or 197; tel./fax 661 196), on Jabal al-Weibdeh. Only 100m northwest of Abdali Station, located across the street from the King Abdullah Mosque. Looking uphill, the entrance is one block to the left of the mosque, across from an Orthodox Church. Spacious rooms with green carpeting are spotless, and the beds are spongy-soft. For true luxury, ask for a balcony. Ihsan Twal will nourish your stay with Arabic food custom-cooked to fit your budget. Special *Let's Go* rates with breakfast included: Singles JD15; doubles JD20; triples JD24.

Shahin Palace Hotel, Muhammad Tash St., P.O. Box 921575 (tel. 648 138 or 139), Jabal al-Weibdeh. Take your first left off Sa'id bin al-Harith St. onto Beit Nouba St. Follow the circle around the park, and take a right on Muhammad Tash St. The hotel is 1½ blocks on the right. Serene place with plush, red-carpeted rooms and refrigerators, TVs, and clean bathrooms, all within a block of a lush park. Singles JD14; doubles JD18; triples JD20.

Remal Hotel, 4 Sa'id Bin al-Harith St., P.O. Box 910477 (tel. 630 670; fax 655 751). Look downhill from the Abdali bus station for the police station on the right; the hotel is a good olive-pit-spit up the small street next to the station. Small rooms are brightened by fresh paint and balconies, but noise from the street can be distracting. Attached restaurant offers traditional Arab fare. Singles JD14; doubles JD18, plus a 10% service charge.

Al Monzer Hotel, King Hussein St., P.O. Box 926595 (tel. 639 469; fax 657 328). From the bus station, it's on the left when looking downhill. Upstairs waiting area has enormous lounge chairs. Clean rooms come with ceiling fans and balconies. Mattresses are thin, but the rooms facing away from the bus station are quiet enough to ensure a good night's sleep. Singles JD12-14; doubles JD16; triples JD18; quads JD20. Cash only.

Sunrise Hotel, King Hussein St. (tel. 621 841 or 428). To the left of Abdali as you face downhill. Cool marble halls and complimentary flip-flops may entice late arrivers to Amman. Rooms are clean and quiet and come equipped with a fan. Singles JD8; doubles JD12; triples JD18, plus a 10% service charge. Cash only.

Merryland Hotel, King Hussein St., P.O. Box 9122 (tel. 615 441, 654 052, or 657 393; fax 657 392). Look downhill from the Abdali bus station and you will see the black walls and large yellow sign on the right. A bit more expensive, but the place to go to splurge. Rooms feature overstuffed mattresses, refrigerators, and sparkling new bathrooms. Singles JD20; doubles JD25; triples JD30.

OUTLYING DISTRICTS

Nefertiti Hotel, 26 Al Jahiz St. (tel. 603 865), in Shmeisani, in front of the Ambassador Hotel. Finding the Nefertiti will be a challenge, but worthwhile. A uniformed attendant will guide you down wide, well-lit corridors to your room, which may have a small terrace. Spacious accommodations and a relaxing, manicured courtyard. Restaurant attached to the hotel. Singles JD11.550; doubles JD14.850; triples JD26.400; quads JD29.700.

■ Food

The better sit-down restaurants in Amman cluster near Third Circle, in Shmeisani, and along Mecca St.; these places usually add a 10% service charge to the bill. The jewel of the city's offerings, however, are the various street foods, which are cheap, plentiful, and safe. If the listings are in Arabic, ask the vendor to translate. For more information about food in Amman and Jordan, see page 466.

Shawerma is always available for about 250fils; the most succulent stuff comes from the stands on Prince Muhammad St., on Second Circle, near the Lebanese Embassy, but it has also been rumored that the **Al Faris Restaurant,** around the corner from the Turino Hotel and Restaurant in Shmeisani, has the best chicken *shawerma* in Jordan. **Falafel** and **corn on the cob** go for 110fils and 250fils respectively. Sides include **hummus** plates, *fuul,* and salads for 250-350fils.

Bread is a staple. *Khoubez* is pita bread; rise at the crack of dawn to sample the freshest *ka'ik* (yummy, crunchy sesame rings). Both are available at stands for 100-200fils. Ask for *za'atar* (dried thyme, sesame seeds, and other spices) to sprinkle on top. Also try cheese or lamb *sfiehah* (Arabic pizzas) or *mana'eesh* (bread baked with olive oil and *za'atar*), sold in many small restaurants and shops.

In the **downtown** area, rolled falafel sandwiches are 110fils. Two busy stands opposite Al Husseini Mosque are open until 11pm. Freshly squeezed **juices,** found in stands throughout the city, are too refreshing to miss (250-350fils). Options range from tomato and orange to banana, carrot, and delicious brown tamarind. A "cocktail" is a blend of bananas, mangos, and strawberries with a pineapple wedge on top. **Ranoush,** off of Firas Circle in Jabal Hussein, serves up the best "cocktail" in Amman.

If you're in **Sweiffiyeh,** check out the **Crema Creme** on Paris St. This popular spot is the place to go for ice cream, and is usually packed with people who triple-park their cars to get a taste of gelato and chat with friends. **Frosti** down the street offers 60-calories-per-scoop ice cream. Anyone who is anyone mingles at the **Caffe Moka.** This Abdoun hangout serves delectable strawberry tarts (JD1.250) and frothing Italian cappuccino (JD1). Prices aren't rock bottom, but the people-watching elite aren't looking for a bargain.

The up-and-coming district of **Umm Uthaina,** by Sixth Circle past Amra Hotel, offers a variety of appetizing, cheap foods. Grab some grilled *halloomi* (white cheese) wraps or stop in at **Al Baron** for tasty sandwiches. Purple neon signs and sidewalk cafes contribute to a festive atmosphere.

Westerners in Amman swear by the giant **Safeway** (tel. 685 311) on the edge of Shmeisani. Any taxi driver will get you there in no time—everyone knows where it is. This island of abundance stocks all of your favorite brand name foods and offers dry cleaning, shoe repair, and a hardware store (open 24hr.). The **Amman souq** is a huge vegetable market located by the Al Husseini Mosque (with your back to the mosque, turn left and then look left for the huge stands overflowing with produce). Fruit and veggie prices have recently been deregulated by the government. More than ever, don't forget to bargain, and bargain hard (open Sun.-Thurs. 8:30am-sundown).

Hashem Restaurant, Prince Muhammad St., in the alley directly across from the Cliff Hotel. The Jordanian choice for hummus since the 50s, Hashem is a great place to see, hear, and feel Amman's pace. Hummus and *fuul* served with an amazing pickled pepper concoction; bread freshly baked across the street; everything garnished with mint leaves and onions grown fresh in their garden. Tea, hummus, and evening's conversation with locals totals well under 500fils. Open daily 24hr.

Al Quds Restaurant, King Hussein St. (tel. 630 168), around the corner from the post office and across from the Cliff Hotel. Though it looks like an American pancake house, serves authentic Arabic food. Mounds of tempting, artistically-arranged sweets. Try their variation on *mensaf,* made with chicken instead of lamb (JD2). *Kebab* JD1.900, french fries 400fils, hummus 500fils. Open daily 7am-11pm (until 10pm in the winter).

Beefy Restaurant (tel. 643 755), in the alley by Andalus Jewelry, downhill from Al Quds. This American-style diner is the only place downtown to get down-home milkshakes (500fils), pizzas (JD1.650), and cheeseburgers topped with cucumbers and onions (600fils).

Abu Ahmad's New Orient Restaurant, 10 Orient St. (tel. 641 879). Take the last right before 3rd Circle as you approach it from 2nd. The first left is Orient St. A luxurious dining experience among vines, green checkered tablecloths, and a hyper-attentive staff. Award-winning charcoal-grilled dishes JD2-2.750. An order of *men-*

Kentucky Fried Jordan

Craving American fast-food diet staples? They're easy to find in Amman now that grease-to-go has invaded Jordan. The culinary coup culminated with the 1997 opening of **McDonald's** in Shmeisani. Along with **Pizza Hut** and **Kentucky Fried Chicken,** it draws crowds from all over the world; tourists and locals gather at all hours to enjoy the culture and smell of these ubiquitous chains. You can't miss the neon signs in Shmeisani (taxis know the route well). For a real taste of Americana, head to **Cheers Elite Cafe** in Sweifiyyeh's stylish Turino Hotel, where everyone knows your name. Authentic blues and Top 40 music will serenade you while you chow on affordable buffalo wings, pizzas, and gourmet burgers.

saf (JD3) is enough for 2. Generous *mezzeh* dishes 400fils. Traveler's checks accepted. Open daily noon-midnight.

Cairo Restaurant, on a side street on the left 2 blocks away from the Al Husseini Mosque. With your back to the mosque, head left past the clothes booths, looking for the big red and white sign. Fill up inexpensively: roasted ½-chicken 1.150fils, *kebab* 1.150fils, *fasulya* (green beans cooked with lamb in tomato sauce) 300fils, breakfast *fuul* plates 300fils, and a ½ head of lamb (including eyes and tongue) JD1.100. Vegetarians beware: this place is a flesh orgy. Open daily 5am-10pm.

Salaam Restaurant, King Faisal St. (tel. 622 626), ½ a block away from the Al Husseini Mosque on the left-hand side of the street, next to the Bata shoe store. No English sign; look for spitted chickens in the window. The colorful crowd, tasty food, and A/C may lure you inside, but the pastries will make you stay. JD3.300 buys bread, bird, and fries. *Sfiebah* and *manaish* 200fils each. Menu is in Arabic but servers can describe the dishes in English. Open daily 7am-10pm.

Abu Saleh Restaurant, King Faisal St. (tel. 622 782), a minute's walk downhill from the "SEIKO" sign, in the alley on the right. English translations opposite the Arabic dishes listed on the menu, but prices are conveniently left untranslated. Half-chicken and *kebab* go for about JD1 each. Open daily 7:30am-9pm.

Romero, 3rd Circle, Jabal Amman (tel. 644 227). This romantic outdoor cafe with a sunny Mediterranean ambience serves the best Italian food in Amman. Entrees JD2.500-7. Open daily noon-midnight.

Indian Restaurant, 8th Circle (tel. 819 829). True to its name, this place serves Indian food. No hummus or *mensaf* here: feast on vegetarian curry, basmati rice, and fresh-squeezed juice. The food is spicy and delicious. Entrees JD1.500-3. Open daily noon-4pm and 6:30pm-midnight. Visa, MC accepted.

Pizza Italiano Alreef, Al Madina Almunawra St., near University Hospital Bridge, a 10min taxi ride from downtown. With its polished wood interior and cool brick floors, this new pizzeria is a great place to escape your millionth falafel sandwich. Family-size *pizza margherita* a mere 800fils. Open Sun.-Fri. 11:30am-midnight.

Milano, Shmeisani (tel. 680 670). Johnny Depp and Jean-Claude Van Damme preside over a teenage clientele guzzling generous portions of pizza and pasta in this perennial Amman institution. Entrees JD1.200-3. Outdoor dining in the summer.

■ Sights

The **Roman Amphitheater,** downtown on Jabal al-Qala'a, is the most renowned of Amman's historical sights. Built by Antonius Pius (138–161 CE), the amphitheater could once accommodate 6000 spectators, the entire population of the city (open Wed.-Mon. 9am-5pm). It's free, but you'll be met by a line of eager "guides" who charge JD2 or your best price. Ignore them—you won't need help to find it.

Two museums are built into the foundations of the amphitheater on either side of the enclosed stage area. The **Folklore Museum** (tel. 651 742) displays exhibits of the diverse heritages of the Jordanian people, with Circassian military weaponry, Palestinian embroidery, and Bedouin encampments (open Wed.-Mon. 9am-5pm; admission JD1). The **Museum of Popular Traditions** (tel. 651 760) shows off attire and accessories from the country's past. The gallery to the right of the entrance displays 6th-century mosaics from Madaba and Jerash (open Wed.-Mon. 9am-5pm; admission

JORDAN

JD1). Students can beg for free admission, which often works if there aren't many other visitors. Otherwise, the hefty JD1 fee is far from worth it for either museum.

From the Roman Amphitheater, or any downtown locale, you can climb the steep steps and streets to the flat top of **Citadel Hill.** This is better done with a friend, especially for women traveling alone, in order to avoid harassment from locals who are a bit overzealous in their hospitality. On the southern slope of Jabal al-Qala'a, the citadel is the site of ancient Amman, called Rabbath-Ammon, or the "Great City of the Ammonites." The Ammonites make frequent guest appearances in the Bible. King David besieged Rabbath-Ammon twice, the second time improving his chances of marrying the already pregnant Bathsheba by putting her husband Uriah in the front line of battle. A few Byzantine and Umayyad ruins remain.

A trip to the top of Citadel Hill is a good idea for your first day in Amman. The view will give you the best perspective on the city's labyrinthine ups and downs. The **Archaeological Museum** (tel. 638 795), on Citadel Hill, contains a chronologically organized series of finds from ancient sites throughout Jordan. 200,000-year-old dinner leftovers share the limelight with Iron Age anthropomorphic sarcophagi, minimalist Nabatean portraits, and a Roman marble statuary (open Wed.-Thurs. and Sat.-Mon. 9am-5pm, Fri. 10am-4pm; JD2). In front of the museum are the foundations of a 2nd-century CE Roman temple that housed a 10m statue of Hercules, to whom the temple was likely dedicated. Three of the statue's giant marble fingers hint at the shrine's former glory.

The best-preserved and most intriguing of Amman's ruins lie behind the museum. Vaulted chambers tower 10m over a spacious courtyard where elaborate floral decorations can still be seen in the stonework. The 7th-century structure once supported a huge stone dome and was used as a mosque, audience hall, and residence. Below the Roman walls directly to the north, an open pit leads into the underground passageway that connected the fortified city to a hidden water supply. With a flashlight and fancy footwork you can enter the cavernous rock-hewn **cistern** by this route. The more conventional approach is from the gate on the street below.

The Citadel was the heart of ancient Amman; today the pulse emanates from downtown, in and around **Al Husseini Mosque.** The Ottoman-style structure was built in 1924 on the site of an ancient mosque, probably also the site of the Old Cathedral of Philadelphia. The nearby **Nymphaeum** was a sacred fountain and bathing ground for the ancient city.

The area around the Al Husseini Mosque is full of second-hand shoe shops. At the center of the triangle formed by the Citadel, the Mosque, and the post office is Amman's glittering **gold market,** featuring row upon row of gold jewelry. One or two shops vend antique Bedouin silver jewelry. Although bargaining is a way of life in much of Amman, prices in the gold market are fixed, as jewelry is priced strictly by weight (open Sat.-Thurs. 9am-9pm, Fri. 9am-1:30pm).

Barely out of a good *muezzin*'s range from Al Husseini Mosque is Abdali's own **King Abdullah Mosque.** Constructed in seven years in memory of the late King, 3000 Muslims can kneel in prayer under its huge blue mosaic dome. Perched atop Jabal Ashrafiyyeh is the black-and-white checkered dome of the **Abu Darwish Mosque.** Built in the 1940s by Circassians, this is one of the most unusual religious structures in the Middle East. The mosque was constructed entirely from black basalt, brought from quarries in the northern part of the country, and white rock. The two colors were used not only for the structure of the building, but for its decoration and ornamentation as well.

The **Jordan Craft Center** (tel. 644 555), downhill from the Lebanese Embassy (Second Circle) and on the left, exhibits rugs, silver, glass, jewelry, embroidery, caftans, and pottery (open Sat.-Thurs. 9am-5pm; in winter Sun.-Thurs. 9am-1pm and 3-6pm; free). The **Jordan National Gallery,** (tel. 630 128) on Jabal al-Weibdeh at Muntazah Park, displays contemporary artwork from throughout the Islamic world. The range of art makes this place worth a visit. Modern Islamic pieces contain a surprising amount of criticism of daily life. The guy at the front desk may tell you to pay for a ticket, but donations are optional (open Wed.-Mon. 10am-1:30pm, 3:30-6pm; free).

Amman's finest Byzantine artifact is the **Sweifiyyeh Mosaic,** found during construction at the western edge of the city in 1970. This 46 sq. m. mosaic floor illustrates the passing of the four seasons, and once belonged to a 6th-century church. Ask the caretaker to hose down the floor for a better look at the bizarre creatures, including leaf-bearded men, eagles with ears, and eely fish-men. This is possibly the most worthwhile sight north of Madaba. Follow the signs from the first left west of Sixth Circle (open Sat.-Thurs. 9am-4pm, Fri. 9am-1:30pm; free). The **Martyr's Monument** and **Military Museum** (tel. 664 240) are in an odd square building overlooking the Hussein Sports City. The museum houses a chronological display of military memorabilia, dating from the Arab revolt in 1916 to the present (open Sun.-Fri. 9am-4pm; free). Call ahead: both are closed to visitors when the Royal Family is entertaining.

■ Entertainment

During the late afternoon and early evening, Amman's central **souq** (market) becomes the city's most happening spot, swallowing several blocks southwest of Al Husseini Mosque. Most people rest between 2 and 4pm (*service* and buses become scarce), but cafes allow homeless budget travelers to linger over coffee in the shade. Try **Ma'atouk's,** outside the *souq,* on Third Circle (coffee 300fils).

Amman's **nightlife** thrives in the summer. When the sweltering days give way to cool evenings, nocturnal enthusiasts find fulfillment in bars or on dance floors. But Amman is not Cairo—even glamour boys and fly girls here bed down by 1 or 2am. Celebrating its fifth successful year, **Salute,** between First and Second Circles (under the Villa d'Angelo Italian restaurant), remains the favorite amongst the younger members of Amman's privileged class, especially on Monday and Thursday nights, this city's "weekend nights." If you can squeeze yourself onto their breezy patio, consider yourself a member of the "in" clique (Unaccompanied men will not be admitted. No cover. Drinks around JD2-4.) Overflow from Salute and stylish Euroclub dancers head to the **Roof Garden,** between the First and Second Circles, upstairs from Gengisghan Restaurant. The view of the city is spectacular, but can only be enjoyed by those 18 and over with ID (cover JD3.500 on Mon. and Thurs.). **Cavalier,** above the Olivier Restaurant down the street from Coconut Grove, is scheduled to reopen after renovations. Cavalier used to be a contender, and probably will continue to compete.

Still the most popular dance club in Amman, **Scandal,** in the basement of the **San Rock Hotel** (Sixth Circle), has security people frisking club-goers at the door, mirrored walls, black upholstered booths, purple neon lights, and 40-year-old men trying to pick up airline stewardesses. On the far side of Shmeisani (about twice as far as the Ambassador Hotel, on the same road) is the **Middle East Hotel,** which hosts the **Talk of the Town** disco on Monday and Thursday nights. The crowd is mostly made up of twenty-something Jordanians and foreigners; the tunes range from techno to reggae. (Both open until 3am, and people don't arrive until 10 or 11pm.)

The Cellar, in the cozy basement of **Al Qasr Hotel** (Shmeisani, between the Ambassador and Nefertiti Hotels) is mellower. The American-style jazz bar features terrific live music, mixed drinks, and potato skins—enough to please any hep-cat abroad. Expats and beer drinkers cluster at the **Irish Pub** (downstairs in the **Dove Hotel,** between Fourth and Fifth circles). All the Guinness you can drink is here, but no singles are admitted (men or women). The **Caesar's Palace Restaurant** on Jabal al-Weibdeh offers more traditional Jordanian music and dancing, including belly dancing on Thursday nights.

At first glance, the city center seems to lack the traditional Middle Eastern constellation of cafes and tea houses. Look up: they're mostly perched on second floors. The **Hilton Cafe** (across from the Cliff Hotel) overlooks the royal intersection of King Hussein and King Faisal St. (above the Seiko watch sign). There's a crowded and noisy *al fresco* hangout on the second floor, where you can learn local card games over a cup of Amman's sludgiest Arabic coffee (100fils and up) and entertain your recently acquired best friends by choking on the dense charcoal and tobacco smoke of an *argeileh* (300fils). Jordanian society reserves such entertainments for members of the male gender; women probably will feel more comfortable elsewhere. **Babiche Cafe, Geneva,** and the new **Caffe Moka** in Shmeisani serve coffee, drinks, and pastries to a co-ed chi-chi crowd. **Reem al-Bawady** (Tla' al-Ali, Al Ubeel circle) offers fruit-flavored tobacco for smoking *argeileh* in traditional Bedouin camel-hair tents. Women, with male friends, are welcome.

There are three **cinemas** that show English-language films: the **Philadelphia,** Third Circle (tel. 634 149), **Concord,** Shmeisani, opposite the Forte Grande Hotel (tel. 677 420), and **Plaza,** at the Forte Grande in Shmeisani (tel. 699 238). The **Nabil & Hisham's Theater,** Rainbow St., First Circle (tel. 625 155) sometimes produces English-language plays. Call for more information.

NEAR AMMAN

■ Wadi Seer وادى السير

Burgeoning Amman has poked its urban tentacles westward into the quiet valley of Wadi Seer. Like much of the fertile hill country to the north and west of Amman, Wadi Seer was first settled by Circassians. These fair-skinned Muslims came from Russia during the Czarist persecutions of the 1870s and account for most blonde and red-headed Jordanians. Amman's **Folklore Museum** displays the traditional Circassian costume, a cylindrical fur cap and black waistcoat with red trim (see p.477).

At Wadi Seer, the high desert plateau suddenly gives way to the **Jordan Valley.** Here, a little stream snakes through the countryside on its way to the Dead Sea. The narrow asphalt road that follows this valley out of town is ideal for daytripping motorists and tramping backpackers, but be prepared for scorching summer days. Verdant pomegranate plants and olive trees, along with a bevy of children, line the 12km road which runs southwest to the remains of Qasr al-Abd.

Soon after leaving Wadi Seer you'll pass **Al Bassa Springs,** the source of the valley's fertility and a swimming pool for the area's children. Above the left bank of the *wadi*, **Ad-Deir** (the monastery) is carved into the face of the cliff. This extraordinary building merits the 20-minute climb, even if you don't find any of the Roman gold which villagers claim is buried under the floor. Each of the ossuary's thousands of triangular wall-niches once cradled a skull, the remnants of monks.

Local legend holds that **Qasr al-Abd** (Castle of the Slave), better known as **Qasr Iraq al-Emir** (Castle of the Prince's Rock) was built by a love-smitten slave named Tobiah. While his master was away on a journey, Tobiah built a palace and carved lions, panthers, and eagles into its walls in order to win the hand of the master's daughter. Unfortunately, the master returned before Tobiah could finish the work, and the slave's efforts went unrewarded. This story is given credence by the Aramaic inscription "Tobiah" carved near the entrance of one of the eleven caves, 500 meters back up the valley road. These caves, **Iraq al-Emir,** are believed to have been dug by hand and used to house horses.

Kill-joy historians explain the inscription and the castle remains with references to Tobiah the Ammonite Servant. This Tobiah was a rich priest in Jerusalem, and the name of the castle refers to his occupation as a servant of God. Ancient historian Josephus also records the wealth of a Tobiah family and the exploits of the young son Hyrcanus, who built a strong fortress constructed entirely of white marble and enclosed by a wide, deep moat. Several red stone lions remain intact, though there is no roof. The most impressive is the lioness on the northwest corner, but both lions have a unique twist: the male (with the flowing mane) is breast-feeding a baby with its female nipples—and the female lioness, prowling the corner alone, has male genitals. The guard or his son should let you in for free; a small donation of 100-200fils, however, is appreciated.

The easiest way to get to Wadi Seer begins at Al Husseini Mosque. As you face out of the mosque, turn left and walk past the screeching taxis until you arrive at a fork in the road (10 minutes). Head left at the fork and look for lines of minibuses; they'll drop you off at Wadi Seer for 100fils. You can also catch the Wadi Seer bus from either Fifth or Sixth circle. Just hail the driver when you see the bus going north, away from downtown. From Wadi Seer, catch a minibus headed down the valley road (150fils). The whole trip can take between 45 minutes and 1½hr., depending on the wait between buses and the number of times they stop for stray chickens in the road. These buses leave when they are full, so bring water and plenty of patience— you may have a bit of a wait for the return trip.

■ Salt السلط

Salt (pronounced like "SULTry") was the thriving administrative center of the surrounding *vilayet* during Ottoman rule. In the late 1920s, it seemed a likely choice for the capital of the new mandate of Transjordan; eventually, however, it was bypassed for the smaller but centrally located village of Amman. Because of that lost opportunity, Salt is better known today for its history than its political prowess. In the second half of the 19th century, industrious Saltis built Jordan's first hospital and its first modern church. In 1925, Salt established Jordan's first secondary school; by now, the swank preparatory establishment boasts almost all of Jordan's ministers and prime ministers as alums.

A church destroyed during a war in Ottoman times was picked apart and used to construct local houses: look for whole sections of archways that are now cozily integrated into the yellow homes that date from that time. The Ottoman barracks, still intact, were built over a 13th-century fortress that was destroyed to prevent its capture by Crusaders. Salt is also known for its large Christian community, and church towers pepper the hillsides.

If the adventurous spirit moves you, wander downhill from the bus station into **Wadi Sh'eib.** Look for the natural streams bubbling out of the ground, both breaking through the pavement of the main road and off the beaten track. These can be refreshing to dip your hands into, but are unsafe to drink. Unexplored caves and abandoned stone houses dot the *wadi,* and numerous dirt paths lead you further down. Pink flowers and fruit trees line the narrow stream that winds through the bottom of the valley. Leave a trail of bread crumbs, or you might not find your way back.

Practical Information Taking a **minibus** up Wadi Sh'eib is the most dramatic approach to Salt. Lush, terraced farmlands and eucalyptus groves tumble down the *wadi* to the southwest of town, descending to Shuneh Nimrin (South Shuneh) on the busy route from Amman to the King Hussein/Allenby Bridge (Jordan Valley Highway). From Amman, corner an Abdali bus driver to find the minibus going to Salt (30min., 175fils). Be prepared to wait until the bus has enough passengers to depart. The **post office** (tel. 554 96 85) is located uphill on the main road, a good 10-minute walk from the circle at the bottom (open Sat.-Thurs. 7:30am-7pm, Fri. 7:30am-1:30pm). As in every town in Jordan, in case of **emergency,** dial 192. For a **medical emergency,** dial 193. Salt's **telephone code** is 05

Accommodations and Food Although Salt has no hotels, Saltis are proud to uphold the Arab Bedouin tradition of *khuttar,* whereby prominent (and not-so-prominent) local families take it upon themselves to host any visitors that cross their paths or knock on their doors. The tourist office, across the hall from the archeological museum, is empty more often than not, but the municipal building, up the street from the **Abu Jaber** house, is a good source of information on the city.

Delicious food is easy to find; for the best *kebab* north of Amman, eat at **Al Amad's,** established by Radi Al-Amad in 1927 and inherited by his son, who runs it today. JD1.25 will buy you *kebab* as well as the privilege of seeing his guest book, which has been signed by the head of the Central Bank and other dignitaries, all of whom ate there as students in Salt. There is also detailed documentation of what they ate. For good hummus, *fuul,* and the like, the **Canam Restaurant** (down past the

Archaeological Museum) is a good bet, and cheap (hummus, *mezze*, and tea, 300fils). Finish up with some freshly-baked pastries at **Al Habiba,** up the road from Canam. Especially good is the *warbaht*. If you can only afford minimal food, go here. It may not be the healthiest dinner, but the sweets are too honey-fresh to pass up.

Sights The famous Abu Jaber house, located across from the Jordan Gulf bank, was constructed in 1894. Even if you can't get in to see the ceilings covered with Italian frescoes, a street-side perspective is enough to appreciate why this building is one of Jordan's finest architectural works. The highest point in Salt is the mosque on **Jabal Yushah** which, according to Muslim legend, covers the site of the tomb of the prophet Hosea (Yushah), and is a JD2 round-trip taxi ride from downtown Salt. The awe-inspiring view of the West Bank will make the trip up the hill worth your while. In the morning, you can see from the Dead Sea to Lake Tiberias.

To get to the **Salt Archaeological Museum** (tel. 555 651), go left where the road splits uphill from the bus station. On the right hand side, you'll see a white building with red stone around the outside, with a rather obscure blue sign on the second floor. It consists of two rooms with lots of coins, pottery, and jewelry dating from the Chalcolithic period (4000BCE) to the Islamic period (1516CE). Open Sat.-Thurs. 8am-4 or 5pm; free. The **Salt Folklore Museum** (tel. 553 653) is one flight up from the Archaeology Museum. Both are open Wed.-Mon. 8am-6pm.

■ Azraq and the Desert Castles

الازرق و القصور الصـحـراوية

The springs at Azraq are the only permanent bodies of water in over 2500 sq. km of barren sand-and-scorpion desert. Unfortunately, the water is being pumped to parched Amman throats, so the area has dried up significantly. As recently as last year, the palm trees were green, the animals abundant, and the hundreds of species of exotic birds that rest at Azraq colored the sky. Sadly, what was once green is now a crunchy brown, and the only movement is of trucks passing through.

The discovery of an enormous cache of flint hand-axes indicates that either Paleolithic settlers or extremely sophisticated camels hunted in the area 500,000 years ago. Even so, the most remarkable records of human habitation are the scattered Umayyad castles, a group of structures that originally formed a chain from the north of Damascus to Khirbet al-Mafjar, near Jericho. Built in the 7th and 8th centuries CE by the Umayyads, the castles were mysteriously abandoned a century later. The imposing stonework of **Qasr Kharaneh** and strategic location of **Qasr Azraq** and **Qasr Mushatta** support speculation that the castles sheltered caravans along the trade route between Syria, Arabia, and the Far East. The baths near **Qasr al-Hallabat** and the magnificent frescoes at **Qasr Amra** brought creature comforts to the desert.

Orientation and Practical Information A trip to Azraq oasis and the Desert Castles is fraught with uncertainty and annoyingly difficult to arrange, but worth every annoyance. Still relatively tourist-free, these quietly majestic ruins will awe you with the strength of their standing arches and the warmth of their Bedouin gatekeepers. There are only three options for transportation to the castles. First, you can hire a **taxi** from Amman for the official rate of JD24 (try bargaining it down to JD20). This will provide half a day's wheels and someone who knows the route (full day over JD30). Second, you can **rent a car** in Amman for JD25-35 or more for a day, with unlimited mileage and the option to return it in Aqaba or at the airport. **Reliable Rent a Car** (tel. 819 676) offers the best deals. Finally, JETT **buses** do full day group tours of the desert castles; arrange this through a travel agent.

As always, **hitchhiking** is discouraged and potentially suicidal. If you decide to attempt it, you'll need an immense supply of food and water and an excessive appetite for adventure. There are only a few hitchers and cars on the Damascus highway from Amman to Zarqa (30km). Alternatively, *service* from Abdali Station in Amman can take you to Zarqa quickly and cheaply (300fils). Accepting rides from the army is **illegal,** and anyway will take you only as far as some lonely desert depot. The highway passes right by Qasr al-Hallabat (30km from Zarqa) before reaching Azraq (87km from Zarqa). From the Azraq junction, you'd have to hitch 13km north to reach Qasr Azraq and then return to Azraq. If you take the southern highway back to Amman, you will pass near Qasr Amra (25km from Azraq), then Qasr Kharaneh (40km from Azraq), and Qasr Mushatta (about 90km from Azraq and 40km from Amman).

The following description of the castles and Azraq details a road trip that takes the northern route from Amman to Azraq and the southern highway on the return trip (a **clockwise tour**). Going the other way is deadly for hitchhikers, since cars come as frequently as snowstorms. If you have a car, you could go as easily in either direction. Drivers beware: the road from Amman to Zarqa passes through several notorious speed traps, where unforgiving cops dispense fines of JD50 even if you're only doing 1km over. Make sure you wear your seat belt; unprotected driving fines are hefty, too. The desert **telephone code** is 06, the same as in Amman.

QASR AL-HALLABAT قصر الحلابات

Qasr al-Hallabat's ruined arches appear approximately 30km east into the desert from Zarqa. Angle off at the right, turn onto the paved road, and turn left up the track to the gate. The gatekeeper's tent is to the left of the crumbling castle; you're free to roam around whatever is left. Keep in mind that any gatekeeper who provides you with information will expect a few hundred fils in return. Originally built by Caracall (198-217 CE) as a Roman fort, it was reused by the Byzantines as a monastery during the reign of Anastasius (491-518), and then rebuilt and used by Umayyads as a residential palace in the 8th century. The Umayyad conquerors added a mosque just meters away from the 2nd-century main defense structure. Look for the Byzantine carvings on what is left of the walls and fallen slabs of stone.

Back on the main highway, the sand and limestone desert to the south contrasts sharply with the gray volcanic desert to the north. Just off the road to the south is **Hammam As-Sarh,** the ruined bathhouse modeled after Amra (below). A 1000-year-old **well** lurks next to a shallow pool. *Let's Go* recommends admiring the well from above ground—be careful not to fall into the unmarked hole.

AZRAQ الأزرق

On the long and grinding road east of **Hallabat,** you'll hear nothing but the entreaties of your overheating engine. After ages of drab desert, you'll suddenly come upon the formerly lush gardens of **Azraq Oasis,** Jordan's only permanent body of fresh water, which is quickly drying up. Relax and reassemble your bearings (both mental and mechanical) at **Azraq Junction,** where the highway to the northeast goes to Iraq and the southeastern road leads to the southern castles and on into Saudi Arabia.

About 13km north of Azraq Junction, on the highway to Iraq, squats **Qasr Azraq.** Most of the castle is in excellent condition thanks to extensive restoration. The black basalt fort, built by the Romans in 300 CE and later rebuilt by the Ayyubids in 1237, rose to three levels. Only parts of the second level survived the 1926 earthquake, including a ceiling that exposes a web of huge basalt beams. The Druze gatekeeper will haul open the three-ton portal of the castle and, if he's feeling friendly, will show you his **Lawrence of Arabia** photograph collection (many of the photographs look suspiciously like the gatekeeper himself). The most interesting attractions lie within a few meters of the entrance. Looking up from the main door, you'll see the *machicoulis* (holes) through which boiling oil and molten lead were poured on invaders' bald spots. Carved into the pavement behind the main gate is a Roman board game. In the center of the courtyard lies a small cube of a mosque, thought to have been built originally as a Roman church. Just above the entrance is the room used by Lawrence himself during his short stay on the premises. He used the fort as his headquarters during the Arab revolt against Ottoman rule in 1917.

Located on the north side of Azraq, down a tree-lined road, is the **Azraq Resthouse** (tel. 647 611, ext. 6). Rooms include bath, air-conditioning, color TV, minibar, and a view of the pool, which non-guests can use for JD1 (singles JD23.500; doubles JD29). The overpriced restaurant serves usual fare (complete meal JD5). There are many small markets and stands in town that provide cheaper nourishment. You'll also find a **post office** (open Sat.-Thurs. 7:30am-7pm, Fri. 7:30am-1pm) and a **Housing Bank** (open for exchange Sat.-Wed. 8:30am-1pm and 4-5pm, Thurs. 8:30am-1pm).

Throughout the trip, keep an eye out for desert wildlife, now making a comeback since Jordan started protecting the fragile habitat. In the **Shaumari Wildlife Preserve,** near Qasr Amra, the government is reintroducing armadillos, Himalayan dwarf hamsters, ostriches, **Syrian wild asses,** and Arabian oryxes. Cheetah and desert wolves roam in regions to the northeast and southwest of Azraq (preserve admission 500fils, students 300fils).

QASR AMRA قصر عمرة

Constructed under the auspices of Umayyad Caliph al-Walid ibn 'Abd al-Malik, the hunting lodge and bath complex of Qasr Amra impress visitors with the elegant simplicity of their designs. The interior is also the best preserved of the desert palaces; its vaulted stucco ceilings are splashed with lively frescoes, and mosaics grace two of the floors. As you walk in, on the right is a **mural** depicting the enemies of Islam, among them the emperors of Byzantium, Persia, and China. The mural also names Roderique, then King of Spain. The face's similarity to traditional depictions of Jesus suggests a Roman rather than Muslim artist. An early portrayal of the zodiac covers the domed ceiling of the *caldarium* (hot room). Since they ignore the Muslim tradition forbidding the pictorial representation of human beings, the **frescoes** are all the more riveting. Especially surprising are the many portrayals of nude women, which somehow escaped the decree of Umayyad Caliph Yazid II (720-724 CE) ordering all human images and likenesses destroyed. Some say he came here on the weekends to relax. You can reach Qasr Amra on the road heading southwest of Azraq Junction, about 28km from Qasr Azraq. The gatekeeper expects a small *bakhsheesh.*

QASR KHARANEH قصر الخرانة

One of the best preserved of the desert castles, Qasr Kharaneh is named for the small black stones that blanket the area. Some experts believe Kharaneh was a defensive fort; they point to the four corner towers and the square plan of a Roman fortress, as well as the appearance of arrow slits through the enigmatic fort. Others believe these slits were part of an elaborate ventilation system and argue that it served as a retreat for Umayyad leaders to discuss matters of state. Most historians believe it was a *khan,* or inn—the first of the Islamic world. This is further evinced by the architectural style of the castle, which would come to typify the Umayyad inn. A painted Arabic dedication in a second-story room dates the building's construction to 710-711 CE. Greek inscriptions on the doorjambs imply that the Umayyads built upon an earlier structure. For a good view of the courtyard, climb the staircase on your left as you enter. You'll also see the neighboring military base and the maneuverings of Jordanian troops. When you've finished exploring, the gatekeeper will let you ride his camel for some *bakhsheesh* (500fils should do). As he leads you around the castle, listen carefully; he insists that ghosts of horses, camels, and even people roam the ruins.

QASR MUSHATTA قصر مشتة

To reach this final castle, take any turn-off to Queen Alia International Airport. Hitchhikers often hire *service* from the village of **Muwaqaar** in the north to reach the castle. The castle is on the left as you approach the airport from the north, but the public access road turns off to the right and loops about 4km around the airport. If you're walking from the airport, don't take this marked turn-off. Instead, continue to the left of the airport, past the Alia cargo terminal, until Mushatta appears on the left (a 30min walk). Soldiers and guards at checkpoints will ask to see your **passport,** or even take it temporarily. The entrance to the 8th-century castle once beckoned travelers with wonderfully carved floral designs. Most of the carved stones, however, were delivered to Kaiser Wilhelm II as a gift from Ottoman Sultan Abdulhamid II, and only fragments remain. An entire piece of wall now resides in the Berlin Museum: an odd switch; usually Berlin contributes the wall. Although the size of the ruins attest to the ambition of the construction, the castle, for unknown reasons, was never completed. Mushatta was constructed with smaller, weaker bricks than other castles. It is a testament to the architect's skill that his work still stands. From Qasr Mushatta you can catch a **taxi** (JD10) or **bus** (850fils) to Amman via the airport. Hitchers reportedly find it an easy trip back into town.

South of Amman

Three roads link Amman and Aqaba: the Wadi Araba (Jordan Valley) Highway, the Desert Highway, and the Kings' Highway. The **Wadi Araba Highway** hugs the Dead Sea Coast. Enormous trucks rumble impassively along the **Desert Highway,** the artery that ties the cities of the north to the port at Aqaba. Since the Iran-Iraq War, the Desert Highway has been the chief link between Europe and Turkey and the Persian (Arabian) Gulf. Major construction has made the highway smooth and swift, but even the King can do little about the scenery—three and a half hours of unchanging desert to Petra, an hour and a half more to Aqaba. Only the antics of bored drivers playfully bumping the narrow shoulders or squeezing between oncoming cars break the monotony. Gas and phones along the way are scarce.

The **Kings' Highway** (Wadi Mujib Road) is the ideal way to travel the length of Jordan. This ancient route journeys through spectacular canyons, passing Biblical sites, Crusader castles, and Byzantine churches and mosaics along the way. Known by the same name in Biblical times, this road was supposedly traveled by the Israelites during their exodus from Egypt. Caravans filled with cinnamon and myrrh crept from Arabia to Palestine and Syria on their way to Europe.

Service run most of the way from Amman to Petra, as do minibuses, but generally in the mornings only. Karak is a convenient overnight stop. **Hitchhiking** south of Amman is possible, but involves the risks inherent in hitching anywhere. Hitching along the sometimes deserted Kings' Highway is said to be difficult. It is illegal to hitchhike on the Wadi Araba Highway, which runs alongside the Israeli border. Since roadside bystanders often wave at passing cars in salutation, hitchers generally stick their right arm out, palm down.

To get to the Desert Highway from downtown Amman, hitchhikers head south on Jerusalem St. (in Jabal Nadhif across Wadi Abdoun), which metamorphoses into Rte. 15 (the Desert Highway). To get to the Kings' Highway, hitchers take a *service* from Amman's Wahdat Station to Madaba (330fils) and then try their luck on the road to Karak, which passes out of Madaba by the Apostles' Church. Small groups of hitchers stand by the mini-obelisk marking the intersection of the Kings' Highway and the Desert Highway, 18km south of Amman. People reach the intersection by taking a Madaba-bound *service* from Wahdat Station or by hitching south from Seventh Circle.

The distances are manageable: 33km from Amman to Madaba, 98km from Madaba to Karak, and 150km from Karak to Petra. The total distance from Amman to Petra is 282km along the Kings' Highway or 262km along the Desert Highway. Many people camp in the *wadis* north of Karak or in the desert regions between Karak and Petra. The only indoor accommodations are in Karak and Madaba. The easiest route is to see Madaba, before heading to Karak for the night. Leaving early in the morning from Karak, the trip to Petra can be done comfortably in a day, stopping in Shobak and at the Dana nature reserve along the way.

JORDAN

■ The Dead Sea البحر الميت

More than 400m below sea level, the Dead Sea is the lowest point on earth. Now a serenely quiet shore, the Dead Sea region is thought by many to be the site of five biblical cities: Sodom, Gomorrah, Admah, Zeboin, and Zowr. Indeed, a dried pillar of salt nearby is believed to be the remains of Lot's wife, who, upon fleeing the damned city of Sodom, disobeyed God's command to not look back (and was unceremoniously turned into a pillar of salt). Four times as salty as regular sea water, the peculiar buoyancy of this briny water forces even the densest swimmer into a back float, and the wealth of salts and minerals gives it its renowned curative powers, recognized for over 2000 years. The salt water makes a tiny paper cut feel like an amputation and it tastes awful. Don't get any in your eyes, or you'll have to beg to use one of the eye-flushing plastic water bottles that those in the know tote along to the beach. See **Israel: Dead Sea,** p. 406 for geographical information.

After a minibus descent through rolling hills that will rival your 747's approach to Queen Alia airport, prepare to come as close to walking on water as is humanly possible. The Dead Sea's northeastern shore, 1 to 1½ hours from Amman or Deir Alla, hosts the only stretch of sand open to visitors on the Jordanian side. During the middle of the day, the sun reflects off the sea's still surface, creating the illusion that the entire body of water is about to spill into the Jordan Valley.

The greatest obstacle in reaching the Dead Sea is getting to the highway that runs along its edge. Once there, hop on one of the many **buses** or *service* shuttling up and down the road. Buses from the Ras al-Ayn area in Amman go to the Dead Sea Rest House/Suweimeh (1-2hr., 600fils). To reach this area, begin at Al Husseini Mosque. With your back to the mosque, make a left, and walk for about ten minutes. When the road forks, go left and cross the busy intersection. Take a right on the big street and stay to the left. The buses are 20 minutes up the road. Don a panama, bring plenty of water, and don't forget your passport—you'll need it at several military roadblocks along the way. There are buses leaving every 30 minutes. Some go to Shouna (1hr., 400fils), where you can catch a second bus to the Rest House (30min., 200fils). Group daytrips can also be arranged with the JETT and Alpha bus companies for JD10-20. A taxi to the Dead Sea from Amman is about JD25, but you may be able to get a slightly lower price by bargaining.

The **Dead Sea Rest House** (tel. (05) 546 110) offers showers to relieve you of Lot's wife's encrusted fate. Unless you swim around the barrier on the north, which closes off the nicest section of beach, you'll have to pay JD2 to enter the resort enclave. The complex contains showers, the air-conditioned Rest House (bungalow with A/C, bathroom, TV, and telephone JD33), and an overpriced restaurant (main courses JD3-7, soft drinks 700fils, water 800fils). The rocky walk into the water can be tough; you may want to wear some form of foot protection. The beach also has shelters for those who prefer shade to the merciless sun. The last bus leaves at 6pm. If you do get stranded, the sunset over the West Bank will almost make it worth it. (Rest House open daily 8am-11pm. Swimming allowed until sundown.) Several new hotels are scheduled for completion by the end of 1998.

About 12km south of the Rest House is the natural spring of **Zara,** nestled between the colorful Jordan Valley cliffs. Under 30km south on the highway to Aqaba (Rte. 35) is **Zarqa Ma'in,** a cascading hot spring (see **Near Madaba,** p. 488). A road connecting the Dead Sea Rest House and Zarqa Ma'in is rumored to be in the works.

■ Madaba مادبا

Madaba is located on a plateau of orange groves overlooking the Jordan Valley. The scanty Roman columns next to the government Rest House hardly evoke visions of the flourishing trade center that was once the size of Jerash, but American archaeologists at work in the newly formed "Archaeological Park" downtown are quickly revealing past glories. A Roman road, burnt palace, and several churches have been discovered only meters away from the Church of St. George, home of the famous mosaic map of the Holy Land. The elaborate mosaics scattered throughout the "City of Mosaics" attest to Madaba's importance as a Byzantine ecclesiastical center; the town received its own bishop as early as the 5th century CE. Persians attacked Madaba in 614 CE, slaughtering the residents and damaging many Roman and Byzantine artifacts. Most of what still stood was leveled by an earthquake in the 8th century, leaving Madaba untouched for nearly 1100 years until Christian clans from Karak reinhabited the city in the late 1800s.

Practical Information Minibuses shuttle between Madaba and Amman's Wahdat (180fils), Raghadan (220fils), and Abdali Stations (260fils) regularly until 7pm in summer and 5pm in winter. No *service* run between Amman and Madaba. To reach the city center from Madaba's bus station, take a *service* (70fils) or hike up the hill toward the ever-visible Church of St. George (20min.). The **tourist office** (tel. 545 527), around the corner from St. George's in a newly restored building, has colorful brochures (open Sat.-Thurs. 8am-2pm). The **Bank of Jordan** (open Sat.-Thurs. 8:30am-12:30pm and 4-6pm) and **Housing Bank** (open Sat.-Thurs. 8am-1pm and 4-5:30pm) are on King Abdallah St. around the corner from the tourist office. The nearest public hospital, 1km from Madaba, is **Nadim Hospital** (tel. 541 700). **Mahabba Hospital**, a new private institution, is located near the entrance to the town. In a **medical emergency,** dial 193; dial 192 to reach the **police**. The central **post office** (open Sat.-Thurs. 7:30am-7pm, Fri. 7:30am-1:30pm) is on King Abdallah St., around the corner from the tourist office. Madaba's **telephone code** is 08.

Accommodations and Food Madaba's increasing popularity among tourists has undermined the monopoly power of **Lulu's Pension** (tel. 543 678), a gorgeous home-turned-bed and breakfast. Lulu's features full clean bathrooms and a cute kitchen with tablecloths, doilies, and fake flowers. The pre-bargaining price for a royal room with a king-sized bed is JD15 (JD10 for students). Ring the bell if the door is locked. The **Madaba Hotel** offers more affordable, still-spotless rooms, extremely hospitable management, and a mosaic-friendly location around the corner from the Church of St. George (singles JD5; doubles JD8; Arabic or continental breakfast JD2).

Join short-shorts-clad Germans at the **Rest House** (tel. 544 069), next to the tourist office. The Rest House caters mainly to groups, but individuals are welcome to join the party; their buffet lunch is for anyone who can pay the JD6 bill. A hummus and coke snack costs JD1.500, but prices are negotiable in the off-season (open daily 7:30am-approx. 10pm; buffet lunch daily noon-4pm). The **Agola Coffee Shop,** on Yarmouk St., serves deli-style sandwiches (350-750fils) in a pleasant Bedouin restaurant full of Madaba's young hipsters. For the best falafel in town (150fils), **Shaheen's Restaurant,** off of King Abdullah St., is a great alternative.

Sights Built in 1896 atop the foundation of a Byzantine church, the prominent, yellow-brick Greek Orthodox **Church of St. George** stands in the center of town, right off the square. Inside, parts of the 6th-century CE **Map of the Holy Land,** originally composed of 2.3 million tiles, remain intact. The map includes the Palestinian cities of Byzantium, most notably Nablus, Hebron, and Jericho. At one time the map depicted the entire Middle East, as shown by the few remaining tiles of Turkey, Lebanon, and Egypt. A map of Jerusalem, with representations of the buildings existing in the 6th century CE, including the Church of the Holy Sepulchre, is the most renowned section. Ask one of the postcard-selling faithful to point out some landmarks. The church is also known by some devout local Christians and Muslims for hosting the Virgin Mary in 1978. She made an appearance to heal the sick, according to faithful townsfolk. A small shrine in the crypt pictures Mary with a third arm and blue "healing hand" supernaturally imprinted on the icon during the Madonna's visit (open Mon.-Thurs. and Sat. 8:30am-6pm, Fri. and Sun. 10:30am-6pm; admission JD1).

Madaba's **museum,** tucked in an alley down the hill from the Apostles' Church off of Prince Abdullah St., features an extensive collection of mosaics, including a well-preserved depiction of the Garden of Eden, traditional dresses representative of the different regions in Jordan, and jewelry and pottery dating as far back as 4500 BCE.

JORDAN

The museum was made from several adjoining houses, some of which had mosaic floors. The complex is divided into three sections—the Old House of Madaba, a Folklore Museum, and an Archaeological Museum (open Wed.-Mon. 9am-5pm, holidays 10am-4pm; admission JD3 includes the Archaeological Park and Apostles Church).

Excavations and growing tourism have spawned new projects in Madaba. The **Archaeological Park,** around the corner from the Church of St. George, is a 1000 square meter playground of archaeological finds, featuring the **Church of the Virgin Mary** and **Hippolytus Hall.** In addition to a recently uncovered **Roman Street,** the park is home to mosaics dated from the days of Herod the Great (1st century BCE) until the Umayyad period (8th century CE). The **Apostles Church,** on the southern edge of town, houses the remains of the original church, dated 578 CE, as well as Madaba's largest intact mosaic (open Wed.-Mon. 8am-7pm; 8am-5pm in winter; JD3).

■ Near Madaba

MT. NEBO

Moses' last request to God was for a view from Mount Nebo. The Bible says of Moses: "no man knows the place of his burial to this day" (Deuteronomy 34:6), but his grave is rumored to be in a secret cave somewhere along **Ain Musa.** On the **Siyagha Peak** of Nebo, the Christians of Madaba built a three-nave **Memorial Church,** next to which looms an imposing serpentine cross. Archaeological work has revealed a complete mosaic floor in the church dating from 531 CE, as well as foundations of monasteries from the 3rd century CE. In the 7th century, the chapel of the Theotokos, or Mary, mother of God, was added, with lavish decorations adorning the walls. The buildings (admission JD1 or your best price, depending on tourist traffic) close at 7pm. No buses go to Mt. Nebo; **taxis** are JD4 round-trip (including a 30min. stay at the site), or take a *service* from Madaba to the village of Feisaliyyeh (150fils), and then bargain with the driver once the other passengers get off. For JD2.500, he should take you the extra 3km up, wait 30 minutes, and bring you back to any point in Madaba. Without a prearranged ride, the only way off Mt. Nebo is to walk back to Feisaliyyeh. Siyagha Peak closes at 7pm, unless you pay the guard 500fils to see the sunset.

Just beyond Feisaliyyeh, a marked turn-off leads to **Khirbet al-Mukheiyat,** the ancient village of **Nebo** on the southern base of the mountain. A one-hour hike (round-trip) will allow you to see the secular scenes of fishing, hunting, and winemaking that decorate another finely preserved Byzantine church floor. Cigarettes are the preferred *bakhsheesh* for the Bedouin gatekeeper who lives next on the hill at the end of the paved road (open till dusk, or whenever the gatekeeper leaves).

ZARQA MA'IN

Herod the Great, Governor of Judea in 40 BCE, frequented the hot mineral springs at **Zarqa Ma'in** to relieve his rheumatism. As he lay dying, he was carried here from his breathtaking hilltop fortress at nearby **Mukawer**—where Salome later danced and John the Baptist lost his head (Matthew 14:1-12). For a fee, both men and women can swim in **Hammam az-Zarqa,** a hot indoor pool sunk in a cliff face, or bathe under the voluptuous torrents of hot waterfalls. Reach Zarqa Ma'in by **bus** from Madaba (100fils). The JETT Bus Company in Amman occasionally offers daytrips for JD8 with lunch (depart 8am, return 6pm; see **Intercity Transportation,** p. 472).

DHIBAN AND SOUTH

Further south on the road to Karak lies the Biblical **Dhiban,** where Mesha, King of Moab, erected a stele celebrating his country's independence won from Omri, King of Israel, around the year 850 BCE. The basalt block now resides in the Louvre, but copies may be seen in both the Karak and Madaba Museums. An ancient **Roman mile marker** is on the road approaching the modern town of Dhiban. Just beyond town, the road descends into the vast **Wadi Mujib,** 4km wide and 1km deep. Cut from the rock by water and time, this is Jordan's version of the Grand Canyon. Although getting from Madaba to Karak along the Kings' Highway can be difficult, the breathtaking sights are worth the effort. Few buses run from Madaba to Karak along the highway. Some travelers say the easiest way to go is to hitch. Alternatively, a bus from Madaba to **Al Qasr** runs several times per day. After stepping off the bus in Al Qasr, you can see a very ruined Nabatean temple (c. 350 CE) before getting on a bus to Karak (200fils).

■ Karak الكرك

Once the ancient capital of Moab, Karak now humbles itself in the shadow of **Karak Castle,** the largest of the mountaintop Crusader castles which stretch from Turkey to the Sinai. Home to some of Jordan's most influential clans, the prosperous modern town of Karak extends away from the castle on its northern and eastern slopes and serves as an ideal resting place for travelers on the Kings' Highway.

Orientation and Practical Information Travel to Karak from Amman's Wahdat Station by **minibus** (1 hr., 750fils) or **service taxi** (JD1.200) along the desert highway. To reach Petra from Karak, take a minibus from the city center to Tafilah (30min., 500fils), and from Tafilah to Shobak (30min., 250fils). At times, no buses run to Shobak; those who hitch say it's easy, although *Let's Go* does not recommend hitchhiking. Minibuses sometimes run from Shobak to Petra (Wadi Musa). A direct bus from Karak to Petra leaves at 9am, depending on the volume of tourist traffic. No *service* travel these routes, but a **private taxi** will take you directly from Karak to Petra for a hefty JD40. **Buses** also run from Karak to Petra through Ma'an (JD1.050), although they may take longer than if you try your luck going through Shobak.

The two main landmarks in town are the castle and the town's center circle, which has a statue of horse and rider in the middle. To get to Karak's **tourist office,** take the first right turn downhill from the castle onto a small side street (sometimes open Sat.-Thurs. 8am-2pm). The **Housing Bank,** uphill (first right, then left) from the Italian Hospital, will change traveler's checks and cash, but may not open for exchange until as late as 10am (open Sat.-Thurs. 8:30am-1pm and 4-5:30pm; winter 3:30-5pm).Karak's **Italian Hospital** (tel. 351 045 or 145), is downhill from the road up to the castle, or in the direction of the dagger if you orient yourself using the manic horseman in the center circle. For **medical emergencies,** dial 193. The **police station** is located down the street and on the right of the tourist office, next to the huge radio tower. Facing the manic horse in the center of town, take the street on the left. From here, the second street on the left will take you to Karak's **post and telephone office** (open daily 7:30am-7pm, Fri. 8am-noon). The **telephone code** is 03.

Accommodations and Food The best room for your dinar is at the **Castle Hotel** (tel. 352 489). The Castle offers comfortable clean rooms, some with a view (singles JD3.300; doubles JD8). Across the street, the **Towers Hotel** (tel. 354 293) under the same management, is cozy, spacious, spotless, and slightly more upscale. The manager of the Castle and Towers is more helpful than the tourist office and will make your stay worth more than you pay (singles JD8; doubles JD15, more with private baths. Prices negotiable during the off-season. The **Rum Hotel** (tel. 351 351; fax 351 105), around the corner from the Castle Hotel, has newly carpeted singles for JD4. (Doubles with private bath JD6, with private bath, TV, and small refrigerator JD8.) A few tiny hotels near the center of town offer less comfortable rooms for less.

For a tasty sit-down meal without inflated prices, try the **Rum Restaurant** (tel. 353 789), across the street from the police station and the radio tower. Pizza costs JD1.500, and the bidding for a tasty grill or *mensaf* with salads and coffee or tea starts at JD2.500 (open daily 7am-10pm). **Fida' Restaurant,** across the street from the Rum Hotel, serves an open buffet luncheon (JD3) popular with tourist groups (open 11am-3pm). A lunch or dinner at the government **Rest House,** near the entrance to the castle, offers a great view of the Jordan Valley's descent to the Dead Sea, if you can afford the food (open until 10pm). Pocket change will get you falafel and fruit—stalls line the street to the left of the Rum Restaurant. Nothing beats a picnic atop the ruins.

Sights Karak Castle is full of secret passageways and hidden rooms; bring a flashlight for easier exploration and allow at least two hours. Steep, jagged walls atop a steeper hill turn even a guided tour of the windblown ruins into a challenge. In 1142, Baldwin I of Jerusalem built the castle midway between his capital and Shobak on the site of an iron age citadel mentioned in the Mesha Stele in 850 BCE. The castle was renovated in 1188 under Salah ad-Din. Although the fortress wall has mostly collapsed, its building blocks remain large enough to inspire starry-eyed wonder. Inside, vaulted stone ceilings span only a few meters, resulting in a network of long, narrow halls and barracks. You can still see the bolt holes for mammoth stone doors that have since turned to dust. To the west across the dry moat are battlements from which the charming Renauld de Chatillon cast prisoners 40m to their deaths (with wooden boxes fastened around their heads so that they would not lose consciousness too quickly). When Salah ad-Din took the castle after the 1187 Battle of Hittin, he personally saw to it that Chatillon's head was removed. Below, a 50m tunnel leads out of town through an arched gateway (castle open daily 8am-5pm). To the right of the castle entrance, a stone staircase descends to the **Archaeological Museum,** with Nabatean, Roman, and Mamluk artifacts, as well as a copy of the Mesha Stele (open Wed.-Mon. 9am-5pm; admission to castle and museum JD1).

■ Near Karak

Highway 49/80 (for added confusion, maps may say 50) west from Karak drops 20m from the Kings' Highway to the Dead Sea "port" of **Mazra'a** and the Al Lisan (tongue) Peninsula. Five kilometers before reaching Mazra'a and the Wadi Araba Highway to Aqaba, Highway 49/80 passes **Baab adh-Dhira.** The cemeteries here contain some 20,000 shaft tombs enshrining 500,000 bodies (an unfortunate 25-to-1 body-to-tomb ratio) and over three million pottery vessels. The length of the bones indicates that the average height in Baab adh-Dhira was a sturdy 2m, over 6½ft.

Hitchers report that there is very little traffic between Mazra'a and Karak. Stop in at the **Mazra'a Police Post,** 5km north of the junction, if you need assistance. Heading out of Mazra'a the Wadi Araba highway runs alongside Israel and is sometimes closed to civilian travel; hitchhiking here is always prohibited.

In the towns surrounding Karak, tourist services are non-existent. If you're lost or need a ride or a place to stay, approach a friendly looking store owner or businessperson and ask for help. It's a good idea to offer a tip (500fils or JD1) in return. Although it may be refused, they will appreciate your gesture. Solo women should refuse hospitality from single men. The mosques at **Mu'tah** and at the nearby village of **Mazar** (bus 150fils) commemorate the Islamic generals who died in the first great battles between the forces of Islam and Byzantium in 632 CE. The green-domed mosque in Mazar houses a small **Islamic museum** on the first floor (usually open 9am-4pm).

SHOBAK شوبك

King Baldwin's first castle at Shobak pales in comparison to his later creation at Karak. **Shobak Castle,** 4km from the marked turn-off at the northern edge of Shobak town, fell to Salah ad-Din in 1189, just 74 years after it was built. In 1260, the Mamluks gained possession of the castle, restored it, and inscribed records of their work on its main walls and towers. Although most of the castle is gone today, the view from the approach road across the natural moat is inspiring: colossal white stones silhouetted against desert brush and a cobalt sky. Villagers who lived inside the castle walls depended upon the water from the rock-hewn well, 375 steps deep. They have abandoned the area, leaving a secluded spot for free **camping.**

You can reach Shobak on an Amman-bound **minibus** (500fils) from Wadi Musa (near Petra), departing from Wadi Musa gate at 7 and 8am. If you hire a **taxi** (from

Petra

Ad-Deir, 1
Amoud Far'aun
(Pharaoh's Pillar), 16
Conway Tower, 4
Corinthian Tomb, 13
Djin Blocks, 24
Garden Tomb, 20
High Place, 28
Katuteh, 27
Khazneh (The
Treasury), 23
Lion Fountain, 21
Lion's Tomb, 2
Mughar an-Nasara

(Caves of the
Christians), 5
Museum, 7
Nabatean Baths, 29
Nymphaeum, 15
Obelisk Tomb, 25
Palace Tomb, 12
Petra Visitor's
Center, 26
Qasr Bint Far'aun, 8
Qasr Habis
(Crusader Castle), 6
Rest House, 30
Roman Theater, 17

Snake Monument, 22
Temenos Gate, 9
Temple of Al Uzza
(Atargatis) or Temple
of the Winged
Lions, 10
Tomb of the Roman
Soldier, 18
Tomb of Sextus
Florentinus, 11
Triclinium, 19
Turkmaniya
Tomb, 3
Urn Tomb, 14

JORDAN

Karak not more than JD3, from Wadi Musa not more than JD7), make sure the driver waits while you explore.

■ Petra البتراء

Match me such marvel save in Eastern clime,
a rose-red city 'half as old as Time'!

—Dean Burgon

The once-lost city of Petra is now easy to find, but access has not lessened its magnificence. Peeking out from n the walls of a natural 3m-wide fissure are towering sculptures, raw mountains fashioned by human hands into impossibly delicate structures. Petra, meaning "stone" in ancient Greek, is perhaps the most astounding ancient city left to the modern world, and certainly a must-see for visitors to the Middle East.

For 700 years, Petra was lost to all but the few hundred members of a Bedouin tribe who guarded their treasure from outsiders. In the 19th century, Swiss explorer Johann Burkhardt heard Bedouin speaking of a "lost city," and he vowed to find it. Though Burkhardt was initially unable to find a guide, he guessed that the city he sought was the Petra of legend, the biblical Sela, which should have been near Mount Hor, the site of Aaron's tomb. Impersonating a Christian pilgrim, Burkhardt hired a guide and, on August 22, 1812, walked between the cliffs of Petra's *siq* (the mile-long rift which was the only entrance to Petra). Awed and driven to sketch the monuments and record his thoughts, the "pilgrim" aroused the suspicion of his Bedouin guide. The guide warned him of the spiritual significance of the ancient rocks, and a chastened Burkhardt left—to announce his discovery to the rest of the world. In the nearly two centuries since, Petra has become a feature tourist attraction. Admired by visitors from all over the world, including the film crew of *Indiana Jones and the Last Crusade,* Petra now has its own camel corps to protect the ruins from the many overzealous pilgrims who are following in Burkhardt's footsteps.

The area's principal water source, **Ain Musa** (Spring of Moses), is one of the many places where Moses supposedly struck a rock with his staff and extracted water (Exodus 17). Human history in the area dates back to the 8th millennium BCE. By the 6th century BCE, the Nabateans, a nomadic Arab tribe, had quietly moved onto land controlled by the Edomites and had begun to profit from the trade between lower Arabia and the Fertile Crescent. Over the next three centuries the Nabatean Kingdom, secure in its easily defended capital, flourished. The Nabateans carved their monumental temples out of the mountains, looking to Egyptian, Greek, and Roman styles for inspiration. Unique to the Nabateans are the crow-step (staircase) patterns that grace the crowns of many of the memorials. The crow-steps so decidedly resemble inverted stairways that the people of Meda'in Salih (a miniature Petra in Saudi Arabia) were able to sustain the claim that God threw Petra upside down and turned it to stone to punish its people's wickedness.

More historically verifiable evidence suggests that in 63 BCE the Nabatean King Aretas defeated Pompey's Roman Legions. The Romans controlled the entire area around Nabatea, however, prompting the later King Rabel III to strike a deal: as long as the Romans did not attack during his lifetime, they would be permitted to move in after he died. In 106 CE the Romans claimed the Nabatean Kingdom and inhabited the city of rosy Nubian sandstone.

In its heyday, Petra may have housed 20-30,000 people. But after an earthquake in 363 CE, a shift in the trade routes to Palmyra (Tadmor) in Syria, the expansion of the sea trade around Arabia, and another earthquake in 747 CE, much of Petra had deteriorated to rubble. The city fell under Byzantine and then Arab control for a few centuries before the Crusaders tried to resurrect it by constructing a new fortress. Shortly thereafter, Christian Petra declined so much that even its location was forgotten. A few explorers searched in vain for the city, but not until Burkhardt schemed his way in was the city visited by anyone other than the Bedouin.

For decades, the Bedouin adapted to the influx of tourists by providing them with food and accommodations inside Petra, a practice which was outlawed in 1984-85 out of concern for the monuments. While many of Petra's Bedouin have been relocated to a housing project near Wadi Musa, a large portion still make their homes in the more remote caves and hills of the city (spanning 50km, most of which the average tourist never sees). Many Bedouin sell souvenirs and drinks amidst the ruins; others tend goats—don't be surprised to hear a baaa emanating from inside an ancient tomb. If you venture on paths that go beyond the standard one-day itinerary, you will notice stones piled into neat columns. As long as these markers are in sight, you're near a trail, and Bedouin will pass by.

GETTING THERE

Petra lies in the rocky wilderness near the southern extreme of the Kings' Highway, about 282km from Amman (262km via the Desert Highway). **JETT buses** leave Amman daily (6:30am, 3[hr., JD5; complete round-trip tour including lunch, guide, and horse, JD32.500). Reservations should be made at JETT stations well ahead of time, especially during the busy fall and spring seasons; these must be made in person, but questions can be handled by phone (tel. 664 146). You'll be dropped off at the Petra Visitor's Center. More than one day is needed to do longer hikes, but the JETT tour will cover the most impressive (and frequented) sights.

Service to Petra from Wahdat Station in Amman takes about five hours, plus a wait in Ma'an (JD2). Drivers will drop you off at either the Al-Anbat or the **Musa Spring Hotel;** from Wadi Musa you can walk the 5km or take a **private taxi** (JD1) to Petra. From Aqaba, a two-hour **minibus** trip costs JD2. Start early in the morning to make any of these connections.

To leave Petra, you can catch minibuses or *service* to Aqaba (JD1.500) or Amman (JD2) at the center of Wadi Musa near the post office or at the Musa Spring Hotel. Buses leave at 6, 7, and 8am and 3:30pm. A local bus to Ma'an leaves at 6am and returns at 2pm (500fils one way).

To reach Petra from the Kings' Highway, take the well-marked turn-off and head west into the colorful, steep-sided town of Wadi Musa. Halfway through Wadi Musa on the way to Petra, you'll pass the main traffic circle and travel through the main market area. A tortuous 5km from the traffic circle, the spur road leaves town and ends at the entrance to Petra. The cluster of buildings here includes the visitors center, the government Rest House, the lavish Forum Hotel, and the gatehouse to the valley that leads to the *siq* and Petra proper.

PRACTICAL INFORMATION

The **tourist police** munch on cigar ends at the **Petra Visitor's Center** (tel. 215 60 60; open Sat.-Thurs. 7am-5pm), where you can hire an official guide for a "low tour" of the city center (JD8). More comprehensive guided tours go to Al Madbah (JD8), Ad-Deir (JD9), and Jabal Harun (JD35). Trips to more remote areas should be arranged with the guide directly; a full day tour costs JD35. You can rent a horse (you're also responsible for renting the guide's horse), but it's more interesting to remain on foot. It's easy to tag along behind a group with a guide or to form a group of your own. The various guidebooks available at the visitor's center are helpful, but there's no substitute for the expertise of an official guide, especially for the more remote sites of Al Barid or Al Madras. On the other side of the visitor's center are the Rest House and the swinging gate marking the beginning of the trail down to the *siq*. The three **banks** open for exchange Sat.-Thurs. 8:30am-12:30pm all extract exorbitant commissions: the **Arab Bank** and the **Housing Bank** are in the town center, and the **Cairo Amman Bank** is in the Mövenpick Hotel just outside the entrance to Petra. You can get a Visa **cash advance** from any bank.

Wadi Musa has no hospital, but the **government health center** (tel. 215 60 25), a 15-minute walk uphill from the main traffic circle, is open 24 hours. The **Petra Polyclinic** (tel. 215 66 94) at the traffic circle is more expensive, but has modern equipment, including an x-ray unit. The **Wadi Musa Pharmacy** (tel. 215 64 44) is on the main traffic circle (open 24hr.). Wadi Musa has a **post office** with **poste restante** (tel. 215 62 24) next to the Musa Spring Hotel (open Sat.-Thurs. 7:30am-7pm, Fri. 7:30am-1:30pm). A second branch is behind the visitor's center by the entrance to the *siq* (tel. 215 66 94; same hours). Petra's **telephone code** is 03.

Admission to the ancient city is JD20 for one day, JD25 for two days, and JD30 for three days. Children under 12 pay JD12.5 for one day, 50% off for two or three days. Those who can't afford a ticket have found ways in the back door. Beware, though, as scary guards in green robes and ammunition belts abound. Guides are expensive but recommended for four of the more remote hikes in Petra, although it is possible to do without them. Petra is open daily 6am-6pm, but these hours are only loosely enforced. If you choose to stay to see the sun set, you should have no problem getting out.

ACCOMMODATIONS

Since the peace treaty between Jordan and Israel was signed, visitors from all over the world have flooded the Jordanian hillside, and construction has boomed in Wadi Musa. Most of the development revolves around luxury resorts, but there are enough cheapies to go around. Prices become extremely negotiable in the off-season (May-July and Dec.-Feb).

Musa Spring Hotel and Restaurant, Wadi Musa Gate (tel. 215 6310; fax 215 69 10). The first hotel as you enter town from Amman, but a trek from Petra proper. Renowned for evening showings of *Indiana Jones* and *Lawrence of Arabia;* plenty of budget traveler companionship. Free shuttle to Petra at 7 and 8am, returning 6pm. Free use of kitchen. Rooftop mattresses with facilities including hot showers JD2; singles JD5; doubles JD8, with private bath JD10. Breakfast JD1.500; lunch or dinner all-you-can-eat buffet JD3.

Al-Anbat I Hotel (tel. 215 62 65; fax 215 68 88). Follow the trough down from the spring until you see the hotel with the best view of the descent to Petra. Witness the most beautiful sunset in Wadi Musa from mattresses in the "greenhouse" (JD2). Camping facilities (tents and showers) available for JD2. The basement of this 2-star hotel offers cavernous student rooms (JD4) and clean communal baths. Upstairs singles JD7; doubles JD10; triples JD15. Free and frequent buses to Petra.

Sunset Hotel (tel. 215 65 79; fax 215 69 50), about 200m uphill from the visitor's center. If your feet are sore and your bottom hurts from a Petra camel ride, this place is for you—the first inexpensive and clean option outside of the Mega-hotel complex. Doubles JD10, JD15 with private bath. Breakfast JD2.

Araba Hotel (tel. 215 61 07), 200m uphill from the main circle in Wadi Musa. Pastel-hued rooms with small private baths and soft, colorful mattresses make this hillside hotel worth a look; the free towels and soap may convince you to stay. Rooftop mattresses JD2; singles JD6; doubles JD8. Breakfast JD2.

Al-Rashid Hotel (tel. 215 68 00; fax 215 68 01). Right on the main traffic circle, this sea-foam green palace has the most luxurious rooms in its price range. Gold chandeliers, high ceilings, and plush carpeted rooms are a bargain at JD8 per person, JD10 with breakfast. MC, Visa, and Diner's Club.

Orient Hotel and Restaurant (tel./fax 215 70 20), to the left of the traffic circle facing downhill. Small, cozy rooms have sparkling, white tiled baths. The two neighboring mosques and their competing *muezzins* make for an interesting aural experience. Singles JD6; doubles JD9; triples JD14. Breakfast JD2.

Cleopetra Hotel (tel./fax 337 090), 50m uphill from the main traffic circle, on the left. Colorful rooms with relatively clean private baths. Genuinely friendly manager provides maps and info. Singles JD9; doubles JD12; triples JD18. Breakfast JD1.

Petra Gate Hotel (tel. 215 69 08), about 100m uphill from the main circle in Wadi Musa. Bed in a shared room JD2. Relatively clean rooms with soft, pink beds and private baths JD3-6. Breakfast JD1.500.

Camping inside Petra is illegal, but lingering explorers may receive invitations for overnight stays from hospitable Bedouin. It's also very possible to pick an off-the-beaten-path cave for a night, although explaining yourself to Jordanian police could turn you pinker than the ruins.

FOOD

The farther you go from the ruins, the less you'll pay for falafel. The best bargains are in Wadi Musa, especially in the streets to the right of its main circle as you approach from Petra. Many hotels have all-you-can-eat buffets at reasonable prices. The **Musa Springs Hotel** offers a filling meal with pasta, rice, chicken, salad, and bread for JD3 (daily 6-9pm). The **Star Supermarket** (on the left, uphill from the traffic circle) has the cheapest water at 300fils and the most reasonably priced basics for bag lunches. If you want something non-Jordanian, you'll have to pay. **Papazzi,** uphill from the visitor's center, is a chain Italian restaurant with great pizza (medium JD5-7).

Rose City Restaurant (tel. 215 73 40), just uphill from the site. Attentive staff serves delicious grills (JD2.500-3) and energy for the hike uphill. Hummus 600fils, soda 500fils. Open daily 7am-10pm.

Al-Janoub Restaurant and Sweets, on the first street on the right before reaching the main circle from Petra. Modest *kebab*s are the cheapest in town at only JD1. Hummus 300fils, falafel 150fils, soda bottles 150fils. Open daily 6am-11pm.

Khan Checken, across from the Treasury Restaurant, has falafel sandwiches for 250fils and hummus for 500fils.

Cleopatra Restaurant, to the left to the main circle facing downhill. Friendly Egyptian cooks will serve you rice, salad, bird, and bread for JD1.500. Falafel 200fils, *shawerma* 300fils, soda 300fils. Open daily 6am-midnight.

SIGHTS AND HIKES

The Nabateans worshipped only two deities: Dushara, the god of strength, symbolized by sculpted rock, and Al Uzza (or Atargatis), the goddess of water and fertility. Still, the number of temples and tombs in Petra seems infinite. Climbing will allow you to escape the tour groups crowding the inner valley. Many spectacular monuments are close enough to be viewed in one day, but a few require multi-day expeditions. Bedouin sell water throughout the park, but at JD1-1.500 per bottle, you'll need to empty the Treasury to stay hydrated—it's best to bring bottles from outside.

Even before you reach the narrow canyon-like *siq,* caves staring from distant mountain faces and large *djinn* monuments (ghost tombs) will draw you in. On the left, built high into the cliff, stands the **Obelisk Tomb.** Closer to the entrance of the *siq,* rock-cut channels once cradled ceramic pipes which brought Ain Musa's waters to the inner city and the surrounding farm country. A nearby dam burst in 1963, and the resulting flash flood killed 28 tourists in the *siq.* While designing a new dam, the Nabateans' ancient dam was uncovered and used as a model.

As you enter the *siq,* walls towering 200m on either side begin to block out the light, casting enormous shadows on the niches that once held icons of the gods meant to protect the entrance by hexing unwelcome visitors. The *siq* winds around for 1.5km, then slowly emits a faint pink glow at the first peek of the **Khazneh** (Treasury). At 90m wide and 130m tall, the Khazneh is the best preserved of Petra's monuments, although bullet holes are clearly visible on the upper urn. Believing the urn to be hollow and filled with ancient pharaonic treasures, Bedouin periodically fired at it, hoping to burst this petrified piñata. Actually, the treasury was a royal tomb and, like almost everything else at Petra, is quite solid. The Khazneh's rock face is like a geological mood ring: in the morning, the sun's rays give the monument a rich peach hue, in late afternoon it glistens rose, and by sunset, it drips blood red.

Down the road to the right as you face the Khazneh, Wadi Musa opens up to the 7000-seat **Roman Theater.** The long row of Royal Tombs on the face of Jabal Khubtha is on the right. The Romans built their theater under the red stone Nabatean necropolis, and the ancient carved caves still yawn above it. The theater has been restored to its 2nd-century appearance and audiences are returning after a 1500-year wait. A marble Hercules (now in the museum) was discovered just a few years ago in the curtained chambers beneath the stage.

Across the *wadi* are the **Royal Tombs.** The **Urn Tomb,** with its unmistakable recessed façade, commands a soul-scorching view of the still-widening valley. The two-tiered vault beneath the pillared façade is known as the **prison,** or *sijin.* A Greek inscription on an inner wall describes how the tomb, originally dedicated to the Nabatean King Malichus II in the first century CE, was converted to a church 400 years later. Nearby is the **Corinthian Tomb,** allegedly a replica of Nero's Golden Palace in Rome, and the **Palace Tomb** (or the Tomb in Two Stories), which literally juts out from the mountainside. The latter tomb had to be completed by attaching preassembled stones to its upper left-hand corner. Around the corner to the right is the **Tomb of Sextus Florentinus,** who was so enamored of these hewn heights that he asked his son to bury him in this ultimate outpost of the Roman Empire.

Around the bend to the left, a few restored columns dot either side of the paved Roman **main street.** Two thousand years ago, columns lined the full length of the street, shielding markets and residences. At the beginning of the street on the right, the **Nymphaeum** ruins outline the ancient public fountain near its base. On a rise to the right, before the triple-arched gate, recent excavations have uncovered the **Temple of Al Uzza (Atargatis),** also called the **Temple of the Winged Lions.** In the spring you can watch the progress of American-sponsored excavations which have already uncovered several workshops and some cracked Nabatean crocks.

Also recently excavated by a joint Jordanian-American team is an immense mosaic-rich **Byzantine church.** The site lies several hundred meters to the right of the Roman street, near the Temple of the Winged Lions, from which some of the church's column bases and capitals were probably lifted. Each of the church's side aisles is paved with 70 square meters of remarkably preserved mosaic, depicting native as well as exotic or mythological animals, humans of various professions, and representations of the four seasons. The church is thought to have been a major 5th- and 6th-century cathedral, likely the seat of the bishop of the Byzantine province of Palaestina Tertia, and challenges the belief that Petra was in decline by 600 CE.

Across the street, a team from Brown University is in the process of unearthing the **Southern Temple.** White hexagonal paving stones cover an extensive tunnel system marking the importance of this holy site. Farther along, the triple-arched **Temenos Gate** was once the front gate of the **Qasr Bint Far'aun** (Palace of the Pharaoh's Daughter), a Nabatean temple built to honor the god Dushara. On your left, just before the gate, are the **Nabatean Baths.** On the trail leading off behind the temple to the left, a single standing column gloats beside its two fallen comrades—**Amoud Far'aun** (Pharaoh's Pillar) marks the entrance to the ancient Roman city. To the right of the Nabatean temple, a rock-hewn staircase leads to a small **archaeological museum** which holds the spoils of the Winged Lions dig and carved stone figures from elsewhere in Petra. On the way to the monastery, the **Nabatean Museum** has nice artifacts, and air-conditioned **restrooms** with probably the **world's best toilet seat view** (both museums open daily 9am-4pm; free).

Hikes to Remote Sights

Many people, content with daytrip dosage, will go home raving about Petra's first 10%. Few see the rest. You'll need two days to do the following seven treks, but you can easily spend a week wandering, especially if you venture beyond the ancient city limits. The Bedouin say that to appreciate Petra you must stay long enough to watch your nails grow long. Four places require a guide (JD35): **Sabra,** the **Snake Monument, Jabal Numair,** and **Jabal Haroun.** The requirement is not enforced, but it's not a good idea to hike the remote hills alone.

Wadi Turkimaniya وادى تـركمانية

The shortest and easiest of the hikes leads down the *wadi* to the left of and behind the Temple of the Winged Lions. Fifteen minutes of strolling down the road that runs through the rich green gardens of **Wadi Turkimaniya** guide you to the only tomb at

Petra with a Nabatean inscription. The lengthy invocation above the entrance beseeches the god Dushara to safeguard the tomb and to protect its contents from violation. Unfortunately, Dushara took an interminable sabbatical and the chamber has been stripped bare.

Qasr Habis قصر حابس

A second, more interesting climb begins at the end of the road that descends from the Pharaoh's Pillar to the cliff face, a few hundred meters left of the museum. The trail dribbles up to the **Qasr Habis** (Crusader Castle). The steps have been restored recently, but they don't lead up to much. A path winds all the way around the mountain, however, revealing gorgeous canyons and (you guessed it) more tombs on the western side. The climb to the top and back takes less than an hour.

Jabal Harun جبل هارون

This climb begins just to the right of Jabal Habis, below the museum. A sign points to **Ad-Deir** (the Monastery) and leads northwest across Wadi Siyah, past the Forum Restaurant to Wadi Deir and its fragrant oleander. As you squeeze through the narrowing canyon you will confront a human-shaped hole in the façade of the **Lion's Tomb.** A hidden tomb awaits daredevils who try to climb the cleft to the right; less intrepid wanderers backtrack to the right and find the tomb a few minutes later. Back on the path, veer left to get to Petra's largest monument.

Ad-Deir, 50m wide and 45m tall, is larger, though less ornate, than the Khazneh. With a single inner chamber dating back to the first century CE, most scholars believe that Ad-Deir was originally either a Nabatean temple or an unfinished tomb dedicated to one of the later Nabatean kings. It picked up its orthodox appellation in the Byzantine period. On the left, a lone tree popping through a crack in the rock marks more ancient steps, which continue all the way up to the rim of the urn atop the monastery. Straight across the *wadi* looms the highest peak in the area, **Jabal Harun** (Aaron's Mountain or Mt. Hor). On top of the mountain, a white church reportedly houses the **Tomb of Aaron.** The whole trip takes a few hours, a few more if you detour into **Wadi Siyah** and visit its seasonal waterfall on the way back.

Jabal Umm al-Biyara جبل أم البيارة

A grueling three-hour hike climbs **Jabal Umm al-Biyara** (Mother of Cisterns Mountain), which towers over the Crusader castle on Jabal Habis. Follow the trail from the left of the Nabatean temple past the Pharaoh's Pillar and down into the *wadi* to the right. If you scramble 50m up the rock chute to the left of the blue sign you'll reach the beginning of a stone ramp that leads to the top. It was here, at the site of Petra's original acropolis and the biblical city of Sela, that a Judean king supposedly hurled thousands of Edomites over the cliff's edge. The gigantic piles of shards, over 8000 years old, are the only remnants of the mountains' first inhabitants.

If instead of climbing Umm al-Biyara you continue south along Wadi Tughra, which runs by its foot, you'll eventually reach the **Snake Monument,** one of the earliest Nabatean religious shrines. From here it's about two hours to Aaron's Tomb on Jabal Harun. The path meanders around Mount Hor before ascending it from the south. When it disappears on the rocks, follow the donkey droppings. As you start to climb Jabal Harun you'll see a lone tent. Inside, a Bedouin, the official holder of the keys, will escort you the rest of the way and open the building for you to explore. The entire trek takes five or six hours.

The High Place الاماكن العليا

One of the most popular hikes is the circular route to the **High Place** on Jabal al-Madbah, a place of sacrifice with a full view of Petra. A staircase sliced in the rock leads to the left just as the Roman Theater comes into view. Follow the right prong when the trail levels and forks at the top of the stairs. On the left, **Obelisk Ridge** presents one obelisk to Dushara and another to Al Uzza. On the peak to the right, the Great High Place supports a string of grisly sights: two neatly cut altars, an ablution cistern, gutters for draining away sacrificial blood, and cliff-hewn bleachers for an unobstructed view of the animal sacrifices. Head downhill past the Pepsi stand, leaving the obelisks behind you, and backtrack under the western face of the Great High Place. If you hunt around you'll find a staircase leading down to a sculptured **Lion Fountain.** The first grotto complex beyond it is the **Garden Tomb.** Below it is the **Tomb of the Roman Soldier** (named for the tough guy carved in the façade) and across from it a rock **triclinium** (feast hall), which has the only decorated interior in Petra. The trail then leads into Wadi Farasa and ends near the Pillar. The circle, followed either way, takes about an hour and a half.

Al Madras and Al Barid المدرس و البارد

Beyond Petra, tourist groups and commercialism disappears. Bedouin here have been unaltered by modernity, and the wildlife roam free. The isolated antiquities can only be reached by donkey or foot—all roads lead back to the Kings' Highway.

A trail branching to your left just past the Obelisk Tomb and just before the entrance to the *siq* leads to **Al Madras,** an ancient Petran suburb with almost as many monuments as Petra itself. On the way, watch for the short-eared desert hare and a full spectrum of long lanky lizards—purple, fuchsia, and iridescent blue. Come with water, a snack, and a guide. The round-trip takes four to eight hours.

Past the Tomb of Sextus Florentinus and the **Mughar an-Nasara** (Caves of the Christians), a trail chisels into the rock leading to the northern suburb of **Al Barid.** A road passing the new hotel in Wadi Musa also approaches this archaeological site. Al Barid is a curious miniature of Petra, complete with a short *siq,* several carved tombs, and caves. If you don't feel like hoofing it, a Wadi Musa taxi will take you there and wait for you at the entrance for an hour (JD7). Also off the new road past the hotel is **Al Beidha.** Excitement runs high among the members of the excavating expedition here; they've uncovered traces of a pre-pottery Neolithic village, a sedentary society dating to the 8th millennium BCE. This find would make Al Beidha, along with Jericho, one of the oldest known farming communities in the world. A Bedouin guide can lead you here via a painless trail (about 3hr. each way). Bring an extra JD2-3 or some of your own native trinkets to trade.

■ Aqaba العقبة

Set in a natural amphitheater beneath a crescent of rugged hills, Aqaba is Jordan's sole link to the sea. Beneath the water, legions of brilliantly colored creatures flit through a surreal universe of coral. Aqaba's reefs are a world apart from the damaged reefs of Eilat, mainly due to a lesser tourist impact. Above (and as a result of) the water, Aqaba is an important trade and military center and has become the darling of the Arab elite in need of a periodic escape from dry cityscapes.

At the tip of the gulf of the same name, Aqaba's strategic setting has been apparent since Biblical times, when King Solomon's copper-laden ships sailed from here. The Romans stationed their famous Tenth Legion at this point, and the Crusaders fortified the port and Pharaoh's Island 7km off the coast (now in Egyptian territory). During the 1917 Arab Revolt, Faisal Ibn Hussein and T.E. Lawrence staged a desert raid on the Ottoman fortifications and captured the port. In 1965 King Hussein shrewdly traded the Saudis 6000 square kilometers of southeastern desert (before he knew there was black gold beneath the sand) for 13km of coastline, and started developing the city. After the reopening of the Suez Canal in 1957 and the increased traffic caused by the Iran-Iraq War, the harbor became packed with huge leviathans bulging with cargo. During the 1991 Gulf War, Aqaba was Iraq's chief illicit outlet, but a blockade slowed traffic considerably. Aqaba has bounced back in recent years—trade has resumed under international supervision, and the open border with Israel has exposed the city to tourism.

ORIENTATION

Aqaba is one elongated beach extending from King Hussein's villa on the Israeli border to the huge, fenced-in port facilities 4km down the arching corniche to the south-

Ash Sharif Shakir Ibn Zayd St.

Al 'Istiqlal St.

Ali Ibn Abi Talib St.

Ash Sharif al-Hussein Ibn Ali St.

Mu'ta St.

Khalid Ibn al-Walid St.

King Abdullah Ibn al-Hussein St.

Umar Ibn al-Aziz St.

Qansuwa al-Ghuri St.

Al Farabi St. (Gazza St.)

Al Hashimi St.

Ar Rashid St.

An Nahda St.

Al Yarmouk St.

Ar Reem St.

King Talal St.

Abu Hanifa an-Nu'man St.

Ar Ramadan St.

Ar Razi St.

Prince Muhammad St.

Makka Mukarrama St.

Aqaba Gulf

King Hussein St.

Ar Rida St.

AQABA BORT

JORDAN

N

65

0   300 yards

0   300 meters

Aqaba

Bus Station, **4**
Egyptian Consulate
and Embassy, **1**
Hussein Ibn Ali
Mosque, **3**
Post Office, **2 & 5**

east. Luxury hotels and military complexes have gobbled up a good part of the beach near town. **Four countries** come together in the small northern tip of the Gulf of Aqaba: Egypt meets Israel near the conspicuous resort hotels at Taba, Israel's Eilat faces Jordan's Aqaba across the border, and Saudi Arabia looms to the southeast (for information on **border crossings**, see p. 264, p. 436, and p. 503).

Shops line the streets of central Aqaba branching around the post office and behind the **Hussein Ibn Ali Mosque.** South of the port and 10km from central Aqaba, the **ferry dock** handles the thousands of Egyptian workers and occasional foreign travelers who cross the Gulf of Aqaba to Nuweiba' in Egypt. One kilometer past the ferry port you'll come to the **Marine Research Center** building, past which you'll find Aqaba's finest coral reefs and a sandy beach that stretches south to the Saudi border.

Hitching around Aqaba is reportedly easy, as an army of trucks serves the port. Herds of six-wheeled beasts cover vast stretches along the highway two kilometers north of town. **Truck stops** make strategic starting points for hitching trips to the north. Taxi fare out to the truck stops is about JD2; the road to the port, which bumps the eastern side of town, has closer hitching points. **Hitching** is inherently risky, especially for women.

PRACTICAL INFORMATION

Aqaba's tree-lined streets and circles and the anchored ships offshore give a first impression of a sleepy seaside town. Don't be fooled; this city can be as hectic as the rest of Jordan. People don't change their driving habits just because they're in a seaside municipality. There are road signs telling drivers to lay off their horns, which are about as effective as telling King Hussein to stop printing posters of himself.

Visitors' Center: tel. 313 363 or 731, on the grounds of the new Islamic Museum, about halfway to the port from the town center. A long hike or a JD1 taxi ride. Maps, brochures, and information on travel to nearby cities. Open Sat.-Thurs. 8am-1pm and 5-7pm.

Tourist Police: tel. 313 513.

Egyptian Consulate: tel. 316 171, on Al Istiqlal St.; turn right along the curve about 800m northwest of the Aquamarina II Hotel and look for the guard booth in front. Same-day service for **Egyptian visas.** Bring your passport, a photo, and JD12. Open Sat.-Thurs. 9am-2pm. Apply for visa 9am-noon, pick-up at 2pm.

Currency Exchange: Bank hours are normally Sat.-Thurs. 8:30am-12:30pm, with some banks reopening Sat.-Wed. 4-6pm. Money exchanges are open in the morning and some stay open until midnight. Bring a passport to exchange traveler's checks. The **Jordan National Bank** in the Commercial Center on Al Yarmouk St., near the Jordan Flower Hotel, allows withdrawal with MasterCard. Open Sat.-Thurs. 8:30am-12:30pm and 5-6:30pm. Most banks accept Visa. Beware the hefty JD5 commission on traveler's checks.

American Express: International Traders Travel Agency Office, P.O. Box 136 (tel. 313 757). Walk downhill from the post office, take your first left, and continue for 30m—the office is just before the Ali Baba. Will hold mail for anyone. Open Sat.-Thurs. 8am-1pm and 4-7pm, and occasionally a few hours Fri. mornings.

Flights: Royal Jordanian (tel. 314 477) has 2 regular flights per day to and from **Amman** (1hr., JD22 one way). Their office is a ten-minute walk northeast of town on Ash Sharif al-Hussein Ibn Ali St., just past the rotary. Some hotels run buses from Aqaba International Airport to the center of the city. Taxis cost JD2 per person.

Buses and Service: To reach the station, go uphill past the post office, turn right on King Talal St., and walk two blocks. Daily minibus to **Petra,** leaving at roughly 8:30am, but really when it is full (2½hr., JD3). Sometimes another bus in the early afternoon—check in advance. Another way to Petra is to take a minibus from Aqaba to **Ma'an** (1½hr., JD1) and catch a Petra bus from there (1½hr., JD1). Bus to **Wadi Rum:** at 8:30am, and during the busy season sometimes after noon also. Check times in advance. **JETT bus station** (tel. 315 222), just north of the Miramar Hotel. Service to **Amman** (7 buses 7am-4pm, 4hr., JD4).

Taxis: Regular taxis offer groups (max. 4 people) quick transport to **Petra** (JD30), **Wadi Rum** (1¼hr., JD20), and the Aqaba **ferry terminal** (10km, JD3).

Car Rental: Prices are controlled by the government and range from US$25-80 per day, plus 44-88¢ per km. Call around for specials and unlimited-mile options. Rental agencies include **Rum** (tel. 313 581), across from the Post Office, which is perhaps the cheapest, **Avis** (tel. 322 883), downhill from the Jordan National Bank, and **Hertz**, across from the Aquamarina II.

English Bookstore: Yamany Bookshop (tel. 312 221) opposite the post office. Excellent selection of newspapers, magazines, and tourist guides. Also sells film, snorkeling equipment, sunscreen, and odds and ends. Open daily 8:30am-2pm and 5:30-10:30pm. Accepts MC, Visa, Discover.

Laundry: Most hotels provide expensive laundry service. **Al Abbi Dry Cleaning** (tel. 315 722), 1 block down from the bus and *service* station on King Talal St., is cheaper. Shirts 300fils, pants 400fils. Open Sat.-Thurs. 9-11am and 2-8pm.

Pharmacies: Aqaba Pharmacy (tel. 312 237), next to the Jordan National Bank. Open 24hr. except Fri., when it is closed 8am-8pm. Accepts Visa and MC. **Jerusalem Pharmacy** (tel. 314 747), on Tunisiyya St. next to the Az-Zeitouna Hotel. Open Sat.-Thurs. 7:30am-midnight. Many other pharmacies in the city.

Emergency: Medical: tel. 193. **Hospital: Princess Haya el-Hussein** (tel. 314 111), near the Royal Jordanian Office. One of Jordan's best hospitals, with decompression chambers and a staff capable of dealing with diving accidents. **Police:** tel. 191. Police station across from the bus station.

Post Office: Turn left out of the bus station, and take the next left. Next to the large radio tower. **Poste Restante** and **EMS.** Open Sat.-Thurs. 7am-7pm, Fri. 8am-1pm.

Telephones: Next to the post office. Open daily 7:30am-10pm. Cheap rates after 8pm and on Fridays. **Telephone Code:** 03.

ACCOMMODATIONS

While Aqaba has some of the highest prices in Jordan (after Petra), there are several good values. The usual rules apply: shop, bargain, walk out a few times, and the prices will come down. In the summer, air-conditioning is worth the extra dinar. The only legal **camping** north of the port is in the lots beside some of the larger hotels. The **Aqaba Hotel** has a small site and the JD6 fee admits you to the private beach and showers.

Nairoukh Hotel I (tel. 319 284 or 285), behind Ata Ali and Ali Baba restaurants. There are 2 Nairoukhs, next door to each other—this one is on the left. Employees constantly clean, and the hotel sparkles. Spacious rooms with A/C, TV, fridge, fluffy towels, and phone. Singles JD12; doubles JD18; triples JD25. Breakfast JD2.

Al-Shuala Hotel, Raghadan St. (tel. 315 153; fax 315 160), behind the Hussein Ibn Ali Mosque. A luxury hotel with semi-budget prices. Color TV, refrigerators, bidets, balconies, and a charming view of Eilat. Singles JD20; doubles JD28.

Amira Hotel (tel. 318 840; fax 312 559), next door to Nairoukh I. Small rooms with lots of amenities: TV, small towel, fridge, private toilet, and A/C. Singles JD14; doubles JD18; triples JD22.

Red Sea Hotel (tel./fax 312 156). Next door to Nairoukh I. Somewhat dark, with basic rooms and bathrooms. Be sure to get a room with a "Western toilet." Singles with bath JD5; doubles JD7. Singles and doubles with A/C, TV, and fridge JD12.

Al Khouli Hotel (tel. 312 207), in the square behind the Al-Shuala Hotel. Small entrance, bigger rooms. Some with A/C, fan, and phone. Singles JD7; doubles JD8; triples JD12. With A/C and amenities: singles JD8; doubles JD10.

Jordan Flower Hotel (tel. 314 377; fax 314 378), in the commercial area near the Arab Bank. Rather dreary entrance but comfortable rooms, some with balcony view of the sea. Ceiling fans and outside bathrooms: singles JD6; doubles JD8; triples JD12. Rooms with A/C and fridge: singles JD10; doubles JD12; triples JD18.

FOOD

Fresh fish, the obvious staple of a seaside town, is actually not that abundant. Because of the low plankton content in the clear northern waters of the Gulf of Aqaba, there are few edible sea creatures. Jordanians are not permitted to fish the richer Saudi waters, and the Egyptian export tax is outlandish. There is a **market** (open daily 7am-11pm) in the area behind the Al Shuala Hotel where you can fill up on fresh fruit, bread, and cheese, though your snout may be overwhelmed on windless summer days. Shops on the street surrounding the square sell everything from ice cream to **fried sloth.** Lamb, beef, and falafel are everywhere around the Hussein Ibn Ali Mosque. Many restaurants cluster around the Aquamarina II Hotel. **Gelatto Uno,** near Tikka Chiken, serves frozen treats (10am-midnight).

Captain's Restaurant, An-Nahda St. (tel. 316 905), by the Aquamarina II Hotel. Look for the blue-and-white veranda. One of Aqaba's best, and the restaurant of choice for tour groups. Spaghetti with fresh cheese (JD1.500), meat dishes (JD2.500-5.500), and simple omelettes (500fils) are served. Open daily 9am-11pm.

Ali Baba Restaurant (tel. 313 901), near the Nairoukh Hotel and next door to Hani Ali Restaurant. Ali Baba's outside terrace is a great place to people-watch. Top-notch *baba ganoush* (500fils), hamburgers (JD1.750), and a huge variety of steaks. Open daily 8am-11pm. Visa, MC, AmEx.

Hani Ali Restaurant (tel. 315 200), near the Nairoukh Hotel and Ali Baba Restaurant. Always busy, Hani Ali serves up tasty meals and sticky pastries. Hummus (600fils), spaghetti (JD2), omelettes (JD1.200). Open daily 7am-10pm.

China Restaurant (tel. 314 410), behind the post office. Gaudy red interior and varied menu of quality food (entrees JD2-4). Open daily 11:30am-3pm and 6:30-11pm.

Tikka Chicken, An-Nahda St. (tel. 313 633), 100m west of the Aquamarina II Hotel on your right. Seven different chicken dishes (BBQ, fried, etc.) with various side dishes (JD1.750-2.500). Herbivores will enjoy the veggie salad (500fils) and hummus (500fils). Open daily noon-midnight.

SIGHTS

Yemeniyyeh Reef, just south of the Marine Research Center beyond the port, ranks among the world's best for scoping fish. The **Royal Diving Center** (tel. 317 035; fax 317 097) in the Yemeniyyeh area will help you get into the water. They rent out snorkeling gear for JD5 and conduct **beach dives** (JD10 for one, JD17 for two). Novices can enroll in a four-day dive course for JD200. Entrance fee to the center costs JD2, which includes use of the beach next to the center. A bus runs to and from all major hotels in Aqaba (to the diving center at 9am, back to Aqaba at 4-5pm) for JD1. Otherwise, it is a 15 minute taxi ride south of the city. Most luxury hotels rent out equipment and organize outings. With a mask, snorkel, and pair of fins it is possible to wander off on your own to some of the more isolated spots near the Saudi border, where the fish run on super-octane. For important information on snorkeling and scuba diving, see **Underwater Adventures,** p. 248.

The **Seastar Watersports Center** (tel. 314 131 or 132; fax 314 133), in the Al-Cazar Hotel, conducts dives daily at 9am and 2pm (arrive 30min. early). One dive costs JD26, two dives JD38, with discounts for multiple dives. JD7 will rent snorkeling gear for a day (prices include transportation). Beginners can take a test dive for JD50; a full PADI scuba course costs JD265. Independent snorkelers can buy or rent their own equipment and go solo to the reef area. The **Yamani Bookshop** has a good selection of masks and fins (see **Practical Information,** p. 501). The **Aquamarina Club** (tel. 314 333) at the Aquamarina Hotel offers a number of **watersports.** Get your exercise by waterskiing (JD4), wind surfing (JD5 per hour), or tubing (JD2).

There is an **aquarium** (tel. 315 145), in the Marine Research Center beyond the port, which is home to a number of local fish living in small tanks (open daily 8am-5pm; JD1; taxis to the aquarium JD3)—but you'll see more in your first five minutes of snorkeling.

Near the Miramar Hotel is a free and relatively clean **public beach.** The majority of Aqaba's more scenic, clean, and empty free beaches are quite far away. The Aqaba Hotel has a gorgeous white sand beach, but will gouge you JD2.200 for the privilege of burning your feet—shade and lounge chairs are reserved for guests. Southeast of downtown, there's a free pebble beach behind a "Restricted Area—No Camping" sign. It's mostly a male scene, and women may become the focus of more attention than they may want. The beaches south of the port off the road leading to Saudi Arabia are more remote but they have beautiful views and great snorkeling.

Aqaba should thank its lucky starfish for its aquatic splendors, because the sights above sea level are totally dry. The recently discovered ruins of **Aila** are the only exception; in a plain beachside lot across from the Miramar Hotel, archaeologists have uncovered the original 120m by 160m city. In the 7th to 10th centuries CE, Aila ("god" in Aramaic) was an early Islamic port trading as far away as China. The sight is always open and visitors are free to wander amidst signs explaining the paltry ruins. Items recovered in the excavations, including Greek and Arabic inscriptions, pottery shards, and other small items are displayed in the recently completed **Aqaba Museum,** in the same building as the visitors center, between the castle and the southern waterfront (museum open Wed.-Mon. 8am-1pm and 4-6pm; JD1). The **Medieval Castle,** built in the 16th-century CE by Sultan Ganswa al-Ghouri, behind a dilapidated mosque and a palm grove, is gradually being restored by the Department of Antiquities, and is another semi-interesting spot for the truly bored.

An accord between Jordan and Egypt has recently opened up the Egyptian **Pharaoh's Island** (known in Arabic as Jaziret Far'aun), 7km off shore, to tourists from Jordan. The **Aquamarina Hotel** (tel. 316 250) runs full day trips to the island for JD20 (see p. 265 for more on Pharaoh's Island). Reservations must be received at least two days ahead. The Aquamarina also runs daytrips to **Wadi Rum** for JD38.500.

GOING TO ISRAEL

To cross from Aqaba to Eilat, all nationalities must pay the JD4 exit fee. The border crossing is quick, and money can be exchanged on both sides. There is no entrance fee into Israel and free visas are given at the border. The Israeli border authorities will call you a taxi to get into Eilat (NIS15-20).

GOING TO EGYPT

A **ferry** shuttles between Aqaba and Nuweiba' (US$19). You'll need an Egyptian visa (2-week or 1-month), which can be obtained in one day at the Egyptian Consulate and costs JD12 (see **Practical Information,** p. 500). Visas can also be obtained on board the ferry for an extra charge or upon arrival in Nuweiba' if you're willing to wait in line. Visitors planning on staying only on the Sinai coast can get a free Sinai-only visa. Taxis to the ferry terminal from Aqaba center cost JD2-3. As in Nuweiba', nobody really knows what time the ferries leave, and even if they did, the boats wouldn't leave on time. The slow ferry leaves somewhere between 10am and noon and again around 4pm. The ride takes 3½ hours or more. A faster, less crowded, and more punctual **speedboat** leaves around 10:30am and again around 2:30pm (1hr.; US$32; JD4 departure tax). Show up a few hours before departure. Tickets can be purchased at any travel agency in Aqaba.

■ Near Aqaba: Wadi Rum وادي رام

Two tectonic plates split to create the wide desert valley of Rum. At the northern end of the Wadi lies the village of Rum, home to hundreds of Bedouin, the Desert Police, and the Government Rest House. At the southern end of the valley is the fort of the **Desert Camel Corps,** the descendants of the British-trained Arab Legion. The unabashed members of the Desert Patrol are proud to be photographed in their green robes and red *kafiyas.* When not posing for visitors, they chase smugglers and renegade Bedouin or offer nighttime desert jaunts to beautiful star-gazing areas.

Just beyond the village of Rum, a vast wilderness of sand and rock begins. Massive, rust-colored cliffs tower over the desert floor, some shooting up to heights of 1700m. Though there is little escape from the sun during the day, the evening brings fantastic shadows, transforming the desert into a vast jigsaw puzzle of light and dark. The

A Rockin' Good Time

A fabulous but little known way to enjoy Wadi Rum is by **rock climbing.** Many Europeans (especially French) arrive each year with their gear for days of climbing in this spectacular region. Experienced climbers will take people with their own equipment on trips for very little money. Inquire at the Rest House for the rock climbing book, containing descriptions of a number of different climbing routes and visitors' accounts of their adventures. If you want to climb but don't have equipment, you can rent some from a Bedouin guide. One day of climbing, including equipment rental and a guide, will probably cost around JD35.

whopping slabs of granite and sandstone erupted through the desert floor millions of years ago; it's easy to imagine that Wadi Rum has not changed a day since then.

In *Seven Pillars of Wisdom*, **T.E. Lawrence** wrote that when he passed between these rusty crags his "little caravan fell quiet, ashamed to flaunt itself in the presence of such stupendous hills." The hills and dunes are still as stupendous as they were in Lawrence's time, and provide a magnificent setting for a few days of desert exploration and camping. Wadi Rum is easily reached from Aqaba or Petra—there are one or two **buses** per day to Wadi Rum from both cities, and taxis run all the time (1hr. from Aqaba, 2hr. from Petra, JD15-20). Buses and *service* along the Desert Highway can drop passengers off 25km north of Aqaba at the turn-off marked "Rum 30km." From there it is possible to hitch a ride east and south to the **Government Rest House** within Wadi Rum. Hitching, always dangerous, is not a feasible option in the summer due to the lack of traffic in the area. Another option is to rent a car—Avis, Rum, and Budget all have offices in Aqaba (see **Aqaba Practical Information,** p.501). Four-wheel drive vehicles are not necessary unless you plan on exploring the desert by yourself. The Aquamarina Hotel in Aqaba arranges day trips to Wadi Rum (see p. 503). Wadi Rum admission is JD1, which includes a complimentary cup of tea or coffee, plus JD4 if you bring in your own car.

The other-worldly lavender mountains against the empty sky have earned Wadi Rum the name **Valley of the Moon.** For JD5, a Bedouin will lead you on a camel to a crack in the rocks, the origin of the springs that support all of the *wadi*'s life. Dark stains point out the conduits carved by the ancient Nabateans to conserve the precious water. You may also be shown **Lawrence's Well,** a small spring that bursts forth from the rocks where T.E. used to doze. The Bedouin can point out the many mammoth boulders inscribed with millennia-old Thamudic graffiti. Other sights include the **Rock Bridge,** a massive rock with an arch through the middle, and the elusive **moving sand dune,** an enormous red mountain of sand.

The village is the base for desert explorations by jeep or camel. While a camel ride certainly gets you and your butt into the spirit of things, cars cover more ground. A sign in the Rest House lists the possible destinations. Camel rides start at JD7 for a two-hour trip to the Well, and continue up to JD40. Trips can be arranged through the tourist police at the Rest House. For jeep trips, try to gather a group of up to six at the Rest House to try to share the cost. A full day jeep itinerary, with climbs through narrow *siqs* and hikes up sand dunes, can go for JD40. A good option is to take a 4-5 hour jeep/truck trip that visits a number of the sights. Try to plan your visit at dusk, when the *wadi* explodes with color.

The only place to stay in the village is the **Government Rest House** (tel. 318 867). Guests can sleep on the roof (JD2) or in one of the tents (JD3). Breakfast costs JD3, other meals JD2-5. A large tent beside the Rest House is often the site of traditional Bedouin music and singing in the evenings. You can also arrange an **overnight** in the desert for the official Rest House price of JD30-40—save JD10-15 by arranging a trip directly with a Bedouin (they'll find you). A night in the desert is unforgettable.

Buses leave Wadi Rum daily for Petra and Aqaba—inquire about the times the day. Some travelers find it possible to get a ride with taxis and private cars.

North of Amman

■ Jerash جرش

Stumbled upon by German traveler Ulrich Seetzen in 1806, Jerash is one of the most extensive provincial Roman cities still in existence. Dubbed Gerasa in ancient times, this city was a member of the famed Decapolis, a loose association of trading cities allied with Rome (see **The Ancient Levant,** p. 47). Because of Jerash's isolation in a remote valley, it survived long after the other nine cities were destroyed.

Unlike the other great classical cities in this area, Jerash is typically Roman in design. The city's builders trampled over earlier settlements, so little evidence of pre-Roman days remains. Inscriptions calling the town Antioch reveal that the Seleucid king of that name had a prominent outpost here, but Jerash entered its golden age only after its conquest by the Roman general Pompey in 63 BCE. Over the following three centuries, Jerash experienced a period of prosperity rivaled only by the city's tourist boom of the 1990s. Granite was brought from as far away as Aswan and old temples were razed and rebuilt according to the latest architectural fads. The Emperor Trajan annexed the surrounding Nabatean lands in 106 CE and built a highway from Damascus to Aqaba that passed through Jerash. Hadrian visited the town in 129; the Triumphal Arch built for the occasion still stands. The town was converted to Christianity and had a bishop by the mid-4th century.

Following the destruction of the Syrian trading center at Palmyra and the decline of the Nabatean kingdom, trade routes shifted from the desert to the sea. Frantic construction continued through the 6th century, but without their former wealth, the citizens of Jerash could only replace the older monuments with inferior structures which were plundered by invading Persians in 635 CE. The great earthquake of 747 left few remnants for the Muslim Arabs who controlled the city at that time. The Crusaders described Jerash as uninhabited, and it remained abandoned until its rediscovery in the 19th century. After the invasion of the Ottoman Turks, Circassians built the modern town in what was once the main residential area.

Orientation and Practical Information Jerash will dazzle you along the 1km walk from the South Gate down the Street of Columns to the North Gate. The tiny Chrysoras (Golden) River separates the ancient ruins on the western bank from the new town on the eastern bank. The **Visitors Information Center** (tel. 451 272; open daily 8am-6:30pm in summer, 8am-5pm in winter) is west of the main road, about 400m north of the Triumphal Arch. Groups can hire guides for JD4 (a JD1 tip is also expected). Booklets including maps and explanations of the sights invite leisurely exploration (JD1-6). There is a **post office** in town, behind the bus station (open daily 8am-7pm). The **telephone code** is 04.

Buses and **service taxis** leave from the Jerash bus station on the western edge of the new city in front of the mosque. Buses to Amman's Abdali Station cost 270fils (350fils with A/C), and the ride takes about an hour (bus to Ajlun 250fils, to Irbid 320fils). *Service* generally cost 50% more than buses. Public transportation shuts down at around 7pm in summer and 5pm in winter. Hitchers to Amman, Dibbin, or Ajlun are known to walk south about 1km from the visitors center to the intersection with Highway 20. Turning right (west) leads to Ajlun and Dibbin National Park. Going straight will lead to Amman, and the main road continues through town, north to Irbid. Buses pass frequently toward Amman and are reportedly easy to flag. Hitchers should stand back from the road as they signal the bus; drivers consider time and speed infinitely more important than toes.

Accommodations and Food Because Jerash is such an easy daytrip from Amman, there are no accommodations in the town. You might consider either **camping** at Dibbin National Park, about 8km away, or taking a room at the Dibbin Rest

House (see **Near Jerash,** p. 507). One might also "camp" in the backyard or basement of the **Jerash Rest House** (tel. 451 146), a stomping ground for tour bus groups. Rest House soft drinks are a rip-off at 600fils, and bottled water goes for a throat-drying JD1. At the **Al Khayyam Restaurant,** just past the visitor's center on the main road, JD3.500 buys bread, salad, and grilled meat (open daily 8am-10pm or 11pm). Street stands surrounding the bus station sell cheap falafel and *fuul* (100-200fils).

Sights Jerash's captivating claim to fame is its extensive ruins, even though the best ones are probably lying beneath your feet (over 90% of ancient Jerash awaits excavation). The ruins are open daily 7am-7pm in summer, 7am-5pm in winter (admission JD2), and are described here from south to north.

The **Triumphal (Hadrianic) Arch,** 400m south of the ancient walls, was built to honor the arrival of Emperor Hadrian in the winter of 129 CE. Examine the spare parts strewn about to get a feel for how big the structure once was. After your own majestic passage through the arch, you'll come upon the remaining stables and spectator seats of the **Hippodrome.** This arena hosted chariot races and other contests of skill for the amusement of up to 15,000 spectators. Continuing north, you'll see the **visitor's center** and enter the site proper.

Entering the **South Gate,** you arrive at the **Forum** or **Oval Plaza,** the most photographed part of the city. The Ionic Columns ringing the plaza have been reconstructed to first century CE form. The central podium was once topped with a statue. The Forum opens onto a main street intersected by two avenues.

A footpath to the left in the forum leads to the **South Theater.** Greek doodles reveal that 4000 of Jerash's wealthiest citizens could reserve seats here. The two-story backstage was once furnished with curtains and marble statues. Find "the spot," the groove in the floor of the stage where your voice will carry and magnify to several times its regular volume. The circular niches below the first row of seats are ancient telephones—speak into any one and your voice will be audible at any other "receiver." The best view of the ruined **Temple of Zeus,** which lies between the theater and the South Gate, is probably from the top row of theater seats. Although only its outer walls remain, archaeologists swear that it was glorious in the late 2nd century CE. Renovation efforts are currently underway.

The **Cardo** (Street of Columns) runs from the forum to the **North Gate.** Its 260 pairs of columns are Corinthian replacements for earlier Ionic columns and were once capped by aqueducts carrying water throughout the ancient city. The huge paving stones show grooves worn by chariots. The holes in the floor drained rainwater into a sophisticated sewer system. Massive sidewalk coverings protected pedestrians from the sun, but only traces of these metropolitan parasols remain. The **Jerash Antiquities Museum** is on the right, halfway down the pillared promenade. Tall display cases mounted along the walls show neatly arranged artifacts from the Neolithic to the Ottoman periods. Coins, jewelry, theater "tickets" made of stone, and other household items highlight the museum's small collection (open Sat.-Thurs. 7:30am-5pm, closed on holidays; free). Opposite from the museum is the city's **Agora,** a newly restored meeting place with a central fountain. This small area served as the city's meat and fish market.

The main avenue's first intersection is named the **South Tetrapylon** after its four huge slabs of stone once accompanied by pillars and a large statue. Going west (left) at the cross street brings you to the remains of a 7th century Umayyad building. Back on the Cardo, look for frescoes depicting lizards, cats, and turtles on the floor of the 4th-century **Cathedral** to the left, unsanctimoniously built from, and on top of, the remains of a 2nd-century temple to Dionysus. Next along the street is the **Nymphaeum,** built in 191CE. Intricate stone carvings and the incorporation of marble and gypsum indicate that this two-story fountain was assembled at the height of Jerash's fortune, and was later used in an annual reenactment of the Miracle at Cana, where Jesus changed water into wine (John 2:1-11).

To the west, behind the Cathedral and Nymphaeum, lie a series of Byzantine churches built in the 6th century CE. One especially worth the walk is the **Church of**

St. Cosmos and St. Damius, dedicated to a twin brother team of doctors who treated their patients for free. The church's mosaic floor, depicting the do-gooders surrounded by animals, is one of the few pieces of art to survive Umayyad Caliph Yazid II's attempt to destroy all "images and likenesses" of God's creations in 720CE.

The ominous columned structure at the top of the hill to the left of the Cardo is the **Temple of Artemis.** Dedicated to the patron Goddess of Jerash, the daughter of Zeus and the sister of Apollo, Artemis held special significance throughout the Decapolis, once the territory of similar goddesses Ishtar and Anat. Her temple consisted of a Great Gate, two flights of stairs leading up to a shrine-topped podium, and a courtyard surrounded by giant pillars. Opposite the Temple of Artemis are the **West Baths,** including a 2nd-century cold bath *(frigidarium),* warm bath *(tepidarium),* hot bath *(caldarium),* and changing rooms. The **East Baths,** across the *wadi* by the bus station, were built on an even larger, more majestic scale. Farther north along the Cardo, past the **North Tetrapylon** is the **North Theater** (under renovation).

Entertainment Occasionally during the summer months (April-October), there is an hour-long **sound and light show** among the ruins, with special JETT buses to get you there. Check with the JETT office in Amman (tel. 664 146) for details.

Jerash is undergoing eternal restoration as the government attempts to raise the city's profile. The **Jerash Festival,** instituted in 1981, takes place under royal patronage every summer beginning in the second half of July. Check with the Jerash Festival office in Amman for details (tel. 675 199) or see *The Jordan Times* for complete coverage. The South Theater and Artemis Steps provide a dramatic setting for musical, theatrical, and dance groups from all over the world. Shows range from the Gary Burton Quintet to the Royal Jordan Orchestra to the Azerbaijan State Ballet to modern interpretations of *The Taming of the Shrew.* Recently, more Jordanian artists, such as renowned composer Yousef Khaso, are appearing on the schedule along with international performers. The famous Lebanese singer, Majdah ar-Roumi, has delighted the crowds at the theater more than once. Ticket prices vary; if you arrive after 7:30pm you won't have to pay the JD2 entrance fee to the ruins.

Transport to and from Jerash during the festival is chaotic. The best option is to form a group and share a private taxi. *Service* are crowded. Hitchhikers have trouble finding rides, especially if they leave after 4pm; coming home at about 10pm is less of a problem, but hitchhikers still report difficulty because most cars are full. *Let's Go* urges you to consider the risks before hitchhiking.

■ Near Jerash

The Aleppo pines and oaks of the fertile woodland are a remarkable sight in this desert country. Located in the hills 10km southwest of Jerash and 65km north of Amman, the **Dibbin National Park** encompasses some 20km of forest stretching south from the town of the same name.

On the old road to Jerash near Dibbin village is the **Dibbin Rest House** (tel. (04) 452 413; fax 813 246), offering semi-budget accommodations. The access road leaves the Amman-Jerash Highway about 2km south of Jerash; look for the signs. You'll have to take a car, as neither buses nor *service* access the park. Another option is the bus from Jerash to the nearby village of Dibbin; the hike from the village to the park is about 2km uphill. The park offers campgrounds free of charge and equally free of facilities. Call ahead to make sure the park is open.

■ Ajlun عجلون

Loosely translated from Arabic as "the cattle that straddles a camel's hump," **Qal'at ar-Rabadh** (Ajlun Castle) is true to its name. This huge Arab castle built in 1184 by Izz ad-Din Ibama, nephew of and commander under Salah ad-Din, sits atop the highest peak overlooking the town. Built to contain the progress of the Latin kingdom in Transjordan, the original building was erected to outdo the Castle of Belvoir on Lake Tiberias. With its four corner towers and seven floors, Qal'at ar-Rabadh closely resembles Karak Castle, south of Amman. Filled with secret passages, winding, crumbly staircases, and dark corridors, the castle makes every explorer feel like Indiana Jones.

The castle controlled a long stretch of Jordan's northern valley, protecting communication lines between Jordan and Syria. Crusader knights spent decades unsuccessfully trying to capture the castle and nearby village. The name Kufranjah, a town in the area famous for its olive trees, suggests that the Franks (*Franjis* in Arabic) spent some time here, if only as prisoners. After the Crusader threat dissipated, Salah ad-Din used the castle as a base from which to work nearby iron mines and to transmit messages by beacon and pigeon; from Baghdad to Cairo, day or night, the relay could be made in 12 hours. During the Ottoman period, 50 soldiers were stationed in the castle at all times, and during the first quarter of the 17th century, Prince Fakhr ad-Din al-Ma'ni II, a relative of Salah ad-Din, used it during his fight against Ahmad ibn Tabay. The castle was mostly uninhabited after that time until the Swiss explorer J.L. Burkhardt (better known for discovering the lost city of Petra that same year) found 40 members of the Barakat family living there in 1812. Two major earthquakes in 1837 and 1927 did the damage that the Crusades never could. While the castle is in very good condition today, parts of it are still under restoration by the Department of Antiquities (open daily 8am-6 or 7pm, until 5pm in winter; JD1).

Orientation and Practical Information Ajlun lies a hilly 24km west of Jerash, and is also an easy bus ride from Amman (73km) or Irbid (88km). The **bus** from Abdah Station in Amman (1 1/2 hr., 450 fils) will drop you off a few streets down from the main circle. Follow the sounds of honking cars and the smells of roasting *shawerma* uphill to the center of town. From the circle, the castle is four km up a gently sloping road. You can catch a taxi for 500 fils one-way or a minibus for 50fils. Especially on Fridays, public transportation can be slow—start walking uphill and flag the bus on the way. Generous passers-by may also give you a lift if you're looking tired. Exchange money at the **Arab Bank,** next door to the post office, the **Housing Bank,** on the center circle, or the **Bank of Jordan,** on Irbid St. uphill from the circle (all three open Sat.-Thurs. 8am-12:30pm, closed Fri. and holidays). The **Directorate of Tourism** in Ajlun (tel. 462 115), located about 200m downhill from the castle, gives out free maps and brochures, and can arrange for a guided tour of the castle. Ajlun's **post office** is located on Amman St., to your right as you enter the town, a few hundred yards from the circle (open Sat.-Thurs. 7:30am-7pm, Fri. until 1:30 pm).

Accommodations and Food There are two hotels in Ajlun, both within short walking distance of the castle along the road to town. The **Ajlun Hotel** (tel./fax 462 524), closer to the castle, offers clean, bright singles and doubles with breakfast for the post-bargaining prices of JD15 and JD23, respectively. At the **Ar-Rabad Castle Hotel** (tel. 462 202) new rooms come with a TV, phone, patio with chairs for watching the sunset, and immaculate bathrooms. Unless you plan on staying longer than a week, the management will not stray from official rates (singles JD24; doubles JD32, including breakfast). The restaurants of both hotels offer a view with a side order of lunch for a whopping JD4-5. The Ar-Rabad sports an outdoor café with a fountain and umbrellas, while the Ajlun Restaurant looks like a fully-enclosed ski chalet. The view is affordable if you stick to the 300-400fils *mezze* plates. Those who prefer to fill their bellies rather than their eyes should stop in at the **Green Mountain Restaurant** (open daily 6:30am-8:30pm) in Ajlun's center circle. A half-chicken goes for JD1.050, *kebab* JD1.120, and hummus or *fuul* 280fils; 700fils buys a complete meal including rice, meat, and a vegetable. The **Abu al-Izz Restaurant** (tel. 462 625) is in front of the Green Mountain. This sprawling outdoor cafe with leafy trellises offers the usual Middle Eastern food for higher prices than the Green Mountain, but with more ambience.

■ Irbid اربد

Like Amman, Irbid (1hr. north of Jerash) is an industrial center which has overwhelmed the site of its ancient predecessor (in this case the Decapolis city Dion). Irbid's streets are stuffed with merchants and Kung Fu theaters. The fluorescent maze is the home of Yarmouk University, one of the biggest institutions of higher learning in Jordan. The university gives Irbid the feel of a college town. Its charm makes Irbid an enjoyable base from which to plan a trip to Umm Qeis, Al Himma, or Damascus.

ORIENTATION AND PRACTICAL INFORMATION

Facing downhill from the **main circle** (next to the Al Ameen Hotel), the town **mosque** and **market** are located down the street to the right. The Hotel al-Wehdeh al-Arabiyyeh, Bank of Jordan, and Abu Bakr Hotel are up the street to the left. To get to the post office, walk downhill 10m and take the first left onto Baghdad St. after the Al Ameen Hotel. On your right you will see another big circle with a monument. Continue down Baghdad St. past the Omayed Hotel.

ANZ Grindlay's Bank, across from the post office, exchanges cash and traveler's checks (open Sat.-Thurs. 8am-12:30pm). Many travelers hitch to Irbid via Jerash, but the quickest and safest way to the city from Amman is by the **Arabella** or **Hijazi** bus companies (75 min., with A/C 820fils). Taxis from the private bus station to the main circle downtown cost 500fils. **Minibuses** from Amman, Jerash, and Ajlun are cheaper but slower; they drop you off at Irbid's New South Station, from which you can take a *service* taxi downtown (60fils). Taxis to Yarmouk cost 500fils (JD1 after midnight).

To leave Irbid, go to the New South Station (ask for *Bas ila Amman*). From here a minibus runs regularly to Ajlun (250fils) and to Amman's Abdali Station (500fils). The last buses depart for Amman at about 8pm (in winter as early as 5pm). *Service* also leave New South Station for Syria. The trip to Damascus costs JD4 and takes 4-5hr., depending on border crossings. Bring your visa for the border crossing (see **Visas and Visa Extensions**, p. 8). *Service* run regularly from downtown to Yarmouk and to North Station. *Service* to Yarmouk (70fils) leave from Abu Bakr as-Siaddiqa St. Cross the street at the Omayed Hotel and take a left down one of the small streets off of Baghdad St. The *service* line up in front of the Chicken Palace Restaurant. For a *service* to North Station, take the first left after the Omayed Hotel facing toward the post office. Continue straight, across the street, until the road ends at a diagonal intersection. Turn right, walk for about 5min., then go right again when you see the big purple sign on your left. *Service* line up here and will drop you off one street up from the station. Buses to Al Himma and Umm Qeis leave often from North Station. Taxis between the two bus stations cost 700fils.

Irbid's **post office** is open Sat.-Thurs. 7:30am-7pm, Fri. and holidays 8am-1:30pm. **FedEx** and **TNT** services are available at the travel agent located on Baghdad St. downtown, across from the Omayed Hotel (open Sat.-Thurs. 8am-7:30pm, Fri. 10am-2pm). The **telephone office,** with international phone and telex services, is open Sat.-Thurs. 7:30am-10pm; hours vary Fri. and holidays. Irbid's **telephone code** is 02.

ACCOMMODATIONS

Al-Ameen al-Kabir Hotel (tel. 242 384), on Midan Malek Abdallah St., one block from the city center and the Ministry of Antiquities building. Bright, breezy rooms with beautiful bedspreads and exceptionally courteous management, but no fans. Singles JD5; doubles JD6; triples JD9. Bargain in off-season. Hot shower 500fils.

Hotel Al-Wehdeh Al-Arabiah (tel. 242 083), at the top of Al Jaish St. Dark but homey. Look for the "bedouin tent" on your right as you enter. Clean rooms, some with balconies, have spongy mattresses. Egyptian management is friendly and ready to bargain. Singles JD4; doubles JD6.500. Extra bed JD2. Free showers.

Abu Bakr Hotel (tel. 242 695), around the corner from the Al Ameen on Wasfi Et-Tal St., in the same building as the Bank of Jordan. Orange curtains, fans, and free flip-flops grace the quiet rooms upstairs. Earthy bathrooms. Singles JD3; doubles and triples JD6. Bed in the communal room JD2. Free showers.

Omayed Hotel (tel./fax 245 955) on Baghdad St., one block down from the post office. All rooms have television, telephone, fan, private bathroom, and bidet. Receptionist Ahmad Mansour can tell you how to get anywhere you want to go. Single JD14; doubles JD18 plus 10% tax.

FOOD

The colorful streets around Yarmouk University are lined with wall-to-wall restaurants to tempt any palate. Around dinner time, everyone from students to local fortune-tellers crowd the outdoor cafes looking for food and a chance to argue about politics. If you've been unimpressed with falafel and *shawerma* so far, give the food stands on the main street a second chance. Fresh and hot, with no spice spared, the cheapest food in Irbid is some of Jordan's best (falafel sandwich 120fils, *shawerma* 200-250fils). The local market, held around the mosque visible from the main circle, is a great place to get lost while stocking up on fresh fruit (including the best peaches in the world), bread, and sweets. For a sit-down meal, the local favorite is the **Den of Happiness Restaurant** (*mat'am 'ush al-hana'*). The big red and yellow sign is in Arabic only; look for tables across from the mosque. The food is cheap and plentiful, and the menu includes hummus and cheese omelettes for 350fils.

Assufara Restaurant, on the main circle, offers reasonable local fare and drinks on sprawling patios. Entrees JD1-3. Open daily 8am-1am, 11pm in winter.

Italian Café Amon, next door, serves spaghetti for JD1. Open daily 8am-12pm.

Yarmouk University Cafeteria, accessible at the North Gate. Go straight, then take a right just before the big sculpture. Look for a little round birdhouse chalet crammed with studious types inhaling huge meals for under JD1. Open 8am-8pm.

Andalus Cafeteria, by the post office. Good falafel and *shawerma* (120-220fils), and fresh juices for 500fils. A swell lunchtime hangout for local shopkeepers.

Palestine Restaurant, on Palestine St. past the main circle. The late-night hummus and *fuul* joint where mostly male customers play backgammon and dine.

SIGHTS

The **Museum of Jordanian Heritage,** provides a narrative of Jordan's history from prehistoric times to the present. It is the best and biggest museum in Jordan and should not be missed. The tiny **Natural History Museum** houses many stuffed birds and animals indigenous to Jordan, but the area's animate wildlife is more interesting. Both museums are free and are open Wed.-Mon. 8am-5pm, 8am-3pm in June and July. To get to the Museum of Jordanian Heritage, enter the Yarmouk campus at the North Gate. Turn right at the second white monument and the museum will be on your left. The stationary birds and animals are to the left of the same white monument.

■ Near Irbid

UMM QEIS أم قيس

Umm Qeis was the Biblical Gadara, where Jesus exorcised a sinner's demons into a herd of pigs which stampeded down the hill to drown in the Sea of Galilee. This thriving city was one of the ten cities of the Decapolis, founded by Pompey after his conquest of Syria and Palestine in 64 BCE. Once a resort for Romans vacationing at Al Himma's therapeutic hot springs, Umm Qeis was renowned for its arts and its legendary orgiastic extravagances. The epitaph on the grave of Germanus the Roman in the courtyard of the museum says it all: "To you I say, passerby, as you are now, I was. And as I am, you will soon be, so enjoy your mortal life."

The city was probably founded in the 4th century BCE. Its name comes from a Semitic word meaning "stronghold," reflecting the city's role as a fortified border town guarding the crucial land routes between southern Syria and northern Palestine. Earthquakes and plagues in the 7th and 8th centuries left Umm Qeis nothing more than a hamlet. Most of the standing structures date from the 2nd century CE.

Before paying the entrance fee (JD1), step inside the Roman tombs located just outside the guard's booth. The first one is **Germanus' Tomb,** the second **Modestos' Tomb.** The heavy stone doors with ornate carving are still intact, even though these tombs were used as barracks by the Jordanian army in the 1967 war.

After paying the entrance fee, follow the path past the **Eastern Necropolis,** a cemetery just outside the city walls where the Greco-Roman and later Arab residents of Umm Qeis were interred. On your left will be the entrance to the Roman **aqueduct,** which brought water from Ezra in Syria. Just before the aqueduct, the **Temple of Zeus** is being restored. The mass of Ottoman Buildings on the top of the hill covers what used to be an **acropolis** and the most important quarter of ancient Gadara.

Today, the two-story white limestone **museum** is the main building of interest. Check out **Tyche,** the Goddess of Gadara, who is missing a few important appendages but still holds onto her fruit-filled cornucopia, a symbol of fertility (open daily 8am-5pm; free). The white marble statue served as a sharp contrast to the black basalt **West Theater** in which it was once enshrined. In front of the museum, the shape of the **North Theater,** once accommodating 5000, is apparent. The Ottomans took the actual stones of the structure to build the village on the hill, but German archaeologists are attempting to reconstruct parts of it.

Before the west theater, to the left of the **Decumanus Maximus** (main road), lies the **Basilica Terrace.** Its black basalt Corinthian columns surround the octagonally arranged white limestone columns of what was a Byzantine church. Farther along the main road, built into the perimeter of the Basilica Terrace, are fourteen barrel-vaulted rooms, that used to be street-front shops. The shops have been reconstructed to look as they did in Roman times. Farther down the road lie the weed-embraced **East Baths** and **Nymphaeum.** At the end of the Decumanus sits a circular building of basalt rocks and, adjacent to that, an **underground mausoleum,** the only completely intact structure from **Ancient Gadara.** Holes in the ceiling of the mausoleum were used to drop food to the spirits of the interred, and now provide enough light to peek through the locked gate into the underground caverns. The main burial room, with six chambers on each of three walls, was expanded and re-used by the Christian Byzantines.

The **Um-Qeis Hotel** (tel. 217 081, ext. 80) is about 100m up the hill from the ruins, on the left. Rooms (JD5 per person without bathroom, JD8 with bathroom) are new, freshly-painted, and sparsely furnished. Breakfast costs JD3, dinner JD4. The beautiful **Umm Qeis Rest House** (tel. 217 555) serves overpriced refreshments to desperate travelers and overlooks the Golan Heights and the Sea of Galilee. For JD3-4 you can eat your fill of soup, salad, or pasta; an ice cream drips for 750fils. The **Mount Hermon Restaurant**, next door to the gift shop, serves a full gourmet meal, including appetizers, mineral water, and tea or coffee, for JD4. Traditional Middle Eastern food is available at a few cheap places along the main road before the ruins. There is a **post/telephone office** (tel. 217 210) along the main road through modern Umm Qeis (open 7:30am-7:30pm). If the door is locked, knock with aplomb. You can get stamps, post cards, and loads of invaluable historical information from Abd as-Salam at the reasonably-priced **Umm Qeis Gift Shop** (tel. 07 956 202). Start your tour of Umm Qeis here. Credit cards are accepted at the hotel, rest house, and gift shop.

AL HIMMA الحمة

A minibus runs from Irbid to Al Himma, which is 10km away. Just past Umm Qeis, a soldier will check your **passport** and may want to search your bags. Beyond the military roadblock gapes the valley of the Yarmouk River. Looming quietly across the wide green vale are the glorious Golan Heights.

After an exquisite descent, the bus will drop you at the entrance to the **mineral springs** complex. Swimming costs JD1.100, JD6.600 if you reserve a private bath with slightly cooler water (open daily 6am-8pm). Two-hour shifts alternate between the sexes (men first, 6-8am). After 8pm, you can reserve the mineral springs complex for JD8.800 per hour if you don't mind the stench of sulphur. Women are not allowed to swim in the cool outdoor pool. Their baths are fully-enclosed and can get uncomfortably steamy and smelly in summer. Groups of men and women may use a new, secluded outdoor pool for around JD9 per hour (price negotiable). The **Hotel al-Hamma al-Urdun** (tel. (02) 249 829, ext. 11), built like a staircase around the springs, has no-frills rooms, some of which are getting moldy from disuse (doubles JD8; triples JD10; "chalet triples" with fridge and rusty gas cooker JD25, plus 10% service tax). The **Jordanian Hammi Restaurant** (tel. (02) 249 829, ext. 12) on the east side of the complex serves *kebab* for an outlandish JD1.800 and juice for 500fils. Pack a lunch or head back to Umm Qeis for affordable snacks. **Buses** travel to Umm Qeis (200fils) and Al Himma (300fils) from Irbid's North Station. The last minibus to Umm Qeis/Al Himma leaves at 5:30pm.

SYRIA سوريا

US$1=41.85 Syrian Pounds (S£)	S£100=US$2.39
CDN$1=S£30.07	S£100=CDN$3.33
UK£1=S£67.27	S£100=UK£1.49
IR£1=S£61.69	S£100=IR£1.62
AUS$1=S£31.30	S£100=AUS$3.20
NZ$1=S£27.10	S£100=NZ$3.69
SAR1=S£8.93	S£100=SAR11.20
JD1 (Jordanian Dinar) =S£59.11	S£100=JD1.69
L£1 (Lebanese Pound) = S£.0273	S£100=L£3600

> For important information on travel in general and some specifics on Syria, see the **Essentials** section of this book. Syria's **international phone code** is 963.

The Syrian Ministry of Tourism claims that "every cultured man belongs to two nations; his own, and Syria." Other than its exclusion of women, the claim isn't too far off: the origins of language, art, and architecture are all part of this area's archaeological treasure chest. Syria's unique position at the meeting point of Asia, Africa, and Europe has always made it a center of civilization. More than seven empires have left their mark on this land between the Caspian Sea, the Indian Ocean, the Black Sea, and the Nile River. The silk route ran through Syria, a strong thread linking China with the Mediterranean and making Doura Europos (Salhieh) an ancient center of trade. Syria's role in the evolution of civilization is mind-boggling: it was here that copper was made pliable and bronze was invented. The kingdom of Ugarit (Ras Shamra) on the Mediterranean coast developed the first alphabet in history, and at Ebla (Tel Merdikh) a royal palace was discovered containing one of the largest and most comprehensive documentary archives of the ancient world.

After a more recent history of closed regimes and enmity with Israel, Syria is now open to travelers. Backpackers are passing through with increasing frequency and organized tour groups are becoming more common. Independent travel is easy; public transportation is abundant and a strong tradition of hospitality provides bottomless resources. From the sparsely populated Syrian Desert in the east to the west's balmy seashore, the country's natural beauty and friendly inhabitants remain unmolested by the hordes. Get there before they do and discover magnificent Roman ruins, medieval castles, and prices that haven't changed since the dawn of time. Syria is one of the last frontiers of budget adventure in the Eastern Mediterranean.

ONCE THERE

▓ Getting Around

Taxis Private taxis are yellow, easy to use, and relatively cheap. Hail one by holding out your arm, hand outstretched with palm down. Most taxis have meters; drivers usually don't feel the need to use them. If you can negotiate a fair price before you get into the car, don't worry about using the meter. If a driver refuses to bargain or tries to rip you off, you can always point to the meter as a last resort and you will get a fair rate. Many taxi drivers specialize in cheating newly arrived tourists; be firm when deciding on price (we list approximate fares for most common trips).

Service (pronounced ser-VEES) are shared taxis, usually large white American cars from the 50s and 60s. They drive on set routes within Damascus and to outlying areas, which are sometimes written in Arabic on the side of the vehicle. They usually depart only when full, and fares vary based on where you get off. They are cheaper than taxis, but they can be difficult to figure out at first. For shorter, local rides, a taxi is probably a better bet. For intercity travel, *service* are largely being replaced by the cheaper microbus, a white minivan (see below).

Buses **Karnak** (tel. (11) 222 14 92) is the government-run bus company. Routes go everywhere and fares are low. Buses tend to be ramshackle wrecks, but they sometimes depart on schedule. Reservations are required and can be made at bus stations in the cities. **Pullman** buses are even a step down from Karnak. Over 50 **private bus companies** now operate in Syria; they have ship-shape coaches and competitive prices. Reservations are a good idea for these buses as well. Usually, Karnak, Pullman, and private buses leave from different stops—make sure you're at the right one. All tickets must be bought at the stations, as drivers do not handle money.

Microbuses (MEE-cro-bas or MEE-cro) are an easy, cheap, and relatively hassle-free way to travel between cities. They are different from the clattery old **minibuses** which are becoming less frequent on the roads. *Micros* are usually white Japanese minivans that seat around 14 people and run on specific intercity routes. The most difficult part of *micro* travel is finding the one going to your destination. Payment is made during the ride via one passenger who volunteers to be conductor. You can relax and enjoy the ride until you see people beginning to pass money toward the front. Wait and see what other people are paying in order to figure out your fare. Just remember that people pay more or less depending on where they get off. The trust system virtually guarantees that you will not be ripped off, and saves you the trouble of hassling with a driver.

Trains Strictly speaking, trains connect some cities in Syria. Frankly speaking, roller skates would serve you better. Trains are slow, crowded, and dirty, and in most places they drop you off about 30km out of town. Use the buses.

Cars Very few people in Syria own private cars, which is why the public transportation is so good. If you want to risk your life driving one, cars can be rented at a few places in Damascus for US$37 per day plus mileage; unlimited mileage costs US$59 per day. Special weekly rates are only slightly cheaper. All the sights you could possibly want to see are easily accessible via cheap public transportation; the freedom of having a car is not worth the expense. For negotiable prices, some *service* drivers will be your private chauffeur for the day. If you want the security and freedom of your own driver when visiting out-of-the-way places, this is still a better option than renting a car, and will probably cost the same or less.

Hitchhiking There is no need to hitchhike in Syria. If you stand by the side of a road, a *micro* will eventually stop and cost only pocket change. It is not unusual, however, for truck drivers to pick up passengers in order to subsidize their trips (they usually expect S£1-2 per km). Travelers that are caught by the police may be taken in for questioning or given a stern warning not to do it again. *Let's Go* does not recommend hitchhiking.

■ Money Matters

Currency and Exchange The basic unit of currency in Syria is the Syrian pound, abbreviated S£. Each pound is divided into 100 piasters, or qirsh (plural qurush), abbreviated pt. Paper currency comes in denominations of S£500, 100, 50, 25, 10, 5, and 1. Coins come in 100, 50, 25, 10, and 5pt values.

If you are in Cairo or Amman before coming to Syria, you can **exchange** money there for Syrian pounds at the free market rate, a bit higher than the official rate. You may bring as much foreign currency into the country as you like but may not leave with more than you bring in. Amounts up to US$5000 do not have to be declared. Once in Syria, you can change money at the Commercial Bank of Syria, which has exchange desks in most of the major hotels as well as at all branches, at the rates

Syria

listed above. There is a S£25 commission fee on all exchanges involving **travelers' checks,** but there is no fee for changing cash. US$ are the preferred currency for exchange. UK£ are also accepted, although not as widely.

Credit cards cannot be used to obtain a cash advance, although major cards like Visa, MasterCard, and American Express are increasingly accepted at large hotels and stores for purchases. If you are in a bind, some shopkeepers in the Damascus *souq* will disguise a cash advance as a purchase, although the exchange rate will be lower than the official bank rate (around S£40 per US$).

Black market exchange is most common in Damascus, where a thriving trade flourishes beneath the thumb of secret service agents on the lookout for offenders. Some hotels will unofficially change money for you at the black market rate, usually up to S£8 per US$ more than the bank rate. Transactions using US$ except to pay a hotel bill are illegal: in 1986, a law was passed making illegal exchange or possession of hard currency punishable by up to three years in prison. Syrian prison is scary—be discreet when changing money on the black market. You may be approached in a *souq* or near Al Marjeh Sq. in Damascus, but be aware that there are undercover government officials waiting for you to take their bait. Hotel employees are usually the safest bet. You can haggle for a higher exchange rate: often, an offer starts at S£45 per dollar. You should get S£50 for US$ cash, a little bit less for travelers' checks.

Business Hours In Syria, the work week begins on Saturday and ends on Thursday. Friday is the official day off. Stores are generally open from 8am to 1:30pm, and then again from 4 to 8pm (7pm in winter). Some stores stay open all day in winter. Government offices are open from 8am to 2pm. Some offices (telephone, post) are open on Friday. Museums are generally open from 8am to 2pm every day but Tuesday. Restaurants open for lunch around 1pm and for dinner at 8pm. Hours are not always followed to the letter.

Tipping and Bakhsheesh It used to be the case that nothing would get done in Syria without a bit of **palm-greasing.** Now, increased contact with the world market is changing the general attitude towards *bakhsheesh*. While bribes are no longer necessary to accomplish the smallest task (and are inappropriate when dealing with high government officials and police officers), tipping is expected. Taxi drivers, waiters, and movie theater employees should be given at least a 10% tip. If you stay multiple nights at a hotel that cleans its rooms daily, a small thank-you (S£20-40 per day) to the person responsible is appropriate.

■ Accommodations

There are no hostels in Syria. Instead, there are two options of opposite price and quality: international chain-style (more expensive) hotels and basic hole-in-the-wall, bed-and-a-roof crash sites. The higher the quality of a room, the more likely it is that you'll have to pay in US$; all two-star or higher hotels carry this requirement. In most places there is an even split between hotels that charge US$ and S£, but in the more touristed places like Palmyra, prepare to part with the dead Presidents. Different employees of one establishment often quote contradictory rates; bargaining can save some money. Damascus and Aleppo hotels are less likely to haggle, but if they look empty, give it a shot. Even posted rates can sometimes be brought down, if only by a few pounds. Unmarried couples may have a difficult time getting a room together; generally this is less of a problem in the more expensive establishments.

■ Keeping in Touch

Mail Mail from Syria is inexpensive but slow (letters to the U.S. can take 3 weeks to arrive). It costs about S£20 to mail letters overseas, S£8 for postcards (rates vary). Take packages to a post office for inspection before wrapping them for delivery to another country. **Poste Restante** service is available in Damascus's main post office.

Bring your passport and S£10 per letter. The American Express office in Damascus will hold mail.

Telephone Trials and tribulations abound. Damascus has a 24-hour telephone office, where you can place international calls, but you'll need your passport, lots of money, and patience (at least an hour's worth). Some other cities have offices as well. Most hotels have direct-dial international capabilities, but rates from Syria are exorbitant to begin with (US$12 for a 3min. call to the U.S.), and hotels charge at least double the phone office rates. It's much cheaper to have your party call you back or to call collect. The access code for **MCI's World Phone** program is 0800, for **AT&T's USADirect** it is 0801, and for **Sprint** 0888. You can now use phone cards to make local calls; they are available in denominations of S£200 and S£500. Syria's **international phone code** is 963.

■ Dress and Etiquette

Conservative dress is the norm in Syria; shorts, tank tops, and short skirts will invite stares, comments, and possibly unwanted sexual advances. Pants and skirts should fall to at least mid-calf and shirts should cover the shoulders and upper arms (for more information, see **Travel Etiquette**, p. 45 and **Women and Travel**, p. 33)

It is impolite in Syria to point directly at someone or to point the sole of your shoe at someone (as when sitting down and placing an ankle on one knee). When a Syrian tips his or her head up and makes a clucking noise, this means "no," although Westerners have been known to mistake it for a sign of acknowledgment or a "get in the back seat" gesture by a taxi driver. No means no.

LIFE AND TIMES

■ Religion and Ethnicity

Islam is the dominant religion of Syria, with about 82% of the populace following the teachings of the **Qur'an.** 68% of the total population is Sunni, 14% Shi'a. The Shi'a branch is splintered into sects such as the Isma'ilis (1.5%), and the Alawites (11.5%), who include President Asad among their adherents. Another 13-14% of Syrians belong to the Catholic or Eastern Orthodox churches; 3% are Druze.

The statistics on Syria's ethnic composition vary, with different sources setting the percentage of Arabs in the country between 82% and 90%. The remainder of the population is Kurdish, Turkish, Armenian, or Circassian. Part of the Kurdish minority in Syria would like to create an independent Kurdish state, which would also include the Kurds in Turkey, Iran, and Iraq, but as of yet, their grievances have not been accompanied by positive action. Pamphlets distributed in 1992 advocating this proposal brought about the arrest of 200 Kurdish activists; some remain in prison today. Only about 5% of the world's Kurdish population lives within Syrian borders.

■ Government and Politics

Before Asad's ascent to power, the centralized Ba'th party system had no provisions for local governance, which meant that a complaint about the size of street signs in Ma'alula would end up on the desk of the prime minister. Asad mandated the election of local government councils and required them to be at least 51% workers or peasants. With representatives in every village, the government decentralized, but the party still maintains a presence in local affairs. Asad has also stabilized government (mainly through elevating Alawites and his childhood friends to positions of authority throughout the nation) and continues to maintain a vaguely socialist infrastructure.

Today all political parties are associated with the National Progressive Front (NPF), a coalition dominated by the Ba'th party and run by Asad himself. The People's Council, a 250-member legislative body, has political power in theory, but is controlled by the NPF, meaning Ba'th policies are passed with a minimum of opposition. The cabinet advises Asad on policy, but they would probably have "Ba'th" tattooed on their foreheads if Asad asked them to. Syria has three vice-presidents (including Asad's brother, who attempted to take control of the country in 1984 and was exiled; he was later allowed to return to his post). President Asad is essentially a dictator, controlling everything he can, from foreign policy to information flow.

As with all dictatorships, Syria's future beyond Asad's reign is uncertain. There is no question about the present; in 1992, Asad was elected to his fourth seven-year term as president, with 99.9% of the vote. A generous person could attribute Asad's success to his policies, which have certainly improved the quality of life in Syria since 1971 when he took power. Another explanation for his political longevity is his aggressive suppression of his enemies (some of whom were arrested in 1971 and remain incarcerated) through the omnipresent internal security forces looking to quell anti-Asad sentiment. The spy industry, combined with an abysmal human-rights record, has created an atmosphere of fear in Syria and invited the displeasure of foreign countries. Additionally, Syria has only recently begun to curb its nasty habit of harboring (some say training) terrorists.

Lately, Asad has been seeking Western aid in an attempt to revitalize his country's plodding economy. The government enthusiastically supported the allies during the Gulf War; and is even periodically engaged in talks with Israel. These talks may lead to the establishment of diplomatic relations between the two countries, the return of part or all of the Golan Heights to Syria, and, eventually, economic benefits.

When traveling in Syria, **do not get involved in political discussions.** If you just can't avoid the topic, offer vaguely enthusiastic praise for Asad and quickly change the subject. Mentioning Israel is also a *faux pas*—many travelers refer to it as "Disneyland" among themselves.

■ Economy

Syria is blessed with black gold (oil). The oil money of the early 1970s allowed Asad to go forward with a program of capital formation, including investments in agriculture, heavy industries, health services, and education. A drive toward speedy modernization shaped the mid-70s, also characterized by rebuilding after the destructive October War and taking advantage of the oil boom. Unfortunately, industries were haphazardly chosen and designed for development, leaving Syria with a legacy of wasteful, inefficient factories. Some industries were profitable, including light crude oil, natural gas, phosphates, iron and steel, and light industries including rubber, glass, tobacco, and paper.

The Syrian economy also suffers from the two-headed monster of rapid population growth and massive inflation. In 1994 in Damascus, the population grew at a 3.8% annual rate: an extra 40,000 people to feed each year in that city alone. Inflation in 1987-88 reached 100%, and in November 1991, prices jumped 300% when the government relaxed price controls. Since then, inflation has dropped to a less stratospheric level (22%), but the Syrian pound is still far from a good investment option.

With such restraints on economic growth, Syria has had trouble improving the economy. Asad's uninspired attempt to reduce unemployment (which reached 35% in the 70s and 80s) created the situation today in which 1 of every 5 workers gets a paycheck signed by the government. Many of these government workers are unnecessary, unmotivated, and inefficient. The Syrian government no longer releases unemployment figures. In the 80s, government ministries encouraged private investors to support import substitution, tourism, and agricultural projects, but investors didn't share the state's enthusiasm for capital investment; instead, they put their money into real estate. Consequently, property prices rose dramatically, further worsening the Syrian economy.

As a country in the midst of the politically unstable Middle East, Syria maintains a large standing army, accounting for about 60% of its total expenditures. The result of these expenditures, Syria's past connections with terrorist groups, its support of Iran, and sporadic skirmishes with Jordan, have translated into low levels of foreign aid; but Asad has begun to change all this. In 1991, Syria's opposition to Iraq in the Gulf War garnered a great deal of aid from Saudi Arabia, Japan, and European nations, while talks with Israel and the loosening of travel restrictions for Syrian Jews (95% of whom had left the country by the end of 1994) curry favor with Western governments and investors.

■ Festivals and Holidays

Muslim holidays (see **When to Go,** p. 2) are official days off in Syria; Christmas and Easter are celebrated by Christians but not legislated as holidays. Political holidays close everything down; they are **New Year's Day** (Jan. 15), **Revolution Day** (March 8), **Women's Day** (March 21), **Evacuation Day** (April 17), **Martyrs' Day** (May 6), **Security Force Day** (May 29), **October War Day** (Oct. 6), **Flight Day** (Oct. 16), **Correction Movement Day** (Nov. 16th), and **Peasant's Day** (Dec. 14).

■ Language

The oldest phonetic alphabet in the world, the **Ugarit alphabet** was discovered in Syrian ruins dating from the 14th century BCE. The find gives Syria a valid claim to the world's-earliest-civilization throne.

Although only 82-90% of Syrians claim Arab ancestry, all speak **Arabic,** which is the official language. **French** has long been a second language, and a fair amount of Syrian literature, if it has been translated into any Western tongue, will be in French. English is steadily replacing French as the second spoken language. The various minority groups in Syria maintain their own languages to a degree; Kurds in the east speak Kurdish, and the Armenian population, centered in Aleppo, continues to use their own language. In some villages you may encounter Turkish, or possibly even Aramaic, the language spoken during Jesus' time. Travelers with even a small amount of Arabic knowledge should be able to communicate anywhere in Syria. For some handy phrases, consult the **Language Glossary,** p. 575.

■ The Arts

Despite the wonders of Ugarit, Syria has not been a hotbed of modern literary activity. In the late 7th century CE, **Jacob of Edessa** wrote many theological, historical, grammatical, and philosophical works. Early in his life he studied Greek and worked as a translator, which encouraged him to write studies of the Bible, as well as the books *Enchidron* and *The Book of Treasures.* He is best known, however, for codifying the Syrian language; his *Syriac Grammar* became the seminal work on the subject. In the middle of the 13th century, the philosopher **Bar Hebraeus** began writing philosophical treatises. His later work, *Book of the Pupils of the Eyes,* discussed logic; *Book of the Speech of Wisdom* explored physics and metaphysics. Mathematics and astronomy were also enriched by Hebraeus's research, as was hermitism: the *Book of the Dove* was a manual written by Hebraeus for the ascetically inclined. Other late-13th-century philosophers in Hebraeus's tradition were Abhd-Isho bar-Berikhou, Yabh-alaha III, and Timothy II.

While some works have been written in French or English, those written in Arabic have only recently begun to be translated for Western consumption. In *The Desert and the Sown,* Gertrude Bell writes about her travels through Syria and Jordan, and Ross Burn's *Monuments of Syria*, available in English-language bookstores, provides an excellent historical overview of the area.

Traditionally, Arab **visual arts** are works of abstract beauty, focusing on color and geometric design; Syrian art is no exception. Islamic law prohibits the depiction of human beings, though modern artists are beginning to bypass that law. In mosques and other buildings, you are most likely to encounter traditional art.

SYRIA

■ Food and Drink

With a few exceptions, Syrian food is the same as that of the rest of the Levant. Foods that are considered snacks are consumed morning, noon, or night. Two of the most popular snack foods, which have made massive inroads into Western culture, are hummus and falafel. **Hummus** is the Big Brother of Middle Eastern foods—chickpeas are ground into a paste seasoned with lemon, garlic, salt, and *tahini*, which is then scooped up with pieces of bread and consumed in mass quantities. **Falafel** starts with a similar paste of chick peas and fava beans, mixed with spices and fried, and is then rolled into a piece of bread with vegetables and *tahini* sauce. If you want a little meat in your diet or a little lining on your arteries, try delicious *shawerma*, lamb (sometimes chicken) cooked beneath dripping fat, rolled in bread with vegetables and spices. There are other kinds of *shawerma* as well, including liver, brains, etc.

If you get tired of eating food from roadside stands, or if a long-lost uncle unexpectedly leaves you a small fortune—say, US$4—why not blow it all on a main dish? You could start with *shish kebab*, lamb chunks on skewers, grilled, and served with bread. *Shish tawouq* is similarly treated chicken. A dish uncommon in other Arab countries is *farooj*, roasted chicken served with chilis and onions. Also common at local restaurants and in homes are bean, spinach, and potato stews cooked with lamb in tomato sauce and ladled over rice. Fish, except on the Mediterranean coast, tends to be spiced to the hilt and saltier than a grumpy old sailor.

Don't leave Syria without trying one of its most unusual and delicious offerings. You'll find *bybil*, an exotic desert banana, in *souqs* and fancy restaurants. Its short growing season (culminating in a harvest around the first of October) and limited availability make it one of the most prized and beloved, though mysterious, fruits in the world. You'll recognize *bybil* by its soft, honey hue and elegant shape. One taste and you'll be hooked forever.

For dessert, Syrians favor pastries that are very, very sweet. Most of these *halawiyyat* have a fair amount of sugar and butter baked into them and are then drenched in syrup or honey. *Ba'laweh* is made of pistachios or almonds in fillo dough, *burma* of pistachios in shredded fried dough, and *basbouseh* of wheat and syrup. *Booza* is not alcohol but ice cream. Eat, drink, and be merry.

Speaking of drink, Syrians like their *ahwa* (coffee) like they like their *ba'laweh*—strong and sweet. Both s*hay* (tea) and *ahwa* are consumed frequently creating caffeine highs that rival cocaine rushes (espresso has a lot to learn from *ahwa*). Stalls with bags of fruit hanging out front are an oasis of cool liquid refreshment. Here you'll find *aseer* (juice) in abundance. Sometimes Syrians add milk to drinks—stay away from the dairy additives. Syrian milk is not always pasteurized. *Mandarin* is the Syrian-brewed soft drink. Alcohol in Syria ranges from locally brewed beers (Sharq and Barada are two) and Amstel smuggled into Damascus from Lebanon to *'araq*, an anise-seed flavored liquor mixed with water and consumed slowly from shot glasses.

Damascus دمشق

Damascus' monumental, centuries-long past wraps around an enigmatic present to create one of the most intriguing cities in the Middle East. Unchecked pollution and a frenetic city pace make Damascus look like any other urban jungle, but the city's *souqs*, the Umayyad Mosque, and the National Museum, not to mention the Qur'an and the Bible, uncover an overwhelmingly rich history.

Although Aleppans will try to convince you otherwise, the Damascus area has been continuously inhabited longer than any other city in the world. Early historical references to the city include the Ebla tablets, written in 3000 BCE, as well as 15th-century BCE pharaonic inscriptions and records of the city as the capital of the Aramaic kingdom. Centuries later, Roman invaders left their mark, most notably in the form of the Temple of Jupiter, built by Apolodor the Damascene. During the Byzantine era, Christians converted the temple into a church and built other monuments that remain standing today. In 636 CE, Khaled Ibn al-Walid, the "sword of God," conquered Damascus in the name of Islam.

The city served as the capital of the Islamic Umayyad Empire for close to a century, at a time of enormous growth for the Islamic community. It was during the Umayyad period that Muslim rule spread as far as Transoxania in the East and Spain in the West. Damascus began to suffer when the Abbassids replaced the Umayyads and moved the capital of the Islamic empire to Baghdad.

In the ensuing centuries, Damascus fell under various Muslim dynasties and empires, including the Ottoman Turks, whose influence is quite visible in existing Damascene architecture. During World War I, German and Turkish armies used Damascus as a base. The League of Nations mandate gave France control of Syria in April of 1920. Resistance to French rule flamed until 1925, when the French crushed a popular revolt in Damascus. In 1946, Syria won its independence, and Damascus became the capital of a modern nation-state.

Today, the pulse, physical appearance, and odors of the city reflect contemporary realities rather than historical splendor. Damascus is a city of many faces: large fountains, parks, and wide avenues grace the newer parts of town, while the winding cobblestone streets of the Old City are home to Damascus' Christian population and a plethora of small craft shops and bakeries. A diverse population in class, race, and religion, Damascenes are bound together by a fierce pride in their country and history.

■ Orientation

With the help of a few landmarks, it is easy to navigate on foot. The **Hijaz Railway Station** is located at the intersection of **An-Nasr Street** and **Sa'ad al-Jabri Street,** and has an old railway car on display in front of its stone steps and crowded stone water fountain. Facing away from the station, Sa'ad al-Jabri St. is directly in front of you. Walking down this street, the **post office** and **exchange bank** are directly on your left-hand side. Across the well-traveled footbridge crossing **Quwatli Street,** Sa'ad al-Jabri St. becomes **Port Said Street.** Continuing on Port Said St. brings you to **Yousef al-Azmeh Square.** Just beyond this landmark are the **Tourist Information Center** and the five-star **Cham Palace Hotel.** Continuing past the Cham Palace brings you to **Abu Roumaneh Street,** one of the nicer residential areas of Damascus, and several embassies and cultural centers.

Another important area, especially for those seeking cheap eats and hotels, pistachio desserts, money changing, or Russian prostitutes, is **Al Marjeh Square** (also named, but never called, Ash-Shuhada' or Martyr's Square), two blocks off An-Nasr St. In the center of the square, the **Barada River** surfaces from its underground lair in the form of a big fountain. Continuing right on An-Nasr St. from the Hijaz Station takes you to the entrance of the **Souq al-Hamidiyyeh.** A walk through the covered *souq* brings you to the **Umayyad Mosque** (at the very end of the *souq*) and, behind the mosque, to the **Old City** entrance.

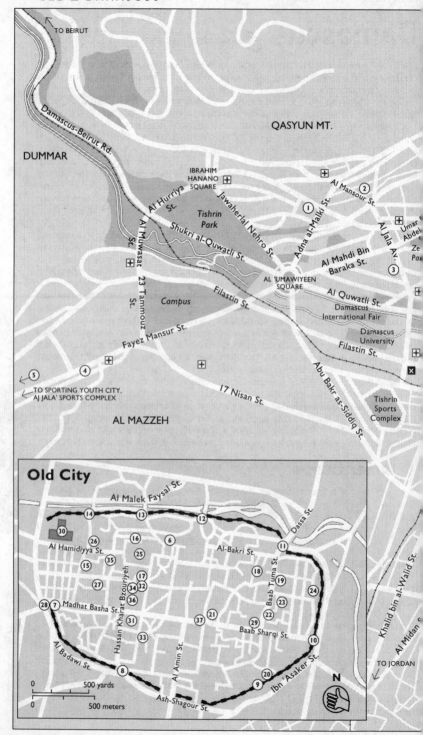

TO BEIRUT

Damascus-Beirut Rd.

DUMMAR

QASYUN MT.

IBRAHIM HANANO SQUARE

Al Mansour St.

②

①

Al Hurriya St.

Jawaherial Nehro St.

Tishrin Park

Adna al-Malki St.

Al Jala Av.

Umar Abdel Ze Pa

Al Muwasat St.

Shukri al-Quwatli St.

Al Mahdi Bin Baraka St.

③

23 Tammouz St.

Campus

Filastin St.

AL 'UMAWIYEEN SQUARE

Al Quwatli St.

Damascus International Fair

Damascus University

Fayez Mansur St.

Filastin St.

⑤

④

Abu Bakr as-Siddiq St.

TO SPORTING YOUTH CITY, AJ JALA' SPORTS COMPLEX

17 Nisan St.

Tishrin Sports Complex

AL MAZZEH

Old City

Al Malek Faysal St.

⑭ ⑬ ⑫

Dassa St.

㉚

⑯ ⑥

Al Hamidiyya St.

㉖

Al-Bakri St.

⑪

㉟ ㉕

⑮

⑱

Hassan Kharat Bzouriyeh

⑰ ㉜ ㉞ ㊱

⑲

Baab Tuma St.

㉗

⑦ ㉘ Madhat Basha St.

㉑ ㉓

㉔

㉛

㊲ ㉒

⑨ ⑳

Baab Sharqi St.

Khalid bin al-Walid St.

㉝

㉙

⑩

Al Badawi St.

⑧

Al Amin St.

Ibn 'Asaker St.

Al Midan

TO JORDAN

0   500 yards

0   500 meters

Ash-Shagour St.

⑳ ⑨

N

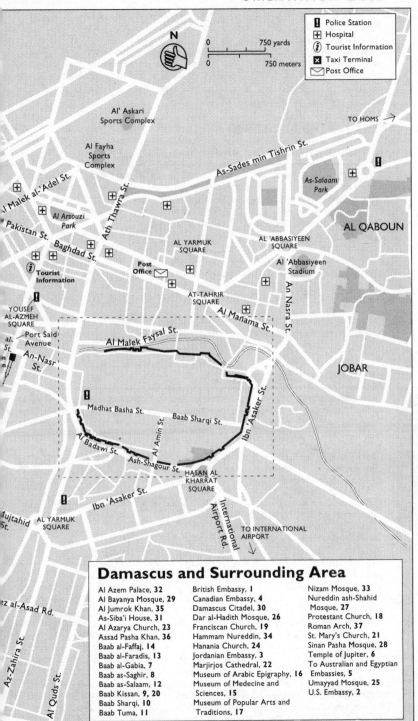

Damascus and Surrounding Area

Al Azem Palace, 32
Al Bayanya Mosque, 29
Al Jumrok Khan, 35
As-Siba'i House, 31
Al Azarya Church, 23
Assad Pasha Khan, 36
Baab al-Faffaj, 14
Baab al-Faradis, 13
Baab al-Gabia, 7
Baab as-Saghir, 8
Baab as-Salaam, 12
Baab Kissan, 9, 20
Baab Sharqi, 10
Baab Tuma, 11

British Embassy, 1
Canadian Embassy, 4
Damascus Citadel, 30
Dar al-Hadith Mosque, 26
Franciscan Church, 19
Hammam Nureddin, 34
Hanania Church, 24
Jordanian Embassy, 3
Marjirjos Cathedral, 22
Museum of Arabic Epigraphy, 16
Museum of Medecine and
 Sciences, 15
Museum of Popular Arts and
 Traditions, 17

Nizam Mosque, 33
Nureddin ash-Shahid
 Mosque, 27
Protestant Church, 18
Roman Arch, 37
St. Mary's Church, 21
Sinan Pasha Mosque, 28
Temple of Jupiter, 6
To Australian and Egyptian
 Embassies, 5
Umayyad Mosque, 25
U.S. Embassy, 2

A left turn from the Hijaz Station onto **Al Baroudi Street** leads eventually to the **Foire Internationale de Damas,** the site of the annual international exposition, where the Barada River flows and numerous fountains shoot high into the air. The **Takkiyeh as-Suleimaniyyeh Mosque** and the **Military Museum** are on the right as you walk away from the station. The **University of Damascus** and the **National Museum** border the river. Farther down, under the **President Hafez al-Assad Bridge,** lurks the huge **bus and service station** at the end of the street.

■ Transportation

GETTING AROUND TOWN

Private taxis have meters and are required by law to use them. If the meter isn't turned on (starting fare S£3), either demand that the driver use it or negotiate a fair price before beginning the trip. Longer trips, like the one from Hijaz station to Karajat Hararta, shouldn't cost more than S£50. Most drivers will give you an honest rate and appreciate a small tip (S£5-10) (see **Getting Around,** p. 513).

Service taxis (white minivans) have predetermined routes and pick up passengers along the way. The routes are written in Arabic on the sides. If one is going your way, flag it down and jump in. *Service* run to Mezzeh from the beginning of Ath-Thaura St. and to Muhajereen and Aba Roumaneh from under the President's Bridge (Jisr az Rais). A *service* also connects Baramkeh Station with Karaj Halab (all fares S£5). For only S£2-5 per ride, even a short ride is usually worth it. Rap on the window when you want out.

There is an extensive **city bus** system stationed with the *service* taxis past the National Museum, at the end of An-Nasr Ave. Crowded and dirty buses go everywhere for S£4 per ride, or you can buy tickets in packs of five for S£20. The ticket seller can help you find the right bus.

GETTING OUT OF TOWN

For **intercity transportation,** the 30 private bus companies that operate out of Karajat Hararta, on the eastern edge of the city, have fairly competitive rates. The **Damas Tour Co.** (tel. 511 90 67; open 24hr.) at Hararta has a big, beautiful, blue fleet of buses and is among the most reliable. Following are some common destinations:

Aleppo: 6am, 9:15am, 11am, 1pm, 2:30pm, 5:30pm, 8pm, 1am; 4hr.; S£150.
Homs, Hama: 6am, 9:15am, 11am, 1pm, 2:30pm, 5:30pm, 8pm, 1am; 2hr.; S£75.
Tartus: 6am, 8am, 9:30am, 10:30am, noon, 1:30pm, 2:30pm, 4:30pm, 6:30pm, 8pm; 4hr.; S£110.
Lattakia: 6am, 8am, 10am, 12pm, 1:30pm, 3pm, 5:30pm, 8pm, 10pm; 5hr.; S£150.
Palmyra: 9:30am, 1pm, 3pm, 4:30pm, 10pm, 11pm; 4hrs.; S£150.
Safita: 12pm, 6pm; 3hrs.; S£100.
Deir ez-Zor: 9:30am, 1pm, 3pm, 6:30pm, 10pm, 11pm; 6hrs.; S£175.

The government-run **Karnak Bus Company** (tel. 212 2499 or 215 0340) is located behind the Hijaz station, down the first street on the right. Smoky, run-down buses serve **Aleppo** (7:30am, noon, 4pm; 4hr.; S£130); **Bosra** (noon, 3pm, 6pm, 8pm; 1½hr.; S£40); **Homs** (hourly 7am-7pm; 2hrs; S£60); **Lattakia via Tartus** (7:30am, 8:30am, 2pm, 3pm; 4hr.; S£125); **Tartus** (1:30 pm; 5hrs; S£100); **Palmyra** (8:30am, 9am, 10am, 11am, 4pm, 5pm; 4hr.; S£125); **Amman** (7am, 9am, 3pm, 4pm; 4-6hr.; S£250); **Beirut** (7:30am, 8:30am, 9:30am, 2:30pm, 3:30pm, 4:30pm; 2-3hr.; S£150). All domestic trips depart from Karajat Hararta; trips to Amman and Beirut depart from Baramkeh station. **Pullman buses, minibuses ("micros"),** and **service taxis** also have intercity service. Departing to **Aleppo** (S£90), **Lattakia** (S£100), and **Deir ez-Zor** (S£120) from Baramkeh Station. The Pullmans are even less comfortable than Karnak and have sporadic schedules. Minibuses and *service* are cheap and leave when full. Service fares and destinations to: **Aleppo** (5hr., S£150), **Amman** (4-5hr., S£400), **Beirut** (2-3hr., S£300), **Sidon** (3½hr., S£275), and **Tripoli** (4½hr., S£425).

■ Practical Information

Tourist Office: 29 Mai Ave. (tel. 222 23 88). From Yousef al-Azmeh Sq., walk to the right of the white modern building. The poster-coated center will be on your right. Maps and information in English. Open Sat.-Thurs. 9am-7pm.

Tourist Police: tel. 222 68 10.

Embassies: Australia, 128 Al Farabi St. (tel. 666 43 17). **U.K.** (tel. 371 25 61), on Malki-Kurd Ali St. **U.S.,** 2 Al Mansour St. (tel. 333 23 15), in Abu Roumaneh. Take Al Jala'a Ave. away from Al Quwatli until Rawdat Abilalan Sq. You'll see the Stars and Stripes flying off to the left. Consular section open Sun.-Thurs. 8am-4pm. Observes all U.S. federal holidays and most Syrian holidays. **Egypt** (tel. 333 35 61), on Al Jala'a Ave., Abu Roumaneh. **Jordan** (tel. 333 46 42), on Al Jala'a Ave., Abu Roumaneh. **Turkey,** 48 Ziad Ben Abi Sufian St. (tel. 333 14 11).

Visa Extension Office: Off Sa'ad al-Jabri St. near the Barada Hotel. A near-flawless display of inefficiency. Travelers staying in Syria for longer than 2 weeks must register with the police and apply for a visa extension. You will be sent to various places, including a photocopy store (if they forget to use carbon paper) and possibly to a very special room downstairs where a uniformed man with your passport in his hand asks you for a tip. It is not required. Open 9am until sometime in early afternoon, usually just before you show up. Go in the morning.

Currency Exchange: Always a chore. Even though it's illegal, many shop owners and travel agents in Damascus will offer to change foreign currency at higher rates than the banks. If you don't want to incur the risk of getting dragged to a Syrian detention center, stick with the banks (see **Money Matters,** p. 514). Banking hours are Sat.-Thurs. 8:30am-noon. The **Commercial Bank of Syria,** at Yousef al-Azmeh Sq., has a foreign cash exchange window (open Sat.-Thurs. 8am-7pm). The branch in front of the Hijaz Station exchanges cash or traveler's checks (Sat.-Thurs. 10am-6pm and Fri. 10:30am-3pm). To change traveler's checks, bring your passport, your purchase record, and S£25 per check cashed.

American Express: tel. 221 78 13 or 224 65 00; fax 222 37 07, on Belkis St. From Hijaz St., take a left on Fardous St. Belkis St. is the first left; AmEx is in the Sudan Airways office. They hold mail and serve tea. One lump or two? Open Sat.-Thurs. 8:30am-8pm, Fri. 9am-1:30pm and 5-8pm.

Airport: Damascus International Airport, southeast of Damascus. Buses to the airport leave from the Victoria Bridge on Al Quwatli St. (S£100) and *service* leave from the station near the Hijaz railway station (S£300). A taxi to the airport costs around S£300. Regular flights to European and Arab capitals; domestic one-way flights daily to **Aleppo** for only S£600. There is a S£100 exit fee if you leave Syria by air. The **SyrianAir** office (tel. 222 07 00) is on Sa'ad al-Sabri St., across from the post office. Open daily 8:30am-8pm.

Car Rental: There are a few places around the post office, but English is rare. For helpful driving information in English, try the agency at the Cham Palace Hotel. Rent for a day (US$37, unlimited mileage US$59) or a week (US$238/US$378).

English Bookstores: The **Librarie Universelle** (tel. 223 23 00), near the Cham Palace Hotel in Azmeh Sq., has 2 big shelves full of paperbacks, including Ludlum, Clancy, and Asimov. Yesterday's *International Herald Tribune* and last week's *Time* and *Newsweek* also available. Open daily 9am-9pm. Ritzy hotels such as the **Cham Palace** and the **Meridien Hotels** offer less extensive selections. Most Arabic bookstores have simple **photocopiers** (S£2 per copy).

Cultural Centers: American Cultural Center, 87 Rue Ata Ayoubi (tel. 333 18 78). Frequent film screenings and concerts. **British Council** (tel. 333 84 36), Place Adnan al-Malki. A/C reading room. Open 9am-2pm.

Laundromat: The **Al-A Krameen** laundry service near the Al Haramain Hotel will clean and press your clothes for the lowest prices in town (pants S£35, shirts S£25, socks S£5, underwear S£10). Open Sat.-Thurs. 7am-8:30pm. **Aous ash-Sharq** (tel. 222 45 76), off Salam al-Barudi St. Facing out from the Hijaz Station, the laundromat is on the 2nd street on the left, across from the Sultan Hotel (pants S£40, shirt S£25, socks/underwear S£20). Open Sat.-Thurs. 9am-7pm.

Pharmacies: Hours are generally Sat.-Thurs. 9am-1:30pm and 5:30-9pm. Try **Kassar** (tel. 222 73 47), near the Hijaz Station on Sa'ad al-Jabri St., or **Al-Halabi** (tel. 221 55

50), closer to Azmeh Sq. Pharmacies rotate late hours; lists are posted in Arabic outside most pharmacies; or, inquire at one of the larger hotels. The **Central Pharmacy**, on Saba' Abhar Square across from the Central Bank, is always open at night, although it closes for lunch from 1-3pm.

Emergency: U.S. citizens can call the embassy (tel. 333 32 32). The embassy nurse (tel. 333 50 74, in emergencies 333 91 30), makes medical referrals, usually to Shami Hospital. **Ambulance:** tel. 110. **Police:** tel. 112.

Post Office: tel. 119 000, on Sa'ad al-Jabri St., in front of the Hijaz train station. Open Sat.-Thurs. 8am-7:30pm and Fri. 8am-12:30pm. **Poste Restante** S£10 per letter. The **EMS** office is directly behind the post office, in a little building in the parking lot. Open Sat.-Thurs. 8am-7pm, but letters can only be sent until 5pm.

Telephone Office: On An-Nasr Ave., 1 block down from the Hijaz Station. The office doesn't have a telephone number, but it's open 24hr. For international calls, bring your passport, lots of cash, and a good supply of patience—placing calls can take up to an hour. **Telephone Code:** 11.

■ Accommodations

In two-star or better hotels, prices for foreigners are listed in US dollars. The Syrian government, eager to grab greenbacks, charges "wealthy" tourists two to three times what Syrians and those with residence permits pay in Syrian pounds. Most hotels accept traveler's checks and will give change in dollars, but it's a good idea to have small bills on hand to simplify exchange and avoid horrible hotel exchange rates. The best two-star hotels are located near the Hijaz Station and the post office, but there are cheaper, equally comfortable options around Al Marjeh Sq. Many "hotels" in this area moonlight as brothels and may turn you away if you're not going to pay extra for a bedmate, but don't let the sleazy places keep you from finding jewels. Damascus does indeed have cheap hotels with high ceilings, clean bathrooms, and bug-free beds. Never forget to bargain, especially in the off-season or if a place looks empty.

AL MARJEH SQUARE

Al Haramain Hotel (tel. 231 94 89), on Bahsa St. From Al Marjeh Sq., head away from An-Nasr St. and go down the small street by the Omar al-Khayyam Hotel. Cross the big street and go right, looking for the signs; the hotel is down an alley on the left. By far the best place to stay in Damascus. Open courtyard with tiled floors and fountain. Cool, high-ceilinged rooms with fan and soft beds. Laundry service and restaurant. Singles S£200; doubles S£325; triples S£425. Hot showers S£35.

Ar-Rabie Hotel (tel. 231 83 74), next door to the Al Haramain and similar in style (although not as well maintained), with a spacious green court and fountain. You can avoid the hectic telephone office by placing international calls here. 3-bed dorms S£150 per person; singles S£200; doubles S£375; triples with bath S£475.

Hotel Najmit Sharq (tel. 222 91 39), above the juice and *shawerma* stands. Shut the window and turn on the fan to avoid noise from the square below. Nice TV lounge and no prostitutes. Great rooftop with fountain, plastic tables, and chairs. The few rooms on the roof have negotiable prices, but no windows. Rooftop room S£200; rooftop mattress S£150; singles with fan S£300; doubles with shower and toilet S£500.

Hotel Basman (tel. 221 80 03; fax 224 66 89), up Rami St. in front of the column in Marjeh Sq. Beautiful facade and lobby. Rooms with mini-fridge and TV are spacious and pleasant with fans and bath. Singles US$15; doubles US$24.

Al-Tal Hotel (tel. 231 55 83), on Al Shuhada'a St., with an unmistakable yellow and green sign. Clean, A/C rooms are popular with Russian business people—so is the restaurant downstairs, which serves Russian dishes. Laundry service available. Singles US$24; doubles US$31.

Imad Hotel (tel. 231 42 25), next door to the Al-Tal. Sparkling marble halls lead to rooms with bright orange bedspreads, spotless private baths, fan, and phone. Beware of the street noise. Singles US$20; doubles US$23; triples US$28.

NEAR HIJAZ STATION

Barada Hotel (tel. 221 25 46 or 224 14 45), on Sa'ad al-Jabri, down the street on the right. Relatively clean rooms with bath. Nice first floor lounge. Singles US$14; doubles US$20; triples US$25; quads US$30. Private bath US$2 extra. Breakfast US$2.

Al-Afamia Hotel (tel. 222 91 52 or 89 63), off Joumhouriyyah St. Walk straight down al-Jabri past the post office and take the first left. Enormous, high beds, TV, and private bathrooms. Pleasant management. Singles US$18, with bath US$21; doubles US$21, with bath US$24.

Al-Hamra Hotel (tel. 221 07 17), on Furat St. around the corner from Al Afamia. Rooms have TV and some have private bath. A good alternative if the Al Afamia is full. Singles US$15; doubles US$20; triples US$25. Private bath US$3 extra.

Sultan Hotel (tel. 222 57 68 or 221 69 10; fax 224 03 72) on Al Barudi St. Turn left from the station, and the Sultan is ½ block down across the street. Rooms are passably comfortable, with lamps, telephones, desks, and hard mattresses. Singles with bathroom US$17; doubles US$20, with bathroom US$23; triples US$25, with bathroom US$28. Rooms with A/C US$1 extra. Breakfast included.

■ Food

Hummus, falafel, and *shawerma* are Damascene staples—there are almost as many food stands around **Marjeh Square** as there are portraits of the big man. Fresh fruit stands serve juice drinks that are meals in themselves. Prices are fairly low (hummus S£30, falafel S£10, *shawerma* S£15, large juice S£40-50). Be sure to sample the various honey-shellacked pistachio pastries. The best pastry shops are around Marjeh Sq.

Maysaloun Street, just off Yousef al-Azmeh Sq. past the Cham Palace Hotel, is home to numerous sit-down restaurants and ice cream parlors. In the evenings, the street is crawling with cologne-scented sweets-lovers, strolling with a sundae or large juice in hand. The best ice cream in Damascus is at **Damer Patisserie** on Maysaloun St. (open Sat.-Thurs. 10am-1am). If you've had enough hummus, there are some good pizzerias on Abu Roumaneh St., one block down from Damer.

The Christian quarter in the Old City (Baab Touma Sq.) has great falafel, atmosphere, and a genuine fast-food pizza joint.

Al Ezz (tel. 222 42 11). Take the last left off Souq Al Hamidiyyeh before the ruins—the restaurant will be on your left. Modest, cramped entrance gives way to an Islamic palace, a built-in Bedouin tent, and the voice of Umm Kulthum. Best place in Damascus to soak up Syrian atmosphere and food. Enticing menu includes Sheep Eggs (S£70), Sheep Tongue (S£50), and the usual Middle Eastern fare (*shish tawouq* S£100). Open daily 8am-12:30am. Live music in the tent after 8:30pm.

Al Shamiat (tel. 222 72 70), An-Nijma Sq. This local favorite also caters to an eclectic crowd of expats and Damascene intellectuals. Beaded lamps, hanging woven baskets, and embroidered tablecloths make even hummus an exquisite dining experience (appetizers S£25-50, meat entrees S£120-150). Open daily 24hr.

Umayyad Palace Restaurant (tel. 222 08 26 or 224 89 01), behind the mosque. Walk to the right of the mosque, turn right, and follow the many signs. The restaurant, once an antique shop, is downstairs. The owners have gone all-out to make this a truly amazing dining experience. Lunch buffet S£350, dinner S£700. Whirling Dervishes perform every night. Open daily 12:30pm-midnight. Visa, MC.

Nadi al-Ummal (tel. 231 87 69). Turn off 29 May St. near Agmeh St. to the right when you reach Cinema Al-Sufara (near red sign). This "Workers' Club" serves up excellent appetizers (S£30) and grills (S£100-150) in a spacious, lush garden, complete with huge fountain. Bottle of Barada Beer S£50. Open Sat.-Thurs. 1pm-1am.

Ali Baba (tel. 222 54 34), Azmeh Sq., in the basement of the Ministry of Labor building on the corner of Fardous St. The lights get dimmer as you descend, and there's a waterfall in the corner. Excellent meat, fish, and chicken dishes (S£100-200), and appetizer menu. Open daily 8am-1am. Visa, MC.

Abou Kamal (tel. 221 11 59 or 224 48 80), Azmeh Sq., upstairs in the same building as Ali Baba. The dirt of Damascus' streets is nowhere to be found in this white, polished, tropical palace. Appetizers from S£30, entrees from S£140 (*shish tawouq* S£225). Open daily 24hr. Visa, MC.

Al Arabi (tel. 221 40 18), Marjeh Sq., in a little alley as you head toward the Citadel from the Square. The cafe portion of the restaurant displays all sorts of meat and vegetable dishes, as well as Syria's own Double Cola. You can get an appetizer, meat, and drink for S£180. Full breakfast with eggs, cheese, toast, and tea S£75, omelette S£40. Open daily 24hr.

White Horse Restaurant (tel. 333 81 28), on Abu Roumaneh St. Renowned since 1973 for its pizza and "lazanya," this brick and wood Italian bistro adds pizzazz to a Middle Eastern diet. Pizzas S£125-185, with discounts for groups. Open daily 1-5pm and 7pm-1am.

Station One (tel. 333 45 75 or 62 24), Abu Roumaneh St. Hop aboard the "Luxury Wagon" (restaurant), the "Economy Train" (snack bar), or the "Express" (take away). For S£45-55, you get a burger and fries, chicken, or steak. The three "trains" are right next to each other, and those riding the Luxury Wagon or the Economy Train can park their caboose at the beautiful outdoor cafe. Open daily 1pm-1am.

■ Sights

The **Citadel,** located next to the entrance to the Souq al-Hamidiyyeh, was built by the Seljuks in 1078 CE, and once housed elaborate baths, mosques, and schools. During the crusader invasions, it was a headquarters for Egyptian and Syrian sultans, including Salah ad-Din. The Ayyubid Sultan Malek al-'Adel demolished and rebuilt the Citadel in 1202 because he felt it was no longer suitable for contemporary warfare. The new fortress has 300 arrow slits and was once surrounded by a deep moat. Now, the moat is filled in and serves as a *souq* floor. The Citadel itself is currently undergoing extensive renovation and will eventually open as a war museum and cultural center.

The **Souq al-Hamidiyyeh** is one of the busiest and most diverse in the region. It begins next to the Citadel and stretches to the Temple of Jupiter and the Umayyad Mosque. Children and store owners may want to bring you through the jumble of overcrowded stalls to have tea in their shops. Bargaining for a set of Bedouin knives or a backgammon board can become an entire afternoon's entertainment.

Just before the Umayyad Mosque at the end of Souq Al Hamidiyyeh is the 3rd-century CE **Temple of Jupiter,** now a source of shade for magazine and Qur'an sellers. The few remaining pillars now blend into the chaos of the *souq*. To the left of the mosque on the way to the visitors' entrance is **Salah ad-Din's Tomb,** built in 1193 and restored by Kaiser Wilhelm II of Germany in the late 19th century. The famed fighter's body lies under a red dome in a peaceful garden mausoleum. Inside the building, both a wooden and a marble tomb occupy the place of honor. The marble was a gift from the Kaiser; Salah ad-Din chose to stay in the wooden one (open daily 10am-4pm; free with paid entrance to the mosque).

The Caliph Walid Ibn Abd al-Malek supervised the building of the **Umayyad Mosque** in 705. Originally the site of an ancient temple dedicated to Hadad (an Aramaean god revered circa 1000 BCE), it was later the temple of Jupiter the Damascene. In the 4th century, a Byzantine church dedicated to St. John the Baptist was erected on this site. The church was destroyed to make room for the grand mosque; the only relic that survived was the head of St. John (known by Muslims as the prophet Yahia), now resting in its own shrine in the mosque's prayer hall. The shrine is a site of veneration for both Christians and Muslims. The mosque's three minarets were built in different styles and touched up by various empires since their original construction. The walls of the mosque are decorated with intricate mosaics; on the central dome are the names of some of the most significant figures in early Muslim history. In the courtyard stands the treasury, also covered with remarkable mosaics (mosque open daily 8am-8pm; S£10 includes entrance to Salah ad-Din's Tomb). Use the visitors' entrance left of the main entrance. Robes are available.

On the side of the mosque (to the right when approaching from the Souq al-Hamidiyyeh) is the **Azem Palace.** Built in 1749, the palace was the official home of As'ad Pasha al-Azem, the Ottoman governor of Damascus. Through the modest door, a

SYRIA

Photo: R. Olken

Greetings from Let's Go Publications

The book in your hand is the work of hundreds of student researcher-writers, editors, cartographers, and designers. Each summer we brave monsoons, revolutions, and marriage proposals to bring you a fully updated, completely revised travel guide series, as we've done every year for the past 38 years.

This is a collection of our best finds, our cheapest deals, our most evocative description, and, as always, our wit, humor, and irreverence. Let's Go is filled with all the information on anything you could possibly need to know to have a successful trip, and we try to make it as much a companion as a guide.

We believe that budget travel is not the last recourse of the destitute, but rather the only way to travel; living simply and cheaply brings you closer to the people and places you've been saving up to visit. We also believe that the best adventures and discoveries are the ones you find yourself. So put us down every once in while and head out on your own. And when you find something to share, drop us a line. We're **Let's Go Publications,** 67 Mount Auburn St., Cambridge, MA 02138, USA (email: fanmail@letsgo.com; http://www.letsgo.com). And let us know if you want a free subscription to **The Yellowjacket,** the new Let's Go Newsletter.

When in 172-1011,
do as the 172-1011's do.

All you need for the
clearest connections home.

Every country has its own AT&T Access Number which makes calling from overseas really easy. Just dial the AT&T Access Number for the country you're calling from and we'll take it from there. And be sure to charge your calls on your AT&T Calling Card. It'll help you avoid outrageous phone charges on your hotel bill and save you up to 60%.* For a free wallet card listing AT&T Access Numbers, call 1 800 446-8399.

It's all within your reach.

courtyard with a fountain leads into the palace's specialized rooms: the bride's chamber, mother-in-law's chamber, instrument room (with a phonograph imported from New York), king's room, room of the pilgrimage (featuring tiny Qur'ans), arms room, bath, and reception room. Above each room are painted and engraved wooden ceilings. A **Museum of Popular Traditions** is inside (palace and museum open Wed.-Mon. 9am-5:30pm; S£200, students S£25).

Behind the Umayyad Mosque, the narrow streets of the Old City begin their winding journey to the Christian quarter, centered around Baab Touma Sq., at the end of Midhat Parka St., on the border of the Old City. There you'll find the **Chapel of Ananias,** dedicated to the Christian disciple who restored sight to Saul of Tarsus (later St. Paul), and **St. Paul's Chapel,** from which that same saint was lowered out of a window in order to escape arrest by his Jewish enemies. Entrance to these buildings may involve knocking at the gate; the friendly multilingual staff will be happy to let you in and give you a religious history lesson. The Old City itself, crammed with craft shops, restaurants, and cafes, is a great place to get lost.

Modern Damascus holds many wonders as well. The **Taqiyyeh as-Suleimaniyyeh Mosque,** on Salam al-Barudi St., is a fascinating example of Ottoman architecture. Built in 1554 by the famed architect Sinan, its two lofty minarets frame a huge dome reflected in a courtyard fountain. Outdoor patios are crowned with archways where the faithful pray. The surrounding *madrasa* was converted into the **Artisanat,** an Ottoman market offering silver jewelry, oil paintings, and mother-of-pearl inlaid backgammon boards (most shops open daily 9am-9pm; Visa and MC accepted). Next door to the mosque and the market is the **Military Museum.** You can get a taste of the exhibits without going in: the area around the mosque is littered with old fighter planes. The museum is a memorial to Syria's military past, displaying both ancient and modern weapons and photos that pay homage to those who perished for their country (open Wed.-Mon. 9am-2pm; S£5).

One street over from the military museum, the **National Museum** has a shady green courtyard and an excellent collection of Ugaritic writings (Ugarit was the first alphabet, dating from the 14th century BCE). The museum contains Syrian sculpture, a Qur'an collection, Palmyran textiles from the first three centuries CE, and an entire reconstructed underground tomb from Palmyra. Beyond the door at the end of the last hall you will find the frescoed walls of a synagogue excavated from the 3rd-century CE town of Doura Europos. You may need to ask a guard to let you in (open Sat.-Thurs. 9am-6pm, Fri. 9am-12:30pm and 2-6pm; S£200, students S£25).

■ Entertainment

As the evenings cool, Damascenes take to the streets. The area behind the Umayyad Mosque is peppered with outdoor cafes. By the end of the evening, the place grows into a big street party as people pull up chairs to drink or smoke *argeileh.* **Maysaloun St.,** past the Cham Palace Hotel, hops until 1am, when the ice cream stores and juice stands close.

Most of the late-night and early-morning activity in Damascus takes place in the bars of the larger hotels, where women are welcome. Women will not be received warmly at local bars. **Le Piano** (tel. 543 03 75), is on the last left off of Hanamia St. before Bab Sharqi in the Old City. It serves beer (S£100-150) and plays karaoke amidst classy Middle Eastern decor. There's no cover charge, but reservations are necessary and singles (men or women) are not admitted. The **Pig and Whistle Pub,** located near the British Embassy, is full of expats and backpackers kicking back with pitchers of beer. Several embassies rotate hosting parties on Thursday nights; call the American or British embassies for details.

The high-quality Cham Palace Theater has regular showings of American films at 3:30, 7:30, and 9:30pm (S£60). There are numerous **swimming pools** in Damascus, where you can take a dip for S£200. Maps of the city list their locations. For a steamier time, you might consider one of several hammams (Turkish baths) that gurgle around the *souq.* The **Hammam Nour ed-Din** (tel. 229 513), close to Azem Palace, is the most recently renovated establishment. Full massage, bath, soap, and sauna cost S£225. The baths here are for men only (open daily 9am-midnight).

■ Near Damascus

BOSRA بصرة

Bosra, 20km from the Jordanian border, was the northern capital of the Nabatean kingdom 19 centuries ago. The Romans annexed the city in 106 CE, renamed it Neatrajana Bustra, and made it the capital of the Province of Arabia. They left the town with grand monuments, including a 15,000-seat theater. Muslim control began in 634, and over the next six centuries, the Roman theater was slowly converted into a citadel. Bosra remained an important crossroads and Muslim pilgrimage site until the 17th century, when increasing banditry made its trading routes unsafe.

The **Roman Theater-Arab Citadel** is today the most impressive structure in Bosra. The first walls of the Citadel were built during the Umayyad and 'Abbassid periods, with further fortification tacked on by the 11th-century Fatimids. The Roman theater inside the fortress walls is one of the best preserved in the world, with secret stairways and an undamaged stage (admission S£200, S£25 for students). Bosra is also home to the 8th- (some say 12th-) century **Mosque of Omar** and the 4th-century **Al Mabrak Mosque/Monastery,** where Muhammad met the Nestorian monk Boheira, who predicted the prophet's potential.

Although many people sleep in the theater for a night, the tiny town of Bosra is best as a daytrip. Karnak **buses** from Damascus leave for Bosra (noon, 3, 6, and 8pm, S£40) from Karajat Haraita. Microbuses from Karaj Dar'a on the southern edge of Damascus go to Dar'a for S£45 (it's S£15 more to get to Bosra).

MA'ALULA معلولا

Forty-five km northeast of Damascus, the tiny town of Ma'alula lies hidden in the Al Qalamoun Mountains. Ancient churches and old mosques nestle among the blue houses that crowd the slopes. Ma'alula seems to linger in timeless stagnation. Townsfolk still speak **Aramaic,** the language in which Jesus preached and the **Lord's Prayer** was authored.

Carved into the face of a barren cliff, **St. Taqla's Monastery** is a destination for both Christian and Muslim pilgrims. Built in the 4th century, it now holds the remains of St. Taqla, daughter of a Seleucid prince and pupil of St. John. A convert to Christianity before such behavior became popular, the young Taqla was alerted by a servant that her father had plans to kill her. On the night that she was to be burned, Taqla escaped. While being pursued, an angel pointed her toward safety: a mountain opened up for her and then quickly closed, crushing her father's soldiers. Luckily this same mountain path has opened up again, leading visitors to another 4th-century monastery, the mountaintop **Mar Sakis.** Built on the remains of a pagan temple, it is named after St. Sarkis, a Syrian horseman during the reign of King Maximus in 297 CE. When you come to the end of the mountain path, turn right to get to the monastery. A left turn will take you to cliffs which provide spectacular views of the town below, marred only by the five-star Safir Hotel (the lone overnight option in Ma'alula). The town is an easy daytrip from Damascus, with frequent **buses** from **Karaj Ma'alula** on the east side of town (50min., S£20). To get to the *karaj*, take a *service* to Abasseyeen Sq.; it's down An-Nasra St., on the left.

SEYDNAYA صيدنيا

Seydnaya, which means "Our Lady" in ancient Syriac, is located halfway between Damascus and Ma'alula, a 20km, 25-minute ride from either city. The hilltop convent in the center of town was built in 547 CE to honor the place where the Virgin Mary appeared before a wealthy hunter. Within a maze of stone stairways, a shrine to the Virgin contains an icon said to have been painted by St. Luke. Beside the church is the entrance to a small, underground sanctuary where Mary supposedly stood. It is adorned with Oriental rugs, gold-engraved icons, and portraits of the Virgin, all dimly lit by the glow of candles. The inscription outside the entrance echoes the commandment Moses was given before the burning bush: "Take off your shoes, for the ground you are treading on is sacred" (Exodus 3:5). To get to Seydnaya take a bus from Karaj Ma'alula (45min., S£15; see **Ma'alula** above for directions). Those who have come to pray (or respectful passers-through) may spend one night in the clean, spacious rooms of the convent for free.

QUNEITRA قنيطرة

The word Quneitra is a diminished form of *quantara,* meaning bridge. The war-ravaged town owes its misfortune to its strategic location beside the Golan heights, at an intersection of roads leading to four countries.

Quneitra was destroyed during the Syrian-Israeli conflict of 1967, and has recently been opened by the Syrian government as a "museum" and memorial to those who perished during the Israeli bombing. Your guide may be spewing out the scripted Syrian party line, but the visit is nonetheless a moving insight into the effects of Middle East conflicts. Visitors are given a guided tour of the modern ruins, including a walk through the crumbled main street, now overgrown with weeds. From the blatantly out-of-place Quneitra Restaurant, a spacious new dining facility, binoculars are provided to gaze out over the U.N. Military Security zone and then to Israel, 500m away. Visitors must obtain **permission** from the Syrian Tourist Police before going to Quneitra. You can do this in ten minutes at the office behind Place Adnan al-Malki, up the stairs of the white monument, across the street to your left (look for two plainclothes men with rifles out front). **Buses** leave from Baramkeh Station for Khan Arnabeh (1½hr., S£12) and then from Khan Arnabeh to Quneitra (15min., S£5). You will pick up your mandatory guide/security officer between Khan Arnabeh and Quneitra. Bring your **passport**—it will be checked often along the way.

Northwest Syria

■ Palmyra تدمـر

Once the capital of Queen Zenobia's renegade province of the Roman Empire, the city of Palmyra maintains its former majesty, standing proudly in a lush oasis surrounded by miles of uninhabited desert. Palmyra's grand column-lined avenues seem more monumental and glorious with every step. The ruins, weathered by centuries of war and sandstorms, remain among the most spectacular in the Middle East, and certainly a Syrian must-see. Because of its well-deserved fame, Palmyra (City of Palms) or Tadmor (City of Dates), as it is locally known, has not managed to resist the claws of tourism. Visitors are coming in increasing numbers, and new hotels are going up every year. Nonetheless, sunsets over the castle are still sublime, and strolls among the spectacular ancient temples still awe with imperial silence.

Mentioned briefly in 19th-century BCE tablets, Palmyra first flourished in the first century BCE as a stop for caravans passing from the Gulf to the Mediterranean. Its residents prospered on tax revenues collected from hot, thirsty traders taking advantage of Palmyra's green oasis. Palmyrans became even wealthier after their city was turned into a Roman colony in 129 CE. Most of the surviving remains date from this period of prosperity, when Palmyra was the keystone of the thriving trade between the Roman Empire, the Middle East, and India.

During the mid-2nd century CE, reduced trade and increasing Persian power inspired the Palmyran Odenathus to overthrow the city's senate and declare himself king. Odenathus and his son were assassinated in 267 after defeating the encroaching Persians, and his multi-lingual and strikingly beautiful second wife Zenobia took control of the city on behalf of her young son. Said by 18th-century historian Edward Gibbon to possess "manly understanding," this Greek-Arab woman achieved full independence from Rome, then actually attacked Roman territories, taking possession of lower Egypt and much of Asia Minor. Minting coins emblazoned with her image was the last straw; an infuriated Roman emperor Aurelian successfully attacked Palmyra and carted Zenobia to Rome—his most triumphant accomplishment. The rebellious spirit of Zenobia lived on among the residents of Palmyra long after her departure, but continued resistance only brought the city destruction. In succeeding years, Palmyra served as a Roman border fortress and, in the 7th century, was conquered by Muslims. Local emir Fakhr ad-Din built the castle overlooking the ancient site in the early 1600s, but the ruined city itself was only sporadically inhabited.

The modern lazy town was centered in the courtyard of the Temple of Bel, but between 1929 and 1932 was relocated northeast of the ruins. Clusters of hotels, restaurants, and antique shops have sprung up in the new town, catering to a growing number of travelers who stop to admire the famed site.

ORIENTATION AND PRACTICAL INFORMATION

The **tourist office** (tel. 910 574) is on the highway, between the ruins and the new city (open daily 8am-2pm and 5-8pm). They give out one informative brochure and a few backgammon hints; more helpful books and guides are at the entrance to the Temple of Bel. **Change money** before coming, though some hotels will change money if you're in a crunch. The **pharmacy** (tel. 910 455) is next to the Palmyra Hotel. For **medical emergencies,** call the **hospital** (tel. 551) or contact the police. The **police station** (tel. 112) is on the main street off the highway as you get to the first hotels in the new town. The **post office** (tel. 910 255) is near the circle on the highway (open daily 8am-2pm). Two 24-hour **telephones** are outside the post office; purchase your calling card inside during office hours. Palmyra's **telephone code** is 31.

The **Karnak Station** (tel. 910 288) is near the circle by the post office. Karnak has service to Damascus (noon, 1:30, 3:30, and 5pm, S£100), Homs (6pm, S£65), and Deir ez Zor (11:30am, 1, 1:30, 3:30, 5, 6:30, and 7:30pm, S£75). The **Furat** bus company in the Al-Fhaian Restaurant goes to Damascus three times daily (9:30, 11:30am, and 5:30pm, S£100); other private bus companies down the street in the **Pullman station** service Damascus, Homs, and several smaller towns.

ACCOMMODATIONS

The town of Palmyra has been steadily encroaching upon the ruins for years; hotels are being renovated and prices are continually on the rise. There are still a good number of friendly cheapies, although they are slowly becoming an endangered species. Most hotels and good food options are on the main street starting at the highway. The hotels that charge in dollars are more comfortable and luxurious, but about six times as expensive. You can **camp** under one of the backyard olive trees at the luxury **Hotel Zenobia,** just yards away from the ruins, for S£250. Peak season is March to May; bargaining may work in the off-season, when simply walking away may be enough to lower a price by half.

Ummayad Palace Hotel (tel. 910 755), down the main street to the right of the fountain. Beautiful, pastel-hued lobby and a spacious courtyard make this Palmyrene house an inviting place to stay. Clean, high-ceilinged rooms are quiet and comfortable. Singles S£300; doubles S£450; triples S£550. Breakfast S£75.

New Tourist Hotel (tel. 910 333), on the main street. Decent rooms, unbeatable hospitality, and more free tea than you can drink. The effusive guest comment book confirms this place as a backpackers' haven. Singles S£200; doubles S£325. Some rooms have private bath.

Afqa Hotel (tel. 910 386), off the main street, before the Karnak station. Big fans and the thickest mattresses in Palmyra. Singles S£200 with private bath; doubles S£500 with bath and breakfast; luxurious upstairs doubles S£600 with breakfast.

Citadel Hotel (tel. 910 537), across the street from the Karnak station and the museum. The first hotel you'll see when you get off the bus, but probably not the

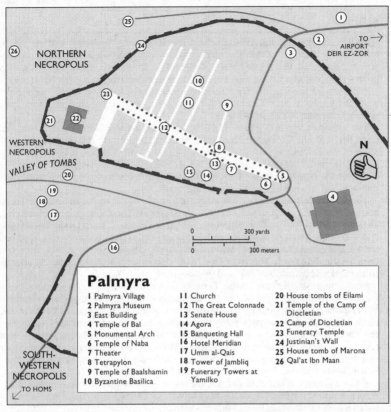

Palmyra

I Palmyra Village	II Church	20 House tombs of Eilami
2 Palmyra Museum	12 The Great Colonnade	21 Temple of the Camp of
3 East Building	13 Senate House	Diocletian
4 Temple of Bal	14 Agora	22 Camp of Diocletian
5 Monumental Arch	15 Banqueting Hall	23 Funerary Temple
6 Temple of Naba	16 Hotel Meridian	24 Justinian's Wall
7 Theater	17 Umm al-Qais	25 House tomb of Marona
8 Tetrapylon	18 Tower of Jambliq	26 Qal'at Ibn Maan
9 Temple of Baalshamin	19 Funerary Towers at	
10 Byzantine Basilica	Yamilko	

best. Clean and cramped upstairs rooms, or dark, monastic, journey-to-the-center-of-the-earth "student rooms." Doubles with bath S£700, without bath or window S£400; student rooms S£100 per person, with free upstairs bathtubs and toilet.

Tower Hotel (tel. 910 01 16; fax 910 273), on the main street. Grand entrance leads to cool, tiled lobby modeled after a Parisian cafe. Soft beds, high ceilings, views of ruins, and spacious blue bathrooms. Singles US$17; doubles US$23; triples US$28. TV, heat, A/C, and fridge extra. Breakfast US$2.

FOOD

Palmyra's main street is lined with restaurants that attempt to cater to tourists' every desire. Each has a special feature (student discounts, free tea, spaghetti), but value and quality don't differ greatly. Most places offer mediocre meals—prices vary depending on tourist traffic. Some of the two-star hotels serve beer for S£50 until 11pm, and almost all are open from 8am-midnight. Up the street, the local diners will be just as ready to feed you. They also may try to rip you off.

The **Palmyra Tourist Restaurant** (tel. 910 346) is the most refreshing oasis for a reasonably priced sit-down meal. Surrounded by fountains, canopies, and an in-house boutique, you can get a *mezze* with chicken, mineral water, and salad for £250 (enough for two). Beer, wine, and *'araq* served (open daily 8am-midnight). The **Palmyra Traditional Restaurant** on the main street offers unappetizing appetizers on less-than-spotless tablecloths.

SIGHTS

Palmyra takes at least a full day to explore. The Ministry of Tourism would like you to begin at the **Temple of Bel,** the mammoth building enclosed by a largely reconstructed high wall. In the gate house, you'll find books on Syria and Palmyra as well as guides who may charge as much as S£1000 for one day. Bargaining can halve prices, and the guides are worthwhile for a more in-depth appreciation of the ruins, especially the tombs and the Temple of Bel (gatehouse open daily 8am-1pm and 4-6pm; winter 8am-4pm; S£200, students S£15).

The existing temple, begun in 32 CE, was built on the site of a Hellenistic site. Bel, identified with the Greek god Zeus and Roman god Jupiter, is a Babylonian pronunciation of the Semitic word "Ba'al," meaning master, and designated as the supreme god. In the middle of the temple, a **sacrificial altar** was used to slaughter animals. The blood ran into the drain in the floor, next to which are remnants of a large stone pipe that was part of a sophisticated plumbing system.

The **Great Colonnade** once led from the Temple of Bel to the monumental arch and the rest of the city, but is now cut by the highway. The **Ethnographic Museum** is an ill-fated attempt to make a "Museum of Popular Tradition" sound more interesting. It displays the usual wax statues and campfire scenes (admission S£100, students S£15). The oft-photographed **Monumental Arch,** constructed in 200CE, puts you back on the right track. The arches are richly decorated with rows of pearls, acorns, palm trunks, and acanthus, oak, and grape leaves.

Continuing, you'll come to the **Temple of Nabo** on the left. Raised about two meters off the ground and dedicated to the Babylonian god of writing (later identified with Apollo), this 1st-century CE construction, along with **Zenobia's Baths** to the right, is largely in ruins today. Up the colonnade and to the left is a newly (and overly) renovated **theater.** You can see the stage, the paved, semi-circular orchestra where the chorus performed, and the foundations of the actors' **dressing rooms** on either side of the stage. Adding a modern, personal touch, the Arabic script above the shiny new eastern door is a dedication to President Hafez al-Asad.

Farther down the street to the left are the not-so-distinguishable remains of the **Agora,** a public forum, and the **Senate House.** Placement in the Agora was based on societal role: Palmyran or Roman officials in the northern portico, senators in the eastern portico, military persons in the western portico, and merchants and caravan leaders in the southern portico. Next door to the Agora is the **Banqueting Hall,** where religious fraternities congregated on holidays.

The prominent structure consisting of four groups of poorly rebuilt columns is the **Tetrapylon.** The pedestals in the center of each group of columns once supported statues, including the likenesses of the great Zenobia and her husband, Odenathus. To the right of the Tetrapylon, near the Zenobia Hotel, is the **Temple of Baalshamin,** dedicated to Zeus Baalshamin, Du-Rakhlun (the god of Rakhleh on the Hermon). Baalshamin, whose name means "Master of the Heavens," was the god of storms and fertilizing rains. The vestibule of the temple has six columns with platforms serving as bases for statues. Further to the right, in the ruins partially covered by the Zenobia Hotel, you can envision a **colonnaded courtyard** surrounded by rooms, one of them a **chapel.** This complex's role within the temple is unknown.

The imposing **Qal'at Ibn Maan,** or Arab Castle, is attributed to Fakhr ed-Din the Ma'nite, once the ruler of the area between Mt. Lebanon and the Syrian desert. This fortress, built in the 12th or 13th century to protect Palmyra from eventual Crusader attacks, is *the* place to be at sunset. You can climb the 150m slope for free (about 30-45min.) or bargain for a ride from town (about S£150 with a 2hr. wait). The gatekeeper at the castle expects a S£10 tip.

To the left of the castle, are **funerary towers,** known as "eternal houses" in Palmyra. There are individual sepulchres, but each of the most important families had its own mausoleum. Guides may charge as much as S£300 for a trip out to the towers; cheaper rides without a guide can be found in front of the Palmyra Museum in town. From the main city, the tombs are a 30-minute walk, but the more interesting ones are locked—the keymaster hangs out at the Palmyra Museum, where tickets can be purchased (S£200, students S£15). Once at the towers, most guides will let you latch on to their group for S£20. The **Tomb of Elahbel,** belonging to a rich Palmyran family, has stairs to the roof for a good view of the Valley of the Tombs. The impressive **Tomb of the Three Brothers** is located southwest of the city (you'll need transportation to this one). The interior is painted with **colorful frescoes:** in the center panel, Achilles is depicted in feminine dress among the daughters of Lycomedes, king of Skyros, where he hid after the Delphic oracle foretold his death in the Trojan War. Upon seeing Ulysses, however, he suited up and fought until an arrow fatally pierced his now-famous left heel.

The **Palmyra Museum,** located at the entrance to the new town, displays statues taken from various family tombs, coins with godly depictions, a tacky model of an ancient Palmyran cave and its semi-naked inhabitants, and two very impressive mummies. An attendant with a key to the Tomb of the Three Brothers waits here at 8:30, 10, 11:30am, and 4:30pm, but you must arrange for transportation in town (open April-Oct. Wed.-Mon. 8am-1pm and 4-6pm, Nov.-March. Wed.-Mon. 8am-1pm and 2-4pm; S£200, students S£15).

■ Homs حمص

Homs, Syria's third largest city, was built in 2400 BCE. Known in ancient times as Emesa, it was an important metropolis during the Roman era and a vital stop along the trade route that made Palmyra an important city. Unlike those in Palmyra, though, most buildings of historical interest have been destroyed by wars and earthquakes, leaving Homs an industrial wasteland strewn with bent telephone poles, hanging electrical wires, and rank streets. An oil refinery that processes the most sludge in Syria is now its claim to fame. "Homsies," as residents are called, experienced a similar decline, in reputation at least; many jokes in Syria and all over the Levant claim that they are notoriously stupid. As much as tourists may try to avoid the smoke-spewing city, Homs is often a mandatory transit point—roads from Hama, Palmyra, Damascus, and Tartus converge here, and Crac des Chevaliers is only a short bus ride away.

ORIENTATION AND PRACTICAL INFORMATION

The **bus station** is located at the intersection of two large streets, **Al Corniche Street** and **Hama Street.** A right turn out of the station brings you around the intersection to Hama Street, where you'll find food vendors and small, cheap restaurants. Hama St. intersects **Quwatli Street** past the Khalid Ibn al-Walid Mosque, at a bus stop and fountain. A right on Quwatli brings you to most of Homs' meager accommodations.

Tourist Office: tel. 473 898. In a booth on Quwatli St. in a small park past the hotels, toward the clock tower. Open daily 8:30am-2pm and 5-8pm.

Passport Office: On the right side of Ibn Khaldoun St., at the Quwatli St. intersection. Open 9am-1pm for visa extensions. You'll need 4 passport-sized photos.

Currency Exchange: Take the first right after the clock tower, at Quwatli St. The booth is at the end of the short block on the right. Open Wed.-Thurs. 8am-7pm.

Buses: The bus station is past the small clock tower circle on Hama St. and the Khalid Ibn al-Walid Mosque. Minibuses from the station go to Crac des Chevaliers (Qal'at al-Hosn) hourly until 5pm (1hr., S£25). **Microbuses** make frequent runs to: **Damascus** (2hr., S£50); **Aleppo** (2½hr., S£50); **Palmyra** (2hr., S£60); and **Hama** (1hr., S£17). The Karnak station next door sends buses daily to: **Damascus** (6 per day, 2hr., S£65); **Hama** (6 per day, 1hr., S£20); **Lattakia** (5 per day, 3hr., S£65) via **Tartus** (1½hr., S£40); and **Palmyra** (9:30am, 2hr., S£65). Also daily buses to: **Cairo** (S£2150), **Istanbul** (S£1500), **Amman** (S£2500), and **Beirut** (S£125).

Pharmacy: Umaliyya **Pharmacy** (tel. 226 464), across from the mosque on Hama St.

Hospital: The government **hospital** is on Al Corniche St., a left turn out of the bus station; at the intersection with As-Salamiyeh St.

Emergency: Medical: tel. 110. **Police:** tel. 112. Headquarters in the government building on Hashem al-Atasi St., a sharp left turn at the clock tower on Quwatli St.
Post Office: On Quwatli St., past the tourist information office at the large clock tower circle. **Poste Restante** available. Open daily 8am-2:30pm.
Telephone Code: 31.

ACCOMMODATIONS

Hotel options in Homs are not great, especially if you're traveling solo. Most rooms are in large, old buildings on Quwatli St. in varying states of disrepair.

Hotel Naser al-Jadid (tel. 227 432), in the middle of Quwatli St. Huge sitting room with high ceilings, comfy couches, and a breezy balcony. Rooms are relatively clean and sport supercool fans. The "single single" S£200; doubles S£300; triples S£450; quads S£550. Cold showers S£25, hot showers S£50.

Ghazi Hotel (tel. 222 160), 1 block from the Naser al-Jadid (English sign says HOTEL). If you can't get a single at the Naser, the Ghazi has the only other one in town—a stuffy shoebox with no window or fan. Doubles are more pleasant, with windows and high ceilings. Stuffy single S£175; doubles S£275. Hot showers S£35.

Basman Grand Hotel (tel. 225 009), on Abu Alaa St., parallel to Quwatli St. Take a left at the Hotel al-Khayam and the Basman will be on your right. Decent private baths, but privacy costs. Doubles US$22; triples US$25.

Hotel al-Khayam (tel. 223 959), next door to the Ghazi. A last resort, with grimy floors and less than sparkling bathrooms. Rooms come with sinks and brown towels. Doubles S£300.

FOOD

Falafel, *shawerma,* and pastry shops, some open until midnight, line Hama St. between the bus station and Quwatli St. Roving merchants hawk fresh-roasted corn on the cob, fruits and vegetables, and nuts here. Several **juice and snack shops** squeeze on the street parallel to Quwatli St., behind the Hotel Naser al-Jadid. They are open late and offer affordable sandwiches (S£15) and cocktails (S£25). The diners between the park and the hotels are the stomping grounds of army officers from the Homs military headquarters. The **Nile Restaurant's** special is *fatteh,* a huge bowl of hummus with pita, lemon juice, and olive oil (S£17). Across the park from the tourist office, Syrians crowd into the semi-outdoor **al-Bawdah,** serving cheap, simple meat dishes for S£100. A **cafe** next door showcases *argeileh* smokers, tea sippers, and coffee addicts. For a sit-down meal try the **Toledo Restaurant,** behind the tourist office and park. Appetizers begin at S£20, entrees at S£80.

SIGHTS

The **Khalid Ibn al-Walid Mosque** is on Hama Street between the city center and the bus station. The imposing mosque is dedicated to the Arab commander who brought Islam to Syria in the year 636 CE and was dubbed "the Sword of God" for his martial ability; his tomb lies inside. Built at the time of King adh-Dhaher Baybars and rebuilt in 1910 at the end of the Ottoman period, the mosque mixes Byzantine, Ottoman, and Arab styles. Its nine silver domes are surrounded by a pleasant park.

The **Great an-Nouri Mosque** is near the gate of the *souq,* at the intersection of Hama St. and Quwatli St. Built in 1162 by Ayyubid commander Nour ad-Din Zanki (Nuraddin), it is famous for its square minaret and wooden pulpit. The nearby *souqs* date back to the Ayyubid, Mamluk, and Ottoman periods, and are easy to get lost in.

In the old city, the fifth major right off of Al Hamidiyyeh St. brings you to the **Umm az-Zunnar Church,** built in 59 CE. Homs's earliest Christians worshipped here secretly, in fear of their pagan rulers' persecution. Expanded during the Christian era, it holds the so-called **Belt of the Virgin Mary,** found under the altar in 1953.

Homs's **museum,** located on Quwatli St. across from the hotel block, displays the usual pottery, jewelry, Ottoman swords, and handwritten Qur'ans. (Open Wed.-

Thurs. 8am-4pm; S£100, students S£15. If you look interested they may turn on the lights and let you in for free.)

Crac Des Chevaliers قلعة الحصن

The Crusader castle **Crac des Chevaliers** (Qal'at al-Hosn in Arabic) is one of the best sights in Syria, and arguably the greatest castle in the world. Crac is really a castle within a castle, with a moat separating the two and a larger moat surrounding the entire structure. A governor of Homs built it in 1031, leaving a Kurdish garrison in the castle for defense against enemy attacks on the Tripoli-Homs-Hama road. In 1110, Crusaders nearly destroyed the fortress while capturing it. They built a new castle on the ruins of the old and used it to control the "Homs Gap," a narrow pass linking the coast with the Orontes Valley. The Crusaders held the medieval fortress for 161 years; Salah ad-Din supposedly withdrew his troops upon viewing the castle. It finally fell to the Mamluk army under the command of Sultan Baybars in 1271 after a month of intense fighting. The Crusaders were allowed to leave the country peacefully. Perched on a hill 750m above sea level and spreading over 30,000 square meters, the castle's high towers afford panoramic views of the Mediterranean, the Port of Tripoli, the Tower of Safita, and Homs Lake.

Upon entering through the main door, continue up the ramp past the **guard rooms** and **stables** on your left. You will come to a tower which leads to a **moat** and the outer wall if you go straight, or to the **main courtyard** if you take a sharp right turn. In front of the courtyard, the **seven-arched facade,** bearing two doors and five windows, is the castle's most aesthetically impressive feature. Behind it is the **main assembly room,** with Gothic, vaulted roofs, where Crusader kings were received by the knights of the castle. The **long room** against the castle's back wall contains a huge oven, five meters in diameter. To the right is a **cathedral** that was converted into a mosque in 1271. In another room, the bases of large clay oil jars still remain. The top floor of the Tower of the Daughter of the King is now a **cafe** serving overpriced coffee and soft drinks (S£25-40). Bring a **flashlight** to explore the secret passages and the dark corridors of the walls and castle (open daily 9am-5pm; S£200, students S£15).

Buses and *service* leave the Homs station for Qal'at al Hosn daily (approx. every hr., 7am-5pm; S£25). The last bus returns to the town at around 6pm. At the **Roundtable Restaurant and Hotel,** 100m to the right of the castle entrance, you can get a passable bed and bath for S£500 and a meal for S£200. The **Restaurant Des Chevaliers,** in front of the main entrance, has similar prices and food (hummus S£25, grills S£125).

▓ Hama حماة

The green Orontes River flows through the heart of Hama, and its slow-moving waters seem to dictate the town's pace. Hama has seen many empires rise and fall on the banks of its river, among them the Amorite, Babylonian, Hittite, Persian, Greek, Hellenistic, and Seleucid. It was not until 638 CE that the Muslim Arabs moved in. Although Hama has been inhabited since the 4th millennium BCE and was once an important trade center, few of its ancient monuments remain—except, of course, for the **norias** (Aramaic for "water wheels"). These impressive structures were built to raise water for irrigation. The low-pitched groaning sound is produced by wood rubbing wood; the same sound has been heard here since the *norias'* construction in the Middle Ages.

Today the constant groaning serves as a reminder of the painful events the town suffered in February 1982, when a small uprising by the Muslim Brotherhood was brutally quelled by the Syrian government. Nevertheless, life in Hama, like the beautiful *norias,* has gone on. The Orontes River and the numerous parks on its banks make the town an ideal place to spend a relaxing couple of days.

ORIENTATION AND PRACTICAL INFORMATION

Getting around the small city of Hama is easy. The intersection of **Quwatli Street** and **Sadiq Avenue** marks the city center. Most budget hotels and restaurants are on

Quwatli St., on the opposite side of the intersection from the bank and post office. This direction also leads to Al Murabet St. and the city's second major intersection. If you ever get lost, walking toward the grinding sound will bring you to the river.

Tourist Office: tel. 511 033. On Sadiq Ave., across the river from the central intersection. Open daily 8am-2pm.

Passport Office: Take a right at the intersection of Murabet and Quwatli St. Bring 4 passport-sized photos to renew visa. Open Wed.-Thurs. 9am-12pm.

Currency Exchange: Commercial Bank of Syria, next to the post office. Cash and traveler's checks exchanged. Open daily 9am-2pm and 5-8pm.

Buses: Al Ahliah bus station (tel. 522 551) has service to all major Syrian cities in big, beautiful buses. Go past the Basman Grand Hotel, and take a left after the large, white government building—the station is on your left around the corner. Frequent service to: **Damascus** (S£90); **Aleppo** (S£65); and **Homs** (S£20). The daily bus to **Lattakia** (S£100) via **Tartus** (S£70) departs at 6am. The **Karnak** bus station (tel. 229 985) is on the corniche in the middle of town, doubling as the Afamia Restaurant and pastry shop. Frequent service to **Damascus** (S£75), **Aleppo** (S£60), and **Homs** (S£25).

Minibuses: A left turn away from the river at the intersection of Mubaret and Quwatli. Conquer the hill by foot (20min.) or take a city bus headed in that direction (S£2). Minibuses to: **Damascus** (4hr., S£32); **Aleppo** (3hr., S£25); and **Homs** (1hr., S£11) depart when full. **Service** leave from the station across the street to: **Damascus** (S£40); **Aleppo** (S£35); **Homs** (S£17); and **Suqelbia** (S£20).

Pharmacy: Hala Pharmacy is on the small street behind post office building. Open Wed.-Thurs. 8:30am-2pm and 6-9:30pm. **Ummalia Pharmacy** is on 8 March St.

Hospital: Medical Center Hospital (tel. 222 012), just uphill from the Al Ahliah bus station.

Police: tel. 11.

International Express Mail: FedEx is located across from the post office. Open Wed.-Thurs. 9am-2pm and 5-7pm. **DHL** is on the second left with your back to the Cairo Hotel. Open Wed.-Thurs. 9am-2pm and 5:30-8:30pm.

Post Office: A right on Quwatli St. when facing the river from the town center. Minimal services. Open daily 8am-2pm and 4-6pm.

Telephones: Around the corner from the post office; looks like a hot dog stand. Open daily 8am-9:30pm. Phone booths available 24hr. **Directory Assistance:** tel. 147. **Telephone Code:** 33.

ACCOMMODATIONS

Hotel prices in Hama vary drastically between summer and winter (high season and low season), and according to how well business has been going. Listed prices are only meant to give an idea of each hotel's range.

Cairo Hotel (tel. 222 280; fax 511 715), on Quwatli St. near its intersection with Jamal Abd en-Nasr St. Manager Anas is a gracious host; rooms are spotless and some have A/C. Roof mattress S£100; bed in a shared room S£150; singles S£200, with private bath, S£300; doubles S£400, with bath and A/C S£500; triples S£500, with bath and A/C S£600. Breakfast S£75.

Riad Hotel (tel. 239 512), next door to the Cairo Hotel. Similar quality, but most of their single rooms are windowless. Rooftop mattress and facilities S£100; singles S£300, with bath S£350; doubles S£600; triples S£750. Breakfast S£100.

Noria Hotel (tel. 512 414; fax 511 715), on Quwatli St. towards Al Murabet St. across from the Riad and Cairo. Luxurious and welcoming, the Noria is under the same impeccable management as the Cairo, but is much more upscale than its budget-conscious cousin. All rooms come with A/C and continental breakfast. Singles US$18; doubles US$28; triples US$36. Magnificent suites with kitchen, living room, and views of the *norias* are US$60 for 3 or 4 people. Visa, MC.

FOOD

Most of the restaurants in Hama are of the chicken, meat, and fulafel variety. Those scattered among the hotels on Quwatli St. have plump chickens and large portions. A full meal, complete with salad, soda, and meat, won't cost more than S£100. More expensive restaurants line the waterfront. The **Sultan Restaurant** (tel. 235 104), behind the Hama Museum on the river, provides an excellent riverside meal in an Ottoman insane asylum, if the grinding noise from the neighboring *noria* doesn't drive you mad. Try Hama's specialty, *batirsh,* which consists of layered eggplant, mincemeat, and *tahini* sauce eaten with bread (S£100). The **Al Rawdah Restaurant** (tel. 239 890), along the pier in the center of town, offers *kebab* (S£80), *tabouli* (S£15), and ice cream (S£17). A 15-minute walk from the center of town with the river on your left takes you to **Four Norias** (tel. 221 013), an upscale riverfront restaurant. A complete Middle Eastern meal here costs S£200-250; *'araq* and Sharq beer are available (open daily 8am-2am).

SIGHTS

Most of Hama's sights can be seen by taking a stroll along the river. When facing the Orontes from the center of town, walk left along the bank and enter the cobblestone road of the **Old City.** The narrow, winding streets were built to provide protection from the sun at all hours. A small Arabic sign above an old door on the left marks the entrance to **Hammam Othmania,** a Turkish bath from the Ottoman era. A bath with soap and a massage is only S£100 (open for men 7am-noon, women noon-7pm).

The **Hama Museum,** located in the Old Azem Palace, is a bit farther on the right. As'ad Pasha al-Azem, governor of Hama from 1700 to 1742, built the palace as his residence. When he was promoted to a post in Damascus, he built an even grander structure of the same name. The palace had a men's section (the *Salamlek*) and a women's section (the *Haramlek*), which conveniently joined at the baths (open Wed.-Mon. 9am-6pm; S£125, students S£15).

After passing the Al Jabariyya water wheel (home of late-afternoon daredevil diving kids), the road opens up at the **An-Nouri Mosque.** Built in 1162 by Ayyubid commander Nour ad-Din Zanki (Nuraddin), the mosque is famous for its square minaret and wooden pulpit. The pulpit is housed in the Hama Museum while the mosque undergoes reconstruction.

A left turn at the mosque brings you to the **Citadel,** the center of the old city and a popular spot for evening strolls. Supposedly, relics from the 6th millennium BCE were unearthed from under this hill. Today, the only digging is done by kids playing in the huge park planted on top. You may be asked to pay a S£5 entrance fee.

The **Grand Mosque** behind the Citadel used to be one of Hama's biggest attractions, although you won't find it listed in the official literature anymore. This Umayyad structure, along with the tombs of Hama's 13th-century emirs, was destroyed during the 1982 uprising. Greek writing from a previous edifice still marks some of the fallen stones. The structure is currently being rebuilt.

■ Near Hama

APAMEA

Apamea lies 55 kilometers north of Hama on a hill overlooking the lush Ghab Valley and the Orontes River (Nahr al-Aussi). The Macedonians called it Barnakeh; its present name was given to it by Sahicos in 310 BCE, in honor of his Persian wife Afamia. A military stronghold of Sahicos, Apamea fell to the Romans in 64 BCE, who supplied the city with an impressive water canal carved into rock. The Romans also ornamented the stone colonnades, the longest of which is 1850 meters, and built a Roman **amphitheatre** and a **public bath.**

The **Cathedral** has well-preserved mosaic floors, and contains a cross and a set of jewels that was given to the King of Persia in 540 CE in the vain hope of staving off a Persian invasion of the city. The Persians invaded and razed Apamea 33 years later and enslaved almost 300,000 Apameans. The Muslim Arabs entered the city on peaceful terms under the leadership of Abu Obeida Bin Jarrah. The city is likely to have been abandoned as a result of a series of earthquakes that struck between 1137 and 1170. One of the more impressive structures in Apamea is the circular Al-Madiq Castle. The Ottoman Stan Pasha built a great *khan* inside the castle containing an inn, a stable, and a market. Now a "museum," the echoing domes of the *khan* are well worth the S£200 admission (students S£25).

To get to Apamea, take a **microbus** from Hama to Suqelbia (S£20), and then a service from Supelbia to Qasr al-Madiq (S£5).

■ Aleppo حلب

Aleppo (*Halab* in Arabic), the "second capital of Syria" 350km north of Damascus, has been a flourishing city since the 3rd millennium BCE. Abraham is said to have milked his grey cow on the acropolis here—hence the name *Halab ash-Shahba*, or "he milked the grey." The famous Citadel sits on the same *tel* today.

Situated at the crossroads of several vital trade routes, Aleppo has been of great commercial and military importance since the 2nd millennium BCE. The city controlled "The Great Syrian Passage" connecting Mesopotamia and Persia with the Mediterranean Sea. Such stellar positioning made Aleppo appealing to many kingdoms, and the Hittites, Egyptians, Assyrians, Persians, Greeks, and Romans all laid an occasional siege on the city. After the division of the Roman Empire, Aleppo became part of the Byzantine Empire; its early Christian atmosphere is still tangible. The conflict between Byzantium and Persia resulted in Persian occupation and plundering of the city in 440 CE.

Arab armies stormed the city in 636 CE. Aleppo flourished under the Umayyads and Abbassids, but it was not until the days of the Hamadanis that Aleppo reached its peak. Sayf al-Dawla, who established the Hamadani state in 944 CE, built the city's towering citadel and kept in his court the great poets Al Mutanabbi and Abu al-Firas. During this period, Aleppo was an architect's playground filled with splendid mosques, schools, and tombs. The city's *khans* (or caravanserai) were built later to accommodate the many traders passing through; several still stand. Building continued during Ottoman rule, and increased trade with Europe added Western style to Aleppo: the cafes and outdoor restaurants which crowd the city's wide, tree-lined streets make today's Aleppo a cosmopolitan metropolis. Expanded trade in textiles and glassware has brought this ancient city an air of sophistication and a freewheeling sense of fun not felt in the bigger, older capital to the south.

ORIENTATION

Mastering Aleppo's layout is simple. You'll find all budget accommodations and some restaurants in the area bounded by **Al Ma'ari** and **Quwatli Streets** (running east/west), and **Baron** and **Bab al-Faraj Streets** (running north/south). Late-night walks in this area can be unpleasant, especially when the Kung Fu and porn movies let out. Starting from the **National Museum** and going up- (then down-) hill, you'll pass the tourist information office, private bus services, travel agents, the **Karnak bus station,** the Commercial Bank of Syria, and a few expensive restaurants. The city's wealthy residents strut their stuff in and around the restaurants and cafes of the **Christian Quarter.** Walking is cheap and enjoyable in the cool evenings, especially in the enormous **Public Garden.**

Several branches of the Commercial Bank of Syria remain closed most of the time on congested **Al Mutanabbi Street** between the hotel district, the **souqs,** and the **Citadel.** The easiest way to get a perspective on Syria's second-largest city is to hike up the Citadel's bridge and climb the western wall.

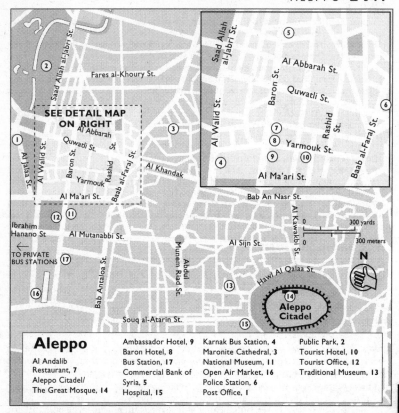

Aleppo

Al Andalib Restaurant, 7
Aleppo Citadel/ The Great Mosque, 14

Ambassador Hotel, 9
Baron Hotel, 8
Bus Station, 17
Commercial Bank of Syria, 5
Hospital, 15

Karnak Bus Station, 4
Maronite Cathedral, 3
National Museum, 11
Open Air Market, 16
Police Station, 6
Post Office, 1

Public Park, 2
Tourist Hotel, 10
Tourist Office, 12
Traditional Museum, 13

PRACTICAL INFORMATION

Tourist Office: tel. 221 200, on Al Ma'ari St. at the intersection with Baron St., across from the National Museum. Get their map with bus and transportation information. The policemen who occupy the building in the afternoon may be able to help you. Open Sat.-Thurs. 8:30am-2pm.

Tourist Police: tel. 119.

Currency Exchange: Changing anything but cash in Aleppo is a hassle. The **Commercial Bank of Syria** Branch #6, on Baron St. just past the Ugarit theater, accepts traveler's checks for a small commission; bring your passport and your waiting-in-line shoes. Other branches on Al Mutanabbi St. only change cash. All branches open daily 8am-noon. An **exchange booth** at the intersection of Quwatli and Bab al-Faraj St. changes cash only. Open Wed.-Thurs. 8am-8pm, Fri. 9am-7pm.

Buses: To ride a local bus, purchase a card valid for 4 rides (S£10). A bus leaves regularly during the day for the airport from a station across from the tourist office. **Minibuses** depart from the Pullman Station to **Homs** (S£30), **Hama** (S£25), **Damascus** (S£58), **Tartus** (S£75), **Lattakia** (S£30), **Ma'aret en-Noman** (S£13) and **Deiret 'Ezzeh** (S£5). Many **private bus companies** have offices on Ibrahim Hanano St. (a few minutes' walk to the right when facing the Amir Palace), and in the parking lot across the street from the Baron hotel. The **Pan bus company** (tel. 224 276) has daily services to just about any destination in **Turkey,** including **Antakya** (6am and 2pm, S£300); **Iskenderun** (6am and 2pm, S£550); and **Istanbul** (6am and 2pm, S£900). US$20 gets you a visa at the border. The **Karnak** station (tel. 210 248) faces the Baron; buses to: **Lattakia** (7am and 3pm, 3hr., S£65); **Homs** (every hr., 3½hr., S£75); **Hama** (every hr., 3hr., S£60); and 2 to **Damascus** (5am and 10:30am, 5hr., S£130).

Taxis: Service stop next to the **Pullman Station,** behind the palatial Amir Palace Hotel.

English Bookstores: Follow Baron St. away from the sleazy theaters toward the park. The **Omnia Bookshop,** on the left side of the street near the corner of Faris al-Khoury St., carries some international news magazines and a few English paperbacks. Open Wed.-Thurs. 8am-2pm and 5-9pm.

Pharmacies: The **Ummal An-Nagl Pharmacy** (tel. 758 478), next to the entrance of Baghdad Station, is open 24 hr. **Al Mughrabi** (tel. 237 231), near Cham Palace Hotel, and **Al Mathaf** (tel. 246 419), across from the National Museum. Most pharmacies in Aleppo open 9:30am-1:30pm and 5-9pm. They rotate late-night duties.

Medical Assistance: English-speaking Dr. Faher (tel. 215 252), offers the best medical assistance.

Emergencies: Medical and Police: tel. 112.

Post Office: tel. 221 200, on Al Jala'a St. near Quwatli St. and the park; a green-shuttered building with postcard sellers blocking the entrance. Open daily 8am-8pm. **EMS** available Sat.-Thurs. 8am-5pm. Bring your passport.

Telephones: Inside the post office. Bring your calling card and pay at the desk after your call. Open daily 8am-10pm. 1min. to the U.S. S£100; to the U.K. S£90. **Telephone Code:** 21.

ACCOMMODATIONS

Hotels in Aleppo range from the seat of sleaze to the lap of luxury, with enough in between to satisfy any budget. Higher-priced options cluster on Baron St. in the center of town; more affordable places are scattered among the spare car parts of the streets behind the Baron and Al Ma'ari St. Those searching for very cheap hotels should be warned that many are frequented by Russian prostitutes. Look carefully before letting go of your cash.

Tourist Hotel (tel. 216 583), off Yarmouk St. across from the museum. Head down Al Ma'ari St. and go left at the Syria Hotel. Spotless rooms are inspected by Madame Olga, the distinguished owner. Singles S£350; doubles with shower S£650.

Hotel Najem Akhdar (tel. 239 157). When facing the library from the clock tower, take a left and then a right around the mosque; the hotel is on your right. Not as nice as the Tourist Hotel, but cheaper and also has friendly management. A basic bed in a basic room with a fan goes for S£150.

Hotel Yarmouk, Al Ma'ari St. (tel. 217 510), across from the National Museum. An elevator on its last legs carries you high above street noise. Quiet rooms are often reserved for Russian groups. Singles S£250; doubles S£400; triples S£550.

Baron Hotel (tel. 210 880 or 881), on Baron St. Aleppo was once the end of the line on the Orient Express, when the Baron was a stopover for such illustrious guests as T.E. Lawrence, Agatha Christie, Kemal Ataturk, and Hafez al-Asad. It still exercises a certain majestic charm and grandiose prices. Singles US$29; doubles US$39.

Ambassador Hotel (tel. 211 833), on Baron St. next to the Baron Hotel. Cool rooms with blue beds. Some have balconies overlooking Baron St. Singles US$14, with bath US$17; doubles US$20, with bath US$23; triples US$23, with bath US$29.

FOOD

For great inexpensive restaurants and cafes, go around the corner from the exchange booth on Quwatli St. onto Bab al-Faraj St. Take a right at the fruit shake stands and you'll see six or seven places on your right. Baron Street is lined with rooftop restaurants with bird's-eye-views of the crowds. The Christian neighborhood near the park off Sa'adullah al-Jabri St. is home to almost-Americana: **Pizza House** (small with unlimited toppings S£150) and **MicMac,** a golden arch-bedecked imposter.

Abu Nouwas (tel. 210 388). From Al Ma'ari St., take the last left before Bab al-Faraj St. This clean, A/C diner is 2 blocks uphill on the left. Outstanding lentil soup. Tasty *kebab* with warm pita, onions, tomatoes, and peppers. Served with soup, salad, and drink (full meal S£200). Breakfast S£75. Open daily 8am-midnight.

Al Andaleeb (tel. 224 030), just to the left of the Baron Hotel when facing it from the street. Cool, breezy rooftop dining. Al Andaleeb (the nightingale) has a daily lunch or dinner special featuring *kebab* or 2 big *shishes* plus salad and hummus or *mutabbal* for S£150. *'Araq* and beer served. Open daily 10am-midnight.

Ali Baba Restaurant (tel. 215 024). From the clock tower, head up Bab al-Faraj St. and take a left at the "cocktail" stands. This rooftop restaurant's specialty is the *kebab halabi* (S£80). Sharq beer (S£40) and *'araq* (S£50) are sipped by the mostly male dinner guests.

Sage, Sa'adullah al-Jabri St. (tel. 215 870), in front of the park. Cakes, pizzas, cheese sandwiches, banana splits, and all the sugary incentive you need for a stroll away from the city center. Fill up on pastries (S£100-150), or try the best cappuccino in Aleppo (S£45). Open daily 8:30am-midnight.

Patisserie Mousattat, Bab Al-Faraj St., next to the exchange booth. Can't stomach *shawerma* before noon? Bring your morning munchies here and ask for *ma'moniyya:* a yummy cream-of-wheat-like starch, drenched in warm syrup and eaten with pita bread.

SIGHTS AND ENTERTAINMENT

Begin your sightseeing tour of Aleppo at the **Citadel** for an outstanding view of the city. Its enormous entrance gate is fortified with three sets of steel doors. Built in the 10th century CE by Sayf ad-Dawla, the Citadel stands 50m above the city on a hill heightened by the remains of prior civilizations (these kinds of hills are known in both Arabic and Hebrew as *tels,* and are all over the Middle East). In times of war, Aleppans equipped themselves with plentiful provisions and took refuge in this fortress. The 12th-century moat is 20m deep and 30m wide, lined with smooth stones to make climbing difficult (some of these tiles are still in place today). The once watery defense is now full of garbage, though not for the first time. Historical accounts gruesomely, if hyperbolically, recount how in 1400, Timor's Central Asian forces couldn't penetrate the Citadel until the moat was brimming with fallen soldiers' bodies.

To the immediate left of the main path inside lies a **bath** that was at one time used as a metal-working studio. Beyond that is the **small mosque** (with a well in the middle of its courtyard), the **great mosque** (only slightly bigger than the small mosque but with a fountain instead of a well), and a cafeteria. To the right of the main path are **storage rooms** for keeping food and water to be consumed during sieges, followed by stairs which lead to the **Royal Palace.** One of the most interesting sections of the Citadel, this area has its own baths and a courtyard paved with black and white marble. From the Palace, a passage leads to the opulent but overly restored **Throne Room,** which sits directly above the main entrance. In front of the main path and connected to the cafeteria are the **barracks,** now a museum displaying objects found during the Citadel's excavation (Citadel open Wed.-Mon. 9am-6pm; S£200, students S£25; museum S£100, students S£15).

Outside the Citadel, the **Hammam Yalboagha An-Nasiri** waits to steam, wash and massage the sweat and grime off dirty, sore bodies. This restored 14th-century bath is now heavily marketed by the Ministry of Tourism (open for women Sat., Mon., and Thurs. 10am-6pm; for men Sat., Mon., and Thurs. 7pm-midnight and every other day 9am-2am; S£365 for soaping, massage, and cup of coffee or tea).

Between the Hammam/Citadel area and the hotel district is the best **souq** in the Eastern Mediterranean. All nine kilometers of ancient and winding covered passageways are bursting with leather goods, wool, backgammon boards, carpets, tablecloths, Qur'ans, *argeilehs,* brass goods, and gold and silver jewelry. Several **khans** (caravanserais) in the *souq* once housed international traders during the Mamluk and Ottoman periods (*souq* open Sat.-Thurs. early morning until 7 or 8pm).

Situated in the center of the gold market, **Al Jami' al-Kabir,** the Great Mosque of the Umayyads (also known as Zacharias's Mosque, after the Father of John the Baptist), was built on top of a Byzantine cathedral in the 8th century. To the left of the main entrance is a 600-year-old **insane asylum,** in good condition (though empty). Wander through to see where the insane, the not-so-insane, and the very rich were kept locked up by their families. The clean smell emanates from two **soap factories** around the corner—Aleppo's soap is known all over the Middle East for its excellent quality. Both factories have been in the same spotless families for generations.

The **National Museum,** across from the tourist office on Baron St., is second only to the Damascus museum in exhibit quality. Several 100,000-year-old flint axes from Ugarit, a basalt altar from the 3rd millennium BCE city of Ebla, and a stone guard lion from an 18th-century BCE temple will leave you reeling with wonder at the relative insignificance of your own temporal existence. The third floor includes a modern art wing; you may have to ask a guard to open it for you (open Wed.-Mon. 9am-6pm; S£200, students S£25).

The narrow streets of the **Christian Quarter** are lined with fabulous 17th- and 18th-century homes. Within a few blocks, churches from four different denominations attract worshippers. Walk down Quwatli St. past Baab al-Faraj St. and take a left at a weird-looking stone gate. Down a narrow alley to the right is a 19th-century **Maronite Cathedral.** To the right is a gorgeous **Greek Catholic Church.** When you get to the store with underwear hanging in the window, take a right to visit the **Greek Orthodox Church** and the **Armenian Church of the Forty Martyrs.** These magnificent buildings feature 3rd-century artwork, engraved marble altars and sanctuaries, and antique chandeliers. The tiny **Museum of Popular Traditions** shows clothes, tools, and furniture from the area's historic homes (open Wed.-Mon. 8am-2pm; S£200, students S£25).

■ Near Aleppo

THE BASILICA OF SAINT SIMEON قلعة سمان

Born in a small mountain village in 386 CE, Saint Simeon of Stylites acquired the first and last parts of his name by spending decades preaching from atop a "stylite" (from the Greek *sylos*, meaning "pillar"). Simeon, a shepherd, had chained himself to a railing atop the pillar after receiving divine instruction in a dream. Local peasants heard about his actions and began coming to the chained man for advice. Before long, people came from all around to hear Simeon preach. With so many fans, Simeon had to find higher and higher pillars to sanctify, eventually ending up 15m in the air. Simple Simeon would accept only two supplies of rations a week, and, while he would gladly answer male pilgrims' spiritual questions, he refused to talk to women—not even his beaming mom.

Simeon's death in 459 did not stop pilgrims from coming, and the emperor Zenon had a cathedral, now considered a masterpiece of pre-Islamic architecture, built around his home. A large dome covered the octagonal courtyard in which the pillar stood, surrounded by four basilicas which formed a giant cross. One basilica was a chapel, the other three housed pilgrims. The rear wall of the chapel was decorated with delicate acanthus leaves and Byzantine crosses, widespread decorations of the time. An earthquake destroyed the structure less than 50 years after its completion, causing pilgrims to question the site's holiness and deterring pious investors from rebuilding the cathedral. The 5th-century remains are impressive nonetheless. In the 10th century, the site was converted to a Byzantine fort with 27 towers along an enclosing wall. The fortifications are easily distinguishable from the cathedral ruins.

To reach St. Simeon from Aleppo, take a **microbus** to **Darret 'Azzay** (S£5). From this small town, you can negotiate with locals for the 15km ride to the cathedral. The *service* minivans will ask for S£100 for one way, but locals in brightly colored Suzuki three-wheelers might do a round trip for S£150-200 (cathedral open Wed.-Thurs. 9am-3pm; S£200). If the driver is unyielding with the price, ask for a side trip to **Qatura**. This Roman tomb is carved into rock about 1km off the road to St. Simeon. Above the entrance to the main tomb, an eagle with spread wings symbolizes the soul; it's identical to one in Palmyra's Temple of Bel, carved around the same time.

EBLA أبلا

This *tel* 60km south of Aleppo was the discovered in 1964, and excavations are still in progress. Ebla is thought to have been the oldest city in Syria, dating back to the 3rd millennium BCE. Over 17,000 cuneiform tablets have been recovered in an ancient palace library, revealing much about Syria's early history. Apparently, Ebla was the center of an important north Syrian empire around 2000 BCE, but a 17th-century BCE Hittite invasion ended its rule.

From the Aleppo station, take a microbus headed to **Maaret En-Noman** (S£15) and ask to get off at the road to Ebla. It's a half-hour walk to the site and there is no food or water available (S£100, students S£15, when the guy is there to collect it). Back on the highway, it's easy to catch a bus back to Aleppo; they come often from both Maaret En-Noman and Hama.

MEDITERRANEAN COAST

▦ Lattakia اللاذقية

Lattakia is a decidedly practical city. Far from being the Mediterranean resort the Ministry of Tourism would have you believe, Lattakia's tall buildings and crowded streets have a congested, big-city feel. Lattakia is Syria's largest seaport and serves as the country's major import-export center. It is equipped with plenty of cheap eats and budget accommodations, and is a base for exploring the ruins at Ugarit and the castle of Salah ad-Din. The only clean beach is at the 5-star Cham Palace Hotel (accessible by *service* from the station near the mosque), where for S£250, you can enjoy the white sands and shimmering sea seen in the brochures.

Constructed in the second century BCE by the Seleucids, Lattakia was named after the mother of its architect (her name was Laudetia). The only ancient remains are a few columns, a Roman arch from 200 CE, and some Ugarit artifacts. You can see them at the **museum**, housed in the Ottoman Khan ad-Dukhan (open Wed.-Mon. 9am-6pm; S£200, students S£25).

Orientation and Practical Information The main street in Lattakia is 14 **Ramadan Street,** running northeast away from the water and ending at the **tourist office** (tel. 416 926; open daily 8am-2pm). At its intersection with Hanano St., the **Place Hanano** is home to an Asad statue and many budget accommodations. A little bit inland, running north and south from the beginning of 14 Ramadan St., is **8 Azar Street,** which turns into **Baghdad Avenue** south at the **Al Quds Street** intersection. Exchange money at the **Commercial Bank of Syria** on the right side of 8 Azar St. before reaching the traffic circle (open 8am-2pm and 5-8pm; traveler's checks not exchanged in evening). The **Sani Daker Pharmacy** (tel. 476 979), on 8 Azar St. before the Karnak office, has excellent, multi-lingual service (open Sat.-Wed. 9am-1:30pm and 5-8:30pm). To find out which pharmacy is open late, ask at one of the larger hotels. In case of **emergencies,** call the **Asad Hospital** (tel. 487 782), on 8 Azar St., or the **police** (tel. 112). To get to the new **post office**, take a *service* from the far right corner of the Asad statue to the beach (*shati'*), and ask to be dropped off at the post office (*bareed*). Across the street is **DHL international** (open Sat.-Thurs. 8:30am-8:30pm, Fri. 9am-2pm). From Baghdad Ave., a right on Sayf al-Dawla St. (after Baghdad intersects Al Quds St.) brings you to the surprisingly efficient **telephone office** (open daily 8am-10pm; 1min. to the U.S. S£100, to the U.K. S£90, to Australia S£115). The **telephone code** is 41.

The **Karnak bus station** (tel. 233 541) is on the corner of Baghdad Ave. and Sayf al-Dawla St. (turn left off Baghdad Ave. opposite the post office). Buses to **Damascus** (5hr., S£120) via **Homs** (3hr., S£65) leave at 7, 8am, 2:30, and 3:30pm (reserve a day ahead or get to the office by 7am). There's also daily service to **Aleppo** (3pm, 3hr.,

S£60) and **Beirut** (6pm, 4hr., S£175). **Private buses** off of 14 Ramadan Street frequently depart to **Aleppo** (S£100) and **Damascus** (S£140). The **Al-Shati'** transport company (tel. 467 149), on 14 Ramadan St., has daily 6am buses to **Antakya** (S£400), **Adana** (S£800), **Mersin** (S£600), **Iskenderun** (S£500), **Istanbul** (S£1500) and **Ankara** (S£1300). Bring your passport and US$20 to the border to get a visa.

Travel within the city by **taxi** for S£20-30 or by *service* (white minivans). To get to the **microbus station,** with regular departures to neighboring areas, walk down Ramadan St. toward the tourist office, break left on Al Maghreb al-Arabi Street at the big traffic circle, then take your first right and continue for about 500m.

Accommodations and Food The **Hotel Lattakia** (tel. 239 927) is to the right when facing the outdoor cafe from the Asad Statue. Walk down the right-hand street and take your first right; look for the yellow "Hotel" sign. The friendly management provides fan, balcony, a clean bath, and a welcoming cup of tea for S£150 per person. The **Dounia Hotel** (tel. 421 296) is also a great value. Facing away from the Asad statue and outdoor cafe, take your second right after the gas station; the small hotel is on your left. A bed in a clean room and a pair of slippers for the walk to the cold shower are yours for S£175. The **Riad Hotel** (tel. 479 778), on the right-hand side of the Asad statue, has quiet rooms with clean private baths for those willing to spend hard currency (singles US$24; doubles US$28).

Eating meals in Lattakia works the usual way—walk around enough and the raw meat and overcooked chicken in the windows start to look appetizing. Before seeking out their 317th falafel sandwich, herbivores should check out the **Alexandria Restaurant** on the corner of Ramadan St. near the Dounia Hotel, where a spicy plate of beans and rice goes for S£40. Next door, the **Sindbad Restaurant** makes a pizza-like dish with ground beef, onions, and green peppers for S£55. The **Tea Room,** near the Commercial Bank of Syria on Azar St., is a the perfect place for an after-dinner cup (tea or coffee S£25). They have honey-drenched sweets, a pleasant terrace, and the best lemonade in the known world (S£35).

■ Near Lattakia

RAS SHAMRA AND UGARIT رس الشمرة

This tiny town 16km north of Lattakia is the site of the historic Kingdom of Ugarit. In 1928, an unsuspecting peasant farmer unearthed a few slabs of stone marking a spot originally settled in the 7th millennium BCE. Ugarit's greatest gift to our time is its twenty-eight letter **alphabet,** preserved in a stone tablet from the 14th century BCE. The oldest phonetic alphabet in the world, Ugaritic is the probable ancestor of both the Phoenician and Hebrew alphabets (though not the languages), and from there those of Latin and Greek. You can see the tablet in the National Museum in Damascus (see p. 529). The maze of ruins is mostly overgrown with weeds, and a professional guide is necessary to truly appreciate the structures. English and French-speaking guides hanging out at the entrance can be hired for half a day for about S£250, or your best offer, depending on demand. As you enter, the **royal palace** (where the alphabet was found) is to the right; the **residential quarters** and **acropolis** are further down along the main path. To get to Ugarit, take a *service* from Sheikh Daher Sq. to the beach service station (*ash-shati'*); then take another service from the beach to Ras Shamra (S£5 each trip) and ask the driver to drop you off at the ruins (open daily 9am-6pm; S£200, students S£25).

QAL'AT SALAH AD-DIN قلعة صلاح الدين

Situated 35km east of Lattakia, this fortress is named for the exalted warrior who took the "impregnable" castle from the Crusaders in 1188. Perched on a plateau flanked by two deep gorges, the site's most impressive feature is the 156km long, 18m wide, and 28m deep trench that was cut by hand to completely isolate the fortress from the adjacent land. The lone column of rock in the gorge was used to support a lowering drawbridge. Inside the walls, you'll find the arched entry to a stable on your right, and a dungeon in the drawbridge tower. Holes in the dungeon walls mark where prisoners' chains were drilled into the stone. Inside the next tower up the path, a hollow column conceals a secret staircase, which soldiers on the roof used to descend and attack the enemy from behind. Across from the entrance is a huge cistern that collected rain water for 4000 soldiers' teas. To the left are remains of Byzantine and Crusader churches, and directly in front is the mosque (castle open daily 9am-5pm; S£200, students S£25).

From Lattakia, take a microbus to Al Haffeh (S£10, 45min.). The easiest ride from there is to hire the services of one of the Honda mopeds across the street. For S£100 they take you to the castle, wait for an hour, and bring you back to the bus stop. Taxis will ask for S£100 one-way, and they know how few cars there are along the 7km road to the castle (hitchers should think twice).

■ Tartus طرطوس

Tartus is Syria's second major seaport, 90km to the south of Lattakia and much more charming. This Mediterranean town was called Antardus by the Phoenicians and Tortusa by the Byzantines, and is referenced in cuneiform texts dating back to the 2nd millennium BCE. Tartus was one of the main supply ports for the Crusaders and an important military base until its capture by Salah ad-Din in 1188; the patchwork architecture of the medieval city underscores its diverse past. Modern-day Tartusians still inhabit the narrow lanes and arched buildings of the old town.

Orientation and Practical Information The downtown area of Tartus is bounded by three main streets and the corniche, forming a rectangle. **First Street** and **Ibn al-Walid Street** run from the sea to **Ath-Thawra Avenue.** Most of Tartus's reasonably priced hotels and many restaurants line **First Street,** running east from the corniche at the **Arwad dock.** At the **clock tower circle,** a left on **Ath-Thawra Avenue** sends you in the direction of another circle near the **police station.** A block farther and to the right of Ath-Thawra is the **telephone office** (open daily 8am-midnight). A left turn on Ibn al-Walid St. past the traffic circle brings you to the new **post office** (open daily 8am-5pm). A right turn at the circle onto Ibn al-Walid St. takes you past the **Commercial Bank of Syria** and the **tourist information office,** and deposits you back on the corniche in front of the **Old City.**

The **Kadmous Transportation Co.,** on Ibn al-Walid St. next to the information office, has daily buses to Damascus (4hr., S£110), Aleppo (5hr., S£115), and Lattakia (1hr., S£30). The **microbus station,** a good 15-minute walk from the town center, services nearby destinations. To get there, take either of the two main streets away from the sea, pass Ath-Thawra Ave. and turn right on Tichrin Ave.

Accommodations and Food Tartus has enough budget hotel and restaurant options to make any brief stay a pleasant one. The **Daniel Hotel** (tel. 220 581), a block and a half up from the beach on First St., has spotless rooms with fans and private baths (S£300 for a bed, S£400 with breakfast; S£400 for a double room, S£500 with breakfast). Up the street on the right of the next intersection is the **Republic Hotel** (tel. 222 580). Clean rooms come with a fan and a sink (singles S£225; doubles S£300; shower included). Rooms are cheaper, though less inviting, farther up First St. at the **Hotel Tourism** (tel. 221 763), where they have telephones and either a balcony or a fan (singles S£100; doubles S£200). On the more expensive end, the **Blue Beach Hotel** (tel. 220 650), on the corner of the corniche and First St., will exchange a room with a few amenities and a balcony over the sea for a close-up view of more than a few greenbacks (singles US$13; doubles US$17; triples US$21).

The **Venicia Restaurant,** near the Blue Beach Hotel, sells the usual meat, chicken, and *mezze* dishes for reasonable prices. Fresh fish is a catch at S£500-700. If you come after 7:30pm, the pizza (S£75 per slice) that the sign advertises may be ready. Tables for two on the balcony overlook the sea and Arwad dock. Just across First St., the **Al Nabil Restaurant** (tel. 220 959) offers similar cuisine at similar prices (fresh fish S£500 per kg; meat, salad, and soda S£125-150). Up the street from Al Nabil and just past the pharmacy is a cheap, delicious restaurant called **Nabil.** Gobble and gab with the local fishermen: a filling meal of hummus or *fuul* and *mezze* goes for S£20. For a more luxurious dining experience, explore **The Cave,** on the waterfront by the Old City. Chef Ahmed spent 18 years as a cook on a Greek ship and brews his own *araq.* Local fish with all the trimmings costs S£700-800 but serves two.

Sights The medieval **Old City** bustles with modern life. Almost entirely unrenovated, the sturdy walls enclose a hive of activity and chronologically jumbled architecture. The fortified, 12th-century **cathedral** claims to be the location of the world's oldest altar dedicated to the Virgin Mary. Now a **museum,** the cathedral houses an eclectic collection of artifacts from all over coastal Syria (open Wed.-Mon. 9am-6pm; S£200, students S£25). For evening entertainment, nothing beats a sunset stroll along the corniche.

■ Near Tartus

ARWAD ارواد

Syria's sole island, Arwad is positioned just 3km from the coast of Tartus. In ancient times Arwad served as a sanctuary for those seeking protection from foreign invaders. As such, it was the last Crusader stronghold to return to Muslim hands. More recently, its citadel was used by the French as a prison for Syrian nationalists. The Phoenician kingdom of Aradus was centered on the island, and though its renowned defensive walls no longer stand, two medieval forts remain, one of which now calls itself a museum (S£200, students S£25). Your time would be just as well spent wandering the narrow lanes or enjoying a sea-side cup of tea.

Ferries run every 15 minutes or so from Arwad port in Tartus. The round-trip costs S£20, which you pay on the island before returning. The last boat leaves at 8:30pm, and there are no formal lodgings available on the island.

SAFITA سفيتة

Of the once majestic **Castle le Blanc,** only one remaining tower stands guard over the tiled roofed houses and olive trees of the small mountain town of Safita. The tower's entrance level is graced by a beautiful chapel that has never been deconsecrated and is still used for services today. Upstairs are the spacious living quarters, and above them the roof, offering panoramic views (open daily 8am-1pm and 4pm-7:30pm; winter 8am-1pm and 3-6pm).

To get to Castle le Blanc, take a microbus from Tartus to Safita (S£7, 45min.). Round-trip *service* and minibuses leave every 15 minutes or so from the town center. Alternatively, you can hoof it from the town center: walk up the steepest street and look for the cobblestone side-road on the right leading up to the tower. Admission is free, but a tip (around S£10) may be expected on the way out.

QAL'AT AL-MARQAB قلعة المرقب

Arabic for "control," al-Marqab Citadel holds a dominant position over the surrounding mountain range and sea. The enormous black basalt citadel has 14 imposing towers and was designed to house 1000 soldiers. Built by Muslims in 1062 CE, the castle was occupied by Crusaders in the 12th century before being retaken by the Mamluks in 1285. To reach the Citadel, take a microbus to Baniyas (S£12, 30min.) and then a local *service* (S£5) to the castle's entrance. You can also hire a moped for a thrilling ride up to the castle and back (S£100, the driver should wait an hour). Ask the guard to show you the Byzantine frescoes in the church—S£10 tip should suffice (open 9am-6pm; in winter 9am-4pm; S£200, students S£25).

LEBANON لبنان

US$1=1535.25 Lebanese Pounds (L£)	L£1000=US$0.65
CDN$1=L£1103.27	L£1000=CDN$0.91
UK£1=L£2468.76	L£1000=UK£0.41
IR£1=L£2259.50	L£1000=IR£0.44
AUS$1=L£1148.06	L£1000=AUS$0.87
NZ$1=L£994.23	L£1000=NZ$1.01
SAR1=L£327.56	L£1000=SAR3.05
JD1 (Jordanian Dinar) =L£2168.43	L£1000=JD0.46
S£100 (Syrian Pounds) =L£3668	L£1000=S£27.26

> Despite lifting the U.S. travel ban, **the U.S. State Department does not consider travel in Lebanon to be safe** (see p. 17). For more information on travel in general and some specifics on Lebanon, see the **Essentials** section of this book. Lebanon's **international phone code** is 961.

Lebanon (from the Arabic *loubnan,* white) has emerged from over 15 years of civil war with its spirit intact. The country covers an area of only 10,450 sq. km, and the small area heightens the concentration of hospitality, passion, and diversity in its population. Before the war, Lebanon was known as the "jewel of the Middle East"—it offered clean *souqs,* ritzy hotels, Parisian fashions, and dirt-cheap prices accessible to both royalty and backpackers. It is now welcoming a growing number of tourists back to its elegant shores. Much of Lebanese self-proclaimed sophistication is tied to French influence; France controlled the area from 1918 to 1943, leaving lasting impressions on the cuisine, language, and traditions of Lebanon and adding to an already cramped cultural melange. Four major religious groups are constantly vying for power and status—Sunni and Shi'ite Muslims, Druze, and Christians of different denominations. In times of peace, the diversity adds flavor to the historical sights and natural splendor of the country, but added to political tensions, it can be explosive.

Lebanon, especially Beirut, is rising from the ashes of its internal strife rejuvenated and more alive than ever. Large areas of the capital city are being rebuilt and restored. Baalbeck's international arts festival, world-famous in the 60s, has begun again, and Lebanon's youth is on a patriotic mission to discover previously inaccessible countryside. Visitors will be awed by ancient Roman cities, pristine mountains, Mediterranean beaches, natural springs, and other monuments of history and nature—but most of all by the spirit of an ambitious, resilient, and stylish people. Share in the exhilaration and bittersweet emotion of a nation recreating itself for the 21st century.

ONCE THERE

■ Getting Around

Buses and *service* to points north of Beirut leave from Barbir Bridge (bar-BEER); transportation to points south and east leaves from the Cola Bridge.

Taxis Service taxis (ser-VEES) are white or gray Mercedes similar to those in Jordan and Syria. They pass by at breakneck speeds, but will stop en route if flagged from the side of the road. As the car slows, yell your destination at the driver. If he is going your way, he'll stop—if not, he'll speed away. *Service* rides cost L£1000 or L£2000 within Beirut and are negotiable for intercity trips. Within Beirut, drivers can be trusted to charge the standard fare. For longer trips, negotiate the price before getting in. *Service* usually stop running around 11pm or midnight.

Private taxis are more expensive than *service* and can be called 24 hours. There are no meters; tariffs are predetermined by location. If there is no posted list in the taxi, ask the driver for the "tariff" and he should give you a printed chart of prices for common trips. For taxi rides outside of Beirut, negotiate the price before getting in.

Buses Most buses are privately owned and very efficient. Some are Pullman buses, large "luxury" vehicles. Others are a smaller, older variety with vinyl school bus-type seats, no A/C, and tacky, colorful interiors. Unfortunately, none of the companies have come up with the brilliant idea of printing bus schedules, so the only way to find out when buses leave is to ask locals.

Cars While it is possible to rent a car in Beirut, it is not advisable. There are few universally understood traffic signals in Lebanon, which is one of the reason why cars are like bats out of hell. Trusting a *service* driver with your life is much safer and more convenient. For daytrips outside of Beirut, hire a *service* driver for the day at an agreed-upon flat rate.

Hitchhiking While hitchhiking is common in some rural mountain areas, it is dangerous and not advisable. Most places are accessible by *service* or bus. *Let's Go* does not recommend hitchhiking, especially given the sometimes tense political situation in Lebanon.

▓ Money Matters

Currency and Exchange The basic unit of currency is the Lebanese pound (L£), sometimes known locally as the lira. Bills come in denominations of L£50, 100, 250, 500, 1000, and 10,000. No coins are in circulation because the currency was devalued so much during the war (see **Economy,** p. 552). U.S. dollars are widely accepted, especially at most restaurants and hotels, although the government, aiming to stabilize the post-war economy, has declared that all official transactions must be made in Lebanese pounds.

Business Hours Government offices are open Monday through Saturday 8:30am-2pm and Friday 8-11am. Banks are open Monday through Saturday 8:30am-12:30pm. Shops and commercial businesses vary, but are usually open Monday through Saturday 9am-6pm. While some Muslim businesses may close on Fridays, the Lebanese week ends on Sunday. As elsewhere in the Middle East, official hours can be misleading.

Tipping and Bakhsheesh *Bakhsheesh* (see p. 77) may be necessary to get into an out-of-the-way sight or two, but is not as widespread as in Egypt, Jordan, and Syria. Unfortunately, since Lebanese prices are higher and tourists here are generally wealthier than in other countries, spoiled door guards and tourist officials may expect more in each palm-grease than elsewhere. Liberal tipping at restaurants is expected; *service* drivers do not expect tips, but taxi drivers should get a little something extra (especially for long rides or ones that include many military checkpoints).

▓ Accommodations

Lebanon does not offer plentiful, cheap accommodations. Wartime inflation has made prices skyrocket, and budget travelers feel this most when sleepy. There seem to be three unofficial lodging categories: uninhabitable but very cheap, "middle range" establishments which start at around US$20 per night, and luxury resort havens patronized mostly by visiting dignitaries, non-starving artists, and vacationing Gulf Arabs. There are some affordable campsites, but they are not well publicized: the best are north of Beirut, on the beach, and near Jbail. Be insistent at the tourist office and they may help you reserve a spot.

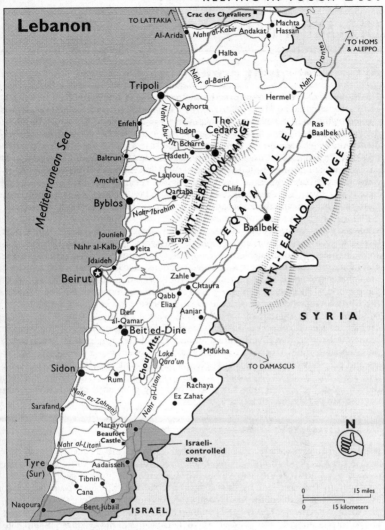

Lebanon

TO LATTAKIA
Crac des Chevaliers
Al-Arida Nahr al-Kabir Andakat Machta Hassan
Halba TO HOMS & ALEPPO
Tripoli
Aghorta Hermel
Enfeh Ehden The Cedars Ras Baalbek
Bcharrê
Baltrun Hadeth Mt. LEBANON RANGE
Amchit Laqlouq Chlifa ANTI-LEBANON RANGE
Qartaba
Byblos Nahr Ibrahim
Jounieh Faraya Baalbek
Nahr al-Kalb Jeita
Jdaideh
Beirut Zahle
Qabb Elias Chtaura
Deir al-Qamar Aanjar
Beit ed-Dine SYRIA
Mdukha
Lake Qara'un TO DAMASCUS
Sidon Rum Chouf Mts.
Nahr az-Zahrani Rachaya
Sarafand Ez Zahat
Marjayoun Beaufort Castle Israeli-controlled area
Nahr al-Litani
Tyre (Sur) Aadaisseh
Tibnin
Cana
Naqoura Bent Jubail ISRAEL

Mediterranean Sea

BEQA'A VALLEY

Nahr Abu Ali Nahr al-Barid Orontes Nahr

N

0 — 15 miles
0 — 15 kilometers

LEBANON

■ Keeping in Touch

Poste Restante is not the reliable service it was before the civil war. Mail sent to the main post office in Beirut may disappear. There are many **DHL** offices for express mail, but no Federal Express. Packages take up to four days for international express delivery. At press time, mail to the United States took longer than to Europe because there were no direct trans-Atlantic flights to or from Beirut. Although its snail-mail system may be on the fritz, Lebanon compensates with **Internet access.** You can get on the infobahn from Beirut for reasonable prices (see **Beirut: Practical Information,** p. 560). **International calls** can be placed from public telephone offices—there is one in every Beirut district, though not in every city in Lebanon. AT&T operators can be accessed from any phone, public or private. For now, they can help you make collect but not calling card calls. In Beirut, dial 426 801 (costs the same as a local call). Out-

LIFE AND TIMES

■ Government and Politics

The Republic of Lebanon is governed by a President, a Prime Minister, and a unicameral Parliament, called Majlis Alnuwab (or Assemblee Nationale). The President is elected by the legislature for a non-renewable six-year term, and he, in turn, appoints the Prime Minister. Ethnicity and religion are major concerns of the Lebanese government—until 1990, an unwritten agreement called the National Pact required that the President be a Maronite Christian, the prime minister a Sunni Muslim, the speaker of parliament a Shi'ite Muslim, and the Chief of the Armed Forces a Druze. These categorizations were based on ethnic percentages in the Lebanese population determined by a 1932 census. The President of Lebanon since 1989 is **Ilyas Harawi,** a moderate Maronite Christian, and the Prime Minister is **Rafiq al-Hariri.**

Political apathy in men is discouraged by law; voting is mandatory for all males 21 years and over. Apathy in the other half of the population is discouraged quite a bit less—a woman can petition for the right to vote when she reaches age 21 if she has an elementary-school education. The constitution stipulates that elections for the Assemblee are to be held every four years. Elections have been irregular, but in 1991 the Cabinet appointed 40 "deputies" to fill empty seats due to resignation or death of the members. These new appointees also balanced discrepancies between Muslim and Christian representatives. A decade ago, the president would have appointed the deputies, but a 1990 international agreement created the half-Muslim, half-Christian cabinet and gave it many Presidential powers. The same agreement gave the Muslim Prime Minister greater governmental authority, including the right to countersign presidential decrees. This disempowering of the president was a result of the sectarian and religious concerns of small political parties, which in Lebanon often have their own militias. Political clashes have led to military clashes, and the lessening of the Christian President's power was seen by many as an appeasement to militant Islamist parties (see **Recent History,** p. 553).

■ Economy

Because Lebanon possesses virtually no natural resources, the Lebanese economy has always been dependent on banking, commerce, and tourism. Before the war, the country was known as the "gateway to the Mediterranean," where backpackers and Saudi royalty frolicked side by side. It was also banking capital of the Middle East, holding half the wealth of the Arab world in secret bank accounts even more clandestine than Switzerland's. Eighty banks operate in the country today. Wartime inflation forced the economy to adopt a more stable currency than the Lebanese pound, and the invisible hand chose the U.S. dollar. Today's government has dictated that all official transactions must be conducted in pounds, and it has lowered income taxes to provide investment incentive and increase disposable income. Agriculture in the Beqaa valley thrives when there is relative peace in the area, and Lebanese *'araq* is famous all over the Arab world—but the country is really dependent upon tourism and banking rising from the rubble left after the war.

■ Religion and Ethnicity

Maronite Christians are rare throughout the rest of the world, but they are the most prevalent Christian denomination in Lebanon and were once even the Lebanese religious majority. The beginnings of Maronite Christianity are unclear; the sect is named after St. Maron, a fifth-century hermit from Syria, and St. John Maron, a monk who later preached St. Maron's theological works. Early Maronites isolated themselves on the peaks of Mount Lebanon to avoid persecution by other Christian groups and Muslim conquerors.

Islam split when the death of Prophet Muhammad left a power vacuum because he had not designated a successor. One group of followers believed that the leader should be chosen among the community of believers (these became the **Sunni Muslims**), and the other group demanded that the successor be a direct decendant of the Prophet; these became the **Shi'a**, or **Shi'ite Muslims** (see **The Rule of the Caliphs,** p. 49). There are more Sunni Muslims than Shi'ites worldwide, but Shi'ites are more common in Lebanon (and in a few other Arab nations, including Iran).

Lebanon also has a sizeable **Druze** population of about 300,000. The religion was founded in 1017 by Ad-Darazi, an Egyptian who believed that God would be repeatedly incarnated in human form. Little is known about Druze theology or religious practices; the Druze have cultivated secrecy in order to avoid persecution (see **The Druze,** p. 69). Druze communities also endure in Syria and northeastern Israel (see **Isfiya & Daliyat Al Karmel,** p. 361, and **Metulla,** p. 399).

Lebanon's political turmoil is inextricably tied to the population's religious and ethnic identities. In the early half of the 20th century, Maronite Christians were the majority in the country, and for that reason, common law stated that the Lebanese president had to be a Christian. Other government positions were also reserved by religious denomination, all due to the incisive 1932 census (see **Government and Politics,** p. 552). Due to high Muslim birth rates and Christian emigration, Muslims began to outnumber Christians, and the Muslim population became discontented with Christian minority rule; the stage was set for Civil War. The religious groups have been for the most part geographically separate; differences were reinforced, and group cohesion strengthened. Before 1975, when the Civil War began, Shi'ite Muslim communities dominated southern Lebanon, including Sur (Tyre), and the northeast part of the country along the Syrian border, including the city of Baalbeck. The Maronite Christian population held the majority in central Lebanon, including Eastern Beirut, as well as the northwestern coastline approaching Tripoli. Tripoli, northern Lebanon, and western Beirut were populated primarily by Sunni Muslims.

▓ Recent History: The Civil War

After the 1948 War, the State of Israel was formed, and many Palestinians fled to Lebanon. By the 60s, Beirut had become the home of Yassir Arafat's Palestine Liberation Organization (PLO) and a center of Palestinian activity. The influx of often-vocal Palestinian Arabs added to Lebanon's burgeoning Muslim population, which then outnumbered the Christian population. Christians feared that loss of majority status would weaken their political voice (see **Religion and Ethnicity** and **Government and Politics,** above).

The PLO's activity in Lebanon widened the fissure between Christians and Muslims. The Muslim population, on the whole, supported the actions of the PLO with increasing Pan-Arabic sentiments, but Christians worried that PLO guerrilla activity would threaten Lebanese security and turn international sentiment against them. The Christian population used their entrenched but outdated "majority" government rule (see **Religion and Ethnicity,** above) to counter guerrilla activity with the Lebanese national army. Many Lebanese Muslims saw this as a direct act of aggression by their own government.

Meanwhile, Israel had begun to shell the south of Lebanon, where PLO guerrilla forces were stationed. Much of the predominantly Shi'ite population of the south migrated to Beirut to escape the danger. These 30,000 poverty-stricken Muslim refugees formed a "Belt of Misery" across the western half of the city, suffering at the doorstep of their wealthy Maronite neighbors to the east.

Through the mid-70s, soldiers in the National Army had continued to defect to their sectarian ethnic and religious groups—by the late 80s, the national army was only the fifth or sixth most powerful military organization in the country. The army had trained soldiers who had then divided among the warring factions, leaving the national government with little military power.

On June 6, 1982, Israel initiated "Operation Peace for Galilee" (see **The Israeli Invasion of Lebanon,** p. 57). The invasion, an effort to eradicate guerrilla activity from southern Lebanon, significantly weakened the PLO. However, it also angered and radicalized Shi'ite Muslim militias throughout the country. With the help of Iran, the fundamentalist Hizbullah (Party of God) was founded, determined to act with more immediacy and extreme measures than the PLO had.

When Israeli troops partially withdrew their forces, Druze and Christian militias fought to take control of the mountains near Beirut. Western peace-keeping forces that had been brought in during the Israeli siege of Beirut were now targets of terrorist attacks, and finally withdrew from Lebanon. When Shi'ite-Druze fighting erupted in 1987, Syrian troops moved in to enforce peace, and they stayed. Despite the disagreements of the various sectarian militias, most concurred that the Syrian soldiers were unwelcome occupiers. After Syria helped reinstate the Lebanese National Army, both the Syrians and the Lebanese national government were seen as unwelcome intruders. Nonetheless, parliamentary elections were held in 1992, with Hizbullah, no longer only a military organization, winning the largest number of seats. The now-centralized Lebanese government is doing much to rebuild the country and its infrastructure, even though fighting between Hizbullah troops and Israeli soldiers on the southern border continues. Although its internal politics seem to be normalizing, Lebanon's place in the international community is still uncertain.

THE HOSTAGE CRISIS

In 1982, militant Islamic factions began taking hostages as a method of gaining publicity for their cause and getting various demands met. The most conspicuous victims of kidnapping were Western expatriates who lived and worked in Beirut, usually for international organizations. In July, David Dodge, the president of the American University of Beirut, became the first foreign hostage. Most hostages were kidnapped in the Beirut's Hamra district, a center of urban cultural activity where many Westerners lived and worked. By the time the last hostage was released in June 1992, fifty foreigners had been taken hostage, some kept chained and blindfolded for up to five years. In some ways, the terrorists were successful because the Western world paid attention to Lebanon when Western citizens were in danger. Until summer 1997, the United States government, afraid of losing more people to kidnappers, made it illegal for American citizens to travel to Lebanon. The U.S. government has now lifted that ban, though they still do not consider travel in Lebanon to be safe (see **Terrorism,** p. 16). European tourists had been returning to tour the country for several years before the U.S. ban was lifted.

■ Language

The official language is Arabic, but Lebanon is unique among its neighbors in the degree of French spoken. Many people speak English as well; some are fluent in all three languages. French is taught in predominantly Christian areas, while English is more common as a second language among Muslims. **Street signs** are written in Arabic and French.

■ The Arts

LITERATURE

Largely because of its liberal political history, Lebanon has one of the richest and most diverse literary traditions in the Arab world. In the 19th century, Beirut led a broad Arab cultural renaissance; the movement re-examined old Arab texts and explored new styles. The 20th century has produced brilliant novelists who write in Arabic,

French, and English. **Gibran Khalil Gibran** was a mystic and metaphysical poet, novelist, and artist. He is most famous for his novel *The Prophet*, which has been translated into numerous languages. A museum in his home village of Bcharré is devoted to his life and works (see **Bcharré,** p. 567). **Amin Maalouf** has published four historical novels in French that have established his presence as a writer in Lebanon. He made history when his novel about a 19th century Lebanese village, *The Rock of Tanios*, won the distinguished French *Prix de Goncourt* in 1993. He is the first Lebanese and only the second Arab to win the literary prize, which has been awarded since 1903. **Amin Rihani** is another well-known twentieth-century writer. Influenced by American poet Walt Whitman, Rihani introduced free verse into Arabic poetry. His major novel, *The Book of Khalid,* grapples with issues of prophecy and religious unity. Lebanese **poetry** has developed a distinctive form—the *zajal,* which are verses sung rather than recited. Poets often meet to help each other create; lots of *'araq* usually helps along the spontaneous singing and composing.

Recently, world literature has started to contemplate Lebanon's civil war. Kamal Salibi's *A House of Many Mansions—The History of Lebanon Reconsidered* recounts events of the war. Robert Fisk's *Pity the Nation: Lebanon at War* gives a British journalist's first-hand account of the war and its major players. The international **media** has an established presence in Lebanon that dates from pre-war days. *Time, Newsweek, The International Herald-Tribune,* and other papers, including *L'Orient-Le Jour,* a respected French newspaper, are available in Beirut.

PERFORMING ARTS

Lebanon's cities and villages come alive with annual festivals which feature traditional folk dancing and music. The largest festival is in Baalbeck (see **Baalbeck,** p. 555), but others are held in Sur, Saida, and at other ancient Roman sites. **Belly dancing** is a popular form of entertainment at nightclubs and even at private parties. One form of provincial dance is the **dakle,** in which dancers wearing traditional mountain garb enact themes from village life. The national dance is the **dabke.**

Modern **theater** in Lebanon took off in the 1950s and 60s, and was featured in many of the annual festivals around the country. The luxurious Hotel al-Bustan in Beit Meri, a suburb in the mountains above Beirut, hosts Lebanon's main dramatic and musical festival—the **International Festival of the Performing Arts**—for five weeks in February and March. Performances are also staged at university theaters. The war has colored theatrical themes: most contemporary theater ponders the effects of conflict.

Cinema in Lebanon has undergone a similar post-war evolution, and now consists largely of documentaries about the war. Popular movie theaters play mainly American and European films.

▦ Food and Drink

Lebanese food is known all over the Middle East for its variety, flavor, and quality. Since there are no Bedouin in Lebanon, the national cuisine lacks the Bedouin influence present in the rest of the region's cuisine. Vegetarian dishes are common, and recipes tend to use less fat than those in other parts of the Levant. Staples like falafel and *shawerma* can be found as commonly as in Jordan and Syria, but some specialties are specific to Lebanon. *Tabbouleh* is the national dish; it is a salad made with parsley, *burghul* (cracked wheat), onions, tomatoes, lemon juice, and spices. *Fattoush* is a salad of lettuce, tomato, and cucumber with small pieces of toasted pita mixed in to soak up the dressing. Lebanese *mezze* is a mixture of green peppers, cucumbers, radishes, scallions, olives, pickles, hummus, *baba ghannouj,* and fuzzy raw almonds. Stuffed squash (*mehshe koosa*) and stuffed eggplant (*mehshe betenjein*) are common also. *Mujeddra* is a lentil stew cooked with sauteed onions and spices, and eaten with bread and salad. Salad dressings are made with lemon juice, olive oil, salt, and enough garlic to repel Transylvania. *Kibbeh naye* is raw beef and spices, whipped into a dip and eaten with pita. There are different varieties of pita as well: *marqooq* is a paper-thin bread cooked on a metal dome in a wood fire and is very common both in the mountains and at stands in Beirut. *Ka'ak* is a sesame bread, made either into little round balls or breadsticks. Unlike the soft sesame rings of the same name found in Jordan, these are crunchy and customarily dipped into coffee as a morning snack.

Lebanese meals usually finish with huge cornucopias of fresh fruit, but sweets are also popular. The best ones are made with secret recipes closely guarded by those who possess them (mostly Sunni Muslims). Tripoli is especially famous for sweets like *halawat al-Jibn:* unsalted cheese is kept in a warm place for a few days and then rolled out with semolina into long sheets. Sugar and syrup are then added, followed by a layer of *'ashta* (sweet cream). Ice cream is well-loved, and comes in fresh-fruit flavors like apricot, mango, and peach.

Lebanon is most famous for its *'araq,* an anise-flavored liquor similar to Greek *ouzo.* It is produced in small villages by families that have passed on techniques for years. The non-alcoholic specialty is *jellab,* made from raisin syrup and served with pine nuts.

Meals may "begin" two or three hours before the main courses are served. Drinks are consumed, a game of backgammon or two is played, conversations become arguments and are resolved, and snacks are served before the main courses arrive. It is customary to wish guests good health during a meal: in Arabic, *"sahtein"* should be returned with *"a'alback"* to a man or *"a'albick"* to a woman.

Beirut بيروت

Beirut in the 60s was the gateway to the Mediterranean, the meeting point of East and West. Europeans could enjoy the flavor of the Orient while lounging in familiar comfort, and wealthy Arabs could slip away to a hedonistic world condemned by their conservative nations. International jet-setters, journalists, socialites, and spies unwound at cafes, casinos, and resorts on the sea. Home to people of many religions and ethnicities, Beirut during its golden years seemed like a paradise shared by all. The reality, however, was that a growing underclass of disaffected Shi'ite Muslims and Palestinian refugees was barely surviving on the edges of the city, silently witnessing the extravagant lifestyle of Beirut's *chi-chi* crowds.

The civil war blew away the illusion of the city as a content, multicultural melting pot, but an overriding sense of nationalism survived the class and ethnic conflict. Beirut has been dubbed "The City That Would Not Die" by the Ministry of Tourism, and the epithet is well-earned. Some parts of the city were ravaged more than others, but a decade and a half of constant conflict took its toll on every district. A rebuilding effort is under way, managed by the Lebanese-owned company Solidere, and teams of archaeologists from all over the world have been working with their Lebanese counterparts to unearth the city's treasures before roads pave over ancient sites. Astounding evidence has confirmed that Beirut has actually been destroyed seven times: by a tidal wave, fire, several earthquakes, and war. Its history of strength and long-term survival lends perspective to the recent past. Starting out as a small fishing village, Beirut gained fame in the 3rd century BCE when it was chosen as the site for a Roman law school. The school and the entire Roman city were destroyed by earthquakes, killing 30,000 city-dwellers. Rather than fading into obscurity, Beirut continued to grow. Buildings are springing up at an astounding pace, and Beirut is blossoming again.

▓ Transportation

Buses and **service** leave Beirut from two bridges: Barbir (bar-BEER) for points north, and Cola for points south and east (Syrian Karnak buses run to and from Damascus from the Cola bridge). Many intercity *service* also congregate at Dawra, on the outskirts of the city. Within the city, *service* run regular routes until 11pm or midnight (most cost L£2000). Private **taxis**, usually old Mercedes-Benz with red license plates, are available 24 hours and are more expensive. It is sometimes difficult to distinguish between *service* and taxis; ask the driver. Rather than using a meter, taxi companies have set rates between common pick-up and drop-off points. Ask to see the "tariff" (price list) if it is not posted in the back of the cab. Taxi prices should be approximately five times the price of a *service*. The **New Taxi, Radio Taxi,** and **Lebanon Taxi** companies are the cheapest and most reliable.

There are many reasonably priced **car rental** companies in Beirut. If you drive, you have decided to risk life and limb among people who may have *never* experienced a traffic light. **Europcar** (tel. 48 04 80) has an office in the Saarti building on Hayek Ave. in Sin el-Fil. **Budget Rent-a-Car** (tel. 36 45 34; fax 60 21 65) is in the Minkara building on Rue Clemenceau.

Buses, like *service*, depart when full, so bus schedules are unpredictable. Buses and *service* leave from the Cola bridge to: **Damascus** (twice daily, 3½hr., L£10,000); **Amman** (US$20); **Sur** (3½hr., L£5000) via **Saida** (2hr., L£1000); and **Baalbeck** (3hr., L£7000). They leave from Barbir to **Tripoli** (A/C Pullman bus, 3hr., L£2000) and **Byblos** (*service* via Nahr al-Mawt, L£1000). Buses stop running at 8 or 9pm. For more general information about transportation, see **Getting Around,** page 549.

Beirut International Airport has regular flights to Damascus, Amman, and London. Many international routes are accessible by **Middle East Air** (see p. 39). Taxis to the **airport** should cost no more than L£8000.

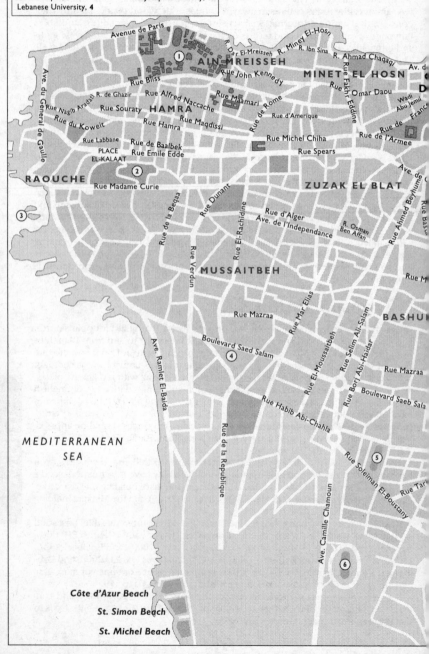

Beirut

American University of Beirut, 1
Arab University of Beirut, 5
Archaeological Excavations, 7
Hippodrome, 10
LAU Campus, 2
Lebanese University, 4

National Museum, 9
Pigeon Rock, 3
Place Sassine, 11
Sport City, 6
St. Joseph University, 8

Avenue de Paris
R. Dar El-Mreisseh
R. Miney El-Hosn
R. Ibn Sina
R. Ahmad Chaqaqi
Av. de
AIN-MREISSEH
MINET EL HOSN
D
Rue Bliss
Rue John Kennedy
Rue Fakhr Eddine
Omar Daou
Wadi
Abu Jemil
Av. de
France
R. de Ghazir
Rue Alfred Naccache
Rue Miamari
Rue de Rome
Rue d'Amerique
Rue Nagib Aradati
Rue Souraty
HAMRA
Rue Maqdissi
Rue Michel Chiha
Rue de l'Armee
Rue du Koweit
Rue Hamra
Rue Spears
Rue Labbane
Rue de Baalbek
PLACE
EL-KALAAT
Rue Emile Edde
Ave. de
RAOUCHE
Rue Madame Curie
ZUZAK EL BLAT
Rue Ahmed Beyhum
Rue Bas
Rue de la Beqaa
Rue Dunant
Rue d'Alger
Ave. de l'Independance
R. Osman
Ben Affan
Rue El-Rachidine
Rue Verdun
MUSSAITBEH
Rue M
Rue Mazraa
Rue Mar Elias
BASHU
Rue El-Moussaitbeh
Rue Selim Ali-Salam
Rue Borj Abi-Haidar
Rue Mazraa
Boulevard Saed Salam
Boulevard Saeb Sala
Ave. Ramlet El-Baida
Rue Habib Abi-Chahla
Rue Soleiman El-Boustany
Rue Tari
Rue de la Republique
MEDITERRANEAN
SEA
Ave. Camille Chamoun
Côte d'Azur Beach
St. Simon Beach
St. Michel Beach

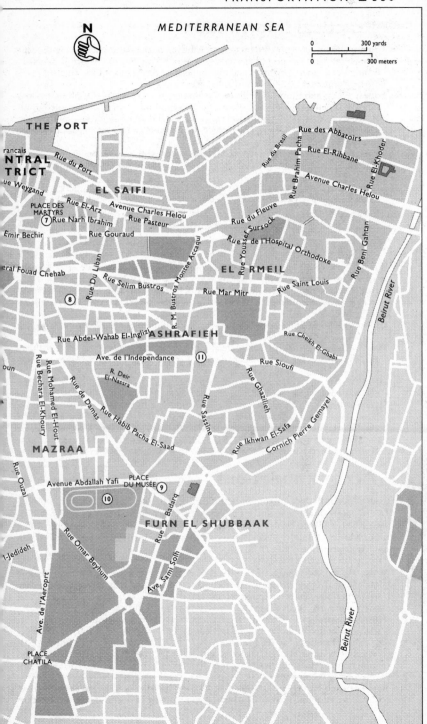

MEDITERRANEAN SEA

N

0   300 yards
0   300 meters

THE PORT

rancais

NTRAL
TRICT

ue Weygand

Rue du Port

EL SAIFI

Rue El-Arz

Avenue Charles Helou

PLACE DES
MARTYRS
⑦ Rue Narh Ibrahim

Rue Pasteur

Emir Bechir

Rue Gouraud

eral Fouad Chehab

Rue Du Liban

Rue Selim Bustros

⑧

oun

Rue Abdel-Wahab El-Ingliz

Ave. de l'Independance

Rue Mohamed El-Hout

Rue Bechara El-Khoury

Rue de Damas

R. Deir
El-Nassra

⑪

MAZRAA

Rue Habib Pacha El-Saad

Rue Ouzai

Avenue Abdallah Yafi

PLACE
DU MUSÉE ⑨

⑩

FURN EL SHUBBAAK

l-Jedideh

Rue Omar Beyhum

Ave. de l'Aeroprt

Ave. Sami Solh

PLACE
CHATILA

Rue des Abbatoirs

Rue du Bresil

Rue Brahim Pacha

Rue El-Rihbane

Rue El-Khoder

Avenue Charles Helou

Rue du Fleuve

Rue Youssef Sursock

Rue de l'Hospital Orthodoxe

Rue Beni Gahtan

EL RMEIL

Rue Mar Mitr

Rue Saint Louis

R.M. Bustros Moniee Accaqui

ASHRAFIEH

Rue Cheikh El-Ghabi

Beirut River

Rue Sioufi

Rue Ghazilieh

Rue Sassine

Rue Ikhwan El-Safa

Cornich Pierre Gemayel

Badaro

Beirut River

■ Practical Information

Tourist Office: tel. 34 09 40, on Central Bank St., to the right when facing the Ministry of Tourism. The best of its kind in the Middle East. Fluent English-speakers distribute sleek, up-to-date maps and brochures for every region of the country.

Tourist Police: tel. 35 09 01. Available 24hr.

Tours: The **Nakhal and CIE Tour Company** (tel./fax 38 92 82) offers five-day tours of Lebanon leaving from Beirut for US$45-50 per day (lunch included), one-day tours to Baalbeck, Aanjar, and other sights, and week-long tours to Syria, Jordan, Cyprus, Egypt, Turkey, and Greece. Other tours can be arranged through the tourist office.

Embassies: Australia (tel. 34 70 80), in Ras Beirut. **U.K.** (tel. 40 36 40), in Rabyeh. **U.S.** (tel. 40 22 00), in Awkar. **Egypt** (tel. 83 03 14), in Ramlet Baida. **Jordan** (tel. 46 85 88), on Elias Helou St.

Currency Exchange: Foreign currency can be exchanged at any bank or currency exchange shop. **Fransabank** (tel. 34 01 80) is centrally located on Rue Hamra, where it intersects Central Bank St. The **Credit Lyonnais Liban** (tel. 34 03 50) is also in Hamra, on Rue Artois. Both exchange traveler's checks. Both open Mon.-Fri. 8am-1:30pm, Sat. 8am-noon.

American Express: tel. 34 18 25, in the Gefinor Center on Rue Clemenceau. Will hold mail if notified in advance.

Buses, Taxies, Car Rental and Flights: See **Transportation,** above.

English Bookstore: Nawfal Booksellers, on Rue Artois. An excellent English-language magazine and travel guide selection. **Librairie Antoine,** on Rue Hamra, has an extensive collection of books and magazines in French, with a smaller selection of English books.

Laundry: Five Star Cleaners (tel. 74 28 56), on Rue Nehme Yafet just off Jeanne d'Arc St. Laundry and dry cleaning services.

Pharmacies: Pharmacie Rishani (tel. 84 28 31), on Rue Artois in Hamra. A multilingual staff speaks English, French, and Arabic. Open Mon.-Fri. 8am. **Mazen's Pharmacy,** in Mazra'a, is open 24hr.

Hospital: American University of Beirut Hospital (tel. 34 04 60), in Hamra. The best in Beirut.

Internet Access: You can have your web and eat it too at **University Snack,** on Bliss St. and **Web Cafe,** on Makhoul St. See **Food,** below, for prices and hours.

Telephones: The telephone office in Hamra is located in a small, glassy room under the Ministry of Tourism. To the U.S. or U.K. L£3000 per min.; to Australia or New Zealand L£3600 per min. Open daily 8am-10pm. **Telephone Code:** 01.

■ Accommodations

Finding decent budget lodging in Beirut can be difficult. There are a few "hostels" that are barely inhabitable and a full host of luxury resorts, but little in the middle range. All hotels listed here are centrally located in the Hamra district, near the American University of Beirut (AUB) campus, an area with lots of cheap eats and frequent public transportation.

West House Residence (tel. 35 04 50), near the corner of Rue Artois and Rue Abdel-Aziz. During the academic year, many AUB students call this reputable establishment home. Fully equipped rooms with mini-fridge, A/C, private bath, TV, and kitchenette. Streetside rooms are noisy. Private room for 1 or 2 is US$40.

Mushrek Hotel (tel. 34 57 73). Breezy terrace and relatively clean rooms, but less-than-sparkling bathrooms. Singles L£33,000; doubles L£44,000; triples L£66,000.

Embassy Hotel (tel. 34 08 14, fax 34 08 15), Rue Makdissi, across from the post office. Pleasant lobby. Dark rooms with A/C, TV, mini-fridge, private bath, and springy mattresses. Singles L£50,000; doubles L£70,000; triples L£82,000. When considering your options, add a 14 percent service charge—they do.

San Lorenzo Hotel (tel. 34 86 04 or 05), on Rue Hamra just above the Taverne Suisse Restaurant. Sparsely furnished rooms have fans and bright fluorescent

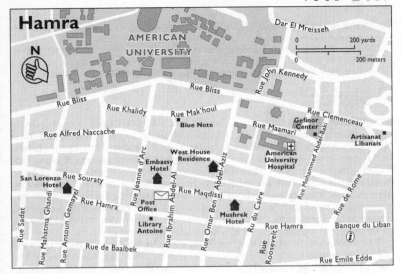

Hamra

AMERICAN
UNIVERSITY

Dar El Mreisseh

0   200 yards
0   200 meters

N

Rue Bliss
Rue Bliss
Rue Khalidy
Rue Mak'houl
Rue John Kennedy
Rue Clemenceau
Gefinor
Center
Rue Maamari
Blue Note
Rue Alfred Naccache
Artisanat
Libanais
Rue Jeanne d'Arc
West House
Residence
Embassy
Hotel
American
University
Hospital
Rue Mohammed Abdel-Baki
San Lorenzo
Hotel
Rue Souraty
Rue Hamra
Post
Office
Rue Maqdissi
Rue Omar Ben Abdel-Aziz
Rue du Caire
Rue de Rome
Rue Mahatma Ghandi
Rue Antoun Gemayel
Rue Ibrahim Abdel-Al
Rue Sadat
Library
Antoine
Mushrek
Hotel
Rue Hamra
Banque du Liban
Rue de Baalbek
Rue Roosevelt
Rue Emile Edde
(i)

lamps. Singles L£30,000, with bath L£35,000; doubles L£35,000, with bath
L£45,000.

■ Food

European pub grub, cafe fare, and Lebanese favorites are all part of Beirut's food
scene. "Snacks" are sandwich shops with little ambience but good value. The Hamra
district, especially around AUB, is packed with small, affordable eateries.

Hamadeh Snack, at the corner of Rue Jumblatt and Central Bank St. in Hamra—
look for the Arabic Pepsi sign. Delicious *mana'ish* with *za'atar,* lamb, and cheese
L£1000-2000. Try the *"beetza"* with olives and mushrooms for L£3000. Open daily
8am-11pm.

Flying Pizza, on Rue Makhloul, next door to the Web Cafe. Make-your-own Italiano-
Lebanese pizza, thick or thin crust, featuring a special secret-recipe spicy tomato
sauce (small pizza L£5500; toppings L£1250 each). Open daily noon-midnight.

Eagle's Nest Pub and Grill, Rue Jeanne d'Arc. Oak paneling with greasy pub food
to match. Buffalo wings (L£6000), chicken tenders (L£8000), and burgers
(L£6000). Local beer L£3000, imports L£5000. Open Mon.-Sat. noon-2am.

Four Meals Snack, on Rue Artois. Serves Lebanese sandwiches (L£750-2500) and
appetizers (L£1500). Huge portions of lasagna can be yours to go (L£5000). Serves
the only hummus *fatteh* to be found in Beirut (L£5000). Open Mon.-Sat. 7am-8pm.

Bakkar, on Rue Nehme Yafet next to the Napoleon Hotel. Fresh falafel and *shawerma* sandwiches (L£1500-2500), as well as *"rosto,"* a Lebanese rendering of the
roast beef sandwich (L£3000).

Euro Cafe, Rue Artois under the Elegant Suites. This outdoor Parisian wannabe has
great selection and attitude you'll pay for. Salads and sandwiches (L£6000-8000),
fettucine alfredo (L£8000), and traditional Lebanese breakfasts (L£7000). Fresh
fruit juice (L£2500) and local beer (L£3500). Top it all off with a *creme caramel*
(L£3000).

University Snack, Rue Bliss. This AUB institution serves fresh falafel and *shawerma*
with appetizing salads (L£1000-3000). Get on-line while you munch: Internet
access L£1000 for 5min. Open Mon.-Fri. 7am-11pm.

Web Cafe, on Rue Makhoul, in Hamra. For caffeine and Internet addicts. Gourmet
sandwiches (L£5000-8000) and espresso drinks (L£2000-3000). Ask about student
discounts. Open daily noon-midnight.

Henry J. Bean's, on Rue Madame Curie. Junkyard decor adorns this London-based
franchise. "Hank's," as it is popularly known, offers burgers, huge sandwiches, and

legendary hot dogs (entrees L£8000-15000; L£2000 cover charge). Also see **Entertainment,** below.

720 is easily mistaken for a misplaced runway off the coastal highway between Beirut and Jounieh. A unique opportunity to eat gourmet food in a real plane. Decent burgers L£8000, complemented by a great view of Harissa Mountain.

■ Sights

Beirut's archaeological heritage goes back at least 5000 years. Since the war ended in 1991, the reconstruction effort, combined with urban archeological digging initiatives, has peeled back otherwise inaccessible layers of destroyed cityscape. Lebanese and foreign teams have uncovered ancient ruins that are in process of being catalogued and, in some cases, taken apart to be deposited in city parks. Behind Central Bank Street near the Port, are the remains of a large **Roman bath.** Originally discovered in 1968, it underwent a thorough excavation and cleaning over the past two years. Near Central Bank St., the Solidere Company's **reconstruction project** is renovating and restoring over 265 existing structures. Solidere (tel. (01) 646 129) has been known to offer **tours** of the rebuilding sites upon request.

The wealthy suburb of Raouche, on Beirut's western tip, boasts cliff-side cafes and a Promenade with beautiful views of one of Beirut's landmarks, **Pigeon Rocks.** The two rocks are huge formations just off the coast; one has a hole in the center through which boats pass. The shores near Pigeon Rocks have yielded the oldest evidence of human existence in Beirut. The flints and basic tools that were found are now displayed in the American University of Beirut **Archaeological Museum.** Small but chock full of local history, it is definitely worth a visit. The AUB and the Museum are on Rue Bliss, in the Hamra district (museum open 10am-4pm, except on academic holidays). The AUB campus is a nice place for a picnic, as well.

The **National Museum** was ready to open its doors in 1938, but tension leading to World War II delayed the opening until 1942. When the war broke out in 1975, the museum closed, and it is still undergoing restoration and renovation. Most of the treasures were sent to Germany for safekeeping or kept in the National Bank vaults. Large pieces that could not be moved were cased in concrete boxes. The front of the museum, once pocked with bullet holes, has now been completely fixed, although at press time the inside was closed to the public. The first floor is scheduled to open within the next year.

■ Entertainment

BARS, CLUBS, AND DISCOS

Lebanese who can afford it support a thriving dance and party scene. During the war, clubs in the northern suburbs of Jounieh and Kaslik helped Beirutis forget about life for a while. When the darkest years of conflict ended, discos and bars filled up with optimistic youth, newly mobilized by the end of sniper threats and car bombings. Recently, Ras Beirut (downtown West Beirut) has become a club mecca that rivals the suburban scene. Downtown is throbbing with a new beat after years of boarded-up silence, making it a convenient place to mingle at local watering holes. Unfortunately, after-hours public transportation to suburbia is limited to private taxis, which makes excursions to some hotspots prohibitively expensive. All of the places listed below are accessible from Beirut by bus or *service* before midnight and should cost no more than US$10 for return taxi fare to Beirut.

In the City

Orange Mechanique (formerly BO-18), Sin el-Fil. The most popular and notorious discotheque in Beirut, as well as one of the very few that tend to attract gay patrons. Follow the eclectic crowds and professional dancers for a melange of New York City techno, acid jazz, and rave. No cover. Drinks L£7000-10000. Drinking starts at 10pm; dancing at midnight.

Henry J.Bean's, "but his friends call him Hank." Located across from the Terra Sancta College on Rue Madame Curie. The bar and its English-speaking bartenders hold happy hour daily 4-8pm, when imported beers can be consumed at half-price (L£4000-8000).

L'Escroc (also known as **Cheap Shots**), on Rue Al-Inglisi. True to its nickname, cheap shots, massively consumed, make this Achrafiyyeh favorite a great place to start the night. If you'd rather inhale smoke than alcohol, you can suck on an *argeileh* here. Shooters L£4000-6000.

Miles' Ras Beirut palace has plush sofas, thick carpets, and an outdoor fountain that create the perfect setting for mellow jazz and occasional live music on weekends. No cover. Drinks L£10,000.

Pacifico, off Rue Monot in Achrafiyyeh. A cocktail menu that will keep you giggling till dawn (shooters L£5000-7500, mixed drinks 8500-11,000). They also supply cigars (L£9500-33,500), Latin American food (L£9000-11,000), Almaza beer (L£4000), and Corona (L£6000). Happy hour Mon.-Sat. 7-9pm.

Hard Rock Cafe, Ain Mreisseh. This American original serves the usual over-priced burgers (L£10,000-12,000) and beers (L£4500-8000), in a glassy, paraphernalia-littered hall.

Blue Note, on Rue Makhoul, Hamra. An excessively ambient jazz joint, serving pasta lunches (L£8000-13000). Live music Friday and Saturday nights. Cover L£6000. Local beer L£3900, imported L£6000.

Monkey Rose. A younger crowd, mostly hip 16-18 year olds, grooves the night away to rave, trance, and acid jazz. No cover. Drinks L£6000-10,000.

Jounieh and environs

Oliver's, in Old Jounieh. The first disco to open in the area, this mirrored *boîte* is often crowded to capacity. The US$12 cover charge buys two drinks and the privilege of bouncing to mostly commercial hip-hop and dance music.

Crazy/Duplex, on the main road in Kaslik. This dance complex is divided into two huge dance floors. The loud music at Crazy attracts "alternative," cellular-toting Beirutis—strictly rave, with cage dancers everywhere. Duplex plays hip-hop and reggae music for a more diverse clientele. US$15 cover admits you to both. Mixed drinks L£10,000.

Janneh, Beit Meri. A tropical food and drink complex that lives up to its name, which means "heaven" in Arabic. Waterfall, pond, and crossbridge flow through 2 restaurants specializing in Oriental and Western cuisine (entrees L£10,000-18,000). The 2 bars serve beer (L£4000-8000) and mixed drinks (L£7000-10000) to get you started.

SHOPPING AND OTHER SPORTS

Beirut is known for its cheap, high-quality gold and silver jewelry, traditional crafts, perfume, embroidery, intricate inlay work, and gold-leaf calligraphy. Beautiful and affordable Lebanese crafts can be found at the **Artisanat Libanais,** on Rue Clemenceau opposite the old French embassy, and at the branch next to the St. Georges Hotel downtown. "*Les Artisans,*" as these cooperative craft unions are also called, are non-profit—all revenue goes to the artists themselves. There are jewelry shops on every corner in Beirut, but it is a good idea to ask a trustworthy local for directions to an honest shop. Bargaining for gold and silver is usually acceptable, but prices are

LEBANON

Leave It to Beaver

The Beirut Golf Club is famous for its members' stubborn insistence on maintaining their daily routine during the war, despite the nuisances that bombing and an Israeli invasion posed. Calmly dodging bullets and swinging clubs around fallen shells, dozens of golf fanatics (some say lunatics) showed up on the green during Beirut's worst conflicts, carrying only their equipment and a will to live. BGC legend has it that one Mr. George Beaver, an 82 year-old retired English expat and a club member, refused to let the war gain the upper hand—he played every single day, whether the sky was clear or raining artillery.

fixed at the Artisanat. Beirut's *souqs* were once world-renowned, but were destroyed during the war and have not yet been restored.

More virile sporting urges may be quelled at the **Beirut Racetrack,** where pure-bred Arabian horses run every Sunday. Beirut's posh **Golf Club** is open to foreigners who can use the nine-hole course, swimming pool, and squash and tennis courts for a fee (varies with activity; around L£20,000). The Club survived some difficult times: in 1982 the Israeli army bulldozed the gold club pavilion, and in 1989 alone 360 shells landed on the course. The Mediterranean is too polluted for swimming, but there are several **swimming pools** open to visitors. The cleanest and best is at the St. George Hotel downtown (L£20,000 for use of pool and facilities for 1 day).

NEAR BEIRUT

■ Beit ed Din

The Beit ed Din palace is a breathtaking example of early 19th century Lebanese architecture, located 17km up the coastal highway, 26km inland, and 850m above Beirut. It was built over a thirty year period by the dashing Emir Bechir el-Chehab II, ruler of Mount Lebanon for over half a century.

In the Middle Ages, Lebanon was divided into autonomous fiefs, each with its own ruler. In the early 17th century, Emir Fakhr ed Din II Maan wasn't satisfied with just one fief, so he enterprisingly set out to annex his neighbors' land. Such were his abilities of persuasion that, after a decade or so, he controlled an area corresponding to the present-day boundaries of Lebanon. His first capital was at Baaqline, but a water shortage there sent him scurrying to Deir el-Qamar (Monastery of the Moon), a village 5km from Beit ed Din. When the Maan dynasty finally died out, the lucky emirs of the Chehab family inherited all of their hard-earned spoils. Emir Bechir, perhaps haunted by the ghost of his overachieving forbearers, decided to leave the old capital at Deir el-Qamar and build his own posh pad at Beid ed Din (House of Faith). Beit ed Din was at that time a Druze hermitage, which is still part of the palace. Determined not to repeat the inconveniences of the past, the newly-empowered Emir drafted healthy male subjects in 1812 and signed them up for two days of unpaid labor working to make sure he would never be thirsty. Within two years, the palace had plumbing.

Lacking the *je ne sais quoi* of Fakhr ed Din, Emir Bechir was unable to smooth-talk the invading Ottomans, who forced him into exile in 1840. By 1942, the palace and its plumbing had been put to use as the Ottoman government residence. Under the French Mandate following World War I, it was again used for local administration. Beit ed Din was declared a historic monument in 1934, and then a national monument after Lebanon's independence in 1943. Lebanon's first president began a tradition of spending summers in the palace; President Bechara el-Khoury thought it would be a nice touch to bring Emir Bechir's remains back home from Istanbul, where he had died in 1850—too late to enjoy his ingenious plumbing (palace open Tues.-Sun. 9am-6pm; L£4000). Beit ed Din is accessible by *service* from Beirut. The tourist office in Beirut provides a detailed floor plan and sight map that is worth picking up. The **Beit ed Din Festival** is held annually in July and August in the outdoor courtyard of the palace. It draws thousands and features international performers, usually including one Egyptian or other Arab performer. Ask at the tourist office for details.

The **Emir Amine Palace** perches just up the hill to the right of Beit ed Din. Emir Bechir liked to spoil his children; he built three palaces, one each for his sons Qassim, Khalil, and Amine. Qassim's is now in ruins and Khalil's is used as the Serail (seat of local government) of Beit ed Din, but Amine's estate has proved to be Bechir's greatest investment. It is now a fully restored super-luxury hotel with 24 rooms, each with a private terrace and hanging garden. Not quite budget accommodations, but looking is free and worthwhile.

■ Jeita Grotto

The Jeita Grotto, one of the largest and most intricately carved caverns in the world, is located 20km north of Beirut off the coastal highway near the village of Zouk Mikael. The entire inside of a wooded mountain has been hollowed out by Nahr el-Kalb (Dog River). The caverns house the source of the river, and the soaring cathedral of latticed stalactites and stalagmites is perhaps the most spectacular sight in Lebanon. The grotto has been known to humans since the Paleolithic age according to archaeologists, but credit for the most recent and well-publicized discovery goes to an American, Reverend William Thomson, a missionary who ventured 50 meters into the cave. Once he reached the underground river, he fired his gun and the echoes told him of the immensity of his find—the still water in the lower gallery of the cavern is named Thomson's Pool.

Minister of Tourism Nicolas Fattouche, responsible for reopening the grotto after the war, decided to hire a German company, Mapas, to overhaul the attraction and make it kitschy enough to draw Disney-lovers. Mapas did not disappoint—a little replica of a steam engine can now tug you the 50 meters to the entrance from the parking lot if you don't feel like taking one of the four "Austrian" cable cars. (Open Tues.-Thurs. 9am-6pm, Fri.-Sun. 9am-7pm. L£13,500 admission includes entrance to the upper and lower grottos, train or cable rides, a boat tour of Thompson's Pool, and a short film in the language of your choice.)

NORTH OF BEIRUT

■ Tripoli

Tripoli (*Trablos*) is the "capital of the North," a time capsule that preserves a way of life all but gone from the rest of the region. The city's mellow flavor is a complete reversal from the tart modernity of Beirut. The progressive capital is forever pushing to get ahead of its own latest trends, while Tripoli comfortably basks in its long traditions.

Tripoli's rich history began when the Phoenicians established a small port in the Al-Mina area in 9th century BCE. It was taken over by the Persians, the successors of Alexander the Great, and then the Romans in 64 BCE. In 551 AD, an earthquake and a tidal wave completely destroyed the port town. In 638 AD, the Mamluks settled the area and ruled until 1109, when the Crusaders took the city. The 11th century, before the Crusader invasion, is widely regarded as the city's golden age, a time when Tripoli flourished as an intellectual center, complete with library. After staving off one Crusading leader by bribery and persuasion in the 1090s, its leaders succumbed to the fierce Crusader Raymond Saint-Gilles in 1099. The occupation lasted for 180 years. In 1289, the Mamluks had their revenge: years of scheming and minor skirmishes paid off when they were finally able to send the Crusaders packing, and they set to work fortifying the peninsula from further attacks. Mamluk Sultan Qalaoun razed the old Crusader city to the ground and built a new one, now known as Al-Madina, at the foot of the hill near the castle. The Mamluks ruled until 1516. The *khans, hammams,* mosques, and *madrasas* that dot the city today remain from this period, the city's second golden age. When the Ottomans came to power in the region, Sultan Suleiman I, ruling from 1520 to 1566, kept the city unchanged, and even restored many of its treasures. The Ottomans ruled for 400 years until the 1918 French Mandate.

Today, Tripoli's rich past is reflected in the continuing use of ancient soap factories, *hammams*, and *souqs*. The smell of its famous sweets wafts through the air with a lethargy that Beirut has never experienced. Wandering through the twisted streets may lead to hidden treasures you weren't even looking for, whether it be a Roman column supporting a vendor's stall in the *souq* or a relaxing scrub-down in a historic *hammam*.

PRACTICAL INFORMATION

The **tourist office** is located in Karami Square, the first main square if you enter the city from the south. It provides a historical map and some pamphlets. Excellent English is spoken at **Pharmacie Hajar,** on the east side of Tall Sq. (tel. 434 939; open Mon.-Fri. 8am-8pm, Sat. 8am-1:30pm). Send mail fast at the **DHL office** on Fouad Chehab St. in Helou Plaza, about 1km north of Tall Sq. (tel. 433 205; 1kg. of paper to any destination, US$50). The main **post office** is on Fouad Chehab St., north of Tall Sq. (open Mon.-Sat. 8am-2pm).

Buses to **Beirut** (L£2000) leave every 30 minutes from the Ahdam Bus Station, just west of Tall Sq. *Service* to Beirut (L£4000) depart from the south side of the square. *Service* to **Bcharré** (L£5000) and the mountains leave from Koura Sq., near the Ahram Hotel. The **Karnak Bus** office is located around the right-hand corner from Ahdam, and runs daily buses to **Damascus** (S£250), **Homs** (S£200), **Hama** (S£220), **Aleppo** (S£250), and **Lattakia** (S£250). Tripoli's **phone code** is 06.

ACCOMMODATIONS AND FOOD

Accommodations are generally much less crowded and less expensive than in Beirut. Many tourists make Tripoli a long day trip from Beirut, but a few nights' stay allows more leisurely exploration of the northern half of the country.

Tall Hotel (tel. 628 407), on Tall St., about 1km east of Tall Sq. By far the best value in Tripoli. Genuinely friendly management. Spotless, carpeted rooms US$15 per person; deluxe rooms with A/C, TV, and mini-fridge US$20.

Palace Hotel (tel. 432 257), on Tall St., just off Tall Sq. The Palatial reception area with attractive Orientalist ceilings seems to earn the hotel its name, but the rooms are anticlimactic, with spotty floors. Beautiful stained-glass windows throughout the hotel. Singles US$10, with bath US$15; doubles US$20, with bath US$30.

Ahram Hotel, in Koura Sq. Less-than-sparkling rooms and even worse bathrooms are hard on the nose, but there is a pleasant lounge area that catches nice breezes. Mostly men. Bed in a shared room L£5000; singles L£10,000; doubles L£15,000.

Fast food with a Middle Eastern twist can be found at **Big Bite,** on the corner of Tall St. and Fouad Chehab St. Falafel meets French fries at this bustling fast food haven, where you can get a burger (L£3000) with a side of hummus (L£1500). For a pleasant and affordable Middle Eastern sit-down meal, try the **Continental Rest,** on Tall St., where *kebab* and hummus can be yours for under L£5000.

Tripoli is famous for sweets containing a special kind of cream, called *'ashta* (see **Food**, p. 555). Some of the best sweets in town are at **Hallab Brothers,** on Tall St. Try their syrupy baklava (L£1500 per ¼kg.), or Tripoli's scrumptious specialty, *halawat al-jibn* (L£250 per ¼kg.; open daily 5:30am-10pm). (See also al-Mawiyye, below.)

SIGHTS

Tripoli is divided into two sections, **Al Mina** (the old area around the port) and **Al Madina** (the new). The old city, centered around the fortified Citadel, was built by Mamluk Sultan Qalaoun in 1289, when the Mamluks regained control of Tripoli after 180 years of Crusader occupation. To get to Al Mina, head east, to the right of the clock tower in Karami Square. The green-domed **Taynal Mosque,** the most beautiful mosque in Tripoli, was built in 1336 by Saif ed Din Taynal on the site of a ruined Crusader Carmelite church. This location was outside the limits of the Mamluk city, and was originally a Roman Temple to Zeus, then a Byzantine church, and finally the Crusader structure. Visitors are sometimes allowed to climb the minaret (free; women must wear a full-length cloak; no shoes).

After leaving the mosque, turn right and then left towards an area called Bab al-Hadeed, and you will pass **Ahwa Moussa,** one of the oldest coffee houses in the city. Just before you reach **Hammam al-Jadeed,** you will reach **al-Mawiyye,** paradise disguised as an ordinary sweet-shop. Their speciality is *halawet al-jibn.* The Hammam is the largest in Tripoli, built in 1740 but non-functional since the 1970s.

Through the arch in the same direction is a **souq,** crammed full of baskets, overflowing stalls, and the smell of rotting organic matter underfoot. Don't slip on the fish heads, beef entrails, or chicken claws that litter the cobblestones. A street running perpendicular to the *souq* leads to two *madrasas* (Qur'anic schools): the Madrasa al-Khatuniyyah, built in 1373, and the Madrasa al-Saqraqiyyah, built in 1359. The inscriptions above the Khatuniyyah door list the details of the *waqf,* or endowment left by the founder for the students and the poor. On the other wall is the image of a cup, a symbol that recalls the Mamluks' days as slaves. The Madrasa al-Saqraqiyyah was founded by a soldier, and its dome stands over a former Mamluk tomb.

Continuing on to the right is the **Great Mosque.** It was built from 1294 to 1315 on the remains of a ruined 12th-century Crusader cathedral. Remains of Western architecture from the old church have been incorporated into the mosque structure; most notably, the Lombard style bell tower was transformed into the minaret (free; modest dress; women must cover themselves with a full-length cloak available at the entrance; no shoes). Near the mosque are two *madrasa,* the Madrasa al-Shamsiyat and an unnamed madrasa from the same period.

Beyond the Great Mosque, the **Hammam al-Abd** (bath of the slave) is still in use. After the road forks on the left, it leads to the Khan al-Sabun, the soap factory. It was an Ottoman construction, and although it was used as recently as 1970, it looks tired. At the end of the small alley, a right and then a left leads you back to the main north-south *souq.* At the end of the main street is the brass *souq.* A right turn after that takes you to the Hammam Izz al-Din, completed in 1298, which is the oldest and largest Turkish bath in the city. The *souq* to the right of the *hammam* leads to vendors who can give you directions to another soap factory, this one still in use, producing colorfully psychedelic, swirly soap bars.

A visit to the **Citadel** takes you to the heart of Al Mina. The Citadel, at the heart of the *souqs, hammams, mosques,* and *madrasas,* is known as **Qal'at Sinjil** (Saint Gilles). Raymond Saint-Gilles was the Crusading tough guy who took the city from the Mamluks in 1099. The castle has been renovated and changed many times during its history; today's remaining features include an octagonal Fatimid construction converted to a church by the Crusaders and some visibly layered Mamluk and Ottoman additions from the 14th and 16th centuries, respectively. A stroll to the top of the building yields an impressive view of Tripoli (open Sun.-Tues. 10am-6pm; L£2000).

■ Near Tripoli

BCHARRÉ

Bcharré is the birthplace of Gibran Khalil Gibran, one of the greatest Lebanese writers in history. At 1400 meters above sea level, the quiet mountain air of the small village is a refreshing break from the noise and pollution of the bigger cities. The **Gibran museum** in itself is worth the trip. It houses the author's personal library and many of his drawings, paintings, manuscripts, and letters (open daily 9am-5pm; in winter closed Mon.; L£3000, students L£2000). Gibran was a romantic, fascinated by the interplay of humans with each other and with God. Born in Bcharré in 1883, he immigrated to Boston, Massachusetts at a very young age with his mother, his two sisters, and his half-brothers. In 1898 he returned to Lebanon to spend the summer with his father in Bcharré and then attend the Sagesse College in Beirut, where he studied Arabic and French. In 1902 he returned to Boston. In the next two years, his sister and brother died of tuberculosis and his mother of cancer. After traveling through Paris, where he met artist Auguste Rodin in 1908, Gibran returned to Boston. In Boston, he wrote his masterpiece, *The Prophet,* in English. By the time he died in 1931, he had published seventeen works in Arabic and English. His body was returned to the hermitage in Bcharré, an old hermit's cavern, for burial.

Bcharré is best reached by *service* from Tripoli (about L£3000). Since the town's two budget hotels closed, the only reasonably priced accommodations are at the **Palace Hotel,** which sports clean, simple rooms with amazing mountain views (tel. 671 460; singles US$25; doubles US$35). **Shallal Rest,** next to the waterfall up the road from the museum, serves pizzas (L£5000), burgers (L£6000), and potato salad (L£1500) in a pleasant outdoor setting. **Les Copains Cafeteria,** next door, offers excellent *mana'ish* and meat pizzas (L£1500), as well as burgers and grills (L£2500-3500). The **telephone code** is 06.

THE CEDARS

The Cedars of Lebanon (*Arz el Rab;* literally, Cedars of God) are more than just groves of immense, rare trees perched in the mountains. They are an image of national pride, resort for winter skiing, and symbol of history. The cedars can be reached by *service* via Bcharré, or from Deir al Ahmar in the Beqaa valley. The trees are what remain of a once-thick blanket of primeval forest. They were decimated for timber trade with Egypt (they used the resin for mummification), for Phoenician shipbuilding, and for Roman temple and tomb construction. The few remaining patches have been protected since 1876. Although a stroll through the grove near Bcharré is free, donations toward the preservation of this national treasure are happily accepted. The tourist office in Beirut has detailed information on winter skiing and snowboarding in the area.

SOUTH OF BEIRUT

■ Saida (Sidon)

Now therefore command that cedars of Lebanon be cut for me...for you know that there is no one among us who knows how to cut timber like the Sidonians.

-1 Kings 5:6

Saida (Sidon was the Phoenician name) is located 48km south of Beirut and is the middle of the three great Phoenician city-states (the other two are Byblos and Tyre). Although many of Saida's ancient artifacts were plundered and sold by treasure hunters in the 19th century (some have even turned up on the black market recently), there is a lot left to see in southern Lebanon's largest city. Saida has a rich history, with evidence of habitation dating from 4000 BCE. The port flourished in the Phoenician era (10th-12th centuries BCE), and the city peaked during the Persian Empire (550-330 BCE). Although glass manufacture was Sidon's biggest industry, it became most famous for its **purple dye,** made from the small shell of the Murex snail. The dye was so beautiful and so rare that it became the mark of royalty. Like other Phoenician city-states, Sidon suffered under a succession of conquerors, including Alexander the Great in 333 BCE, the Romans, the Crusaders, and Salah ad Din in 1187 CE. Skirmishes between Mamluks and Crusaders continued until 1291, when the city was finally conquered by the Mamluks. It fell into obscurity during the French Mandate, and then revived as an urban center as recently as in the last 100 years.

The **old city** developed at the end of the Crusader period and contains *souqs, khans,* and other Medieval remnants. The most interesting sight is the **Sea Castle,** a Crusader fortress built on a small island, connected to the shore by a stone walkway (open Tues.-Sun. 9am-6pm; L£5000). Fishermen mend their nets on the beach by the entrance. The **souqs** lie between the Sea Castle and the **Castle of St. Louis** (*Qal'at el Muizz*), a 13th-century structure that was erected on top of a Fatimid fortress during a Crusade led by French King Louis IX. The **Great Mosque** is south of the *souq* on the way to the Castle of St. Louis. **Murex Hill** is just south of the Castle of St. Louis; the

Hill is a 50m mound of snail-shell refuse left by ancient Sidonians who didn't clean up after their dye factory. The three main **Necropoli of Sidon** (Magharat Abloun, Ayaa, and Ain el Helwe) lie outside the old city limits. Located in residential areas, they have not yet been excavated. Buses and *service* to Saida leave regularly from the Cola bridge in Beirut (L£2000). Saida's **telephone code** is 07.

∎ Sur (Tyre)

> *Behold, I am against you, O Tyre, and will bring up many nations against*
> *you, as the sea brings up its waves. They shall destroy the walls of Tyre,*
> *and break down her towers; and I will scrape her soil from her, and make*
> *her a bare rock.*
>
> —Ezekiel 26:3

The modern city of Sur and the remains of the ancient Phoenician city-state of Tyre are located 79km south of Beirut. Originally, Tyre was a mainland settlement with a city on an off-shore island. **Herodotus,** "Father of History," visited Tyre in the 5th century BCE and described the famous but now long gone **Temple of Melqart** (better known as Heracles). The city-state's King Hiram is known for providing the cedar wood for Solomon to build his temple, as recounted in the Bible. Tyrenians' many successes—as renowned traders, Murex purple dye producers, and glass manufacturers—attracted the usual empire-building conquerors. The city staved off invaders for 13 years before being toppled by Babylonian troops in 685 BCE. After the Persians, Alexander the Great captured Tyre by building a causeway between the mainland and the island city. The most interesting remains today are of Roman origin and can be found at the mainland sight, just over 1km from the coast.

The Roman city begins with a **monumental archway** and *cardo* (main street), and includes the remains of large civic buildings, an **aqueduct, baths,** and a **theater.** The **necropolis** has yielded hundreds of ornate stone and marble sarcophogi. A few of the most important were taken to the National Museum in Beirut, but many were left in their original locations. The necropolis today looks like a vandalized graveyard, with open sarcophogi littering the grounds—some still contain **skeletal remains.** Tyre's larger-than-life **hippodrome** is one of the largest and best preserved in the world. It was discovered around 70 years ago under 6m of windswept sand. During Roman times it seated over 20,000 spectators who gathered regularly to witness and place bets on madcap chariot races. *Service* are available from Beirut (L£7000) and Saida (L£2000). Sur's **telephone code** is 07.

EAST OF BEIRUT

∎ Baalbeck

Baalbeck, 86km from Beirut, is Lebanon's greatest Roman treasure, a majestic temple complex towering over the fertile Beqaa plain. It was originally named after the Phoenician God Ba'al. Greeks and Romans called the city Heliopolis (City of the Sun), and the Romans chose it as the site for a major center of worship for three of their Gods: Jupiter (the Roman version of Ba'al), Venus (the Roman version of Astarte, Ba'al's consort), and Mercury (the messenger of the gods). When Christianity became the official religion of the Roman Empire in 313 CE, Emperor Constantine closed the Baalbeck temples. At the end of the 4th century, Emperor Theodosius tore down Jupiter's altars in the **Great Court** of the complex and built a **basilica** using the temple's stones. The remains of the three apses of this basilica, originally oriented to the west, can still be seen in the upper part of the stairway in the Temple of Jupiter. After the Arab Conquest in 636 CE the temples were transformed into a fortress (*qal'aa*). Baalbeck then fell successively to the Umayyad, Abbasid, Toulounid, Fatimid and Ayyoubid dynasties. Although sacked by the Mongols around 1260, it eventually enjoyed serenity under the Mamluks.

The **Temple of Jupiter** is easily recognizable because of its six remaining 22m-high Corinthian columns. The columns hint at the immensity of the original standing structure, which was completed in about 60 BCE. Jupiter's **Propylaea** and **Hexagonal Court** were added in the 3rd century CE. The small, circular **Temple of Venus** dates from this time as well. The **Temple of Bacchus** is the most well-preserved building in the complex. While the great monuments were clearly dedicated to the Heliopolitan trio, exquisite reliefs of grapes and poppies on the main door indicate that this newer place of worship (completed in the 2nd century CE) was consecrated to a small cult of Bacchus, which drank wine and smoked opium in rituals. Bacchus's temple is the site of the world-famous **Baalbeck Festival.** The festival began in 1955 and continued until 1974, drawing performers like Ella Fitzgerald, Rudolf Nureyev, and Margot Fonteyn. Since the war ended, the festival has revived and has been wildly successful. Get tickets in advance for next year's July-August bash—almost the whole country attends, and **buses** are available there and back from Beirut for around US$6. *Service* run to Baalbeck from both the Cola and the Barbir bridges in Beirut (L£10,000). Baalbeck's **telephone code** is 08.

APPENDIX

HOLIDAYS AND FESTIVALS

All festivals and holidays in Israel last from sundown the night before to nightfall the next day. For longer holidays, businesses are closed for the first day (and in the case of Passover, the last day) but remain open for the rest of the duration. Be aware that Friday (*Juma'a*) is the holy day in the Muslim world and that Saturday (*Shabbat*) is the holy day in Israel; expect many businesses to be closed on these days. Jewish holidays are celebrated by in Israel. Islamic holidays are celebrated in Egypt, Jordan, Syria, Lebanon, and the West Bank, and by the Arab population in Israel. Businesses and services may be inaccessible during these holidays, as well as during national holidays, also listed below. Christian holidays listed are those of the Eastern Orthodox or Maronite Church and celebrated among Christians in Syria and Lebanon.

Date	Festival	Type
Nov. 28, 1997	Isra' and Miraj	Islamic
Dec. 14	Peasant's Day	Syrian
Dec. 23	Victory Day	Egyptian
Dec. 24-25	Christmas	Christian
Dec. 24-31	Hanukkah, 1997	Jewish
Dec. 31	First Day of Ramadan	Islamic
Jan. 15, 1998	Tree Day	Jordanian
Jan. 16	Nuzulul Qur'an	Islamic
Jan. 30	'Eid al-Fitr (end of Ramadan)	Islamic
Feb. 9	Mar Maroun	Christian (Lebanon)
Feb. 28	Union Day	Egyptian
Mar. 8	Revolution Day	Syrian
Mar. 12	Purim	Jewish
Mar. 21	Women's Day	Syrian
Mar. 22	Arab League Day	Syrian, Jordanian
April 8	'Eid al-Adha	Islamic
April 11-17	Passover	Jewish
April 17	Evacuation Day	Syrian
April 17	Good Friday	Christian
April 19	Easter	Christian
April 22	Yom Ha-Shoah	Israeli
April 25	Sinai Liberation	Egyptian
April 28	Islamic New Year	Islamic
April 29	Yom Ha-Zikaron	Israeli
April 30	Yom Ha-Atzmaut	Israeli
May 1	May Day	Egyptian
May 6	Martyr's Day	Syrian
May 7	Ashoora	Islamic
May 24	Yom Yerushalayim	Israeli
May 25	Labour Day	Jordanian
May 29	Security Force Day	Syrian
May 31	Shavuot	Jewish

June 7	Pentecost	**Christian**
June 10	Army Day and Anniversary of the Great Revolt	**Jordanian**
June 18	Evacuation Day	**Egyptian**
July 7	Mawlid Nabi	**Islamic**
July 23	Revolution Day	**Egyptian**
Aug. 2	Ninth of Av	**Jewish**
Aug. 11	Hussein's Accession	**Jordanian**
Aug. 15	Assumption of the Virgin Mary	**Christian**
Sept. 8	The Virgin's Birthday	**Christian**
Sept. 21-22	Rosh Ha-Shanah	**Jewish**
Sept. 30	Yom Kippur	**Jewish**
Oct. 5-11	Sukkot	**Jewish**
Oct. 6	National Day	**Egyptian**
Oct. 6	October War Day	**Syrian**
Oct. 12	Simhat Torah	**Jewish**
Oct. 16	Flight Day	**Syrian**
Oct. 24	Suez & National Liberation Day	**Egyptian**
Nov. 14	King Hussein's Birthday	**Jordanian**
Nov. 16	Correction Move Day	**Syrian**
Nov. 17	Isra' and Miraj	**Islamic**
Nov. 22	Independence Day	**Lebanese**
Dec. 13-20	Hanukkah	**Jewish**
Dec. 14	Peasant's Day	**Syrian**
Dec. 20	First Day of Ramadan	**Islamic**
Dec. 23	Victory Day	**Egyptian**
Dec. 24-25	Christmas	**Christian**

CLIMATE

The following chart gives the average high and low temperatures in degrees centigrade (Celsius) and the average rainfall in centimeters during four months of the year.

Temp in °C Rain in cm	January		April		July		October	
	Temp	**Rain**	**Temp**	**Rain**	**Temp**	**Rain**	**Temp**	**Rain**
Aleppo	10/2	8.9	24/9	2.8	34/21	0	27/12	2.5
Alexandria	19/11	4.8	23/15	.3	30/23	0	28/20	.5
Amman	16/4	6.9	23/9	1.5	32/18	0	27/14	.5
Aqaba/Eilat	21/10	0	31/18	.5	40/25	0	33/21	0
Aswan	25/10	0	36/19	0	42/26	0	37/22	0
Beirut	15/7	5.0	23/16	1.5	32/23	0	27/20	1.0
Cairo	18/8	.5	28/14	.3	36/21	0	30/18	.3
Damascus	12/2	4.3	24/9	1.3	36/18	0	27/12	1.0
Haifa	17/8	17.5	25/14	2.5	30/20	0	29/20	2.5
Jerusalem	11/6	13.2	23/10	2.8	29/19	0	27/15	1.3
Tel Aviv	19/10	20.2	27/15	3.0	37/25	0	32/20	2.0

To convert from °C to °F, multiply by 1.8 and add 32. For an approximation, double the Celsius and add 25. To convert from °F to °C, subtract 32 and multiply by 0.55.

°C	-5	0	5	10	15	20	25	30	35	40
°F	23	32	41	50	59	68	77	86	95	104

APPENDIX

TIME ZONES

The countries in this book reside entirely within one time zone, exactly two hours ahead of Greenwich Mean Time (GMT). During standard time, they are normally eight hours behind Sydney, two hours ahead of London, seven hours ahead of New York and Toronto, and ten hours ahead of California and Vancouver. During Daylight Savings time, however, such calculations are easily confused.

MEASUREMENTS

The metric system is used throughout the Middle East.

1 inch = 25 millimeter (mm)	1mm = 0.04 inch (in.)
1 foot (ft.) = 0.30 meter (m)	1m = 3.33 foot (ft.)
1 yard (yd.) = 0.91m	1m = 1.1 yard (yd.)
1 mile = 1.61kilometer (km)	1km = 0.62 mile (mi.)
1 ounce = 25 gram (g)	1g = 0.04 ounce (oz.)
1 pound (lb.) = 0.45 kilogram (kg)	1kg = 2.22 pound (lb.)
1 quart = 0.94 liter (L)	1 liter = 1.06 quart (qt.)

TELEPHONE CODES

EGYPT	
Alexandria	03
Aswan	097
Bahariyya	010
Cairo	02
Dakhla	092
Hurghada	065
Kharga	092
Luxor	095
Port Said	048
Sinai (all)	062
Suez	062

ISRAEL	
Akko/Haifa	04
Be'er Sheva	07
Eilat	07
Golan	06
Jerusalem	02
Nazareth	06
Tel Aviv	03
Tiberias	06
Tzfat	06

JORDAN	
Amman	06
Aqaba	03
Dead Sea	05
The Desert	06
Irbid	02
Madaba	08
Petra	03

SYRIA	
Aleppo	21
Damascus	11
Hama	21
Homs	31
Lattakia	31
Palmyra	34

LEBANON	
Baalbeck	08
Bcharre	06
Beirut	01
Saida	07
Sur	07
Tripoli	06

W. BANK	
North (Nablus)	09
Central (Ramallah)	02

APPENDIX

Country Codes

Egypt	20
Israel	972
Australia	61
Canada	1

Jordan	962
Lebanon	961
N. Z.	64
S. Africa	27

Syria	963
W. Bank	972
U. K.	44
U. S.	1

ARABIC (EL 'ARABI) العربى

Today's Arabic is actually two (some say three) distinct languages, and many, many dialects. **Classical Arabic (Fus-ha),** was the language of pre-Islamic Arabs and the Qur'an. Its complex rules of grammar were not fully developed until the Umayyad period, when the Islamic Empire rapidly expanded to include people of non-Arab origin (i.e., Turks and Persians). Today, the intricate complexity of the Classical, rigorously taught in schools and used for Qur'anic recitation, is every student's horror. A simplified version is used for writing, public speeches, and even cartoons on television. This less rigid form of classical Arabic has been packaged and sold to Westerners as "Modern Standard Arabic." Newspapers and television broadcasts throughout the Arab world are in Modern Standard. As its name suggests, the language is a modern invention—Classical Arabic taken down a notch and updated with terms like تكسى (taksee, taxi). The other species of the language is the **Colloquial ('Amiyya),** the speech of daily life. Dialects are so diverse that an Iraqi and a Palestinian meeting for the first time would sound like a Monty Python sketch. Educated Arabs can always fall back on the Classical, however stilted it may sound in conversation.

Arabic uses eight sounds not heard in English. *Kh* (خ) is like the Scottish or German *ch*; *gh* (غ) is like the French *r*. There are two "h" sounds; one (ه) sounds like an English "h" and the other (ح, in Mohammed) is somewhere between *kh* and plain *h*. The letter *'ayn* (ع) comes from the throat; it is indicated by an apostrophe in transliteration. Finally, *s, d, t, th,* and *k* have two sounds each, one heavier than the other.

The heavy *k* (ق), represented by a "q" in transliteration, is not commonly pronounced (one exception is in the word Qur'an). Instead, city people replace it with a glottal stop (the hard vowel sound heard in English when a vowel begins a word). Upper Egyptians and *fellaheen* ("peasants") use a "g" sound instead of the glottal stop. So a word like *qamar* (moon) is pronounced "gamar" by, say, Mubarak.

Vowels and consonants can be either long or short, often an important distinction. Although *jamaal* is "beauty," *jamal* means "camel." Extended vowels can mean the difference between finding a *ham-mam* (bathroom) and finding *hamam* (pigeons).

R is pronounced as a trill, similar to Spanish. In Egypt, all *g*'s (ج) are pronounced hard (as in "giddy"); Palestinians, Jordanians, and Syrians say *j* (as in the French *"je"*). Thus "hill" is spelled *gabal* in Egypt, *jabal* elsewhere. The definite article is the prefix *al*, in Egypt pronounced more like *el*. When *al* comes before the sounds t, th, j, d, dh, r, z, s, sh, or n, the *l* is not pronounced. Never say *"ihna fee al-nar"* (we are in Hell); a more correct pronunciation is *"ihna fee an-nar."*

Although Arabic is read from right to left, numerals are read from left to right.

NUMERALS

٠	١	٢	٣	٤	٥	٦	٧	٨	٩	١٠	٢٠
0	1	2	3	4	5	6	7	8	9	10	20
sifr	waahid	tinein	talaata	arba'a	khamsa	sitta	sab'a	tamanya	tis'a	'ashara	'ishrin

PHRASEBOOK

English	Arabic
	Greetings, etc.
Hello	Marhaba
Hello (formal)	Salaam aleikum
(response)	Aleikum as–salaam
Welcome	Ahlan/Ahlein/Ahlan wa sahlan
(response)	Shukran/Ahlein feek (m)/Ahlein feekee (f)
Good morning	Sabah al-kheir
(response)	Sabah an-nour/Sabah al-ishta (cheesy)
Good evening	Masa' al-kheir
(response)	Masa' an-nour
Good-bye	Ma' as-salaama
Yes	Eeh (Levant)/Aiwa (Egypt)
Yes (formal)	Na'am
No	La/La-a (for emphasis)
Thank you	Shukran
Please	Min fadlak (male), Min fadlik (female)
I'm sorry	Ana aasif (male), Ana aasfa (female)
Excuse me (to get attention)	'An iznak (male), 'An iznik (female)
God willing	In sha allah (shortened to inshaala)
Praise God	Al hamdu lillah
What is your name? (Levant)	Shoo ismak (male), Shoo ismik (female)
What is your name? (Egypt)	Ismak eh (male), Ismik eh (female)
My name is...	Ismi...
How are you? (in Levant only)	Keefak? (male), Keefik? (female)
How are you? (in Egypt only)	Izzayyak (male), Izzayyek (female)
I'm fine (in Levant only)	Mabsuut (male), Mabsuuta (female) (I'm happy)
I'm fine (in Egypt only)	Kuwayyis (male), Kuwayyisa (female)
I'm tired	Ana ta'baan (male), Ana ta'baana (female)
I feel like I'm about to die	Rah a moot (Levant), Ha moot (Egypt)
student (male)	Talib
student (female)	Taliba
Never mind, No big deal	Ma'lish
	Directions
Let's Go!	Yalla! or Yalla beena!
Where? or Where is ...?	Fein? / Wein? / Ayna?
When?	Eimta
Why?	Leish (Levant)/Leih (Egypt)
I'm going to ...	Ana rayih (male)/Rayha (female) ila...
There is ... or Is there ... ?	Fee ... ?
There is no ... or Isn't there any ... ?	Mafeesh ... ?
restaurant	mat'am
post office	maktab al-bareed (Levant)/bosta (Egypt)
street	share'
market	souq or sou'
museum	mat-haf

mosque	masjed/jaame' (Levant), masgid/gaame' (Egypt)
church	kineesa
university	jaam'a (Levant), gaam'a (Egypt)
hotel	funduq or (h)otel
room	oda or ghurfa
airport	mataar
station	mahatta
traffic circle, public square	midan
right (direction)	yameen
left	shmal or yasaar
straight	dughree
bus	baas (Levant), utubeese (Egypt)
automobile	sayyaara (Levant), 'arabiyya (Egypt)
tourist	saa-ih (male), saa-iha (female), suwwaah (pl)

Bargaining

How much?	Addeish? (Levant) Bikaam? (Egypt)
No way!	Mish mumkin!
Will you take half?	Taakhud nuss? (male) Taakhdee nuss? (female)
money	masaari (Levant), fulous (Egypt)
change	fraata (Levant), fakka (Egypt)
I want…	Biddee (Levant), 'Ayiz (Egypt, m), 'Ayza (Egypt, f)
I'm not a dumb tourist (Egypt only)	Ana mish khawaga

Date and Time

What time is it?	Addeish as-saa'a? (Levant) Es-saa'a kaam? (Egypt)
hour, time	saa'a
day	yoam
week	usbuu'
month	shaher (Levant), shahr (Egypt)
year	sana
today	al-yoam
yesterday	imbaareh, ams (formal)
tomorrow	bukra
Sunday	yoam al-ahad
Monday	yoam al-itnein
Tuesday	yoam at-talaat
Wednesday	yoam al-arba'a
Thursday	yoam al-khamees
Friday	yoam aj-jum'a (Levant), eg-goum'a (Egypt)
Saturday	yoam as-sabt

Emergency

Do you speak English?	Bitihkee inglizi? (Levant), Bititkallim inglizi? (Egypt, m), Bititkallimee inglizi? (Egypt, f)
I feel like I'm about to die.	Rah a moot (Levant), ha moot (Egypt)
I don't speak Arabic.	Ana ma bahki 'arabi (Levant), Ana mish batkallim 'arabi (Egypt)
tourist police (Egypt only)	bolees es-siyaaha
hospital	mustashfa
doctor	duktoor
passport	basbor/jawaz (Levant), gawaz (Egypt)
embassy	safaarah
water	mayya

Do you speak English?	Bitihkee inglizi? (Levant), Bititkallim inglizi? (Egypt, m), Bititkallimee inglizi? (Egypt, f)
I feel like I'm about to die.	Rah a moot (Levant), ha moot (Egypt)
I don't speak Arabic.	Ana ma bahki 'arabi (Levant), Ana mish batkallim 'arabi (Egypt)
tourist police (Egypt only)	bolees es-siyaaha
hospital	mustashfa
doctor	duktoor
passport	basbor/jawaz (Levant), gawaz (Egypt)
embassy	safaarah
water	mayya

HEBREW (IVRIT) עברית

See **Israel: Language,** on page 275, for historical background. The transliterations *ḥ* (ח) and *kh* (f and l) are both guttural, as in the German word *ach*. The Hebrew *r* is close to the French *r,* although an Arabic (or even English) *r* is also understood. Hebrew vowels are shorter than English ones, which leads to discrepancies in transliteration. The definite article is the prefix *ha.* Feminine adjectives add an "-ah" at the end; feminine verbs usually add an "-at" or an "-et.".

Although Hebrew is read from right to left, numerals are read from left to right.

NUMERALS

0	1	2	3	4	5	6	7	8	9	10	20
efes	eḥad	shtayim	shalosh	arba	ḥamesh	shesh	sheva	shmoneh	teisha	eser	esrim

PHRASEBOOK

English	**Hebrew**
	Greetings, etc.
Hello/Good-bye	Shalom
Good morning	Boker tov
Good evening	Erev tov
See you later	L'hitra'ot
What's up?	Ma nishma?
(response) Everything's good	Kol tov
Yes	Ken
No	Lo
Thank you	Toda
Excuse me/I'm sorry	Sliḥa
Please/You're welcome	Bevakasha
What is your name?	Eikh korim lekhah? (m) Eikh korim lakh? (f)
My name is...	Shmi...
How are you?	Ma shlomkha? (male) Ma shlomekh? (female)
Fine, OK	B'seder
Not good	Lo tov
Excellent	Metzuyan
I'm tired	Ani ayef (male)/Ani ayefa (female)
student	student (male)/studentit (female)

Directions

Where is…?	Eyfoh…?
When	Matai
Why	Lama
I'm going to…	Ani nose'a l'…
There is…	Yesh…
There is no…	Ain…
Do you know where… is?	Ata yodea (Female: Aht yoda'at) eifoh nimtza…?
Wait (for authenticity, bring fingertips together and gesture as you say this)	Rega
restaurant	mis'adah
post office	do'ar
street	reḥov
boulevard	sderot
market	shuk
museum	muzaion
synagogue	beit knesset
church	knaissia
central bus station	taḥana merkazit
hotel	malon
hostel	akhsaniya
room	ḥeder
university	universita
beach	ḥof
grocery store	makoleet
right (direction)	yamin
left	smol
straight	yashar
taxi	monit, taxi
automobile	mekhonit
train	rakevet
bus	otoboos

Bargaining

Do you have…?	Yesh lekha…? (male) Yesh lakh…? (female)
How much is this?	Kama zeh oleh?
I want…	Ani rotzeh… (male) Ani rotzah… (female)
I don't want… (male/female)	Lo rotzeh … (male) Ani rotzah… (female)
Go away	Tistalek
Go to hell	Lekh l'azazel
money	kesef
change (literally "leftovers")	odef
waiter	meltzar (male), meltzarit (female)
water	mayim
coffee	kafeh
tea	teh

Date and Time

What time is it?	Ma hasha'a?
hour, time	sha'a
day	yom
week	shavua
month	ḥodesh

year	shana
today	ha'yom
yesterday	etmol
tomorrow	maḥar
Sunday	Yom rishon
Monday	Yom shaini
Tuesday	Yom shlishi
Wednesday	Yom revi'i
Thursday	Yom ḥamishi
Friday	Yom shishi
sabbath (Saturday)	Shabbat

Emergency

Do you speak English?	Ata medaber Anglit? (m) At medaberet Anglit? (f)
I don't speak Hebrew	Ani lo medaber (m)/medaberet (f) Ivrit.
police	mishtara
hospital	beit ḥolim
doctor	rofee
passport	darkon
airport	s'deh te'ufa

Index

A

Aaron's Tomb 497
'Abbasids 49
Abdallah 53, 441
abortion 21
Abraham 47, 62, 416, 456
Abraham's Well 418
Abu Bakr 49
Abu Darwish Mosque 478
Abu Ghosh 319
Abu Jaber house 481
Abu Jaber, Kamel 457
Abu Qir 161
Abu Simbel 210
Abu Sir 138, 141
Abydos 46, 61
Ad-Darazi 69, 115
Afula 385
Aga Khan 208
Aghurmi 173
'Agiba 169
Agnon, Shmuel Yosef (Shai) 275
ahwa 127
AIDS. See HIV.
Aila 503
Ain Musa 492
airplane tickets 38–40
airports
  Aqaba 500
  Aswan 204
  Ben-Gurion 325
  Cairo International 72
  Damascus International 525
  Eilat 430
  Hurghada 240
  Kharga 226
  Luxor 180
  Marsa Matrouh 166
  Queen Alia International (Amman) 472
Akhenaton 123
Akhzibland 371
Akhziv 371
Akhziv National Park 371
Akko (Acre) 364–369
Al Azariyyeh 448
Al-Azhar University 27, 92, 113

Al Bab 69, 358
Al Balad 468
Al Barid 498
Al Hakim 49
Al Hakim Mosque 115
Al Himma 386
Al-Madina 565
Al Madras 498
Al Mina 566
Al Uzza (Atargatis) 495
alcohol
  and Islam 467
  'araq 467, 520, 553, 556
  Egyptian 86
  Israeli beer 277
Aleppo 540–544
Alexander the Great 47, 148, 169, 185, 569
Alexandria 148–161
al-Hariri, Rafiq 552
alligator park 387
Alma Cave 396
alternatives to tourism 23–32
  in Egypt 27, 154
  in Israel 27–31
  in Jordan 32
  in Syria 32
  in the West Bank 32
  study 23
  volunteering 25
  work 25
American Field Service (AFS) 27
American Society of Haifa University 31
American University of Beirut (AUB) 32
American University of Cairo (AUC) 27, 91, 92, 100, 130
Amman 467–480
Ammonites 478
Amoud Far'aun 496
Amr, Mosque of 121
Amun 47, 61, 184
ankh 65
An-Najah University 455
Annunciation 376
Antioch 505
Antony, Marc 47, 148, 169

Apamea 539
'Apiru 47
Aqaba 498–503
Arabic 574
Arad 420–421
Arafat, Yassir 54, 58, 59
Aramaic 399, 530
'araq 467, 520, 553, 556
archery, desert 427
Ark of the Covenant 319
aromatherapy 130
Artisanat Libanais 563
Arwad 548
Asad, Hafez al 54, 56
Ashdod 340
Ashkelon 340–342
Ashkelon National Park 341
Ashkeluna water park 342
'ashta 556, 566
Assyrian empire 48
Aswan 203–209
Asyut 229
Ataturk, Kemal 542
Avdat 425
Avivi, Eli 371
Avshalom 320
Ayyubids 50, 90
Azraq 483

B

Ba'al 534
ba'laweh 520
Ba'th Party 517
Baab adh-Dhira 490
Baab Zuweila 112
Ba'al 362
Baalbeck 569
baboons 214
backgammon boards 126
backpacks 36
Baha'i 69
Baha'i Gardens (near Akko) 369
Baha'i Temple (Haifa) 358
Bahariyya 218–220
Baha'u'llah 69, 368, 369
bakhsheesh 77, 108, 550
Balaat 225
Baldwin I 50

Balfour Declaration (1917) 52
banana, inflatable 384
Banyas 404
Bar Hebraeus 519
bargaining tips 125, 318
Baris 228–229
Bar-Kokhba, Simon 410
Barquq, Mausoleum of 116
Bar-Yohai, Rabbi Shimon 374, 379, 395
Basata 265
basbouseh 520
Bashendi 225
Basilica of St. Simeon 544
Basilica of the Nativity 446
batirsh 539
Baybars el-Gashankir 115
Bayn el-Qasrayn 114
Bcharré 567
Be'er Sheva 414–419
Beach of Love 169
beatitudes 389
Beaver, George 563
Bede 440
Bedouin 246, 260, 262, 378
Bedouin market, Be'er Sheva 418
Begin, Menahem 56
Beirut 557–564
Beit ed Din 564
Beit es-Suheimi 115
Beit Guvrin National Park 343
Beit She'an 385
Beit She'arim 362
Beitin 454
Bell, Gertrude 519
belly dancing 129, 131, 161, 196, 555
Ben-Ezra Synagogue 119, 120
Ben-Gurion, David 52–53, 422–424
Ben-Gurion Institute 424
Ben-Gurion University 31, 419

Benjamin 448
Ben-Yehuda,
  Eliezer 275
Bethany 448
Bethel 454
Bethlehem 444–448
billiards 130
bird watching 434
birth control 21
Birzeit University 32,
  441, 455
bisexual
  resources 34
Bitash 163
Bke'ah 374
Black Hebrews'
  Village 421
Black September 55,
  457
Blue Mosque 111
*The Bold and the
  Beautiful* 465
Bond, James
  Bond 124, 248
*Book of the
  Dead* 82, 83, 190
booza 520
border crossings 41
  Egypt to Israel 266
  Egypt to
    Jordan 264
  Israel to Egypt 435
  Israel to
    Jordan 385, 436
  Israel to West
    Bank 438
  Jordan to
    Egypt 503
  Jordan to Israel 503
  Jordan to Syria 471
  West Bank to
    Jordan 438
Bosra 530
Bouleuterion 341
Boutros-Ghali,
  Boutros 59
Bow Cave 373
Bubastis 142
Burkhardt,
  Johann 492
burma 520
Burning Bush 253,
  254
bybil 520

C

cable cars,
  Austrian 565
Caesar, Julius 148,
  185
Caesarea 347–349
Cairo 86–131
  accommodations 1
    02–104

entertainment 127
  –129
food 105–107
history 86–90
museums 123–125
orientation 90–92
practical
  information 99–
  102
shopping 125–127
sights 107–123
transportation 93–
  99
Cairo University 122
Cairo Zoo 123
Camel Corps 503
camel market
  (Daraw) 202
Canaan 48
Canada Centre 400
Capernaum 389
Captain Hook 236
Carmel Mizrahi 338,
  351
Carmelite Order of
  monks (Haifa) 359
Carter, Howard 190
Casablanca 366
Castle le Blanc 548
Catholicism. See Ro-
  man Catholicism.
Cave of the
  Makhpela 62
The Cedars 568
Central Negev 414
Chagall, Marc 311,
  315
Chapel of
  Hathor 202
Cheops 134
Chephren 134
children 35
Christ. See Jesus.
Christianity 63–66
Christie, Agatha 209,
  542
Church of St. Cosmos
  and St. Damius 507
Church of St.
  Paul 239
Circassians 480
Citadel Hill
  (Amman) 478
Citadels
  Akko 368
  Aleppo 543
  al-Marqab 548
  Bosra 530
  Damascus 528
  Hama 539
  Islamic Cairo 110
Cities of the
  Dead 116–118
Cleopatra 47, 148,

169
Cleopatra's Bath 169
climate 3, 572
Club Med 371
con artists 16, 92
condoms 22
Constantine 49, 253
Coptic Cairo 119–
  120
Coptic Church 65,
  87, 143, 145, 150
cotton candy 154
Crac Des
  Chevaliers 537
credit cards 14
Crimean War 447
Crocodopolis 145
Crusades 49, 364,
  447, 498, 548
cuneiform 545, 547
currency. See mon-
  ey.
customs 10–11
cybercafes 45

D

Dada 363
Dahab 260–262
Dakhla 221–225
  Eastern 225
  Western 224
Daliyat Al
  Karmel 361–362
Damascus 521–530
Daraw 202
Darret 'Azzay 544
David 48, 399, 409,
  444, 448
Dayan, Moshe 387
Dead Sea
  (Israel) 406–411
Dead Sea
  (Jordan) 486
Dead Sea Scrolls 311,
  408
*Death on the
  Nile* 209
Decapolis 49, 386
Dendera 197
Dengue Fever 19
Devil's Head 265
Dhiban 488
diarrhea 20
Diaspora
  Museum 333
Dibbin National
  Park 507
Dimona 421
Diocletian 65, 150,
  158
disabled travelers 35
doll museum 402
Doura Europos 529
driving permits and

insurance 12
driving, desert 217
drug laws 17
Druze 69, 115, 361,
  399, 405, 553
Dush 229
Dushara 495
dwarf hamsters,
  Himalayan 484

E

Early Dynastic
  Period 46
Ebla 545
Ebla tablets 521
Ed-Daba 225
Edfu 200–201
EGYPT 71–266
Egyptian
  Museum 123
Eid al-Adhah 2
Eid al-Fitr 2
Eilat 428–436
Ein as-Sultan 452
Ein Avdat Nature
  Reserve 424
Ein Bokek 414
Ein Feshka 409
Ein Gedi 409–411
Ein Hod 363
Ein Kerem 314
El Agami 163–164
El Alamein 163, 165
El Ghouri 112
El Kab 199
El Mu'allaqa 119
El Qahira 86–90
electric current 36
Elephantine
  Island 207
Eliahou Hannabi
  Synagogue 159
Elijah 252, 362, 378,
  404
Elijah's Cave 359
email. See internet.
embassies 5
Emperor
  Justinian 253
En-Nasr
  Muhammed 114
entry 6
  into Egypt 72
  into Israel 267
  into Jordan 457
Eretz Yisrael
  Museum 332
Eshkol, Levi 54, 314
Esna 198
Essenes 409
ESSENTIALS 1–45
  alcohol and
    drugs 17
  alternatives to

tourism 23–32
bisexual, gay, and lesbian travelers 34
children 35
climate 3
customs 10
disabled travelers 35
documents and formalities 5
embassies and consulates 5
entrance requirements 6
health 17–22
insurance 22
internet resources 4
keeping in touch 43
mail 43
money 12–15
older travelers 34
packing 36
passports 6
safety and security 15
telephones 44
tourist and information offices 3
travel etiquette 45
visas 8
women and travel 33
Euclid 148
Exodus 368
extraterrestrials 194, 422

F

falafel 520
Faqus 143
Farafra 220–221
farooj 520
Fatimid Cairo 111
faxes 45
Fayyum 145–147
felucca 131, 178, 203
festivals. See holidays or music festivals.
film 36
Finch, Samuel 454
First Intermediate Period 46
fish farm 174
Flaubert, Gustave 296
Flavius, Josephus 402, 412
food and drink Egypt 84–86

Israel 277
Jordan 466–467
Lebanon 556
Lebanon (sweets) 566
Syria 520
forest fires, help prevent 374
Forster, E.M. 150, 155
Fort Qaytbay 158
Fourth of July 131
fried sloth 502
Fustat 108, 120–122
futbol 131

G

Gabal el-Mawta 172
Gabriel (Angel) 377
Galilee 374–400
Galilee, Sea of 386–389
gallabiyya 217
gambling 128
Gamla 400, 402
Gan Ha-Eim 358
gay resources 34
Gayer-Anderson, Major 124
Geziret en-Nabatat 208
Gibran, Khalil 555, 567
Giv'at Ram 310
Giza 132–136
Godfrey I 50
Golan Heights 400–405
Golan hikes 403
Goldstein, Robin 454
The Good Fence 399
Gulf Crisis 442

H

Ha-Tikva 362
Ha-Ari. See Luria, Rabbi Isaac.
Hadrian 229, 505
Ha-Gader Ha-Tova (The Good Fence) 399
Ḥai Bar Biblical Nature Reserve 437
Haifa 351–361
Haifa University 358
hajj 68, 319
Hama 537–539
Hamas 59, 442
Ḥammat Gader 386
handicapped diving 259
handicapped. See disabled travelers.
Hannah 394

Hannoville 163
Harawi, Ilyas 552
Hasmonean Dynasty 48
Hathor 195, 196, 215
Hatshepsut 186, 192
health 17–22
AIDS, HIV, STDs, and birth control 21
Dengue Fever 19
food and water 18
hepatitis 20
immunization 18
malaria 19
mosquitoes 19
Pharaoh's Revenge 20
women and health 21
Hebrew 577
Hebrew Israelite Community 421
Hebrew University 312, 313, 315
Hebrew University of Jerusalem 31
Hebron 441
Heb-Sed Court 139
Heliopolian Theogony 61
Heliopolis 87
hepatitis 20
Hermit's House 344
Herod 48, 379, 411, 450, 453, 456, 488
Herodion 450
Herodotus 142
Herzl, Theodore 51
Herzliya 343–344
High Dam (Aswan) 210
High Place 497
Hijra 66
Hilla 373
Hisham's Palace 452
history
Ancient Egypt (7000 BCE-451 CE) 46–47
The Ancient Levant (1400 BCE-559 CE) 47–49
The Rule of the Caliphs (632-1260 CE) 49–50
The Ottoman Centuries (1500-1882 CE) 50–51
Zionism and the British Mandate (c. 1800-1945

CE) 51–53
The 1948 (Independence) War and the Unification of Jordan (1947-1951) 53
The Suez Crisis and Pan-Arabism (1948-1964) 53
The 1967 Six-Day War 54
War and Peace (1970-1988) 55
The Israeli Invasion of Lebanon (1982-1985) 57
The Intifada (1987-1989) 57
The Peace Process (1991-1996) 58
This Year's News (1997) 60
hitchhiking
in Egypt 75
in Israel 268
in Jordan 460
in oases 216
in Syria 514
HIV 21
Hizbullah 17, 61, 397, 554
holidays 2, 571–572
Christian 519
Coptic Christian 82
Druze 69
Egypt 82
Islamic 82, 519
Jordan 464
Sufi 82
Syria 519
Syrian 519
Holocaust 267, 299, 310, 314, 369
Holy of Holies 213
homosexual. See gay resources.
Homs 535–537
Ḥorshat Tal Nature Reserve 399
Horus 46, 61, 202
Hosea 394
Hostelling International-American Youth Hostels (HI-AYH) 41
Hostelling International-Canada (HI-C) 43
hot spring (really hot) 386
House of Gamal ed-Din 112
Ḥula Valley 398

hummus 520
Hurghada 239–245
Hussein, King of
Jordan 53, 56, 457
Hussein, Saddam 58
hydroponics 406
Hyksos 46
hyrax, endearing 409
hyrax, furry little 386

I

Ibn Tulun
Mosque 108
ice skating 400
Imber, Naftali
Hertz 362
*Indiana Jones and
the Last
Crusade* 492
infitah 55
insurance 22
International Student
Identity Card
(ISIC) 4, 11
International Teach-
er Identity Card
(ITIC) 4, 11
internet 4, 45
intifada 57, 438,
441, 455
Iraq al-Emir 480
Isaac 456
Isfiya 361–362
Isis 61, 229
Islam 66–68
Ismailiyya 233–235
ISRAEL 267–437
Israel Defense Forces
(IDF) 411
Israel Museum 310
'Izz al-Din 50

J

Jabal al-
Ashrafiyyeh 468
Jabal al-Madbah 497
Jabal al-Qala'a 467
Jabal al-Weibdeh 468
Jabal Amman 468
Jabal Harun 497
Jabal Hussein 468
Jabal Umm al-
Biyara 497
Jacob 454, 456
Jacob of Edessa 519
Jaziret Far'aun 503
jazzercise 131
Jeita Grotto 565
jellab 556
Jerash 505–507
Jerash Festival 464,
507
Jericho 450–452
Jerusalem 278–319

accommodations 2
88–292
entertainment 315
–317
food 292–296
history 278–283
orientation 283
practical
information 286–
288
shopping 317–319
sights 296–315
transportation 283
–286
Jerusalem Forest 314
Jesus 63–65, 228,
313, 347, 374, 377,
379, 388, 388–389,
404, 444, 448, 457
Annunciation 377
loaves and
fishes 388
Nativity 447
the Passion 64
Transfiguration 37
8
*Jesus Christ
Superstar* 425
jihad 66
John the Baptist 64,
314, 374, 457, 528
Johnson, Nick 454
Jones, Indiana 363,
492
*Indiana Jones and
the Last
Crusade* 492
*Raiders of the Lost
Ark* 143
JORDAN 457–512
Joseph 145, 377
Joshua 396, 450
Judaism 62–63
Judin Fortress 373
Justinian 65

K

Kakhalon,
Nissim 344
Kanafani,
Ghassan 443
Karaites 70
Karak 489–490
Karak Castle 489,
490
Karnak Temple 185
Katzrin 401
Kfar Giladi 398
Khaled Ibn al-
Walid 521
Khan el-Khalili 113,
126
Kharga 226–228
khawaga 77

Khazneh 495
Khnum 198
Khonsu 61, 184, 228
Kibbutz 51, 274
Adamit 373
Avnei Eitan 404
Ayelet Ha-
Shahor 397
Beit Guvrin 343
Dan 399, 404
Deganya Alef 387
Ein Karmel 350
El-Al 404
Ga'ash 346
Ginnosar 388
Kfar Blum 398
Kfar Giladi 398
Lohamei Ha-
Geta'ot 369
Ma'agan
Mikha'el 350
Nachsholim 350
Samir 437
Sasa 395
Sdeh Boker 422
Sdot Yam 348
Senir 399
volunteering 29
Yad
Mordekhai 342
Yehi'am 373
Yotvata 437
Kidron River 449
Kikkar Ha-
Atzma'ut 342
Kinneret. See Lake
Kinneret.
Kiryat Gat 342
Kiryat Shmona 397
Kissinger, Henry 56
Kitchener's
Island 208
kitty litter 142
Klil 373
Knesset 311
Kom Ombo 201
Kook, Avraham 278
Korazim 389
Kulthum, Umm 84
Kurds 517
Kursi 389
Kuwait 58

L

Lake Kinneret 386–
389
Lake Nasser 210
Latrun 320
Lattakia 545
*Lawrence of
Arabia* 217
Lawrence, T.E. (of
Arabia) 52, 483,
498, 504, 542

Lazarus 449
LEBANON 549–
570
lesbian resources 34
Levant, Ancient 47
Library of
Alexandria 148
Libya 170
Lighthouse of
Alexandria 148
lions,
hermaphroditic 480
lookalikes
Jackson,
Michael 183
Lawrence of
Arabia 483
Lord Cromer 51
Louis IX, King of
France 348
love-cow 195
Luke xiii
Luria, Rabbi
Isaac 390, 394, 395
Luxor 179–196
Luxor Temple 184

M

Ma'alula 530
Maas'ada 405
Maccabees 48
Mahfouz, Naguib 80,
83
mail 43
Maimonides,
Moses 383
Majdal Shams 405
Majlis Alnuwab 552
Makhtesh Ramon
(Ramon Crater) 425
malaria 19
Malik es-Salih
Ayyub 114
Mamluks 50, 90, 364
Mamshit 422
Map of the Holy
Land 487
Mar Saba
Monastery 449
Maronite
Christianity 553
Marsa Matrouh 163,
165–169
Mary 447, 448
Mary Magdalene 388
Mary, the Virgin 314,
359, 362, 374, 376,
383, 388
Masada 49, 411–414
Mausoleum of El
Ghouri 112
Mawlid an-Nabi 2
Mazar 490
Mazra'a 490

Me'a She'arim 310
measurements. See
  weights and mea-
  sures.
Mecca 68
Meir, Golda 56, 314
Memphis 46, 61, 87,
  141
Memphite
  Theogony 61
Mendelssohn,
  Erich 312
Menes 46
Meron 395
Mesha Stele 465
Metulla 399
Miami Beach 151
Middle Egypt 16, 81
Migdal 388
Mi'ilya 373
Milk Grotto
  Church 448
Mishkenot
  Sha'ananim 313
Mishnah 363, 378
Mitzpeh
  Ramon 425–428
mock flood 421
Monastery of St.
  Jeremiah 140
money 12–15, 16
  Egypt 71, 76
  Israel 267, 270
  Jordan 457, 460
  Lebanon 549, 550
  Syria 513, 514
  West Bank 440
monophysitism 65
Montfort 372
Moore, Henry 311
Moses 62, 250, 251–
  252, 400
  and the Burning
  Bush 253
moshavim 29, 51,
  274, 397
Mosque
  Architecture 68
Mosque of Al-
  Jazzar 367
Mosque of Qijmas el-
  Ishaqi 111
mosquitoes 19
Mount
  Hermon 405
  Gerizim 456
  Herzl 314
  Meron 395
  Nebo 488
  of Beatitudes 389
  of Temptation 452
  Scopus 313
  Sinai 251–252
  Tabor 378

Zion 306
Mount Carmel Na-
  tional Park 358
Mu'tah 490
Mubarak, Hosni 57
Muhammad 49
Muhammad Ali 50,
  90, 172
Muhraqa 362
Mukawer 488
murex 568
music
  Egyptian 84
  Israeli 318
  Jordan 465, 472
  Lebanon 555
music festivals
  Baalbeck 555, 570
  Beit ed Din 564
  Haifa Blues
  Festival 360
  Hebrew (Arad) 421
  Hebrew Rock 435
  International
  Festival of the
  Performing Arts
  (Beit Meri) 555
  Jerash 464, 507
  Klezmer and
  Hasidic rock 395
  Red Sea Jazz 435
  Reggae
  (Akhziv) 371
  Sea of Galilee 385
Muslim
  Brotherhood 537
Mussolini,
  Benito 389
Mut 61, 184, 228
Mut (Dakhla) 222
Mycerinus 134

N
Na'ama Bay 258–260
Nabatean
  Kingdom 492
Nabatean
  Museum 496
Nabateans 48, 422,
  495
Nablus 455
Nahal Betzet Nature
  Reserve 373
Nahal Keziv 372
Nahal Me'arot Nature
  Reserve 350
Nahal Yehi'am Na-
  ture Reserve 373
Nahariya 369–371
Nahman of
  Breslev 394
Nakht 194
Napoleon 50, 90,

150
Narmer 46
Narmer Palette 123
an-Nasser, Gamal
  Abd 53–56
Nazareth 374–378
Nebo 488
Nebuchadnezzar 48
Nefertari 215
Negev Museum 418
Nekhbet 199
Netanya 344–346
New Kingdom 47
Nile Cruiser 176
Nile Delta 142
Nile Valley 175–215
Nilometer
  Aswan 207
  Cairo 122
  Kalabsha 213
  Philae 212
Nimrod 404
Nimrod's
  Fortress 404
Nubia 203
nude beach 347
Nut 61
Nuweiba' 263–264

O
oases
  Bahariyya 218–220
  Dakhla 221–225
  Farafra 220–221
  Fayyum 145–147
  Kharga 226–228
  Siwa 148, 169–174
Obelisk,
  Unfinished 210
Octavian 47, 150
Odenathus 531
Old Kingdom 46
older travelers 34
oldest
  church 446
  city 450
  continuously-
  inhabited city 521
  synagogue 414
  university 113
Oliphant, Sir
  Lawrence 362
Oracle of Amun 148,
  170, 173
Orthodox
  Christianity 65
Osiris cycle 61
Oslo Accord 59
Ottoman Empire 50

P
packing 36
Palestine Liberation
  Organization

(PLO) 54–61, 553
Palestinian National
  Theatre 317
Palmyra 531–535
Pan 404
papyrus 126, 143
the Passion 64
passports 6–8
Paul 64
Peki'in 374
Pepi I 123
Pepi II 46
Persian dynasty 47
Persian Tombs 139
Pesah 2
Petra 48, 492–498
Pharaoh's Island 265,
  503
Pharaoh's
  Revenge 20
Pharaonic
  Village 131
Philospher's
  Circle 140
phrasebooks
  Arabic 574
  Hebrew 577
Picasso, Pablo 311
Pilate, Pontius 347
Pillars of Islam 67
Place de la
  Concorde 184
Poleg Nature
  Reserve 346
Pompey 48, 148,
  505
Pool of Fatnas 174
Port Said 230–233
Port Tawfik 235
post. See mail.
Poste Restante 43
prostitutes,
  Russian 521, 542
Protestantism 65
Ptah 61
Ptolemy 47, 62, 148
puppet theater
  (Cairo) 130
Pyramid Texts 62,
  139
Pyramids at
  Giza 132–136
pyramids, other
  Step Pyramid of
  Djoser-
  Netcherikhe 138
  Titi 141
  Unis 139

Q
Qal'at al-Marqab 548
Qal'at Ibn Maan 534
Qal'at Salah ad-
  Din 546

Qalawun 114
Qanatir 142
Qasr al-Abd 480
Qasr al-Hallabat 483
Qasr Amra 484
Qasr Bint
  Far'aun 496
Qasr Bishtak 115
Qasr el-Gowhara 111
Qasr Habis 497
Qasr Kharaneh 484
Qasr Mushatta 484
Qaytbay, Mausoleum
  and Mosque of 117
Qumran 311, 408
Quneitra 531
Quneitreh 405
Qur'an 66, 68, 517

R
Rabbi Akiva 347
Rabin, Yitzhak 56,
  59, 314, 322, 331,
  442, 457
Rachel 448
*Raiders of the Lost
  Ark* 143
Ramadan 2, 68, 127
Ramallah 453–454
Rambam. See Mai-
  monides, Moses.
Rambo III 343
Ramla 339
Ramon Crater 425
Ramses II 184, 214
Ramses IX 190
Ras as-Sana 2
Ras Muhammad Na-
  tional Park 257
Ras Shamra 546
Rashid (Rosetta) 162
Rashidun 49, 66
Real World 178
reflexology 130
Rehania 396
Rehavia 312
Rehovot 339
Rekhmire 194
religious history
  Ancient Egypt 61–
    62
  Baha'i 69
  Christianity 63–66
  Druze 69
  Islam 66–68
  Judaism 62–63
Rifa'i 109
Rihani, Amin 555
Rishon Le Zion 338
Rodin, Auguste 311,
  567
Roman
  Catholicism 65
Rommel, Erwin

("Desert Fox") 165
Rosh Ha-Nikra 372
Rosh Ha-Shana 2
Rosh Pina 397
Rothschild
  Family 311, 350,
  397
Russian
  Compound 315
Ruth 449

S
Sabastiya 456
Sabil Kuttab of Abd
  er-Rahman
  Kathuda 115
Sabil Umm
  Abbas 109
sabra 277
es-Sadat, Anwar 55–
  57
Safed. See Tzfat.
safety 15–17
Safita 548
Saida (Sidon) 568
Saint
  Catherine's 253–
    255
Salah ad-Din 50, 87,
  90, 117, 279, 373,
  528, 546, 547, 568
Salt 481–482
Samaritans 70, 456
San el-Hagar 143
sand baths 173
Sandomirsky,
  Nick 454
sandstorms 217
Sanhedrin 313
Saqqara 137–142
  Abu Sir 141
  Memphis 141
  North Saqqara 138
  South Saqqara 141
  Western North
    Saqqara 140
Saul 48
scuba diving 244
Sdeh Boker 422–424
Seleucids 48
senior citizens 34
Sennofer 194
Septuagint 150
Serapis 229
Seth 43, 61
sexually-transmitted
  disease 21
Seydnaya 530
Shabbat 2
Shali 172
Shamir, Yitzhak 58,
  442
Sharm el-Sheikh 256
Shaumari Wildlife

Preserve 484
Shavu'ot 2
shawerma 520
sheep's liver,
  cheap 446
sheesha 83
Shekhem 455
Shepherd's Field 449
Shi'a 49, 57, 66, 517,
  553
shirwal 405
shish kebab 520
shish tawouq 520
Shmeisani 468
Shobak 490
Shobak Castle 490
Shomron 456
Shomron Valley 456
shopping
  Beirut 563
  Cairo 125–127
  Jerusalem 317–319
Shuk Ha-Carmel 331
Sigothersuck 52
Simhat Torah 2
Sinai 245–266
  Gulf Coast 256–
    266
  High Sinai 255
  Mount Sinai 251–
    252
  Western Sinai 250
Siwa Oasis 148, 169–
  174
skiing 405, 568
Snake
  Monument 497
Sobek 202
soccer 91, 131
Solar Boat 136
Solomon 48, 498
Soreq Cave 320
sound and light
  shows
  Ben-Gurion's life
    (Sdeh Boker) 424
  Jerash 507
  Karnak 185, 196
  Masada 414, 420,
    421
  Sphinx 134
Sphinx 134
*The Spy Who Loved
  Me* 134
St. Anthony 239
St. Joseph 377
St. Nicodemus 339
St. Paul 239
St. Paul, Church
  of 239
St. Paul's
  Monastery 239
St. Simeon 544
St. Taqla 530

stala-
  ctite 320, 565
  gmite 320, 565
Stallone,
  Sylvester 343
Stella Maris 359
student ID cards 11
study abroad. See al-
  ternatives to tour-
  ism.
Suez 235–236
Suez Canal 230
  historical
    significance of 51
Suez Crisis 210
Sufi 67, 82, 129, 130
Sukkot 2
Suleiman I 565
Sultan Hasan 109
Sultan's Pool 313,
  317
sunna 66
Sunni 49, 66, 517,
  553
Sur (Tyre) 569
Sussiya 421
*Sweet Valley
  High* 154
Sweifiyyeh
  Mosaic 479
Sykes-Picot Agree-
  ment (1916) 52
SYRIA 513–548

T
Tabgha 388
Talmud 379
Tanis 143
tanzimat 51
Tarabin 263, 265
Tartus 547–548
Technion 358
Tel 385, 543, 545
  Abu Alayia 453
  Arad 421
  as-Sultan 452
  Basta 142
  Be'er Sheva 419
  Dan 399
  definition 1
  Dor 350
  ephone codes 573
  ephones 44
  Hai 398
  Hazor 396
  Jericho 452
  Maresha 343
Tel Aviv 321–336
Tel Aviv
  University 31, 332,
  333
telegrams 45
telephone codes 573
telephones 44

Temenos Gate 496
Templars 351, 372, 373
Temple Mount 297–299
temples
    Baha'i Temple (Haifa) 358
    Karnak Temple 185
    Luxor Temple 184
    Temple of Artemis 507
    Temple of Bacchus 570
    Temple of Horus 200
    Temple of Isis 212
    Temple of Jupiter 569
    Temple of Kalabsha 213
    Temple of Kom Ombo 202
    Temple of Venus 570
Ten Commandments 45 6
Tenth Legion 498
terrorism 16
testicles, ox 356
The Prophet 555
Thomson, Reverend William 565
Tiberias 379–385
time zones 573
Timna National Park 436
Titus 48, 455
Tobiah the Ammonite Servant 480
Tombs
    Corinthian Tomb 496
    of Ankhma-Hor 141
    of Mereruka 141
    of Rachel 448
    of Sextus Florentinus 496
    of the Apis Bulls 140
    of Ti 140
    Palace Tomb 496

Persian 139
    Tutankhamun's 12 3
    Urn Tomb 496
Torah 63
Trajan 48, 229, 505
Transfiguration 378
travel agencies 37
traveler's checks 13, 13–14
Tree Lovers' Association (Cairo) 131
Trinity 64
Tripoli 565–567
Trumpeldor, Yosef 397, 398
Tutankhamun 190
    his tomb 123
Tzfat 389–395

U

U-boat 169
Ugarit alphabet 519, 529, 546
ululation 466
Umayyad Dynasty 49
Umayyad Mosque 528
United Arab Republic (UAR) 54
universities
    Al-Azhar 27, 92, 113
    American Society of Haifa 31
    American University of Beirut (AUB) 32
    American University of Cairo (AUC) 27, 91, 92, 100, 130
    An-Najah 455
    Ben-Gurion 31
    Birzeit 32, 455
    Cairo 122
    Damascus 524
    Haifa 358
    Hebrew University of Jerusalem 31
    State University of New York at New Paltz 23
    Tel Aviv 31, 332, 333
    University of

Jordan 32
    Yarmouk 32, 509
Uyoun Mussa 250

V

Valley of the Kings 189
Via Dolorosa 64
visas 8
visas, Sinai-only 435
volunteering. See alternatives to tourism.
voyeurs, gastronomic 156

W

Wadi Kid 260
Wadi Natrun 143–145
Wadi Qelt 453
Wadi Rum 503
Wadi Seer 480
Wadi Sh'eib 481
Wadi Turkimaniya 496
Wafd party 52
Wakala of El Ghouri 112
water parks
    Ashkeluna 342
    Ein Feshka 409
    Luna Gai 385
waterwheels
    Fayyum 147
    Hama 537
weather. See climate.
weights and measures 573
Weizmann House 339
WEST BANK 438–456
Western Union 15
Whirling Dervishes 67, 129, 130
Whitman, Walt 555
wild asses
    Asiatic 426
    Israeli 437
    Syrian 484
wineries
    Golan Heights 402
    Rishon Le Zion 338
    Zikhron

Ya'akov 351
women travelers 33
    and health 21
    in Egypt 79
    in the oases 217
working abroad. See alternatives to tourism.
world wide web. See internet.

Y

Ya'ar Yehudiya Nature Reserve 403
yachts 236
Yad La-Yeled 369
Yad Mordekhai 342
Yad Va-Shem 314
Yahweh 62
Yam L'Yam hike 373, 388
Yarmouk University 32, 509
Yehi'am Fortress 373
Yemeniyyeh Reef 502
Yemin Moshe 313
Yo Mama 126
Yom Ha'Atzma'ut 2
Yom Ha-Sho'ah 2
Yom Ha-Zikaron 2
Yom Kippur 2

Z

Zagazig 142
Zaghloul, Sa'ad 52, 87
zajal 555
Zamalek 122
Zarqa Ma'in 488
Zawiya of Sultan Faraj 112
Zenobia, Queen 531, 534
Zenon 544
Zikhron Ya'akov 350
Zionism 51–53
Zippori 378
zoos
    Allenby 58 (Tel Aviv) 334
    Cairo 123
    Haifa 358, 359
    Ramat Gan Zoological Center 332